THE ANIME ENCYCLOPEDIA

THE ANIME ENCYCLOPEDIA

A Guide to Japanese Animation since 1917

Jonathan Clements

Helen McCarthy

Stone Bridge Press • Berkeley, California

Published by
STONE BRIDGE PRESS
P. O. Box 8208, Berkeley, CA 94707
TEL 510-524-8732 • sbp@stonebridge.com • www.stonebridge.com

We want to hear from you! Updates? Corrections? Comments? Please send all correspondence regarding this book to **animeinfo@stonebridge.com**.

Book design and layout by Linda Ronan.

Printed in the United States of America.

10 9 8 7 6 5 4 3   2006 2005 2004 2003 2002

LIBRARY OF CONGRESS CATALOGING-IN-PUBLICATION DATA
Clements, Jonathan.
    The anime encyclopedia: a guide to Japanese animation since 1917 /
Jonathan Clements, Helen McCarthy.
        p. cm.
    Includes bibliographical references and index.
    ISBN 1-880656-64-7
        1. Animated films—Japan—Encyclopedia. I. McCarthy, Helen. II.
Title.
  NC1766.J3 C53 2001
    791.43'3—dc21

                                                2001042819

To Peter Goll, anime's unsung hero

CONTENTS

THE ANIME ENCYCLOPEDIA

ILLUSTRATIONS

INTRODUCTION

Japanese animation started in the early years of the last century and is sustained by the largest animation industry in the world, with strong links to its Asian, European, and American counterparts. Despite the worldwide commercial success of **POKÉMON**, many critics still judge anime on the basis of the violent and pornographic titles widely promoted by Western distributors. We have always argued for a broader perspective. Our aim in this book is to show the diversity of anime production in its cultural context and to indicate some of the main trends and creative influences.

The prospect was daunting from the outset—merely listing all the shows we could name took 64 pages. In the interests of making a book you can lift without a hoist and afford without a mortgage, we have omitted approximately 1,000 titles and incorporated 500 more into other entries. We have given priority to anime with English-language releases and anime currently available on Japanese video.

The period up to 1945 is covered in two generic sections, **EARLY ANIME** and **WARTIME ANIME**. The period 1945–79 is represented by around 300 titles, including all major films and TV series. The 1979 landmark **WORLD MASTERPIECE THEATER** series has its own entry.

The advent of video created a whole new subset of anime, and we have listed the last quarter of the 20th century in depth. The year 1979 was our watershed year; most titles released after that date were marked for inclusion, though those designed to teach English to preschoolers, arbitrary spinoffs of music over recycled footage, and some of the more transient porn films may not have survived. Many connected series are listed together, so although there are no separate entries for *Kiramekiman* and *Ippatsuman*, both can be found under the **TIME BOKAN** umbrella. Also omitted are several titles on the periphery of the anime field—*Armageddon* and *Red Hawk*, sold as anime despite being Korean, and Tsui Hark's *Chinese Ghost Story*, which was made in Hong Kong, albeit with a Japanese animation director. Stop-motion animation and puppetry, often filed with anime in Japanese sources, have also been left out.

Although our cut-off point is the year 2000, we have included those shows announced for 2001 about which we had significant information. For reasons of available space and editorial sanity, we have had to remove most references to voice actors and voice acting from this edition—tempting though it is to reveal that the authors provided the voices for V-Daan and Akumako in **BEAST WARRIORS**, we couldn't afford the space, or the embarrassment. We have also limited references to merchandising, the engine that drives the entire industry, to items of particular significance or international interest such as the **GODAIKIN** line.

Following are additional points about our listings and how they are presented.

TITLES

We have included as many Japanese titles as possible, but owing to space limitations, many episode titles, TV specials, and minor films have simply been left in English. We give variant titles but have indexed by Western release where possible—hence *Space Cruiser Yamato* is filed as **STAR BLAZERS**. The "three-dimensional" typography of many anime titles leaves them with a foreground name and a background qualifier, which plays havoc with filing: is it **MACROSS**, or is it *Super-Dimensional Fortress Macross*? Where possible we have used the Western title most recognizable—few fans in the U.S. *or* Japan speak of *Neon Genesis Evangelion*; instead they refer to it as **EVANGELION**, though both variants will be found in our index. Similarly, the anime known in Japan as *Shojo Kakumei Utena* (and translatable as *Revolutionary Girl Utena*) is often given the French title *La Fillette Revolutionnaire* on Japanese merchandise and was mystifyingly renamed *Ursula's Kiss* in some studio sales documents (press releases whose tenuous relation to the shows they purport to sell has confused many attempts to determine names and plots). We have filed it simply as **UTENA** but indexed it by all its variants.

For consistency, we have replaced the ampersand (&) with the word "and,"

although box typography and "official" titles may offer variant forms.

Titles printed in **BOLDFACE CAPITAL LETTERS** refer to main entries elsewhere in the book. The indexes can be used to find titles that are referred to but that do not have their own entries.

Note that in our commentaries we often (but not always) space-savingly refer to the anime under discussion by its initials or a shortened form: in the text about **CREAM LEMON**, for example, we refer to it as *CL* and to a related work as *New CL*, and we refer to the film **EVANGELION** as *Eva*.

Titles appear in the listings in alphabetical order using the alphabetize-by-word system. Thus, **BOY WITH CAT'S EYES** comes before **BOYFRIEND**. If you are unfamiliar with this system (the one favored by computers and databases), you may need to turn a page or two to find the title you're looking for. Some variant titles known to exist appear in the index as well, although they may not be in the main listings. Finally, if a title contains a numeral, it is alphabetized as if the numeral were spelled out in English: 2 = Two, in other words.

See also the note on romanization, below.

INTERNATIONAL RELEASES

An asterisk (*) by a title heading denotes the existence of a *legal* English-language release of at least part of a show at some point, though not all titles are internationally available. The U.S. has **THE SECRET OF BLUE WATER** to itself, **HUMMINGBIRDS** is not available outside the U.K., and **KEN THE WOLF BOY** was only broadcast in Australia. Furthermore, while an English edition may exist, some, such as **MEMORIES**, were only seen as subtitled prints at film festivals or on Japanese DVD with English subtitles. Since this is an English-language book with limited space, we have avoided discussion of other languages, although a few well-known French title variants have been included for the benefit of readers in Canada, and there is occasional reference to Spanish-language versions.

FORMATS AND RUNNING TIMES

The nature of the medium has changed radically through technological and economic influences. Animation was an obscure cottage industry until its use as military propaganda led to the first full-length feature, **MOMOTARO'S DIVINE SEA WARRIORS**, in 1945. Television created a larger medium during the 1960s, which came to be dominated by merchandising tie-ins in the 1970s.

The arrival of the video recorder in the 1980s allowed for the targeting of smaller niches in the audience, beginning the process whereby anime studios held on to their audiences as they left childhood behind. Before video recorders became widely available in the 1980s, producers could expect a reasonable number of fans to pay to see repeat performances of TV shows in theaters, leading to holiday reruns, erroneously credited in some sources as genuine "movies." Furthermore, many shows made for video, such as **BELOVED BETTY**, were also shown theatrically as second or third features. We have listed these shows as video productions, though some other sources describe them as movies. **APPLESEED**, for example, is listed as a video work because that was its original format, even though it was shown in theaters outside Japan.

The 1990s saw many more developments—the "retro" revival as studios tried to appeal to former fans *and* their children, the advent of digital animation, and the use of satellite/cable as an even cheaper preview medium than video (the studio only has to pay for one tape!).

We have had to piece together some entries, especially for older shows, from sources with time listings that do not account for commercial breaks. Sometimes the difference can be drastic: the *Animage 25 Years of Television Cartoons* gives the broadcast time of **BAGHI** as 120 minutes, whereas the *Newtype Animesoft Complete Catalog* entry lists it as only 86 minutes, and the *Animation Filmography of Osamu Tezuka* infuriatingly disagrees with both. We have also had to consider different companies' editing and compilation policies, which can affect published running times.

We have given full episode counts of shows *made*, even if the complete runs of shows such as **ULYSSES 31** and **ALICE IN WONDERLAND** were only ever seen outside Japan. We have tried to distinguish among multiple versions of an anime using different abbreviations, and also by using a short-form of the title after the time and episode count. Finally, where we have had to cram several incarnations of a title into one entry, pertinent changes in staff or running time are separated by semicolons or denoted by numbered abbreviations, e.g., "m1" for the first movie, "TV2" for a second TV series, or "v2" for a second video series. See the list of abbreviations on page 2.

CREATIVE CREDITS

We have listed as many crew members as space allowed. Though not exhaustive, we have included the most important parties responsible for the five major areas of production on each anime. The period under study is so vast that meanings have changed over time. As well as lead animators (ANI) and composers (MUS), we have listed directors (DIR), scriptwriters (SCR), and designers (DES), though these last three job titles have had over 12 definitions during the last 50 years.

A "series producer," for example, is sometimes a "story editor" (i.e., a lead writer—SCR) and sometimes a "supervising director" (DIR), depending on the whims both of the studio and the English translators, who may not know as much about film terminology as they do about Japanese. Similarly, "supervising director" is sometimes an honorary title for a producer, but it is also occasionally used for the chief among several directors on a long-running series. We have done our best to pin down exactly what a staff member did and place him or her in the right slot, but sometimes we had to admit defeat—Frederik L. Schodt *himself* is not quite sure why he is credited as a "planning brain" on SPACE FIREBIRD.

In cases where a manga has been adapted into anime, we have followed the Japanese practice and credited the original creators as the writer/designer where no alternative is given.

Those who check our credits against Western releases may notice discrepancies; this is often because some distributors use the same set of credits for long-running shows, though writers and animators may change with each episode. Where possible, we have checked the credits of the Japanese originals, and though we have had to admit defeat on many occasions, jobs go uncredited (N/C) only after a trawl through every available option, including several Japanese-language listings and studio histories.

ABOUT JAPANESE NAMES

Japanese names are particularly troublesome, as they are generally written with non-phonetic *kanji* characters. Even the Japanese themselves are not always sure how to pronounce a particular *kanji* in every context. Matters are not helped by the proliferation of pseudonyms, often deliberately hard to read.

Watching every anime made, end-to-end, in order to catch the names of all the staff and all the fictional characters would have taken over 18 years. We have been necessarily frugal with our time and utilized other sources where possible. Sometimes we have had to wing it, as in THUNDERBIRDS 2086, where not even ITC-approved publications can agree on spellings. However, where we know Western credits to be in error, we have replaced them with our own.

We have elected to present Japanese names in Western order, that is, family name last, because this is generally how they are presented in English-language credits. This has resulted in the names of some well-known historical characters being given unconventionally as, for example, Nobunaga Oda or Musashi Miyamoto.

Doubtful names have been passed on to our research assistant Motoko Tamamuro and her mystified family, who have provided the best pronunciations they could. Where a guess is the best we can manage, we have opted for a guess made by Japanese native-speakers.

TERMINOLOGY

Some points remain the same across cultures—more money is spent on a film than a TV episode. Movies "made for television" tend to be cheaper and more conservative in their execution. Shows that go "straight to video" are generally for a smaller, niche audience. We have avoided the spin-doctor's term OAV—an "Original Anime Video" made for direct sale rather than theatrical or TV airing. In some cases, especially many musical spinoffs and porn, "OAVs" aren't particularly animated, and with the advent of LD and DVD, still more are not technically videos. We found ourselves questioning the "original" part more than once, too.

We have, however, included mentions for several "manga videos"—comics on VHS in which voice actors read to the viewer, and even save them the bother of turning the pages. Though these are the lowest-tech "animation" imaginable, they are likely to turn up in video store bargain bins and are included here to save would-be buyers' blushes. These are not to be confused with Manga Video, the *brand name* that led many (including the *Oxford English Dictionary*) to confuse "manga" (Japanese comics) with "anime" (Japanese animation).

Beyond the words "manga" and "anime," we have tried to avoid the obstructively arcane jargon of fandom. We intend to make anime accessible to every reader, so as much as possible we have used terms traceable in any good dictionary. Anime is increasingly targeted at an international audience and can be described in any of the wide variety of languages into which it's translated—the abuse of terms such as *hentai, shojo,* and *otaku* only serves to alienate the general reader.

ROMANIZATION

We have adopted a strategy for handling Japanese words: keep it simple. Purists and language scholars may be unhappy at some of the choices we have made, but our first impulse has been to serve the needs of our readers, most of whom have no particular expertise in speaking or pronouncing Japanese.

Our job has been made more difficult because the Japanese and American studios that release anime into English-language markets do not follow the same or even consistent romanization rules. And some Japanese anime and Japanese names are already known outside Japan by their "incorrect" English spellings.

So what we have done is made the best of an inherently confusing situation.

1. We almost always favor the "official" spellings of anime titles as provided by their studios, nonstandard though they may sometimes be. Names, too, can be rendered in the romanized form preferred by the particular individual: Joe (not Jo) Hisaishi, for example.

2. Japanese titles, when we provide them, are romanized consistently, except that "English" words adopted into the Japanese anime title are rendered back into English: thus, the film known in English as **BLOCKER CORPS** is in fact known in Japanese as *Burokkaa Guntan IV Masheen* but is listed here as *Blocker Guntan IV Machine.*

3. The syllabic nasal *n* is written as *n* before *b, m,* and *p* (Shinbashi); in other texts, *m* is frequently seen here (Shimbashi). We have dropped the apostrophe used in specialized texts to indicate

syllabic division involving the nasal *n*; thus we write Junichiro, not Jun'ichiro.

4. We do not indicate the extended vowels *o* and *u*, either by "long signs" (macrons) over the vowels or by spelling out as *ou, oo,* or *uu.* Extended vowels are usually either ignored or mispronounced by those unfamiliar with Japanese, and are in any case not provided at all or are provided inconsistently by those who prepare staff credits and English-language materials. Rather than litter this book with mistakes and inconsistencies we have simply decided to adopt a leaner style of romanization. For later editions we may decide to rethink this choice.

PARENTAL ADVISORIES

Like any mass medium, anime can soar to great heights of creative expression or plumb the depths of human depravity. Some anime you want to share with your family; some you might need to watch in a room with the door locked. Whatever your tastes, far be it from us to cast judgment. But at the request of our publisher, and in the interest of making this book of practical use for fans as well as guardians, teachers, librarians, and shop owners, we have provided some simple icons to indicate those anime that have language, violence, or nudity of the sort that one might not wish children or other sensitive souls to be exposed to. Not all violence is gratuitous;

not all nudity is exploitative. Our "ratings" are merely a guide to content, and we hope a useful one.

* * *

Anime is an ever-expanding medium, and though we include over 2,000 titles in this book, we estimate the total number of anime to be around twice that figure. We have done our best to pick the most important shows and to include honorable mentions for many others, but there will always be omissions, shows whose importance will only be realized with hindsight. Despite this, we are confident that every anime fan in the world can learn something from this book—a quarter of the titles we include have never been discussed in the West before, while details on the foreign treatment of anime are absent from Japanese sources.

If there is anything that will date this encyclopedia in years to come it is the absence of interactive animation—Production IG's animation for the computer game *Scandal* (2000) lasted three hours and used 30,000 cels, ironically making it longer and better made than many of the "normal" anime titles we *have* included. Perhaps such interactive works, along with voice actor data, translation credits, personalities, organizations, and extra entries can wait for a revised edition, when our long-suffering editor Peter Goodman has stopped weeping.

ACKNOWLEDGMENTS

Thanks to:

Our overworked, underpaid research assistants, Fred Patten, Motoko Tamamuro, and Steve Kyte.

And, for sundry help and advice:

Brad Attwell, Jerry Beck, Chris Bottone, Anna Bowles, Lee Brimmicombe-Wood, Ardith Carlton, John T. Carr III, Stephen Cremin, Ben Carter, Jeremy Clarke, Edwin de la Cruz, Paul Corrigan, Robert Fenelon, Chelsey Fox, Mark Frodsham, Simon Furman, Simon Gale, Marcus Hearn, David Hughes, Simon Jowett, Alden Harbour Keith, Mary Kennard, John Ledford, Cam Lufkin, Michael Mallory, Alex McLaren, Avi Melman, Brett Mermer, Chrys Mordin, Adam Newell, Kate Pankhurst, Bill Paris, Gilles Poitras, Richard Reichman, Brian Robb, Mee-Lise Robinson, Linda Ronan, Anneli Rufus, Ake Sasaki, Frederik L. Schodt, Julia Sertori, Rod Shaile, Jerry Shaw, Steven Smet, Toren Smith, J. Michael Straczynski, Jim Swallow, Akiko Tamamuro, Jason Taylor, Miki Terasawa, Emmanuel van Melkebeke, Brad Warner, Wendell Washer, Aki Watanabe, Paul Watson, Amos Wong, Jeff Zitomer. Also publisher Peter Goodman—for knowing a good thing when he saw it, both when we came to him with the original proposal, and a year later when we decided to write 160,000 extra words.

And last, but not least, thanks to our partners Kate and Steve, who endured an entire year of conversations on topics including the merits of *Learning English with Dinosaurs*, where to file GALAXY ADVENTURES OF SPACE OZ, and Yukio Mishima's relationship to CATGIRL NUKUNUKU.

J. C., H. M.

PUBLISHER'S NOTE

We are grateful to the following companies for generously granting image permissions:

A.D. Vision Inc., AIC/Tripeaks, Bandai USA, Central Park Media, Enoki Films Co. Ltd., Sandy Frank Syndication, Inc., Fuji Creative Corporation, Harmony Gold, Kodansha Ltd., Manga Entertainment, Media Blasters, Mushi Production Co. Ltd., Nintendo of America Inc., Nippon Animation Co., Ltd., The Right Stuf, Studio Ghibli, Tezuka Productions Co., Ltd., Voyager Entertainment

Thanks are also due to the following individuals, some of them from the above companies, who were particularly helpful with information and materials:

Jason Alnas, Ricki Ames, Anna Bechtol, Sara Bush, Libbie Chase, Gamal Hennessy, Rena Ikeda, Yoshi Inoki, Tomoko Kanai, Kris Kleckner, Shawne Kleckner, Minoru Kotoku, Junko Kusunoki, Cindy Ledermann, Chieko Matsumoto, Yasuhiko Matsuoka, Phil Oldman, Tak Onishi (and Japan Video & Media), Fred Patten, Matt Perrier, Patty Pfister, Gilles Poitras, Roland de la Rosa (and Movie Image), Shigehiko Sato, John Serabet, Mikiko Takeda, Natsumi Ueki, Robert Woodhead, Steve Yun

We have tried diligently to obtain permissions for all copyrighted images used in this book. If we have inadvertently omitted or incorrectly listed the name of a rights-holder, we will gladly correct the error in the next edition. We honor the rights of creators and acknowledge their work.

The companies acknowledged here were helpful in many ways: suggesting images, sending high-quality materials for scanning, and providing the authors with updated information for inclusion in the text. However, we were unable to include several important examples of anime art because the studios that held the rights either never responded to us or, for reasons known only to them, flatly refused to have their material included in this book. Rights issues are complicated, and we'd like to think that legal circumstances prevented their participation. But we suspect that in some cases studios simply couldn't be bothered to reply or to do the necessary paperwork. We'd like again to thank those companies who *do* see the value in this book, and urge the other companies to perhaps review their own attitudes about permissions requests. Books like this provide essential information in reference form for hungry and thirsty fans as wells as dealers, reviewers, and filmgoers.

One final note about the illustrations. Owing to schedule and permissions uncertainties, we have opted to insert images at random but regular points throughout the main text. (That is, we sometimes did not know until the last minute whether an image could or could not be used!) Page references in the anime entries and image captions will help you find your way from one to the other. In addition, all illustrations are listed alphabetically after the contents page and in the indexes.

We'd like to hear from you! Please send comments, corrections, complaints, information updates, and letters via e-mail to:

animeinfo@stonebridge.com.

STONE BRIDGE PRESS

THE ANIME ENCYCLOPEDIA

ABBREVIATIONS AND KEY

The following abbreviations are used throughout the listings:

*	available in English
JPN	released in Japan as
AKA	"also known as" (alternative title)
DIR	directed by
SCR	script by
DES	design by
ANI	lead animation by
MUS	music by
PRD	production by
N/C	not credited
N/D	no data available
(b/w)	black and white
(m)	movie
(TV)	[made for] TV
(TVm)	TV movie
(v)	video
?	uncertain (data; usually episode count)
ca.	circa, approximately
ep., eps.	episode(s)
mins.	minutes
BOLDFACE TYPE	cross-reference to main entry
Ill. p. ##	see illustration on page ##
L	language advisory
N	nudity advisory
V	violence advisory

A.LI.CE *

1999. Movie. DIR: Kenichi Maejima. SCR: Masamitsu Yoshimoto. DES: Hirosuke Kizaki. ANI: N/C. MUS: N/C. PRD: Gaga Communications. 85 mins.

Time paradoxes, snowy wastes, and new developments in computer graphics are on display in this story of a 21st-century tour shuttle from the moon that crashes leaving the 16-year-old Alice and the robot flight attendant, Maria, the only survivors. When strangely clothed scavengers chase them from the wreckage, Alice and Maria meet Yuan, a young boy who is half-Eskimo, half-Finn. They have fallen 30 years into the future to a world ruled by the evil Nero. They delve back into the archives only to discover that many years ago, a girl called Alice became a famous pop star, and that the trip through time is a (somewhat illogical) attempt to change history.

Dogged by the standard problems of time-travel stories (such as how an older version of Alice can exist when the younger version was sent into the future), this sci-fi film looks not unlike a long game cut-scene, predictably so since one of the writer's former projects was the game *Shen Mue*. By all accounts, however, a surer step into digital animation than the disappointing VISITOR.

ABASHIRI FAMILIES *

1991. JPN: *Abashiri Ikka*. Video. DIR: Takashi Watanabe. SCR: Takashi Watanabe. DES: Shigenori Kurii. ANI: Shigenori Kurii. MUS: Takeo Miratsu. PRD: Dynamic Planning, Studio Pierrot, Soeishinsha, NEXTART. 75 mins.

Papa Abashiri, leader of one of the most notorious criminal syndicates in history, decides it's time for his super-powered family to retire so his daughter, Kukunosuke, can have a normal existence. However, her "normal" school turns out to be a hunting ground for crazed perverts and brawlers, who have no intention of teaching the students anything. As the violence escalates, Kukunosuke calls in her family to fight against the principal in a final showdown of bone-crunchingly epic proportions.

Recalling SUKEBAN DEKA, with its tale of a bad girl trying to go straight, and DEBUTANTE DETECTIVES, with its well-connected students, *Abashiri Families* was originally released as four short chapters in the RENTAMAN video magazine. It was soon compiled into this omnibus edition, which is the version circulated in the English language. Its cartoonish comedy angle gives it more in common with creator Go Nagai's KEKKO KAMEN and HANAPPE BAZOOKA than with his more serious stories, but the disjointed nature of the original production makes for an inferior offering. Director Watanabe would go on to adapt another Nagai story, BLACK LION.

ABENO BRIDGE MAGICAL MALL

2001. JPN: *Abeno Hashi Maho Shotengai*. TV series. DIR: Hiroyuki Yamaga. SCR: Hiroyuki Yamaga, Satoru Akahori. DES: Kenji Tsuruta. ANI: Tadashi Hiramatsu. MUS: N/C. PRD: Gainax. 25 mins. x 12+ eps.

Two average Japanese kids, Satoshi and Arumi, discover that the architects of their local shopping district were sorcerers so the entire area is crawling with ghosts and otherworldly spirits. This comedy was designed as Gainax's TV follow-up to their successful video FLCL.

ACROBUNCH

1982. JPN: *Makyo Densetsu Acrobunch*. AKA: *Haunted Frontier Legend Acrobunch*. TV series. DIR: Masakazu Yasumura, Satoshi Hisaoka. SCR: Masaru Yamamoto. DES: Shigenori Kageyama, Mutsumi Inomata, Masakazu Higuchi. ANI: Kazuhiro Taga, Masakazu Yasumura, Hideki Takayama, Yutaka Arai, Kazuhiro Ochi. MUS: Masaji Maruyama. PRD: Nippon TV. 30 mins. x 24 eps.

Half-Japanese amateur inventor Tatsuya Lando talks his five *almost* all-American children into piloting his latest project, a transforming super-robot called Acrobunch. Older boys Hiro and Ryo pilot the two Buncher Hornets, while twin girls Miki and Rika ride the Buncher Arrow flying motorcycles. Middle-child Jun is the 15-year-old boy who gets to pilot the Acrobunch unit formed from the combination of all the vehicles with dad's Falcon Buncher main craft. Tatsuya is searching for the ancient treasure of Quaschika, which was the true inspiration behind the ancient stories of Atlantis. But Lando is not the only one—Emperor Delos of the undersea Goblin empire is also searching for the Quaschika, and the Acrobunch robot becomes the last line of defense between them and Earth. Each week, it must fight against the robots of the Goblin armies, one of which is led by Delos's own daughter, Queen Shiira, who develops a crush on her enemy Hiro.

Shunted around the schedules and between two different production studios, the troubled *Acrobunch* ("a robot controlled by a *bunch* of *acro*bats!") nevertheless served as a training ground for a group of new talents who would find fame in the decades to come. It was the first anime job for future **TEKKAMAN**-designer Rei Nakahara. Among the animators, Arai would work on **CITY HUNTER**, Ochi would make **HIKARIAN**, and Takayama would become the director of the notorious **UROTSUKIDOJI** series. Two decades later, Inomata produced similar character designs for **BRAIN POWERED**.

AD POLICE *
1990. Video, TV series. DIR: Akihiko Takahashi, Akira Nishimori. SCR: Noboru Aikawa. DES: Tony Takezaki, Fujio Oda, Toru Nagasuki. ANI: Fujio Oda, Hiroyuki Kitazume. MUS: Kaoru Mizutani. PRD: Artmic, Youmex, AIC. 40 mins. x 3 eps., 25 mins. x 12 eps.
A dark spinoff from Toshimichi Suzuki's **BUBBLEGUM CRISIS**, *AD Police* concentrates on the AD(vanced) antirobot crime division of Mega Tokyo's police force. Leon McNicol, a minor character in the original series, is partnered here with butch lady-cop Gena in several investigations that play with ideas of humanity in a high-tech society. The "voomer" robots here are all female in the man's world of the ADP, where only women who are prepared to become one with machines stand a chance in it. Whereas this device was used in *Bubblegum Crisis* as an excuse for girls with impressive high-tech kits, here it is far more misogynistic, as femininity is gradually eroded by bionics and prosthetics, taking characters' humanity with it. A businesswoman, for example, is only successful in the boardroom after she has a hysterectomy, but the trauma turns her into a serial killer. There are shades of *Blade Runner* in the sex-android stalker that locks onto the man who injured her, and there are also blatant steals from *Robocop* in the final chapter, wherein one of Gena's ex-boyfriends receives so

much augmentation that his tongue is the only part of his original body that remains.

Canceled after just three of the planned five episodes, the franchise was not revived until 1999, in the wake of the *Bubblegum Crisis 2040* remake, as a 12-part TV Tokyo series directed by Hidehito Ueda. The new *AD Police* was a far shallower affair, ditching many of the old characters in favor of a buddy-movie cliché between rapid-response robot-crime cop Takeru Sasaki and his new partner, Hans Krief. Clearly made with half an eye on the overseas market (all the other leads have foreign names like Paul Sanders, Liam Fletcher, and Nancy Wilson), the melting-pot remake is something of a disappointment. *Ill. p. 365.* ❶❷❸❹

ADRIFT IN THE PACIFIC *
1982. JPN: *Jugo Shonen no Hyoryuki*. AKA: *15 Boys Adrift; Deux Ans de Vacances*. TV special. DIR: Yasuji Mori, Yoshio Kuroda. SCR: Shunichi Yukimuro. DES: Hiroshi Wagatsuma, Rumiko Takahashi. ANI: Tatsuo Ogawa, Hideo Maeda. MUS: Katsutoshi Nagasawa. PRD: Toei, Fuji TV. 75 mins., 84 mins.
When bad weather causes her to slip her moorings and drift out to sea, the British schooner Sloughi is left in the hands of the 15 schoolboys on holiday. Without officers or sailors on board, the French boy Briant manages to organize the group and beach the ship on a deserted island they name Cherman after their school. The upper-class British boy, Doniphan, begins to argue with Briant about who should be in charge, and problems are multiplied a hundredfold when a 16th castaway washes up on the shore—a schoolgirl called Kate.
Deux Ans de Vacances, Jules Verne's low-rent copy of **SWISS FAMILY ROBINSON**, remains immeasurably more popular in Japanese than in English. This TV movie included a young design assistant called Rumiko Takahashi, whose growing success with **URUSEI YATSURA** would make her rich and

unlikely to work in animation again.
In 1987, the story was remade as another TV movie to cash in on the popularity of the Hollywood movie *Stand By Me* (which also featured several boys going exploring and getting mildly upset). Directed by Masayuki Akehi, the new version featured Maria Kawamura, shortly to find fame as Jung Freud in **GUNBUSTER**, as the troublesome Kate. This second TV movie was released in English as *Story of 15 Boys*, a pedantically faithful translation of the Japanese title suggesting the U.S. distributor knew little of Verne's original. See also **VIDEO PICTURE BOOK** and **VIFAM**.

ADULT FAIRY TALES
1999. JPN: *Otono no Dowa Series*. Video. DIR: Soichi Masui. SCR: Shige Sotoyama. DES: Kaoru Honma. ANI: N/C. MUS: Miki Kasamatsu. PRD: Tac, Toei. 50 mins.
A deliberate attempt to take **GRIMMS' FAIRY TALES** away from their cuter modern image and back to their darker roots, this series comprises three short versions of popular tales augmented with copious horror and flavor-of-the-moment computer graphics. The tales include *Hansel and Gretel*, *Blue Beard*, and *Cinderella*, all chosen because they presented an opportunity for the crew to depict stories of love and obsession.

ADVANCER TINA *
1996. Video. DIR: Kan Fukumoto. SCR: Wataru Amano. DES: Hironobu Saito, Kenji Teraoka. ANI: Dandelion. MUS: Ann Fu. PRD: Dandelion, Green Bunny, Beam Entertainment. 45 mins.
Three thousand years after pollution renders Earth uninhabitable, the human race is a space-faring people in search of new planets to settle. Elite super-scouts called Advancers blaze trails for the rest, but Omega 13 is one world proving difficult to conquer. Nine teams have failed to return, prompting high-ranking executive Mugal to make convict Tina Owen an offer she can't refuse. If she can solve the mystery of Omega 13, he'll knock a

whole millennium off her 2,000-year sentence for an undisclosed crime.

Tina only spends five tedious minutes on Omega 13; the rest of the story involves the pointless hunt for a crew (telepath/alien/comic relief Frill and Japanese love interest/sidekick Akira), and the rescue of fellow Advancer Garuda from a beleaguered ship. The alien menace turns out to be a multi-tentacled creature with acid saliva that burns through bulkheads and clothes but not through girls' skin. The alien murders all the disposable members of the cast (three concubines whose sole role is to be sexually assaulted in different locations) before being summarily executed as it tries to rape Tina. This, apparently, makes the planet safe and avenges Akira's dead parents all in one shot, allowing Tina to fly off to her next mission, though a sequel was never made.

Despite promising beginnings that unite the last-chance mission of *The Dirty Dozen* with the interstellar trouble-shooting of **DIRTY PAIR**, *Advancer Tina* soon collapses into a tacky exploitation movie. With an icthyphallic menace that gestates in human stomach cavities and a predictable, false ending, its debt to the *Alien* series is obvious, but the film is shoddily assembled from start to finish. Fukumoto, Saito, and Teraoka, the real-world perpetrators of this anime crime, are still at large and can be found elsewhere in this book in the entries for **VENUS FIVE**, **SEXORCIST**, and **GIGOLO**. 🅛🅝🅥

ADVENTURE BOY SHADAR

1967. JPN: *Boken Shonen Shadar*. TV series. DIR: Juzo Kataoka. SCR: Masaki Tsuji. DES: Shinichi Kuwajima. ANI: Takashi Saijo, Nobukazu Kabashima. MUS: Atsutoshi Soda. PRD: Nippon TV. 10 mins. x 156 eps.
When Earth is threatened by the invading Ghostar, a young boy with nerves of steel and the strength of 50 men appears from a cave on Mount Fuji. He is Shadar, a boy of unknown origin who, with his faithful dog, Pinboke, fights each week to save the world in several ten-minute installments, guaranteeing a final showdown for Japanese viewers each Saturday.

Ghostar actor Kenji Utsumi's voice would come to represent the ultimate in evil to a Japanese audience, and he would go on to play the title roles in **DRACULA: SOVEREIGN OF THE DAMNED** and **DON DRACULA**.

ADVENTURE KID *

1992. JPN: *Yoju Sensen Adventure Kid*. AKA: *Demon-Beast Battle Line Adventure Kid*. Video. DIR: Yoshitaka Fujimoto. SCR: Atsushi Yamatoya, Akio Satsugawa. DES: Dan Kongoji, Ryunosuke Otonashi, Yuji Takahashi. ANI: MW Films. MUS: Masamichi Amano. PRD: MW Films. 40 mins. x 3 eps.
Wartime Japanese scientist Professor Masago devotes himself to his research, ignoring his beautiful wife, Michiyo. In 1945, he is murdered by the dastardly Captain Matsubara's soldiers, after first being forced to watch them rape her. Fifty years later, the husband and wife are reincarnated as students Norikazu and Midori. Norikazu unearths Masago's prototype dimension-hopping device, and it propels them into a parallel universe where Masago's bitter psyche has created a world of marauding zombie soldiers. Eventually Norikazu (good side) defeats Masago (bad side) by dropping him into the Hiroshima bomb blast. The couple then find themselves in Hell Zone, where lusty elf-girl Eganko latches onto Norikazu and accompanies him back to Earth. Back at Norikazu's school, the reincarnation of Captain Matsubara, college-boy Yukimoto, wants Midori for himself and schemes with Eganko's mother, Queen Dakiniten, to make Norikazu fall in love with Eganko. The plan goes awry when love potions are mixed up and given to the wrong victims.

A pornographic tale of rape and domination that suddenly turns into a farce, *Adventure Kid* contains erotic musings on the alien girlfriend-squatter setup of **URUSEI YATSURA**, a clumsy attempt to integrate computers into horror (also seen in **DIGITAL DEVIL STORY**), and a final episode that pokes merciless fun at the excesses of both itself and creator Toshio Maeda's earlier **UROTSUKIDOJI**. In an attempt to draw in new crowds, the producers hired live-action erotic "actresses" to provide some of the voice roles, a move which backfired spectacularly when they couldn't actually act. In the U.K., the series was heavily cut and renamed *Adventure Duo*. 🅛🅝🅥

ADVENTURE OF KOTETSU *

1996. JPN: *Kotetsu no Daiboken*. Movie. DIR: Yuji Moriyama. SCR: Yuji Kawahara. DES: Yoko Kikuchi. ANI: Tetsuya Watanabe. MUS: Kuniaki Haishima. PRD: Daiei, Tokuma Japan. 30 mins. x 2 eps.
Hot-headed Linn "Kotetsu" Suzuki is an accomplished martial artist at 14 and the last in a long line of warriors. Running away from her old-fashioned Kyoto home to look for her brother in Tokyo, she helps a shapely private eye, Miho, defeat two possessed street thugs. The two soon move in together, and Kotetsu inadvertently saves Miho's life once again when Tetsuya, the man hired by a corrupt businessman to kill her, instead falls in love with her new roommate. Settling their differences at a hot-springs resort, the trio are attacked by a tree demon, sent by Tetsuya's boss. Upon defeating it, Kotetsu's grandmother tells her she can stay in the big city.

Recalling both **DEVIL HUNTER YOHKO** and **LA BLUE GIRL** with its female inheritor of a family martial arts tradition, this silly affair was based on the best-selling 1992 adult manga by MEE (aka Mikun). Though featuring atmospheric music from **SPRIGGAN**'s Haishima and direction from **PROJECT A-KO**'s Moriyama, the fan-service nudity and setups make it less than the sum of its parts—one assassination attempt involves a nude clone of Miho in the bath simply to arrange a lesbian scene between the two girls. Despite undeserved popularity for its nude heroine's resemblance to **RANMA 1/2**, the series stopped after the experimental two-part opener. MEE would have better success with his next anime project, the TV series **HYPER POLICE**. **◐**

ADVENTURE ON KABOTEN ISLAND

1967. JPN: *Boken Kaboten Shima*. TV series. DIR: Motokazu Watanabe. SCR: Aritsune Toyota, Masaki Tsuji, Arashi Ishizu, Junichi Yoshinaga. DES: Fumio Hisamatsu. ANI: Shizuko Komooka, Toyoo Ashida, Kazuo Mori. MUS: Various. PRD: TBS, Eiken. 30 mins. x 39 eps.
SUPER JETTER–creator Fumio Hisamatsu's 1967 comic in *Shonen Sunday* magazine featured a group of boys and girls marooned on a South Sea island in an imitation of Jules Verne's **ADRIFT IN THE PACIFIC**. The anime version reduced the female cast to a single comic relief little sister called Tomato, preferring instead to concentrate on the male characters as they explore their new home.

ADVENTURES OF PINOCCHIO *

1972. JPN: *Kashi no Ki Mokku*. AKA: *Mokku (Woody) the Oak Tree*. TV series. DIR: Ippei Kuri, Yukihiro Takahashi. SCR: Junzo Toriumi, Akiyoshi Sakai. DES: Yoshitaka Amano. ANI: Masayuki Hayashi. MUS: Nobuyuki Koshibe. PRD: Tatsunoko, Fuji TV. 25 mins. x 52 eps.
Finding driftwood that has been struck by lightning, toy-maker Gepetto constructs a puppet that comes alive but wants to be a real boy. Based on the 1881 children's story by Carlo Collodi, it was also animated as **PICCOLINO**. Yoshitaka Amano's first work in character design. Shown on HBO in the U.S.

AESOP'S FABLES *

1983. JPN: *Manga Aesop Monogatari*. TV series. DIR: Eiji Okabe, Jun Hagiwara, Fumio Kurokawa. SCR: Michiru Tanabe, Asami Watanabe, Ryo Nakahara. DES: Yu Noda. ANI: Hirokazu Ishino. MUS: Pegumo, Toko Akasaka. PRD: Nippon Animation, Transarts. 25 mins. x 52 eps.
Aesop, an ancient Greek storyteller

thought to have lived in the 6th century, has been a staple of anime since the beginning with **EARLY ANIME** such as Sanae Yamamoto's *Tortoise and the Hare* (1924) and *Frog's Belly* (1929). The 1983 TV series added the term "manga" to accentuate the children's-picture-book quality of the presentation, running through tales such as *The Ants and the Grasshopper*, *The Sun and the North Wind*, and *The Thirsty Crow*. Eight of the stories were combined to make the theatrical feature *Aesop's Fables* (1983, U.S. release 1985), with a framing device of young Aesop tricking his fellow villagers into believing that a wolf is attacking. When a real wolf comes, nobody believes him, and he is chased down a magic hole into a kingdom of animals. As he looks for a way out, he meets a tortoise, a hare, an ant, and other creatures who tell him their stories. Several of Aesop's fables were also used as part of the *Shogo Hirata's Picture Book* series (1995). See also **VIDEO PICTURE BOOK**.

AFTER-SCHOOL LOVE CLUB ÉTUDE

1997. JPN: *Hokago Ren'ai Club Koi no Étude*. Video. DIR: Moritaka Imura. SCR: N/C. DES: Yoshiaki Hatano. ANI: Yuki Mine. MUS: N/C. PRD: Pink Pineapple, KSS. 31 mins. x 2 eps.
Originating in Libido's mildly titillating computer role-playing game in the same genre as **TOKIMEKI MEMORIAL**, this is the story of Shunichi and Sanae, who are attracted to each other, but whose relationship seems to go nowhere. Neither does the plot until episode two, when the members of the "love club" start to get into the sex scenes promised on the box. In the original game, the player had to manage his resources to ensure he could get the most out of 12 sex-starved female members of a dating club in just 30 days. The anime doesn't retain its appeal for quite that long. **◐**

AFTER-SCHOOL TINKERBELL

1992. JPN: *Hokago Tinkerbell. Video*. DIR: Kiyoshi Murayama. SCR: Akira Oke-

tani. DES: Yasuhide Maruyama. ANI: Yasuhide Maruyama. MUS: N/C. PRD: Life Work, Ashi Pro. 45 mins.
In this animated adaptation of two novels in Shoichiro Hinata's *After School* series, high-school investigators Kenichi and Misako get on the case when the popular Broadcast Club disc jockey, Ryoko, goes missing.

AGE OF THE GREAT DINOSAURS

1979. JPN: *Daikyoryu no Jidai*. TV special. DIR: Shotaro Ishinomori with Hideki Takayama. SCR: Shotaro Ishinomori, Makoto Naito. DES: Shotaro Ishinomori. ANI: Kozo Morishita. MUS: Shogun. PRD: Ishi(no)mori Pro, Toei, Nippon TV. 73 mins.
CYBORG 009–creator Ishinomori (just plain Ishimori at the time) was heavily involved in this anime shot on 35mm film, in which naïve boy Jun, his female companion, Remi, and her little brother, Chobi, are whisked away to the Cretaceous Period by a flying saucer. There they hobnob with Cro-Magnon men, which would be damage enough to the program's educational merit even without the suggestion that aliens wiped out the dinosaurs when their population became too great—a dark portent for the expanding human race and a typical touch from the dour Ishinomori. Dinosaurs were a regular feature in children's entertainment, also cropping up in Makoto Noriza and Shigeru Omachi's one-shot video *Dinosaur Guide* (1989), in which Professor Doctor (*sic*) escorts children Tai and Ayumi on a trip to the prehistoric past. Aliens would return to do away with the dinosaurs in **LAWS OF THE SUN**.

AGEDAMAN

1991. JPN: *Genji Tsushin Agedama* [sic]. TV series. DIR: Masato Namiki. SCR: Takashi Yamada, Shigeru Yanagawa, et al. DES: Hatsuki Tsuji. ANI: Hiroaki Sakurai, Hideyuki Motohashi, et al. MUS: Toshihiko Sahashi. PRD: Studio Gallop, TV Tokyo. 25 mins. x 51 eps.
Average boy Genji can use his warp key to transform into the superhero Agedaman, the last line of resistance

against the evil 11th-century scientist Nostradamus and his equally evil granddaughter, Kukirei, in a brightly colored show that mixes action and comedy.

AGEMAN AND FUKU-CHAN

1991. Video. DIR: Teruo Kigure. SCR: Susume Yoshiike. DES: Masamichi Yokoyama. ANI: Masamichi Yokoyama. MUS: Jiro Takemura. PRD: Knack. 30 mins.
Mantaro Nishino is obsessed with money and women, but his schemes invariably fail in this satire of Japan and the Japanese in the late 1980s bubble economy. The sexy strumpet Fuku-chan is Mantaro's eventual undoing in this erotic fable based on a manga by Masamichi Yokoyama, who also created **MISTER HAPPY**. The title recalls that of Juzo Itami's live-action *Ageman: Tales of a Golden Geisha* (1990). **ⓝ**

AGENT AIKA *

1997. JPN: *Aika*. Video. DIR: Katsuhiko Nishijima. SCR: Kenichi Kanemaki. DES: Noriyasu Yamauchi, Hidefumi Kimura, Yoko Kikuchi. ANI: Noriyasu Yamauchi. MUS: Junichi Kanezaki. PRD: Graviton, Bandai Visual. 30 mins. x 6 eps.
Aika Sumeragi is a freelancer who lifts artifacts and data from the submerged ruins of Tokyo in the year 2036. She is a friend and business partner to the father-daughter team of Gozo and Rion Aida and has a love-hate relationship with Gust Turbulence, her spiky-haired male rival. Hired to go after the Ragu, an energy source reputed to be the cause of the global catastrophe, Aika must compete against evil super-bitch Neena Hagen, Neena's incestuous brother, Rudolf, and their army of women inexplicably dressed as French maids. Her only advantages: high-tech vehicles and transforming underwear that is really a weapon.

Envisaged by director Nishijima as a replay of **PROJECT A-KO**, with Aika, Neena, and Rion as A-Ko, B-Ko, and C-Ko, *Agent Aika* fast becomes the ultimate in peekaboo anime, as almost every camera angle conspires to get an eyeful of cleavage or panties. Worm's-eye views and gratuitous nudity soon drag the plot far off course, though exactly where Kanemaki's story of a treasure-huntress with a sentient bodice was originally headed is anyone's guess. Compare to the same team's later **NAJICA**. **ⓝ**

AI CITY *

1986. AKA: *Love City* (U.K.). Movie. DIR: Koichi Mashimo. SCR: Hideki Sonoda. DES: Chuichi Iguchi, Tomohiko Sato. ANI: Chuichi Iguchi, Nobuyoshi Habara, Satoru Utsunomiya, Kenichi Maejima, Hiroyoshi Okawa, Hiroshi Kawamata. MUS: Shiro Sagisu. PRD: Toei, Movic, Ashi Pro. 100 mins.
Young girl Ai and her protector, Kei, are on the run from rival gangs of "Headmeters"—humans with DNA recombined through nanotech viruses to give them psychic powers. Rival leaders Leigh and Lyrochin want Ai for the terrible secrets she contains, so she and failed Headmeter Kei join forces with an ex-cop turned private eye, an amnesiac ex-enemy, and a gratuitous cute cat (a design rip-off of Lucifer from Disney's *Cinderella*).

A poor man's **AKIRA**, even down to blue-skinned mutants with numerical foreheads, *AC* is much more than the sum of its parts, with surreal sequences of giant heads melting out of sidewalks, a plot revolving around multiple universes, and visceral scenes of psychic violence as Headmeters trump each other with ever-higher power levels. Based on the *Action Comics* manga by Shuho Itabashi (who would go on to draw one of the *X-Files* manga adaptations) but made just that little bit too early to benefit from the higher budgets of the sci-fi anime boom of the early 1990s, it was eclipsed by its successors and relegated to the anime B-list despite a plot far superior to contemporaries such as **LOCKE THE SUPERMAN**. Masterfully feeding the audience scraps of plot one bit at a time, it throws the viewer into the story without explaining a thing, slowly piecing together the reasons why Ai and Kei

The live-action *Zeiram* took place on boring old Earth, but its prequel **IRIA** was animated, allowing for exotic locations and effects impossible to achieve with the live action's budget. *See entry p. 184.*

Iria

© 1994 CROWD, BANDAI VISUAL, MITSUBISHI CORPORATION, BANPRESTO

are on the run, who is after them, and where they are from. Sonoda's script, loaded with careful English neologisms like "Headmeter," "tuned man," and "metapsychic phase wall," is truly excellent and even features a serious contender for one of the best endings in anime, later swiped for the grand finale of **UROTSUKIDOJI**. Available in separate U.K. and U.S. versions.

AIM FOR THE ACE

1973. TV series. JPN: *Ace o Nerae*. Movie. DIR: Osamu Dezaki, Masami Hata. SCR: Kazuaki Okamura. DES: Akio Sugino. ANI: Yoshiaki Kawajiri, Kazuo Yamazaki, Sadao Tomonaga, Shinichi Kato, Katsuhiko Yamazaki. MUS: Akira Misawa. PRD: TMS, A Pro, Takara, Madhouse, NET. 25 mins. x 26 eps.
Hiromi Oka is a new girl at Nishitaka tennis club, swiftly making a friend in the chatty Maki Aikawa and a deadly enemy in Reika "Madame Butterfly" Tatsuzaki, the undisputed queen of student tennis. Sacrificing her personal life (and her chances with lovelorn local boy Todo), Hiromi resolves to become the greatest tennis player in the world.

A second series of 25 episodes followed in 1978, with a new coach bringing new problems to the Nishitaka tennis students. With additional animation, this spawned a 1979 theatrical outing (still directed by **TOMORROW'S JOE**'s Dezaki). There was a renewed interest in the story in 1988, resulting in another movie, *AftA 2*, and a 12-part video series directed in part by former designer Akio Sugino. Dezaki did make some episodes and also provided some storyboards under the pseudonym Makura Saki. Revolving around the death of Hiromi's original coach, the final series featured her in many more foreign tournaments, finishing at Wimbledon itself. A bit part as a neighbor in a New York scene proved to be the first anime role for future **SAILOR MOON**–voice actress Kotono Mitsuishi.

The series has inspired several other anime, notably **YAWARA**, which follows a similar story progression but uses judo as its sport of choice. It also has the questionable distinction of both SF and erotic pastiches, in **GUNBUSTER** (subtitled "Aim for the Top") and *Aim for the A* in the **TALES OF . . .** collection.

AIRBATS *
1994. JPN: *Aozora Shojotai 801 TTS*. AKA: *Blue Sky Girl Squad 801 TTS*. Video. DIR: Yuji Moriyama. SCR: Yuji Kawahara, Soya Fujiwara. DES: Yuji Moriyama. ANI: Yuji Moriyama, Osamu Mikasa, Junichi Sakata. MUS: Seiko Nagaoka. PRD: Studio Fantasia. 30 mins. x 7 eps.
Geeky Takuya Isurugi is a fan of anime and machinery assigned as a mechanic to the 801 "Airbats" Tactical Training Squadron. Far from being a training ground for elite female pilots, it's a dead-end posting for burnouts—Miyuki Haneda has been sent there for striking a superior officer, Sakura Saginomiya is an inveterate gambler, Arisa Mitaka has an attitude problem, and Yoko Shimorenjaku is the world's worst pilot. Haneda and Mitaka both fall in love with Isurugi, and as bureaucrats try to disband the unit, they all try to hold onto their jobs in this wacky military comedy.

Plane fever struck Japan in the wake of *Top Gun*, inspiring the live-action Japanese rip-off *Best Guy*, *Airbats*, and its sharper, more satirical predecessor **HUMMINGBIRDS**. A cute contemporary of **TENCHI MUYO!**, employing similarly crowd-pleasing tactics of fanboy-meets-fawning-females, *Airbats* has its origin in a 1990 manga by Toshimitsu Shimizu, creator of **REI REI**. The six episodes and the *Airbats in Snow Country* vacation spinoff were later edited into the omnibus volumes *First* (episodes 1–3), *Second* (4 + holiday special), and *Third Strike* (episodes 5–6). It was supposedly made with the cooperation of the Japanese Air Force, which accounts for the loving aircraft detail but does not explain why a military organization would consent to be portrayed as misfits, desk-jockeys, and nuts whose main concern is winning a year's supply of free noodles. Whereas such inanities helped reinforce the realism of the long-running **PATLABOR**, in a short comedy series such as this they only demonstrate how wacky waters so often run shallow.

AKAI HAYATE *
1991. AKA: *Red Gale*. Video. DIR: Osamu Tsuruyama. SCR: Osamu Yamazaki. DES: Chiharu Sato, Koichi Ohata. ANI: Chiharu Sato, Masayoshi Sato. MUS: Takashi Kudo. PRD: NEXTART, Pony Canyon. 30 mins. x 4 eps.
The real rulers of modern Japan are the Shinogara clan, whose base is in a hidden valley at the base of Mount Fuji. The leader's son, Hayate, is executed for patricide but transfers his soul into the body of his sister, Shiori. Hiding out from Shinogara assassins in Tokyo, Shiori is able to call up her brother's skill in battle but loses a part of her own soul each time she does. As the power struggle continues between several factions of his clan, Hayate must save himself before he kills another member of his own family.

Originally serialized in the **RENTAMAN** video magazine, *Akai Hayate* was later compiled into two 60-minute volumes—the version released abroad. One of a large subset of anime in which the past bubbles to the surface in modern Japan, including writer Yamazaki's own **TAKEGAM**, it features **GENOCYBER**-creator Ohata as a guest designer for the MacGuffin "Shadow Armor" over which the ninja are fighting.

AKANE-CHAN
1968. TV series. DIR: Fusahito Nagaki, Yasuo Yamaguchi, Yugo Serikawa, Takeshi Tamiya. SCR: Shunichi Yukimuro, Masaki Tsuji. DES: Shinya Takahashi. ANI: Masamune Ochiai. MUS: Keiichi Honno. PRD: Fuji TV. 30 mins. x 26 mins.
Young Akane moves to the country and soon becomes popular with the other children in her class, befriending the troublesome local rich-kid Hidemaru and leading her gang into all sorts of scrapes. Tetsuya Chiba's original manga *Miso Curds* in *Shojo Friend* magazine was deliberately designed to evoke a distant, carefree time of rural childhood for city kids deprived of the opportunity, placing it in the same spirit as **MY NEIGHBOR TOTORO**. Renamed for its TV outing, it was the first of many Chiba titles to be adapted for anime—the creator is better known for more manly tales such as **TOMORROW'S JOE** and **I'M TEPPEI**.

AKANUKE ICHIBAN
1985. JPN: *Showa Aho Soshi Akanuke Ichiban*. AKA: *Showa Era Idiot Storybook: Most Refined; City Boy*. TV series. DIR: Hidehito Ueda. SCR: Takao Koyama, Hiroko Naka. DES: Hiroshi Hamazaki, Ammonite. ANI: Hidehito Ueda, Shinya Sadamitsu, Tetsuya Komori. MUS: Toshiyuki Watanabe. PRD: Tatsunoko, TV Asahi. 30 mins. x 22 eps.
Kojiro moves to Tokyo from Japan's northernmost island of Hokkaido and insists on bringing his favorite horse, Hikarikin, with him. The alien king Rel arrives from planet Wedelun and gives him a belt that will allow him to transform into a Miracle Hero and to protect the world from alien menaces. He is more interested, however, in impressing the pretty Yuka, though his rival,

Michinari, wants her for himself.

Yu Azuki, creator of **IGANO KABA-MARU**, enjoys as a reputation an artist who is able to straddle the divide between boys' and girls' comics. Though *Akanuke Ichiban* looks on the surface like a typical superhero story for a male audience, it originally ran in *Margaret* magazine—perhaps it appeared more palatable to male producers and fulfilled some form of girl/boy quota. The ratings, however, did not bear out the theory, and the series was canceled before reaching the end of its second season.

AKIHABARA CYBER TEAM

1998. JPN: *Akihabara Dennogumi*. TV series. DIR: Yoshitaka Fujimoto. SCR: Katsumi Hasegawa, Hiroshi Yamaguchi. DES: KA-NON, Tsukasa Kotobuki, Seiji Yoshimoto. ANI: Yuji Takahashi, Seiji Yoshimoto. MUS: Nobuyoshi Mitsumoto. PRD: Ashi Pro, TBS. 22 mins. x 26 eps.

Early in the 21st century, the combination of personal data-organizers and virtual pets results in a new piece of essential equipment. These "patapi" robots are friends, guardians, and personal computers, but to Hibari Hanakogane, they are more than that. Her patapi, Densuke, has been sent to Earth by a handsome prince to defeat the evil sorceress Blood Falcon. With her friends Suzume, Tsugumi, and their own patapi companions, Hibari forms the titular squad to fight cybercrime.

Tsukasa Kotobuki, who had formerly drawn a **GUNDAM** spinoff comic, collaborated with the pseudonymous Ka-non to create this tale of girls and gadgetry for *Nakayoshi* magazine, soon riding the coattails of the Tamagotchi craze to make the jump to radio drama, computer games, and this anime series. A mysterious clash of genres results in a cloyingly cute show for girls that somehow manages to have an evil character with giant breasts.

AKIKO

1995. Video. DIR: Kaoru Tomioka. SCR: Kaoru Tomioka. DES: Mitsuru Fujii. ANI: Mitsuru Fujii. MUS: Simon Akira. PRD: Fairy Tale, Pink Pineapple. 30 mins. x 2 eps.

Lust and forbidden fruits at an all-girls school, as a beautiful female agent poses as a researcher at the Nobel Academy only to become the victim of a cavalcade of rape, bondage, and sexual abuse. Based on a Japanese PC game with publicity about particularly unpleasant scenes of sex and violence—supposedly strong even by the standards of Japanese pornography. **NV**

AKIRA *

1988. Movie. DIR: Katsuhiro Otomo. SCR: Katsuhiro Otomo, Izo Hashimoto. DES: Toshiharu Mizutani. ANI: Takashi Nakamura. MUS: Geino Yamashiro. PRD: Akira Committee, Mash Room, Toho, Hakuhodo, TMS. 124 mins.

In 2019, Tokyo has been rebuilt after World War III. As the city prepares to host the Olympics, it is rocked by antigovernment terrorism secretly organized by power-brokering politician Nezu. Juvenile delinquent Tetsuo is out racing against a rival gang when he crashes his bike into a child with the face of an old man. He is swiftly taken away by the military, while his friend Kaneda allies with a cell of the terrorists to track him down. Tetsuo begins to develop psychic powers and discovers that he is just one of many experimental subjects in a secret government program to replicate Akira, the human bioweapon that obliterated Tokyo in 1988. Tetsuo escapes to the Olympic stadium, where the remains of Akira are kept in a hidden chamber. Losing control of his powers and absorbing several of his colleagues, Tetsuo causes the return of Akira and a second destruction of Tokyo. Kaneda is one of the survivors, while Tetsuo absconds to create his own universe.

Adapted from the early part of the long-running manga by director Otomo, *Akira* is almost singlehandedly responsible for the early 1990s boom in anime in the English language.

Echoes of the seminal *Blade Runner* are undeniable (the film is even set in the same year), but *Akira* owes less to an alleged "cyberpunk" sensibility than it does to the young Otomo's perspective on 1960s counterculture—rioting students, crazed biker gangs, and corporate intrigue. The military conspiracy in *Akira* carries elements of the 1963 live-action film *Japan's Longest Day*, while other themes include the wartime Unit 731 human guinea pigs and nuclear contamination covered more directly in **BAREFOOT GEN**. Even the Olympic stadium is a historical marker—Tokyo was due to host the games in 1940 but only got to do so after postwar reconstruction in 1964. In many ways, *Akira* is also a retelling of Otomo's *Fireball*, an unfinished 1979 story about scientists fighting terrorists for control of an apocalyptic energy source.

Akira was a visual tour-de-force, including experiments in digital and analog animation that were to stun audiences worldwide, enjoying greater success abroad than in its country of origin. With a production budget that ran wildly out of control, it was defeated by its very success—few of its lower-budget imitators compare favorably and Western distributors have difficulty replicating its success. Otomo became the first "name" in Japanese animation abroad, but he is not *of* the anime industry. His output has been comparably tiny, even when one includes (much to the annoyance of his collaborators) those films in which his role has been negligible, such as **PERFECT BLUE**. After *Akira*, he made the live-action *World Apartment Horror* (1990) on a shoestring, wrote the script for **ROUJIN Z**, shared the **MEMORIES** anthology with two other directors, and provided designs for **SPRIGGAN**. A decade after *Akira*, he announced he would direct another feature-length anime, the Victorian SF thriller *Steam Boy*, though the production has since been delayed for years. In 2001, *Akira* was rereleased with a new dub, closer in meaning and tone to the original Japanese version. *Ill. p. 287.* **V**

ALADDIN AND THE WONDERFUL LAMP *

1982. JPN: *Aladdin to Maho no Lamp.* AKA: *Aladdin and the Magic Lamp.* Movie. DIR: Yoshinori Kasai. SCR: Akira Miyazaki. DES: Dale Baer, Jane Baer, Shinya Takahashi. ANI: Shinya Takahashi. MUS: Yukihide Takekawa, Godiego. PRD: Toei, Rankin-Bass. 65 mins.

Aladdin is a poor Arab boy asked by a mysterious stranger (an evil wizard) to help him retrieve an old lamp from an underground cavern. The wizard traps Aladdin in the cavern, but he accidentally releases a jinni from a magic ring and makes a wish to escape. When Aladdin tries to clean up the old lamp, a second jinni appears to grant him unlimited wishes. Aladdin falls in love with the sultan's daughter, Badraul, and uses the Slave of the Lamp to disguise himself as a rich prince. However, the wizard gains possession of the lamp and orders the jinni to transport the princess inside Aladdin's new palace to his own home in Africa. The angry sultan gives Aladdin three days to return her. The Slave of the Ring dies in the initial assault on the African palace, and Aladdin and Badraul must use their own wits to defeat the wizard.

There have been many all-Japanese productions spun off from ARABIAN NIGHTS, but in this case the Baers, former staffers on Disney's *Snow White*, contributed to a Rankin-Bass coproduction that also featured music from Godiego, best known outside Japan for the unforgettable theme tune to the *Monkey* series. The story would be revisited in 1993 in the Sanrio PEKKLE video *Aladdin and the Magic Lamp*. In 1995, several Japanese animators would also work on the Disney *Aladdin* TV series—enough to qualify it as an anime coproduction in some sources.

ALEXANDER *

1999. JPN: *Alexander Senki.* AKA: *Alexander War Chronicle.* TV series. DIR: Yoshinori Kanemori. SCR: Sadayuki Murai. DES: Peter Chung. ANI: N/C. MUS: Ken Ishii, Haruomi Hosono, Inheil. PRD: Madhouse, WOWOW. 25 mins. x 13 eps.

In the midst of a bitter war, King Philip's wife, Olympias, gives birth to a son, Alexander. Reared amid intrigue in the palace, he proves himself on the battlefield at Chaeronia at the age of 16. After his father's death under mysterious circumstances, Alexander declares war on Darius III of Persia and goes on to become master of the known universe.

Despite its sci-fi sheen, this is a surprisingly faithful retelling of the life of Alexander the Great based on a novel by DOOMED MEGALOPOLIS–creator Hiroshi Aramata. Featuring a techno-magic based on Pythagorean solids and vast alien armies, it bears more resemblance to *Dune* or *Stargate* than a classical biopic. Character designs from the Korean-born Chung contain echoes of his work on *Aeon Flux*, and some of the visual conceits (such as a swimming pool in the shape of the Mediterranean) are simply superb. The historical Alexander is known in the Middle East as "Iscander," a name appropriated for STAR BLAZERS.

ALIBABA'S REVENGE *

1971. JPN: *Alibaba to Yonjubiki no Tozoku.* AKA: *Alibaba and the Forty Thieves.* Movie. DIR: Hiroshi Shidara. SCR: Motohisa Yamamoto. DES: Reiko Okuyama, Katsuya Koda. ANI: Hideki Mori, Hayao Miyazaki, Yoichi Otabe, Yasuji Mori. MUS: Seiichiro Uno. PRD: Toei. 55 mins.

Alibaba became rich by defeating the 40 thieves. Now his distant descendant Alibaba XXXIII has inherited the fiefdom and become the worst sultan in history, squandering his ancestor's wealth and the good will of the jinni of the lamp. Al Haq, descendant of the original leader of the thieves, is a good honest boy who resolves to get back his father's fortune, enlisting the aid of 38 cats and a lone mouse. Another of the many anime loosely based on ARABIAN NIGHTS, this short film featured Hayao Miyazaki as a key animator and a flashback sequence using nothing but shadow puppetry. It was not, however, the first anime adaptation of the story—that honor goes to Takeo Ueno's 17-minute EARLY ANIME *The 40 Thieves* (1928).

ALICE IN CYBERLAND

1996. Video. DIR: Kazuyoshi Yokota. SCR: Chiaki Konaka. DES: Daisuke Moriyama. ANI: Fumio Shimazu. MUS: N/C. PRD: Warner Vision Japan, Bandai. 28 mins. x 2 eps.

Fourteen-year-old Alice Rena is a 21st-century schoolgirl from Miskatonic College who is dragged into Cyberland, the computer network that connects vast Data Colonies of information. She and her friends are mistresses of the Dive System that allows them to access the treasures within, but all hell breaks loose when one of them falls in love with the prince who rules Cyberland.

A curio dashed off to cash in on a PlayStation game, released along with a radio drama and a PC version of the original, *AiC* mixes various parts of Lewis Carroll's original with large chunks of *Tron*, courtesy of writer Chiaki Konaka, who used cyberspace for more dramatic purposes in SERIAL EXPERIMENTS LAIN. Konaka's love of H. P. Lovecraft, as shown in the name "Miskatonic," would reappear in ARMITAGE III.

ALICE IN WONDERLAND

1983. JPN: *Fushigina Kuni no Alice.* AKA: *Alice in the Mysterious Kingdom.* TV series. DIR: Taku Sugiyama. SCR: Fumi Takahashi. DES: Yu Noda. ANI: Yu Kumada, Takao Kogawa. MUS: Reijiro Komutsu. PRD: Apollo, Nippon Animation, TV Tokyo. 30 mins. x 26 eps.

One fine summer's day, the seven-year-old Alice chases a white rabbit down a hole and finds herself in the underground kingdom of Wonderland. Spending 13 episodes each on *Alice in Wonderland* and its sequel, *Alice through the Looking Glass*, this series ran through all the high points of Lewis Carroll's original stories, though the final two parts were only broadcast in the Tokyo area. To see the series in its entirety, you had to go to Germany, a major financial contributor to this coproduction. In the Japanese version, Alice was played by Tarako, the voice actress behind another children's favorite, CHIBI MARUKO-CHAN. Masako Nozawa, who provided the voice of the white rabbit, went on to play Son Goku in DRAGON BALL.

In 1998, an unofficial sequel by Ryo Nakahara was adapted by director Shingo Kaneko into the 14-episode *Alice SOS*, which featured further adventures in Dinosaur-land, Cookery-land, Topsy-turvy-land, Cactus-land, Bully-land, Salad-land, Edo-land (old-fashioned Tokyo), God-land, Ghost-land, Backward-land, Santa-land, TV-land, and Devil-land. A far naughtier pastiche was CLAMP's 1995 MIYUKI-CHAN IN WONDERLAND. See also VIDEO PICTURE BOOK.

ALIEN FROM THE DARKNESS *

1996. JPN: *Inju Alien.* AKA: *Lust Alien.* Video. DIR: Norio Takanami. SCR: N/C. DES: Ryu Tsukiyo. ANI: Shin Taira. MUS: N/C. PRD: Pink Pineapple, (KIT). 45 mins.

Sci-fi porn in the spirit of ADVANCER TINA, heavily influenced by the *Alien* films. On their way back from a mining trip to the planet Kerun, the all-female crew of the starship Muze find a vessel drifting in space. The derelict Zogne, carrying an illegal cargo of the narcotic Metrogria, is scattered with naked corpses. The sole survivor, a beautiful girl called Flair, claims to have amnesia. As the Muze continues on its way, the same fate starts to befall members of the crew, and lone scientist Hikari trawls through the Zogne's records in an attempt to stop the carnage. Needless to say, it involves an alien monster that consists of little more than tentacles and a permanent craving for female flesh. ●◐◑

ALIEN 9

2001. Video. DIR: Jiro Fujimoto. SCR: Sadayuki Murai. DES: Yasuhiro Irie. ANI: Yasuhiro Irie. MUS: N/C. PRD: Genco, JC

Staff. 30 mins. x 4 eps.
In 2016, the very reluctant Kasumi Tomine, Kumi Kawamura, and Yuri Otani are picked as Alien Monitors at their Japanese school, in charge of cleaning up the various kinds of messes caused by unwelcome pests. A right-wing POKÉMON, perhaps?

AMAZING NURSE NANAKO *

1999. JPN: *Nanako Kaitai Shinsho.* AKA: *Nanako's Medical Report.* TV series. DIR: Hiroshi Negishi. SCR: Rasputin Yano. DES: Toshinari Yamashita. ANI: Toshinari Yamashita, Kazuya Miura. MUS: Takahiro Negishi. PRD: Save Our Nurse Project, Genco, Pioneer. 30 mins. x 5 eps.

This strange hybrid of 1980s techno-thriller and 1990s geek-meets-girl comedy begins with a pastiche of GHOST IN THE SHELL's copious computer graphics, as brilliant research scientists construct the humanoid superweapon Venus 2000. But Venus is missing a brain, and Dr. Kyoji Ogami decides that he will put the finishing touches on the project by "borrowing" the brain of his large-breasted maid, Nanako. After all, he reasons, it's not like *she* uses it for anything.

Nanako is a bouncy ingenue baffled by the attention of the world's military—as a violent conspiracy unfolds around her, she frets about cooking and underwear, creating a saucy if puerile antidote to the deadly serious EVANGELION and its clones. Those seeking stranger comparisons should note that CATGIRL NUKUNUKU features a girl who has had a small mammal's brain carefully inserted into her skull, whereas the plot of *Amazing Nurse Nanako* involves a concerted attempt to remove one.

AMAZING 3, THE *

1965. JPN: *Wonder Three.* AKA: *W3.* TV series. DIR: Taku Sugiyama, Osamu Tezuka, Ryosuke Takahashi. SCR: Ichiro Wakabayashi, Osamu Tezuka, Sadao Tsukioka, Kunihiko Yamazaki. DES: Osamu Tezuka. ANI: Kazuko Nakamura. MUS: Tatsu Kawai. PRD: Mushi Pro, Fuji

Bigger than big, quicker than quick, and ready to fight for right, against wrong. GIGANTOR "the space-age robot" was an attempt to grapple with Japan's wartime past in a modern context. Only a child born after the war can save the nation from its past misdeeds, which return in the form of military prototypes in the hands of criminals. *See entry p. 143.*

Gigantor

© 1964 DELPHI ASSOCIATES INC. © 1992 ENTERCOLOR TECHNOLOGIES CO.

TV. 25 mins. x 52 eps.
The Galactic Alliance sends three secret agents to Earth with orders to destroy it if the planet's warmongering attitude presents a danger. Masquerading as farmyard animals, Major Boko (Bonnie Bunny), Lieutenant JG Poko (Zero Duck), and Lance Corporal Noko (Ronnie Horse) are discovered by young Shinichi Hoshi (Kenny Carter). The younger brother of international crime fighter Koichi (Randy), Shinichi convinces them to help make the world a better place and to give secret aid to Koichi's Phoenix organization, a group whose aims are approximately equivalent to their own. Based on Osamu Tezuka's 1965 manga in *Shonen Magazine*, this minor series was also adapted for the U.S. market. Tezuka reused similar ideas in BREMEN FOUR.

AMBASSADOR MAGMA *

1993. JPN: *Magma Taishi.* Video. DIR: Hidehito Ueda. SCR: Katsuhiko Koide. DES: Kazuhiko Udagawa. ANI: Kazuhiko Udagawa. MUS: Toshiyuki Watanabe. PRD: Tezuka Pro, Bandai Visual, Plex. 25 mins. x 13 eps.

Long ago, the evil Goa was defeated by the golden giant robot Magma, created to defend this planet and its people.

Now the two warriors are locked in a deep slumber, while on Earth the descendants of the Asuka family are guardians of their spirits. Fumiaki Asuka is kidnapped by aliens and used to awaken Goa. Schoolgirl Miki, the link to Magma, is forced to flee and takes refuge with the Murakami family. Mamoru Murakami meets with the protecting spirit of our planet, who calls himself "Earth," and is drawn into the battle between good and evil, becoming the one who can summon Magma with a magical golden whistle. Based on a minor manga by **ASTRO BOY**–creator Osamu Tezuka, *Ambassador Magma* was one of several projects, along with *Zero Man* and *No Man*, that only reached the pilot stage during their creator's lifetime. When Tezuka failed to sell *AM* as anime, he allowed the company P Pro to make it as a live-action series instead—the poor-quality 1966 52-episode rubber-monster show eventually released in the U.S. as *Space Giants*.

It was only much later, as Tezuka's estate embarked upon a long and ongoing project to adapt all of his works for a new generation, that the series finally got an anime release, deliberately made in the blocky, old-fashioned 1950s style of the original, even so far as using the original artwork in the closing credits screened over an impossibly peppy martial theme. The show itself is never quite as interesting as it could be, alternating between scenes that are too childish to be engrossing and too hard-hitting to be suitable for young children. Despite its camp villains, the story has its scary moments—and is simply bursting with ideas and relationships that *The X-Files* later reprised, such as covert alien takeovers, human sleeper-agents, and time disturbances.

AMON SAGA *

1986. Video. DIR: Yoshikazu Oga. SCR: Noboru Shiroyama. DES: Shingo Araki, Michi Himeno. ANI: Shingo Araki. MUS: Shigeaya Saegusa. PRD: Centre, Toku-ma, Yumemakura, Ten Pro, TMS. 72 mins.

Amon's family is destroyed and his country conquered by the evil Valhiss. Befriending Gaius the giant, Amon joins forces with a number of disgruntled individuals to attack Valhiss's capital city, which is located on the back of a giant turtle. While sneaking into the city, Amon meets and falls in love with the beautiful hostage, Princess Lichia. Captured and thrown into the dungeons to be devoured by Valhiss's savage pet, Amon escapes while one of his companions rescues the princess, only for her to be recaptured when their camp is attacked by werewolves. The final battle is on to defeat Valhiss, avenge Amon's parents, and rescue his love.

Not to be confused with the similarly named **DEVILMAN** sequel, this video was also shown in theaters on a double bill with **BELOVED BETTY**. The manga in *Ryu* magazine was written by Baku Yumemakura and is the only one ever drawn by Yoshitaka Amano, who, dissatisfied with the manga medium, soon returned to straightforward illustration.

ANGEL *

1990. Movie. DIR: Hideki Takayama, Hiromitsu Taida, Kaoru Toyooka. SCR: Wataru Amano, Koji Sakakibara. DES: Rin Shin. ANI: Osamu Tsuruyama, Mitsuru Fujii, Masato Ijuin. MUS: N/C. PRD: Studio Angel, Pink Pineapple. 45 mins. x 2 eps., 30 mins. x 4 eps.

The adventures of Keisuke, a sex-obsessed college boy who's always ready to help damsels in distress, just so long as he gets something special in return. Cue a succession of short stories in which a young, often nameless female comes to him with a problem; he sorts it out, then sorts *her* out.

U-jin is the pseudonymous artist who was made famous in Japan by the efforts of the Association to Protect Children from Comics to have his *Young Sunday* comic *Angel* banned. The video versions of his hard-core comics are not quite as explicit as the originals but are still pretty eyebrow-raising. The original *Angel* video was followed in 1994 by five volumes of *New Angel*, though the running time soon was cut to a mere two-thirds of its former size. The U.S. distributor has made it available in both uncut and edited editions, though your guess is as good as ours as to who would want to watch a porno movie with the porno taken out. Similar erotic stories from the same author can be found in **U-JIN BRAND** and the **TALES OF . . .** series. Ⓝ

ANGEL COP *

1989. Video. DIR: Ichiro Itano. SCR: Noboru Aikawa. DES: Nobuteru Yuki. ANI: Yasuomi Umezu, Satoru Nakamura, Hideki Takayama, Hiroyuki Ochi. MUS: Hiroshi Ogasawara. PRD: Studio 88, DAST, Soeishinsha, Japan Home Video. 30 mins. x 6 eps.

At the close of the 20th century, Japan forms a Special Security force to protect it from foreign terrorists like the fanatical Red May. Angel, the newest officer, loses her partner, Raiden, to psychic vigilantes and suspects that she has more to fear from a secret government cybernetics project than from left-wing activists. Soon all hell breaks loose, as cyborgs and psychics fight for access to the secrets of the mysterious "H-File."

Consisting of long fight scenes stitched together by ham-fisted expository soliloquies, *Angel Cop* wastes loving detail on weapons and machinery but leaves its characters shallow and uninteresting. A nasty bloodbath from **VIOLENCE JACK**–director Ichiro Itano, it fails despite a crew of great talents who would go on to work on **ESCAFLOWNE**, **ARMITAGE III**, and, admittedly, the equally soulless **KITE**.

The original creator, Taku Kitazaki, was only 17 when he sold his first story, shooting to fame thanks to his works' resemblance to flavor-of-the-moment **AKIRA**. As one might expect from the creator whose publications include *War Story Busty*, *Angel Cop* is aimed squarely at the lowest common denominator. Different arms of the military show off their hardware and are then trashed by psionic supersoldiers, while a mad scientist cackles . . . madly. The final showdown is against Lucifer, a glacial blonde seemingly modeled on Brigitte Nielsen, in whose bone-crunching defeat the good guys take an ethnically suspect pleasure—a few of their antiforeign quips have survived the English-language dub, though the original Japanese script is far more antiAmerican and antiSemite throughout. There is, however, an ironic happy ending; by the time *Angel Cop* was made, its 23-year-old creator had already tired of the genre and moved into gentle romance with *Like This Love Song*. **LNV**

ANGEL LEGEND
1996. JPN: *Angel Densetsu*. Video. DIR: Tatsuo Misawa. SCR: Naoyuki Sakai. DES: Nobuyoshi Ito. ANI: Nobuyoshi Ito. MUS: Jun Sky Walkers. PRD: Toei. 45 mins.
New kid in town Shinichiro Kitano is a noble, sensitive boy with "the face of a devil and the kindness of an angel." Pushed into a world of drugs and crime simply because of the way he looks, he tries to make the world a better place without fighting, eventually becoming the leader of the local gang. This adaptation of Norihiro Yagi's manga from *Shonen Jump* only lasted for a single episode—at the time it was released, Japan was obsessed with more compelling "angels" in EVANGELION. **V**

ANGEL LINKS *
1999. JPN: *Seiho Tenshi Angel Links*. AKA: *Stellar Angel Angel Links*. TV series. DIR: Yoshikazu Yamaguchi. SCR: Masaharu Amiya. DES: Asako Nishida, Rei Nakahara. ANI: Hiroyuki Hataike. MUS: N/C. PRD: Sunrise, WOWOW. 25 mins. x 13 eps.
Orphaned 16-year-old Li Mei-Feng inherits the family business from her grandfather, Jian-He—it's the private police franchise for an entire solar system that's simply crawling with pirates. Refusing to be scared away, Mei-Feng assembles the Angel Links team of

troubleshooters, including a weapons expert and the last survivor of a race of dinosaur vegetarians, and sets out to bring the system under the rule of law. A spinoff from Takehiko Ito's OUTLAW STAR, replaying the mood, look, and staff.

ANGEL OF DARKNESS *
1995. JPN: *Inju Kyoshi*. AKA: *Lustful-Beast Teacher*. Video. DIR: Kazuma Muraki, Suzunari Joban. SCR: Yukihiro Kosaka. DES: Kazunori Iwakura, Yuji Ikeda. ANI: Kazunori Iwakura. MUS: Takeo Nakazawa. PRD: Pink Pineapple. 45 mins. x 4 eps.
In a typical girls' boarding school, Atsuko and Sayaka manage to fit in a lesbian affair around their class schedule without too much trouble. But when one of their teachers digs up an ancient artifact and releases a demonic entity, things get a bit more hectic. The entity needs to be fed a steady supply of nubile young women to keep itself alive and build the new form it needs to take over the world (the ancient spirits of Earth oppose this, or would if any of them were more than nine inches high). With the help of an elf who fits in her handbag, Sayaka sets out to save her girlfriend and classmates from a fate worse than death and foil the threat to the world, though similar events wreak havoc in other schools, with the same basic setup and conclusion. Much ripping of underwear, bondage, "comical" characters like the Kuroko from UROTSUKIDO-JI, and sexualized violence to match. The four episodes were also filmed as live-action movies in 1995–96 directed by Mitsunori Hattori and Koji Shimizu. **LNV**

ANGEL SANCTUARY *
2000. JPN: *Tenshi Kinryoku*. Video. DIR: Seiko Sayama. SCR: Mayori Sekijima. DES: Hidekazu Shimamura. ANI: Hidekazu Shimamura. MUS: Hikaru Nanase. PRD: Bandai. 30 mins. x 3 eps.
As a punishment for defying God Almighty and fighting against the

legions of Heaven (led by her brother, Razael), the soul of the fallen angel Alexael is imprisoned in a crystal, doomed to be forever reincarnated as a human being who will die a young and violent death. Born into the body of *male* juvenile delinquent Setsuna Mudo, Alexael realizes that God is dead and the world is ending, just as foretold in the Black Book of Revelation. S/he is the long-awaited Messiah but would rather seduce his/her sister than take up arms in the final battle between Heaven and Hell. Based on the manga by Kaori Yuki, *AS* tries but fails to cram the original story line into three tiny episodes, reducing Yuki's carefully paced original into a mad rush of revelations. Compare to other apocalyptic tales of androgynous young men pouting sulkily, such as X: THE MOVIE and EARTHIAN.

ANGELIC LAYER
2001. TV series. DIR: Hiroshi Nishigori. SCR: Kazushi Okawanai, Reiko Yoshida, Akihiko Inari. DES: Takahiro Omori, CLAMP. ANI: Koichi Horikawa. MUS: N/C. PRD: Bones, TV Tokyo. 25 mins. x 26 eps.
Diminutive junior high-school girl Misaki Suzuhara is separated from her mother at an early age. When her father dies, she must move from her home in Wakayama to her aunt's house in Tokyo. There, she becomes intrigued by the Angel dolls, customizable dolls with "micro-actuator" controls, which are hatched from eggs and appear to be fully alive. The Angels are controlled by their owner's willpower but can only move within the "Layer" battle arena. Misaki gets an Angel called Hikaru, and their battles begin. This anime based on a *Shonen Ace* manga by CARD CAPTORS–creators CLAMP has all the appearance of a game tie-in, just without a real game to tie into.

ANGELIQUE
2000. Video. DIR: Akira Kiyomizu. SCR: Midori Kusada. DES: Kairi Yusa. ANI: Masanori Fujioka. MUS: N/C. PRD: Yumeta Company. 30 mins.

Angelique, Rachael, and Rosaria are three of the nine guardian angels, members of a secret sect called Alios, whose job it is to protect mere mortals from ruining their lives. Angelique is also destined to be the future queen of the universe, which may be why sweet-talking Osaka charmer Charlie is so keen on her. The events of the anime take place a little after *Requiem for the Sky*, the computer game that spawned it.

ANGEL'S EGG *

1985. JPN: *Tenshi no Tamago*. Movie. DIR: Mamoru Oshii. SCR: Mamoru Oshii. DES: Yoshitaka Amano. ANI: Yasuhiro Yukura. MUS: Yuhiro Kanno. PRD: Studio Deen, Tokuma Shoten, Tokuma Japan. 108 mins.

In a timeless, placeless everytown, a boy with a crucifix arrives and meets the sole inhabitant, a young girl. She shows him her most treasured posses-sion, a magical egg, which she believes will hatch one day. When the girl is asleep, the boy smashes the egg open but finds that it contains nothing. The girl dies and the boy heads off alone.

Plotless and highly symbolic with hardly any dialogue, reputedly a stream-of-consciousness exercise by PATLABOR–director Oshii, the film fea-tures his trademark Christian imagery and an inexplicable passage through the town of soldiers with motorized artillery. Surreal elements recall Oshii's work on URUSEI YATSURA, including spaceships full of silent people bearing other eggs and even shadows of fish that swim through the air in the city streets. The animation and design, incorporating work from 1001 NIGHTS–creator and illustrator Amano, is beautifully executed. Parts of the film were plundered for interstitial footage in Carl Colpaert's live-action film *In the Aftermath* (1988).

ANIMAL 1

1968. TV series. DIR: Taku Sugiyama, Yoshiyuki Tomino, Ryosuke Takahashi. SCR: Tadaaki Yamazaki, Shunichi Yukimuro, Masaki Tsuji. DES: Noboru Kawasaki. ANI: Sadao Miyamoto. MUS: Hiroki Takaragi. PRD: Mushi Pro, Fuji TV. 30 mins. x 27 eps.

The seven Azuma brothers have all been raised as fighters by their long-shoreman father. Sent to a new school when the family moves, Ichiro Azuma becomes a great success in the wrestling club. As his prowess gains greater fame, he is soon known as "Ani-mal 1," as you might expect from some-one who's had to fight over the bathroom with six siblings. Based on the true story of Ichiro Azuma, who represented Japan in the 1960 Mexico Olympics, this series about a gold medalist only won silver in the race to become the first sports anime—STAR OF THE GIANTS beat it onto the screens by just a month. Noboru Kawasaki, who created *both* stories, would also supply the original manga for SONG OF THE LADYBUGS. This tale of true-life wrestling included early directorial credits for two future specialists in giant-robot combat, GUNDAM's Tomino and VOTOMS' Takahashi.

ANIMATED CLASSICS OF JAPANESE LITERATURE *

1986. JPN: *Seishun Anime Zenshu*. AKA: *Youth Anime Compendium*. TV series. DIR: Fumio Kurokawa, Akiko Matsushi-ma, Noboru Ishiguro, Eiji Okabe, Isamu Kumada, Hidehito Ueda. SCR: Kenji Yoshida, Shizuo Kuriyama, Haruhiko Mimura, Ryuzo Nakanishi. DES: Hiroshi Motomiya, Tetsuya Chiba, Shotaro Ishi-nomori, Osamu Komori, Hiromitsu Morita. ANI: Yoshio Kabashima. MUS: Koichi Sakata, Hideo Shimazu, Junno-suke Yamamoto. PRD: Nippon Anima-tion, Nippon TV. 30 mins. x 37 eps.

Few Japanese classics make it to the screen in an anime industry obsessed with spectacle and entertainment. This series made some small attempt to redress the balance, adapting some of Japan's most famous stories, including works by Eiko Tanaka, Yasunari Kawa-bata, Shintaro Ishihara, Masao Kume, Sachio Ito, Yasushi Inoue, and Jiro Akagawa.

As one might expect, a nation's liter-ature is not readily sawed into bite-sized chunks for digestion on prime-time TV, and the selections are often arguably off-base. The collection does best with punchy short stories like Junichiro Tanizaki's *Tale of Shunkin*. Longer works often suffer through drastic cutting (Shiro Ozaki's *Theater of Life* is condensed from 530 pages to less than 30 minutes), censorious edit-ing (the prostitution subplot is removed completely from Ogai Mori's *Dancing Girl*), or sloppy translation (the English version makes several silly errors, and explanatory liner notes are unforgivably absent from the video release). The choices for adaptation also seem haphazard or overly conser-vative. It's difficult, for example, to think of something *less* representative of Yukio Mishima than *The Sound of Waves*, and there are duplicates of BOTCHAN and SANSHIRO SUGATA, while THE TALE OF GENJI, HAKKENDEN, and THE SENSUALIST are conspicuously absent. The collection also includes a story by "Koizumi Yakumo" without revealing he was the foreign-born author Lafcadio Hearn. But although this story is not Japanese, others debat-ably "classic" and occasionally barely "animated," it is still a noble failure in its attempt to get couch-potato chil-dren interested in real books. Two episodes, adaptations of Masao Kume's *Student Days* and Musanokoji Saneatsu's *The Friend Who Didn't Believe in Friend-ship*, were not broadcast, appearing instead as two "specials" on TV Asahi the following year. *Ills. pp. 19, 169.*

ANIMENTARY: CRITICAL MOMENTS

1971. JPN: *Animentary: Ketsudan*. TV series. DIR: Fumio Kurokawa, Ip-pei Kuri, Hideo Makino. SCR: Junzo Toriumi. DES: Tatsuo Yoshida. ANI: Sa-dao Miyamoto, Tsutomu Shibayama, Yoshiyuki Tomino, Ryosuke Taka-hashi. MUS: Nobuyoshi Koshibe. PRD: Tatsunoko, Nippon TV. 30 mins. x 26 eps.

This *Anim[ated Docum]entary* details the

various critical moments that brought Japan into World War II and eventually caused the country's defeat, including the battles over Pearl Harbor, Midway, Malaysia, Singapore, Hong Kong, the Philippines, Java, Corregidor, Bataan, the Solomon Islands, Rabaul, and Leyte. The story concentrates chiefly on Isoroku Yamamoto, the "reluctant admiral" who urged his superiors not to declare war on the U.S. but was eventually given command of the fleet that bombed Pearl Harbor. A more dramatic look at some of the same events can be found in Leiji Matsumoto's **COCKPIT**, and the logical conclusion of the "what ifs" implicit in *Animentary* gets an airing in the alternate-universe **DEEP BLUE FLEET**, in which Japan gets to replay World War II and win it.

ANNE OF GREEN GABLES

1979. JPN: *Akage no Anne.* AKA: *Red-Haired Anne.* TV series. DIR: Isao Takahata. SCR: Shigeki Chiba, Aiko Isomura, Isao Takahata. DES: Yoshifumi Kondo. ANI: Yoshifumi Kondo. MUS: Kurodo Mori. PRD: Nippon Animation, Fuji TV. 30 mins. x 50 eps.

Green Gables is the house in Avonlea village on Prince Edward Island in early 20th-century Canada where childless brother and sister Matthew and Marilla bring an 11-year-old orphan, Anne, to live. Though there is some confusion when Anne turns out not to be the strapping male farmhand they were hoping for, she soon makes friends with local girl Diana, and the pair begin a happy, if somewhat tedious, rural existence.

Based on Lucy Maude Montgomery's book, this entry in the **WORLD MASTERPIECE THEATER** series was directed by **GRAVE OF THE FIREFLIES**' Takahata and featured animation from **WHISPER OF THE HEART**'s Kondo. The earlier part of the series contained layouts by Takahata's famous cohort Hayao Miyazaki, although after episode 16 he left to make **CASTLE OF CAGLIOSTRO**.

ANPANMAN

1988. JPN: *Sore Ike! Anpanman.* AKA: *Go for It! Anpanman.* TV series. DIR: Akinori Nagaoka. SCR: Ayako Okina, Jiro Nakajima, Osamu Nakamura. DES: Michishiro Yamada. ANI: Minoru Maeda. MUS: Taku Izumi. PRD: TMS, Nippon TV. 30 mins. x 500+ eps.

A superhero constructed from bean paste by the kindly Uncle Jam, Anpanman fights for justice alongside his ethnically diverse cohorts White-Breadman, Curry-Breadman, and Cheese the Wonderdog against the dirt-obsessed Germ-man.

RINGING BELL and **LITTLE JUMBO**–creator Takashi Yanase's original illustrations for the Japanese chain-store Froebel Kan took 15 years to reach the screen, transforming into stories in publications such as *Mommy, New Baby,* and *Baby Book.* Regularly restored to life through the simple act of getting a new head from the saintly Uncle Jam, Anpanman gives those he rescues something special to remember him by—a piece of his own head for them to eat. This trick has proved to be immensely popular, especially with parents encouraging children to finish their breakfast (although what damage the concept of consuming one's playmates has done to a generation of Japanese, only time will tell). The TV series has also spun off into several short theatrical outings, including *The Disappearance of Uncle Jam, Anpanman in the South Seas, The Secret of Breadrollman,* and *Christmas with the Meringue Sisters.* The twelfth and most recent was *Anpanman and the Mermaid's Tears* (2000), a **LITTLE MERMAID** spoof in which he helps the sea-dwelling Sunny in her quest to become human.

Yanase would also try to duplicate the success of Anpanman with another food-related superhero. *Riceball-man* (1990, *Omusubiman*) was a 27-minute theatrical short featuring a samurai snack, but it could not compete with its bun-headed predecessor.

ANTIQUE HEART

1988. JPN: *Antique Heart: Gakuen Ben-*

Superhero **CUTEY HONEY** doing what she does best—fighting off a bad guy while displaying ample cleavage. Rushed onto television less than a year after her first appearance in manga form, *CH* was the first anime heroine to have a nude transformation sequence. Though controversial at the time, such moments of bare flesh have become relatively commonplace, even in mainstream shows. Loaded, like **DIRTY PAIR**, with wrestling in-jokes, the show featured real women's wrestling stars in voice cameos. *See entry p. 75.*

Cutey Honey

© 1996 GO NAGAI/DYNAMIC PLANNING/TOEI VIDEO CO., LTD.

riya Series. AKA: *Antique Heart: School Handyman Series.* Video. DIR: Chuichi Watanabe. SCR: Asami Watanabe. DES: Minoru Yamazawa. ANI: Takumi Tsukasa. MUS: N/C. PRD: Animate Film. 40 mins.

In this short-lived adaptation of a long-running series from *Wings* magazine, three intrepid school investigators track down ghosts in the restroom, anonymous love letters, and any other mystery they can find. Intended to be the first of a series, this video was ten years too early. The concept of supernatural schools would return in the 1990s with the successful **REAL SCHOOL GHOST STORIES**, **HERE COMES HANAKO**, and **HAUNTED JUNCTION**.

APOCALYPSE ZERO *

1996. JPN: *Kakugo no Susume.* AKA: *Onward Kakugo.* Video. DIR: Toshihiro Hirano. SCR: Akiyoshi Sakai. DES: Keisuke Watanabe. ANI: Keisuke Watanabe, Toshihiro Yamane. MUS: Takashi Kudo. PRD: Ashi. 45 mins. x 2 eps.

On a postapocalyptic Earth prey to monsters, Kakugo and Harara Hagakure have been trained by their father in the ancient Zero fighting technique to protect the last remnants of humanity. Paramount in their arsenal is the Tactical Zero armor, a fighting suit charged with the souls of ancient heroes. But Harara turns to the dark side, killing his father and creating the new Tactical Evils. Left for dead, Kakugo reaches a ruined town and offers to help the few human inhabitants protect themselves from cannibals and depraved mutants. Meeting once again with his insane sister, he fights to save the world in this gory adaptation of Takayuki Yamaguchi's *Shonen Champion* manga. Though *AZ* contains veiled allusions to honor and tradition (the siblings' surname is a famous samurai manual), it has more in common with the mutant maulings of FIST OF THE NORTH STAR. ◑

APPLELAND STORY

1992. JPN: *Appleland Monogatari.* Video. DIR: Kunihiko Yuyama. SCR: Atsushi Takegami. DES: Minoru Yamazawa, Keiko Fukuyama. ANI: Minoru Yamazawa. MUS: Morgan Fisher. PRD: JC Staff. 45 mins. x 2.
On the eve of World War I, Vale Sibelius is a young orphan pickpocket in Appleland, a central European state that could be an important prize in the coming conflict. He befriends Frida, a girl with the secret of a new weapon that could decide the country's future, and the two go on the run from the evil East European duo, Aryana and Attila. Based on a novel from Yoshiki Tanaka, the prolific creator of LEGEND OF GALACTIC HEROES.

APPLESEED *

1988. Video. DIR: Kazuyoshi Katayama. SCR: Kazuyoshi Katayama. DES: Yumiko Horasawa, Takahiro Kishida, Hideaki Anno. ANI: Yumiko Horasawa. MUS: Norimasa Yamanaka. PRD: Gainax, AIC. 70 mins.
In an authoritarian utopia, humanity has handed the reins of power to super-capable robots. But the suicide rate goes up mostly among people from the wastelands outside the city; rehabilitated and brought back to civilization they are unable to cope with paradise.

As the first scene (a suicide freeing her pet before she jumps) makes clear, the inhabitants of Olympus are no freer than birds in golden cages, and a group of human beings (led, in a typical touch of Masamune Shirow irony, by a cyborg) organize a revolt to seize the city back from the robots. Working for the benevolent dictator, Athena, human SWAT team leader Deunan Knute attempts to foil the terrorists before it is too late.

This adaptation of Shirow's best-selling manga was adequate for its time but was soon eclipsed by AKIRA, which permanently raised the stakes on high-quality sci-fi. The next Shirow anime, GHOST IN THE SHELL, had a far higher budget—ironically, the straight-to-video *Appleseed* was often shown in foreign theaters in unfair competition with its richer, better-endowed cousin.

Look out for a couple of in-jokes (a magazine named after Shirow's superior BLACK MAGIC M-66) and some very bad Japlish spelling on signs. There are some sweet touches, such as the loose change falling out of Deunan's pants when she gets in the shower, or the cloying way she starts simpering whenever she sees a child. But for an anime produced by the peerless Gainax studio, *Appleseed* depicts a curiously mundane future—1980s Japan with a few shiny buildings. Tough-girl Deunan uses conventional firearms, drives a normal-looking car, and eats contemporary fast food. Only the robots add any real sense of the future, particularly a "multipede" tank modeled on the Probe Droid from *The Empire Strikes Back.*

Shirow loaded the original story with classical references, of which only Olympus, Gaia, Tartarus, and Athena survive the dub unscathed. Inadequate translation and diction have hidden the true pronunciations of Gyges, Charon Mausolus, and Briareus Hecatoncheires, which is why the English voice actors refer to a robot as "Gudges," a male character named "Karen Mawserus," and a lead cyborg called "Bularios." The uncredited

translator was more successful in spotting references to U.S. cop shows (a police chief called Bronx) and Ridley Scott's ubiquitous *Blade Runner* (the terrorist A. J., not J. F., Sebastian). Although he ignored the author's classical interests, adapter John Volks added much bad language, inspiring critics to invent the term "fifteening" for those U.K. anime dubs that insert swearing purely to attain a more commercial rating. That's not to say that the dub isn't a peppy paragon of cop-show cussing, including such immortal dialogue as, "Half cyborg? He's *all* bastard!" ◑

APPROACH OF AUTUMN, THE

1998. JPN: *Kasho no Getsu Aki no Kyogen.* AKA: *Hot Month Autumn Performance.* Video. DIR: Mamoru Hamazu. SCR: Mari Hirai. DES: Takashi Komori. ANI: Takashi Komori. MUS: Yuriko Nakamura. PRD: SME. 30 mins. x 2 eps.
A strange medieval romance based on a manga by Mari Hirai in which a pretty-boy sorcerer in Kamakura-period Japan begins a relationship with a hermaphrodite creature who is half-human, half-cat. The titular *aki no kyogen* refers to the last performances of the theatrical year, with their undertones of final curtain calls, farewells, and tomfoolery.

AQUA AGE

1996. JPN: *Mizu-iro Jidai.* AKA: *The Water-Colored Years; My Years in Blue.* TV series. DIR: Hiroko Tokita, Shin Misawa, Susumu Kudo, Hiroaki Sakurai, Hiroshi Fukutomi. SCR: Junji Takegami, Tsunehisa Arakawa, Reiko Yoshida. DES: Shinichi Yamaoka. ANI: Takahisa Ichikawa, Tatsuo Otaku. MUS: N/C. PRD: NAS, Comet, TV Tokyo. 25 mins. x 47 eps.
A quaint but uneventful look at the life and loves of average schoolgirl Yuko Kawai as her home life and school life place her under pressure to succeed, and she develops a crush on classmate Hiroshi, whose window faces hers. Named for the "Aqua Age" hair salon where she gets a part-time job and for

the distinctive blue colors of the sailor-suit uniform worn by so many Japanese schoolgirls, this anime was somewhat marginalized in anime sources for committing the heinous crime of featuring no robots, interdimensional gateways, erotic plot twists, or anything out of the ordinary at all. Scratch the surface, however, and you will find a role-reversal of KIMAGURE ORANGE ROAD, with a female lead and an idealized *male* love object without the latter anime's occasional intrusion of psychic subplots. Based on the manga in *Ciao* magazine by Yu Yabuchi.

ARABIAN NIGHTS

1961. JPN: *Senya Ichiya Monogatari.* AKA: *1001 Nights.* Movie. DIR: Eiichi Yamamoto, Osamu Tezuka. SCR: Kazuo Fukuzawa. DES: Osamu Tezuka, Eiichi Yamamoto. ANI: Kazuko Nakamura, Sadao Miyamoto. MUS: Isao Tomita. PRD: Mushi Pro. 128 mins.
Aladdin the water-seller (modeled upon French star Jean-Paul Belmondo) carries the beautiful Miriam away from a Baghdad slave market where she is just about to be sold to Havahslakum, the spoiled son of the chief of police. They spend a night of passion in a house they believe to be deserted but is actually a hideaway for the pervert Suleiman, who has been watching them. The police arrest Aladdin on suspicion of Suleiman's murder, and a heartbroken Miriam dies shortly after giving birth to his child. In fact, the murder was committed by Havahslakum's father's assistant, Badli, who not only covets the chief's job but has also been arranging secret trysts between Kamhakim, leader of the 40 thieves, and the chief of police's wanton wife. Badli plays all sides against each other, allowing the thieves to escape to make his boss look incompetent but also raping Kamhakim's tomboyish daughter, Mahdya, to break her spirit. He has even had sex with a crocodile, believing an ancient prophecy that promises a kingdom to anyone who can manage it. Aladdin escapes from jail, steals some treasure from the

40 thieves, and escapes with Mahdya, who soon deserts him when he succumbs to temptation on an island of nymphomaniacs. Discovering they are really snake-women, Aladdin flees and eventually finds a great treasure after many more adventures.
    Many years later, two interfering jinn cause Aladdin and Miriam's daughter, Yahliz (now Badli's stepdaughter), to fall in love with Aslan the shepherd boy. In search of her lover while disguised as a man, Yahliz is forced to marry a king's daughter, a lesbian who is extremely pleased to discover her new "husband's" secret. The princess helps Yahliz find Aslan, and they return to Baghdad in time for the arrival of "Sindbad," who is really Aladdin in disguise. After a feud with the king (engineered by Badli, of course), Aladdin becomes ruler and Badli his vizier. Badli fakes Aslan's death and persuades Yahliz to join Aladdin's harem. Aslan is saved by the two jinn, one of whom turns into a lioness to pleasure the lions who are supposed to devour him, and returns in time to prevent Aladdin committing incest with his own daughter. Mahdya kills Badli in belated revenge for her father's death, and Aslan and Yahliz become the new rulers, leaving Aladdin penniless but happy once more.
    During a mini-boom of Japanese interest in the *Arabian Nights*, ASTRO BOY–creator Tezuka published his own manga adaptations and subsequently adapted them into this sumptuous film, faithfully including erotic elements often dropped from modern versions. As well as music from composer Isao Tomita (who scored several Tezuka anime), it included early contributions from future big names Akio Sugino, Gisaburo Sugii, and Osamu Dezaki as lowly animators. For reasons known only to himself, Tezuka also invited several famous novelists to contribute to the production as voice actors. Unsung talents included *Silence*–author Shusaku Endo and the science–fiction writers Yasutaka Tsutsui and Sakyo Komatsu. Komatsu would

return to help Tezuka in a more sensible capacity on SPACE FIREBIRD. There have been several other Japanese versions of the same classic cycle of stories, including ALIBABA'S REVENGE, 1001 NIGHTS, ALADDIN AND THE WONDERFUL LAMP, and SINDBAD THE SAILOR. An English-dubbed version, running at approximately 100 minutes and missing the crocodile sex, the lesbian princess, and several other scenes, was reputedly made for foreign distribution, though none of our sources can confirm its existence in translated form. Tezuka went on to make a far less successful erotic movie, CLEOPATRA: QUEEN OF SEX. See also VIDEO PICTURE BOOK. Ⓝ

ARC THE LAD *

1999. TV series. DIR: Toshiaki Kawasaki. SCR: Akimi Tsuraizu. DES: Yoko Kikuchi. ANI: Satoshi Murata, Kenji Teraoka. MUS: Michiru Oshima. PRD: B-train, WOWOW. 25 mins. x 26 eps.
Roughly based on the events of the second *Arc the Lad* PlayStation game, this series, directed by NADESICO's Kawasaki, takes place after the events of the War of the Holy Coffin and features Hunter Erik (or Elk), the last surviving member of a tribe of fire-wielding sorcerers called the Pyrenians. He becomes a mercenary, teaming up with monster-tamer Lena, orphans Shunter and Sanya, exiled prince Grueger, and android Diecbeck. Needless to say, the many quests for revenge on behalf of wronged parents (which accounts for at least four party-members' motivations) are all tied up in an adventure plot in an incoherent but attractively designed world so typical of computer games in the wake of FINAL FANTASY. *Ill. p. 293.*

ARCHA LYRA

1992. JPN: *Aru Kararu no Isan.* AKA: *The Inheritance of Aru Kararu.* Video. DIR: Koichi Ishiguro. SCR: Mayori Sekijima. DES: Satoshi Saga. ANI: Masamitsu Kudo. MUS: N/C. PRD: Tokuma Japan Communications. 70 mins.
In the 26th century, humans discover a

humanoid race living on the distant world GO/7498/2, a dark-skinned, golden-eyed people who seem to eke out a primitive, carefree existence. However, a scout team from Earth discovers that there is more to them than meets the eye—they live in symbiosis with vicious reptilian parasites, and the Terran scientists have upset the delicate natural balance.

Despite the obvious tip of the hat to Ray Bradbury's *Dark They Were and Golden Eyed*, *Archa Lyra* taps into a rich vein of SF concepts and puts them to good use, including the alien symbionts of Hitoshi Iwaaki's *Parasyte* and the addictive allure of Frank Herbert's *Dune*. Original creator Katsumi Michihara is best known in Japan for drawing adaptations of other people's work, including LEGEND OF GALACTIC HEROES and the JOKER series.

AREA 88 *

1985. Video. DIR: Eiko Toriumi. SCR: Akiyoshi Sakai. DES: Toshiyasu Okada. ANI: Toshiyasu Okada. MUS: Ichiro Nitta. PRD: Project 88. 50 mins. x 4 eps.
In a faithful adaptation of Kaoru Shintani's 1979 manga from *Shonen Sunday*, ace pilot Shin Kazama is duped into joining a mercenary air force by his acquaintance, Kanzaki. At airbase Area 88 in the tiny, civil-war-torn Middle-Eastern kingdom of Asran, desertion is a capital offense. Kazama must live through a three-year tour of duty or shoot down enough enemy planes to buy out his contract. Meanwhile back home, the venal Kanzaki moves in on Kazama's girlfriend, Ryoko, trying to force her into a marriage of convenience to save her father's ailing business.

Area 88 is a lively adventure story, featuring a dastardly cad, noble pilots, and star-crossed lovers who, while they may occasionally be within waving distance of each other, are always torn apart by circumstances. Parallel plots of desert storm and urban mischief ask the viewer what either civilization really thinks they are fighting for. The incongruously sweet-faced characters draw a

tense, thrilling picture of the way war, corruption, and simple compromises change people. Few war anime compare, although the following year's GREY: DIGITAL TARGET makes a similarly masterful use of a popular genre.

Made as a four-part series in the earliest days of video anime, the first two chapters were also cut together into a movie in 1985. Several other Shintani stories have been turned into anime— TWO TAKAS, DESERT ROSE, CLEOPATRA DC, GODDAM, and I DREAM OF MIMI. The artist also worked as a designer on GOD SIGMA.

ARGENT SOMA

2000. TV series. DIR: Kazuyoshi Katayama. SCR: Hiroshi Yamaguchi. DES: Shuko Murase, Matsuri Yamane. ANI: Takuro Shinbo, Shuko Murase, Asako Nishida. MUS: Katsuhisa Hattori. PRD: Sunrise, TV Tokyo. 25 mins. x 25 eps.
Mysterious metallic life forms attack Earth in 2054 and also haunt the dreams of Earth boy Kaneshiro Takt, who is unable to show his feelings for his lover, Maki, until it is too late. Maki's laboratory pieces together "Frank," a whole alien made from parts scavenged from wrecks, but when the monster is activated, it destroys the laboratory and kills Maki. Hideously scarred in the accident, Takt changes his name to Ryu Soma and vows to avenge himself on the aliens, only to discover that his new bosses at the "Funeral" organization are now employing one. The damaged but functional Frank resolves to help humankind (although humankind may not necessarily want to be helped in the way Frank intends), but the only human he is prepared to communicate with is the pretty Harriet Bartholomew—a girl who reminds Takt of the dead Maki. Mixing the nihilism of GREY: DIGITAL TARGET with the ambiguous enemies of EVANGELION, *AS* also features curiously lopsided designs for the asymmetric Frank and obvious tips of the hat to the FRANKENSTEIN story. As with many other TV series of the cash-

strapped turn of the century, it also demonstrates a noticeable drop in animation quality, going from reasonable to barely adequate in the space of the first few episodes.

ARIEL *

1989. Video. DIR: Junichi Watanabe. SCR: Muneo Kubo, Yuichi Sasaki. DES: Osamu Tsuruyama, Yuji Moriyama. ANI: Osamu Tsuruyama. MUS: Kohei Tanaka. PRD: Animate Film, JC Staff. 30 mins. x 2 eps., 45 mins. x 2 eps.
Mad scientist Grandpa Kishida builds a giant robot called the All-Round Intercept and Escort Lady, or ARIEL, a convoluted acronym that is the namesake of his dead wife. Earth is attacked by the elfin alien general Hauser, who is searching for the Breastsaver Haagen, a powerful fighter he believes to be somewhere on the surface, but his assault is repelled by the Ariel team. Pilot Kasumi (Kishida's granddaughter) enjoys herself immensely, but her sister, Aya, and friend, Miya, refuse to fly again. The girls have no choice, however, when a second wave of alien attackers pours toward Scebai base, and they are humanity's last line of defense. The two initial sci-fi robot episodes in this low-rent GUNBUSTER clone were swiftly followed by the two longer *Deluxe Ariel* sequels, even though the original series hardly deserved a comeback.

ARION

1986. Movie. DIR: Yoshikazu Yasuhiko. SCR: Akiko Tanaka, Yoshikazu Yasuhiko. DES: Yoshikazu Yasuhiko, Kyoko Yamane. ANI: Yoshikazu Yasuhiko. MUS: Joe Hisaishi. PRD: Sunrise, TMS. 118 mins.
Three brothers, the last of the Titans, divide the world between them, but a quarrel soon breaks out between Poseidon, Lord of the Sea, and the Mountain-god Zeus, engineered in secret by the third brother, Hades. Fearing the wrath of Zeus, goddess Demeter hides Arion, her son by Poseidon, far away from Olympus. Caught up in the power struggles of the gods, Arion

becomes the prisoner of the dangerously unstable Artemis and her capricious brother, Apollo, until he is set free, once more through the machinations of Hades. He is also falling in love with a slave girl, Lesfeena, but fears she might be his sister.

Beginning life in the pages of *Ryu* magazine (which it shared with the similar fantasy **AMON SAGA**), *Arion*, a loose adaptation of classical myth with a distinctly oriental flavor, is a mature and exciting adventure. Though original creator Yasuhiko is credited with most aspects of production, he also recruited some impressive assistants. Miyazaki composer Joe Hisaishi supplies a magnificent score, while **FAIRY KING**'s Ryoko Yamagishi, an artist specializing in myth, helped with the design. Epic battles, perverse cruelty, great heroism, and unselfish love all have their place in this film, which is superior in every way to Yasuhiko's later **VENUS WARS**.

ARMITAGE III *
1994. Video. DIR: Hiroyuki Ochi. SCR: Chiaki Konaka, Akinori Endo. DES: Atsushi Takeuchi. ANI: Kunihiro Abe. MUS: Hiroyuki Nanba. PRD: AIC, Pioneer. 30 mins. x 4 eps.

"Red to Blue" is the motto, but it will be many generations before Mars is truly habitable. The air is still too thin for human beings, so colonists live beneath the roof that now closes off the Marineris Trench. Like Hong Kong and Singapore before it, the city of Saint Lowell has become a bustling metropolis simply because there is nowhere else to go. Although the Trench is hundreds of miles long, the colony has expanded fast, and Saint Lowell resembles much older cities back on Earth, packed with cramped skyscrapers and dark streets. With a shortage of manpower in the mines (and girl-power in the bars), Mars becomes the center of the solar system's robotics industry, pioneering the functional "Firsts" and the lifelike "Seconds."

Discredited cop Ross Sylibus is transferred from Earth to the colonies after he loses his partner to a rogue robot. As the city is terrorized by a brutal flurry of killings, all he's got to help him are his Terran wits and his new partner, the underdressed Naomi Armitage. The victims are all female, but they are also all "Thirds," the state of the art in android technology. Sylibus discovers that the murders are part of a gargantuan conspiracy involving big corporations, scientific cartels, and Earth's feminist government.

Blade Runner comparisons are a dime a dozen in the anime world, but *Armitage* truly deserves it. Wells City (as in H. G. Wells) and the spaceport at Saint Lowell (as in astronomer Percival Lowell) are dead ringers for Ridley Scott's Los Angeles. The frontier feel of newly colonized Mars only arrives in the later episodes, when Ross and Naomi are out in the barren countryside beyond the city standing beneath the glorious red of a Martian sky—an image also purloined for the later **COWBOY BEBOP**. With its high-tech future, android technology, and Martian frontier life, *Armitage* hits many sci-fi hotspots, but it is also a cop-buddy movie, a romance, and a sexy pastiche on several military conspiracy shockers. Writer Chiaki Konaka, who would go on to write the quintessential Internet thriller **SERIAL EXPERIMENTS LAIN**, made *Armitage* conspicuously cyberpunk, including a trip to cyberspace via a painfully messy human interface and meditations on the place of humanity in a high-tech world.

Originally released as part of a multimedia experience that included false newspaper reports to fill narrative gaps, the omission of these items in the English-language release renders Konaka's plot less coherent than it could have been. But there are still hidden depths in his script, the first episode of which was written in collaboration with SF veteran (and author of the **GHOST IN THE SHELL** tie-in novel) Akinori Endo. There is also a sly dig at modern Japanese business; the rival Conception and Hu-Gite cybernetics compa-

Local girl Orin befriends the put-upon Hyokichi, but the childhood friends are separated by circumstances beyond their control. At one point described by its own author as "the urine induced by drinking large quantities of beer," *The Theater of Life* is considered to be the masterpiece of early-20th-century writer Shiro Ozaki. Adapted as one of the **ANIMATED CLASSICS OF JAPANESE LITERATURE**, the long novel was crammed into just 30 minutes. *See entry p. 14.*

Animated Classics of Japanese Literature: The Theater of Life

© 1986 NIPPON ANIMATION CO., LTD.

nies battle to create the first android that is more human than human, continually outperforming each other with new formats and better models in a story line no doubt inspired by the large corporate battles of recent years, such as Sega versus Nintendo and Sony versus Pioneer. The script is also scattered with references to H. P. Lovecraft's *Dunwich Horror* (a favorite of Konaka's), including Professor Armitage, the writer Lavinia Whateley, and a laboratory on Dunwich Hill.

Regarded as the most Americanized "girls-and-guns" example of Pioneer's output, *Armitage* initially got much less attention than it deserved. As with Konaka's later **BUBBLEGUM CRISIS 2040**, it is sometimes easy to miss the fine line between his satirical sexism and the everyday variety prevalent in so many other shows. Following the success of the video, it was rereleased as the movie *Polymatrix* with some cuts, a couple of extra scenes, and a completely new ending. It was also redubbed featuring the voices of Keifer Sutherland and Elizabeth Berkley in the main roles in an attempt to gain extra press attention through star power—a tactic common for Disney but rare in anime until Buena Vista's acquisition of **PRINCESS MONONOKE**. However, the video ending, which looks farther into the future of the lead characters, remains the better of the two—*Armitage* really belongs on the small screen. It was originally made for video, and although the story is compelling, the art does not really survive being enlarged in a theater. But the bright design, powerful sound, and lemon twist of romance all make for a great retelling of one of sci-fi's oldest stories: the machine that wants to be human.

Note: the Roman numerals in *Armitage III* are part of the lead character's name, and not, as some commentators have assumed, evidence of two earlier episodes in the series. It is read "Armitage the Third," not "Armitage Three." **O**

ARMORED CHRONICLE HIO

2000. JPN: *Karakuri Den Hio Senki.* AKA: *Puppetry Legend Chronicle Hio.* TV series. DIR: Tetsuro Amino. SCR: Noboru Aikawa. DES: Kazu Kamiyadera, Junya Ishigaki, Hajime Jinguji. ANI: Koji Aisaka. MUS: Hiroshi Yamaguchi. PRD: Bones, NHK2. 25 mins. x 26 eps. When his humble village is attacked by the cruel Wind Ninja, Hio breaks the ultimate rule of his people and hides within the holy of holies of his village shrine. There, he awakens the Homra, an ancient tribal totem given to Hio's clan by people from another dimension. Hio discovers he has inherited a fabulous power from his ancestors—the ability to summon and control fearsome devices he can only describe as "puppets." And Homra is no ordinary puppet; it is a powerful weapon.

In 19th-century Edo (Tokyo), the emperor is merely a puppet—it is the shogun who truly rules, though not for much longer. Japan is alive with calls for revolution: "Restore the emperor! Expel the barbarians!" Only the noble samurai Ryoma Sakamoto (see **OI RYOMA!**) can turn the tide of history, but with an eye on the children's market, writer Aikawa created this imaginary teenage sidekick to reach a new audience. For good measure, he

throws in two warrior princesses as well.

As the SF benchmark year 2000 became a reality, many anime companies were already firmly focused on the past. Exhausting the early 20th century with **SAKURA WARS** and its fellow martial arts shows, they delved back into the 19th—with suspicious synchronicity, both *Armored Chronicle Hio* and **TREE IN THE SUN** were announced in the same month.

AROUND THE WORLD WITH WILLY FOGG *

1985. JPN: *Dobutsu 80 Nichikan Sekai Icho.* AKA: *Animals Around the World in 80 Days; La Vuelta al Mundo de Willy Fog.* TV series. DIR: Fumio Kurokawa. SCR: Ryuzo Nakanishi. DES: Isamu Noda. ANI: Hisatoshi Motoki, Hirokazu Ishino. MUS: Shunsuke Kikuchi. PRD: Nippon Animation/BRB, TV Asahi. 30 mins. x 26 eps. Wheelchair-bound old goat Lord Guinness believes it is possible to travel around the world in 80 days, but he is too infirm to prove it himself. A lion called Willy Fogg volunteers to put the theory to the test, betting against several other people at the Gentlemen's Reform Club. Accompanied by two circus refugees, Rigadon and Tico, Fogg sets off around the world. However, Sullivan, who has bet against Fogg, hires a jackal thug called Transfer to ensure that the trip is a failure. Fogg is also hounded by two Scotland Yard detectives convinced that he has robbed a bank and has to rescue Romy, a beautiful Indian princess, en route.

This anthropomorphic (but chiefly feline) adaptation of Jules Verne was a companion piece to the canine **DOGTANIAN AND THE THREE MUSKEHOUNDS** made in association with the Spanish studio BRB. Though it charmed a generation in Europe, the Japanese version was not broadcast until 1987 and omitted episodes 14, 18, 21, and 22—curiously, one of the missing chapters was "En Route to Yokohama." Fogg and friends would return in a 30-episode sequel in the early 1990s,

adapting *Journey to the Center of the Earth* and *20,000 Leagues under the Sea* in similarly flamboyant style.

ART OF FIGHTING *

1995. JPN: Battle Spirits: *Ryoko no Ken.* AKA: Battle Spirits: *Dragon Tiger Fist.* Video. DIR: Hiroshi Fukutomi. SCR: Nobuaki Kishima. DES: Kazunori Iwakura. ANI: Kazunori Iwakura, Kenichi Shimizu, Mamoru Taniguchi. MUS: Akira Konishi, SNK Sound Team. PRD: Fuji TV, NAS. 45 mins.

An anime clone of a Neo-Geo game clone of **STREET FIGHTER II**, even to its mismatched leads, except instead of Ryu and Ken, we've got Ryo and Robert. The two heroes witness a gangland slaying and are accused of stealing a valuable diamond by the gang that has kidnapped Ryo's sister, Yuri. The two martial artists are obliged to fight to get her back in a tired story-by-numbers suspiciously like **TEKKEN**, or **TOSHINDEN**, or **VIRTUA FIGHTER**. **O**

ASARI-CHAN

1982. TV series. DIR: Osamu Kasai. SCR: Tadaaki Yamazaki, Masaki Tsuji, Akiyoshi Sakai. DES: Hideyoshi Ito. ANI: Tadashi Shirakawa, Koji Uemura, Nobuyuki Endo. MUS: Hiroshi Tsutsui. PRD: Toei, TV Asahi. 25 mins. x 54 eps. Asari Hamano is a preteen girl who refuses to try at anything except sports. Her elder sister, Tatami, however, is a model student, adored by their mother, who pays Asari no attention at all. As the sisters fight a continual game of one-upmanship, Dad buries his head in his paper and tries to be even-handed. Both girls make life hell for the Morino boys next door—Jiro, who is waiting to retake his exams, and his younger brother, Kakesu.

MISTER PEN-PEN–creator Mayumi Muroyama only changed the names to protect the guilty when she started writing about her own family for *Corocoro Comic* in 1977. *Asari-chan* is still running to this day, but its anime incarnation was less successful. The 54 episodes were shown several times (occasionally split into 100 installments since most could be neatly divided into two shorter stories) and also spun off into a 25-minute film at the Toei Manga Festival in 1982, in which Asari is forced to read a five-volume compendium of fairy tales in order to prove to her aunt that she genuinely does like the gift.

ASSEMBLE INSERT *

1989. Video. DIR: Ayumi Tomobuki. SCR: Mitsuru Toyota, Michiru Shimada. DES: Masami Yuki, Yutaka Izubuchi. ANI: Toyomi Sugiyama. MUS: Kohei Tanaka. PRD: Studio Core. 30 mins. x 2 eps.
Demon Seed, a group of power-suited criminals, has stolen over a billion yen in valuables and caused immense damage while resisting arrest. In a drunken stupor, Police Chief Hattori decides to catch the group by auditioning for a super-idol, a singing girl who can wear Professor Shimokawabe's new giant robot suit, defeat the menace, and keep him from doing too much overtime. The 15-year-old Maron Namikaze, who can bend steel microphone stands with her bare hands, is put to work stopping the Demon Seed gang from stealing an expensive museum exhibit. She defeats the bad guys but destroys the priceless artifacts in the process.

Three months later, the Special Operations group is so discredited that it decides to enter Maron for a talent contest. When an onstage display of strength is caught on camera, Maron becomes a star, and the police become her managers. Annoyed at the change in direction, Professor Shimokawabe secretly gives Demon Seed four new suits, and it stages another heist that coincides with Maron's big concert.

Predating both the showbiz-satire of **HUMMINGBIRDS** and the insane self-referentiality of **DRAGON HALF**, **PATLABOR**–creator Masami Yuki wrote this musical comedy for *Out* magazine, reuniting many of the staff in both offscreen roles and onscreen cameos. The drunken Hattori is based on *Shonen Sunday*–editor Fukuda Takahashi, who

first took a chance on Yuki. His lieutenant, Taka, is based on designer Yutaka Izubuchi, while the three other members of the Special Operations group are caricatures of **MACROSS PLUS**'s sensible Shoji Kawamori, laconic *Patlabor*-staffer Yutaka Yoneda, and a drunken pervert modeled on Yuki himself.

ASTRO BOY *

1963. JPN: *Tetsuwan Atom*. AKA: *Mighty Atom*. TV series. DIR: Osamu Tezuka, Gisaburo Sugii, Daisaku Sakamoto, Eiichi Yamamoto, Osamu Dezaki, Yoshiyuki Tomino, Minoru Okazaki, Fusahito Nagaki. SCR: Osamu Tezuka, Noriyuki Honma, Masaki Tsuji, Kenichi Takahashi. DES: Osamu Tezuka. ANI: Daisaku Sakamoto. MUS: Tatsuo Takai. PRD: Tezuka Pro, Fuji TV. 30 mins. x 193 eps.
In the year 2003 (2000 in the U.S. release), Professor Tenma (Boynton) is distraught when his son Tobio (Astro/Toby) is killed in a car accident. He loses himself in his latest project, creating Atom (Astro), a robot boy programmed to be forever good. Upset that his Tobio-substitute can never grow up, Tenma sells Atom to Hamegg (Cacciatore), the cruel ringmaster of a robot circus. Atom meets the kindly Professor Ochanomizu (Elefun), who adopts him, inspires him to become a crusader against evil, and eventually builds him a robot "sister," Uran (Astro Girl).

Often erroneously described as the first TV anime (see **INSTANT HISTORY**), *AB* began in 1951 as *Captain Atom* in *Shonen Magazine*. Renamed *Mighty Atom* a year later, it became the flagship title of the magazine and was made as a live-action TV show in 1959. A combination of *Pinocchio* and *Superman*, it became the first of many animated adaptations by Tezuka of his own work.

First shown on Fuji TV on New Year's Day 1963 but eventually moving to the NHK network, it was the first anime to be broadcast abroad. Still known around the world as *Mighty*

Atom—the U.S. name change was forced by the existence of a local comic character with a similar name—it was adapted for the English-language market by Fred Ladd, and its success created the first wave of anime abroad. The U.S. version eventually screened 104 of the full Japanese run, including such curiosities as a TV special of Atom fighting the **STAR OF THE GIANTS**—though the latter remains unknown in the English-speaking world. The influence of *AB* extended further than is often realized. On the strength of *AB*, Stanley Kubrick offered Tezuka a job as a production designer on *2001:A Space Odyssey*, though Tezuka declined.

The Japanese series, whose ratings peaked at over 40%, ended with Atom sacrificing his life to save Earth. He also appeared in a feature-length anime movie, *Hero of Space* (1964), directed by Atsushi Takagi. Hamegg, Tezuka's stock villain, was recycled for **KIMBA THE WHITE LION**, and Tezuka attempted to write Atom for an older audience with the more philosophical *Atom Chronicles* for *Shonen Magazine*.

An inferior copy appeared as **JETTER MARS** in 1977, but the original itself returned in a new color format in 1980. These *New Adventures of Astro Boy* featured a younger-looking hero in keeping with audience expectations and scripts written chiefly by Tezuka himself, though Ryosuke Takahashi contributed several and Kenji Terada was credited with "literary assistance," whatever that may be. With many of the original crew now famous in their own right, the new production drafted new faces including directors Noboru Ishiguro, Satoshi Dezaki, Naoto Hashimoto, and Takashi Anno. Perhaps as a result of Tezuka's own dissatisfaction with the series, the *New Adventures* were dark in mood despite their bright colors, featuring many failed missions and dying good guys. There was a greater concentration on Atom's evil twin, Atlas, built from stolen blueprints by Count Walpurgis (Walper Guiss), a European arms manufacturer. Deciding to conquer the world, Atlas opposes the emotional Atom with cold logic, eventually coming to realize over many episodes that it is he who is lacking something. Atlas was not the only one: the series was unsatisfactory to makers and viewers alike, and only lasted for 52 episodes—a quarter of its predecessor's longevity, though still considerably longer than most modern serials.

Despite its failure to live up to the impact of the original, the color *AB* kept the myth alive for a new generation, existing in two separate dubs from Australia and Canada. Homages abound in both the U.S. and Japan, from the obvious *Big Guy and Rusty the Boy Robot* to the desperate stab at legitimacy of **BIRDY THE MIGHTY**. The character's simple, recognizable lines became an icon in U.S. subculture and is currently rumored to be the subject of *two* remakes: a U.S. live-action feature and a Japanese TV anime comeback for a new generation. A third project, a Japanese-Canadian IMAX coproduction, began development but was shelved in 2000. *Ill. p. 189.*

ASUKAS OF FLOWERS, THE *

1987. JPN: *Shin Kabuki-machi no Story: Asuka no Hanagumi.* AKA: *New Story of Kabuki Town: Asuka's Flower Collection.* Video. DIR: Atsutoshi Umezawa. SCR: Kenji Terada. DES: Satosumi Takaguchi, Yuri Handa. ANI: Toei. MUS: Kenji Kawai. PRD: Kadokawa, Tohoku, Toei. 48 mins. x 2 eps.

In this adaptation of a famously sensational girls' manga said to encapsulate the *ennui* of the 1980s, Asuka is a teenage student who wanders the windswept streets of Kabuki Town each evening, dragged into teenage prostitution and gangland violence. She saves fellow schoolgirl Yotsuko from another gang and returns the girl's diary, remaining honorable but distant—even when she subsequently prevents Yotsuko from committing suicide.

The original story, published in a magazine also called *Asuka*, was a huge hit for artist Satosumi Takaguchi, spawning 27 volumes, a six-part spin-

off, a live-action movie, and a TV drama. This two-part series, however, was the only anime appearance. The youth-gone-wild of the following decade were similarly "sensationalized" in the live-action *Bounce Ko-gals*, nicely demonstrating that the more things change, the more they stay the same.

ATTACK NUMBER ONE

1969. TV series. DIR: Fumio Kurokawa, Eiji Okabe. SCR: Masaki Tsuji, Satoshi Dezaki, Haruya Yamazaki, Tsunehisa Ito. DES: Jun Ikeda. ANI: Shingo Araki. MUS: Takeo Watanabe. PRD: TMS, Fuji TV. 30 mins. x 104 eps.

Kozue is a new student transferred to Fujimi College. Though she has a low opinion of her own abilities, she resolves to practice hard to fit in with the school volleyball team. She soon makes a lifelong friend in the kind Midori and a bitter enemy in Yoshimura, the girl who was formerly the school volleyball superstar. She falls in love with a local boy but is prepared to sacrifice everything to please her beloved Coach Honma.

This adaptation of Chikako Urano's 1968 volleyball manga was the first sports anime made specifically for a female audience, generating not only four 1970 movies assembled from reedited footage, but also an entire subgenre that survives to this day. Successors that simply switch the focus to another sport include **AIM FOR THE ACE** and **YAWARA**, while recent years have seen misguided pastiches such as **BATTLE ATHLETES**.

In 1977, Kurokawa, Okabe, and Yamazaki would return on the staff of *Attack on Tomorrow (Ashita e Attack!)*, a cloned TV series timed to cash in on Japan's successes in the volleyball World Cup. Featuring Mimi, a student with just one year of school remaining who decides to revitalize a volleyball team that is still recovering from the accidental death of one of its members, the new series was a shadow of its illustrious predecessor and ceased after just 23 episodes.

ATTACKER YOU!

1984. TV series. DIR: Kazuyuki Okaseko. SCR: Hideki Sonoda, Susumu Yoshida. DES: Jun Makimura, Teruo Kigure. ANI: Satoshi Kishimo. MUS: Shiro Sagisu. PRD: Knack, TV Tokyo. 30 mins. x 58 eps.

Thirteen-year-old Yu Hazuki moves to Tokyo to be with her cameraman father. Bumping into volleyball star Nami Hayase on her first day at her new school, Yu joins the volleyball team and soon trounces the former champion with her brilliant abilities. Teaming up with Eri, an ace attacker, the trio try to realize their dreams of getting to the all-Japan finals.

Though there was a spinoff manga by Jun Makimura, *Attacker You!* was actually based on Shizuo Koizumi's novel *Now the White Ball Is Alive*. While its predecessor, **ATTACK NUMBER ONE,** romanticized school drama and camaraderie, *Attacker You!* concentrated on volleyball as a career in itself, making it less a sports anime than a professional soap opera that happened to revolve around sports.

AURORA

2000. JPN: *Umi no Aurora.* AKA: *Marine Aurora.* Movie. DIR: Yoshinori Kanno. SCR: Michiru Shimada. DES: Katsuya Kondo. ANI: Satoshi Fujiwara. MUS: Masamichi Amano. PRD: Nippon TV. 91 mins.

An action thriller with overtones of *The Abyss* and *Sphere*—a 21st-century drilling team based at the bottom of the South Pacific is searching for age-old bacteria that can synthesize oil. Though the team finds it, the glowing bacteria proves highly combustible in the oxygen-rich atmosphere and can eat through metal. Biologist Oshunru is aware of the potential danger and suspects the bacteria "wishes" to restore Earth to the primeval conditions that created it, wiping out all other life in the process. This hackneyed, predictable sci-fi thriller's CG origins merely make the characters more expressionless than usual. *Aurora* was Japan's first full-length 3-D computer-animated movie, though **VISITOR** and **A.LI.CE** were shorter works that preceded it.

AWOL *

1998. TV series. DIR: Toshifumi Kawase. SCR: Koji Miura, Toshiyasu Nagata, Chika Hojo, Atsuhiro Tomioka. DES: Isamu Imakake, Wataru Abe. ANI: Yoshihiro Yamaguchi, Masahiko Murata. MUS: Shiro Hamaguchi, Kazuhiro Wakabayashi. PRD: BeStock, TV Tokyo. 25 mins. x 13 eps.

Turncoat scientist Dr. Culten turns off perimeter defenses around a military compound just long enough for the Solomon terrorist group to get in and steal several powerful PDB missiles. To demonstrate their zeal, the terrorists detonate one of the bombs, though they do not make any demands. Meanwhile, within the government, a scandal breaks out when it is discovered that Dr. Culten's secret orbital defense network, constructed without presidential approval, can be turned into a weapon and used against its makers. An elite team of commandos sets off to stop the Solomon terrorists before things can get any worse.

From early scenes of partygoers, lovers, and a child blissfully unaware that they are about to be blown to smithereens, to the introduction of a rookie character who might as well have "Dead Meat" tattooed on his forehead, *AWOL* is a low-rent Cold War thriller. Former X-Japan member Hide's theme song was the best-selling anime single of 1998, but this poor effort is otherwise doomed to obscurity. The fact that it's set in space amid a confederation of worlds seems like a last-minute idea designed to justify it as an anime production, though even the cost-cutting tactic of drawing the spaceships and explosions still falls down when faced with such a low budget as this. Given millions of dollars and a Hollywood star, this would have been just as bad, but it would have made it onto a thousand screens as a successor to *Broken Arrow* and *Under Siege*. In the anime world, however, it is simply below par, and few are likely to be fooled by half-hearted sci-fi design fudges like turning the Pentagon into a Triangle.

AYANE'S HIGH KICK *

1996. JPN: *Ayane-chan no High Kick*. Video. DIR: Takahiro Okao. SCR: Isa Shizuya. DES: Kazuo Tatsugawa. ANI: Kazuo Tatsugawa. MUS: Norio Inoue. PRD: Nikkatsu. 30 mins. x 2 eps.

Ayane secretly wants to be a female wrestler but is swindled into fighting as a kickboxer. Despite opposition from the ineffectual school principal (as if expulsion would scare this sports addict), Ayane throws herself into the world of professional martial arts, fighting off a roster of surprisingly stupid opponents, a large number of whom seem amazed that people actually get hurt in the ring.

Originally announced as a six-part series, *Ayane's High Kick* was canceled after only two episodes. To excuse the cartoonish design, the script tries to play for laughs, piling on dozens of Japanese sporting in-jokes that fall flat. What's left is a predictable rags-to-riches tale, ripping-off **TOMORROW'S JOE** and **AIM FOR THE ACE** without any of their charm. The Japanese version relied heavily on a voice cast that included Yuko Miyamura (Asuka from **EVANGELION**, in another fiery red-haired role), but this was not enough to redeem it. Matters are not helped by a truly awful English-language dub that features a cast who cannot even pronounce each other's names, with only Debbie Rabbai as Ayane producing anything like a decent performance.

AZUKI-CHAN

1995. TV series. DIR: Masayuki Kojima. SCR: Shunichi Yukimuro. DES: Yoshiaki Kawajiri. ANI: Katsuyoshi Iizuka. MUS: Akira Tsuji. PRD: Madhouse, NHK2. 30 mins. x 117 eps.

When someone mispronounces her name at age eight, Azusa Nogami finds herself stuck with the nickname Azuki ("Red Bean"). Now in the fifth grade, she makes friends with a transfer student, Yunosuke, when he overhears another boy teasing her and can't help remembering such an original name. Azuki swiftly develops a crush on Yunosuke but doubts he will ever look at her as anything more than a friend, especially with the irritating Ken and Makoto eternally scheming to ruin everything for her.

Based on the comic serialized in *Nakayoshi* by writer Tsukasa Akimoto and artist Chika Kimura, *Azuki-chan*'s timeless school romance has since found great popularity across Europe and East Asia while preparing a whole generation back in Japan for the more cynical yet similarly entertaining high-school antics of **HIS AND HER CIRCUMSTANCES**.

B

BABEL II *
1973. JPN: *Babel Nisei*. TV series, Video. DIR: Takeshi Tamiya, Minoru Okazaki, Kazuya Miyazaki. SCR: Shunichi Yukimuro, Tomohiro Ando, Masaki Tsuji. DES: Shingo Araki, Teruo Kigure, Eimi Maeda. ANI: Shingo Araki, Teruo Kigure, Toshiyasu Okada. MUS: Shunsuke Kikuchi. PRD: Hikari Pro, TV Asahi, Toei. 25 mins. x 39 eps.
In the distant past, a race of aliens lived in the Euphrates basin, where they built the "Three Servants"—Ropros, Rodem, and Poseidon—mighty beings designed to wipe out invading armies. Thousands of years later, when the ancient civilization has turned to dust, red-haired Japanese boy Koichi is troubled by strange dreams of the beautiful Juju, who eventually appears in the flesh and urges him to join a secret cabal of psychics led by Yomi, an alien prince.

When Koichi refuses, he is rescued by the Three Servants and taken to Mesopotamia, where he discovers that Yomi was the chosen inheritor of the powers of Babel. Now that Yomi has turned to the dark side, it falls to Koichi, a distant descendant of intermarriage between the aliens and humans, to put his nascent psychic powers to use defending Earth as the new inheritor, Babel II.

Based on the 1971 manga by Mitsuteru Yokoyama, creator of **GIGANTOR** and **LITTLE WITCH SALLY**, *Babel II* inspired an entire generation of creators, and its effects are still felt today, from the reluctant psychics of **AKIRA** to the biblical archaeology of **SPRIGGAN**. It was reverse-engineered many times to create lesser robot/psychic shows in

the marketing-led decades that followed. Selected parts were rushed onto tape with the coming of video, creating a nostalgic audience in Japan for the inevitable remake.

Yoshihisa Matsumoto's 1992 video version compresses the story into four 30-minute episodes and includes the events of Yokoyama's 1977 manga sequel *His Name is No. 101*, in which Yomi returns and uses Koichi's blood to create an army of cloned soldiers. Released in an English-language version amid confusion over its origins (many buyers were put off when they couldn't find the nonexistent *Babel I*), the new *Babel II* looked too much like its imitators—original crew member Shingo Araki designed a new-look Koichi who lost his red mop in favor of the bland hero-template black hair, and the Three Servants with their air, land, and sea specialties looked like cheap copies of the same year's **BEAST WARRIORS**. Teruo Kigure, an animator on the original, also directed the erotic pastiche **LUNATIC NIGHT**.

BABY AND ME
1996. JPN: *Aka-chan to Boku*. TV series. DIR: Masahiro Omori. SCR: Sukehiro Tomita, Kenji Terada. DES: Takayuki Goto, Yuji Ikeda. ANI: Yuji Moriyama. MUS: Kenji Kawai. PRD: Studio Pierrot, TV Tokyo. 25 mins. x 35 eps.
Thirteen-year-old Takuya Enoki faces unexpected challenges when his mother is killed in a car accident. Father Harumi has to spend extra time at the office, and Takuya becomes a surrogate parent for his two-year-old brother, Minoru. While he cares deeply for Minoru, the constant chores and atten-

tion can be very wearing. His father starts dating Miss Otani, but while Minoru happily believes she is his mother reborn, Takuya cannot come to terms with the idea. As time wears on, he comes to realize that it is *he* who has replaced his mother, and the love between the brothers grows stronger.

Based on Marimo Ragawa's long-running comic in *Hana to Yume* magazine, *Baby and Me* is often compared to **SAZAE-SAN** for its slice-of-life observations, but it also owes a certain debt to **MAMA'S A FOURTH GRADER** with its emphasis on impromptu parenting. *Ill. p. 49.*

BAD BATZ-MARU
1995. Video. DIR: Kazuya Murata. SCR: Kenji Terada. DES: N/C. ANI: N/C. MUS: N/C. PRD: Sanrio. 30 mins.
Batz-maru, a tough-talking, naughty penguin, has a name formed from Japanese school terminology for right (maru) and wrong (batsu), as well as an old-fashioned suffix found in warriors' names—compare with **MAN-MARU THE NINJA PENGUIN**. But unlike his fellow Sanrio merchandise characters **HELLO KITTY** and **PEKKLE THE DUCK**, Batz-maru's commercial success has come without attachment to an anime vehicle, and this one-shot video is his only solo outing. Clearly a pilot for a far longer offering, it features two short tales in which Batz-maru proudly enters his pet crocodile in a contest and then goes off to learn how to be "a man." He also appeared with Hello Kitty in six video specials, *HK&BBM: Everybody Dance, Full of Playtime, Play Together, We Love Dance, Let's Dance*, and *Let's Origami*.

BAD BOYS

1993. Video. DIR: Osamu Sekita, Takeshi Yamaguchi. SCR: Kazuya Miyashita, Kaori Takada, Masayoshi Azuma. DES: Hiroshi Tanaka. ANI: Mitsuharu Kajitani. MUS: Hiroaki Yoshino. PRD: Toei. 40 mins. x 5 eps.

It's tough being a hard, streetwise member of a biker gang, especially if it's called the Paradise Butterflies and its goal is to be the baddest gang in . . . Hiroshima. Such is the lot of Tsukasa, Yoji, Eiji, and friends, boys determined to outgun the engines of every other biker in town. Hiroshi Tanaka's manga was originally intended to be a hard-hitting crime story of warring biker gangs, but he was unable to take the posturing seriously, and it eventually became a tongue-in-cheek pastiche of the genre popularized by **BOMBER BIKERS OF SHONAN**. It was serialized in *Young King* magazine from 1988, eventually running to 23 volumes. These video shows were released once yearly during the manga's final years to drum up interest—a damp squib finale ran for 1 volume in *Glare* magazine after the series was pulled from its original publication.

BAGHI

1984. TV special. DIR: Osamu Tezuka, Kimiharu Ono. SCR: Osamu Tezuka. DES: Osamu Tezuka, Hitoshi Nishimura. ANI: Hitoshi Nishimura, Kazuhiko Udagawa. MUS: Kentaro Haneda. PRD: Toei, Sanrio, Goku, Nippon TV. 86 mins.

With his mother, Dr. Ishigami, absent on a secret science project, Ryosuke rebels against his father and joins a biker gang. They harass a passer-by, who turns out to be a cat-girl and kills everyone in the gang except Ryo. He rears "Baghi," who grows into a sexy adult, walking on two legs and possessing human intelligence. The couple goes in search of her origins. Clues lead to Ryo's mother's original science experiments. Tracking down her follow-up project in South America, the two arrive just in time for Baghi to become the prime suspect in Dr. Ishigami's murder. Baghi flees, and Ryo swears

vengeance, becoming a big-game hunter to track her. Years later, Ryo is hired to shoot a wild animal that has been terrorizing villagers in the Amazon. It is Baghi, who only fled from Ryo because she feared that she was reverting to a feral state and wished to protect the man she loved from harm. It is revealed that Baghi is innocent, and that Dr. Ishigami was murdered by the dictator who funded her illegal research.

Ahead of his time as usual, Tezuka wrote this tale of genetic experimentation on animals for *Shonen Action*, the lead character named in homage to Bagheera as portrayed in Disney's version of Kipling's *Jungle Book*. Though this synopsis has been reordered for clarity's sake, the film is told chiefly in flashback, as Ryo the hunter relates his story to a local boy, and then in flash-back-within-a-flashback, as Ryo the investigator remembers how he first met his feline friend. The anthropomorphic appeal of cat-women would become an anime staple, from **CATGIRL NUKUNUKU** to **ESCAFLOWNE**'s kittenish Meryl, while Tezuka's cautionary zeal would even influence the story of the first **POKÉMON** movie, which featured a similar **FRANKENSTEIN** creation escaping from an Amazon stronghold.

BAKUMATSU SPACIBO

1997. JPN: *Bakumatsu Spacibo*. Movie. DIR: Satoshi Dezaki, Kenichi Maejima. SCR: Shigeo Nakakura. DES: Keizo Shimizu, Setsuko Shibunnoichi. ANI: Keizo Shimizu, Setsuko Shibunnoichi. MUS: Kazuya Moroboshi. PRD: Magic Bus, Toho. 85 mins.

The true story of the arrival of the Russian commander Putyatin in 19th-century Japan during the last days of the shogunate (Bakumatsu). Japan had been closed to the outside world for 200 years, and the arrival of the warship Diana was to cause a major commotion in the sleepy seaside villages. After making friends with the Japanese during treaty negotiations, the Russians are left stranded when their ship runs aground during an 8.4 magnitude

Arriving in a futuristic Tokyo slum like a refugee from a 19th-century novel, the dark, handsome stranger Darkside is the personification of revolution itself. His role, however, is undefined in a film so loaded with similar heavy-duty symbolism that it lacks the running time to explain all. This strange mix of brooding gothic and high-tech combat was based on a novel by Hideyuki Kikuchi, who would concoct similarly fantastical no-go areas of Tokyo in **WICKED CITY** and **DEMON CITY SHINJUKU**. See entry p.82.

Darkside Blues

earthquake. The Japanese bring help to the beleaguered Russians, who leave with a grateful "thank you" (*spacibo*). The timing of the production suggests it was inspired by the Kobe earthquake in 1995. See also **THE DAY THE EARTH SHOOK**.

BALTHUS: TIA'S RADIANCE *

1988. JPN: *Balthus: Tia no Kagayaki*. Video. DIR: Yukihiro Makino. SCR: N/C. DES: Shoji Furuta. ANI: Murasaki Katano, Shinnosuke Kusama. MUS: N/C. PRD: Kusama Art. 30 mins.

In the factory-city of Balthus, human workers are little more than slaves to the ruling overlord, Morlock. Eud is a young boy in the resistance, part of a plot to use the warrior-robot Klaatu to defeat Morlock. The resistance fails, and when his coconspirator, Alphonse, is killed, Eud is hidden by Alphonse's beautiful sister, Tia. Both are captured by Morlock, and Eud is thrown into the dungeon. Tia is ravished by the sadistic overlord and taunted with the news of her brother's death, until she is saved in the nick of time by Eud, and both are saved by the timely arrival of Klaatu.

More from the people who brought you **LEGEND OF LYON**, in a frantically rushed erotic pastiche of the same year's CASTLE IN THE SKY, but with a fraction of the budget, talent, or commitment. It also features a pointless musical interlude from an off-key vocalist when it badly needs the time for matters of greater importance, such as plot—or, indeed, a little more sex. Sprinkled with sly references to great science fiction, including Morlock (*The Time Machine*), Klaatu (*The Day the Earth Stood Still*), and a plot that crashes *Metropolis* into a porno film. Only in anime! **N**

BANDAR BOOK: ONE MILLION A.D.

1978. JPN: *Bandar Book: Hyakuman-nen Chikyu no Tabi*. AKA: *Bandar Book: 1 Million Year Earth Journey; Bander Book; Bander's Book*. TV special. DIR: Hisashi Sakaguchi. SCR: Osamu Tezuka. DES: Hisashi Sakaguchi. ANI: Hitoshi Nishimura. MUS: Yuji Ono. PRD: Tezuka Pro, Nippon TV. 86 mins.
Shortly before an explosion tears their spacecraft apart, Professor Kudo's wife places their newborn son in an escape capsule. The baby drifts across space and eventually lands on planet Zobi, where he is adopted by the ruling prince as his own. The Zobians can shapeshift at will, and the young Prince Bandar is teased for his inability to do so. Years later, a grown Bandar agonizes as to whether his "handicap" should disqualify him from marrying Princess Mimulu. His world is attacked by the space pirate Black Jack, and he and Mimulu are captured. Dumped by Black Jack on another world, the distraught Bandar believes Mimulu to be dead. Teaming up with shapeshifting steed Muzu, he rescues the beautiful princess Marina, who is being held prisoner by Dracula and the Cyclops. Taking Marina to her home world, Bandar is betrayed by a Terran military adviser, Dokudami, who has Prime Minister Hamegg throw him in jail. There he is helped by Sharaku, a scientist who has patented a scheme of extracting hatred from people's souls and bringing peace. Bandar escapes, but Dokudami steals Sharaku's distilled

Elixir of Evil and threatens to scatter it. He is stopped by the timely arrival of Black Jack, who has discovered that he is Bandar's long-lost elder brother. The new allies pursue the fleeing Dokudami through hyperspace back to prehistoric Earth, where his ship crashes and scatters evil throughout the atmosphere. Using Black Jack's time machine (built with the proceeds of piracy), the group returns and destroys the totalitarian computer that had ordered their father killed. Black Jack is killed in the final conflict, and a dying Marina reveals that she is really a chlorophyll life form whose final stage is a tree. Muzu reveals that she is really Mimulu, adopting a disguise to be close to the man she loves. Earth is finally at peace, and Bandar sits with Mimulu beneath the tree that has grown from what was once Marina.

Like the other early TV specials, the anime featured several cameo appearances by characters from other Tezuka stories, including BLACK JACK, Hamegg from KIMBA THE WHITE LION, Sharaku the THREE-EYED PRINCE, ASTRO BOY in a crowd scene, and Professor Ochanomizu as a servant to Dracula. There are also walk-on visual parodies of Edward G. Robinson and Linda Blair, who played the possessed girl in *The Exorcist*. First broadcast during the 24-hour NTV Super Special commemorating the 25th anniversary of Tokyo's fourth TV channel, it became the first of a series of annual Tezuka TV specials for NTV, including later productions such as MARINE EXPRESS, FUMOON, BREMEN 4, PRIME ROSE, BAGHI, and GALAXY SEARCH 2100.

BANNERTAIL THE SQUIRREL *

1979. JPN: *Risu no Banner*. AKA: *Banner the Squirrel*. TV series. DIR: Yoshio Kuroda. SCR: Toshiyuki Kashiwakura. DES: Yasuji Mori. ANI: Seiji Okuda, Tatsuo Ogawa. MUS: Akihiro Komori. PRD: Nippon Animation, TV Asahi. 23 mins. x 26 eps.
Banner is captured by humans and raised by a domesticated cat, whom he

believes is his real mother. Separated from his "parent" by a village fire, he meets a stray cat who tells him the truth—he is a squirrel. Going back to his original home in a New Jersey forest, Banner meets a female of the same species called Sue, who helps him get back to his squirrel roots.

The second of SETON'S ANIMAL TALES series to be animated (the first was MONARCH: THE BIG BEAR OF TALLAC), *Bannertail* was to be the most successful. The series was notable at the time for the large number of cels used in the animation—a successful attempt to impart realistic motion to the animals. The story received a very limited U.S. subtitled broadcast on some Japanese-community TV stations shortly after its Japanese release, much to the annoyance of anime fans expecting more giant robots.

BAOH *

1989. JPN: *Baoh: Raihosha*. AKA: *Baoh: The Visitor*. Video. DIR: Hiroyuki Yokoyama. SCR: Kenji Terada. DES: Michi Sanaba, Masayoshi Tano. ANI: Michi Sanaba, Jin Kaneko. MUS: Hiroyuki Nanba. PRD: Toho, Studio Pierrot. 50 mins.
Seventeen-year-old Ikuro is implanted with BAOH, an experimental organism that will defend itself and its host at all costs. Escaping from the Doress corporation with the telepathic girl Sumire, he returns to rescue her when she is recaptured by the evil Dr. Kasuminome.

One of many psychic espionage stories rushed straight to video in the wake of AKIRA, *Baoh* takes the well-traveled route of symbiotic weaponry in the style of GUYVER, relegating telepathic powers to the possession of a supporting character. A violent, visceral show prefiguring GENOCYBER, it also features mid-combat posturing in the style of martial arts movies, as characters pause to announce their next "special move" before striking. Hirohiko Araki's original manga in *Shonen Jump* only lasted for two volumes in 1984, though the creator would find more enduring success with **JOJO'S BIZARRE ADVENTURES**. ⊙

BAREFOOT GEN *
1983. JPN: *Hadashi no Gen*. Movie. DIR: Mori Masaki. SCR: Keiji Nakazawa. DES: Kazuo Tomizawa. ANI: Kazuo Tomizawa. MUS: Kentaro Haneda. PRD: Gen Pro, Madhouse. 85 mins.

It's 1945, Japan is losing the war, and times are particularly hard for Gen's pacifist family. Gen, only six years old, has had to grow up fast, and each day is a struggle to get enough food for his pregnant mother, older sister Eiko, and younger brother Shinji. Then the Allies drop a new kind of bomb on Gen's hometown of Hiroshima. People are vaporized by the intense blast, but in a way, they are the lucky ones. Gen's house collapses on its occupants, and he and his mother cannot lift the rubble off their family. Forced to watch their loved ones burn alive, they wander through a world in which survivors succumb to the effects of radiation poisoning, their hair falling out and their bowels bleeding away.

A hard-hitting tale of the horrors of war based on Keiji Nakazawa's 1973 manga, *BG*'s only shortcomings lie in the nature of the original material. Since it is semiautobiographical, it chronicles events instead of subsuming them to a narrative—the bombing of Hiroshima is the central event of Nakazawa's life and work, but once past the immediate aftermath, the film falls into a selection of vignettes. This style was used to better effect in **GRAVE OF THE FIREFLIES**, where such scenes denoted the characters' slow decline, but since the hero of *BG* survives, the use of these scenes in this film often seems to depict the passing of time for its own sake. Nevertheless, *BG* is a terrifying snapshot of one of the most horrific events in human history, perhaps all the more harrowing because it is presented in the cartoon medium so often associated with children's entertainment.

A 90-minute sequel by future **RAIL OF THE STAR**–director Toshio Hirata followed in 1986. Set three years later, it continues the story as Gen tends to his mother with his adopted little brother Ryuta, who also lost his family in the bombing. The film was twice revived as a part of TV specials with a nuclear subject—1992's *Never Forget BG: A Promise to the Children of Chernobyl*, and again in 1995, the 50th anniversary of Hiroshima, when it was shown along with the live-action/CG pieces *Our Playground Was the Genbaku Dome* and *From Hiroshima to America*. Nakazawa's Hiroshima was also the subject of **BENEATH THE BLACK RAIN, FLY ON, DREAMERS!** and the setting for his feature-length 45th anniversary video, *The Summer with Kuro*, in which a black cat charms the lives of two Hiroshima children. Curiously, only one anime, 1995's *Goodbye to Mother's Perfume*, documented the later bombing of Nagasaki, telling the story from the point of view of a 15-year-old apprentice cook.

BARK, BUNBUN
1980. JPN: *Hoero Bunbun*. Movie. DIR: Shigeru Omachi. SCR: Yuji Amemiya, Akira Nakahara. DES: Moribi Murano. ANI: Eiji Suzuki, Yasuhiko Suzuki, Yasuo Mori. MUS: Kazuhito Mori. PRD: TV Tokyo, Wako Pro. 30 mins. x 39 eps.

Bunbun the mastiff puppy climbs into a wooden box and floats down the river, eventually drifting into Tokyo. There he meets a stray dog who teaches him "the commandments" – how to live life without human interference. Based on a manga by former **MOOMIN** animator Moribi Murano, the plot and timing of this anime suggest a jump to TV in the wake of the success of **BANNERTAIL THE SQUIRREL**. An initial 84-minute TV movie was followed six months later by a TV series with the same cast and crew. In 1987, Bunbun returned in a 65-minute theatrical release directed by Toshio Hirata and animated by the Madhouse Studio.

BASARA *
1998. JPN: *Legend of Basara*. TV series. DIR: Nobuhiro Takamoto. SCR: Takao Koyama. DES: Keizo Shimizu. ANI: Hideaki Matsuzaki. MUS: N/C. PRD: KSS, Chiba TV. 30 mins. x 13 eps.

In a postapocalyptic future the Gold King of Kings splits his land into quarters for his color-coded children to rule. In the domain of the youngest, the Red King, the blind prophet Nagi predicts that a desert village will bring forth twins, a boy and a girl, and that the boy shall depose the ruler. The Red King hears the prophecy and sends his army to the village—he boy, Tatara, is killed, but his sister, Sarasa, takes on his prophetic role by cutting off her hair and putting on his clothes. Impersonating Tatara, she convinces the villagers that there is still hope and sets off to retrieve her brother's sword, Byattsuko.

Wounded by the Red King, she is taken to a secluded lake by Kakuji (one of the few villagers who knows her secret). There, she falls in love with a young man called Shuri, though she is unaware that "Shuri" is the Red King, and he is unaware that his new love is the woman who has sworn to destroy him.

Already a success with **THERE GOES TOMOE**, manga artist Yumi Tamura turned to fantasy in 1990. A one-shot "image video" was released in 1993 after *Basara* won the Shogakukan Manga Prize, but the story only became a full-fledged TV series in 1998. The theme of a girl taking on a boy's mission also appears in **YOTODEN**, though the ancestor of all such shows is Osamu Tezuka's **PRINCESS KNIGHT**.

BASEBALL CLUB NUMBER THREE
1988. JPN: *Meimon! Daisan Yakyu Bu*. AKA: *Noble! Baseball Club Number Three*. TV series. DIR: Hiroshi Fukutomi. SCR: Ryuji Yamada. DES: Hiroshi Kanezawa. ANI: Hiroshi Kanezawa. MUS: Yusuke Honma. PRD: Fuji TV, NAS. 25 mins. x 40 eps.

The struggles of a particularly bad baseball team as it fights to win against other schools and the far superior "Number One" and "Number Two" teams at its own Sakura High School. Toshiyuki Mutsu's gag manga in *Shonen*

Magazine obviously hit the market at the right moment, lasting for ten volumes and spawning this relatively long-running series. More romantic takes on baseball would come in a slew of other anime, including **NINE** and **SLOW STEP**.

BASTARD *

1992. JPN: *Bastard: Ankoku no Hakkaijin*. AKA: *Bastard: God-Destroyer of Darkness*. Video. DIR: Katsuhito Akiyama. SCR: Hiroshi Yamaguchi. DES: Hiroyuki Kitazume. ANI: Moriyasu Taniguchi, Hiroyuki Ochi. MUS: Kohei Tanaka. PRD: AIC, Anime R. 30 mins. x 6 eps.

Humanity lives a quasi-medieval existence on an Earth in the midst of apocalypse. Dark Schneider, a powerful sorcerer, causes such havoc that high priest Dio traps him inside the body of a newborn baby, Rushe Renren. Fifteen years later, Schneider's former henchmen (Abigail the dark priestess, Kall-Su the king of ice, Gara the ninja master, and Arshes Nei the empress of thunder) return on a campaign to conquer the world for the fallen angel Anthrasax. Dio must bring Schneider back from limbo and orders his virgin daughter Tia to kiss the lovestruck boy in order to free the man. Their savior arrives, and he is a complete bastard.

Creator Kazushi Hagiwara began as an assistant to Izumi Matsumoto on **KIMAGURE ORANGE ROAD** before becoming a solo artist in his own right. Though the anime *Bastard* stops before the final showdown with Kall-Su, the manga series would continue far beyond, with Schneider assembling his four horsemen of the apocalypse and fighting a final war between Satan and the angels, all while trying to come to terms with Rushe's boyish love for princess Tia.

Many of the names in the *Bastard* series come from Western rock, including the kingdoms of Metallicana, Judas, Aran Maiden, and Whitesnake, the high priest Dio, the battleship King Crimson Glory, and the names of spells include Megadeth, Slayer, Guns'n'Ro, Venom, Tesla, Kiss, Raven, and Exodus. "Bastard" was the original name planned for Motorhead, and Dark Schneider himself is named after Udo Dirkschneider, the lead singer of Accept. Such blasé jokiness seems to work in *Bastard*, though if tried too often, it can grate painfully—just compare with the sausage-machine attitude of Satoru Akahori's shows in a similar vein, such as **MAZE** or **SORCERER HUNTERS**. **Ⓝ**

BASTARD WARRIOR

1990. JPN: *Ajin Senshi*. Video. DIR: Tsuneo Tominaga. SCR: Kazumi Koide. DES: Yoshiaki Matsuda. ANI: Tsuneo Tominaga. MUS: Yuki Nakajima. PRD: Magic Bus. 100 mins.

During a war in 2200, in which both sides utilize psychic weapons, Zero is born of mixed parentage, a Terran mother and an alien father, the last survivor of the Mint clan of sorcerers. In this adaptation of the SF novel by Chiaki Kawamata, it is Zero's destiny to fight the Manjidara Empire and prevent it from seizing control of the galaxy. **Ⓥ**

BATS AND TERRY

1987. Movie. DIR: Tetsuro Amino. SCR: Yasushi Hirano. DES: Noriyasu Yamauchi, Indori-Koya. ANI: Noriyasu Yamauchi, Kenichi Maejima. MUS: Tatsumi Yano. PRD: Sunrise, Matsutake, Magic Bus. 80 mins.

Batsu and Terry ("battery," as in the baseball sense) are a pitcher and catcher devoted to sports, bikes, girls, and good times. When they try to console Anne, a pretty girl who loses her biker boyfriend in a traffic accident, they are dragged into gangland intrigue and must rescue the damsel in distress before the next day's game. Set in Yokohama's Shonan district, home to other road-knight tales such as **BOMBER BIKERS OF SHONAN** and **GTO**, this feel-good crime caper was shown as a double bill with the **DIRTY PAIR** movie *Project Eden*. The first Sunrise production to be adapted from a manga, it had its origins in Yasuichi Oshima's serial in *Shonen Magazine*.

BATTLE ANGEL ALITA *

1993. JPN: *Gunmu*. AKA: *Gun-Dream*. Video. DIR: Hiroshi Fukutomi. SCR: Akinori Endo. DES: Nobuteru Yuki. ANI: Nobuteru Yuki. MUS: Kaoru Wada. PRD: Animate Film, KSS, Movic. 35 mins. x 2 eps.

Though the floating island of Zalem is thought to be a heavenly paradise, few have been there. Instead, the poor scavenge from the giant scrapheap where Zalem throws its garbage. Daisuke Ido and his ex-girlfriend, Chiren, are two experts in cybernetics, forced to ply their trade in the scrapyard after falling out of favor on Zalem. Chiren will do anything to get back home and builds bigger and better modifications for cyborg gladiators. Ido prefers to work as a cyberdoctor for impoverished cyborgs, moonlighting as a bounty hunter. Poking around in Zalem's trash, Ido finds the remains of a cyborg, complete with the irreplaceable spinal cord. He fixes "her" up, names her Alita (Gally in the original), and has his very own robot "daughter" to keep him company. Alita develops a crush on local odd-job boy Yugo, pesters her adoptive dad when he's trying to work, and accidentally reveals that she has superhuman kung-fu skills.

This short-lived spinoff from Yukito Kishiro's 1991 *Business Jump* manga never explains what life on Zalem is really like, why Ido was thrown out, or who the amnesiac Alita was before she was scrapped. The scene is set for a couple of fight scenes and some mawkish flirting between Yugo and Alita before the innocents of the story realize that the corrupt adults have been stringing them along, and it all ends in tears. Highly regarded in the early 1990s by an anime audience punch-drunk on **FIST OF THE NORTH STAR**, *Alita* wasn't particularly original – it takes little to substitute drugs for cybernetics and the scrapheap for an LA ghetto before you have *Boyz N the Hood*. A postholocaust world where one has to buy social betterment was covered more interestingly in GREY: DIGITAL TARGET, whereas Earth as a celestial race's garbage dump was first suggested in Shinichi Hoshi's 1970s short story "Hey! Come On Out!" Initially inspired by MICROMAN toys, Alita herself began life as an illustration around which Kishiro had to work up a story in a hurry, elements of which survive in the anime's fuzzy plotting: she doesn't know much about her past because, at this stage in the story's history, her creator wasn't that sure himself.

Director Fukutomi does the best he can here with the limited budget, but there simply isn't the time to do the story justice, and one amazing image of a paradisiacal city hovering above a disgusting junkyard does not a successful series make. Viewers can take solace, however, in a high amount of immortal dialogue, including, "How long am I going to have to wait for my new spine?"

BATTLE ATHLETES *

1997. JPN: *Battle Athletess* [sic] *Daiundokai.* AKA: *Battle Athletess Great Sports Meet.* Video, TV series. DIR: Kazuhiro Ogawa, Katsuhito Akiyama. SCR: Hideyuki Kurata. DES: Ryoichi Makino. ANI: Shinji Ochi, Nobuyuki Kitajima. MUS: Takayuki Hattori. PRD: Pioneer, TV Tokyo, Aeon. 30 mins. x 6 eps. (V), 25 mins. x 26 eps. (TV).
In the year 4998, athletes strive for the glittering Cosmo Beauty prize on University Satellite. Akari Kanzaki is one such candidate, and the daughter of a former Cosmo Beauty. With little confidence in her own abilities, she still gains the respect and friendship of her multinational teammates. But University Satellite is not merely a sports club, it is a training ground where generations of humans have been secretly honed to perfection for the ultimate battle against a race of sports-loving aliens.

Despite a passionless and cynical execution, this 1990s comedy update of GUNBUSTER still contains moments

of subtle humor, such as an invading alien queen delivering a message of conquest to a pair of bewildered giraffes. The original video series, based on an idea by EL HAZARD's Hiroki Hayashi, stumbles amateurishly through several pointless prologues about World War III, a natural disaster, and still another war before settling down to the story. The later TV series *Battle Athletes: Victory* does a more coherent job, throwing the viewer straight into comedy training setups such as cycling on a roller-coaster track or pulling giant garden rollers across a minefield. Akari works hard (a staple of all such anime, since being a "natural" implies one is lazy) and befriends a plucky Osaka girl, assorted Caucasian also-rans, a comic-relief Chinese rich-bitch, and a feral African girl who is supposed to be cute. The characters laugh at their own jokes and intone antiquated pep talks and clichés from classic shows like AIM FOR THE ACE.

In the grand finale held before a giant headless statue of the Goddess of Victory, Akari is forced to compete against the aliens' champion, the rejuvenated form of her own mother, while her ailing coach (and father) looks on. The Pioneer English dub is excellent as usual, though it is a mystery why the company squandered such riches on a mediocre hybrid of *The Last Starfighter* and *Triumph of the Will.*

BATTLE CAN CAN *

1987. Video. DIR: Kazuya Sasaki. SCR: Kazuhiro Kasai. DES: N/C. ANI: Joji Oshima. MUS: N/C. PRD: Studio G7, Nikkatsu. 30 mins.
The Battle Can Can investigation team is sent out to halt pirate incursions in the space-year 2087. Sophia, Diane, Jill, Marina, and Lily (with a comic–relief robot, Harold) must retrieve the Cosmic Firefly, a fragile jewel worth literally billions. With so much at stake they must subdue space pirates, have sex with aliens, and confront a traitor from within. Nikkatsu was surprisingly ahead of its time with this sci-fi porno; it would take another decade for

Street Fighter II V

© 1996 CAPCOM/GROUP TAC, AMUSE, YOMIURI TELECASTING CORP., MANGA ENTERTAINMENT, INC.

ADVANCER TINA and ALIEN FROM THE DARKNESS to prove that there truly was no hope for the genre. Ⓝ

BATTLE OF THE PLANETS *

1972. JPN: *Kagaku Ninjatai Gatchaman.* AKA: *Science Ninja Team Gatchaman, G-Force, Eagle Riders.* TV series, movie, video. DIR: Junzo Toriumi, Eiko Toriumi, Fumio Kurokawa, Hiroshi Sasakawa, Katsuhisa Yamada. SCR: Junzo Toriumi, Toshio Nagata, Akiyoshi Sakai. DES: Tatsuo Yoshida, Kunio Okawara. ANI: Miyamoto Sado. MUS: Bob Sakuma. PRD: Tatsunoko, Fuji TV. 30 mins. x 205 eps. (TV), 110 min (m), 45 mins. x 3 eps. (v)
Only five young heroes and their giant God-Phoenix aircraft can save Earth from the invading legions of the alien Gallacter. In each episode, Gallacter would send a mechanized menace to terrorize the planet, and the Gatchaman team would stop him, graphically slicing through the enemy minions with weapons such as their *shuriken* and yo-yo bombs, all the while inexplicably dressed in bird costumes.

Though preceded by the five-strong teams of SKYERS 5 and *Thunderbirds* (see THUNDERBIRDS 2086), *Battle of the Planets* was a watershed show, with strong leader Eagle Ken, loose cannon

Condor Joe, love interest Swan June, big-guy Owl Ryu, and little Swallow Jinpei setting up group dynamics that would dominate anime character rosters for decades to come. Episodes 22 and 37, *The Fiery Phoenix vs. the Fire-Eating Dragon* and *Electron Beast Renzilla*, were shown theatrically in 1973 as part of Toho's summer and winter holiday film anthologies. In 1978, acclaimed live-action director Kihachi Okamoto made a genuine anime movie version in which Gatchaman joined forces with the mysterious pilot Charm Red Impulse (Red Specter), who would eventually be revealed as Ken's estranged father.

Eighty-five of the original 105 episodes were adapted for the Sandy Frank English-language version broadcast in the U.S. in 1978. The enemy was renamed Spectra, a dying planet whose Great Spirit had ordered the evil Zoltar to conquer Earth and neighboring worlds in the Federation of Planets. The characters' names were also changed—Mark, Jason, Princess, Tiny, and Keyop were now fighting "attacks by alien galaxies beyond space." With much of the violence cut, additional footage was commissioned to bridge continuity gaps. This included a babbling robot controller, 7-Zark-7, a mascot, 1-Rover-1, shots of the team off-duty in their Ready Room, and, since the group was now supposedly traveling around the universe, several sequences of the Phoenix flying through space.

When Sandy Frank's rights lapsed in 1986, the original series was completely redubbed as *G-Force* by Turner Broadcasting, which dispensed altogether with the 7-Zark-7 footage and selected many episodes from the original run that had not previously been seen outside Japan. The series included more deaths and was more faithful to the original, though the names were again replaced with the awful Ace Goodheart, Dirk Daring, Agatha June, Hootie, and Pee Wee. A ratings disaster, the new show was quietly buried and only seen in its entirety in Australia, though it did eventually return to American TV when Turner established the Cartoon Network in 1995.

The 1979 Japanese sequel *Gatchaman II* featured early design work from Akemi Takada and Yoshitaka Amano, adding another 52 episodes to the original, along with the female foil Professor Pandora and a cyborg replacement for the deceased Joe. This was followed in 1979 by another 48 episodes, *Gatchaman F(ighter)*. Both serials were eventually bought by Saban Entertainment in 1996, cut down to 65 episodes, and released as *Eagle Riders*. The characters were renamed for a third time, as Hunter Harris, Joe Thax, Kelly Jenar, Ollie Keeawani, and Mickey Dougan. Their mission: "To defend the global good."

In 1994, the series was remade in Japan, compressed into a three-part video outing called simply *Gatchaman* by director Hiroyuki Fukushima with character designs by Yasuomi Umezu. The show was swiftly dubbed for an American anime market now more aware of its origins. The original Japanese names were retained, and in a bizarre coincidence, the voice actor who played Ken, Richard Cansino, also lent his talents in *Eagle Riders* as Joe. *Ill. p. 395.*

BATTLE ROYALE HIGH SCHOOL *

1987. JPN: *Shinmajinden*. AKA: *Tale of True Devilry*. Video. DIR: Ichiro Itano. SCR: Ichiro Itano. DES: Nobuteru Yuki. ANI: Nobuteru Yuki, Satoshi Urushihara, Hideaki Anno. MUS: Shiro Sagisu. PRD: DAST. 55 mins.
A time-traveling security officer must prevent an extradimensional demon lord from taking over the world. But the demon-lord in question has taken over the body of a high-school karate teacher in modern-day Tokyo. The demon-hunter sent to get him has also been possessed, but by an evil fairy queen who wants the planet for herself.

Shinichi Kuruma's original manga in *Shonen Captain* was based on a story by **AMON SAGA**'s Baku Yumemakura.

Looking like a toned-down version of the later **NIGHTMARE CAMPUS**, the anime version simply restored much of the gore for a straight-to-video audience. Animator Anno and composer Sagisu would later work together again on **EVANGELION**. No relation to the live-action Kinji Fukasaku film *Battle Royale* (2000). **LNV**

BATTLE SKIPPER *

1995. Video. DIR: Takashi Watanabe. SCR: Hidemi Kubota. DES: Takashi Kobayashi, Kimitoshi Yamane. ANI: Takashi Kobayashi, Toshiko Sasaki. MUS: Kenyu Miyotsu. PRD: Artmic, Tokyo Kids. 30 mins. x 3 eps.
"In the Etiquette Club, the first rule is strength! The second rule is strength! There is no third or fourth rule, but the fifth rule is strength!" Rivalries at St Ignacio's Catholic girls' school get out of hand when rich-bitch Sayaka starts using giant "battle skipper" robots to dominate those who oppose her Debutante Club. Only a group of unknown vigilantes foils her plans, and little does Sayaka know that the Exstars vigilantes are actually the unassuming freshmen of the undersubscribed Etiquette Club—current membership, two.

Rie and Reika are looking for recruits, but it's difficult when they are not allowed to tell new arrivals that their deserted clubhouse is really an underground base containing their secret arsenal. New girls Kanami, Saori, and Shihoko sneak into the clubhouse, where they stumble across the color-coded battlesuits that almost seem made for them. . . .

Initially created to promote Tomy's MRV toy line, *Battle Skippers* mixes elements of *Thunderbirds* and **BUBBLEGUM CRISIS** with the school satire of **PROJECT A-KO** and **DEBUTANTE DETECTIVES**. The three episodes were edited into a "movie" compilation for the U.S. video market and resolicited after director Watanabe became better known for **SLAYERS**.

BATTLE TEAM LAKERS EX *

1996. JPN: *Seishojo Sentai Lakers EX*.

AKA: *Holy Girl Battle Team Lakers EX.* Video. DIR: Takashi Kawamura. SCR: Ryusei. DES: Koichi Fujii, Mitsuharu Miyamae. ANI: Koichi Fujii. MUS: Kazuya Matsushita, Hideo Kuroda. PRD: Beam Entertainment, Animate Film. 30 mins. Five exiled space warriors live undercover as Tokyo college girls, sworn to use their Laker power to defend Earth from the evil queen Oleana of the Godram empire. Would-be singer Reiko (Star), hot-headed Chiaki (Kung Fu), bespectacled Yayoi (Soul), big-chested tomboy Natsumi (Judo), and baby-faced Yuka (Bunny) all lust after their team leader, the handsome Akira (Blade Knight). After a rehearsal for Reiko's forthcoming concert, Akira convinces Reiko to try out a sex toy to help amass greater energy for battle. Meanwhile, Oleana sends four robot doppelgangers to pose as Akira and seduce the other girls. The next day, the girls assume that Akira has swindled them and refuse to follow orders when one of Oleana's giant monsters attacks the school. They are captured and taken to Oleana's spaceship but rescued by Akira. Lacking the energy to transform, they stage an impromptu orgy to regain their powers and escape.

A soft-core pastiche of the all-girl team shows that began with SAILOR MOON, even to the extent of posing as just one episode in a long-running saga, *Lakers EX* barely has time for a setup and showdown. Not quite hitting the ludicrous heights of VENUS FIVE (though the voice acting is superior to many other erotic anime dubs), the careful duplication of hack genre conventions ironically leaves little time for the sex. Based on a computer game. **N**

BAVI STOCK

1985. Video. DIR: Shigenori Kageyama. SCR: Kenji Terada. DES: Mutsumi Inomata, Takahiro Tomoyasu. ANI: Masahiro Shida, Ryunosuke Otonashi. MUS: Yasuaki Honda. PRD: Hero Media, Kaname Pro, Studio Unicorn. 45 mins. x 2 eps.
Agent Kate Lee Jackson of the GPP (space police) frees the mute girl Muma from a space prison on a huge satellite called the Bentika Empire. She also frees Bavi Stock, a young boxer jailed after accidentally killing an opponent. The prison doctor, Sammy, who has been trying to ensure that Bavi stays alive, joins them, and they head for GPP HQ. But bad guys from Benti-ka, the psionic Ruth Miller and her henchman, Eyesman, disintegrate the GPP home world. With nowhere else to go, our heroes head for Sammy's home world, arriving on the eve of a big sky-sled race. Sammy and Bavi enter and face off against Eyesman, while Ruth Miller tries to sabotage the control computers, and Kate and Muma have to stop her. In the aftermath, Ruth is trapped in an alternate dimension, and Muma is revealed as the key to the downfall of the Bentika Empire.

Cherry-picking the destruction of planet Alderaan, the rescue of Princess Leia, and the Endor speeder-bike chase from the early *Star Wars* films, *Bavi Stock* is a deliberate attempt to reverse-engineer U.S. space opera. It even features Americanized names, though some of them are altered beyond recognition in transit—Bavi is a mutation of Bobby, "as in Bavi Kennedy," according to producer Hiro-masa Shibazaki. Less innocent *Star Wars* rip-offs can be found in BONDAGE QUEEN KATE.

BAYBRADE *

2001. JPN: *Bakuten Shoot Baybrade.* AKA: *Flashpoint Shoot Baybrade.* TV series. DIR: Toshifumi Kawase, Jun Takada, Masahiko Murata. SCR: Toshiyasu Okubo, Kiyoshi Mizugami, Tatsuhiko Urahata, Kazuyuki Fudeyasu. DES: Takao Aoki. ANI: Shigeru Kato, Kiyoshi Nakahara. MUS: Yoshihisa Hira-no. PRD: Madhouse, TV Tokyo. 25 mins. x 51 eps.
Takao Kinomiya wants to be a master of the gladiatorial Baybrade contest, but only the chosen few can truly control the Pit entities that live inside the spinning-top-like fighting devices. His friend Kai uses the Transor Pit, but Takao discovers a Pit of his own, the creature known as Dragoon, who has lived inside the family's heirloom sword for generations.

An anime based on the *begoma* toy craze, fighting gyroscopes from TRANS-FORMERS-creators Takara. The last gyro standing within the ring is the winner, and each has five component parts that can be customized to create (almost) unique toys. The post-POKÉMON generation in Japan set aside its Pikachus and Jigglypuffs in favor of the arcane design of Pit Chips, Attack Rings, Weight Discs, Spin Gears, and Blade Bases. At least it got them out of the house. Released in the U.S. as *Beyblade*.

BEAST CITY *

1996. JPN: *Inju Dai Toshi.* AKA: *Lust-Beast Great City.* Video. DIR: Shinichiro Watanabe. SCR: Naomi Hayakawa, Yuri Kanai. DES: Naomi Hayakawa. ANI: Hitoshi Imazaki. MUS: N/C. PRD: Com-stock, Karasu Communications. 45 mins. x 3 eps.
Tokyo is held for ransom by the demonic Beasts that stalk its streets. Born into a family of vampires, Mina has vowed to destroy all of the creatures with her Beast-hunter sword.

Sex and violence galore as Mina and her bisexual vampire associates from Draculon get their daily fix by having oral sex with a sleeping human and sinking their teeth into his engorged penis, all without waking him up. Then they go looking for a fight, get knocked about a bit, and kill some demons.

Though its premise is distantly related to VAMPIRE HUNTER D, *Beast City* removes all the subtextual tension of vampire stories. A heroine named for Bram Stoker's original and a home world poached from *Vampirella* do little good when the rest of vampire lore is taken with a pinch of salt—these creatures still fear crucifixes but happily immerse themselves beneath running water in long shower scenes. In Japan, the series was partly sold to the public on the basis that sharp-eared viewers would hear several famous voice actresses grunting and groaning behind pseudonyms, a sure-fire sign of a lack of faith in other aspects of production (see **ADVENTURE KID**). Two other Naomi Hayakawa creations have been animated: *Binding* (as part of **COOL DEVICES**) and **MELANCHOLY SLAVE**. Similar liberties were taken with legends about werewolves to create **MIDNIGHT PANTHER**. **🅛🅝🅥**

BEAST WARRIORS *

1992. JPN: *KO Seiki Beast Sanjushi*. AKA: *KO Century Beast Three Beastketeers; KO Century Beast Warriors*. Video. DIR: Hiroshi Negishi. SCR: Satoru Akahori, Tetsuko Watanabe, Mayori Sekijima, Koji Masunari. DES: Zero-G Room, Rei Nakahara, Takehiko Ito. ANI: Takuya Saito, Makoto Matsuo. MUS: Nick Wood. PRD: KSS. 30 mins. x 7 eps.

On an Earth literally broken in two, the evil Humans have invaded the territory of the heavily mutated Beast tribes. Though they possess powerful totem weapons, the Beasts cannot stand against the Humans' high-tech might. Wan Dabada, who can transform into a tiger when angry, is captured when his tribe is destroyed and thrown into jail with three other Beasts: Meima, the mermaid princess; Mekka, the turtle boy; and Badd Mint, the transforming chicken. Professor Password, a human scientist ashamed at his race's behavior, is killed helping them escape but not before entrusting the group with his granddaughter, Yumi Charm. Searching for the mythical Gaia system that could turn the battle, they find one of its outposts by draining a lake—elements here not only of **TREASURE ISLAND**, but also of director Negishi's earlier **LADIUS**. With Yumi's help, they learn how to combine their totems into a superweapon, though a power supply proves harder to come by.

As with other Akahori creations like **MAZE** and **KNIGHTS OF RAMUNE**, the hackneyed but entertaining *Beast Warriors* has a flimsy plot concealed by tongue-in-cheek humor and loud, brash designs—here including costumes by **OH MY GODDESS!**–creator Kosuke Fujishima. The initial series is clearly the setup for a TV version that never came, and the final four episodes (renamed *Beast Warriors II* and written, in part, by future **PHOTON**-director Masunari) simply adds some new designs and an extra subplot similar to that surrounding Rini in **SAILOR MOON**. As the first and only release of the ill-fated Anime U.K. label, it was also a failure in its English version— never making enough money to justify the release of the final four episodes and never distributed in the U.S.

BEAT SHOT

1989. Video. DIR: Takashi Akimoto. SCR: Hidemi Kamata. DES: Satoshi Ikezawa. ANI: Hiroyuki Oka. MUS: N/C. PRD: Gainax, AIC. 30 mins.

Expert linksman Akihiko joins the university golf club at the same time as maverick golfer Akikazu. The pair often tee off against each other, though Akikazu is distracted by the charms of his opponent's beautiful caddy, Misako. A heady mix of sex and golf in this adaptation of a manga from *Monthly Playboy* (no relation to the U.S. magazine). Creator Satoshi Ikezawa normally specializes in racing stories like **CIRCUIT WOLF** but here replaces the tension of fast cars with furtive fumblings in the rough.

BE-BOP HIGH SCHOOL

1990. Movie. DIR: Toshihiko Ariseki, Hiroyuki Kadokane, Junichi Fujise. SCR: Kazuhiro Kiuchi, Tatsuhiko Urahata. DES: Kazuhiro Kiuchi. ANI: Junichi Haneyama. MUS: Ginjiro Ito. PRD: Toei. 45 mins. x 7 eps.

School tough-guys Toru and Hiroshi have impossibly wedge-shaped haircuts and a deep love of pretty girls. Forever fighting against the authority of the weak-willed principal they refer to as Turtle Man, they live only to scrap with rival gangs like the Hitman Brothers in this anime spinoff of the 1987 live-action film based on a manga by screenwriter Kazuhiro Kiuchi. The cartoonish nature of the original story made the anime infinitely preferable to the movie, which was hampered by poor acting and a cripplingly low budget (director Hiroyuki Nasu would make the equally bad *Pinch Runner* in 2000). The series also spawned the three-part *Be-Bop Pirate Edition*, a humorous spinoff supposedly written by "Memeoka Manhiro" in 1991. In 1991, four years after the sixth episode of the video, a final chapter was released in which the same amount of time had passed onscreen for the leads, taking them out of school and into the real world along with their audience.

BE-BOY KIDNAPPIN' IDOL

1989. Movie. DIR: Kenichi Yatsuya. SCR: Michiko Onuki. DES: Kazumi Oya, Naoyuki Onda. ANI: Naoyuki Onda. MUS: Katsunori Ishida. PRD: AIC. 30 mins.

Comical adventures of beautiful boy pop-idol Kazuya Shinohara and his dear friend, Akihiko Kudo. Featuring significant design input from girls' manga artist Kazumi Oya (creator of **OTOHIME CONNECTION**), this one-shot video was sold to the anime audience on the strengths of its two leads, Nozomu Sasaki (Tetsuo from **AKIRA**) and Takeshi Kusao (Pern from **LODOSS WAR**), in uncharacteristically romantic roles.

BELLE AND SEBASTIAN *

1981. JPN: *Meiken Jolly*. AKA: *Famous Dog Jolly*. TV series. DIR: Keiji Hayakawa, Shinji Okada, Kazuyoshi Yokota, Fumio Ikeno, Seiji Endo. SCR: Toshiyuki Kashiwakura, Soji Yoshikawa, Kunio Nakatani. DES: Shuichi Seki. ANI: Nobuyuki Kitajima. MUS: TT Nescebance. PRD: Toho, Visual 80, NHK. 25 mins. x 52 eps.

Named for the saint's day on which he was born and abandoned by his gypsy mother, Sebastian has been raised by Old Seasal, who may or may not be his grandfather. Rejected by the village children for having no parents, he befriends Jolly (Belle), a large Great Pyrenees dog hated and reviled as "the white devil." In search of somewhere to call home, the pair (and their comic-relief puppy, Poochie) journey across the Pyrenees in search of Sebastian's mother, which is similar to a quest seen in FROM THE APENNINES TO THE ANDES. Though they find many places to live (the Pyrenees seem to be littered with kindly childless couples willing to adopt a boy and his dogs), they are always forced to move on by the relentless pursuit of Garcia, an officer of the law who believes them to have committed a crime. Based on the children's books by Cecile Aubrey, this series was picked up by Nickelodeon in the 1980s.

BELOVED BETTY: DEVIL STORY
1986. JPN: *Itoshi no Betty: Ma Monogatari*. Video. DIR: Kazuo Koike, Masahito Sato. SCR: Hideo Takayashiki. DES: Kazuo Ohara. ANI: Michio Shindo. MUS: Haruki Mino. PRD: Big Bang, Cosmos, Toei. 53 mins.
A devil-girl with the face of an angel and a heart of gold, blonde Betty falls in love with an earthbound gangster, Danpei Kimogawa, when they meet in a rainstorm. They end up living together in a Tokyo highrise apartment, though Danpei has trouble coping with his new witch and demon in-laws dropping in at inopportune moments. Betty has actually been sent to the human world on a mission to defeat the demon Lutan. While Betty continues with her task, her skeletal grandmother sends nubile nymphs to tempt Danpei and see if he is suitable husband material. A Japanese knockoff of *Bewitched* but with a lowlife husband and considerably more sex, *Beloved Betty* thrived amid a 1980s Japanese fad for domestic magic. The same year saw the release of GOING STEADY WITH A WITCH, though both titles would soon be eclipsed by another alien lover more suitable for the mass market, URUSEI YATSURA's Lum. In this short video, also shown theatrically on a double bill with AMON SAGA, the henpecked Danpei was played by Yuji Miyake, a pop star from the group Set. Director Koike also wrote the original

1980 manga, drawn by Seisaku Kano for *Big Comic*, though by the time the anime version was released, he was making more of a name for himself with CRYING FREEMAN. **Ⓝ**

BENEATH THE BLACK RAIN
1984. JPN: *Kuroi Ame ni Utarete*. Movie. DIR: Takeshi Shirato, Kazuhiko Udagawa. SCR: Motokazu Hara, Keiji Nakazawa, Takeshi Shirato. DES: Keiji Nakazawa. ANI: Kazuhiko Udagawa. MUS: Kitaro. PRD: Gen Pro, Tsuchida Pro. 90 mins.
BAREFOOT GEN–creator Keiji Nakazawa wrote an even darker series of tales for this anthology movie about several characters reacting in different ways to the ongoing effects of the atomic bomb. Yuri attempts a one-woman crusade against the U.S. by giving syphilis to servicemen; Yuko becomes a human museum, baring her burned and distorted skin as a testament to the effects of the bomb; while Eiko frets over whether she should get pregnant, since she is a child of bomb victims and may still carry mutant genes. **Ⓝ**

BENKEI VS. USHIWAKA
1939. JPN: *Benkei tai Ushiwaka*. Movie. DIR: Kenzo Masaoka. SCR: Kenzo Masaoka. DES: Kenzo Masaoka. ANI: Ryotaro Kuwata. MUS: N/C. PRD: Nippon Doga Kenkyu Tokoro. 10 mins.
Ushiwaka (aka Minamoto no Yoshitsune) lives in the forest and is trained in the martial arts by *tengu* crow spirits. One day he is walking through Kyoto when his path is blocked by a giant monk, Benkei, who has sworn to take the swords of a thousand defeated foes and now has but one left to collect before he can retire. The diminutive Ushiwaka, however, refuses to hand his sword over and trounces the giant monk on the Gojo bridge. Recognizing his true master, Benkei swears eternal loyalty. Often termed the "Robin Hood and Little John" of Japanese legend, stories of Yoshitsune and Benkei often crop up in JAPANESE FOLK TALES. However, sightings of them are curiously rare in anime despite a rich tradition

The Secret of Blue Water

that could easily fill a series the size of RANMA 1/2. Apart from this single antique two-reeler, they can only be found in oblique references in other shows and in a couple of tales in the series JAPANESE HISTORY and MANGA PICTURES OF JAPAN. *Ill. p. 207.*

BERSERK
1997. JPN: *Kenpu Dengi Berserk*. AKA: *Sword-Wind Chronicle Berserk*. TV series. DIR: Naohito Takahashi. SCR: Yasuhiro Imagawa, Atsuhiro Tomioka. DES: Yoshihiko Umakoshi, Tokuhiro Matsubara. ANI: Tokuhiro Matsubara, Yuriko Senba. MUS: Susumu Hirazawa. PRD: OLM, Nippon TV. 25 mins. x 25 eps.
Guts, a mercenary, rises fast through the ranks of the Midland army. Worried at intrigues behind the scenes, he decides to leave, but his leader, Griffiths, does not allow him to go, forcing Guts to best him in combat. After seducing the king's daughter, the disgraced Griffiths is thrown in jail. Joining forces with the other mercenaries, including his lover, Casca, Guts attempts to rescue Griffiths, only to discover he has made a pact with God Hand, interdimensional beings who demand human sacrifice. Guts loses an eye and his left arm in the ensuing

fight and is forced to watch as his comrades die, while Casca is raped by the creature that was once Griffiths. Hellbent on revenge, Guts sets off to hunt down God Hand.

With a hero whose magical wound will not heal, baddies named after SF greats (Conrad, Ubik, Slan, and Boskone), fighting on and off the battlefield, and no punches pulled in its savagery and devilry, *Berserk* was a manga hit with both readers and critics when it appeared in *Young Animal* magazine. Told chiefly in flashback, the anime series covers the early chapters of Kentaro Miura's manga. The series was lampooned in an episode of the **OH MY GODDESS!** comedy show, *Adventures of Mini-Goddess*, in which Skuld and Urd, dressed as Guts and Griffiths, must rescue Belldandy from a castle. There were rumors of a U.S. release following the publication of the *Sword of the Berserk* game on the Dreamcast, but negotiations were reportedly incomplete at our deadline. ●

BETTERMAN *

1999. TV series. DIR: Yoshitomo Yonetani. SCR: Hiroshi Yamaguchi. DES: Masahiro Kimura, Kunio Okawara, Masahiro Yamane. ANI: Masahiro Kimura. MUS: Kohei Tanaka. PRD: Sunrise, TV Tokyo. 25 mins. x 14 eps.
The year is 2006. Keita Aono is a bespectacled schoolboy in Yokohama who is surprised to meet childhood sweetheart Hinoki Sai when she transfers to his school. The rainbow-haired Hinoki now works for Akamatsu Industrial Company (AIC—as in the anime studio), piloting the large robots called Neuronoids. These machines run on a kind of artificial blood called Linker Gel and patch directly into their pilots' nervous systems. When Hinoki's fellow pilot Cactus is killed in a battle with monsters called Algernons, Keita is talked into taking his place and discovers that he is one of the rare Dual Kind, able to synchronize almost perfectly with the complex machine. He becomes a full-fledged pilot, though Hinoki's activities alongside him are

often suspiciously supported by "Betterman Lamia," a man with the same hairstyle as her and an uncanny ability to turn up in the nick of time and save the day by transforming into the bioweapon Betterman Nebula.

In the grand tradition of **GUNDAM**, Sunrise filed the serial numbers off its standard story template and punched it out again post-**EVANGELION**—evidence, if ever it was required, that two years after you do something in the anime business, you can do it all over again and nobody will notice.

BIG O, THE *

1999. TV series. DIR: Kazuyoshi Katayama. SCR: Chiaki Konaka. DES: Keiichi Sato. ANI: Masami Osone, Kenji Haneyama. MUS: Toshihiko Sahashi. PRD: Sunrise, WOWOW. 25 mins. x 13 eps.
In 2099, beneath the overarching dome of Paradigm City, amnesiac humanity has lived for 40 years without any contact with the outside world. But there's trouble in Paradigm, and the government has been forced to use increasingly harsh measures to keep the restless citizenry in check. Criminal Negotiator Roger Smith finds himself in over his head when he becomes involved in the race to activate Big O, one of the last surviving examples of the super-advanced technology that led to humanity's self-immurement in the first place.

Big O has a distinct resemblance not only to director Katayama's earlier **GIANT ROBO**, but also to Warner Bros.' *Batman Beyond*, for which Sunrise had been a Japanese subcontractor. Beyond its crime-fighting millionaire, *Big O*'s roots extend much further back into science fiction, with settings and cybernetics inspired by Isaac Asimov's *Caves of Steel* (1954) and impressive Art Deco costumes and architecture. With the introduction of R.(obot) Dorothy Wayneright, an android almost indistinguishable from real humans, who may hold the secret to humankind's amnesia, the show gains elements that also tie it to a Japanese antecedent,

Osamu Tezuka's **METROPOLIS**. Retrospirited action in the spirit of **GIANT ROBO** and **STEAM DETECTIVES**.

BIG WARS *

1993. Video. DIR: Toshifumi Takizawa. SCR: Kazumi Koide. DES: Satomi Mikiyura, Kow Yokoyama. ANI: Keizo Shimizu. MUS: Michiaki Kato. PRD: Tokuma, Magic Bus. 70 mins.
Many centuries ago, aliens calling themselves Gods visited Earth and subjugated the primitive peoples. When they left, the vestiges of their technology helped humanity become civilized. The aliens return in A.D. 2416 to find mankind unwilling to serve them again, so they unleash a mind-control plague. Haunted by Catholic imagery and a carrier called Hell, Captain Akuh of the battleship Aoba is worried that his girlfriend is showing the first signs of infection (nymphomania, would you believe), but he needs to pull himself together in time for the coming fight— which is as carefully detailed as one might expect from Yoshio Aramaki, who also gave us **DEEP BLUE FLEET**. This anime was made straight to video but given a limited theatrical release to boost its credibility. *Ill. p. 141.* ●

BIG X

1964. TV series. DIR: Mitsuteru Okamoto, Osamu Dezaki. SCR: Jiro Kadota, Mami Murano, Tadashi Hirose. DES: Osamu Tezuka. ANI: Eiji Suzuki, Renzo Kinoshita. MUS: Isao Tomita. PRD: TMS, TBS. 30 mins. x 59 eps.
During World War II, the Nazis force pacifistic Japanese Professor Asagumo and German Professor Engel to develop Big X, a genetically engineered formula to turn men into giant, invincible soldiers, as a superweapon for Hitler. As Berlin falls in 1945, the researchers are murdered to preserve the secret, but not before Asagumo hides the formula with his son, Shigeru, who returns to Japan. Twenty years later, Hitler's underground neo-Nazi movement revives the war. Gestapo agents in Tokyo attack Shigeru in the midst of an experiment and kill him, but the

intruders are thwarted by his son, Akira, who injects himself with the Big X serum, transforming into a 60-foot giant, a Big X intent on fighting for good. The Nazis scheme to bring Akira/Big X to Carthago, a north African state recently conquered by Germans under the command of Hans Engel, grandson of the serum's coinventor. Hans, the victim of Nazi brainwashing, believes that his grandfather was the sole inventor of Big X and that the Asagumos have stolen his birthright from him. In Carthago, Akira meets his love interest, Nina Burton, a sweet young girl who can communicate telepathically with animals. After the liberation of Carthago, Akira and Nina move on to fight the Nazis in other parts of the world, where they are operating through a seemingly neutral international political movement that they control, the Cross Party.

The first production for Tokyo Movie Shinsha, this was the second anime to be made from the works of **ASTRO BOY**–creator Osamu Tezuka. Rethinking Japan's wartime association with Nazism for a more juvenile audience than the same author's *Adolf*, *Big X* ran in *Shonen Book* in 1963 and presaged another Tezuka genetics plot in **BAGHI**. Akira would transform by injecting himself with the serum from a disguised fountain pen, a dangerously tempting idea for a juvenile audience, outclassed perhaps only by **8 MAN**'s radioactive cigarettes and the pyromaniac pleasures of **GOLD LIGHTAN**.

BIKKURIMAN

1987. AKA: *Surprise-Man*. TV series. DIR: Yukio Misawa. SCR: Sukehiro Tomita, Asami Watanabe. DES: Mitsuru Aoyama. ANI: Hiroyuki Kadokane, Masahiro Ando. MUS: Takanori Arisawa. PRD: Toei, TV Asahi. 25 mins. x 48 eps.
At a time when Earth is about to be cleansed of the old order, the princes of the gods return to fight for the new. Super Zeus, lord of the God-World, orders Saint Phoenix, Prince Yamato, the divine Ali Baba, and their dizzying array of pals to journey to the "edge of the West" and set up a new peaceful land called Jikai. Lined up against them are the minions of Super Devil, king of Devil-World. An incredibly popular tie-in featuring characters from the Bikkuriman Chocolate packets, Bikkuriman also made it into theaters in 1988 with the screening of the time-travel side-story *First Armageddon* and a 45-minute special entitled *Secret Treasure of the Abandoned Zone*. A 44-episode sequel, *Super Bikkuriman*, followed in 1993, written by Aya Matsui with sharper, brighter designs in the style of other 1990s shows.

BILLY DOG

1988. JPN: *Billy Inu*. TV series. DIR: Hiroshi Sasakawa, Junji Nishimura. SCR: Noboru Shiroyama, Masaru Yamamoto. DES: Yayoi Takihara. ANI: Chuji Nakajima. MUS: Tetsu Inakawa. PRD: TV Asahi, Shinei. 20 mins. x 44 eps.
Tatsuo Yumori leaves on Hanabibi Hill with his dog, Billy, who followed the boy home one day and just stayed. But Billy is a talking dog with the mind of a human being, and he soon brings his friend, Gary Dog, into the lives of Tatsuo, his family, and his friends. Based on a manga by Fujiko-Fujio.

BIOHUNTER *

1995. Video. DIR: Yuzo Sato, Yoshiaki Kawajiri. SCR: Yoshiaki Kawajiri. DES: Hiroshi Hamazaki. ANI: Hiroshi Hamazaki. MUS: Masamichi Amano. PRD: Madhouse. 60 mins.
A virus transforms people into monsters with demonic powers. Two molecular scientists, Koshigaya and Kimada, who moonlight as psychic researchers, are approached by the beautiful Sayaka Murakami, whose fortuneteller grandfather has gone missing after an appointment with a prominent politician. Based on a manga serialized in *Comic Burger* by **JUDGE**-creator Fujihiko Hosono, this anime was partly bankrolled by the U.S. distributor Urban Vision, whose Mataichiro Yamamoto is credited as a producer. Under the charge of the Madhouse studio and **WICKED CITY**'s Yoshiaki Kawajiri, it looks just like every other demons-among-us tale that characterized so many successful anime in the U.S., which probably explains the foreign money. **NV**

BIRDY THE MIGHTY *

1996. JPN: *Tetsuwan Birdy*. Video. DIR: Yoshiaki Kawajiri. SCR: Chiaki Konaka. DES: Kumiko Takahashi, Yutaka Izubuchi. ANI: Kumiko Takahashi. MUS: Yuki Otani. PRD: Madhouse. 35 mins. x 4 eps.
Loser schoolboy Tsutomu is fatally wounded in the crossfire between an alien criminal and an intergalactic bounty hunter. To preserve his life, officer Birdy Cephon Altirra merges with him, living *inside* his body, helping him through teenage troubles but forcing him to transform at humorously inappropriate moments.

A sex-swap farce à la **RANMA 1/2**, with a tip of the hat to Tezuka's "Mighty" **ASTRO BOY**, *Birdy*'s true roots lie in the live-action **ULTRAMAN**, with aliens defeated by low-budget gimmicks like dish soap and a hapless Earthman forced to share his body with an invisible, controlling alien. Birdy straddles separate subplots as a vengeful bounty hunter, magical girlfriend, and confidante, contrasting with Tsutomu's spiteful real-life sister. Based on a short-lived manga from **PATLABOR**'s Masami Yuki, this disappointing series features a dream-team of anime creators, all working below par. Writer Konaka, brother of *Ultraman*-director Kazuya, manages a few tongue-in-cheek observations, such as why ugly aliens never get to be space cops, but these are outnumbered by the very genre conventions they lampoon—for example, the evil-yet-beautiful alien mastermind Revi, who wants to turn humans into bioweapons. Matters are not helped by a lead actor in the dub who is forced to pitch his voice so high that, in the words of someone from the U.S. distributor, "he sounds like Mr. Hanky the Christmas Poo."

BIRTH OF JAPAN

1970. JPN: *Nihon Tanjo*. TV series. DIR: Eiichi Yamamoto. SCR: Eiichi Yamamoto. DES: N/C. ANI: Yoshifumi Seyama. MUS: Isao Tomita. PRD: Tezuka Pro, Nippon TV. 26 mins. x 5 eps.

Liu Fa is a kappa, an amphibious humanoid creature who lives in the south of China. He meets the lovely Kozara, a girl from a distant land. Eventually, he follows her to Japan, bringing iron weapons and rice cultivation to the island of Kyushu. Because kappa live for a thousand years, he is able to watch as his inventions spread, creating the foundations of the state that will become Japan. With characteristic Japanese vagueness about historical origins, this fantasy was shown beneath the slogan "Nonfiction Theater," though with its mixture of the supernatural and quasi-historical it is no truer to life than its distant cousins PRINCESS MONONOKE and DARK MYTH.

BIT THE CUPID *

1995. TV series. DIR: Tameo Ogawa. SCR: Soji Yoshikawa. DES: Susumu Matsushita. ANI: Toshiyasu Okada. MUS: Ko Suzuki. PRD: B2 Pro, TV Tokyo, 25 mins. x 48 eps.

In the realm of the Greek gods, where Zeus and Poseidon aren't talking, Narcissus is falling in love with himself, and Icarus is taking flying lessons, the titular Bit is a young demigod of uncertain parentage (though possibly the son of Apollo) who is able to make characters fall in love, though his aim is not always true. As he mixes it up with Hyacinth, Galatea, Atlas, and the gang, many Greek myths are intermixed with tales of more contemporary origin—such as Frisbee the Golden Assassin and Lee of Birdland. One of the earliest anime to be made inside a computer, it was broadcast in English on Fox Kids in the Netherlands—it's a wacky world.

BITE ME! CHAMELEON *

1992. JPN: *Chameleon*. Video. DIR: Mitsuo Hashimoto, Takao Yotsuji. SCR: Takao Yotsuji. DES: Tamiyoshi Yazaki. ANI: Tamiyoshi Yazaki. MUS: Saburo Takada. PRD: Victor. 50 mins. x 6 eps.

Eikichi Yazawa is a thug determined to be top dog at Narita High, so he does his best to convince love interest Asaoka that he used to be the toughest kid in junior high. Local bully Aizawa doesn't believe it for a moment, and Eikichi is forced to fight a battle with whatever is at hand, including urine, farts, and bloody napkins. Proud of its puerile nature, each episode would introduce a new challenger, whom Eikichi would have to outsmart or outgross. The final two releases were directed by former scriptwriter Yotsuji and had not previously appeared as stories in the manga, although they were little different from those that had.

Taking the stained mantle of the similar BRAT COP and moving the action to a school, Atsushi Kato's 33-volume manga from *Shonen Magazine* sold 1.3 million, but adding the words "Bite Me!" to the title couldn't save it in the U.S., where it bombed after just one episode. 🅛🅥

BLACK HEAVEN *

1999. JPN: *Kacho Oji*. AKA: *Section Chief Oji, Legend of Black Heaven*. TV series. DIR: Yasunori Kikuchi. SCR: Narihisa Arakawa. DES: Kazuto Nakazawa. ANI: Hiroshi Hashimoto. MUS: Koichi Korenaga. PRD: AIC, APPP, Pioneer, WOWOW. 25 mins. x 13 eps.

Oji Tanaka, a henpecked, middle-aged salaryman with a dull wife and a mewling infant, still thinks fondly of his teenage years when he was "Gabriel" Tanaka, lead guitarist with the hard rock group Black Heaven. He is contacted by a beautiful blonde agent, Leila Yuki, and hired to play his particular brand of music for use as a sonic weapon in an interstellar war.

The space war is curiously underused, the script concentrating instead on Tanaka's hapless attempts to enlist his old band in his secret mission and his wife's attempts to discover whether he is having an affair with Leila. But with a focus on farce and everyday life not unlike Nigel Kneale's *Kinvig, BH* resembles a live-action production that cannot afford the special effects rather than an anime that can go anywhere in the galaxy for the price of a pot of paint. *BH* has much in common with other short-lived TV serials of the late 1990s—the backgrounds are sparse and reused often, and the animation is cheap, flat, and digital. The filmmakers attempt to distract the viewer's attention with occasional flashy graphics and rotoscoping, especially over the opening credits featuring footage of Whitesnake's John Sykes, who sings the theme tune. It's music as power, à la MACROSS, but expanding the audience to include disenchanted thirty-somethings, with many 1970s heavy metal in-jokes.

BLACK JACK *

1993. Movie, video. DIR: Osamu Dezaki. SCR: Eto Mori, Kihachi Okamoto. DES: Akio Sugino. ANI: Akio Sugino. MUS: Osamu Shoji, Kiyoshi Suzuki. PRD: Tezuka Pro. 50 mins. x 9 eps. (v), 93 mins. (m).

Black Jack was one of Osamu Tezuka's most popular creations, a scar-faced doctor-for-hire with a deep-set sense of honor and justice. His sole confidante is Pinoko ("pinochle," a companion card-game to "blackjack" in a typical Tezuka wordplay), a diminutive, lisping girl carried for decades in the womb of her unsuspecting twin sister and found by Black Jack during an operation to remove what he thought to be a cyst. Although she looks like a toddler, she is as old as her grown-up twin and becomes Black Jack's surrogate daughter and assistant.

The original *Black Jack* ran in *Shonen Champion* magazine from 1973 to 1978. It reached a wider audience through Nobuhiko Obayashi's 1977 live-action film *Stranger in Her Eyes*, in which Black Jack (Daisuke Ryu) uses a drowned girl's corneas to restore sight to a female patient who is then haunted by visions of the donor's last moments. Reissued after lying dormant for most of the 1980s, the manga was followed in 1993 by an anime version on video from the GOLGO 13–team of Dezaki and Sugino. Undertaken as part of an ongoing plan to produce animated versions of all of Tezuka's work, the videos suffer from faithfulness to the letter rather than the spirit of the originals, creating a sanitized nostalgia instead of the series' famously dark mood.

In *Chimaera Man*, Black Jack must operate to save his old acquaintance Crossword before traveling to Hokkaido to revisit a former patient who has become the victim of a mob-run medical conspiracy in *The Procession Game*. In *The Decoration of Maria and Her Comrades*, he is called to save the life of a South American rebel ousted by foreign-backed conspirators; then he tries to save the life of a traumatized movie star in *Anorexia*, where he faces his old adversary, "dark doctor," and euthanasia-advocate Kiriko. Events take a more paranormal turn in *The Owl of San Merida*, in which Black Jack aids a man with stigmata and false memory syndrome, and in *Night Time Tale in the Snow*, a variation on an old Japanese folktale of doomed love found in many other anime including KIMAGURE ORANGE ROAD.

Black Jack returned to live-action cinema in 1995, with a trilogy directed by Kazuya Konaka and written by AKIRA's Izo Hashimoto, with Daisuke Ryu reprising the lead role. The first two films chart Black Jack's initial fall from grace (only revealed in flashbacks in the original manga) and first encounter with Pinoko (the manga chapter *Teratogenous Cystoma*). The final installment replays the Kiriko encounter from the anime, and the cross-promotion was reinforced in 1996 when the last live-action movie was followed by a feature-length anime. Set in 1998 as Tezuka would have imagined it, with a UN that includes off-world colonies, *Black Jack the Movie* dumps the condescending attitude that crept into the video series. Two years after the appearance of superhuman child prodigies at the Atlanta Olympics, the same children are sud-

denly succumbing to accelerated aging. Black Jack is blackmailed into helping the ice-cool Doctor Jo Carroll, who kidnaps Pinoko to secure Black Jack's cooperation in what turns out to be a viral conspiracy.

Black Jack continued as a straight-to-video anime after the movie with *Green Memories*, *The Face in the Affliction*, and *Sinking Woman*, though these episodes have yet to be released in English. A TREE IN THE SUN, a very different kind of Tezuka medical drama, was also animated in 2000.

BLACK LION
1992. JPN: *Jigen Sengoku-shi: Kuro no Shishi*. AKA: *Dimension Civil War Chronicle: Black Lion*. Video. DIR: Takashi Watanabe. SCR: Noriko Hayasaka. DES: Hideyuki Motohashi, Koichi Ohata. ANI: N/C. MUS: Masami Anno. PRD: Tokyo Kids. 45 mins.
In 1580, Nobunaga Oda united Japan with the aid of foreign guns, but *Black Lion* has a more fantastic view of these events, suggesting that he used rapid-fire machine guns, lasers, and missiles. His ultimate weapon is Ginnai Doma, a ninja said to be immortal who carries out the command to eradicate dissident temples with extreme prejudice. A warrior monk is the sole survivor of one such massacre, and he swears to avenge the deaths of his friends and lover.

In taking contemporary items and hurling them into the past, Go Nagai's 1978 manga from *Shonen Magazine* is a reversal of his SHUTENDOJI, which dragged ancient concerns into the present day. Supervising producer Osamu Yamazaki directed several similar retellings of Japanese history, including YOTODEN, which depicted Nobunaga as being in alliance with demons.

BLACK MAGIC M-66 *
1987. Video. DIR: Masamune Shirow, Hiroyuki Kitakubo. SCR: Masamune Shirow, Hiroyuki Kitakubo. DES: Hiroyuki Kitakubo, Toru Yoshida. ANI: Hiroyuki Okiura, Hiroki Hayashi. MUS: Yoshihiro

Monster Rancher

Katayama. PRD: Animate Film, AIC. 45 mins.
A military transport crashes and loses its cargo, two top-secret military androids whose unerased test program instructs them to terminate their inventor's granddaughter, Ferris. When the first of the robots is destroyed, snooping reporter Sybel decides to track down Ferris and warn her. In a showdown that costs the lives of 18 soldiers, Sybel saves Ferris, though the reporter's feckless partner, Leakey, tries to pass off the news footage of the incident as his own.

Black Magic began life as a fanzine, a sprawl of loosely linked manga that gained Shirow his first professional contract. The anime adapted *Booby Trap*, the most coherent chapter, drawing heavily from James Cameron's *Terminator* and the final act of *Aliens*. Sybel and Ferris replay Cameron's Ripley/Newt relationship in several scenes, most notably with an elevator chase and last-minute rescue, but *Black Magic* is entertaining despite the steals. The only disappointment in watching the acrobatic androids decimate a roadblock comes in wondering how it could have looked if the makers had had the budget to include the original's six-armed M-77 prototype, which is only referred to offscreen. Another vestige of the manga is the allegorical Cold War standoff between North and South, misinterpreted by some oversensitive Japanese critics as a slur on Korea. Also note Sybel's **APPLESEED** T-shirt, an in-joke that would be repaid when that other Shirow title was animated the following year.

The fallout from *Black Magic* is remarkably similar to that of Katsuhiro Otomo's **AKIRA**, another case of a creator's perfectionism driving an anime over budget. *Black Magic* used over 20,000 cels, an extravagance on video that, ironically, has caused it to age very gracefully—it could easily pass for a show ten years younger. Shirow's first and last work as anime director, it ended so acrimoniously that he refused to associate himself with any future adaptations. In some ways, this is an indirect cause of the later monstrosities **LANDLOCK** and **GUNDRESS**, for which his name was appropriated to secure unwarranted publicity. As well as **BLOOD**-director Kitakubo, two future big names worked as lowly animators on the project—Hiroki Hayashi would make **BUBBLEGUM CRISIS 2040**, and Hiroyuki Okiura would eventually direct **JIN-ROH** after contributing to the superior Shirow adaptation **GHOST IN THE SHELL**. The production was the debut of future voice star Chisa Yokoyama as Ferris. **Ⓥ**

BLOCKER CORPS

1976. JPN: *Blocker Guntan IV Machine Blaster.* AKA: *Blocker Corps IV Machine Blaster.* TV series. DIR: Masami Anno, Takashi Anno. SCR: Akira Hatta, Susumu Takahisa. DES: Tomosuke Takahashi, Kunio Okawara. ANI: Mamoru Tanaka. MUS: Hiroshi Tsutsui. PRD: Nippon Animation, Fuji TV. 25 mins. x 38 eps.

Hellqueen V and Kaibuddha, rulers of the devilish undersea Moghul Empire, launch an all-out assault on the surface world. From Astro Base, Professor Yuri sends out Robocles, Thundaio, Blue Caesar, and Vospalda, four "blocker" robots piloted by young boys with

Elpath powers, Earth's last-ditch defenders against the people of the sea.

The first production for Ashi, a studio founded by former Tatsunoko-member Tatsuhiko Sato, *Blocker Corps* used many Tatsunoko alumni, including **BATTLE OF THE PLANETS**–designer Okawara. This simple robot show with a *Stingray* feel gains added drama halfway through when lead character Tenpyo Tobidori discovers he is the offspring of a union between a Moghul man and an Earth girl.

BLOOD: THE LAST VAMPIRE *

2000. AKA: *Blood.* Movie. DIR: Hiroyuki Kitakubo. SCR: Kenji Kamiyama. DES: Katsuya Terada. ANI: Shinji Takagi. MUS: Yoshihiro Ike. PRD: Production IG. 50 mins.

On the eve of the Vietnam War, a secret organization sends Saya, a young Japanese girl, to destroy vampires ("Chiropterans") on a U.S. air base at Yokota in Japan. Neither human nor vampire, she uses her skills with a sword to dispatch these unearthly menaces.

Seemingly combining the plot of **DEVIL HUNTER YOHKO** with an alternate past similar to coproducer Mamoru Oshii's **JIN-ROH**, this is likely to be regarded in the U.S. as a Japanese rip-off of *Buffy the Vampire Slayer.* However, it features simply stunning animation and, in a first for anime, was made chiefly in English with Japanese subtitles to ease its progress into foreign markets. Mysteriously, however, this "film" is not feature-length, with the studio promising to complete the story with a manga and game—a suspicious sign of trouble behind the scenes and liable to leave the film forever inconclusive in much the same way as **ARMITAGE III**. An impressive action movie, but lacking in substance.

BLUE BIRD

1980. JPN: *Maeterlink no Aoi Tori.* AKA: *Maeterlink's Blue Bird.* TV series. DIR: Hiroshi Sasakawa, Akira Kurooka, Kazuo Terada, Takashi Anno, Makoto

Mizutani, Shigeru Omachi, Shinji Okada, Kenji Yoshida, Seiji Endo, Fumio Ikeno, Kunihiko Okazaki. SCR: Yoshinori Nishizaki, Keisuke Fujikawa. DES: Toyoo Ashida. ANI: Toyoo Ashida. MUS: Yasushi Miyagawa. PRD: Westcape Corporation, Fuji TV. 25 mins. x 26 eps.

A fairy named Bérylune visits brother and sister Tyltyl and Mytyl and tells them of the blue bird, a magical creature that brings good fortune to those who capture it. The children, accompanied by their dog Tylo and cat Tylette, search for it to help their ailing mother. They fly on a slipper to the Land of Memory, the Palace of Night, and the Kingdom of the Future before discovering that the blue bird (and the charity it represents) has been at home all along.

Maurice Maeterlinck's 1908 play *L'Oiseau Bleu* has been adapted for the screen several times—a 1918 silent film, a 1940 Shirley Temple vehicle, and a 1976 U.S.-Soviet coproduction. With a fairy-tale quality not dissimilar to the works of Kenji Miyazawa such as **NIGHT TRAIN TO THE STARS**, the story remains immensely popular in Japan. The series was also edited into a 120-minute movie-length version for video, *Maeterlinck's Blue Bird: Tyltyl and Mytyl's Great Adventure*, which retained many of the musical interludes that appeared sporadically in the TV version. A character called Tyltyl Mytyl appears in the book sequel to **KIMAGURE ORANGE ROAD**, where he befriends Madoka in New York. The story was retold in the **KIKI AND LARA** video, *Kiki and Lara's Blue Bird.*

BLUE BLINK

1989. TV series. DIR: Osamu Tezuka, Seitaro Hara, Hideki Tonokatsu, Naoto Hashimoto. SCR: Osamu Tezuka, Shigeru Yamagawa. DES: Osamu Tezuka, Kazuhiko Udagawa, Kimitoshi Yamane, Kazuo Okada. ANI: Kazuhiko Udagawa, Seiji Endo, Yasuhiko Suzuki, Megumu Ishiguro. MUS: Hiroaki Serizawa. PRD: Tezuka Pro, NHK. 25 mins. x 39 eps.

This last series in which **ASTRO**

BOY–creator Tezuka was directly involved before his death features Alexander, a young boy who helps Blink, a magical blue mule-colt, out of trouble; in return, Blink (combining the attributes of a best friend and a pet) promises to come whenever Alexander calls. Alexander returns home to find that his father, a writer, has been kidnapped by the Black Emperor. He and Blink are transported to an alternate world, and after many adventures, they face the emperor, only to discover that he is Alexander's father in disguise, who has set the whole thing up to demonstrate the wonder of books.

BLUE BUTTERFLY FISH

1993. JPN: *BB Fish*. Video. DIR: Mamoru Hamazu. SCR: Mamoru Hamazu. DES: Takayuki Sato. ANI: Takayuki Sato, Nobuyoshi Habara. MUS: Yoichiro Furukawa. PRD: Pioneer. 30 mins.
On a southern island, a swimmer who has wasted his potential gradually regains his confidence after meeting a beautiful girl. NINETEEN-creator Sho Kitagawa's 1990 manga, a girls' romance cunningly concealed within the pages of a boys' magazine, ran for 15 volumes in *Young Jump*. Eschewing the humdrum struggle and victory of sports training stories, it concentrated instead on emotion, underwater scenery, and the mechanics of marine sports for a sumptuous tale that often forgot it was supposed to be about an athlete.

BLUE FLAMES

1989. JPN: *Aoki En*. Video. DIR: Noboru Ishiguro. SCR: Norikazu Imai. DES: Masao Nakada. ANI: Masao Nakada. MUS: N/C. PRD: Nippon Animation. 50 mins.
Sex and romance are found in this adaptation of Kimio Yanasawa's 1987 manga from *Young Sunday*. The handsome teenager Ryuichi falls into life on the edge of the criminal world, but despite offers from hostesses to become his "sex friend," falls instead for a girl called Emi at the hospital. But his criminal leanings return after her

father discovers evidence of their affair and offers him ten million yen to disappear.
Yanasawa is known for hard-boiled manga such as *The Mayor* and *Self-Portrait of a Man* but also specializes in strange romance, such as his *A Formal Marriage*, about a sexless contract between a gay man and an abused woman. *Blue Flames* mixes the two with its handsome boy hero who is offered a fantasy gigolo job but only wants the girl next door. The idea of an erotic picaresque receives more salacious coverage in many other anime, including JUNK BOY and GOLDEN BOY.

BLUE GENDER *

1999. TV series. DIR: Koichi Ohata, Masashi Abe. SCR: Katsumi Hasegawa. DES: Bunji Kizaki, Kunio Okawara. ANI: Bunji Kizaki. MUS: Kuniaki Haishima. PRD: AIC, TBS. 25 mins. x 13 eps.
At the turn of the 21st century, subatomic research finds a way of rewriting human DNA, a leap in science that produces powerful new benefits and insidious viral hazards. With mutating superviruses that can destroy people from the inside out, the world faces an epidemic that makes AIDS look like a runny nose. Those who discover they are suffering from the deadly disease elect to go into cybernetic hibernation until medical science can catch up and deliver a cure. A generation later, they awake on an Earth ruled by the "Blue," who range in size from 2 feet small to 24 feet tall. The remnants of humanity are crammed into a space station called Second Earth, desperately trying to invent a drive that will allow them to escape to the stars, and now they need the help of the "sleepers." Director Ohata has toyed with postapocalyptic adventure before in **MD GEIST** and **GENOCYBER**.

BLUE REMAINS

2000. Movie. DIR: Masanori Ikeda. SCR: Masatoshi Kimura, Toshio Sakuma. DES: Haruhiko Mikimoto, Tatsuya Tomosugi. ANI: Toshifumi Takizawa, Hisaya Takabayashi. MUS: N/C. PRD: Gaga, Oki-

nawa Prefecture Industry Promotion Plc. 30? mins.
After a major war in 2142, the last remnants of the human race dwell on the sea floor in computer-controlled habitats ruled by Mother systems. One of the computers, Mother Six, decides that humanity does not deserve to survive the war it started and commences killing off all the humans it can find (see GREY: DIGITAL TARGET). Meanwhile, officer Marose is on patrol when his ship rescues a young girl called Amamic. She is the only survivor of a spaceship sent out during the war in order to return and reseed the barren Earth in the event of an ecological cataclysm. This fully computer-animated film was originally designed to be the centerpiece of the Okinawa Digital Power Film Festival.

BLUE SEED *

1994. TV series. DIR: Jun Kamiya, Kiyoshi Murayama, Shinya Sadamitsu. SCR: Toshihisa Arakawa, Masaharu Amiya. DES: Yuzo Takada, Kazuya Yokose. ANI: Kazuya Yokose, Nobuyoshi Habara, Akio Takami. MUS: Kenji Kawai. PRD: King Record, TV Tokyo. 25 mins. x 26 eps.
Schoolgirl Momiji has been raised by a shrine priestess in Izumo, Japan's spiritual heartland. Ancient demons, the Aragami, are returning to wreak havoc, and only a priestess of the Kushinada bloodline can stop them. Momiji is saved from an Aragami attack by Mamoru Kusanagi, a half-Aragami defector who has sworn to protect the protectors. Kusanagi works alongside the TAC organization, a secret project to save Japan for the invaders. TAC's director, Daitetsu Kunikida, explains that only the Kushinada bloodline (see LITTLE PRINCE AND THE EIGHT-HEADED DRAGON) can put the Aragami to sleep and Momiji's long-lost twin, Kaede, is missing, presumed killed in action. Momiji trains hard to live up to her sister's peerless example, all the while fighting new mythological menaces including Orochi (also seen in YAMATO TAKERU), Susanoo (see TAKEGAMI), the

giant Mukade centipede (see **USHIO AND TORA**), and kappa sprites (see **BIRTH OF JAPAN**). The titular "blue seeds" are comma-shaped *mitama* talismans common to Japanese archaeology, also found adorning the shell of the monster turtle in *Gamera: Guardian of the Universe.*

Created by **3x3 EYES'** Yuzo Takada for *Comic Gamma* in 1992, *Blue Seed* has superpowered schoolchildren, invading menaces-of-the-week, lost family, mythological roots, apocalyptic patriotism, mawkish romance, government intrigue, humor, *and* tragedy in quantum doses—all suspiciously similar to the later **EVANGELION**. Influenced by the mid-1990s ambiguity of the *X-Files*, it also features a government cover-up opposed by its own employees; Momiji discovers that the last-ditch plan to stop the ancient threat is for her to become a human sacrifice.

The show exists in two formats, a TV series for general consumption and a video version "director's cut" that included extra nudity and violence. A three-part video sequel, *Blue Seed 2: Operation Mitama,* followed in 1996–97, set two years later when a new Aragami threat looms on the horizon. Other *Blue Seed* releases include the original *Making of* prequel featuring voice-actor interviews and a two-part video spinoff, *Blue Seed Ver 1.5,* which collected the humorous bumpers added to the TV series. *Ill. p. 453.*

BLUE SONNET *

1989. JPN: *Akai Kiba Blue Sonnet.* AKA: *Red Fang Blue Sonnet.* Video. DIR: Takeyuki Kanda. SCR: Seiji Matsuoka. DES: Katsuichi Nakayama. ANI: Katsuichi Nakayama, Hisashi Abe. MUS: Go! PRD: Mushi Pro. 30 mins. x 5 eps.
Blue Sonnet is the codename of a street urchin rescued from the slums and rebuilt as a superpowered cyborg. Working for the kindly Dr. Merikus, she is pitted against psychic threats to the new world order and soon finds herself in Japan investigating the entity known as Red Fang. But Sonnet's main problem is the Talon organization,

which is hellbent on world domination. They capture Blue Sonnet's friend Lan Komatsuzaki and limit her powers with a restraining collar. Now Sonnet has the dual mission of defeating Talon and rescuing her friend before she can be used in a breeding program to create a master race of telepaths.

Blue Sonnet is what a lot of English-speaking viewers have come to expect from anime: pubescent young ladies with uncontrollable powers, massive collateral damage, and a Japanese angle on the whole superhero/secret-agent idea so beloved of television series writers all over the world. It also displays hints of Japanese culture's long-term fascination with the sorcerous powers of women. The onset of menstruation is also the onset of true power for Red Fang, although that wasn't something that Manga Entertainment mentioned in their press release when they released this series.

As one can guess from the lack of a proper ending, *Blue Sonnet* began life as a manga. The creator, Masahiro Shibata, remains relatively unknown in the West, but his 1987 *Sledge* was a major inspiration for Kenichi Sonoda's **GUNSMITH CATS.**

BLUE SUBMARINE NO. SIX *

1998. JPN: *Aono Rokugo.* AKA: *Blue Six.* Video. DIR: Mahiro Maeda. SCR: Hiroshi Yamaguchi. DES: Mahiro Maeda, Range Murata, Takehito Kusanagi, Shoji Kawamori. ANI: Toshiharu Murata. MUS: The Thrill. PRD: Production IG, Bandai. 30 mins. x 4 eps.
With the ozone layer destroyed, mankind is moving into dome cities or underwater. Rogue scientist Zorndyke decides that humanity has lost the right to survive on the planet it has ruined and breeds a race of mer-people, the Mutio, to repopulate Earth. Young officer Mayumi Kino retrieves Tetsu Hayami, the navy's best pilot of yesteryear, now a junky in the flooded ruins of Tokyo. Although he at first refuses to return to help humanity, Hayami saves Kino when Zorndyke's

forces attack, joining with the remnants of the navy to fight for humanity's last stand.

Though the adaptation of Satoru Ozawa's **SUBMARINE 707** sank without a trace in 1996, this follow-up to his 1960s manga rushed into production thanks to the number of underwater scenes, which allowed the animators to hide the joins between computer and cel animation with a blue sheen. Heavily influenced by Gerry Anderson's *Stingray,* particularly in the non-romance between Hayami and the mute Mutio mermaid he rescues, *Blue Six* is an **EVANGELION** clone only insofar as it possesses brassy music and echoes of the Pacific War. Taking the boys' adventure of the original manga and adding the shapely-but-shrill female lead Kino, *Blue Six*'s aquatic basis plays to the strength of its digital animation and coloring. While often obvious or just plain showy, the pros of the cel/CG combination far outweigh the cons. The characters are marvelous, including a cybernetic whale, an idea last seen in the ill-fated **LADIUS.** Zorndyke in particular is a wonderful creation, an "evil genius" who occupies the moral high ground, whose tripod-crustacean war machines broadcast apologetic rationalizations, even as they wipe out human settlements. If there is any problem at all with *Blue Six,* it is the choice of format—the four "episodes" are so obviously a partitioned movie edition that it seemed dishonest not to release the "series" in feature-length from the outset. *Ill. p. 53.*

BOBBY'S IN DEEP

1985. JPN: *Bobby ni Kubittake.* AKA: *Bobby's Girl.* Movie. DIR: Toshio Hirata. SCR: Shiro Ishinomori. DES: Akimi Yoshida. ANI: Gaku Ohashi. MUS: Keiichi Oku. PRD: Madhouse. 44 mins.
Akihiko "Bobby" Nomura, a student whose love of motorcycles has led him to write a column for a biker magazine, receives a letter from Sakiko Nakahara, a girl in distant Okayama. She likes his work, and the two begin a correspondence about bikes, which soon

becomes more personal. The months pass as they coyly circle around the issues of whether they should meet and whether each has fallen in love with someone they have never seen.

Using a cut-up technique to summarize Yoshio Kataoka's short story, *Bobby's in Deep* was shown as part of a double bill with **DAGGER OF KAMUI**. The involvement of the Madhouse studio led to many famous names behind the scenes, including producers Rintaro and Masao Murayama, who would later cooperate on **ALEXANDER**. The same year, character designer Akimi Yoshida would begin her most famous creation, the manga *Banana Fish*.

BODYJACK

1987. Video. DIR: "Dojiro." SCR: Takashi Tanigawa. DES: To Moriyama. ANI: Makoto Kaneda. MUS: N/C. PRD: AIC. 35 mins.

Dr. Toyama takes control of the body of a beautiful high-school girl, Komaba, with his strange invention. He lets the randy young Asagedani "slip into" her body so he can see how it really feels to be a girl. Then Komaba's classmate, the equally beautiful Nakano, surprises "him" and mistakes his activities for a sexual advance from her friend, beginning a lesbian scene that isn't really a lesbian scene because one of them is a man trapped in a woman's body, and enjoying every minute of it.

Bodyjack began as an erotic manga by **CREAM LEMON**'s pseudonymous To Moriyama, known today as Mori Toyama and, in more mainstream publications, as Naoki Yamamoto, the creator of **DANCE TILL TOMORROW**. An original incorporation of sex into SF since imitated in **SEXORCIST** and the **SECRET ANIMA** episode *Dream Hazard*. 🚫

BOES

1987. JPN: *Geragera Bus Monogatari*. AKA: *Chuckling Bus Story*. TV series. DIR: Hiroshi Sasakawa. SCR: Kaoru Toshina, Satoshi Ohira, Sachiko Ushida, Hisashi Furukawa. DES: N/C. ANI: Susumu Ishizaki. MUS: Shinsuke Kato. PRD: Telescreen, Studio Cosmos, TV

Tokyo. 25 mins. x 52 eps.

Only the Dutch could come up with the idea of a talking bull in red dungarees who can fly when he puts on his magical wooden clogs, for such is the hero of this Netherlands coproduction based on the comic-strip character created by Wil Raymakers and Thijs Wilms that has been syndicated in ten different countries.

BOMBER BIKERS OF SHONAN *

1986. JPN: *Shonan Bakusozoku*. AKA: *Explosive Racers of Shonan*. Video. DIR: Nobutaka Nishizawa. SCR: Kenji Kurata, Naoko Takahashi, Kisei Cho. DES: Satoshi Yoshida. ANI: Takashi Saijo. MUS: Yasaku Kikuma, Koichi Hirai, Haruo Kubota. PRD: Ashi, Toei. 50 mins. x 11 eps.

Yosuke Eguchi is cool, brave, enigmatic, and the star of the school's embroidery club. With his pals in the Shonan Bomber Bike gang, he just wants to ride his motorcycle after school without any trouble, following in the footsteps of former schoolmate and current king of the road, Noboru Ishikawa. A rival gang tries to force Eguchi off the road and, when that fails, send in its out-of-town friends to finish the job, but Eguchi's impassioned speech about the Way of Biking convinces everyone they should live in peace. Later episodes concentrate on other members of the gang, including Yoshimi's ham-fisted courting of Nagisa and Eriko's surfer boyfriend, Seiji, falling into depression after a bad performance, and asking Eguchi to help him arrange a rematch. The third installment, a 1987 *Rocky* pastiche where the gang must pick a champion to fight the boxer Kondo, was also screened in theaters on a double bill with **VICTORY PITCHER**.

Keeping closely to Satoshi Yoshida's original 1983 *Shonen King* manga, combined sales of which topped 20 million volumes, the series lasted ten years, mixing romance and racing, with gang-members pairing off and even the sound of wedding bells. Eguchi falls for an American girl, Samantha, in the

Sky Over the Shanghai Battle Line

penultimate installment, and the finale includes his homegirl Yoshiko's last-ditch attempts to show her feelings.

An immensely successful production throughout the 1980s, the video series did not disgrace its manga predecessor, selling almost a quarter of a million tapes and inspiring a successful imitator in Toru Fujisawa's *Shonan Pure Love Gang* and **GTO**. Its English-language performance was less impressive—only a single episode made it to a U.S. video market that couldn't see the appeal of lovelorn Hell's Angels.

In 1997, barely a year after the original coasted to a halt, the same staff would return with *New Bomber Bikers of Shonan: Stormy Knight*. Featuring all-new bikers but with cameo appearances by the original cast, the series consisted of two videos, each split into two faux-TV episodes detailing new gang leader Katsuhiko and his feud with the Tigers.

BOMBERMAN

1995. JPN: *Bomberman B-Daman Baku Gaiden*. AKA: *Bomberman B-Daman Explosive Tales*. TV series. DIR: Nobuaki Nakanishi, Takafumi Hoshikawa, Yasuo Iwamoto. SCR: Tatsuhiko Urahata, Tomoyasu Okubo, Toshiki Inoue. DES: Koji Sugiura. ANI: Junko Abe. MUS:

Jun Chiki Chikuma. PRD: Madhouse. 25 mins. x 48 eps.

In the wake of the Kobe earthquake, the game character Bomberman was dragged out to make a 25-minute program on safety measures called *Thank You to Heroism: Lend Me Your Ears*. This one-shot from director Norio Kawashima was the precursor to a full-fledged series featuring the attempts of the evil Dark B-Da to seize control of B-Da City, opposed only by Bomb, the round-headed agent of justice. B-Daman would return in 1999 with the series *Super B-Daman*, animated by the Xebec studio for breakfast television on TV Tokyo. Writer Urahata would go on to direct **MASTER KEATON**.

BONDAGE QUEEN KATE *

1994. JPN: *Nessa no Wakusei*. AKA: *Desert Planet*. Video. DIR: Takashi Asami. SCR: Yuji Kishino. DES: Ryoichi Oki. ANI: N/C. MUS: N/C. PRD: All Products, Beam Entertainment. 45 mins. x 2 eps.

Kate Curtis is a young, virginal police officer sent undercover to Doune, the desert planet where getting raped by one of the locals is supposedly the highlight of any trip. Her mission is to find out who's raping all the tourists. Her disguise is a skimpy costume with the words "RAPE ME," emblazoned on it in big letters. Kidnapped on arrival by some men clad in incongruous 1970s fashions, she is assaulted during a desert drive and subjected to toilet-training torture while hanging from a chain above a pit full of monsters—including a thinly disguised Sarlacc from *Return of the Jedi*. She is then taken into their lair, where she confesses that she secretly enjoys rape in an anime that manages to demean women not only with what is done to them but also in how they react to it.

Produced by "Dr. Pochi," perpetrator of several of the **CREAM LEMON** series, *Bondage Queen Kate* recalls the *Story of O* with its heroine's adoration of her abusive captors and a salacious interest in invading the female body not just with the usual suspects, but

also with diuretics and the surgeon's knife. The science fiction elements are perfunctory—Doune is a Middle Eastern airport departure lounge only cosmetically related to Frank Herbert's *Dune*; the spacecraft has the engines of a Star Destroyer turned on its side; the desert is a glorified sand pit; and if there was ever a time to use a pseudonym, **ORGUSS 02**–writer Kishino and several famous voice actors should have realized that this was it. **NV**

BONOBONO

1993. Movie, TV series. DIR: Hitoshi Nanba. SCR: Tetsuo Yasumi. DES: Michishiro Yamada. ANI: Michishiro Yamada, Yuka Kubodani. MUS: Gonchichi. PRD: Amuse, Tac, TV Tokyo. 94 mins. (m), 15 mins. x 48 eps. (TV).

Bonobono the otter, along with his friends the raccoon and chipmunk, first appeared in a children's manga by **MUKA-MUKA PARADISE**–creator Mikio Igarashi in 1986. With the gentle stories' sales topping the five million mark, the artist directed and wrote the 1993 film, which featured the woodland pals having fun and debating simple points of philosophy (à la *Winnie the Pooh*), leaving director Nanba to helm the subsequent 1994 TV series. By this time, the corporate giant Bandai was involved, and Japan was deluged with *Bonobono* toys, games, and merchandising.

BOOGIEPOP PHANTOM *

2000. JPN: *Boogiepop wa Warawanai*. AKA: *Boogiepop Does Not Laugh*. TV series. DIR: Takashi Watanabe. SCR: Sadayuki Murai. DES: Koji Ogata, Shigeyuki Suga. ANI: Minoru Tanaka. MUS: N/C. PRD: Madhouse. 25 mins. x 12 eps.

The god of death has manifested in a Tokyo high school and killed one of the boys, Saotome. His girlfriend Yasuko has kept their liaison secret but confides in Moto, a terminally shy girl at her school. Moto keeps her own crush on Saotome secret, but it comes back to haunt her when Saotome's ghost traps her in an alleyway. Mean-

while, a shadowy figure wanders the night defending the pupils from further attacks. Though based on earlier novels by Kohei Kadono, *Boogie Pop Phantom* is very much a product of the 1990s anime scene. A deliberate attempt to reverse-engineer the appeal of **SERIAL EXPERIMENTS LAIN**, but, considering that at its basic level it is simply one more tale of a mystic warrior fighting cases of demonic possession in modern-day Tokyo, the look and feel are a welcome glimpse of originality in an already crowded genre. *Ill. p. 173*.

BORDER

1991. JPN: *Meiso o Border*. AKA: *Running King Border*. Video. DIR: Noboru Ishiguro. SCR: Akira Sata. DES: Kiyotoshi Aoi. ANI: Kiyotoshi Aoi. MUS: Nojin. PRD: Artland. 45 mins.

Akio Tanaka's 1986 manga in *Action Comics*, based on a story by Karibu Marai, features a modern-day odd couple, the naïve virgin Kubota and the handsome charmer Hachisuka, who meet up by accident in a Middle Eastern desert and return to Japan to hustle their way through life. The animated excursion comprises their involvement in shady TV dealings, where they get jobs making fake documentaries, although the manga would continue for another 14 volumes of scheming.

BORN FREE

1976. JPN: *Kyoryu Tankentai Born Free*. AKA: *Dinosaur Investigators Born Free*. TV series. DIR: Koichi Takano, Haruyuki Kawajima. SCR: Keiichi Abe, Tomoyuki Ando. DES: Haruyuki Kawajima. ANI: Shigeyuki Kawashima. MUS: Toru Fuyuki. PRD: Tsuburaya, Sunrise, NET. 25 mins. x 25 eps.

In 1996, Comet Arby's approach to Earth causes major upheaval. Dinosaurs, long thought extinct, begin to wander the planet. In the Japanese outpost of an international alliance devoted to controlling the problem, Professor Tadaki forms the Born Free group, a team of dinosaur catchers that aims to protect the creatures from the evil hunter King Battler and deliver them safely to a preserve on Saron Island.

Mixing live action and animation in much the same way as Tezuka's **VAMPIRE**, *Born Free* features an animated cast inserted into Tsuburaya model footage of the team's mobile base and stop-motion dinosaurs. Twenty years later in the *real* 1996, Sunrise would make the **BRAVE SAGA** series *Daguon*, in which evil aliens enter the solar system on a rogue asteroid. Coincidence?

Tsuburaya followed the series with the 38-episode *Dinosaur War Eisenborg* (1977, *Kyoryu Daisenso Eisenborg*) on TV Tokyo, in which dinosaurs are found to have survived until the present day in subterranean caves. Ulul, the 300-IQ king of the dinosaurs, decides it is time for his race to reclaim the surface. Professor Tachibana tries to stop them but is killed. His children, Ai and Zen, are mortally injured in the same accident but receive cyborg bodies in the style of **8 MAN** from Tachibana's fellow inventor Professor Torii. Joining the antidinosaur task-force Team D, the Tachibana kids can also fuse into the Super Aizen Cyborg for that typical Tsuburaya last-minute transformation to save the day. From episode 20 onward, the dinosaur threat is replaced by Goddess the Evil Witch-Queen and her aliens from planet Gazaria. As with *Born Free*, the anime action (this time from the Oka studios, not Sunrise) is spliced in with stop-motion and live-action footage in the style of **ULTRAMAN**.

BOSCO ADVENTURE

1986. TV series. DIR: Taku Sugiyama. SCR: Nobuyuki Fujimoto, Shoji Yoshikawa. DES: Shuichi Seki. ANI: Takao Kogawa. MUS: Toshiyuki Watanabe. PRD: Nippon Animation, Yomiuri TV. 25 mins. x 26 eps.
The evil Hoodman hears the prophecy that a princess will become Queen of Fontaine Land at the time of a total solar eclipse. His minions kill the elfin king and queen, but Princess Apricot is spirited away by loyal animal subjects

and grows up in their enchanted forest. At age 14, she is told of her destiny by the old man Ender, who reveals that the time of the eclipse is at hand. Apricot is captured by Hoodman but is rescued by her woodland friends, Croak the frog, Tati the turtle, and Otter the otter, in their experimental airship, the Bosco. Pursued by Hoodman across a land of dragons, unicorns, and giants, Apricot and her friends gather the inhabitants of the enchanted land for a final battle, fought at Hoodman's castle itself as the eclipse begins. If Apricot does not sit on the throne in time, the Fountain of Life will run dry. This magical quest was an immense success all over Europe but not in the English language, despite being inspired by Tony Wolf's *Woodland Folk* series of children's books.

BOTCHAN

1980. AKA: *The Young Master*. TV special. DIR: Osamu Dezaki, Toshio Takeuchi. SCR: Yoshiyuki Fukuda. DES: Monkey Punch. ANI: Akio Sugino. MUS: Takeo Watanabe. PRD: TMS. 70 mins.
"The Young Master," a brash young graduate from Tokyo named Uranari, comes to teach at Matsuyama Middle School on the island of Shikoku, where he gets into trouble with the surly locals. The hapless English assistant falls in love with a local maid, Madonna, and proposes to her, only to discover that she has already had another offer from the local boy known as Red Shirt. Eventually, Madonna returns to Red Shirt.

One of the best-selling Japanese books ever, the original 1906 novel by **I AM A CAT**–creator Soseki Natsume contained strong elements of autobiography. He once taught in Matsuyama himself, though his experiences were less troublesome than his protagonist's. There may have been strife behind the scenes of the anime, too, since **LUPIN III**–creator Monkey Punch's designs were "cleaned up" by Akio Sugino, and Osamu Dezaki is credited as the director's "assistant" in some sources. Another, shorter version of *Botchan* was

made in 1986 as part of the **ANIMATED CLASSICS OF JAPANESE LITERATURE**. **Ⓝ**

BOUNTY DOG *

1994. Video. DIR: Hiroshi Negishi. SCR: Mayori Sekijima. DES: Hirotoshi Sano. ANI: Hirotoshi Sano. MUS: Sho Goto. PRD: Zero-G Room. 30 mins. x 2 eps.
Freelance troubleshooters Yoshiyuki, Shoko, and Kei are sent to the moon to check up on a suspected military project. Far from human habitation beneath the lunar surface, they find an alien observation post run by the good Yayoi and the bad "Darkness." Both they and their minions are all clones of the same original, who fell in love with Yoshiyuki on one of her sightseeing trips to Earth. With the original Yayoi dead, the troubleshooters must fight to save the balance of the universe.

Like many modern anime, *Bounty Dog* began as a radio drama and has difficulty shaking off its origins. Yayoi, Darkness, and the alien army are all clones of the same girl, which makes for cheap casting in radio but unimaginative visuals. Much of the story unfolds over still frames and static pans, while director Negishi plunders shots and sound effects from his own **BEAST WARRIORS**. Scenes are bathed in a limited palette of yellows and greens, while subsurface sequences are all shot in red. The final showdown in Darkness's blue hideaway completes the pattern, but though one paint costs much the same as another, the avant-garde color scheme actually makes the film look even cheaper.

Stealing great chunks of plot from *2001: A Space Odyssey* and **PLEASE SAVE MY EARTH**, *Bounty Dog*'s real failing lies in sloppy science and sloppy fiction. The moon, we are told, has been terraformed, which must have been difficult without an atmosphere. The plot calls for spacesuits intermittently and illogically, while temperature and gravity are inexplicably like Earth's. As for the good-vs.-evil alien setup, it appears to be an ill-conceived MacGuffin from the production committee that cooked up the original story, and it is simply dismissed with a "how weird" voice-over at the end.

BOUNTY HUNTER: THE HARD

1995. Video. DIR: Yoshikazu Oga. SCR: Megumi Hiyoshi. DES: Masami Suda. ANI: Masami Suda. MUS: Shinichi Kida. PRD: JC Staff. 47 mins.

Keiji "The Hard" Nando, the toughest bounty hunter in New York, acquires a floppy disk full of names, which drags him into a conspiracy to buy and sell human organs. This one-shot tale reputedly added *extra* violence to STORY OF RIKI–creator Tetsuya Saruwatari's mean-streets manga from *Business Jump*. Postdating MAD BULL 34, which also had a Japanese fish out of water in the U.S., this New York hard-man was eclipsed in the same year by the success of a Chicago crime story. Ironically, GUNSMITH CATS starred Michiko Neya, a minor voice in *The Hard*, as the bounty hunter Rally Vincent. **LNV**

BOY WHO SAW THE WIND, THE *

2000. JPN: *Kaze o Mita Shonen*. Movie. DIR: Kazuki Omori, Toshiya Shinohara. SCR: Shu Narijima. DES: Minoru Maeda. ANI: Minoru Maeda. MUS: N/C. PRD: N/C. 90 mins.

Amon is a boy who has the power to control the wind. Branich, the ruler of the world, needs Amon's power to complete the ultimate weapon and sends his minions to bring the boy in. Though Amon's parents have forbidden him from using his talents, the arrival of Branich's men leaves him with no choice—giving them the slip, Amon runs away with Maria, one of the People of the Sea. Maria agrees to help Amon find his own tribe.

The Boy Who Saw the Wind is "a plea for good people to stand up and say 'no' to fascism and dictatorship," according to its creator, the Welsh-born author C. W. Nicol, whose writings are said to have inspired Hayao Miyazaki to set CASTLE IN THE SKY in a Welsh mining village.

BOY WITH CAT'S EYES, THE

1976. JPN: *Yokaiden Nekome Koso*.

AKA: *Ghost Story: Boy with Cat's Eyes*. TV series. DIR: Keinosuke Shiyano. SCR: Yuji Amemiya. DES: Tasuteru Hakumori. ANI: N/C. MUS: Masahiko Nishiyama. PRD: Wako Pro, TV Tokyo. 15 mins. x 22 eps.

Short ghost stories from MAKOTO-CHAN–creator Kazuo Umezu, all linked by the titular feline-featured youth, including *The Girl Who Cried in the Night*, *Eyes of the Dryad*, *Portal to Hell*, *Witch of Misty Valley*, and *Enigma of the Dark Sorcerer*. Umezu's trademark misogyny is greatly in evidence here— though his only tale available in English is the live-action adaptation of his bitchy brain-swapping revenge tragedy *Baptism of Blood*. Two further horror shorts, *There's Something on the Video Camera* and *Haunted House*, were released on a single 45-minute tape as *Incantation* (1990, *Umezu Kazuo no Noroi*). These later stories featured animation from Shingo Araki and direction by Naoko Omi. Another Umezu story, *Orochi*, was released in 2000 as a "manga video" (see CRUSHER JOE).

BOYFRIEND

1992. TV special. DIR: Satoshi Dezaki. SCR: Kazumi Koide. DES: Yukari Kobayashi. ANI: Yukari Kobayashi. MUS: Hiroshi Ikeda. PRD: Magic Bus, TV Tokyo. 94 mins.

After an accident, teen basketball star Masaki is transferred to a new school, where he immediately falls in love with local girl Kanako. After helping her home through her drunken stupor one night on the train, he can think of nobody else but her, though she is already interested in a beautiful blond basketball player, the handsome Akiro.

Originally broadcast as a TV special then split in two halves and rereleased on video, this gentle love story began as a 1985 manga by Soryo Fuyumi. A similar high-school sports love triangle can be found in SLOW STEP.

BOYS BE . . .

2000. TV series. DIR: Masami Shimoda, Eiji Suganuma, Shinji Kasai. SCR: Kenichi Kanemaki, Hiroyuki Kawasaki.

DES: Itsuko Takeda. ANI: Michinori Chiba. MUS: Be Factory. PRD: Hal Filmmaker, WOWOW. 25 mins. x 13 eps.

Makoto is a brash, loud little charmer at his school, but deep down he's just a shy little boy who lives at home with his adoring mother. And as he and his three friends flirt and spar with the school's three girls most likely to put out, will one of them notice what a delicate little flower he really is? This series takes Masahiro Itabashi and Hiroyuki Tamakoshi's 1991 manga from *Shonen Magazine* but simplifies the picaresque plot to concentrate on a single boy and a mere trio of girls. The final episode, "Let it Be," was not broadcast but is included on the video.

BRAINPOWERED *

1998. TV series. DIR: Yoshiyuki Tomino. SCR: Yoshiyuki Tomino. DES: Mutsumi Inomata, Mamoru Nagano. ANI: Atsushi Shigeta. MUS: Yoko Kanno. PRD: Sunrise, WOWOW. 25 mins. x 26 eps.

The meek shall inherit the Earth. The rest of us shall escape to the stars. Such is the belief of those who are trying to raise Orphan ("the ruin with a woman's face") from the watery depths. On a devastated world, they see Orphan as their last, best chance for survival, but they need the assistance of the Grand Chers, organic machines that are "born" from spinning plates (not unlike the creatures in MONSTER RANCHER). On a routine recovery mission, brash pilot Yu faces off against Hime, a girl who has accidentally bonded with an Anti Body, a particularly powerful form of organic machine. The meeting inspires Yu to defect from Orphan a year later, but his former colleagues are in hot pursuit.

An incoherent EVANGELION clone, *Brainpowered* is still curiously watchable, thanks largely to Yoko Kanno's wonderful music. It's as if Tomino and his crew were thrown in at the deep end and told to wing it. Nothing is explained, but all the details fill the viewer with the vain hope that somehow they will all make sense—until the disappointingly anticlimactic ending. Naked nymphs dance around Buddhist temples, flame-haired pilots keep their tresses down because their machines "like it that way," and nobody seems fazed by the groinal hatches on the Grand Chers. ◑

BRAT COP

1989. JPN: *Gaki Deka*. TV series. DIR: Yuzo Yamada. SCR: Keiji Terui, Yoshio Urasawa, Hideki Mitsui. DES: Tatsuhiko Yamagami. ANI: Takeaki Natsumoto, Yuri Handa, Michishiro Yamada. MUS: N/C. PRD: Tokio Animation Film, Asia Do, Fuji TV. 12 mins. x 43 eps. Tatsuhiko Yamagami's surreal 1974 comic about a boy/cop who liked playing with his testicles, sentencing people to death, and occasionally transforming into a deer or elephant ran in *Shonen Captain* for 26 volumes until 1981. This 1989 revival was seemingly timed to cash in on the child readers becoming old enough to purchase videos, with a straight-to-video special directed by Junichiro Nakamura, released a month after the TV series began. A spiritual ancestor of the 1990s hit CRAYON SHIN-CHAN.

BRAVE FROG, THE *

1973. JPN: *Kerokko Demetan*. AKA: *Ribitty Demetan; Adventures on Rainbow Pond*. TV series. DIR: Tatsuo Yoshida, Seitaro Hara. SCR: Akiyoshi Sakai, Hiroshi Sasakawa. DES: Tatsuo Yoshida, Yoshitaka Amano. ANI: Masayuki Hayashi, Hiroshi Kawabata. MUS: Nobuyoshi Koshibe. PRD: Tatsunoko, Fuji TV. 25 mins. x 39 eps. Demetan (Jonathan Jumper) is a frog too poor to attend school in Rainbow Pond, but he's good friends with Ranatan (Hillary Hopper), daughter of the rich Lord Frog (Maxwell/Big Max). Though Big Max tries to break them apart, they persevere and try to help him become a nicer person. The community is united by a common threat when menaced by a giant catfish who steals the frogspawn. Jonathan heads for the sea with his friend Cheepy the bird, and there they per-

suade an electric eel to accompany them back to the pond and drive out the catfish. Hillary's father finally approves of Jonathan, and they all live happily ever after.

BRAVE RAIDEEN *

1975. JPN: *Yusha Rydeen*. AKA: *Heroic Rydeen*. TV series. DIR: Yoshiyuki Tomino, Takeyuki Kanda, Yoshikazu Yasuhiko, Kazuo Terada. SCR: Fuyunori Gobu, Masaru Yamamoto, Masaki Tsuji. DES: Yoshikazu Yasuhiko. ANI: Yoshikazu Yasuhiko. MUS: Akihiro Kobayashi. PRD: Tohoku Shinsha, NET. 25 mins. x 50 eps., 25 mins. x 38 eps. (remake). After a slumber of 12 millennia, the Demon Empire returns to seize control of Earth, plotting evil from its secret volcano base, from which its high priest regularly sends out fearsome Fossil Beasts to attack humanity. Raideen, the giant robot-like protector of the lost continent of Mu (see SUPER ATRAGON), senses the evil presence and awakes within its golden pyramid, revealing to young Japanese boy Akira Hibiki that he is the one descendant of the ancient Mu people who must help Raideen save Earth. He can call on Raideen whenever he needs him and ride his "Sparker" motorcycle into the robot's chest, where it can be stored during missions. The Demon Empire seeks control of Mutoron, the powerful element that allows Raideen to self-repair in its cliff-face hideaway. Akira also has the assistance of his friends, token girl Mari Sakirada (daughter of a scientist fighting the Demon Empire) and several members of his high-school soccer team—with suspicious echoes of BATTLE OF THE PLANETS. This early giant-robot story was based on a manga by Ryohei Suzuki and united the Tomino and Yasuhiko team that would work so well together on the later GUNDAM, where they would replay the well-matched rivalry of Akira and the blond Demon Prince Sharkin as the later serials' Amuro Ray and Char Aznable. Subtitled (poorly) in Hawaii by Kiku-TV, it was shown on the New York Japanese

A million light years from home, Japanese schoolboy Makoto must fight off bug invaders and impersonate a lesbian princess. His girlfriend's brother decides to turn to the Dark Side. Meanwhile, his teacher frets over his dwindling supply of cigarettes. An amusing mix of Edgar Rice Burroughs and the Marx Brothers, **EL HAZARD** featured a distinctly Arabesque setting and a refreshingly honest appraisal of how normal people might behave in a fantasy setting. *See entry p. 111.*

El Hazard

© AIC/PIONEERS LDC/TV TOKYO

community channel 47, thereby becoming the first giant-robot show to reach a large U.S. audience. As Raideen, it also formed part of the SHOGUN WARRIORS collection. The series was remade as *Reideen: The Superior* (1996), directed by Toshifumi Kawase, which similarly featured a boy assembling a five-man team of warriors to pilot cool vehicles and save the planet.

BRAVE SAGA

1990. JPN: *Exkaiser; Fyvard/Fighbird; Da Garn; Might Gine/Might-Gaine; J-Deka; Goldoran; Daguon; Gaogaigar*. AKA: (see below). TV series. DIR: Katsuyoshi Yutabe, Shinji Takamatsu. SCR: Yasushi Hirano, Hiroyuki Hoshiyama, Fuyunori Gobu, Hiroyuki Kawasaki, Takao Koyama, Yoshitomo Yometani. DES: Kunio Okawara, Atsuko Ishida, Akira Oguro. ANI: Masami Obari. MUS: Toshiyuki Watanabe, Takashi Kudo. PRD: Sunrise, Nagoya TV. 25 mins. x 20 eps. (*Exkaiser*), 48 eps. (*Fyvard*), 46 eps. (*Da Garn*), 47 eps. (*Might Gine*), 48 eps. (*J-Deka*), 20 eps. (*Goldoran*), 48 eps. (*Daguon*), 30 mins. x 2 eps. (*Daguon* v), 44 eps. (*Gaogaigar*). Almost matching Tatsunoko's TIME BOKAN and Tokyo Movie Shinsha's

LUPIN III for sheer endurance, the Sunrise "Brave" series (each title contains the word *yu:* "brave/hero") of giant-robot shows may look like an endless stream of formulaic pap, but not to its target audience. In the fiercely hierarchical world of childhood, last year's show is passé by definition—this year's toys and this year's heroes are what counts. The heroes of **ULTRAMAN** and **BATTLE OF THE PLANETS** have been reverse-engineered and refined over the years to create a set template of series construction, and "Hajime Yadate," the house pseudonym that assigns half the credit for new shows to the Sunrise studio itself, has realized that there is a point in every boy's life when he has never seen a giant robot before. Each and every "Brave" show represents a whole age group's first evening viewing, first hot-headed hero, first crush, and first battle-cry of improbable-sounding attack names. There is also an important technical issue in the construction of TV anime involving a transformation sequence— the same footage can be reused in every episode, effectively cutting production costs. And though one could argue that Sunrise should invest in one decent series and repeat it, that would destroy the entire industrial complex that grows up around each show. The nature of merchandise-driven entertainment for a young audience requires constant upgrades and renewals built around the same basic templates of colors, action figures, and, unfortunately, plotting.

The "Brave" phenomenon began in 1990 with *Heroic Exkaiser* (*Yusha Exkaiser*), in which a giant galactic police robot fights to protect humanity from the predations of the Gaistar space pirates. In an attempt to create an ongoing franchise separate from the same studio's ongoing **GUNDAM** series, the same crew returned in *Sun Hero Fyvard* (1991, *Taiyo no Yusha Fyvar*), in which Professor Amano convinces his grandchildren, Kenta and Haruka, to combine with the Fyvard android in order to save Earth. Work-

ing on the principle that if something isn't broken, it doesn't need fixing, they were back in 1992 with another "Brave" anime, *Legendary Hero Da Garn* (*Densetsu Yusha Da Garn*), where Earth is attacked by the alien Orbus invaders, and only a group of young kids in a giant robot can save it. Ever the optimists, Sunrise returned in 1993, retaining the "Brave" name in the title to reassure viewers that nothing was really going to change. This time, the series was *Heroic Express Might Gine* (*Yusha Tokkyu Might Gine*), which, with dazzling originality, concentrated on a team of young kids in a giant robot saving Earth from invading aliens. By 1994, the "Brave" slot on Japanese TV was well established, and the template was punched out once more as *Heroic Cop J-Deka* (*Yusha Keisatsu J-Deka*), in which the hot-headed young hero, Yuta, pilots a giant robot cop, fighting giant robot criminals. In 1995, the franchise was back with tiresome predictability in *Golden Hero Goldoran* (*Ogon no Yusha Goldoran*), featuring three young boys in a transforming robot, who go in search of the fabled lost treasure of Rajendra. *Goldoran*, however, was taken off the air very quickly, possibly because it pushed the envelope a little too far, but more likely because it didn't push it far enough in a year when everybody was watching **EVANGELION**. In 1996, the studio returned to the tried-and-true alien-invasion story line with *Heroic Order Daguon* (*Yusha Shirei Daguon*), featuring five young kids, their Daguon vehicles, and their allies from planet Bravestar defending Earth from the invading hordes of Sandor, who have piggy-backed into the solar system on a wandering asteroid—perhaps a homage to the similar story of the studio's earlier **BORN FREE**, which was set in the "future year" of 1996. Regaining its old level of popularity, the franchise also picked up a substantial female audience by imitating the success of its sister-franchise's *Gundam Wing* pretty-boy line-up. No prizes for guessing that 1997 saw another series, *Gaogaigar: King of*

Bravery (*Yusha o Gaogaigar*), featuring alien invaders held off by young children piloting transforming robots. By 1998, however, robots had been replaced in a generation's affections by **POKÉMON** and its clones, and the "Brave" series was laid to rest for a while, though robot shows themselves show no sign of disappearing.

BREAK-AGE

1999. Video. DIR: Tsuneo Tominaga. SCR: Tsuneo Tominaga. DES: Zhiemay Batow. ANI: Akira Kano. MUS: N/C. PRD: Panasonic/Beam Entertainment. 45 mins.

In 2007, the inhabitants of Danger Planet III fight their battles using remote-controlled robots or "virtual puppets." Kirio Nimura is a high-school student and the strongest puppeteer on the planet, until he falls for Sairi Takahara, who insists that nobody may make advances until they have beaten her puppet, Benkei.

After running for seven years in *Comic Beam*, Zhiemay Batow's manga *Break-Age* was adapted into an anime video by Panasonic, belatedly realizing that there might be some money in customizable robots, combat, and teen romance.

BREMEN FOUR

1981. JPN: *Bremen 4: Jigoku no Naka no Tenshitachi*. AKA: *Bremen Four: Angels in Hell*. TV special. DIR: Osamu Tezuka, Hiroshi Sasakawa. SCR: Osamu Tezuka, Katsuhito Akiyama. DES: Osamu Tezuka. Hisashi Sakaguchi. ANI: Kazuhiko Udagawa. MUS: Yasuo Higuchi. PRD: Tezuka Pro, NTV. 90 mins.

Rondo, a flower-child alien, is sent down to bring peace to Earth but unfortunately lands in the middle of a blitzkrieg orchestrated by the evil Colonel Karl Presto, a Nazi-style military leader who is massacring the local peasantry with storm troopers and Martian war machines. The mortally wounded Rondo uses the last of her powers to transform Allegro the dog, Coda the cat, Largo the donkey, and

Minuet the hen into human teenagers to carry on her mission. The kids form a band to sing for peace but let success go to their heads and devolve into an arrogant punk band. At a command performance for the evil, Wagner-loving Colonel Presto, they witness a machine-gun massacre and remember their mission of saving the world, but it's at the price of sacrificing their human forms and becoming animals once more.

As with so much in anime and manga, Tezuka blazed the trails for others. Distantly inspired by one of GRIMMS' FAIRY TALES, *The Musicians of Bremen*, but with comic Nazis that led some to describe this little-known TV movie as Tezuka's *Springtime for Hitler*, the peace-through-music message would be taken up the following year by the runaway success of MACROSS.

BRIDE OF DEIMOS

1988. JPN: *Akuma (Deimos) no Hanayome*. AKA: *Bride of Satan (Deimos)*. Video. DIR: Rintaro. SCR: Etsuko Ikeda. DES: Yuho Ashibe. ANI: Hirotsugu Hamazaki. MUS: N/C. PRD: Madhouse. 30 mins.

DARKSIDE BLUES–artist Yuho Ashibe also drew the original 1975 manga for *Princess* magazine based on a story by *Witches' Bible* author Etsuko Ikeda. A story of incestuous love between the divine beings Deimos and Venus—the latter is aggravated by the former's adoration of the Earth girl Michiko. This perverse love triangle ends up in a spooky mansion from which people never return. In a similar setup to Chie Shinohara's *Anatolia Story*, Michiko must die to save Deimos, but he has fallen for her. 🅝

BRIGADOON

2000. JPN: *Brigadoon: Marin to Melan*. TV series. DIR: Yoshitomo Yometani. SCR: Hideyuki Kurata. DES: Masahiro Kimura. ANI: Masahiro Yamane, Takuro Shinbo. MUS: N/C. PRD: Sunrise, WOWOW. 25 mins. x 26 eps. Marin, a happy but inept student who lives in world loosely modeled on

1970s Japan, is the first to notice the giant floating city hovering above her town. Brigadoon, for so it is called, fast becomes a personal project for Marin as she meets Melan, a large blue super-robot who befriends her and takes her up to the magical city.

With its resemblance to the story of Urashima Taro (see JAPANESE FOLK TALES), the original *Brigadoon* story about a Scottish village that only appears once every century is not unknown in Japan. However, this show seems to owe more to Miyazaki's CASTLE IN THE SKY, aimed squarely at the pretty but vacant audience that warmed to Kurata's earlier BATTLE ATHLETES.

BROTHER DEAREST

1991. JPN: *Oniisama e*. AKA: *To My Elder Brother*. TV series. DIR: Osamu Dezaki. SCR: Hideo Takayashiki. DES: Akio Sugino. ANI: Akio Sugino. MUS: Kentaro Haneda. PRD: NHK, Visual Book. 25 mins. x 39 eps.

ROSE OF VERSAILLES–creator Riyoko Ikeda wrote this take of life in Seiran Academy, a school for privileged young ladies. Professor's daughter Nanako writes many letters to the titular brother, outlining her life at the school, especially with regard to the intense relationships she has formed within the elite sorority. Her new friend Mariko does her best to ruin Nanako's friendship with her old friend, Tomoko. The tall, boyish Saint Juste carries a torch for the sorority leader, Miya, while Nanako calls on the assistance of the consumptive girl "Prince" Kauro to help her get closer to Miya, for whom she herself is falling. Intense desires bubble under the surface in this beautifully animated series, which, despite its languid pace, deals sensitively with incest, bullying, young love, obsession, conspiracy, suicide, jealousy, and death in the style of SONG OF WIND AND TREES. Its broadcast in English is doubly unlikely, not merely for its subject matter, but also because of the scandal caused when it was yanked off the air in France. Not all anime, as

broadcasters discovered, are "kids' stuff." 🅝🅥

BRYGAR

1981. JPN: *Ginga Senbu Brygar*. AKA: *Galactic Whirlwind Brygar; Galaxy Cyclone Brygar; Cosmo Ranger; Cosmo Runner*. TV series. DIR: Takao Yotsuji, Teppei Matsuura, Hideki Takayama. SCR: Masaru Yamamoto, Shunsuke Kaneko, Hiroshi Hamazaki. DES: Kazuo Komatsubara. ANI: Masami Yamazaki. MUS: Masayuki Yamamoto. PRD: Kokusai Eiga, TV Tokyo. 25 mins. x 39 eps. (*Brygar*), 25 mins. x 39 eps. (*Baxinga*), 25 mins. x 43 eps. (*Sasrygar*). King Carmen Carmen wants to destroy the planet Jupiter in order to create a new star and irrevocably change the solar system forever. Only the J9 Cosmo Rangers, comprised of Razor Isaac, Blaster Kid, Flying Bowie, and token girl Angel Omachi, can stop him. This energetic and popular series was supposedly inspired by real-life scientific research and used a lot of Korean talent at the lower ranks of production.

The following year saw a sequel, *Galactic Stormwind Baxinga* (*Ginga Reppu Baxinga*, aka *Cosmo Rangers*), set 300 years after the destruction of Jupiter, in which the solar system has enjoyed a period of relative peace under the Bakufu government. In much the same way that RAI adapted the events of Japan's civil war, *Baxinga* retold the fall of the 19th-century Bakufu government (or shogunate) in an SF setting, placing its cast in the role of the Shinsengumi organization (see OI! RYOMA). The J9 group takes on a new role, with Don Condole, Schutteken, Billy, Thauma, and token girl Laila fighting to keep the Bakufu alive. However, like their historical counterparts, they eventually fail, ending with a climactic battle that sees the entire central cast killed.

As the popularity of the franchise waned, it returned for a final lighter-hearted series in 1983 with *Galactic Hurricane Sasrygar* (*Ginga Shippu Sasrygar*). This time, the historical reality warped for SF purposes is Prohibition-era America, while the plot is supplied in a pastiche of Jules Verne's *Around the World in Eighty Days*. IC Blues, a card shark operating in the asteroid belt, bets mob leader Bloody God that he can visit all 50 inhabited worlds in the de-Jupitered solar system within a year. He sets off to do so in his transforming robot ship Sasrygar accompanied by his faithful friends, though he soon discovers that members of the Bloody Syndicate are out to make him forfeit the bet, and will stop at nothing to do so. Jupiter suffers another unpleasant fate in Hideaki Anno's **GUNBUSTER**.

B'T X

1996. TV series. DIR: Mamoru Hamazu. SCR: Sukehiro Tomita, Yasushi Hirano. DES: Hideyuki Motohashi. ANI: Hideyuki Motohashi. MUS: Fence of Defense. PRD: TMS, TBS. 25 mins. x 25 eps.
Teppei's elder brother, the brilliant scientist Kotaro, is kidnapped by the forces of the evil Machine Empire, who have been lying in wait in the Gobi Desert for centuries. Local girl Karen, who turns out to be a rebel against the Machine Empire, has taken a sample from the body of Raphael, the last of the great "B't" (pronounced "Beat") devices.

Singled out by the cross-shaped scar on his forehead, the result of a childhood encounter with the Machine Empire, Teppei gains "X," the greatest of the B't machines. Teaming up with the riders/pilots of other B'ts built to resemble a dragon, a phoenix, and a turtle, he sets off to rescue his brother. Masami Kurumada's earlier **SAINT SEIYA** also featured pretty boys and semimythical machines fighting to save the world. *B't X* wasn't quite as successful as its predecessor, only racking up a single TV series before coming off the air. A 14-episode sequel, *B't X Neo*, was directed by Hajime Kamegaki and released straight to video in 1997. That show's swift arrival and strange taxonomy (a total of 39 episodes making three complete seasons) prompted speculation that the "video" series was actually the unbroadcast remainder of

an axed TV show. Other heroes similarly marked with the scars of destiny include the lead in **RURO NI KENSHIN**, the lead characters of **DARK MYTH** and **ARGENT SOMA**, and, most famously, Char Aznable from **GUNDAM**.

BUBBLEGUM CRISIS *

1987. Video, TV series. DIR: Katsuhito Akiyama, Hiroki Hayashi. SCR: Toshimichi Suzuki, Hidetoshi Yoshida, Arii Emu. DES: Kenichi Sonoda, Shinji Makino. ANI: Masahiro Tanaka, Jun Okuda. MUS: Koji Makaino. PRD: Artmic, Youmex, AIC. 30 mins. x 8 eps. (v), 25 mins. x 22 eps. (TV).
In the postquake city of Megatokyo, sentient robots, or "voomers," are a part of everyday life, but these androids can be used for evil as well as good. Sylia Stingray fights a private war with the evil corporation that murdered her scientist father (inventor of the voomers). With her "Knight Saber" companions Priss, Linna, and Nene and their powerful "hard-suit" armor, they attempt to prevent the Genom Corporation from seizing control of the world with voomer agents.

A fan favorite in its day, *BGC* was one of the earliest openly Japanese anime to reach the West (as opposed to "invisible" kiddie cartoons), in a subtitled edition from AnimEigo. With babes in battlesuits designed by **GUNSMITH CATS'** Sonoda and a sprawling high-tech cityscape, the retention of Japanese dialogue caught the oriental flavor of the cyberpunk zeitgeist, and, it should be said, blinded the audience to the show's flaws: variable animation quality, cheesy rock music, steals from Hollywood (particularly *Robocop* and *Blade Runner*), and the camp *Buckaroo Banzai* pop-star-as-crime-fighter conceit. Though still well-regarded to this day, a lot of the series' popularity seems to stem from the hazy memories of old-school fans, who were grateful in the early days that anything was translated at all, so much the better if it was science fiction.

In 1988, the voice actresses shot the live-action *Hurricane Live 2032/3* con-

cert videos, featuring extra animated footage over music. Three final episodes appeared the following year, directed by Hiroshi Ishiodori and Hiroyuki Fukushima and called, owing to a split between Artmic and Youmex, *Bubblegum Crash*. In these episodes, the Sabers have gone their separate ways but reform when an old enemy (guess who?) reappears. The pseudonymous Arii Emu ("REM") provided the script, but the *BGC* magic had already faded. It's true that *Crash* has its moments (particularly the arrival of little-robot-lost Adama, who turns out to be an ingenue-assassin), but its vision of the future has aged quite badly. The punks and techno music that would have impressed the *Terminator* generation look out of place, as do the chunky mobile phones. There are moments in *Crash* when the robot-slave-society spins into some really interesting ideas, but much of it is marred by the ridiculously contrived team of female vigilantes and lame attempts at humor.

A more stylistically successful version of the franchise appeared in **AD POLICE**, which focused on the early years of supporting character Leon McNicol, but it only lasted for three episodes. A plan was briefly mooted for a video special about the Knight Sabers off-duty—when it was canceled, the proposal was heavily rewritten and eventually filmed as **TENCHI MUYO!**

In 1998, after **EVANGELION** turned TV serials into a new growth area, *BGC* was revived along with many other old favorites. Hayashi directed a remake, *Bubblegum Crisis 2040*, written by Chiaki Konaka, whose **ARMITAGE III** had made far better use of robot-slave setups. *BGC2040* dumped the humor in favor of sexual politics—Sylia sells lingerie at the Sexy Doll clothes shop, but the outfits she forces on the girls are little different. With much stretching of rubber, teetering on high heels, and inserting of "plumbing," the trademark hard-suits demean even as they empower. The characters, too, possess interesting flaws, and many situations draw on U.S. superhero comics—Sylia

Stingray is remodeled as a cold-hearted neurotic like Tim Burton's *Batman*, while wide-eyed country-girl Linna has a Clark Kent existence as a humble secretary, troubled by both the office Lothario and the robotic manageress. Tomboy fan pinup Priss is remade as a mercenary bitch, whose new band, Sekiria, is named after Konaka's own, though with EVANGELION-inspired launch sequences and a *very* 1990s drum & bass soundtrack, much of *BGC2040* will date just as swiftly as the original. *Ill. p. 433.*

BUNNA! COME DOWN FROM THE TREE!

1986. JPN: *Bunna yo, Ki kara Orite Koi.* TV special. DIR: Eitaro Ozawa. SCR: Yuji Tanno. DES: Yoshio Kabashima. ANI: Yoshio Kabashima, Michiru Suzuki. MUS: Nisaburo Hashimoto. PRD: DAX, Shigoto, NHK. 55 mins.

Bunna the frog lives in a pond within a temple precinct, where he sees himself as a "watchfrog." Announcing that he intends to seek a new home, he ignores his girlfriend and father and climbs the pasania tree close to his pond. Commissioned to celebrate the 30th anniversary of the United Nations, this adaptation of Ben Mizugami's children's story was designed to show that cooperation is better than selfishness—hardly a radical departure from any other children's show.

BURN UP *

1991. Video, TV series. DIR: Yasunori Ide. SCR: Jun Kanzaki. DES: Kenjin Miyazaki. ANI: Kenjin Miyazaki. MUS: Kenji Kawai. PRD: AIC, DirecTV. 50 mins. (orig.), 30 mins. x 4 eps. (*W*), 25 mins. x 13 eps. (*X-cess*).

Frustrated traffic cops Maki, Reimi, and Yuka interfere in a *real* detective's investigation of a white slavery ring. Infiltrating the network of prominent businessman Samuel McCoy, Yuka is captured, and her two friends mount an all-out assault on the villain's headquarters.

Little more than an excuse for large-breasted girls with guns, *Burn Up*'s

biggest fans appeared to be AD Vision, the U.S. distributor that was prepared to help fund the lame sequel *Burn Up W(arrior)* in 1996. Keeping to the AIC studio policy, best seen in TENCHI MUYO!, of throwing in more girls whenever possible, the sequel dumped most of the old characters in favor of the "Warrior" team, a police squad monitoring computer crime.

Heavily influenced by GHOST IN THE SHELL, *W* revolves around the Cerebus cartel's attempts to supply a virtual drug with mind-altering capabilities, as well as the disappearance of a virtual idol from the company mainframe—is it theft, or kidnapping? Maria, the AI in question, is an innocent creature in a computer but has superhuman strength in the real world, not dissimilar to Adama in the BUBBLEGUM CRISIS spinoff *Bubblegum Crash*. But despite music from ARMITAGE III's Yasunori Honda, *Burn Up W*'s roots have less to do with sci-fi than with the "zany" cookie-cutter concepts of producer Satoru Akahori. Despite its minimal running time, plot and characterization are sacrificed for setups to exploit the bouncing breasts of new-girl Rio. In the opening episode when terrorists seize hostages at a peace conference, one of their demands is that Rio must perform a nude bungee jump—police work taking a very distant second place to girls and guns.

This, it would seem, is all it takes, since the franchise was resurrected as *Burn Up X-cess* in 1997. One of the first shows on digital TV in Japan, the show was finally able to break from the confines of video—*X-cess* is twice as long as its combined predecessors, which allows for *slightly* more character depth. The new director was Junichiro Kimura. **CLNV**

BURNING ALPINE ROSE: JUDY AND RANDY

1985. JPN: *Hohoe no Alpen Rose: Judy and Randy.* AKA: *Passionate Alpine Rose.* TV series. DIR: Hidehito Ueda. SCR: Sukehiro Tomita, Shigeru Yanagawa, Hiroko Naka. DES: Akemi Takada.

Takuya and Minoru. *See entry p. 24.*
Baby and Me

© 1996 MARIMO RAGAWA/HAKUSENSHA • TV TOKYO • STUDIO PIERROT

ANI: Hidehito Ueda. MUS: Joe Hisaishi. PRD: Tatsunoko, Fuji TV. 25 mins. x 20 eps.

At the close of the Second World War, Judy is seeking her lost parents. The handsome Randy offers to help, though the only clue Judy has is her distant memories of hearing a song called "Alpine Rose." Judy escapes from the feckless Baron Guillermon and heads for Salzburg, where she believes the song's composer, Leonhardt Aschenbach, can be found.

Based on the comic in *Ciao* by Michiyo Akaishi, this was the first anime made by the Tatsunoko Studio specifically for girls. Hisaishi's score was so popular that the series was recut into two half-hour music videos purely to showcase the compositions. The story itself was edited into a 90-minute feature-length version on video. Compare to HONEY HONEY and HEIDI.

BURNING BLOOD

1990. AKA: *BB.* Video. DIR: Osamu Dezaki. SCR: Machiko Kondo. DES: Akio Sugino. ANI: Akio Sugino. MUS: N/C. PRD: Magic Bus. 45 mins. x 3 eps.

After killing a man in a fight, a Japanese down-and-out changes his name and moves to America, where he becomes a mercenary. Realizing that if he has a talent for anything, it's for fighting, he drifts into a career as a professional boxer. This adaptation of Osamu Ishiwata's 1985 comic from *Shonen Sunday* was directed by one better known for the original boxing anime TOMORROW'S JOE. ⓥ

BURNING BROTHER

1988. JPN: *Moeru Oniisan*. TV series. DIR: Osamu Kobayashi. SCR: Kenji Terada, Noboru Aikawa. DES: Michishiro Yamada. ANI: Michishiro Yamada, Kazunari Kume. MUS: Koji Makaino. PRD: Pierrot, Nippon TV. 25 mins. x 24 eps. Japanese boy Kenichi wanders the mountainous hinterland of Japan in search of his father and his sister, Yukie. Swept away by a river as a baby, he was raised in the country by the old man Cha Genmai, but he eventually wanders back into human society accompanied only by a mangy wolf called Flipper. Reunited with his family, he falls in with the local gangster crowd, but life seems to go well, until Cha Genmai and Kaede (Kenichi's adopted sister) turn up to stay. Based on the *Shonen Jump* comic by Tadashi Sato and adapted by the production team behind KIMAGURE ORANGE ROAD, *Burning Brother* was praised at the time for the high quality of its comedy acting and characterization.

BURNING EXCHANGE STUDENT

1991. JPN: *Hohoe no Tenkosei*. Video. DIR: Katsuhiko Nishijima. SCR: Toshio Okada. DES: Yuji Moriyama. ANI: Katsuhiko Nishijima. MUS: Kohei Tanaka. PRD: Gainax. 25 mins. Noboru Takizawa is the new kid in school, determined to apply the raging fire of his talent to success in all sporting arenas. He also falls for local girl Yukari, an interest which compels him to fight for her hand in the boxing ring. Featuring the writer and composer from GUNBUSTER with the director and designer from PROJECT A-KO, here is an anime whose Western release would have been guaranteed were it

not for the subject matter of sports. Creator Kazuhiko Shimamoto would go on to write the martial-arts soccer manga *Red Card*, a contender for the most insane ever written. ⓥ

BURNING VILLAGE

1989. Video. DIR: Fusahito Nagaki. SCR: Fusahito Nagaki. DES: N/C. ANI: Chukai Shimogawa. MUS: Masahito Maekawa. PRD: Clover Art, Tama Pro. 12 mins. x 10 eps. Animal folk tales set in the titular community, in which local eccentric Oharai retells several popular fairy tales with considerable license, including the LITTLE MERMAID and the *Musicians of Bremen*.

BUSHBABY, THE *

1992. JPN: *Dai Kusahara no Chiisana Tenshi Bushbaby*. AKA: *Little Angel of the Savannah: Bushbaby*. TV series. DIR: Takayoshi Suzuki, Takashi Kaga. SCR: Akira Miyazaki. DES: Shuichi Seki, Hiromi Kato. ANI: Nobuhiro Hosoi, Hiroshi Ito. MUS: Akira Miyagawa. PRD: Nippon Animation, Fuji TV. 25 mins. x 40 eps. Jackie Leeds, a British game warden's daughter in Kenya, gets into adventures with her bushbaby companion, Murphy, in this adaptation of William Stevenson's 1965 book. After initial high jinks, the time comes for her to return to England, but Jackie refuses to leave Murphy and sneaks off the ship. Going on the lam with her father's manservant, Tenbo, she spends the latter part of the series on the run from poachers and policemen, who believe she has been kidnapped. This remarkable change in tone may have been part of the reason for the serial's immense success in Japan, where it peaked at a 20% TV rating. It was later cut into four feature-length edits for video release, and there is also a 1970 live-action movie version directed by John Trent, starring Margaret Brooks and Louis Gossett, Jr. Shown on Canadian TV in the 1990s. *Ill. p. 87.*

BUSINESS COMMANDO YAMAZAKI

1997. JPN: *Kigyo Senshi Yamazaki: Long Distance Call*. Video. DIR: Tsuneo Tominaga. SCR: Tsuneo Tominaga. DES: Akira Kano. ANI: Akira Kano. MUS: N/C. PRD: Ripple Film, Beam Entertainment. 40 mins. Jun Tomozawa's lighthearted 1992 manga in *Super Jump* took the premise of Roland Emmerich's *Universal Soldier* and moved it to a typically Japanese arena—the business world. A 42-year-old salaryman is made to serve his company beyond the grave when his brain is installed in a superpowered android body in order to carry out corporate espionage. ⓝⓥ

BUTCHIGIRI

1989. AKA: *Take It to the Limit*. Video. DIR: Katsuyoshi Yatabe, Takashi Imanishi, Noboru Ishiguro. SCR: Norio Masuhara. DES: Eiichi Endo. ANI: Eiichi Endo. MUS: N/C. PRD: Nihon Eizo, Creative Bridge, Life Work. 50 mins. x 4 eps. Takahara, leader of the notorious seven-man Silver Wolf gang, also dabbles in baseball, in this short series based on Yu Nakahara's 1987 comic in *Shonen Sunday*. Mixing bikes with school life in a similar fashion to BOMBER BIKERS OF SHONAN, the story shares SLOW STEP's idea of a bad seed redeemed by a hidden sporting talent. ⓥ

B-YOND

1998. Video. DIR: Hiroyuki Kurimoto. SCR: Atsuhiro Tomioka. DES: Toshiya Yamada. ANI: Toshiya Yamada. MUS: N/C. PRD: Pink Pineapple, KSS. 36 mins. x 2 eps. Satan, an alien creature who has lain dormant on Earth for many years, awakens and causes havoc. Fay is a female bounty hunter searching for Satan's younger brother, although that is soon forgotten in favor of more sex scenes in this lackluster replay of UROTSUKIDOJI. ⓝ

C

CALIFORNIA CRISIS: GUN SALVO

1986. JPN: *California Crisis: Tsuigeki no Juka*. Video. DIR: Mizuho Nishikubo. SCR: Mizuho Nishikubo. DES: Matsuri Okada. ANI: Matsuri Okada. MUS: Masami Kurihara. PRD: Hero Media, Studio Unicorn. 45 mins.

Noera and his new-found girlfriend, Marsha, become mixed up in a secret U.S.–Soviet space mission project. On the run from rival gangs in California, they gain possession of a round object that directs them to Death Valley, where an alien contact is being covered up by the government's men in black. This arbitrary plot, however, is of less importance to the filmmakers than a long, lingering tour of Californian beaches, possibly since location-hunting would be more fun on this project than on, say, something called *New Jersey Crisis*. *CC* ends with a cliffhanger, but no sequel was made due to lack of audience interest—the first of many straight-to-video anime to leave their fans without a proper conclusion.

CALIMERO

1974. TV series. DIR: Yugo Serikawa, Kazuya Miyazaki, Fusahito Nagaki. SCR: Taichi Yamada, Takeshi Yoshida, Osamu Kagami, Mayuko Takakura, Hamakichi Hirose. DES: Shinya Takahashi. ANI: Fusahito Nagaki. MUS: Tadashi Kinoshita. PRD: K&S, NET (TV1); TV Tokyo (TV2). 12 mins. x 84 eps. (1974), 23 mins. x 36 eps. (1992).

Calimero, a little black chick with an eggshell for a hat, was created in 1963 by Nino and Tony Pagot for an Italian advertisement. Taken up by a Japanese production company, the original ani-mation was expanded into a long series. The series was revived for TV Tokyo in 1992 under director Tsuneo Tominaga, with new scripts by Jiro Takayama and Mayori Sekijima. If anything, the availability of the new series on video made it an even bigger success in the children's market than its predecessor.

CALL ME TONIGHT

1986. Video. DIR: Tatsuya Okamoto. SCR: Tatsuya Okamoto, Toshimichi Suzuki. DES: Kumiko Takahashi, Chuichi Watanabe. ANI: Kumiko Takahashi, Osamu Yamazaki. MUS: N/C. PRD: AIC. 30 mins.

Schoolgirl Rumi Natsumi moonlights as the boss of a phone contact club, hired by Ryo Sugiura to help him through a strange fetish. Ryo is an intergalactic nexus, and his body is subject to possession by various aliens and monsters whenever he becomes overexcited. Ryo wants Rumi to excite him *so* much that he gets used to the idea and can control his urges—though their wanderings through the city soon attract the attention of press photographer Maki, and Rumi's schoolmate Yuki, who is head of the "Sukeban" orgy club and wants Ryo and his transformations for herself. With a *Beauty and the Beast* subplot and demonic transformations brought about by frustrated teen lust, this plays like the junior comedy version of **UROTSUKIDOJI**. This and **SECRETS OF THE TELEPHONE CLUB** demonstrate that the scandal of schoolgirl "date-clubs" in the late 1990s came a little late. **Ⓝ**

CALL OF THE WILD *

1981. JPN: *Arano no Sakebi Koe: Howl, Buck*. AKA: *Call of the Wild: Howl, Buck*. TV special. DIR: Kozo Morishita. SCR: Keisuke Fujikawa. DES: Seiji Kikuchi. ANI: Seiji Kikuchi. MUS: Takeo Watanabe. PRD: Seisaku, Toei. 85 mins.

California, 1897. Buck, a domesticated mongrel who lives in the Santa Clara valley, is kidnapped by the family gardener, Manuel, and sold to a gold prospector. Soon he is a sled-dog in the harsh winter of the Klondike, and his civilized exterior swiftly falls away, awakening a wildness buried deep in his genes for centuries. This anime adaptation of Jack London's novel (**WHITE FANG** followed in 1982) kept close to the original, eschewing the talking animals one might expect for a cartoon audience and leaving the dogs in silence while the humans (shiftless Manuel, swarthy Francois) are the only ones who speak.

A second, unrelated *Call of the Wild (Anime Yasai no Sakebi)* was a 26-part series shown intermittently on TV Tokyo between 1982 and 1984. Directed by Shigeru Omachi, this was a show in the spirit of **SETON'S ANIMAL TALES**, based on stories by Japanese author Muku Hatoju, including *Taro the Mountain Bear, Little Monkey Brothers*, and *The Disappearing Stray*.

CALLING ALL STUDENTS

1986. JPN: *Seito Shokun*. TV special. DIR: Mitsuo Kusakabe. SCR: Ryo Ishikawa, Azuma Tachibana. DES: Yoko Shoji. ANI: Kazuo Imura. MUS: Toshiyuki Watanabe. PRD: Toei, Ashi Pro, Fuji TV. 81 mins.

In this adaptation of Yoko Shoji's 1977 manga from *Friend* magazine, Naoko, a new girl in town , has trouble fitting into life at the local middle school but comes to terms with jealousy and broken hearts. Believing her parents to be dead, Naoko discovers the twin sister she never knew she had, who soon develops a heart condition and dies. Despite pulling no punches, the 24-volume manga series was unceremoniously crammed into a single TV special, which made it unlikely to draw as large an audience on TV. The similar BROTHER DEAREST was more successful as a TV *series* a few years later.

CAN CAN BUNNY *

1996. JPN: *Can Can Bunny Extra.* Video. DIR: Katsumaki Kanezawa. SCR: Tetsuya Ozeki. DES: Nanako Shunsai. ANI: N/C. MUS: Pika Pika. PRD: Pink Pineapple, KSS. 25 mins. x 6 eps. Suwati, the Goddess of Happiness, falls in love with Japanese boy Kenta and indulgently grants him the power to seduce seven women. True love, of course, is not always that easy—the first girl is a virgin on the run from a street gang. As with the superior VIDEO GIRL AI, Suwati is only using her powers because she wants Kenta to fall in love with *her*, but her cousin Shuree is also on his case.

The *Can Can Bunny* PC seduction game was very successful and was followed by *CCB Superior*, *CCB Spirits*, *CCB Blue Honey*, and *CCB Extra*—this fifth incarnation, with a greater emphasis on adventure over sex, provided the basis for the anime version. Cashing in on the hiatus between the OH MY GODDESS! videos and movie, this porno retread also spun off into radio dramas, comics, and three novels. ◐

CANDY CANDY *

1976. AKA: *Candy White, Candice.* TV series. DIR: Yugo Serikawa. SCR: Shunichi Yukimuro, Noboru Shiroyama. DES: Yumiko Igarashi. ANI: Keisuke Morishita, Kazuo Tomizawa. MUS: Takeo Watanabe. PRD: Toei, TV Asahi. 25 mins. x 115 eps.

A girl is left outside the Pony's Home orphanage. A note says that her name is Candice, and she is christened Candice White after the snow that is falling outside. Candice grows up in the orphanage, where she watches her friends leave to be fostered by other families. She is helped by a mysterious stranger and yearns for him to return to her. Sent to work as a servant for the Ragham family, she is bullied by the Ragham children, Eliza and Neil. She develops crushes on many nice young men, especially the charming gentleman Anthony Brown, though he dies suddenly on a fox hunt. His cousin, Alastair "Stair" Audrey, is another potential suitor, but he is killed in World War I. Candice falls in love with a man called Terence in London but steps aside to allow him to marry a woman whose need is greater than hers.

Equal parts CINDERELLA and DADDY LONG-LEGS mixed with a doomed love out of *Romeo and Juliet*, *Candy Candy* was one of the great successes of the 1970s. Begun as a manga in *Nakayoshi* magazine in 1975, Kyoko Mizuki and Yumiko Igarashi's weepy tale of self-sacrifice ended ironically with the two creators' acrimonious dispute over copyright. The speed of adaptation caused the animated version to deviate from the original in later chapters—Candice's hospital job from episodes 102 to 109 is not present in the manga, which instead dispatches her to New York to be an actress, and Toei insisted on the introduction of a mascot character, Clint the albino raccoon. *CC* provides moments of inadvertent comedy in its portrayal of early 20th-century America, with servants making Japanese-style bows, and English-style foxhunts in the Midwest. The newly moneyed Raghams are beastly to their social underling Candice, but she is regularly rescued from a fate worse than death (exile to Mexico, signified by a Pancho Villa–lookalike bandito onscreen) by the interference of the distant William, a British royal who inexplicably lives in America, where

the upper classes fawn over him. William, however, is later revealed to be far closer to Candy than anyone realizes.

Candice would return in *The Voice of Spring/Candy's Summer Holiday*, a 40-minute theatrical outing in 1978. A 26-minute short, inexplicably titled *Candy Candy: The Movie*, was directed by Tetsuo Imazawa in 1992 and concentrated on her abuse at the hands of the Raghams.

Another Igarashi manga, LADY GEORGIE, was animated in 1983, but *Candy Candy* was a watershed production in the Japanese industry. After the animated version led to $45 million of merchandising spinoffs and boosted the sales of its parent magazine by a million copies, *Nakayoshi* would actively seek to recreate such success in the girls' market from the ground up. The eventual result would be the market-led SAILOR MOON franchise. Candice's distant memories of a "handsome prince" helping her in early life were also lifted for UTENA. The show received a very limited partial broadcast on U.S. local TV for the Japanese community, with English subtitles. True to the political climate of the times, the nasty Raghams were renamed the Reagans in this version.

CAPRICORN *

1991. AKA: *Joji Manabe's Capricorn.* Video. DIR: Takashi Imanishi. SCR: Takashi Imanishi, Joji Manabe. DES: Moriyasu Taniguchi. ANI: Moriyasu Taniguchi. MUS: Ikuro Fujiwara. PRD: Aubec. 48 mins. Teenager Taku Shimamura is transported to the parallel world of Slaphrase, a world of anthropomorphic animals, where evil General Zolba plans to usurp the imperial throne. Realizing that Zolba's next conquest, planet "Capricorn," is really Earth, Taku joins forces with Mona, the last of the Yappy race of dragon-people, to defeat Zolba and save both worlds.

This video features a similar plot to manga creator Manabe's OUTLANDERS and the cookie-cutter character designs that distinguish (or rather, *don't* distinguish) his other works such as *Caravan Kidd* and *Drakuun*—in which *Capricorn*'s Zolba also makes a cameo appearance. Manabe had more luck with **RAI**.

CAPTAIN

1980. TV series. DIR: Satoshi Dezaki. SCR: Noboru Shiroyama. DES: Akio Chiba. ANI: Shigetaka Kiyoyama, Keizo Shimizu, Isao Kaneko. MUS: Toshiyuki Kobayashi. PRD: Eiken, NTV. 84 mins., 82 mins. (TVm), 93 mins. (m), 25 mins. x 26 eps. (TV).
Takao Taniguchi enters the Nakano baseball club and fights his way to the top, determined to lead his team to victory in the national finals. Manga artist Akio Chiba specialized in baseball (his other big hit was 1973's *Play Ball*) and this adaptation of his 1972 manga was soon followed by a second TV movie later the same year. The two incarnations were recut into a 95-minute movie release in 1981, and the story finally received a full-length TV series in 1983, supposedly because of a "great critical reception," though a serial had been planned from the beginning.

CAPTAIN FUTURE *

1978. TV series. DIR: Tomoharu Katsumata, Hideki Takayama, Noboru Ishiguro, Yasuo Hasegawa. SCR: Masaki Tsuji, Hiroyuki Hoshiyama. DES: Sadao Noda. ANI: Toshio Mori. MUS: Yuji Ono. PRD: Toei, NHK. 25 mins. x 52 eps.
Brilliant young scientist Curtis Newton (aka Captain Future) brings peace and justice to the galaxy with his sidekicks Android Otho, alien robot Grag, and "living brain" Simon Wright. Known collectively as the "Future Men," they keep their flagship, The Comet, hidden in a lunar crater and launch it to help Earth's government, which communicates with them through the beautiful agent Joan Randall.

The sci-fi novels of Edmond Hamilton were optioned for anime production in record time when George Lucas mentioned that they were a major inspiration for *Star Wars* (1977). Beginning with an adaptation of *Captain Future and the Space Emperor* (1940), the anime series is remarkably faithful to the original, especially compared to the license taken with E. E. Smith's **LENSMAN**. Hamilton's work was surprisingly well-served in Japan; his later *Starwolf* series was also spun off into a live-action TV show, itself reedited for the 1978 movie *Fugitive Alien*.

Four episodes were released on video in the U.S. as *Captain Future* 1 and 2, which chart the events of *The Lost World of Time*, where Newton must travel back to save the inhabitants of planet Prometheus (Kaitan) that is just about to disintegrate and form the asteroid belt. A third video, confusingly titled simply *Captain Future*, was a truncated digest of *Captain Future's Challenge*, in which Newton must stop "King Wrecker" from destroying all the gravium mines in the solar system. The other 14 hours or so of the Japanese version remain untranslated.

Captain Future also had a 60-minute TV special in 1978, in which an experimental spaceship goes missing on Mercury shortly before the start of the Interplanetary Yacht Race. In order to infiltrate a criminal network, Future must pose as a test pilot at the notorious Venusian "Suicide Base," before a showdown in the "Sargasso" Graveyard of Space. In an intershow homage, a character called "Curtis Newton" has a cameo in the later **SOL BIANCA** series.

CAPTAIN HARLOCK *

1978. JPN: *Uchu Kaizoku Captain Harlock*. AKA: *Space Pirate Captain Harlock, Albator*. TV series/special. DIR: Rintaro, Kazumi Fukushima. SCR: Masami Uehara, Haruya Yamazaki. DES: Leiji Matsumoto. ANI: Kazuo Komatsubara. MUS: Toshiyuki Kimori. PRD: Toei, TV Asahi. 25 mins. x 42 eps.
Leiji Matsumoto's tale of space piracy began in *Shonen Sunday* in 1977 and was set a thousand years in the future. 2977—Captain Phantom F. Harlock of the Solar Federation refuses to surrender his warship Deathshadow. He scut-

One of the genetically engineered Mutio seapeople created by rogue scientist Zorndyke in Mahiro Maeda's **BLUE SUBMARINE NO. SIX**. The second adaptation of a Satoru Ozawa manga to be rushed into production in the 1990s, *Blue Six* cleverly mixes old and new animation techniques—the blue sheen of underwater scenes hides many of the joins between traditional cel animation and the show's copious computer graphics. One of the better post-**EVANGELION** anime, due to both its impressive style and its sympathetic adversary. See entry p. 40.

Blue Submarine No. Six

tles his vessel, refusing a post with the Illumidas race that has conquered Earth. Joining forces with the engineer Tochiro, who has just completed the pirate ship Arcadia, Harlock swears to overthrow the invaders.

Harlock also teams up with Tadashi Daiba, a disaffected orphan who hates Earth's new government, and discovers that the Illumidas invasion is a front for the Mazone, a race of alien plants that have adopted the form of human women. Mortally wounded in battle, Tochiro's dying wish: that his daughter, Mayu, a character created for the anime, should be able to live on a free Earth, and Harlock promises to protect her (doing so eventually costs him his eye). Harlock assembles a crew that includes Mime, the last of an alien race whose home world was destroyed by the Mazones; Yattaran, an obsessed model-maker based on Matsumoto's friend and **AREA 88**–creator Kaoru Shintani; and Maji, the unwitting father of a half-Mazone child. Tochiro's widow, Emeraldas, leaves to grieve among the stars in her own ship, the titular **QUEEN EMERALDAS**. Eventually, Harlock wins a duel with Queen Lafressia of the Mazone (who has fallen in love with him) and leaves with just Mime for company to sail around the universe in search of a place to die. The series received a very limited partial broadcast on U.S. local TV for the Japanese community, with English subtitles.

After a cameo with Emeraldas' sister, Maetel, in the latter part of GALAXY EXPRESS 999 in 1978, Harlock returned in 1982 for a 22-episode prequel *Arcadia of My Youth: Endless Orbit SSX* (an arc included in the above synopsis). Concentrating on the story of his love for Maya, the female Voice of Free Earth, it also features a new enemy in the soulless Machine People. Tomoharu Katsumata's 130-minute movie version the same year, known variously as *My Youth in Arcadia* or *Vengeance of the Space Pirates*, added flashbacks to one of Harlock's ancestors, a 20th-century aviator with a biplane called, coincidentally, the Arcadia.

Though the various *Harlock* serials, the spinoffs starring Emeraldas or Maetel, the distant cousins QUEEN OF A THOUSAND YEARS and DNA SIGHTS 999.9, and even lookalikes such as Rheindars in THE COCKPIT are supposedly related, the discrepancies make this hard to believe. Dates and characters vary wildly (the suicidal Harlock who leaves the original series is maniacally cheerful when he reappears in *Galaxy Express*), and two serials have a gap of several centuries between them. Matsumoto himself has constantly revised and rewritten over the years, and many inconsistencies are irreconcilable. Paramount amid the confusion is the claim that Harlock is really Mamoru Kodai (Alex Wildstar) from STAR BLAZERS, but, although Mamoru does indeed disguise himself as a space pirate called Harlock in the original manga (not the anime), he is copying a character from a comic by Leiji Matsumoto.

Harlock in modern times is no less confusing. Twenty-seven episodes of the original TV series were rearranged into feature-length chunks to make an eight-video digest version at the close of the 1990s. For an idea of the mind-boggling complexity, the first tape consists of episodes 1, 4, and 9, the second merely episode 17, with ten minutes of all-new bridging footage. Needless to say, episode 13, which was also shown theatrically in 1978 as the short film *Witch Castle in the Sea of Death: Mystery of Arcadia*, is absent from the modern rerelease. The series was also reissued in an LD collection under the umbrella title of *Leiji Matsumoto Theater* along with DANGARD ACE, *GE999*, and Matsumoto's SF version of JOURNEY TO THE WEST, *Starzinger*.

The hero returned *again* in 2000 with Nobuo Takeuchi's six-part video series *Harlock Saga: Ring of the Nibelung* (also available in the U.S.), discarding much of the previous continuity for a retelling of Wagner's Ring Cycle. Harlock, Tochiro, and Emeraldas are called to planet Rhine to help Mime, the guardian of the planet's gold, prevent her brother, Alberich, from forging the gold into a ring and becoming the ruler of the universe. With the aid of the goldsmith Tadashi, and despite the opposition of *Galaxy Express 999*'s Maetel, Alberich gets his wish and departs for his home planet Valhalla to confront his father, Wotan. Harlock and the crew of the *Arcadia* must head him off to save the universe once more. The hero also appeared in the 2000 "manga video" *Herlock* (see CRUSHER JOE). Herlock is just one of many alternate transliterations for proper nouns in the series, many of which have become canonical despite their lack of relation to the author's intent. Laffresia, for example, should really be Rafflesia—the queen of the plant-people named after the world's largest flower, while Maetel, the surrogate mother of the Galaxy Express, takes her name from the Latin *mater*. Such transpositions of letters, however, are common in anime, not just from translators ignorant of the sources, but also from those who are all too cognizant but wish to tone down certain creators' embarrassing English puns and in-jokes (see GUNDAM). The pirate was first sighted in the new millennium in the TV anime *Cosmo Warrior Zero* (2001), which tells the story of the man sent to capture him. *Ill. p. 165.*

CAPTAIN TSUBASA
1983. TV series. DIR: Hiroe Mitsunobu, Ken Hibari, Katsumi Minoguchi, Hiroshi Yoshida, Norio Yazawa. SCR: Naoko Miyake, Yoshiyuki Suga, Yasushi Hirano, Ken Hibari. DES: Yuichi Takahashi, Kazuhiro Okaseko. ANI: Nobuhiro Okaseko. MUS: Atsumoto Tobisawa. PRD: Shida Pro, TV Tokyo. 25 mins. x 128 eps. (TV), 45 mins. x 4 eps. (m), 30 mins. x 13 eps. (v).

Tsubasa Ozora has literally been playing soccer since he was a baby. Moving to a new town, he immediately joins the junior team, which has former Brazilian international player Roberto Honma as a coach. Much like his tennis counterpart in AIM FOR THE ACE, Tsubasa progresses through the various levels of his chosen sport until he and his friends (a superfast striker, a wily tactician, and a gifted goal-keeper) face the best in the world.

CT was not the first soccer anime; that honor goes to *Red-Blooded Eleven* (1970, *Aki Ketsu no Eleven*), but it remains the best-known. Even though only 4% of the Japanese population participated in soccer at the beginning of the 1980s, Yuichi Takahashi's *CT* manga polled twice as high as FIST OF THE NORTH STAR in the pages of *Shonen Jump*. The TV series was a foregone conclusion, cunningly kept alive by a periodic resetting to zero of the hero's achievements. Fifty-six episodes into the series in 1984, Tsubasa graduated to middle school, allowing the earlier, junior victories to be set aside for a clean slate and a new set of struggles that would take a further 72 weeks. Four short theatrical outings followed—*CT: Great European Challenge* and *CT: Japanese Junior Championship* in 1985, *CT: Run Toward Tomorrow* and *CT: The Junior World Cup* in 1986. This last film was the beginning of an updated series, *New CT*, directed by Osamu Sekita and eventually going straight to video in 1989. Now playing for the national youth team, Tsubasa learns many trick shots from his foreign opponents, including the Italians and French, before finally playing for the ultimate prize against West Germany.

In 1993, reality caught up with fiction, as a professional Japanese soccer league was finally established, an opportunity exploited in **SHOOT!**, **KICKERS**, and **FREE KICK FOR TOMORROW**, but surprisingly not by *CT*—after the one-shot video *Holland Youth* (1995) Tsubasa faded away, only to return in a new 2001 TV series, cashing in on the 2002 World Cup.

CARDCAPTORS *

1998. JPN: *Card Captor Sakura*. TV series. DIR: Akitaro Daichi, Morio Asaka. SCR: Nanase Okawa, Jiro Kaneko. DES: CLAMP, Kumiko Takahashi. ANI: Kumiko Takahashi. MUS: Takayuki Negishi. PRD: Madhouse. 25 mins. x 70+ eps.
Created by CLAMP shortly after the success of **RAYEARTH**, *CardCaptors* combines the long tradition of magical-girl shows like **LITTLE WITCH SALLY** with the collection-oriented computer games such as **POKÉMON**. In her father's basement study, ten-year-old Sakura Kinomoto discovers the Clow, which looks like a book but is really a prison for sorcerous cards. She accidentally allows all the cards to escape, and Cerberus, the Guardian of the Cards, persuades her to hunt them all down. Each card represents a particular kind of spirit (e.g., elemental or seasonal) that Sakura can use once she acquires it, so her progress through the story amounts to a series of game-style power-ups—a point often made by Cerberus himself, who spends most of his time in his "cute" Kero-chan form. Other problems besieging Sakura include her best friend, Tomoyo, a rich girl who insists on designing new costumes for her and taping her missions. She must also compete against her Chinese rivals Li Meiling and Li Xiaolang (who also becomes Sakura's would-be boyfriend, though at first she much prefers her brother's indifferent best friend).

The 1999 *Card Captor Sakura: The Movie* sees Sakura win a trip to Hong Kong, where she competes with the Li siblings on their home turf. In a plot suspiciously similar to that of the final **TENCHI MUYO!** movie, Sakura is haunted by dreams of a strange woman, an old flame of the original Card Captor, Clow Reed. She must convince the phantom that Clow Reed is dead without angering her and causing her to destroy the parallel world in which they have become trapped. A second movie, *CCS: The Sealed Card*, followed in 2000, in which someone begins to steal Sakura's cards as she prepares to celebrate the Nadeshiko festival—an occasion doubly dear to her since Nadeshiko (see **NADESICO**) is also the name of her late mother.

The series came to the U.S. in late 2000 dubbed by the Nelvana Studios, though, as with many other ill-fated anime, the inertia of network "demands" ruined much of what made the series initially so interesting. As if the name change were not already a hint, the translation of the series attempted to move the focus to a more acceptable protagonist (see **SABER RIDER AND THE STAR SHERIFFS**), beginning with episode eight ("Sakura's Rival") and implying that she and Li Xiaolang are equals, in a futile attempt to gain more male viewers. *Ill. p. 269.*

CAROL

1990. Video. DIR: Satoshi Dezaki, Tsuneo Tominaga. SCR: Tomoya Miyashita, Yun Koga. DES: Yukari Kobayashi, Yun Koga. ANI: Yukari Kobayashi. MUS: Tetsuya Komuro. PRD: Animate Film, Magic Bus. 60 mins.
Carol is a teenage girl who notices music disappearing from the world—at first minor annoyances like the chimes of Big Ben or the sound of her father's cello, but then a major crisis when her favorite band, Gaball Screen, loses its music. Transported to the alternate dimension of Lapaz Lupaz, she joins forces with heroes Clark, Tico, and Flash to prevent monsters from stealing songs from Earth.

Naoto Kine, guitarist with the Japanese prefab pop band TM Network, supposedly wrote the original novel of *Carol* himself. Filtered through **EARTHIAN**-creator Koga and scenarist Miyashita before it was ready for the screen, the end result still became the best-selling anime video of the year in Japan. The sunglasses-wearing Tico is modeled on Kine himself, with lead singer Takashi Utsunomiya providing the model for Flash, and keyboardist-producer Tetsuya Komuro inspiring Clark. As with the Beatles' *Yellow Submarine*, but unlike the similar pop-promo anime **HUMANE SOCIETY**, the band's voices are provided by actors. Another of Kine's literary outpourings, **JUNKERS COME HERE**, was animated in 1994.

CASSHAN: ROBOT HUNTER *

1973. JPN: *Jinzo Ningen Casshan*. AKA: *Android Casshan*. TV series, Video. DIR: Hiroshi Sasakawa. SCR: Junzo Toriumi, Akiyoshi Sakai, Takao Koyama, Toshio Nagata. DES: Tatsuo Yoshida, Yoshitaka Amano. ANI: Masayuki Hayashi, Chuichi Iguchi. MUS: Shunsuke Kikuchi. PRD: Tatsunoko, Fuji TV. 25 mins. x 35 eps. (TV), 30 mins. x 4 eps. (v).
As an artificial human project nears completion, robot BK-1 is activated early by a bolt of lightning that damages its sense of morals. It leads a group of killer robots in the attempted destruction of the world, and its remorseful creator Kotaro Higashi cybernetically augments his son, Tetsuya, to fight them, with his canine companion, Friender, and love interest, Luna, whose passion for the hero is doomed to frustration because he is technically no longer human. Meanwhile, Tetsuya's mother is turned into Swanee the electronic swan to deliver messages and increase his angst. In the follow-up to Tatsunoko's successful **BATTLE OF THE PLANETS**, though, instead of a fiery phoenix warplane, Friender would transform into a variety of vehicles to suit his master's needs.

After the similar stories of *Terminator* and *Robocop* reached Japan, a sequel of sorts followed in the video series

New Android Casshan (1993), directed by Hiroyuki Fukushima from a screenplay by Fukushima and Noboru Aikawa, with Yasuomi Umezu as designer. The new series, which was the one released in the U.S., picks up the story after "Black King" and his robot army have defeated humanity's main forces. Tetsuya, still tortured over the loss of humanity no matter how good the cause, is forced to rescue Luna when she is captured by the Black Gang.

CASTLE IN THE SKY *

1986. JPN: *Tenku no Shiro Laputa*. AKA: *Laputa: The Castle in the Sky*. Movie. DIR: Hayao Miyazaki. SCR: Hayao Miyazaki. DES: Hayao Miyazaki. ANI: Tsukasa Tannai. MUS: Joe Hisaishi. PRD: Nibariki, Tokuma, Studio Ghibli. 124 mins.

Orphan Pazu dreams of following in his father's quest for the legendary flying city of Laputa. Another orphan, Sheeta, is linked to the city by the power of her strange necklace, which saves her life when she falls from an airship. Sheeta's necklace is a fragment of the legendary Levitation Stone that keeps cities like Laputa in the air, and chief of secret police Muska, a fellow descendant of Laputans, wants it for his own ends. Muska steals the stone to guide him to Laputa, and the children join forces with Ma Dola, matriarch of the Dola pirate clan—Sheeta in search of her stone, and the Ma Dola pirates in search of treasure. Laputa turns out to be a peaceful ruin that seems to have been abandoned by its inhabitants with only three extant robots still operational and tending the overgrown gardens (shades here of Douglas Trumbull's *Silent Running*). Muska seizes control of Laputa's weapon system, which he claims was the original device used to smite cities in Biblical times. Realizing he cannot be stopped, Sheeta and Pazu speak the magical words to destroy the city, though the core of the city floats off to a higher, safer altitude where humans cannot reach it.

Taking themes from an aborted earlier project that was eventually made in his absence as SECRET OF BLUE WATER, Miyazaki mixed these with elements of GULLIVER'S TRAVELS and images from his tour of Wales after the miners' strike. With a believably human cast bickering over the remnants of the old order, only to eventually destroy it, it shares many elements with both its predecessor NAUSICAÄ and Miyazaki's later PRINCESS MONONOKE. Shown on a double bill with two episodes of Miyazaki's TV series, SHERLOCK HOUND.

CASTLE OF CAGLIOSTRO *

1979. JPN: *Lupin III: Cagliostro no Shiro*. Movie. DIR: Hayao Miyazaki. SCR: Hayao Miyazaki, Haruya Yamazaki. DES: Yasuo Otsuka. ANI: Yasuo Otsuka. MUS: Yuji Ono. PRD: TMS. 100 mins.

One year after *The Secret of Mamo* (see LUPIN III), the master thief Lupin has successfully evaded Inspector Zenigata's clutches and is planning a new heist. When he inadvertently steals fake money, Lupin realizes that the high-quality printing plates are worth more than the money itself. He tracks down the counterfeiters to the tiny European state of Cagliostro but is soon distracted by the approaching wedding of Count Cagliostro and Clarice, the last princess of the ruling family.

As strings strike up straight out of "Papa Was a Rolling Stone," and amid filmic nods to *The 39 Steps* and other famous caper movies, it's Lupin and his gang against the world, with cross and double-cross, as the thieves shop each other to the cops and change their minds about what they should be stealing (Lupin alone goes from money to plates to a bride in the course of the film). Supposedly inspired by the wedding of Grace Kelly to Prince Rainier of Monaco, the film also draws on one of Kelly's most memorable movies, *To Catch a Thief*, and Maurice Leblanc's 1924 Lupin novel *Countess Cagliostro*. From the opening casino heist to the Chaplinesque duel inside a giant clock, this is a superbly paced crime caper and Lupin's best screen outing. First-time movie director Miyazaki would reuse many of the ideas later in his career, including the Mediterranean Riviera setting of PORCO ROSSO, a courageous nature-loving princess in NAUSICAÄ, a friendly hound in KIKI'S DELIVERY SERVICE, and the mossy ruins in CASTLE IN THE SKY. The film also lifted an idea from Miyazaki's work on TREASURE ISLAND—the fabled Cagliostro treasure is hidden at the bottom of an artificial lake. Surprisingly, the *Lupin* franchise lay dormant for several years afterward, not revived until the third TV series in 1984. *Ill. p. 333.*

CATGIRL NUKUNUKU *

1992. JPN: *Banno Bunka Neko Musume Nukunuku*. AKA: *All Purpose Cultural Cat Girl Snuggly-Wuggly*. Video, TV series. DIR: Yuji Moriyama, Hidetoshi Shigematsu. SCR: Yuzo Takada, Katsuhiko Chiba. DES: Yuzo Takada. ANI: Yuji Moriyama. MUS: Hiro Matsuda and Beat Club. PRD: Animate Film. 30 mins. x 6 eps.

Ryunosuke (Ryan) loses his beloved pet kitten in an accident, and his scientist father, Dr. Natsume, places the creature's brain inside a sexy android body. This is just one of many treats designed to keep the boy's mind off his parents' acrimonious divorce, but Ryunosuke and his new pal Nukunuku are soon caught up in a bitter custody battle between his crazy inventor father and his mother, Akiko, who owns a weapons factory. She regularly sends her minions, Arisa and Kyoko, to kidnap Ryan, only to be foiled by the innocent activities of Nukunuku, also intended as a bodyguard for her endangered master.

With the massive collateral damage of PROJECT A-KO, an anime ingenue whose feline origins go right back to Tezuka's BAGHI, and a surprisingly accurate study of marital breakup that still has bite even if played for laughs, *Catgirl Nukunku* was based on a minor work by 3X3 EYES–creator Yuzo Takada, and it is one of a limited number of anime that exist in two translations. A British dub of episodes 1–3 was the sole release from Crusader Video, who aimed to dispel the U.K. media's view that all anime were perverse, although they had to excise a masturbation scene before they could achieve the general rating their PR required. U.S. distributors AD Vision were less coy, running the entire series both uncut and in a feature-length "movie" edit.

Nukunuku jumped to TV Tokyo in 1997 for a 12-part series directed by Yoshitaka Fujimoto that retold the story from the beginning. In 1998, the franchise was revived with the same crew for the 12-part straight-to-video *Nukunuku Dash*, looking suspiciously like the tail end of a canceled TV series.

CATNAPPED! *

1995. JPN: *Totsuzen! Neko no Kuni Banipal Witt.* AKA: *Suddenly! Catland Banipal Witt.* Movie. DIR: Takashi Nakamura. SCR: Chiaki Konaka, Takashi Nakamura. DES: Takashi Nakamura. ANI: Takashi Nakamura, Mamoru Kurosawa. MUS: Naruaki Mie. PRD: Triangle Staff, Pioneer. 75 mins.

When his pet dog, Papadoll, goes missing, Toriyasu is inconsolable. He is taken to the magical world of Banipal Witt, where both he and his sister, Miko, are transformed into cats. Dodo, the brightest pupil of high-priest Sandada, has been turned to the dark side and now serves Bubulina, the cursed witch-queen whose touch turns people into balloons. The pair have kidnapped Papadoll and turned him into a monster that menaces the whole kingdom, and Toriyasu must stop him before sunrise, when he too will be transformed. Earthlings (including dogs) can only be in Banipal Witt for two days before the sunlight will turn them into monsters. Toriyasu and Miko are there for two days before Sandada completes his magic pill that will restore Papadoll. Returning Papadoll to canine form, the children use the magic cat's-paw talisman to restore normalcy and are rushed home before sunrise on the third day by the feline trio that brought them to Banipal Witt

in the first place. Only three minutes have passed on Earth, but as the kids head off for a normal day at school, they are accosted once more by cats from Banipal Witt in search of help with another crisis.

Featuring a 3D-rendered fondant world spinning in the light of a gold paper sun, featuring marshmallow skies, balloon cats, giant floating mice, and even a girl with kaleidoscope eyes in Bubulina, *Catnapped!* is a hallucinogenic mixture of *Yellow Submarine* and **ALICE IN WONDERLAND** that ultimately fails through its dispassionate precision. The candy-striped design and childish worldview seem almost calculatedly endearing, but no amount of brainstorming and focus groups can make up for true magic such as Miyazaki's **MY NEIGHBOR TOTORO**, which *Catnapped!* would very much like to be. For its U.S. release, Pioneer preferred to play up the writers' connections to **AKIRA** and **ARMITAGE III**, a sure sign that they doubted its stand-alone status within the children's cartoon market.

CAT'S EYE

1983. TV series. DIR: Toshio Takeuchi, Yoshio Hayakawa, Hiroshi Fukutomi. SCR: Keisuke Fujikawa, Tomoko Konparu. DES: Akio Sugino. ANI: Satoshi Hirayama, Nobuko Tsukada. MUS: Kazuo Otani. PRD: TMS, Nippon TV. 25 mins. x 73 eps.

Artist Michael Heinz disappears along with his antique collection, parts of which keep turning up in the holdings of criminal connoisseurs. His three daughters, Rui, Hitomi, and Ai Kisugi, secretly become the "Cat's Eye" team to steal the artworks back, hoping to locate their father in the process. Detective Toshio Utsumi is assigned to crack the cat-burglar case, unaware that his girlfriend, Hitomi, is one of the thieves he is tracking. Only his lovelorn assistant, Mitsuko, suspects, though since the coffee bar opposite the police station, run by Hitomi, is called the Cat's Eye, it's difficult to see how Toshio qualified for detective.

Compared by *Animage* to an all-girl

© 1991 YUJIN/SEIYO/ANIMATE FILM CO., LTD.

LUPIN III, Tsukasa Hojo's sexy trio of leotard-wearing cat burglars struck a chord in *Shonen Jump*, where they ran for 18 manga volumes between 1981 and 1984. The series was no less successful netting male as well as female viewers, albeit for different reasons, with its mix of crime and passion. The theme song was also a hit in its own right, selling 800,000 copies. The initial 36 episodes were followed in 1985 by a second season, directed by Kanetsugu Kodama, which gradually refocused on the farcical love comedy between Hitomi and Toshio and was played more for laughs. Though there was no real ending to the TV series, the manga eventually closed with the girls revealing their identities and running for the U.S. Belatedly demonstrating a genuine skill in detection, Toshio leaves his job and tracks them down, "capturing" his true love with a wedding ring where handcuffs had failed.

The girls would return for a live-action TV special in 1988 and a live-action feature in 1997, directed by *Zipang*'s Kaizo Hayashi. Presumably with an eye on the Hong Kong market, the film adds a Triad boyfriend for Ai (**STREET FIGHTER II** *Zero*'s Kane Kosugi), who is ordered kill off the Cat's Eye team, and a climactic shootout at the Triad's restaurant headquarters, where the elusive Heinz is held prisoner. *Cat's Eye* characters would also have occasional cameos in Hojo's later **CITY HUNTER**. There was also a porno pastiche, *Cat's Ai [Love]: Milky Girl* (1985), released straight to video.

CAT'S NIBBLES

1992. JPN: *Yoyo no Neko Tsumami*. AKA: *Yoyo's Cat Nibbles*. TV series. DIR: Masami Annai, Yorifusa Yamaguchi, Katsumi Arima. SCR: Takao Koyama, Makoto Narita. DES: N/C. ANI: Yorifusa Yamaguchi. MUS: N/C. PRD: Visual 80, Nippon TV. 2 mins. x 15 eps.

Six cats introduce unusual snacks in this compilation of short culinary program bumpers, featuring a map of the cats' home island and data on each character.

CERES: CELESTIAL LEGEND *

2000. JPN: *Ayashi no Ceres*. AKA: *Mysterious Ceres*. TV series. DIR: Hajime Kamegaki. SCR: Shikichi Ohashi. DES: Hideyuki Motohashi. ANI: Hideyuki Motohashi. MUS: Ryo Sakai. PRD: Studio Pierrot, Bandai, WOWOW. 25 mins. x 24 eps.

Long ago, a man fell in love with the goddess Ceres when she came down from Heaven. He stole her winged cloak, and, trapped on Earth for eternity, she became his wife. In time, a child was born to the mismatched couple, and the wheels of fate began to turn. After many generations, Ceres tired of her Earthbound existence and sought to regain her wings from their guardians, her distant descendants, the 16-year-old Japanese twins Aya and Aki Mikage. Based on **FUSHIGI YUGI**–creator Yu Watase's manga, serialized in *Weekly Shojo Comic*, and featuring many staff from the *FY* anime.

CHALK-COLORED PEOPLE

1988. JPN: *Chalk-iro no People*. Video. DIR: Akira Kamiyama. SCR: Seizo Watase. DES: Seizo Watase. ANI: Keizo Kira. MUS: Astrud Gilberto. PRD: 3D. 54 mins.

Five short episodes from **HEART COCK-TAIL**–creator Seizo Watase's romantic manga set to bossanova music for reasons unknown. The stories include *Building without Tide, Brother and Sister, Sometimes I'm Happy, I've Saved the Sidecar for You,* and *The Santa Quartet*. The music is from Latin lounge legend Astrud Gilberto. A similar music/animation combination was tried the previous year with Watase's **MY ALL-DAY ALL-COLOR**, and later with **TWO ON THE ROAD**.

CHAMPION OF GORDIAN

1979. JPN: *Toshi Gordian*. AKA: *Gardian*. TV series. DIR: Shigeru Yanagawa, Masamune Ochiai. SCR: Masaru Yamamoto. DES: Ippei Kuri. ANI: Kazuhiko Udagawa. MUS: Masaaki Jinbo, Masayuki Yamamoto. PRD: Tatsunoko, Tokyo 12 Channel. 25 mins. x 73 eps.

Daigo Otaki and his pet mechanical leopard, Clint, are transferred to the Mecha Con Unit that protects the computer-run Victor Town from the predations of the Madoctor Gang. However, he is abducted by the giant robot Gordian and meets his "sister," Saori, at Fort Santore, where he hears the voice of his own father issuing from the central computer that is making all the decisions. The run of this transforming robot story was extended several times, with Daigo eventually heading out for adventures in space with his robots Protteser, Delinger, and Garbin, whose similarity to the **MACHINE ROBO** line prompted Bandai to retool its existing molds in order to imply a relationship that wasn't there.

CHANCER PRINCESS

1997. JPN: *Detatoko Princess*. Video. DIR: Akiyuki Shinbo. SCR: Mayori Sekijima, Masashi Kubota. DES: Hiroko Sakurai. ANI: Hiroko Sakurai. MUS: Shinken Kenra. PRD: JC Staff. 30 mins. x 3 eps.

Transported by a magic mirror to a distant fantasy world, Princess Lapis tries hard to impress the people of Saucerland with her nascent powers, fighting Topaz, the fearsome North Witch who is invariably late for any occasion.

Former **TENCHI MUYO!**–manga artist Hitoshi Okuda created this Jell-O-mold successor seemingly in an attempt to secure his own franchise after drawing for someone else's for so long. The preceding *Chancer Princess* radio drama featured a gimmick in which Lapis would sing her spells but was inexplicably replaced in the animated version by a magic wand that simply transforms her into a "cute" version of herself. Why not just watch **DRAGON HALF** again?

CHARGE AHEAD! MEN'S SCHOOL

1988. JPN: *Sakikage! Otoko Juku*. TV series. DIR: Nobutaka Nishizawa. SCR: Susumu Takahisa. DES: Masami Suda. ANI: Masami Suda. MUS: Shunsuke Kikuchi. PRD: Toei, Fuji TV. 25 mins. x 34 eps.

Otoko Juku is the juvenile hall where men are sent for being too honorable and too manly, the kind of rough, tough academy one might expect from the team who made **FIST OF THE NORTH STAR**. Newcomers Momotaro, Genji, and Taio endure bullying and harsh treatment at the hands of class leader Onihige and the evil teachers.

Like Akira Miyashita's original 34-volume 1985 *Shonen Jump* manga, this show starts as a comedy but soon devolves into fights, the quality of animation dropping along with the story. It retained elements of its comedic past right to the end, however, with Momotaro reading out fake fan mail over the "next episode" shots and pretending to take requests. There was also a 1988 movie directed by Tetsuo Imazawa, in which the gang gets to trash Hawaii, Alaska, Niagara Falls, and Manhattan in a battle of wills with an evil mastermind. **❾**

CHARLOTTE

1977. JPN: *Wakakusa no Charlotte*. AKA: *Charlotte the Young Grass/Green Shoot*. TV series. DIR: Eiji Okabe. SCR: Shunichi Yukimuro. DES: Shinya Takahashi. ANI: Tetsuo Shibuya, Nobuyuki

Kitajima, Hiroshi Yoshida. MUS: Yoshimasa Suzuki. PRD: Nippon Animation, TV Asahi. 25 mins. x 30 eps.
Charlotte grows up on a Canadian cattle farm and has a happy life until her 12th birthday, when her father André reveals that he is really a French aristocrat, hiding out in the colonies to escape persecution. Her mother, believed dead, is actually still alive, and André sets off to bring her back, but he is killed en route. Charlotte struggles to keep the farm going, encouraged by her friend Sandy, and, in the tradition of almost every girls' anime from CANDY CANDY onward, aided by a "mysterious stranger" called Knight. Nippon Animation's first homegrown series for girls deliberately alluded to LITTLE HOUSE ON THE PRAIRIE and LITTLE WOMEN in its look and feel but was considered a failure and taken off the air after a relatively short run.

CHARM POINT
1999. JPN: Sister's Rondo: Charm Point 1. Video. DIR: Yoshimaro Otsubo. SCR: Tedokoro Imaike. DES: Maron Kurase. ANI: N/C. MUS: N/C. PRD: Beam Entertainment, Akatonbo. 30 mins.
In this typical tale of anime abuse replaying the vengeful student/teacher setup from ADVENTURE KID, new teacher Serina Kawano strikes up a very strange relationship with her pupil Masaya, submitting to his sadistic demands. Meanwhile, Serina's little sister, Yumi, is having boyfriend "troubles" of her own and doesn't understand how to keep her man. Needless to say, Serina has some advice for her. ◐

CHIBI MARUKO-CHAN
1990. AKA: Cute Little Maruko. Movie, TV series. DIR: Tsutomu Shibayama. SCR: Momoko Sakura. DES: Yuji Shigeta. ANI: Michishiro Yamada, Yoshiaki Yanagida, Masako Sato. MUS: BB Queens. PRD: Nippon Animation, Fuji TV. 94 mins. (m), 25 mins. x 321+ eps (TV).
Maruko is a nine-year-old schoolgirl who spends most of her time day-

dreaming, particularly that she is a noble princess, her parents are divorced, or both. Inexplicably talking like an old woman despite her tender years, she continually pesters her parents, elder sister, and relatives to answer questions, and "amusing" misunderstandings ensue. Momoko Sakura's 1986 manga, loaded with 1970s nostalgia, was christened a "new SAZAE-SAN" by some Japanese critics for its gentle humanity and interminable run.

CHICKEN TAKKUN
1984. TV series. DIR: Keiji Hayakawa. SCR: Masaru Yamamoto, Kazuyoshi Ohashi. DES: Yoshihiro Owada. ANI: Mitsuru Honma, Tetsuro Hagano, Shigeru Omachi. MUS: Masami Anno. PRD: Ishinomori Pro, Studio Pierrot, Studio Gallop, Fuji TV. 25 mins. x 23 eps.
The Walchin Dictionary, a computer packed with evil ideas from Planet R, falls into the hands of Doctor Bell, who plans to use it to rule the world. Prince Chicken enlists the help of his alien friends to get the dictionary back and lands his flying saucer on the roof of the Minamita family's house in Japan. Miko Minamita and her four friends offer to help Chicken. This anime was adapted from Shotaro Ishinomori's manga run in the educational magazine Science for Grades 1–6.

CHILD'S TOY
1995. JPN: Kodomo no Omocha. TV series. DIR: Akira Suzuki, Akitaro Daichi, Hiroaki Sakurai. SCR: Tomoko Konparu, Ryosuke Takahashi, Miho Maruo. DES: Hajime Watanabe. ANI: Nobuyuki Tokinaga. MUS: Hiroshi Koga, Tokio. PRD: Pony Canyon, TV Tokyo. 25 mins. x 102 eps.
Sana Kurata is a child star who attends a normal school, initially at odds with the bullying Akito Hayama, until he reluctantly becomes her friendly rival ("my enemy and my boyfriend," she describes him with a typically innocent oxymoron). Originally turned into a video as part of the 40th anniversary celebrations of Ribbon magazine in 1995, Miho Obana's 1994 manga

became a full-fledged TV series the following year. With a sixth-grader who is already a star (appearing in the self-referentially titled Child's Toy TV show), it takes the aspirations of magical-girl shows like CREAMY MAMI as given, preferring instead to concentrate on school one-upmanship like that in GOLDFISH WARNING.

CHIMERA *
1997. JPN: Seikimatsu Reima Chimera. AKA: End of the Century Demon Beauty Chimera. Video. DIR: Mitsuo Kusakabe. SCR: Narihiko Tatsumiya. DES: Asami Tojo. ANI: Taeko Sato. MUS: N/C. PRD: Toei. 47 mins.
Sex and violence in the Hong Kong underworld, as pretty assassin Rei leaves a wake of death and grief behind her as she carries out jobs for the Mob. Her codename: Chimera. Based on the girls' manga by Asami Tojo, and not to be confused with KIMERA. ◐◑◒

CHINA NUMBER ONE
1997. JPN: Nekketsu Ryori Anime: Chuka Ichiban. AKA: Hot-blooded Cookery Anime: China Number One. TV series. DIR: Masami Annai. SCR: Nobuaki Kishima. DES: Yoshinori Kishi, Tsuneo Ninomiya. ANI: Eikichi Takahashi. MUS: Michihiko Ota. PRD: Nippon Animation, Pony Canyon. 25 mins. x 52 eps.
In this adaptation of Etsuji Ogawa's manga for Shonen Magazine, a gifted teenage cook travels late 19th-century China in search of rival chefs worthy of his cooking prowess. Like RANMA 1/2 before it, it was immensely successful in East Asia, where its Japanese origins were swiftly forgotten. Episodes 9–14 were edited into a 30-minute digest version.

CHIRORIN VILLAGE
1992. JPN: Chirorin Mura. TV series. DIR: Yasuo Yamakichi. SCR: Osamu Nakamura, Riko Hinokuma. DES: Takao Kasai. ANI: Takao Kasai. MUS: Tatsumi Yano. PRD: C&D Distribution, Bandai Visual, NHKEP. 8 mins. x 170 eps.
Chirorin Village and Walnut's Tree was a children's puppet show broadcast on

NHK between 1956 and 1964 featuring the adventures of three junior high-school children: Tonpei the Onion, Kurumi the Walnut, and Peanut (the Peanut) in the titular village. Brought back to cash in on parents' nostalgia, it was remade as a TV anime with famous voice actresses, such as Noriko Hidaka and Minami Takayama, and far-fetched episodes, including *I'm Not a Criminal*, *The Sound of a Vampire*, *Come Out You Monsters*, and *Back to the Secret Base*.

CHISTE: THE GREEN THUMB

1990. JPN: *Chist: Midori no Oyayubi*. Movie. DIR: Shumon Miura, Yuji Funano. SCR: Ryu Tachihara. DES: Masahiro Kase. ANI: Shinya Sadamitsu, Kazuya Ose. MUS: Marc Berriere, Francoise Legrand, Jean-Michel Ervé. PRD: Dax International. 73 mins.

In this adaptation of the book by Maurice D'Orleans, Chiste is a boy with the strange ability to make flowers grow wherever he places his thumb, a power which he puts to use bringing love and peace to the world. For more peace-loving florists, see **WEISS KREUZ**.

CHOBIN THE STARCHILD *

1974. JPN: *Hoshi no Ko Chobin*. TV series. DIR: Rintaro, Hiroyuki Hoshiyama, Noboru Ishiguro, Shinji Okada. SCR: Shunichi Yukimuro, Hisashi Ito, Keisuke Fujikawa, Yukiko Takayama, Soji Yoshikawa. DES: Shotaro Ishinomori. ANI: Norio Yazawa. MUS: Tetsuaki Hagiwara. PRD: Watanabe Planning, Ishinomori Pro, TBS. 25 mins. x 26 eps.

Chobin, king of planet Fairystar, arrives from his home world in a spaceship and lands at the house of Professor Amagawa and his assistant, Ruri. Enlisting the help of terrestrial creatures (including a frog, rabbit, and butterfly from the nearby forest), Chobin searches for his missing mother and dreams of the day when he and his family can return to Fairystar and depose the usurper Brungar.

Invented by producers at Watanabe Planning in cooperation with **CYBORG 009**–creator Shotaro Ishinomori,

Chobin's adventures were serialized in a number of magazines, including *Shojo Friend* and *Terebi* magazine, to drum up support for the TV series. The story received a very limited broadcast on U.S. Japanese community TV stations shortly after its release.

CHOCOLATE PANIC PICTURE SHOW, THE

1985. Video. DIR: Kazuyoshi Hirose. SCR: N/C. DES: Kamui Fujiwara. ANI: Mamoru Sugiura. MUS: TV Asahi Music. PRD: CBS, Taurus, Filmlink. 33 mins.

Jaw-droppingly racist musical in which grossly caricatured Africans Manbo, Chinbo, and Chonbo cause chaos in civilization despite the efforts of their pretty tour guide/bedmate to tame their zany, grass-skirted cannibal ways. This video was based on a manga by Kamui Fujiwara in *Super Action* and partly inspired by Jamie Uys's *The Gods Must Be Crazy* (1980).

CHOPPO THE MISCHIEVOUS ANGEL

1970. JPN: *Itazura Tenshi Choppo-chan*. TV series. DIR: Takashi Aoki, Fumio Ikeno. SCR: Noboru Ishiguro, Tomohiro Ando. DES: N/C. ANI: New World Pictures. MUS: Yuki Tamaki. PRD: Fuji TV Enterprise. 5 mins. x 240 eps.

Slipping off his cloud and falling out of heaven, Choppo, a naughty angel, lands in the food store owned and run by Kantaro Fujino's parents. Unable to fly home because his wings are not yet fully grown, he stays with the family, though his inability to understand the meaning of danger soon leads him into numerous accidents. The same crew had previously worked on Fuji TV Enterprise's *Pinch and Punch*, a 1969 tale of naughty twins that was otherwise very similar.

CHRISTMAS IN JANUARY

1991. JPN: *Ichigatsu ni wa Christmas*. Video. DIR: Satoshi Dezaki. SCR: Setsuko Shibunnoichi, Toshiaki Imaizumi. DES: Yukari Kobayashi. ANI: Yukari Kobayashi. MUS: Takashi Ui. PRD: For Life Record, Media Ring. 45 mins.

Nobumasa is a boy who works part-time in a shoe store, where he meets Mizuki, a girl whose abusive family life has left her unable to trust other people. Meanwhile, Nobumasa is unaware that another girl, Seiko, has a crush on him but is unable to express her feelings.

A love triangle straight out of **VIDEO GIRL AI** or **KIMAGURE ORANGE ROAD**, but this time presented for the female readership in *Margaret* magazine, Mariko Iwadate's 1984 manga made it to the screen in this one-shot video.

CINDERELLA

1996. JPN: *Cinderella Monogatari*. TV series. DIR: Hiroshi Sasakawa, Takaaki Ishiyama, Yuji Asada. SCR: Masaaki Sakurai, Hiroko Naka, Tsunehisa Arakawa. DES: Tatsunoko Planning Office. ANI: Masami Suda, Chuichi Iguchi. MUS: N/C. PRD: Tatsunoko, Marubeni, NHK2. 25 mins. x 26 eps.

Forced to scrub the floor in her wicked stepmother's kitchen, Cinderella refuses to let her situation get her down. Her fairy godmother, Palette, casts a spell so that she can understand the speech of animals, and Cinderella's life is made easier by her friendships with Wanda the dog, Pappy the bird, and mice Chuchu and Bingo. She falls in love with a man called Sharrol whom she meets in town, unaware that he is actually *Prince* Sharrol, traveling in disguise, and that the "real" Prince Sharrol back at the palace is an imposter.

Straight after finishing **SNOW WHITE**, Tatsunoko added a pirate attack, funny animal business, and a subplot straight out of the *Prince and the Pauper* in order to pad out the running time of this adaptation. Since Cinderella and her prince charming are *both* in disguise each time they meet, it adds to the tension, but once all the intrigue is resolved, the last three episodes end traditionally with the ball, glass slipper reunion, wedding bells, and happy-ever-after. Other versions of *Cinderella* have appeared in **GRIMMS' FAIRY TALES** (1987), *Famous World Fairy Tales* (1989), as part of the **HELLO KITTY** series (*Hello Kitty's Cinderella*, 1992), and, in a more risqué incarnation, in ADULT FAIRY TALES (1999). See also VIDEO PICTURE BOOK.

CINDERELLA EXPRESS

1989. Video. DIR: Teru Moriboshi, Nanako Shimazaki. SCR: Kenji Terada. DES: Moriyasu Taniguchi. ANI: Moriyasu Taniguchi. MUS: N/C. PRD: Nippon Eizo. 50 mins.

Everyday salaryman Yuji Shimano meets and beds a pretty young girl at his bachelor party. Meeting her again at his wedding, he realizes that he has just begun an affair with his sister-in-law, in this erotic farce from Hikaru Yumizuki found in the pages of *Young Jump*. A decade later, TEACHER'S PET would demonstrate that nothing ever changes. ◐

CIPHER THE VIDEO

1989. Video. DIR: Tsuneo Tominaga. SCR: Machiko Kondo, Yuko Sakurai. DES: Yukari Kobayashi. ANI: Kenichi Maejima, Takeshi Koizumi, Minoru Yamazawa. MUS: Wags, Thompson Twins. PRD: Victor Entertainment. 40 mins.

In this adaptation of Minako Narita's 1985 manga from *Lala*, pretty-boy Cipher goes to high school in New York, sometimes posing as his twin brother, Shiva, a famous actor who often needs to cut classes. Shiva wanders moodily through the streets of New York before the scene shifts to the set of his latest movie, an American football tale called *Winning Tough*. We see a fake "making of" documentary featuring interviews of him and his costars before being shown the trailer for the film and an image video based on it. Eventually, Shiva returns from his wanderings and cooks breakfast, revealing that his wanderings were just wanderings, not the result of a fight with his brother.

Cipher the Video is a true curiosity, featuring English-language dialogue with Japanese subtitles for that extra touch of exoticism, although it was never released outside Japan. Deliberately shot in an MTV pop-video style, much

of it is simply overlaid with songs from American movies contemporaneous with the manga—Phil Collins' title song from *Against All Odds* (1984), as well as the title song and "Let's Hear It for the Boy" from the same year's *Footloose*, all in relatively poor versions from the group Wags. As an additional bonus, there's also the original version of the Thompson Twins' "Kamikaze." The running time is bulked out with the self-indulgent "Making of *Cipher the Video*," recycling some footage for a third time, featuring interviews with the crew and live-action shots from the New York location hunt that informed some of the admittedly picturesque images of the city. As a bonus, the video also includes Cipher's other animated appearance, a short 1986 Japanese commercial for Sumitomo Insurance. An earnest and ultimately touching treat for fans of the manga. Narita specialized in a fantasy America—her earlier manga *Alien Street* (1980) is set at a U.S. college where a beautiful, blond Arab prince flirts with liberal Western ways.

CIRCUIT ANGEL

1987. JPN: *Circuit Angel: Ketsui no Starting Grid*. AKA: *Circuit Angel: Resolving Starting Grid*. Video. DIR: Yoshikazu Tochihira, Hideki Tonokatsu. SCR: Asami Watanabe. DES: Chuichi Iguchi, Boomerang. ANI: Hiroshi Kazawa. MUS: N/C. PRD: Studio Unicorn. 45 mins.

Mariko is a downtown schoolgirl who loves motorcycles and wants to graduate from the street-racing circle of her friends to the world of pro racing. But despite poaching LEGEND OF ROLLING WHEELS-writer Watanabe and concentrating hard enough on machinery to justify a "Mariko's Bike Designed by" credit for the Boomerang agency, little can disguise this show's true nature as a rip-off of the far more successful BOMBER BIKERS OF SHONAN.

CIRCUIT WOLF II

1990. JPN: *Circuit no Okami II: Modena no Ken*. AKA: *Circuit Wolf II: Ken*

Hapless sword master, Lina Inverse, with her sometime traveling companion, Amelia, the self-proclaimed Champion of Justice. Beginning in print as a lighthearted antidote to the deadly serious RECORD OF LODOSS WAR, Hajime Kanzaka's popular SLAYERS endured through the 1990s in anime form. After a long run on TV, it was put out to pasture on video and the occasional short movie. Accidents of rights acquisition led to the movie and TV versions being picked up by different U.S. distributors. See entry p. 358.

Slayers

© 1995 HAJIME KANZAKA/R. ARAIZUMI/TV TOKYO/SOFTX/MARUBENI

[Sword] of Modena. Video. DIR: Yoshihide Kuriyama. SCR: Dai Kuroyuki. DES: Satoshi Yamaguchi. ANI: Satoshi Yamaguchi. MUS: GL48. PRD: Gainax, CBS. 45 mins.

Qualified racing-driver Satoshi Ikezawa's *Circuit Wolf* comic ran in *Weekly Playboy* magazine for 18 volumes in 1975, reputedly gaining considerable praise through its author's appreciation of the realities of racing. This is a sequel to the manga, rather than a nonexistent anime predecessor, and features a young racer, Ken, arriving in Italy in search of his missing Ferrari Dino. Car chases and road rages soon ensue against the fearsome "White Wolf of Stuttgart." ◐◐

CITY HUNTER *

1987. AKA: *Nicky Larson*. Movie, TV series/special. DIR: Kanetsugu Kodama, Takashi Imanishi, Tetsuro Amino, Kiyoshi Egami. SCR: Hiroyuki Hoshiyama, Yasushi Hirano, Akinori Endo. DES: Yoshiko Kamimura. ANI: Takeo Kitahara. MUS: Ryoichi Kuniyoshi. PRD: Sunrise, Yomiuri TV. 25 mins. x 140 eps.

Ryo (Joe, in some U.S. dubs) Saeba is a professional "sweeper," an Equalizer who packs a .357 Magnum and specializes in bodyguard details in the Tokyo district of Shinjuku, where he can be reached through coded messages on the train station billboard. Promising his dying partner, Hideyuki, that he will look after Kaori, Hideyuki's sister, the terminally lecherous Ryo is lumbered with a prim female assistant, who nevertheless remains eternally jealous of his conquests.

Tsukasa Hojo's 1985 *Shonen Jump* comic proved even more successful than his CAT'S EYE, running for a total of 35 volumes. The regular cast of characters, including Ryo, surrogate wife/daughter Kaori, policewoman Saeko, and rival investigator Reika (both gorgeous, of course) would be reprised for TV directed by *Cat's Eye* alumnus Kodama. The TV edition kept Ryo's relationships with his female clients unconsummated, preferring instead to truncate many seductions with farce and slapstick.

Steadily gaining popularity (the closing theme "Get Wild" became a hit in its own right), the series moved from seven to six o'clock after 51 episodes. An 87-minute theatrical feature, *Magnum of Love's Destiny* (1989), was released in the U.S. as *.357 Magnum* and featured beautiful European pianist Nina trying to track down her father amid a then-topical backdrop inspired by the reunification of East and West Germany (here renamed Galiera). In a typical *City Hunter* setup, Nina is the unwitting mule for a vital microchip planted on her by a communist agent shortly before his own death. Ryo takes one deceptively simple mission only to find himself deep over his head in another.

With new theme music but otherwise unchanged, seasons two and three introduced occasional hour-long "special" episodes that were eventually to become the franchise's medium of choice. *Bay City Wars* (1990) features a Central American dictator using drug money to take over the world and reprogramming U.S. nuclear missiles, all from the titular Shinjuku hotel. Ryo's natural lechery is brought to the fore when he must stop the general's

beautiful daughter from destroying the world. *Million Dollar Plot* (also 1990) pits Ryo against a CIA conspiracy to liquidate a beautiful rogue agent.

City Hunter '91 was the fourth and final TV series, ending after just 13 episodes. However, in 1993, the franchise was rejuvenated by Wong Jing's live-action film, which cleverly exploited the show's popularity abroad by casting big Chinese names in the lead roles—Jackie Chan as Ryo and *A Chinese Ghost Story*'s Wang Zhuxian as Kaori. One of the few anime series brought back regularly for TV specials (another is LUPIN III), Ryo's more recent one-shot TV adventures have included *The Secret Service* (1996), in which he teams up with a pretty secret agent to protect the leader of a banana republic, and *Goodbye My Sweetheart* (1997—released in the U.S. as *City Hunter "The Movie"*), which imitates PATLABOR 2 with its tale of a disgruntled soldier bringing his war experiences to Tokyo. *The End of Ryo Saeba* (1999) quite patently wasn't—it's likely that *City Hunter* will be back before long. In the meantime, the "special" format has been retroactively imposed upon the original series in Japan, now shuffled into 20 video compilations designed to showcase the best TV episodes, out of chronological order but in a semblance of feature-length editions. At least part of the *CH* franchise lives on in Hojo's manga *Angel Heart* (2001), in which a former assassin receives a prominent character's heart in a transplant operation. *Ill. p. 403.* 🅝🅥

CLAMP SCHOOL DETECTIVES *

1997. JPN: *Clamp Gakuen Tanteidan*. TV series. DIR: Osamu Nabeshima. SCR: Mayori Sekijima, Masaharu Amiya. DES: Hiroshi Tanaka. ANI: Toshikazu Endo, Yuki Kanno. MUS: Michiya Katakura. PRD: Studio Pierrot. 25 mins. x 26 eps. Nokoru, Suoh, and Akira are the Elementary Division Student Council, leaders of the sixth, fifth, and fourth grades in a private urban school for ten thousand of Japan's smartest (read:

richest) children. Moonlighting as private investigators in the fashion of CONAN THE BOY DETECTIVE, they solve mysteries (missing school records found, feckless bullies caught) and troubleshoot in affairs of the heart for their fellow students. A minor work from CLAMP, creators of CARDCAPTORS (who seem to have realized that only the inclusion of their brand name in the title would guarantee any attention), this harmless series was originally aimed at a female audience that was expected to be charmed by polite, well-mannered rich boys solving minor problems.

CLAN OF PIHYORO

1988. JPN: *Pihyoro Ikka*. Video. DIR: Satoshi Dezaki, Tsuneo Tominaga. SCR: Kazumi Koide. DES: Akio Sugino, Setsuko Shibunnoichi. ANI: Akio Sugino, Setsuko Shibunnoichi, Yukari Kobayashi. MUS: Noriaki Yamanaka. PRD: Bandai, CBS, Movic. 60 mins. Kyota, Sabatta, Q-ta, and Kyonta are the guardian spirits of our age, protecting Earth from evil spirits while masquerading as humble students at the Seiwagi ("Holy Japanese Citadel") middle school. Suspecting supernatural involvement in the suicide of female student Maiko, Kyota and Kyonta investigate, only to discover that their school is built on a prehistoric crematory, and the restless dead are haunting the students.

Kaori Himeki's fantasy manga from *Princess* magazine was originally going to be adapted into a video series, but its chances were destroyed when AKIRA was released barely a week later. Fantasy anime fell out of favor, and this abortive first episode never got further than its theatrical double bill with the digest edition of AIM FOR THE ACE 2. A few years later, the likes of POLTERGEIST REPORT made *Clan of Pihyoro* more appealing, but it was too late. Note director *Satoshi* Dezaki, working here with designer Sugino, who is normally associated with his brother, Osamu.

CLAN OF THE KAWARAZAKI

1996. JPN: *Kawarazaki-ke no Ichizoku.* Video. DIR: Shungyo Makokudo. SCR: Shungyo Makokudo. DES: Seifun Yamahatei. ANI: Harashu Suzuki. MUS: N/C. PRD: Triple X, Pink Pineapple, KSS. 30 mins. x 2 eps.

Mukuro, a college boy working through the vacation as a servant of the aristocratic Kawarazaki family, explores a mysterious pavilion on the grounds of the family mansion. Tempted by gorgeous women and "forced" to commit sexual acts, he is dragged into an alternate world of passion and free love. Or is it just a dream?

This otherwise unremarkable erotic anime was based on a 1993 computer game (from Silkies) that was one of the first in Japan to have multiple endings instead of a single narrative—hence the hallucinatory aspect of the story line as the pseudonymous crew tries to cram in as many finales as possible. ◑

CLASS FULL OF GHOSTS

1998. JPN: *Kyoshitsu wa Obake ga Ippai.* Video. DIR: Toshiya Shinohara. SCR: Makiko Sato. DES: Yutaka Hara. ANI: Yoko Furumiya, Yumiko Kanehara. MUS: N/C. PRD: Toei. 23 mins. x 2 eps.

Writer Sato and illustrator Hara, creators of HOLY THE GHOST, returned for this children's tale of a haunted classroom. Guaranteed high sales and a video release when selected, like COBBY THE CUTE LITTLE CAT, by the Japanese Library Council as a core title, the second episode features computer graphics of our hero banishing the spooks from his school. See HERE COMES HANAKO for the full story of Japanese school ghouls in the 1990s.

CLASSMATE

1998. Video. DIR: Satoshi Kato. SCR: Yuka Kurokawa. DES: Yoshihito Murata. ANI: N/C. MUS: N/C. PRD: Five Ways. 28 mins.

Not to be confused with END OF SUMMER, another anime whose Japanese title can also be translated as "Classmate," this later release is a surprisingly old-fashioned CREAM LEMON clone, fea-

turing a schoolgirl, Nami, who wants to have sex. Surprise, surprise—she gets some. ◑

CLEOPATRA DC *

1989. Video. DIR: Naoyuki Yoshinaga. SCR: Kaoru Shintani, Sukehiro Tomita. DES: Nobuteru Yuki. ANI: Tai Fujikawa. MUS: Hiroaki Suzuki. PRD: Agent 21, JC Staff. 30 mins. x 3 eps.

Cleo, the Chairwoman of the Cleopatra financial conglomerate, is so rich that she controls much of the U.S. economy and is described as the "moving capital of the world." When a light aircraft crash-lands in her bedroom, the delirious pilot can only give her the message "Mary Anne." Investigating with her assistant, Surei, Cleo determines that he is referring to the daughter of the Oil Minister, rumored to have been kidnapped by the sinister Junior.

After bungling a hit on Cleo, Junior's discredited henchman Apollo turns on his former boss, who is forced to seek help from Cleo herself. The final episode features Cleo going to Nice on holiday, where she is embroiled in an android plot, in a lightweight adventure series from AREA 88's Kaoru Shintani.

CLEOPATRA: QUEEN OF SEX *

1970. JPN: *Cleopatra.* Movie. DIR: Osamu Tezuka, Eiichi Yamamoto. SCR: Shigemi Satoyoshi. DES: Ko Kojima. ANI: Kazuko Nakamura, Gisaburo Sugii, Yoshiaki Kawajiri. MUS: Isao Tomita. PRD: Mushi Pro. 112 mins.

Three young people from the 21st century have their minds sent back into the past, into the bodies of people living in Alexandria at the time of Julius Caesar's first meeting withCleopatra. One of the two young men is a lecher who vows that he will seduce Cleopatra instead of just watching. Having won over Caesar (depicted as a cigar-chomping American politico riding in a horse-drawn Edsel) and Mark Antony, Cleopatra is defeated by Octavian's homosexuality and takes her own life.

Screened in U.S. cinemas, where it was the first animated film to receive an "X" rating, *Cleopatra*'s release coincided with a temporary suspension of business at Mushi Pro. A financial disaster in Japan and misleadingly marketed in the U.S. as hard-core erotica, *Cleopatra* was ASTRO BOY–creator Tezuka's last-ditch to recoup money for his troubled company, though the production was reportedly characterized by defecting animators, who had realized that little could save Mushi and stole anything that was not nailed down. The production's salability was not helped by Tezuka's own artistic experiments, including the opening scenes set in the future as an ironic reversal of the distinctive animation style of the U.S. series *Clutch Cargo.* Whereas *Clutch Cargo* featured live mouths matted onto animated faces, *Cleopatra*'s future scenes were shot as live-action but with anime faces matted onto the human actors. Other art-house experiments included foolhardy anachronisms such as gladiatorial combat staged as TV events and the murder of Caesar presented as a kabuki drama (a famous scene from *Chushingura*—see WOOF WOOF 47 RONIN), bringing the story to a screeching halt for several minutes. Compare to Tezuka's earlier success with ARABIAN NIGHTS. *Ill. p. 273.* ◑

CLIMBING ON A CLOUD

1990. JPN: *Kumo ni Noru.* Video. DIR: Osamu Sekita. SCR: Shoji Imai. DES: Eiichi Endo. ANI: Eiichi Endo. MUS: Masanori Iimori. PRD: JC Staff. 50 mins. x 2 eps.

GOODFELLA-creator Hiroshi Motomiya wrote this very different tale of gang warfare for *Comic Morning* in 1988. Set in a Buddhist heaven where saints fight over turf in the clouds, it features Niomaru, a man searching for the younger sister torn from him in an aircraft accident back in the human world. Motomiya is better known today for the manga *Salaryman Kintaro*, which has been adapted as a live-action TV series and film.

COBBY THE CUTE LITTLE CAT

1998. JPN: *Chibi Neko Cobby*. Video. DIR: Yumi Tamano. SCR: Miyuki Takahashi. DES: Konomi Sakurai. ANI: Konomi Sakurai. MUS: N/C. PRD: Toei. 20 mins. x 2 eps.

Eiko Kadono, who also created KIKI'S DELIVERY SERVICE, collaborated with artist Mako Taruishi for this tale of a female black-and-white kitten born to a cat called Meme. The original was selected as a core title for Japanese libraries, guaranteeing a long shelf life and leading to sales of over 100,000 copies, but these simple stories of mischief and friendly animals flew no further on video.

COCKPIT, THE *

1993. Video. DIR: Yoshiaki Kawajiri, Takashi Imanishi, Ryosuke Takahashi. SCR: Yoshiaki Kawajiri, Takashi Waguri, Ryosuke Takahashi. DES: Yoshiaki Kawajiri, Toshihiro Kawamoto, Hironobu Saito. ANI: Yoshiaki Kawajiri, Toshihiro Kawamoto, Hironobu Saito. MUS: Kaoru Wada. PRD: Madhouse, Jamco Video, Visual 80. 30 mins. x 3 eps.
This trilogy retells three stories from Leiji Matsumoto's long-running *Battlefield (Senjo)* series, here retitled at the author's request and assigned to three different studios.

The first, *Slipstream*, is a Faustian tale, handled by WICKED CITY–director Kawajiri, about the Luftwaffe in August 1944. Nazi ace Rheindars (a lookalike of CAPTAIN HARLOCK) is asked to escort an atomic bomb to Peenemunde, where it is to be loaded onto a V-2 rocket. However, he eventually sabotages the project, even though it will mean the death of his ex-lover Marlene, a twin of QUEEN EMERALDAS. Rheindars's plight is depicted as a pact with Satan and comes loaded with arch antinuclear messages—Marlene warns that only the truly evil would ever use atomic weapons, while Rheindars's commander anachronistically describes the V-2 as the world's first missile. In the final scene, as Rheindars saves Britain from nuclear holocaust, he describes himself as "the man who

did not sell his soul to the Devil," though this line was absent from the original Japanese script and appears to have been improvised on the day of the recording.

Pointedly shifting ahead a year to the day before Hiroshima in August 1945, *Sonic Boom Squadron* is a naval story focusing on Nogami, a Japanese kamikaze rocket pilot. As in director Imanishi's GUNDAM stories, men are slaves to their machines, both sides suffer, and, in one scene, a Japanese pilot is found to have an exact double on the U.S. aircraft carrier he is attacking. The futility of the navy pilots, sacrificing their lives to carry human bombs to targets they will never reach, is echoed by their American counterparts, who mourn a promising comics artist shot down by the "crazy Japs." The hero, for his part, wants to be a rocket scientist and fly to the moon, but now finds himself piloting a human bomb.

The final part leaps back to 1944 (presumably to make Hiroshima the worthy centerpiece) and the Allied assault on Leyte in the Philippines. Directed by SPT LAYZNER's Ryosuke Takahashi, *Knight of the Iron Dragon* features Japanese army officers, all of whom have sworn never to surrender, realizing that they will have to retreat. A young motorcyclist goes to fetch the last artillery group but finds them almost completely wiped out. Despite the attractive prospect of desertion, he resolves to return to his base. A mechanic who used to be a motorcycle racer offers to help out, and there are shades of *The Great Escape* as they rush across the war-torn island to reach the base in time. Once again there is an element of tragedy; the base has already fallen, but it becomes a matter of honor that they go to die with their comrades.

With Nazis and Japanese soldiers for heroes, this could have easily added to anime's bad press, but, though Matsumoto is clearly in love with the idea of defeat, the superb animation and thoughtful script make this one of the triumphs of anime. It is also available

in two excellent translations, in the U.K. from Kiseki (1995) and in the U.S. from Urban Vision (1999). ❶

COERCION *

1999. JPN: *Kyohaku*. Video. DIR: Katsumasa Kanezawa. SCR: Sakura Momoi, Taifu Kanmachi. DES: Teruaki Murakami. ANI: Teruaki Murakami. MUS: N/C. PRD: Pink Pineapple. 30 mins. x 1 ep (3 eps. planned).
Japanese teenager Asuka is touched to receive a love letter from a boy in her class. However, she makes the mistake of confiding in her "friend" Aya, who secretly desires the boy herself. The jealous Aya ensures that Asuka pays the price in pain and bondage—salutary relationship advice. Released in the U.S. as *Black Mail* (2001). ❶❶

COLD GEHENNA

2001. TV series. DIR: N/C. SCR: N/C. DES: N/C. ANI: N/C. MUS: N/C. PRD: Public & Basic, Animax. 25 mins. x 12+ eps.
The moon is destroyed in a terrible cataclysm, forming a ring around the Earth and bringing drastic climate changes. The world is now chiefly desert and frozen wastes, while fearsome "dragons" have occupied what little of the temperate zones remain. Humans, eking an existence in the barren areas, build the Deadly Drive, an 18-meter robot designed to rid them of the dragon menace. Cue Barn, the hero, who will pilot it, and Alice, the tiresomely predictable "mysterious girl" who holds the key to victory.

COLLEGE CHRONICLE MURYO

2001. JPN: *Gakuen Senki Muryo*. TV series. DIR: Tatsuo Sato. SCR: Tatsuo Sato. DES: Takahiro Yoshimatsu. ANI: Takahiro Yoshimatsu. MUS: Yuji Ono. PRD: Madhouse. 25 mins. x 8+ eps.
In the year 2070, the Japanese government finally admits the existence of aliens after an "unidentified" flying object in Tokyo identifies itself as "the Seeker." A few days later, new student Subaru Muryo transfers to a school in Tenmo, a new town in Kanagawa Pre-

fecture. He dresses and behaves oddly, inspiring fellow student Hajime Murata to investigate further—no prizes for guessing that Subaru is not of this Earth.

COLLEGE INVESTIGATOR HIKARUON

1986. JPN: *Gakuin Tokuso Hikaruon.* Video. DIR: Kazuhiro Ochi. SCR: Kazuhiro Ochi. DES: Kazuhiro Ochi. ANI: Mutsumi Inomata, Osamu Nabeshima. MUS: Michiaki Watanabe. PRD: AIC. 30 mins.
In a school under attack from the evil demon Ura, mild-mannered Hikaru can transform into Hikaruon, a super-powered hero dedicated to battling monsters. Along with his beautiful assistant, Azumi, he fights off the bad guys in this spinoff of the long tradition of superhero shows that stretches all the way back to ULTRAMAN.

COLLEGE SUPERGIRLS

1991. JPN: *Za [The] Gakuen Chojotai.* Video. DIR: Satoshi Dezaki. SCR: Noriko Hayasaka. DES: Jumu. ANI: Yukari Kobayashi. MUS: Nobuo Ito. PRD: Magic Bus. 45 mins.
In this short-lived adaptation of Tatsuhiko Dan's novel that was originally serialized in *Shonen Jump*, Yumi, Kei, and Mai are three schoolgirls who moonlight as a secret crime-fighting team ever since experiments at the school Superpower Society went drastically awry and gave them all amazing abilities.

COLORFUL

1999. TV series. DIR: Ryutaro Nakamura. SCR: Kazushi Sato. DES: Takahiro Kishida. ANI: Takahiro Kishida. MUS: Moka. PRD: Triangle Staff, TBS. 7 mins. x 16 eps.
Torajiro Kishi's manga from *Young Jump*, full of panty-flashing gags and jiggling female flesh, was brought to late-night TV as part of the *Wonderful* program. The show enjoyed a second lease on life as one of the first to go straight to DVD in Japan—all 110 minutes were released on a single disc without a prior VHS appearance. Ⓝ

COLUMBUS

1992. JPN: *Columbus no Daiboken.* AKA: *Les Aventures de Christophe Columbe.* Movie. DIR: Yorifusa Yamaguchi. SCR: Thibault Chatel, Anne Colé. DES: Masahiro Kase. ANI: Masahiro Kase. MUS: N/C. PRD: Telescreen (SPO). 70 mins.
As he nears the New World, Christopher Columbus tells cabin boy Paco about his youthful hardships, the difficulties of convincing others of his vision, and the final victory when King Ferdinand and Queen Isabella agreed to sponsor his trip. The sailors are doubtful, though Columbus is vindicated when they arrive on land, but it's not the planned destination of Japan. This Franco-Japanese coproduction was made to commemorate the 500th anniversary of Columbus's "discovery" of America but not released in Japan until January 1993. Columbus was also profiled in GREAT PEOPLE and *Stories of Greatness*, making him and HELEN KELLER the only historical figures whose lives have been the subject of three anime.

COMBATTLER V

1976. JPN: *Cho Denji Robo Combattler V.* AKA: Super Electromagnetic Robot Combattler V; Combattra. TV series. DIR: Tadao Nagahama. SCR: Masaki Tsuji, Keisuke Fujikawa, Masaru Yamamoto. DES: Makio Narita, Yoshikazu Yasuhiko, Studio Nue. ANI: Satoshi Dezaki, Yoshiyuki Tomino, Shinji Okada. MUS: Hiroshi Tsutsui. PRD: Hiromi Pro, Toei, NET (eps. 1–46); TV Asahi (eps. 47–54). 24 mins. x 54 eps.
Hyoma, Juzo, Daisaku, and token brat Kosuke are four boys handpicked from Earth's finest for their mental and physical prowess and trained to fly Professor Nanbara's Combattler superrobot. Invaders from Planet Campbell have awoken from their subterranean slumber and are threatening the inhabitants of the surface world. In a story that will be original to anyone who has never heard of BATTLE OF THE PLANETS, it's up to the four boys, with the professor's daughter, Chizuru, as

The lovestruck Urara washes her cousin's back, though his thoughts are of another woman. U-Jin's best and most mature work, walking a careful line between believable characterization and erotic wish fulfillment, SAKURA DIARIES sadly loses some of its original appeal in the anime incarnation. Instead of a truly faithful adaptation, the anime favors the prurient eroticism and sexual setups that characterize U-Jin's shorter works, and it ultimately fails to make its characters lovable. *See entry p. 339.*

Sakura Diaries

© SHOGAKUKAN/KITTY FILM/VICTOR ENTERTAINMENT

the chaste love interest, to use their giant electric yoyo to protect Earth from the Campbell General Garuda. Toys from the show reached the U.S. as part of the GODAIKIN line.

COMET-SAN

2001. TV series. DIR: Mamoru Kobe. SCR: Akira Oketani. DES: Kazuo Makida. ANI: Miho Nakajima, Masamitsu Kudo. MUS: Kaba Konishi. PRD: Nippon Animation, TV Tokyo. 25 mins. x 12+ eps.
Comet, a princess from planet Harmonica, is invited to a party with a princess from Castanet, where they discover that the prince of Tambourine, largest world in the Triangle Nebula, is trying to decide which of them he should take as his bride. Comet stomps off to Earth (which, when you think about it, is just as stupid a name for a planet), where her arrival brings magic and joy into the lives of a Japanese family. *Comet-san* has a convoluted pedigree, dating back to Mitsuteru Yokoyama's 1967 manga in *Margaret* magazine, itself an attempt to do a more grown-up version of his earlier LITTLE WITCH SALLY. A *Bewitched* clone, originally featuring a magical housekeeper from planet Beta, its 1967 TV adaptation was live-action but featured animated sequences directed by Tsuto-

mu Shibayama. The 21st-century fully animated version is a product of its time, playing up the "magical-girl" feel with a far younger protagonist and showing lots of pretty eye-candy girls.

COMIC PARTY

2001. TV series. DIR: Norihiko Sudo. SCR: Hiroshi Yamaguchi. DES: Hirokazu Taguchi. ANI: Mima Yoshikawa, Masao Nakada. MUS: N/C. PRD: OLM, KBS. 25 mins. x 12+ eps.

Eighteen-year-old high-school student Waki has already been accepted by a university and only has to wait for graduation. When this proves to be too boring to endure, he wanders into a manga convention and is dragged into the world of amateur comics. He befriends three young fanzine creators who are, of course, all pretty girls. This lighthearted comedy, a Dreamcast tie-in, is an ominous sign of the increasingly self-referential nature of the anime/manga market—compare to KUROMI-CHAN. In one pointed moment, a character bemoans America's domination of popular culture, announcing that it is time for Japan to take over with anime.

COMPILER *

1994. Video. DIR: Takao Kato, Kiyoshi Murayama. SCR: Michitaka Kikuchi. DES: Yasuhiro Oshima. ANI: Yasuhiro Oshima. MUS: Toshiyuki Omori. PRD: Movic. 45 mins. x 3 eps.

In a remarkably three-dimensional "2D Universe," female agents are dispatched to destroy the 3D Earth. Instead, they decide to stay with two Japanese boys and live a happy life of unwedded bliss and teen angst. One day, they decide to go on holiday in Osaka, a city long-neglected in anime since being buried under a mass of tentacles and spooge in UROTSUKIDOJI. In this anime based on SILENT MÖBIUS–creator Kia Asamiya's 1991 love-comedy in *Comic Afternoon*, Osaka becomes the venue for two naked female assassins sent from the 2D universe to terminate the turncoat terminators. They attempt to blend in by

loading Osaka language chips, which turns them into a pair of bitchy game-show hosts, but their gags will fall flat on an audience ignorant of Osaka's *manzai* comedy tradition (see JARINKO CHIE).

Much of the humor rests on the unique attitude and accent of Osaka's people—which could be described as Chicago gangster-talk and New York sarcasm combined with a ludicrous love of yen. The dubbing script tries to approximate the Osaka accent as a mix of Valley girls, Jersey longshoremen, and cretins, but, although there is a lengthy discourse on the history of Osaka baseball, this episode is almost incomprehensible without a set of liner notes, sadly lacking in AD Vision's translation.

Once the shapely Terminators (*"We put the ass in Assassins!"*) have been defeated, the unfeasibly thick-haired Compiler fights with would-be beau Nachi about his flirting ways. Meanwhile, the innocent Assembler tries (unsuccessfully) to seduce Nachi's brother in a simple tale of Tokyo marital discord that was originally the first episode, switched by the U.S. distributor with the zanier second presumably to hold viewers' attention.

Redeeming features include a score from GOLGO 13's Omori that pastiches the *Godzilla* theme as Osaka food franchise logos turn into giant monsters and smash up "famous" landmarks, including the Hanshin Expressway, that would be destroyed for real in the following year's Kobe earthquake. HUMMINGBIRDS-director Murayama also provides clever moments such as background fountains that spurt in time with Compiler's anger and rubbernecking passers-by that add a really human touch to her argument with Nachi. But even these finesses can't rescue a show whose original raison d'être was not to entertain so much as to advertise.

A marketing tool designed to remind Japanese viewers of a manga that remains untranslated in English, *Compiler* has little purpose in the U.S.

market. It follows late on the heels of *Music Clips in Trackdown*, a 1990 music video also designed to promote the *Compiler* characters but without the pretense of a plot. Sections from this early work are used in the closing credits to *Compiler Festa* (released as just plain *Compiler 2* in the U.S.), the final episode in which the 2D universe sends White Compiler, a deadly upgrade of our heroine, who is defeated once again by homespun Earth boys and wisecracking alien girls. **Ø**

COMPUTOPIA

1968. JPN: *Computopia Seireki 2000-nen no Monogatari*. AKA: *Computopia: A Tale of the Year 2000 A.D.* TV special. DIR: Yoshikazu Kawamura. SCR: Masaki Tsuji. DES: Masami Shimoda. ANI: Sadao Tsukioka. MUS: N/C. PRD: Knack, Nihon TV. 30 mins. x 2 eps.

After the success of FIFTH ICE AGE, the *Wonderful World Travel* staff returned with this sci-fi documentary about the way New York might be in the distant year 2000, using real photographs of computer innards as backdrops for the cel animation—the first low-tech form of "computer animation," perhaps?

CONAN THE BOY DETECTIVE

1996. JPN: *Meitantei Conan*. AKA: *Famous Detective Conan*. Movie, TV series, specials. DIR: Kanetsugu Kodama. SCR: Hiroshi Kashiwabara, Kazunari Kouchi, Shuichi Miyashita. DES: Masaaki Sudo. ANI: Masaaki Sudo. MUS: Katsuo Ono. PRD: TMS, Yomiuri TV (Nippon TV). 25 mins. x 232+ eps; 90 mins. x 4 movies.

High-school student Shinichi Kudo accidentally takes a drug that gives him the appearance of a seven-year-old child. He takes the name Conan Edogawa (conjoining Arthur Conan Doyle and Ranpo Edogawa, the best of both occidental and oriental detective traditions) and specializes in cases that the adults just can't handle, using his childish guise as a means of avoiding criminal reprisals.

First appearing in 1994 manga in *Shonen Sunday* magazine by YAIBA-creator Gosho Aoyama, Conan has the body of the child but commands the thinking power (and respect) of an adult. He also has a band of young friends, the Juvenile Detective Club, who aid him in his investigations. As with the YOUNG KINDAICHI FILES, this caught a post-*X-Files* wave of interest in supernatural sleuthing and would make Aoyama Japan's highest-paid manga artist by 1999. The series was dubbed in the U.S., but into *Spanish*, where the hero was renamed Bobby Jackson (he may be known under this name to some viewers).

Many of the TV story lines, such as the *Ski Lodge Murders* and the *First Love Murders*, spanned two episodes, so it was a simple step to expand into 90-minute movies. Conan's first theatrical outing, *Clockwork Skyscraper* (1997), pits him in a battle of wits against a thief who has stolen high explosives from a military base. *The 14th Victim* (1998) has a stalker picking off members of the family who own the Aquacrystal restaurant and leaving playing cards pinned to their corpses. In *End of the Century Sorcerer* (1999), a child steals a priceless Fabergé egg, and the relatively simple quest to return it leads to a series of murders rooted in a historical vendetta. *Captured in Her Eyes* (2000), pits Conan against an enemy from within after the murder of a police officer turns all his associates into suspects. His most recent movie is *Countdown to Heaven* (2001), in which a secret society causes mayhem at the inauguration party of the new high-tech Twin Towers.

Conan's father starred in several Aoyama short pieces, including *The Wandering Red Butterfly* and *Summer's Santa Claus*. These, along with the Conan-Shinichi team-up tale *10 Planets in the Night Sky* and the unrelated stories *Investigator George's Little War, Play It Again*, and *Wait a Moment* were animated as 20-minute specials for TV by Osamu Nabeshima in 1998.

CONDITION GREEN

1991. JPN: *Inferious Wakusei Senshi Gaiden Condition Green*. AKA: *Inferious Interplanetary War Chronicle Condition Green*. Video. DIR: Shigeyasu Yamauchi. SCR: Yoshihisa Araki. DES: Shingo Araki, Michi Himeno, Eisaku Inoue. ANI: Eisaku Inoue. MUS: Kazuhiko Ito. PRD: Hero Communications, KSS. 50 mins. x 3 eps.

Keith, George, Edward, Yang, and Sho are Platoon #801, the five-man team formed to protect their home world in the Inferious galaxy from alien invasion. Gazaria's evil emperor Vince conquers the neighbor worlds of Kal and Granad and suddenly only Platoon #801, also known as Condition Green, stands between him and the conquest of Emerald Earth. Made straight to video despite the false appearance of two "25-minute TV episodes" per tape, *Condition Green* missed the point made all too well by GUNBUSTER, that only real TV could afford to be cheesy. The paying audience of the video market demanded more but didn't get it here from former CRYING FREEMAN–animator Yamauchi.

CONFUCIUS

1995. JPN: *Koshi-den*. AKA: *Life of Kong Zi*. TV special. DIR: Osamu Dezaki. SCR: N/C. DES: N/C. ANI: Noboru Furuse. MUS: N/C. PRD: NHK, NHKEP21, PTS, KBS, Image K, C&D. 45 mins.?

Born in the Chinese state of Lu in 551 B.C., Confucius is raised by his mother after his father dies when he is only three. He marries at 19 and enters the service of the local nobility. At 32, he becomes tutor to the Prince of Lu's children, eventually becoming a politician at 51. His peaks are the roles of Lu's justice minister and eventually prime minister. The land prospers for four years, but Confucius grows disenchanted with court intrigues. For the following 12 years, he wanders the neighboring states, offering advice to their rulers.

Mystifyingly dropped from the earlier GREAT PEOPLE series in favor of such luminaries as Babe Ruth, China's most famous son was nevertheless considered a worthy subject by the many anime companies that cooperated on the TV movie. But since his life was uneventful and his victories disappointingly intellectual, it has but a single one-line mention in our Japanese sources.

COO OF THE FAR SEAS

1993. JPN: *Coo: Toi Umi kara Kita Coo*. AKA: *Coo: Coo Who Came from the Far Seas*. Movie. DIR: Tetsuo Imazawa. SCR: Kihachi Okamoto. DES: Masahiko Okura. ANI: N/C. MUS: Nick Wood. PRD: Toei. 116 mins.

Excitedly if weakly hyped in *Newtype* as "the best film for all the family, apart from something by Disney," this Christmas feel-good movie was based on a novel by Tamio Kageyama and written for the screen by live-action director Okamoto. A scientist's child on an idyllic Pacific island befriends the titular creature, a baby plesiosaur whose mother has died. Other, less scrupulous people are searching for this relic of the dinosaur age, and our hero teams up with a beautiful female journalist to keep Coo safe until he can be released into the wild.

This charming film, greatly helped by ravishing backgrounds researched on real-life Pacific islands at great expense to the sponsors at the Fiji Tourist Board, marries the 1990s ecological fad of *Free Willy* and FLY PEEK to the eternal guarantee that dinosaurs will get children into theaters.

COOK DADDY

1990. JPN: *Kyukyoku Chef Oishinbo Papa*. AKA: *Ultimate Chef Gourmet Papa*. Video. DIR: Kazuo Tomozawa. SCR: Kazuo Tomozawa. DES: Kazuo Tomozawa. ANI: Hiroaki Mizorogi. MUS: N/C. PRD: Agent 21. 45 mins.

Kenzo Nishikata, an everyday chef in the Chinese restaurant Chin-Chin Ken, moonlights as an assassin. Disposing of his victims by serving them up as dishes of the day, he is sidetracked one day by the amorous attentions of Sai, the pretty college girl who works part-time as a waitress. Based on a manga by TALES OF . . . and SAKURA DIARIES–creator U-

Jin, and not to be confused with **OI-SHINBO**. **Ⓥ Ⓝ**

COOL COOL BYE

1986. Video. DIR: Yukien Kogawa. SCR: Yukien Kogawa. DES: Yukien Kogawa, Akihiko Yamashita. ANI: Yukien Kogawa, Hidetoshi Omori. MUS: Ken Sato. PRD: Toyo Links. 45 mins.
Lek and Flena Han are a brother and sister on a mission to defeat the Big Machine, a giant robot that attacked their village and killed the inhabitants, in this forgettable title from **DUNBINE**'s Kogawa, which adds insult to injury by bulking out its running time with a 15-minute "making of" special.

COOL COUPLE

1999. JPN: Iketeru Futari. TV series. DIR: Takeshi Yamaguchi. SCR: Masayoshi Azuma. DES: Ryoichi Oki. ANI: N/C. MUS: N/C. PRD: JC staff. 7 mins. x 16 eps.
A **HIS AND HER CIRCUMSTANCES** clone based on Takashi Sano's manga from Young King magazine, in which high-school student Kyosuke Saji falls in love with class valedictorian Aki Koizumi. Though she is beastly to him at first and her friends equally cruel, eventually he breaks through and makes her his girl. Shown, like **COLORFUL**, as part of the late-night TV show Wonderful, it was eventually compiled into two omnibus editions. **Ⓝ Ⓥ**

COOL DEVICES *

1996. Video. DIR: Osamu Shimokawa, Megumi Saki, Yasuomi Umezu, Hiroshi Matsuda. SCR: Mon-Mon, Masamichi Kaneko. DES: Mon-Mon, Hiroyuki Utatane, Protonsaurus, Yasuomi Umezu, Naomi Hayakawa. ANI: Hiroshi Mori. MUS: N/C. PRD: Beam Entertainment. 30 mins. x 11 eps.
An umbrella title for disparate erotic stories from a number of mainly pseudonymous creators, the Cool Devices brand name was clearly valued highly enough by distributors Critical Mass to be kept for the U.S. release; compare this to Anime 18's treatment of the **SECRET ANIMA** series, which was broken

up and released as stand-alone titles.
The subject matter often crosses the boundary of good taste—cartoon characters are more pliant actors than human beings, and though the sexualized violence of 1980s shows like **RAPE-MAN** are less in evidence, there are still many sadomasochistic tales of women volunteering for abuse. One such example is Curious Fruit (#1), based on a manga from former **CREAM LEMON**–designer Mon-Mon, in which an innocent girl discovers her deep, dark desires to be dominated. Incest is another recurring theme, as seen in Sacred Girl (#2), from **COUNT DOWN**–creator Hiroyuki Utatane, in which a rich orphan attempts, and fails, to overcome his longing for his sister by holding orgies at their mansion. It was back to bestiality and domination for Lover Doll, the lecherous male gaze in Winter Swimsuit, and toilet training in Enema (all #3). It's far shorter tableaux from Secret Anima's Protonsaurus, little more than sex scenes and all but devoid of plot. For Kirei (#4), the setting moved to a summery beach for the seduction of a Japanese girl by a local lothario.
Seek (#5–6) was based on a computer game from Hiroshige Tadokoro, retaining its origins even to the extent of keeping the male lead's face hidden to aid player/viewer identification. Although stretching across two 30-minute episodes, its chapters are only tenuously related—the innocent young Marino discovers how her "mostly unwilling body" is secretly crying out to be dominated by a smug male abuser. Once she has been taught her lesson, she is dragged in for another cavalcade of torment, alongside several other girls, in scenes of domination and electrocution that the U.S. distributor proudly claimed to be the "most disturbing tape of the entire Cool Devices series."
For Yasuomi Umezu's Yellow Star (#7), which looks and often plays like a prequel to his later **KITE**, a young girl is drugged and raped by her policeman stepfather, who uses the titular narcotic

to ensure her cooperation. Slave Warrior Maya (#8–9), based on a manga by Konodonto, covers ground similar to the previous year's **FENCER OF MINERVA**. An innocent girl is transported to a magical world, where she is immediately captured by lizard-men and sold into slavery. Sold to a robot king (presumably because robots are not human and consequently cannot legally have genuine genitalia that need to be censored), she is subjected to slave training before revealing that she is really a warrior. The second volume is a far simpler tableau of bondage and domination, in which Maya's extra "appendage," revealed at the end of episode one, is put to considerable use.
Binding (#10) is another game spin-off, featuring character designs from **BEAST CITY**–creator Naomi Hayakawa. For once it is the male character who gets the raw deal, as hack writer Masaki loses his luggage and his wallet leaving his train after an earthquake and follows a pretty girl to a dark mansion. There he is welcomed by an all-female community who turn into dominatrixes at sundown, tying him up and tormenting him, though in a far more playful and consensual fashion than in other chapters.
The final volume to date is another Mon-Mon story, Fallen Angel Rina (#11). Recalling its contemporary **PERFECT BLUE**, Rina is a singer, fallen on hard times due to her father's profligacy, whose new manager makes her discard a wholesome girl-next-door image in favor of skimpy outfits and provocative appearances—resulting in her molestation by passers-by in the street, and even her own audience—before the makers' consciences are salved by an ending in which Rina gets her revenge. **Ⓛ Ⓝ Ⓥ**

CORAL INVESTIGATES

1979. JPN: Coral no Tanken. TV series. DIR: Seitaro Hara, Gen Mizumoto. SCR: Hideo Anzai, Tomoyuki Miyata. DES: N/C. ANI: N/C. MUS: Akihiro Komori. PRD: Chikara, Zak, Nippon Columbia, TBS. 25 mins. x 50 eps.

An animated show based on Albert Berié's French puppet show, in which Hector the Rat teams up with his fellow denizens of Pretty Wood, including the titular Coral (a young girl) and the unimaginatively named Crow (a crow), to head off to Holland. With many musical scenes, the voice actors were chosen for their singing ability above other considerations.

CORRECTOR YUI

1999. TV series. DIR: Yuji Muto. SCR: Satoru Nishizono. DES: Fumie Muroi. ANI: Shintaro Muraki, Miko Nakajima. MUS: Kenji Kawai. PRD: Nippon Animation, NHKEP. 25 mins. x 52 eps.
The young Yui is a manga fan who wants to be an anime voice actress when she grows up. One day, she is sucked into her computer, where she discovers that the gigantic computer Grosser intends to rule the human race from within cyberspace. The only way to stop Grosser is to join forces with pieces of mystic software (Eco, Rescue, Control, Peace, Follow, and Synchro) and her assistant, IR, combining to form the greatest debugging program known to man.

Mixing elements of his earlier COMPILER with Disney's *Tron* (a film conveniently old enough to be unknown to the target audience), Kia Asamiya's first anime for girls is a surprisingly old-fashioned affair. Though set in 2010, its heroine carries a magic wand and must assemble a team of mismatched trouble-shooters, pausing regularly to hector her audience about computer terminology and keeping parks tidy. And like SAILOR MOON before it, the first season ends with the baddie defeated, but the plot resets to zero for a repeat performance. A curious combination of the preachy conservatism to be expected from a state-owned education channel like NHKEP and the formulaic, marketing-led appeal of a corporate creator like Bandai.

COSMIC FANTASY

1994. Video. DIR: Kazuhiro Ochi. SCR:

Kazuhiro Ochi. DES: Kazuhiro Ochi. ANI: Keisuke Watanabe. MUS: Tatsuya Murayama. PRD: Tokuma. 45 mins.
A one-shot cash-in on a computer game in which the heroic Yu leads a team of interstellar crime-fighters against evil space pirates, in this case, the female buccaneer known as the Galactic Panther.

COSMOS PINK SHOCK

1985. Video. DIR: Yasuo Hasegawa, Keisuke Matsumoto. SCR: Takeshi Shudo. DES: Toshihiro Hirano, Rei Yumeno. ANI: N/C. MUS: N/C. PRD: AIC. 36 mins.
An anime parody about Michiko dreaming of a promise her boyfriend, Hiroshi, made to her and then being whisked off into space on the Pink Shock spaceship, in which she rescues the denizens of a prison planet. The original was serialized as original content on the *Animevision* video magazine that otherwise consisted of trailers for other shows and assorted voice-actor gossip, eventually being compiled into a one-shot video the following year.

COTTON STAR

1984. JPN: *Wata no Kuniboshi*. AKA: *Planet of Cotton*. Movie. DIR: Shinichi Tsuji. SCR: Masaki Tsuji, Yumiko Oshima. DES: Katsumi Aoshima. ANI: Katsumi Aoshima, Shinya Takahashi, Jun Kawagoe, Kuni Tomita. MUS: Richard Clayderman. PRD: Mushi Pro. 96 mins.
Cuteycat, a two-month-old kitten, is taken in by a young man called Tokio, who takes pity on her on a rainy day. Cuteycat becomes one of the family, though she has trouble winning over Tokio's mother, who is allergic to cats. Cuteycat is heartbroken when Tokio falls in love with a girl in the park, only to be rescued from despair when she meets the handsome, silver-haired tomcat Raphael, who explains that humans and cats can never truly be together.

Richard Clayderman's twee piano hits just the right note in this weepy romance. Yumiko Oshima's 1978 manga for *Comic Lala* was adapted here by its original author with veteran scenarist Tsuji. Years later, animator Tomita

Benisato, a shape-shifting snake succubus—just one of the supernatural adversaries ranged against the warrior Jubei in Yoshiaki Kawajiri's NINJA SCROLL. Samurai-era dramas remain eternally popular on Japanese TV, where stock props and sets can easily be exchanged between shows, but budgetary necessity keeps the live-action drama earthbound. The more fantastic aspects of samurai-era folklore, flourish in anime, where the only limit is the artist's imagination. *See entry p. 276.*

Ninja Scroll

would defect to the U.S. to work on homegrown animation like *Invasion America.*

COUNT DOWN *

1995. JPN: *Yuwaku Countdown*. AKA: *Temptation Countdown*. Video. DIR: Shoichi Masuo, Naohito Takahashi. SCR: Hiroyuki Utatane. DES: Sanae Chikanaga, Ryunosuke Otonashi. ANI: Ryunosuke Otonashi. MUS: Kanji Saito. PRD: Pink Pineapple, KSS. 35 mins. x 6 eps.
Creator Utatane, best known in the mainstream for his SF manga *Seraphic Feather*, made an early name for himself drawing erotic short stories that were eventually compiled into the anthologies *Count Down 54321* and *Temptation.*

The first three are simple tales: a modern-day subway encounter leads to erotic confusion; a sword-swinging macho man meets his match in a girl who can tie anything down; and a bride has a last-minute fling before taking that walk to the altar—quite literally. The final three episodes encompass a single story arc, *Akira*, featuring designs from END OF SUMMER's Otonashi, a replay of the faux-incest of CREAM LEMON's *Ami* stories. Akira carries a torch for his stepsister, a supermodel, and fantasizes about her even when making love to the other women in his life. When she eventually returns from decadent Europe, she has brought a "special" friend with her, and Akira must come to terms with the fact that the affair between them was never going to last. **LNV**

COWBOY BEBOP *

1998. TV series. DIR: Shinichiro Watanabe. SCR: Keiko Nobumoto, Michiko Yokote, Ryota Yamaguchi, Sadayuki Murai, Dai Sato. DES: Toshihiro Kawamoto, Kimitoshi Yamano. ANI: Yoichi Ogami. MUS: Yoko Kanno. PRD: Sunrise, TV Tokyo. 25 mins. x 26 eps.
Spike Spiegel and ex-cop Jet Black are bounty hunters who range across the whole solar system. Teaming up, albeit reluctantly, with mystery woman Faye Valentine, hacker brat Ed (who's a girl), and a super-intelligent Welsh corgi called Ein, they remain perpetually on the lookout for criminals on the run.

From such a simple premise springs one of the most entertaining anime shows of the 1990s. Made with a deliberate 1970s retro style, it posits a solar system that is one part Chinese diaspora and two-parts Wild West. Cityscapes straight out of kung-fu movies jostle with neo-architecture in the style of *Blade Runner* and one-horse frontier towns in the middle of the Martian desert.

Spike is a hero cast in the mold of **LUPIN III**, a good-hearted man operating at the edge of the law, betrayed by an old flame and still nursing his wounded heart. The show itself varies wildly in tone, from comedy to tragedy, but maintains its believability throughout. From the outset, director Watanabe cut much of the exposition from the original script, preferring to give the impression that the viewers were watching the show *in* 2072, and that no explanations would be necessary. The idea of watching a pulp TV show from 100 years in the future truly adds to the experience—a mood retained for the fake Martian radio broadcast *Music for Freelance*, released on CD. The tactic also helps disguise the

show's few flaws—at its core, *Cowboy Bebop* is little more than *Route 66* in space, with plots ripped off from generic U.S. crime shows. Space truckers, space mafia, and space hippies would be hack conventions in another series, but they seem to work here because the world seems so believable.

Though complete in its foreign edition, the entirety of *Cowboy Bebop* was not shown on Japanese terrestrial TV. The opening episode, featuring scenes of drug-taking and John Woo–inspired shootouts, was only broadcast on the more forgiving satellite networks, and the censorious climate post-**EVANGELION** meant that, eventually, only 12 episodes of the complete 26 in the series were seen by the first-run audience. The movie, *CB: Knockin' on Heaven's Door* (2001), takes place between episodes 22 and 23 of the TV series. *Ill. p. 129.* **V**

CRAYON SHIN-CHAN *

1992. TV series, Movie. DIR: Mitsuru Honma, Keiichi Hara. SCR: Mitsuru Honma, Keiichi Hara, Ryo Motohira, Keiichi Hara. DES: Masaaki Yuasa. ANI: Shizuka Mori, Katsue Hara. MUS: Toshiyuki Arakawa. PRD: Shinei, TV Asahi. 25 mins. x 391+ eps. (TV), ca. 90 mins. x 7 eps. (m).
Shinnosuke "Shin-chan" Nohara is the ultimate brat—a loud, nosy kid prone to impersonating elephants with his genitals, peeking up teachers' skirts, and tormenting his stupid dog. His harassed mother turns a blind eye, his teachers despair, and a cast of zany regulars turn this nasty cartoon into a hellish look at the world through the eyes of a spoiled child. Most episodes are divided into three smaller, unrelated chapters, giving just enough time to set up accidents with snot, panty-flashing, and bratty behavior. At school, two prissy female teachers are engaged in a constant war of one-upmanship, not realizing that their pupils are manipulating their jealousies for their own ends. A bright, bouncy new teacher refuses to be downhearted at the utter

chaos that confronts her, and the headmaster gets angry at being constantly mistaken for a gangster. Out in the wider world, Shin's family and neighbors are also the subject of ceaseless torment. He even persists in getting the teenager Shinobu fired from every job she takes, and, though he is the bane of her life, he can never remember her name. There are even parodies of anime shows—school super-jock Kawamura is obsessed by the nonexistent show *Action Kamen* (*Action Mask*), while Shin religiously watches an insane **GUNDAM** parody called *Kuntam Robo*.

Created by Yoshihito Usui for *Manga Action* magazine in 1990, *Shin-chan* caused a stir in Japan when it was claimed that up to 68% of children under 12 were avid viewers of this show, supposedly made for adults who would get the joke. Unfortunately, the joke backfired, with complaints in the Japanese media that an entire generation of Japanese children was growing up to be lecherous, evil menaces.

The *Crayon Shin-chan* movies were genuinely aimed at a juvenile audience, albeit one that had grown up watching the series. In *Action Kamen vs. Evil High-Leg* (1993), the entire cast is forced to wear skimpy swimsuits by a bad king, while in *Secrets of Buriburiland* (1994), they are packed off to the South Sea island of Buriburi (Japanese for "annoying"). In *Adventures in Henderland* (1996), a simple trip to the titular amusement park finds Shin foiling a gay warlock's bid to become ruler of the world. Shin-chan's baby sister, Himawari, had her debut in *The Search for the Black Balls* (1997), which also featured a cameo role for creator Usui. *Attack! War of the Pig's Trotter* (1998) embroiled the Nohara family in a vendetta between two secret societies. *Dazzling Hot Spring Wars* and *Paradise Made in Saitama* (1999) split the feature format into two chapters: a traditional vacation episode and a cyberspace pastiche. In *Storm in the Jungle* (2000), Shin-chan's family is kidnapped on a southern island, leaving him and Himawari to rescue them from the Afro-haired Funky Monkey Army—nicely demonstrating that Shin would have the ability to insult foreign audiences, too, if only his English-language appearances went further afield than a limited number of subtitled broadcasts on a Hawaiian Japanese community station. His most recent outing is *The Storm Is Calling! The Adult Empire Strikes Back* (2001), in which Shin-chan and his iconoclastic bunch run amok in a 20th-century theme park, ruining their elders' nostalgia trip—somewhat ironic, considering the series has been around for so long that some of the original "under-12" audience may now have brats of their own. **CLMV**

CREAM LEMON *

1986. Video. DIR: Kazuya Miyazaki, Bikkuri Hako, Ayako Mibashi, Yuji Motoyama, Toshihiro Hirano. SCR: N/C. DES: Masako Nitta, Mon-Mon, Kei Amaki, Yuji Motoyama, To Moriyama, Toshihiro Hirano, Ayako Mibashi, Hiroyuki Kitakubo, Nekoda Nyan. ANI: Hiroshi Tajima, Mamoru Yasuhiko, Bikkuri Hako. MUS: N/C. PRD: Fairy Dust. 25 mins. x 36 eps.

One of anime's most notorious serials, and, though only 7 episodes were translated into English, it is one of the most significant shows of the 1980s. *CL* wasn't the first erotic anime video (that was the similar **LOLITA ANIME**), but the brand survived for over a decade as an umbrella for several subseries, eventually becoming synonymous with anime pornography. The original spanned 16 episodes, followed by assorted specials, the nine-part *New CL*, and two epilogues, shuffled here into some semblance of order.

Its first and biggest star was Ami Nonomura, an 11-year-old girl who seduces her older brother, Hiroshi, in *Be My Baby* (#1). When Hiroshi is banished to London in *Ami Again* (#5), an older but hardly wiser Ami dreams that she is having sex with him again, only to wake and discover that she is drunk in bed with a stranger. Hiroshi returns in *Now I Embrace You Ami* (#13) only to tell her that the affair is over, at which point she returns to the arms of her one-night stand. The 1986 movie *CL: Ami's Journey* came next, in which her friends drag her off to Hokkaido to take her mind off things. Shown on a double bill with the first **PROJECT A-KO** movie, the film was noticeably more mainstream than its erotic predecessors, and, surprisingly for a theatrical version, of lower-grade animation. Ami becomes an idol singer, squeezing in a clandestine tryst with Hiroshi when her entourage passes through London. Her adventures ended in the miniseries *Ami: From Then On* (#31–34), in which Ami is forced to choose between Hiroshi and her fiancé, eventually choosing neither and electing to stay single.

In *Escalation* (#2), the bisexual Rie is banished to a strict Catholic school when she is found in bed with her piano teacher. Predictably, she soon ends up in a lesbian ménage à trois with her roommate, Midori, and dominated in a series of power games by the senior girl Naomi. After graduation, Naomi would invite the girls to her mansion for a repeat performance (#6), and the girls would return in a third installment (#16) to initiate a new recruit.

SF Legend Rall (#3) is a space fantasy in which Carol, an underdressed, sword-wielding warrior-maid, stands against an evil overlord who intends to sacrifice the beautiful Princess Orgasma. She would take up the call to adventure in *Lamo Ru Strikes Back* (#15). Both episodes were distributed in the U.S. as *Gonad the Barbarian* and *The Search for Uranus* in the Brothers Grime animation series.

Pop Chaser (#4) was directed by **PROJECT A-KO**'s Yuji Moriyama under the pseudonym Yuji Motoyama and has early designs by Hiroyuki Kitakubo. It features interstellar Wild-West lesbian antics inside a giant robot suit, as biker chick Rio liberates her woman from a rival gang only to discover that the distressed damsel has agreed to marry the leader. Under the title *Offenders of the Universe*, it was combined with *Star Trap* (#10), an unrelated *Star Trek* spoof starring the lesbian crew of the USS Mischief, and released in the U.S. as another two-part video.

Don't Do It Mako: Sexy Symphony (#7 and #12) presaged **SPRITE** by introducing a timid girl possessed by a knowing, sexual personality—the quintessence of the *CL* series in its assurance that inside every child, there is a sex kitten waiting to get out. In another mainstream cameo, it was directed by **ICZER-ONE**'s Toshihiro Hirano.

Further sci-fi antics awaited in *Super Virgin* (#8) in which another Mako, a psychic, falls in love with one of the schoolboys who torment her. It was followed by another one-shot, *Happening Summer* (#9), in which naughty Yuki seduces her big sister's boyfriend—a man who, in a series in-joke, is found reading a porn magazine featuring photographs of *Escalation*'s Naomi.

In *Black Cat Manor* (#11), student Masaki leaves wartime Tokyo to escape the bombings, staying with the widow Saiko, her daughter, and maid. When the *CL* series eventually ground to a halt in 1993, it would be with *Return to Black Cat Manor* (#36).

Parodying **PROJECT A-KO** and foreshadowing **KEKKO KAMEN**, *Nalice Scramble* (#14), which closed the first season of *CL*, features a heroine in battle armor fighting three lesbian Nazis for control of a school. It was back immediately in 1987 with *New CL*, a straightforward continuation of some of the earlier stories with a few new one-shots and an increased concentration on the artwork and manga origins. *Five-Hour Venus* (#17), for example, was one of several shows by "To Moriyama," a pseudonym for **DANCE TILL TOMORROW**'s Naoki Yamamoto. Heroine Shimeji is blackmailed into posing nude for an art class when her porn past is revealed, and she would return in *Afterschool XXX* (#18) to save a younger classmate from a similar fate.

The supernatural began to take over with *White Shadow* (#19), in which a gymnast is possessed by a demon and seduces the boy who loves her. For *Visions of Europe* (#20), taken from Toshiki Yui's *Mermaid Junction* manga, two frisky female tourists lose their passports and money at the airport and are whisked off to an alternate Europe where passion rules. Kei Amaki's *Cherry Melancholy* (#21) has a couple of man-hunting girls giving up the chase and settling for each other, but the series soon returned to fantasy with *Astalot* (#22), a tale of swords and sorcery with the requisite sex, running almost twice as long as most other videos in the series. A boy finds a gun in *I Guess So* (#23) and uses it to compel a girl to have sex with him, while in *Dream-Colored Bunny* (#24), a trip to the pet shop nets a sexy companion for one lucky pervert.

The Dark (#25), based on a story by Nicholas Lloyd, features two men offered shelter by a woman in a castle, where she seduces and kills one of them, a priest. This episode, *Magic Doll* (#26), in which a kindly man is tempted away from his family by a sexy ghost, and the aforementioned *Black Cat Manor* (under the title *The Black Widow*) were compiled into the feature-length *Pandora: An Erotic Adventure* in the U.S. Similar supernatural goings-on await in *Summer Wind* (#27) for a bereaved boyfriend who meets a girl named Mina (like the heroine of **BEAST CITY**, a reference to Dracula).

E-tude (#28 and #29) is a classic star-crossed romance between the genteel pianist Yurika and the rough tough jazz-playing biker Ryo, who are separated by her father and set up with new partners only to long for each other. *Heartbreak Live for Two* (#30) parodies magical-girl shows like **CREAMY MAMI** as a fox grants a lovelorn girl's wish to become the idol singer that the boy she loves so adores. *Angie and Rose* (#35), the tale of a boy seduced by a Canadian mother and daughter, came out as a bonus for the *CL: Climax* boxed set in 1992, but that is by no means all there was. The *Ami* series also boasts the *Ami Graffiti* digest edi-

tion and the *Ami: White Shadow* teaser for the movie. Other abridgments include *CL Junior*, which cut a third of each episode's running time to survive in a tougher censorship climate. The series was repackaged again with two episodes per tape as *CL Twin* (aka *CL Best Coupling*), which is the version now on DVD. There are also several versions arranged by artist rather than story, collecting the "best" works from To Moriyama, Kei Amaki, and Toshiki Yui. **LNV**

CREAMY MAMI
1983. JPN: *Maho no Tenshi Creamy Mami*. AKA: *Magical Angel Creamy Mami*. TV series. DIR: Osamu Kobayashi, Tomomi Mochizuki, Naoto Hashimoto, Takashi Anno. SCR: Kazunori Ito, Michiru Shimada, Shigeru Yanagawa, Shunsuke Kaneko. DES: Akemi Takada. ANI: Hideo Kawauchi, Shinya Takahashi. MUS: Koji Makaino. PRD: Studio Pierrot, Nippon TV. 25 mins. x 52 eps. (TV), 90 mins. x 1 ep. (v), 53 mins. & 150 mins. (m).
Posi and Nega, two spacefaring aliens posing as harmless kittens, give 11-year-old Yu Morisawa a magic wand so she can transform at will into Creamy Mami, idol singer and magical being, but for just one year. Her parents and her friend Toshio don't notice this double identity, even though they are all huge fans of Mami. But when Toshio sees her transform partway through the story, Yu loses her magic powers, and the friends go on a quest to recover them. They succeed, and Creamy comes back to her fans, but Toshio loses his memory.

Mami returned straight to video in 1983 with *Eternity Once More*, a two-part finale in which she gives a first-anniversary concert, Toshio regains his memory, and Yu finally loses Mami's magical powers. It was so well received that she came back for another encore with *The Long Goodbye* (1985), in which she, now 13, is transported to an alternate world while helping Toshio make an SF film. The 53-minute story was shown on a triple bill with a *Minky Momo* (see **GIGI**)

short and the film *CM vs. Minky Momo*, in which the girls use weapons and special attacks named after the show's staff, including an "Ito Flash" and a "Watanabe Cutter."

In 1985, she also starred in the music compilation *CM: Curtain Call*, and she returned again for Takashi Anno's 1986 TV special *Three Magical Girls*, with *Magical Fairy Pelsha* and **MAGICAL EMI**. Immensely influential in the magical genre, she is much imitated to this day in shows such as **FANCY LALA**, and parodied in the **TENCHI MUYO!** spinoff *Pretty Sammy*. In 1996, she appeared once more in a computer game, *CM: Tale of Two Worlds*.

CREST OF THE STARS *
1999. JPN: *Sekai no Monsho*. AKA: *Celestial Crest*. TV series. DIR: Yasushi Nagaoka. SCR: Aya Yoshinaga. DES: Takami Akai. ANI: Takuro Shinbo. MUS: N/C. PRD: Sunrise, WOWOW. 25 mins. x 13 eps. (TV1), 25 mins. x 13 eps. (TV2).
In Space Year 172, peace-loving Planet Martine is occupied by the Abh Human Reich, the genetically engineered descendants of Terran exiles. Now the immortal, elfin rulers of their own empire, they demand Martine's surrender. President Lock Rin deactivates the defenses to avoid a war, and his family is sent back to rule Martine as Abh aristocrats. Years later, the president's son, Jinto, prepares to journey to the heart of the Abh territory to complete his studies, accompanied by the beautiful 16-year-old Abh military cadet Rafeel.

Despite the promising concept of a collaborator turning against his masters and the painstaking recreation of the Abh's alien language, *Crest of the Stars* fails through misplaced loyalty to Hiroyuki Morioka's original novels, resulting in a succession of uneventful debates not unlike the slower portions of **LEGEND OF GALACTIC HEROES**. Squandering much of the budget on showy computer graphics for the first episode, it is soon reduced to cut-rate animation, which further stretches viewers' patience. **IDOL PROJECT**–director Nagaoka attempts to compensate by making Rafeel an elfin space-bimbo, forever bending over and jiggling, a sop to the adolescent audience that devalues much talk of Abh war crimes and conquests, as if Britney Spears had been cast as an SS officer. But there's no accounting for taste, and a sequel, *Celestial Banner*, duly followed in 2000.

CRIMSON WOLF *

1993. JPN: *Hon Ran*. AKA: *Hong Lang* (orig. Chinese). Video. DIR: Shoichi Masuo. SCR: Shoichi Masuo, Yasuhito Kikuchi, Isamu Imakake. DES: Kenji Okamura. ANI: Kazuya Kuroda, Yasuhito Kikuchi, Isamu Imakake. MUS: Kunitoshi Tojima. PRD: APPP. 60 mins.
A scientific expedition finds the hidden tomb of Genghis Khan in Mongolia. Supernatural apparitions destroy the expedition and proclaim a curse that in a thousand days a great natural disaster will devastate the whole world unless three young people bearing a wolf-shaped birthmark or scar are found and killed. Kei, a martial-arts student in Beijing, is identified as the first of the Crimson Wolves. He survives an assassination attempt, but his old teacher is murdered. Kei tracks the killers for revenge and is shocked to learn that he has been targeted by every government espionage agency in the world. Refusing to believe the "curse," Kei teams up with the other Crimson Wolves, nubile Japanese love interest/distressed damsel Mizuho Washio and the handsome, rakish "adversary" of the team Ryugen, a Chinese tong boss.
Genghis Khan is just one of three Great Kings, Oriental undead who will become supreme masters of the world unless stopped by the Crimson Wolves a thousand days after the opening of the tomb, with the other two being the Qin Emperor (China's unifier and the ward of the famous Terracotta Army) and Communist leader Mao Zedong. In scraps of clumsy plotting typical of such matinee adventures, the Crimson Wolves only become aware of the

threat they pose when assassins are sent to stop them—if the Great Kings left them in ignorance, the thousand days would have passed without opposition! The Crimson Wolves are told they have great powers (not surprising since Kei has his eyes poked out in prison and is miraculously healed by the time he is rescued). Eventually, the Great Kings take over the Chinese government's supercomputer, Goku, in a finale that implies the Crimson Wolves have saved China from its cruel first emperor, its Mongol conqueror, the architect of the Great Leap Forward, *and* the future spread of Communism! Entertainingly bad "yellow peril" hokum, unlikely to be as popular in the People's Republic as **RANMA 1/2.** **⚏⚍**

CROWS

1993. Video. DIR: Masamune Ochiai. SCR: Shunsuke Amemura. DES: Koichi Kagawa. ANI: N/C. MUS: N/C. PRD: KSS, Knack. 45 mins. x 2 eps.
Shundo is the new kid in town, ready to fight with anyone. After beating more than ten opponents, he gets a reputation as the toughest kid around, but he uses his strength to help those who cannot help themselves, soon gaining a following of grateful youngsters.
Transferring the honor of samurai drama to a school setting, Hiroshi Takahashi's 1990 manga from *Shonen Champion* was a more serious take on the teenage tough guys of shows like **BE-BOP HIGH SCHOOL** and **ANGEL LEGEND**, although Shundo's alma mater, "The Edge of Badness," is named with a pomposity that might perhaps have benefited from a little humor. **⚏⚍**

CRUSHER JOE *

1983. AKA: *Crushers*. Movie, video. DIR: Yoshikazu Yasuhiko, Toshifumi Takizawa. SCR: Haruka Takachiho. DES: Yoshikazu Yasuhiko, Shoji Kawamori. ANI: Naoyuki Yoshinaga, Ichiro Itano, Gen Sato. MUS: Tadao Maeda. PRD: Studio Nue, Sunrise. 131 mins. (m), 60 mins. x 2 eps. (v).

Orguss 02

© 1993./1995 BIGWEST/ORGUSS 02 PROJECT

The Crushers are a loose federation of trouble-shooting space mercenaries. The crew of the ship Minerva is led by teen Joe (son of head Crusher Dan), with teammates Alfin (cute tomboy), Talos (hulking muscle, much smarter than he looks), and Riki (bratty kid), plus Dongo the comical robot. Joe and crew agree to transport a frozen heiress to a distant world's medical facility, but their ship is attacked en route and the cryogenic capsule is stolen. Pursued by the galactic police while simultaneously trying to regain their cargo, the Crushers stumble into the lair of notorious space pirate Murphy, who intends to use a doomsday weapon to rule the universe.
Haruka Takachiho's famous character first appeared in the 1977 novel *Crisis on Planet Pizan* with a gang named after two of the author's wrestling heroines, the Crush Gals. The anime version is also riddled with minor characters lifted from *Go for It, Alfin-chan!*, a manga by animator Gen Sato. Several background film clips also showed two characters from another Takachiho series who were so popular they got their own show: **DIRTY PAIR.**
Joe and his gang returned in 1989 for two video adventures also released

in the U.S. In *The Ice Hell Trap*, they are framed by the despotic Ghellstan, who hires them to save the prison planet Debris without revealing that the entire world is rigged to blow as part of an insurance scam. Once again, the Crushers' mission is twofold; save the planet *and* bag the bad guys. In *Ash: The Ultimate Weapon*, they must team up with Tanya, a military officer determined to track down a conspiracy to steal yet another doomsday device. On a planet overrun with self-replicating killing machines, they have yet another race against time as the titular device is activated, leaving 20 minutes to turn it off and rescue Tanya.

In 2000, two *Crusher Joe* stories, *Legend of the Saint Jeremy* and *Pandora II*, were illustrated by JUDGE-artist Fujihiko Hosono and released on VHS as the first in the new (and rather pointless) "manga video" format, featuring voice actors reading the manga aloud.

CRY FOR OUR BEAUTIFUL WORLD

1992. JPN: *Utsukushii Chikyu o Yogosanaide*. AKA: *Don't Spoil the Beautiful Earth*. Movie. DIR: Yasuyuki Mori. SCR: Koji Takahashi. DES: N/C. ANI: Masami Furukawa. MUS: N/C. PRD: Asmik. 28 mins.

A little girl called Nana learns about how to keep Earth safe from pollution. Based on a 1985 British collection of poems and pictures on ecological themes by children from 70 different countries that was edited by Helen Exley.

CRY OF THE DRAGON

1988. JPN: *Nageki no Ryu*. Video. DIR: Satoshi Dezaki. SCR: Kazumi Koide. DES: Keizo Shimizu. ANI: Keizo Shimizu. MUS: N/C. PRD: Gainax, Magic Bus. 45 mins. x 4 eps.

Ryu ("Dragon") is a master of mahjong who becomes embroiled in gangland gambling and murders in eastern Japan. Selling over two million copies after it was serialized in *Modern Mahjong* magazine, *Cry of the Dragon* made creator Junichi Nojo one of the two most successful manga creators of

the 1980s; the other, Katsuhiro Otomo, also had a manga turned into an anime that year—AKIRA. The anime adaptation was the first show to portray mahjong games onscreen, a task no doubt made less boring by the murder subplots.

CRYING FREEMAN *

1989. Video. DIR: Daisuke Nishio, Shigenori Yamauchi. SCR: Higashi Shimizu, Ryunosuke Ono. DES: Ryoichi Ikegami. ANI: Koichi Arai, Satoshi Urushihara. MUS: Hiroaki Yoshino. PRD: Toei. 45 mins. x 6 eps.

Yo Hinomura is an internationally acclaimed potter, until he becomes involved with the 108 Dragons crime syndicate, gets brainwashed, and is turned into the assassin Crying Freeman. When the lonely Emu Hino witnesses one of his missions, he is sent to terminate her, but she seduces him, and the two eventually devote their lives to the 108 Dragons. Successive episodes featured a number of rivals and evil syndicates trying to oust Yo, including the 108 Dragons' own Bayasan, the granddaughter of a former leader. Yo fights off an African syndicate, while Emu, who acclimates rather well to life as a gang member after giving up being a virginal artist, takes on a Chinese criminal hellhole. Freeman's old enemies return to haunt him in the fourth episode (part five in the U.K.), with crooked cop Nitta and former moll Kimie teaming up with a professional wrestler to help replace Yo with a brainwashed cultist. The fifth episode featured a sex-starved female gang leader kidnapping a rival boss's family in order to make Yo become her sex slave. The final part, in which Yo defeats yet another rival, this time from the Russian syndicate, received such heavy cuts in the U.K. that it and chapter four were released on a single tape.

Based on the 1986 manga in *Big Comic Spirits* by MAD BULL 34's Kazuo Koike and SANCTUARY's Ryoichi Ikegami, *Crying Freeman* exists in a passable dub from Streamline Pictures and Manga Video, which comes complete

with deeply offensive phony Chinese accents. Like Christophe Gans' later live-action remake starring Mark Dacascos, the animated series suffered from being overly faithful to the original. Effort expended in recreating the original artwork and characters might have been better spent on actual animation, which had degenerated to extremely cheap levels by the final installments; ironic considering that PLASTIC LITTLE's Urushihara was one of the talented staff. In addition to Gans' 1997 remake, there was an unofficial Chinese version directed by Clarence Ford and released as *Dragon From Russia* (1991). **LNV**

CRYSTAL TRIANGLE *

1987. JPN: *Kindan no Mokushiroku Crystal Triangle*. AKA: *Forbidden Revelation: Crystal Triangle*. Video. DIR: Seiji Okuda. SCR: Junji Takegami. DES: Kazuko Tadano, Toyoo Ashida. ANI: Kazuko Tadano. MUS: Osamu Totsuka. PRD: Animate Film. 86 mins.

Dr. Koichiro Kamishiro, along with assistants Mina and Hisao and priestess Miyabi, is searching for "messages from God"—coded messages written on the titular crystals, relics of the distant past. However, other powers are searching for these ancient artifacts, and the plucky archaeologists must fight the CIA (pretty blonde Juno Cassidy), the KGB (Rasputin's grandson Grigori Efemovich), and the yakuza (sword-wielding gangster Genji) for the crystals in a battle that takes them across the Middle and Far East to the deep north of Japan. As with the later SPRIGGAN, these ancient messages turn out to be connected to a crashed alien spaceship and ecological catastrophe, as the rogue star Nemesis, whose last passing destroyed the dinosaurs, is returning to wreak more havoc, and the messages contain information on how to survive it.

CUBITUS

1988. JPN: *Dondon Domeru and Ron*. TV series. DIR: Hiroshi Sasakawa, Keiichiro Mochizuki, Hidehito Ueda, Yukio

Okazaki, Junichi Sakata. SCR: Kaoru Toshima. DES: Dupa. ANI: Michiru Suzuki, Shinnosuke Mina. MUS: Takanori Arisawa. PRD: Telescreen, TV Tokyo. 25 mins. x 104 eps.

Ron is an inventor who loves to tinker around with machines. His loyal friend and companion is Domeru (Cubitus), a talking dog who helps him in trying out his many new inventions, much to the annoyance of Cherry, the pretty girl next door, her husband, Beatrik, and their cat, Blacky.

In 1968, the Dutch artist "Dupa" created a new character for *Tintin* magazine—a fat white dog that looked like a ball of hair with paws. This kindly mutt became his most successful creation (others included a truck driver who fell in love with a crate) and is so famous in his native Netherlands that the dog even has his own postage stamp. Note: Dupa's European publishers claim that the *Cubitus* series was released in the U.S., but we can find no record of its broadcast under this title.

CUTEY HONEY *

1973. TV series, video. DIR: Tomoharu Katsumata, Masamune Ochiai, Hiroshi Shidara, Takeshi Shirato. SCR: Masaki Tsuji, Keisuke Fujikawa, Susumu Takahisa. DES: Shingo Araki. ANI: Shingo Araki, Kazuo Komatsubara, Masamune Ochiai, Satoshi Kamimiya. MUS: Takeo Watanabe. PRD: Toei, Dynamic, NET. 25 mins. x 25 eps. (TV), 30 mins. x 8 eps. (v), 25 mins. x 39 eps. (TV).

Based on a short-lived *Shonen Champion* manga from KEKKO KAMEN–creator Go Nagai, the breast-fixated *Cutey Honey* was animated for TV before its rookie year in manga was over. In a pastiche of ASTRO BOY, a bereaved professor creates an android facsimile of his murdered daughter, implanting a superpowerful device into her ample bosom. The "airborne element solidifier" can reassemble matter in the vicinity, effectively giving Honey anything she needs to help her in her fight to save the world—including specialized bodies such as the Hurricane Honey and Flash Honey. It also ensures that

all her clothes disappear every time she transforms, a controversial innovation at the time, now commonplace in shows such as SAILOR MOON. Her enemy in the original TV series is Panther Zora, leader of the all-female Panther Claw crime syndicate.

The immense success of the TV series rejuvenated the manga, allowing this very male appreciation of the female form to appear in girls' magazines such as *Nakayoshi*, and titles for younger readers such as *Happy Zoo*. Honey would return in 1994 for *New CH*, directed by Yasuchika Nagaoka and released straight to video. With new designs by Osamu Kasai, the new series picked up where the TV series left off, with Honey returning after a decade to discover that Panther Zora and her accomplice, Dolmeck, are still menacing civilization. She also gains an entire family of assistants, the Hayami clan, whose son, Chohei, provides viewer identification, while granddad Denbai provides heavy violence. Other Go Nagai characters put in cameo appearances, including DEVILMAN Akira as a wrestler, alongside real-life women's wrestling stars Cuty Suzuki and Mayumi Ozaki.

As the video series was translated, bringing Cutey to the West for the first time, the character's popularity in Japan peaked with a new TV series. The same year saw a *CH Flash* movie, an all-new story in which Honey battled Panther Claw for the key to an ancient treasure (the posters boasting that there would be "all-new transformation scenes," too) and two digest videos consisting of highlights—one, *Birth of Love's Warrior CH*, retelling her origin story, and the other, *Battle for W Honey Destiny* repeating the season-two finale. In 2001, it was announced that the character would return in a fully 3-D CG animated video directed by Hiroyuki Kitakubo. *Ill. p. 15.* ●NV

CUTTER'S STORY

1998. JPN: *Cutter-kun Monogatari*. Movie. DIR: Kenji Yoshida. SCR: Kenji Yoshida, Saburo Kaniguchi. DES: Tameo

Ogawa, Yasuhiro Matsumura. ANI: Hajime Matsuzaki. MUS: Toshiyuki Watanabe. PRD: Toei, Nabe, Aubec. 75 mins.

"Dreams and adventure" await in this movie funded by the state coffers of Yamaguchi Prefecture, although how the local government thought it was helping its taxpayers by producing this fictional tale about a giant genetically engineered, peach-colored pelican at the local zoo, who can say?

CYBER CITY OEDO 808 *

1990. Video. DIR: Yoshiaki Kawajiri. SCR: Akinori Endo. DES: Yoshiaki Kawajiri, Takashi Watanabe, Hiroshi Hamazaki, Masami Kosone. ANI: Hiroshi Hamazaki. MUS: Yasunori Honda, Kazz Toyama. PRD: Madhouse. 45 mins. x 3 eps.

Three loosely linked tales of a cyberpunk stripe, caught up in the post-AKIRA popularity of SF futures. In the year 2808, three criminals are offered conditional release. Even though they have each stacked up several life sentences, they may work off their terms by performing secret missions against the clock. If the mission succeeds, years are taken off their sentences. If the mission fails or they try to escape, the explosive collars around their necks will take their heads off.

For the first mission, *Virtual Death* (*Ancient Memory* in the original), tough-guy Sengoku must fight his way into the Kurokawa Tower, a self-aware skyscraper, to discover who is hacking into its systems. Presaging the first PATLABOR movie, he discovers that the "hacker" is in fact the original programmer, who has long since departed from this world. More hackery abounds in *Psychic Trooper*, in which bespectacled computer expert Goggle must outwit a cybernetic soldier while fighting his hidden feelings for an old flame who once betrayed him. The final episode, *Bloodlust* (originally *Crimson Medium*), focuses on Benten, the androgynous dandy who must track down a vampire who is using a beautiful android to entice young victims into his lair. The final showdown, in a cryogenic chamber (i.e., coffin) at the top of a space elevator, neatly encapsulates the old/new culture clash of the series. The pretty-boy cross-dresser Benten is inspired by a popular character from the 19th century, the protagonist of the kabuki play *Benten the Thief.* Since Sengoku's name means literally "civil war," the characters all carry *jitte* parrying weapons modeled on those used by samurai-era police, and the titular 808 recalls the **808 Districts** of old Edo (Tokyo), we can assume that the anime was originally intended as an SF pastiche of old stories (possibly in the style of **Samurai Gold**), which never quite got off the ground. It is just one of several superior video serials from creator Juzo Mutsuki, whose **Phantom Quest Corp** and **Devil Hunter Yohko** were similarly luckless in their quest for TV remakes. ❶❿❷

CYBER SIX *

1999. TV series. DIR: Hiroyuki Aoyama, Toshihiko Masuda, Atsuko Tanaka, Nobuo Tomizawa, Kazuhide Tomonaga. SCR: N/C. DES: Keiichi Takiguchi. ANI: Nobuo Tomizawa. MUS: Robbi Finkel. PRD: TMS, NOA, Telecom, Kid's Station. 25 mins. x 13 eps.

Cyber Six is one of many genetically engineered warriors created during World War II by the German scientist Von Reichter. The titular heroine is the only one to escape alive when Reichter destroys his creations. She hides out in the city of Meridiana, where she disguises herself as the mild-mannered *male* librarian Adrian Seidelman during the day, donning a skintight catsuit to leap across the rooftops at night. She is accompanied by Data Seven, formerly warrior Cyber 29, who was mortally wounded and whose brain was transplanted into a large black panther. Meanwhile, Reichter sends Jose, a child clone of himself, to track down and destroy his errant creation. Jose does so with an army of mutants, whose green "substance" (not blood, the producers assured U.S. networks!) Cyber Six must drink to stay alive. As with any

superheroes worth their salt, there are identity crises back in the real world, with Adrian's work buddy Lucas lusting after the female form of Cyber Six, not realizing that he shares an office with her alter ego, and schoolgirl Lori developing a crush on Adrian, not realizing that "he" is a she.

This international coproduction was based on the Argentinian comic written by Carlos Trillo and drawn by Carlos Meglia, but seems, however coincidentally, to be a belated cross between **Big X**, **Cyborg 009**, and *Batman*, with a little existential musing of the **Ghost in the Shell** variety thrown in for good measure. One of the rare anime, like **Alexander**, that premiered abroad—it was not shown in Japan until late in 2000.

CYBERFORMULA GPX

1991. JPN: *Shin Seiki* [New Century] *GPX Cyber Formula Future Grand Prix.* TV series, video. DIR: Mitsuo Fukuda, Satoshi Nishimura. SCR: Hiroyuki Hoshiyama, Tsunehisa Ito, Michiru Shimada. DES: Mutsumi Inomata, Takahiro Yoshimatsu. ANI: Takahiro Yoshimatsu, Atsushi Aono. MUS: Yuki Otani. PRD: Sunrise, Nippon TV. 25 mins. x 37 eps. (TV), 30 mins. x 30 eps (v). In the year 2016, 14-year-old Hayato Kazami enters the Cyberformula Grand Prix, in which superpowered, super-advanced cars race to determine the best team in the world. He drives a computerized car designed by his father, in a high-concept that takes the "dad's robot" formula of other Sunrise shows and puts it on wheels.

After qualifying in local championships in Fujioka and Niseko, Hayato and his teammates get to travel the world. Mixing local color (Grand Canyon, Peru) with an off-track romance developing in exotic locations (Peru, Brazil), the show also incorporates sporting rivalry and derring-do. By the time the world tour reaches Canada and England, Hayato's rivals are well-established characters in their own right, such as the cold British racer Knight Schumacher and the

Aryan tactician Karl Richter von Randall. After a race in Kenya, the crew heads into the home stretch for a lightning-fast series of races in Spain, Germany, and Japan—in succession rapid enough to imply that the TV series was canceled early.

As with the soccer antics of **Captain Tsubasa**, the sporting angle allows for regular resets of the characters' positions. The following year, Hayato reenters the championships to retain his crown in the six-part video series *CF 11 (Double One)*, driving a car designed by the beautiful blonde foreigner Claire Fortran. As romance develops between Hayato and Asuka Sugo, the daughter of his team's rich backer, he beats Schumacher and races to a "double-win" in his "double one" car in the "11th" annual championship in a highly improbable set of numerological coincidences.

The situation changes for Hayato's third championship in the 8-part *CF Zero* (1994), when an accident loses him a race *and* fiancée Asuka, who walks out on the injured driver. Though she eventually returns, Hayato must best Japanese rival Shinjo both on and off the track. This was soon followed by the eight-part *CF Saga* (1996), in which Alzard, an android driver, defeats both Shinjo and Hayato's best friend, the green-haired Bleed Kaga. While Asuka frantically searches behind the scenes for Alzard's weak spot, rival teams set traps off the race track to keep Hayato from even trying. Needless to say, he wins in the end, and a 19-year-old Hayato, who has grown up along with his target audience, gets behind the wheel once more for eight more episodes in *CF Sin* (1998), though this most recent outing focused more on his teammate Bleed.

CYBERNETICS GUARDIAN *

1989. JPN: *Seijuki Cyguard.* AKA: *Holy Beast Machine Cyguard.* Video. DIR: Koichi Ohata. SCR: Mutsumi Sanjo. DES: Atsushi Yamagata. ANI: Jun Okuda. MUS: Norimasa Yamanaka. PRD: AIC. 45 mins.

Top brains at the future city of Cyberwood attempt to come up with a solution to Cancer, the aptly named slum district. The Cybernetic Guardian unit is sent to patrol the streets, unaware that the secret Doldo Brethren organization is engaged in an attempt to bring back the death-god Saldor by implanting young men with the "seeds" to become hosts for the second coming. One such unwitting host is Cyguard technician John Stalker, whose abduction leads chief scientist Leyla (Laia in the original) Rosetta to risk everything to save him.

A directorial debut for GENOCYBER's Ohata, this claustrophobic horror tale suddenly widens out at the end for a monstrous showdown in the tradition of the GUYVER series. ●NV

CYBORG 009 *

1966. Movie, TV series. DIR: Yugo Serikawa, Ryosuke Takahashi, Saburo Sakamoto. SCR: Yugo Serikawa, Masaki Tsuji, Akiyoshi Sakai, Masaaki Sakurai. DES: Shotaro Ishinomori. ANI: Kazuhiro Yamada. MUS: Daiichiro Kosugi. PRD: Toei, Sunrise, NET. 64 mins., 60 mins., 25 mins. x 26 eps. (b/w), 25 mins. x 50 eps (color), 130 mins. World-class sprinter Joe Shimamura is seriously injured in an accident and taken away by the Black Ghost, an agent of the sinister Merchants of Death, who intend to take over the world. The kind-hearted Professor Gilmore saves his life, and in so doing, turns him into the ninth of a series of cyborg warriors that were originally designed to carry out the Merchants' bidding all over the world but are now dedicated to stopping them at all costs.

Marrying ASTRO BOY to the James Bond movies, but also far ahead of *The Six Million Dollar Man* and *X-Men*, Shotaro Ishinomori's 1964 *Cyborg 009* manga in *Shonen Sunday* was one of the original Cold War warriors—he was even succeeded in 1967 by the manga adventures of a female cyborg called *One of 009*. The debut of the animated version was swiftly followed by another short feature film, *C009: Kaiju Wars* (1967). Here, the Black Ghost uses a resurrected plesiosaur to terrorize the world, while Joe must fight spy-cyborg 0010 and the newest recruit, Plus Minus (0011).

The TV series followed in 1968, introducing many other enemies and allies, including 006, who runs a Chinese restaurant, and the wisecracking 007. In addition to the superfast Joe, each of the other cyborgs possesses one special talent, including telepathy, underwater breathing, flight, superhuman strength, the ability to breathe fire, and psychokinesis. The story was revived in 1979 for a color series, reintroducing the characters for a new audience, directed by VOTOMS' Takahashi and adapting previously unused story lines from the original, such as 009's adventures in space and the "Neo Black Ghost" chapters.

Much of the same crew stayed on for the 1980 movie to celebrate Ishinomori's 25th anniversary in manga publishing. *C009: Legend of the Super Galaxy* (aka *Defenders of the Vortex*) was directed by Masayuki Akehi and is the only part of the 009 franchise available in English. Featuring the tragic death of 004 (who keeps weapons stashed all over his body), the 130-minute color feature pitted Joe's gang against the evil Zoa, who intends to use a space vortex to control the world. *Star Wars* comic author Jeff Segal contributed to Ryuzo Nakanishi's script, though his involvement was deviously hyped in Japan as that of "the writer of *Star Wars*." The series was revived in 2001 on TV Tokyo.

CYBOT ROBOTCHI

1983. TV series. DIR: Kazuyuki Okaseko. SCR: Tomohiro Ando, Hideki Sonoda. DES: Dynamic Pro. ANI: Takao Suzuki. MUS: N/C. PRD: Dynamic, Knack, TV Tokyo. 25 mins. x 39 eps. Professor Deco creates Robotchi, an android with a TV set in his stomach. With a number of the other robots created by the professor, he causes havoc for the evil Dr. Highbrow, in this lighthearted comedy from GETTER ROBO–creator Ken Ishikawa and scenarist Tomohiro Ando.

D

D-1 DEVASTATOR

1992. Video. DIR: Tetsu Isami. SCR: Masashi Sogo. DES: Nasatomi, Masami Obari, Yukiji Kaoru. ANI: Masaki Taihei. MUS: N/C. PRD: Dynamic. 50 mins.

A manga serialized in *Ascii Comics* by "Sphios Lab" and Toshi Yoshida provided the basis for this one-shot anime, in which Ryu, a young boy, must pilot the titular Devastator to defend the planet from the invading Varsus warriors.

D4 PRINCESS

1999. TV series. DIR: Yasunori Ide. SCR: Yasunori Ide. DES: Shinji Ochi. ANI: Tatsuo Iwata. MUS: Kenji Kawai. PRD: Canyon, Domu, WOWOW. 10 mins. x 24 eps.

Based on Shotaro Harada's manga, serialized in *Dengeki Daio*, in which princess Doris Rurido turns up at a school famed for its fighting "Panzer League" and soon becomes its leader through the use of the transforming drill on her arm. The original short episodes, screened as part of the satellite channel WOWOW's *Anime Complex II* anthology show, were eventually compiled into four videos for retail release.

DAA! DAA! DAA!

2000. TV series. DIR: Hiroaki Sakurai. SCR: Tomoko Konparu, Shingo Arakawa. DES: Masayuki Onchi. ANI: Ryoichi Oki. MUS: Toshio Masuda. PRD: JC Staff, NHK2. 25 mins. x 78 eps.

When her mother qualifies as an astronaut and must travel abroad with her scientist father, Miu is sent to live with her uncle in an old temple. Forced to share a dwelling with her handsome classmate Kanata, Miu's embarrass-ment is compounded when the "couple" is "adopted" by an alien baby, Ru. The reluctant foster parents must cope with a baby who can levitate and with the additional annoyance of their child's alien protector, Wannya.

Based on Mika Kawamura's manga in *Nakayoshi* magazine, this comedy combines the odd-couple romance of HIS AND HER CIRCUMSTANCES with an SF excuse for playing mommies and daddies straight out of MAMA'S A FOURTH GRADER.

DADDY LONG-LEGS

1979. JPN: *Ashinaga Ojisan*. TV special. DIR: Masakazu Higuchi. SCR: Akira Miyazaki. DES: Shinichi Tsuji. ANI: Shinichi Tsuji. MUS: Makoto Kawaguchi. PRD: Herald Enterprise, Tatsunoko Pro, Fuji TV. 75 mins. (TVm), 25 mins. x 40 eps (TV).

When she turns 18, the stories Judy Abbot publishes about her life in the orphanage secure her a place at university. She writes many letters to her mysterious benefactor "Daddy Long-Legs" unaware that he is Jervis Pendleton III, an adoring millionaire who has already met her (and fallen in love with her) in disguise. This musical one-shot anime is only the most recent adaptation of Jean Webster's 1912 children's book—Hollywood movies of the same story include one with Mary Pickford as Judy (1919), Janet Gaynor taking the role in 1931, and a 1955 version with Leslie Caron and Fred Astaire. There is also a Dutch adaptation, *Vadertje Langbeen* (1938), but this inversion of CINDERELLA, in which an unusual girl seeks a "normal life" (with a millionaire, of course), was also immensely influential in Japan's girls' manga market, where it inspired CANDY CANDY and its many imitators. The story was remade by Kazuyoshi Yokota as a WORLD MASTERPIECE THEATER anime TV series, *My Daddy Long-Legs* (1990, *Watashi no Ashinaga Ojisan*), featuring new character designs by Shuichi Seki. Also see VIDEO PICTURE BOOK.

DAGGER OF KAMUI *

1985. JPN: *Kamui no Ken*. AKA: *Blade of Kamui*. Movie. DIR: Rintaro, Susumu Ishizaki. SCR: Mamoru Masaki. DES: Murano Moriyoshi. ANI: Atsuo Noda, Kyoko Matsuhara, Yoshiaki Kawajiri, Koji Morimoto, Osamu Nabeshima, Yasuomi Umezu. MUS: Ryudo Uzaki, Eitetsu Hayashi. PRD: Algos, Madhouse. 132 mins.

Jiro, a foundling boy, loses his adoptive parents to an assassin. Avenging their death by murdering a one-armed man, he falls in with the priest Tenkai, who trains him in the black arts of the ninja. Learning that the one-armed man was really his true father, a distraught Kamui searches for his true mother, an Ainu princess. He also goes in search of Captain Kidd's treasure in order to take from Tenkai the only thing that he values. Tenkai wishes to use the treasure to overthrow the antiisolationists and close Japan once more to the outside world—the action takes place just before the Meiji Restoration that would throw Japan open once and for all. Jiro's quest takes him all the way to the American West, with time out for a brief meeting with TOM SAWYER–creator Mark Twain, where he is saved by a defecting servant of Tenkai's (who turns out to be his long-lost sister) before returning to exact revenge for all his family.

This Kamui is no relation to Sanpei Shirato's MANUAL OF NINJA MARTIAL ARTS; it was based on a series of novels by *Legend of the Paper Spaceship*—author Tetsu Yano, who was also Robert Heinlein's Japanese translator. Though not one of his best works, *Dagger of Kamui* contains much of the clash of old and new that distinguishes his writings—the idea of foreign assistance in sending Japan back into the past would be reused by animator Kawajiri in NINJA SCROLL. *Blade of Kamui*, an earlier U.S. dub of the series, rewrites the plot completely, claiming that it is set on an alien world, where Kamui's dagger is a "powerful weapon [that] controls the future of the universe." **NV**

DAGON

1988. JPN: *Ikinari Dagon*. TV series. DIR: Kazuyoshi Yokota. SCR: Nobuyuki Fujimoto. DES: Noboru Takano. ANI: Tetsuya Ishikawa. MUS: Kazunori Ishida. PRD: Nippon Animation, TV Asahi. 25 mins. x 12 eps.
Dagon is the pilot of the starship Digital whose daughter, Meryl, is always getting into trouble. In the middle of an investigation, a shipboard accident causes the Digital to crash-land on a planet ruled by a race of giants called the Sapiens (i.e., Earth). Dagon and his crew, however, are helped by the bee doctor Marilyn, Jisamu the cockroach, Floppy the spider, and Skipper the ant. They return the favor by saving Marilyn from Geppo the evil frog. This short-lived anime recalls the Fleischer brothers' *Mr. Bug Goes to Town* (1941, aka *Hoppity Goes to Town*) and features the contribution of non-Japanese creators Dennis Bond and Ken Morton.

DAIGUARD *

1999. JPN: *Chikyu Boetai Kigyo Daiguard*. AKA: *Earth Defense Enterprise Daiguard*. TV series. DIR: Seiji Mizushima. SCR: Hidefumi Kimura. DES: Hiroyuki Kanno. ANI: Michiru Ishihara. MUS: Kohei Tanaka, Kenji Kawai. PRD: Sotsu,

Xebec, TV Tokyo. 25 mins. x 13 eps.
In A.D. 2030, 12 years after the extra-dimensional Heterodyne invasion was repelled by the people of Earth, the planet has settled into a time of relative peace. The chief weapon against them, the giant robot known as Daiguard, is now performing police PR duties in Japan with a new pilot—the hot-headed 25-year-old Shunsuke Akagi. But during one of Daiguard's routine publicity appearances, the Heterodyne strike again, and the old war horse is brought back into service without a moment to lose. Announced as forthcoming in the U.S. from ADV at our deadline.

DALLOS *

1983. Video. DIR: Mamoru Oshii. SCR: Hisayuki Toriumi, Mamoru Oshii. DES: Toshiyasu Okada, Masaharu Sato. ANI: Toshiyasu Okada, Takemi Tanemoto, Masahiro Neriki. MUS: Hiroyuki Nanba. PRD: Bandai, Yomiuri, Studio Pierrot. 30 mins. x 4 eps.
The grandchildren of the original lunar colonists, toughened by generations in the mines on the dark side of the moon, fight to gain their independence from an exhausted and oppressive Earth, as guerrilla leaders Shun and Dog oppose the ruthless Terran commandant Alex Riger's group, complete with armed heavies and robot dogs.

This unremarkable rip-off of Robert Heinlein's *The Moon Is a Harsh Mistress* will go down in history for being the first anime made specifically for direct video release. The series, later released in a 120-minute feature-length edition, was cut down to form the 85-minute *Dallos Special*, which added 50 extra shots and was the only incarnation to be released in the U.S. Before we even get to the opening *Star Wars*–inspired crawl of expository scene-setting, there's a lengthy narration over stills of concept art, a sure-fire sign (as in the much later JIN-ROH) that the makers mistakenly feared the audience would be bewildered. As with writer Toriumi's later SALAMANDER, the script is actually

Lemnear from Kinji Yoshimoto's swords-and-sorcery **LEGEND OF LEMNEAR**. She is the long-awaited Champion of Silver, fated to lead the people against the Dark Lord in a by-the-numbers fantasy adventure—though the blame ultimately lies in a glut of Western fantasy movies providing lackluster inspiration. Like **PLASTIC LITTLE**, *LoL* is high on gorgeous imagery and low on plot, a feature of creative control resting in the hands of Yoshimoto and fellow artist Satoshi Urushihara. *See entry p. 215.*

Legend of Lemnear

better than the crew seem to realize (much of the 5-minute voice-over seems to consist of his rather sensible production notes), but his writing is badly served by hackneyed setups and execution by staff members who had yet to realize that the video audience would be slightly older than the viewership for TV serials such as GUNDAM. The final conceit, in which an awestruck colonist gazes upon the distant Earth that spawned him, *almost* makes up for the cheap animation and lazy world-building that gives a lunar city a blue sky and Earth-normal gravity.

DANCE TILL TOMORROW

1990. JPN: *Asatte Dance*. AKA: *Dance the Day after Tomorrow*. Video. DIR: Teruo Kigure, Masamune Ochiai. SCR: Sheila Nakajima, Tomohiro Maruyama. DES: Jiro Sayama. ANI: Jiro Sayama. MUS: Tetsuya Nakamura. PRD: Knack. 45 mins. x 2 eps.
Country boy Suekichi only has to graduate from his Tokyo college to inherit his late grandfather's fortune. He'd rather be working in a deadbeat experimental theater troupe in the hope of getting into its earnest, pretty leading light's good book, not to mention panties, but there are two major obsta-

cles. One is that Granddad, not content with setting up a stony-faced lawyer to try and keep his descendant on the straight and narrow, materializes in Suekichi's apartment at awkward moments to dispense totally useless advice. And the other is Aya Hibino (or is it Munakata?), a wild child with an attitude problem who keeps breaking into his apartment and forcing sex on him. She also forces reluctant tenderness, responsibility, and a realization that there's more to adult life than he'll ever find in his drama group, in this short-lived adaptation of Naoki Yamamoto's seven-volume 1989 manga from *Big Comic Spirits*. The same creator contributed to the **CREAM LEMON** series under the pseudonym To Moriyama. Ⓝ

DANCING WITH DAD

1999. JPN: *Papa to Odoro*. TV series. DIR: Akira Yoshida. SCR: Chuya Chikazawa. DES: Masaaki Kawanami. ANI: Hirohide Shikishima, Moriyasu Taniguchi. MUS: N/C. PRD: Studio Deen, TBS. 8 mins. x 13 eps.
A gag comedy depicting the everyday life of a lustful, lazy, and indecent father and his strait-laced son and daughter. Chuya Chikazawa's 1991 comic from *Young Magazine* was adapted for short slots on the *Wonderful* show.

DANCOUGAR *

1985. JPN: *Choju Kishin Dancougar*. AKA: *Super-Bestial Machine God Dancougar*. TV series, movie, video. DIR: Nobuyoshi Habara, Seiji Okuda. SCR: Keisuke Fujikawa, Kenji Terada, Junji Takegami. DES: Indori-Koya, Hisashi Hirai, Masami Obari. ANI: Akira Saijo, Osamu Tsuruyama. MUS: Takeshi Ike, Osamu Totsuka. PRD: Ashi Pro, TBS. 25 mins. x 38 eps. (TV), ca. 90 mins. x 2 (v), 30 mins. x 4 eps. (v).
Earthman Shapiro Keats betrays his own race and switches his allegiance to the space emperor Muge Zolbados. Earth's last hope is the Dancougar team, which harnesses the power of Terran beasts to fight with its combin-

ing giant robot. Carefully repeating the formula established by **BATTLE OF THE PLANETS** and director Okuda's earlier **GOBARIAN**, *Dancougar* features leader Shinobu (pilot of the Eagle Fighter), love interest Sarah and her Land Cougar, youngster Masato in the Land Liger, and big-guy Ryo, pilot of the Mammoth. Battles rage across the Amazon Basin, New York, and Europe before a final showdown between Sarah and Shapiro in the asteroid belt.

As the series closed, 60 minutes of recycled footage was augmented with 30 new minutes to make the *Requiem for Lost Heroes* video. Toshitaro Oba's all-new *God Bless Dancougar* was the best-selling anime video of 1987 (released in the U.K. as plain *Dancougar*), foreshadowing **PATLABOR** 2 with its postseries look at the team training new recruits. Framed by a military cartel, they are imprisoned but rescued by their students and short-lived suicide squad of black knights (who also appeared in episode 26 of the TV series). The usual robot action is punctuated by completely incongruous musical interludes (Shinobu wants to be a pop star), perhaps recycled footage from the 1985 *Songs from the Beast Machine Team* video special.

The team's last appearance was in the four-part 1989 video series *White Hot Final Chapter*, when they are dragged out of retirement to resist a new threat from planet Delado, with Shapiro pulling strings from behind the scenes.

DANGAIOH *

1987. JPN: *Hajataisei Dangaio*. AKA: *Star Destroyer Bullet-Criminal-Investigation-Phoenix*. Video. DIR: Toshihiro Hirano. SCR: Noboru Aikawa. DES: Shoji Kawamori, Masami Obari, Koichi Ohata. ANI: Hideaki Anno. MUS: Michiaki Watanabe. PRD: AIC. 45 mins. x 3 eps.
Four kids (Mia, Pai, Lamda, and token male Roll) are abducted and brainwashed by the kindly (!) Professor Tarsan and trained to become warriors in the fight against the pirate Galimos. They later discover that their planets

were destroyed by the invaders (who keep their armor on indoors so the animators don't have to move their lips) and that the kids' powers are the last thing that prevents the end of the universe.

The 1980s anime industry, still taking tottering steps into the world of straight-to-video science fiction, had a lot of trouble working out what to give its audience. Boys who had grown up watching kiddie shows that featured giant transforming robots were now grown-up twenty-somethings with VCRs, and this was one of the many experiments aimed at bringing them back. But the amnesia subplot is a lame excuse for long exposition scenes and huge holes in the plot, and it contains many of the flaws of children's shows without exploiting their appeal. The end result is a show that imitates the big-robot fights (originally designed to sell toys) and halfheartedly includes a psychic-weapon subplot influenced by **AKIRA**. Ultimately too childish for an adult audience and too complex for kids, *Dangaioh* is an also-ran in Japanese sci-fi.

Originally sold as *Dangaio* (*sic*) in a subtitled edition in the U.S., the first episode was dropped from Manga Entertainment's compilation dub, which added the final "h." The dub is the usual shrill mess that characterizes translations of the period; listen for the telltale "bloodies" and occasional asides like Pai's darts slang ("One hundred and *eighty*!") that mark this as a British dub made with American accents to secure U.S. distribution.

Note also the careful balancing of the sexes. Producer Toru Miura realized early on that that a primarily male audience would prefer to watch a lone boy amid a gaggle of gorgeous girls rather than a load of sweaty men in spacesuits. Miura went on to perfect this eye-candy formula in **TENCHI MUYO!**

The video series was remade for television as the 13-episode *G Dangaio* (2001), which begins with Miya Alice crash-landing on Earth in the 1980s and sending a telepathic message to teenager Miya Shikitani that warns her of the approach of Banger Invaders. The Terran Miya starts developing a Dangaioh unit to defend Earth, and ten years later they are ready to defend the planet with the aid of the combining Dangaioh Burst, Dangaioh Flail, and Dangaioh Cross, piloted by angst-ridden teens Takaya Tenjo, Manami Umishio, and Hitomi Jido.

DANGAIZER THREE

1999. JPN: *Choshin-hime Dangaizer Three*. AKA: *Super-Divine Princess Dangaizer Three*. Video. DIR: Masami Obari. SCR: Masami Obari, Reimu Aoki. DES: Yasuhiro Oshima, Natsuki Mamiya, Masami Obari. ANI: Masami Obari. MUS: N/C. PRD: Kaos Project. 30 mins. x 4 eps.

The arrival of a giant crystal causes havoc in the future city of Neo Hong Kong, sucking the pretty martial artist and games fan Hina Mitsurugi into an alternate world. There, she finds the four kings of this parallel Earth facing destruction at the hands of the evil Sapphire and teams up with big-sister figure Sindy Shahana on a quest for some of the mythical Protect Gear.

Directed, scripted, designed, *and* animated by VIRUS's Obari, with plenty of fan-service cleavage to make up for the absent characterization. **N**

DANGARD ACE *

1977. JPN: *Wakusei Robo Dangard A.* AKA: *Planetary Robot Danguard Ace*. TV series. DIR: Tomoharu Katsumata. SCR: Haruya Yamazaki, Soji Yoshikawa. DES: Shingo Araki. ANI: Shingo Araki, Akira Saijo. MUS: Shunsuke Kikuchi. PRD: Toei, Fuji TV. 25 mins. x 56 eps.

Dr. Oedo organizes a scouting mission, led by the elite young pilot Takuma (Winstar), to the rogue tenth planet Prometheus as it nears Earth. Approaching the planet in the super-fast carrier Jasdam, the crew rescues Captain Dan (Captain Mask), who has escaped from the evil Commissar Krell. The captain assumes duties with the Dangard A robot team, ready to put

them through the toughest training in order to save Earth from invasion. Based on an idea by STARBLAZERS' Leiji Matsumoto (reputedly in answer to the giant-robot shows made by his fellow big-name manga artists, Go Nagai and Shotaro Ishinomori) and Dan Kobayashi (who appears to have lent his own name to the show and to the heroic Captain Dan), 26 episodes of this series were shown in the U.S. as part of the FORCE FIVE anime compilation, and the first 2 episodes were re-rereleased on video to capitalize on the new boom in anime. The characters also appeared in an episode made specifically for theatrical release in Japan called *Dangard A: Great War in Space* (1978). The series was reissued in an LD collection under the umbrella title of *Leiji Matsumoto Theater*.

DARK CAT *

1991. Video. DIR: Akira Suzuki. SCR: Toshiki Inoue. DES: Masami Suda. ANI: Hirohide Shikishima. MUS: N/C. PRD: Nikkatsu. 60 mins.

Human beings carry a seed of evil within them that demonic creatures wish to nurture and exploit. Other paranormal beings, the "dark cats," seek to protect humanity from its own heritage. Two such feline angels are Hyoi and Ryoi, who are spying on strange events in a Japanese school. Hyoi has transmuted into human form, while Ryoi has invited himself in cat form into the life of female student Aimi. As the evil spirit Jukokubo possesses the teachers and turns them to violence, Hyoi and Ryoi must protect their charges with the aid of their magical Dark Cat sword.

Based on a manga serialized in *Halloween* magazine by Naomi Kimura, *Dark Cat* crashes the pretty boys of girls' manga such as TOKYO BABYLON with the tits-and-tentacles ghostbusting of innumerable horror anime like WICKED CITY. **NV**

DARK MYTH *

1990. JPN: *Ankoku Shinwa*. Video. DIR: Takashi Anno. SCR: Takashi Anno. DES:

Yoshiaki Yanagida. ANI: Kazuo Kawauchi, Tomomi Mochizuki. MUS: Kenji Kawai. PRD: Asiado. 50 mins. x 2 eps.

Ten years ago, Takeshi's father was murdered. The weeping boy was found by his side in the forest, nursing a strange shoulder wound. Takeshi suspects that the scar is a symbol of an ancient snake cult and teams up with some acquaintances to track down relics of the era. He discovers that ancient clans from Japanese prehistory are fighting to preserve their secrets in the present day. These secrets include the elixir of life, a great treasure, and a savage immortal hidden beneath a mountain.

Daijiro Moroboshi's original one-volume 1976 *Shonen Jump* manga is tied into a much larger universe both of "real" myths and his personal revisions. He already treated a similar subject the previous year in *Maddomen*, in which a scholar discovered secrets of Japanese history at a lost New Guinea temple, and would return to it again with the linked story *Confucius's Dark Myth* (1977) and a rewrite of the Monkey-King tale in *Phantom Monkey's Journey to the West* (1983). The stories all take their cue from the fact that the supposedly homogenous Japanese are a melting pot of several different races, the earliest of which are only known from a handful of archaeological relics. The Jomon, Yamatai, Ainu, Chinese, Koreans, Manchurians, and Southeast Asians all brought elements of their own cultures to Japan. Compare this to PRINCESS MONONOKE, in which several of these cultures fight each other at the birth of Japan. *Dark Myth* suggests that before the coming of humans, an ancient race of Indian gods also fought over the land, and that today's legends are fragmented race memories of this great war. Similar liberties are taken with history in many other anime from PSYCHIC WARS to YAMATO TAKERU.

There is a clever economy of animation (especially a scene where Takeshi alone is animated in a whited-out world) and some suitably arcane music from **Ghost in the Shell**'s Kawai, but *DM* is ultimately disappointing. That place in Japanese history where real events elide into myth is truly fascinating. Even today, the emperor can supposedly trace his lineage back to Amaterasu, the Sun Goddess mentioned in *DM*, and the sorcerous Princess Himiko is the semihistorical figure mentioned in Chinese histories as the Queen of Wa, who appears in other guises in **Zeguy**, **Flint the Time Detective**, and **Steel Jeeg**. But much of the plot is a tour of Japanese antiquities, and while director Anno turns up the tension with waving grasses at the scene of a murder, action is slow to arrive and difficult to follow. The names are too cumbersome for non-Japanese speakers and the stories are too complex, especially when they require the viewer to know exactly what old legends are being slyly adapted. Takeshi's quest takes him all over modern Japan, though to the uninitiated, one temple looks very much like another.

For the dub, Manga Entertainment does its best, but John Wolskel's rewrite still has to stumble through lines like, "The head of the Kikuchi clan is always called Kikuchi-hiko. It is a very old name. It is recorded as Kukuchi-ku of the country of Kuna, in the *Gishiwajin-den* in the third century A.D." Matters aren't helped by a cast that can't pronounce this stuff half the time. **V**

DARK NIGHT'S DRAMA
1995. JPN: *Yamiyo Jidaigeki*. AKA: *Dark Night's Period-Drama*. TV series. DIR: Takashi Imanishi, Yoshiyuki Tomino, Ryosuke Takahashi. SCR: Takashi Imanishi, Yoshiyuki Tomino. DES: Norio Shioyama, Kazuhiro Soeta. ANI: Kazuhiro Soeta. MUS: N/C. PRD: Sunrise, Nippon TV. 15 mins. x 4 eps.
Four tales of old-time horror in the anthology spirit of **Pet Shop of Horrors** and **The Cockpit** from directors best known for giant-robot shows. Tales include *The Hill of Old Age*, which tells of a conspiracy hatched against Japan's unifier, Nobunaga Oda; *Seeing the*

Truth, about the assassin sent to murder Nobunaga's successor, Ieyasu Tokugawa; a wandering swordsman saving a damsel in distress from evil spirits in *The Ear of Jinsuke*; while the final chapter, *Prints from the Fall of the Bakufu*, features a tomboy from a woodcut works charged with making a print of the young warrior Okita Soji. Broadcast as part of the *Neo Hyper Kids* program. **NV**

DARK SOLDIER D *
1999. JPN: *D*. Video. DIR: Tatsuya Ishii. SCR: N/C. DES: N/C. ANI: N/C. MUS: Michael Barter. PRD: KSS. 30 mins. x 3 eps.
A computer-animated series from the director of the live-action *Acri: Homo Aquarellius* involving the escalation of East-West Cold War conflict, two protagonists running to Russia with military secrets *and* invading aliens.

DARK WARRIOR *
1991. JPN: *Maku Senjo*. AKA: *Demon Pavilion Battleground*. Video. DIR: Masahisa Ishida. SCR: Masaru Yamamoto. DES: Kenichi Onuki, Osamu Tsuruyama. ANI: Keisuke Morishita. MUS: Teruo Takahama. PRD: Daiei, Tokuma Japan Communications. 50 mins. x 2 eps.
When computer genius Joe Takegami hacks into a top-secret computer system in search of information on a mysterious girl, he discovers he is a clone created at the command of David Rockford, CEO of America's largest electronics company. Forced to run for his life from the secret government project that created him, he must rely on his newly discovered psychic powers for protection. He meets another psychic, Aya Lee Rose, and the pair face the combined might of Rockford Electronics in a fight for truth and justice.

Author Sho Takejima (who also created **Phantom Heroes**) was killed in a motorcycle accident in the year of *DW*'s Japanese release, a tragedy cynically exploited to drum up interest in this awful anime adaptation of his novel. With shades of *Blade Runner* and

Total Recall in its implanted memories and confused identities, *DW* (known by its Japanese title *Maku Senjo* in the U.K.) would have been years ahead of **Perfect Blue** were it not for the stultifying ineptitude of its execution.

It starts as it means to go on, with a pompous voice-over vainly attempting to justify another story of musclemen hitting each other. *DW* would like to play mind games with the viewer but has such a ham-fisted grasp of the real world that it's hard to notice where the unreal comes into effect. The direction is lazily inexact, with characters "crossing the line" between shots so that they appear to be going in separate directions. The artwork is dreadful, including a laughably lopsided "Pentagon," and the animation is criminally cheap, often below TV standards (Joe drives down one street which consists of just two buildings on a loop). Such travesties compound the shoddy script—we are just as shocked as Joe when we see a "double" of his former lover, since the two girls could not look more different! Genetically engineered superwarriors shrug off bullets but cower from flames. With incoherent nimbyism masquerading as environmental angst, Joe thinks that the world's pollution problems can be solved simply by moving all the computer companies out of Silicon Valley, where, incidentally, it is always either foggy or raining. But in an anime where a character can continue to function after his brain has been punched out through the back of his head, it's perhaps unsurprising that the production crew could manage a similar feat. **LNV**

DARKSIDE BLUES *
1994. Movie. DIR: Nobuyasu Furukawa. SCR: Mayori Sekijima. DES: Hiroshi Hamazaki. ANI: Hiroshi Hamazaki. MUS: Kazuhiko Sotoyama. PRD: Toho. 83 mins.
The future belongs to one company: the "family" business of the Persona Corporation. Only a few places on Earth hold out against its dominion; one is in Kabuki Town, a ramshackle

part of Shinjuku known as the Tokyo Darkside. Tatsuya is a terrorist on the run, aided by a sorcerous stranger (also called Darkside). Tatsuya is a revolutionary, but Darkside is revolution personified, a messianic figure born of oppression.

Replaying AKIRA with supernatural elements, *DB* is a beautifully designed but confused Gothic tale with a slow pace and nonexistent ending, based on the 1985 novel by DEMON CITY SHINJUKU's Hideyuki Kikuchi and filtered through a 1993 manga adaptation by BRIDE OF DEIMOS's Yuho Ashibe. Concerned with the soul rather than the body, it takes many liberties with place and time, such as doors that don't necessarily lead to the same room twice. This is a film loaded with symbolism—flowers shedding petals, people turning into statues, spiders spinning red webs—but like its rebels without a cause, it says a lot but doesn't really mean anything. Its best creation is Darkside himself, even down to his voice in the Japanese edition, which was done by male impersonator Natsuki Akira. Even the foley editing of his footsteps implies the sound of hooves, most noticeable when he's walking up to a seedy hotel. His first appearance, a hell ride through the dimensions, is a masterly touch, but one that was done better in the opening scenes of SHUTENDOJI.

Despite lush designs and a moody, suspenseful beginning, the animation and color palette get progressively cheaper as the film goes on. The same can be said for the meandering plot, which begins with a compelling mystery but soon finds itself sprinting for the finish, failing to cram the original story into the running time. *Ill. p. 25.* **NV**

DARTANIUS

1979. JPN: *Mirai Robo Dartanius.* AKA: *Future Robot Dartanius; Daltanias.* TV series. DIR: Katsutoshi Sasaki, Norio Kabeshima, Akira Suzuki. SCR: Fuyunori Gobu, Masaki Tsuji. DES: Yuki Hijiri, Akehiro Kaneyama, Yutaka Izubuchi.

ANI: Akehiro Kaneyama. MUS: Hiroshi Tsutsui. PRD: Y&K, Toei, Tokyo 12 Channel. 25 mins. x 47 eps.
Ten years after the alien Akrons invade Earth, the last remnants of humanity live in savage gangs in the ruins of the world's cities. Street urchins Kento, Danji, Sanae, Mita, Tanosuke, Jiro, and Manabu find the entrance to a secret underground base where Professor Earl, a scientist from Planet Helios, has been working on a plan to stop Earth from suffering the same fate as his own world, already conquered by the Akrons. Kento and Danji are made the pilots of Atlas and Gumper, a robot and a spaceship, and in their first battle against the Akrons, they awaken the lost "third component," the robotic lion Beralios. Earl realizes that Kento is the lost son of Harlin, King of Helios, and that with all the pieces in place, the three machines can combine to form the super-robot Dartanius. Though the robot was originally named after the hero of the THREE MUSKETEERS, the GODAIKIN release of the toy in the U.S. used the Daltanias spelling listed above as an alternative.

DASH KAPPEI

1981. TV series. DIR: Masayuki Hayashi, Akehira Ishida, Keiichiro Mochizuki, Hiroko Tokita, Katsuhito Akiyama. SCR: Shigeru Yanagawa, Masaru Yamamoto, Haruya Yamazaki, Takeshi Shudo, Akiyoshi Sakai, Osamu Sekiguchi, Sukehiro Tomita. DES: Noboru Rokuda. ANI: Sadao Miyamoto. MUS: Koba Hayashi. PRD: Tatsunoko, Fuji TV. 25 mins. x 65 eps.
Kappei is a male student who is always hanging around the girls' locker room. Because this anime was shown on TV at six in the evening, his reason for doing so is that he wants to collect white panties. This "harmless" but annoying fetish eventually lands him a place on the school basketball team, which he only accepts because of his interest in the underwear of the coach, Miss Natsu. Though the series soon veered into the standard tropes of sports anime like AIM FOR THE ACE, this adapta-

The worldwide success of POKÉMON, a multimedia phenomenon of which anime is but one facet, created an unprecedented boom in new translations, and created vast potential for anime in the 21st century. The children who watch *Pokémon* today could become the anime buyers of tomorrow. *See entry p. 302.*

Pokémon

POKEMON PROPERTIES USED WITH PERMISSION

tion of Noboru Rokuda's 1979 manga from *Shonen Sunday* often deviated from the original story, even to the extent of an episode set in space. Other anime adapted from Rokuda's work include **F** and TWIN. **N**

DASH SHIKIRO

1989. TV series. DIR: Hiroshi Sasakawa, Hitoshi Nanba. SCR: Takashi Yamada, Hiroko Naka, Kiichi Takayama. DES: Oji Suzuki. ANI: Oji Suzuki. MUS: N/C. PRD: Aubec, TV Tokyo. 25 mins. x 25 eps., 35 mins. (special).
Shikiro and his friends like racing their cars and outwitting their rivals in Team Horizon. Their vehicles look uncannily like the plastic model "shiki" kits on sale in Japan at the time.

Though allegedly based on a manga by "Saurus Tokuda" in *Corocoro Comic, Dash Shikiro*'s origins are in the same toy tie-in genre as BATTLE SKIPPER and the later POKÉMON. Among a largely pseudonymous crew, former BATTLE OF THE PLANETS–director Sasakawa is prepared to stand up and be counted. A 1990 TV special, *Team Shikiro vs. Team Horizon,* featured the ultimate race, which was moved to South America for a bit of local color.

DAY THE EARTH SHOOK, THE

1997. JPN: *Chikyu ga Ugoita Hi.* Movie. DIR: Toshio Goto. SCR: Ayako Okina. DES: Takashi Saijo. ANI: Takashi Saijo. MUS: N/C. PRD: Tama Pro. 80 mins.

In 1995, an earthquake strikes the city of Kobe, and Tsuyoshi must swiftly adapt to the new danger brought into his sheltered life. Amid the destruction, he observes Japanese people pulling together and helping each other. Based on a story by Etsuko Kishigawa, this feel-good movie was rushed out to capitalize on the real-life events, and even real-life participants. Tetsuya Okazaki, who plays Tsuyoshi, supposedly experienced the quake himself as a middle-school student. The Kobe earthquake was also the indirect cause of several other anime—BOMBERMAN's first appearance was in a safety video, and the postquake financial climate transformed the planned live-action PERFECT BLUE into a cheaper anime version. Doubtless it also inspired the same year's BAKUMATSU SPACIBO, which showed the Japanese coping with a historical natural disaster but bringing aid to troubled foreigners.

DEAD HEAT

1987. Video. DIR: Toshifumi Kawase, Shinji Takamatsu. SCR: Akinori Endo. DES: Toshimitsu Kobayashi. ANI: Toshimitsu Kobayashi. MUS: Appo Sound Concept. PRD: Sunrise. 36 mins.

Claiming to be "Japan's first 3D anime," this curio using the VHD-3D system features 21st-century youngsters racing "FX" machines—predictable crosses between motorcycles and giant robots. Failed driver Makoto is ready to quit the business until he is approached by Hayami Go, who offers him a hyper-engine to change his fortunes. In other words, it's CYBERFORMULA GPX but with clichés that stick out of your screen.

DEBUT

1994. JPN: *Tanjo.* AKA: *Birth.* Video. DIR: Tomomi Mochizuki. SCR: Go Sakamoto. DES: Hiroshi Tanaka. ANI: Hiroshi Tanaka. MUS: Shinichi Kyoda. PRD: Movic. 29 mins. x 2 eps.

Saori, Aki, and Kumi are three schoolgirls who want to become actresses, but they are beset by showbiz pressures and by the lure of handsome boys. In this short-lived series made to cash in on the success of the original computer game (itself a clone of GRADUATION), once the girls take their first steps in their chosen career, they meet a female time-traveler who knows the secrets of their futures.

DEBUTANTE DETECTIVES CORPS *

1995. JPN: *Ojosama Sosa Ami.* AKA: *Lady Investigator Network.* Video. DIR: Akiyuki Shinbo, Masami Shimoda. SCR: Juzo Mutsuki. DES: Shinji Ochi. ANI: Shinji Ochi. MUS: Takeshi Haketa. PRD: Toho. 30 mins.

The five richest girls in the world attend Japan's richest, most privileged school, where posing as international crime-fighters is one of their many high-class pursuits. After arriving at their new school, where they outdo each other with their modes of transport, a terrorist organization decides to assassinate them for their hubris and conspicuous consumption—an event that ironically forces the spoilt madams to cooperate with each other for the first time in their lives. With Japanese twins Kimiko and Miyuki Ayanokoji in charge, the rest of the team comprises gun-crazy blonde Russian sharp-shooter Nina Kirov, Chinese martial artist and gambling addict Reika Shu, and Adolf Hitler's illegitimate granddaughter, Yoko.

Put into protective custody for their own good, the girls escape thanks to Miyuki's electronics expertise and Yoko's cunning disguises. Faced with terrorist attacks by plane, rifle, and fists, the girls dispatch their adversaries with weapons (Nina), martial arts (Reika), and psychic powers (Kimiko), only to discover that the entire hazard has been engineered to trick them all into demonstrating what they can accomplish as a team.

Based on an idea by DEVIL HUNTER YOHKO's Juzo Mutsuki, *Debutante Detectives* was conceived as a vehicle to showcase a group of minor voice actresses collectively known as Virgo. It is thus little more than an excuse to put the girls into the public eye in order to sell spinoff games and albums. Frivolously throwing away its limited character routines in just half a shallow hour, its original raison d'être is completely destroyed by the removal of the Japanese voices for the English dub, leaving nothing but an orphaned "episode one" of a series that was never going to happen. Compare to its predecessor GIRL DETECTIVES' CLUB.

DEEP BLUE FLEET

1993. JPN: *Konpeki no Kantai.* Video. DIR: Takeyuki Kanda, Hiromichi Matano, Shigenori Kurii. SCR: Ryosuke Takahashi. DES: Masami Suda, Noriyasu Yamauchi. ANI: Masami Suda. MUS: Koji Makaino. PRD: JC Staff. 45 mins. x 28 eps.

Isoroku Takano, a Japanese pilot shot down over Bougainville island in 1943, is thrown through a time slip and allowed to relive his life, retaining all the memories of his former existence. Teaming up in 1941 with another time-traveler, Yasaburo Otaka, he seizes power in the Japanese government. With Otaka as prime minister and Takano leading the armed forces, the Japanese demand that Western powers pull out of Asia. When the Americans refuse to comply, the Japanese declare war and bomb Pearl Harbor.

Foiling the evil American plans for the atom bomb, the Japanese push the enemy back to Christmas Island, using the foe's own weapons against them. As the fighting rolls down from the Torres Strait to the Tasman Sea, U.S. President Roosevelt has a heart attack and dies. Scared at the Japanese victories, Hitler declares war on his one-time allies. The Japanese navy blows up a Third Reich atomic facility on Madagascar, and, in a desperate attempt to curb Nazi advances, launches suicide attacks in the Red Sea. By 1946, a stalemate leads to espionage operations in California and Manchuria, and the

Nazis launch a U-boat counterattack in the Indian Ocean.

Based on the long series of novels by Yoshio Aramaki, *Deep Blue Fleet* takes a very different approach toward the pacifist posturings more commonly seen in English-language anime. Ironically, this "alternate history" has more in common with genuine **WARTIME ANIME**, but it coyly extricates itself from the real issues of WWII. Mixing the second chances of **EMBLEM TAKE 2** with the historical reenactment of **ANIMENTARY**, the series dispenses with the Allied enemy relatively quickly—there is just enough time to self-righteously shoo them out of the Pacific before more acceptable foes enter the fray. From that point on, the story is an excuse for a series of battles utilizing Axis weapons and vehicles that never left the drawing board. Compare to Ted Nomura's U.S. comic *World War II:1946*, which places similar emphasis on "what-if" technology.

A one-shot special, *Secret Launch of the Sorai* (1997), features two engineer brothers working on a secret project, who see American planes in the air and launch ahead of schedule to thwart the 1942 Doolittle bombing raid on Tokyo. It is *Deep Blue Fleet* in a nutshell—a famous Japanese defeat turned into a victory. Though some may claim that the series' value lies in its painstaking research, the Doolittle raiders are flying B-30s instead of historically accurate B-25s.

After the initial 19 episodes, the series continued as *Fleet of the Rising Sun (Kyokujitsu no Kantai)*, directed by Hiromichi Matano and backtracking a year to 1945 and the launch of Japan's latest battleship, the Yamato Takeru, which immediately trounces Germany's Bismarck II. The flagship soon leads a fleet to Europe, where, amid its spats with Hitler, it takes time out to shell Britain. As with earlier episodes, the result is an unnerving window on a very different world, one that holds the sick fascination of a traffic accident. ❸

DELINQUENT IN DRAG *

1992. JPN: *Oira Sukeban*. AKA: *I'm Ban Suke*. Video. DIR: Yusaku Saotome. SCR: Fumio Saikiji. DES: Satoshi Hirayama. ANI: Nobuhiro Nagayama. MUS: Keiji Kunimoto. PRD: Studio Signal. 45 mins. Banji Suke's parents want the best for their son, but only if the price is right. When he is expelled from all the local schools, they decide the cheapest option is to dress him up in women's clothes and send him to a girls' school. **SHAMELESS SCHOOL**–creator Go Nagai piles on the transvestite trauma, as Banji must learn how to wear bras and makeup, avoid the locker-room spies, and harbor a secret love for a fellow student.

Surprisingly devoid of nudity and sex, this "comedy" began life as a manga in *Shonen Sunday*, home of the similarly gender-bending **RANMA 1/2**. Featuring the Pantyhose Brigade (girls who fight in their underwear) and an oedipally paranoid father convinced that his son will elope with his wife, it also has evil school staff like those of Nagai's **KEKKO KAMEN**—a principal who wants to steal Banji's jewelry. However, unbelievably cheap animation makes the show look far older than it really is. The best joke in the whole sorry affair is the title, since "Oira Suke Ban" can mean either "I'm Ban Suke" or "I'm a bad girl," as in the feisty females of **SUKEBAN DEKA**.

DELPOWER X

1986. JPN: *Delpower X: Bakahatsu Miracle Genki*. AKA: *Delpower X: Explosion Miracle Happy*. Video. DIR: Masahito Sato. SCR: Sumiko Tsukamoto, Aki Tomato. DES: Ayumi Chikake, Hidekazu Shigeno, Mutsumi Inomata, Yutaka Izubuchi, Haruhiko Mikimoto, Mamoru Nagano, Masami Yuki, Iruka Tabi. ANI: Ayumi Chikake. MUS: Takahiro Negishi. PRD: Big Bang. 40 mins. As video took over with the arrival of **MADOX-01** and **ASSEMBLE INSERT**, numerous famous designers lent their names to this giant-robot comedy one-shot in which the feckless robot designer Hosogetzel tries to demonstrate that

German ingenuity can conquer the world. However, both he and his bitchy American sidekicks, Suzy and Lola, are defeated by the plucky Japanese schoolgirl Manami who pilots her grandfather's prototype robot, the Delpower X.

DEMON BEAST INVASION *

1990. JPN: *Yoju Kyoshitsu*. AKA: *Demon-Beast Classroom*. Video. DIR: Jun Fukuda, Yoshitaka Fujimoto, Juki Yoma, Kan Fukumoto. SCR: Joji Maki, Wataru Amano. DES: Mari Mizuta, Junichi Watanabe, Rin Shin, Hisashi Ezura, Toshikazu Uzami. ANI: N/C. MUS: Teruo Takahama. PRD: Daiei. 45 mins. x 6 eps., 30 mins. x 6 eps. Earth's former inhabitants return to reclaim their home world after 100 million years' absence, planning their conquest by sending rapist-agents to breed an invading army with young women. The Interplanetary Mutual Observation Agency sends three agent sisters to stop them, including the beautiful Ash, who is perhaps named for *Hunting Ash*, the 1992 live-action tentacle film from **ANGEL OF DARKNESS**–director Mitsunori Hattori. Meanwhile, Terran schoolgirls are overwhelmed by attacking space-demons, who mix violence with plaintive cries for maternal affection. Ash falls in love with an Earth boy, eventually sacrificing her own life to destroy the beast within him.

Based on a story by **UROTSUKIDOJI**'s Toshio Maeda, *DBI* repeats his insidiously clever storytelling—beneath the horrific sex and violence is a masterful exploitation of adolescent fears. Hero Muneto and sometime girlfriend Kayo pay the price of sex when she gives birth to a monster. As with the subtext of much of the **CREAM LEMON** series, most of the remaining action involves their attempts to turn back the clock to the days before the loss of innocence. The series also cleverly survives multiple endings; the threat is defeated in episode four, but returns to haunt the young lovers on vacation in Hong Kong. Muneto teams up once more with the IMO Agency, only to discover that its plan is to end the threat forever by killing Kayo. The "final" episode, with the lovers on another vacation, reveals that the Demon Beast's spirit can live on even after its body is killed.

Three two-part spinoffs were released after the original series in 1995. *Revenge of the Demon Beasts* (also available in the U.S.) featured the return of Ash's sisters, BB and Dee, with a plan to bring their sister back from the dead to fight a new enemy. *Descent of the Goddess* and *Ecstasy of the Holy Mother* continued the story in Japan, with the last of the IMO, Captain "O," helping Kayo destroy her horrific past.

DBI features a dramatic drop in quality of animation and music when compared to Maeda's earlier work and, like the similar **ADVENTURE KID**, attempted to compensate for these shortcomings by using real-life erotic stars as voice actresses. It also inadvertently contributed to anime's reputation abroad as child pornography. The American release from Anime 18 (for which the long-suffering "Moe I. Yada" turned in a thanklessly superior translation) removed the blurs, dots, and mosaics of the Japanese version, although the original animators had never intended the images to be seen uncensored. The genitals revealed are thus incompletely drawn, devoid of hair or distinguishing marks, and give the false impression that all the sexually active characters are underage. **LNV**

DEMON-BEAST PHALANX

1989. JPN: *Maju Sensen*. Video. DIR: Shunji Oga. SCR: Noboru Aikawa. DES: Hideyuki Motohashi. ANI: Eiji Takaoka, Keiichi Sato, Satoshi Saga. MUS: Hiroya Watanabe. PRD: Magic Bus, Dynamic. 45 mins. x 3 eps.
Replaying **FRANKENSTEIN** for a Japanese audience, 13 scientists seek to tap genetic powers by creating a hybrid of man and beast. Years later, 13 of their children are embroiled in a battle to undo their handiwork, while Shinichi, the son of one of the scientists, teams

up with Christian super-beings to save the world.

Often confused with **ADVENTURE KID** because of their similar Japanese titles, *DBP* is actually based on a manga by **GETTER ROBO**–cocreator Ken Ishikawa, whose inspiration was the Book of Revelation. **NV**

DEMON CITY SHINJUKU *

1988. JPN: *Makai Toshi Shinjuku*. AKA: *Hell City Shinjuku, Monster City*. Video. DIR: Yoshiaki Kawajiri. SCR: Kaoru Okamura. DES: Yoshiaki Kawajiri. ANI: Naoyuki Onda. MUS: Motoichi Umeda, Osamu Shoji. PRD: Madhouse. 80 mins.
Ten years ago, the evil Levi Ra killed Kenichiro Izayoi and cast him into a fiery pit. Ra is the earthbound emissary of the demon world and is preparing to open the portals for all his devilish allies. Only Kenichiro's son, Kyoya, can stop him, assisted by Sayaka, the daughter of an elder statesman who has just abolished nuclear weapons and solved the Arab/Israeli problem, and Chibi, a midget on roller skates. Kyoya and friends must walk into the demon-infested wasteland at the heart of Tokyo and stop Levi Ra before it is too late.

Based on a novel by **WICKED CITY**'s Hideyuki Kikuchi and directed by Yoshiaki Kawajiri, the passionless, perfunctory *DCS* (known as *Monster City* in the U.K.) is at least partly responsible for the popular mainstream notion that "all anime are the same." Opening with the stark red/blue color palette so beloved of Kawajiri, its lead character is a dead ringer for his **GOKU MIDNIGHT EYE**. Its plot is not dissimilar to the second **UROTSUKIDOJI**, which also features both a demon world trying to enter our own and a climactic battle at the Shinjuku skyscrapers. One apparent steal, however, is no such thing. An early shot that shows Levi Ra almost split in two then repair himself was two years ahead of a similar image in James Cameron's *Terminator 2*.

Strangely paced, with long spells of silence broken by cheesily awful music,

its ending is surprisingly anticlimactic, though perhaps nobody should expect too much from the story of a Ben Kenobi clone telling a Luke Skywalker clone to avenge the "death" of an Anakin Skywalker clone with a magic sword. One gets the impression that the crew were all working on autopilot, a feeling unchanged by the listless English-language dub, which inexplicably gives half the cast Tex-Mex accents while the pale Sayaka is played as a blue-blooded British consumptive. Listen for some classic Manga Entertainment "fifteened" dialogue (added to raise the rating to 15-year-olds and up in the U.K.), including, "I'm gonna tear his head off and shove it up his ass!" **LV**

DEMON WARRIOR KOJI *

1999. JPN: *Gokuraku Satsujin Choken Kan*. AKA: *Koji: Paradise Assassin Investigator, Sex Crime Detective Koji*. Video. DIR: Yasunori Urata. SCR: Takaro Kawaguchi. DES: Ayato Muto. ANI: Ayato Muto, Teruaki Murakami. MUS: Masamichi Amano. PRD: Phoenix Entertainment, Sepia. 41 mins. x 3 eps.
Koji Yamada is a man of many talents—a stuntman by day and a demon-hunter by night, he also has the ability to transform into a demon himself. With the aid of a mismatched band of superpowered assistants, he fights supernatural crimes that normal police can't even begin to touch.

Koji plumbs new depths in Toshio Maeda's futile quest to outdo his own **UROTSUKIDOJI**. Featuring a hokey gang of costumed crime-fighters, seemingly inspired by *Doc Savage*, and the usual cavalcade of demonic assaults, *Koji* is also the least well-animated of Maeda's many works. As with other later Maeda anime such as **DEMON BEAST INVASION**, there are desperate attempts to create interest through gimmickry, including "guest appearances" by the voices of erotic stars, and even uncensored shots of pubic hair. Meanwhile, bored voice actors yawn their way through scenes of depravity enacted by characters whose designs are noticeably uglier than the Maeda norm. With comedy jailbait, death by oral sex, and a rack of childhood family traumas, this replays many of Maeda's earlier themes, but the law of diminishing returns has reached such a low level by this point that these are even likely to annoy his fans. Director Urata even teases his audience, framing one scene as a flashback of his own NINJA RESURRECTION, only to reveal that it is from one of the films for which Koji is performing stunts. In other words, even the crew wish it was somewhere else. In a final irony, the distributor's attempt to cover up naked breasts with daubs of blood on the U.S. box art actually made the series look even more violent and unpleasant than it really was. ⓒⓃⓋ

DEMONIC LIGER
1989. JPN: *Jushin Raigar.* TV series. DIR: Norio Kabeshima. SCR: Noboru Aikawa, Yoshiaki Takahashi, Toshiki Inoue. DES: Miku Uchida. ANI: Miku Uchida. MUS: Hiroshi Tobisawa. PRD: Sunrise, Nagoya TV. 25 mins. x 42 eps.
Bold Earthmen in suits of "bio-armor" hold off an alien invasion in a series created by DEVILMAN's Go Nagai for the GUNDAM-studio Sunrise. Eventually the good robots, Raigar and Dolgar, are heavily damaged but still defeat the evil robot Drago, as if you couldn't guess.

DESCENDENTS OF DARKNESS
2000. JPN: *Yami no Matsuei.* TV series. DIR: Satoshi Otsuki, Hideki Okamoto. SCR: Masaharu Amiya. DES: Yumi Nakayama. ANI: Yumi Nakayama, Kazuo Yamazaki. MUS: N/C. PRD: JC Staff, WOWOW. 25 mins. x 13 eps.
Tsuzuki Asato and Kurosaki Hisoka are members of the *shinigami* (elite undead), who can use the Book of the Dead to reanimate the deceased. Based on the manga by Yoko Matsushita in *Hana to Yume* magazine.

DESERT ROSE
1993. JPN: *Suna no Bara.* AKA: *Rose of the Sands.* Video. DIR: Yasunaga Aoki. SCR: Kaoru Shintani. DES: Minoru

Yamazawa. ANI: Minoru Yamazawa. MUS: Jun Watanabe. PRD: JC Staff. 45 mins.
When Mariko Rosebank's husband and child are killed in a terrorist bombing, she is left with nothing but a rose-shaped scar and a thirst for revenge. In this one-shot adaptation of the 1989 *Young Animal* manga from AREA 88's Kaoru Shintani, Mariko joins the tactical assault squad C.A.T. The story was revived for a "manga video" visual comic in 2000. ⓝⓥ

DESTRUCTION DEVIL SADAMITSU
2001. JPN: *Hakaima Sadamitsu.* TV series. DIR: Shoichi Ohata, Yukihiro Matsushita. SCR: Masanao Akahoshi. DES: Akira Kikuchi, Tamotsu Shinohara. ANI: Masaaki Kawanami, Koichi Ohata. MUS: N/C. PRD: Studio Deen, WOWOW. 25 mins. x 10 eps.
Sadamitsu Tsubaki is a self-proclaimed vigilante armed with a wooden sword. The Exiles are a group of interstellar criminals cast into space on a long and eternal orbit that unfortunately has Earth right in the middle of its trajectory. Earth is threatened by 20 million exiles, but Sadamitsu has an important ally—Junk, his sentient helmet, made by the race who exiled the Exiles. However, Sadamitsu and Junk must also contend with Vulture, an intelligent spaceship sent to Earth to police Exile activity but which rejects Sadamitsu's help. ULTRAMAN meets GUYVER, based on a manga in *Ultra Jump* by Tadahiko Nakadaira.

DETECTIVE *
1999. Video. DIR: Akihiro Okuzawa. SCR: Takuhiro Fukuda. DES: N/C. ANI: N/C. MUS: N/C. PRD: Beam Entertainment, Akatonbo. 30 mins. x 2 eps.
Detective Higashino rescues a beautiful girl from a gang of strange men. Discovering that Ayane Akimoto was *sold* to them by her parents, Higashino begins an investigation into the modern world of slavery, tracking the life of Ayane's dead older brother, with time out for gratuitous scenes of bondage and abuse. Released in the U.S. as *Bondage Room* (2001). ⓝⓥ

British game-warden's daughter Jackie Leeds, with her pet Murphy, the eponymous **BUSHBABY**. Based on a British book, its only English broadcast was in Canada. *See entry p. 50.*

The Bushbaby

© 1992 NIPPON ANIMATION CO. LTD.

DETONATOR ORGUN *
1991. Video. DIR: Masami Obari. SCR: Hideki Kakinuma. DES: Michitaka Kikuchi. ANI: Masanori Nishii. MUS: Susumu Hirasawa. PRD: AIC. 60 mins. x 3 eps.
Tomoru skips school to hang out at the aviation museum, where he harbors secret dreams of becoming a pilot. He gets what he wants when Earth is attacked by invaders, and he signs up with the Earth Defense Force.

Despite such a hackneyed opening, *DO* plays some neat tricks with the traditions of robot shows. Tomoru lives 200 years in our future but has the problems and worries of any teenager. Despite living in a sci-fi fan's dream world, he's bored at the idea of a career in lunar finance and thinks the floating equatorial city he calls home is too uncool for words. An early scene in which Tomoru argues with a friend is a stunningly accurate prediction of that common modern malaise: a roommate who "helpfully" finishes all your computer games for you while you're out. Look out, too, for Kakinuma's tongue-in-cheek adverts for the Defense Corps, shown here long before *Babylon 5* or *Starship Troopers* got the hang of postmodern irony. Finally, there's a sweet epilogue in which we discover that

Tomoru has gotten exactly what he wished for, the chance to fly with the other pilots and someday inspire another wide-eyed museum visitor.

Scenarist Kakinuma draws the full benefit of writing directly for three hour-long episodes; without a TV series, comic, or console game to muddy the creative waters, *DO* has none of the compression or hurried storytelling of lesser shows. The robot battles and dream sequences are artfully done, though director Obari would use similar material to even better effect in his later VIRUS. Future YOU'RE UNDER ARREST–director Kazuhiro Furuhashi also worked on *DO* as a humble storyboarder.

Unfortunately, the dub is another mediocre effort from Manga Entertainment's mercifully short-lived cost-cutting experiments in a Welsh studio, and elements that are deliberately evocative (such as Hirasawa's sub-Vangelis music) will strike many as just plain unimaginative. It's also a little jarring to see that the young Tomoru's idols are actually pilots in the Luftwaffe—one of those moments when anime and Japan suddenly seem incredibly alien. *Ill. p. 161.*

DEVADASY *

2001. Video. DIR: Nobuhiro Kondo. SCR: Naoshi Tokimura. DES: Masako Goto. ANI: N/C. MUS: N/C. PRD: AIC. 70 mins. In 2012, aliens attack an overpopulated Earth ravaged by global warming, ingesting humans for their energy. The UN is helpless against the onslaught unless the SPIRIT organization's giant robot Devadasy, powered by the "sexual energy" between its selected male and female pilots, can stand firm. Unlike EVANGELION's Shinji, 15-year-old Kei needs little convincing to ditch schoolwork and climb into a cockpit with the attractive Misako, though he is dogged by schoolmate Naoki, who also carries a torch for him. Featuring giant robots, a love triangle, and a lone boy in a dormitory of girls, AIC's press notes for *Devadasy* sheepishly promised "the same as usual" but with more bla-

tant excuses for titillation. Announced as forthcoming in Japan at our deadline.

DEVIL AND THE PRINCESS

1981. Movie. DIR: Ryosuke Takahashi. SCR: Shunichi Yukimuro. DES: Yasuhiro Yamaguchi. ANI: Yasuhiro Yamaguchi. MUS: Haruo Chikada. PRD: Toei. 32 mins.
The 18-year-old princess of Tomorrow Castle has a beauty famed far and wide but a less-attractive penchant for daytime drinking. Despite this, she has plenty of suitors, including a devil wearing a cunning disguise. One day, the princess meets Snow White at her teahouse in the forest, and while the girls get acquainted, the devil kidnaps them both.

Shown in a double bill with DOOR INTO SUMMER, this adaptation of a weird "beauty and the beast" fairy tale by *Banana Fish*'s Akimi Yoshida was also the directorial debut for VOTOMS-director Takahashi.

DEVIL HUNTER YOHKO *

1992. JPN: *Mamono Hunter Yoko.* AKA: *Devil Hunter Yoko.* Video. DIR: Katsuhisa Yamada, Hisashi Abe, Akiyuki Shinbo. SCR: Sukehiro Tomita, Tatsuhiko Urahata. DES: Takeshi Miyao. ANI: Tetsuro Aoki. MUS: Hiroya Watanabe. PRD: Madhouse, NCS, Toho. 45 mins. x 1 eps., 30 mins. x 3 eps., 45 mins. x 2 eps.
Yohko Mano is the latest in a long line of devil-hunters. Torn between her grandmother's insistence that she carry on the tradition (for which she must remain a virgin) and her mother's urging to get knocked up as soon as possible, she is beset by demons who use any means possible to dispel the threat she presents. After a promising opener in which a local nice-guy is possessed and turned into a bad-boy in an attempt to seduce Yohko, later episodes fast decline in quality. She acquires a manager, Azusa (presaging a similar relationship in the later CARD-CAPTORS), calms angry spirits at a construction site, appears in her own

music video (the pointless *Yohko 4-ever*, which is sensibly bundled with other episodes in the U.S. release), then dies and rises from the dead. The sixth episode, confusingly called *Yohko2* in Japan, has Yohko defending the family honor from her lookalike cousin, Ayako. An inferior translation of the first three episodes was released in the U.K. in 1995 as *Devil Hunter Yoko* (*sic*). Producer Juzo Mutsuki would create a similar clash of traditional and contemporary ghostbusting in PHANTOM QUEST CORP. 🐱🐱

DEVILMAN *

1972. TV series, video. DIR: Tomoharu Katsumata, Nobutaka Nishizawa. SCR: Masaki Tsuji, Tadaaki Yamazaki, Susumu Takahisa. DES: Go Nagai. ANI: Kazuo Komatsubara, Takeshi Shirato, Kazuo Mori, Shingo Araki, Makoto Kunihara, Masamune Ochiai. MUS: Go Misawa. PRD: Dynamic, Oh Pro, NET. 25 mins. x 38 eps. (TV), 43 mins. (m), 50 mins. x 3 eps. (v), 25 mins. x 26 eps. (TV).
Devilman and two other demons are sent to Earth to possess humans and cause chaos. Finding two Japanese families nearby when they awake from their long slumber in the Himalayas, Devilman chooses to possess Akira Fudo (his first choice, Akira's father, having died from fright), and the bedeviled boy is adopted by the kindly Makimura family. Falling in love with his stepsister Miki, Akira forgets his original mission. His former demon overlord, Zenon, sends a succession of creatures to kill him, and Akira must call on his ill-gotten powers.

When a Japanese TV network wanted to adapt Go Nagai's *Devil-King Dante* for TV in 1972, the artist instead offered them his new *Devilman* project, already running in *Shonen Magazine*. An uneasy combination of superhero serial and macabre horror, it featured a schoolboy forced to become an agent of good by using the powers of evil. Following his TV series, Devilman would appear in Tomoharu Katsumata's theatrical short MAZINGER Z *vs. Dev-*

ilman (1973), in which Dr. Hell tries to recruit him to defeat the robot warrior of the title.

In 1987, *Devilman* was revived for a two-part video adventure directed by Tsutomu Iida, which altered much of the designs and origins while keeping a retro 1970s look. In the video Akira is a shy boy who lives with his simpering childhood friend Maki while his parents are away on a business trip. His tough friend, Ryo (the hermaphroditic son of Satan) tells him of the existence of demons, and that Earth was once occupied by this evil race. The only way to defeat a demon is to fuse with one, and Ryo convinces Akira to allow this to happen. Ryo slaughters human beings at a nightclub to summon a demon, lucking into Amon, the Lord of Darkness. Because Akira is pure of heart, he is able to control the demon within him, turning his evil powers to good use. The second episode (as in the original TV series) features a battle with Amon's former lover, Sirene, though no further episodes were made. *Devilman*'s best moments are the flashback scenes of a prehistoric, demon-infested dreamtime that owed nothing to East *or* West, but it was the messy confluence of Japanese and European mythology that brought *Devilman* down (not helped by the U.K. dubbers Manga Entertainment's inability to get some of the classical references right, though they did find the time to write new lines like, "I'm gonna rip off your head and shit down your neck!"). The same director would make the three-part *Chibi Character Go Nagai World* (1990) featuring squashed-down versions of several Nagai characters fighting at Armageddon. Akira Fudo also put in a cameo appearance in Nagai's later CUTEY HONEY.

Nagai returned to the franchise in 1997 with *Devilman Lady*, retelling the story for the more adult *Comic Morning* magazine by altering the sex of his protagonist and introducing evolutionary angles. VAMPIRE PRINCESS MIYU–director Toshihiro Hirano and ARMITAGE III–writer Chiaki Konaka adapted it

into a 26-episode TV series in 1998. Though characters from the earlier versions make cameo appearances, the remake centers on Jun Fudo, a shy fashion model (a schoolteacher in the manga) who begins to develop mystic powers. As part of Mother Nature's answer to overpopulation, a "Devil Beast Syndrome" is afflicting the world's poor, transforming them into rapacious cannibal demons. Jun, however, has been genetically engineered by her scientist father to retain her former memories after infection and uses her power to fight off further incursions.

Devilman was revived again for *Amon Devilman Revelation* (2000), a 50-minute video released to cash in on the millennium, supervised by FIST OF THE NORTH STAR's Toyoo Ashida and directed by Kenichi Takeshita. Featuring creatures designed by Yasushi Nirasawa, this chapter tied up many loose ends from the earlier versions, spooling forward in the original story to the final Armageddon. Akira now leads the demon-hunting Devilman Army, while a traumatized Miki wanders through a Tokyo in the grip of apocalyptic violence and rapine. Exploiting Akira's somewhat schizophrenic position as a force of good possessed by the ultimate evil, *Amon* is a vicious, sadistic anime in the spirit of UROTSUKIDOJI, and even features a one-on-one fight between Devilman and Satan.

The epilogue to all the *Devilman* stories was written in 1973 (only a year after the original manga) in Nagai's VIOLENCE JACK, which begins with a remorseful Satan's decision to remake the world, to reincarnate as a cripple, and to create the Slum King to punish himself, though this relationship is not apparent in the 1986 anime version. In 2000, an issue of the *Devil King Dante* manga that inspired *Devilman* was released as a "manga video." **LNV**

DIARY OF ANNE FRANK

1979. JPN: *Anne no Nikki: Anne Frank Monogatari*. AKA: *Diary of Anne: Story of Anne Frank*. TV special, movie. DIR:

Eiji Okabe. SCR: Ryuzo Nakanishi. DES: Yu Noda. ANI: Seiji Endo. MUS: Koichi Sakata. PRD: Nippon Animation, Trans Arts, Tomi Pro, Studio Orc, TV Asahi. 82 mins. (TVm), 102 mins. (m).

In 1940, Amsterdam is occupied by the Nazis. Persecuted for their Jewish faith, the Frank family is forced into hiding in a secret annex concealed in a canal-side house. The young daughter Anne begins to write down her thoughts in a diary, escaping from her situation by writing fantastic stories. Eventually, the family is discovered by the Nazis and taken away to a concentration camp.

This earnest but pretentious TV movie about the famous diarist uses four of Anne's stories (published as *Tales from the Secret Annex*) as interludes to break the monotony of her confinement: *Fear, The Wise Dwarf, Henrietta,* and *The Adventure of Bralee the Bear Cub.* Such a decision may have made cinematic sense, but it somehow trivializes Anne's plight. After the broadcast of this film, a child's viewpoint becomes a regular feature in anime about WWII, since it permits the use of Japanese characters who, like the baby-boom audience itself, had no part in the war that so dramatically altered the course of their country's history.

A second anime version was released in Japanese theaters in 1995, directed by Akinori Nagaoka. This production, from KSS and the Madhouse studio, was much more lavish than the original TV movie, featuring more realistic character designs from Yoshinori Kanemori and music by Michael Nyman, composer for *The Piano.*

DIGI CHARAT

1999. TV series. DIR: Hiroaki Sakurai, Masayuki Kojima, Tatsuo Sato. SCR: N/C. DES: Yoshiki Yamagawa. ANI: N/C. MUS: N/C. PRD: Madhouse, TBS. 25 mins. x 16 eps., 30 mins. x 4 eps. (special).

Adorning merchandise and commercials as the mascot character for the Gamers chain of stores in Japan, the cartoon ten-year-old Digiko is reputedly from the planet Digicarrot, from whence she was enticed to Earth by her love of broccoli. Landing with her friends in Tokyo's Akihabara district, she takes a job at a Gamers store with her friend Puchi Charat and leporine rival Rabi En-rose. Difficult customers and occasional adventures follow.

A four-part *DC: Summer Special* (2000) pits Digiko against new nemeses from the Black Gamer Gang, whose poverty-stricken leader Piyoko intends to kidnap her and hold her for ransom. The Black Gamers open their own shop in competition with Digiko's own, though they use sinister means to keep their customers. Digiko also appeared in cameos in **PIA CARROT**, **EXCEL SAGA**, and **FIRST KISS STORY**.

DIGIMON *

1999. JPN: *Digimon Adventure*. AKA: *Digital Monsters*. TV series. DIR: Mamoru Hosoda, Hiroyuki Kadono, Takashi Imamura, Tetsuo Imazawa. SCR: Satoru Nishizono, Hiro Masaki. DES: Kappei Nakatsuru. ANI: Hiroki Shibata. MUS: Takanori Arisawa. PRD: Toei. 20 mins. x 54 eps. (*01*), 3 x 25 mins. (m), 20 mins. x 50 eps. (*02*).

Goggle-wearing hero Taichi (Tai) and friends Izzy, Joe, Matt, Mimi, and Sora are at a summer camp like no other, where snow can fall in June and the Northern Lights appear far from the Arctic. The pals fall through a magic portal into the very different world on the pink sandy beaches of File Island, where they become embroiled in a battle between strange creatures. The kindly "digi[tal] mon[sters]" that inhabit the parallel world are being corrupted by an evil force, who inserts Black Gears into good digimon to turn them bad. As the children try to solve the mystery, their digimon companions "digivolve" into better and stronger fighters.

After a handover engineered one of the three holiday special minifeatures (2000, cut together for U.S. release as the *Digimon Movie*), a second season followed, rebranded as *Digimon 02* and set three years later, with the return of the evil Devilmon in control of a pow-

erful new energy source. Our heroes, who attend the same soccer club with the gang from the first series, team up with a new digital monster, the blue Buimon, to fight back. A third series, renamed *Digimon Tamers*, began in April 2001, moving the action into the "near-future" year of 200X.

Optioned for U.S. release in the post-**POKÉMON** gold rush, *Digimon* was inadvertently one of the most faithful translations of TV anime; the U.S. and Japanese schedules were so close together that there was little opportunity to do too much rewriting or cutting. Technically speaking, as the descendants of the *original* virtual pets featured in **TAMAGOTCHI VIDEO ADVENTURES**, Digimon have a better pedigree than Pokémon, despite only achieving approximately half the latter's ratings. The series was also dogged by legal wrangles in the U.S., when the Screen Actors Guild challenged production company Saban over the rights to residuals for the *Digimon* movie. The irony was not in SAG's claim that voice acting was a creative and skilled task that warranted better conditions, but that they had never brought it up before.

DIGITAL DEVIL STORY *

1987. JPN: *Digital Devil Story: Megami Tensei*. AKA: *DDS: Goddess Reborn*. Video. DIR: Mizuho Nishikubo. SCR: Mizuho Nishikubo. DES: Hiroyuki Kitazume. ANI: Naoyuki Onda. MUS: Usagi-gumi. PRD: Tokuma Shoten, Animate. 45 mins.

Computer geek Tamami uses the school's computer center to summon the "digital devil" Loki, soon enlisting teachers and fellow students in a dark cult. Only new-girl Yumiko is unaware of this secret, though she soon discovers that she is the reincarnation of an ancient goddess and, consequently, the only person who can put an end to Loki's violent rampages.

Based on a novel by Aya Nishitani and featuring character designs by original illustrator Hiroyuki Kitazume, this inferior horror anime enjoyed an

inferior British release, using the original spotting list from Kiseki, which retains the Japanese translator's creative romanizations of otherwise well-known mythological creatures, including Loki and Set. In Japan, it was screened on a theatrical double bill with **I GIVE MY ALL**. The story was also adapted into a computer game, which in turn was adapted into *another* anime, **TOKYO REVELATION**. **◐**

DIOXIN SUMMER

2001. JPN: *Inochi no Chikyu: Dioxin no Natsu*. AKA: *Life's World: Summer of the Dioxin*. Movie. DIR: Satoshi Dezaki. SCR: Kazuo Koide. DES: Setsuko Shibunnoichi. ANI: Setsuko Shibunnoichi, Keizo Shimizu. MUS: N/C. PRD: Sotsu Agency, Sunrise. Ca. 85 mins.

The true story of an accident in Italy in 1976, when an explosion at a biological research laboratory threatened the surrounding area with deadly dioxins and ruined the happy existence of a group of 11-year-old children. Adapted from a book by Kei Hasumi. Compare to **SEA OF THE TICONDEROGA**.

DIRTY PAIR *

1985. TV series, movie, video. DIR: Katsuyoshi Yatabe, Toshifumi Takizawa, Tsukasa Dokite, Norio Kabeshima, Masaharu Okuwaki, Koichi Mashimo. SCR: Hiroyuki Hoshiyama, Kazunori Ito, Tsukasa Tsunaga, Haruka Takachiho, Yasushi Hirano, Fuyunori Gobu, Masaaki Sakurai, Go Sakamoto. DES: Tsukasa Dokite, Fujihiko Hosono, Yoshito Asari, Katsuhiko Nishijima, Studio Nue. ANI: Kazuo Tomisawa, Tsukasa Dokite. MUS: Toshiyuki Kimori, Yoshihiro Kunimoto. PRD: Nippon Sunrise, Studio Nue, Nippon TV. 25 mins. x 26 eps. (TV) 50 mins. x 3 eps. (v), 80 mins. (m), 25 mins. x 10 eps. (*Original*), 30 mins. x 16 eps. (*DPF* videos).

Kei and Yuri are the "Lovely Angels," Trouble Consultants for the World's Welfare Work Association (3WA), a federal police force that serves the United Galactica government. Wearing skintight spacesuits that happen to be almost completely transparent (thereby looking just like bikinis) and accompanied by their "pet" ursoid Mughi and R2D2 clone Nammo, the girls are sent on missions that often end in massive explosions and collateral damage, resulting in the unkind nickname of the "Dirty Pair."

At the time they first appeared onscreen in the anime adaptation of Haruka Takachiho's CRUSHER JOE, the Dirty Pair had already featured in two novels of their own, including *The Great Adventures of DP*, which won the Seiun (Japanese Nebula) Award. The year after their anime debut, the characters won another Seiun for the book *DP Strike Back*. They were named for one of the author's favorite female wrestling teams, the Beauty Pair, while the 3WA is a reference to the World Women's Wrestling Association. The real-life Beauty Pair inspired many imitators in the wrestling field, including the Black Pair, Golden Pair, and Queen Angels—a roster that influenced several other series, including MARIS THE CHOJO and METAL FIGHTER MIKU.

Designer Dokite adapted Yoshikazu Yasuhiko's illustrations from the original novels, the third of which was timed to come out simultaneously with the debut show. Though the series was canceled early after 24 episodes, the last two parts were immediately rushed out onto video in 1985 as *DP: From Lovely Angels With Love*. The franchise stayed on video with *DP: Affair on Nolandia* (1985), directed by Okuwaki and written by PATLABOR's Ito, in which the girls are sent to an arboreal planet where they must stop an illegal genetic experiment. *Nolandia* is notable for being the only occasion in the entire anime adventures that alludes to Kei and Yuri's telepathic abilities, a major feature of the novels.

The 1987 *DP* movie, known in the U.S. as *DP: Project Eden*, pastiched Frank Herbert's *Dune* by revealing that warp travel is impossible without the rare metal vizorium. Sent to planet Agerna to stop two rival nations from destroying each other in a war over the element, the girls meet Professor Wattsman, a scientist intent on using vizorium to bring forth a powerful new life form. The same year saw the publication *The Great Adventures of DP* in English, but the duo's greatest impact on the U.S. market came in 1988 with the publication of the first of many American *DP* comics produced by Toren Smith and Adam Warren.

Though it would be several more years before the movie and video versions of *DP* would reach the U.S. through Streamline Pictures, the original TV series sold well in Europe, and ten extra shows were made in 1989 specifically to bulk out the TV run to 36 episodes for the Italian market. Stuck straight onto two-part videos in the Japanese market as *DP Wink, Masterworks, Complete, Mystery, Birth, Special, Variety, Investigation, First Final,* and *Last Fantasy*, these "bonus" episodes were released abroad by AD Vision as *Original DP*, the distributor's argument being that although they were not the initial (untranslated) TV series, they were still truer to the original than *DP Flash* (see below).

The video *DP Flight 005 Conspiracy* (1990) concentrated less on zany antics and more on a serious thriller story, as the pair are sent to investigate a space liner explosion that kills 300 passengers, though nobody attempts to claim insurance. It was to be the last anime outing to date for the original Kei and Yuri.

Takachiho would revise the characters in 1994 for *DP Flash*, which portrayed the Lovely Angels as younger, dumber, cuter investigators rendered in sharper (and cheaper) animation. Though many (including the production staff!) often assume *DPF* to be a Flashback to the characters' early years, it is actually set over a century later, starring young girls called Kei and Yuri, who look very similar to the originals but are only the latest in a series of duos to use the codename. These two new Lovely Angels undo all the good work done by the last holders of the title (Molly and Iris, some 15

Officer Natsumi Tsujimoto puts out an APB in YOU'RE UNDER ARREST!, a cop show with all the grit and realism of a dancing kitten. Despite featuring a mismatched buddy premise common to American shows, *YuA* glorifies the car chase above all other elements, except perhaps the childish interactions of its leads. A gentle situation comedy in the spirit of KAMEARI PARK PRECINCT, with excessive attention to automobile detail thrown in. Mostly harmless. *See entry p. 457.*

You're under Arrest!

years earlier), returning the codename to infamy.

Despite this convoluted back story, *DPF* struggles to recreate the fun of the original. With a complex numbering system obscuring one long succession of stand-alone episodes (there is no "story arc" worth repeating in the "serials" separately named *DPF1, 2,* and *3*), the characters of *DPF* spend very little time investigating, preferring instead to parody other anime with a visit to a 20th-century theme park or to experience minor difficulties in their attempts to have a vacation. The *DPF* video adventures play up the girls' eye-candy qualities (admittedly, not entirely absent in the appeal of the original), giving them nude transformation sequences and missions such as winning a volleyball tournament, designed as little more than an excuse to spool through a line of sports-show training clichés, leavened with regular wobbles of fan-service cleavage. But while Takachiho's originals continue in their novel form with the most recent *DP: A Legend of Dictator*, *DP*'s most successful incarnation abroad remains the U.S. comic rather than the anime that inspired it. *Ill. p. 447.* Ⓝ

DISPATCHES FROM THE SPIRIT WORLD

1996. JPN: *Jigoku Reikai Tsushin*. AKA: *Spiritual Report: Occult Shop from Hell*. Video. DIR: Junichi Sato. SCR: Miyuki Takahashi. DES: Akihito Maejima. ANI: N/C. MUS: N/C. PRD: Toei. 23 mins. x 2 eps.

Three young boys are chased by a ghost and run to an occult shop for help. There, they are given a selection of magical items that will allow them to send malevolent spirits back to hell. After successfully dealing with their initial assailant, they go into business as professional ghostbusters, righting wrongs all over Tokyo.

Beginning as a best-selling children's book by Karin Kagetsu and illustrated by Akihito Maejima, this *Ghostbusters* rip-off became a live-action film directed by **BE-BOP HIGH SCHOOL**'s Hiroyuki Nasu in 1996. Controversial for introducing scary themes in what was supposedly a children's film, the live version was refused a general rating, and its original target audience was forced to settle for the anime.

DIVINE CHANGELING ENCHANTMENT

1988. JPN: *Shinshu Sudamahen*. AKA: *Fantasy Kingdom War*. Video. DIR: Satoshi Dezaki. SCR: Tetsuaki Imaizumi, Kazumi Koide. DES: Keizo Shimizu. ANI: Keizo Shimizu. MUS: Yukari Omori. PRD: Magic Bus. 30 mins. x 6 eps.

In medieval Japan's Genroku era, the young warrior Yoshiyasu Yanasawa approaches Takaharu, the leader of the Hazuki clan in search of the power of the "Golden Dragon," unaware that the power of the dragon flows within the very bloodstream of the maiden Orie. The quest broadens out into a fight over a line of gold ore in the Nasu mountains, and the Tokugawa lord Tsunayoshi learns of the Golden Dragon's magical powers when he tries to rape Orie. The samurai Kageshichiro Hagetsu tries to dispel Tsunayoshi's evil spirit before it awakens the dragon completely and brings chaos to Japan. The animated version of a period drama by Tsuneo Tani.

Director Dezaki also made the two-part spinoff series, *Cold Moon Spirit Cutter* (1989), a samurai-era detective saga starring the popular supporting character Itto Kanzuki, who has a constant quest to help those in need. **NV**

DNA SIGHTS 999.9 *

1997. JPN: *Fire Force Danasight Four-Nine*. Video. DIR: Takeshi Shirato, Masayuki Kojima. SCR: Tatsuhiko Urahata. DES: Leiji Matsumoto. ANI: Aki Tsunaki. MUS: Katsuo Ono. PRD: Madhouse. 45 mins.

After Earth is devastated in an apocalyptic meteor shower, it is taken over by a military cartel calling itself the Trader Forces, which is secretly supplied by an alien woman called Photon. A second woman, Mellow, "casts her cosmic consciousness" at Earth, where it crashes in 2024 with the impact of another meteorite. Daiba, a local boy, investigates the crash site but is arrested by the Traders. Contacted telepathically by Mellow, he is told that he, an Earth girl called Rei, and a third party whom they will have to find themselves (who turns out to be a cat) are all examples of the next stage in evolution. Aided by Mellow, the three must overthrow the Traders.

"This contains the essence of all my previous works. It's a space opera that also focuses on Earth's environmental problems," said creator Leiji Matsumoto at the time of this anime's release; neatly sidestepping the issue of yet another rewrite of his standard character templates reusing ideas and imagery from his **GALAXY EXPRESS 999** and **QUEEN EMERALDAS**.

There are a few new ideas, such as the magma-dwelling "underlife" creatures briefly encountered, but essentially this is a run-of-the-mill teen adventure using familiar-looking characters in an attempt to drag in longer-standing fans of Matsumoto's other work. That was certainly the way it was sold in Japan, where press releases could not resist hinting that both **CAP-TAIN HARLOCK** and the Yamato spaceship from **STAR BLAZERS** would make cameo appearances.

DNA^2

1994. JPN: *DNA2 (Dokokade Nakushita Aitsuno Aitsu)*. AKA: *(Dumb Nerd Always Astray)*. TV series. DIR: Junichi Sakata. SCR: Tatsuhiko Urahata. DES: Kumiko Takahashi, Masakazu Katsura, Takeshi Koike. ANI: N/C. MUS: Eiji Takano. PRD: Powhouse, Nippon TV. 25 mins. x 12 eps. (TV), 25 mins. x 3 eps. (V).

Junta Momonari is a hapless boy with a real complex about sex—the merest thought of it makes him physically sick. But one day he will become a Mega-Playboy, siring 100 equally fecund children, and agent Karin Aoi is sent back from the future to stop his genes from causing an uncontrollable baby boom. Unluckily for her, she shoots him with the wrong drug and ends up creating the very Mega-Playboy she was sent back to prevent.

Despite the popularity of similar boy-meets-dozen-girls shows like **TENCHI MUYO!**, this adaptation of **VIDEO GIRL AI**–creator Masakazu Katsura's 1994 *Shonen Jump* manga underperformed in its anime incarnation. Even though *DNA2* contains all the elements thought to guarantee success, including a geeky-Jekyll-and-macho-Hyde subplot as Junta's playboy persona takes periodic control of his body and libido, the series was taken off the air early and ignominiously forced to finish its run on video. With revisionist hindsight, the video episodes were shuffled among the actual TV episodes and now comprise the second, third, and final chapters in the 15-chapter (5-tape) series available in Japanese stores. It was parodied in the pornographic computer game *Timestripper*. **N**

DOCTOR CHICHIBUYAMA

1988. Video. DIR: Tetsuro Amino, Masa Watanabe. SCR: Yoshio Urasawa. DES: Yutaka Kawasuji. ANI: Yutaka Kawasuji. MUS: The Chichibuyama Band. PRD: Studio Ship, Pony Canyon, Ashi Pro, Fuji TV. 30 mins. x 2 eps.

In this short-lived black comedy based on a 1983 manga by Keiichi Tanaka originally serialized in *Comic Gekiga Murajuku*, Dr. Chichibuyama, the perverse, sunglasses-wearing head of a hospital way out in the mountains, terrorizes patients with the help of his lover and a sexy young nurse. Though the manga rode the fad of "Lolita Complex" titles typified by **CREAM LEMON**, the anime version appeared at the end of the boom and failed to ignite much interest. Two five-minute sections were broadcast on Fuji TV's midnight *All Night Fuji* program, presumably to promote the video. **Ⓝ**

DOCTOR DOLITTLE

1990. JPN: *Dolittle Sensei Monogatari*. AKA: Stories of Doctor Dolittle. Video. DIR: Seiji Okuda. SCR: N/C. DES: Tom Ray. ANI: N/C. MUS: N/C. PRD: Knack, My Video. 48 mins. x 3 eps.

Hugh Lofting's famous children's story about a doctor who could genuinely talk to the animals was animated here in a U.S.–Japan coproduction featuring input from designer Tom Ray, who worked on famous Western cartoons such as *Tom and Jerry* and *The Pink Panther*.

DOCTOR FABRE THE DETECTIVE

2000. JPN: *Fabre Sensei wa Meitantei*. AKA: *Dr. Fabre Is a Famous Detective; Inspector Fabre*. TV series. DIR: Osamu Nakamura, Masami Yoshikawa. SCR: Osamu Nakamura. DES: N/C. ANI: Nobuteru Tanaka, Masashi Shiozawa, Scott Frazier. MUS: N/C. PRD: Enoki Film, IG Film. 25 mins. x 26 eps.

The adventures of a detective modeled on *Sherlock Holmes* but dwelling in 19th-century Paris, where he solves mysteries centering around the great exhibition, the invention of cinema, and other new developments, rubbing shoulders with the famous people of the age in the manner of *Young Indiana Jones*. A fittingly fin-de-siècle mixture of the detective boom of the **YOUNG KINDAICHI FILES** with the new retro craze of **TREE IN THE SUN**.

DOCTOR MAMBO AND JIBAKO THE THIEF

1982. JPN: *Doctor Mambo to Kaiketsu Jibaki: Uchu yori Ai o Komete*. AKA: *Doctor Mambo and Jibako the Thief: From Space with Love*. TV special. DIR: Yoshio Yabuki. SCR: Akinori Matsubara. DES: Toyoo Ashida. ANI: Kiichiro Suzuki. MUS: Kazuo Sugita. PRD: Toei, Fuji TV. 84 mins.

In this one-shot adaptation of one of Morio Kita's *Dr. Mambo* SF novels, the dashing Dr. Mambo and his unlikely sidekick, Jibako the thief, help Princess Laura, former ruler of Eden, regain her birthright from the usurping president Capo.

DOCTOR SLUMP

1981. JPN: *Doctor Slump and Arale-chan*. TV series/special, movie. DIR: Minoru Okazaki, Yoshiki Shibata, Daisuke Nishio, Akinori Nagaoka. SCR: Masaki Tsuji, Shunichi Yukimuro, Tomoko Konparu, Michiru Shimada. DES: Shinji Koike. ANI: Shinji Koike. MUS: Takeo Watanabe. PRD: Fuji TV, Toei. 25 mins. x 243 eps., 90 mins. (m), 52 mins., 48 mins., 38 mins. (m), 25 mins. x 26? eps. (TV).

In the wacky hamlet of Penguin Village, Dr. Senbe "Slump" Norimaki decides to put together the perfect robot woman from data collected in pop idol photos and porno mags. Instead of perfection, he ends up with Arale-chan, a bespectacled and inquisitive tyke with superhuman strength, and the odd couple get into many wacky adventures. They are helped in their quest for the weird by Slump's penchant for crazy inventions, such as time machines, quantum cloning devices, an invisible gun, and X-Ray spectacles.

Akira Toriyama's original 1980 manga ran in *Shonen Jump* for 18 volumes. This anime version came about after an abortive attempt at a live-action show made producers realize that the only way to capture the cartoony spirit of the original was by making a cartoon. The other occupants of Penguin Village provide a menagerie of amus-

ing characters in the fashion of Toriyama's later **DRAGON BALL**, including a pig that does a rooster's job of waking everyone up in the morning, a superhero that must eat prunes to transform, and Gatchan, a metal-eating flying creature.

Dr. Slump is one of anime's most successful shows, scoring a massive TV rating of 36.9 at its peak (the "mega-hit" **EVANGELION** managed a paltry 7.1). It has also been a hit abroad, particularly in the large anime markets of Hong Kong and Italy, but has yet to make it to the English language. The series also spun off several "TV specials" often premiered in theaters during summer festivals. Since the TV episodes often consisted of small vignettes, these "movies" consisted of little more than extended anthologies, like *Hello! Mysterious Island* (1981), which often spoofed other films of the day such as **QUEEN OF A THOUSAND YEARS** (*Who Is the Real Queen of a Thousand Years!?*, 1981) and **DON QUIXOTE** in *Heroic Legend of Penguin Village* (1986), which is about Slump undertaking a dangerous quest to the supermarket to get more toilet paper.

The first true *DS* movie, called simply *Dr. Slump* (1982), sends the characters on a space mission to planet Takeyasaodake, a mission loaded with parodies of the *Star Wars* movies, **STAR BLAZERS**, and **GALAXY EXPRESS 999**. Later "movies" were closer in length to the TV specials they replaced, including *The Great Race Around the World* (1983) and *The Secret Treasure of Nanaba Castle* (1984), both glorified episodes at little more than 50 minutes. Though straggling TV specials would make it a lingering death, the official grand finale was *Megapolis the Dream City* (1985), a "movie" of only 38 minutes, in which Arale and company befriend some monsters from outer space.

The series returned for several New Year's TV specials in 1992, although only two of the vignettes, *The Tearful Film Director* and *The Day New Year Didn't Arrive*, were actually new; the other episodes were old *DS* "movies." The franchise was properly revived in 1997, when a new TV series, without the direct involvement of Toriyama, became the first anime to use computer coloring instead of cels.

DOCTOR SURPRISE

1998. AKA: *Dokkiri Doctor*. TV series. DIR: Kazunori Mizuno. SCR: Satoru Nishizono, Aya Matsui, Yoshiyuki Suga, Tsutomu Kaneko. DES: Mari Kitayama. ANI: Masaya Onishi, Shinsuke Terasawa, Manabu Fukusawa. MUS: Yoshimoto Hizawa. PRD: Visual Works, Studio Pierrot, Fuji TV. 25 mins. x 27 eps.

The prestigious Shirabara Clinic has had four previous directors since its founding in the 19th century, but none have been quite so memorable as the fifth incumbent, Haruka Nishikikoji. With a fat face, "a jaw like FRANKENSTEIN," a gentle manner, and a genius way with patients, he's a mad scientist working for the side of justice. Lumbered with a cute nursing assistant after the lovely Miyuki's parents go off on a round-the-world trip, Haruka finds himself with a surrogate family, soon becoming embroiled in her younger sister's trials at the local primary school. But Haruka has always carried a torch for Miyuki, although he cannot think of a way to confess his true feelings, in this lighthearted adaptation of JUDGE-creator Fujihiko Hosono's original manga. *Ill. p. 411.*

DOG OF FLANDERS *

1975. TV series, movie. DIR: Yoshio Kuroda. SCR: Ryuzo Nakanishi, Yoshiaki Yoshida, Shunichi Yukimuro, Tsunehisa Ito, Aki Matsushima, Yukiko Takayama, Tomohiro Ando. DES: Yasuji Mori. ANI: Toshikazu Sakai, Shinya Takahashi. MUS: Takeo Watanabe. PRD: Nippon Animation, Fuji TV. 25 mins. x 52 eps., 25 mins. x 24 eps. (TV), 103 mins. (m).

In 19th-century Europe, Nello, a young Flemish boy, loves to draw and is inspired by the art of Rubens to become a painter. One day, Nello adopts the dog Patraasche and nurses

the ailing animal back to health. He falls in love with the local girl Alois, whose family will never let her marry him because he is too poor. Meanwhile, his grandfather dies, and soon Nello and Patraasche are all that are left of the family. Eventually, they too die and are buried together.

Based on the 1872 book by Marie-Louise de la Ramée, an Englishwoman of French extraction who confusingly wrote under the Flemish pseudonym Oui'da Sebestyen, this miserable tale of death and despair remains much-loved for its sheer emotional extremes. With a maudlin love of sacrifice and a weepy ending in which the faithful pair freeze to death on Christmas Eve amid the majestic works of art in Bruges Cathedral, it is perhaps no surprise that it has proved so popular with the sentimental Japanese (though there have also been several live-action U.S. versions, the first as early as 1914, the most recent in 1999). This anime version was the first of the WORLD MASTERPIECE THEATER series.

Remade as a 15-minute episode of the *Manga World Fairy Tales* series in 1976, *DoF* came back again as a 24-part TV series in 1992. This Tokyo Movie Shinsha version was directed by Kanetsugu Kodama and "set in the small French village of Flanders," according to one Japanese source. Not to be put out by such geographical fudging, the tale was resurrected again in 1997, this time for a lavish feature film directed by the original series' Kuroda, with the location now officially "Belgium." This version was released in the U.S. by Pioneer, although the distributor inexplicably removed 11 minutes of footage and the entire Japanese language track for the DVD edition.

DOG SOLDIER: SHADOWS OF THE PAST *

1989. JPN: *Dog Soldier*. Video. DIR: Hiroyuki Ebata. SCR: Noboru Aikawa. DES: Masateru Kudo. ANI: Motomu Sakamoto. MUS: Hitomi Kuroishi. PRD: Movic, Animate Film, JC Staff. 45 mins.

Japanese-American commando John Kyosuke Hiba is forced to face ghosts from his past when he is sent in to steal back an AIDS-like virus from the clutches of a criminal syndicate. His mission becomes more than simply saving the world on behalf of the Pentagon; he takes the opportunity to avenge the deaths of his parents. Based on a manga by STORY OF RIKI–creator Tetsuya Saruwatari, this Rambo clone was released in America by U.S. Manga Corps. ⬤NV

DOGTANIAN AND THE THREE MUSKEHOUNDS *

1981. JPN: *Wan Wan Sanjushi*. AKA: *Dogtanian and the Three Invincible Musketeers*. TV series. DIR: Taku Sugiyama, Shigeo Koshi. SCR: Taku Sugiyama. DES: Shuichi Seki. ANI: Shuichi Seki, Takao Kogawa. MUS: Katsuhisa Hattori. PRD: Nippon Animation, TBS. 25 mins. x 24 eps., 25 mins. x 10 eps.

D'Artagnan (Dogtanian) is a young dog who wants to be one of the fabled musketeers, but his hot-headed ways get him into trouble when he challenges the Earl of Rochefort (Black Moustache) on the way to Paris. Eventually he becomes a musketeer, teaming up with three experienced guard dogs, Athos, Porthos, and Aramis. When war breaks out between France and England, Dogtanian and his friends must undertake a mission to save the honor of the French queen, who has befriended the English ruler—a King Charles Spaniel, of course. The spiteful feline spy Milady, however, is on their trail at every turn.

This touching, funny, and exciting retelling of the THREE MUSKETEERS in the canine spirit of WOOF WOOF 47 RONIN became a much-loved serial on British children's television, though its Japanese origins were completely obscured and one "Dave Mallow" was credited as the director. The excruciating pun in the title was a direct translation of the original Spanish coproducers' *D'Artacan y los Tres Mosqueperros*. As well as four separate

TV compilations on video in the U.S., a movie-length edit, *One for All and All for One*, was released in the U.K. Ten extra episodes were made solely for foreign broadcast by Shigeo Koshi but never shown in Japan, though they are presumably a major part of the "second series" seen abroad as *The Return of Dogtanian*.

DOKABEN

1976. AKA: *Lunchbox*. TV series. DIR: Hiroe Mitsunobu, Eiji Okabe. SCR: Tatsuo Tamura. DES: Eisuke Endo. ANI: Nobuhiro Okaseko. MUS: Shunsuke Kikuchi. PRD: Nippon Animation, Fuji TV. 25 mins. x 163 eps.
Compulsive eater Taro "Lunchbox" Yamada is a new transfer student at Takaoka (Hawk Hill) middle school. A gentle and kind individual, he soon shows his incredible strength in the school judo club. The baseball team soon realizes that he could be useful and brings him onto the team as its "little giant." Before long, Dokaben is the ace hitter on the team, but this brings forth bad feelings in some of his teammates. This typical sports anime was based on a 31-volume manga by Shinji Mizushima, creator of SONG OF THE BASEBALL ENTHUSIAST. Dokaben also has a cameo appearance in GO FOR IT, TABUCHI.

DOLLIMOG

1986. JPN: *Dollimog Da!* AKA: *It's Dollimog!; Mock and Sweet*. TV series. DIR: Hiroshi Fujioka. SCR: Yasunori Kawauchi, Seiji Matsuoka, Ryuji Yamada. DES: Susumu Shiraume. ANI: Yoshihiko Takakura, Masami Abe, Teruo Kigure. MUS: Goro Nogi. PRD: Japan Comart, NTV. 25 mins. x 49 eps.
In 8th-century Europe, the Frankish king Charlemagne sends out his paladins to invade the neighboring countries. In the midst of this chaos, Dollimog the mole and his sister, Hanamog, come to the aid of humans in trouble. They understand human speech and are walking the "dollimog road" on a quest to bring down Charlemagne and his evil sorcerer, Babar.

Based on a story by writer Kawauchi in which underground dwellers try to preserve peace in their own world by interfering in ours, this original piece of medieval moling only stayed with the Charlemagne plot for 23 episodes—the rest of the series leaps 300 years ahead to the time of the Crusades.

DOMAIN OF MURDER *

1992. JPN: *Hello Harinezumi: Satsui no Ryobun*. AKA: *Hello Hedgehog: Domain of Murder*. Video. DIR: Akira Suzuki. SCR: Akinori Endo. DES: Masaaki Kawanami. ANI: Masaaki Kawanami. MUS: Noriyoshi Matsuura. PRD: Animate Film. 51 mins.
Private investigator Goro Nanase, whose nickname "Hedgehog" is a pun on "Watchman" and "Bed-head," is hired by Mrs. Toyama to locate her missing husband. The only clue, his face on a poster proclaiming that he's wanted for murder. The race is on, Nanase against the Tokyo Police, through the snowbound Japanese countryside to the slush and dirty sleet of small-town Japan.

Sadly, *Domain of Murder* was the only episode from the 24-volume manga in *Young Magazine* to be animated. Artist Kenshi Hirokane also created the bestselling *Section Chief Kosaku Shima* and the manga masterpiece for the over-60s, *Shooting Stars in the Twilight*. This is the Japan familiar to Hirokane's adult audience, a lower-middle-class suburb of hard-drinking salarymen and smoking mothers. The production was ill-served in English (with a distributor who managed to mistranslate the names of the creator, writer, main cast, *and* director!), though the subtitled edition retained the excellent voice of Shigeru (ARION) Nakahara in the lead, and there's a wonderful cameo from Yo Inoue (PATLABOR's Kanuka Clancy) as a bar-girl past her prime. Endo's script contains some beautifully observed moments, such as a reverse interrogation when Nanase and his ally double-team the cop they find in her apartment. The subtitles leave the mar-

Despite the evil plots of a scarred lion and his laughing hyena minions, a young cub, who just can't wait to be king, is the hero of this first anime TV series to be broadcast in color. Osamu Tezuka's KIMBA THE WHITE LION was partly funded by the American network NBC and widely syndicated in the U.S. during the 1960s. A movie reedit was nominated for a Golden Lion at the Venice Film Festival. The series returned as the subject of controversy in the 1990s, when Disney representatives denied it had any influence on *The Lion King*. See entry p. 204.

Kimba the White Lion

© TEZUKA PRODUCTIONS • MUSHI PRODUCTIONS

velous Japanese-style Raymond Chandler–inspired dialogue untouched, and linguists should watch for the timeless moment when Inoue changes from polite-friendly to superpolite-hostile.

DOMINION *

1988. AKA: *Dominion:* Tank Police. Video. DIR: Koichi Mashimo, Takaaki Ishiyama, Noboru Furuse. SCR: Koichi Mashimo, Hiroshi Yamaguchi. DES: Mitsuharu Miyamae, Koji Ito. ANI: Hiroki Takagi, Osamu Honda. MUS: Yoichiro Yoshikawa. PRD: Agent 21. 40 mins. x 4 eps., 30 mins. x 6 eps.
Newport City, an artificial island in Tokyo Bay, is already overcrowded with giant bioengineered termite mounds for buildings by 2010. Nanotechnology gone wrong chokes the city with a bacterial fog, and the unhappy citizenry is besieged by high-tech crime syndicates. To combat this spree, the government forms the self-explanatory Tank Police.

Dominion was the first professional manga by APPLESEED-creator Masamune Shirow, published in *Comi-Comi* in 1988, and displays a sense of humor that tails off in his later works. Like PATLABOR, it has a lowly lady cop, Leona Ozaki, who works for a paramilitary police force, bestows a pet name on her machine, and spars flirtily with her partner, though the show concentrates more on comedy than slice-of-life drama. Thus we have Leona's immediate boss, the *Dirty Harry*—wannabe Brenten constantly arguing with his hypertense Chief, as well as the standard semi-love interest Al and computer nerd "Megane" Lovelock.

After a prequel beginning with Leona joining the Tank Police and the creation of her beloved tank Bonaparte out of spare parts, the anime series draws on early chapters of the manga, pitting the police against Buaku, a rogue android, who is accompanied by the infamous, scantily clad Puma Twins, Annapuma and Unipuma. Taking the piss is the order of the day—the Buaku gang wants to steal urine samples from uncontaminated citizens and attempts to deter pursuit by throwing inflatable dildoes all over the street. As in the manga, there are hints that Buaku's motives are secretly honorable; in a *Blade Runner* pastiche, he is searching for information about his creator, and his urine thefts may be part of a plan to deal with the pollution (less ecologically damaging than in the manga but still there). Buaku and Leona are forced to team up against the Red Commando terrorists in the next two episodes as they try to recover a valuable painting, and, at the finale, Buaku seemingly reforms his evil ways.

In 1992, Shirow revisited the franchise in *Comic Gaia* with a parallel story, dropping Buaku and Al, promoting Leona to Squad Leader, and giving her command of an entire fleet of Bonaparte-model tanks. Adapted into anime by Noboru Furuse as *New Dominion Tank Police* (1993), the new, slightly darker series brought Al back, restored the Puma Twins to a life of crime (they had reformed in the manga and joined the squad), and told a far darker story as the squad battles the evil corporation Dai Nippon Gaiken, which is developing a virtual drug as a spinoff from its weapons research. These new episodes were renumbered for the U.K. release and are hence sometimes known as episodes 7–12 of the "old" *Dominion*, rather than 1–6 of the "new." **LNV**

DON CHUCK

1975. JPN: *Don Chuck Monogatari*. TV series. DIR: Yukizo Takagaki, Tsutomu Yamamoto. SCR: Tomohiro Ando, Susumu Yoshida, Tsutomu Yamamoto. DES: Eiji Tanaka, Yasuo Ikenodani. ANI: Eiji Tanaka, Yasuo Ikenodani. MUS: MAC. PRD: Knack, TV Tokyo. 25 mins. x 26 eps. (TV1), 25 mins. x 73 eps. (TV2).

Deep in the Zawazawa Forest by the Jub-Jub river lives Don Aristotle the beaver and his child, Don Chuck. Aristotle frets that his son will grow up strange without a mother, and Chuck starts to associate with beaver girl Lala, a rabbit called Mimi, and Daigo the bear cub. The quartet gets into all sorts of trouble as Chuck slowly grows into an adult.

Don Chuck began as the mascot character for a fairground before starring in children's books by Shizuo Koizumi and Makio Narita and eventually gaining this anime outing. The measure of the series' success is in the fact that the "real" Chuck mascot began to take on attributes of the anime character in the months that followed. A second series, *New DC* (1976), lasted even longer and introduced a family of out-of-place koalas.

DON DRACULA

1982. TV series, video. DIR: Masamune Ochiai. SCR: Takao Koyama. DES: Osamu Tezuka. ANI: Masayuki Uchiyama. MUS: Masayuki Yamamoto. PRD: Jin Pro, TV Tokyo. 30 mins. x 4 (orig., 8 total) eps., 90 mins. (v).

Count Dracula, his daughter Chocula, and servant Igor move from Transylvania to Tokyo, where Dracula has trouble finding enough victims on his night sorties. Chocula helps her father, though it also interferes with her studies at night school. Trouble arrives in the form of famed vampire-hunter Dr. Rip van Helsing, who comes to Tokyo in search of his archenemy. An anime adaptation of Tezuka's manga serial in *Shonen Champion* that was truncated by the bankruptcy of its production house. Of the planned 26 episodes, only 4 were shown on Japanese TV. The 8 episodes completed were eventually released straight to video in a feature-length movie edit. Similar light-hearted treatment of vampire folklore can be found in **PHANTOM QUEST CORP.** Dracula's voice actor Kenji Utsumi played the same role in the more serious **DRACULA: SOVEREIGN OF THE DAMNED.**

DON QUIXOTE

1980. JPN: *Zukkoke (Bumbling) Knight Don de la Mancha*. TV series. DIR: Kunihiko Yuyama, Shinya Sadamitsu, Soji Yoshikawa, Osamu Sekita. SCR: Akiyoshi Sakai, Soji Yoshikawa, Tomomi Tsutsui, Junzo Toriumi, Masaru Yamamoto. DES: Noa Kawai. ANI: Kazuo Tomisawa, Kunio Watanabe, Satoshi Hirayama, Osamu Nabeshima. MUS: Nobuyoshi Koshibe. PRD: Ashi Pro, Tokyo 12 Channel. 25 mins. x 23 eps.

Don Quixote sets out in search of his beloved Princess Dulcinea, but the girl he desires is only a "princess" insofar as she is the daughter of Carabos the pirate "king." In order to impress Carabos, Quixote carries out several criminal missions on behalf of his would-be father-in-law. Discovering that "Dulcinea" is an imposter, Quixote sets out once more in search of her, accompanied by his faithful servant, Sancho Panza, and his horse, Rozinante. Miguel de Cervantes's classic knight who tilted at windmills is brought to life here in this action-comedy, with the character's insanity brought to the fore by a manic performance from **DON DRACULA'S** Kenji Utsumi, who positively foams at the mouth.

DON! BRUTAL WATER MARGIN

1992. JPN: *Don! Gokudo Suikoden*. Video. DIR: Osamu Sekita. SCR: Tadashi Hirose. DES: Masafumi Yamamoto. ANI: Takeshi Osaka. MUS: Manako Nonoyama. PRD: JC Staff. 50 mins. x 2 eps. Takekichi and Masakazu are two tough guys who are forced to go underground when they lose their boss in a turf war. This modern update of the classic Chinese novel *Water Margin* (see **SUIKODEN**) is another gangster tale from **GOODFELLA**'s Hiroshi Motomiya, originally published in *Big Comic*. **NV**

DONKIKKO
1965. TV series. DIR: Koichi Ishiguro. SCR: Koichi Ishiguro, Yoshio Nunogami. DES: Shotaro Ishinomori. ANI: Yoshio Nunogami, Yoshikazu Inamura. MUS: Kiyoko Yamamoto. PRD: B Pro, Fuji TV. 25 mins. x 21 eps.
Short tales of Donkikko, his boy assistant, Dondon, and their pet duck, Gonbei, as they search the town for missing items, help Grandpa run an antique shop, and eventually go to live in an old abandoned train. An adaptation of **CYBORG 009**–creator Shotaro Ishinomori's manga from *Shonen Book* magazine.

DON'T GIVE UP: WAY OF THE MAGIC SWORD
1995. JPN: *Don't Give Up: Ma Ken Do.* Video. DIR: Kazuya Murata. SCR: Yasuo Komatsuzaki. DES: NAO Shimizu, Sayuri Isseki. ANI: Sayuri Isseki. MUS: Koji Sakuyama. PRD: OLM. 29 mins.
Officer Doro, a good demon, attempts to recruit Mai Tsurigino as a demon-hunter to police the activities of less scrupulous creatures from the Other Side. Mai refuses but gets dragged in anyway when her little sister, Hikari, takes the job. Doctor Mad (a mad scientist) operates on juvenile delinquent Rei Kamiyoji to turn him into a super-weapon to conquer both the human and demon worlds. Rei kills his creator and goes on the rampage, and it's up to the newly recruited demon-hunters to stop him. A **DEVIL HUNTER YOHKO** rip-off originating in an SNES console game.

DON'T LEAVE ME ALONE DAISY *
1997. JPN: *Misutenaide Daisy.* TV series. DIR: Yuji Muto. SCR: Satoru Nishizono, Ryota Yamaguchi, Kazuhisa Sakaguchi. DES: Atsuko Nakajima. ANI: Shigeru Ueda, Naoki Hishikawa. MUS: Kazuhiro Wakabayashi. PRD: Studio Deen, TV Tokyo. 25 mins. x 12 eps.
Reijiro Tekuno (Techno) is a super-rich recluse who lives in a nuclear bunker. He uses his IQ and bank balance to build walls of technology around himself and his fantasy world, where net-surfing is as physical an experience as the real thing. One day (in a scene reminiscent of **KIMAGURE ORANGE ROAD**) Hitomi's hat is blown away by the wind and lands in Techno's garden. He is immediately smitten with her and insists on calling her Daisy, claiming her as his property, much to her distress. This new twist on geek-meets-girl, intercut with survivalism-by-Microsoft, has a *deus ex machina* in the bearded form of Grandpa fulfilling a promise to Techno's dead parents, and a fly in the ointment in the butch senior classmate, Ani, who appoints herself to ride shotgun on Techno's schemes. A salutary message about how life won't always comply just because you point money or a computer at it is buried beneath a lighthearted school romance in the spirit of **JUBEI-CHAN THE NINJA GIRL**. Strangely endearing despite being a comedy about a stalker, Noriko Nagano's original 1988 manga somehow caught the "virtual" spirit of the times, though it was by no means her most popular—unadapted geek-meets-girl tales from the same creator include *Otaku Master* and *God Save the Sugekoma-kun.*

DOOMED MEGALOPOLIS *
1991. JPN: *Teito Monogatari.* AKA: *Capital Story.* Video. DIR: Rintaro, Kazuhiko Katayama, Koichi Chigira. SCR: Akinori Endo, Takaichi Chiaki. DES: Masayuki. ANI: Shinji Tanaka, Yumiko Kawakami, Osamu Kobayashi. MUS: Kazz Toyama. PRD: Madhouse. 47 mins. x 4 eps.
In 1908, the ghost of Yoshinori Kato, a soldier killed in the Sino-Japanese War, kidnaps the beautiful Yukari and offers her as a human sacrifice to Masakado, Tokyo's unofficial guardian deity. Masakado refuses Kato's offer, but Yukari gives birth to Yukiko, assumed to be Masakado's spiritual heir. The years pass, and Kato tries again to seize power at the death of the emperor in 1912. Child-prodigy Yukiko fights him off and he retreats to the underworld. By 1923, the traumatized Yukari and her daughter live with Yukari's brother, Tatsumi, and his new wife, Keiko, who is an undercover priestess charged with defeating Kato. Another coup attempt by Kato almost succeeds, resulting in the 1923 Tokyo earthquake (found in many anime, including **UROTSUKIDOJI**, **OSHIN**, and **SMART-SAN**). Tatsumi confesses that Yukiko is *his* daughter, and that Yukari's madness is the result of her rape by her own brother. Keiko goes out to face Kato one final time, revealing herself to be the Goddess of Mercy. She fuses with Kato, and Tokyo is saved, leaving Tatsumi to wonder that if even Kato can be forgiven, there might be hope for him.

With a virginal, sleepwalking heroine in jeopardy, a powerful, predatory sorcerer, and a wise old man seeking to keep them apart, **ALEXANDER**-creator Hiroshi Aramata's original novel is a Japanese retelling of Bram Stoker's *Dracula*. Though often labored and unnecessarily slow, the series still has many good points, notably a well-handled incest subplot and a surreal palette of colors, textures, and set pieces. Later episodes move into *Omen* territory, as Yukiko struggles with her alleged destiny as the child of the Devil, though the finale is pure anime, with hallucinogenic visions and mass destruction à la **AKIRA**. The story is loaded with historical references—not only does Kato hail from the birthplace of medieval magician Abeno Seimei (hero of *Master of Yin and Yang*), but the period background also shows many of Tokyo's familiar landmarks under construction. Tokyo's guardian Masakado is a genuine historical figure, a 10th-century rebel from the region, just one of the real figures in a story that views the century since Tokyo became Japan's capital as an era in which the country itself was demonically possessed. The year 1940, as Japan prepared for WWII, was the thousandth anniversary of Masakado's death. Kato represents a modern malaise, a soldier forged in the fires of Meiji Japan's first foreign war, who dies in the battle of Dalian in 1894, returns to stoke nationalist arrogance after the defeat of Russia in 1905, and observes the "dark valley" of 1920s militarism. In this regard, he is a distant cousin of the prodigal soldier who terrorizes Tokyo in PATLABOR 2. In a further subtext, the death of the Meiji Emperor had a recent parallel for a home audience that had just mourned his grandson Hirohito.

There are separate U.S. and U.K. dubs, each with their own merits. Manga Entertainment's uses British accents, which work well with the overpolite, middle-class characters but still leave them sounding unsettlingly twee. Streamline's U.S. dub, however, doesn't put quite as much effort into duplicating the haunting folksongs that carry much of the suspense in the middle episodes.

The story was also made into the live-action movies *Tokyo: The Last Megalopolis* (1988) and *Dictator of the City* (1989), directed by Akio Jissoji and Takashige Ichinose. A third film, *Capital Story: Secret Report* (1995), was a live-action epilogue set in the present day, when evil spirits use the traumatized survivors of the earlier films to return to our world. **OM**

DOOR INTO SUMMER, THE

1981. JPN: *Natsu e no Tobira*. Movie. DIR: Mamoru Masaki, Toshio Hirata. SCR: Masaki Tsuji. DES: Keiko Takemiya, Yoshiaki Kawajiri. ANI: Kazuo Tomisawa. MUS: Kentaro Haneda. PRD: Toei. 59 mins.
In 1864 France, Marion is a young man forced to spend the summer at his boarding school because his uncaring mother has recently remarried and does not want him around. Stuck with a small number of companions for the long vacation, Marion soon becomes involved in a series of duels, brawls, and romantic entanglements, such as

falling in love with the mayor's daughter, Ledania, but also developing strong feelings for Claude, a boy in his class. Based on the romance manga in *Hana to Yume* by TOWARD THE TERRA–creator Keiko Takemiya, this story was published later than the author's similar SONG OF WIND AND TREES but beat it to anime adaptation, thus gaining some notoriety. This is one of the very rare cases of a mass-market release for a gay anime. Even in supposedly more liberal times, such stories tended to go straight to video, e.g., FAKE or MY SEXUAL HARASSMENT. **N**

DORAEMON

1973. TV series. DIR: Nobuo Onuki, Hiroshi Fukutomi, Hideo Nishimaki, Tsutomu Shibayama, Takeyuki Kanda. SCR: Ryohei Suzuki, Masaki Tsuji, Seiji Matsuoka, Masaaki Sakurai, Kazuyoshi Okubo. DES: Fujiko-Fujio, Kunio Okawara. ANI: Fusahito Nagaki, Sadao Tominaga, Hidekazu Nakamura. MUS: Nobuyoshi Koshibe, Shunsuke Kikuchi. PRD: Studio Take, Studio Joke, NTV Animation, Shinei, Nippon TV. 25 mins. x 26 eps., 10 mins. x 617 eps., 25 mins. x 900+ eps., films approx. 90 mins. each.
In the 22nd century, the impoverished descendants of Nobita Nobi pool their resources and send Doraemon, a cut-rate, blue robot cat, back in time to turn him into a more successful person. Doraemon dazzles the schoolboy Nobita and his friends with his endless array of futuristic gadgets, including a portable dimension-door and head-mounted rotor-blades. However, Nobita's great-great-grandchildren are so poor that they have sent a malfunctioning mentor whose plans often go awry. Though Doraemon always saves the day, it's normally his fault it needs saving.

Often credited Lennon-and-McCartney-style to the Fujiko-Fujio duo who created QTARO THE GHOST, *Doraemon* was actually a solo project for Hiroshi "Fujiko" Fujimoto. An ongoing series fully expected to top 2,000 episodes by the end of 2004, the simple stories and

almost timeless animation have kept the series a perennial favorite. Like LUPIN III, it is an original "retro anime" that never had to be revived and has reared several generations of Japanese children. The lineup never changes—Nobita and his cat, along with prissy love interest Shizuka, sneaky intellect Suneo, and hulking lummox Jaian play in their neighborhood (which, with its open spaces and woodlands, is perhaps the only part of the series to have dated), boast about their abilities, and call each other's bluff. With the threat of undesirable forfeits, such as stuffing an entire plateful of spaghetti up the loser's nose, Nobita turns to Doraemon for help, and the cat's techno assistance causes more trouble than it is worth.

Doraemon movies have become a regular feature of the Japanese spring break. In *Nobita's Dinosaur* (1980), a harmless prehistoric pet assumes gargantuan proportions and must be returned to its proper era before it eats Tokyo. When Doraemon returns it to the wrong group of dinosaurs, it has to be rescued, only to need rescuing *again* when it is kidnapped by a hunter from a 24th-century zoo (note how even this feature version can easily break into three episode-length chapters). This was followed in successive years by *Nobita the Space Colonist, Nobita's Magic Tower, Nobita's Undersea Fortress, Nobita Goes to Hell, Nobita's Little Star Wars*, and *Nobita and the Iron Warrior*, the latter released in the year of creator Fujimoto's death, 1986. After a one-year hiatus, Doraemon was back again in 1988 with *Nobita's Parallel* JOURNEY TO THE WEST, then *Nobita at the* BIRTH OF JAPAN, *Nobita's Animal Planet, Nobita's Animal* ARABIAN NIGHTS, *Nobita in Snow Country, Nobita's Tin-Plate Labyrinth*, and *Nobita's Fantastic* THREE MUSKETEERS. After this rash of pastiches, perhaps more conservative choices in the absence of Fujimoto, a slight change of emphasis came with the 1995 movie, *2112: The Birth of Doraemon*, which cleverly recapped the series' origins for another new generation before returning to form with *Nobita's Galactic Express*, *Nobita's Clockwork City*, *Nobita's South Sea Adventure* (which has the biggest box office to date and is the eighth-highest-grossing animated film in Japan), *Nobita Gets Lost in Space*, the Aztec-themed *Nobita and the Legend of the Sun King*, and, in the year 2001, *Nobita's Winged Heroes*.

The robot cat has also appeared in literally dozens of TV specials over the last 20 years, many of which were combined with other specials to create still more "movies," including *It's New Year!*, *It's Summer!*, *It's Autumn!*, *It's Winter!*, *It's Spring!*, *Summer Holiday*, *Doraemon Meets* **Hattori the Ninja**, *Featherplane*, *What Am I for Momotaro?*, *Come Back Doraemon* (which was, ironically, repeated several times), *Doraemon and Itchy the Stray*, *Doraemon's Time Capsule for 2001*, and *Treasure of Shinugami Mountain*. Later outings also featured cameos from Doraemon's "little sister" from the future, Dorami-chan, who got several short films of her own, starting with *Dorami-chan: Mini-Dora SOS* (1981). The concept was employed many times by other creators, most notably in the saucy time travels of **DNA²** and **Visionary**.

DORATARO
1981. JPN: *Fusen no Dorataro*. AKA: *Wandering Taro and His Balloon*. TV series. DIR: Tomohiko Takano, Kozo Kusuba. SCR: Kozo Kusuba. DES: Yasuji Mori. ANI: Takao Kogawa. MUS: Masayuki Chiyo. PRD: Nippon Animation, Fuji TV. 25 mins. x 13 eps.
After many years of wandering, Taro returns to Cat Island to meet his sister, Sakura, who has stayed on the island with their adoptive parents, and to woo the beautiful ship captain, Haruko. Though his family is pleased to see him, they all come to realize that the long separation has seen them grow into different people, and the return of the prodigal son has only emphasized how far apart they have all become. An anime pastiche of the long-running live-action **Tora-san** series.

DORORO
1969. TV series. DIR: Gisaburo Sugii, Osamu Dezaki, Yoshiyuki Tomino, Ryosuke Takahashi. SCR: Ryohei Suzuki, Toru Sawaki, Taku Sugiyama. DES: Osamu Tezuka. ANI: Hideaki Kitano. MUS: Isao Tomita. PRD: Mushi Pro, Fuji TV. 25 mins. x 26 eps.
A warlord promises 48 demons that he will donate the body parts of his unborn son in exchange for power. The baby is born as little more than a lump of flesh and is cast into a river, from which it is rescued by a kindly physician. He replaces the missing parts with prostheses, and the child, now a grown man called Hyakki-maru, resolves to slay the 48 demons and regain each of his missing limbs and organs. As he sets off, he teams up with Dororo (baby-talk for *dorobo*, Japanese for thief), a girl thief whose parents once tried to lead an uprising.

Dororo began as a 1967 manga by **Astro Boy**–creator Osamu Tezuka. Inspired in part by Shirato's **Manual of Ninja Martial Arts**, which featured similar Marxist undertones, it incorporates elements of Tezuka's **Black Jack**, another driven, patchwork hero with a little-girl sidekick. The manga series was canceled early, before Tezuka's planned shift in focus to Dororo's coming-of-age, and the anime version retains the slightly misleading title—the stories broadcast remain primarily the tale of Dororo's *companion*. From episode 14 onward, this was reflected in a name change, to *Dororo and Hyakki-maru*. Director Sugii and a roster of future big-names emphasized a realistic look, making a virtue out of the monochrome production. Tezuka originally intended to make the show in color (and even made a color pilot) but was prevented from doing so by the low budgets approved by Fuji TV. The story has been cited as a major influence on one of the 1990s' best-selling manga, Hiroaki Samura's *Blade of the Immortal.*

DORORON ENMA
1973. JPN: *Dororon Enma-kun*. TV

See entry p. 331.
Romeo's Blue Sky
© 1995 NIPPON ANIMATION CO., LTD.

series. DIR: Kimio Yabuki, Keisuke Morishita, Takeshi Shirato, Fusahito Nagaki, Tomoharu Katsumata, Satoshi Dezaki. SCR: Masaki Tsuji, Tadaaki Yamazaki, Shunichi Yukimuro, Masami Uehara. DES: Kimio Yabuki. ANI: Kazuhide Tomonaga, Kazuo Mori, Yoshinori Kanemori. MUS: Hiroshi Tsutsui. PRD: Dynamic Planning, Toei, Fuji TV. 25 mins. x 25 eps.
All the obvious hallmarks of a production from Go Nagai, creator of **Devilman**, as the King of Hell discovers that several of his Earthbound minions are not causing mayhem but secretly plotting to overthrow him. He sends his nephew, Little Enma, to solve the problem, and Little Enma teams up with miniskirted Yukiko, daughter of the Snow Princess (see **Japanese Folk Tales**), and Kappael the water-demon (a kappa) to form the Japanese Monster Patrol. Enma also has a sentient hat called Chapeau, a coward who always advises against danger but will always help out his young master in the end. Hiding out at the house of manga fan Tsutomu, who christens them, the group hunts down those who have abused the laws of Hell. Their guide is Count Dracula himself, a disgraced demon who failed to report the conspiracy, and who sulkily acts as Enma's

Tokyo guide despite resenting having to take orders from a little brat. "Doro-ron" is Japanese onomatopoeia for the sound of a spell occurring, loosely approximated by "Kapow!"

DOTANBA'S MODERN MANNERS

1984. JPN: *Dotanba no Manner*. AKA: *Last-Minute Manners*. TV series. DIR: Hiroshi Yoshida. SCR: Tomoko Misawa, Osamu Murayama, Saburo Goto. DES: Sanpei Sato. ANI: Tadao Wakabayashi. MUS: N/C. PRD: Fuji TV, Eiken. 6 mins. x 284 eps.

An introduction to etiquette through the hapless antics of Mr. Dotanba, who manages to put his foot in it in innumerable social situations. Gems of life-saving wisdom include tips on how to use a toilet, what *not* to say to your co-workers, how to avoid getting slapped by pretty girls, and exactly what to do to make foreign business trips go wrong. Based on a four-panel strip by Sanpei Sato in the *Asahi Shinbun* newspaper. Another Sato strip was released as *Video Manga: Yuhi-kun* (1984), although it was not technically "anime," consisting of narration over still panels. The same team would go on to make the even more successful **KOTOWAZA HOUSE**, a series of tips for health and well-being.

DOTERAMAN

1986. TV series. DIR: Shinya Sadamitsu, Hiroshi Yamada, Yoshiyuki Suga. SCR: Takao Koyama, Toshiki Inoue, Yoshiyuki Suga. DES: Mayori Sekijima, Yoshio Mizumura. ANI: Yoshio Mizumura, Chuichi Iguchi. MUS: Kohei Tanaka. PRD: Tatsunoko. 25 mins. x 20 eps.

Shigeru Suzuki is an everyday salaryman at an everyday Tokyo company in an everyday part of town with an interdimensional gateway to a world of demons. As devils with punning names try to invade the planet, Shigeru and the demon-hunter Zukan-Socknets recruit Hajime Sato and his friend Mariko Nakamura to don superhero costumes and fight back.

DOUGRAM: FANG OF THE SUN

1981. JPN: *Taiyo no Kiba Dougram*. AKA: *Fang of the Sun Dougram; Sun Fang Dougram*. TV series. DIR: Ryosuke Takahashi, Takeyuki Kanda. SCR: Ryosuke Takahashi, Hiroyuki Hoshiyama, Yuji Watanabe, Ryohei Suzuki, Sukehiro Tomita. DES: Soji Yoshikawa, Kunio Okawara. ANI: Kaoru Izumiguchi. MUS: Toru Fuyuki. PRD: Sunrise, TV Tokyo. 25 mins. x 75 eps.

Planet Deroia claims independence from Earth, and Terran forces set out to put down the revolt. Kurine, son of the chairman of Earth's Federal Congress, sides with the Deroians and becomes a terrorist. Forming the "Fang of the Sun" organization with his friends Rocky, Chico, and Cavina, he operates the Dougram giant war robot designed by the guerrilla leader, Dr. Samaline. Meanwhile, Kurine's father, Donan Kashim, is under threat from internal machinations as his secretary plots to seize power for himself, and the adoring Lady Daisy sets off to follow Kurine, for whom she has fallen in a big way.

One of many clones of **GUNDAM**, but one that was a robot debut for **VOTOMS**-creator and father of "real robot shows" Ryosuke Takahashi.

DOWNLOAD

1992. JPN: *Download: Namu Amida Butsu wa Ai no Uta*. AKA: *Download: Song in Loving Homage to Amida Buddha*. Video. DIR: Rintaro. SCR: Yoshiyuki Suga. DES: Yoshinori Kaneda. ANI: Takao Noda. MUS: Hiroshi Kamiyatsu. PRD: AIC, Artmic. 47 mins.

Shido, a priest, is a genius in two fields—computer hacking and lechery. For the sake of the beautiful Namiho, he takes on evil corporate president Echigoya in a battle of wits and skill. Based on the PC Engine game created by Wataru Nakajima.

DOWNTOWN

1997. TV special. DIR: Kenji Shimazaki. SCR: N/C. DES: Toyoo Ashida. ANI: Toyoo Ashida. MUS: N/C. PRD: Toei, Fuji TV. 30 mins.

Two class clowns take their humor out into the streets, terrorizing members of the public. Falling behind at school, they join the Yoshimoto Talent Agency and become the "fists of Yoshimoto," better known as the comedy duo "Downtown." They make their first TV appearance in 1987 and their own series, *No Job for Kids*. In 1996, they become Japan's richest comedians and are honored the following year by this anime biopic.

DRACULA: SOVEREIGN OF THE DAMNED *

1980. JPN: *Yami no Teio Kyuketsuki Dracula*. AKA: *Dracula: Vampire Emperor of Darkness; Tomb of Dracula*. TV special. DIR: Minoru Okazaki, Akinori Nagaoka. SCR: Tadaaki Yamazaki. DES: Hiroshi Wagatsuma. ANI: Hiroshi Wagatsuma. MUS: Seiji Yokoyama. PRD: Toei, TV Asahi. 81 mins.

In modern-day Boston, Domini (Delores) is offered in sacrifice as a bride of Lucifer by the occultist Lupeski, but she is stolen away by Dracula. At first intending to drink her blood, the vampire instead falls in love with her. Wheelchair-bound Quincy (Hans) Harker and Rachel van Helsing, the son and granddaughter of Dracula's old enemies, realize that some Boston "murders" are his handiwork. They recruit Frank Drake, a descendant of Dracula ashamed at his ancestor's evil, as a vampire-hunter. Months later, on Christmas Eve, Domini gives birth to Dracula's son, Janus. Lupeski, who has been informed of Dracula's true identity, offers to baptize Janus, cornering Dracula in a church. Dracula evades the attack, but Lupeski accidentally shoots and kills the infant Janus. Dracula flees, and, having lost her son and lover, Domini plans to kill herself. However, God brings Janus back from the dead (as a fully grown man) in order to create the ultimate vampire-hunter. Before Janus can kill his father, Dracula and Domini are transported to Hell by Satan, for whom their love is an unbearable abomination. Satan blasts Dracula into ashes, but Domini's holy love resurrects Dracula once more, this time as a *mortal*. When Lilith (Lila), a New York vampire created by Dracula, refuses to bite him to restore his immortality, Dracula flees to Transylvania. Dueling with the new Lord of the Vampires, Dracula reasserts his authority and saves peasant children from walking corpses. Despite signs that Dracula has rejected evil, the vampire-hunters locate him, and Harker kills both himself and Dracula with a bomb hidden in his wheelchair. Frank and Rachel admit their feelings for one another, and Janus flies home to tell Domini the news. His divine mission accomplished, Janus is restored to infant form to be raised by Domini.

A remarkably faithful adaptation of the first 50 or so issues of the Marvel Comics *Tomb of Dracula* series. The designs look unorthodox for anime, chiefly because they adhere to the original comic artwork by Gene Colan, though neither Colan nor the comic-writer Marv Wolfman are credited in the animated version. Less serious takes on Dracula appear in **DON DRACULA** and **DORORON ENMA**. Toei negotiated with Marvel in the 1970s about producing animated versions of several superheroes, though the only product of this was the eventual live-action *Spider-Man* team show. **FRANKENSTEIN** would follow the next year.

DRAGON BALL *

1986. TV series, movies. DIR: Minoru Okazaki, Daisuke Nishio, Kazuhisa Takenouchi, Katsumi Endo, Haruki Iwanami, Akinori Nagaoka. SCR: Yasushi Hirano, Toshiki Inoue, Takao Koyama, Michiru Shimada, Yuji Endo, Tetsuo Imazawa, Tatsuo Higashino, Mitsuo Hashimoto. DES: Tadamasa Tsuji, Yuji Ikeda. ANI: Minoru Maeda, Ryukichi Takauchi, Masayuki Uchiyama. MUS: Shunsuke Kikuchi. PRD: Fuji TV, Toei. 25 mins. x 153 eps., 45 mins. x 3 films, 25 mins. x 291 eps. (*DBZ*), Ca. 45–70 mins. x 14 films, 25 mins. x 64 eps. (*DBGT*).

Son Goku (Sun Wu-Kong) is an orphan martial artist, taught by the Master Kamesennin (Roshi) and enlisted by Bulma, a pretty girl whose father owns the Capsule invention corporation, to help her search for the seven legendary Dragon Balls. If brought together in the presence of the dragon god, Shen Long (Shin Long), these balls will grant a single wish. The two assemble a band of pilgrims, and, with time out for many martial arts tournaments and fights with divine beings, slowly gather the seven orbs. Members include Yamcha the highwayman; his shapeshifting feline partner, Pooal; Oolong the pig; Goku's future wife, Chichi; and Goku's Buddhist classmate, Krilyn. They must also fight off other groups, including the Red Ribbon organization, which wishes to change the space-time continuum by destroying Goku. Eventually, the high demon Piccolo uses the Dragon Balls to rejuvenate himself then kill Shen Long, while Goku and his gang travel to another world to use *their* Dragon Balls instead and prevent the alien overlord Frieza from getting them himself.

Tiring of his **DOCTOR SLUMP** and seeking a clean break from Western inspirations, creator Akira Toriyama plucked elements from **JOURNEY TO THE WEST** for this follow-up. Redeveloping his early strip *Dragon Boy*, which incorporated Jackie Chan homages, he published *Dragon Ball* in 1984, and the series was soon animated. With a reset-to-zero gimmick in the balls' unerring habit of scattering themselves throughout the universe and taking a year to recharge, the anime was able to stretch itself out for a formidable run, becoming one of the smashes of the late 1980s. It was less successful in the U.S., where only 26 episodes were shown before the distributors Funimation ditched the rest of the series and relaunched with *DBZ* (see below, though in 2001 they announced they would go back and fill in the gap).

Short "movie" versions followed as part of double and triple bills, beginning with Nishio's *DB: Legend of the Dragon* (1986), in which Goku fights the evil Pasta and Pongo. The same director made *DB: Sleeping Beauty in the Magic Castle* (1987), while Takenouchi took over for the final film, *DB: Marvelous Magical Mystery* (1988), in which the cast of *DB* wanders into *Doctor Slump*'s Penguin Village for a crossover. All formed parallel stories designed not to interfere with the continuity of the series, which eventually finished in 1989.

The *DB* sequel, *DBZ*, jumps three years into the future when an older Goku is now married with a son, Gohan. Because this is where many foreign-language versions begin, early episodes often seem like a massive class reunion at which the viewer knows nobody. Goku is attacked by the alien Raditz, who reveals that Goku is his brother, a Sayajin alien, sent to destroy the planet many years ago. Goku refuses to blow up his adopted home and opposes the invading Sayajin, dying and then being reborn as a blond-haired "Super Sayajin." Violence and some nudity were cut for the U.S. release, but even in this bowdlerized form, the series remained popular.

This series also had a thriving series of short "movie" spinoffs, beginning with *DBZ* (1989) and then following with two a year, one for each major school holiday. These included *The World's Strongest* and *Dead Zone* (both 1990, and released in the U.S. following the success of the *DBZ* TV series), *Super Sayajin Son Goku* and *Tree of Might* (both 1991, and U.S. releases), *Collision: Billion Powered Warriors* and *Extreme Battle: Three Super Sayajin* (both 1992), *Ignite! Burning Fight! Greater Fight! Super Conflict Fight!*, and *Galaxy Flex! Very Threatening Guy* (both 1993), *Dangerous Duo! Super Warriors Never Rest* and *Super Warrior Destructive Fist: I Am the Victor* (both 1994), *Return Fusion! Goku and Vegeta* and *Strike Out Dragon Punch: Who'll Get Goku?* (both 1995), and, at last, the 80-minute feature *The Strongest Way* (1996).

DBZ came off the air in 1996, a few months after Toriyama pleaded exhaustion and stopped drawing the manga. Rebranded as *Dragon Ball G(rand) T(our)* the following month, it featured the return of arch-nemesis Emperor Pilaf with yet another set of Dragon Balls. The emperor accidentally wishes for Goku to be a child once more, so the new kiddie-friendly Goku sets out on another galactic adventure with Pan (his granddaughter) and an older version of Trunks (son of Bulma and Goku's alien nemesis-turned-buddy Vegeta). Directed by Osamu Kasai, the new series seemed to have lost the magic and ended in November 1997. Tellingly, this was also the same time as Toriyama's *Doctor Slump* was brought back on air, perhaps showing that the artist wasn't quite so tired of his original creation after all. The story also exists in a tacky live-action 1996 Cantonese adaptation, *DB: The Movie*, directed by Joe Chan.

DRAGON CENTURY *

1988. JPN: *Ryuseiki*. Video. DIR: Hiroyuki Kitazume. SCR: Noboru Aikawa. DES: Hiroyuki Kitazume. ANI: Hiroyuki Etsutomo. MUS: Michiaki Kato. PRD: AIC. 30 mins. x 2 eps.

Miserable teenager Riko wishes for her city to be destroyed. Dragons appear in the sky from an unknown dimension but are killed by government forces. A lone survivor, the baby dragon Carmine, is reared in secret by Riko and former soldier Shoryu. Demons appear in the sky, summoned by the impurity of human hearts, and Carmine reveals that with the dragons sent to oppose them now dead, Riko will soon get her apocalyptic wish. Riko changes her mind and rides Carmine to defeat the demon king. As Riko breathes her last, the sky cracks open, filled with dragons come to defeat evil.

With teen angst and interdimensional holocaust, this forerunner of **EVANGELION** had an afterthought sequel set 300 years after the invasion. On a traumatized Earth, another young girl, Lucillia, wishes to avenge her father's death in the dragon-fighting tournament and enlists the help of

Carmine (now known as Vermilion) in doing so. From an idea by Ryukihei, creator of the *Dragon Wars* manga.

DRAGON CHRONICLE

1989. JPN: *Maryu Senki*. AKA: *War Chronicle of Magical Dragons*. Video. DIR: Tatsuya Okamoto. SCR: Chuichi Watanabe. DES: Naoyuki Onda. ANI: Naoyuki Onda. MUS: Tadamasa Yamanaka. PRD: AIC. 30 mins. x 2 eps.

A mixture of Oriental history and legend in the spirit of **YOTODEN** and **DARK MYTH**, as Miki Chiyoko, modern-day descendant of an ancient clan expunged from Japanese history books by a jealous emperor, summons one of the four Chinese creatures responsible for defending Earth. Conjoining with the Blue Dragon, he discovers that the three other beasts have scattered into other bodies, and he must find them if he wants to join forces with them. The others are revealed as drunken priest Gendo (Black Warrior), handsome potter Hiyu (White Tiger), and pretty Japanese teenager Shizue (Vermilion Sparrow), who all stand against Miki as he tries to enlist them in a scheme of evil. **NV**

DRAGON FIST

1991. Video. DIR: Shigeyasu Yamauchi. SCR: N/C. DES: Shingo Araki, Michi Himeno. ANI: Hideki Kazushima. MUS: Kenji Kawai. PRD: Agent 21. 40 mins.

Chinese transfer student Ling Fei-Long is attacked by boys at his new school and saved by the female martial arts student Yuka. Later, at a karate tournament, Ling discovers that Yuka is a clone, part of a secret military project. But Ling has a secret of his own—he is a member of one of four clans in the Chinese mountains, descended from mythical beasts (in his case, the White Dragon) and endowed with psychic powers. He has been banished to Japan for killing a human, but his past is catching up with him. Based on a manga by Shu Katayama, serialized in *Wings* magazine, mixing romance and rough stuff.

DRAGON HALF *

1993. Video. DIR: Shinya Sadamitsu. SCR: Shinya Sadamitsu. DES: Masahiro Koyama. ANI: Masahiro Koyama. MUS: Kohei Tanaka. PRD: Production IG. 30 mins. x 2 eps.

Ruth the dragon-slayer falls in love with a dragon, and they settle down and produce a manic offspring called Mink, the titular dragon-half. The evil king plots to murder Ruth and take his wife for himself. Mink and her friends are obsessed with Dick Saucer, an idol singer who moonlights as a dragon-slayer. They try to get into his concert but are thwarted by Mink's rival, Princess Vina, a half-blob girl resentful of her genetic inheritance. Eventually, Saucer squares off against Mink and is defeated with a laxative potion that sends him scurrying to the toilet. Based on a 1989 manga by Ryusuke Mita, *Dragon Half* is a fan favorite and deservedly so, with an energetic sense of fun that switches constantly between normal and squashed-down cartoon versions of the characters, playful satire straight out of Warner Bros. cartoon comedies like *Road Runner*, and a very Japanese sense of humor that includes children in a medieval village having to forage for food before they can go shopping for CDs. Remembered less for its genuinely zany action than for the closing theme, which features Mink (played by **SAILOR MOON**–actress Kotono Mitsuishi) singing a song about cooking to the tunes of Beethoven's fifth, seventh, and ninth symphonies. It still makes the authors laugh even now; what can we say?

DRAGON KNIGHT *

1991. Video. DIR: Jun Fukuda, Kaoru Toyooka. SCR: Akira Hatta. DES: Ako Sahara, Akira Kano. ANI: Yuma Nakamura. MUS: N/C. PRD: Agent 21. 45 mins. x 2 eps.

The knight Yamato Takeru must rescue a number of damsels in distress imprisoned in a demonic castle near Strawberry Fields. Although he has a reputation for ogling the naked charms of the women he saves, he wishes to save the one he genuinely loves. Based on the Masato "elf" Hiruta computer game in which defeating monsters was rewarded by pictures of girls in various states of undress. Not to be confused with the unrelated LORD OF LORDS: DRAGON KNIGHT or with YAMATO TAKERU, which is slightly less unfaithful to Japanese myth. 🅝🅥

DRAGON LEAGUE *
1993. TV series. DIR: Nobuhiro Takamoto, Takashi Yamaguchi. SCR: Hideki Mitsui, Kenichi Araki. DES: Kazuyuki Kobayashi. ANI: Kazuyuki Kobayashi, Hideo Kudasaka, Junichi Tokaibayashi. MUS: N/C. PRD: Studio Gallop, Fuji TV. 25 mins. x 39 eps.
In a fantasy world populated by humans, animals, and dinosaurs, religion is based on soccer. Amon boasts that he is the greatest player in the world and trains his son, Tokio, in the forest until the boy is good enough to be considered "the second-greatest." Amon takes his son to the kingdom of Elevenia, whose soccer team has won the Dragon League five years in a row. Settling an old rivalry, Amon is challenged to a rematch by Elevenia's star player, Leon Legacius, who defeats him with the Golden Ball and turns him into a small dragon. If Tokio is ever to see his father in human form again, he must take over the local junior team and transform its players into winners, in a bizarre combination of DRAGON BALL and CAPTAIN TSUBASA. Tokio's relationship with Leon undergoes a transformation after Tokio defeats him in sudden-death overtime playoffs— Leon becomes Tokio's mentor and later team coach when they are called upon to play against the hellspawn Warriors of Darkness. A similar angle on sports-as-worship appears in GALACTIC PIRATES, though later episodes take a far darker turn. Presaging BATTLE ATHLETES, the entire religion is ˜ revealed as an attempt to hold off invasion—*real* dragons from an alternate dimension have given King Win of Elevenia a single generation to train a team that can hold off their champion

players. The grand finale features a literal death match, as stone "Death Dragons" destroy a city every time the dragon-team scores a goal, while Tokio's team desperately fights a losing battle.

DRAGON PINK *
1994. Video. DIR: Wataru Fujii, Hitoshi Takai. SCR: Itoyoko. DES: Itoyoko. ANI: N/C. MUS: N/C. PRD: Pink Pineapple, AIC. 35 mins. x 3 eps.
A fantasy sex romp about slave girl Pink putting on the cursed Panties of Torajima and literally becoming a sex kitten. Pink and her master, Santa the swordsman, must fight their way through the forest of Tajif with elfin sorcerer Pierce and Bobo the barbarian. The gang track a monster in episode two, but have to leave Pink as a security deposit at an inn when they run out of jewelry to barter. The final part has the heroes rescued by Pierce's magic, but from an unexpected source.
Based on the Itoyoko manga, serialized in *Penguin Club* and *Hot Shake* magazines, that quickly spawned a computer game, a garage kit, this inevitable anime adaptation, and the question on everyone's lips—was "dragon" '90s Japanese slang for "soft-core"? 🅛🅝🅥

DRAGON RIDER *
1995. Video. DIR: Katsumasa Kanezawa. SCR: Tetsuya Taiseki. DES: Tomo Kino. ANI: N/C. MUS: N/C. PRD: Pink Pineapple. 30 mins. x 2 eps.
In Carnus village, the beautiful Callis is powerless to prevent the death of her mother, though she herself is saved by Ryke, a would-be dragon-rider searching for a suitable mount. In this porno anime based on a manga in *Comic Papipo*, Callis transforms into a Red Dragon when she gets passionate or angry, and a different kind of mounting soon ensues. 🅝🅥

DRAGON SLAYER *
1992. JPN: *Dragon Slayer: Eiyu Densetsu: Oji no Tabitachi.* AKA: *Dragon Slayer: Legend of Heroes: Voyages of*

When the goddess Belldandy offers to grant a wish to lonely Japanese boy Keiichi, he wishes for *her*. Hey presto, instant girlfriend, but also instant banishment from his boys-only dorm and instant in-laws in the form of her divinely intervening sisters. This mix of *Bewitched* and the magical-girlfriend genre, which stretches back to COMET-SAN, was based on the manga by Kosuke Fujishima. The production of an anime movie of the series was reputedly delayed by the prophecies of Nostradamus. *See entry p. 282.*

Oh My Goddess!

the Prince. Video. DIR: Tadayuki Nakamura. SCR: Kenichi Matsuzaki. DES: Ken Ishikawa, Hisashi Hirai. ANI: Hisashi Hirai. MUS: Fujio Sakai. PRD: Amuse Video. 30 mins. x 2 eps.
Faaren is a peaceful and happy realm ruled by a wise king, until the Demon Lord Ackdam invades with his black legions and terrifying dragon, killing the king and capturing the queen. Aswel's last brave old knight, Rias, spirits young Prince Sirius to safety. Ten years later, the teenaged Sirius returns to help Faaren's peasants overthrow Ackdam, slaying Ackdam's demon-baron Zanji at a mine. In revenge, Ackdam sends his chief henchman, Zagi, who transforms into a giant fire-breathing dragon. Zagi slays Rias and captures Sirius. But Sirius is rescued from Ackdam's dungeon by Ryunan, a brave knight from a neighboring kingdom, who is organizing Faaren's peasant rebellion. Sirius is taken to the rebellion's headquarters under the command of Rias's twin brother, Aaron (a good way to have a tragic death scene without losing the character). Aaron's granddaughter, the tomboyish Sonya (combination comic relief and love interest), a wizard-intraining, nurses Sirius back to health and demands to join the boys in slay-

ing Ackdam's orcish minions. The rebellion grows so serious that Ackdam threatens to execute Queen Felicia the next day if Sirius does not surrender. This sets the deadline for the final attack on Ackdam's castle. In preparation, Sonya has Sirius escort her to "the abandoned Temple of the Old Ones" (apparently copied from photos of Mayan temple ruins) where she can get a mystic weapon that will ensure Ackdam's defeat. She does not tell Sirius that the weapon is a dragon that she will animate with her soul, giving up her human form forever.

At the grand climactic battle, supporting-character wizard Roe reveals that he and Ackdam were classmates in magic school, and it is his duty to personally destroy Ackdam for betraying his vows to use his powers for good. The Sonya-dragon kills the Zagi-dragon, and the strength of Sirius's love for Sonya restores her human body. At the last minute, Ackdam breaks free of Roe and flees. While the rest of the party sets off in pursuit, leading-man Sirius elects to stay behind with his mother and help rule the kingdom, in the only unexpected twist to a standard fantasy template.

An early release for the U.S. company Urban Vision, *DS* features an early example of so-bad-it's-good dialogue, with priceless gems such as, "Your reign of terror is nearing its end, you dog!", and the unforgettable, "Now you die, hellspawn creature!"

DRAGON WARRIOR *

1989. JPN: *Dragon Quest*. TV series. DIR: Rintaro, Takayuki Kanda, Katsuhisa Yamada, Nobutaka Nishizawa. SCR: Takashi Yamada, Sukehiro Tomita, Nobuaki Kishima. DES: Akira Toriyama, Yasushi Nagaoka. ANI: Takeyuki Kanda, Hiroshi Kanezawa. MUS: Koichi Sugiyama. PRD: Studio Comet, Toei, Fuji TV. 25 mins. x 32 eps., 25 mins. x 48 eps., 40 mins. x 2 films.
Sixteen-year-old Abel, sorcerer Janac, and Daisy the swordswoman are in search of eternal life, for which they will have to drink a dragon's blood.

Baramos is their enemy, a creature from the undersea kingdom of Estarkh so accustomed to pollution that it is unable to tolerate clean water. Seeking to summon the Great Dragon to lay waste to the world, Baramos kidnaps Abel's childhood sweetheart, Tiala, who is the guardian of the summoning jewel "the Red Stone."

Based on the 1985 *Dragon Quest* computer game created for the MSX computer and NES console game, several games and the first part of the anime, *DQ: Legend of Abel*, were released in the U.S. by Saban but sank without a trace. In Japan, anime and game were far more successful, kicking off the vogue for computerized "role-playing games" that would culminate in **FINAL FANTASY** and **POKÉMON**. The U.S. dub by Saban ended after 13 shuffled episodes, with the party reaching the Tower of Najimi. It also replaced the soundtrack and some of the series' more adult elements: a scene in Port Myla where Abel is propositioned by a whore is altered to an unconvincing conversation about bullfighting.

The series went much further in Japan, following the *Legend of Abel* story arc in 1991 with the *Adventure of Dai*. Set, like **LODOSS WAR**, suitably long after an earlier legend, it features Dai, a young boy raised on the island of Demurin, where many monsters were said to have been banished by an ancient hero. The sorcerer Aban and his apprentice Poppu arrive on the island, looking for the demon lord Hadora, who is coming back from the dead. Aban sacrifices himself to save Dai and Poppu, and the boys continue Aban's quest. Dai's adventures were much longer-running than his predecessor's and also spun off into Yoshiki Shibata's 40-minute feature version *DQ: Disciple of Aban* (1992). Much later, the manga published to explain the plot of another *DQ* game was also made into a feature, *DQ: Crest of Roto* (1996), directed by Tsukasa Sunaga.

DRAGONAR

1987. JPN: *Kiko Senki Dragonar*. AKA:

Armored Chronicle Dragonar; Metal Armor Dragonar. TV series. DIR: Takeyuki Kanda. SCR: Fuyunori Gobu. DES: Kenichi Onuki, Kunio Okawara. ANI: Hirokazu Endo, Masami Obari. MUS: Toshiyuki Watanabe, Kentaro Haneda. PRD: Sunrise, Nagoya TV (TV Asahi). 25 mins. x 48 eps.
The Imperial Giganos Empire is invading planet Earth, and the multiethnic Kain, Tapp, and Lyte, with their female foils, Linda and Rose, steal the Dragonar Metalli-Armor from the enemy and turn it against them. The pesky kids are then "bonded" to their weapons, and the Earth military is forced to work with them, in this series which Sunrise hoped would be the "new **GUNDAM**." It wasn't.

DRAGON'S HEAVEN

1988. Video. DIR: Makoto Kobayashi, Shigeru Fukumoto. SCR: N/C. DES: Makoto Kobayashi, Toshiyuki Hirano, Kimitoshi Yamane. ANI: Itaru Saito. MUS: N/C. PRD: Artmic, AIC. 45 mins.
A great war in 3195 destroys most of civilization when the robot servants of human armies run out of control. The robot Shaian lies dormant for a thousand years after the death of its operator but is accidentally reactivated by a girl, Ikaru, while she scavenges for a living after her family's death at the hands of the Brazilian army. Shaian wishes to avenge himself on the Brazilians' leader, Elmedyne, and enlists the help of the human in order to ensure he operates at top capacity. The victorious couple go off into the ruins together, in an anime with the weirdest robot designs until **EVANGELION**.

DRAGOON *

1997. JPN: *Ryuki Dengyo*. AKA: *Legend of the Dragon Machine*. Video. DIR: Kenichi Maejima. SCR: Ryota Dezaki. DES: Shino Takada, Satoshi Nishimura. ANI: Masami Nagata. MUS: Harukichi Yamamoto. PRD: KSS. 30 mins. x 3 eps.
May has blue hair, red eyes, a corpselike pallor, and is the key to a powerful military device controlled by her

father. She escapes from her captors and bumps into Sedon Calibre, a noble squire who takes up his father's sword and leads her to her destiny. This, it would seem, involves giving her an incongruous stripey hat to wear and some low-rent swashbuckling as they run away from Incompetent Soldiers and The Man Who Almost Killed His Father, while an Annoying Little Sister tags along for comic relief. Characters say things like, "He destroyed my village. He murdered my entire family. He's evil incarnate," and there's a bit of sub-Jedi bullshit about wielding a sword with your heart.

Harmless hokum, marred only by stingy cost-cutting that renders almost all the battle sequences as freeze-frames or close-ups (presumably the savings were used to throw in a little more fan-service nudity since it seems May has a magical ability that causes her clothes to fall off). Sadly, it only ends with a partial resolution, revealing its origins as a marketing tool designed to drum up interest in the sequel to the original PC game. While the Japanese audience was able to enjoy the spinoff novel, both PC adventures, *and* a radio drama based on the story, U.S. fans are left with a bum deal, though distributor ADV wisely crammed all three episodes onto a single tape. The virtual absence of the titular "dragon machine" artifact is also rather disappointing, as if **AKIRA** had failed to make an appearance in the film that bears his name. Not much better than **PANZER DRAGOON**, but three times as long. **Ⓝ**

DREAM CRAYON KINGDOM

1997. JPN: *Yume no Crayon Okoku*. TV series. DIR: Junichi Sato. SCR: Takashi Yamada, Yumi Kageyama. DES: Akira Inagami. ANI: N/C. MUS: N/C. PRD: Toei, TV Asahi. 25 mins. x 65 eps.
Princess Crayon must journey to 12 magical points to help her parents from the mountains to the seaside. She meets queens in different kingdoms, all the while traveling through space and time. Each four or five episodes

constitute a "month" of both show and broadcast time, and Crayon's adventures are timed to coincide with real events, such as Christmas, New Year's, and the arrival of spring. Based on a children's book by Reimi Fukunaga and drawn by *Moon Bunny Egg Princess*–manga artist Michiru Kataoka. Not to be confused with **CRAYON SHIN-CHAN**!

DREAM DIMENSION HUNTER FANDORA *

1985. JPN: *Mu Jigen Hunter Fandora*. Video. DIR: Kazuyuki Okaseko, Shigenori Kageyama. SCR: Hirokazu Mizude, Takashi Yamada. DES: Hideki Tamura, Eiko Yamauchi. ANI: Masahiro Shita, Hiroyuki Ikegami. MUS: Nozomu Aoki. PRD: Hero Media, Kaname Pro. 45 mins. x 3 eps.
In dimensional year 2002, the ability to warp between new dimensions has created new customs and new criminals. The overworked Dimensional Police Force turns to bounty hunters for help, including Fandora and her partner, Quest (a shape-shifting dragon), who go to the oppressed dimension of Lem in search of rogue crook Red-Eye Geran. Later episodes center on lovers Soto and Fontaine, who are separated when galactic criminal Yog Sothoth destroys the Deadlander dimension. Desiring Fandora's Red Rupee gem, Sothoth tricks Soto into stealing it by telling him that balance can be restored if it is brought to him. Fandora stops Soto before he can unite the Red Rupee with the "Blue God's" Blue Rupee, but she is trapped in Sothoth's lair. Created by **DEVILMAN**'s Go Nagai specifically for video. Yog Sothoth is a sly nod to the works of H.P. Lovecraft, also referenced in **ICZER-ONE** and **ARMITAGE III**.

Using many crew members from Go Nagai's Dynamic Productions (hence the Nagai-esque look), *DDHF* was released in an English-dubbed version, by **BAVI STOCK**–producer Hiromasa Shibazaki, who hoped to jump-start an American commercial anime video market by selling an English dub by

mail order *from* Japan. The lack of advertising, paucity of U.S. fans at the time, and the high price killed that experiment. However, *DDHF* was not particularly helped by the horrible quality of the dub itself—Fandora and Quest have very artificial, haughty English accents; a medieval innkeeper's voice is a bad W. C. Fields imitation; and the Chief of the Dimensional Police talks like a rural cop from the American South. Compare to **CIPHER**, which was also released in English in Japan but with no intention of reaching the U.S. market.

DREAM HUNTER REM

1986. Video. DIR: Satoru Kumazaki, Kiyoshi Nagao, Shinji Okuda. SCR: Shinji Okuda. DES: Kazuaki Mori, Masami Aisakata, Akira Inoue. ANI: Moriyasu Taniguchi, Masahide Yanasawa. MUS: Heitaro Manabe. PRD: Project Team Nagahisa Kikan, Studio Zain. 45 mins. x 5 eps.
The insomniac little girl Rem develops the power to enter other people's dreams and earns a living as a private investigator, accompanied by her dog, Alpha, and cat, Beta, who appear as a puppy and kitten in the real world but transform into a fierce giant wolf and cougar when Rem enters people's dreams. Her first mission is against the "Death God" who appears to be possessing a young girl's dreams and driving Rem to commit murder. In episode two, she investigates a series of murders at a high school rumored to be the work of the ghost of a girl who was held prisoner and died in the clock tower. The first series ends with a traditional ghost story, as Rem must fight the jealous spirit of a Taira warrior executed there many centuries earlier. Two further episodes that were pastiches of famous horror novels, *New DHR*, followed in 1990 and 1992, with Okuda writing *and* directing. In the first, a *Dracula* rip-off, Rem must discover why the pretty young Mina has developed sleeping-sickness. In the second, she journeys to the small Alpine city-state of Franken, where a Dr. Victor is trou-

bled by dreams of a robot man called Julian.

Like **PROJECT A-KO**, *DHR* was originally planned as an erotic video series but released into the mainstream without undue nudity as the creative climate changed during the 1980s. She gets her name from the acronym "Rapid-Eye-Movement," a phenomenon of deep sleepers. A combination of the magical girl and teen ghost-hunter genres.

DREAM-STAR BUTTON NOSE

1985. JPN: *Yume no Hoshi Button Nose*. TV series. DIR: Masami Hata, Toshio Takeuchi, Katsuhisa Yamada, Kazuyuki Hirokawa. SCR: Tomoko Konparu, Hideo Takayashiki, Kenji Terada. DES: Akiyo Hirose, Masami Hata. ANI: Maya Matsuyama, Kazuyuki Omori. MUS: Kohei Tanaka. PRD: Sanrio, TV Asahi. 25 mins. x 26 eps.

The first TV series from the merchandise-led Sanrio studio, *Button Nose* was two years in the making. Button is an eight-year-old girl who lives at the Ichigo research institute. Her father invites space travelers from Hookland on planet Kalinto, but they arrive while he is away, so Button takes his place, accompanied by her pet, Franklyn (a pink kangaroo/mouse). With King Fastener of Hookland, Button sets off on the long journey to Kalinto.

DRIFTING CLOUDS

1982. JPN: *Ukigumo*. Movie. DIR: Mamoru Masaki. SCR: Chiku Yamatoya. DES: George Akiyama. ANI: Kazuo Tomisawa, Kuni Tomita, Nobuko Yuasa. MUS: Seiji Yokoyama. PRD: Madhouse, Toei. 91 mins.

A period-drama with real historical figures, in the style of the later **TREE IN THE SUN**. Ukigumo, a merchant in old-time Tokyo, leaves the running of his company to his wife and assistant and drifts "free as a cloud." He saves Ryoma Sakamoto (see **OI! RYOMA**) from an attack in the street, and Sakamoto entertains Ukigumo's family with his vision of a future Japan. Ukigumo's son, Shinnosuke, is inspired by Ryoma,

but Ryoma is inspired by Ukigumo, and announces that he plans to renounce his way of life and leave the Shinsengumi organization. Later that year, Ukigumo hears that Ryoma has been assassinated. Based on George Akiyama's monstrously long-running 1973 manga, still going in *Big Comic*, and placed incongruously on a double bill with the **GOSHOGUN** movie.

DT EIGHTRON

1998. TV series. DIR: Tetsuro Amino. SCR: Hideki Kakinuma, Toshimitsu Himeno. DES: Yoshi Tanaka. ANI: Yoshi Tanaka. MUS: Hiroyuki Nanba. PRD: Sunrise, Fuji TV. 25 mins. x 26 eps.

In the computer-controlled state of Datania, schoolboy Shu resolves to escape from the oppressive city life and joins the resistance movement known as the Returners. He fights Datania with the super-android Eightron, which was created by applying powerful energies to a pile of junk. *Logan's Run* meets **EVANGELION** in this earnest but hackneyed replay.

DU ZIQUN

1981. JPN: *To Shishun*. TV special. DIR: Hideo Nishimaki. SCR: Takeshi Shudo. DES: Yoshio Kabashima. ANI: Yoshio Kabashima. MUS: Naoki Yamamoto. PRD: Tohoku, TBS. 84 mins.

In late Tang-dynasty China, Du Ziqun's mother, Bailian, is abducted by robbers. Twelve years later, the teenage Ziqun is leading a gang of thieves in nearby Luoyang, but he despairs of humanity and decides to become a hermit, putting himself through many trials, including a vow of utter silence. Based on the 1920 short story by Ryunosuke Akutagawa, the story was animated a second time for the *Classic Children's Tales* series (1992) as a 30-minute stop-motion short released straight to video.

DUAL *

1999. JPN: *Dual! Parallel Trouble [Run-run] Adventure*. TV series. DIR: Katsuhito Akiyama. SCR: Yosuke Kuroda. DES: Atsushi Okuda, Kenji Teraoka, Yasushi

Muraki. ANI: Atsushi Okuda. MUS: Seiko Nagaoka. PRD: AIC, Pioneer, WOWOW. 25 mins. x 13 eps., 25 mins. x 1 ep (V).

When he uncovers a strange artifact at a construction site, a worker accidentally splits the universe into two parallel continua. In one universe, the artifact is used to develop human technology in strange and new directions; in the other, life continues as normal. Twenty-two years later in the everyday world, Professor Sanada tries to prove the existence of a parallel universe. His daughter, Mitsuki, tells him about the visions of schoolboy Kazuki, who claims to see giant robots fighting in the streets. Accidentally triggering the professor's device, Kazuki finds himself in the parallel-world where the evil Rara is trying to conquer the world. Kazuki also learns that the parallel Prof. Sanada has gotten the UN's backing to create an Earth Defense Command to stop Rara, and that Mitsuki transported to this world the month before. She has had time to introduce herself to the parallel of her father, who is a bachelor in this world and has been too busy fighting evil to develop a similar parallel world technology to send her home. Sanada accepts the obligation of adopting Mitsuki, also making her a robot pilot in the EDC. When they find that Kazuki has arrived and can also fly a robot, they enlist him, too.

Dual was Pioneer's entry in the race to duplicate **EVANGELION**, stealing plots, moods, characters, shots, and even set designs from the 1995 smash and adding half a dozen pretty girls straight out of their own **TENCHI MUYO!** franchise. The show adds some clever identity crises—Kazuki is the only person who does not exist in the parallel world that includes evil versions of love interest Mitsuki and her mother. With a passionless, suicidal girl (the cyborg D, last remnant of a lost civilization), young pilots forced to share a house, and Eva-like robots, its reverse-engineered origins are clear, but the slick marketing savvy of producers Toru Miura and

Kazuaki Morijiri ensure that nothing gets taken *too* far. People don't get killed (at least not permanently), jokiness often takes precedence over drama, and a happy ending restores everything to *almost* normal, with Kazuki surrounded by adoring girls. Careful integration of computer graphics makes for some good robot battles, but much of the design in *Dual* seems a little too sparse; the scenes often seem too uncluttered, giving the show a sanitized look to match its sanitized plot. Thankfully, it also lacks *Evangelion*'s messy ending, though after a denouement seemingly shot on the same roadbridge that closes SERIAL EXPERIMENTS LAIN, a final episode on video threatens an as-yet-unmade sequel.

DUNBINE *

1983. JPN: *Seisenshi Dunbine*. AKA: *Holy Warrior Dunbine, Aura Battler Dunbine*. TV series, video. DIR: Yoshiyuki Tomino, Toshifumi Takizawa. SCR: Yoshiyuki Tomino, Sukehiro Tomita, Yuji Watanabe. DES: Yukien Hirogawa, Yutaka Izubuchi. ANI: Hiroyuki Kitazume. MUS: Katsuyuki Ono, Tatsumi Yano. PRD: Sunrise, Nagoya TV (TV Asahi). 25 mins. x 49 eps., 75 mins. x 3 eps., 25 mins. x 3 eps.
Japanese boy Sho Zama is transported to the alternate world of Byston Well because his human "aura" will make him a powerful robot pilot in Drake Luft's quest to rule the planet. However, Sho defects to the other side and leads the resistance, until his former employers, fighting a rearguard action, open a gateway through to our world and begin a second conquest.

Inspired by *Wings of Lin*, an earlier novel by GUNDAM-creator Yoshiyuki Tomino, *Dunbine* shares its stablemate's concentration on big robots (a studio addition not in the original) and heavy character development. It was soon remade by Toshifumi Takizawa as a three-part video series incorporating designs from PATLABOR's Yutaka Izubuchi. The new series, *Aura Battler Dunbine: Tale of Neo Byston Well* (1987), featured more expensive animation and robots with literally scintillating armor. The original Dunbine designer Shott Weapon is thrown through a time warp at the end of the TV series to arrive in Byston Well 700 years later. He brings with him a veritable battalion of Earth weaponry, including a fully laden aircraft carrier, and the locals must form a new resistance to stop him. Although the video series only consisted of 75 minutes of footage, the series was stretched out three times as long with the aid of digest versions of the previous TV episodes.

Much later, in the wake of the similar ESCAFLOWNE, Tomino would adapt the robot-free *Wings of Lin* itself into a video anime, the truly awful three-parter *Garzey's Wing* (1996). Chris, a Japanese teenager, loses half his soul when he is summoned to Byston Well by the priestess Hassan. The Meitomias tribe wishes to escape from Ashigaba slavers, and Chris is to be their champion. He guides them through their flight to their promised land, fighting off Roman-armored, dinosaur-riding Ashigabas, while the Tokyo half of his soul sends telepathic messages about such topics as how to make gunpowder. This show is very cheaply animated and shoddily written, and, though this was the only part of the series to be released in the U.S., the poor quality of the dub makes it almost unwatchable.

DYNAGIGA

1998. JPN: *Chokido Densetsu Dynagiga*. AKA: *Super Robot Legend Dynagiga*. Video. DIR: Naoyuki Yoshinaga. SCR: N/C. DES: Tada Miura. ANI: Yoshiko Sugai. MUS: N/C. PRD: Studio Deen. 30 mins. x 2 eps.
An anime series that began life on the TV variety program *What's Up, Shibuya?*, it's set in a near future when robots are commonplace and follows the lives and loves of a group of high-school girls as they try to get their robot licenses—driving school with giant robots. Allegedly an experiment to discover new talent in voice acting and design, though cynics might suggest that amateur nights always have cheaper staff.

E

EAGLE SAM

1983. TV series. DIR: Hideo Nishimaki, Kanetsugu Kodama. SCR: Masaaki Sakurai, Tetsu Hirata, Kazunobu Hamada, Kazuo Yoshioka. DES: Yoshio Kabashima. ANI: Yoshio Kabashima, Yukio Otaku. MUS: Harumi Ibe. PRD: DAX, TBS. 25 mins. x 51 eps.

All-American private investigator Sam is transformed into an eagle one day as he prepares to open for business. With his shapely assistant, Miss Canary, and her little brother, Gooselan, he must fight the corrupt Chief of Police Albatross and somehow regain his true form. He travels all around the world and solves problems with his Eagle Hat, which contains many useful items à la **DORAEMON**, chiefly the glowing Olympic Rings that give Sam the extra confidence he needs to save the day. Other members of the mostly human cast included Pelican the hippie, Thunderbird the weightlifter, and dim-witted, donut-eating cop Bogie (presumably a Humphrey Bogart reference amid all the avian names). Though set in "Olympic City," the location is clearly modeled on Los Angeles, even down to LAPD uniforms, though these have incongruous Stars of David instead of the traditional sheriffs' badges. When not fighting corruption within the force itself, Eagle Sam chases Gokiburi, a skateboarding, jive-talking cockroach in shades. Made to cash in on the "Eagle Sam" mascot of the 1984 Los Angeles Olympics—compare to the Moscow equivalent, **MISHA THE BEAR CUB**.

EAR OF THE YELLOW DRAGON

1995. JPN: Koryu no Mimi. Video. DIR: Kunihiko Yuyama. SCR: Kenji Terada. DES: Arimasa Ozawa. ANI: Masayuki Goto. MUS: Hiroki Nakajima. PRD: Vap. 25 mins. x 2 eps.

An SF tale of intrigue in which agent Kiro, who can call on the mystic powers of "the yellow dragon" through his earring, falls in love with Kanako, daughter of the mob family he is trying to bring down. Based on just one story arc in a manga from *Young Jump* that won the coveted Naoki Prize for its creator Arimasa Ozawa. **NV**

EARLY ANIME

The first Japanese animated film, *Mukuzo Imokawa the Doorman* (1917, *Imokawa Mukuzo Genkanban no Maki*), was a five-minute short by Oten Shimokawa, a 26-year-old amateur filmmaker who had formerly been an editorial assistant on *Tokyo Puck* magazine. The Okinawa-born Shimokawa drew in ink straight onto the film, making five short films in a single six-month period before returning to newspaper cartoon illustration.

Another early animator, Seitaro Kitayama, preferred fairy tales and legends to humor, producing early versions of **MONKEY AND THE CRAB** (1917), **MOMOTARO** (1917), and *Taro the Guardsman* (1918, *Taro no Banpei*), though these were all lost in the 1923 Tokyo earthquake. Other notable silent-era animators include another *Tokyo Puck* alumnus, Junichi Kouchi, who made *The Sword of Hanawahekonai* (1917, *Hanawahekonai Meito no Maki*), and Sanae Yamamoto, whose *The Mountain Where Old Women Are Abandoned* (1924, *Obasuteyama*) is the earliest anime still extant. Animation

remained a cottage industry throughout the 1920s, with most pioneers working in small home studios, though they came to be financed by Japanese theatrical companies, which provided production money in exchange for distribution rights.

Legends and funny animal stories were the trend in the 1920s, including Nobuo Ofuji's early animations of **JOURNEY TO THE WEST** (1926) and *Urashima Taro* (1928), which were made by animating paper cutouts, and Yasushi Murata's *Animal Olympics* (1928, *Dobutsu Olympic Taikai*). Anime's first "sequel" was *The Pirate Ship* (1931, *Kaizoku-bune*), a continuation of the previous year's *Monkey Island* (*Sarugashima*), in which a young child cast adrift has adventures on the high seas. By this time, however, filmmakers were feeling the pressure of militarism, and Yasushi Murata's *Aerial Momotaro* (1931) was the first of the **WARTIME ANIME**.

After the release of the talkie *The Jazz Singer* (1927) in the U.S., it was only a matter of time before anime also experimented with sound. The first was Ofuji's *Whale* (1927, *Kujira*), a silhouette animation synchronized to the *William Tell Overture*. He followed this up with the cutout-animation *Kuro Nyago* (1930), using Tojo's Eastphone sound system—anime's first genuine "talkie," and only 90 seconds long. The first talkie to use an optic track (as with modern films) was Kenzo Masaoka's *World of Power and Women* (1933, *Chikara to Onna no Yo no Naka*), the tale of a henpecked salaryman husband who begins an affair with a younger woman. Nobuo Ofuji was also a pioneer in the development of color anime, but, although he made a two-color version of his *Golden Flower* (1929, *Ogon no Hana*), the version released to the public was still in monochrome. The first color anime actually *released* was Megumi Asano's *My Baseball* (1948, *Boku no Yakyu*). *Ill. p. 329.*

EARTH DEFENSE FAMILY
2001. JPN: *Chikyu Boei Kazoku.* TV series. DIR: Satoshi Kimura. SCR: Shoji Kawamori. DES: Kazuaki Mori. ANI: Kazuaki Mori. MUS: Shigeo Naka. PRD: Tac, WOWOW. 25 mins. x 13 eps.
Troubled family man Mamori Daichi is on the verge of divorce when he and his wife are disturbed mid-argument by a mysterious fax commanding them to protect planet Earth. Soon afterward, a giant comet smashes into Earth, releasing a space monster that only Mamori can stop. He, his wife, Seiko, and their children, Dai and Nozomi, discover that when they insert their special magic cards into a computer, they are teleported into superpowered battle suits, complete with user manuals on how to save Earth. An **ULTRAMAN** pastiche from Shoji Kawamori, best known in recent years for his work on **MACROSS** and **ESCAFLOWNE**, deliberately using "old-fashioned" techniques of cel animation in contrast to the contemporary fashion for digital animation and effects.

EARTH GIRL ARJUNA
2001. JPN: *Chikyu Shojo Arjuna.* TV series. DIR: Shoji Kawamori, Eiichi Sato, Tomokazu Tokoro, Yoshitaka Fujimoto. SCR: Shoji Kawamori, Hiroshi Onogi. DES: Takahiro Kishida. ANI: Manabu Fukusawa, Haruo Sotozaki. MUS: Yoko Kanno. PRD: Satellite, TV Tokyo. 25 mins. x 12 eps. + 1 bonus video ep.
Young teenager Juna Ariyoshi is in an accident and receives a vision of life on Earth in the future. She sees that humans have been raised to a higher state of consciousness but are still victims of predatory raids from evil Rajah invaders, who must be held off by the wearer of the "Aura Suit." She is soon

enlisted by local boy Chris Horken in a mission to save both worlds. Or in other words, **ESCAFLOWNE**, but traveling in time instead of space. Ichiro Itano, former anime director, adds another string to his bow here as director of the CG motion-capture sequences, while director Kawamori claimed in press releases that the show was designed to encourage a return to nature and renunciation of material things. We'll see what the merchandising department has to say about that.

EARTH STORY: TELEPATH 2500
1984. JPN: *Chikyu Monogatari Telepath 2500.* Movie. DIR: Nariyuki Yamane. SCR: Yoshimi Shinozaki. DES: Ammonite, Yoshitaka Amano, Masashi Sato. ANI: Ippei Kuri, Sadao Miyamoto. MUS: Hiroshi Ogasawara. PRD: Tatsunoko. 105 mins.
On the fifth world of the Tolphan system in the year 2500, a supercomputer chooses marriage partners to find the best matches. Eighteen-year-old Will flies to an orbital facility to discuss his fate with his elders but receives telepathic SOS messages from the winged Flora. He deviates from his course and goes to help this damsel in distress, slowly coming to realize that he has fallen in love with her before they have even met. A star-crossed love story with an SF twist. **N**

EARTHIAN *
1989. Video. DIR: Nobuyasu Furukawa, Kenichi Onuki. SCR: Hiroyuki Kawasaki. DES: Kenichi Onuki. ANI: Kenichi Onuki. MUS: Shinnosuke Uesugi. PRD: JC Staff. 40 mins. x 4 eps.
Optimistic Chihaya and pessimistic Kagetsuya are two angels sent from Planet Eden to walk among mankind (the "Earthians") and determine whether the race deserves to survive. This interesting premise is then stretched in all kinds of hack directions by a crew that seems unable to decide what to do with it. The boys bicker constantly about humanity, though since both have been chosen for their good-cop/bad-cop attitudes, each is unlikely

Left to right: space pirate Ryoko, hapless teenager Tenchi, and the insufferably perky princess Sasami at one of **TENCHI MUYO!**'s many dinner scenes; it is otherwise difficult to cram his extended family into one place! Focus-group writing taken to extremes, *TM* features an unthreateningly average guy who gains an alien space-harem, royal pedigree, and occasional galactic trip by simply remaining idle. A strangely enduring combination of *The Waltons* and *Star Wars*. See entry p. 395.

Tenchi Muyo!

to convert the other. Like a fey version of *Highway to Heaven*, they simply wander in and out of what could almost be episodes from other shows—a London music biz soap opera, for example (featuring a dark angel), or an SF tale of psychics (when Chihaya rescues a runaway psionic in Hong Kong). Yun Koga's original 1987 pretty-boy manga was given a considerable amount of screen time for a video release, and the whistle-stop international setting would have been very difficult to achieve in a live-action budget. However, matters were not helped in the U.S. market by a distributor that coquettishly refused to number the tapes, forcing many potential fans to watch episodes in a random order. *Ill. p. 369.*

EASY COOKING ANIMATION
1989. JPN: *Seishun no Shokutaku.* AKA: *Youth's Dining Table.* Video. DIR: Toshio Hirata. SCR: N/C. DES: N/C. ANI: N/C. MUS: N/C. PRD: Kitty Film, Madhouse. 30 mins. x 5 eps.
A set of handy hints for basic cooking, including advice on preparing noodles, salad, hot-pots, and pizza. From the studio that gave you **WICKED CITY**.

EAT WITH BAGETSU
1996. JPN: *Bagetsu de Gohan.* AKA:

Meal with Bagetsu. TV series. DIR: Satoshi Dezaki. SCR: Kiriko Kubo. DES: Yukari Kobayashi. ANI: Yukari Kobayashi. MUS: Shinichi Kyoda. PRD: Magic Bus, Yomiuri TV. 25 mins. x 20 eps.

The animals at Uenohara Zoo love their jobs, and their jobs involve acting like animals when the human beings are watching and getting on with very human lives when they're not. Paramount among them is Ginpei the penguin, who is eternally getting into trouble with the giraffes, lions, and pandas. Based on a manga by *Cynical Hystery Hour*–creator Kiriko Kubo.

EAT-MAN *

1997. TV series. DIR: Koichi Mashimo, Toshifumi Kawase. SCR: Akemi Omode, Aya Matsui, Hiroshi Nomoto. DES: Satoshi Murata. ANI: Masaaki Kawanami. MUS: Taifu Kamigami. PRD: Studio Deen, TV Tokyo. 25 mins. x 24 eps.

Bolt Crank, a mercenary who can eat metal objects and then rematerialize them in times of need, wanders from city to city in a futuristic wasteland helping people in trouble.

Based on a manga by Akihito Yoshitomi that is similarly high in concept and low in plot, *E-M* takes the raw material of pulp TV and remolds the wandering heroes of *The Incredible Hulk* and *The Running Man*, adding a dash of Clint Eastwood and Ken from FIST OF THE NORTH STAR. However, it lacks the believable background of its similarly pulp-inspired contemporary COWBOY BEBOP—the world it creates is little more than a desert backlot, and it soon sinks into a quagmire of episodic setups and showdowns.

E-M shows both the good and bad aspects of a limited budget. Art director Jiro Kono deliberately uses flat, uniform colors (like TENCHI MUYO! without the shine) to exploit the talents of his Chinese animators, and it works well. There are some neat compositions (a face in a cracked mirror, the sky in a puddle), but also some blatant corner-cutting. A cheap loop of a girl's running silhouette is used for a total of three and half minutes. A staring match reaches ridiculous levels of stillness, which may be fine for free on late-night TV, but stretches the patience of video buyers.

Paramount among the series' problems is Bolt's peculiar ability itself, mystifying a succession of writers who push the titular "eating" into the background. Setups are drawn from the staples of U.S. law shows (a would-be dancer is forced to work as a stripper), SF (a clone hunts down all her sisters), and fantasy (a feisty young lady is a lost heiress), but Bolt merely watches the action unfold before producing a gun out of thin air instead of a holster for the finale. As *Manga Max* famously observed, "he could have pulled it out of his ass for all the difference it made."

The second season, *Eat-Man 98*, replaces director Mashimo with EHRGEIZ's Kawase and injects hints about Bolt Crank's past. In rip-offs from GENOCYBER, GHOST IN THE SHELL, and AKIRA, it suggests that Bolt was somehow involved in a genetic experiment, and that the titular "98" is the percentile of subjects who did not survive the process. Though the new direction is at least a plot of sorts, Bolt's habit of munching on metal objects is still little more than a display of macho toughness—you'd get the same effect if he regularly smashed a bottle over his own head. Though the animation is still limited, *E-M98* at least duplicates the look of Bolt's powers from the manga, but much of the storytelling remains shoddy and illogical despite a high-quality translation in the English-language version far better than this show really deserves. **OV**

EDEN'S BOY

1999. TV series. DIR: Tsukasa Sunaga. SCR: Masashi Sogo. DES: Hiroko Kazui. ANI: Hiroko Kazui, Yoshiaki Tsuhata. MUS: N/C. PRD: Studio Deen. 25 mins. x 26 eps.

On a world where a floating city rules over groundling farmers, humble peasant boy Yorun becomes the target of a group of assassins. He is protected by Ellysis, a girl with healing powers, who can also transform into a warrior version of herself called Sita. She reveals that Yorun is a "god-hunter" in hiding, a human with the ability to destroy unruly deities such as the one who now rules over the floating city of Eden. Based on a manga from *Shonen Ace* by Kitsune Tennoji, who was previously known for the adult story *Rape + 2πr*, *EB* soon transforms into a bizarre love triangle in the spirit of CREAMY MAMI, with Yorun falling for Sida while Ellysis falls for Yorun.

EFFICACE

1998. Video. DIR: Shigeru Motomiya. SCR: Shigeru Motomiya. DES: Hideaki Shimada. ANI: Hideaki Shimada. MUS: N/C. PRD: Magic Bus. 40 mins. x 2 eps.

Sisters Maply, Sucre, and Parte live in the magical kingdom of Efficace. In a cash-in of the video game of the same name, the girls are forced to find other sources of income after sales of buns go into decline. The second episode takes the girls to a haunted house to face an old adversary.

EHRGEIZ *

1997. JPN: *Next Senki: Ehrgeiz.* AKA: *Next Chronicle: Ehrgeiz.* TV series. DIR: Toshifumi Kawase. SCR: Atsuhiro Tomioka, Koji Miura, Toshiyasu Nagata, Chika Hojo. DES: Isamu Imakake, Tetsuya Yanasawa, Takahiro Yamada. ANI: Naoki Hishikawa. MUS: Kazuhiro Wakabayashi. PRD: BeStack, TV Tokyo. 25 mins. x 12 eps.

The Next orbital colony declares independence from Earth, starting a war of secession fought with giant robots called Metal Vehicles. Meanwhile, the terrorist organization Tera, led by the telepathic boy Hal, fights the Earth government from within, as the Next forces search desperately for the legendary "S" superweapon that will turn the tide of the war. On a wrecked colony satellite, a group of part-time pirates turn out to be the best pilots of the lot, and the scene is set for a blatant **GUNDAM** rip-off. Originally broadcast on Japanese late-night TV, the production may well have been dumped in the graveyard shift as a cheaper alternative to video; certainly, there is no "adult" content to otherwise justify its broadcast time. Though the English-language translation tries to spice up the language somewhat, it is a perfectly mundane children's robot show with animation so cheap that the robots slide everywhere instead of walking. And no matter how old the original target audience, it was bound to be bewildered by the baffling array of sides in the war, with two nations, two freelance groups, and, as the plot advances, a newly arrived alien civilization to boot. Supposedly amusingly referential and parodic but really just plain dull, the series is best remembered for spawning a PlayStation game in which characters from *Final Fantasy VII* made cameo appearances, which is hardly a recommendation.

808 DISTRICTS

1990. JPN: *Ishinomori Shotaro no 808 Hyori*. AKA: *Shotaro Ishinomori's 808 Districts*. TV series. DIR: Hiroshi Fukutomi. SCR: Kaneto Shirasu. DES: Shotaro Ishinomori. ANI: Masuji Kinoue. MUS: N/C. PRD: Shinei, TBS. 10 mins. x 16 eps.

A series of costume-dramas in which **CYBORG 009**–creator Shotaro Ishinomori plays out modern situations against the backdrop of samurai-era Japan. Linked by the wandering character, Kosanma, the stories include a man's desire to light up the sky with fireworks, a battle between a freelancer and a large company, a girl growing up in the Edo-period version of a massage parlor, and a man searching for a way to get a girl to love him.

The first episode was a 30-minute special, with subsequent parts screened irregularly as part of the *Gimme a Break* show on TBS. For an SF update of the same mean city streets, see **CYBER CITY OEDO 808**, which also takes its name from the 808 city blocks of old-time Tokyo.

8TH MAN *

1963. JPN: *8 Man* [sic]. AKA: *Tobor the Eighth Man*. TV series, video. DIR: Haruyuki Kawajima. SCR: Kazumasa Hirai, Ryo Hanmura, Tsunehisa Tomita, Tetsuyoshi Onuki, Masaki Tsuji. DES: Jiro Kuwata. ANI: Yukizo Takagaki, Kazuhide Fujiwara. MUS: Tetsuaki Akibara. PRD: Eiken, TBS. 25 mins. x 56 eps., 30 mins. x 4 eps. (v).

Police officer Hachiro Azuma (Peter Brady) is murdered by a criminal gang, but Professor Tani (Genius) installs his memories in a robot body, the 008 military prototype model from the Republic of Amarco. With his new body, he takes on the cyborgs and mutants of an international crime syndicate in a show partly inspired by James Bond 007 but way ahead of its spiritual descendants **CYBORG 009** and *Robocop*.

Based on a story by **HARMAGEDON**-author Kazumasa Hirai that was previously adapted into a manga in *Shonen Magazine* by Jiro Kuwata, the TV series was notable for the script contribution of real SF authors such as Hirai himself and Ryo Hanmura, though much of the original impact was lost in the U.S. dub *Tobor the Eighth Man* (1965), in which our hero must defeat such creatively named adversaries as Saucer Lips (the man who "killed" Peter Brady), as well as Armored Man, Baron Stormy, Dr. Spectra, the Satan Brothers, and the Intercrime spy ring. The TV series has since been rereleased on video in the U.S., though the later video compilations downplay Azuma's novel way of recharging his batteries—smoking nuclear isotope cigarettes.

After the success of the *Robocop* films, the story was remade as the live-action *8 Man* (1992, aka *8 Man Returns*). Nobuyasu Furukawa's belated anime video sequel, *Eight Man After* (1993) plays up the drug subculture, as gangsters receive cybernetic prostheses with built-in weapons. Cybernetic implants, however, require stimulants, and the criminal fraternity is soon fighting a new turf war over control of its own drugs. Detective Azuma is sent

to investigate the disappearance of a scientist from the Biotech Corp, but he is killed trying to save pretty Sachiko. He is brought back to life by Dr. Tobor, who makes him the new "Eight Man." The video series was also released in the U.S. in a dubbed version from Streamline Pictures.

EIJI

1990. Movie. DIR: Mizuho Nishikubo. SCR: Kazuya Miyashita, Yasuyuki Suzuki. DES: Takayuki Goto. ANI: Satoshi Murata. MUS: Rogue, Go-Bangs, Passengers, Rabbit, Mari Iwata, J-Bloods. PRD: Animate Film. 50 mins.

Legendary boxer Keijiro Akagi's second son, Eiji, is a high-school dropout and the world's worst rock guitarist. Though his father and elder brother are both boxers, he hates the sport but suddenly takes an interest in it when he meets the local champion's little sister. This movie was based on a one-volume 1984 manga from *Fresh Jump* magazine by Hisashi Eguchi and features a rock soundtrack by the bands of the moment. Two other works by the same author were animated straight to video soon after—*Something's Going to Happen* (1990) and *The Hisagoro Show* (1991), directed by Rintaro and Osamu Nabeshima, and both consisting of several short comedy pieces.

EL HAZARD *

1995. JPN: *Shinpi no Sekai El Hazard*. AKA: *The Magnificent World of El Hazard*. Video, TV series. DIR: Hiroki Hayashi, Katsuhito Akiyama. SCR: Ryoei Tsukimura. DES: Kazuto Nakazawa. ANI: Jun Okuda. MUS: Seiko Nagaoka. PRD: AIC, Pioneer. 45 mins., 30 mins. x 6 eps., 50 mins. (v), 25 mins. x 26 eps. (TV), 45 mins. x 4 eps. (v), 25 mins. x 13 eps. (TV).

Whisked off to a faraway world, schoolboy Makoto has to impersonate a princess and fight the forces of evil. Spunky love interest Nanami and schoolteacher Mr. Fujisawa, a booze-swilling chain-smoker who inexplicably develops superhuman powers, are also dragged along. They must save the world from attacking insect armies led by Nanami's brother, school bully Jinnai, who has taught the locals how to lie, cheat, and steal.

Two TENCHI MUYO! staffers, Marx Brothers fan Hayashi and *John Carter of Mars*–fan Tsukimura, decided to combine their interests to create a screwball pulp adventure series, rooting their comedy in the culture clash of 20th-century people and fantasy characters. With a teacher trying to maintain school discipline in an Arabesque paradise, a cross-dressing hero, an evil general who names all his soldiers after his favorite film stars, and Mr. Fujisawa's eternal quest for more cigarettes, *El Hazard* is a masterly comedy. With fish-out-of-water characters in a world inspired by the ARABIAN NIGHTS, it remains more popular outside Japan than some of Pioneer's more ethnocentric productions such as HAKKENDEN and KISHIN CORPS. Arguably one of the most seamless anime translations ever, the English-language dub by Jenny Haniver and John Pierce is a perfect translation of the original Japanese version, even down to the background improvisations by talented voice actors.

The video series was remade for TV Tokyo in a version known abroad as *El Hazard: The Wanderers* (1996), which stretched the material of the original video series thinly over a longer timeframe. A video sequel to the original *video* series, *El Hazard 2* (1997), was similarly disappointing as it merely replayed some of the old gags, though, typically for the series' sense of humor, even the production team inserted "here-we-go-again" jokes. A final incarnation of the series *El Hazard: The Alternative World* (1997), directed by Yasunori Kikuchi, reunited the video characters in a new adventure, shipping them off to the Kingdom of Creteria to fight Ajrah, the self-proclaimed ruler of the universe. The newly crowned priestess of water, Qawool, falls for Makoto with leaden predictability, and the old setups are rehashed once more with a few new

characters and slight tweaks—in other words, a slow decline into hackery that mirrors the disappointing performance of the same studio's TENCHI MUYO! The thirteenth version and final episode of the *Alternate* series was never broadcast but was included as a "bonus" with the video release. *Ill. p. 45.*

ELEMENTALORS
1994. JPN: *Seirei Tsukai*. AKA: *Elemental Master*. Video. DIR: Katsuhito Akiyama. SCR: Takeshi Okazaki. DES: Hidenori Matsubara. ANI: Hidenori Matsubara. MUS: Masanori Sasamichi. PRD: Sony. 48 mins.
Kagura fails to save his brother-in-law in an accident. His sister accuses him of deliberately allowing the accident to happen because he harbors secret incestuous desires for her. She commits suicide, and Kagura is consoled by his neighbor, Asami, but *then* the world is invaded by "elementalors." Shiki, the leader of the water elementals, freezes most of the inhabitants of Earth, kidnaps Asami, and kills Kagura. However, Kagura is an elementalor himself, and he rises from the dead with help from Tsuyuha, the elemental of wood who resembles Kagura's sister, and Koimura, the elemental of metal. Shiki, only wanting to save his own daughter, leads an assault on Kagura's base, where Kagura's elementalor powers reach their full levels during a fight with Shizuku, the elemental of ice. Based on a 1989 manga by Takeshi Okazaki, serialized in *Newtype* magazine.

ELEVEN CATS
1981. JPN: *Juichibiki no Neko*. Movie. DIR: Shiro Fujimoto. SCR: Yoshitake Suzuki. DES: Noboru Baba. ANI: Akihito Kamiguchi. MUS: Hitoshi Komuro. PRD: Tac. 83 mins.
Eleven naughty cats on the run from the neighborhood police chief hear that a "giant fish" is nearby for the taking. They go on a hazardous quest to find it, learning that they must work as a team to reach their goal. Based on a children's book by Noboru Baba, this movie was followed by a 90-minute

sequel, *Eleven Cats and an Albatross* (1986), directed by Tameo Ogawa, in which the cats set up a croquette potato restaurant, lose all their customers, and agree to provide croquettes for a kingdom of albatrosses, while secretly hoping that albatross drumsticks will be on the menu.

ELF 17
1987. Video. DIR: Junichi Sakata. SCR: Sukehiro Tomita, Toshimichi Suzuki. DES: Takumi Tsukasa. ANI: Takumi Tsukasa. MUS: Kohei Tanaka. PRD: JC Staff, Agent 21. 30 mins.
Mascat Tyler (Masakado Taira, see DOOMED MEGALOPOLIS), the 108th Galactic Emperor, holds a competition to determine who will accompany him on a secret mission. After some comedic mishaps, soldier KK and the beautiful elfin Lu win the contest and set off on their quest. Based on one part of a long-running manga by Masahide Yamamoto in *Comi Comi* magazine.

ELF PRINCESS RANE *
1995. JPN: *Yosei Hime Rane*. AKA: *Fairy Princess Rane*. Video. DIR: Akitaro Daichi. SCR: Hitoshi Yamazaki. DES: Toshihide Sotodate. ANI: Toshihide Sotodate. MUS: Harukichi Yamamoto. PRD: KSS. 30 mins. x 2 eps.
Teen slacker Go Takarada wants to be an archaeologist like his parents. He meets the titular Rane, who is on a quest for magical objects to save her homeland. Meanwhile, in this genuinely funny comedy from the director of CARDCAPTORS, Go's sisters (just three of a veritable army of siblings, who even have their own rock band) are taking sibling rivalry to extremes of collateral damage, and corporate plans for a local theme park threaten everything. Though loaded with anime sight gags (such as a pretty-boy baddie whose hair keeps getting in his eyes), the show's real strength lies in its script, which has multiple onscreen speakers yelling abuse at each other in several Japanese dialects. Despite these hellish complexities, Anime Works'

English-language dub artfully captures the spirit of the original and preserves much of the show's wacky humor. Sadly, however, this was just one of many mid-1990s video comedies that never made it past episode two.

ELFY

1986. JPN: *Aoi Umi no Elfy.* AKA: *Elfie of the Blue Seas, Legend of Coral Island.* TV special. DIR: Yoshihide Terai, Yoshio Kuroda. SCR: Nobuyuki Fujimoto. DES: Yoichi Otabe. ANI: Takao Kogawa. MUS: Toshiyuki Watanabe. PRD: Nippon Animation, OH Pro, Fuji TV. 75 mins.
Four hundred years after a catastrophic rise in sea levels, the inhabitants of Earth live in giant floating cities. Twelve-year-old Elfy is raised by Nereus, one of the Seven Sages who rule over the city of Neptune. She discovers that her own black hair turns green when she swims and that she can breathe underwater. Expansion of Neptune's undersea farms meets with resistance from the local dolphins, among whom Elfy sees a merman with a strange shell necklace like her own. Investigating with Nereus and her brother, Alcus, Elfy discovers that the dolphins were responding to warning signals from the undersea empire of Mu (see **SUPER ATRAGON**), and that the expansionist plans of the Sage Charisma will be Neptune's doom. Nereus confesses that Elfy is adopted, and the distraught girl is arrested for releasing captured dolphins. Charisma leads a force from Neptune out against the merpeople, but Elfy intervenes and forms a psychic link between the two cultures. In a TV movie that cynics might call a marine replay of **NAUSICAÄ**, Elfy saves the day, but the strain proves too much, and she becomes one with the waters.

ELLCIA *

1992. JPN: *Genso Jodan Ellcia.* AKA: *Fantastic Tales of Ellcia.* Video. DIR: Noriyasu Furukawa. SCR: Noriyasu Furukawa. DES: Yasuomi Umezu. ANI: Yasuomi Umezu. MUS: Tatsumi Yano. PRD: JC Staff. 45 mins. x 4 eps.
In a pseudo-medieval society, the peo-

ple of Megaronia stumble on the relics of a lost civilization and leap ahead of their neighbors. Soon, the nation has conquered all the surrounding kingdoms, and the king's evil daughter, Crystel, sets out to find Ellcia, the legendary Ship of God, before the prophesied Fall of Megaronia can come to pass. In doing so, she inadvertently rouses the Chosen One who will destroy her kingdom, a young pirate girl called Eira.
The only remarkable thing about this tedious fantasy is that all aspects of production are uniformly poor, from lackluster designs by the famous Umezu to Yano's sub–*Raiders of the Lost Ark* music. The dub similarly disappoints with risible attempts at British dialogue, riddled with pronunciation howlers and remedial grammar. But who can blame the crews on both sides of the Pacific for merely cashing their paychecks? With its unconvincing pirates, pretentious philosophizing, and hackneyed plot, *Ellcia* was doomed from the scripting stage. **V**

ELVEN BRIDE, THE *

1995. JPN: *Elf no Waka Okusama.* Video. DIR: Hiroshi Yamakawa. SCR: N/C. DES: Kazuma G-version. ANI: Inatsugi Kiyomizu. MUS: N/C. PRD: KSS, Pink Pineapple. 27 mins. x 2 eps.
Town guardsman Kenji marries the elfin Milfa despite hostility from their families and friends. On their wedding night, Milfa reveals that although she may look 18, in elf years she is only 5 and too underdeveloped for full sexual intercourse. Kenji resolves to go on a quest for Harpy Ooze, said to be the ultimate sexual lubricant. He discovers that harpies cannot breed with other harpies and is "forced" to sire triplets with the angelic Pyully before he can obtain any Ooze. Milfa goes to see the local gynecologist, who attempts to molest her, but she is saved in the nick of time by Kenji and his grandmother.
Mixing magic with the mundane in the style of **BELOVED BETTY**, this sex-comedy is set in a pseudo-medieval world that recalls **DRAGON HALF**, where

Anime insanity taken to extreme levels in **THOSE WHO HUNT ELVES**, the everyday story of a group of misfits transported to a fantasy land by accident and forced to hunt down and strip naked the elven beauties who have parts of the Return Spell tattooed on their bodies. Luckily, our heroes have their own tank to ride around in. The *Wizard of Oz* retold with humor, nudity, and armor-piercing shells, with a novel excuse for undressing its guest stars, courtesy of original creator Yutaka Yagami. See entry p. 397.

Those Who Hunt Elves

© YU YAGAMI/MEDIA WORKS • AMUSE • SOTSU AGENCY

there are faucets in the kitchen, but characters still brush their teeth outside at a well. But while it and the original manga by "Kazuma G-Version" on which it was based may contain subtextual musings on miscegenation and the perils of modern marriage, ultimately it is simply an excuse to see what **LODOSS WAR**'s Deedlit would look like with her clothes off. **NL**

ELVES OF THE FOREST

1984. JPN: *Mori no Tontotachi.* TV series. DIR: Masakazu Higuchi, Norio Yazawa, Osamu Inoue. SCR: Yoshiaki Yoshida, Ryoko Takagi. DES: Susumu Shiraume. ANI: Akihito Kato. MUS: Takeo Watanabe. PRD: Zuiyo, Fuji TV. 25 mins. x 23 eps.
Deep in the forests of Finland live the "little people," or Tontos, the elves who work all year round to keep Jorpikki (Santa Claus) supplied with toys for Christmas Eve. Based on the Finnish book *The Story of Santa Claus* and featuring a very Western look in the animation, *Elves of the Forest* also features one of anime's youngest actresses— one character was played by the designer's four-year-old daughter.

EMBLEM TAKE TWO

1993. Video. DIR: Tetsu Imazawa. SCR:

Tatsuhiko Urahata. DES: Hideyuki Motohashi. ANI: Hideyuki Motohashi. MUS: Kazuhiko Sotoyama. PRD: Toei. 50 mins. x 2 eps.

Gangster Susumu is betrayed in the backstreets and lies dying in a pool of his own blood. He wakes up to find a time warp has transported him ten years back into the past, returning him to a younger, healthier version of his former self who is ready to take on the world once more. In a tale of time travel revisionism similar to **DEEP BLUE FLEET,** Susumu is equipped with indelible memories of the people who will fall into and out of favor, who will rise to power in the organization, and who will betray him, and he begins a revenge vendetta before his opponents realize he's there. Based on the 1990 manga from *Young Magazine*, written by Kazumasa Kiuchi and drawn by Jun Watanabe, that cleverly combines nostalgia with modern savvy and gangster chic, the anime version was made to cash in on the success of a 1993 live-action film and TV series, directed by the creators.

EMERALD PRINCESS

1992. JPN: *Ruri-iro Princess*. Video. DIR: Takeshi Mori. SCR: Jiyu Watanabe. DES: Tetsuhito Saito. ANI: Tetsuhito Saito. MUS: Yoshiaki Matsuzawa. PRD: Studio Pierrot. 28 mins. x 2 eps.

High-school girl Ruri is dragged into a battle over the fate of the Pulsean Moon when the princess Leila sends assassins to dispense with her. Ruri's lover, Toru, is wounded protecting her, and Ruri must leave the real world behind and journey to the Pulsean Moon to save him. Based on the manga in *Omajinai Comic* by Mito Setsuhara, who also wrote the theme song.

EMPEROR OF THE SOUTH SIDE

1993. JPN: *Minami no Teio*. Video. DIR: Yoshitaka Fujimoto. SCR: Yoshitaka Fujimoto. DES: Masayuki Watanabe. ANI: Masayuki Watanabe. MUS: N/C. PRD: SHS Project, KSS. 45 mins. x 2 eps.

Ginjiro is a gangster in South Central Osaka who has just ten days to get back

a massive debt. This hard-hitting yakuza tale was based on the 1992 manga by Dai Tennoji (pseud. for **THERE GOES SHURA**–author Yu Kawanabe) and Rikiya Go in *Manga Goraku* magazine and was also adapted into a live-action video movie. **V**

END OF SUMMER *

1994. JPN: *Dokyusei Natsu no Owari ni*. AKA: *Classmates until the End of Summer*. Video. DIR: Kinji Yoshimoto. SCR: Sukehiro Tomita. DES: Masaki Takei, Ryunosuke Otonashi. ANI: Yoshiyuki Okuno. MUS: Tomas Unit. PRD: KSS, Pink Pineapple. 30 mins. x 4 eps., 30 mins. x 12 eps.

Wataru really loves Mai, but there's temptation all around and he just can't resist. The typical teenage-boy dream: lots of gorgeous women just throwing themselves at you, and a girl-next-door who believes you when you say you couldn't help yourself. The artwork, under the direction of **PLASTIC LITTLE**'s Yoshimoto, is really lovely, and you can observe the artists' skill with flesh tones in some detail. This series was based on the computer game *Classmates* by **DRAGON KNIGHT**–creator "elf" (Masato Hiruda). A 12-part sequel, *Classmates 2* (1997), was released in Japan on video and later cut into two toned-down TV movies. It focused on new-boy Makoto, who enjoyed a similar succession of encounters with the traditional female archetypes of anime porn: an older woman, a prissy rich-bitch, a foreign girl, a tomboy, a maidenly doormat, jailbait, and, finally, the girl next door. See also **FIRST LOVES**. **N**

EQUATION OF THE ROTTEN TEACHER

1994. JPN: *Kusatta Kyoshi no Hoteishiki*. AKA: *Fish in the Trap, Bad Teacher's Equation*. Video. DIR: Nanako Shimazaki. SCR: Hiromi Akino. DES: Akira Koguro. ANI: Yumi Nakayama. MUS: N/C. PRD: Daiei, Tokuma Japan Communications. 30 mins. x 2 eps.

In this adaptation of another gay-love manga from Kazuma Kadoka, the creator of **KIZUNA**, ten years after being

forced to suppress his feelings for the beautiful boy next door, a young man meets the object of his desires and gets a second chance. But Atsushi, whose unrequited love still burns, now finds himself in a classroom where Ma-chan, the object of his youthful affections, is now the teacher. A humorous homosexual variant on the school shenanigans of **HOMEROOM AFFAIRS**. **N**

EROTIC TORTURE CHAMBER *

1994. JPN: *Princess Lord: Bara to Rosoku no Monsho*. AKA: *Princess Lord: The Mark of Rose and Candle*. Video. DIR: Yoshitaka Fujimoto. SCR: Akira Oketani. DES: Masakatsu Sasaki. ANI: Masakatsu Sasaki. MUS: Torsten Rasch. PRD: Taki Corporation. 45 mins.

After 30 happy years, the twin kingdoms of Asronia and Gostania are awaiting the wedding of Prince Elias and Princess Yurie when the royal family is decimated by the army of Maryuo, the "Demon Dragon Lord." Elias is captured, Yurie is enslaved, and while the two supporting players who will save the day in the as-yet-unavailable second episode mooch around in their own subplot, the princess is taught the meaning of submission and obedience. The dark armor of Maryuo hides a well-spoken young man called Andreas, who wears half a bathrobe for no apparent reason and is exactly the kind of Bad Boy we know that Yurie has been waiting for. Yurie "reluctantly" offers her body to her captor in order to save her people.

A roster of well-known voice talents but with animation and design of a poor quality one has come to expect from a production crew just trying to pay the bills. The in-betweening often falters and the characters are lifted from other shows. The ninja bodyguard Maya borrows elements from both Ayanosuke of **YOTODEN** and Oscar of **ROSE OF VERSAILLES**, while the other leads are a standard cluster of anime archetypes.

The story's origin in Pierce Hoshino's erotic novel is betrayed in a languorous pacing that takes a good 20 minutes to get down to the nitty-gritty and so much back story that you can feel the original straining to squeeze itself into the format. Sex was clearly not the be-all and end-all of the original story, resulting in an anime version that takes too long to get going and then ends on a cliffhanger just when it does. **◎**

ESCAFLOWNE *

1996. JPN: *Tenku no Escaflowne*. AKA: *Heavenly Escaflowne; Vision of Escaflowne*. TV series, movie. DIR: Kazuki Akane, Shinichiro Watanabe, Takeshi Yoshimoto, Hiroshi Osaka, Takuro Shinbo, Tetsuya Yanasawa, Hiroyuki Takeuchi. SCR: Shoji Kawamori, Ryota Yamaguchi, Akihiko Inari, Hiroaki Kitajima. DES: Nobuteru Yuki, Kimitoshi Yamane, Mahiro Maeda. ANI: Shigeki Kobara, Yuki Kanno, Takahiro Omori, Yoshiyuki Takei. MUS: Yoko Kanno, Hajime Mizoguchi. PRD: Sunrise, TV Tokyo. 25 mins. x 26 eps. (TV), 98 mins. (m).

Hitomi Kanzaki is transported to an alternate Earth when a dragon appears on her school's running track. On Gaea, Earth is called the Mystic Moon, beast-men rub shoulders with knights in giant robots, and Earth girls are respected and feared for their sorcerous powers. Her companion, Van, is the disinherited prince of Fanelia and owner of the robot-armor Escaflowne, with which he resists the evil Zaibach Empire. Hitomi is witness to the uneasy alliance between Van and another nobleman, Asturia's roguish ladykiller Allen, but she is also the object of their competing affections. Tortured family ties writhe beneath the surface, with missing or disinherited siblings galore and revelations of dark or forgotten pasts. In only the first of several major plot twists, it is revealed that one of the leaders of the Zaibach armies is Folken, Van's disgraced brother. As war sweeps Gaea, Hitomi is revealed as the crucial key to victory, a role she is tempted to swap for a simple, carefree life back on Earth.

Deliberately designed to appeal to male and female viewers in equal measure, *Escaflowne* is genuine family entertainment, both in and out of the anime world, and arguably the best TV anime of the 1990s. Its ambiguous nature is reflected in *two* spinoff manga, Katsu-Aki's *Vision of Escaflowne* for the male readership of *Comics A*, and Yuzuru Yashiro's *Messiah Knight* for the female readership of *Asuka Fantasy DX*.

Five years in the planning, with something of a debt to SECRET OF BLUE WATER, it and UTENA were the two highly romantic shows that flourished in the morbid vacuum left by EVANGELION. In retaining its coherence throughout, and its earnest devotion to fantasy ideals instead of arch irony, posterity may well decide that *Escaflowne* is the best of them all. Reputedly passed over by Manga Entertainment for being "too childish," it starts off looking like a school romance or girls' sports anime before transforming into high fantasy adventure. As with GUNBUSTER, its first episode is a red herring, a school soap opera where Hitomi pines for her handsome senior Amano. In a steal from the stage version of PETER PAN AND WENDY, the actors of Earth scenes also play doubles in the fantasy world—Shinichiro Miki provides the voice of both Amano and *real* prince charming Allen. One of the few shows to continually outdo itself, *Escaflowne* is a triumph—though the dub sadly missed the opportunity to differentiate between accents on the two worlds by making all the Gaeans British.

Though it was reduced in size from a planned 39-episode run partway through production, the only evidence is the absence of opening credits from the first episode in order to allow the crew time to cram in extra exposition. This was remedied in the Japanese video release, the retail version of which also restored deleted scenes to the first 7 episodes. As the inevitable consequence of its popularity, it exists in bastardized versions, including the incoherent three-part *Best Collection* that unsuccessfully crams the entire

story into just 180 minutes. The series was further bowdlerized for the American TV market, with Yoko Kanno's beautiful music torn out in favor of humdrum techno, and the first episode removed in a version that, with bitter irony, was taken off the air after just 10 episodes because of "low ratings."

The movie version *Escaflowne: A Girl in Gaea* (2000) is a complete remake that redesigns the characters for the big screen and plays up the Asian feel of the series—the earlier TV version allowed elements of European fantasy to creep in. *Ill. p. 357.*

ESPER MAMI

1987. AKA: *Malicieuse/Mischievous Kiki*. TV series, movie. DIR: Pak Kyon Sun, Keiichi Hara, Tsukasa Sunaga, Atsuhide Tsukata, Osamu Inoue, Mitsuru Honma, Shinya Sadamitsu, Tomomi Mochizuki. SCR: Sukehiro Tomita, Ryo Motohira, Akira Higuchi. DES: Fujiko-Fujio. ANI: Sadao Tominaga, Chuji Nakajima. MUS: Kohei Tanaka. PRD: Shinei, TV Asahi. 25 mins. x 119 eps., 40 mins. (m).

Schoolgirl Mami Sagura discovers that she has superpowers. She can sense other people in trouble and teleport to help them, but she keeps her secret double-life hidden from her parents with the help of her schoolfriend, Kazuo Takahata. Based on the 1977 manga in *Corocoro Comic* by DORAEMON-creators Fujiko-Fujio, the series also spawned a short film, *EM: Midnight Dancing Doll* (1988), featuring Mami using her powers to make a puppet show for deprived children.

ETCHIIS

1997. Video. DIR: Kazunari Kume. SCR: Yokihi. DES: Yokihi. ANI: Toshimitsu Kobayashi. MUS: N/C. PRD: Pink Pineapple, KSS. 30 mins. x 2 eps.

Two short comedies, *Unio Familia* and *Normal Human Relations*, reputedly praised for "realistic female characterization" and lots of sex scenes. Based on the 1995 manga anthology by Yokihi, though *2x1*, the original's most popular story, was animated as part of the SECRET ANIMA series the following year and released in the U.S. as *Four Play*. Ⓝ

ETERNAL FILENA

1992. JPN: *Eien no Filena*. Video. DIR: Naoto Hashimoto, Yoshikata Nitta. SCR: Takeshi Shudo, Yasuko Hoshigawa. DES: Akemi Takada, Akiyuki Shinbo. ANI: Chuji Nakajima. MUS: Jinmo, Noriyoshi Matsuura. PRD: Pierrot Project. 30 mins. x 4 eps.

The Devis Empire offers gladiatorial games to keep the masses happy. It's the only way for a commoner to make any kind of living, and the lucky few who last long enough are made citizens. Filena poses as a man to enter the arena and fight to support her ailing mother, but as time passes, she begins to prefer the life of a poor revolutionary to that of a rich slave. Based on a novel serialized in *Animage* by POKÉMON-writer Shudo. Compare to GREY: DIGITAL TARGET.

EVANGELION *

1995. JPN: *Shinseiki Evangelion*. AKA: *Neon Genesis Evangelion; New Century Evangelion*. TV series, Movie. DIR: Hideaki Anno, Kazuya Tsurumaki. SCR: Hideaki Anno, Akio Satsugawa. DES: Yoshiyuki Sadamoto, Ikuto Yamashita. ANI: Masayuki, Kazuya Tsurumaki, Tadashi Hiramatsu. MUS: Shiro Sagisu. PRD: Tatsunoko, Gainax, TV Tokyo. 25 mins. x 26 eps., 102 mins. (m), 97 mins. (m).

At the turn of the millennium, a "meteorite strike" on Antarctica wipes out half of Earth's population. The NERV project fights the real danger—aliens called the Angels who are sending bioengineered weapons to destroy the rest of humanity. The experimental Evangelion project fights the outsized invaders with giant cybernetic organisms, but only children born after the Antarctica incident can pilot the machines. With Rei, the original test pilot, critically ill after an accident, head scientist Gendo Ikari summons his estranged son, Shinji, to take the first mission. Shinji is taken in by the

sisterly Misato, an alcoholic burnout with a passionate hatred for the Angels, and the arrival of the hot-headed pilot Asuka Langley creates a dysfunctional surrogate family.

With this novel excuse for young, audience-friendly protagonists and giant fighting robots, Gainax incorporates many of its favorite staples from classic anime and monster movies—the Evas themselves even have a five-minute timer in homage to ULTRAMAN. A deeply personal, psychological odyssey that allowed Anno to remake his earlier GUNBUSTER at a slower pace, *Eva* similarly replayed the Pacific War from the Japanese point of view, specifically the apocalyptic final events. Cosmetic use of Western religious imagery, such as Angel weaponry exploding in cruciform patterns, may appear to suggest that Western beliefs themselves are an alien invasion, but this owes more to Anno's own readings in Jungian psychology and archetypes as he coped with creative doldrums post-*Gunbuster*.

Like *Gunbuster*, *Eva* also piles on the parodies, particularly from Gerry Anderson shows (see THUNDERBIRDS 2086), with hidden fortresses launching superweapons and uniforms lifted from Anderson's live-action *UFO* (1969). It also features innovative casting, allowing famous voice actors to shine in unusual roles, especially RANMA 1/2's Megumi Hayashibara as the schizoid Rei and SAILOR MOON's Kotono Mitsuishi as the tragic Misato.

Ultimately, however, *Eva* ended in a series of disappointments. Gainax was criticized for later scenes broadcast without network approval, indirectly causing the more censorious climate that hurt COWBOY BEBOP. Later episodes ran visibly low on funds, with overlong pauses to stretch the animation budget and two concluding episodes that were glorified radio plays. Rumors abounded that Gainax had run out of money and/or time, and that the final chapters were thrown together in just two weeks when Anno's hard-hitting original finale was disallowed. However, *Gun-*

buster similarly ended with a montage of stills rather than the promised climactic battle, leading some to suggest Anno had always planned it this way and that the violent nature of the theatrical sequels reflected his annoyance that his "intellectual" ending was unappreciated by the audience. A succession of *Eva* movies followed, seemingly designed to leach the last cash and goodwill from remaining fans. An audio drama, *The Conclusion Continues* (1996), joked that having saved the world, the *Eva* cast would consider placing it in fake peril to get their old jobs back; though the gag was ironically close to the mark. The promised "real" finale turned out to be a double bill—*Death and Rebirth* (1997), a recap of the first 24 episodes with the first reel of the true ending. Audience patience was tested a second time with *Death (True)2*, which added tantalizing scraps of extra footage, including the moment of "Second Impact" and bonus sequences that also appeared in the Japanese (but not U.S.) video releases of the TV episodes. The genuine movie edition, *End of Evangelion* (1997), was a truly shocking apocalypse, taking the themes of the original to their logical conclusion presented as the two "missing" episodes that should have closed the series in the first place. These multiple endings have since been repackaged in another edition, *Revival of Evangelion*.

Despite this confused denouement, *Eva* was the most critically successful TV anime of the 1990s, drawing back many fans who had given up on the medium, and even inspiring *Newtype* to test market a new magazine for "intellectual" anime viewers. But like another of Anno's 1960s favorites, *The Prisoner*, it teased viewers with the illusion of hidden depths that weren't necessarily there, and though designed to be the last word on the giant-robot genre, its success merely ushered in a succession of imitations. Its influence, however, can also be seen in some of the better shows of the years that followed, BLUE SUBMARINE NO. SIX's Japan fighting a morally superior foe, **NADESI-CO**'s tongue-in-cheek homage to old shows, and **GASARAKI**'s mixture of militarism and theatrical passion. In the wake of *Eva*, TV became the growth medium for anime, in turn damaging the U.S. anime market, with distributors forced to risk more money for longer series when they would prefer shorter movies or video productions.

In the aftermath of *Eva*, Anno reused many of its stylistic conceits (such as multiple onscreen titles) in the live-action *Love and Pop* (1999) and the anime romance **HIS AND HER CIRCUMSTANCES**. Sagisu's score was also recycled when parts of it were lifted for Katsuyuki Motohiro's live-action TV series *Bayside Shakedown*. In a final irony, two members of the Gainax studio were indicted for tax evasion over the films' profits—the impoverished filmmakers who finished on a shoestring were now the new fat cats. *Ill. p. 153.*

EVEN MORE GHOST STORIES

1995. JPN: *Zokuzoku Mura no Obaketachi.* AKA: *Even More Village Ghosts.* Video. DIR: Tameo Ogawa. SCR: Masatoshi Kimura. DES: Konomi Sakurai. ANI: Konomi Sakurai. MUS: Koichi Hiro. PRD: Toei. 40 mins. x 6 eps.
A succession of tales taken from the 1.3-million-selling children's books by Akiko Sueyoshi and Mako Taruishi, including *Ram the Mummy, Obatan the Witch, The Childish Goblin,* and *Kitten Ghosts Goo, Soo and Pea.*

EVERY DAY'S A SUNDAY

1991. JPN: *Mainichi ga Nichiyobi.* Video. DIR: Hidehito Ueda. SCR: Hidehito Ueda, Kazuko Ueda. DES: Kazuya Ose. ANI: Kazuya Ose. MUS: Hiroya Watanabe. PRD: Animate Film. 30 mins. x 6 eps.
Yumi Takeshita is saved from a car accident but her rescuer is injured. When she meets him again a year later, she's a rookie police officer with the twin aims of working for justice and finding a boyfriend. His name is Toru Ichidai, and he's a conjuror. He would have

gone to Hollywood by now, but the accident has held him back. And now that he's met her again, he may as well stay in Japan to form half of an unusual crime-fighting team. Based on an idea by **3X3 EYES**–creator Yuzo Takada.

EVOCATION

1997. JPN: *Trouble Evocation.* Video. DIR: Masakazu Amiya. SCR: Ryoga Ryuen. DES: Ryoga Ryuen. ANI: Inatsugi Kiyomizu. MUS: N/C. PRD: Pink Pineapple, KSS. 30 mins. x 2 eps.
Hideya is visited every night by the cute sex-kitten Leah, who falls in love with him. One day she is ordered back to Hell by Satina, but Hideya begs her to stay. In this erotic variant on **OH MY GODDESS!** based on **ZANKAN**-creator Ryoga Ryuen's manga originally serialized in *Kitty Time,* Leah is so shocked by the strength of his feelings that she starts to take off her clothes.

EXCEL SAGA *

2000. JPN: *Heppoko [Silly] Animation Excel Saga.* TV series. DIR: Shinichi Watanabe, Akihiko Nishiyama, Jun Fukuda, Takafumi Hoshikawa, Ken Ando, Masahiko Murata. SCR: Kumi Jigoku, Yosuke Kuroda. DES: Satoshi Ishino. ANI: Satoshi Ishino. MUS: Toshio Masuda. PRD: JC Staff, TV Tokyo. 25 mins. x 26 eps.
In the fortified section of a heavily fortified underground fortress (he's taking no chances), Acros company boss Il Palazzo continues his ongoing attempt to conquer the world. Working for him are the two beautiful agents Excel and Hyatt, but protecting the world isn't a well-paying job, and the girls have to share a flat and travel to work on the subway. They also have to work part-time as bounty hunters to make ends meet, accompanied by their pet dog, Mensch, who is also an emergency food supply. A truly insane comedy in the spirit of **DRAGON HALF** (featuring the same voice actress, Kotono Mitsuishi), with time out for cameo appearances from director Watanabe in his trademark giant afro, assassination attempts on the author of

A murderous Mima, or perhaps someone who thinks he or she is Mima . . . or who the victim *believes* to be Mima. A brilliant example of how a film can be improved by budget cuts—originally planned as a live-action B-movie, the financial climate after the Kobe Earthquake *downgraded* **PERFECT BLUE** to an A-list anime. Director Satoshi Kon places the viewer inside the insanity by cutting all transition scenes between reality and dreams, forcing the audience to doubt the veracity of previous scenes. A masterful psychological thriller. *See entry p. 296.*

Perfect Blue

the original manga, Rikado Koshi, a theme song barked by a dog with Japanese subtitles, and a "flexible" attitude toward the deaths of main characters, perhaps inspired by the tribulations of Kenny from *South Park.* The final episode was not broadcast but included on the video release. **PUNI PUNI POEMI** is a spinoff from the show. Announced as forthcoming from ADV Films at the time of our deadline.

EX-DRIVER D

2000. AKA: *Ex-D.* Video. DIR: Jun Kawagoe. SCR: Shinzo Fujita. DES: Kenichi Hamazaki, Kosuke Fujishima, Hidefumi Kimura, Takeshi Takakura, Shunji Murata. ANI: N/C. MUS: N/C. PRD: Sunrise. 30 mins. x 6 eps.
A century in the future, travel has been made perfectly safe by the introduction of fully automated AI-cars. But when these electrically powered, computer-controlled cars run amok, it's the mission of the EX-Driver team to rev up their engines and give chase. It takes a particular kind of person to drive one of the temperamental gasoline cars, and the perky Risa and laidback Rhona think they have what it takes. This is a predictable SF rehash of Fujishima's earlier **YOU'RE UNDER ARREST**.

EXPER ZENON

1991. Video. DIR: Yuji Moriyama, Hiroaki Hayase. SCR: Yuji Moriyama, Yasushi Hirano, Shigeru Yamamoto. DES: Yuji Moriyama, Satoshi Hashimoto. ANI: Yuji Moriyama. MUS: Kenji Kawai. PRD: Studio Fantasia. 60 mins.

Tadashi is a high-school student and computer-game addict. After a long day spent playing the game Zenon, he is visited in a dream by the heroine, Sartova. In an anime replay of *The Last Starfighter*, she takes him to the world of Zenon, where the game is played with human lives at stake.

EXPLODING CAMPUS GUARDRESS

1994. JPN: *Bakuen Campus Guardress*. AKA: *Combustible Campus Guardress*. Video. DIR: Toshihiko Nishikubo. SCR: Satoru Akahori, Kazushi Hagiwara. DES: Kazuya Kose. ANI: Kazuya Kose. MUS: Fumitaka Anzai. PRD: Production IG. 30 mins. x 4 eps.

Thirty thousand years ago, Takumi, Hasumi, and Kasumi were tragic lovers who vowed to finalize their romance in another life. Thirty thousand years after these heroic Guardians defeated the evil Remnant invaders from the Dark World and sealed them behind an interdimensional Gateway, their reincarnations return once more to save the world. The site of the ancient battle is now in downtown Tokyo, hidden under the somewhat conspicuously named Gateway High School. When the cosmic moment comes for the Guardians and the Remnants to do battle once more, the reincarnations create some confusing blends of ancient and modern personalities and priorities, as our noble warriors are forced to choose between Armageddon and the senior prom, and they must fight enemies who were their friendly teachers only the day before. To make matters *incredibly* complicated, the Guardians have been reincarnated as brother, sister, and mother. Mom and Sis do not see any problems with trying to get into Takumi's pants when they are not battling the Remnants. However, Takumi seems to be more attached to his girlfriend from this life, Hime-chan, a total airhead who may fatally distract him from his duty. Based on a manga in *V Jump* magazine by **KNIGHTS OF RAMUNE**'s Akahori and **BASTARD**-creator Kazushi Hagiwara, this anime combines the gags and sauciness of the two.

EXPLORER WOMAN RAY *

1989. AKA: *The Explorer*. Video. DIR: Yasuo Hasegawa, Hiroki Hayashi. SCR: Mayori Sekijima. DES: Hiroyuki Ochi. ANI: Hiroyuki Ochi. MUS: Norimasa Yamanaka. PRD: Animate Film, AIC. 60 mins. x 2 eps.

Ray Kizuki is an archaeology student and a black-belt martial artist, bequeathed a mysterious mirror by her father that turns out to be the key to a newly discovered temple. She sets off to find it, accompanied by twins Mai and Maki and pursued by the mysterious "Rig Veda," who eventually reveals himself as her late father's assistant. Based on a manga in *Comic Nora* by **ELEMENTALORS**-creator Takeshi Okazaki. **Ⓥ**

F

F
1988. TV series. DIR: Koichi Mashimo, Katsuyoshi Yatabe, Kunihisa Sugishima, Nobuyasu Furukawa. SCR: Hideo Takayashiki. DES: Masamitsu Kudo, Tomohiko Sato. ANI: Masamitsu Kudo, Ryunosuke Otonashi. MUS: Wataru Yahagi, Masaru Hoshi. PRD: Kitty, Fuji TV. 25 mins. x 31 eps.
After the death of his mother, Gunma Akagi discovers his real father is a professional racer. After befriending pit boss Tamotsu, Gunma is inspired to join his father's world and becomes a driver himself, staying at his grandmother's place in Tokyo. The "F" stands for "formula," and with a fish out of water, a surrogate family, and a sporting quest, formula is exactly what you get.

F³: FRANTIC, FRUSTRATED AND FEMALE *
1994. JPN: Nageki no Kenko Yuryoji. AKA: The Lament of an Otherwise Perfectly Healthy Girl, Ménage à Trois. Video. DIR: Masakazu Akan. SCR: N/C. DES: Koji Hamaguchi. ANI: Koji Hamaguchi. MUS: Bang Heads. PRD: Pink Pineapple, KSS. 30 mins. x 3 eps.
A sapphic satire about Hiroe, who is unable to achieve orgasm with her boyfriend and seeks a remedy for her teenage frustrations. Her sister, Yayoi, helps with Chinese medicine, scientific inventions, and even a lesbian biker orgy. The trilogy ends with a haunted-house spoof in which demonic possession allows Yayoi to grow a penis for a replay of the hermaphroditic sex of **LA BLUE GIRL**. The script backtracks on the incestuous characters of episode one, later claiming that they only *look*

as if they are related. Based on the manga by Wan Yan A Gu Da, published in *Penguin Club*. **⚫⊕**

FABLED UNDERGROUND PEOPLE, THE
1989. JPN: Kore ga Uwasa no Chiteijin. Video. DIR: Kazuyoshi Hirose. SCR: Hisaichi Ishii. DES: Hisaichi Ishii. ANI: Kazumi Nonaka. MUS: Yukadan. PRD: Balk. 30 mins. x 2 eps.
In this spinoff from the *Action Comics* manga by **MY NEIGHBORS THE YAMADAS**–creator Hisaichi Ishii's serial, the Underground People desire to leave their overcrowded cavern and seize control of the surface world, but they never quite succeed. A second episode, *Christmas Aid*, soon followed, in which the brainless Undergrounders' second futile escape attempt is set to music by the popular group Yukadan. The first volume also included two unrelated stories by Ishii: *101 Ninja* and *Ken-chan's Space Exploration Adventure*.

FAIRGROUND IN THE STARS
1989. JPN: Hoshi no Yuenchi. Video. DIR: Nobuhiro Aihara. SCR: Nobuhiro Aihara. DES: Ryutaro Nakamura. ANI: Junichi Tokaibayashi. MUS: Koichi Hirai. PRD: Gakken. 18 mins.
A kindly teacher demonstrates origami to his elementary class, but when he gives a paper crane to a child, it is stolen from him by Takeshi, the class bully. Takeshi discovers that the crane is really a talking spaceship that takes him and his friends to visit a fairground in the stars. A girl falls through a hole into Space Hell, and the children cooperate to rescue her. Takeshi

wakes up, wondering if it was all a dream. The next day, he returns the magic crane to its rightful owner. This tale is from **RAINBOW ACROSS THE PACIFIC**'s Daisaku Ikeda, the leader of the Buddhist Sokagakkai organization, although it lacks a particularly religious or moral message, playing like a sanitized version of **NIGHT TRAIN TO THE STARS**. Note the presence of future **SERIAL EXPERIMENTS LAIN**–director Nakamura as a character designer. Ikeda also wrote **PRINCE OF SNOW COUNTRY**.

FAIRY KING
1988. JPN: Yosei O. Video. DIR: Katsuhisa Yamada. SCR: Tomoko Konparu. DES: Atsuo Noda. ANI: Atsuo Noda. MUS: Yuriko Nakamura. PRD: Madhouse. 60 mins.
Sickly high-school student Taka journeys to Hokkaido in search of a magical cure and falls in with Khoo Fu-Ling, the king of the fairies. Ninfidia, the land of the fairies, is under attack from the evil Queen Mab, and Taka must save it. Based on the 1978 girls' manga by Ryoko Yamagishi, which incorporated elements of legends of **KING ARTHUR AND THE KNIGHTS OF THE ROUND TABLE**, as well as scraps of Celtic, Greek, and Ainu myth.

FAKE *
1996. Video. DIR: Akira Suzuki. SCR: Akinori Endo. DES: Nagisa Miyazaki. ANI: Nagisa Miyazaki, Tomo Omota. MUS: Kix-S. PRD: Nippon Columbia. 60 mins.
Sanami Mato's original manga is a *Lethal Weapon* pastiche about fey New York cop Ryo being forced to partner up with Dee, a streetwise macho detec-

tive who wants to bed him. For this anime teaser to drag in new readers, Dee and Ryo are packed off to a British country hotel where guests are being murdered, and the supporting cast of the original manga drop by when they're least needed. While Dee's trying to seduce Ryo and idly mulling over the details of unsolved local killings, their teenage sidekicks serve little purpose except to play happy families with Ryo and Dee as mommy and daddy. The children turn what could have been a queer case of Agatha Christie into a pointless holiday farce, with much swapping of rooms and indoor roller-blading—because it's raining outside.

Ryo and Dee are the world's worst detectives, for whom solving a case involves gossiping for a while and waiting for the criminals to reveal themselves. Faced with a murder case that the *real* police would solve in roughly ten seconds, *Fake* throws in more cameos from the manga to pad out its running time, including the detectives' future boss, Berkley Rose, and Dee's unrequited admirer, JJ, who waste a few more minutes with comedy business before the script reluctantly returns to the murders at hand.

Fake often walks an uneasy line between comedy and tragedy. A bit of cop-on-cop banter fits fine with mayhem and chaos, but not when people are watching their friends die from multiple stab wounds. As one might expect from a story with its pedigree, it ultimately has too many characters and too little time, making the murder mystery unengaging and turning an original romantic farce into humdrum formula. Far from breaking new ground in gay characterization, Ryo is simply a man playing a stereotypical female role; he gets to be an intuitive sidekick, a maternal figure, an unattainable romantic prize, and, as the show rushes to an insane conclusion, even a damsel in distress.

FANCY LALA

1998. JPN: *Maho no Stage Fancy Lala.*

AKA: *Magical Stage Fancy Lala.* TV series. DIR: Masahiro Omori, Takeshi Yamazaki, Miko Shima. SCR: Tomomi Mochizuki. DES: Akemi Takada. ANI: Masako Onishi, Kazuhiro Sasaki. MUS: Michiru Oshima. PRD: Studio Pierrot, TV Tokyo. 25 mins. x 26 eps.

Miho is an eight-year-old girl with a secret: using her two magical pets, Pig and Mog, and her magical sketchpad, she can turn into the beautiful teenage fashion model known as Fancy Lala. As might be expected in a rehash of CREAMY MAMI, she attracts the attention of 19-year-old local wiseguy Hiroya, who falls in love with her adult version, not realizing she is only a child underneath.

FAR EAST OF EDEN

1990. JPN: *Tengai Makyo.* AKA: *Evil World beyond Heaven.* Video. DIR: Oji Hiroi, Toshio Takeuchi. SCR: Toshio Takeuchi. DES: Kotaro Tsujino. ANI: Yasuo Otsuka. MUS: Kohei Tanaka. PRD: TMS. 50 mins. x 2 eps.

In the alternate world of Xipangu, hero Jiraiya defeats local pirates and heads off in search of the fabled treasure of the death god, Hiruko, but Jiraiya is opposed by an equally evil sorcerer. Joining forces with the beautiful princess, Yuki (who has the power to seal Hiruko away), Jiraiya must confront a gang of renegades, led by a female impersonator, that intends to conquer the entire kingdom. Based on a game for the PC Engine console, designed by Red Company, who would eventually make SAKURA WARS with director Hiroi. Though the vampiric Hiruko is defeated at the climax, in the original, the end-of-game boss was Masakado—see DOOMED MEGALOPOLIS. Note the presence of CASTLE OF CAGLIOSTRO's Yasuo Otsuka as animation director and a crew roster that brought a great look to an otherwise forgettable cash-in.

FATAL FURY *

1992. JPN: *Battle Fighters: Garo Densetsu.* AKA: *Battle Fighters: Legend of the Hungry Wolf; Mark of the Wolf.*

Movie, TV special. DIR: Kazuhiro Furuhashi, Masami Obari, Hiroshi Fukutomi. SCR: Takashi Yamada. DES: Masami Obari. ANI: Masami Obari. MUS: Toshihiko Sato, Toshiro Masuda. PRD: Asahi International, Pony Canyon, Fuji TV, NAS. 45 mins. (TVm) 73 mins. (TVm), 90 mins. (m).

As with its contemporary STREET FIGHTER II, this adaptation of a beat-'em-up console game struggles and ultimately fails to make the jump to non-interactive media, though not without some incidental pleasures on the way. Viz's dub is perfectly serviceable, albeit with some unplaceably alien accents from the supporting cast that only add to the fun as one tries to guess whether someone is supposed to come from Oirlend or Scutlund. With overmuscled men meeting, greeting, indulging in strange acts, and then parting, it has a strangely homoerotic charge, peppered with sanctimonious moral messages about the nobility of fighting for what is right but without questioning whether anyone should be fighting at all.

FF: Legend of the Hungry Wolf (1992) sets up the original back story to the game, in which Terry and Andy Bogard witness their father's murder and become bare-knuckle fighters, in a tournament plot not unlike TEKKEN, eventually avenging him by defeating his murderer Geese Howard. Mere months later in *FF: The New Battle* (1993), Howard's half-brother, Wolfgang Krauser, returns to challenge Terry. With time out to reunite a street urchin with his mother in a halfhearted subplot, Terry soon hunts Krauser down to a showdown in a German castle, while other characters pop out of the woodwork for a few rounds to please their fans. The franchise reached theaters at its peak with *FF: The Motion Picture* (1994), which dumped at least part of the "you killed my father" plotting in favor of an Indiana Jones rip-off. Laocoön Gaudeamus is searching for the legendary Armor of Mars, lost by his ancestors during the Crusades. His estranged sister,

Sulia, hires Terry to stop him before he can use the armor's magical powers, in a plot that presages SPRIGGAN, though it was too late to save the tired and formulaic *FF* franchise. **V**

FENCER OF MINERVA *
1995. JPN: *Minerva no Kenshi*. AKA: *Knight of Minerva*. Video. DIR: Takahiro Okao, Tadayoshi Kusaka. SCR: Sukehiro Tomita, Yuji Kishino. DES: Takashi Wada. ANI: Tadashi Hirota, Nobuaki Shirai. MUS: Kanae Wada. PRD: All Products, Beam Entertainment. 45 mins. x 5 eps.
The beautiful, willful Princess Diana is betrothed to a handsome prince but is captured by nomads, who refuse to believe her royal protestations because out of her clothes she looks just like any other wench. After a brief initiation in the amatory arts, she is rescued from a gang bang by a masked man, her childhood sweetheart Prince Sho, who is returning to claim his rightful kingdom from the man who usurped it, Princess Diana's evil father.

Believe it or not, from the tacky designs that replace original ideas with two-legged horses and flying piranhas (sorry, water lizards) to USMC's faithfully camp translation of some of the world's worst dialogue, *Fencer of Minerva* genuinely is so bad that it's good. But what do you expect when the CREAM LEMON team try to imitate B-movie sword-and-sandal fantasy, complete with lost kingdoms, lovably chauvinist heroes, and breathless slave-girls in diaphanous veils? A guilty pleasure, as if John Norman had written an episode of RECORD OF LODOSS WAR. Compare to the similarly risible EROTIC TORTURE CHAMBER. **NV**

FIFTH ICE AGE
1967. JPN: *Subarashii Sekai Ryoko: Alaska no Tabi: Daigo Hyogaki*. AKA: *Wonderful World Travel: Alaskan Journey: Fifth Ice Age*. TV special. DIR: Masahiro Mori. SCR: Mamoru Sasaki. DES: Hiroshi Manabe. ANI: N/C. MUS: Kiyoshi Iwami. PRD: Mushi Pro. 30 mins. x 2 eps.

In the near future, Earth is engulfed in a new ice age as snow falls ceaselessly in summer and glaciers advance with uncharacteristic speed. In this SF spin-off of the live-action *Wonderful World Travel* series, humanity must decide whether to use science to fight the ice or to adapt to it. The same anime team would also peer into the future in COMPUTOPIA.

FIGHT! OSPA
1965. JPN: *Tatakae! Ospa*. TV series. DIR: Masami Aragura, Nobuhiro Okaseko, Yoshiyuki Tomino. SCR: Koichi Yamano, Teru Nagashima. DES: N/C. ANI: Mami Murano, Nobuhiro Okaseko. MUS: Isao Tomita. PRD: NTV. 25 mins. x 52 eps.
The inhabitants of the sunken Pacific continent of Mu (see SUPER ATRAGON) yearn to leave their undersea dome and return to the surface world. After many centuries beneath the waves, they are threatened with destruction by the power-hungry Dorome. The good people of Mu send Ospa, their finest man, to find help on the surface world, where he assembles an international team to fight for justice. Based on an idea by TAKE THE X TRAIN–author Koichi Yamano, this series is a combination of the *Dolphin Prince* (see MARINE BOY) and PRINCE PLANET.

FIGHT! PUTER
1968. JPN: *Fight Da!! Pyu-ta*. TV series. DIR: Hiroe Mitsunobu, Jun Nagasawa, Kunitoshi Shiraishi. SCR: Yoshitake Suzuki, Kenichi Ogawa, Kuniaki Hatanaka. DES: Tsunezo Murotani. ANI: Tameo Ogawa. MUS: Tetsuaki Hagiwara. PRD: MBS. 25 mins. x 26 eps.
Pyuta Imano helps his grandfather, Professor Tsulury, with his experiments. The evil Walther VII and his sidekick, Glocky, try to seize control of the world. While trying to stop them, an accident gives Pyuta a super-computer for a brain. Airing the day after the first episode of CYBORG 009, this younger version was based on a manga in *Shonen Sunday* by Tsunezo Murotani,

whose *Piccory Bee* (the tales of a "Thunder Child" who falls from the sky) had also been animated in 1967.

FIGHT: SPIRIT OF THE SWORD *
1993. JPN: *Fight!!* Video. DIR: Akira Koson. SCR: Akira Koson. DES: Kenichi Onuki. ANI: Masanori Nishii. MUS: Taikai Hayakawa. PRD: Pony Canyon. 45 mins.
High-school student Yonosuke Hikura is the latest in his family to protect the harmony between Heaven and Earth. With the help of the magical sword Chitentai, and Tsukinojo Inbe, a Protector sent to him by the High Priests of Earth, he courageously battles the demons, sending them back to the Earth World from which they have escaped. Another tale in the tradition of DEVIL HUNTER YOHKO, but it's played disappointingly straight.

FIGHTER
1990. JPN: *Kentoshi*. Video. DIR: Yoichiro Shimatani. SCR: Ranko Ono. DES: Kuniaki Tsuji. ANI: Kuniaki Tsuji. MUS: Takahiko Kanemaru. PRD: Apple, Miyuki Pro. 45 mins. x 3 eps.
Kenji is a heavyweight boxer who wants to learn from the legendary Tokyo trainer Eddie Williams and win the American championships. In New York, he takes on the heavyweight Joe

Roman, before fighting another American, George MacGregor, for the title at Madison Square Garden. In this predictable adaptation of Takashi Tsukasa's series from *Manga Club,* it is needless to say that, in the tradition of innumerable sports anime from **TOMORROW'S JOE** to **AIM FOR THE ACE**, by the time of the big fight, coach Eddie is on his deathbed. **ⓥ**

FIGURE 17: TSUBASA AND HIKARU

2001. TV series. DIR: Naohito Takahashi. SCR: Yasuhiro Imagawa, Masashi Komemura. DES: Yuriko Senba. ANI: Yuriko Senba. MUS: Toshihiko Takamisawa. PRD: OLM, Anime Theater X. 60 mins. x 12 eps.
Interstellar traveler "DD" is transporting the Magua energy source when he crash-lands on Earth. He enlists the help of Hokkaido ten-year-old Tsubasa in getting it back, giving her a mysterious capsule containing the doll-like superheroine Figure 17. A predictable rerun of the transforming superhero of **ULTRAMAN** and **BIRDY THE MIGHTY**, pretentiously billed in Japan as "smashing the broadcast paradigm" just because the episodes were twice as long as usual.

FINAL FANTASY *

1993. AKA: *Legend of the Crystals: Based on Final Fantasy.* Video. DIR: Rintaro, Naoto Kanda. SCR: Satoru Akahori, Mayori Sekijima. DES: Yoshinori Kanemori, Kunihiko Sakurai. ANI: Naoto Kanda, et al. MUS: Masahiko Sato. PRD: Madhouse. 30 mins. x 4 eps.
Two hundred years after the elimination of the evil Exdeath, reckless swordsman Prettz and the summoner Linaly are the youngsters who must save their world from Ra Devil, a biomechanical being from the dark moon. Set several centuries after the end of the game, this series is a distant spinoff from *Final Fantasy V,* whose character Batts is supposedly Linaly's ancestor.

The plot is similar to a computer game—after a few random encounters with wandering monsters, the leads must unite two warring parties to create a suitably mismatched party of fearless heroes. Pirate queen Rouge, the whip-wielding mistress of an airship crewed by leather-clad fat girls, falls in love with her sworn enemy, Valcus, leader of the Iron Wing squadron. After some mild tortures (Prettz is tickled and Linaly has to drink prune juice), the former enemies unite to fight Ra Devil, destroying both him and his Bond-villain hideout.

FF's hackneyed quest to save four elemental crystals is upstaged by its backgrounds. As in the games, a good image wins out over the practicalities of physics or geography. With a large number of Chinese and Korean staffers, *FF* lifts design ideas from all over the Orient, with the tall, thin mountains of Guilin forming a backdrop for *klong* canals from Thailand, and old-world Chinese houses from Canton providing hangars for pseudo-Miyazaki giant airplanes.

As later *FF* games achieved fame abroad, this anime was dusted off and released in English with undue prominence given to the words *Final* and *Fantasy* and rather less to its origins as a spinoff from an untranslated prequel.

Hironobu Sakaguchi's fully computer animated *Final Fantasy: The Spirits Within* (2001) features a quest to obtain eight organic specimens, whose "spirit signatures" will cancel out the energies of alien ghosts. Made in Hawaii, it boasts an all-star cast and the anime version's voice director, Jack Fletcher.

FIRE EMBLEM *

1995. JPN: *Fire Emblem: Aritia no Oji.* AKA: *Fire Emblem: Prince of Aritia.* Video. DIR: Shin Misawa. SCR: Yosuke Kuroda. DES: Yuji Moriyama. ANI: Yuji Moriyama. MUS: N/C. PRD: KSS, Studio Fantasia. 30 mins. x 2 eps.
Pacifist prince Mars reluctantly tools up when his homeland, Aritia, is conquered by the evil Druans. On the run with his faithful knights and a reformed mercenary in the neighboring kingdom of Taris, he enlists the aid of the king's only daughter, the Pegasus-riding Princess Cedar. Originating

in a "Fantasy Simulation Game" for the Nintendo Famicom (NES) console, this is a predictable spinoff—just enough episodes to drag back hardcore game fans then rerelease as a one-shot for rental and the export market, which cannot be expected to be as forgiving.

FIRE FIGHTER DAIGO

2000. JPN: *Megumi no Daigo.* Video. DIR: Akira Nishizawa. SCR: Akihiko Inari. DES: Hideyuki Motohashi. ANI: Hideyuki Motohashi. MUS: Shiro Hamaguchi. PRD: Sunrise. 45 mins.
Maverick fireman Daigo Asahina risks disciplinary action by bodily throwing civilians from a high window, but he's exonerated when the building blows up seconds later. Running a gauntlet of girlfriend trouble, he is caught in a fire at a local concert hall and is forced to leave people behind. Outside, he steals a fire engine and rams through a wall, carrying the victims out to public acclaim.

Despite a five-minute closing credit sequence with only three minutes of credits and under-animated moments pretending to be dramatic slow-mo, *FFD* overcomes its low budget thanks to a stirring orchestral score and clever design. Fire and water surround Daigo, even in humdrum scenes of everyday life, with the camera zooming in on a hose at a car wash or a scarlet sunset that looks as if the sky itself is aflame. The fire-fighting scenes themselves are similarly well observed, with incongruous pillars of water falling down through an inferno, and a no-win scenario that finds Daigo knee-deep in water inside a burning building, dodging falling debris and sparking electric cables. Based on the 1995 *Shonen Sunday* manga by Masahito Soda that was itself doubtlessly inspired by Naoto Takenaka's 1994 live-action fire-fighting film *119,* this video traces a thematic line back to the 1991 Hollywood movie *Backdraft.*

FIRE TRIPPER *

1985. JPN: *Rumic World: Fire Tripper.*

Video. DIR: Motosuke Takahashi. SCR: Tomoko Konparu. DES: Katsumi Aoshima. ANI: Junko Yamamoto, Mami Endo. MUS: Keiichi Oku. PRD: Production Ai, OB. 47 mins.

Modern Japanese girl Suzuko and a neighbor's child are thrown back in time by a gas explosion. Meeting the handsome Shukumaru, Suzuko searches for the lost neighbor boy, not realizing that Shukumaru is the adult version of the 20th-century child who accompanied her, and that she herself is an exile from the 15th century. This adaptation of one of Rumiko Takahashi's *Rumic World* manga shorts (which also include MERMAID'S FOREST, MARIS THE CHOJO, and LAUGHING TARGET) cleverly exploits the conventions of time-travel stories as well as the shifting age boundaries put to more lascivious effect in CREAM LEMON. Released on a theatrical double bill with THE HUMANOID. Takahashi would return to medieval time travel in her later INU YASHA.

FIRST KISS STORY
2000. JPN: *First Kiss Monogatari*. Video. DIR: Kan Fukumoto. SCR: Gaku Hoshino. DES: Hiroki Mizugami, Tatsuo Yanagino. ANI: Tatsuo Yanagino. MUS: N/C. PRD: Yaryu, Broccoli. 30 mins. x 4 eps. (planned, only 1 so far).

Yoshihiko is in his busy sophomore year at college while love-interest Kana is stuck back in high school. Her life takes a turn for the surreal when a new teacher at her school turns out to be the spitting image of her dead father. Set two years after the end of its PlayStation origins, Gaku Hoshino's screen adaptation of his game was released on Valentine's Day in a futile attempt to drum up business. The presence of LA BLUE GIRL's Fukumoto as director invites the question, Is he trying to disentangle himself from tentacle porn or is the name an "Alan Smithee" credit used by others on titles of questionable value?

FIRST LOVES *
1995. JPN: *Kakyusei*. AKA: *Underclass-

mates*. Video. DIR: Koichi Yoshida, Kan Fukumoto. SCR: Masaru Yamamoto. DES: Yuji Takahashi. ANI: Yuji Takahashi. MUS: N/C. PRD: Pink Pineapple, KSS. 30 mins. x 4 eps., 30 mins. x 4 eps.

The protagonists in this sequel to END OF SUMMER are younger teenagers, though of course the U.S. version is at pains to assure us that they're not legally minors. Kakeru follows Wataru's lead, trying to make it with his dream girl, Urara, but getting distracted here and there, through no fault of his own of course, when love blooms at a tennis club and another student reveals that she has a sideline as a nude model. These teen titillations were followed in 1997 by a four-part sequel, the special "elf" edition, named for the DRAGON KNIGHT–creator involved in the original game. Set once again in the high-school dreamtime of a final summer vacation, it depicts new-boy Toru's attempts to bed girl-next-door Miho. **N**

FIRST STEP
2000. JPN: *Hajime no Ippo*. AKA: *First for Ippo*. TV series. DIR: Satoshi Nishimura, Nanako Shimazaki. SCR: Tatsuhiko Urahata, Shoji Sugiwara, Hiroshi Mori. DES: Koji Sugiura. ANI: Noriyuki Fukuda. MUS: Tsuneo Imahori. PRD: Madhouse, TV Tokyo. 25 mins. x 31+ eps.

When high-school student Ippo backs out of seeing his friends in order to help his mother with the family business, the other kids at school start pushing him around. Looking for a way of fighting back, Ippo approaches a boxing trainer, Mamoru Takamura, and asks for his help. He begins a tough exercise regime, and, as he learns to stand up for himself, decides that he would like to make boxing his career. Based on the ongoing 1989 manga serialized in *Shonen Magazine* by Joji Morikawa, this is a lighter-hearted take on the sports-drama genre stretching right back to TOMORROW'S JOE. **V**

FIST OF THE NORTH STAR *
1984. JPN: *Hokuto no Ken*. AKA: *Ken the Great Bear Fist—Legend of a

Karate Warrior*. TV series, movie. DIR: Toyoo Ashida, Hiromichi Matano, Hideo Watanabe, Masahisa Ishida. SCR: Susumu Takahisa. DES: Masami Suda. ANI: Masami Suda. MUS: Katsuhisa Hattori, Nozomu Aoki. PRD: Toei, Fuji TV. 25 mins. x 109 eps., 25 mins. x 43 eps., 110 mins. (m).

Rival gangs fight for supremacy in a postholocaust wasteland. Out of the dust walks Kenshiro, a young martial artist in search of his fiancée, Julia, who has been kidnapped by his brother Shin. In the opening story arc (complete in the U.S., truncated in the U.K.), Ken must hunt down the disparate members of his estranged martial-arts family before he defeats Shin and finds, and then loses, the love of his life.

Thrilling a teen audience with its hyper-violence and repetitive menace-of-the-week, the 1983 *Shonen Jump* manga by Tetsu Hara and Buronson was a timely retread of *Mad Max 2: The Road Warrior*. Continuing long after the initial "Julia" story was resolved, the series became a staple of 1980s Japanese pop culture, with Ken lampooned as the hulking Mari in PROJECT A-KO, and his booming voice actor Akira Kamiya becoming a star in his own right. But as the series wore on, drastic budget cuts forced the animators to improvise, sometimes with mind-boggling results. The crew constantly found creative new ways to dispatch villains, such as smearing wet paint on a cel between two pieces of glass, or shooting in real-time through the churning waters of a half-empty fish-tank. The show similarly exploited surreal perspectives—everyone seems giant and impossibly muscled seen through the eyes of children Bart and Lynn but appear smaller from Ken's point of view. The show's star waned even in Japan, and though the second series ended sooner than expected, the franchise was kept alive by foreign sales. A movie-length remake of series one encompasses Ken's search for and defeat of Shin, Shin's admission that the more powerful Raoh has already kidnapped Julia to be *his* bride, a battle between Ken and Raoh, and the revelation that Julia has disappeared once more. Though Julia had committed suicide by this point in the original series, the movie edition leaves it open-ended, with Ken wandering into the desert in search of her again, believing her to be still alive. The movie version of series one, dubbed in the U.S. by Streamline, was Manga Entertainment's first U.K. release and became the cornerstone of their martial-arts-fueled, "beer-and-curry" marketing plan. Riding the coattails of AKIRA, it became one of the U.K.'s best-selling anime videos, though more through its length of tenure in stores than its overt quality.

In 1998, the company tried to capitalize on the anime's "success" by releasing the full 15-year-old TV series. This version featured a good actor as Ken, but it was clumsily cut together with no appreciation of story breaks and mixed so shoddily that Bart ends up playing a silent harmonica. The series was also "augmented" with a drum & bass music track, which, to be fair, couldn't have made it any worse. After predictably disappointing sales, the distributor pulled the TV edit only partway into the schedule, though by this time its "foreign popularity" had inspired a Japanese satellite network to rerun it every day. Like its hero, *Fist of the North Star* simply refuses to die. The series is more likely to be known in the mainstream for its 1995 live-action remake, directed by Tony Randall and starring Gary Daniels. A manga prequel, *Fist of the Blue Sky* (2001), features the adventures of Ken's namesake uncle in 1930s Asia. ●**V**

FIVE STAR STORIES
1989. JPN: *Five Star Monogatari*. Video. DIR: Kazuo Yamazaki. SCR: Akinori Endo. DES: Mamoru Nagano, Nobuteru Yuki, Mika Akitaka. ANI: Nobuteru Yuki. MUS: Tomoyuki Asagawa. PRD: Sunrise. 60 mins.
The Joker Cluster consists of five star systems in close proximity, where human pilots (headliners) are bonded

with sentient androids (fatimas) to control giant robots (mortar heads). Dr. Chrome Ballanche, the greatest of the genetic engineers, completes his two most perfect creations, the fatimas Lachesis and Clotho. Their sister, Atropos, has vanished. The fatimas go to the castle of the local lord Uber to be "impressed," a ceremony at which they select their future partners from among the ranks of headliners. Most pilots have to make do with "etrimls," low-grade subhuman versions, so the beautiful fatimas are highly prized, not only by the assembled pilots, but also by several notables who are attending the ceremony in disguise.

Condensed from just one segment of Mamoru Nagano's sprawling 1986 manga that's still occasionally serialized in *Newtype*, *FSS* duplicates the original's baroque feel, as well as its near impenetrability. With mount-rider relationships that presage BRAIN POWERED and sumptuous science-fantasy conceits, the look of the characters and machinery is as marvelous as one might expect from a fashion-designer-turned-rock-musician such as Nagano. ●

FLAG!
1994. JPN: *Sakidama Hassai Saizen Sen Flag*. AKA: *Sakidama Racing Pole Position Flag*. Video. DIR: Satoshi Dezaki. SCR: Machiko Kondo. DES: Mutsumi Inomata. ANI: Hideki Takahashi. MUS: N/C. PRD: Vap, Magic Bus. 45 mins.
Sixteen-year-old Noboru Yamazaki and Akira Maruyama join the Moonlight bike gang at the Sakidama Biker Meet, although they don't actually own any motorcycles. A rival gang, the Asian Tigers, uses its gangster connections to take out a hit on the Moonlight gang's leader. Noboru inherits his leader's motorcycle, and the attentions of biker chick Hisami. Based on Akio Hotta's manga in *Young King*, this is a latecomer to the anime subgenre established by BOMBER BIKERS OF SHONAN. ●

FLAME OF RECCA
1997. JPN: *Recca no En*. TV series. DIR:

Noriyuki Abe, Kazunori Mizuno. SCR: Hiroshi Hashimoto, Satoru Nishizono. DES: Mari Kitayama, Atsushi Wakabayashi. ANI: Yoshiyuki Kobe, Minoru Yamazawa. MUS: Yusaku Honma. PRD: Studio Pierrot, Fuji TV. 25 mins. x 42 eps.
Contemporary teenage ninja fan Recca Hanabishi becomes embroiled in the activities of real-life ninja. The beautiful Yanagi is targeted by an evil industrialist who wants to use the girl's power to become immortal, and Recca must team up with his school friends to learn the secrets of the martial arts before it is too late. Adapting Nobuyuki Anzai's 1995 manga from *Shonen Sunday*, this series owes a great debt to POLTERGEIST REPORT, with plenty of fighting, some off-color humor, and acrobatics to rival NINJA SCROLL's. However, despite early promise, a low animation budget takes its toll, as does the series' disappointing decline into endless martial-arts bouts. ●**V**

FLCL *
2000. JPN: *Furi Kuri*. Video. DIR: Kazuya Tsurumaki. SCR: Yoji Enokido. DES: Yoshiyuki Sadamoto. ANI: Tadashi Hiramatsu, Hiroyuki Imaishi. MUS: The Pillows. PRD: Gainax, Production IG. 25 mins. x 6 eps.
Left alone in the house with his older brother's 17-year-old girlfriend, Mamimi, Naota Nandaba is concerned that her flirting ways will place him in a difficult situation. The arrival of the scooter-riding, guitar-swinging tomboy Haruko Haruhara swaps one set of problems for another, as Naota is forced to share his life with an alien, a grumpy robot, and the uncontrollable Mamimi. Mixing a narrative inspired by the same studio's HIS AND HER CIRCUMSTANCES with characterization and designs influenced by their earlier EVANGELION, *FLCL* represents a determined effort by Gainax to both supercede its successes of the late 1990s and incorporate elements of the one title that competed with them in fans' polls as the show of the moment. UTENA-writer Enokido brings a surreal

tinge to the whole operation. All but episode one were released in Japan with English subtitles on DVD.

FLIGHT OF THE WHITE WOLF

1990. JPN: *Hashire Shiroi Okami*. AKA: *Run White Wolf*. Movie. DIR: Tsuneo Maeda, Masuji Harada. SCR: Wataru Kenmochi. DES: Isao Kumata, Marisuke Eguchi, Satoshi Matsuoka. ANI: Marisuke Eguchi. MUS: Antonín Dvořák. PRD: Tac, Toho. 84 mins.

Lasset has grown up with a wolf called Gray since they were both babies. Lasset's father found the cub and reared it, but, as he grows, the neighbors become understandably concerned. Gray kills a local dog that belongs to the sheriff, and his days seem numbered. Lasset sets out with Gray, determined to get him to a wolf sanctuary where he can live in peace. Unfortunately, it's several hundred miles away, so the pair face a long road and many adventures in the tradition of **BELLE AND SEBASTIAN**. Based on the novel by Mel Ellis.

FLINT THE TIME DETECTIVE *

1998. JPN: *Jiku Tantei Genshi Kun*. AKA: *Time Detective Genshi*. TV series. DIR: Hiroshi Fukutomi, Koichi Takada, Shinji Okuda. SCR: Hideki Sonoda. DES: Yoshiko Ohashi. ANI: Takashi Yamazaki, Munekatsu Fujita. MUS: Tadashi Nanba. PRD: Pioneer, Tac, TV Tokyo. 25 mins. x 43 eps.

Petrafina Dagmar (accompanied by her two stooges, Might and Dyno) wants to loot the past so that the Dark Lord can destroy the Land of Time. Each period contains a special critter called a time-shifter, each of which possesses a magical power. To coin a phrase, Petra wants to "catch 'em all." Time-shifters keep the very fabric of time together, and their theft is policed by the Bureau of Time & Space Investigations. In one million B.C., Petra demands that caveboy triceratops-herder Flint Hammerhead (Genshi) and his father hand over Getalong (a penguin-like time-shifter whose power is to ensure that everyone gets along).

When they refuse, she turns her fossilizer ray on them then returns to the 25th century to dig them up. Using her modern-day disguise as schoolteacher Miss Aino (pronounced and spelled "Iknow"), she encourages her class to go out and find fossils for her. However, twins Sarah and Tony take their fossil to their uncle, Bernie Goodman, at the Bureau. Bernie, with a little behind-the-scenes help from the Dark Lord's adversary the Old-Timer, defossilizes Flint with one of his gizmos. The process has given Flint superhuman strength, so he is enlisted in the Bureau. Flint's father remains a talking rock, so Bernie carves him into a stone axe for Flint and installs a fossilizer/defossilizer ray in the haft. Each week, Flint is called upon to foil Petra's latest scheme in a different time period. Some of her temporal interferences include imprisoning and taking the place of Japan's ancient queen Himiko (see **DARK MYTH**) and instilling a lust for gold into the Conquistadors. A rehash of the successful **TIME BOKAN** series but with a monster-collecting angle bolted on for the 1990s, *Flint* was snatched up in the tidal wave of post-**POKÉMON** anime interest and brought to the U.S. in record time by **DIGIMON**-producers Saban Entertainment.

FLOWER ANGEL *

1979. JPN: *Hana no Ko Lunlun*. AKA: *Lunlun the Flowergirl*. TV series/special, movie. DIR: Yuji Endo. SCR: Noboru Shiroyama. DES: Michi Himeno. ANI: Tatsuhiro Nagaki. MUS: Hiroshi Tsutsui. PRD: Toei, TV Asahi. 25 mins. x 50 eps.

Lunlun is the 12-year-old daughter of a flower seller in the French countryside. Nouveau, her talking dog, and a cat called Cateau are emissaries from the king of the floral planet Flowern. The bad queen, Toginicia, has seized control of the kingdom and sent her servant Yaboki (a disguised *tanuki*, see **POMPOKO**) to seize the seven colors of magical flowers found on Earth. Lunlun, who can transform into a girl with special powers with her flower key, must travel the world with Nouveau

Irresponsible Captain Tylor

IRRESPONSIBLE CAPTAIN TYLOR joins the military because he wants an easy life. He rises through the ranks simply by loafing, until his lazy attitude brings him prestige, his own command, and the adoration of an alien empress. Conceived as a space-age parody of a famous 1960s farce, in which a salaryman comedian achieved similar successes, albeit without sci-fi trappings. Creator Hitoshi Yoshioka would further lampoon the Japanese military in his privatization farce **HUMMINGBIRDS**. *See entry p. 185.*

© 1997 HITOSHI YOSHIOKA/KADOKAWA SHOTEN/TYLER PROJECT

and Cateau to collect the plants before Yaboki. Flower lore, a magical girl à la **CREAMY MAMI**, and an early collector's quest that presaged **CARDCAPTORS**, all dressed up in a European setting variously described by distributors as Switzerland or France, depending on their mood. There was also a short 15-minute movie version screened in Japanese theaters in 1980.

FLOWER WITCH MARYBELL

1992. JPN: *Hana no Maho Tsukai Marybell*. TV series, movie. DIR: Tetsuya Endo. SCR: Yasunori Yamada. DES: Kenichi Onuki, Shigenori Kanatsu. ANI: Tadashi Hirota, Yuriko Senba. MUS: Takako Ishiguro. PRD: Ashi Pro, TV Tokyo. 25 mins. x 39 eps.

The adventures of a girl with a magical tambourine who works in her parents' flower shop but rights wrongs in her superheroine disguise, often with the help of her friends, Julia and Ribbon. Magic and music in the everytown of Sunnybell, this was also released as a 40-minute theatrical short, *Marybell: The Movie* (1992), in which Marybell is transported to a fantasy world after reading the story of the phoenix in her aunt's book.

FLOWERS BEFORE BOYS

1996. JPN: *Hana yori Dango*. TV series, movie. DIR: Shigeyasu Yamauchi. SCR: Yumi Kageyama, Reiko Yoshida, Aya Matsui. DES: Yoshihiko Umakoshi. ANI: Chuji Nakajima, Tomoko Ito, Tomoyuki Kawano. MUS: Michiru Oshima. PRD: Toei, TV Asahi. 25 mins. x 51 eps. (TV), 25 mins. (m).

Sixteen-year-old Makino Tsukushi is a girl from a poor family who gets a scholarship to attend the prestigious Eitoku Academy. Though she tries to keep a low profile, she is soon singled out for hazing by "F4," an elite group at the academy composed of the sons of the richest families in Japan. When she stands up to them, their leader, Domyoji, becomes attracted to her, though she finds herself falling for his lieutenant, Rui. Rui, however, loves Shizuka, a gorgeous fashion model. This gentle romantic comedy was based on Yoko Kamio's 1992 manga in *Margaret*, which was also adapted into a live-action film and Taiwanese TV series *Meteor Garden*. The same crew also made the theatrical short *FBB: The Movie* (1997), a musical in which Makino travels to New York to become a star, replaying the **CINDERELLA** story even as she appears in a stage version of it.

FLY ISAMI!

1995. JPN: *Tobe Isami*. TV series. DIR: Gisaburo Sugii, Tatsuo Sato. SCR: Hideo Takayashiki, Tomoko Konparu. DES: Kazuaki Mori. ANI: Kazuaki Mori, Yoshiko Sakurai. MUS: Hiroaki Serizawa. PRD: Tac, NHK. 25 mins. x 50 eps.

Isami, a 12-year-old girl with a newscaster mother and research-scientist father, fights against a secret organization, the "Black Tengu," that is trying to take control of the world. Eventually, the Black Tengu joins forces with the Serizawa industrial conglomerate, and Isami must recruit her friends and her father's inventions to fight back.

FLY ON, DREAMERS!

1994. JPN: *Kattobase! Dreamers!* Movie. DIR: Yoshinori Kanemori, Morio Asaka. SCR: Hideo Takayashiki. DES: Yuzo Sato. ANI: Yuzo Sato. MUS: N/C. PRD: Hiroshima Film Center, Madhouse. 86 mins.

In an original story by **BAREFOOT GEN**–creator Keiji Nakazawa, a group of children orphaned by the bombing of Hiroshima fulfill their dream of playing with the professional baseball players of the Hiroshima Carp.

FLY PEEK! *

1992. JPN: *Tobe! Kujira no Peek*. AKA: *Fly! Peek the Whale; Peek the Baby Whale; The Boy and the White Whale Calf*. Movie. DIR: Koji Morimoto. SCR: Keiko Nobumoto, Koji Morimoto. DES: Satoru Utsunomiya. ANI: Satoru Utsunomiya, Hideo Okazaki. MUS: Yoshihisa Tomabechi. PRD: Toho. 80 mins.

After a storm, two young brothers find a baby white whale, the titular Peek, trapped by a rock in a shallow inlet in the Spanish coast. The boys decide to help it return to its mother on the open sea, but one of the boys, Kei, is tormented by older children until he lets the secret out. The whale is taken away by circus owner Odeon, and Kei journeys to the big city to set Peek free. Based on an original story by Hidehito Hara and predating the 1993 Hollywood movie *Free Willy*, beautiful settings and charmingly retro-styled character designs combined in a high-quality children's film that was badly served in the U.K. market, where distributors Kiseki only released a subtitled print.

FLY PEGASUS!

1995. JPN: *Tobe! Pegasus: Kokoro ni Goal ni Shoot*. AKA: *Fly! Pegasus: Shoot for the Goal of the Heart*. Movie. DIR: Shinji Okuda. SCR: Hideki Sonoda. DES: N/C. ANI: Junji Aoki. MUS: Masahito Suzuki. PRD: EG, Victor. 74 mins.

A high school for blind children fields a soccer team using a ball that emits a noise so it can be located. The potential for accidental fouls is mind-boggling, but only in anime could you find such a bizarre combination of **HELEN KELLER** and **CAPTAIN TSUBASA**.

FLYING GHOST SHIP

1969. JPN: *Soratobi Yurei Kan*. Movie. DIR: Hiroshi Ikeda. SCR: Masaki Tsuji, Hiroshi Ikeda. DES: Shotaro Ishi(no)mori. ANI: Yoichi Otabe, Hayao Miyazaki, Hideki Hayashi. MUS: Takasuke Onosaki. PRD: Toei. 60 mins.

A ship carrying a load of the prized "Boar Juice" soft drink is attacked by restless spirits. At the same time, the teenage Atsuhito saves the Kuroshaku drinks company president and his wife from a cycling accident and experiences a vision of the ship's skeletal captain. Atsuhito soon discovers that Kuroshaku is concealing secrets in the basement, and, as a giant robot lays waste to the city center, Atsuhito confronts the company about the truth behind its popular drink. Another cautionary tale from the creator of **CYBORG 009**, with animation and design work on the "golem" giant robot by Hayao Miyazaki.

FLYING SHADOW

1985. JPN: *Ninja Senshi Tobikage*. AKA: *Ninja Warrior Flying Shadow; Tobikage*. TV series. DIR: Masami Annai, Hiroyuki Yokoyama, Takashi Akimoto, Kazuyoshi Katayama. SCR: Sukehiro Tomita, Hideki Sonoda, Hideo Takayashiki. DES: Shigeru Kato, Toshihiro Hirano, Yasushi Moriki, Koichi Ohata. ANI: Takeshi Osaka. MUS: Koji Kawamura. PRD: Studio Pierrot, Magic Bus, Nippon TV. 35 mins. x 43 eps.

Soldiers from the evil planet Zaboom invade the peace-loving world of Radorio, forcing princess Romina to flee on the starship Elshank in search of the fabled "ninja" warrior who can save her people. Arriving in the solar system, she recruits several Earthlings to become the ninja warriors of old—the Black Lion, Fiery Dragon, and Thunder Phoenix. They return to pilot the Flying Shadow giant robot against the minions of Zaboom, in spite of the distinctly ungrateful population of Radorio, who refuse to believe they can do it. A mix of a team show and giant-robot combat,with an alien starship whose interior is modeled on samurai-period Japan.

FOBIA *

1995. JPN: *Mirai Choju Fobia*. AKA: *Future Superbeast Fobia*. Video. DIR: Shigenori Awai. SCR: Narihiko Tatsumiya. DES: Yoshinobu Yamakawa. ANI: Yoshinobu Yamakawa. MUS: Arcadia Studio. PRD: Tec, Gaga. 45 mins. x 2 eps.

Replinoids, creatures who thrive on human blood and have a preference for young girls, exhaust the supply in 2112 and come back to 1990s Japan to harvest more female flesh. They are pursued by Megumi, a time-traveling agent instructed to find a hero who can wield a magic sword of justice to destroy them. Replinoids murder several members of Enoshima College's drama group, and Megumi teams up with class geek Mutsumi, who inevitably turns out to be the Chosen One.

With a heroine resembling a younger version of Urara from his SAKURA DIARIES and a school background redolent of ANGEL, manga creator U-Jin makes a rare foray into SF for a tits-and-tentacles story line that combines the story of *Terminator* with the face-huggers and adult beasts of *Aliens*. However, the attempts at both murder-mystery and questing subplots are somewhat stillborn. Time and cast are so limited that there is only one suspect for the murders and only one candidate for hero, while the contemporary setting is under-used in favor of a school that is conveniently deserted by all but the central cast every time something interesting happens. The overuse of flashbacks cleverly, but also obviously, recycles footage to save money. Compare to DEMON BEAST INVASION. **NCLV**

FOR REAL

1990. JPN: *Maji*. Video. DIR: Kazuya Miyazaki. SCR: Shigeo Nakakura. DES:

Ayumi Tachihara. ANI: Chuji Nakajima. MUS: Hideo Shimazu. PRD: Creative Bridge, Transarts, Nippon Animation. 50 mins. x 2 eps.

Maji is a young punk in the Nagisa criminal organization whose name is synonymous with loyalty and truth. He falls for a local high-school girl, Kumiko, but their affair is as doomed as any meeting of different worlds—when the tattooed boy and his moll go out on the town, they run into the rival Kikuchi gang looking for trouble. A gangster story based on the first two volumes of the 50-part 1986 *Shonen Champion* manga by JUSTICE-creator Ayumi Tachihara. The first episode was screened theatrically. **NV**

FORCE FIVE *

1980. TV series. DIR: Kenneth Feuerman. SCR: Mike Haller. DES: N/C. ANI: N/C. MUS: N/C. PRD: Toei, Jim Terry Productions. 25 mins. x 74 eps. (*Grandizer*), 44 eps. (*Gaiking*), 39 eps. (*Starvengers*), 56 eps. (*Dangard Ace*), 64 eps. (*Spaceketeers*).

Five separate anime serials bought and repackaged for stripped U.S. syndication by Jim Terry so that each could be shown on a different day of the week, every week. The separate series have their own entries in this book as DANGARD ACE (Mondays), *Starvengers* (i.e., GETTER ROBO, Tuesdays), SPACEKETEERS (Wednesday), GRANDIZER (Thursday), and GAIKING (Friday). Though many of the *FF* serials had figures that were included in the SHOGUN WARRIORS line, Mattel had lost its license for the toys by the time *FF* was broadcast. Jim Terry Productions also tried to sell a feature-length edit of each series, some of which made their way to U.K. video as the *Krypton Force* line.

FORTUNE QUEST

1994. Video, TV series. DIR: Takeshi Yamaguchi, Takashi Watanabe. SCR: Keiko Maruo, Yumi Kageyama, Reiko Yoshida. DES: Yumi Nakayama. ANI: Kazuhiro Okaseko, Susumu Ishizaki. MUS: N/C. PRD: Victor, Beam Entertain-

ment, MBS. 30 mins. x 4 eps. (V), 25 mins. x 26 eps. (TV).

A group of adventurers on a parallel world seek their fortunes in a story whose debt to role-playing games is so great that the press notes even describe the characters as "low-level." Teenage "mapper" Pastel leads a party comprising young swordsman Clay, bandit chieftain's son Trapp, blue-blood "walking dictionary" Kitton, gentle giant Knoll, baby dragon Shiro, and infant elf sorceress Rumy. After their latest quest, they call in at the Adventurers Support Group, which stamps their ID cards and evaluates their experience, both pastiching and predicting the inevitable console game version of the story. Originally based on a best-selling 1991 novel by Michio Fukuzawa, who also wrote the *Duan Surk* prequel set in the same universe, the story was also adapted into a manga by Natsumi Mukai, in turn adapted into the sequel anime TV series *Fortune Quest L* by Eiichi Sato and SLAYERS-director Takeshi Watanabe. The series added the gaming experience by featuring hidden items and monsters, as well as unexpected dialogue from certain characters. Though hardly anything new, it prepared the ground for the success of POKÉMON, for which exploiting the game tie-in was the sole raison d'être.

FOXES OF CHIRONUP

1987. JPN: *Chironup no Kitsune*. Movie. DIR: Tetsuo Imazawa. SCR: Fukuo Matsuyama. DES: Yoshinao Yamamoto. ANI: Noriko Imazawa. MUS: Etsujiro Sato. PRD: Tac, Herald. 72 mins.

Foxes Ken and Chin become the proud parents of cubs, Koro and Kan, who enjoy a carefree life on the northern Japanese island of Chironup. They befriend a fisherman and his wife but are forced to run for their lives when soldiers on a military exercise decide to take home some fox pelts as souvenirs. A sweet little film that obliquely symbolizes the plight of Japan's aboriginal Ainu people and the northern islands that have been contested with

Russia since they were occupied by Stalin's soldiers in 1945. Based on a book by Yoshiyuki Takahashi.

FOXWOOD TALES

1991. Video. DIR: Seiji Endo. SCR: Seiji Endo. DES: Brian Paterson. ANI: Maya Matsuyama. MUS: Osamu Tezuka (not *the* Osamu). PRD: Grouper Productions. 25 mins. x 3 eps.

Harvey, Rue, and Willie are a hedgehog, rabbit, and mouse who live in a windmill in the peaceful town of Foxwood, where they have several adventures in this short-lived series based on the children's picture books by the British creators Cynthia and Brian Paterson.

FRANKENSTEIN *

1981. JPN: *Kyofu Densetsu Kaibutsu: Frankenstein.* AKA: *Mystery! Frankenstein Legend of Terror.* TV special. DIR: Yugo Serikawa. SCR: Akiyoshi Sakai. DES: Toyoo Ashida. ANI: Toyoo Ashida. MUS: Kentaro Haneda. PRD: Aoi Productions, Toei Animation, TV Asahi. 111 mins.

After the success of **DRACULA: SOVEREIGN OF THE DAMNED**, the same team made this bewildering version of Mary Shelley's novel. For reasons unknown, the setting was moved to North Wales, where Frankenstein conducts his experiments amid the mountainous splendor of Snowdonia. His creature, Franken, is brought to life by a lightning bolt and runs for Switzerland, where he is pursued by police inspector Belbeau. Franken befriends a little girl called Emily and her blind father, saving Emily from a wild bear before succumbing to his fate and committing suicide.

FREE KICK FOR TOMORROW

1992. JPN: *Ashita e no Free Kick.* TV series. DIR: Tetsuro Amino, Toshiaki Suzuki. SCR: Masaru Yamamoto, Nobuaki Kishima, Akira Oketani. DES: Noboyushi Habara. ANI: Takahiro Omori, Masami Suda. MUS: Satoshi Tozuka. PRD: Ashi, Nippon TV, Shizuoka TV. 25 mins. x 50 eps.

Shun arrives in Italy with his disabled friend, Roberto, to live with his rich grandfather who also emigrated from Japan many years ago. He becomes passionate about soccer, but Grandfather wants him to take over the family business and resents the time he devotes to sports. Eventually, though, he has to accept that Shun will become a professional player. Roberto, meanwhile, succeeds as an architect and wants to build a great stadium in their town, a project that Shun's grandfather very much opposes. The series has an open ending—a big competition with top teams comes to the town, but we never know if Shun's team wins. A series that reflects the reality of a modern sports business, where few players were born anywhere near the town they represent, and corporate interests can make or break a team.

FRIED OCTOPUS MAN

1998. JPN: *Takoyaki Manto Man.* AKA: *Fried Octopus Cloak Man.* TV series. DIR: Masami Annai. SCR: Yoshio Urasawa. DES: Midori Nagaoka. ANI: Tsugenobu Kuma. MUS: N/C. PRD: Studio Pierrot, TV Tokyo. 25 mins. x 12 eps.

Evil priest Baobao is intent on ruling Earth, and a lone woman in a *takoyaki* (fried octopus dumplings) diner prays for a savior to protect the planet. In a series that owes a lot of its comedy and inspiration to the earlier **ANPANMAN,** the woman's request is answered, sort of, when a hero arrives draped in an edible cloak.

FRIGHTFUL NEWS

1991. JPN: *Kyofu Shinbun.* Video. DIR: Takashi Anno. SCR: Masaaki Sakurai. DES: Koji Uemura. ANI: Koji Uemura. MUS: Takashi Tsunoda. PRD: Pierrot Project. 50 mins. x 3 eps.

Junior high-school student Rei Onigata finds a newspaper, *The Frightful News,* that cuts one's life short by a hundred days whenever it is read. It also, however, contains much interesting information about the spirit world and future events, and Rei is the only one who can read it. Realizing he has been tricked by an evil spirit, he offers his services to psychic Jo-un Hoshi. Rei, his love interest, Midoriko, and her sister are stalked by the ghost of an old man in a dark cloak. This short series is based on the 1973 *Shonen Champion* manga by Jiro Tsunoda, who also drew **HYAKUTARO** and **KARATE-CRAZY LIFE**. In 1996, the story was remade as a live-action movie, directed by Teruyoshi Ishii. Perhaps in the wake of the not-dissimilar live-action film *Ring* (1998), it was brought back in 2000 for a one-shot "manga video," in which voice actors narrated the story over still images from the manga onscreen.

FRITEN-KUN

1981. Movie. DIR: Taku Sugiyama, Kazuyuki Okaseko. SCR: Noboru Shiroyama, Tsunehisa Ito, Haruya Yamazaki. DES: Takamitsu Mitsunori. ANI: Takamitsu Mitsunori, Haruo Takahashi, Keiji Morishita. MUS: Haruo Matsushita. PRD: Knack. 75 mins.

Gambling japes from Friten, a Tokyo gangster whose sense of humor was screened on a double bill with the diametrically opposed Osaka-based comedy of **JARINKO CHIE**. Based on the manga by Masashi Ueda, serialized in both *Modern Mahjong* and *Gamble Punch* magazines, the seven vignettes here include Friten demonstrating his winning gambling tactic and the wrong way to play mahjong. Among the stories are more far-fetched incidents such as his trip back in time to Edo-period Japan, his attempts to get involved in real sports, and his hapless tries at seducing the pretty Ikue-chan.

FROM THE APENNINES TO THE ANDES

1976. JPN: *Haha o Tazunete Sanzan Ri.* AKA: *3,000 Leagues in Search of Mother.* TV series, Movie. DIR: Isao Takahata, Hajime Okayasu. SCR: Kazuo Fukuzawa. DES: Yoichi Otabe. ANI: Yoichi Otabe. MUS: Koichi Sakata. PRD: Nippon Animation, Fuji TV. 21 mins. x 51 eps.

Italian boy Marco lives in the town of

Genoa, which has been hard hit by heavy taxes and recession. His mother leaves for Argentina, where her husband runs a clinic for the poor, but Marco cannot bear to be parted from her and pursues her ship. So begins a long quest that will ultimately take him to Bolivia, in the company of the Peppino puppet theater, and Fiorina, the daughter of a local chieftain. The story was reedited into a 107-minute movie version in 1980 by Hajime Okayasu and completely remade by director Kozo Kusuba as *Marco* (1999). Based on part of the novel *Cuore* by Edmondo de Amicis, which was also adapted in its entirety as HEART: AN ITALIAN SCHOOLBOY'S JOURNAL. The moving story was also mercilessly lampooned in the 1991 GENIUS IDIOT BAKABON–movie *3,000 Leagues in Search of Osomatsu's Curry* (1991), directed by Akira Saito, in which the quest for Mother was replaced by a zany search for a decent meal.

FROM TODAY ON, THIS IS ME

1992. JPN: *Kyo kara, Ore wa!* Video. DIR: Takeshi Mori. SCR: Shikichi Ohashi. DES: Masaya Onishi. ANI: Masaya Onishi. MUS: Kimio Morihari. PRD: Studio Pierrot. 61 mins.
Teenagers Takashi Mitsubashi and Shinji Ito move to a new high school in "C" Prefecture near Tokyo and resolve to pretend to be the toughest kids around, dyeing their hair into threatening tough-guy blond hairdos. Forced to cooperate simply because each could rat out the other, they outwit genuine tough guys with elaborate bluffs and deceits. This movie is based on a comedy in the 1988 manga in *Shonen Sunday* by Hiroyuki Nishimori. Compare to BITE ME! CHAMELEON.

FRUIT BASKET

2001. TV series. DIR: Akitaro Daichi. SCR: Rika Nakase. DES: Akimi Hayashi. ANI: N/C. MUS: N/C. PRD: Studio Deen, Fuji TV. 25 mins. x 26 eps.
Happy-go-lucky orphan Toru Honda has to move in with the family of Yuki, the high-school boy she secretly adores. However, she is not expecting to discover that they are a family of sorcerers and shape-shifters. Fluffy animals, magic, and schoolgirl crushes, based on the manga by Natsuki Takaya in *Hana to Yume* magazine.

FUJIKO F. FUJIO'S LITTLE WEIRDNESS THEATER

1990. JPN: *Fujiko F. Fujio no Sukoshi Fushigi (SF) Tanben Theatre*. Video. DIR: Satoshi Dezaki, Tomomi Mochizuki. SCR: Toshiaki Imaizumi. DES: Keizo Shimizu. ANI: Keizo Shimizu. MUS: N/C. PRD: Studio Gallop. 50 mins. x 5 eps.
A series of SF short stories by the cocreator of DORAEMON made for adults but in the spirit of fondly remembered shows from childhood. The punchy one-shots include *Tomorrow in the Letterbox*, in which a man receives a message from the future warning of impending danger for his friends; *A Dish for the Minotaur*, about a crash-landed astronaut who finds himself on a planet where the roles of men and cows are reversed, and finds that he is to be eaten at a royal banquet; *Green Guardian*, a pastiche of *Day of the Triffids* in which Tokyo is overrun by man-eating plants; *Island of Extinction*, about the population of Earth being all but wiped out by invading aliens; and the lighthearted superhero pastiche, *Ultra Super Deluxe Man*.

FUKU-CHAN

1982. JPN: *Fuku-chan: Yokoyama Ryuichi no Kessaku Anime*. AKA: *Fuku-chan: Ryuichi Yokoyama's Anime Masterpiece*. TV series. DIR: Mineo Fuji. SCR: Masaki Tsuji, Toshiyuki Kashiwakura, Noboru Shiroyama, Hiroko Naka. DES: Ryuichi Yokoyama. ANI: Michishiro Yamada. MUS: Hiroshi Tsutsui. PRD: Shinei, TV Asahi. 25 mins. x 71 eps.
Childish goings-on for Fukuo Fuchida (also known as Fuku-chan), a small boy who attends nursery school with his "girlfriend," Kumi, and hangs out with his playmates Namiko (whose parents own a china shop), her younger broth-

Cowboy Bebop

© 1998 SUNRISE INC.

er, Kiyo, naughty twins Doshako and Garako, and school bully Ganchan.

FUKUYAMA THEATER: SUMMER SECRETS

1990. JPN: *Fukuyama Gekijo: Natsu no Himitsu*. Video. DIR: Michiyo Sakurai. SCR: Michiyo Sakurai. DES: Keiko Fukuyama. ANI: N/C. MUS: N/C. PRD: Urban Project. 60 mins.
Several short animated films based on the short stories and four-panel manga of Keiko Fukuyama, including *My Father the Mouse*, *The Rabbit Brothers*, *Summer Secret*, *The Mysterious Fairy*, *How Very Strange*, and *Kuro*.

FUMOON

1980. TV special. DIR: Hisashi Sakaguchi. SCR: Hisashi Sakaguchi. DES: Hitoshi Nishimura, Hisashi Sakaguchi. ANI: Hitoshi Nishimura. MUS: Yuji Ono. PRD: Tezuka Pro, Nippon TV. 91 mins.
Nuclear-bomb tests near Horseshoe Island have mutated the locals, creating a new breed of psychic humans called the Fumoon. Dr. Yamadono reports on the new species at an international conference attended by representatives from the nuclear superpowers, Star and Uran (a thinly disguised U.S. and USSR), but nobody listens to his dire warnings. Star and

Uran go to war, while the Fumoons constitute a third front, attacking all humans while a cloud of dark gas closes in around Earth. By the end, as the Fumoons flee into space, the warring nations join forces to save the planet and discover that the dark gas is a benign phenomenon that turns into harmless oxygen—though who is to say that next time the human race will be so lucky? A cautionary tale from **ASTRO BOY**–creator Osamu Tezuka based on his 1951 manga *Next World*, itself inspired in equal parts by the Korean War and nuclear testing in the Pacific. As with other TV specials from Tezuka, many characters from his other stories appear in cameo roles. See also **METROPOLIS**, to which *Fumoon* is a distant sequel.

FUSHIGI YUGI: THE MYSTERIOUS PLAY *

1995. JPN: *Fushigi Yugi*. AKA: *Mysterious Game*. TV series/special, video. DIR: Hajime Kamegaki, Nanako Shimazaki, Akira Shigeno. SCR: Yoshio Urasawa, Kazuhisa Sakaguchi. DES: Hideyuki Motohashi. ANI: Hideyuki Motohashi, Hisatoshi Motoki, Mayumi Hiroda. MUS: Tatsumi Yano. PRD: Studio Pierrot, TV Tokyo. 25 mins. x 52 eps., 56 mins. x 2 eps. (TVm), 30 mins. x 3 eps. (v), 45 mins. x 6 eps. (v).

Fifteen-year-old Miaka accompanies her friend Yui to Tokyo's national library, where the girls find an ancient Chinese book called *The Universe of the Four Gods*. They are transported to the world of the book, though Yui is soon thrown back to Earth, leaving Miaka temporarily stranded. Miaka finds herself in a fantasy version of ancient China, where she is rescued from slavers by the handsome Tamahome and becomes a ward of the emperor. The land of Konan ("Southern Scarlet," as it is called) is threatened by invaders from Kotuo, and Miaka volunteers to be the long-awaited priestess of Suzaku ("Vermilion Sparrow"), who will assemble the legendary heroes known as the Seven Stars of Suzaku and save the world.

Though Yu Watase's original manga in *Flower* magazine dated back to 1992, *Fushigi Yugi* was swamped by the later success of the superior **ESCAFLOWNE**, making *FY* look like a lackluster copy. This anime's problems include an intensely irritating heroine, Miaka, with all the charm of a spoiled child, conspicuously cheap animation that often has to resort to static pans, and a forgettable plot assembled from off-the-peg clichés. The Emperor Hotohori falls in love with Miaka, but she loves Tamahome, a predictable love triangle which causes a falling-out with her friend Yui. Nevertheless, *FY* clearly struck a chord with an audience too young to remember *The Neverending Story* or the **WIZARD OF OZ**, and the series gained an enthusiastic fan following in both Japan and the U.S. The second season (episodes 27–52) changes slightly, with the death of one of Miaka's guardians, the removal of some of the risqué humor that occasionally lightened the first season, and an endless succession of arbitrary magical obstacles to stretch out Miaka's journey.

Two TV specials were little more than clip shows of the highlights of the first 33 episodes, but a true sequel soon continued the series on video. The first video series was set a month after the close of the TV version, with the events in Konan returning to haunt the cast back on Earth in both serious and parody versions on the same tapes. Looking suspiciously like a third TV season consigned to video after falling ratings, 1997's second "video" series plunged the cast into a new conflict over the mystic Jewel of Memory. A later Yu Watase work, **CERES: CELESTIAL LEGEND**, soon followed in both Japan and the U.S.

FUTURE BOY CONAN

1978. JPN: *Mirai Shonen Conan*. AKA: *Conan the Boy in Future*. TV series, movie. DIR: Hayao Miyazaki, Isao Takahata, Keiji Hayakawa. SCR: Takaaki Nakano, Soji Yoshikawa. DES: Hayao Miyazaki, Yasuo Otsuka. ANI: Yoshiaki Kawajiri, Hideo Kawauchi. MUS: Kenichiro Ikehama. PRD: Nippon Animation, NHK. 25 mins. x 26 eps. (TV), 123 mins. (m).

Twenty years after a devastating nuclear war in 2008, only scattered communities of humans are left living on the small islands that were once mountaintops. Conan grows up on his island with his grandfather, believing themselves to be the last survivors of their race until a young girl, Lana, is washed up on their shore. She is a refugee from the evil military kingdom of Industria, which is trying to revive the use of dangerous energy sources. A first-time directing job for Hayao Miyazaki that incorporated elements he would later reuse in his **NAUSICAÄ** and **CASTLE IN THE SKY** (though the original genesis of *FBC* lay in the novel *The Incredible Tide* [1970], by Alexander Key). The series was also edited into *FBC: The Movie*, which was released three months before **CASTLE OF CAGLIOSTRO** and, hence, could be argued on a technicality to be Miyazaki's first "movie."

The franchise was revived as *FBC 2: Taiga Adventure* (1999), directed by Miyazaki's former assistant Keiji Hayakawa, though its relationship to the original is extremely tenuous. The eponymous Taiga and his archaeologist father, Professor Dyno, are searching for ancient artifacts in South America, where there was supposedly a mysterious culture that could build great metallic birds 20 thousand years before. As he fights with treasure hunters for control of the ancient power-stones, Taiga discovers that the ancient O-Parts devices can power land, sea, and air machines that are each designed to look like a giant animal. In other words, it's a rehash of **BABEL II** and **MYSTERIOUS CITIES OF GOLD** with a name designed to promise more than it actually delivers. *Ill. p. 177.*

FUTURE COP URASHIMAN

1983. JPN: *Mirai Keisatsu Urashiman*. AKA: *Rock 'n' Cop*. TV series. DIR: Koichi Mashimo, Shinya Sadamitsu, Takaaki

Ishiyama. SCR: Hirohisa Soda, Haruya Yamazaki, Kenji Terada. DES: Takashi Nakamura, Shigeru Kato, Chuichi Iguchi. ANI: Takashi Nakamura, Kunihiko Yuyama. MUS: Shinsuke Kazato. PRD: Tatsunoko Pro. 25 mins. x 50 eps. An SF adaptation of *Urashima Taro* (see **JAPANESE FOLK TALES**) about Ryo Urashima, a young private investigator from 1983 Tokyo who is whisked to the year 2050 by Professor Q, a mad scientist working for the evil, blue-skinned Führer. The trip into the future subjects Ryo to the "Urashima Effect"—he loses his memory and develops superhuman powers. Führer plans to use Ryo for his own ends, but Ryo is found by the police, who enlist him in their robot police unit, Magnapolice 88, along with a handsome wiseguy, Claude Mizusawa, and token girl Sophia Nina Rose. A witty sci-fi spectacle, it begins with comedy business (as Ryo insists on using his 1983 Volkswagen Beetle instead of a 2050 police car) that soon takes a more serious turn as Ryu tracks down Führer's Necrime group and becomes involved in the power struggle between Führer and his assistant, Adolph von Ludovich.

FUTURE WAR 198X

1982. Movie. DIR: Toshio Masuda, Tomohiro Katsumata. SCR: Yuji Takada. DES: Masami Suda. ANI: Masami Suda. MUS: Seiji Yokoyama. PRD: Tokkyu Agency, Toei. 125 mins.
American scientist Bart, a specialist in Star Wars orbital antimissile lasers, defects on a Russian submarine, which is sunk by the U.S. Navy. His best friend, Mikumo, is ordered to come out of mourning to finish Bart's work, while U.S. president Gibson tries to calm the volatile diplomatic situation. His efforts fail, and border troubles between East and West Germany escalate into full-scale war. When American Secretary of Defense Bugarlin murders Chief Secretary Orlof of the Soviet Union, all negotiations break down, and atomic war breaks out.

A controversial anime production inspired in part by the best-selling *The Third World War, August 1985* by General Sir John Hackett, *FW198X* was based on actual projections from contemporary government reports and statistics. During production, there were protests about the "aggressive content" of the story, creating something of a media stir in Japan.

G

GAIKING *

1976. JPN: *Ozora Maryu Gaiking*. AKA: *Great Sky Dragon Gaiking; Daiking; The Protectors*. TV series. DIR: Tomoharu Katsumata, Takeshi Shirato, Masamune Ochiai, Hideo Takayashiki. SCR: Kunio Nakatani, Masao Murayama, Masaru Yamamoto, Soji Yoshikawa. DES: Takeshi Shirato, Akio Sugino, Dan Kobayashi. ANI: Takeshi Shirato, Moriyasu Taniguchi, Akio Sugino. MUS: Shunsuke Kikuchi. PRD: Toei, Fuji TV. 25 mins. x 44 eps.

Sanshiro Tsuwabuki's dream of becoming a professional baseball player is crushed by an invasion of mysterious bird-men, the Dark Horror Army, sent by Prince Darius of Planet Zera (Zala) to kill any psychics who could be obstacles to their plans of world conquest. Zera needs Earth because Zera is just about to be engulfed by a black hole. In Toei Animation's first robot animation not to be based on a manga, Sanshiro is invited by Dr. Daimonji (Professor Hightech) to join the Great Sky Magic Dragon (Gaiking Space Dragon) combat force to fight back, and he duly does so. Shown as part of the FORCE FIVE series on U.S. television, for which Sanshiro's name was changed to Ares Astronopolis, which the producers must have deemed nicely inconspicuous.

GALACTIC PATROL PJ

1981. JPN: *Ginga Patrol PJ*. TV series. DIR: Eiken Murata. SCR: Hideo Takayashiki, Masamichi Nomura. DES: Lune Valgue, Manchu. ANI: Tetsuo Shibuya, Jiro Tsuno. MUS: Koji Makaino, Michel Legrand. PRD: Eiken, Fuji TV. 27 mins. x 26 eps.

A Franco-Japanese coproduction that, like ULYSSES 31, was not shown in Japan until several years after it was made, *GPPJ* is virtually unknown in Japan, where it was buried in an early-morning TV slot. The story supplied by the French for the Japanese to animate involves Captain Jumbo and his loyal servants Jim, Putty, and Metro the robot, who work to keep law and order in the Omega Alliance of Peaceful Planets. Sworn to abstain from using deadly weapons, as befits the representatives of a multiracial coalition of space-faring life forms, they must solve every hazard they meet by negotiation and quick thinking. Perhaps the absence of much fighting might have also contributed to the series' swift disappearance.

GALACTIC PIRATES *

1989. JPN: *Teki wa Kaizoku: Neko no Kyoen*. AKA: *The Enemy Is the Pirate: Banquet of Cats*. TV series. DIR: Shinya Sadamitsu, Kazuo Yamazaki. SCR: Akinori Endo. DES: Takayuki Goto. ANI: Takayuki Goto, Hiroshi Hamazaki. MUS: Air Pavilion. PRD: Madhouse, Kitty Film, Mitaka Studio, NHK2. 30 mins. x 6 eps.

Apollo the jive-talking cat and his human sidekick, Latell, are working in the AntiPirate Division of the police force sent to Mars to put a stop to the activities of the space raider Yomei. The officers are intent on convincing each other to resign but eventually manage to solve a case involving piracy, double-cross, people turning into cats all around them, and an interlude in which they discover that the Martians have built up a militaristic religion that practices ritual games of hyperviolent baseball. Based on a comedy SF novel by Chohei Kanbayashi, this is one of the earliest video series to be given a satellite TV broadcast to recoup costs, a practice that would become commonplace in the late 1990s. "Air Pavilion," who provides the soundtrack, is a supergroup comprising former members of Whitesnake, Iron Maiden, and Motorhead.

GALAXY ADVENTURES OF SPACE OZ

1992. JPN: *Space Oz no Boken*. TV series. DIR: Soji Yoshikawa, Yoshiaki Okumura, Katsumata Kanezawa, Shinichi Suzuki. SCR: Soji Yoshikawa, Yasuko Hoshikawa, Seiji Matsuoka, Hirokazu Mizude. DES: Yoshiaki Okumura. ANI: Ichiro Fukube, Osamu Kamijo, Seiji Kikuchi. MUS: Ryuichi Katsumasa. PRD: E&G, Enoki, TV Tokyo. 25 mins. x 26 eps.

Eight-year-old blonde Dorothy Gale and her genetically enhanced dog, Talk-Talk, are swept off planet New Kansas and land in the distant galaxy of Oz. There, she joins forces with Dr. Oz, Mosey (a boy companion), Chopper (the Tin Man as a C-3PO rip-off), Lionman (the Cowardly Lion posing as Rambo), and Plantman (the Scarecrow) in order to defeat the evil witch Gloomhilda. This involves a race to obtain the three magic crystals of Love, Wisdom, and Courage, before Gloomhilda's minions Bungle, Skumm, and Sludge. A rehash of WIZARD OF OZ that ends with the acquisition of the Rainbow Crystal, allowing Dorothy to return home (there being no place like it). *Ill. p. 157.*

GALAXY ANGEL

2001. TV series. DIR: Morio Asaka, Ryo Mizuno. SCR: N/C. DES: Kanan, Kikaku Design Kobo Sensen. ANI: Kunihiko Hamada, Masaru Kitao. MUS: N/C. PRD: Madhouse, Animax. 25 mins. x 25 eps.

A century after the fall of the Galactic Network, the Transvaal Empire has risen on the ruins. However, the "lost technology" of the GN, looked after by priestesses called Moon Maidens, appears semimagical to the people of the Transvaal. Exiled prince Eonia kills King Gerrare and seizes control of the empire, but he is opposed by five pretty girls, the Angel Troopers, who steal a spaceship and team up with the young commander of the local militia. This is one of the last entries written before this encyclopedia was sent to press—which would seem to imply that little is going to change in the 21st century.

GALAXY EXPRESS 999 *

1978. JPN: *Ginga Tetsudo 999*. TV series, movie. DIR: Nobutaka Nishizawa, Masayuki Akehi, Kunihiko Yuyama. SCR: Hiroshi Yamaura, Keisuke Fujikawa, Yoshiaki Yoshida. DES: Leiji Matsumoto. ANI: Kazuo Matsubara. MUS: Nozomu Aoki, Godiego. PRD: Toei, Fuji TV. 25 mins. x 114 eps., 114 mins. (TVm1), 60 mins. (TVm2), 114 mins. (TVm3); 129 mins. (m1), 17 mins. (m2), 130 mins. (m3).

After his mother is killed by the evil count Kikai (Count Mecca), Tetsuro Hoshino (Joey) resolves to get an immortal metal body. Impossibly expensive on Earth, they are reputedly given away free to anyone who reaches Megalopolis, the last stop on the Galaxy Express. A ticket on the GE is also impossibly expensive, but the ethereal beauty Maetel (who looks uncannily like his mother) offers him one for free. She helps him to board the Galaxy Express 999 on the understanding that he must accompany her on her travels. In a long-running series based on Leiji Matsumoto's 1977 manga (distantly related to the same author's **CAPTAIN HARLOCK** series continuity), after

killing the Count to avenge his mother, Tetsuro sets off with Maetel on a journey across the galaxy. After the movie edition, *Galaxy Express* (1979), the second movie was the super-short featurette *GE999: Through a Glass Clearly* (1980, *Gurasu no Clear*), a partial remake of the third TV episode. A third movie, *GE999: Last Stop Andromeda* (1981, *Andromeda no Shuchakueki*), is set two years after the series, when Tetsuro, now a freedom fighter on Earth, receives a distress call from Maetel and heads out to help her one last time. Fuji TV also broadcast three specials, beginning with *GE999: Can You Live Like a Warrior* (1979, *Senshi no Yo ni Ikirareru ka*), which combined scenes from episodes 12 and 13. *GE999: Emeraldas the Eternal Wanderer* (1980, *Endo no Tabibito Emeraldas*) expanded episode 22, which featured Maetel's sister, **QUEEN EMERALDAS**. The final TV movie, *GE999: Can You Love Like a Mother* (1980, *Kimi wa Haha no Yo ni Aiseru ka*), adapted parts of episodes 51 and 52, adding 47 minutes of all-new footage. The series received a very limited partial broadcast on local New York TV for the Japanese community with English subtitles. The first movie was released in the U.S. by Roger Corman's New World, which incurred the wrath of fans by renaming Harlock "Warlock" and giving him a John Wayne accent for his cameo appearance. He would also claim that Joey was searching the universe for revenge, that being a little easier to take than an upgraded cybernetic body, at least back then. Maetel would return for the video series *Maetel the Legend* (2000).

GALAXY FRAULEIN YUNA *

1995. Video. DIR: Yoshinobu Yamaguchi. SCR: Satoru Akahori, Masashi Noro. DES: Katsumi Shimazaki, Mika Akitaka, Makoto Yamada. ANI: Ryoichi Oki. MUS: N/C. PRD: Animate Film, JC Staff. 30 mins. x 2 eps., 30 mins. x 2 eps.

A beauty contest is staged in present-day Tokyo with ulterior motives—as with **BATTLE ATHLETES**, it is really a

Anime's first full-length feature. *See entry p. 259.*

Momotaro's Divine Sea Warriors

front for choosing a champion to save the world. Yuna, the blond winner, is informed that, long ago, the Queen of Light fought the Queen of Darkness and lost the battle. All the remaining goodness of light was concentrated in one of the good android survivors, Elna, whose duty it was to carry the Light forward for the next battle. As Elna's successor, Yuna has three android doubles for use on land, sea, and air, as well as a super-transformation ability that allows them to turn into the mighty El-Line robot.

Based on a 1992 game for the PC Engine, the combination of giant war machines and cloyingly cute girls was resurrected for *GFY: Fairy of Darkness* (1996, released in the U.S. as *GFY Returns*), in which the evil Princess Mirage spreads false rumors that Yuna is fighting on the wrong side, sending the mysterious Fraulein D to ravage a few cities in Yuna's name just to make sure that GP Officer Misaki will find lots of incriminating evidence. Yuna and her orally fixated friend Yuri must then fight off "D" and several of Mirage's minions. Yuna turns one of the three evil Apparition Sisters to the side of good by introducing her to the joys of shopping, and then the stage is set for a final, noisy showdown. Sold to the Japanese as "the last word in girls' anime," though thankfully that was a complete lie.

GALAXY SEARCH 2100

1986. JPN: *Ginga Tanken 2100: Border Planet.* TV special. DIR: Osamu Uemura, Mamoru Hamatsu. SCR: Osamu Tezuka. DES: Shinpei Ohara. ANI: Shinya Takahashi, Nobuhiro Okaseko. MUS: Ryotaro Haneda. PRD: Tezuka Pro, NTV. 79 mins.

A doomed romance from **ASTRO BOY**–creator Osamu Tezuka about sworn friends Subaru and Procyon almost falling out over their love for the pretty Mira. Eventually, Subaru steps aside, but Procyon contracts a deadly space disease soon after his wedding. Subaru discovers that the widow, whom he still loves, has contracted the disease that killed her husband. Subaru sets off across the galaxy in search of a cure, while Mira remains back on Earth in suspended animation. His quest takes him to a world of automated agricultural machinery, where humans are being turned into planet fertilizer. The next world he finds is ruled by "the Boss," who maroons travelers so he can salvage their spaceships. With the help of local girl Michelle, Subaru organizes a revolt and builds an escape vessel from salvaged parts. Further adventures follow on a planet of humanoids that go through a chrysalis stage, but Subaru finally returns with a cure for Mira. She is restored to life, but, though she is still young, Subaru's journey has aged him 50 years. Mira falls in love with the doctor who woke her, who is the spitting image of his father, Subaru. The aged Subaru comments to his wife, Michelle, that they make a lovely couple. A bittersweet romance from Tezuka—compare to the similar **BANDAR BOOK: ONE MILLION A.D.**

GALL FORCE *

1986. Movie, video. DIR: Katsuhito Akiyama, Jun Fukuda, Koji Fukushima.

SCR: Sukehiro Tomita, Kenichi Matsuzaki, Hideki Kakinuma. DES: Kenichi Sonoda, Jun Okada, Kimitoshi Yamane. ANI: Nobuyuki Kitajima, Masaki Kajishima. MUS: Ichizo Seo, Etsuko Yamakawa, Takehito Nakazawa. PRD: Animate, Artmic, AIC. 86 mins. (m), 45 mins. (*Destruction*), 60 mins. (*Stardust*), 60 mins. (*Rhea*), 45 mins. x 3 eps. (*Earth Chapter*), 45 mins. x 2 eps. (*New Era*), 30 mins. x 4 eps. (*Revolution*).

Elsa, Catty, Rabby, Pony, Patty, and Rumy are the crew of the Starleaf, a spaceship in the Solnoid Navy, at war with the alien Paranoids. Unknown to any but the highest-ranking officers, the Solnoid leaders have decided that the two species must unite to preserve the best qualities of both—the Solnoids are all female clones, so their gene-pool is self-limiting (compare to **VANDREAD**). Fighter pilot Lufy joins the Starleaf when her ship crashes onto the flight deck. Though she is a hostile, hot-tempered loner, the real source of danger is elsewhere. When Patty is injured in an encounter with the enemy, her "injury" is revealed as an accelerated pregnancy. She is about to become mother to a new race, providing they survive long enough to get her and her child to safety.

Based on a series of model features in *Model Graphix* magazine and illustrated with photos of the plastic cuties that inspired the characters, the original story for *GF* was accompanied by a manga from Hideki Kakinuma. Replaying both the sci-fi horror of *Alien* and its use of conspiratorial androids (Catty), the U.S. movie audience had Sigourney Weaver in a role written for a man, but the Japanese had an all-female crew whose heroism was counterbalanced by dollops of fluffiness. **GUNSMITH CATS**–creator Sonoda's designs for *GF* would establish him as a fan favorite. Subsequent parts of the saga were released on video, starting with *GFII: Destruction* (1987). Years after the violent conclusion of the movie, Lufy is found floating in space by the crew of the Solnoid ship Lorelei—as in

Aliens. Most of the crew are androids, and one is identical to Catty. Lufy learns that the original Catty is the prime mover of the plan to interbreed the species, and her rescuers are en route to see if the plan is working. On Terra, Patty's half-Solnoid, half-Paranoid child and his mate, Starleaf-survivor Rumy, are starting a new race, but the war is still raging, and not everyone wants the plan to succeed. By *GFIII: Stardust War* (1988), the last remnants of both armies are still determined to annihilate each other and thwart the Unification Plan. A new *GF* team is set up, with *another* android Catty joining Lufy and some old friends to try and avert the final conflict. The plots were stuck in a rut by this time, but the theme of heroically cute young women fighting military boneheadedness and political machinations still had mileage in it.

Rhea Gall Force (1989) moves the action eons into the future, when Patty's descendants have repopulated the ruined wasteland of Earth. On Earth's moon, an ancient crashed Paranoid spacecraft has "bred" cybernetic MMEs (Man-Made Existences). These cybernetic creatures turn on their creators and, à la *Terminator*, force a nuclear war. The only hope is to evacuate the survivors to Mars, regroup, and plan the repopulating of Earth. A small group led by Sandy Newman and her best friend Melodi resolves to save Earth's population. Though conceived as the first of a four-part series, the "Rhea" prefix was a victim of the same acrimonious split between the producers that plagued **BUBBLEGUM CRISIS**. Consequently, episodes 2–4 were released under a new title, renumbered 1–3 as the *GF: Earth Chapter* (1989) videos. The war machines led by computer entity Gorn, who wants to eliminate humankind, are opposed by Sandy and her comrades, while Catty is still pulling all the strings behind the scenes. Once again, two different species must come together if the best of both is to survive, and once again military forces are conspiring to annihilate everything in a vain quest for victory. Later episodes of the franchise hint further at the series' cleverest conceit—it is implied that the narrative is completely cyclical (a true "eternal story"), with lookalikes of the original cast continually reappearing, and Catty living through the entire process. Asides in the original reveal that the Solnoids' home world was planet "Marsus," whence they had fled to avoid a catastrophe on their real home world—the similarity to *Earth Chapter*'s "Mars" likely to be more than mere coincidence. By *GF New Era* (1991), the action moves to 2291, when the humans live in peace on Earth with the machine entities now called Yuman, but Yuman leader Gorn is not convinced it's over and plans a preemptive strike. Android Catty, still planning for survival, selects six young women for a dangerous mission. Catty still has a few secrets in store—she's been around the human race for longer than anyone knows and has always worked to prevent its extinction. But if this last remnant of humanity is wiped out, the galaxy will be left to the machines.

A final lackluster outing came in the form of *Gall Force: Revolution* (1996), a flashback to the time of the original *Gall Force*, with the crew (now played by different actresses) caught in the crossfire between the East and West Solnoids. However, it could be argued that this final chapter is not an inexact remake, but instead the beginning of another cycle—compare to the similarly mind-bending continuity of **UROTSUKIDOJI**. See also **SUPER-DEFORMED DOUBLE FEATURE**. ○NV

GALS
2001. JPN: *Super Gals Kotobuki Ran.* TV series. DIR: Tsuneo Kobayashi. SCR: Masashi Kubota. DES: Yoshiko Kuzumoto, Hirohito Tanaka. ANI: Keiichi Ishiguro, Takahiro Kitano. MUS: N/C. PRD: Studio Pierrot, TV Tokyo. 25 mins. x 12+ eps.
Ran Kotobuki is the girliest girl in the fashion-conscious, shopping-crazy

Tokyo district of Shibuya, but her parents and elder brother desperately want her to be a police officer like themselves. Based on the manga in *Ribbon* magazine by Miho Fujii.

GALVION
1984. JPN: *Cho-kosoku Galvion.* AKA: *Superfast Galvion.* TV series. DIR: Akira Kamano. SCR: Tsunehisa Ito, Yoshihisa Araki, Yoshiyuki Suga, Haruya Yamazaki. DES: Yoshihisa Tagami. ANI: Hiroshi Negishi, Yoshinobu Shigeno. MUS: Masao Nakajima. PRD: Kokusai Eiga, TV Asahi. 25 mins. x 22 eps.
In the 23rd century, aliens seal off Earth with the impenetrable Sigma Barrier, ready to begin their conquest. United Nations police chief Ray Midoriyama sets up Circus, a team of robot pilots charged with fighting off the would-be world rulers of the Shadow Society. Unable to find anyone foolhardy enough to take the job, he offers it to convicted criminals Mu and Maya on the understanding that each task they perform will earn them days off their sentences. A similar setup to the later **CYBER CITY OEDO 808**, and just as truncated, it was pulled off the air at short notice, with the rest of the plot hastily reported in a voice-over at the end of episode 22. A rare anime job for **GREY: DIGITAL TARGET**-creator Yoshihisa Tagami, whose distinctive snub-nosed style can be seen in all the main character designs.

GAMBA AND HIS SEVEN FRIENDS
1986. JPN: *Bokentachi Gamba to Nanbiki no Nakama.* AKA: *The Adventurers Gamba and his Seven Friends.* Movie. DIR: Osamu Dezaki. SCR: Atsushi Yamatoya. DES: N/C. ANI: Yoshio Kabashima. MUS: Takeo Yamashita. PRD: Tokyo Movie Shinsha. 100 mins.
When a badly injured mouse staggers off a ship in Tokyo Harbor, he tells the local mice that he has escaped from Devil's Island, where Norio, the evil white weasel, has crushed the mice with his reign of terror. Tough-guy Gamba rashly promises to help depose Norio and leads a group of rodents on

a long odyssey that eventually brings them to Devil's Island—they are hindered in the early stages by not actually knowing where Devil's Island is. A reedit of an earlier 1975 TV series, itself based on children's books by Atsuo Saito.

GAMBLER LEGEND TETSUYA
2000. JPN: *Gambler Legend Tetsuya.* TV series. DIR: Nobutaka Nishizawa, Yuji Endo, Satoshi Nakamura. SCR: Yoshiyuki Suga. DES: Hidemi Kuma. ANI: Junichiro Taniguchi. MUS: Kuniaki Haishima. PRD: Toei, TV Asahi. 25 mins. x 20 eps.
In 1946, in a Shinjuku still reeling from the effects of the Pacific War, young Tetsuya Asada learns the secrets of mahjong from an old man. He meets his mentor Boshu and becomes a famous mahjong player and novelist, eventually earning the title Jong Sei (Jong Saint) and becoming the subject of a manga in *Shonen Magazine*, which goes on to win the Kodansha Manga Award. Then his life story is adapted into an anime, shown in the graveyard slot on Japanese TV.

GAME CENTER ARASHI
1982. TV series. DIR: Tameo Ogawa. SCR: Soji Yoshikawa. DES: Mitsuru Sugiyama. ANI: Kazuyuki Okaseko. MUS: Koji Makaino. PRD: Shinei, Nippon TV. 25 mins. x 26 eps.
An early spinoff of the craze for computer games, as Japan's national Invader Game champion Arashi ("Storm") Ishii discovers that while he is bottom of the class at school, he is unmatched with a joystick. Slowly developing a friendship with his rivals Satoru and Ippeita, he treats computer games with the reverence of martial arts, developing special attacks such as the Blazed Top, Vacuum Hurricane Shot, and Fish Stance. In other words, **AIM FOR THE ACE**, but less athletic.

GANBALIST HAYAO
1996. AKA: *"Persevere-ist" Hayao.* TV series. DIR: Hajime Kamegaki, Shinichi Watanabe. SCR: Katsuhiko Chiba. DES:

Hideyuki Motohashi. ANI: Hideyuki Motohashi. MUS: Hiroaki Arisawa. PRD: Sunrise, Yomiuri TV. 25 mins. x 30 eps.

A boy in the first year of junior high decides to become an Olympic-class gymnast despite having no clue about the amount of effort and hard work involved. An uninspired retread of **AIM FOR THE ACE** and other sports anime, given extra clout because the author of the original *Shonen Sunday* manga was Shinji Morisue, himself a former Olympic gymnast.

GANBARUGAR

1991. JPN: *Genki Bakuhatsu Ganbarugar*. AKA: *Happy Explosion Ganbarugar*. TV series. DIR: Toshifumi Kawase. SCR: Kenichi Kanemaki, Manabu Nakamura. DES: Takamitsu Kondo, Akira Kikuchi, Takahiro Yamada. ANI: Masamitsu Hidaka. MUS: N/C. PRD: Sunrise, TV Tokyo. 25 mins. x 47 eps.

Eldoran, the Knight of Light, gives teenage Torio a giant robot as long as he promises to use it to defend the Earth from alien invaders. In this typical Sunrise robot show, he luckily gets his chance, as flying space-whales, magical dimension holes, and time slips test his mettle and his ability to persevere (*ganbaru* in Japanese). The *Ganbarugar Encyclopedia* (1992) was a parody episode released straight to video, directed by Kunio Ozawa.

GANDHARA

1998. JPN: *Nessa no Ha-o: Gandhara*. AKA: *Lord of the Desert: Gandhara; Gandalla*. Video. DIR: Hidehito Ueda, Toshifumi Kawase. SCR: Akiyoshi Sakai, Kazuhiko Kobe. DES: Haruhiko Mikimoto, Junichi Haneyama, Yasushi Moriki. ANI: Masami Nagata. MUS: Toshiyuki Watanabe. PRD: Ashi Pro, Yoyogi Animation Gakuin, WOWOW. 25 mins. x 26 eps.

A group of teenagers struggles to make the big time with their amateur band, though their fortunes improve considerably when they take on a new lead vocalist, Emma Branton. As the group ducks and dives through seedy agents

and dangerous deals in the media world, lead guitarist Yuki begins to wish he had never agreed to support Emma, but he reluctantly helps her career out of his own feelings of responsibility for her missing brother, presumed dead. Meanwhile, deep in the sand dunes, the people known as the Sunlight are busily resurrecting an ancient demon, the titular Lord of the Desert, master of Lovecraftian horrors, who may be supplicated and partly controlled by music. The band is drawn into the conflict, in a desperate attempt to create a new music-led anime franchise defeated by cheapskate 1990s production values. "Superior to **MACROSS**," was the unfounded claim of the ads at the time, a boast as risible as the characters' own comparison of themselves with the early Doors. Though looking suspiciously like a retread of Clive Smith's *Rock and Rule* (1983), the anime was supposedly inspired by the song "Gandhara," a 1980s favorite that closed the live-action series *Monkey* (see **JOURNEY TO THE WEST**), though this impoverished anime sadly lacks any other relation.

GARAGA *

1989. JPN: *Hyper Psychic Geo Garaga*. Movie. DIR: Hidemi Kuma. SCR: Hidemi Kuma. DES: Moriyasu Taniguchi. ANI: N/C. MUS: Tatsumi Yano. PRD: AVN, Asmic. 100 mins.

The year is 2755, and humanity has traveled out to the stars with the aid of the jump-gate known as God's Ring. The starship Xebec is forced to crash-land on a world inhabited by psychics who use intelligent apes as warriors. Based on a manga by Satomi Mikuriya, whose other SF works include *Legend of Darkness*, **NORA**, and *Broken Passport*, as well as the manga that inspired **KING ARTHUR AND THE KNIGHTS OF THE ROUND TABLE**.

GARDURIN

1990. Video. DIR: Toyoo Ashida, Takao Kado. SCR: Michiru Shimada. DES: Mari Toyonaga. ANI: Kenichi Endo. MUS: N/C. PRD: Ashi Pro. 45 mins.

Ryu, an intergalactic trader, and his robot sidekick, MOS, are forced to make an emergency landing on planet Gardurin. Initially keen on repairing his ship and returning home, Ryu adopts the new world as his own and becomes a hero by righting wrongs among the locals. Based on a computer game.

GASARAKI *

1997. TV series. DIR: Ryosuke Takahashi. SCR: Toru Nozaki, Chiaki Konaka. DES: Shuko Murase, Shinji Aramaki, Yutaka Izubuchi, Atsushi Yamagata. ANI: Tatsuya Suzuki, Takuya Suzuki. MUS: Kuniaki Haishima. PRD: Sunrise, TV Osaka. 25 mins. x 25 eps.

As NATO forces fight a minor war against the new Middle Eastern nuclear power of Belgistan, the ancient Japanese Gowa arms-trading dynasty makes preparations to sneak its new humanoid combat robots (Tactical Armor) into the conflict as a "live" testing ground. In cahoots with the black operations division of the Japanese Self-Defense Force, the Gowas have a secret of their own—they also intend to road-test their private top-secret weapon. Family scion Yushiro Gowa is a psychic warrior who displaces his energies through a form of enhanced Noh performance. However, as the weapons go into action, Yushiro encounters Miharu, a beautiful, mysterious psychic, working for the tip-top-secret organization Symbol.

One of the best of the **EVANGELION** clones of the late 1990s, *Gasaraki* successfully duplicates its predecessor's confused kids, military conspiracy, and electrifying action. Miharu is an obvious respray of Rei Ayanami (the words "mysterious girl" appearing depressingly often on 1990s press releases), while Yushiro's peculiarly dramatic powers are a welcome change from nebulous "natural" abilities. Director Takahashi, renowned since **VOTOMS** as the father of realistic robot shows, does not stint on the gritty action, a tactic aided greatly by the script's use of actual Gulf War events and news reports with the names changed, which adds a subtle note of realism. *Ill. p. 309.*

GATE KEEPERS *
2000. TV series. DIR: Junichi Sato, Koichi Chiaki, Yasuhiro Takemoto. SCR: Hiroshi Yamaguchi, Hideki Mitsui, Aya Matsui. DES: Keiji Goto, Mahiro Maeda. ANI: Inao Takahashi. MUS: Kohei Tanaka. PRD: Gonzo, WOWOW. 25 mins. x 26 eps.
In 1969, Japanese schoolboy Shun Ukiya is co-opted into AEGIS (Alien Exterminating Global Intercept System), an international organization founded to hold off invading aliens. These creatures feed on human selfishness, possessing human hosts and transforming them into rampaging monsters. They can only be held off by operatives with "Gate" powers, young psychics whose latent abilities are awakened by trauma or powerful emotions. *GK* is an artful combination of the Cold War paranoia of *The Invaders* with the desperate battle and psychological angst of EVANGELION and the large female supporting cast of TENCHI MUYO! The show was previewed in a manga version by NADESICO-designer Keiji Goto.

GEAR FIGHTER DENDO
2000. JPN: *Gear Senshi Dendo.* TV series. DIR: Mitsuo Fukuda. SCR: Chiaki Akizawa. DES: Hirokazu Hisayuki, Masaharu Amiya, Hiroyuki Yoshino. ANI: Akira Takahashi. MUS: Toshihiko Sahashi. PRD: Sunrise, TV Tokyo. 25 mins. x 38 eps.
In a peaceful 21st-century Earth, it has been 17 years since humanity first learned of the spacefaring alien race of the Galfar Machine Empire. GEAR is the name of the organization to fight off the Galfar with specially adapted giant robots (oh, that's a change). Computer-geek Hokuto and gung-ho scrapper Ginga both want to pilot the Dendo robot, but with fading powers, the robot needs to feed on the boys' friendship to keep going. Strangely parasitic goings-on, directed by former CYBERFORMULA GPX–artist Fukuda.

GEMINI PROPHECIES *
1982. JPN: *Andromeda Stories.* TV special. DIR: Masamitsu Sasaki. SCR: Masaki Tsuji. DES: Keiko Takemiya. ANI: Shigetaka Kiyoyama. MUS: Yuji Ono. PRD: Toei. 105 mins. (U.S. version 85 mins.).
A sentient computer disrupts the lives of the inhabitants of planet Lodorian (Geminix in the U.S. version) in its attempts to create a machine world. The young queen, Lilia, flees with the help of a small band of survivors including the warrior-princess Il, who hails from another planet destroyed by the same entity. Lilia gives birth to telepathic twins, Gimsa and Afl, who are fated to return with Il's people to avenge the death of their father the king.
 Based on a manga by TOWARD THE TERRA–artist Keiko Takemiya and SF author Ryu Mitsuse, *Andromeda Stories* was rushed into production before the story had even finished running in its magazine incarnation. The big twist is the final revelation that the wanderings of the Lodorians were over when they finally settled on a new world—planet Earth. In the wake of *Battlestar Galactica,* this was unlikely to be too much of a surprise for a Japanese audience— the bulk of Mitsuse's work formed a far more serious, long-running "future history," though only this short story was ever adapted for the screen.

GENE SHAFT
2001. TV series. DIR: Kazuki Akane. SCR: Kazuki Akane, Hisashi Tokimura, Miya Asakawa. DES: Yasuhiro Oshima, Takeyuki Takeya. ANI: Junji Takeuchi. MUS: N/C. PRD: Satellite, WOWOW. 25 mins. x 13 eps.
In the 23rd century, human gene therapy is incredibly advanced, but a population imbalance has resulted in nine women to every man (blame TENCHI MUYO!). Life is discovered on Ganymede, but Earth is encircled by a mysterious ring, perhaps of alien manufacture. Terrorists blow up the survey team sent to investigate, and the incident triggers a weapon on the ring that

See entry p. 321.
Ranma 1/2

© 1989 RUMIKO TAKAHASHI/SHOGAKUKAN/KITTY FILM/FUJI TV

devastates Earth. Terran girl Mika Seido is the planet's last hope, with only the incomplete robot prototype Shaft to help her. Director Akane's follow-up to ESCAFLOWNE, preceded by the tie-in manga *Lunar Shaft* in *Ace Next* magazine.

GENEDIVER
1996. TV series. DIR: Masami Furukawa, Takuo Suzuki, Akira Natsuki, Masakazu Amiya. SCR: Masami Furukawa, Riko Hinokuma, Yoshi Nowata, Toshiaki Komura. DES: Akihiro Taniguchi, Michio Mihara. ANI: Keiyo Nagamori. MUS: Masaaki Igawa. PRD: Juno, NHKEP2. 25 mins. x 56 eps.
Sneaker is an evil entity from a time before the Big Bang, but currently it can only manifest itself in the virtual world. The peace-loving inhabitants need help, but the "heroine" they get to save them is nothing more than average schoolgirl Tada. Falling into the virtual world like ALICE IN WONDERLAND, Tada fights evil in the style of the later CORRECTOR YUI. This is one of the first 1990s TV series to combine cheaper cel animation with flashy computer graphics—a mixture much imitated by the end of the century.

GENERATOR GAWL *
1998. TV series. DIR: Seiji Mizushima. SCR: Hidefumi Kimura. DES: Yasushi Moriki, Takashi Tomioka, Kenji Teraoka. ANI: Akira Ogura. MUS: N/C. PRD: Tatsunoko, Victor, TV Tokyo. 25 mins. x 12 eps.
In 2007, new students Koji, Ryo, and Gawl arrive at Oju Academy Town in Japan, but they are not like the other students at this elite institution. They are time-travelers from a future in which humanity has been enslaved by GUYVER-esque mutants called the Generators. After a hellish training program, the resistance movement has sent them back in time to prevent Professor Nekasa from inventing the Generator process at the Academy. However, the professor proves elusive, while the trio is opposed by agents from its own era, sent back to ensure Nekasa's activities are not interrupted. Their one hope in their struggle is Gawl himself, who has reluctantly submitted to the monstrous Generator process, allowing him to transform into a creature that can fight their enemies on their own terms. A mixture of the chronological espionage of *Terminator* and the unwilling, angst-ridden hero of CYBORG 009, Tatsunoko's first TV series since TEKKAMAN replaced the short-lived video outings of the 1990s with a *slightly* longer series, which featured themed monsters-of-the-week just like the same studio's BATTLE OF THE PLANETS and an ambiguous, conspiratorial secret society inspired by EVANGELION's NERV. *Ill. p. 199.*

GENESIS SURVIVOR GAIARTH *
1992. JPN: *Sosei Kishi Gaiarth.* AKA: *Genesis Machine-Warrior Gaiarth, Genesis Surviver* [sic] *Gaiarth.* Video. DIR: Hiroyuki Kitazume, Shinji Aramaki, Hideaki Oba. SCR: Shinji Aramaki, "REM." DES: Hiroyuki Kitazume, Hiroyuki Ochi. ANI: Jun Okuda. MUS: Kazunori Ashizawa, Takehito Nakazawa. PRD: Artmic, Kuma, AIC. Ca. 45 mins. x 3 eps.
In the aftermath of a cataclysmic war, one of the last Imperial cyborgs trains a young boy, Ital, among the ruins of an old military base. Republican forces kill Ital's mentor, and the boy's quest for vengeance leads him to team up with Sahari, the pretty female leader of the Junk-hunters, and an amnesiac war robot called Zaxon. The attacking Republicans are looking for the dormant Sakuya, a young girl who is the central intelligence system of a doomsday device. Ital kills the evil "General" who wishes to use Sakuya for his own ends, and Sakuya drives the device into the desert where she self-destructs. Ital, Sahari, and Zaxon set off into further adventures, although none were forthcoming for this competent but unremarkable science fantasy saga by future big names including ARMITAGE III's Ochi.

This postholocaust plot in the style of GREY: DIGITAL TARGET collapses in the face of humdrum pop-video interludes, and two pointless animal sidekicks. But despite massive steals from *Return of the Jedi, Beast Master,* and *Star Wars,* there are still moments when the world of Gaiarth shows true promise, particularly in technology so ancient it is treated as magical by its operators/summoners. The bright, flat colors were an early example of the simpler anime shading popularized by outsourced Korean animation studios during the 1990s that would eventually define the look of TENCHI MUYO! and other AIC shows.

GENIUS IDIOT BAKABON
1971. JPN: *Tensai Bakabon.* AKA: *Genius Bakabon.* TV series. DIR: Hiroshi Saito. SCR: Yoshiaki Yoshida, Chikara Matsumoto, Yukinobu Komori, Masaki Tsuji, Shunichi Yukimuro. DES: Fujio Akatsuka. ANI: Tsutomu Shibayama. MUS: Takeo Watanabe. PRD: Fujio Pro, TMS. 25 mins. x 40 eps. (TV), 25 mins. x 103 eps. (TV2), 25 mins. x 10 eps. (TV3), 10 mins. x 88 eps. (TV4).
The insane Bakabon family—eccentric Papa, gentle Mama, genius Hajime, and absent-minded Junior—are constantly trying to outdo each other with wacky schemes, but with the exception of the baby, they're all stupid. Shown after STAR OF THE GIANTS in a prime slot, the series soon deviated from the original as sponsor pressure increased—with Father getting a respectable job and the introduction of previously unseen characters to fill out the otherwise small cast.

Fujio Akatsuka, who wrote the original 1967 gag manga on which all the series were based, also created the comedy OSOMATSU-KUN and the girls' series SECRET AKKO-CHAN. The series returned in 1975 with *Original Genius Idiot Bakabon,* a title chosen by its creator to demonstrate that it was truer to the manga from which it came. The new version included the manga favorite Eel-Dog (whose mother is an eel and father is a dog), and Lelele, the Bakabons' next-door neighbor who is obsessed with sweeping, and several crazy classmates from Bakada University.

It came back once more in 1990 with *Heisei-era Genius Idiot Bakabon* and an all-new cast except for Mother, played by Junko Yamazawa. The series was brought back yet again in 2000 in a version from Studio Pierrot, reuniting the family with old favorites like the trigger-happy policeman and the grumbling old man Wanagin. The *Genius Idiot* cast would also team up with Akatsuka's other creations for the 1991 movie spoof *3,000 Leagues in Search of Osomatsu's Curry,* directed by Akira Saito. Father and son Bakabon go on a quest for the most delicious curry in the world in a spoof of both FROM THE APENNINES TO THE ANDES and JOURNEY TO THE WEST.

GENJI
1992. Video. DIR: Akira Koson. SCR: Akira Koson. DES: Michitaka Kikuchi, Masafumi Yamamoto. ANI: Masafumi Yamamoto. MUS: Kentaro Haneda. PRD: Somi, Tee-Up, JC Staff. 45 mins. x 2 eps.
Time-traveling lovers Katsumi and Sakura are thrown into the midst of Japan's medieval Heike-Genji civil war, which is not quite as the history books remember it, complete with sorcerers and unearthly beasts. Based on the

manga in *Wings* magazine by **Earthian**-creator Yun Koga, and not to be confused with the **Tale of Genji**.

GENOCYBER *

1993. Video. DIR: Koichi Ohata. SCR: Noboru Aikawa, "REM." DES: Atsushi Yamagata, Kimitoshi Yamane. ANI: Kenji Kamiyama. MUS: Michinori Matsuoka. PRD: Artmic. Ca. 46 mins. x 3 eps. (released as 5 eps. but on 3 tapes).

Diane is a cripple who relies on a cybernetic body. She lost her limbs in the same accident that killed her father, maimed her mother, and permanently altered her unborn sister, Elaine, a feral child with incredible psychic powers. Not content with stealing the credit for his work, Professor Kenneth adopts his dead friend's children and uses them in his experiments. Elaine goes on the run in Hong Kong, and the evil Kowloon corporation (misnamed "Kuron" in the Manga Entertainment dub) goes after her. She befriends Shorty, a street kid, but is then forced to fight Kowloon's minions and her own sister. Eventually, the two girls combine to form the terrifying Genocyber creature, and Hong Kong is destroyed.

An incoherent mish-mash of **Urotsukidoji**'s demon apocalypse and the psychic weapons of **Akira** held together with technobabble about "qi" energy and "vajra" force amid blatant steals from *Robocop* and *Aliens*. Beyond the idea of military experimentation on children, *Genocyber* also plunders later chapters of the *Akira* manga, in which Tetsuo's biomechanics take over a U.S. aircraft carrier. Though there are some nice ideas here (a science based on Hindu myth and a demonic machine that looks like the praying hands of a Hindu priest), *Genocyber* is far too derivative for its own good. Matters aren't helped by English dialogue like "You stupid, ignorant fucking piece of shit," which, needless to say, is a rather free translation of the original.

The idea of bitter sibling rivalry and a retarded girl with godlike powers has

much potential, but *Genocyber* does little with it. With bone-snappingly horrific fights and incredibly gory splashes of violence, it plays like **Guyver** with girls, trying and failing to use many of the same ideas as the later **Macross Plus**. It throws in computer graphics and icky live-action shots of offal, but these experimentations, along with several pans that use genuine photographs instead of artwork, just make the series look cheaper than it really is. Similarly, Elaine is a telepath, but *Genocyber* just makes it look like a cheap excuse for not moving her lips.

Later episodes are barely connected, as the action jumps a decade to the Middle Eastern republic of Karain, where the ageless Elaine is mistaken for a refugee by the UN. Taken to an aircraft carrier, where everyone decides to confuse things by calling her Laura, she witnesses the arrival of Kowloon's latest machine, a cyborg plane that uses vajra technology. She fights it and destroys Kowloon's latest plans, but not before she drives a woman insane by revealing that the child who saved her life is also the monster who killed her parents in Hong Kong.

The finale (released as two "episodes" on a single tape in both the U.S. and Japan, and not released at all in the U.K.), featured Genocyber laying waste to the world before falling dormant. The Kowloon group puts a doomsday device into orbit to await the creature's return. A hundred years later (or 300 in the U.S. version), the postapocalyptic world develops a religion that worships Genocyber as a god and prays for its return, which eventually occurs with predictably gory results. **LNV**

GENTLEMAN MUGEN

1987. JPN: *Mugen Shinshi*. AKA: *Dreaming/Mugen Gentleman*. Video. DIR: Hatsuki Tsuji. SCR: Izo Hashimoto. DES: Hatsuki Tsuji. ANI: Hatsuki Tsuji. MUS: N/C. PRD: Studio Gallop. 49 mins.

In this one-shot video based on the 1981 *Shonen Captain* manga by Yosuke Takahashi and set in the 1920s, 15-year-

old boy detective Mamiya Mugen gets involved with beautiful girls and solves fantastic mysteries. On this occasion, the case involves the kidnapping of a ballerina and several other girls by a criminal organization. Mamoru deduces that a beautiful concert pianist will be next, but not that the criminals need young girls' energy to power a resurrection machine. In replaying the classic murder mysteries of Ranpo Edogawa and injecting a hard-edged sense of humor, it was a forerunner for **Conan the Boy Detective**.

GEOBREEDERS *

1998. JPN: *Geobreeders: File X: Chibi Neko no Dakkan*. AKA: *Geobreeders: File X: Get Back the Kitty*. Video. DIR: Yuji Moriyama. SCR: Yosuke Kuroda, Yuji Moriyama. DES: Yasuhiro Oshima. ANI: Yasuhiro Oshima. MUS: Motoyoshi Iwasaki. PRD: Victor. 30 mins. x 3 eps., 30 mins. x 4 eps.

A disastrously incompetent supernatural security agency is called in to stop an epidemic of feline ghosts in this anime adaptation of Akihiro Ito's manga. Perhaps for legal reasons, the original "File X" prefix was dropped from the title for the U.S. release, though *Geobreeders* owes just as great a debt to *Scooby-Doo* as it does to Mulder and Scully. Five feisty females in a dilapidated mystery machine run rings around the show's squashed-down Duchovny-clone, facing off against sulking military "allies" and a secret conspiracy.

A predictably madcap mix of ghost-busting tomfoolery in the spirit of **Phantom Quest Corp** and **Ghost Sweeper Mikami**, complete with light-heartedly gratuitous nudity, snappy dialogue, and some really big guns. Even distributors USMC rise to the occasion for the U.S. dub. Considering the output of their sister-brand Anime 18, it must be a refreshing change for a voice actress to shout "Get on your knees, pussies" to an audience that genuinely does consist of cats.

Sight-gags show a return of the **Project A-Ko** spirit from chief director

Moriyama: fake ads separate the episodes, characters must play soccer with hand grenades, and in one scene someone backs into a giant poster for *Geobreeders: The Movie*. Though the series wasn't quite *that* successful, it did spawn the four-part *Geobreeders 02* on video in 2000, reuniting the staff under new director Shin Misawa. **N**

GESTALT *

1996. JPN: *Choju Densetsu Gestalt*. AKA: *Superbestial Legend Gestalt*. Video. DIR: Osamu Yamazaki. SCR: Mamiya Fujimura. DES: Takashi Kobayashi. ANI: N/C. MUS: N/C. PRD: SMEJ, TV Tokyo. 30 mins. x 2 eps. Father Olivier, a young priest, learns of a god that will grant a wish to anyone who can find him on his hidden island of "G." Teaming up with the mute Oli, Olivier sets out to find "G" but is thwarted by his old enemy, Suzu the Dark Elf. A comedy manga serialized in *G Fantasy* magazine by **EARTHIAN**-creator Yun Koga, *Gestalt* includes many jokes at the expense of fantasy role-playing games, including moments of dialogue done deliberately in the *non-sequitur* style of console RPGs. Though clearly an attempt to capitalize on the success of the similar **SLAYERS**, *Gestalt* foundered after only two episodes, despite flashy computer graphics and the contemporary selling point of being made completely inside a computer.

GET A GRIP TSUYOSHI

1993. JPN: *Tsuyoshi Shikkari Shinasai*. AKA: *Get a Grip, Tsuyoshi*. Movie. DIR: Shin Misawa. SCR: Takashi Yamada. DES: Kiyoshi Nagamatsu. ANI: Takahisa Kazukawa. MUS: Kuniaki Haishima. PRD: Toei, Fuji TV. 30 mins. (m), 25 mins. x 112 eps. (TV). Kiyoshi Nagamatsu's original 1993 manga in *Comic Afternoon* and the TV series that followed were critically acclaimed for their "American-style humor," whatever that may be. Tsuyoshi is a typical high-school student, good at sports but bad at study, victimized at home by two sisters who hide their evil natures behind their angelic exteriors. The short cinema release removes him from the eternal feud with his mother and sisters, sending him back 12 years in time for a replay of *Back to the Future*.

GETTER ROBO *

1974 AKA: *Starvengers*. TV series, movie, video. DIR: Tomoharu Katsumata, Yasuo Yamaguchi, Takeshi Tamiya, Takeshi Shirato. SCR: Shunichi Yukimuro, Seiji Matsuoka. DES: Kazuo Komatsubara. ANI: Kazuo Komatsubara, Atsuo Noda, Kazuo Nakamura, Takeshi Shirato. MUS: Shunsuke Kikuchi. PRD: Dynamic, Fuji TV, Toei. 25 mins. x 51 eps., 25 mins. x 39 eps. (*G*), 25 mins. x 50 eps. (*Go*), 25 mins. x 13 eps. (*Change*), 25 mins. x 4 eps. (*Neo*).
Professor Saotome creates the fearsome Getter Machine series of war robots and hires the nobly named Ryoma (see **OI! RYOMA**), Musashi (see **YOUNG MIYAMOTO MUSASHI**), and Benkei (see **BENKEI VS. USHIWAKA**) to pilot the three vehicles, the aerial Getter-1, land-based Getter-2, and seafaring Getter-3, that can be combined to form a giant humanoid robot—the first "transformer."

Based on a collaboration between **DEVILMAN**'s Go Nagai and **DEMON-BEAST PHALANX**–creator Ken Ishikawa, the show returned in 1975 as *Getter Robo G*. The destruction of the evil Dinosaur Empire left the way open for a new enemy, the Clan of 100 Devils, and since the original machinery had been destroyed in the climactic fight of the previous series, it was also time for new vehicles: Getters Dragon, Rygar, and Poseidon (Star Dragon, Star Arrow, and Star Poseidon). Along with the other anime in the **FORCE FIVE** interlinked shows, *Getter Robo G* was redubbed for the U.S. market as *Starvengers*, and several of the vehicles were also included in the **SHOGUN WARRIORS** line. For the English-language version, the horned enemies were renamed the Pandemonium Empire, led by Emperor Ramzorch and his Hitler-lookalike commander, Captain Fuhrer. Back in Japan, *Getter Robo G* also appeared in short theatrical outings alongside other Go Nagai creations including *Great Mazinger vs. Getter Robo G* (1975) and *Great Mazinger / Grandizer / Getter Robo G: Battle the Great Monster* (1976).

After a long hiatus, the franchise hit a low point in 1991 with *Getter Robo Go!* directed by Yoshiki Shibata, featuring the same machines but an all-new team. Though long-running by modern standards, the series was considered a noncanonical flop. The original, however, remained a favorite among fans and professionals, demonstrated by the **NADESICO** staff in their spoof show-within-a-show *Gekiganger 3*. For most of the 1990s, the franchise was kept alive by computer games, and eventually the redesigned machines as used in the *Getter Robo* and *Super Robot Battle* games were resurrected for a new series. Poaching staff from the successful retro series **GIANT ROBO**, Jun Kawagoe's straight-to-video *Change Getter Robo* (1998) presented itself as the "true" sequel to the original 1974–75 serials, beginning with the death of Professor Saotome and Ryoma's arrest for his murder. Three years later, the two remaining team members are forced to contend with a cloned "evil" Saotome, hellbent on avenging his own death and leading an army of Getter Dragons. In a sequel that exploited the limited budgets of late-1990s video productions to recreate the rough-edged look of 1970s television animation, Ryoma is recalled from prison to resist the invasion. This version was scheduled for release in the U.S. in 2001 as *Getter Robot: The Last Day*. The same staff returned for the four-part video sequel *Change Getter Robo vs. Neo Getter Robo* (2000), clearly made with an eye to foreign sales, in which another madman, Emperor Gaul, sends an army of robotic dinosaurs to destroy New York, and Professor Saotome's new lantern-jawed protégé, former wrestler Tetsuhito, leads the underground resistance. See also **MAZINGER Z**. *Ill. p. 215.*

GHOST IN THE SHELL *

1995. JPN: *Kokaku Kidotai*. AKA: *Armored Riot Police/Ghost in the Shell*. Movie. DIR: Mamoru Oshii. SCR: Kazunori Ito. DES: Hiroyuki Okiura, Shoji Kawamori. ANI: Hiroyuki Okiura, Tensai Okamura, Toshihiko Nishikubo. MUS: Kenji Kawai. PRD: Studio IG. 83 mins.

A top-secret military project goes horribly wrong, and a sentient computer virus runs out of control. Its creators disperse in search of political asylum before the mistake is spotted, while the program itself tries to defect to the other side. Calling itself the Puppet Master, it hacks into government systems to gain extra leverage in negotiations. It takes control of gun-freaks, robot bodies, and even a tank, but what it really wants is a permanent, physical home. Meanwhile, Section Nine, agents for the Ministry of Internal Affairs, are forced to clear up after the mess left behind by Section Six (Foreign Affairs), even as the two departments contest jurisdiction in the case. Major Motoko Kusanagi is an angst-ridden platoon leader in Section Nine who can't leave the service because, like the original *Bionic Woman*, parts of her are government property. Her body is just a mass-produced "shell" (note the scene where she sees a twin working as a secretary) and the only part of her that is real is her "ghost," her soul. When seemingly random events all over the city turn out to be crimes committed by the Puppet Master's unwitting accomplices, Motoko realizes that there is a pattern, and that it eventually leads to her.

GitS is one of the best anime available in English, and one of the few that could reasonably claim to be a true cyberpunk film. It is a superb action film with marvelous moments, such as Motoko's final duel with a robot tank, and accomplished use of computer graphics, especially for Motoko's cloaking device. Unlike the many anime "movies" that are really nothing of the sort, it was genuinely made for the big screen, and the budget and dedication really show. It was also a coproduction

partly funded by Manga Entertainment, and it kept the company's reputation afloat in the search for a new **AKIRA**, though at the time it was regarded by many as a money pit for ME's beleaguered boss Andy Frain.

While **APPLESEED**-creator Masamune Shirow set his original 1991 *Young Magazine* manga in the sprawling future metropolis of Tokyo, director Oshii deliberately relocated to Hong Kong for the film to create a lived-in, exotic look with Chinese-language street signs. This was a perfect film for the idiosyncratic Oshii, allowing him to replay **PATLABOR** with clueless "little people" dwarfed by events beyond their ken.

The original manga's intense philosophizing is artfully simplified by screenwriter Ito, who streamlines it into a perverse "romance" between Motoko and the Puppet Master, their final marriage eventually producing a new life form. Kenji Kawai's music is a haunting ceremony in arcane Japanese ("A god descends for a wedding and dawn approaches while the night bird sings"), two separate musical themes that slowly advance on each other during the film, until they marry to form a completely new synergy over the closing credits, adding a final coda to Ito's plot. Or rather, they did—the English-language version replaced the closing music with a mediocre effort from the Passengers CD. Such a gimmick may well have gained *Ghost in the Shell* more mainstream interest, but it wasn't necessary. This is a film that needed no marketing spin. A manga sequel, *Man-Machine Interface*, has been running intermittently for several years in *Young Magazine*, regularly prompting rumors of an anime follow-up. *Ill. p. 227.* 🅛🅝🅥

GHOST SWEEPER MIKAMI

1993. AKA: *GS Mikami*. TV series, movie. DIR: Atsutoshi Umezawa. SCR: Aya Matsui, Nobuaki Kishima, Masaharu Amiya. DES: Takashi Shiina. ANI: Mitsuru Aoyama, Kenji Yokoyama, Yoshiyuki Kawano, Masayuki Uchiyama. MUS: Toshihiko Sahashi. PRD: Toei,

Featuring quasi-naval battles fought on the Martian sand dunes, as well as the suggestion that human "gods" were actually intervening aliens, Toshifumi Takizawa's **BIG WARS** incorporates a heady mix of Ray Bradbury and Arthur C. Clarke, courtesy of science fiction author Yoshio Aramaki. Despite the futuristic trappings, it still retains the feel of a WWII movie, Aramaki is better known for his alternate-history works such as **DEEP BLUE FLEET**. Though the plot is clear enough (a suicide mission on the alien mothership), *BW* suffers like many anime adaptations, from only having the time to tell part of a much longer preexisting story. *See entry p. 34.*

Big Wars

TV Asahi. 25 mins. x 45 eps. (TV), 60 mins. (m).

Reiko Mikami is a sexy penny-pinching exorcist who forces her adoring assistant, Tadao, to work for a pittance. While the snobbish, self-regarding Reiko spars with the lecherous Tadao, Okinu the gentle ex-ghost tries to keep them calm enough to do their ghost-busting job. With an unlikable heroine who persists in selling out her friends, the show spoofs the mercenary do-gooder of Osamu Tezuka's **BLACK JACK**, as well as the miniskirted, "body-conscious" girls of Tokyo's 1990s club scene. There are also occasional moments of social commentary, as it is revealed that Tokyo's ghost epidemic has been caused by urban sprawl pushing previously unseen spirits into the open. The chief emphasis, however, is on comedy, with a subsidiary cast including Pietro the shy half-vampire, impoverished Father Karasu, sexy voodoo ghost-sweeper Emiko, mad scientist Dr. Chaos, and his robot assistant, Maria (see **METAL ANGEL MARIE**). Reiko and her gang also appeared in Atsutoshi Umezawa's anime movie *GS Mikami: War in Heaven* (1994, *Gokuraku Taisen*).

GS Mikami's failure to reach the U.S. is a real mystery. Based on a long-running manga by Takashi Shiina in *Shonen Sunday*, it has all the lighthearted adventure and sex appeal of **URUSEI YATSURA**, and in the hands of Viz Communications, it might have even outperformed the same publisher's **RANMA 1/2**. In the Japanese market, where it peaked at a 14.6% TV rating, it swiftly sent the lookalike video anime **PHANTOM QUEST CORP** packing and outlasted most of its contemporaries in the harsh mid-1990s market. Rumors abound that it was picked up by a well-known distributor as part of a bulk deal then left to fester because the lighthearted banter didn't sit well with the company's more action-based titles. This may have damaged it irreparably, as its cheap animation style will probably lead it to date faster than other anime from the same period—it already looks slightly older than its years.

GHOSTS

1982. JPN: *Obake*. TV special. DIR: Yasunori Kawauchi, Tameo Ogawa, Gisaburo Sugii, Tsutomu Shibayama. SCR: Yasunori Kawauchi. DES: N/C. ANI: N/C. MUS: N/C. PRD: Ai Planning Center, Tac, TBS. Ca. 85 mins.
An omnibus of four ghost stories from famous directors, beginning with *Comparing Transformations*, set at a ghoulish convention somewhere in the Japanese mountains. The scene moves to a seaside cave for *The Two-Eyed Goblin*, in which a family of Cyclopes adopts a human child. A villager at a local festival meets a beautiful girl who suddenly disappears in *Divine Secret*, and in the final story, *Amulet*, Buddha punishes the behavior of Taira no Kiyomori by releasing evil spirits into the world.

GIANT GORG

1984. JPN: *Kyoshin; Giant Gorg*. TV series. DIR: Yoshikazu Yasuhiko, Norio Kabeshima. SCR: Masaki Tsuji, Sumiko Tsukamoto. DES: Yoshikazu Yasuhiko. ANI: Mayumi Ishigaki. MUS: Mitsuo Hagiwara. PRD: Sunrise, TV Tokyo. 25 mins. x 26 eps.
Tectonic activity on the Pacific island of Austral reveals highly advanced technology. The Gail Corporation, an immensely powerful conglomerate that has been carefully manipulating the Cold War, wants the technology for itself and sends its chief executive's grandson, Rod Balboa, to get it. Opposing Balboa is Yu Tagami, the son of a Japanese researcher murdered by the Gail Corporation, who has teamed up with his father's associate, Doctor Wave. Pursued from New York across America and down to the South Seas by Gail's henchmen (and by other interested parties, including the soldier-of-fortune known as the "Captain," and Lady Lynx, queen of the Las Vegas casinos and underworld), Yu, Wave, and Wave's pretty sister Doris finally reach Austral. There, they discover that the island is a time capsule of artifacts from a lost civilization, and that Gorg, the "fearsome sea monster" that terrorizes shipping in the area, is actually a giant robot protecting its creator from interference. Manon, the pilot of a second guardian, is awakened from cryogenic slumber but cannot bear the thought that his civilization has been supplanted by humanity. Instead, he plans to destroy the world. Ronald Reagan and Yuri Andropov decide to launch a joint nuclear attack on Austral before Manon's doomsday device can go off; unfortunately for Yu's gang and the other treasure hunters, they are trapped on the island by Manon's forcefield and have only seven days to escape. Foreshadowing both **SPRIGGAN**, with its corporate conflict over ancient artifacts, and the antediluvian adventure of **SECRET OF BLUE WATER**, *GG* is also renowned for its comic-relief Professor Wave, who looks uncannily like Woody Allen.

GIANT ROBO *

1992. Video. DIR: Yasuhiro Imagawa. SCR: Yasuhiro Imagawa, Eiichi Sato. DES: Makoto Kobayashi, Toshiyuki Kubooka, Akihiko Yamashita, Takashi Watabe. ANI: Akihiko Yamashita. MUS: Masamichi Amano. PRD: Mu Film. 40 mins. x 7 eps.
The Shizuma drive, a clean energy source that has revolutionized world energy and eliminated pollution, has a fatal flaw. The evil Professor Franken von Folger and his associates, would-be world dictators Big Fire, dispatch a black orb to float across the world, draining the energy from all major cities and causing global chaos. Fearing a replay of the Tragedy of Bashtarlle, when faulty Shizuma prototypes wiped out an entire city, the Experts of Justice set out to stop Big Fire. Their members include martial artists, scientific geniuses, secret agents, Folger's own estranged daughter, Ginrei, and a young boy called Daisaku Kusama. Only the voice of Daisaku, the son of a scientist murdered by Big Fire, can control Giant Robo, a 90-foot-tall war machine originally designed for Big Fire but now devoted to fighting crime.
GR began life as a short-lived 1967 manga by **GIGANTOR**'s Mitsuteru Yokoyama and was also adapted into a live-action TV series known in the U.S. as *Johnny Sokko and His Flying Robot* (1968). Director Imagawa's *GR* was the first of the 1990s "retro" boom, a number of anime made in a deliberately old-fashioned style that recalls the imagery of the Golden Age of sci-fi and also reminds baby-boomers of their carefree childhoods during Japan's economic miracle, before the Oil Shocks of the 1970s. Its style was copied in other shows, including **SUPER ATRAGON**, **KISHIN CORPS**, **SAKURA WARS**, and **AMBASSADOR MAGMA**, and also created the environment that allowed Tezuka Pro to seriously consider new versions of previously "dated" classics such as **BLACK JACK**. Imagawa himself became so involved in the development work for another retro anime, **GETTER ROBO**, that the final episode of *GR* only appeared in 1997, when most of the voice actors had forgotten their roles and needed a refresher course.
In addition to changing the manga's Franken to Franken von Folger (his own homage to *The Rocky Horror Picture Show*'s Frank-N-Furter), Imagawa pastiched characters from many of Yokoyama's other works, including **GODMARS**,

BABEL II, and even LITTLE WITCH SALLY. Most notable among these is the presence of characters dressed like medieval Chinese rebels and an HQ in "Ryozanpaku," which *GR*'s U.S. translators failed to note was Japanese for Liang Shan Po, the famous marshes of the *Water Margin* (see SUIKODEN). Yokoyama's *Water Margin* was never animated but was turned into an extremely popular live-action TV series during the 1970s—however, many of its main characters were lifted wholesale for *GR*.

As implied by its Japanese subtitle, *The Day the Earth Stood Still*, *GR* also carries a subtle antinuclear message nestled amid the robot combat and gunfights, with a "safe" energy source put to evil use, ironically against all the major cities of Japan's enemies in WWII, including London, New York, San Francisco, and Shanghai. Featuring great music from UROTSUKIDOJI-composer Amano, it also has the recurring theme, "A Furtive Tear," taken from Donizetti's comic opera *The Love Potion* (1832), which tells a similar tale of mankind putting too much faith in technology, albeit of a different kind!

The show also spun off into three 30-minute videos (perhaps to distract fans during the last-episode hiatus) featuring the undisputed microminiskirted star of the show, starting with the music clips of *Barefoot Ginrei* (1993). *The Mighty Ginrei* (1994) featured two short stories, *Forbidden Fruit* and *War in Heaven*, while the final episode, *Ginrei's Blue Eyes* (1995), was a parody of the rest of the show, set in a desert. *Ill. p. 353.*

GIGANTOR *

1963. JPN: *Tetsujin 28-go*. AKA: *Ironman Number 28*. TV series. DIR: Yonehiko Watanabe, Tadao Wakabayashi. SCR: Yoshikazu Okamoto. DES: Mitsuteru Yokoyama. ANI: Tadao Wakabayashi, Kazuo Nobara. MUS: Hidehiko Arashino. PRD: Eiken, TMS. 25 mins. x 96 eps., 25 mins. x 51 eps. (*New*), 25 mins. x 24 eps. (*FX*).

Before Japan's experimental robot weapon project can be used against the Allies, U.S. bombers destroy the labora-

tory, killing its creator, Dr. Haneda. A decade after the war, several crimes are found to have been committed by remote-controlled giant robots, the 26th and 27th prototypes of a long-forgotten military project. Haneda's detective son, Shotaro (Jimmy Sparks), discovers that the syndicates are searching for a mythical 28th prototype, rumored to be even more powerful. He beats them in figuring out its whereabouts, finding both it and Professor Shikashima (Bob Brilliant), another researcher thought dead in the same attack that killed his father. Shikashima and Shotaro decide to use Ironman #28 for peace, not war. The final 13 episodes, broadcast after a hiatus of several months in which the Eiken team concentrated on PRINCE PLANET, featured a change of direction, with Shotaro having a vision that aliens from Planet Magma are about to invade and piloting Ironman against the Magmans' robot champions Magma X and Gold Wolf.

Based on a 1956 *Shonen Magazine* serial by GIANT ROBO–creator Mitsuteru Yokoyama, and thereby predating Osamu Tezuka's similar BIG X in both anime and manga forms, Ironman's design is not dissimilar to that of Ryuichi Yokoyama's propaganda manga *The Science Warrior Appears in New York* (1943), suggesting perhaps this is indeed the way that WARTIME ANIME might have turned out if the war had gone on any longer! However, the postwar Ironman was considered peaceful enough for 52 of the early episodes to get a U.S. release courtesy of Fred Ladd, who toned down some of the death and violence and ensured that almost every villain in the show sounded like a Nazi or a Chicago mobster. The old show is probably best remembered for its classic theme tune from Lou Singer and Gene Raskin redundantly announcing that our hero was "ready to fight for right against wrong." There was also a short-lived 1960 live-action series in Japan.

The franchise was revived for *New Ironman 28* (1980), directed by Tetsuo

Imazawa, in which Interpol agent Shotaro works for the antirobot crime division, Branch Robo, and occasionally repels alien invaders, too. The new series removed the wartime angle by beginning in the 1990s with the death of Professor Haneda and did not appear in the U.S. as *New Gigantor* until 1993, after the "future year" in which it was originally set.

Super-Electric Robo Ironman 28 FX (1992) was another, less successful TV series from Imazawa that moved the action to 2030 and starred the grandson of the original Professor Haneda, fighting adversaries such as the "Pink Mafia" and the evil Franken organization, as well as the office politics within Interpol that find him arrested at one point by his own staff. Hong Kong's Tsui Hark, of WICKED CITY fame, announced he would be producing a remake of *Gigantor*, scheduled for release in 2002. *Ill. p. 11.*

GIGI AND THE FOUNTAIN OF YOUTH *

1982. JPN: *Maho no Princess Minky Momo*. AKA: *Magical Princess Minky Momo*. TV series, video. DIR: Kunihiko Yuyama, Junji Nishiyama, Kenjiro Yoshida, Hiroshi Watanabe. SCR: Takeshi Shudo, Tomomi Tsutsui, Jiyu Watanabe. DES: Toyoo Ashida, Noa Misaki, Ayumi Fukube. ANI: Mamoru Tanaka, Hiroshi Watanabe, Kazuo Imura. MUS: Hiroshi Takada. PRD: Ashi Pro, TV Tokyo. 25 mins. x 61 eps. (TV), 25 mins. x 62 eps. (v), 25 mins. x 3 eps. (v).

Minky Momo (Gigi) is a princess from the magical dreamland of Fenalinasa who has been sent to Earth where she poses as the daughter of two vets, albeit one who can transform (in the style of CREAMY MAMI) into a grown-up magical heroine, accompanied by her magical companions, Sindbook the dog, Mocha the monkey, and Pipil the bird. Perhaps unnaturally popular in the midst of the "Lolita complex" fad that also produced CREAM LEMON, she returned on several occasions, including the three-minute short *Creamy*

Mami vs. Minky Momo (1985) and *Minky Momo: La Ronde in My Dream* (1985), released in the U.S. as *Gigi and the Fountain of Youth*. In this 80-minute video, also screened theatrically, her human parents' plane crashes in the sea, and Momo discovers a tropical island, above which floats a children's paradise where nobody ever ages. The island's ruler Peter (an obvious reference to PETER PAN AND WENDY) enlists Momo's help in holding off unsavory outsiders, including the original master thief Lupin (not his grandson LUPIN III).

After the original's apparent death and the destruction of Fenalinasa, a new Momo appeared in the 1991 TV series about a princess from the undersea kingdom of Marinnasa taking up the previous Momo's mantle and masquerading on Earth as the daughter of archaeologists searching for the ruins of Fenalinasa. Though the new Momo lost her powers in episode 62, she had three extra unbroadcast adventures that were included when the TV series was released on video in 1993, comprising *SOS Marinnasa*, *Momo Goes to School*, and *A Favor from the Stars*.

GIGOLO *
1993. JPN: *Dochinpira: Onna Daisuki*. AKA: *Vulgar Punk: I Love Women*. Video. DIR: Hiromitsu Ota. SCR: Wataru Amano. DES: Hironobu Saito. ANI: Shigetaka Kiyoyama. MUS: Beyond Two. PRD: Pink Pineapple, KSS. 45 mins.
Jin drops out of college to become a gigolo, selling his favors to bored rich women in Tokyo while still living with his true love, the long-suffering Ranko. After some disastrous jobs that bring him into contact with the Hazakura gang, he is propositioned by Ai, a female contract killer. After he is the first man to "take her to heaven and back" (naturally), she reveals that she works for the rival Konatsu gang, whose boss adopted her after her original parents were killed in gangland cross-fire. After also losing her stepfather to criminal intrigue, she has sworn revenge on Mr. Hazakura him-

self, who is in hiding after the last attempt on his life. Realizing that Jin has serviced Hazakura's mistress, Ai forces him to take her there, where both she and Hazakura die in a shootout. Jin buries her at sea in her beloved Shelby Cobra automobile, then returns to Ranko, who reveals that it is their anniversary, and takes him to bed.

Considering the liberal tastes of the Japanese video porn market, it is bizarre that *Gigolo* wasn't made as a gay anime like FAKE. If the lead characters had been male, the macho posturings and pompous codes of honor would be more believable, as would the appetites and attitudes of the "female" characters, but presumably such a narrative switch wouldn't have pleased the authors of the original manga, Makio Hara and Tetsumi Doko. Better plotted than most porn anime, if only because there is a semblance of story that bolts together the halfhearted (and half-animated) sex scenes, *Gigolo* rivals GOLGO 13 in both its contemptuous attitude toward women and its juvenile take on sex and crime. It also contains the cheesiest of dialogue, played absolutely straight in the U.K. dub. 🄻🄽🅅

GINNAGASHI
1992. JPN: *Ginnagashi: Terajima-cho Kidan*. AKA: *Ginnagashi: Strange Tales of Terajima District*. Video. DIR: Osamu Kobayashi. SCR: Yu Takita. DES: Masaya Fujimori. ANI: Takaichiro Nakamura. MUS: Hiroshi Ogasawara. PRD: Toei, Tac. 41 mins.
Ten-year-old Kiyoshi watches as a tramp transforms himself into a rich imposter at a stand-up bar in the Tamanoi district. Amusing tales from prewar Tokyo based on the 1968 autobiographical manga *Strange Tales of Terajima* and written by Yu Takita for the alternative magazine *Garo*.

GIRL DETECTIVES' CLUB
1986. JPN: *Katsugeki Shojo Tanteidan*. Video. DIR: Masaharu Okuwaki. SCR: Yuho Hanazono. DES: Isamu Eguchi.

ANI: Masako Goto. MUS: "The Girl Detectives' Club." PRD: Tokyo Movie Shinsha. 30 mins.
Yuriko Edogawa, Midori Ichinotani, and Ingrid Shizuka Gruber are ordinary students at the high-class Gautama School for Girls who moonlight as super-sleuths. Midori disappears soon after discovering that her scientist father is working on a weapon, and the other girls track her down. They discover that she has been kidnapped by Akiko Jitsusoji, a bad-girl with her own gang working for the school principal, who is planning to conquer the world with Dr. Ichinotani's doomsday device. This very early multimedia offensive, including a tie-in manga in *Out* magazine, ended with a very early disappointed audience, as *GDC* turned out to be a lackluster affair. Compare to the suspiciously similar DEBUTANTE DETECTIVES.

GIRL FROM PHANTASIA *
1993. JPN: *Fantasia*. Video. DIR: Jun Kamiya. SCR: Katsuyuki Sumizawa. DES: Kazuya Kise. ANI: Kazuya Kise. MUS: Toshiyuki Watanabe. PRD: Production IG. 30 mins.
College boy Akihiro's girlfriend, Michiko, doesn't like his apartment enough to come over, and that seriously reduces his chances of getting her into bed. He buys a bargain rug to improve the decor, only to discover that it is a magical gateway to the fantasy land of Phantasia. Akihiko becomes the object of attention from the feisty sprite Malon. This video is a replay of a dozen other magical-girlfriend tales from URUSEI YATSURA to OH MY GODDESS!, this time with an eye on the soft-core porn market. Based on Akane Nagano's manga in *Comic Gamma*. 🄽

GIRL WITH THE WHITE FLAG, THE
1988. JPN: *Hakuki no Shojo Ryuko*. Movie. DIR: Satoshi Dezaki. SCR: Satoshi Dezaki. DES: Yukari Kobayashi. ANI: Reizo Kiyomizu. MUS: Yuse Nakajima. PRD: Magic Bus. Ca. 80 mins.
In 1945, American troops land on the island of Okinawa. The Japanese fight

a guerrilla war against the invaders, and little Ryuko is forced to leave her grandparents behind and flee with her mother and younger sister, who are eventually killed. Ryuko heads on alone across the war-torn island. Eventually she reaches safety in Japanese-occupied caves, only to witness the Japanese troops committing suicide with hand grenades. Based on a children's book by Akira Aratagawa and Hikuji Norima, itself inspired by real American footage of an Okinawan girl, Tomiko Higa, waving a white flag at the island's surrender. Shown in some theaters on a double bill with MY NEIGHBOR TOTORO instead of the similar GRAVE OF THE FIREFLIES. Another Okinawan war story was filmed as VOYAGE OF THE TSUSHIMA.

GIRLS IN SUMMER DRESSES

1988. JPN: *Natsufuku no Shojotachi.* TV special. DIR: Keiko Sugiura. SCR: Makiko Nakadate. DES: Yoshiyuki Momose. ANI: Toshio Hirata, Masao Murayama. MUS: N/C. PRD: Madhouse. 50 mins.

In 1945, the second- and third-year students of a Hiroshima girls' school are taken away to work in war factories. The remaining 220 girls of the first year try to make the best of their new-found status as the only teenagers in an almost deserted town, even amid the deprivations of wartime. On the 7th of August, an American bomber changes their lives forever. Broadcast on the 43rd anniversary of Hiroshima in memory of "the girls who lost their lives to the atom bomb," this is in the spirit of the earlier BAREFOOT GEN.

GLASSY OCEAN *

1998. JPN: *Kujira no Choyaku.* AKA: *The Whale's Leap.* Movie. DIR: Shigeru Tamura. SCR: Shigeru Tamura. DES: Shigeru Tamura. ANI: Masaya Sato. MUS: Yutoro Teshiume. PRD: Bandai. 23 mins.

On another world where time works differently, the ocean has turned to glass. In an impressive feat of digital animation shown at several film festi-

vals and broadcast on the U.K.'s Channel Four, people gather on the shore at a particular place to watch the group of whales that has arrived preparing to leap out of the water. Creator Shigeru Tamura also made the earlier *Galactic Fish* (1993), which also played with watery themes, this time visualizing a dimension where our world appears to be at the bottom of someone else's sea. He was also associated with Akiyuki Terajima's Japanese DVD compilation *A Piece of Phantasmagoria* (1995), which comprised 15 short animated films of a similar nature.

GLICK'S ADVENTURE

1981. Movie. DIR: Hideo Nishimaki. SCR: Yasuo Tanami. DES: Yoshio Kabashima. ANI: Takeshi Yamazaki. MUS: Reijiro Komutsu. PRD: Studio Koryumi. 82 mins.

Glick the squirrel and his friends leave their urban house and head off for the forest, meeting Gamba the vole on the way. After many hardships, Glick gives up and collapses in the snow, only to be rescued by his friends and arrive in the forest safely. Based on a story by Atsushi Saito that won a Best Newcomer award from the Association for the Study of Japanese Children's Books. Compare to BANNERTAIL THE SQUIRREL.

GLORIA: FORBIDDEN RELATIONS *

1998. JPN: *Glo.ri.a: Kindan no Ketsuzoku.* Video. DIR: Yasuhiro Kuroda. SCR: Akira Yokusuga. DES: Yasuaki Yoshino. ANI: Yasuaki Yoshino. MUS: N/C. PRD: Pink Pineapple, KSS. 30 mins. x 3 eps.

Kira and Gyorg (Beowulf in the U.S. dub) are selected to be personal tutors to the super-rich Gloria family in the U.S., whose five daughters turn out to be in need of an unexpected kind of "education." The tutors settle into the easy life, cosseted by servants and servicing their pupils, only to discover that the family hides a dark secret, and that the teachers will be in deadly danger if they do not leave immediately. Based on the C's Ware computer game *Forbidden Relations.*

Pure Love

© 1998 LIBIDO / DAIEI

GLORIOUS ANGELS

1978. JPN: *Pink Lady Monogatari Eiko no Tenshitachi.* AKA: *Glorious Angels: The Pink Lady Story.* TV series. DIR: Katsuhiko Taguchi. SCR: Masaru Yamamoto. DES: Yuji Hosoi. ANI: Ichiro Dannohara. MUS: Kyosuke Onosaki, Pink Lady. PRD: T&C, Toei, Tokyo 12 Channel. 25 mins. x 35 eps.

Mitsuyo Nemoto and Keiko Masuda, two girls from the backwoods of Shizuoka, meet at school, share the same dream of becoming pop stars, and win the district talent contest. They specialize in the performing arts at school, persevering at ballet and music. One day, they hope they'll make it to the top. This school-days biography of the singers who would eventually become Pink Lady, Japan's most famous duo in the late 1970s, was made at the height of their fame and a clever means of keeping the pair in the public eye without occupying their precious time—other actresses provided the girls' voices. An animated pop star tie-in similar to CAROL and HUMANE SOCIETY, in aims if not execution.

GLORIOUS TALES OF OLD EDO

1989. JPN: *Manga Edo Erobanashi.* AKA: *Glorious Manga Tales of Edo.* Video. DIR: Tsutomu Shibayama, Hajime Oedo,

Hideo Kawauchi. SCR: N/C. DES: N/C. ANI: N/C. MUS: N/C. PRD: Studio Jump. 44 mins. x 10 eps.

Several tales of old-time Tokyo from well-known directors, mainly concentrating on the courtesans of the Yoshiwara and prostitutes in premodern Shinjuku but also on the merchants and the impoverished samurai class of the period, with star-crossed lovers, chirpy artisans, and human-interest stories. Compare to the altogether more accomplished SENSUALIST. Other olde-worlde porn preceded the series with *Classical Sex-Zone* (1988), featuring erotic moments from the wars of the Heike and the Genji, and from the TALE OF GENJI itself. Ⓝ

GLORY TO THE ANCESTORS

1989. JPN: *Gosenzosama Banbanzai*. Video. DIR: Mamoru Oshii. SCR: Mamoru Oshii. DES: Satoru Utsunomiya. ANI: Satoru Utsunomiya. MUS: Kenji Kawai. PRD: Studio Pierrot. 30 mins. x 6 eps.
Maroko, a girl from the future, decides to learn more about her ancestors and travels back in time to modern Japan, only to discover that they are a sorry single-parent family, struggling to make ends meet without Mother around. She tries to help out and soon runs afoul of the Time Police. A show that mixes homespun situation comedy with the chrononautical goings-on of DORAEMON, it was reedited with some extra footage and released as the 90-minute movie *Maroko* (1990).

GO FOR IT, GENKI

1980. JPN: *Ganbare Genki*. TV series. DIR: Rintaro, Masahiro Sasaki, Akinori Nagaoka. SCR: Shunichi Yukimuro. DES: Shigetaka Kiyoyama. ANI: Kazuo Komatsubara, Masami Suda, Kazuo Mori, Tsukasa Abe. MUS: Koichi Morita. PRD: Fuji TV, Toei. 25 mins. x 35 eps.
When young Genki expresses an interest, his father decides to stage a comeback to regain his own featherweight title. Genki becomes a trainer for his own father, and the two take on the world as they struggle to relive past glories and create future ones. Based

on a 1976 *Shonen Sunday* manga by Yu Koyama, who also created OI! RYOMA.

GO FOR IT, GOEMON!

1991. JPN: *Anime Ganbare Goemon*. Video, movie, TV series. DIR: Shigeru Omachi, Katsuyoshi Yatabe. SCR: Shigeru Omachi. DES: Masayuki Hiraoka. ANI: Katsuyoshi Kobayashi. MUS: Yasuo Tsuchida. PRD: Public & Basic, TBS. 30 mins. (v), 25 mins. x 26 eps. (TV), 30 mins. (m).
Goemon, the hero of a fantasy computer game from Konami, is transported from his magical medieval world to become a superhero on Earth. First appearing in Yasunori Iguchi's video *GFIG: Nightmare Dimension* (1991), Goemon returned in earnest for a 1997 TV series, fighting enemy Seppuku-Maru and his army of computer-beasts. The series soon followed the standard plotting of many others: Goemon saves the day at a sports stadium, fights on a train, thwarts a forest fire at a summer camp, meets Santa Claus, helps out an idol singer, etc. For the short movie version *GFIG: Battle to Rescue Earth* (1998), Japan is threatened by a growing mountain of trash, which duly turns out to be the work of evildoers, not humanity in general.

GO FOR IT, KONBE

1980. JPN: *Ganbare Konbe*. TV series. DIR: Hiroe Mitsunobu, Hidenori Kondo, Susumu Ishizaki, Noboru Ishiguro, Tameo Ogawa. SCR: Yukio Izumi. DES: Shunji Sonoyama. ANI: Kenjiro Yoshida. MUS: Kenjiro Hirose. PRD: Production Roots, Anime City, Tokyo 12 Channel. 15 mins. x 56 eps.
Believing himself to be a descendant of Sun Wu-Kong, the hero of JOURNEY TO THE WEST, mountain monkey Konbe and his sister, Monko, run away from school. Pursued by their schoolmates Sanjiro, Benkei, Gataro the bird, and frog couple Mr. and Mrs. Kerosuke, Konbe soon finds that there is much to learn out in the big wide world. Based on an educational eight-panel manga strip from the *Mainichi Shogaku Shin-*

bun by Shunji Sonoyama, who also created GON THE FIRST MAN.

GO FOR IT, TABUCHI: VIOLENT PENNANT CONTEST

1980. JPN: *Ganbare Tabuchi-kun: Gekito Pennant Race*. Movie. DIR: Tsutomu Shibayama. SCR: Hideo Takayashiki, Masaki Tsuji, Tomoko Konparu. DES: Michishiro Yamada. ANI: Osamu Kobayashi, Minoru Maeda. MUS: Hidenori Mori, Hiroki Inui, Kensuke Kyo. PRD: TMS, Kitty Film. 94 mins.
The Seibu Lions baseball team makes it to the next round of a baseball tournament thanks to the heroic efforts of its star player, Tabuchi, but the next stage will involve hard work and cooperation. In a sports anime that pitches caricatures of real-life players against cartoon characters, the Lions (whose real-life mascot is the grown-up KIMBA THE WHITE LION), keep losing games due to Tabuchi's poor condition—his shadow is getting paler. A group of fellow players turns up at the stadium, accompanied by DOKABEN, and they encourage Tabuchi to pull through. They organize a Tabuchi Day to show him how appreciated he is, but it is a miserable failure. Eventually, he is brought out of his depression by the arrival of a girl called Miyoko, who obliges by dressing up as a cheerleader. Based on the 1979 *Action* manga by Hisaichi Ishii, who also created MY NEIGHBORS THE YAMADAS.

GO GOSHOBEN

1991. JPN: *Uttchare Goshobei*. Video. DIR: Kazuyoshi Kozawa. SCR: Noboru Hirose. DES: Mitsuharu Kajiya. ANI: Mitsuharu Kajiya. MUS: N/C. PRD: Nippon Eizo, JC Staff. 50 mins.
Benkyo Gosho is the only dedicated martial artist at his high school, so he is forced to represent the school at the intercollegiate championships in both wrestling and judo. He tries to enlist help from his schoolmates, scouting among the local fat kids for a possible wrestling buddy, eventually deciding he's probably going to have to make it

on his own. Based on the 1988 *Shonen Sunday* manga by Ben Nakajima.

GOAL FIELD HUNTER
1994. AKA: *Goal FH*. TV series. DIR: Masakazu Higuchi, Shinichi Watanabe, Akira Kiyomizu. SCR: Hiroshi Terajima. DES: Yuki Iwai. ANI: Yuki Iwai, Akihiro Kaneyama. MUS: N/C. PRD: Dog Fight, NHK2. 25 mins. x 39 eps.
A standard tale of a soccer team overcoming the odds to become the champions of the J-League. Concentrating on an adult, professional cast instead of the amateurs of CAPTAIN TSUBASA, this series also boasts professional "soccer advisers" among the crew to ensure realism.

GOD SIGMA
1980. JPN: *Uchu Taitei God Sigma*. AKA: *Space Emperor God Sigma*. TV series. DIR: Takeyuki Kanda, Katsuhiko Taguchi. SCR: Masaki Tsuji. DES: Kaoru Shintani, Kazuhiko Udagawa, Yutaka Izubuchi. ANI: Kazuhiko Udagawa, Akira Saijo. MUS: Hiroshi Tsutsui. PRD: Toei, Tokyo 12 Channel. 25 mins. x 50 eps.
In the year 2050, the alien Eldar finally complete their 2,300-year journey to a new world, only to find it occupied by human colonists. Second-generation colonists Toshiya and Kensaku see their homeworld of Io destroyed but are recruited by Professor Kazumi to pilot one of the two "Thunder God" war robots in order to stop the Eldar general Teral reaching Earth. The robots also have a secret (can you possibly guess? . . .): the Earth and Sky Thunder robots can combine with the Sea Thunder Robot piloted by the professor's beautiful assistant, Julie, to form the invincible robot God Sigma.

GODAIKIN *
1982.
This is not an anime show. It is the name for the U.S. release (or rerelease) of a line of diecast and plastic toys from Bandai and its subsidiary company, Popy. In Japan the toy line was known as *DX Chogokin (De luXe Super Alloy)*, *Chogokin* being a term

coined by Go Nagai to describe the metal used to build MAZINGER Z. The *Godaikin/Chogokin* range consisted of a mix of robots from both live-action *sentai* and anime shows, but only the anime robots included are listed here. The Godaikin range included Tetsujin 28 (see GIGANTOR), GOD SIGMA, Gardian (see CHAMPION OF GORDIAN), Daltanias (DARTANIUS), Golion (see VOLTRON), Combattra (COMBATTLER V), Voltes V (VOLTUS), DANCOUGAR, LASERION, and Abega (LIGHTSPEED ELECTRON ARBEGAS). The range enjoyed a Japanese revival in the late 1990s with a range of high-end diecast toys for the collector market entitled *Soul of Chogokin*.

GODDAM
1990. Video. DIR: Noboru Furuse. SCR: Tomo Fujikawa. DES: Noboru Furuse. ANI: Noboru Furuse. MUS: Eri Kani. PRD: Signal. 47 mins. x 2 eps.
The Seiyo racing team enters the world-famous Safari Rally, led by Japanese hero Todohara and his American navigator Rob Lowe(!). Based on the 1988 *Big Comic* manga by AREA 88–creator Kaoru Shintani. The two-part series was unnumbered, but *G: Survival Chaser* is the first, followed by *G: Go Ahead*.

GODMARS *
1981. JPN: *Rokushin Gattai Godmars*. AKA: *Hexademonic Symbiote Godmars; Six-God Union Godmars*. TV series, movie. DIR: Tetsuo Imazawa, Hideyuki Motohashi, Satoshi Dezaki, Junji Nishimura. SCR: Keisuke Fujikawa, Noboru Shiroyama. DES: Hajime Kamegaki. ANI: Hideyuki Motohashi. MUS: Kei Wakakusa, Reijiro Komutsu. PRD: Hikari Pro, TMS. 25 mins. x 64 eps. (TV), 97 mins. (m), 56 mins. (v), 30 mins. x 2 eps. (v2).
In the year 1999, humanity starts to advance beyond the confines of the solar system, encountering the evil Emperor Zaul of Planet Gishin. Takeru Akigami of the Earth Defense Force "Cosmocrushers" discovers that he was sent from Gishin as a sleeper agent 17

years previously. He is forced to choose between his two homes, deciding to defend Earth as one of the pilots of the six-part Godmars robot, which forces him into a tragic conflict with his elder brother Mark, who has chosen the other side.

This series was very loosely based on Mitsuteru Yokoyama's 1976 *Mars* manga from *Shonen Champion* magazine, itself a retelling of Yokoyama's earlier BABEL II. The shows were recut to make a 1982 movie (released in the U.S. as *Godmars*), and Masakazu Iijima also directed *GM: Legend of Seventeen* (1988), a one-shot video retelling the life of the doomed Mark.

After the success of "retro" series like GIANT ROBO, the story was remade on video with greater faith to Yokoyama's original as *Mars* (1994) by Junji Nishimura, who had also worked on *Godmars*. It restored the original manga's story line of a young boy in suspended animation inside a South Sea volcano who awakens a century before his alien masters planned to use his powers to reduce human civilization to a manageable low-tech level. As with his *Godmars* counterpart, however, he chooses to adopt the human race as his own and fight the invaders.

GOING STEADY WITH A WITCH
1986. JPN: *Majo de mo Steady*. Video. DIR: Hiroshi Kobayashi. SCR: Reiko Nakada. DES: Tori Miki. ANI: Hideo Kawauchi. MUS: Hiroshi Ogasawara. PRD: Tokyo Media Connections, Asiado. 42 mins.
Hisashi Seki lives a gray, dull salaryman's life, living alone in an old apartment building that happens to be built over a dimensional warp. He wakes up to find the nude girl Mami in his room. They fall in love and decide to stay in Hisashi's world, but then an accident shoots Hisashi into another world: one occupied by everyone's ideal partners. Compare to OH MY GODDESS!, URUSEI YATSURA, and a zillion other stories in which a passive man gets a gorgeous girl just by loafing. Ⓝ

GOKU: MIDNIGHT EYE *

1989. Video. DIR: Yoshiaki Kawajiri. SCR: Buichi Terasawa, Ryuzo Nakanishi. DES: Yoshiaki Kawajiri, Hirotoshi Sano. ANI: Hiroshi Hamazaki, Hirotoshi Sano. MUS: Yukihide Takekawa, Kazz Toyama. PRD: Madhouse, Toei. 50 mins. x 2 eps.

In the year 2014, private investigator Goku Furinji is contacted by former associates on the police force who are being picked off by a mysterious assailant. Left for dead after an encounter with a female hypnotist, a mysterious force gives him a high-tech stick that can change sizes and a link to every computer on the globe through his left ("midnight") eye. He uses both devices in his ongoing fight against crime. But apart from the magic staff, the name ("Goku" being Japanese for "Wu Kong"), and some luxuriant sideburns, the story bears little resemblance to the Monkey King of JOURNEY TO THE WEST, which supposedly inspired it. It owes more to James Bond films, with the plush locations, silly plots, and breathless girls in tight dresses looking for a Real Man to sort out their problems. With the concentration on that super-duper eye of his, it also recalls the *Six Million Dollar Man*.

Based on a 1988 manga in *Comic Burger*, *GME* is a typical work from Buichi Terasawa, who gave us SPACE ADVENTURE COBRA, KABUTO, and the as-yet-untranslated RED BRAND TAKERU. It was the babes that really appealed to his audience, and the anime doesn't scrimp on regularly wheeling out a beautiful, scantily clad, eye-candy girl, normally with some incredibly theatrical shtick like peacock feathers or a pair of motorcycle handlebars on her back. Other designs are similarly impressive, from flying metal devil-dogs to motorized unicycles. It's not every day you get to see a fully robed Mandarin tycoon roller-skating down the side of a skyscraper, either. **L N V**

GOKUDO: SWORDSMAN EXTRAORDINAIRE

1999. JPN: *Gokudo no Manyuki*. AKA: *Gokudo's Dissolute Wanderings; Jester the Adventurer*. TV series. DIR: Kunihisa Sugishima, Akihiko Nishiyama. SCR: Koji Miura, Sumihiro Tomioka, Masamichi Sugawara, Hirokazu Mizude. DES: Miho Shimokasa. ANI: Masayuki Hiraoka, Michiaki Sugimoto. MUS: N/C. PRD: Trans Arts, Pioneer, TV Tokyo. 25 mins. x 26 eps.

Gokudo is reckless, greedy, and ambitious, the crown prince of Esharott, and self-proclaimed treasure hunter. Exiled after Satan, Emperor of the Darkside, usurps his father's throne, he is saved by Satan's wife, Mora. Disguised as an old fortuneteller, she turns him into two people—Jester and Justice, wielders of the swords of Fire and Ice. After they overthrow Satan and his puppet king, Jester realizes that Justice would make the best ruler, leaves the kingdom to him, and sets out in search of adventure with tomboy Roubett and Mora's son, Prince—banished from the Darkside Empire and ordered to learn the ways of the world. This series, based on a novel by Usagi Nakamura, is part JOURNEY TO THE WEST, part RANMA 1/2.

GOLD LIGHTAN

1981. JPN: *Ogon Senshi Gold Lightan*. AKA: *Golden Warrior Gold Lightan*. TV series. DIR: Koichi Mashimo, Mizuho Nishikubo. SCR: Akiyoshi Sakai, Takeshi Shudo, Masaaki Sakurai, Tomomi Tsutsui. DES: Ippei Kuri. ANI: Sadao Miyamoto, Takashi Nakamura. MUS: Masaaki Shinbo, Masayuki Yamamoto. PRD: Tatsunoko, Tokyo 12 Channel. 25 mins. x 52 eps.

King Ibaldar of the Mecha Dimension sends alien invaders to attack Earth, not realizing that his enemies have already sent a champion to defend it. The invincible Mecha superhero has joined forces with the 12-year-old boy Hiro, hiding unobtrusively inside his cigarette lighter. In times of trouble, he can use the lighter as a dimensional gate to call upon Gold Lightan's power to transform into a giant robot. With a heavy debt to the early ULTRAMAN shows, Lightan and his five-robot team, who hide inside lighters carried by other members of Hiro's Naughty Rangers (a Bic, a Zippo, etc.), fight off the alien invaders in a mind-bogglingly inappropriate series that must have inspired teenage smokers and pyromaniacs all over Japan. A fine example of what can happen if a show is governed solely by the contents of the animators' pockets.

GOLDEN BAT

1967. JPN: *Ogon Bat*. AKA: *The Phanta Man*. TV series. DIR: Kujiro Yanagida, Seiji Sasaki, Tadao Wakabayashi. SCR: Mitsuhide Shimauchi. DES: Tatsuo Nagamatsu. ANI: Nobuhide Morikawa. MUS: Masashi Tanaka. PRD: Daiichi, Yomiuri TV (Nippon TV). 25 mins. x 52 eps.

Golden Bat is the warrior who looks like a golden skeleton, sent from ancient Atlantis to protect the people of our own time. He appears whenever his presence is requested by the Japanese girl Mari, with her associates Professor Yamatone and schoolboy Takeru, in their ongoing fight against attacking robots and monsters. Based on Tatsuo Nagamatsu's manga. In 2000, the studio AIC announced that they were planning a remake for the new century.

GOLDEN BOY *

1995. Video. DIR: Hiroyuki Kitakubo. SCR: Tatsuya Egawa. DES: Toshihiro Kawamoto. ANI: Toshihiro Kawamoto. MUS: N/C. PRD: KSS. 30 mins. x 6 eps.

The wanderings of a college boy who prefers to learn at the university of life, as Kintaro cycles from job to job, charming the local lovelies everywhere he goes. Seducing the sexy boss of a computer company in the first episode, only to bed the daughter of a politician whose campaign he is supposed to be managing, Kintaro never gives up. Other jobs where Kintaro gets to try out his seduction skills include noodle chef, swimming instructor, biker boy, and, finally, working in an animation studio. Based on a minor work by Tatsuya Egawa, better known for MAGICAL TALRUTO and the manga *Tokyo University Story* and *Be Free.*

GOLDFISH WARNING

1991. JPN: *Kingyo Chuiho*. TV series. DIR: Junichi Sato, Atsutoshi Umezawa, Kunihiko Ikuhara. SCR: Keiko Maruo, Yumi Kageyama, Hiroko Naka, Aya Matsuyama. DES: Satoru Irizuki. ANI: Satoru Irizuki, Tomoyoshi Koyama. MUS: N/C. PRD: Toei, TV Asahi. 25 mins. x 54 eps.

Snooty rich girl Chitose Fujinomiya is left in poverty after the death of her father. Thrown out of the elite City Academy with nothing but her valuable pink goldfish, Gyopi, for company, she is found on the premises of the rundown Country High School where children and animals attend classes together. Regaining some of her inheritance from an embezzling family lawyer, Chitose uses some of the money to rebuild the struggling school, making herself chairperson of the school board *and* student-body president. With completely selfish motives, she tries to improve her new school in order to bring a little "urban sophistication," and, she hopes, trounce the feckless City Academy and its prissy student president, Yurika. Her classmates are less keen, with the likable red-head Wapiko mediating between Chitose and the irate animals, while simultaneously fending off the advances of Yurika's assistant, Takapi. A madcap comedy and long-term fan favorite, incorporating meditations on how CANDY CANDY would have worked out if its heroine were a bitch, coupled with surreal visuals and designs that presaged the more abstract moments of director Ikuhara's later UTENA. Based on Neko Nekobe's 1989 manga in the magazine *Nakayoshi*.

GOLGO 13: THE PROFESSIONAL *

1983. JPN: *Golgo 13*. Movie, video. DIR: Osamu Dezaki. SCR: Hideyoshi Nagasaka. DES: Shichiro Kobayashi. ANI: Shichiro Kobayashi. MUS: Toshiyuki Omori. PRD: TMS. 94 mins. (m), 60 mins. (v).

Golgo 13, one of Japan's longest-running manga series, has been drawn by Takao Saito since 1969. Its unsmiling hero, Duke Togo, has never revealed anything about his past. Instead, he wanders the world and kills people for a living, a modern *ronin* with a code name constructed from purest evil: the unlucky number 13 and the first two syllables of "Golgotha." An immense hit with middle-aged businessmen, Duke gets to travel the world, screw foreign chicks, and shoot unpleasant people. Although inspired by the James Bond films, he doesn't even pretend to be working for good. He is totally amoral.

In the 1983 film, Duke is hired by a mystery client to kill the heir of a wealthy businessman. The businessman offers the sexual favors of his newly widowed daughter-in-law to a psychotic killer on the understanding that the son's death will be avenged. And so begins a series of tit-for-tat escalations, risible dialogue, embarrassing characterizations, and a ludicrous procession of gunfights, as the two assassins kill and shag their way toward a final confrontation.

Director Dezaki treats Duke's quest as a modern samurai adventure, with improbable leaps and slices replaced by improbable marksmanship and setups (watch the moment Duke shoots someone through a building). He also experimented with computer graphics in a helicopter assault scene, inserting now-dated CG that makes it not unlike watching an old Atari console. But Dezaki would retain his obsession with out-of-place CG, using it once again in his later BLACK JACK. Duke would return in a video sequel, *Golgo 13: Queen Bee* (1998), in which Duke is assigned to kill Sonia, the titular South American nymphomaniac drug baroness, before she can carry out her own threat to murder a presidential candidate running on a Just-Say-No platform. ●L●N●V

An anime series with a history to rival *Star Trek*, GUNDAM's most famous characteristic is its reliance on "mobile suits"—robotic battle armor distantly inspired by Robert Heinlein's STARSHIP TROOPERS. The series regularly introduces new characters and situations chiefly as an excuse to introduce new robots and their inevitable spinoff toys. Gundam merchandise is so popular that it is estimated there is a Gundam toy for every person in Japan. *See entry p. 158.*

Gundam

© SOTSU AGENCY • SUNRISE

GON THE FIRST MAN

1996. JPN: *Hajime Ningen Gon*. TV series. DIR: Yutaka Kagawa, Takashi Yamazaki, Hiroyuki Yokoyama. SCR: Yoshio Urasawa, Megumi Sugiwara. DES: Shunji Sonoyama. ANI: Masaaki Iwane. MUS: Yusuke Honma. PRD: KSS, NHK2. 25 mins. x 39 eps. (each ep. has 3 stories).

The wacky adventures of Gon the little caveman, as his family tries to cope with prehistoric life. Beginning as a simple comedy featuring Gon and his gang trying to hunt mammoths, running from saber-tooth tigers, and cowering from thunder, later episodes became more satirical of modern times, with Gon's trip to the prehistoric equivalent of summer camp. In the final stage, it developed an SF angle not unlike Shotaro Ishinomori's AGE OF THE GREAT DINOSAURS, with the arrival of aliens in a flying saucer. Based on a manga by GO FOR IT KONBE's Shunji Sonoyama, who also created an earlier caveman anime, *The Gardles* (1974). Gon's adventures made it to the screen in the wake of the live-action Hollywood *Flintstones* (1994) and were of no relation to the diminutive *dinosaur* hero of Masashi Tanaka's 1991 manga *Gon*. Compare to KUM KUM.

GON THE FOX

1989. JPN: *Gongitsune*. Movie. DIR: Yasunari Maeda. SCR: Tsunehisa Ito. DES: Shoji Ikehara. ANI: Nobukazu Otake, Tsukasa Abe, Yoko Tsukada. MUS: Yasuo Tsuchida. PRD: Ai Planning Center, Magic Bus, Orions, Radical Party. 76 mins.

Gon the orphaned fox cub is washed downstream into a small village in Aichi Prefecture. Making his home there, he steals some fish intended for the sick mother of a local villager. After the mother dies, an apologetic Gon brings offerings of mushrooms and fruit to the bereaved villager. One night, thinking Gon is an intruder, the villager kills him as he approaches the house. A Japanese tragedy rich in karmic misery, based on a story by Nankichi Nimi, though the early scenes depicting the death of Gon's mother were added by screenwriter Ito. Made to celebrate the tenth anniversary of the JAPANESE FOLK TALES series.

GOOD MORNING ALTHEA

1987. Video. DIR: Hideki Tonokatsu. SCR: N/C. DES: Michitaka Kikuchi. ANI: Moriyasu Taniguchi. MUS: Nobuhiko Kashiwara. PRD: Animate, Studio Pierrot. 50 mins.

Far in the future, the galaxy is ruled by a race of warrior-mages who have cast aside much of humankind's earlier follies in cybernetics. However, the infamous "Automaton" robot that defended humanity from the Stemma Empire is rumored to be still operational, and three brave young teenagers go on a quest to shut it down . . . or perhaps steal it for themselves. For this they will require Althea of the Seal, a human symbiont. Based on a manga from *C-Live* magazine written by a collective of fans called "Black Point," this video begs the question, "It took more than one person to come up with that plot?"

GOODBYE LITTLE HIPPO

1989. JPN: *Sayonara Kaba-kun*. Movie. DIR: Yutaka Ozawa. SCR: Yoko Yamamoto. DES: Katsumoto Saotome. ANI: Shiro Nakagawa, Toshiki Saida. MUS: N/C. PRD: Asmik, OH Production. 25 mins.

A mixture of live action and animation telling the true story of the animals of Tokyo's Ueno Zoo during the harsh days of bombing raids and shortages that took their toll during World War II. Focusing on the hippos, who were eventually butchered for food in the closing days of the conflict, *Newtype* called the story, "a study of the tragedy of war and a prayer for peace." No hippos were available for comment. See also ZOO WITHOUT AN ELEPHANT.

GOODFELLA

1990. JPN: *Danki*. Video. DIR: Osamu Yamazaki. SCR: Noboru Hirose. DES: Masami Suda. ANI: Masami Suda, Masafumi Yamamoto. MUS: N/C. PRD: Nichiei, JC Staff. 50 mins. x 3 eps., 40 mins. x 2 eps.

After his father leaves when he is very young, Kyosuke Murata grows up under the thumb of his overprotective mother, Shizuko. When he reaches adulthood, he is thrown into the harsh, violent world of Japanese gangland when his mother becomes involved in a gang-related crime. He goes up against the Murata-gumi organization, only to find that his estranged father is its head. Rising up through the ranks, Kyosuke eventually unites half the gangs in Japan beneath his own leadership, only to find that the other half have also combined to resist his new power, starting the greatest gang war in Japanese history. Based on a 1979 manga in *Big Comic Spirits* by Hiroshi Motomiya, who also created CLIMBING ON A CLOUD and MY SKY. The first episode was also screened theatrically.

Shigeru Ueda directed a two-part sequel, *New Goodfella* (1998), in which gang members attempt to arrange a jailbreak by infiltrating a prison disguised as guards. **NV**

GORILLAMAN

1992. Video. DIR: Yoshinori Nakamura. SCR: Noboru Hirose. DES: Koichi Endo. ANI: Mitsuharu Kajiya, Koichi Endo. MUS: N/C. PRD: JC Staff. 50 mins.

A school comedy about a mute transfer student, Tadashi Iketo, who is constantly shuffled from school to school for his "violent nature," though he really is a mild-mannered boy constantly taunted into fights over his simian appearance. Based on a 1989 manga in *Young Magazine* by Harold Sakuishi. Compare with the more dramatic ANGEL LEGEND.

GORSCH THE CELLIST

1982. JPN: *Cello Hiki no Gorsch*. Movie. DIR: Isao Takahata. SCR: Isao Takahata. DES: Shunji Saita. ANI: Shunji Saita, Suemi Nishida, Mariko Nomura, Kumiko Tsukada, Yoko Tomizawa, Takashi Namiki, Taeko Otsuka, Nobuhiro Aihara, Kazuhide Tomonaga. MUS: Yoshio Mamiya, Beethoven. PRD: OH Productions. 63 mins.

A mediocre cellist is forced to practice late at night and "dreams" that he is visited by talking animals. A cat, cuckoo, badger, and field mouse each offer their opinions on his music and keep him company during the lonely sessions, but later on Gorsch discovers that his music, while terrible to human ears, has been healing sick animals all around the neighborhood. The knowledge that even his ability does *some* good brings heart and soul to his music and improves his performance the next time he faces a human audience.

Though most likely to be known in the West through this striking 1982 film, the story was first animated in 1949 as a 19-minute short directed by Kiji Tanaka, and based originally on a short story by NIGHT TRAIN TO THE STARS–creator Kenji Miyazawa. The story was animated a third time for the *Classic Children's Tales* series (1992) as a 30-minute stop-motion short released straight to video.

GOSHOGUN *

1981. JPN: *Sengoku Majin Goshogun*. AKA: *Civil War Devil-God Goshogun*. TV series, video. DIR: Kunihiko Yuyama, Tetsuro Amino, Junji Nishimura. SCR: Takeshi Shudo, Jiyu Watanabe, Sukehiro Tomita. DES: Studio Z5, Mutsumi Inomata, Shunsuke Kasahara. ANI: Hiroshi Tanaka, Etsuko Tomita, Hideaki Matsuoka. MUS: Tachio Akano. PRD: Ashi Pro, Tokyo 12 Channel. 25 mins. x 26 eps. (TV), 65 mins. (m1), 90 mins. (m2).

Professor Masada is killed by the evil Docougar organization, which wants to steal the secrets of his latest invention, the Super Energy Vimra. His son Kenta takes the research to the mobile secret base of the God Thunder organization, assembling the "Goshogun" team of warriors to fight against the minions of Docougar.

Kunihiko Yuyama's movie *Goshogun* (1982) takes the cast to the South American republic of Felcona, where president Santos requires their assistance against Docougar agents. A reedit of episodes 17 and 20 of the TV series, the "movie" adds scraps of extra footage, including an introductory sequence and false interstitial advertisements for nonexistent products endorsed by the cast—Kernagul's Fried Chicken, Kutnall's Tranquilizers, Gitter's 35-section Combining Robot, and Docougar Total Training. The film also used images of characters' previously unseen childhood years in the closing credits, a device that foreshadowed the subplot of the final *Goshogun* release (see below).

In 1985, the *Goshogun* series was combined with SRUNGLE and released in the U.S. as *Macron One.* As with its contemporary ROBOTECH, the series was given a completely new story line, in this case about a teleportation experiment that hurls test pilot David Jance into a parallel universe, where he leads the Beta Command robot team against alien menaces. Meanwhile, the evil overlord Dark Star has been transported by the same experiment into our own universe, where another team must hold back his army of robotic warriors. With the U.S. market interest in SF buoyant after *Return of the Jedi* (1983), *Macron One* boasted a successful mix of alien crew, prattling robots, and enemies who looked suspiciously like Imperial Storm Troopers. The

show's appeal was augmented further with contemporary pop music, not just Duran Duran's "Reflex" over the opening titles, but other chart-toppers strewn around the battle scenes. These additions gave the show a feel not unlike an MTV pop video but inadvertently damaged its long-term salability, since rights were not cleared for the same tunes to be used on video.

Back in Japan, the original had a last hurrah in the video *Goshogun: Time Étranger* (1985), often confused with the unrelated TIME STRANGER. Also shown in Japanese theaters, this is the incarnation of the series best known today through the dub made by Manga Entertainment. Recycling the plot from the *Goshogun* novels, *Time Étranger* added a framing device set 40 years later in a world that looks like Chicago with taller buildings and hover-cars. Much of the footage is wasted on a pointless car chase, leaving little time for anything but a few shots of beeping machines and hand-wringing bedside vigils. The strangely ageless Remi, infamous for refusing her medals, is mortally injured in a crash and looks back on her life while the rest of the old team (including three of her former foes, now pals with their one-time enemies) bickers around her comatose form. Using the world's most irritating French accent, Remi recalls an incident when she fell down a well as a child, and she also hallucinates a surreal "mission" involving those who are assembled around her bed. The film then cuts to the team trapped in a city of confused religious fundamentalists (they worship like Muslims but have crucifixes in their graveyard), who are convinced that the God Thunder team's day of destiny has arrived, and that Remi will be the first of them to die. Remi and her friends fight off the seething locals in quietly racist scenes of the God Thunder team, with vastly superior firepower, shooting into wave after wave of stick-waving towelheads. They steal a tram (yes, a tram, driving it off its rails, not unlike the plot), mess around with hang-gliders,

and have a fight in a bar while pontificating about destiny and fate. All this, it transpires, is a metaphor for Remi's critical condition in the present day, since she must confront the demons of her childhood and psyche if she is to awaken from her coma. However, her fate is left unclear in an ending that is either a ham-fisted metaphor for her death or a reunion scene riddled with continuity errors and poor writing. So Remi either makes a miraculous recovery, springs out of bed, and chases after her comrades, or dies, recovers, and dies again, depending on your interpretation.

GOTTAMAN
1994. JPN: *Dengeki Oshioki Musume Gottaman.* AKA: *Electro Punisher Girl Gottaman.* Video. DIR: Akira Suzuki, Hiroshi Kishida. SCR: Masaru Yamamoto. DES: Toyomi Sugiyama, Eisaku Inoue. ANI: Toyomi Sugiyama, Eisaku Inoue. MUS: N/C. PRD: Movic, Hero, Animate, All Products. 45 mins. x 2 eps.
A normal high-school girl moonlights as the superhero Gottaman, who battles the lusty minions of the sinister Black Buddha organization while wearing nothing but a skimpy loincloth. Tits and tentacles in the style of LA BLUE GIRL, based on the manga in *Shonen Champion* by Masakazu Yamaguchi. ✪✪

GRADUATION *
1994. JPN: *Sotsugyo.* Video. DIR: Katsuhiko Nishijima. SCR: Asami Watanabe, Kenichi Kanemaki. DES: Kazuko Tadano, Kazuaki Mori. ANI: Kazuko Tadano. MUS: Kingo Hamada. PRD: Head Room, Animate. 30 mins. x 4 eps., 30 mins. x 2 eps. (*Marriage*), 30 mins. (*MVP*), 30 mins. x 2 eps. (*M*).
Mami, Reiko, Kiyomi, Shizuka, and Mika are five girls who have mixed feelings about their high-school graduation day. They decide to hold a final celebration, but the clumsy Mami gets lost buying food, and the rest of the girls have to look for her. In a surprisingly heartfelt spinoff from a computer game, the girls decide on their future

careers and say farewell as their school days come to a close. In the PC version, the player took the role of a career guidance counselor, steering the girls through their school days and into the right careers—the anime dramatizes a situation in which Mami and Reiko are undecided and need the advice of their fellows.

Exhausting the potential of the original, the series changed direction for the third and fourth episodes, renamed *Sailor Victory* (no relation to the proto–SAILOR MOON). A spoof that placed the archetypal women of *Graduation* in an SF setting, it features the girls as a team of superheroes in "hard suits," battling not only cybernetic criminals and invading creatures from another dimension (à la BUBBLEGUM CRISIS or SILENT MÖBIUS), but also the entire police force (à la AD POLICE or PATLABOR).

In a cleaner satire than the naughty BATTLE TEAM LAKERS EX, the girls take all of the familiar tropes of SF anime to their logical extremes, forgetting to use their secret identities, spending so long delivering pompous speeches that the crime scene is already secure, and even transforming in scenes of comedically gratuitous nudity.

The original game spawned several sequels and spinoffs, some of which were also adapted into anime. Kazuhiro Ozawa's *Marriage* (1996), also available in the U.S., is set several years after the original, with the same characters replacing their quest for the right grades with the search for the right man. This time, they are recast as five sisters, each one a year younger than the next. With the release of an all-male spinoff featuring a prefabricated pop group, Akiyuki Shinbo directed the one-shot pop promo *MVP EMU Music Video* (1996). In Hajime Kamegaki's inevitable two-part follow-up *Graduation M* (1998), the story of the game itself was retold, with a group of pretty young boys deciding to form a band and play at their school's 50th-anniversary celebrations. ◐

GRANDAR

1998. JPN: *Grandar Buzo RV.* AKA: *Grandar Armory Revolution.* TV series. DIR: Takayoshi Suzuki. SCR: Nobuyuki Fujimoto, Machiko Ikeda. DES: Masayuki Hiraoka. ANI: Masamitsu Kudo, Masami Abe. MUS: Goro Omi. PRD: Nippon Animation, TV Tokyo. 25 mins. x 39 eps.

In order to stop seven legendary lures scattered around the world from falling into evil hands, teenager Musashi and his best friends, Suguru and Mio, set out to save the world, defeating their opponents in a series of martial angling competitions. Based on a manga by Takashi Teshirogi and Hajime Murata, who was once, predictably, a champion angler. Just when you thought you'd seen it all.

GRANDEEK

1999. Video. DIR: Shige Sotoyama. SCR: N/C. DES: Toshiko Baba. ANI: N/C. MUS: N/C. PRD: Tac, Movic, SPE Visual Works. 45 mins. x 2 eps., 45 mins.

Swords and sorcery as the young warrior-woman Tia Allbright and her hapless assistant, Luke, battle demon assassins in a fantasy land. Based on a manga by the pseudonymous Koki Osc, the story continues in *Grandeek: Side Story* (2000), in which their companion Yuri has to be stopped from killing her former lover Ehlen, who has been transformed into a demon assassin.

GRANDIZER *

1975. JPN: *UFO Robo Grendizer* [sic]. AKA: *Goldorak.* Movie, TV series. DIR: Tomoharu Katsumata, Masamune Ochiai, Masayuki Akehi, Kazuya Yamazaki. SCR: Shozo Uehara, Keisuke Fujikawa, Tomohiro Ando. DES: Kazuo Komatsubara, Shingo Araki. ANI: Kazuo Komatsubara, Keisuke Morishita. MUS: Shunsuke Kikuchi. PRD: Dynamic, Toei. 25 mins. x 74 eps.

Young Duke Fleed (Orion Quest) of Planet Fleed (Antares) is forced to leave his homeworld when it is attacked by the forces of the evil King Vega. Fleed, together with his Grendizer spacecraft that can transform into a giant robot, reaches planet Earth, where he hides from Vega's forces and is adopted by the kindly Professor Umon (Bryant), who calls him Daisuke (Johnny). "Daisuke" works happily on a local farm, until the arrival of Vega's forces on Earth forces him to take a stand, together with his friends Koji Kabuto, Hikaru Makiba, and Duke's sister, Maria Grace.

The 30-minute anime movie *War of the Flying Saucers* (1975) introduced the character of Fleed alongside other creations of Go Nagai, such as Danbei from the same author's CUTEY HONEY, and pilot Koji Kabuto, whose inclusion effectively makes *Grandizer* another sequel to MAZINGER Z. The pilot movie features the same basic plot, with the mild-mannered Daisuke Umon appearing as the only son of Dr. Umon of the Umon Space Science Laboratory. To capture both him, his flying saucer, and his combining robot Gattaidar, Princess Teronna from Planet Yarban attacks Earth with the Yarban Flying Saucer Unit.

In the series proper, before Fleed and Maria returned in triumph to their homeworld, *Grandizer* also appeared in two short Go Nagai crossover movies: *Great Mazinger / Grandizer / Getter Robo G: Battle the Great Monster* (1976) and *UFO Robo Grandizer vs. Great Mazinger* (1976). Twenty-six episodes were released as part of the FORCE FIVE series on American TV.

GRANDOLL *

1997. JPN: *Chokosoku Grandoll.* AKA: *Supralight Grandolls; Hyperspeed Grandoll.* Video. DIR: Hideki Tonokatsu. SCR: Katsumi Hasegawa, Yuko Nakada. DES: Toshinari Yamashita, Yoshinori Sayama. ANI: Toshinari Yamashita. MUS: N/C. PRD: Zero G Room, Bandai. 30 mins. x 3 eps.

Sixteen-year-old anime fan-girl Hikaru has a mad scientist for a father, a crush on a high school senior, and a passionate obsession with the anime hero Rockin' Dorger. She dreams of becoming a real-life anime heroine, only to discover that she already is. Recovering her memories of her childhood, she realizes that she is the Crown Princess of Planet Gran, sent away during a civil war to live a life in exile on Earth. However, the evil alien Lord Friedshalf plans to use her Grandoll Armor for himself, sending minions to fight her for it, including his own lover, Sigil, who comes to Hikaru's school disguised as a transfer student. Switching in the style of **DRAGON HALF** from normal to squashed-down cartoon mode in the blink of an eye, *Grandoll* is either a lighthearted spoof of anime clichés or a cynical trawl through them, depending on how charitable you feel today.

GRANDZORT

1989. JPN: *Mado-o Grandzort*. AKA: *Sorcerer King Grandzort*. TV series. DIR: Hideji Iguchi. SCR: Hideji Iguchi, Hiroko Naka, Takashi Yamada, Ryosuke Takahashi. DES: Toyoo Ashida, Kunio Okawara. ANI: Takahiro Yoshimatsu. MUS: Kohei Tanaka. PRD: Sunrise, Nippon TV. 25 mins. x 41 eps. (TV), 30 mins. (TVm), 30 mins. x 5 eps. (v).
Twelve year olds Daichi, Gus, and Rabi are heading off for a lunar holiday but get dragged into an ancient conflict between two forgotten tribes on the moon, who are trying to resurrect ancient evil powers to seize control of Earth itself. A popular giant-robot show whose robots were powered by "magic," it was created in part by **SAKURA WARS**' Oji Hiroi. The final episode was celebrated with a 30-minute TV special, *Grandzort: Non Stop Rabi* (1990). The series continued on video with the two-part *Final Magical War* (1990), in which the children fight off Grunwald, their most powerful enemy. It clearly wasn't final enough for the producers, who came back again with Nobuhiro Kondo's three-part *Grandzort: Adventure* (1992), in which the world turned out to be not quite saved enough. A magical stone in an ancient lunar monument begins emitting energy pulses toward Earth, attracting the attention of the Norman Bates space

pirates, who steal it and decide to blow up a lunar city. The story was also released in a 110-minute feature-length edition under the same title.

GRAPPLER BAKI *

1994. Video. DIR: Hirokazu Ikeda. SCR: Yoshihisa Araki. DES: Keisuke Itagaki. ANI: Yoshihiko Umakoshi. MUS: N/C. PRD: Toei. 80 mins.
Baki Hanma is the youngest martial artist to enter an underground free-for-all fighting tournament. He bests a karate opponent, then fights in the ring against someone whose specialty is ripping out opponents' nerves. The end. Devoid of even the merest hint of plot, Baki simply fights; instead of a damsel in distress to rescue or evil bad guy to defeat, Baki hits people until the ending credits roll. This anime takes the action-oriented plotting of **STREET FIGHTER II** and gruesome acts of **STORY OF RICKY** to extremes. Baki even comes across as something of a sado-masochist, grinning his way through nasty beatings. Based on Keisuke Itagaki's long-running 1991 manga in *Shonen Champion*, whose *actual* plot was Baki's quest to find who genuinely is the toughest person on the planet. His quest takes him to gangsters, biker gangs, and mercenaries, and the karate sequence in this anime represents just a fraction of his search. The story was brought back for a 2001 TV series, directed by Hitoshi Nanba, beginning with a 13-year-old Baki fighting a hundred men at once, but only beating 37 of them. He trains at a number of martial arts, hoping to eventually become the best of the best, all so that he can beat Yujiro Kurama, who, just a wild guess, is the man who killed his father. The TV series adds extra material not in the manga, particularly concerning Baki's relationship with his mother, Emi, who keeps on finding new trainers to teach her little rugrat how to kick ass. **LV**

GRAVE OF THE FIREFLIES *

1988. JPN: *Hotaru no Haka*. Movie. DIR: Isao Takahata. SCR: Isao Takahata. DES:

An EVA unit, designed to protect Earth from attacking "angels" and force humankind in a new evolutionary direction. The success of Hideaki Anno's **EVANGELION** led to a glut of short-lived TV serials, often with suspiciously similar features. Many old video shows were also resuscitated on television. Though many foreign distributors preferred one-time or short-run titles, in the late 1990s they were offered many longer, riskier TV shows as a result. *See entry p. 116.*

Evangelion

© GAINAX/PROJECT EVA • TV TOKYO

Yoshifumi Kondo. ANI: Nobuo Koyama. MUS: Yoshio Mamiya. PRD: Shinchosha, Ghibli. 85 mins.
Seita and his little sister Setsuko are left homeless by the firebombing of Kobe in 1945, which claims their mother's life. Unable to contact their father in the forces and knowing of no other place to turn, they move in with a shrewish aunt who constantly upbraids Seita for not contributing to the war effort. Eventually, they move to an air-raid shelter in the country, begging and stealing what food they can, but both starve to death.

Based on a semiautobiographical novel by Akiyuki Nosaka, who lost his own sister to malnutrition during the war, this is an eerily quiet, sepia-toned apocalypse, accompanied by powerful subliminal messages. Throughout the entire film, we regularly return to the ghosts of Seita and Setsuko, lit in red, as they gaze accusingly at the countrymen who let them die, though these scenes are so fleeting as to pass most viewers by. Similarly, director Takahata loads on subtle guilt as to what might have been "if only" the slightest chance had been taken to make a difference. The firebombs seem almost laughable at their first appearance: tiny sputtering flames, leaning against a water trough and a fire bucket, but Seita doesn't stay to fight them. Instead, he runs to safety with his sister, only to see his old home burn from a distance, like the heroine of **KAYOKO'S DIARY**. He doesn't mumble a simple apology to the shrewish aunt who has taken him in, forcing his own exile. And as his sister dies, he turns to nobody for help, since he has given up hope that help would be forthcoming. A crushingly sad story, beginning by revealing both characters will die and then daring the viewer to hope they won't. Tragedy in the truest sense of the word: every moment of Takahata's masterpiece is loaded with portents of the suffering to come.

Much imitated in anime about World War II, most noticeably in **RAIL OF THE STAR** and **RAINING FIRE**, the film shows a very normal life wiped out by the horrors of war, however indirect. There are no frontline heroics here, merely two innocent children wasting away before our eyes, while an elder brother dutifully tries to assure his sister that everything will be all right. It is all the more effective for being animated, not only because the ruin and deprivation appears so insanely unreal, but because Seita and Setsuko destroy a raft of anime stereotypes. No perky victory in the face of overwhelming odds for these two; instead, they are crushed and left to gaze down on the lights of modern Kobe, expressionless, but ultimately condemnatory of something. Perhaps it is the Allies who defeated Japan (as with so many other anime of its ilk, it makes no mention of the reasons Japan is being bombed), perhaps the Japanese people who, as in **BAREFOOT GEN**, refused to see the light. More likely it is warfare itself, roundly rejected by just two of its many victims.

Producer Toshio Suzuki reputedly used the original novel's educational value to sell theater tickets to schools, thereby allowing him to also release a second film of doubtful potential as part of the same double bill: **MY NEIGHBOR TOTORO**. Some of Nosaka's other works would also form the basis for the

ten-episode anime TV series *Akiyuki Nosaka's Tales of Wartime That Cannot Be Forgotten* (1997, *Nosaka Akiyuki Senso Dowashu: Wasurete wa Ikenai Monogatari*).

GRAVITATION

1999. Video, TV series. DIR: Shinichi Watanabe, Bob Shirahata. SCR: Hiroyuki Kawasaki, Michiko Yokote, Akemi Omote, Mamiko Ikeda. DES: Hiroya Iijima, Miho Shimokasa. ANI: Hiroya Iijima. MUS: Daisuke Asakura. PRD: Studio Deen, SPE Visual Works. 26 mins. x 2 eps. (v), 26 mins. x 13 eps. (TV). The ups and downs of a band of prettyboy musicians called Bad Luck, who spend less time rehearsing than they do indulging in moody stares and doomed loves. This anime was run-of-the-mill on video but somewhat risqué on evening TV. Based on a manga by Maki Murakami that ran in *You and Me* magazine, the original video production was upgraded to TV status after the success of similar boy-band adventures in **WEISS KREUZ**.

GREAT COMPOSERS

1989. JPN: *Meikyoku to Daisakkyokuka Monogatari*. AKA: *Great Composers and Their Compositions*. Video. DIR: Yasuaki Ebihara. SCR: Madoka Hino. DES: Kumiko Shishido. ANI: Masahito Sato. MUS: Various. PRD: Mushi Pro, Big Bang. 22 mins. x 9 eps.
Brief lives of some of the Western world's most famous composers, including Beethoven, Schubert, Mozart, Chopin, Vivaldi, Johann Strauss, and Tchaikovsky. Bizarrely, the obscure Stephen Foster, composer of "Beautiful Dreamer" (see **URUSEI YATSURA**) and "I Dream of Jeannie" (see **JEANNIE WITH THE LIGHT-BROWN HAIR**), gets a whole episode to himself, while Bach and Handel are forced to share. Several composers would also feature in **GREAT PEOPLE**.

GREAT CONQUEST: ROMANCE OF THE THREE KINGDOMS *

1982. JPN: *Sankokushi*. AKA: *Romance of the Three Kingdoms*. TV special x 3,

TV series, movie. DIR: Masaaki Sugatani, Hideo Watanabe (TVm), Seiji Okuda (TV), Tomoharu Katsumata (m). SCR: Masaaki Sugatani (TVm), Junzo Toriumi (TV), Kazuo Kasahara (m). DES: Hiroshi Wagatsuma (TVm), Shingo Araki (TV), Koichi Tsunoda (m). ANI: Keishiro Kimura (TVm), Moriyasu Taniguchi (TV), Koichi Tsunoda (m). MUS: Seiji Yokoyama. PRD: Shinei Doga (m), Enoki Films, TV Asahi. 85 mins. x 3 eps. (specials), 25 mins. x 47 eps. (TV), 90 mins. (m).
It's A.D. 220 as the Han Dynasty of China disintegrates into three warring states. The last Han emperor hands his throne over to the son of his protector, Cao-cao, who becomes the ruler of a fragment of the former empire known as the Kingdom of Wei. Two other former generals set up their own states in the West (Shu-Han) and South (Wu). Liu Bei, who claims to be a descendant of an early Han emperor, fights to bring a measure of liberty and justice to the people and ensure good government.

Based on Luo Guanzhong's novel, itself relatively faithful to actual historical events and one of the most important texts of Chinese literature, along with **JOURNEY TO THE WEST** and **SUIKODEN**. The story was given the full fantasy-legend treatment by Shinei Doga in an effort to grab audience share with lots of battle action, while doing its best to present costumes, architecture, and known historical fact as accurately as possible. It was so popular that they made a new version in 1985, and followed it up with *Romance of Three Kingdoms II—Heroes Crowned in Heaven* (1986). *Mitsuteru Yokoyama's Romance of Three Kingdoms* (1991) retold the story as a TV series, drawing on the manga retelling of the original by Mitsuteru Yokoyama, also known for **GIANT ROBO** and a manga *Suikoden*. The 1992 movie version by Enoki was released in the U.S. as *Great Conquest: Romance of the Three Kingdoms*, with narration by Pat "Karate Kid" Morita. Once again the producers made much of their return to the historical record for details of design and architecture, while focusing on the battles in order to capture theater and video audiences.

GREAT PEOPLE

1977. JPN: *Manga Ijin Monogatari*. AKA: *Manga Tales of Greatness*. TV series. DIR: Masakazu Higuchi, Kenjiro Yoshida, Ryosuke Takahashi, Hitoshi Sakaguchi. SCR: Ryohei Suzuki. DES: Susumu Shiraume. ANI: Toshiyasu Okada. MUS: Osamu Tokaibayashi. PRD: Tac, TBS. 25 mins. x 46 eps.

A similarly educational sequel to JAPANESE FOLK TALES, introducing famous people from history, bundled two to an episode. Classes of greatness include inventors and scientists such as Darwin, Copernicus, Galileo, the Wright Brothers, Bell, Newton, Curie, and Nobel; GREAT COMPOSERS Beethoven and Mozart, as well as Schumann and Foster (again!); explorers Livingstone, MARCO POLO, Scott, Amundsen, and Cook; several writers also covered in ANIMATED CLASSICS OF JAPANESE LITERATURE, including Hearn and Soseki, as well as the creators of HUCKLEBERRY FINN, DON QUIXOTE, THE TALE OF GENJI, and TREASURE ISLAND; poets Li Bo, Du Fu, Ryokan, and Basho; artists Hokusai, Hiroshige, Rodin, Millais, Gauguin, Leonardo da Vinci, and Michelangelo. There is space for baseball legend Babe Ruth, though surprisingly few religious figures beyond Shotoku Taishi. Military heroes are limited to the safely distant ALEXANDER and Genghis Khan, while political greats reflect an inevitable bias toward American and Japanese statesmen, such as Washington and Ryoma Sakamoto (see OI! RYOMA), or the philosopher of the Japanese Enlightenment, Yukichi Fukuzawa. Though such lists can rarely please everybody, one can only wonder at a series of historical giants that includes IKKYU but not CONFUCIUS, or that deems Ernest Seton, creator of SETON'S ANIMAL TALES, as somehow more noteworthy than Shakespeare.

An unrelated six-part video series, *Stories of Greatness* (1989), was directed by Yasuaki Ebihara and featured

COLUMBUS, HELEN KELLER, Edison, Hideyo Noguchi, Lincoln, and Marie Curie, all of whom had already been showcased in the earlier series.

GREED

1985. Video. DIR: Yukien Kogawa. SCR: Yukien Kogawa, Aiko Hanai. DES: Yukien Kogawa. ANI: Yukien Kogawa, Hidetoshi Omori. MUS: N/C. PRD: Film Link, Be Bo. 57 mins.

Upstanding youngster Rid and his four friends stand up against the evil Vai, who wishes to seize control of the world, even though Rid's father tried and failed to resist Vai many years before. A sci-fi action one-shot from the creator of SPACE RUNAWAY IDEON.

GREEN LEGEND RAN *

1992. Video. DIR: Satoshi Saga, Kengo Inagaki, Junichi Watanabe. SCR: Masaru Yamamoto. DES: Yoshimitsu Ohashi. ANI: Yoshimitsu Ohashi. MUS: Yoichiro Yoshikawa. PRD: MTV, AIC, Pioneer. 45 mins. x 2 eps., 60 mins. x 1 ep.

As natural resources on Earth become scarcer, the six alien "Holy Mothers" land from space and drain the world of most of its water and plants. Earth becomes a desert, forcing people to huddle in the small oases of greenery at the base of the Holy Mothers. The Lodo, a religion worshiping the Holy Mothers, becomes the new government, opposed by the Hazzard, a group of freedom fighters. Meanwhile, Earth-boy Ran is determined to find the man who killed his mother. He rescues the silver-haired girl Aira, a servant of the Holy Mothers. In a final showdown, the Holy Mothers release all the life force they have hoarded, the Earth returns to green again, and water falls from the sky.

An above-average video anime, well-served in the U.S. release by Pioneer's usual high-quality dubbing, though ultimately *Green Legend Ran* never does anything that Hayao Miyazaki hasn't done earlier and better. There are moments of simply awesome design, as if Frank Herbert's *Dune* were illustrated by artists of the Golden Age of science

fiction, but other parts simply play like low-rent versions of NAUSICAÄ or CASTLE IN THE SKY and aren't helped by a confused plot that has trouble deciding whether the Holy Mothers are alien invaders or avuncular saviors. Whatever they are, both their policy of making things worse on the off-chance they feel like making things better one day and Aira's baseless faith that humanity, if given a second chance, won't ruin things again, display a naiveté of plotting that sits badly with the accomplished artwork. *Ill. p. 399.*

GREEN MAKIBAO

1996. JPN: *Midori no Makibao*. TV series. DIR: Noriyuki Abe. SCR: Satoshi Hashimoto. DES: Hidekazu Ohara. ANI: N/C. MUS: N/C. PRD: Studio Pierrot, Fuji TV. 25 mins. x 61 eps.

Two prize-winning racehorses, Midoriko and Tamakeen, become the proud parents of a white foal called Makibao, who is determined to live up to their achievements. With a rat for a trainer, he perseveres in this spoof sports anime based on Tsunomaru's 1995 manga in *Shonen Jump* that used funny animals to tell a story of human trials. As with CAPTAIN TSUBASA and CYBERFORMULA GPX, the nature of Makibao's sport allows for a permanent underdog status: it takes him 20 episodes of struggle to qualify for his first race, but winning that merely places him in a more challenging arena with more experienced horses. Makibao develops a deadly rivalry with the Mongolian horse Tourdevil that occupies the later episodes as they compete in France and America, before Makibao finally becomes the world's fastest horse.

GREY: DIGITAL TARGET *

1986. Movie. DIR: Satoshi Dezaki. SCR: Yasushi Hirano, Kazumi Koide, Satoshi Dezaki, Toshiaki Imaizumi. DES: Setsuko Shibunnoichi, Kenichi Maejima. ANI: Yukari Kobayashi. MUS: Goro Omi. PRD: Magic Bus. 73 mins.

On a desolate future Earth, isolated communities fight a ritualized war, scoring points with every confirmed kill. Survivors are allowed to advance through the ranks from class F to A, with the aim of eventually becoming a Citizen. Grey's lover, Lips, joins the forces after being raped by soldiers but dies on her first mission. A distraught Grey joins up himself and gets a formidable reputation as the "God of Death" for being the sole survivor of several missions. When his mentor Red goes missing in action, Grey steals a plane with his new-found accomplice, Nova, and goes to look for him. Red has joined the Resistance, a group fighting the Big Mama computer that, it transpires, pits human towns against each other because it believes the human race wants to die. Grey discovers that the Resistance itself is just another front for Big Mama, and he destroys its floating citadel, which crashes in the supposed location of the Citizens' paradise, itself nothing but a ruin. Determined to destroy Big Mama, Grey and Nova march on the computer's Tower complex in the distance, as countless robots come out to stop them.

Despite antique animation that has forever condemned it to the B-list, *Grey* is still an excellent film, a nihilistic romance in the spirit of COCKPIT, satirizing the unwinnable rules of computer games with ever-multiplying enemies. It also features some truly nutty designs, from traditional giant robots to flying knights' helmets and a city inside a giant floating statue of the Goddess of Mercy. Keeping closely to KARUIZAWA SYNDROME–creator Yoshihisa Tagami's original manga in *Shonen Captain*, the anime only changes one major plot point, keeping Nova alive to the end. In the style of GUNBUSTER, it also shies away from showing the cataclysmic final battle, leaving the viewer to fill in the gap between the final shot and the epilogue that follows the closing credits. Like the ant that is stepped on in the opening scene, only to struggle out of the footprint and continue on its way, life itself refuses to give up without a fight, even though the seas are red and the planet is dying. In its thesis that life is a sick computer game,

it is a forerunner of *The Matrix*, though its actual roots extend back into Tagami's own love of Westerns, with Grey as a lone gunslinger righting wrongs because he has nothing better to do. **ⓁⓃⓋ**

GRIMMS' FAIRY TALES

1987. JPN: *Grimm Dowa*. TV series. DIR: Hiroshi Saito, Takayoshi Suzuki, Shigeru Omachi. SCR: Masaru Yamamoto, Nobuyuki Fujimoto, Akira Miyazaki. DES: Shuichi Seki. ANI: Hidekazu Ishii. MUS: Hideo Shimazu. PRD: Nippon Animation, TV Asahi. 25 mins. x 48 eps. A selection of just a few of the 200 stories collected by the German brothers in their compendium of fairy tales, some of which have also been animated as stand-alone anime in their own right. Stories include CINDERELLA, SNOW WHITE, *Blue Beard, The Princess and the Frog, Hansel and Gretel*, PUSS IN BOOTS, *Rapunzel*, and many others, sometimes two or three to an episode, and sometimes serialized across two to do the longer stories justice. The Brothers Grimm were also profiled in GREAT PEOPLE, unlike their Danish colleague, who had to settle for TALES OF HANS CHRISTIAN ANDERSEN. See also VIDEO PICTURE BOOK.

G-TASTE: MOE YAGISAWA

1999. Video. DIR: Shunsuke Harada. SCR: Yoshiki Imamura. DES: Masaki Yamada. ANI: Masaki Yamada. MUS: N/C. PRD: Beam Entertainment, Mybic, AIC. 30 mins. x 3 eps. A fun-filled day in the life of alleged real-life office lady Moe, from the moment she wakes up from a cozy dream about having sex, through her train-journey fantasies about having sex, to her office activities, which involve a lot of sex. Based on an erotic manga by Hiroki Yagami, who also created *Dear Boys*. Two successive episodes offered similar delights starring different central characters. **ⓁⓃⓋ**

GTO *

1999. AKA: *Great Teacher Onizuka*. TV series. DIR: Noriyuki Abe, Hiroyuki Ishi-

do. SCR: Masashi Sogo, Yoshiyuki Suga. DES: Koichi Usami, Mari Kitayama. ANI: Kumiko Rokunohe. MUS: Yusuke Homma. PRD: SPE, Studio Pierrot, Fuji TV. 50 mins. x 1 ep., 25 mins. x 42 eps. Twenty-two-year-old former biker Eikichi Onizuka decides to go straight and become a schoolteacher, though his old life often comes back to haunt him. He uses his criminal smarts to pass the entrance exams but ends up at a school for no-hopers where teenage pregnancies, drugs, and crime are rife. Despite his hard exterior, he genuinely cares about his students, and he uses his streetwise past to put them on the right track.

With a teacher who is little older than his charges, *GTO* traces a line through SLOW STEP to Soseki Natsume's BOTCHAN, though its true success lies in the conservative media's need to sanitize subculture thuggery—and what better way than by showing that even gangsters and bikers can rejoin the system? *GTO* has a convoluted pedigree that also stretches back to the meteoric success of the BOMBER BIKERS OF SHONAN, which inspired manga author Toru Fujisawa to create his own version, the *Shonan Pure Love Gang*, in 1990. Featuring the school and street-gang activities of Onizuka and Danma, it was adapted into a four-part anime series in 1996 by Katsumi Minoguchi. The following year, Fujisawa began *GTO* as a sequel in *Shonen Magazine*, with Onizuka announcing his intention of becoming a teacher so he can chase girls. The series also spun off into a live-action TV version and theatrical outings, starring heartthrob Takashi Sorimachi as Onizuka. It is this live version that is the quintessential *GTO*, with its handsome loner fighting injustices on his motorcycle like an educational lawman, but the anime incarnation still has considerable bite, mainly because its cartoon origins allowed for slightly more violence and menace than its prime-time live-action counterpart. It also features unobtrusive use of computer graphics that add realistic cloud and water effects to lead the viewer's eye away from the cheap TV animation, and a moody monochrome opening sequence that sums up the series' sardonic attitude, playing the sound of a revving motorcycle while showing the handle of a toilet.

GUDE CREST *

1990. JPN: *Onna Senshi Efe and Jeila: Goude no Monsho.* AKA: *Female Soldiers Efe and Jeila: Crest of Gude; Jun and Sarah.* Video. DIR: Kazusane Kikuchi. SCR: Isao Seiya. DES: Tsukasa Dokite. ANI: Masamitsu Kudo. MUS: Shoji Honda. PRD: JC Staff. 45 mins.
In a one-shot based on Reiko Hikawa's fantasy novel in the spirit of the later SLAYERS, a pair of sexy, sassy swordswomen, modeled rather obviously on the DIRTY PAIR, must rescue a royal orphan, overthrow a cruel tyrant, and destroy an evil goddess. The leads were renamed Efera and Jiliora for ADV's U.S. dub.

GUDZULLA

1967. JPN: *Araa, Gudzulla da to.* AKA: *Ah, So It's Gudzulla, Is It?* TV series. DIR: Hiroshi Sasakawa. SCR: Hiroshi Sasakawa, Ryohei Suzuki, Yugo Serikawa, Tsunehisa Ito, Satoshi Dezaki, Yoshiaki Yoshida, Rentaro Sakai. DES: Hiroshi Sasakawa. ANI: Yusaku Sakamoto. MUS: Takasuke Onosaki. PRD: Tatsunoko, Fuji TV. 25 mins. x 52 eps. (b/w), 25 mins. x 44 eps. (color).
After hatching from an egg found on the volcanic island of Bikkura, the monster Gudzulla comes to live in human society, where his predilection for eating iron objects causes problems for the long-suffering Professor Nugeta and his family. A lovable monster show designed to capitalize on the concurrent kiddification of the *Godzilla* movie series. The original black-and-white series was succeeded in 1987 by a color version, directed by Seitaro Hara, but reusing many of the original scripts.

GU-GU GUNMO

1984. TV series, movie. DIR: Akinori Nagaoka, Takenori Kawada, Shigeru Yanagawa. SCR: Keisuke Fujikawa. DES: Takao Kasai. ANI: Takao Kasai. MUS: Hiroshi Ogasawara. PRD: Toei, Fuji TV. 25 mins. x 50 eps. (TV), 45 mins. (m).
A tale of school high jinks from the *Shonen Sunday* manga by the versatile Fujihiko Hosono, who also created the more adult stories that became BIO-HUNTER and JUDGE. Gummo the giant pink bird hatches and befriends Japanese schoolboy Heita. A movie version was released in 1985 that lampooned several JAPANESE FOLK TALES, including that of the Princess Kaguya, which was also spoofed in REI REI.

GULKEEVA

1995. JPN: *Jusenshi Gulkeeva.* AKA: *Beast-Warrior Gulkeeva; Wild Knights Gulkeeva; Galkiba; Galkiva.* TV series. DIR: Masamitsu Hidaka. SCR: Kenichi Kanemaki, Noboru Aikawa, Hiroyuki Kawasaki. DES: Hisashi Hirai, Takahiro Yamada. ANI: Hisashi Hirai, Satoshi Yoshida, Takuro Shinbo. MUS: Kenji Kawai. PRD: Sunrise, TV Tokyo. 25 mins. x 26 eps.
Adaptation of a manga originally serialized in *Shonen Sunday Super*, in which demonic Darknoid invaders from Nosfertia are held off by a group of pretty young boys, who inexplicably work in a noodle bar during their time off. Japanese teenager Toya Shinjo is told by his parents that he is not from Earth at all, but rather he is a Humanoid from the parallel dimension of Eternaliya, reincarnation of an ancient hero, and fated to work together with transforming Animanoid knights from Heavenstia in order to thwart the Darknoids. Unsurprisingly, the Animanoids are a wolf (Greyfas), a hawk (Beakwood), and a gorilla (Gariel), uniting speed, flight, and strength, like so many other shows since BABEL II. A series in the tradition of shows like SAINT SEIYA, although its attempt to integrate boys' and girls' TV anime genres was easily outclassed by ESCAFLOWNE the following year.

GULLIVER'S SPACE TRAVELS: BEYOND THE MOON *

1965. JPN: *Gulliver no Uchu Ryoko.*

See entry p. 132.
Galaxy Adventures of Space Oz

Movie. DIR: Yoshio Kuroda. SCR: Shinichi Sekizawa. DES: Hideo Furusawa. ANI: Hideo Furusawa, Takashi Abe, Hayao Miyazaki. MUS: Isao Tomita (Milton and Anne Delugg, U.S. version). PRD: Toei. 80 mins.
Ted (Ricky in the U.S. dub) meets the aged Professor Gulliver in a deep, dark forest. Accompanied by Mack the dog, a toy soldier called The General, and the unimaginatively named Crow the crow (see CORAL INVESTIGATES), the two set off on a journey to the Planet of Blue Hope in their spaceship the Gulliver. After adventures in the Reverse Time Nebula, which transforms them all into younger versions of themselves, they finally meet the inhabitants of the Planet of Blue Hope, though they have been thrown off their homeworld by the evil Queen of Purple Planet and her robot soldiers. However, Ted and the professor discover that water disintegrates matter in this part of space, and they are able to lead a successful assault on the enemy, armed only with water pistols and balloons full of water. The doll-like princess of Blue Hope is transformed into a real girl by the victory, and she thanks them for saving her world.
A very remote sci-fi sequel to Jonathan Swift's classic satire *Gulliver's*

Travels, which was itself adapted in 1983 as part of the *Famous World Fairy Tales* series, featuring Yoshiaki Kawajiri as art director. The original novel would also inspire in-betweener Hayao Miyazaki's CASTLE IN THE SKY.

GUNBUSTER *

1988. JPN: *Top o Nerae Gunbuster*. AKA: *Aim for the Top: Gunbuster*. Video. DIR: Hideaki Anno. SCR: Toshio Okada. DES: Haruhiko Mikimoto, Koichi Ohata, Kazuki Miyatake. ANI: Yuji Moriyama, Toshiyuki Kubooka. MUS: Kohei Tanaka. PRD: Studio Fantasia, Gainax. 30 mins. x 6 eps.

Noriko's father dies in space in the first encounter with an alien race that is preparing for an all-out assault on Earth. Noriko overcomes great difficulties at her school in Okinawa and qualifies as one of the pilots sent to defend the planet. She falls out with her partner, "Big Sister" Kazumi Amano, and teams up with Smith Toren, a handsome American pilot who soon dies in action. The predicament of the human race looks bleak: the "aliens" are really the galaxy's natural defense mechanisms, and humanity is merely a virus on the face of the universe. Coach Ota devises the Buster Machines to help the reunited girls turn the tables, and the first major assault is held off with heavy losses. Though only a few weeks have passed for the girls, the effects of relativity mean that several years have passed on Earth. Kazumi marries the dying Ota, and Noriko goes on another tour of duty. Six months later (for Noriko, whereas 15 years have passed on Earth), an older Kazumi rejoins her with Buster Machine Three, a super-bomb designed to wipe out the heart of the galaxy in the final conflict.

Beginning as a sci-fi parody of AIM FOR THE ACE, *Gunbuster* eventually transforms into an homage to Kihachi Okamoto's live-action war film *Battle of Okinawa* (1971), complete with onscreen notes detailing the numbers of "ships sunk" and a background cast of dozens of generals, each only gaining the merest moment of screentime.

Foregrounded through all this is the spunky Noriko, who only ages a year as her friends near retirement age and is eternally in a world of childish things, much like the semiautobiographical heroes of the same producers' OTAKU NO VIDEO. Wartime allusions abound: the human race (i.e., Japan) is fighting on the wrong side in a war it cannot win, while the last-ditch attempt to hold the home islands launches from Okinawa, and schoolchildren age before the viewer's eyes in a variant of the "time travel" of 24 EYES. *Gunbuster* is also a loving pastiche of the anime serials of its creators' formative years, from the martial heroism of STAR BLAZERS (seen on one of the posters in Noriko's quarters) to the super-robots of GIGANTOR. The in-jokes reach staggering levels: Smith Toren was, for example, a tip of the hat to future Studio Proteus boss Toren Smith (see DIRTY PAIR), who was staying with the Gainax animators at the time, while shots of spacecraft under construction often show breakaway sprues as if they were model kits. Played deadly straight no matter how silly the onscreen visuals, it is the ultimate video anime, and, though outlines existed for a full 26-episode series, the story seems perfectly suited to its humble three-hour running time. It also set the pace for many 1990s anime, from the jiggling bosoms of PLASTIC LITTLE to the tongue-in-cheek posturing of BATTLE ATHLETES, though none of its imitators came close. Sadly, it never quite achieved its potential abroad, despite an excellent subtitled version. It was never dubbed, hence losing the large audience it truly deserved, a feat achieved by the same studio's later EVANGELION. The series was screened on Japanese TV after Gainax's more famous follow-up and rereleased on Japanese DVD with some bonus footage in 2001. **NV**

GUNDAM *

1979. JPN: *Kido Senshi Gundam*. AKA: *Mobile Suit Gundam*. TV series, movie, video. DIR: Yoshiyuki Tomino, Shinya

Sadamitsu, Ryoji Fujiwara, Fumihiko Takayama, Takeyuki Kanda, Takashi Imanishi. SCR: Hiroyuki Hoshiyama, Kenichi Matsuzaki, Masaru Yamamoto, Yoshihisa Araki, Katsuyuki Sumizawa. DES: Yoshikazu Yasuhiko, Kunio Okawara, Kazumi Fujita, Mamoru Nagano, Hiroyuki Kitazume, Mika Akitaka, Haruhiko Mikimoto, Yutaka Izubuchi, Gainax, Yoshinori Sayama, Toshihiro Kawamoto, Hajime Katoki, Kimitoshi Yamane, Shuko Murase. ANI: Yoshikazu Yasuhiko, Kazuo Tomizawa, Kazuo Nakamura, Kazuo Yamazaki. MUS: Takeo Watanabe, Yuji Matsuyama, Shigeaki Saegusa, Tetsuro Kashibuchi, Yoko Kanno. PRD: Sotsu Agency, Sunrise, Nagoya TV (TV Asahi). 25 mins. x 43 eps. (*First Gundam*), 25 mins. x 50 eps. (*Zeta*), 25 mins. x 47 eps. (*Double Zeta*), 120 mins. (m/*Char's Counterattack*), 30 mins. x 10 eps. (*SD*), 30 mins. (m/*SD*), 30 mins. x 4 eps. (v/*SD ii–iv*); (30 mins. m2/*SD*), 40 mins. x 4 eps. (*SD Side Story*), 30 mins. x 6 eps. (*War In the Pocket*), 30 mins. x 12 eps. (*Stardust Memory*), 115 mins. (m/*F91*, also 120 mins. special edition), 25 mins. x 51 eps. (*Victory*), 30 mins. x 11 eps. (v/*08th Team*), 25 mins. x 49 eps. (*G Gundam*), 25 mins. x 49 eps. (*Wing*), 30 mins. x 3 eps. (*Endless Waltz*), 25 mins. x 39 eps. (*Gundam X*), 25 mins. x 50 eps. (*Turn-A*).

In the "Universal Century" Year 0079, Earth and its space colonies are split between the democratic Federation and the Principality of Zeon. The Earth ship White Base arrives at the Side 7 research facility to pick up some prototype "mobile suits" (humanoid piloted robots), but it is ambushed by Zeon attackers with orders to destroy them. Fifteen-year-old Earth boy Amuro Ray climbs into the cockpit of his father's prototype RX-78 Gundam unit and fights them off. With most of the original military crew dead, the White Base is commandeered by young Side 7 evacuees—as they head for Earth, they are hounded by Zeon forces led by the dashing enemy officer Char Aznable. Touching down in enemy territory, they fight their way out to their own forces, who reveal that they are "newtypes," a new breed of human with nascent psionic powers. Eventually, they lead a final assault on the asteroid fortress of A Baoa Qu, the Zeon forces are riven by internal struggles (Char himself kills one of their leaders as part of a family feud), and the One Year War is over.

Along with STAR BLAZERS and MACROSS, *Gundam* is a cornerstone of anime SF, an ever-present franchise and sprawling saga, still active two decades after its premiere. Its distinguishing features are firmly rooted in merchandising and its own longevity—a vast taxonomy of robot types ready for exploitation in model kits and action figures (compare to POKÉMON) and a long-running future saga that has often collapsed under its own weight only to be brought back with several attempts to reset the continuity. As with other successful franchises like *Star Trek*, keeping track of the characters themselves also requires a sizable concordance. It's bad enough that they often seem named after random words picked from a Scrabble bag, let alone that they switch sides and identities. Matters are not helped by "joke" names that seem like a great idea to the Japanese but have caused endless difficulties to English translators trying to keep romanizations consistent. Most infamously, Char Aznable is named after the French singer Charles Aznavour, which would have been a poor enough gag in a shallow comedy like SORCERER HUNTERS, but it's quite damaging to the tone of an otherwise serious SF saga. The creation of Yoshiyuki Tomino, veteran of ASTRO BOY and BRAVE RAIDEEN, *Gundam* combines elements of *Star Wars* with space-colony politics and a subtle metaphor for Japan's postwar "new breed" baby-boomers—the "newtype" name was appropriated for Japan's most popular anime magazine.

The original series was rereleased in three movie editions—*Mobile Suit Gundam* (1981), *MSG 2: Soldiers of Sorrow* (1981), and *MSG 3: Encounters in Space* (1982), the latter two comprising roughly 50% new material between them, with the bulk of it concentrated in the third movie. Part of the new footage showed Char escaping from A Baoa Qu, setting up the sequel series *Zeta Gundam* (1985—the seventh year of the franchise named for the seventh letter of the Greek alphabet). *Zeta* kept surviving members of the original cast but reorganized their allegiances, with Char and the White Base now on the same side, resisting the Earth Federation's attempts to wipe out remaining rebels. The series' ambiguity toward enemies has come to be another of its distinguishing marks, though much of it may originate less in a desire for foes with feelings, and more from Tomino's own ambiguous attitude toward the series for which he has come to be known. *Zeta* was followed by a second season, *Double Zeta* (1986), with an all-new cast, while the "conclusion" to the long feud between Char Aznable and Amuro Ray came in the movie edition *Char's Counterattack* (1988, *Char no Gyakushu*). Determined that all humankind will join the colonists in space, Char plans to drop the Axis asteroid on Earth but is finally persuaded to work with Amuro to prevent the tragedy both sides have created.

The series was parodied in Tetsuro Amino's 1988 *SD Gundam* video series, which featured "super-deformed" squashed-down cartoon versions of the characters and machines in unlikely comedic situations. The original ten-part video series was followed by two short movies, and video sequels numbered *Mark II–IV*. There was also the two-part video series *SD Warrior Gundam* (1989), and a spinoff of the spinoff—*SD Gundam Side Story* (1990).

Gaps in the continuity of the original, serious *Gundam* were plugged by two video series, Fumihiko Takayama's *MSG 0080: War in the Pocket* (1989), which observed the One Year War from the new viewpoint of a very young child learning the real meaning of war, and *MSG 0083: Stardust Memory* (1991), which bridged the gap between *Double Zeta* and the same year's movie, *Gundam F91*. Following a template no less predictable than that of TIME BOKAN, *Stardust Memory* features a rehashed Char character, Anavel Gato, and a brash young Amuro clone, Ko Uraki. Three years after A Baoa Qu, as the Earth Federation struggles to rebuild its shattered fleet and Zeon plots revenge, the enemy ace once again tries to steal a Gundam. Drawn unwittingly into a conspiracy to wipe out the Earth Federation HQ by crashing a colony onto it, Ko does his utmost to prevent disaster but is still court-martialled and jailed, set free only because further political machinations require that the whole affair be forgotten. *F91* was a stalled attempt to start again with a clean slate, moving the action thirty years into the future with an all-new cast—teenagers Seabrook Arno and love-interest Cecily Fairchild, who discover that Cecily is, like Char before her, a scion of a powerful noble family (in this case the Ronah dynasty), determined to impose a thousand-year Reich on the solar system. Though the story was continued in novel form with the *Crossbone Gundam* follow-up, it did not last as an anime. Aiming itself, like the same studio's successful BRAVE SAGA franchise, at a younger audience, the franchise returned as the TV series *Victory Gundam* (1993), though the director (who had gained the nickname "Kill 'em All" Tomino after ZAMBOT 3) soon asserted his trademark angst and tragedy. Set another thirty years on (in the year U.C. 0153), it featured yet another all-new cast, headed by the 13-year-old wonder-pilot Usso Ebbing. Takeyuki Kanda's video series *MSG: 08th M[obile] S[uit] Team* (1996) returns to the events of the first year in the saga (0079) and the activities of yet another group of characters in and around the events already established in the continuity.

The gap between *Victory* and *08th MS Team* saw several unrelated series that sought to capitalize on the *Gundam* brand without adhering to the future history continuity. Depending on your point of view, these are either interesting speculations on alternate universes or a cavalier attempt to jettison everything from the series except those all-important robot merchandise tie-ins. Released in the same year as STREET FIGHTER II, Yasuhiro Imagawa's completely unhinged *G Gundam* TV series was redolent of Stuart Gordon's *Robot Jox* (1989), with gladiatorial bouts between giant robots used to settle quarrels between nations (culturally stereotyped to ludicrous degrees with an elephant Gundam for India, a windmill Gundam for the Netherlands, and a Viking Gundam complete with its own rowing boat). No one is entirely sure why Neo-Sweden's Nobel Gundam looks like SAILOR MOON. The kids-in-combat premise was rehashed in another "alternate universe," Masashi Ikeda's *Gundam Wing* (1995), in which five 15-year-old teenagers, inspired by the pretty-boys of SAINT SEIYA, are mobile-suit pilots in a new war between Earth and its colonies in space. Once more, political and economic machinations are out to crush the colonists' desire for self-determination. *Wing* was also reedited into the four-part *Operation Meteor* clip-shows and is arguably the most successful alternative universe adventure so far, though its sudden cancellation forced an ending on video as *MSG Wing: Endless Waltz* (1997), itself reissued with extra footage as the *Endless Waltz Special Edition* movie. A third alternate saga, Shinji Takamatsu's *Gundam X* (1996), did not flourish in the post-EVANGELION climate and was ignominiously dragged off the air. The series' next major outing after *Wing* was *Turn-A Gundam* (1999, literally Ɐ *Gundam*), yet another attempt to encompass as many previous serials as possible into one overarching continuity (compare to similar problems that dogged the *Macross* saga, especially post-ROBOTECH). Leaping two millennia into the future (a period guaranteed to make most continuity errors irrelevant), it depicts Earth people who have forgotten about their space-faring

past, rudely awakened into relearning about the mythical Gundam robots (refer to Tomino's DUNBINE) after they are invaded by a highly advanced society that has languished forgotten on the moon. Featuring new music from Yoko Kanno, controversially bizarre robot designs by American futurist Syd Mead (see STAR BLAZERS), and a move to the Fuji TV network, *Turn-A* is the most recent incarnation of the franchise to date, though the story line is constantly revisited through novels, manga, games, and other spinoffs. These have included the live-action game *Gundam 0079: War for Earth* and movie *G Saviour* (2000), the *A Baoa Qu* ride at the Fuji Express Highland amusement park (featuring original animation designs by *War in the Pocket*–designer Haruhiko Mikimoto), and Gichi Otsuka's novel/manga *For the Barrel* (2000), which refashions Tomino's own *Gundam* novels—the most recent attempt to streamline the continuity to date. *Ill. p. 149.*

GUNDRESS

1999. Video. DIR: Katsuyoshi Yatabe. SCR: Kentaro Isaki, Kenichi Sakai. DES: Tetsuro Aoki, Koji Watanabe. ANI: N/C. MUS: Yutaka Tominaga. PRD: Sanctuary, Nikkatsu. 30 mins.

A predictably disappointing one-shot anime from the people who brought you LANDLOCK, which similarly cashes in on the alleged involvement of "planning assistant" Masamune Shirow. The all-female "Bouncer" task force fights crime in the multiracial "Bayside City" that was once Yokohama, implying all sorts of nonexistent connections with other Shirow titles such as DOMINION (the milieu) and APPLESEED (the robot suits). Despite early press hype that talked up the use of "real" voice actresses instead of ones who specialized in anime, it sank without a trace in the Japanese market, probably because not even Shirow can wave a magic wand and make something interesting out of four stereotypical girls conceived for a computer game.

GUNSMITH CATS *

1995. Video. DIR: Takeshi Mori. SCR: Atsuji Kaneko. DES: Kenichi Sonoda, Tokuhiro Matsubara. ANI: Tokuhiro Matsubara. MUS: Peter Erskine. PRD: Vap, TBS. 30 mins. x 3 eps.

Rally Vincent is a gun-seller and bounty hunter in Chicago who works with her bomb-throwing sidekick Minnie-May Hopkins and strait-laced researcher Becky Farrah. She is blackmailed by an agent from the ATF bureau into meeting with a gun-runner, whose main contact turns out to be a Russian assassin, Radinov. A local candidate for mayor decides to reward Rally's vigilante acts as a campaign gimmick, but the assassin is hiding out in the crowd for the final showdown.

A sparky adaptation of Kenichi Sonoda's 1991 manga from *Comic Afternoon* that steps outside the continuity of the original series, giving Rally the roguish ATF officer Bill Collins as her new "boss," and a new enemy in the form of Radinov. There are, however, several references to the manga, including the appearance of prosthetic limbs owned by Rally's manga enemies and a cameo by her Chicago PD contact Roy Coleman. Supporting character Becky becomes a stronger "part of the team" chiefly to satisfy the filmmakers' desire to reprise *Charlie's Angels*—a gambit that works particularly well in the bright, pop-art tones of the opening credits. Despite a setting in a fantasy Chicago like the urban war zone of MAD BULL 34's New York, *GSC* is remarkably lighthearted, complete with gratuitous underwear flashes, myopic bad guys who never shoot straight, and no sign of the manga's forays into drug addiction and child prostitution. The filmmakers made much of their research trips to the real Chicago, but, although intense effort is expended on the right noises for guns and cars, less thought was devoted to more important plot elements, such as how gunsmiths stow dangerous weapons, and what the police might think of an underage girl who collects hand grenades. But, apart from the holes, this is good fun, helped greatly in translation by a streetwise U.S. dub from ADV.

Asides about May's boyfriend, Ken, imply the show was intended to go further, and if anything deserved a TV replay, it was this. *GSC* was presumably hobbled by its contemporary look; there wasn't much call for pulp crime in 1990s anime unless it had a sci-fi sheen like **COWBOY BEBOP**. A very different, earlier version of Rally Vincent also appeared in Sonoda's **RIDING BEAN**. **LNV**

GURU-GURU

1994. JPN: *Maho Jin Guruguru*. AKA: *Magical Treasury Guru-guru*. TV series, movie. DIR: Nobuaki Nakanishi. SCR: N/C. DES: Masahiro Kase. ANI: Kazuyuki Okaseko. MUS: N/C. PRD: Nippon Animation, TV Asahi. 25 mins. x 45 eps. The adventures of the heroic preteens Nike and friend Kukuri the witch deliberately told in a style that mimics the cartoony questing of computer role-playing games, as they defeat wandering monsters, liberate treasure from dungeons, and eternally seek to better themselves through "level-ups." Based on a manga by Hiroyuki Morifuji, serialized in *Shonen Gungun* magazine.

GUTSY FROG, THE

1972. JPN: *Dokonjo Gaeru*. TV series, movie. DIR: Eiji Okabe, Tadao Nagahama, Tsutomu Shibayama. SCR: Masaki Tsuji, Haruya Yamazaki, Yoshiaki Yoshida, Noboru Shiroyama, Tsunehisa Ito, Masaru Yamamoto, Hideo Takayashiki, Tomoko Konparu, Masaaki Sakurai. DES: A-Pro, Yasumi Yoshizawa. ANI: Osamu Kobayashi, Tsutomu Shibayama, Osamu Kobayashi. MUS: Kenjiro Hirose, Reijiro Komutsu. PRD: Tokyo Movie Shinsha, TBS; TMS, Nippon TV. 25 mins. x 103 eps. (TV1), 25 mins. x 30 eps. (TV2), 40 mins. (m).

Noisy, unruly middle-school boy Hiroshi is walking home from school one day when he falls over, landing on top of a frog. The frog, whose name is Pyonyoshi, is flattened and imprinted

onto the front of Hiroshi's shirt—and insists on commenting on everything he does, with humorous results. A wacky variation on the boy-and-his-dog theme based on the 1970 *Shonen Jump* manga by Yasumi Yoshizawa. Many of the original crew were reunited for *New [Shin] Gutsy Frog* (1981), a shorter-lived series that played up the cartoon slapstick even more than the original. Several episodes were also cut together to make the movie *GF: Gutsy Dreaming* (1982, *Dokonjo Yumemakura*) that was shown on a double bill with **HELLO SPANK**.

GUY *

1988. JPN: *Guy: Yoma Kakusei; Second Target*. AKA: *Guy: Awakening of the Devil; Second Target*. Video. DIR: Yorihisa Uchida. SCR: Hiroyuki Kawasaki, Kunihisa Sugishima, Masami Obari. DES: Yorihisa Uchida, Yasuhiko Makino, Yukio Tomimatsu. ANI: Yorihisa Uchida. MUS: Nobuhiko Kashiwara. PRD: Humming, AIC. 40 mins. x 2 eps. Guy and his sexy female sidekick Raina, mercenaries out to make a quick buck, discover that a revolutionary youth drug is being developed on the prison planet of Geo. Prison warden Helga runs a white slavery operation out of her penal colony, where the victims are also sexually abused in a violent, tits-and-tentacles SF extravaganza in the fashion of **ADVANCER TINA**. Guy saves the day by transforming into a super-violent beast, as he does once again in the belated sequel, in which he and Raina discover that the Golden Goddess religious cult is really a corrupt front. The second episode, however, attempted to lighten the poker-faced sex and violence with a few in-jokes about earlier giant-robot shows and a visual reference to the **DIRTY PAIR** movie. The two episodes were combined on a single tape as *Guy: Double Target* in 1992, and it is this version that was released in the U.S. **LNV**

GUYVER *

1989. JPN: *Kyoshoku Soko Guyver*. AKA:

Detonator Orgun

© 1991 DARTS/ARTMIC

Bio-Booster Armor Guyver. Video, movie. DIR: Koichi Ishiguro. SCR: Takashi Sanjo. DES: Hidetoshi Omori. ANI: Sumio Watanabe, Takaaki Ishiyama. MUS: Reijiro Komutsu. PRD: Takaya Pro. 30 mins. x 12 eps. (v), 55 mins. (m).

In ancient times, an alien race tinkered with human DNA to create the ultimate warrior, or zoanoid. Though these creatures were intended for battlefields on distant worlds, the Creators left before the experiment was complete. Zoanoids interbred with the human race in a number of incidents that survive today as stories of demons, vampires, and werewolves. The "bio-booster" suit was an advanced Creator armor that augmented its wearer's strength. Three such units are stolen in the present day by an agent of the Chronos corporation and scattered in an explosion. One ends up in the hands of Japanese schoolboy Sho, who activates it and becomes its designated wearer. Another is activated by Chronos' agent Lisker, whose power module malfunctions during a fight with Sho. Chronos' Commander Gyro arrives in Japan to recover the third Guyver unit and kidnaps Sho's friend, Mizuki, to draw him out of hiding. He also creates a hyper-zoanoid to fight the Guyver unit on equal terms. Agito Makishima, the son of the former head of Chronos Japan, becomes the third Guyver symbiont, and Sho's school is destroyed as Chronos' minions attack it in search of his control medallion. Though Chronos Japan is defeated, Sho learns that there are many other outposts, and he is forced to fight Dr. Valcus, who creates several new zoanoids and even works on "Enzyme," the antiGuyver. Sho's father is transformed into a monster and Sho is forced to kill him. Losing the ability to bio-boost, Sho regains it by asking the spirit of his father for help in a time of dire need. Though the evil is defeated for now, Sho must face several more of the zoanoids' "Zoalord" controllers . . . one day.

Based on the 1985 *Shonen Captain* manga by Yoshiki Takaya, which continued the story long past the non-ending of the anime, this unremarkable sci-fi series remains a recognizable brand in the U.K. market, chiefly due to Manga Entertainment's policy of releasing it at an insanely discounted price that made it affordable for the young boys for whom it was originally made, though if they bought all *twelve* tapes, it would still cost them a pretty penny. An earlier version of the same story was animated as the 55-minute movie *Guyver: Out of Control* (1986), directed by Hiroshi Watanabe and also released in the U.S. It has the same basic plot but a female owner of Guyver Two, and it possesses a brevity that leaves less room for the pointless repetitions of its straight-to-video successor. But neither anime version really does justice to the material—humanity as the descendants of abandoned military experiments may be a clever idea, but it is used as little more than an excuse for visceral transformations and predictable fights against monsters-of-the-week. Two live-action movies retold the same early chapters of the story, Screaming Mad George's *Guyver* (1991, aka *Mutronics*) and Steve Wang's *Guyver: Dark Hero* (1994).

H2

1995. TV series. DIR: Hidehito Ueda.
SCR: Akira Oketani, Hisato Yamashita,
Nobuaki Kishima. DES: Tomoyoshi Hira-
ta. ANI: Hiroki Takagi, Tadashi Hirota.
MUS: Taro Iwashiro. PRD: TV Asahi. 25
mins. x 41 eps.

The lives and loves of four young people, all of whose names begin with the
letter "H," set against a background of
high-school baseball. Pitching ace Hiro
shatters his elbow, seemingly ending a
promising career in baseball and
throwing all his choices (school,
friends, career) into doubt. Power hitter Hideo continues to train in baseball, while the boys' concerned friend
Hikari frets over Hiro's future, and
Hideo slowly falls for Haruka, a girl at
his new school who is not only the
daughter of his father's boss, but also
the new manager of the school baseball club. Hiro and his friend Noda
(who has also been placed on the
injured list by a bad back) destroy the
opposition from Haruka's club and
suggest that she turn it into a proper
competing team. Based on a 1992 manga in *Shonen Sunday* by Mitsuru Adachi,
who used baseball and love polygons
before in NINE and SLOW STEP.

HAKKENDEN, THE *

1990. Video. DIR: Takashi Anno, Yukio
Okamoto. SCR: Noboru Aikawa, Hidemi
Kamata. DES: Atsushi Yamagata. ANI:
Kazuhiro Konishi. MUS: Takashi Kudo.
PRD: AIC. 30 mins. x 13 eps.

Fifteenth-century lord Satomi rashly
promises his daughter Fuse's hand in
marriage to whoever brings him the
head of his enemy, Lord Anzai. But no
one expects Yatsufusa, the family dog,
to win the prize. Fuse and Yatsufusa are
both killed, but their karma lives on in
a group of "dog" warriors, each symbol-
izing a great virtue. A generation later,
the dog warriors are united and begin
their quest to restore the honor of the
house of Satomi.

An adaptation of a multi-volumed
popular serial written from 1814 to
1841 by Kyokutei Bakin, a samurai fall-
en on hard times who wished to retell
Water Margin (see SUIKODEN) for a Japanese audience and instill some decency
in his own merchant son by concentrating on the Eight Virtues of CONFUCIUS:
Benevolence, Righteousness, Courtesy,
Wisdom, Fidelity, Loyalty, Filial Piety,
and Service to Elders. Bakin's original
characters left nothing to the imagina-
tion, and were often ciphers for particular virtues or sins, spouting pompous
mock Chinese dialogue. The animation crew preferred modern heroes
who often doubt their roles and each
other, particularly bad-guy Samojiro
Aboshi who drips foppish charm, far
removed from the one-note voice of
evil in the book.

The 96-part novel had a large number of starting points to draw in new
readers—an occasionally confusing
policy that remains in the anime. Each
of the heroes has an origin story of his
or her own, thus delaying the "beginning" of their team adventures until
episode nine! The first, Shino, must
deliver a magic sword to a nobleman,
while the second, Sosuke, is sworn to
stop him. The third, Dosetsu, is the
half-brother of Shino's betrothed,
sworn to avenge her death, while the
fourth, Genpachi, is a disgraced
guardsman offered his freedom if only

he kills Shino. And so on. Episode six
was director Anno's last, and the
remaining parts were originally
released under a separate subtitle, *New
Hakkenden* (1993), with changes in the
crew that are particularly reflected in
the character design. As with DARK
MYTH, the heavy use of Japanese names
often makes the dub a polysyllabic
mess, but it is the look rather than the
meaning of this series that appeals to
its fans, and it is best watched in Japanese for that fully cultural experience.

More concerned with drama than
with the impressive battle scenes of
NINJA SCROLL, *Hakkenden* was sold
abroad on the strength of its literary
and cultural pedigree, although the
original crew were less likely to have
been inspired by the novel as by the
1973 *Hakkenden* puppet TV show of
their youth or the 1983 live-action film
by Kinji Fukasaku. There are, however,
references to the many woodblock
prints inspired both by the original
novel and the kabuki plays that drew
on it, most obviously in the opening
credits, in which the anime characters
share the screen with their woodblock
predecessors. See also the sci-fi remake
SHIN HAKKENDEN. *Ill. p. 247.*

HAMTARO TALES *

2000. JPN: *Tottoko Hamtaro.* AKA: *Ham-
taro the Hamster.* TV series. DIR: Kazuo
Nogami, Koichi Sasaki, Yusaku Sao-
tome. SCR: Michiru Shimada, Miho
Maruo, Yoshiyuki Suga. DES: Ritsuko
Kawai. ANI: Masaaki Sudo, Junko
Yamanaka, Yukari Kobayashi. MUS:
N/C. PRD: SMDE, TV Tokyo. 23 mins. x
40+ eps.

Hamtaro is a happy hamster who lives

with his owner, a 5-year-old girl called Hiroko (5th-*grader* Laura in the company's foreign sales sheets). He sleeps in a little home kept on the buffet counter in the kitchen of a house on a quiet suburban street. But in the park, across the street, under the roots of the old tree, there is a hideout where the local hamsters go for secret meetings of the "Ham-Ham Friends." Sappy rodent goings-on based on a manga by Ritsuko Kawai.

HANAICHI MONME

1990. Video. DIR: Toshihiko Arimasa. SCR: Norio Hayashi, Hiroshi Kitano, Junichi Sato, Kazuki Hirada. DES: N/C. ANI: Koichi Arai, Satoshi Kushibuchi. MUS: Toshihiro Nakanishi. PRD: Toei. 60 mins. x 3 eps.
Animated versions of tales that won the Short Story Prize in the *Hanaichi Monme* bulletin, including *Noboru and the Wildcat*, *The Misleading Friends*, *Sanma's March*, *Red Mail-Box on the Mountain-Top*, and *One Sunday Morning at the Beginning of May*.

HANAPPE BAZOOKA *

1992. Video. DIR: Yoyu Ikegami. SCR: Fumio Saikiji. DES: Fujio Oda. ANI: Fujio Oda. MUS: Nozomu Aokl. PRD: Studio Signal. 45 mins.
Hapless teenager Hanappe is masturbating in front of a porno film when two demons appear from his TV. The brusque Ophisto Bazooka and his sexy female sidekick, Mephisto Dance, reveal that they can be summoned once a millennium by particular penile jerking. Charged with turning Hanappe into the new messiah, they give him superhuman powers, allowing him to kill the local bullies. Bazooka, however, falls for Hanappe's mother, while Dance develops an unhealthy interest in Hanappe's sister. They pay off his father and turn his house into a party zone for devils, hoping to fob Hanappe off with the power to charm any woman. Hanappe is not convinced, chiefly because his power backfires and he is chased by the inhabitants of a geriatric ward and a transvestite. He

also refuses to use the power on the girl he loves because compulsion would make the love they shared meaningless. Discovering that the girl he adores is sleeping with her professor to get good grades, a distraught Hanappe takes his own life, and his soul is sent to the Fairy of the World's Forest to be judged. She determines that he is well-loved by his acquaintances, and he is rescued at the last minute by Dance and taken back to Earth to be reincarnated.

A forgettable sex romp from Kazuo Koike and Go Nagai, originally published as a manga in *Young Jump*, HB tries to compensate for its flimsiness by piling on the parodies—split-second cameos exist for many other Nagai characters, including KEKKO KAMEN, DEVILMAN, and GETTER ROBO, while Nagai himself has a voice cameo as an irritated priest. A 15-minute "making of" documentary, showing the momentous occasion when Nagai reads out a single line, pads out the running time of the video to 60 minutes. Groping vaguely for a romantic message then giving up and simply groping for hooters, it is a minor Nagai work and nowhere near his best. ⬤Ⓝ

HANAUKYO MAID TEAM

2001. JPN: *Hanaukyo Maid Tai*. TV series. DIR: Yasunori Ide. SCR: Yasunori Ide. DES: Takahashi Osumi. ANI: Takahashi Osumi. MUS: N/C. PRD: Domu, MOE, TVK. 25 mins. x N/D eps.
An insipid TENCHI MUYO! clone about the pathologically shy Taro Hanaukyo becoming the leader of his powerful political family, even though he cannot bear to be touched by women. And guess what, there are loads of them, all dressed as French maids—and only Marielle seems to have the magic touch. The Maid Team consists of four units: the Domestic Unit mothers him, bathes him, dresses him, and sleeps with him; the Security Unit protects him with high-powered military hardware; the Technical Unit develops new robots for him; and the Intelligence Unit runs Memol, the world's

fastest supercomputer. An Oedipally suspect farce with added gadgetry based on Shige Mori's manga in *Shonen Champion*.

HANDMAID MAY *

2000 AKA: *Handmaid Mei*. TV series. DIR: Junichiro Kimura, Tetsuya Yanasawa. SCR: Kazuki Matsui. DES: Yuzo Hirata. ANI: Tetsuya Yanasawa. MUS: Toshio Masuda. PRD: TNK, Pioneer, WOWOW. 25 mins. x 10 eps. (TV), 1 eps. (v).
Nineteen-year-old student Kazuya Saotome is determined to build a robot of his own. Facing fierce competition from college rival Nanbara, a nasty prank goes wrong when a virus sends Kazuya's PC into a spin and (in a weak *Terminator* homage) he accidentally accesses Cyberdyne Systems' latest project, a "cyberdoll" a sixth the size of normal human being. Stuck with a cute little girl who can literally fit in his hand, Kazuya gets a frilly pink friend to help with his housework, but he also becomes the target of Cyberdyne's later models, determined to steal back the prototype at any cost. An OH MY GODDESS! retread for the new millennium, based on an idea by Juzo Mutsuki, creator of DEVIL HUNTER YOHKO.

HANDSOME GIRLFRIEND

1991. JPN: *Handsome na Kanojo*. Video. DIR: Shunji Oga. SCR: Megumi Nichiyoshi. DES: Yumi Nakayama. ANI: Mitsuharu Kajiya. MUS: Marika Haneda. PRD: JC Staff. 35 mins.
Teenage pop star Mie Hagiwara and gifted film director Kazuya Kumagai get off to a bad start when they fight in rehearsals. Selected as the main actress in Kazuya's film, Mie hates him at first but is attracted by Kazuya's passion toward filmmaking. Meanwhile, at a meeting just before shooting commences, the production is called off, and Kazuya decides to fund it with his own money. In this adaptation of Wataru Yoshizumi's manga from *Ribbon* magazine, tragedy looms as he prepares to perform the final stunt himself.

HAPPY FRIENDS

1990. JPN: *Shiawase no Katachi*. Video. DIR: Shinya Sadamitsu. SCR: Takao Koyama. DES: Takayuki Goto. ANI: Takayuki Goto. MUS: Kenji Kawai. PRD: IG Tatsunoko. 30 mins. x 4 eps.

The comedy adventures of a series of squashed-down characters who live in a world that functions on the rules of role-playing games, based on a manga that was originally serialized in the Nintendo gaming magazine *Famicom Tsushin*. The stories incorporate many game themes, from attacking monsters to tennis tournaments, with character designs that presage the later U.S. cartoon *Powerpuff Girls*.

HAPPY HUMPING! BOING BOING

1992. JPN: *Etchi (H) de Happy Pin! Pin! Pin!* Video. DIR: Katsumasa Kanezawa. SCR: Hidemi Kamata. DES: Takeshi Oshima. ANI: Yutaka Arai. MUS: N/C. PRD: E&G Film. 45 mins.

Tokio is an assistant director at TV Aoyama, while his father is an archaeologist. When Dad marries Karuri, a woman of easy virtue, and then heads off to Peru on a research trip, Tokio is stuck with Karuri and her daughter back at home, fretting that his newscaster girlfriend, Noriko, will think he is having an affair with them . . . which he eventually does. Matters are soon complicated further by the attentions of porn actress Kazuka Kurodawara, who also wants a piece of Tokio . . . and we all know what piece. Based on a manga by Takeshi Oshima in the spirit of WEATHER REPORT GIRL. **N**

HAPPY LESSON

2001. Video. DIR: Takafumi Hoshikawa, Takeshi Yamaguchi. SCR: Yoshio Takaoka. DES: Yasuhisa Kato. ANI: N/C. MUS: N/C. PRD: KSS. 30 mins. x 3 eps.

Predictable classroom high jinks, based on the Dreamcast game in which a group of female teachers must nurture a group of female students.

HARBOR LIGHTS

1988. JPN: *Harbor Light Monogatari Fashion Lala Yori*. AKA: *Harbor Light Story from Fashion Lala; Fashion Lala*. Video. DIR: Tadamasa Takahashi. SCR: Kenji Terada. DES: Yoshiyuki Kishi. ANI: Tadamasa Takahashi. MUS: N/C. PRD: Studio Pierrot. 50 mins.

Eleven-year-old Miho wants to be a fashion designer and is eager to make a dress for her little sister, Shuri, to help her win the Dancing Queen contest. When Miho's stupid aunt ruins the dress, the Fairies of Fanland hear her prayer and transform her into the 16-year-old Lala, a top designer. And in the end, it was all a dream: a cop-out that probably helps to explain why this attempt to create a new magical girl in the tradition of CREAMY MAMI never came back for a repeat performance. Not to be confused with FANCY LALA.

HARD AND LOOSE

1992. JPN: *Shiritsu Tantei Doki Seizo Trouble Note Hard and Loose*. AKA: *Private Investigators Down But Not Out: Trouble Notes Hard and Loose*. Video. DIR: Noboru Ishiguro. SCR: Noboru Ishiguro. DES: Noboru Sugimitsu. ANI: Noboru Sugimitsu. MUS: Masaru Watanabe. PRD: Artland. 45 mins.

A detective thriller in which former boxer Shozo is thrown into a web of intrigue when he picks up a ringing phone in a room whose occupant he is supposed to be following. Based on a manga by SILENT SERVICE–creator Kaiji Kawaguchi and BORDER's Karibu Marai and boasting the distinctive square-jawed characters found in Kawaguchi's other work.

HARELUYA II BOY

1997. TV series. DIR: Kiyoshi Egami. SCR: Yasuhiro Imagawa. DES: Takahiro Kishida. ANI: N/C. MUS: Shingo Kobayashi. PRD: Triangle Staff, TV Tokyo. 25 mins. x 25 eps.

When tough-guy Hibino saves wannabe-artist Kyoshiro from a gang of bullies, the two become firm friends. They also befriend Makoto, who wants to be the lead singer of the Fire Guns rock band and find superstardom, and Michiru, a young girl who wants to be a jewelry designer. Each member of the group seeks to find success in his or her chosen field, though Hibino's only wish is to stay out of trouble long enough to graduate from school. Then he wants to conquer the world.

A comedy anime that looks askance on Hareluya Hibino's burgeoning relationship with Michiru, *HB*'s message is that friends, however mismatched, should always help each other strive for their dreams, especially when one of them is the prodigal son of God. Like a modern-day DORAEMON, Hibino can pull useful objects from a seemingly bottomless backpack, including baseball bats, frying pans, and lobsters, as the occasion demands. Based on a 1992 *Shonen Jump* manga by Haruto Umezawa, who began his career as an assistant to CITY HUNTER's Tsukasa Hojo.

HARETOKIDOKI BUTA

1988. AKA: *Fairweather Pig; Clear Day with Occasional Pig*. Movie, TV series. DIR: Toshio Hirata. SCR: Toshio Takeuchi, Hideo Takayashiki. DES: Kazuo Komatsubara. ANI: Kazuo Komatsubara. MUS: N/C. PRD: OH! Productions, TV Tokyo. 45 mins. (m), 25 mins. x 61 eps. (TV).

Eight-year-old Noriyasu writes and draws in his diary, discovering later that *everything* he writes in it comes

Captain Harlock and Tochiro in one of their disappointing recent appearances. A needlessly complex retelling of Wagner's *The Ring* as "space" opera, *Harlock Saga* (2000) does its much-loved, iconic hero no favors by injecting literary pretensions into a sci-fi shootout. There is also something strangely camp in modern times about a hero who insists on wearing a pirate costume complete with garish skull and crossbones, especially when his actions are anything but piratic. *See entry p. 53.*

Captain Harlock

© 1999 LEIJI MATSUMOTO-SHINCHOSHA/BANDAI VISUAL/81 PRODUCE

true, even if it involves talking pigs and strange adventures. This adaptation of the children's picture book by Shiro Yadakara was revived for a TV series in 1997, directed by Shinichi Watanabe and written by Yoshio Urasawa, with Harebuta's ("Sunny Pig"'s) ability to "smell" people's true intentions getting him into many scrapes.

HARMAGEDON *

1983. JPN: *Genma Taisen*. AKA: *Great War with Genma*. Movie. DIR: Rintaro. SCR: Chiho Katsura, Makoto Naito, Masaki Mori. DES: Katsuhiro Otomo. ANI: Mukuo Takamura, Yoshiaki Kawajiri, Takashi Nakamura, Iwao Yamaki. MUS: Keith Emerson, Nozomu Aoki. PRD: Madhouse, Magic Capsule. 131 mins.
An awkwardly paced and overlong film adapted from a long series of books by **WOLF GUY**'s Kazumasa Hirai and filtered through their manga incarnation by Shotaro Ishinomori. Genma ("Phantom Demon"), the personification of entropy, has eaten half the universe and intends to destroy Earth. Its nemesis, good interdimensional being Floy, who has an intensely annoying voice, contacts Princess Luna of Transylvania and warns her of impending doom. Luna is already aware of it, since the plane carrying her on a diplomatic mission has just been struck by a meteor bearing Vega, a cyborg from a world destroyed by Genma in the distant past (compare to Andro in **TEKKAMAN**). Luna and Vega set about recruiting a multinational army of psionics (including Sonny Rinks, a black kid from the New York ghetto), specifically Japanese schoolboy Jo Azuma, who is the most powerful. As Genma's powers lay waste to Earth, his comic sidekicks, Zombi and Samedi, kill his friends and loved ones. They attack Jo's sister Michiko, who reveals her own psychic powers, only to die seconds before Jo can save her. A distraught Jo is saved from an earthquake by Tao, a Chinese psionic, who leads him to Genma's hideaway amid the boiling lava of a newly active Mount Fuji. Jo and several other psionic warriors, who arrive as an after-

thought, then defeat Genma, who comes back in a predictable twist and is defeated again in a final battle. Vega dies in the final conflict but commends his friends on their victory as he prepares for rebirth, along with life on Earth itself.

This first anime film from *Newtype* publishers Kadokawa boasts a fatuous pseudo-religious message, a truly awful English-language song, a cameo appearance by director Rintaro as a flustered artist, and much-hyped character designs from Katsuhiro Otomo. It also features an interesting choice from the animators, who concentrate on drawing high-quality still images at the expense of actual animation and lip-sync. Trying and failing, like **DARKSIDE BLUES**, to cram a complex text into the running time of a mere movie, it nevertheless contained the seeds of the anime business as we know it today. Designer Otomo was so disillusioned by his experience of working on *Harmagedon* that he resolved to do things differently five years later with **AKIRA**. Not to be confused with Lee Hyunse's *Armageddon* (1995), which was distributed by Manga Entertainment as "anime," but actually made in Korea.

HARRIS'S WIND

1966. JPN: *Harris no Kaze*. TV series. DIR: Yoshiyuki Shindo. SCR: Keisuke Fujikawa, Shunichi Yukimuro, Haruya Yamazaki, Tadaaki Yamazaki. DES: Tetsuya Chiba. ANI: Fukuo Watanabe. MUS: Gatchatorian. PRD: B Pro, Fuji TV. 25 mins. x 25 eps.
Kunimatsu Ishida is a regular wild-child, thrown out of every school in his area for fighting. One day he meets the principal of Harris Academy, where he drifts from club to club trying his hand at sports, mainly contact sports like boxing and kendo, though he also brings his own hands-on style to soccer and baseball. Eventually, he becomes a hero of the school by channeling his aggression into improving the school's athletic reputation. Based on a *Shonen Magazine* manga by **TOMORROW'S JOE**–creator Tetsuya Chiba, the same

story was remade by Tezuka Productions as *Kunimatsu's Got It Right* (1971), directed by Masami Hata.

HATTORI THE NINJA

1981. JPN: *Ninja Hattori-kun*. TV series, movie. DIR: Hiroshi Sasakawa, Fumio Ikeno. SCR: Masaaki Sakurai, Noboru Shiroyama. DES: Fujio-Fujiko. ANI: Hiromichi Matano. MUS: Shunsuke Kikuchi. PRD: Shinei, Pan Media, TV Asahi. 10 mins. x 694 eps., 53 mins. (m).
The everyday Sanyo family gets an unexpected surprise in the shape of a new lodger—Hattori is a ninja boy who has come down from the Iga mountains to attend normal school. Befriending Kenichi Sanyo, who is the same age as he, Hattori starts attending school undercover, occasionally accompanied by his brother, Shinzo, Shishimaru the ninja dog, and Kenichi's girlfriend, Yumeko. The gang is also threatened by the rival Koga ninja, Kemumaki, and his evil sidekick, Kagechiyo the Shadow-cat.

Hattori, the lead character in this long-running work from **DORAEMON** creators Fujiko-Fujio, also appeared in an anime movie, *Hattori and the War of the Little Ninja Villages* (1983), directed by Shinichi Suzuki, in which the evil DR. Mekamaro, wishing to be the best ninja in the world, kidnaps Hattori's parents, leaving the little assassin and his friends to save the world.

HAUNTED JUNCTION *

1997. TV series. DIR: Yuji Muto. SCR: Kazuhisa Sakaguchi, Satoru Nishizono, Yuji Hashimoto. DES: Atsuko Nakajima. ANI: Ryoko Hata, Atsuko Nakajima, Satoshi Inoue. MUS: Hayato Matsuo. PRD: Studio Deen, BeStack. 25 mins. x 12 eps.
Haruto, the son of a Christian minister, becomes the president of his high school's Saints Club, where he, Buddhist acolyte Kazuo, and wannabe Shinto shrine maiden Mutsuki must somehow keep their school's epidemic of ghosts under control.

Based on a manga by Nemu Mukudori first serialized in *Monthly Electric Comic GAO*, *HJ* is a genuinely funny look at what school life might be like with fish-monsters in the swimming pool, statues that come to life, and biology lab skeletons that dance like Cossacks. With a Christian who just wants a mundane, boring life and a Buddhist who is easily possessed, there are hilarious setups for cross-dressing and animal impersonations. Mutsuki's "Shouta Complex," however, is an unhealthy obsession with little boys, which may well have appeared like an ironic inversion of CREAM LEMON's Lolita complex to the Japanese crew, but is likely to keep *HJ* forever off U.S. TV. As it was, the show was only shown on Japanese TV very late at night, and elements remain too risqué for children.

As for the ghostbusting, Mutsuki has a sideline in Shinto exorcisms, while Kazuo can write Buddhist charms. Haruto, however, is neglected by a writing team that knows nothing of Christianity, coming across as little more than a blond dummy in a smock who regularly yells "Oh my God!" in exasperation.

Like the later JUBEI-CHAN THE NINJA GIRL, elements of *HJ* rely on ethnocentric jokes liable to fly over the heads of a U.S. audience. Throwaway lines about a girl in the toilets (see HERE COMES HANAKO) are left unexplained, as is an anatomical doll named after novelist Haruo Sato and a talking statue based on a legendarily hard-working student Kinjiro Ninomiya, whose effigy can be found in many Japanese schools. Nonetheless, a fine, fun parody of school spook stories.

HAWAIIAN BREEZE
1992. JPN: *Shin Dosei Jidai: Hawaiian Breeze*. AKA: *New Age of Cohabitation: Hawaiian Breeze*. Video. DIR: Hiroshi Fukutomi. SCR: Takashi Yamada. DES: Fumi Shibama. ANI: Masuji Kinoue. MUS: King Biscuit Time. PRD: Japan Home Video. 45 mins.
In this adaptation of a manga by Fumi Shibama, itself a retelling of a 1972

manga by Kazuo Kamimura (the original *Age of Cohabitation* whose existence is implied by the "new" in this title), Honda has been living with Eri for two years and debates whether or not he should ask her to marry him.

HAZEDON
1972. TV series. DIR: Makura Saki (pseud. for Osamu Dezaki), Fumio Ikeno. SCR: Haruya Yamazaki, Yoshitake Suzuki, Toshiaki Matsushima, Hiroyuki Hoshiyama. DES: Toshiyasu Okada. ANI: Kazuhiko Udagawa, Keisuke Morishita, Satoshi Dezaki. MUS: Hiroshi Tsutsui. PRD: Fuji TV. 25 mins. x 26 eps.
Young fishboy Hazedon wants to be the "strongest fish in the world," fighting against the evil Ankoragon and Samegills, who eternally plague the undersea kingdom with crab attacks, shark thieves, and kidnappers sent to steal away Hazedon's love interest, the mermaid girl Sealan.

HEART: AN ITALIAN SCHOOLBOY'S JOURNAL
1981. JPN: *Ai no Gakko Cuore*. AKA: *Beloved School Cuore*. TV series. DIR: Eiji Okabe. SCR: Ryuzo Nakanishi. DES: Yu Noda. ANI: Fumio Kurokawa, Akira Suzuki. MUS: Katsuhisa Hattori. PRD: Nippon Animation, TBS. 25 mins. x 26 eps.
Enrico Pocchini is a kindhearted fourth-grader with a strong sense of justice who lives in the picturesque Italian town of Torino. But as he starts the new semester at school, he loses his adored teacher, Miss Delcacci, who is replaced by the stern Mr. Pelboni. After some misunderstandings, the boys in Enrico's class come to respect Mr. Pelboni, and learn about love, life, and human kindness.

Though financed by Calpis, original sponsors of the WORLD MASTERPIECE THEATER, and made by Nippon Animation, *Heart* is not one of the *WMT* series, though it could easily pass for one. Two episodes of the series focus on one boy's quest to be reunited with his mother in South America, a chap-

ter from the original novel by Edmondo de Amicis that was already animated in 1976 as the famous FROM THE APENNINES TO THE ANDES.

HEART COCKTAIL
1986. TV series. DIR: Yoshimitsu Morita, Shinpei Wada, Osamu Kobayashi, Akio Hayashi. SCR: Seizo Watase. DES: Seizo Watase. ANI: Yasuko Yamazaki. MUS: Naoya Matsuoka. PRD: Kodansha, Nippon TV. 5 mins. x 77 eps.
CHALK-COLORED PEOPLE–creator Seizo Watase's 1983 series of short manga in *Comic Morning* is adapted into dozens of romantic vignettes, each designed to tell a simple love story in "no more time than it would take to smoke a cigarette," which often means that there is little time for even revealing people's names; many tales simply star "Me" and "Her." Stories include *Emblem of My Father, Two in the Beer Garden, Old Hawaii Corner, My Brother's Zippo,* and *Takeru's Love of Two and a Half Millennia.* The tobacco analogy may sound strange in these politically correct times, but it is better than the alternative, remembering that such short manga stories are *actually* designed to take no longer to read than the average dump.

HEART MARK
1994. JPN: *Cho Kusei ni Nariso*. AKA: *Super Addictive*. TV series. DIR: Tetsuya Endo, Mitsuo Hikabe, Yasuhiro Matsuyama, Yoshiaki Iwasaki. SCR: Yorimichi Nakano, Takeshi Shudo, Tsutomu Nagai. DES: Toshiko Sasaki. ANI: Kazuyoshi Sasaki, Seiji Kikuchi. MUS: Yo Sakamoto. PRD: Studio Sensen, Video Champ, NHK2. 25 mins. x 39 eps.
Idol singer Nagisa Shiratori disguises herself as a boy to attend school, hoping to prove her prowess at fighting and gain applicants for her father's undersubscribed martial arts school. Based on a manga in *Nakayoshi* magazine by Anzu Yoshimura and Yayoi Takano.

HEARTBROKEN ANGELS

1990. JPN: *Kizudarake no Tenshitachi*. Video. DIR: Tsuyoshi Sasakawa. SCR: Tsuyoshi Sasakawa, Takeshi Saito. DES: Masahiko Kikuni. ANI: N/C. MUS: Toshiyuki Ebihara, Masaya. PRD: Studio M. 70 mins.

Thirty-one stories based on the four-panel manga strips drawn by Masahiko Kikuni for *Young Sunday* magazine make up this anime that mixes animation and live action. Possibly intended for TV broadcast like HEART COCKTAIL, though the rude nature of Kikuni's humor may have prevented that part of the plan. *Tetsuo*'s Tomoro Taguchi was among the live-action actors. See also MOST SPIRITED MAN IN JAPAN.

HEART-COLORED KILLER TICKET

1989. JPN: *Satsujin Kippu wa Heart Iro*. AKA: *Killer Ticket Is Heart-Colored*. Video. DIR: Taku Sugiyama. SCR: Akira Miyazaki. DES: Hiroyasu Yamaura. ANI: Tomoko Kobayashi. MUS: N/C. PRD: Nippon Eizo. 50 mins.

A "soft-boiled" detective comedy based on a series of young-adult novels by Hiroyasu Yamaura, in which sweet, unassuming, bullying-victim Seiko is suspended from school and takes the opportunity to go to Nagasaki, where she becomes embroiled in a murder mystery. In keeping with the originals' focus on the female market, sleuthing à la YOUNG KINDAICHI FILES becomes less important in the story than cats and ghosts.

HEAVY

1990. Movie. DIR: Shinya Hanai. SCR: Noboru Ishiguro, Shoji Imai. DES: Masao Nakada. ANI: Masao Nakada. MUS: N/C. PRD: Artland. 50 mins.

Yet another boxing anime, this time based on SWORD OF MUSASHI–creator Motoka Murakami's 1989 manga from *Shonen Sunday* magazine about an impressionable man taking his father's advice to heart and "fighting for as long as he is still breathing." This takes on a double meaning when Dad needs a life-saving operation, and our hero enters the boxing ring to win the money. ◑

HEAVY METAL L-GAIM

1984. JPN: *Jusenki L-Gaim*. AKA: *Heavy War Machine L-Gaim*. TV series. DIR: Yoshiyuki Tomino, Minoru Onotani, Yasuhiro Imagawa, Toshifumi Kawase, Osamu Sekita, Akira Suzuki, Toshifumi Takizawa, Kunihisa Sugishima, Hideji Iguchi. SCR: Jiyu Watanabe, Sukehiro Tomita, Asami Watanabe. DES: Mamoru Nagano, Kunio Okawara, Toshifumi Nagasawa. ANI: Hiroyuki Kitazume. MUS: Kei Wakakusa. PRD: Sotsu Agency, Sunrise, Nagoya TV (TV Asahi). 25 mins. x 54 eps. (TV), 60 mins. x 3 eps. (v).

The immortal Poseidal of Gustgal leads his 24 elite Temple Knights to subdue the Pentagonia System, proclaiming himself Star Emperor. His "second crusade" ends in the year 3975, when he defeats King Camon Wallha V, but Camon hides his heir on the forgotten planet Coam, with a single giant white battle-robot. Fifteen years later, *Prince* Camon, using the name Daba Myroad, leads a revolt on Coam, backed by the arms dealer Amandara Kamanadara, unaware that his supporter is in fact Poseidal himself, supplying weaponry to both sides while a doppelganger sits on his throne.

A giant-robot show that functioned as a dry run for designer Nagano's later FIVE STAR STORIES, *L-G* boasts the creator's trademark mixture of far-future and fantasy-medieval designs, and many lookalikes of characters from his more famous work. A three-part video series followed, with the initial two parts comprising edited footage from the series, and the third, *L-G: Full Metal Soldier*, adding a coda to the series proper.

HEIDI

1974. JPN: *Alps no Shojo Heidi*. AKA: *Alpine Girl Heidi*. TV series. DIR: Isao Takahata. SCR: Yoshiaki Yoshida. DES: Yoichi Otabe, Hayao Miyazaki. ANI: Toshiyasu Okada. MUS: Takeo Watanabe. PRD: Zuiyo, Fuji TV. 25 mins. x 52 eps., 107 mins. (m).

Eight-year-old orphan Adelheid (or Heidi, for short) is taken in by her aunt Dete, who soon packs her off to stay with her old grandfather on Alm mountain in the Swiss Alps. Heidi befriends local goatherder Peter, only to be spirited away once more by Aunt Dete, who takes her to Frankfurt, where she is to be a playmate for the disabled Klara. Pining for her alpine happiness, Heidi heads back to Alm in this famous anime based on the 1881 children's book by Johanna Spyri. An early masterpiece from GRAVE OF THE FIREFLIES–director Takahata, featuring storyboard contributions from his long-term associate Miyazaki and from GUNDAM-director Yoshiyuki Tomino. Much-loved across Europe, the anime version is less well-known in English. In Japan, its CINDERELLA qualities and Alpine pastorals would lead to many similar children's shows, most noticeably JULIE THE WILD ROSE and TREASURES OF THE SNOW. A 1979 movie-edit consists primarily of footage from the Frankfurt episodes with Klara. Of the many live-action adaptations available in English, the most recent is Disney's 1993 version featuring Jason Robards and Jane Seymour. See also VIDEO PICTURE BOOK.

HELEN KELLER

1981. JPN: *Helen Keller Monogatari: Ai to Hikari no Tenshi*. AKA: *Story of Helen Keller: Angel of Love and Light*. TV special. DIR: Fumio Ikeno. SCR: Hiroshi Kitahara. DES: Michiyo Sakurai. ANI: Seiji Yamashita. MUS: Hiroshi Ogasawara. PRD: NOW Planning. 81 mins.

At 19 months, baby Helen succumbs to a fever that leaves her deaf and blind. Refusing to believe her case is hopeless, her parents seek help from all quarters, eventually finding "Miracle Worker" Annie Sullivan. Arriving in Helen's native Tuscumbia, Alabama, when the child is seven, Sullivan teaches Helen to communicate purely through touch and the sensation of writing on the palm of the hand. An anime made for broadcast on Japan's National Day for the Disabled, *HK* celebrates the early life of a remarkable woman (1880–1968) who would eventually graduate from Radcliffe College, champion the causes of the disadvantaged, and win many international honors, including Japan's Sacred Treasure. Thanks to biographies in the **GREAT PEOPLE** series, Keller shares with **COLUMBUS** the distinction of having her life turned into anime on three separate occasions.

HELL TARGET
1986. Video. DIR: Yoshinori Nakamura. SCR: Kenichi Matsuzaki. DES: Hiroshi Yokoyama. ANI: Teruyoshi Nakamura. MUS: Rosa Bianca. PRD: Nakamura Pro. 50 mins.
A spaceship is lost near the forbidding planet of Inferno II. Some years later, a second ship with a crew of nine gets there and encounters a monster that rapidly makes mincemeat of most of them. In an obvious anime retread of James Cameron's *Aliens* (1986), the sole survivor, Makuro Kitazato, must destroy the monster before it can surprise a third ship that is already en route.

HELL TEACHER NUBE
1996. JPN: *Jigoku Sensei Nube.* TV series. DIR: Yoshio Misawa. SCR: Takao Koyama. DES: Yoichi Onishi. ANI: Masami Suda, Ken Ueno. MUS: BMF. PRD: Toei, TV Asahi. 25 mins. x 48 eps. (TV), 25 mins. (TV special), 45 mins. x 3 (m), 30 mins. x 3 (v).
Meisuke Nueno, otherwise known as Nube, is a grade-school teacher whose left hand is possessed by demonic forces, and whose school is constantly beset by apparitions. This anime lightheartedly retells old **JAPANESE FOLK TALES** updated for modern times in much the same tongue-in-cheek fashion as **HAUNTED JUNCTION** and **GHOST SWEEPER MIKAMI**. So it is that Nube is stalked by besotted snow maiden Yukime, must evict a "Hanako" from the toilets (see **HERE COMES HANAKO**), finds a cursed samurai sword in the lost-and-found, and generally busts ghosts in every conceivable part of his

school, from the library to the swimming pool. At the height of Japan's 1990s ghost-story trend, *HTN* made it to theaters with the short anime films *HTN: The Movie* (1996), *HTN: Nube Dies at Midnight* (1997), and *HTN's Scary Summer Vacation: Tale of the Sea Phantom* (1997); each replaying the formula of a TV episode, but with a slightly longer running time. In 1998, a readers' survey chose three previously unfilmed chapters from the original 1993 *Shonen Jump* manga by Sho Masakura and Takeshi Okano to be adapted straight to video as *HTN: Sun God vs. the Wall Man*, *HTN: Bukimi-chan of the Seven Mysteries*, and *HTN: Biggest Battle in History—Attack of the Relentless Demon*.

HELLO KITTY *
1989. Video, movie, TV series. DIR: Tameo Ogawa, Yasuo Ishikawa, Masami Hata, Yuji Nichimaki, et al. SCR: Tomoko Konparu. DES: N/C. ANI: Kanji Akabori, Maya Matsuyama. MUS: Toyomi Kojima. PRD: Sanrio. Ca. 30 mins. x 50+ eps.
A simply drawn icon, Hello Kitty is the most successful image created by the merchandising corporation Sanrio to sell toys, toasters, luggage, dolls, stickers, and just about anything else. Her fellow brands include **KERO KERO KEROPPI** and **PEKKLE THE DUCK**, but Kitty has a bigger international fan base than the rest put together. A complete rundown of her screen appearances, including all the compilations and recombinations of the last 21 years, would require substantially more space than this book allows, but these are the highlights of her anime resume.
A Hello Kitty version of **CINDERELLA** (1989) was originally shown theatrically before initiating the franchise of *Hello Kitty's Fairy Tale Theater*, where the mouthless icon appeared in many adaptations of famous stories, including her own versions of **SNOW WHITE**, **HEIDI**, *Sleeping Beauty*, **ALICE IN WONDERLAND**, *The Dream Thief*, *Kitty and the Beast*, and the **WIZARD OF OZ** pastiche *Wizard of Paws*. Sensibly realizing that the U.S. market would not bear a sin-

Japanese monks wonder at their encounter with the supernatural in *A Ghost Story*, one of the **ANIMATED CLASSICS OF JAPANESE LITERATURE**. Its original author, Koizumi Yakumo, was the Japanese name of Lafcadio Hearn, a European who eventually attained Japanese citizenship. Soon after, he was fired from his Japanese university post by a racist dean. The original folktale was told to Hearn by his Japanese wife. *See entry p. 14.*

Animated Classics of Japanese Literature: A Ghost Story

gle episode to a tape, these were bundled into compilation volumes in America, where they were well received as children's entertainment, and *Santa's Missing Hat* was combined with *Keroppi* crossover *The Christmas Eve Gift*.
Meanwhile, Kitty's popularity continued in Japan—1990 saw a theatrical retelling of **THUMBELINA**, and the Japanese audience was treated to several successive video outings that never made it to the West, including a second *Heidi* pastiche in 1994 and a ten-part series of **JAPANESE FOLK TALES**, including adaptations of *The Hidden Tengu*, **MOMOTARO**, *Kintaro*, *The Snow Maiden*, **THE MONKEY AND THE CRAB**, *Princess Kaguya* (see **REI REI**), and **HERE COMES THE MOUSE BRIDE**. Kitty also featured in several video specials with fellow Sanrio character **BAD BATZ MARU** (see same) and the old-time Japanese adventures *Ratboy* and *Return of the Tanuki* (both 1989).
Other stories were more original, including some set in Kitty's hometown of London, such as *The Day the Clock Stopped* (1992), in which Kitty and sister Mimi have to restart Big Ben, and *HK: Aliens in London* (1992), in which the gullible sisters are convinced that two jewel thieves are visitors from outer space. Other outbreaks of the Kitty

virus were aimed squarely at impressing parents. *HK: Mom Loves Me After All* (1992) deals with a child's jealousy for a newborn sibling, telling the tale of Kitty's mother babysitting for someone else. *We Love Hello Kitty* (1993) explained the wonders that await good little kittens on their birthdays, when they get presents from all their friends and the chance to eat their favorite food. The franchise jumped on the eco-bandwagon in 1994, the same year as **POMPOKO**, with *HK: Everyone Must Protect the Forest*. In 1997, the parental propaganda machine began rolling in earnest with a succession of short informational videos including *Trying Hard, Cleaning up the House, Going to the Toilet Alone, Sleeping Alone, Being Careful Outdoors, Saying Sorry, Table Manners,* and *Enjoying the Bath,* all followed by the winning subtitle *". . . with Hello Kitty."* The late 1990s saw the Kitty team animate a six-part video series of **AESOP'S FABLES** in their own inimitable style. The *". . . with Hello Kitty"* series, combined with *"Kitty Parody Theater"* (possibly a new name for the fables or fairy tales above) was rebroadcast on Japanese TV as the 39-episode *Kitty's Paradise* (1999), which was swiftly snapped up for the U.S. market by Saban Entertainment during the mad rush to option Japanese children's animation post-**POKÉMON**. This was particularly ironic, since it was now sought after because "anime sells," whereas it had clearly been selling rather well without the "anime" tag for several years already.

HELLO SANDYBELL

1981. AKA: *Sandy Jonquille.* TV series. DIR: Hiroshi Shidara, Kazumi Fukushima, Hideo Kozawa. SCR: Noboru Shiroyama. DES: Makoto Sakurai. ANI: Shoji Yanagise. MUS: Takeo Watanabe. PRD: TV Asahi, Toei. 25 mins. x 47 eps.
Sandybell is a happy-go-lucky Scottish girl who lives in the highlands and adores local nobleman Mark Wellington, though he is betrothed to Kitty Shearer, a rich heiress. Sandybell cherishes a dream of becoming an artist,

but when her father, Leslie Christie, falls ill, she discovers that she is adopted. Sensing her real parents are still alive somewhere, she heads for London, where she stays with Can-Can, an old family friend. She becomes a cub newspaper reporter, traveling all over Europe in search of clues about her own past, while the venal Kitty plots to ruin her future. Like its more melancholy predecessor **CANDY CANDY**, *HS* may look European, but has an all-Japanese origin: it is based on a book by Shiro Jinbo, whose illustrator Makoto Sakurai also provided basic designs for the animated version.

HELLO SPANK

1981. JPN: *Ohayo Spank.* TV series. DIR: Shigetsugu Yoshida, Susumu Ishizaki, Satoshi Dezaki, Naoto Hashimoto. SCR: Satoshi Kaneko, Masaaki Sakurai. DES: Shizue Takanishi, Yukari Kobayashi. ANI: Takao Kasai. MUS: Koji Makaino. PRD: TMS, TV Asahi. 25 mins. x 63 eps. (TV), 100 mins. (m).
When teenage Aiko Morimura's father disappears on his yacht, her mother gets a lucrative hat-designing job in Paris. Instead of going with her, Aiko stays with her uncle and his dog, Pappy. With predictable Japanese pathos, Pappy is soon killed in a road accident. The arrival of a new dog, Spank, brings a smile back to Aiko's face, even if Spank is constantly getting her and her friends into trouble. *Spank* began as a 1978 manga in the girls' magazine *Nakayoshi,* drawn by Shizue Takanashi from a script by Shunichi Yukimuro, the writer of dozens of anime including **CANDY CANDY**, but curiously not this one. In 1982, Spank returned for an all-new movie outing about his falling for the mongrel puppy Anna, whose handsome male owner has newly transferred to Aiko's school.

HER NEED FOR EMBRACE

1989. JPN: *Dakaretai Onna.* Video. DIR: Yoshihisa Matsumoto, Akane Yamada. SCR: Milk Morizono. DES: Milk Morizono.

ANI: N/C. MUS: N/C. PRD: Toei. 45 mins. x 2 eps.
Several erotic short stories taken from a manga of the same name by the controversial erotic creator Milk Morizono, featuring high-quality animation and vignettes along such themes as *Hold Me Harder, Hold Me Lustier,* and *Sunday Ecstasy.* See also **MILKY PASSION**. Ⓝ

HERE COMES HANAKO

1994. JPN: *Gakko no Kowai Uwasa: Hanako-san ga Kita.* AKA: *Scary Stories of Your School: Here Comes Hanako; Phantom of the Toilet.* Video. DIR: Tetsuo Yasumi. SCR: Yukiko Matsui, Nobuyuki Hori. DES: Tac. ANI: N/C. MUS: Ko Suzuki. PRD: Tac. 10 mins. x 10 eps.
The granddaddy of all children's anime ghouls remains Shigeru Mizuki's **SPOOKY KITARO**. However, the 1990s were dominated by "Hanako," an iconic figure that came out of nowhere. The indisputable hit of Toru Tsunemitsu's urban myth collection *School Ghost Stories* was the short story *Ghost Toilet,* set in an elementary school in Nagano Prefecture. In the dark, dank toilet on the north side, the fourth stall was said to be permanently locked. Students forcing the door discover the corpse of a girl in a red dress, presumed to have committed suicide, whose ghost is said to haunt the restrooms, eternally trying to lead schoolboys into hell with the temptation "Shall we play?" This tall tale has become the defining spooky story for the Japanese children who grew up in the 1990s, creating a subgenre in children's books beginning with *Hanako in the Toilet: Scary Stories of Your School* (1993). This in turn was adapted into the *Here Comes Hanako* manga by several artists, most of whom also wrote the anime version that was broadcast as part of the TV program *Ponkikki Kids* in 1994. In that special, Hanako, with a deathly pallor like a juvenile Elvira, introduces episodes such as *The Haunted Cinema* and *The Cursed Promise Ring.*
Hanako also appeared in her own

50-minute anime movie, *Hanako of the Toilet* (1996), directed by Akitaro Daichi, which recast the wild-child as a ghostbuster keeping evil spirits at bay. The franchise reached live-action cinema with Joji Matsuoka's 1996 film of the same name and *New Hanako* (1998), which returned to the original story by featuring a group of high-school sleuths contacting Hanako through a Ouija board and saving another classmate from a homeless pervert who is the true cause of all the strange happenings. The phenomenon and its exploitation are parodied in HAUNTED JUNCTION, where Buddhist Kazuo wishes to collect "all the Hanakos" from every school in Japan; DIRTY PAIR *Flash*, which features a Hanako hologram; and HELL TEACHER NUBE, which features a more "traditional" Hanako apparition. REAL SCHOOL GHOST STORIES and SCHOOL SPIRITS are among its many distant relatives. The generation that grew up watching *Hanako* swelled box office receipts for modern horror films such as *Ring*.

HERE COMES THE MOUSE BRIDE
1979. JPN: *Nezumi no Yomeiri*. Movie. DIR: Daisaku Shirokawa. SCR: Daisaku Shirokawa. DES: N/C. ANI: Sadao Tsukioka. MUS: Shingo Asano. PRD: Toei. 13 mins.
A mouse father seeks the ideal husband for his beloved daughter, but the sun refuses on the grounds that he is not the most powerful thing in the universe. A humble cloud blocks his rays, but the cloud concedes defeat to the wind, who can blow it away. The wind, however, is unable to budge a little girl's house, but the house is unable to rid itself of a troublesome mouse. The lucky mouse marries the bride, and they all live happily ever after. Also adapted as one of the many HELLO KITTY retellings of classic folk tales.

HERE IS GREENWOOD *
1991. JPN: *Koko wa Greenwood*. Video. DIR: Tomomi Mochizuki. SCR: Tomomi Mochizuki. DES: Masako Goto. ANI:

Masako Goto. MUS: Shigeru Nagata. PRD: Pierrot Project. 30 mins. x 6 eps.
When his brother marries the woman *he* secretly adores, Kazuya moves out of the family home and into the student dorm of Greenwood. There, the heart-broken loner gains the friendship and support he needs, including his androgynously pretty roommate, Shun Kisaragi, and a gang of sweet-natured but mildly zany boys. With obvious parallels to MAISON IKKOKU, the show also incorporates occasional supernatural moments, such as a ghostly haunting that brings out people's true feelings for each other (compare to similar events in KIMAGURE ORANGE ROAD). In the group's occasional involvement in sports championships, wacky pranks, and personal problems, it also recalls the more sedate installments of PATLABOR. Former students kidnap someone's sister in one episode, while in *Here Is Devilwood*, the characters make a fantasy film about wandering swordsman Lemon Herb having to defeat the evil overlord Clorettes. The final episodes involve the arrival of a gangland badgirl who replaces Kazuya's sister-in-law in his affections, but each of these episodes are merely brief moments from the original 11-volume run of the 1986 manga by Yukie Nasu, serialized in *Hana to Yume* magazine. In a mere six episodes, there is little chance of anything but a general survey of the original's content and themes, which was, of course, exactly what the producers wanted in order to encourage people to go out and buy the manga.

HERMES *
1997. JPN: *Hermes: Ai wa Kaze no Fuku*. AKA: *Hermes: Winds of Love*. Movie. DIR: Tetsuo Imazawa. SCR: Hermes Scenario Project. DES: Yoshiaki Yokota. ANI: Yoshiaki Yanagida. MUS: Yuichi Mizusawa. PRD: Toei. 114 mins.
Hermes, a youth who it is said will one day overthrow the evil King Minos of Crete, falls in love with the beautiful Princess Aphrodite. After two pointless musical interludes, he rescues her

from the tower where she is imprisoned and decides it's time to defeat Minos. To do this, he enlists the help of the Athenian Theseus and Minos' daughter, Ariadne, "the only one who is sane and religious." After a straightforward run through the events of the tale of Theseus and the Minotaur, Hermes turns up at the last moment to kill Minos himself, at which point Theseus and Ariadne sail off into the sunset and out of the story. Hermes is told that he is a reincarnation of the great god Ophealis—though he is told this *by* Ophealis, meaning he spends part of the film talking to himself. He is given a magic staff and does great deeds all over Greece, before rescuing Aphrodite's blind mother from prison and descending into Hell to kill Minos . . . again. Meanwhile, the childless Aphrodite muses that she wouldn't mind if Hermes took a mistress, only to find that her selfless thoughts have reached the ears of the Goddess of Love. The Goddess shoots her with a magic arrow to make her give birth to an heir. After chatting with some fairies, Hermes resolves to unite Greece, but he suspects it might take a while. Then he defeats his enemies through peaceful means by setting up a trade confederacy which they all want to join.

A lavish but clumsily written combination of Greek myth and half-remembered fairy tales, though occasional scenes of contradictory preaching show its true colors as a publicity vehicle for a religious organization. Based on a book by Ryuho Okawa, the founder of the Institute for Research in Human Happiness, who claims to be a reincarnation of the same alien being who was once Hermes and Ophealis. As with the later LAWS OF THE SUN, it received a very limited theatrical release in the U.S., chiefly at screenings for the faithful, though perhaps a few mystified anime fans were also present and guessing just which scenarists wisely declined to be credited for this one. The film limped out onto video in 2001, amid hype that preferred to emphasize the director's previous work on **DIGIMON** rather than the story's origins.

HERMIT VILLAGE

1963. JPN: *Sennin Buraku*. AKA: *Village of Immortals*. TV series. DIR: Fumiaki Kamigami. SCR: Akira Hayasaka. DES: Tsutomu Kojima. ANI: Susumu Nojima. MUS: N/C. PRD: Eiken. 15 mins. x 23 eps.

The ancient Chinese village of Taoyuan is populated solely by Taoist ascetics. The eldest, Lao Shi, conducts research into the mysteries of magic and alchemy, while his disciple Zhi Huang remains more interested in pleasures of the flesh. He has fallen for three pretty sisters who live nearby, much to Lao Shi's annoyance. Based on a manga serialized in *Asahi Geino* magazine by Tsutomu Kojima, this naughty comedy was the first-ever late-night anime, broadcast just before midnight. The graveyard slot would continue to run erotica such as **LEMON ANGEL**, though by the late 1990s it would also be used to premier serials like **AWOL** that would formerly have gone straight to video in an attempt to amortize rising production costs.

HEROIC LEGEND OF ARSLAN *

1991. JPN: *Arslan Senki*. AKA: *Arislan; Chronicle of Arislan*. Video. DIR: Mamoru Hamatsu, Tetsuro Amino. SCR: Tomoya Miyashita, Kaori Takada. DES: Sachiko Kamimura. ANI: Kazuya Kise. MUS: Norihiro Tsuru, Yasuo Urakami. PRD: Animate Film. 60 mins. x 2 eps., 30 mins. x 4 eps.

King Andragoras of Persia (or Parthia, or Parse, or Palse) wars against the invading Lusitanian army, while his son, Arslan, gathers a band of adventurers about him, including the disgraced officer Daryoon. Andragoras is defeated with sorcerous fog and imprisoned by the enigmatic usurper Silver Mask. Meanwhile, Hermes, agent of Silver Mask, searches for the legendary sword of Ruknabard, which once belonged to Kai Hoslo, the first King of Kings. Arslan assembles an army of a hundred thousand and marches on Silver Mask, while a second party tries to stop Hermes, lest he awake the evil snake-king Zahak.

Arslan began as a series of novels by **LEGEND OF GALACTIC HEROES**–creator Yoshiki Tanaka. It was very loosely inspired by several genuine medieval Arslans, most notably the one taken hostage after leading a hundred thousand archers against Mahmud of Ghazna, and whose nephews founded the Seljuk Empire. Other models include Ali Arslan, who founded the Qarakhânid dynasty in modern-day Turkestan, and Alp Arslan, who captured the Byzantine Emperor Romanus IV at the battle of Manzikert in 1071. Tanaka's dates do not match any single historical event (even if we count by the Muslim system), but the maps in the novels are clearly based on historical Persia, stretching from contemporary Baghdad to Kashmir and bordered by the Caspian Sea and the Persian Gulf. Like Robert E. Howard's *Conan* series, *Arslan* mixes history and fantasy with impunity, with the Romanesque "Lusitanians" to the west and Rajendra's "Sind" kingdom to the east—for all the effort, Tanaka might as well have set it in the far future and be done with it, à la **ALEXANDER**. To an uneducated Japanese audience however, it all looks equally exotic, much as Western moviegoers rarely concern themselves with the difference between, say, kung fu and karate.

From its early heyday when the videos were premiered in movie theaters, the *Arslan* series soon declined. Later episodes show a fall in budget, with a different production team, simplified designs, slashed running times, low-quality animation, and the ditching of the earlier diplomacy for a simplistic quest modeled on **KING ARTHUR AND THE KNIGHTS OF THE ROUND TABLE**. The first two parts were translated in the early days of Manga Entertainment, which altered the name to *Arislan* in a futile attempt to avoid "ass" jokes. The company elected to use British voices in an unremarkable dub that nonetheless seems to have impressed a U.S. audience inured to everyone sounding like they attend the same Californian high school (see **ESCAFLOWNE**). However, the British dub takes considerable liberties with the translation, claiming that Andragoras is dead (even though he is later found to be very much alive!) and missing some lines that explain otherwise incomprehensible events. The inferior later episodes passed to Central Park Media, which released them bundled two to a tape. As with **UROTSUKIDOJI**, the different dub location led CPM to hire a completely different set of actors, as well as altering many of the already-confusing names at the request of the Japanese producers, whose whimsical spelling has been completely ignored in this encyclopedia entry. As with many other anime, *Arslan* exists chiefly to promote the novels and their manga spinoff to a Japanese audience, whose access to the textual continuations of the story leaves them less baffled than English-speakers, who are left with a cliff-hanger but little hope of a sequel.

HEY BUMBOO

1985. TV series. DIR: Eiji Okabe, Kenjiro Yoshida. SCR: Juzo Takahashi, Asami Watanabe. DES: Yu Noda. ANI: Yoichi Otabe, Sadayoshi Tominaga. MUS: Nobuyoshi Koshibe. PRD: Nippon Animation, TV Tokyo. 10 mins. x 130 eps.

The adventures of a bright yellow talking automobile who is born from an egg in an unattended vehicle factory and enlists schoolboy Ken to help him find his mother. This vehicular pastiche of **FROM THE APENNINES TO THE ANDES** features a car with an uncanny resemblance to Benny, the talking yellow cab in *Who Framed Roger Rabbit?* (1988).

HIGH SCHOOL AGENT

1988. Video. DIR: Junichi Sakata. SCR: Izo Hashimoto. DES: Takumi Tsukasa. ANI: Takumi Tsukasa. MUS: Scrap. PRD: JC Staff, Agent 21. 30 mins. x 2 eps.

Teenager Kosuke Kanemori is a secret

agent for the international "VN" spy network. Using his computer hacking skills, he tracks international criminals all the way from New York to Spain. In his second outing, he is packed off to the Arctic Circle, where Neo-Nazis are trying to raise a sunken U-boat that holds a sinister WWII secret onboard. Based on a manga by Satoshi Tanimura in *Comic Burger*, this anime foreshadows similar Bond-style adventures in SPRIG-GAN. **◑**

HIGH SCHOOL HONOR

1992. JPN: *High School Jingi*. Video. DIR: Tetsuro Amino. SCR: Keiji Michiyoshi. DES: Hisashi Abe. ANI: Hisashi Abe. MUS: N/C. PRD: JC Staff, Nippon Eizo. 50 mins.

Hiroshima gangster Seiji goes undercover in a Tokyo high school to set up a front for moving large quantities of drugs. However, he falls in love with both his attractive fellow teacher Reiko and with the city of Tokyo itself. Local Shinjuku mobsters, however, want him out of town. An adaptation of Shushi Mizuho's manga in *Young Jump* magazine. **◐◐**

HIGH SCHOOL KIMENGUMI

1985. TV series. DIR: Hiroshi Fukutomi, Shin Misawa. SCR: Takao Koyama, Shigeru Yanagawa. DES: Hikuji Kanezawa. ANI: Hikuji Kanezawa, Kenichi Chikanaga. MUS: Shunsuke Kikuchi. PRD: Studio Comet, NAS, Fuji TV. 25 mins. x 86 eps., 51 eps. (second series).

A Japanese high school is divided into rigid gangs, including Jocks, Seducers, Bad Girls, and Brains. Paramount among them is the Kimengumi, the "Strange Faces," a five-man team with punning names and strange quirks, who lord it over all the other students. Two summer-vacation episodes were also cut together and shown in theaters as a "movie" version before broadcast. The same crew returned with *Regarding Tonchinkan* (1987, *Tsuide ni Tonchin-kan*), a similar series about one particular gang deciding to play at burglary without the knowledge of their school-

mates, each masquerading at different times as the master thief Tonchinkan.

HIGH SPEED JECY

1989 AKA: *Hi-Speed Jecy*. Video. DIR: Shigenori Kageyama. SCR: Sukehiro Tomita, Shikichi Ohashi. DES: Haruhiko Mikimoto. ANI: Hidetoshi Omori, Aki-nobu Takahashi. MUS: Kei Wakakusa. PRD: Studio Pierrot. 30 mins. x 12 eps.

Jecy is an incredibly fast runner who detests all forms of violence but has vowed to avenge the deaths of his parents. He wanders the galaxy in the "living ship" Paolon, which can transform into an elderly gentleman for convenience, accompanied by the love-struck Tiana and a priest from a cult of sadists, searching all the while for the trail of the man who killed his parents. Based on a novel by Eiichiro Saito in the spirit of CRUSHER JOE, this series boasts illustrations from Haruhiko Mikimoto, who also worked as a designer on the adaptation.

HIGH STEP JUN

1985. TV series. DIR: Junichi Sato, Hiroshi Shidara, Yukio Misawa. SCR: Akiyoshi Sakai, Tadaaki Yamazaki, Shu-nichi Yukimuro. DES: Kazuo Komatsu-bara. ANI: Kazuo Komatsubara, Michi Himeno, Mitsuru Aoyama, Hirokazu Ishino. MUS: Nozomu Aoki. PRD: Toei, TV Asahi. 25 mins. x 45 eps.

Jun Nonomiya is a child prodigy who loves tinkering with machines and has even invented some robot companions for herself. But the real companion she desires is Rei ("Zero"), the class biker boy, but Yoko, another girl in her class, claims to be Rei's fiancée. Beginning in an early Sunday morning slot, this love comedy based on a manga by Yasuichi Oshima changed radically in its latter half. Thrown into a new late Wednes-day morning slot, presumably where most of its original audience wouldn't see it, it ditched the love triangle, packing Rei off to boarding school in England, and transforming into a robot comedy centered on Jun's inventions.

Anime for an older audience, once the domain of straight-to-video releases, found a new home on late-night television in the 1990s. One such show is BOOGIEPOP PHANTOM, a confusing but watchable mystery done in the style of SERIAL EXPERIMENTS LAIN. This mix of homeroom romance with demonic battles in the nighttime streets was based on a series of novels by award-winning writer Kohei Kadono and is also available in a live-action incarnation. *See entry p. 42.*

Boogiepop Phantom

© KOJHEI KADONO/MEDIAWORKS. PROJECT BOOGIEPOP.

HIKARIAN

1997. JPN: *Chotokkyu Hikarian*. AKA: *Super Express Hikarian; Hikarian: Great Railroad Protector*. TV series. DIR: Kazuyuki Hirokawa. SCR: Kazuyuki Hirokawa, Toshiki Inoue, Shunichi Yukimuro. DES: Takeshi Miyao. ANI: N/C. MUS: N/C. PRD: Tomy. 8 mins. x 153 eps.

In a bizarre cross between TRANSFORM-ERS and *Thomas the Tank Engine*, Hikari the bullet-train and his robot allies are struck by a "mysterious light" from the heavens that gives them transforming robot powers to defend Earth from the invading Bratcher Force. Broadcast as part of the children's TV show *Nori-mono Kingdom Bubu Kankan* and tied into a line of toys from Tomy, the series was also edited into 51 half-hour episodes.

HIME-CHAN'S RIBBON

1993. JPN: *Hime-chan no Ribon*. TV series. DIR: Hatsuki Tsuji, Hiroaki Saku-rai, Shinji Sakai, Tomohiro Takamoto, Masato Namiki. SCR: Takashi Yamada, Shunichi Yukimuro, Tomoko Konparu, Hiroshi Koda, Shigeru Yanagawa. DES: Hajime Watanabe. ANI: Hajime Wata-nabe, Masayuki Onchi, Yoko Konishi. MUS: N/C. PRD: Victor, TV Tokyo. 25 mins. x 61 eps.

A princess from a magical world appears before Himeko and offers her a deal. As part of her magical training, she must observe the behavior of a human girl who resembles her for a whole year. In exchange, Hime-chan (literally, "little princess") is given a magical ribbon that allows her to transform. A magical-girl story packed full of magic items, talking toys, and problem-solving resolutions in the mold of **CREAMY MAMI**, this anime was based on the 1991 *Ribbon* magazine manga by Megumi Mizusawa and actually ran longer than the original, magically defined time limit.

HIMIKO-DEN

1999. TV series. DIR: Ayumi Tomobuki. SCR: Saburo Kurimoto. DES: Yumi Manosono. ANI: Hirohito Kato. MUS: N/C. PRD: Tac. 25 mins. x 12 eps.
A Japanese teenager discovers that she is the daughter of shrine guardians from the ancient land of Yamatai, flung centuries into the future by an incident that occurred during an invasion of forces from the neighboring kingdom of Kune. Accompanied by her classmate Masahiko, she is dragged back to her original era, where they join forces with the rebels who are still holding out against the undead soldiers born of the Black Mist.

Yet another girl-transported-to-different-world/time anime, tracing its ancestry to **WIZARD OF OZ**, but with more immediate antecedents in **MAZE**, **ESCAFLOWNE** and **FUSHIGI YUGI**. However, considering that *Himiko-den* originated in a 1999 PlayStation RPG, it is remarkably coherent and well-plotted, superior to many other game-based anime. The slightly longer running time afforded by the TV airing is a considerable help, as is the effective opening animation and music. Produced by **SAKURA WARS'** Oji Hiroi.

HIPPO-KEEPER: A ZOO DIARY

1981. JPN: *Kaba-Encho: Dobutsuen Nikki*. TV special. DIR: Masayuki Akehi. SCR: Makoto Naito, Ryuzo Nakanishi. DES: Kozo Masanobu. ANI: Kozo Masanobu. MUS: Nozomu Aoki. PRD: Toei. 75 mins.
Aging zoo keeper Toshio Nishiyama acquires two young trainees: short-tempered former chef Takeshi Ishizawa and gentle vet Ichiro Hasegawa. Both are surprised by the difficulties they face in a deceptively easy job but persevere through troubles such as an escaped pelican, a dying camel, and the birth of a hippo.

A semiautobiographical series of anecdotes from real-life Tobu Animal Park zookeeper Toshio Nishiyama, who appears at the beginning and end of the film to talk about his love for animals—and to reveal that Ishizawa is in fact a projection of his own younger self. Blatant self-promotion for Nishiyama's place of employment, to be contrasted with **GOODBYE LITTLE HIPPO**, which presents a far more negative view of bad times at the rival Ueno Zoo.

HIS AND HER CIRCUMSTANCES *

1998. JPN: *Kareshi Kanojo no Jijo*. AKA: *Tales at North Hills High*. TV series. DIR: Hideaki Anno, Kazuya Tsurumaki. SCR: Hideaki Anno. DES: Tadashi Hiramatsu. ANI: N/C. MUS: Shiro Sagisu. PRD: Gainax, JC Staff, TV Tokyo. 25 mins. x 26 eps.
Yukino Miyazawa is the most popular girl at school and a permanent straight-A student, her frantic home life hidden to preserve her seemingly effortless perfection. Her classroom kingdom is invaded by a newcomer, the handsome Soichiro Arima, who competes with her for every prize and accolade. Both are appointed as class reps and forced to work together. Behind icy masks of politeness, the pair fight a private battle of wills and slowly begin to fall in love.

Based on a 1996 manga by Masami Tsuda in *Hana to Yume* magazine, *H&HC* effortlessly outclasses its lookalike U.S. cousin *Ally McBeal* in its dramatic innovation and use of surreal "cartoon" effects in a contemporary sitcom. In Japan, it owes a debt to earlier comedies of manners such as **GOLDFISH WARNING** and **REIKO SHIRATORI I PRESUME**, throwing in Greek choruses of cynical siblings, split-screens, and squashed-down cartoon versions of the lead characters. In terms of off-the-wall experimentation, it rivals the earlier **FIST OF THE NORTH STAR**—not just stop-motion and live action, but one episode features a character whose head is a photograph of a Gainax staff member, while another is animated with paper cutouts, until Yukino bursts into real flames. As with director Anno's earlier **EVANGELION**, onscreen captions and subtitles comment on the action and warp the characters' meanings, perfectly capturing the adolescent power struggles and hypocrisies of the original. A very funny satire about unlikable people who are nevertheless sympathetic characters. Though an English-language version from Right Stuf is forthcoming at time of writing, the authors doubt whether the show's chaotic onscreen action could survive translation intact. *Ill. p 243.*

HIT AND RUN

1979. JPN: *Ganbare! Bokura no Hit and Run*. AKA: *Go for It! Our Hit and Run!* TV special. DIR: Hiroe Mitsunobu. SCR: Fumi Takahashi. DES: Hikuji Kanezawa. ANI: Hikuji Kanezawa. MUS: Kensuke Kanadome. PRD: Nippon Animation, Fuji TV. 75 mins.
Baseball captain Ran leads his team to victory in another tale of athletes overcoming adversity, this one based on a manga by Hideo Aya originally serialized in *Shonen Sunday* magazine.

HOLEY PANTS: DESIRE ON A STROLL

1987. JPN: *Pants no Ana: Manbo de Ganbo!* Video. DIR: Nobuyuki Kitajima. SCR: (see below). DES: N/C. ANI: Noboru Furuse. MUS: Seiko Ito. PRD: Gahosha. 25 mins.
The ad blurb claims that this is a sweet, humorous look at teen worries, born from the real-life concerns of correspondents for *Bomb!* magazine. An excellent excuse to blame the audience if a project is unsuccessful. Since

there were no follow-ups, we can assume that the experiment was a failure. Less salacious reader input informed the successful OSHIN. Ⓝ

HOLMES THE TORTOISESHELL CAT

1992. JPN: *Mikeneko Holmes no Yurei Jochu*. AKA: *Holmes the Tortoiseshell Cat and the Haunted Castle*. Video. DIR: Nobuyuki Kitajima, Takeshi Aoki. SCR: Arii Emu. DES: Neko Shijisha. ANI: Noboru Furuse, Jun Okuda. MUS: Kentaro Haneda. PRD: AIC. 45 mins.
A tortoiseshell cat (who solves mysteries on the side) decides to question whether or not the police really have solved a murder case at a castle on an uninhabited island. Based on the bestselling novel *Holmes the Tortoiseshell Cat and the Bouquet of Flowers* by Jiro Akagawa.

HOLY THE GHOST

1991. JPN: *Obake no Hori*. TV series. DIR: Minoru Okazaki, Rikuko Yoshida, Masami Furukawa. SCR: Osamu Nakamura, Riko Hinokuma, Megumi Sugiwara, Minori Ikeno. DES: Megumi Watanabe. ANI: Noriko Imazawa. MUS: N/C. PRD: Apollon Create. 10 mins. x 25 eps.
Humorous stories about a weak-willed ghost made of chocolate, whose mild adventures take him to a birthday party, a carnival, a fight with a bullying witch, and so on. In 1992, his best adventures were released on video as the three-part *Holy the Ghost: Special*. Based on *The Cowardly Ghost*, a children's book by Megumi Watanabe.

HOMEROOM AFFAIRS *

1994. JPN: *Tanin no Kankei*. AKA: *Human Relations*. Video. DIR: Osamu Sekita. SCR: Hiroyuki Kawasaki. DES: Minoru Yamazawa. ANI: Minoru Yamazawa. MUS: Hiroyuki Takei. PRD: Jam Creation, JC Staff. 45 mins. x 2 eps.
Young minx Miyako teases older man Tokiro Ebara with views of her underwear at a train station, but both are in for a shock. She is a student at Mitsuba Girls' School, and he is her new home-

room teacher. To make matters worse, Miyako's father then asks the flustered Mr. Ebara to babysit while he is away, forcing the couple to live together. Coy soft-core high jinks ensue, as our teacher nobly resists Miyako's charms, while fantasizing about her all the time. Eventually, she points out that if they were married, they could have sex as often as they liked, and nobody would care—though it is somewhat presumptuous of her to assume that anyone does anyway. Based on the 1992 manga by Ichiro Arima published in *Young Animal* magazine, the most amusing thing about this "comedy" is the distributor's hysterical insistence, at every available occasion, that Miyako is over the age of consent. Quote of the week: "Not to be viewed by minors under 18." As opposed to what? Ⓝ

HONEY HONEY *

1981. JPN: *Honey Honey no Suteki na Boken*. AKA: *Honey Honey's Wonderful Adventure*. TV series. DIR: Takeshi Shirato, Masakazu Yasumura, Minoru Hamada. SCR: Masaki Tsuji, Shunichi Yukimuro, Tomohiro Ando. DES: Yoshiyuki Yamamoto, Kozo Masanobu. ANI: Takeshi Shirato, Akira Okuwara. MUS: Akihiro Komori. PRD: Toei, Fuji TV. 25 mins. x 29 eps.
Teenage Austrian orphan Honey is a waitress in 1907 Vienna whose pet cat, Lily, swallows Princess Florel's precious gemstone, the "Smile of the Amazon." Honey is forced to go on the run with Phoenix the gentleman jewel thief, pursued by Florel's angry suitors. Equal parts LUPIN III and THREE MUSKETEERS, the story eventually transforms into a fairy tale worthy of CINDERELLA, when Honey is revealed to be Florel's long-lost twin and marries Phoenix so they can all live happily ever after. Based on a 1966 manga by Hideko Mizuno and given a partial release on an obscure U.S. video label.

HONEY THE BUG

1986. JPN: *Bug-tte Honey*. AKA: *Honey the Bug Dance Megarom Girl 4622*. TV series, movie. DIR: Akinori Nagaoka,

Minoru Okazaki, Toshio Takeuchi, Yutaka Sato, Kanetsugu Kodama. SCR: Kasumi Oka, Hideki Sonoda, Shunichi Yukimuro, Yasushi Hirano. DES: Minoru Maeda. ANI: Takao Kasai. MUS: Hiroshi Tsutsui. PRD: TMS, Nippon TV. 25 mins. x 51 eps.
Computer-gaming prodigy Harahito Takahashi is whisked off to Game World by Honey the insect girl and her friends, who need his help in a quest that takes them through several different sectors, each suspiciously similar to several Nintendo games, including *The Adventures of Morihito Takahashi* and *Xanadu*. Fast on the heels of the theatrical success of SUPER MARIO BROTHERS, this mixture of *Tron* and *The Last Starfighter* also appeared in a movie version, *Honey the Bug: Mai the Megarom Girl 4622* (1987), featuring Leo, a scientist from Toycom World whose lover, Mai, has been brainwashed by evil forces. A rather quaint relic of the early days of product placement before the hard-sell of more recent series such as POKÉMON.

HUCKLEBERRY FINN

1976. TV series, movie. DIR: Hiroe Mitsunobu, Tameo Ogawa, Keiichi Abe. SCR: Mamoru Sasaki. DES: N/C. ANI: Eisuke Kondo, Teruhito Kamiguchi. MUS: Nobuyoshi Koshibe. PRD: Tac, Nippon Herald, Fuji TV. 25 mins. x 26 eps., 86 mins. (m), 25 mins. x 26 eps.
Huckleberry Finn and his friend Jim, a black slave, make a bid for freedom by floating down the Mississippi River on a raft. Huck is faced with the perilous choice of damnation or saving his friend, choosing friendship. This WORLD MASTERPIECE THEATER adaptation of Mark Twain's 1885 sequel to TOM SAWYER was cut into an 86-minute "movie" version in 1991. A second TV version, *The Story of Huckleberry* (*Huckleberry Monogatari*), was made by Norio Kabeshima for Enoki Films and an NHK satellite channel in 1994.

HUMANE SOCIETY

1992. JPN: *Humane Society: Jinrui Ai ni Mochita no Shakai*. AKA: *Humane Soci-*

ety: A Society in Which Humanity Is Loving. Video. DIR: Jun Kamiya. SCR: Mayori Sekijima, from an idea by Demon Kogure. DES: Kazuya Yokose. ANI: Kazuya Yokose. MUS: Kaimono Matsuzaki-sama. PRD: Animate Film. 57 mins.

In an anime adventure featuring one of Japan's most eccentric pop groups as themselves, the five members of the rock band Seikima-II must save the world from the demonic forces of the Tower of Babel. Claiming to be demons from the other side of the universe, the KISS-lookalikes announced that the apocalypse was coming in 1999 and that ownership of a ticket stub from one of their "Black Masses" would entitle the holder to salvation. Despite a slightly incoherent message (as in **DEVILMAN**, how were demons supposed to save us from Satan?), Seikima-II gained many fans, particularly among young Office Ladies who thought they were cute, with some of their best songs including "Pinky Dinosaur," "Frightful Restaurant," and "Stainless Night" (the latter used in a **BEAST WARRIORS** spinoff CD). They also sang themes to **WANNA-BE'S**, **MAZE**, and one of the **CONAN THE BOY DETECTIVE** movies, while lead singer Demon Kogure was the voice of Munchausen in **UROTSUKIDOJI**. The band's apocalyptic message became more subdued as the 1990s wore on, and they played a farewell concert on New Year's Eve 1999. The music in *Humane Society* is credited to their producer and sometime keyboardist, but it's derived from many of their most famous songs, including "Rosa," the name of their evil adversary.

HUMANOID, THE *

1986. Video. DIR: Shinichi Masaki. SCR: Koichi Minade. DES: Hajime Sorayama, Jinpei Kohara. ANI: Takuya Wada, Osamu Kamijo. MUS: Masao Nakajima. PRD: Toshiba EMI, Hero Media. 45 mins.

A truly awful *Star Wars* rip-off, written solely to showcase the "Sexy Robot" art style of illustrator Hajime Sorayama.

After a crash-landing, two hotshot pilots seek help from Professor Watson, unaware that they are stumbling into an evil man's attempt to rule the world. Pilot Eric falls for the android Antoinette, who sacrifices herself to save him, but only after pathologically obsessive dialogue about coffee, a couple of chase scenes, and painfully geeky flirtation. A dire reprise of Tezuka's **SPACE FIREBIRD** or an amateurish rehearsal for the infinitely superior **ARMITAGE III**, however you look at it, it is a sure contender for one of the worst anime ever made. Also shown theatrically in Japan as part of a triple bill.

HUMMINGBIRDS *

1993. JPN: Idol Boetai Hummingbird. AKA: Idol Defense Band Hummingbird. Video. DIR: Kiyoshi Murayama. SCR: Kiyoshi Murayama. DES: Masahide Yanasawa. ANI: Kenichi Katsura. MUS: Kazuo Otani. PRD: Youmex. 50 mins. x 1 ep., 30 mins. x 3 eps.

Starstruck mother Hazuki Toriishi pushes her five daughters into careers as pop idols in a Japan "the day after tomorrow" that has privatized the armed forces. With only media companies having the finances to invest, the air force has become an entertainment industry, as prefabricated pop groups sing songs and fly jets in bizarre competitions, occasionally breaking off to defend the country from foreign invaders.

A silly spoof of the media from **IRRESPONSIBLE CAPTAIN TYLOR**–creator Hitoshi Yoshioka, combining the siblings and super-vehicles of *Thunderbirds*, from whose Tracy family the Toriishis get their name (see **THUNDERBIRDS 2086**), with pop-song interludes in the style of **MACROSS** to promote the singing careers of the five lead voice actresses. Though the quality of the songs never declined, later episodes lost their satirical edge, with middle sister Satsuki developing a crush on her trainer and competing against the feisty foreign Fever Girls, in a predictable run-through of clichés from sports anime.

The first two volumes were released in the U.K. by Western Connection with rhyming song subtitles. However, they were clumsily cut together in order to avoid paying the BBFC classification authority for two separate releases. The British version is consequently missing two songs and any proper credits—its short "closing credits" actually being the *opening* credits from episode two. The series was never released in the U.S.

HUNDREDTH MONKEY, THE

1986. JPN: Hyakubanme no Saru. Movie. DIR: Kazuo Anzai. SCR: Masaaki Sakurai. DES: Shingo Ozaki. ANI: Shingo Ozaki. MUS: Yuki Takamura. PRD: Tokyo Media Communications, Cinework. 20 mins.

A short cartoon of the 1981 book of the same name by new-age guru Ken Keyes, Jr., based on the story of a 1952 experiment on the southern Japanese island of Kojima. Once one monkey has learned how to wash its food, it is able to teach others the same skill. When a certain number have learned (and Keyes suggests an arbitrary figure of 100), not only do the remaining monkeys suddenly appear to know how to do it, but so too does a completely different group of apes on a completely separate island. Keyes uses this apocryphal tale as a parable for the antinuclear movement, as "proof" that change would come if enough people joined forces. The story has a triple appeal to the Japanese: not only is it "local," it is also antinuclear in the tradition of **BAREFOOT GEN**, and, best of all, copyright-free in accordance with Keyes's wish for it to reach as many people as possible.

HUNTER X HUNTER

1999. TV series. DIR: Kazuhiro Furuhashi. SCR: Nobuaki Kishima. DES: Yoshihiro Togashi. ANI: Masaaki Kawanami. MUS: Toshihiko Sato. PRD: Nippon Animation, Fuji TV. 25 mins. x 61+ eps.

Twelve-year-old orphan Gon lives on Whale Island with his Aunt Mito. A chance forest meeting with Kyte the Hunter reveals that his father is actually still alive and is known throughout the world as the greatest hunter who ever lived. Gon decides to be just like his dad (the all-purpose job description encompassing monster-killing, bounty-taking, treasure-troving, and tomb-raiding), setting off to take the tests of manhood. In this anime based on a manga by **POLTERGEIST REPORT**–creator Yoshihiro Togashi, however, only one in ten thousand makes it through the tough trials.

HURRICANE POLYMAR *

1974. JPN: *Hariken Polymar*. AKA: *Inner Destruction Fist Polymar*. TV series, video. DIR: Eiko Toriumi, Hideo Nishimaki, Yoshiyuki Tomino. SCR: Junzo Toriumi, Akiyoshi Sakai, Masaru Yamamoto, Junichi Shima. DES: Tatsuo Yoshida. ANI: Tsuneo Ninomiya. MUS: Shunsuke Kikuchi. PRD: Tatsunoko, NET. 25 mins. x 26 eps., 30 mins. x 2 eps.

Mild-mannered police chief Takeshi works for the International Crime Division in Washinkyo City (Washington + Tokyo). One night, he is set upon by four thugs and, despite being an expert at karate, is severely injured. In a replay of **8TH MAN**, kindly Professor Oregar gives him the Polymar suit, an experimental project that could save his life. Takeshi becomes a super-cop with a voice-activated suit that fits him like a second skin but can also transform into a plane, a boat, a submarine, and a tank.

A lighthearted and popular superhero show that rode the wave of interest in Bruce Lee and martial arts, with time out for a few in-jokes at the expense of the same studio's earlier **BATTLE OF THE PLANETS**, the series was remade by Akiyuki Shinbo as *New HP* (1996), which is the version available in the U.S. Tatsunoko's remake simplified the original somewhat, moving the action to the man-made island of Tokyo Plus, where Oregar's lab is attacked by the Catshark Squad. The professor is killed, but his beautiful

assistant, Ryoko, manages to get the prototype Polymar Helmet to detective Takeshi before her own death.

HUSTLE PUNCH

1965. TV series. DIR: Hiroshi Ikeda, Kazuya Miyazaki, Hiroshi Shidara. SCR: Hiroshi Ikeda, Hiroaki Hayashi. DES: Yasuji Mori. ANI: Yasuji Mori. MUS: Tsuguhoshi Kobayashi. PRD: Toei, NET. 25 mins. x 26 eps.

Three orphaned animals, Punch the Bear, Touch the Mouse, and Bun the Weasel, try to live a carefree life in a seaside town despite the efforts of their evil enemies, the lupine Professor Garigari and his hench-creatures, Black the Cat and Nu the Pig. Based on a manga in *Manga-O* by prolific animator Yasuji Mori.

HUTCH THE HONEYBEE

1970. JPN: *Mitsubachi Monogatari: Minashigo Hutch*. AKA: *Bee Story: Hutch the Orphan*. TV series. DIR: Ippei Kuri, Seitaro Hara. SCR: Junzo Toriumi, Saburo Taki, Masaaki Yoshida. DES: Tatsuo Yoshida. ANI: Eiji Tanaka. MUS: Nobuyoshi Koshibe. PRD: Tatsunoko, Fuji TV. 25 mins. x 91 eps., 25 mins. x 26 eps., 25 mins. x 55 eps.

Life in the peaceful Bee Kingdom is disrupted by an invasion of wasps, who destroy the eggs and force the queen to flee with her subjects. A single remaining egg hatches, and young Hutch grows up in an environment where his bee-like looks lead to bullying and persecution. In a mixture of **FROM THE APENNINES TO THE ANDES** with the "Ugly Duckling" from the **TALES OF HANS CHRISTIAN ANDERSEN,** Hutch realizes he is really a bee and sets off with his insect companions to find others of his race. This award-winning tale of a bug's life was so successful that it returned for a second series, *New Hutch* (1974), featuring new designs from the Tatsunoko studio's teenage prodigy, Yoshitaka Amano. For the sequel, the wasps return, and Hutch and his sister are exiled and hear that their mother has perished. With nowhere else to go, they search

An early Hayao Miyazaki. *See entry p. 130.*

Future Boy Conan

© NIPPON ANIMATION CO., LTD. 1978

for a mythical "Beautiful Hill," along with insect companions including a firefly, butterflies, and a ladybug. In 1989, the story was completely remade for Tatsunoko by Akira Suzuki using many of the original scripts from the 1970 version but with all-new animation.

HYAKUTARO

1991. JPN: *Ushiro no Hyakutaro*. AKA: *Hyakutaro by My Side*. Video. DIR: Seitaro Hara. SCR: Jiro Tsunoda, Isao Shizudani, Masaaki Sakurai. DES: Koji Uemura. ANI: Seiji Kikuchi. MUS: Hiro Tsunoda. PRD: Pierrot Project. 50 mins. x 2 eps.

Occult researcher's son Kazutaro Ushiro and his guardian spirit, Hyakutaro, investigate paranormal activity. Based on the 1973 manga in *Shonen Magazine* by **FRIGHTFUL NEWS**–creator Jiro Tsunoda, this anime is said to be the indirect inspiration for most of the ghostbusting genre, from **PHANTOM QUEST CORP** to **POLTERGEIST REPORT**.

HYPER POLICE

1997. TV series. DIR: Masahiro Omori, Shinya Sadamitsu, Koichi Chiaki. SCR: Sukehiro Tomita, Shigeru Yanagawa. DES: Keiji Goto. ANI: Keiji Goto, Yoshiyuki Kobe, Kazumi Ikeda. MUS: N/C. PRD:

Studio Pierrot, TV Tokyo. 25 mins. x 25 eps.

Natsuki Sasahara is a human-feline cross-breed, her associate Sakura is an eight-tailed fox-girl (a sure sign she cannot be trusted, since she needs to swindle Natsuki to gain her ninth tail), and both use their magical powers to hunt criminals in a Tokyo crawling with animal hybrids, ghosts, and goblins. Other major cast members are Batanen Fujioka, Natsuki's lycanthrope senior, canine patrolman Tommy, and the two flustered humans: station-chief Mudagami and (initially) beast-hating patrolwoman Naoko Kondo. As befits ensemble cop shows like PATLABOR and YOU'RE UNDER ARREST!, downtime is as important to the show as crime-fighting, and the cast spends an inordinate amount of time at Makoto and Ayami Tachibana's friendly Ranpo Coffee Shop. *HP* has the supernatural urban feel of SILENT MÖBIUS, but it's played for laughs and features a considerable dose of anthropomorphic titillation. Based on a manga by "MEE," who also created ADVENTURE OF KOTETSU. Ⓝ

HYPERDOLL *

1995. JPN: *Rakusho Hyperdoll*. AKA: *Happy Victory Hyperdoll; Hyper-Doll: Mew and Mica the Easy Fighters.* Video. DIR: Makoto Moriwaki. SCR: Ryo Motohira. DES: Satoru Nakamura. ANI: Satoru Nakamura. MUS: Hiroshi Nakano, Masayuki Negishi. PRD: Pioneer, AIC. 40 mins. x 2 eps.

Mica (the cool, sensible one) and Mew (the hotheaded, impulsive one) are two beautiful aliens sent to defend Earth from monsters. Disguised as typical Japanese high-school girls, they befriend Earth girl Shoko and hapless boy Hideo, taking time off (when their boss tracks them down) to fight alien invaders with the aid of an orbiting power converter that harnesses the energy of "zero-space" and beams it to them via their earrings. Unfairly termed "hyperdull" in fandom, this lighthearted superhero comedy features high-quality animation, a good dub, and spoofs of monster shows stretching back to ULTRAMAN, though its dim-witted girls in skimpy costumes accidentally causing massive collateral damage owe a further debt to the DIRTY PAIR. There are also bonus live-action sections in which the petrified voice actresses stammer their way through some minor comedy business, demonstrating why so many Japanese scripts are better performed as anime. Based on a manga from *Shonen Captain* by Shinpei Ito, who also wrote the manga adaptation of MOLDIVER. The live-action sections were written and directed by the Konaka brothers, ARMITAGE III's Chiaki and BLACK JACK's Kazuya.

I

I AM A CAT

1982. JPN: *Wagahai wa Neko de Aru*. TV special. DIR: Rintaro. SCR: Kiyohide Obara. DES: Kazuo Komatsubara, Haruki Yoshimi. ANI: Kazuo Komatsubara. MUS: Antonio Vivaldi. PRD: Toei, Fuji TV. 73 mins.

"I" is a cat without a name who lives with an English teacher, Mr. Kushami (Mr. Sneeze). "I" can't believe how stupid human beings are and chronicles some of their more incredible foibles. In particular, he is fascinated by Kushami's pupil Mizushima, who falls in love with Haruko, only daughter of war profiteer Kaneda. Based on the 1905 novel by **BOTCHAN**-author Soseki Natsume, this adaptation gained a huge 27.8% rating when broadcast. The feline character designs were by **JARINKO CHIE**'s Haruki Yoshimi.

I AM A DOG

1983. JPN: *Wagahai wa Inu de Aru: Don Matsugoro no Monogatari*. AKA: *I Am a Dog: The Story of Don Matsugoro*. TV special. DIR: Kimio Yabuki. SCR: Kiyohide Obara. DES: Haruki Yoshimi. ANI: Takashi Abe. MUS: Hiroki Takaragi. PRD: Toei, Fuji TV. 73 mins.

Mr. Matsuzawa is a novelist who lives in Chiba Prefecture. Only his daughter Kazuko knows that the family dog, Don Matsugoro, can talk. Don is wounded in a fight with the neighbors' dog, King, a nouveau-riche mongrel with ideas above his station. At the vet, however, he falls in love with a little patchwork puppy called Chotaro. A less successful follow-up to the previous year's **I AM A CAT**; some of the same team from that show adapted Hisashi Inoue's novel *The Life of Don Matsugoro*,

changing the title to imply a connection that simply wasn't there.

I DREAM OF MIMI *

1997. JPN: *Buttobi CPU*. Video. DIR: Masamitsu Hidaka. SCR: Atsuhiro Tomioka. DES: Yuriko Senba. ANI: Yuriko Senba. MUS: N/C. PRD: Pink Pineapple, KSS. 30 mins. x 3 eps.

In this erotic comedy based on the *Young Animal* strip from **AREA 88**–creator Kaoru Shintani, a hapless boy finds himself in possession of Mimi, a new model of "sexy computer." Biocomputer Mimi must fend off romantic rivals such as the Nac sisters and the superpowered Performa Girl, while her man Akira looks on shyly like the hero of **HANDMAID MAY**, **METAL ANGEL MARIE**, and any number of similar geek-meets-love-toy shows. **Ⓝ**

I GIVE MY ALL

1987. JPN: *Minna Agechau*. AKA: *I'll Do It with Anyone; Everybody's Doing It*. Video. DIR: Osamu Uemura. SCR: Yutaka Takahashi. DES: Takumi Tsukasa. ANI: Takafumi Hayashi. MUS: Hiromoto Tobisawa. PRD: Animate Film, JC Staff. 45 mins.

Mutsuro has been forced to take a "ronin" year off to study for retaking his university entrance exams. Resorting to self-abuse in his lonely room, he attracts the attentions of lonely neighbor Yuno, the bored daughter of a rich corporate magnate. The two are soon in bed together, though Yuno's interfering grandmother decides that she should make an honest man out of Mutsuro and give him a job in Daddy's company. Based on the 1982 manga by Hikari Yuzuki, serialized in *Young Jump*,

this well-animated soft-core story premiered on a double bill with **DIGITAL DEVIL STORY**. **Ⓝ**

I LIKE THE NANIWABUSHI

1982. JPN: *Naniwabushi Daisuki*. TV series. DIR: Takashi Sawada. SCR: Kiyohiro Yamamoto. DES: N/C. ANI: Norio Takahashi. MUS: N/C. PRD: Kansai TV, Tohan Planning, Fuji TV. 54 mins.

Two stories that mix animation with *naniwabushi* (storytelling accompanied by shamisen playing). One is a tale of General Nogi, the famous suicide, visiting the shrines at Ise on his way to Nagoya, while his wife is mistaken for a commoner as she books into a hotel. The second story is of a sumo wrestling trainee, ridiculed by his fellows, who trains hard and avenges himself—the standard clichés of a sports anime, just with plink-plonky music on top of it.

I SAW THE LAZYBONES

1988. JPN: *Namakemono o Miteta*. Video. DIR: Akinori Nagaoka, Masami Furukawa. SCR: Takashi Murakami. DES: Takashi Murakami. ANI: Kinichiro Suzuki. MUS: N/C. PRD: Toei, Agent 21. 30 mins. x 2 eps.

In this short comedy based on a gag manga by Takashi Murakami originally serialized in *Young Jump*, a koala robs a bank to help poverty-stricken pandas. Listed as a "movie" in some Japanese sources, even though the package clearly states "original video anime."

I WISH YOU WERE HERE

2001. TV series. DIR: Seiji Mizushima. SCR: Natsuko Takahashi. DES: Yasuhiro Oshima. ANI: Yasuhiro Oshima, Yasufumi Soejima. MUS: N/C. PRD: Gonzo. 25 mins. x 4 eps.

In May 2002, a terrorist group sets off a gas explosion in Atlanta, Georgia. It is the first of many incidents across the U.S., though the perpetrators' motives are a mystery. Only unclear photographs of (surprise, surprise) a "mysterious girl" provide any clue. They seem to be linked in some way to Project I, a top secret operation by an international collective of scientists, who are rumored to be working on a "Multipurpose Operative Being" experiment in sentient cybernetics. A mixture of conspiracies and espionage from Gonzo, combining CG elements of the studio's earlier BLUE SUBMARINE NO. SIX with the identity crisis of SERIAL EXPERIMENTS LAIN.

ICZER-ONE *

1985. JPN: Tatakae! Iczer-1; Boken! Iczer-3; Iczer Gal Iczelion. AKA: Fight! Iczer-1; Adventure! Iczer-3; Iczelion; Iczer Saga. Video. DIR: Toshihiro Hirano, Hideaki Hisashi. SCR: Toshihiro Hirano, Arii Emu ("REM"). DES: Toshihiro Hirano, Chuichi Watanabe, Masanori Nishii, Hiroaki Motoigi, Shinji Aramaki, Yasuhiro Moriki, Takashi Hashimoto. ANI: Narumi Kakinouchi, Masami Obari, Hiroaki Ogami, Masanori Nishii, Takafumi Hashimoto. MUS: Michiaki Watanabe, Takashi Kudo. PRD: AIC, KSS, 30 mins. x 2 eps., 48 mins., 60 mins. x 3 eps., 30 mins. x 2 eps.

An alien ship carrying the survivors of the Cthulhu, a race of female clones, is taken over by the sinister entity Big Gold and heads for Earth. The Cthulhu (hastily and ineptly disguised as "Cutowolf" in early Western publicity to avoid copyright problems) seek a new home, and with Big Gold's malign energy driving them, they decide that Earth will suit them nicely once they kick out the current occupants. One of the Cthulhu, Iczer-One, is willing to fight for Earth but must link up with the right human to help her power her mighty fighting machine, Iczer-Robo. The "right human" is Nagisa Kano, an ordinary Japanese schoolgirl who is so

terrified by seeing her parents transformed into alien monsters and her world falling to pieces around her that she can do very little apart from quake in terror. Only when she unleashes the full force of her anger can she power the huge robot, but then she and Iczer-One are an unstoppable combination. The Cthulhu call on all their powers to warp dimensions, transform familiar objects and places into nightmarish threats, and send in gross, drooling monsters. At last, they even throw in Iczer-One's nasty red-haired clone sister, Iczer-Two; but they can't win against the love and trust between Nagisa and Iczer-One, since both are willing to make the ultimate sacrifice to save Earth.

Hirano's dark, dank otherworld was based on a story by Rei Aran, with nightmarish references to the work of H. P. Lovecraft (see ARMITAGE III). However, nameless terrors are hampered by the fact that the "unimaginable," once animated, looks merely nasty, but Watanabe's monsters are as well crafted as Aramaki's fabulous robots. The script is loaded with homoerotic subtexts and sexualized cruelty, all the more effective for being less than completely explicit. Nagisa's helpless terror is an understandable reaction to an extreme situation, rather than being an annoying character trait played up by writer and actress in the mistaken belief that helplessness is cute, and Iczer-One is the ideal heroine—brave, understanding, and determined. A shameless steal from the ending of Superman II doesn't jibe but makes for a rather touching finale in which Nagisa, having given her all to save the world, is rewarded by getting her old life back and forgetting everything else, including the friend who would have died to save her.

Hirano returned to the concept with Iczer-3 (1990), toning down the violence but keeping the fan-service nudity. Big Gold was defeated but left many of her progeny still at large in the galaxy. Iczer-One has tracked them down and destroyed all but one, Neos

Gold. After a terrible battle, both are wounded and agree to a truce to heal, after which they'll settle things with a final fight. As Iczer-One withdraws to recoup her strength, Neos Gold cheats by sending her cohorts to soften up Earth for her attack, so the Cthulhu send prepubescent Iczer-3 to defend the planet until "big sister" recovers. With a descendant of Nagisa Kano and the crew of an Earth battle cruiser, Iczer-3 attempts to hold off the enemy with the Power of Cute. A helium-powered performance from wrestler Cuty Suzuki in the leading role took what had been a tale of nameless horrors into the realms of high camp, grounded by the reappearance of the two older Iczer clones for the final battle.

Hirano reworked the concept again as an armored-girl-team show in the manner of BUBBLEGUM CRISIS, first as a manga and then for the two-part video Iczelion (1994). For this resurrection, production moved to KSS, with Hashimoto and Masanori Nishii joining Hirano for design work. Nagisa Kai is an ordinary teenager until fate intervenes and makes her the chosen combat partner of an intelligent battlesuit. Iczel robots, useful entities in their own right, become Iczelion battlesuits when "fused" with their girl operatives in a nude transformation sequence. Together with three other young women, Nagisa must save Earth from subjugation by an invading alien army headed by Chaos and Cross, who have so far swept across the galaxy defeating all in their path. At first Nagisa is too terrified to fight and even separates from her Iczel in an attempt to escape, but when her friends at school are threatened, she decides she must save them. Once more, affection between girls wins the day, though the explicit lesbian overtones of the first series have been edged into the background. The two later incarnations lack the dark power of the first, moving the original concept in less adventurous directions, but the series remains a firm favorite with older fans. **LNV**

IDOL ANGEL WELCOME YOKO

1990. JPN: *Idol Tenshi Yokoso Yoko.* AKA: *Hello Yoko.* TV series. DIR: Tetsuro Amino. SCR: Takeshi Shudo. DES: Studio Live. ANI: Sanae Kobayashi. MUS: Hideyuki Tanaka. PRD: TSC, Quest, Ashi Pro, TV Tokyo. 25 mins. x 43 eps.
A unique addition to the magical-girl genre of CREAMY MAMI and its ilk, in which real-life idol Yoko Tanaka, along with her anime alter ego (also called Yoko Tanaka, but with different Chinese characters spelling out the name), must solve problems and get to the concerts on time.

IDOL FIGHT SWEETYPIE II

1996. Video. DIR: Yasunori Ide. SCR: Yasunori Ide. DES: Kenichi Sonoda, Yoshiko Sakurai. ANI: Kunihiro Abe. MUS: N/C. PRD: Darts, Domu. 30 mins.
All Sweetypie has to do is wave her Sweetystick, and she turns into an avenging angel of love and justice. And with bondage-freak Cherrypie, alien superhero Milkypie ("Milky Change!"), emissary from Peachyland, Peachypie, and cyborg warrior Lemonpie ("Lemonade Transfer!"), you can bet that the streets are safe. One of many computer-game spinoffs (such as GRADUATION or BATTLE TEAM LAKERS EX) that, perhaps wisely, dumped the gameplay and merely reassigned the characters to a more interesting situation. In this case, the stars of an obscure strip computer game, notable only for designs by GUNSMITH CATS' Kenichi Sonoda, are reassigned roles in a spoof of SAILOR MOON. As with the STREET FIGHTER II franchise, there was no *Sweetypie "I"* in anime form, a fact lampooned in the show's subtitle: "Somehow this feels like the first episode."

IDOL OF DARKNESS *

1997. JPN: *Inju Nerawareta Idol.* Video. DIR: Susumu Aran. SCR: N/C. DES: N/C. ANI: Lion Ginan. MUS: N/C. PRD: Pink Pineapple. 45 mins.
Lesbian goings-on as famous idol singer Rie initiates newcomer Ikumi in the pleasures of the flesh, much to the annoyance of her boyfriend, who always suspected the media was a corrupt world. Soon, onstage jealousies lead to the activation of a cursed wooden idol, which leads to more sex.

IDOL PROJECT

1995. Video. DIR: Yasushi Nagaoka. SCR: Toshimitsu Amano. DES: Noritaka Suzuki. ANI: Masahiko Murata. MUS: Kanji Saito. PRD: KSS. 30 mins. x 4 eps.
Fourteen-year-old Mimu Emilton wants to be an idol singer and applies for the Starland Festival, where the people's next idol will be chosen. Inspired by her hologram pendant, which carries a pep talk from the last idol, Mimu learns from a number of other aspirants the various secrets of being an idol, including the power of a smile and the value of dance. A silly, perky anime based on a computer game in which the player's job was to become the top idol singer.

IF WE MEET IN DREAMS

1998. JPN: *Yume de Aetara.* Video. DIR: Hiroshi Watanabe. SCR: Noriyuki Yamahana. DES: Hiroshi Watanabe. ANI: Hiroshi Watanabe. MUS: N/C. PRD: JC Staff. 30 mins. x 3 eps.
Twenty-four-year-old Masuo has never really talked to a girl, until the fateful day he meets the pretty Nagisa. As he begins a faltering attempt at seduction, illness finds him in a hospital bed on Christmas Eve, the traditional time for shy Japanese boys to pop the question. Nagisa makes it easier for him by visiting and staying till he confesses his love. Based on Noriyuki Yamahana's manga, serialized in *Business Jump.*

IGANO KABAMARU

1983. TV series. DIR: Tameo Ogawa, Akinori Nagaoka, Tsutomu Shibayama, Keiji Hayakawa, Naoto Hashimoto. SCR: Tokio Tsuchiya, Rei Akimoto, Shigeru Yanagawa, Tomomi Tsutsui. Hirokazu Kobayashi. DES: Akio Hosoya. ANI: Akio Hosoya, Kaworu Hirata, Keiko Yoshimoto. MUS: Toshiyuki Omori. PRD: Tohoku, NTV. 25 mins. x 24 eps.
Kabamaru is a new boy at high school, who cannot reveal to anyone that he is really the scion of an infamous ninja clan. He helps the kindly Mrs. Okubo, falls in love with her granddaughter, and is forced against his will to use his ninja skills in struggles against other schools, and his own corrupt principal. Yu Azuki, creator of AKANUKE ICHIBAN, wrote this 1983 manga for *Margaret* magazine as a spoof of Mitsuteru Yokoyama's 1961 ninja story *Kagemaru the Ninja* (*Iga no Kagemaru*).

IKENAI BOY

1990. AKA: *The Boy Who Couldn't.* Video. DIR: Hiroshi Uchida. SCR: Satoichi Moriyasu. DES: Toshio Takahashi. ANI: Toshio Takahashi. MUS: N/C. PRD: JC Staff. 50 mins. x 2 eps.
College boy Shinichi Kamigawa moonlights as the master masseur Doctor K, popular with many young women all around Tokyo for his sexily soothing hands. This anime was based on Yoshihiro Suma's erotic manga in *Business Jump* and features a live-action epilogue from real-life adult video star Ayami Kida, in a futile attempt to make up for the low quality of the rest of the production.

IKKIMAN

1986. JPN: *Hagane Q Choji Ikkiman.*

Five years after the big-budget anime movie STREET FIGHTER II, its sequel went straight to video. The anime business was kept afloat by gaming money during the 1990s, though creators had varying levels of success in their attempts to turn the simple conflicts of beat-'em-ups into a coherent plot. All too often, the result is a half-hearted sermon about martial arts mysticism. *See entry p. 381.*

Street Fighter Alpha

AKA: *Steel Q Armored Child Ikkiman*. TV series. DIR: Nobutaka Nishizawa. SCR: Haruya Yamazaki, Kenji Terada, Yoshiyuki Suga. DES: Takashi Saijo. ANI: Masahiko Imai, Michio Shindo. MUS: Seiji Yokoyama. PRD: Toei, NTV. 25 mins. x 32 eps.

A bizarre combination of sports anime and martial arts, as Ikki leaves behind the woman who broke his heart in Hokkaido, and comes to 21st-century Tokyo to seek his fortune at the violent baseball-fighting game Battle Ball. Gate-crashing a game between the Terran team, Blue Planets, and the off-world team, Satano Blackies, he steps up to bat and is soon the star player. Based on a manga by Yasuo Tanami and Kazuo Takahashi, serialized in *Shonen Magazine*, among others.

IKKYU

1975. JPN: *Ikkyu-san*. TV series. DIR: Kimio Yabuki, Tetsuo Imazawa, Hideo Furusawa, Shinya Miyazaki. SCR: Masaki Tsuji, Satoshi Ishida, Tajio Tamura, Keisuke Fujikawa, Tomoko Konparu, Hiroshi Yamaura, Tomomi Tsutsui. DES: Hiroshi Wagatsuma. ANI: Yasu Ishiguro, Shinya Miyazaki, Takeshi Shirato. MUS: Seiichiro Uno. PRD: TV Asahi, Toei. 25 mins. x 296 eps.

After the Ashikaga shogun unifies Japan, the emperor's son Sengikumaru is sent to the Yasukuni Shrine by family politics—his maternal grandfather opposed the Ashikaga in the conflict. Shaving his head and changing his name to Ikkyu, he tries to live as a good monk, though taking any opportunity he can to outwit the greedy merchant Kikyoya, his daughter Yayoi, and even Yoshimitsu Ashikaga himself.

The series received a very limited partial broadcast, as *Ikkyu the Little Monk*, on U.S. local TV for the Japanese community, with English subtitles. The character had two short theatrical outings: *Ikkyu and Princess Yancha* (1978), in which Ikkyu must talk a tomboy into behaving in a more ladylike manner before her habit of calling herself by the boy's name Tsuyumaru and attacking shogun Yoshimitsu

Ashikaga with a wooden sword gets her into trouble. This was followed by *Ikkyu: It's Spring!* (1981), in which further feudal fun ensued.

An unrelated 26-episode series, *Ikkyu-san* (1978), was a baseball drama on the rival Fuji TV directed by Toshifumi Takizawa, based on a STAR OF THE GIANTS–influenced manga by Shinji Mizushima.

I'M GONNA BE AN ANGEL *

1999. JPN: *Tenshi ni Naru Mon*. AKA: *Let Me Be an Angel; Make Me an Angel*. TV series. DIR: Hiroshi Nishikori. SCR: Mamiko Ikeda, Masashi Sogo. DES: Hiromi Kato. ANI: Hiromi Kato. MUS: Yoshikazu Suo. PRD: Studio Pierrot, TV Tokyo. 25 mins. x 26 eps.

As is the way with so many anime children, Yusuke's father goes away on business and leaves him at home alone (there is no sign of his mother). En route to school, he lands on top of a naked girl with a halo. The "accidental kiss" she receives makes him her husband in her eyes—for similar inadvertent betrothals see URUSEI YATSURA and PHOTON. Yusuke runs a mile but is shocked to discover that his new "wife" Noelle is a new transfer student at his school. Unable to shake her off, he gains a new extended family of supernatural creatures, including a father modeled on FRANKENSTEIN, vampiric elder brother Gabriel, dark-elf sister Ruka, and invisible older sister Sara. The grandmother matriarch, even more opposed to the marriage than Yusuke himself, tries to oppose his presence, though since they have moved into and converted his own house into a supernatural dwelling, this is not so easy. Meanwhile, Noelle is at the center of another anime love polygon with Despair, who wants her for himself, Yusuke, still lusting after girl-next-door Natsume, and the enigmatic Michael, whose book of dreams writes the closure of each episode. A hyper-cute, hyper-silly TV series that crashes together innumerable clichés of unwelcome-guest and magical-girlfriend shows, along with the traditions

of school dramas and a brighter, breezier rip-off of the *Addams Family*.

I'M TEPPEI

1977. TV series. DIR: Tadao Nagahama, Shigetsugu Yoshida, Yoshifumi Kondo, Hiroshi Fukutomi, Tsutomu Shibayama. SCR: Seiji Matsuoka, Shunichi Yukimuro, Soji Yoshikawa, Hirokazu Mizude. DES: Tetsuya Chiba. ANI: Daikichiro Kusunobe. MUS: Michiaki Watanabe. PRD: Shinei, Nippon Animation, Fuji TV. 25 mins. x 28 eps.

Fortune hunters Hiromi Uesugi and his son Teppei are arrested for damaging a field in the Shinshu mountains, though they claim they are only following the directions to buried treasure from an ancient map. Teppei blows up the police station to aid his father's escape, and the case reaches the local newspaper, where it is read by estranged members of the Uesugi clan. The prodigal clan-members return, and Teppei, who has grown up in the wild in the company of animals and his semicivilized father, has trouble adjusting to the genteel culture of the Rin Academy school where he is sent.

Based on a 1973 manga in *Shonen Magazine* by TOMORROW'S JOE–creator Tetsuya Chiba, *I'm Teppei* was soon taken off the air due to low ratings, despite featuring storyboards from future WHISPER OF THE HEART–director Yoshifumi Kondo.

IMMA YOJO: EROTIC TEMPTRESS *

1994. JPN: *Inma Yojo*. AKA: *Lust-Beast Fairies*. Video. DIR: Yukiyoshi Makino. SCR: Tsukasa Tomii. DES: Kazushi Iwakura. ANI: Kazushi Iwakura. MUS: Takeo Nakazawa. PRD: Pink Pineapple, KSS. 45 mins. x 5 eps.

Witchery and bondage as Maya wanders a fantasy landscape inhabited by depraved rapists. She enters a town where the ruling tyrant dwells in a "tower of pleasures" and sends out young ruffians to procure women, whose juices he requires in the manufacture of a dangerous drug. Before long, Maya is captured and abused by a gang of men before leaving to experience several more episodes of assault, including one at the hands of robot women, the seduction of an unsuspecting knight, and even a retelling of one of the oldest JAPANESE FOLK TALES, as two witches lure passers-by to their deaths on a haunted mountain pass. Not to be confused with the COOL DEVICES story *Slave Warrior Maya,* or indeed with ROSE OF VERSAILLES, with which it shares some lookalike characters and costumes, though the costumes don't stay on for long. ✪✪✪

IMMORALITY WARS

1998. JPN: *Inju Dai Kessen.* AKA: *Lust-Beast Great Battle.* Video. DIR: Iwao Zumen, Tai Kikumoto. SCR: Atsuhito Sugita. DES: Shimendoji. ANI: N/C. MUS: N/C. PRD: KSS, Pink Pineapple. 47 mins.
A demonic rapist plagues Japan (for a change), repeatedly dividing itself and reforming in different places. In order to stop Japan becoming "a hell of mad sex," the government initiates a sex-sting operation, predictably encouraging attractive young agents to submit to the rapist for the benefit of world peace and the pornographic consumer. ✪✪✪

IN PRAISE OF JUDO

1974. JPN: *Judo Sanka.* TV series. DIR: Shigetsugu Yoshida, Masami Hata, Tetsuo Imazawa, Hiroshi Fukutomi, Hideo Takayashiki. SCR: Haruya Yamazaki, Tsunehisa Ito, Akio Matsuzaki. DES: Hiroshi Kaizuka. ANI: Takao Kasai, Yoshiaki Kawajiri. MUS: Yukio Takai. PRD: Nippon TV, Tokyo Movie Shinsha, Madhouse. 25 mins. x 27 eps.
This was the last of the TMS sports-themed anime, ending a line that began with STAR OF THE GIANTS. Tosshinta Tomoe grows up by the rough seas of Sotobo in Chiba Prefecture. He goes to high school where he decides to follow in the footsteps of his divorced mother, Teruko, a former judo champion. As with every other sports story, our hero is trained by a tough but kind coach who only wants the best for him, and he eventually

faces up to an opponent who has sworn revenge on the previous generation—in this case, a male judoist defeated by Tomoe's mother in her fighting days. The series was taken off the air due to low ratings before the more touching later episodes of Hiroshi Kaizuka's manga could be adapted. Compare to YAWARA.

IN THE BEGINNING *

1992. JPN: *Tezuka Osamu no Kyuyaku Seisho Monogatari.* AKA: *Osamu Tezuka's Old Testament.* TV series. DIR: Osamu Dezaki. SCR: Osamu Tezuka. DES: Osamu Tezuka, Shinji Seya. ANI: Masaki Yoshimura, Akio Sugino, Junji Kobayashi, Hideaki Shimada. MUS: Katsuhisa Hattori. PRD: NTW, RAI, Tezuka Pro. 25 mins. x 26 eps.
In 1984, the Italian RAI channel approached ASTRO BOY–creator Tezuka and asked him to make a series of Bible stories for this international coproduction that were closer to the originals than the apocryphal SUPERBOOK: VIDEO BIBLE. Tezuka threw himself into adapting his earlier manga version of the *Old Testament,* even to the extent of working as a humble animator on the *Noah's Ark* episode. The series was not completed until 1992, long after the death of its creator, and though it was soon screened in Italy, Germany, and the U.S., it did not receive a Japanese broadcast until 1997, when it was dumped on the WOWOW satellite channel. Coro, a sloe-eyed fox, acts as the viewpoint character for the entire series, witnessing the Fall of Man, the Flood, the rise of King David, and other major events. There was simply no time to allow for the many minor stories included in *Superbook.*

INFINITE RYVIUS

1999. JPN: *Mugen Ryvius.* TV series. DIR: Goro Taniguchi, Akihiko Nishiyama. SCR: Yosuke Kuroda. DES: Hisashi Hirai. ANI: Yoichi Ueda, Asako Nishida. MUS: Katsuhisa Hattori. PRD: Sunrise, TV Tokyo. 25 mins. x 26 eps.
An EVANGELION clone set in a solar sys-

tem 80 years after a solar flare has immersed the system in a massive plasma field that links all the planets like a nervous system. Troubled youth Koji Aibo (who looks just like *Evangelion*'s Shinji) is lured into a quest by the enigmatic Neya (a girl who looks like *Evangelion*'s Rei) to sail to the heart of the plasma field in the titular ship. Later put online for free download, this series blazed a trail for future Internet anime.

INITIAL D

1998. TV series. DIR: Shin Misawa. SCR: Hiroshi Ashida, Nobuaki Kishima. DES: Noboru Furuse. ANI: Noboru Furuse. MUS: Ryuichi Katsumata. PRD: Fuji TV, Prime Direction, OB. 25 mins. x 39 eps. (TV), 30 mins. x 2 eps (v).
In a blighted, soulless town north of Tokyo in Gunma Prefecture, disaffected youths drag souped-up cars in illegal street races. Seventeen-year-old petrol pump attendant Itsuki dreams of saving up enough to buy his own set of wheels and join the Akina Speed Stars gang, fellow garage worker Iketani boasts of his prowess, and their manager occasionally regales them with tall tales about the fastest man on the mountain. This shadowy figure is actually their shy friend Takumi, who breaks the speed limit each dawn to keep the deliveries fresh for his father's tofu shop, enjoying the occasionally unwelcome advances of Natsuki, a pragmatic local girl who pays the bills with "subsidized dating."
Replaying the semifantastic road mythologies of BOMBER BIKERS OF SHONAN and his own earlier LEGEND OF ROLLING WHEELS, Shuichi Shigeno's human interest manga in *Young Magazine* about boys and their toys was snapped up on the cusp of the revolution in digital animation. Featuring car magazine test-driver Keiichi Tsuchiya as a technical adviser, the anime version plays up an anal attention to detail with lectures on driving skill and interior shots of engine activity. Meanwhile the traditional cel animation of the non-racing scenes contrasts jarringly

with the computer-animated racing sequences in the style of the PlayStation game *Gran Turismo*. The second season, unsurprisingly rebranded as *Initial D: Second Stage*, begins with Takumi's car trashed by the rival Akagi Red Suns—a challenge if ever there was for a new duel over who owns the road. When the series gained a 24.5% TV rating, a movie, *Third Stage* (2001), was produced, focusing on the characters' graduation from high school and opportunities to leave the dead-end town of their birth behind.

INSTANT HISTORY

1961. JPN: *Otogi Manga Calendar.* AKA: *Manga Fairy Tales.* TV series. DIR: Ryuichi Yokoyama, Shinichi Suzuki, Michihiro Matsuyama. SCR: Ryuichi Yokoyama, Shinichi Suzuki, Michihiro Matsuyama. DES: Ryuichi Yokoyama, Shinichi Suzuki, Michihiro Matsuyama. ANI: Ryuichi Yokoyama, Shinichi Suzuki, Michihiro Matsuyama. MUS: N/C. PRD: Otogi Pro, TBS. 3 mins. x 312 eps. Anime's very first TV series. This black-and-white series of shorts explains various historical events and notable occasions, normally through a framing device of a character who is not aware "what happened on this day in history," discovering firsthand for themselves. Explanations did not always take a cartoon form, but sometimes included photographs and film footage, often taken from the research archives of the *Mainichi Shinbun* newspaper, where director Ryuichi Yokoyama's **FUKU-CHAN** manga was running at the time. Note: though *IH* was the first TV *series*, it was still not the first anime broadcast on TV. That honor goes to *Three Tales* (1960, *Mitsu no Hanashi*), an experimental anthology broadcast on the NHK channel, comprising adaptations of famous stories—*Oppel and the Elephant* by Kenji Miyazawa (see **NIGHT TRAIN TO THE STARS**), *Sleepy Town* by Mia Ogawa, and the first anime ever truly broadcast on Japanese TV, *The Third Blood*, by Kosuke Hamada, directed by Keiko Kozonoe.

INU YASHA

2000. TV series. DIR: Masashi Ikeda, Akira Nishimori. SCR: Masashi Ikeda, Katsuyuki Sumizawa, Takashi Yamada, Akinori Endo. DES: Eiji Suganuma. ANI: Kazuhiro Soeta, Eiji Suganuma, Shinichi Sakuma. MUS: Kaoru Wada. PRD: Nippon TV, Sunrise, Yomiuri TV. 25 mins. x 38+ eps.
Japanese schoolgirl Kagome is pulled into a well by a centipede monster and through a 500-year time tunnel to Japan's civil-war era. She escapes from the well to discover Inu Yasha, a half-dog demon, pinned to a nearby tree by the priestess Kikyo. The local villagers believe Kagome to be the reincarnation of Kikyo, and she must reluctantly team up with her predecessor's enemy to hunt down the many shards of the "Jewel of Four Souls," which Inu Yasha originally came to steal.

In the unsure economic climate that began the 21st century, with the **POKÉMON** tide ebbing and their **BRAVE SAGA** on hiatus, Sunrise bought into the success of a long-running, best-selling creator, optioning this recent manga from **RANMA 1/2**'s Rumiko Takahashi. A buddy-story in the tradition of **USHIO AND TORA**, with a time-traveling element that bears a close relationship to the creator's earlier **FIRE TRIPPER**.

IRIA *

1994. JPN: *Iria: Zeiram the Animation.* Video. DIR: Tetsuro Amino. SCR: Tsunehisa Arakawa, Tetsuro Amino. DES: Ryunosuke Otonashi, Masakazu Katsura. ANI: Ryunosuke Otonashi. MUS: Yoichiro Yoshikawa. PRD: Bandai. 35 mins. x 6 eps.
Bounty hunter Iria and her associates are charged with rescuing hostages from a deep-space cargo vessel, only to discover that they are already dead. Her brother Gren dies defending her from Zeiram, an unstoppable bioweapon with a carnivorous noh mask built into his head. As the vengeful Iria chases Zeiram across a marvelously well-realized alien planet, she sees that she has been framed in a conspiracy and has accidentally obtained a pendant containing an incriminating data chip.

Featuring excellent music, wonderful designs inspired by Terry Gilliam films such as *The Adventures of Baron Munchausen* (1988), and a rare anime character design job for **VIDEO GIRL AI**–creator Masakazu Katsura, *Iria* is an excellent science-fantasy adventure with a truly alien feel, let down only by a mediocre English-language dub.

The series is a prequel to Keita Amemiya's live-action movie *Zeiram* (1991), in which Iria, played by Yuko Moriyama instead of the anime's Aya Hisakawa, pursues Zeiram to Earth. Set three years earlier, the anime is mercifully free of the mundane constraints of the live version (which primarily took place in deserted Japanese streets), leaping from vast space freighters to alien worlds and cities full of bizarre technologies. More characters are introduced, and the handful of rubber monsters in the original are replaced by an army of clones, causing a degree of carnage that would bankrupt a live-action studio. The franchise continued in its live-action format with *Zeiram 2* (1994) and *Zeiram 3* (1997), directed once more by Amemiya. He would also direct *Moon of Tao* (1997), also starring Moriyama, which moved the general look and feel of *Zeiram* to an unconnected historical-fantasy setting. *Ill. p. 7.*

IRON COMMUNICATION

1998. JPN: *Kurogane Communication.* TV series. DIR: Yasuji Kikuchi. SCR: Mitsuhiro Yamada. DES: Shinya Takahashi. ANI: Toshimitsu Kobayashi, Hideaki Shimada. MUS: Kenji Kawai. PRD: APPP, WOWOW. 10 mins. x 24 eps.
Earth has been ravaged by a devastating war, and one-time robot servants fight in the ruins over spare parts. Haruka, a human girl who might be the last survivor of her race, is found by some kindly robots, who protect her from war machines hellbent on carrying out their programming to wipe

humanity off the face of the Earth. Haruka and her new friends set off in search of other survivors in, if you can believe such a thing, a lighthearted tale of surviving the apocalypse. This series was based on the manga in *Dengeki King* by Yoshimasa Takuma and Hideo Kato and broadcast as part of the satellite TV strip *Anime Complex*.

IRON LEAGUER

1993. JPN: *Shippu Iron Leaguer*. AKA: *Whirlwind Iron Leaguer*. TV series. DIR: Tetsuro Amino. SCR: Fuyunori Gobu, Akihiko Inari, Noboru Sonekawa. DES: Tsuneo Ninomiya, Kunio Okawara. ANI: Hideyuki Motohashi. MUS: Kaoru Wada. PRD: Sunrise, Studio Nue, TV Tokyo. 25 mins. x 52 eps. (TV), 25 mins. x 5 eps. (V).
An inevitable combination of the sports-anime plotting of CAPTAIN TSU-BASA with the giant-robot combat of GUNDAM, as a team of cartoonish armored super-soldiers plays a fusion of soccer and street basketball against cybernetically augmented rivals. With secret attacks, absentee parents, struggles against adversity, and the usual rash of off-the-peg formulae, credited as usual to house pseudonym "Hajime Yadate," the *Iron Leaguer* series survived on video for another handful of episodes but never attained the popularity of its predecessor CYBERFORMULA GPX, in whose sci-fi sports image it was clearly made.

IRON MAN

1991. Video. DIR: Koichi Ishiguro. SCR: Keiji Michiyoshi. DES: Hidetoshi Omori. ANI: Hidetoshi Omori. MUS: N/C. PRD: JC Staff. 50 mins.
Nineteen-year-old university student Yuji decides to become a "host" at a city bar where lonely women will pay a cover charge for the pleasure of his company. He soon becomes a full-fledged male prostitute, claiming all the while that this is all an experiment in order to "better understand the hearts of women." Based on a minor manga in *Comic Morning* by CLIMBING ON A CLOUD–creator Hiroshi Motomiya, this

predated the similar GIGOLO by two years. **N**

IRON VIRGIN JUN *

1992. JPN: *Tetsu no Otome (Shojo) Jun*. Video. DIR: Fumio Maezono. SCR: Fumio Maezono, Tsukasa Sunaga, Akihiko Takadera. DES: Mitsuyoshi Munesaki. ANI: Mitsuyoshi Munesaki. MUS: Hiroki Ishikawa. PRD: Triangle Staff, Animaruya. 46 mins.
A sword-and-sorcery romp from DEVIL-MAN-creator Go Nagai about spunky teenager Jun refusing to accept an arranged marriage and fighting to save her honor. Her mother makes this difficult for her by sending a gang to bring her back and teach her that sex isn't something to be afraid of. After watching the way this porno handles it, you might disagree. **NV**

IRONFIST CHINMI

1988. JPN: *Tekken Chinmi*. AKA: *Ironfist*. TV series, video. DIR: Toshitaro Oba, Kazuhiro Mori. SCR: Junji Takegami, Shikichi Ohashi. DES: Kenichi Onuki. ANI: Kenichi Onuki, Hideyuki Motohashi, Osamu Tsuruyama. MUS: Kei Wakakusa. PRD: Tohoku, TV Asahi. 25 mins. x 12 eps. (TV), 32 mins. (V).
Chinmi is a kung-fu protégé brought to the Dailin temple by the Old Master. There, he learns at the feet of the teacher Ryukai, befriends fellow student Jintan, and plays in the forest with his pet monkey, Goku (see JOURNEY TO THE WEST). He runs errands for the temple, learning all the while about the nature of strength, both physical and mental. This short-lived adaptation of Takeshi Maekawa's 1983 *Shonen Magazine* manga, faithfully depicted the first 12 volumes (all that were available at the time, though the manga itself is still ongoing today) but introduced new characters, kung-fu aspirant Laochu and female foil Lychee, to even out Maekawa's original boy-heavy cast. Chinmi was back the same year with the straight-to-video *Ironfist Chinmi's Kung-fu Picture Book (Tekken Chinmi Kenpo Daizukan)*, a clip-show of his eight best bouts, which, with an

RG VEDA, a distant adaptation of Hindu myth, features the delicate art style of the CLAMP collective. Its incomplete story and sudden ending are features of its production history—it is one of that large set of anime designed to promote ongoing manga stories. The expectation, implicit in a galling number of anime, that viewers should find out what happens next by reading the manga is of little help to most foreign viewers, who would need to learn to read Japanese first. *See entry p. 327.*

Rg Veda

© 1992 CLAMP./SHINSHOKAN/SONY MUSIC ENTERTAINMENT (JAPAN) INC./MOVIC

emphasis on fighting, outlasted the series that spawned it by a mile.

IRRESPONSIBLE CAPTAIN TYLOR *

1992. JPN: *Musukenin Kancho Tylor*. TV series, video. DIR: Koichi Mashimo. SCR: Hiroyuki Kawasaki, Kenichi Kanemaki, Asami Watanabe. DES: Tomoyuki Hirata. ANI: Tomoyuki Hirata. MUS: Kenji Kawai. PRD: Big West, Tatsunoko Pro, TV Setouchi. 25 mins. x 26 eps. (TV), 40 mins. x 2 eps. (V), 35 mins. x 6 eps. (V).
Justy Ueki Tylor is the ultimate slacker, a lazy good-for-nothing who joins the galactic military because he thinks it is the passport to an easy life. Put in charge of a battered hulk called the Soyokaze (Slight Wind), the former captain of which committed suicide due to depression, Tylor finds himself commanding a gang of thugs led by two stuffy officers (named after martial icons Mifune and Fuji) who would like nothing better than to throw him out of the airlock. Tylor, however, continually falls on his feet, accidentally thwarting an enemy double-cross by giving them a parcel bomb meant for him, haphazardly steering his way through a battle so that alien warships shoot each other, and even unknowingly volunteering for a suicide mission

only to escape from danger by leading his would-be destroyers right into the middle of the Terran fleet. In the tradition of Tylor's contemporary **TENCHI MUYO!**, our loser hero is also surrounded by a bevy of beauties, including girl-next-door Lieutenant Yuriko Star, adoring alien ruler Queen Azalyn Goza (who likes Tylor, even though her ministers want her to invade his planet), pretty and vacant twins Eimi and Yumi, and alien spy Harumi, who is planted on the Soyokaze to assassinate Tylor but never quite gets around to it.

The character is a cartoon version of Hitoshi Taira, the lazy protagonist of the 1962 live-action TV series *Japan's Irresponsible Age* who was played by comedian Hitoshi Ueki. This popular satire on Japan's salaryman culture featured a feckless individual who always managed to come out on top, advancing up promotional ladders when accidents befall his superiors, or lucking into important business information simply by malingering and goofing off. The series and its theatrical spinoffs were revived in 1990, suspiciously close to the time when **HUMMINGBIRDS**-creator Hitoshi Yoshioka would have begun work on this anime version.

The series returned in several video outings starting with the two-parter *Tylor: An Exceptional Episode* (1994), followed in 1995 by a six-part series that concentrated in turn on some of the supporting cast—Azalyn, for example, given an episode of her own, followed by one in which the star is Tylor's mad-dog pilot, KB Andressen. The series was rounded off by the two-part video series *Tylor: From Earth to Eternity* (1996), in which the lazy captain once again saves Earth from an alien menace by hoping the problem will go away. *Ill. p. 125.*

ISABELLE OF PARIS

1979. JPN: *Paris no Isabelle*. TV series. DIR: Keiji Hayakawa. SCR: Takeshi Shudo. DES: Nobuyuki Kitajima. ANI: Yoshiyuki Sugawara, Tadayuki Hayashi. MUS: Tsutomu Matsushita. PRD: DAX, TV Tokyo. 25 mins. x 13 eps.

Romance, cross-dressing, and intrigue in 1870s France, which could conveniently imply a relationship (of sorts) to **ROSE OF VERSAILLES**. Fifteen-year-old Isabelle Laustin is the daughter of a wealthy landlord, Leon, and his wife, Marie. She has spent a happy childhood with her friend Jean and sister Genevieve, and she has a suitor in the person of Captain Victor of the French army. However, her life changes when Napoleon III's army is beaten by the Prussians, and Paris is besieged. When the city is sold to the enemy by the feckless Louis Adolphe Thiers, it falls to Isabelle to save France by disguising herself as a boy and heading for London on a secret mission. A short-lived tale of French whimsy drawing on **LES MISÉRABLES** and **THREE MUSKETEERS**, but a solo scripting project for future **POKÉMON**-writer Takeshi Shudo that made little use of the rich historical potential, looked just like every other adventure anime, and sank without a trace. Compare to **STAR OF THE SEINE**.

IZUMO

1991. Video. DIR: Eiichi Yamamoto, Masaya Mizutani. SCR: Yoshihiko Tsuzuki. DES: Masaya Mizutani. ANI: N/C. MUS: Reijiro Komutsu. PRD: Kove, Studio Kumosuzu. 45 mins. x 2 eps.

Izumo, a prince of Nakatsu, hates old-fashioned custom and befriends Sanae, a girl from the rival kingdom of Yamatai. Meanwhile, neighboring countries Asuka and Yamato are plotting to steal the Amenomukumo Sword, a sacred treasure of Nakatsu. The warrior **YAMATO TAKERU** (q.v.) kidnaps Sanae, and Izumo takes up the sword to regain her, but he must first defeat Orochi, a serpent with eight heads and eight tails. This adventure anime combines the Japanese myth of **LITTLE PRINCE AND THE EIGHT-HEADED DRAGON** with a prehistoric meeting of cultures that would be revisited in **PRINCESS MONONOKE**. Based on Yoshihiko Tsuzuki's manga in *Comic Nora*.

JACK AND THE BEANSTALK *

1974. JPN: *Jack to Mame no Ki*. Movie. DIR: Gisaburo Sugii, Naoto Hashimoto. SCR: Kenji Hirami. DES: Shigeru Yamamoto. ANI: Shigeru Yamamoto, Kazuko Nakamura. MUS: Morihisa Shibuya. PRD: Herald, Tac. 98 mins.

Farmer's son Jack believes a traveling salesman (similar to the portrayal of the WIZARD OF OZ back in Kansas) when he tells him that his beans are magical. Willingly exchanging his cow for them, Jack is chastised by his mother and throws the beans away. The beans grow into a massive stalk overnight, and Jack's dog, Crosby, is approached by a mouse, who entreats them to climb up. The beanstalk leads up through the bottom of the well into the courtyard of a castle in the sky that is occupied by the witch Mrs. Noire (Hecuba). Keen on stealing treasure, Jack is eventually convinced by Crosby that he should rescue the imprisoned Princess Margaret (whom Mrs. Noire intends to marry to her ogrish son, Tulip) and break Noire's spell that has turned all the castle's former occupants into mice. After a final confrontation with Tulip, Jack saves the day, though it becomes patently obvious that Margaret is a clearheaded girl of 18, determined to get on with restoring her people's fortunes, while Jack is merely a child in love with the idea of being a hero. In an original and poignant twist on happy-ever-after, Margaret stays on in her castle while Jack returns home (happily) to his farm, where he soon forgets all about her. This feature debut of future TALE OF GENJI–director Gisaburo Sugii is an excellent musical anime that could easily have given Disney's films of the day a run for their money, but one which sank without a trace on a very limited U.S. release.

JACK AND THE WITCH *

1967. JPN: *Shonen Jack to Maho-tsukai*. AKA: *Boy Jack and the Sorcerer*. Movie. DIR: Taiji Yabushita. SCR: Shinichi Sekizawa, Susumu Takahisa. DES: Reiji Koyama. ANI: Akira Okuwara. MUS: Seiichiro Uno. PRD: Toei. 80 mins.

The mischievous Jack and his friends are racing through the forest when they meet Kiki (Allegra), a girl on a mini-helicopter. With Chuko (Squeaker) the mouse and several other companions, he is taken to the Devil's Castle. Kiki is revealed as a Devil-child, working for Grendel (Queen Iliana), the master of Devil's Castle, who uses a Devilization Machine to turn children into monsters (or "harpies," in the U.S. dub). Chuko is turned into a devil, but Jack escapes. Kiki is sent after him but falls out of the sky, where she is nursed back to health by Jack. Accompanied by bear, fox, and dog companions, Jack returns to the castle to confront the witch. Grendel captures the animals and leaves them imprisoned to watch through her crystal ball as she kills Jack. The animals are keen to watch events unfold, but seeing that they are anxious to see what is happening, the spiteful Chuko (who is still devilized) smashes the crystal ball. This breaks Grendel's spell, and she dies trying to escape in a balloon. Chuko, Kiki, and all the other occupants of the castle are restored to normalcy and pile into Jack's car for the journey back to his place.

A bizarre updating of the Old English poem *Beowulf*, originally entitled *Adventure in the Wonder World*, *JatW* was originally commissioned to mark the tenth anniversary of Toei Animation. Pushing the envelope at the time for Japanese animation, it features a striking change in style after Jack enters the "witch-world" and was the first anime work to win a Mainichi Film Award for best score.

JAKOBUS NIMMERSAT *

1980. JPN: *Nodoka Mori no Dobutsu Daisenso*. AKA: *Great War of the Animals of Placid Forest*. TV special. DIR: Yoshio Kuroda. SCR: Toshiyuki Kashiwakura. DES: Yasuji Mori. ANI: Kazuko Hirose. MUS: Tatsumi Yano. PRD: Nippon Animation, Fuji TV. 70 mins.

When people from a nearby village discover a hole in their church roof, they unthinkingly rush into the forest to cut down trees to repair it. Agreeing that they should warn the humans off, Peter the Root Fairy and his animal friends attempt to shoo them from the forest, and when this tactic fails, they embark on a campaign of careful resistance and nuisance—compare to POMPOKO. Based on the book by Boy Lornsen, this TV special reduced the age of the original Peter to make him more appealing to young viewers and dropped all child characters in order to allow the young audience to enjoy watching little people avenge themselves on the folly of grown-ups. Released in English under differing titles, including *Peter of Placid Forest* and *Back to the Forest*.

JANKEN MAN

1991. AKA: *Scissors-Paper-Stone Man.* TV series. DIR: Toshiya Endo, Hiroshi Yoshida, Naohito Takahashi. SCR: Satoru Akahori, Yoshiaki Takahashi, Tsunehisa Arakawa, Takao Oyama. DES: Nobuyoshi Habara. ANI: Nobuhiro Ando, Naoyuki Matsuura. MUS: N/C. PRD: Ashi Pro, TV Tokyo. 20 mins. x 51 eps.

A superhero who defeats adversaries by playing games of scissors-paper-stone with them hardly seems like a pitch for a successful show, but Janken Man's fight against the evil Osodashi Mask kept young viewers hooked for a year.

JAPAN INC.

1987. JPN: *Manga Nihon Keizai Nyumon.* AKA: *Manga Introduction to Japanese Economics.* TV series. DIR: Takenori Kawata, Masamune Ochiai, Yoshimasa Yamazaki, Teruo Kigure. SCR: Takashi Yamada, Shunichi Yukimuro, Miho Maruo. DES: Shotaro Ishinomori. ANI: Nobuhiro Soda. MUS: Sunset Hills Hotel. PRD: Knack, TV Tokyo. 25 mins. x 25 eps.

In the middle of the 1980s, yuppie career girl Sawako Matsumoto graduates from Harvard Business School and returns to Japan. As the country struggles under the export pressures brought by the high yen, she works through the night to produce a business plan that will drag her company out of its rut. Based on the manga by CYBORG 009–creator Shotaro Ishinomori that was originally serialized in the high-class business paper *Nippon Keizai Shinbun* and even published as an economics textbook by the University of California. The anime version was broadcast in a ten-o'clock evening slot when hard-working salarymen stood a better chance of seeing it.

JAPANESE FOLK TALES

1975. JPN: *Manga Nihon Mukashibanashi.* AKA: *Manga Japanese Folk Tales.* TV series. DIR: Rintaro, Norio Hikone, Hidenori Kondo, Gisaburo Sugii, Hiroyuki Hoshiyama, Hiroe Mitsunobu, Isao Okishima. SCR: Isao Okishima, Hiroyuki Hoshiyama, Tsune-

hisa Ito, Ryohei Suzuki. DES: Tsutomu Shibayama. ANI: Masakazu Higuchi. MUS: Jun Kitahara. PRD: Ai Planning Center, Tac. 25 mins. x 1,255+ eps.

Crammed two to an episode, the original *Japanese Folk Tales* series retold many old stories for a children's audience. Some were old anime staples, such as **MOMOTARO** and **THE MONKEY AND THE CRAB**. Others were commonly pastiched in anime but rarely seen in their original form, such as *Snow Woman*, the tale of a sultry siren who lures unsuspecting travelers to their deaths on a snowbound mountain pass. This was first animated as Nobuo Ofuji's *Dream of a Snowy Night* (1947), but snow princesses often appear as characters in diverse anime from **DORORON ENMA** to **URUSEI YATSURA**. Similarly, *Princess Kaguya*, the story of a beautiful woman found inside a strip of bamboo who cannot find a husband on Earth and eventually returns to her home on the moon, was first animated in 1942 by Goro Araiwa and also appears here, but this tale is most likely to be known through oblique references to it in anime such as **REI REI** and **GU-GU GUNMO**. In *Urashima Taro*, first filmed as Nobuo Ofuji's *Cut-Out Urashima* (1928), a Japanese man is carried away to an underwater castle where he lives happily with the daughter of the Dragon King, only to discover that centuries have passed back on the surface when he returns. This early time-travel tale is often referenced in modern anime, including **FUTURE COP URASHIMAN** and **GUNBUSTER**, where time dilation is called the "Urashima Taro Effect."

Shown on several occasions in movie theaters, the series also inspired the *Famous World Fairy Tales* and **JAPANESE HISTORY** serials, as well as imitators such as Hajime Koedo's 28 theatrical shorts *Japanese Fairy Tales* (1988) and Takashi Kurahashi's adult video spinoff *Flirting Japanese Fairy Tales* (1989). Still running in 2001, the *JFT* franchise is anime's second-longest series, after the unstoppable **SAZAE-SAN**.

JAPANESE HISTORY

1976. JPN: *Manga Nippon Shi Series.* AKA: *Manga Japanese History Series.* TV series. DIR: Hidenori Kondo, Norio Yazawa. SCR: Junji Tada. DES: Oji Yutabe. ANI: Oji Yutabe. MUS: Takeshi Sato. PRD: Nippon TV. 25 mins. x 52 eps.

A trawl through the centuries of Japanese history, beginning in myth with the **BIRTH OF JAPAN** then speeding through the early cultures, the rise of the Yamatai nation, the Heian era, the civil war, and finishing with the Meiji Restoration in the 19th century. The series' look was deliberately haphazard, with character designs changing with each historical period in order to give a sense of the passage of time. Ironically, for treatment of Japan's more modern history, the anime medium descends once more into myth-making. Apart from the dramatized historical events of **ANIMENTARY**, Japan's descent into fascism in the 1920s and 1930s is rarely shown in anime except in revisionist shows like **KISHIN CORPS** and **SAKURA WARS** that try to play down the harsh realities in favor of fantastic whimsy. Japanese history was also covered in the **MANGA PICTURES OF JAPAN** series.

JARINKO CHIE

1981. Movie, TV series. DIR: Isao Takahata, Masahiro Sasaki, Tetsu Takemoto, Takashi Anno, Katsuhito Akiyama. SCR: Noboru Shiroyama, Hideo Takayashiki, Kazuyoshi Yokota. DES: Yoichi Otabe. ANI: Kazuhiko Udagawa, Yuki Kishimo, Kazuyuki Kobayashi. MUS: Kiyoshi Suzuki. PRD: Tokyo Movie Shinsha, MBS. 45 mins., 25 mins. x 64 eps.

Eleven-year-old Chie Takemoto runs a restaurant for her father, until the fateful day that the local gang boss comes around to collect her father's gambling debts. In an attempt to scare the girl, the gangster sets his cat Antonio on Chie's cat Kotetsu, but Chie's pet is the toughest, killing the gangster's. The distraught gangster decides to go straight, opening an *okonomiyaki* restaurant and hiring Chie's father Tetsu as a bodyguard. Everything goes well until Tetsu sees Chie having a secret meeting with his estranged wife.

Based on the manga by Haruki Etsuji, who also worked on I AM A CAT, the *Jarinko Chie* film is a loving look at life in Osaka, a city with a very different attitude from the more famous Tokyo (see COMPILER). Featuring Diet politician Chinetsu Nakayama as Chie and the anime debuts of a number of Kansai comedians in other roles, the movie was promoted with a second anime sequence shown as part of the *Kao Master Theater TV* program as the 84-minute TV special *Jarinko Chie: Anime Stand-Up*. The *manzai* comedy tradition of an abusive straight-man and an eternally stupid joker is popular in Japan, and it's mixed with anime here in several scenes of live-action comedians spliced with footage from the anime. The best part is the dream sequence between the anime character Tetsu and his real-life voice actor, the *manzai* comedian Norio Nishikawa. Following the success of the film, *JC* returned to television on the TBS channel, where it survived until 1983.

JEANNIE WITH THE LIGHT-BROWN HAIR

1979. JPN: *Kinpatsu no Jeanie.* AKA: *Golden-Haired Jeanie; Girl in the Wind.* TV series. DIR: Keinosuke Tsuchiya. SCR: Iwao Yamazaki, Kenji Terada, Yasuo Yamakichi. DES: Masami Abe. ANI: Masami Abe, Masahiro Kase. MUS: Harumi Ibe. PRD: Dax, Tokyo 12 Channel. 25 mins. x 13 eps., 25 mins. x 52 eps.

Fifteen-year-old Jeannie Reed has grown up on a farm in Agarta, Virginia, and is disgusted at the outbreak of the American Civil War, when her father uses his position to profit from both sides. Turning her back on her profiteering family, she volunteers to care for orphans and becomes a nurse for the soldiers of the Union army, fretting all the time about the whereabouts of her soldier boyfriend, Robert.

A drama from the same era as LIT-

TLE WOMEN, though this original work owes more to *Gone with the Wind* in its depiction of the Civil War. Popular tunes of the time were interwoven into the scenario, including "Oh, Susanna," "Camptown Races," and the titular "I Dream of Jeannie"—a song by the American Stephen Foster (see GREAT COMPOSERS).

The story would return in a 52-episode run of *Girl in the Wind: Jeannie with the Light-Brown Hair* (1992, *Kaze no Naka no Shojo Kimpatsu no Jeannie*), directed by Makoto Yasumura for Nippon Animation. The new version took considerable liberties, including the introduction of nobleman Count Kurt Russell(!). New Jeannie actress Mitsuko Horie would also star in the ill-fated final remake of NOBODY'S BOY.

JETTER MARS

1977 AKA: *Jet Mars.* TV series. DIR: Rintaro, Sumiko Chiba (pseud. for Toshio Hirata), Noboru Ishiguro, Wataru Mizusawa, Masami Hata, Katsuyoshi Sasaki, Yugo Serikawa. SCR: Masao Maruyama, Masaki Tsuji, Shunichi Yukimuro, Ryohei Suzuki, Hiroshi Yamamoto. DES: Akio Sugino. ANI: Akio Suzuki, Kazuo Mori, Akira Okuwara, Wataru Mibu. MUS: Nobuyoshi Koshibe. PRD: Madhouse, Tezuka Pro, Fuji TV. 25 mins. x 27 eps.

In 2015, Dr. Yamanoue, chief researcher at the Ministry of Science, creates the boy-robot Jetter Mars and prepares to teach him how to fight as a super-soldier. However, he is opposed by the cybernetic specialist Dr. Kawashimo, who is responsible for Jetter's brain. When a storm threatens his island home, Jetter saves the day by cooperating with Kawashimo's robot daughter, Miri. Soon, he becomes a superhero saving the world from harm, though his two mentors war constantly about his true purpose.

A lackluster copy of ASTRO BOY (if Astro was 10–12 years old, Jetter is 6–8) commissioned by Toei from creator Osamu Tezuka, though the studio's interference would lead him to lose all interest in the project and claim that

Fifty years after his first appearance in manga form, ASTRO BOY remains one of the medium's most recognizable characters. A simple combination of the *Pinocchio* story and *Superman*, *AB* is the most famous of Osamu Tezuka's creations, appearing not only in his own serials, but also as a cameo in many of his other stories. *AB* was also the first anime to be broadcast outside Japan, ushering in the first wave of anime exports during the 1960s. *See entry p. 21.*

Astro Boy

they had chipped away everything that made it anything other than a poor imitation. Early episodes involved a will-he-won't-he crisis, as Jetter decided whether to do the altruistic thing as advised by Kawashimo or to follow Yamanoue's more mercenary advice. However, Yamanoue was soon edged out, and the show became an almost carbon-copy of the relationship between Astro and Ochanomizu in *AB*. To compound the resemblance, *JM* featured *AB* voice actors Mari Shimizu and Hisashi Katsuta, and even lifted *AB* scripts wholesale, pausing only to change the names.

JEWEL HUNTER LIME BEM *

1996. JPN: *Takara Ma Hunter Lime.* AKA: *Treasure Demon Hunter Lime.* Video. DIR: Tetsuro Amino. SCR: Kenichi Nakamura. DES: Atsuko Nakajima. ANI: Atsuko Nakajima. MUS: N/C. PRD: Asmik. 30 mins. x 3 eps.

Self-explanatory adventures, as the pretty, scantily clad Lime busts ghosts and steals valuables; based on a computer game but bolstered by designs from RANMA 1/2's Nakajima.

JIBAKU-KUN

1999. AKA: *Bucky the Incredible Kid.* TV series. DIR: Akira Suzuki, Hiroyuki

Tsuchiya. SCR: Atsuhiro Tomioka. DES: Miyuki Shimabuke. ANI: Michiaki Sugimoto. MUS: Gen Sawada. PRD: Trans Arts, TV Tokyo. 25 mins. x 26? eps.

In this madcap **POKÉMON** clone, nasty exploding pink balls called "Trouble Monsters" fall into the hands of spiky-haired hero Baku ("Explosion"), who has his life turned upside-down when he bumps into Great-Child Dan—a traveler through the Twelve Worlds. Featuring a love interest called Pink, a cameo appearance from Ali Baba, and more cute mascots than you can shake a stick at (which also happen to explode). Based on a manga by popular **PAPUA-KUN**–creator Ami Shibata.

JIN-ROH: THE WOLF BRIGADE *

1999. Movie. DIR: Hiroyuki Okiura. SCR: Mamoru Oshii. DES: Hiroyuki Okiura, Tadashi Hiramatsu. ANI: Kenji Kamiyama. MUS: Hajime Mizoguchi. PRD: Production IG. 98 mins.

In a Japan torn apart by riots, an officer from the paramilitary Third Force is almost killed by a suicide bomber from the fanatical Sect. He begins an affair with the bomber's sister, not realizing that they are both pawns in a power-game played out by opposing factions in the government.

Scenarist Oshii has tackled this subject several times before—not only in his manga *Hellhounds*, but also in the live-action spinoffs *Red Lenses* and *Cerberus*. However, it is notable that the acclaimed director of **GHOST IN THE SHELL** should have avoided seeing this particular project through, instead handing it over to the younger Okiura. Although this is Oshii's fourth pass at the same material, it jettisons the authorial input of his **PATLABOR**-cohort Kazunori Ito, leaving a script with a hollow heart. *Hellhounds* had Inui ("Dog"), an officer who is almost killed by a sly female terrorist. It ended with Inui facing the same foe a second time and losing his life. *Jin-Roh* replays this story with Fuse (equally punning, since it is made up of the characters for "man" and "dog") unable to shoot one of the Little Red Riding Hood activist

girls who transport satchel-charges to the rioters.

Oshii's original script employed the Red Riding Hood analogy throughout, retelling the story sympathetically from the wolf's point of view. Elements of this remain in carefully composed shots of Fuse beneath a full moon, and a meeting-place in front of the wolf-pack display at the museum. Fuse himself has a lupine cast to his features, and, in the finale, the fairy tale's use of disguises as bluff and counterbluff assumes **PERFECT BLUE** proportions—within the government, the paramilitary, the elite brigade, and, ultimately, the group that masterminds the whole affair.

Director Okiura, however, does not use the lupine imagery as much as Oshii intended, opting instead for a doomed romance between the softness of the impressionable girl Kei and the impenetrable steel of Fuse's armor. His night-sights are literal rose-tinted glasses through which everything is reduced to straightforward good and evil. In his armor, he can fight the rebels without a thought; out of it, he is a whirl of contradictions. Unfortunately, so is the script, which presents an alternate Japan of the late 1950s, but like *Hellhounds* and *Red Lenses* before it, fails to explain why. Is it a Japan that was not economically rejuvenated by the Korean War? Or simply a Japan with a few more riots? What do the rioters and the wolf-brigade vigilantes want? What is the mysterious Sect fighting for? Advanced technologies like night-sights and tracers jostle with 1940s gear like Volkswagens and German antitank guns, but why? *Jin-roh* was premiered abroad long before its Japanese release in early 2000, possibly to drum up "foreign interest" among audiences who would assume that their failure to comprehend the back story was a cultural problem and not simply lazy plotting—an issue that could be said to haunt the same studio's later **BLOOD**. The end result is a skillfully animated but aimless film, with a desperate opening voice-over

that tries to explain the foundation of the Third Force, in a failed attempt to convince that this is anything more than a Cold War thriller with a respray. **OV**

JOHNNY CHUCK

1973. JPN: *Yamanezumi Rocky Chuck*. AKA: *Rocky Chuck the Woodchuck; Chuck the Beaver*. TV series. DIR: Tadamichi Koga, Seiji Endo. SCR: Keiji Kubota, Takako Omomori, Hikaru Mori, Hiroshi Yamanaka, Hiroshi Saito. DES: Nobuhiro Okaseko. ANI: Nobuhiro Okaseko, Toshio Hirata, Yasuji Mori. MUS: Morihisa Yamamoto, Seiichiro Uno. PRD: Zuiyo, Fuji TV. 25 mins. x 52 eps.

Rocky the adventurous woodchuck is separated from his family and wanders the forests meeting many different animals, including Polly, another woodchuck, Peter Cottontail the rabbit, and the avuncular jaybird Sammy. Based on the output of the prolific Thornton W. Burgess (1874–1965), who wrote a syndicated *Bedtime Story* newspaper column for daily newspapers and was said to have penned 15,000 stories in his lifetime. Many of these involved the adventures of forest animals such as Chatterer the Red Squirrel, Danny the Meadow Mouse, Grandfather Frog, Reddy Fox, and Buster Bear, though it is his ninth book, *The Adventures of Johnny Chuck* (1913), that was used as a framing device for these anime adaptations. Compare to **SETON'S ANIMAL TALES**.

JOJO'S BIZARRE ADVENTURES *

1993. JPN: *Jojo no Kimyo na Boken*. Video. DIR: Hiroyuki Kitakubo. SCR: Hiroyuki Kitakubo. DES: Junichi Haneyama. ANI: Junichi Haneyama. MUS: Marco D'Ambrosio. PRD: APPP. 40 mins. x 6 eps., 40 mins. x 7 eps. (series 2).

Joseph Joestar and his Japanese grandson, Jotaro, fight an ongoing blood feud against Dio Brando, an immortal vampire who caused the death of their ancestor Jonathan. Using the magical powers of the Stand, a deck of tarot cards that bestow psychic attributes on the possessor of each card, the Joestar clan and Brando's minions face off in a violent battle that plays like FIST OF THE NORTH STAR at its most surreal.

With its warring secret elites and magical trumps, *Jojo* owes a considerable debt to Roger Zelazny's *Nine Princes in Amber* (1972), particularly considering the "immortal" undertones of its hero. There are several Jojos stretching from the 19th to the 21st century—a more correct translation of the title might be to put the apostrophe *after* the "s." BAOH-creator Hirohiko Araki's 1987 manga in *Shonen Jump* begins in 1880s, when an Aztec death mask causes trouble for all who come into contact with it. Archaeologist Jonathan Joestar begins a vendetta against Dio, who tries to steal his inheritance and kills his dog. Dio eventually dons the mask and becomes a vampire, causing Jonathan's death as his family flees for the U.S. The story jumps to New York in the 1930s, where Jonathan's descendant Joseph continues the battle through the Second World War, before the story moves into the 1980s with Jotaro Kujo, Joseph's half-Japanese grandson. The anime version deals primarily with the 1980s incarnation, as he and Joseph fight Dio, while he tries to heal his terrible wounds (his disembodied head has been sewn onto the body of Jonathan Joestar) and activate his ultimate trump card—the ability to stop time.

Following the series, the manga moved into the 1990s with Joseph's illegitimate Japanese son, Josuke Higashikata, then the 21st century with the Italian Giorno Giovanna, who, though officially the son of Dio, had been sired using the genitals of Jonathan and is hence the uncle of Joseph. The most recent member of the family to take the Jojo mantle is Jolyne Kujo, Jotaro's daughter, who uses her powers to escape from a Florida prison.

Gripping despite low-grade animation, the 1993 *Jojo* series was overlooked during the anime boom of the 1990s reputedly because of a prohibitively high asking price for the rights. The original *Jojo* remains unreleased in English, perhaps because the anime was always intended to sell the multivolume manga, and one could not be sold without the other. Another possibility is that the license has been considered by U.S. companies but turned down because of the surreal in-jokery of the characters' names—in the style of BASTARD, the series is full of musical references, including psychic warriors Mariah [Carey], [Bette] Midler, [Ronnie James] Dio, Cream, the psychic dog Iggy [Pop], and even the titular character himself ("Jojo was a man who thought he was a loner"), who hails from the Beatles song "Get Back." Despite being one of anime's more original fantasies, *Jojo*, like FIVE STAR STORIES, remains untranslated. In the wake of a Capcom computer game released in the U.S. as *Jojo's Venture* (1998), the Japanese production company began hinting that it would release the anime in the U.S. itself, though at time of writing it has yet to make good its promise. Less convincing or entertaining Aztec sorcery would appear in NAZCA. ❶

JOKER MARGINAL CITY
1992. Video. DIR: Osamu Yamazaki. SCR: Chuichi Watanabe, Hiroyuki Onuma. DES: Chuichi Iguchi. ANI: Takako Sato, Takaaki Ishiyama. MUS: N/C. PRD: Studio Zyn. 45 mins.
Jokers are genetically engineered beings who can switch sex at will, among other, more powerful psychic abilities. A young man escapes from a secret research facility and goes on the run. He is befriended by a reporter, who then has to call on the help of other Jokers to keep the boy safe from his pursuer—a wanted killer known only as the Heartless Assassin. This stylish, well-paced science-fiction video plays with the notions of gender and genetic tinkering, combining the themes of BAGHI with images from the pretty-boy subgenre of gay anime such as FAKE. Based on the manga in *Wings* magazine by ARCHA LYRA–creator Katsumi Michihara. ❶

JOSEPHINA THE WHALE
1979. JPN: *Kujira no Josephina*. TV series. DIR: Kazuyuki Hirokawa, Kazuo Yamazaki, Kazuo Tomizawa. SCR: Hiroshi Yamamoto, Hirohisa Soda. DES: Kazuo Tomizawa. ANI: Satoshi Hirayama. MUS: Hiroshi Kanodo. PRD: Ashi Pro, Tokyo 12 Channel. 25 mins. x 22 eps.
Madrid schoolboy Sante Costas keeps a tiny whale in a bowl, invisible to everyone except him. Josephina takes him on many dreamlike adventures, but when Sante starts taking an interest in the outside world and gets to know his distant father, Josephina herself fades away like the dream she was. However, the final two episodes were unbroadcast in the show's original run. Excerpts were shown in an extended version to rush the plot to a conclusion, but viewers had to wait for repeats in syndication to watch the friends' final farewell.

JOURNEY THROUGH FAIRYLAND, A *
1985. JPN: *Yosei Florence*. AKA: *Florence the Fairy*. Movie. DIR: Masami Hata, Kazuyuki Hirokawa. SCR: Tamanobu Takamasa. DES: Sadao Miyamoto, Noma Sabear. ANI: Sadao Miyamoto, Shigeru Yamamoto. MUS: Naosumi Yamamoto (arranger). PRD: Sanrio. 92 mins.
Michael, a struggling music student not unlike GORSCH THE CELLIST, loves flowers more than he loves music itself. Replacing a begonia in a broken pot, he is visited that night by Florence the flower fairy, who thanks him for his kindness. In this musical fantasy four years in the making, a depressed Michael, cut from the orchestra for the next concert, is whisked away to Flower World by Florence. Naosumi Yamamoto, a conductor with the Tokyo Philharmonic, selected 20 pieces of classical music, which were used in the film itself and, in an imitation of Disney's *Fantasia* (1940), to inspire the surreal

storyboards for the animators. Michael was played by Masaki Ichimura, a leading figure in Japan's leading musical performance troupe, Theater Shiki. Released in the U.S. by Celebrity Home Entertainment.

JOURNEY TO THE WEST *

1967. JPN: Saiyuki. AKA: Xiyouji; Monkey; My Son Goku; Alakazam the Great; Spaceketeers. Movie, video, TV series, TV special. DIR: Gisaburo Sugii, Osamu Dezaki, Hideo Makino, Ryosuke Takahashi, Masami Hata. SCR: Akihiko Kanno, Morihisa Yamamoto, Michio Sano, Michiaki Ichiwa. DES: Osamu Tezuka, Gisaburo Sugii. ANI: Shigeru Yamamoto. MUS: Seiichiro Uno. PRD: Tezuka Pro, Fuji TV. 25 mins. x 39 eps. (1967).

Stone Monkey is born from a rock by the ocean. His boastful, irrepressible nature soon causes a stir on Earth as he makes himself king of all the monkeys. In search of the secret of immortality, he learns martial arts and magic from the Buddhist monk Subhuti, who renames him Sun Wu Kong (in Japanese, Son Goku), meaning "Awakened to Emptiness." Back on his mountain, he finds that demons have taken over his cave, but the skills he has learned from Subhuti enable him to throw them out. The Demon King's brothers trick him into sneaking into the Dragon King's palace and stealing a famous weapon, a miraculous iron staff that can change size on command. Sun Wu Kong is brought before the Jade Emperor for punishment. Wu Kong eats the Peaches of Immortality and is chased from Heaven, only to lose a bet with Buddha. Immured beneath a mountain for 500 years, he is saved by the Buddhist Priest Xuanzang (aka Tripitaka), who invites Wu Kong to accompany him on a pilgrimage to Gandhara in India, the modern Punjab. En route, the pair meet a pig-changeling called Pigze and Monk Sand, a river spirit who was once a Heavenly guard. After Wu Kong defeats them, they both join the pilgrimage.

Possibly inspired by travelers' gar-bled tales of the Hindu monkey-god Hanuman, Wu Cheng-En's 16th-century novel Xiyouji is the Chinese story most often animated in Japan, perhaps because its trickster hero is more appealing to the children's audience than the dour generals of GREAT CONQUEST or the hotheaded revolutionaries of SUIKODEN. Nobuo Ofuji's EARLY ANIME Legend of Son Goku (1926) used cutout figures animated by stop-motion and was soon remade as the two-reel Son Goku (1928), directed by Takahiro Ishikawa. However, Wu Kong's real push into the Japanese market came through foreign influences. Amid the many propaganda WARTIME ANIME, the Wan brothers' Chinese cartoon Xiyouji (1941) was screened in Japan under the title Princess Iron Fan. Featuring one chapter from the legend, when Wu Kong and friends steal a magic fan from Mount Inferno, the film inspired the 16-year-old Osamu Tezuka to write his manga My Son Goku (1952), based on the same Mount Inferno episodes.

Japan's animation business was in ruins after the war, though Taiji Yabushita's New Adventures of Hanuman (1957) was a 14-minute PR exercise funded with American money. Hanuman was chosen over Wu Kong as a subject, presumably because the former Occupying Forces of Japan felt that a character whose main aim in life is revolt against authority was not the most suitable folk hero for the times; for similar reasons during the war, the Japanese censor had lopped 20 minutes off the running time of Princess Iron Fan.

Yabushita returned to the story in 1960 when he directed the anime remake of Tezuka's My Son Goku. Retitled Journey to the West (Saiyuki) in Japan and Alakazam the Great in the U.S., Yabushita's film featured many similarities to the Chinese film that inspired Tezuka. Not only did it keep to the Mount Inferno scenes, but it also played up the moment when Wu Kong, Pigze, and Monk Sand decide to cooperate for the first time and fea-tured a final aerial battle when the characters' feet are surrounded by air-brushed clouds. Substantial name changes were made for the U.S. version, which is set in "Majutsoland," ruled by His Majesty King Amo (Buddha), his wife, Queen Amas, and his son, Prince Amat (Tripitaka). King Alakazam (Wu Kong) tricks Merlin the magician (the Emperor of Heaven) into revealing his secrets and fights past palace guardsman Hercules to confront King Amo, who imprisons Alakazam until he is released to protect Prince Amat's quest to India. Joined by Sir Quigley (Pigze) and reformed cannibal Lulipopo (Sandy), Alakazam defeats King Gruesome (ruler of Mount Inferno) and his wife (Princess Iron Fan), is reunited with his beloved Dee Dee (a new creation in the anime), and all live happily ever after. The film's Japanese origins were further occluded by a big-name voice cast including Dodie Stevens, Jonathan Winters, Arnold Stang, and Sterling Holloway, music by Les Baxter, and the voice of Frankie Avalon whenever Alakazam sang. Released during summer 1961, coincidentally alongside fellow postwar anime MAGIC BOY and PANDA AND THE MAGIC SERPENT, it was Alakazam's commercial failure that led to the perception in the entertainment industry that Americans would not accept Japanese animation at all.

Back in Japan, the experience of making the film further inspired Tezuka to consider repeating the process for TV, indirectly giving birth to ASTRO BOY and the inevitable TV remake of the Wu Kong story, Goku's Great Adventure (1967, Goku no Daiboken). The first three episodes of this series stay close to the legend, but it soon becomes a gag free-for-all filled with surrealistic and adult humor. Viewers were puzzled or irate; the PTA complained about the level of bad language and the series ended after 39 episodes instead of the intended 52.

Leiji Matsumoto's Starzingers (1978) was a science-fiction version that moved the events into outer space;

redubbed as **Spaceketeers**, it was shown in the U.S. alongside the other anime in the **Force Five** series. The next incarnation was the live-action series *Monkey* (1978), featuring scripts from **Japanese Folk Tales**–scenarist Isao Okishima. The music was from the group Godiego, who also provided the theme to Matsumoto's **Galaxy Express 999**—their mournful song about Son Goku's final destination became a hit in its own right, in turn inspiring the otherwise unrelated anime **Gandhara**. The live-action series became well-known in the U.K. and Australia through the BBC dub, supervised by future Manga Entertainment voice director Michael Bakewell, but the period following it produced only one TV movie in Japan, Gisaburo Sugii and Hideo Takayashiki's anime musical *Son Goku Flies the Silk Road* (1982), and a number of SF pastiches, including **Dragon Ball** (1986), the **Doraemon** movie *Parallel Journey to the West* (1988), and Buichi Terasawa's **Goku: Midnight Eye** (1989). Even **Hello Kitty**–creators Sanrio got into the act with *Raccoon Fun Journey to the West* (1991, *Pokopon no Yukai Saiyuki*). At the close of the 20th century, the character reappeared in several new incarnations, including the *very* loose adaptation **One Piece**. Another series, *Monkey Magic* (1999), was released on video and then recommissioned for TV. Based on a computer game, the 13-episode series retells the early part of the legend relatively faithfully, with a hero now named Kongo, though the actual *journey* to the west only begins in the penultimate episode. The same year saw a new *Saiyuki* (a pun on the characters for *Chronicle of Total Fun*, aka *Paradise Raiders*), a two-part video based on Kazuya Minekura's *G-Fantasy* manga that also graduated to a full-fledged 50-episode TV series. The Minekura *Saiyuki* is set long after the evil demon Gyumao is buried by the god of Heaven. After magic and science are mixed by parties unknown, Gyumao is brought back, and the monk Genjo Sanzo, accompanied by

the usual suspects in updated form, is charged with heading west to determine the cause of the trouble.

JUBEI-CHAN THE NINJA GIRL *
1999. JPN: *Jubei-chan: Lovely Metai no Himitsu.* AKA: *Jubei-chan: Secret of the Lovely Eyepatch.* TV series. DIR: Hiroaki Sakurai. SCR: Akitaro Daichi. DES: Mutthuri Moony, Takahiro Yoshimatsu. ANI: Takahiro Yoshimatsu. MUS: Toshio Masuda. PRD: Madhouse, Bandai, TV Tokyo. 25 mins. x 13 eps.
Seventeenth-century warrior hero Jubei fights his last battle, and with his dying breath entrusts his servant Koinosuke with the task of finding his true spiritual heir. Three hundred years later, the magically sustained Koinosuke finds a suitable candidate, the Japanese schoolgirl Jiyu "Jubei" Nanohana, who has the large breasts and pert buttocks that mark her as the Chosen One. Koinosuke must convince Jubei to don the heart-shaped eyepatch that will call forth her spiritual ancestor, but the insufferably perky girl (who has paroxysms of joy if she manages to fry an egg) is a reluctant recruit. Transferring to a new school populated by the descendants of samurai, she is adored by all, even Shiro Ryujoji, whose family, wronged by the original Jubei, insists on sending evil supply-teachers to challenge her to duels.
Jubei-chan must have looked great on paper—a samurai spoof from the same Madhouse studio that produced the kinetic **Ninja Scroll**, featuring school gags, unwelcome guests, historical references, mawkish romance, transformations, and fighting. In other words, reheated **Ranma 1/2**, further damaged by a succession of befuddling ethnocentric in-jokes for the benefit of Japanese parents who remember the 1950s samurai swashbucklers, which also inspired the same scenarist's **Lordless Retainer Tsukikage**.
Without the presence of other Jubei stories in English (the aforementioned *Ninja Scroll*, its illegitimate sibling **Ninja Resurrection**, and the live-action

CLAMP, a pseudonymous collective of female fan artists turned pro, whose **Rayearth** owes something of a debt to **Alice in Wonderland**, previously drew the short-lived **Miyuki-chan in Wonderland** for the Japanese animation magazine *Newtype*. Eventually turned into anime by director Seiko Sayama, the story's chief claim to fame is as a retelling of Lewis Carroll's original children's story but with all the cast, inexplicably, dressed in bondage gear. *See entry p. 257.*

Miyuki-chan in Wonderland

© 1995 CLAMP/SONY MUSIC ENTERTAINMENT/KADOKAWA SHOTEN PUBLISHING CO., LTD./MOVIC

movie *Samurai Armageddon*), there is little chance that this would have even been considered for translation. Its historical roots are too deeply buried; some, like the prissy Sachi Toyama's relationship to Toyama no Kinsan (also parodied in **Samurai Gold**), would be difficult even for a Japanese audience. Others, like the simian Ozaru and Kozaru getting their names from Big Monkey and Little Monkey, could really do with explanatory sleeve notes, sadly lacking in the Bandai English-language release. The result is a nonsensical dub in which a mystified cast and crew hope that the audience will laugh at jokes that they plainly do not find funny themselves. Amid a cynical challenger-of-the-week formula, creator Akitaro Daichi has the temerity to write himself into the story as Jubei-chan's narcoleptic father—somehow appropriate since he could well have written this in his sleep.

JUDGE *
1991. JPN: *Yami no Shihosha Judge.* AKA: *Magistrate of Darkness: Judge.* Video. DIR: Hiroshi Negishi. SCR: Katsuhiko Chiba. DES: Shin Matsuo. ANI: Shin Matsuo. MUS: Toshiro Imaizumi. PRD: Animate Film. 45 mins.
Hoichiro Oma is an everyday salary-

man who is really Enma, the Judge of Hell (see **DORORON ENMA**), meting out nightly justice for those who are wronged back in our world. His first case involves a ruthless executive who has committed murder on his route to the top—with ironic cruelty, Oma makes his punishment fit his crime. The second involves a conflict with Oma's own boss back in the real world, who has hired a supernatural lawyer to get him off a murder charge. Faced with weasly tactics at the bench, Oma appeals to the Court of Ten Kings, presided over by the rulers of Hell. Short tales of the unexpected in a similar style to **PET SHOP OF HORRORS**, based on a manga by sometime **CRUSHER JOE**–artist Fujihiko Hosono.

JUDO STORY

1991. JPN: *Judo Monogatari*. Video. DIR: Junichi Tokaibayashi. SCR: Oki Ike. DES: Junichi Tokaibayashi. ANI: Junichi Tokaibayashi. MUS: Goro Omi. PRD: Nippon Animation. 50 mins. x 2 eps.
Mochi, a complete novice, decides to join the judo club when he begins high school. He must endure many trials before he is accepted—shaving his head, cleaning up after his elders, and enduring their bullying. Eventually, after much blood, sweat, and tears, his fellows select him as a team member for the local championships. Based on the 1985 *Young Magazine* manga by Makoto Kobayashi, creator of **WHAT'S MICHAEL?**

JULIE THE WILD ROSE

1979. JPN: *Nobara no Julie*. TV series. DIR: Keiji Hayakawa, Masami Kigurashi. SCR: Akira Suga, Shina Matsuoka, Tomomi Mochizuki. DES: Masami Abe. ANI: Masami Abe. MUS: Mitsuo Chahata (arranger). PRD: Dax, Tokyo 12 Channel. 25 mins. x 13 eps.
Eleven-year-old Julie Braun lives in the lush green mountain pastures of Austria's Southern Tyrol. Her parents are killed by Italian soldiers, and she is sent to Vienna to live with her relatives, the Clementes. She befriends cousins Johan and Tanya but has trouble

adjusting to life with Uncle Karl and Aunt Klara. As Austria is plunged into World War I, Karl is fired from his job at a glass factory, and Julie's new family is forced into a life of hardship.
A short-lived **HEIDI** clone made with the assistance of the Austrian Tourist Board, though sources are unclear as to whether this was a full-fledged cooperation or merely the provision of a few holiday brochures. The music keeps the Austrian motif, selected from the works of Franz Schubert and Johann Strauss, who had their own anime appearance in **GREAT COMPOSERS**.

JULIET

1998. Video. DIR: Tsukasa Tomii. SCR: Masaru Yamamoto. DES: Kazutoshi Kobayashi. ANI: Akira Takeuchi. MUS: N/C. PRD: Adobe Pictures. 30 mins.
In this adaptation of a minor work by **SAKURA DIARIES**–creator U-Jin, the pretty, young Reina enjoys the advances of her lusty stepbrother and a mysterious stranger. Sold to the Japanese as their one chance to hear Kae Araki, the baby-faced voice of Minnie-May in **GUNSMITH CATS** and Rini (Chibi-Usa) in **SAILOR MOON**, behaving in a more erotic manner than that to which her public was accustomed. **N**

JUMPING *

1988. Video. DIR: Osamu Tezuka, Eiichi Yamamoto, Taku Sugiyama, Shingo Matsuo, Takamitsu Mitsunori. SCR: Osamu Tezuka. DES: N/C. ANI: N/C. MUS: N/C. PRD: Various. 100 mins.
A video compendium of several short films released in Japan to coincide with the Second Image Software Awards. The centerpiece is Tezuka's *Jumping*, a five-minute 1984 short in which a character takes successively higher and higher leaps until he (or is it she?) eventually bounds across the ocean to the middle of a war zone, where an explosion blasts him/her down to Hell. From there, s/he is thrown back out to the beginning of the film, ready to start jumping again. This exercise in perspective is accompanied by another Tezuka short, *Broken Down Film* (1985,

Onboro Film), a playfully postmodern joke showing a supposedly rare print of an old silent cartoon Western in which the condition of the film itself affects the action onscreen. The characters have trouble seeing because the film is so dirty, are confused by abrupt jumps in continuity due to missing footage, and even have to climb to the next frame when the projector jams—compare to Chuck Jones's *Duck Amuck* (1951). These famous but rarely seen anime were accompanied by several other experimental shorts from other animators for an audience who lacked the resources to travel to the film festivals where they are usually only to be seen. Another experimental Tezuka film, the longer **LEGEND OF THE FORESTS**, was released on video the previous year. Conveniently lacking dialogue that requires translation, both *Jumping* and *Broken Down Film* have been screened at English-language film festivals and also on U.K. television.

JUNGLE BOOK, THE *

1989. JPN: *Jungle Book Shonen Mowgli*. AKA: *Jungle Book Boy Mowgli*. TV series. DIR: Fumio Kurokawa, Shinji Takahashi, Akira Kiyomizu, Kazuya Miyazaki, Shigeru Yamazaki, Tatsuya Hirakawa. SCR: Nobuyuki Fujimoto, Kenichi Yoshida, Saburo Sekiguchi, Asami Watanabe. DES: Sadahiko Sakamaki. ANI: Masashi Kojima, Sadahiko Sakamaki, Kazuya Hayashi. MUS: Hideo Shimazu. PRD: Nippon Animation, TV Tokyo. 25 mins. x 52 eps.
An explorer and his wife are killed in the jungle. Their baby son, Mowgli, is raised by wolves, befriending Baloo the bear and Bagheera the panther, who teach him the Laws of the Jungle. Rejected by local humans, who see him as a demon, Mowgli prefers to dwell in the forest, where he must outwit the evil tiger Shere Khan. Eventually, after conflict between the humans and the animals, Mowgli defeats Shere Khan and gets to meet the beautiful human girl he has worshiped from afar for so long, leaving behind his jungle friends as he returns to the world from which

he came. An anime adaptation likely to remain dwarfed by the earlier Disney classic, this version updates Rudyard Kipling's novel for the 20th century—including planes for example, understandably absent from the original. Another old story of a human boy reared by animals was adapted as TA-CHAN: KING OF THE JUNGLE.

JUNGLE DE IKOU *

1997. JPN: Jungle de Iko. AKA: Let's Go with Jungle; Let's Get Jungly. Video. DIR: Yuji Moriyama, Osamu Mikasa. SCR: Jiro Takayama. DES: Yuji Moriyama. ANI: Yuji Moriyama. MUS: N/C. PRD: Kaos Project. 30 mins. x 3 eps.
Ten-year-old Natsumi's father gives her a necklace from the ruins of the Myuginian jungle. Soon afterward, Natsumi dreams that a jungle god is teaching her a powerful ritual dance. Discovering that her father's researchers have also awakened an ancient forest devil, Natsumi must deal with jungle spirits, gigantic whales, and armed fighter pilots. She performs the jungle dance and transforms into Mii, a large-breasted fertility goddess. A cynical combination of the jiggling bosoms of PLASTIC LITTLE and the magical transformations of CREAMY MAMI, Jungle de Ikou comes complete with a childhood pal for Natsumi, who naturally develops a crush on Mii, as well as comic-relief devil-child Ongo and his fiancée, Rongo. Originally based on a segment of voice actress Megumi Hayashibara's Boogie Woogie Night radio show, the series was memorably described by Manga Mania as a "Boogie Woogie Congo Ongo Bongo Jungle Bungle."

JUNGLE WARS

1990. Video. DIR: Yoshio Kuroda. SCR: Mayumi Koyama, Akira Sakuma. DES: Moriyasu Taniguchi, Takayuki Doi. ANI: Moriyasu Taniguchi. MUS: N/C. PRD: Nippon Animation. 25 mins. x 2 eps.
An evil syndicate of hunters attacks a jungle village where animals and humans coexist peacefully. With his parents out of action and his way of life in jeopardy, the imaginatively named

"Boy" swings through the creepers to save the day. Based on the game of the same name for the Nintendo Gameboy.

JUNK BOY *

1987. Video. DIR: Katsuhisa Yamada. SCR: Tatsuhiko Urahata, Hiroyuki Fukushima. DES: Hiroshi Hamazaki. ANI: Hiroshi Hamasaki. MUS: Takashi Kudo. PRD: Madhouse. 44 mins.
A charmless "comedy" in which sex-crazed Ryohei Yamazaki gets a job at the seedy Potato Boy magazine, chiefly because his uncontrollable erection allows the staff to evaluate nude photographs before going to press. He is sent to assist at a fading starlet's photo shoot, where he talks her into baring all by confessing that he spent many happy hours masturbating over pictures of her younger self. Sinking to new depths, he volunteers to conduct an "investigative report" at a local brothel, to which his superiors agree somewhat illogically, since they already have an undercover reporter, the pretty Aki, working there as one of the girls. Ryohei is rebuffed by Aki, and he takes it as a personal challenge that she has never had an orgasm. The way to any woman's heart, it would appear, is to throw on a tuxedo, take her on a bicycle ride through the red-light district, put her into a stolen ballgown, and then get her drunk on your office rooftop. Ryohei then leaves the sexually sated Aki behind so he can file a new story with the treacly moral message of "treating women right." He almost impresses his tough female editor with this change of heart, until she finds him snuffling through her underwear drawer and realizes that he's still a jerk. The authors wonder why she ever doubted it.
Based on a 1985 manga in Manga Action magazine by Yasuyuki Kunitomo, JB would like to think it is a media satire, and occasionally attempts to balance its priapic hero's infantile nature by letting a female character slap him. But since this is hardly a redeeming feature, it also boasts a brief fake com-

mercial interlude made by NINJA SCROLL–director Yoshiaki Kawajiri, as well as a bizarre moment when Ryohei attempts to mate with a plastic effigy of fast-food mascot Colonel Sanders. ⓁⓃ

JUNKERS COME HERE

1994. JPN: Junkers Come Here: Memories of You. Movie. DIR: Junichi Sato. SCR: Naoto Kine. DES: Kazuo Komatsubara. ANI: Keiichi Sato, Mahiro Maeda. MUS: N/C. PRD: Gaga, Triangle Staff. 30 mins.
The carefree life of Junkers, a strange dog who lives with four sisters. Based on a novel by former pop guitarist Naoto Kine (see CAROL), this anime owes a heavy debt to LASSIE and adds just a twist of DOG OF FLANDERS. Originally screened in segments as part of the TV Asahi show Kuni Sanchi Witches, it was given a theatrical showing the following year.

JURA TRIPPER

1995. JPN: Kyoryu Boken Ki Jura Tripper. AKA: Dinosaur Chronicle Jura Tripper. TV series. DIR: Kunihiko Yuyama, Yoshitaka Fujimoto, Naohito Takahashi, Shigeru Omachi, Kunihisa Sugishima. SCR: Isamu Shizutani, Yasushi Hirano, Sukehiro Tomita, Katsuyoshi Yutabe. DES: Kenichi Chikanaga, Mari Tomonaga. ANI: Seiji Kikuchi, Kenichi Chikanaga. MUS: Toshiyuki Omori. PRD: NAS, Ashi Pro, TV Tokyo. 25 mins. x 39 eps.
In a conflation of ADRIFT IN THE PACIFIC and Jurassic Park (1993), fifteen boys and girls are thrown into an alternate world where dinosaurs and humans live alongside each other. Later episodes developed a distant similarity to EL HAZARD, with the adventurers spending more time flirting than fighting, as they pick their way across a desert on the run from a newly awakened golem monster.

JUSTICE

1991. JPN: Jingi. AKA: Humanity and Justice. Video. DIR: Kiyoshi Murayama. SCR: Hideo Nanba. DES: Toshi Kawamura. ANI: Katsushi Matsumoto. MUS: N/C. PRD: JC Staff. 50 mins. x 2 eps.

A kindhearted gangster tries to live by rules of kindness and justice even though he is on the wrong side of the law. When he meets a former college left-winger who has also become a street punk, the two form an unlikely team, bringing their own peculiar code of ethics to the underworld. Based on the 1988 manga in *Young Champion* magazine, this is widely regarded as the masterwork of Ayumi Tachihara, who also created FOR REAL. **OV**

JUSTY

1985. JPN: *Cosmopolice Justy*. Video. DIR: Osamu Uemura. SCR: Hiroyuki Hoshiyama. DES: Tsugo Okazaki. ANI: Kazuya Iwata. MUS: Hiroya Watanabe. PRD: Studio Pierrot. 44 mins.

Justy Kaizard is a Cosmo Police Hunter—his job is to track down rogue psychics and exterminate them before they can harm others. He and his partner, Borba Len, track down the criminal psychic Magnamam Vega, and Justy kills him in front of his 6-year-old daughter, Asteris. The distraught child swears that she would kill Justy herself if she were bigger, and her own psychic powers, triggered by the tragedy, transform her into a 16-year-old, though the shock leaves her with amnesia. Growing up at Cosmo Police headquarters under the care of Justy's friend Jilna Star, she treats him as an adored big brother. But then the Crimina Esper, a group of malicious psychics, decide to dispose of Justy by awakening her memory and her hatred of the man who killed her father. Based on the 1981 manga by Tsugo Okazaki serialized in *Shonen Sunday* magazine, *Justy* was one of the more popular of the 1980s videos in early anime fandom, chiefly because of the short running time and easy-to-follow plot that did not really require subtitles. However, it was not brought to the U.S. as one might have expected, reputedly because the rights were prohibitively expensive.

KABUTO *

1990. JPN: *Karasu Tengu Kabuto*. AKA: *Raven Tengu Kabuto*. TV series, TV special, video. DIR: Takashi Watabe, Kazuya Miyazaki, Akira Kiyomizu, Mamoru Yamamoto, Taku Sugiyama. SCR: Hiroyuki Hoshiyama, Satoru Akahori. DES: Satoshi Urushihara, Buichi Terasawa. ANI: Kinji Yoshimoto, Hideaki Matsuoka. MUS: Seiko Nagaoka. PRD: Hiro Communications. 25 mins. x 39 eps. (TV), 45 mins. (v).

Dohki, the ruler of hell, is summoned to our world by the "evil mood of the age" and sets out to rule the universe with the help of his cronies. Raven Tengu Kabuto, a warrior-mage with the power of flight, magical runes, and a deadly blade, assembles a party of stock characters (a giant warrior, a loyal samurai, a cunning rogue, and the usual token blonde) in order to fight back. He rounds up the old members of his clan, who have been scattered to the four corners of Japan by an undisclosed disaster. Dohki in turn has assembled a group of baddies that represent the "dark halves" of Kabuto's little band, and the battle begins, with plenty of strange techno-fantastic machinery, most notably a flying metal dragon in the shape of a giant swastika.

After GOKU: MIDNIGHT EYE–creator Buichi Terasawa rejected the science-fiction medium for a while, he chose to work on the ALICE IN WONDERLAND—inspired *Black Knight Bat* manga and this decidedly unhistorical fantasy, which began as a 1985 manga in *Fresh Jump* magazine. *Kabuto* seems permanently unsure of whether it wants to be steampunk science fiction or fantastic adventure, with a madly anachronistic clutter of design goofs that polite critics would call eclectic. Kabuto's sword is a double-edged blade, yet he wields it like a single-edged katana, for example (as do the "Greek" warriors of ARION), while any sense of period is compromised by the hard-rock guitar music throughout. Kabuto is a *tengu* warrior, although whether this is a reference to the supernatural crow-demons of JAPANESE FOLK TALES or merely a particular martial arts school is unclear. Kabuto himself claims the latter, but at several points in the story also sprouts wings to fly out of dangerous situations. Suzaku, Kabuto's love interest, wears fishnet tights for no discernible reason, someone uses a semi-automatic musket, and characters can speak and breathe underwater without any effort or explanation. Nevertheless, elements creep in from *actual* Japanese folklore, including the notorious Fuma clan, also seen in LUPIN III and KOJIRO, as well as Kabuto's giant halberd-wielding companion Genbu, a respray of the Little John of Japanese legend, the super-monk Benkei.

The TV series was later edited down into two feature-length videos, *Kabuto: The Warrior* (compiling episodes 1–13) and *Kabuto: The Visitation* (compiling episodes 27–39). The hero returned in the one-shot original video *Kabuto: The Golden-Eyed Beast* (1992), the only incarnation of the series to be released commercially in English. For this story, the beautiful princess Ran is kidnapped by the evil vampiress Tamamushi. Kabuto must then rescue the princess, fighting off typically anachronistic threats such as muskets and medieval helicopters, as well as face-hugging spiders—an arachnid take on the Heike crabs, real-life creatures from Japan's Inland Sea whose shells bear shockingly accurate pictures of samurai-warriors' faces. Eventually, Tamamushi turns out to be a machine herself, which begs the question: If she really is an android, why does she need to sacrifice the souls of young women to keep herself young?

As before, the plot is heavily laden with inconsistencies—dialogue in both language versions switches from ancient idiom ("verily thou art a knave") to modern vernacular ("outta my way, bitch") and back again, while background scenery switches from that of northern Japan to that of southern China. Compare to Terasawa's other big success, SPACE ADVENTURE COBRA.

KAIKAN PHRASE

1999. TV series. DIR: Hiroko Tokita. SCR: Katsuhiko Koide, Reiko Yoshida, Satoru Tsuchiya. DES: Yumi Nakayama. ANI: Hiroaki Shimizu, Kazuhiro Sada. MUS: Takeshi Tsuji, Lucifer. PRD: Studio Unsa, TV Tokyo. 25 mins. x 37? eps.

Realizing that their pop group, Climb, is going nowhere, guitarist Yuki and drummer Santa decide to split and form a new combo. Calling themselves Lucifer, they discover their new vocalist in the form of pretty-boy Sakuya, who takes the job over playing the piano in a hotel bar. Sakuya, however, harbors some dark secrets of his own. This series was based on a manga by Mayu Shinjo serialized in *Shojo Comic* and rushed onto TV to cash in on the success of the earlier boy-band extravaganza WEISS KREUZ. Toning down the sensual original for an early-evening audience, the show nevertheless concentrates on the broody, moody male stars, emphasizing music and drama over the animation itself, which is of a rather cheap digital nature.

KAKKUN CAFÉ
1984. Movie. DIR: Osamu Kobayashi. SCR: N/C. DES: Tsutomu Shibayama. ANI: Tsutomu Shibayama, Hideo Kawauchi, Mitsuru Hongo, Michishiro Yamada, Tomomi Mochizuki. MUS: Takashi Fukui. PRD: Tokio MC, Asia Do, Tokyo Communications. 86 mins.
Kakuei "Kakkun" Tanaka is a superhero who hangs out with his friends Yasuhiro Nakasone (who agrees with everything anyone says), Tokushima yokel Takeo Miki, stingy Takeo Fukuda, and Masayoshi Ohira, who says nothing except "ooh" and "ah." Kakkun's misadventures begin with playing rugby at school, though after graduation he accidentally becomes prime minister of Japan. He visits New York, where he literally causes a stink by grilling dried mackerel, before preventing a nuclear war between hapless superpowers America and Russia. A political satire featuring anime caricatures of several Japanese politicians.

KAMA SUTRA *
1991. JPN: Kama Sutra Kyokyoku no Sex Adventure. AKA: Kama Sutra: The Ultimate Sex Adventure. Video. DIR: Masayuki Ozeki. SCR: Seiji Matsuoka. DES: Shinsuke Terasawa. ANI: Shinsuke Terasawa. MUS: Ken Yashima. PRD: Animate Film. 44 mins.
In 6th-century India, the brave knight Gopal is slain by the Naga cult. His bride Surya is saved from a fate worse than death by the Hindu gods, who transport her to a cavern of ice in the Himalayas. She is found in the 20th century by a team of archaeologists, who thaw her out in a Calcutta hospital by feeding her a mixture of male and female bodily fluids from an ancient relic called the Spermatic Cup. Surya immediately falls for the professor's handsome Japanese grandson, Ryu, who is a reincarnation of her beloved

Gopal. However, she is kidnapped by the Naga cult's present-day leader, Rudracin, who whisks her away to the underground paradise of Shambhala. Realizing that Rudracin intends to take Surya as his bride, drink from the Spermatic Cup, and return to the surface world as an immortal, Ryu pursues them. After pleasuring 48 nymphs in midair, he is allowed to enter Shambhala's temple, where he defeats Rudracin in a trial by combat. Ryu has sex with Surya but must leave her behind in Shambhala—the small print in the immortality contract. Back on the surface, he is reunited with his adoring Japanese girlfriend, Yukari.
A very different take on Hindu myth from the pious RAMAYANA, KS mixes the lovers-across-time theme of ADVENTURE KID with the playful smuttiness that has come to characterize Go Nagai's erotica. Based on an idea by Nagai and Kunio Nagatani, KS is the DEVILMAN creator's answer to the Indiana Jones films, complete with an adventurous archaeologist who is scared of snakes, rooms with crushing walls (which the lovers must halt by taking off their clothes and jamming them in the cracks), chases through Third World marketplaces, and a holy grail whose powers are not all they seem. As if that wasn't enough of a hint, our hero also has an irritating sidekick, seemingly modeled on Nagai himself, who asks to be called Indy. Surprisingly little is made of the central lovers Ryu and Surya, who only get to do the deed once as the closing credits roll, or indeed of Ryu and Yukari, who hardly even meet during the story. Instead, Ryu is educated in the techniques of the Kama Sutra by his father's red-haired Indian assistant Shakti, who escorts him through an elaborate maze of enclosed rooms from which the occupants can only escape by assuming the correct sexual position. Mostly harmless, with some nice sitar music, but not a patch on the oriental eroticism of Tezuka's ARABIAN NIGHTS.
🅛🅝🅥

KAMEARI PARK PRECINCT
1985. JPN: Kochira Katsushika-ku Kameari Koen-mae Hashutsujo. AKA: This Is the Police Station in Front of Kameari Park in Katsushika Ward; "Kochikame." Video, TV series, movie. DIR: Hiroshi Sasakawa (v), Shinji Takamatsu, Shinichi Tabe, Shinichiro Watanabe (TV). SCR: Takao Koyama (v), Takashi Yamada, Satoru Nishizono, Nobuaki Kishima (TV). DES: Ammonite (v), Tsukasa Fusanai (TV). ANI: Tsukasa Fusanai, Akitaro Daichi, Shunji Yoshida. MUS: N/C. PRD: Tatsunoko (v), Studio Gallop, Fuji TV. 30 mins. x 2 eps. (v), 15 mins. x 173+ eps. (TV), 90 mins. (m).
The gently humorous antics of a group of police officers responsible for a sleepy area near a large park. High jinks redolent of YOU'RE UNDER ARREST!, based on a 1976 manga from Shonen Jump magazine by Osamu Akimoto. Mild-mannered cop Ryotsu Kankichi is forever having to apologize for his behavior—as a shop assistant's son, he's a friendly neighborhood cop but eternally at odds with his avuncular boss Chief Ohara. The salt-of-the-earth Kanikichi is forced to share his duties with super-competent officer Reiko Akimoto and rich dandy Keiichi Nakagawa (a setup not unlike that of Goto, Shinobu, and Azuma in the later PATLABOR). The 2000 movie broadened the plot to encompass a bombing campaign by a disguised explosive expert named Benten (refer to CYBER CITY OEDO 808), with the Japanese police forced to cooperate with prissy FBI agent Lisa Hoshino. At over 100 volumes, Akimoto's manga is one of the longest-running in Japan. The anime's similar success, like that of SAZAE-SAN, is a mark of its popularity beyond the standard anime audience—the video versions were made to mark the 10th anniversary of the manga, and the first of the TV broadcasts marked the 20th.

KAMIKAZE THIEF JEANNE
1999. JPN: Kamikaze Kaito Jeanne. AKA: Jeanne de la Cambriole. TV series.

DIR: Atsutoshi Umezawa. SCR: Sukehiro Tomita. DES: Hisashi Kagawa. ANI: Katsumi Tamegai. MUS: Michiaki Kato. PRD: Toei, TV Asahi. 25 mins. x 41+ eps.

Alienated child-of-divorce Marron Kusakabe puts on her brave face and tries not to think about being left alone in Tokyo while her parents work abroad. She is visited by the angel Fin Fish, who reveals that she is the reincarnation of Saint Joan of Arc (known in the French fashion as Jeanne D'Arc in Japan). As the Day of Judgment approaches, it's Marron's job to retrieve important magical items to use in the battle against Satan. In her way stand transfer student Chiaki (who is really the rival angel Sindbad) and his dark angel assistant, Access Time. Meanwhile, since Marron's mission is to steal artifacts, she must keep her secret from her best friend, whose father is the chief of police. Owing more to CAT'S EYE and SAINT TAIL than the legendary liberator of Orleans also depicted in TRAGEDY OF BELLADONNA, this adaptation of Arina Tanemura's manga for *Ribbon* magazine is set in a strange conflation of France and Japan, with European buildings but Oriental lifestyles.

KARATE-CRAZY LIFE, A
1973. JPN: *Karate Baka Ichidai*. AKA: *Life of a Karate Idiot*. TV series. DIR: Eiji Okabe, Osamu Dezaki, Hideo Takayashiki. SCR: Yoshiaki Yoshida, Akinori Matsumoto. DES: Jiro Tsunoda. ANI: Okichiro Nanbu, Keijiro Kimura, Kazuhiko Udagawa. MUS: Mitsuru Kotani. PRD: TMS, MBS. 25 mins. x 47 eps.

Failed kamikaze pilot Ken Asuka becomes a rough, tough hooligan who settles all of his problems with karate, until he learns about the legendary swordsman Musashi Miyamoto in the novels of Eiji Yoshikawa. Resolving to live his life like Musashi, he begins to take karate more seriously. Based on a manga by Ikki Kajiwara and Jiro Tsunoda, itself inspired by the real life of Yasunobu Oyama, the founder of

the "hard-knock" Kyokushin Karate school.

KARUIZAWA SYNDROME
1985. Video. DIR: Mizuho Nishikubo. SCR: Tokio Tsuchiya. DES: Yoshihisa Tagami. ANI: Chuichi Iguchi. MUS: Shinsuke Kazato. PRD: Kitty Film. 76 mins.

In an adaptation of the manga that made a name for creator Yoshihisa Tagami, though radically different in every way from his more famous GREY: DIGITAL TARGET, the sex life of a young man is portrayed in graphic detail, occasionally lapsing into moments of super-deformed silliness. Sections are also shot in live action, directed by Tatsuo Moriyasu. ⊗

KARULA DANCES
1989. JPN: *Hengen Taima Yako Karula Mau*. AKA: *Karula Dances! Nocturnal Phantasm Warders; Garuda Dances*. Movie, video. DIR: Takaaki Ishiyama. SCR: Masaru Yamamoto. DES: Chuichi Iguchi. ANI: Chuichi Iguchi. MUS: Makoto Mitsui. PRD: Agent 21, Picture Kobo. 80 mins. (m), 30 mins. x 6 eps. (v).

Teenage twins Maiko and Shoko Ogi are the 38th generation to inherit the mystic warrior mantle of the holy Karula Shinyo line. They can also switch minds and combine their powers for greater strength against evil. Raised and trained by their grandmother, herself a psychic warrior of awesome powers, they fight the ancient spirits that lurk beneath the surface of modern Japan. Based on Masakazu Nagakubo's manga in *Halloween* magazine, the girls were just two of several anime "inheritors of ancient tradition" from the early 1990s, and they could be said to have inspired DEVIL HUNTER YOHKO and TWIN DOLLS, at least in part. They returned on video in 1990, finishing off demons in Japan's old capital of Nara, before heading up north to the city of Sendai to investigate cases of merpeople, amnesia, and crimes of demonic passion.

KATRI THE MILKMAID
1984. JPN: *Bokujo no Shojo Katri*. AKA:

With Earth enslaved by biomechanical mutants, a trio of boys travel back to the past to prevent Professor Nekasa from inventing the Generator process that will cause the catastrophe. Their secret weapon is Gawl, a boy who is reluctantly submitted to the painful transformation but can now call on the very powers that threaten the world. The result is GENERATOR GAWL, a TV show that combines the temporal espionage of *Terminator* with the weekly monster battle of ULTRAMAN. *See entry p. 138.*

Generator Gawl

© TATSUNOKO PRO • JVC

Katri the Girl of the Pastures. TV series. DIR: Hiroshi Saito, Hiromi Sugimura. SCR: Akira Miyazaki. DES: Noboru Takano. ANI: Noboru Takano, Noriko Moriyoshi. MUS: Toru Fuyuki. PRD: Nippon Animation, Fuji TV. 25 mins. x 49 eps.

When her mother remains in 1915 Germany, little Katri is sent to stay with her grandfather in Finland. Life is hard for the nine-year-old girl as war breaks out, and she is forced to earn money by working as a maid in the Raikola household. She meets various people, including Akki, a campaigner for Finnish independence, and Emilia, a doctor who inspires her to seek a better life for herself. This is another WORLD MASTERPIECE THEATER anime that mines the seemingly limitless vein of stories about little European country girls facing hardships, this one based on the Finnish novel *Paimen Piikamenta* by Auni Nuoliwaara. Compare to HEIDI.

KAYOKO'S DIARY *
1991. JPN: *Ushiro no Shomen Daaaare*. AKA: *Someone at My Shoulder*. Movie. DIR: Seiji Arihara. SCR: Seiji Arihara, Tetsuaki Imaizumi. DES: Takaya Ono. ANI: Takaya Ono. MUS: Reijiro Komutsu. PRD: Mushi Pro. 90 mins.

Kayoko is a nine-year-old girl in 1940 Tokyo, with a poor extended family that includes three brothers and a grandmother. She plays in her neighborhood but is bullied by other children, though she is protected by her kindly big brother Kisaburo. By 1944, Kayoko is caring for another brother, the newest addition to the family, while fear of air raids eventually results in her evacuation to live with her aunt in rural Numazu. From the hilltop, she can see the distant lights of Tokyo, until the night of March 10, 1945, when the city glows with the fires of an American bombing. All Kayoko's family are killed except Kisaburo, and the now-teenage girl returns to her old home one last time to say farewell to her childhood. Based on the autobiography of Kayoko Ebina, who also wrote the novel *Wolf of Downtown*, this tale follows the lead of GRAVE OF THE FIREFLIES, telling a war story through the eyes of a child. It also bears an uncanny resemblance to director Arihara's earlier RAINING FIRE. Shown on a double bill with the short ON A PAPER CRANE and given a limited foreign release through subtitled showings at film festivals.

KEEP IT UP! GUIDE DOG SAAB

1988. JPN: *Ganbare! Modoken Saab*. TV special. DIR: Seiji Okuda. SCR: Fujio Takizawa. DES: Shuichi Seki. ANI: Takashi Saijo. MUS: Hisashi Miyazaki. PRD: Tama Pro, NHK. 27 mins.
The true story of a seeing-eye dog that brings hope to a blind child, based on a novel by Yuichi Tejima. Lifting several tropes from sports anime such as AIM FOR THE ACE, a well-loved puppy's life is turned upside down as he is put through a tough training regime, until he triumphs and makes the world a better place.

KEKKO KAMEN *

1991. JPN: *Kekko Kamen*. Video. DIR: Chuji Iguchi, Nobuyoshi Kondo, Jun Kawagoe, Kinji Yoshimoto. SCR: Masashi Sogo. DES: Satoshi Hirayama. ANI: Masayoshi Sudo, Koji Morimoto.

MUS: Keiji Ishikawa. PRD: Studio Signal, Dynamic, Bee Media. 45 mins. x 2 eps.
The students of Sparta College are terrorized by the perverse regime of the principal, Great Toenail of Satan (aka Satan Tochiz), and his lecherous assistant, Ben. Regularly appointing new teachers to abuse and humiliate the girls (the boys are let off because Tochiz only wants to see the girls with their clothes off), they are thwarted on every occasion by Kekko Kamen, the "naked avenger."
A smutty, saucy adventure based on the 1974 *Shonen Jump* manga from SHAMELESS SCHOOL's Go Nagai, lampooning MOONLIGHT MASK (*Gekko Kamen*) and the sappiest formulae of girls'-school dramas, with liberal doses of female nudity. Though occasionally pushing the boundaries of good taste (the first supply-teacher, S/M queen Gestapa, has just transferred from Auschwitz College), the idea of a superheroine wearing nothing but boots and a mask so that "we see her dumplings, but her face remains a mystery," has plenty of comic potential. The hapless student Mayumi is whipped, tickled, and tortured, while her "big sister" Chigusa tries to offer helpful advice on escaping the teachers' notice. superpowered opponents sent to take care of Kekko Kamen include the muscle-bound Austrian PE teacher, Taro Schwarzenegger, and a samurai cameraman with a hilarious Sean Connery accent in the U.K. dub. Mayumi must also fend off the advances of the Paradicer Mark One, a lesbian android sent to break up her friendship with Chigusa—Kekko Kamen must find Paradicer's off-button, which inventor Ben has put in a predictably sensitive spot. Though never explained in the anime version, the manga reveals that Kekko Kamen is actually Chigusa's twin, allowing the sisters to switch places and keep the superheroine's identity hidden. The story exists in U.S. and U.K. versions, though the British one did not survive the British censor unscathed—a scene

in which Gestapa strips Mayumi by throwing knives at her while she is strapped to a giant rotating swastika was just one of the casualties. The story was also adapted into a live-action film, *Kekko Mask: The Birth* (1991), directed by Yutaka Akiyama, and two sequels, *Kekko Mask* (1993) and *Kekko Mask in Love* (1995). But the live versions, which feature cameos from MAZINGER Z and CUTEY HONEY, suffer from a heroine who is understandably coy about revealing all and lack the slapstick verve of the anime. *Ill. p. 349.* ⬤Ⓛ Ⓝ Ⓥ

KEN THE WOLF BOY *

1963. JPN: *Okami Shonen Ken*. TV series. DIR: Sadao Tsukioka, Kimio Yabuki, Yugo Serikawa, Hiroshi Ikeda, Yoshio Kuroda, Isao Takahata, Taiji Yabushita, Takeshi Tamiya, Masayuki Akehi, Kazuya Miyazaki. SCR: Satoshi Iijima, Yugo Serikawa, Kuniaki Oshikawa, Daisaku Shirokawa, Minoru Hamada, Jiro Yoshino, Aya Suzuki. DES: Sadao Tsukioka. ANI: Takeshi Kitamasa. MUS: Yasei Kobayashi. PRD: Toei, NET. 25 mins. x 86 eps.
Climate changes brought on by a passing comet plunge Africa into chaos, and a group of wolves struggle to survive. However, they have a trump card, the "two-legged wolf" Ken, a boy who lives with them in the jungle. Learning from Jack the wolf-hero and Boss the wolf-elder, Ken protects wolf-cubs Chichi and Poppo. This variant on Kipling's *Jungle Book* was broadcast in Australia but is otherwise unknown in the English-speaking world.

KENNEL TOKOROZAWA

1992. Video. DIR: Hiroshi Sasakawa, Seitaro Hara. SCR: Shikichi Ohashi. DES: Katsumi Hashimoto. ANI: Katsumi Hashimoto. MUS: Ma-ri-ko. PRD: Animation 21. 44 mins.
Pet shop owner's daughter Chika Tokorozawa spends every waking hour with her dog, Rin Tin Tin, who repays her love by watching over her while she sleeps. Based on the manga in *Young Sunday* magazine by Maki Otsubo, who

is better known in the manga world for *Mr. Cinema*.

KENYA BOY

1984. Movie. DIR: Norihiko Obayashi, Tetsuo Imazawa. SCR: Chiho Katsura. DES: N/C. ANI: Hiroshi Wagatsuma, Masami Suda, Kazuo Mori, Shingo Araki, Michi Himeno, Kenji Yokoyama, Hirohide Yashikijima. MUS: Tatsuzo Usaki. PRD: Kadokawa, Toei. 109 mins.
In late 1941, textile trader Mr. Murakami takes his son Wataru on a business trip out of his home base in Nairobi, Kenya. They are attacked by a rampaging rhinoceros and separate to escape it, but Murakami is found by the British. After the attack on Pearl Harbor, the British and Japanese are now at war, so Murakami is arrested. Wataru is taken in by Masai tribesmen and goes native, heading off in search of his father, with time out for *Indiana Jones*-style adventures with lions, elephants, a lost valley of dinosaurs, a giant snake, and a slimy Nazi spy. Based on Soji Yamakawa's novel *The Boy King*, this movie uses heavy rotoscoping techniques from former live-action director Obayashi to impart a more realistic look to many of the scenes. Compare to KEN THE WOLF BOY and BUSHBABY.

KEROPPI *

1989. JPN: *Kerokero Keroppi*. Video. DIR: Masami Hata, Masahito Kitagawa. SCR: Asami Watanabe, Shikichi Ohashi, Satoru Nishizono. DES: N/C. ANI: Tsuchiaki Noma. MUS: Yoshihisa Shirokawa, Richard Niels, Takeshi Ike, Katsuyoshi Kobayashi. PRD: Sanrio. Ca. 30 mins. x 15 eps.
Kerokero ("Ribbit") Keroppi is a friendly green frog with huge eyes and stripy pants, designed on the same Sanrio merchandising production line that created PEKKLE, POCHACCO, and BAD BATZ-MARU. As do his stablemates, he appears in a series of cash-in videos designed to burn brand identity into the retinas of impressionable young children, commencing with cameo spots in other Sanrio videos in 1989. He appeared in the anthology title *KK*

Adventures (1990), comprising his adventures in *In Search of the Pink Mushroom*, *Everybody Say Hello to the Priest*, and *Secrets at the Plum Shop*. Since then, *KK* has flitted between the staple formulae of Sanrio adaptations, including fairy-tale pastiches of *Three Musketeers* (1991), the theatrically shown "movie" *Jack and the Beanstalk* (1991), *Robin Hood* (1993), and *Gulliver's Travels*—these last two released in the U.S. He has also appeared in two moral tales, *Friends Are Fun* (1992) and *Let's Be Friends* (1994), though his educational aspirations never became quite so all-encompassing as those of his brand sister HELLO KITTY. Other *KK* outings are more "original," featuring several adventures for the frog and his friends, including *K's Christmas Eve Gift* (1992), the baseball adventure *Go for It! Keroppies!* (1993), the ghostly *Secrets of KK House* (1993), and the haunted museum chiller *That Dinosaur's Alive!* (1993). More wistful outings came in the form of *K's Flying Dream Ship* (1992) and *If I Could Fly . . .* (1994). In recent years, his anime appearances have waned—his last outing was in *Adventures of the Cowardly Prince* (1997), which was released combined on a tape with the earlier *KK's Flying Ghost Ship*. *Go for It! Keroppies* and *Let's Be Friends* were also released in the U.S., under the title *K: Let's Play Baseball*.

KEY THE METAL IDOL *

1994. Video. DIR: Hiroaki Sato. SCR: Hiroaki Sato. DES: Kunihiko Tanaka. ANI: Keiichi Ishikura. MUS: Minya Terajima. PRD: Studio Pierrot. 25 mins. x 13 eps., 90 mins. x 2 eps.
A dying professor leaves a message for his granddaughter Tokiko "Key" Mima. She is an android, but she is dying, too, and her battery is irreplaceable. If, however, she can make thirty thousand friends, their love will rejuvenate her and turn her into a real girl. Realizing there are not too many ways to reach that many people in a limited time, Key heads for Tokyo, where her friend Sakura helps her begin a career as a pop singer. But she soon discovers that

there is more to her destiny than the simplistic quest outlined by her grandfather—Key's predicament and its solution are tied up in the dark secrets of her own family. The adoration of the crowd can literally free her soul for a moment, but it can also unleash other, more effective powers that other interested parties are keen on gaining for themselves. An uneven but engrossing anime that flips between the attention-hungry desperation of a performance artist and a vampiric military conspiracy, with time out for a number of superior musical interludes. And with a lead character who thinks she is a dying robot but whose friends merely think she is a traumatized, abused little girl, it contains a subtle identity crisis that would be used to greater effect by another Mima, played by the same actress Junko Iwao, in PERFECT BLUE. *Ill. p. 211*.

KICKERS

1986. JPN: *Ganbare Kickers*. AKA: *Go for It! Kickers!* TV series. DIR: Akira Torino, Mutsu Iwata, Shigeru Morikawa. SCR: Sukehiro Tomita, Isao Shizutani, Mitsuo Jushibutsu. DES: Takeshi Osaka. ANI: Takeshi Osaka, Takeshi Nagai. MUS: Jun Irigawa. PRD: Studio Pierrot, Nippon TV. 25 mins. x 23 eps.
The soccer team Kitahara Kickers have lost 22 matches in a row, but all that changes when Sho Oji transfers to the team's school and imbues it with his hot-headed spirit. He inspires the team members to aim to win just a single match to regain their self-esteem. This short-lived series was based on a 1984 *Corocoro Comic* manga by Noriaki Nagai and is uncannily similar to OFFSIDE.

KIKAIDER

2000. JPN: *Jinzo Ningen Kikaider*. AKA: *Android Kikaider*. TV series, video. DIR: Tensai Okamura. SCR: Akemi Omode, Shinsuke Ohashi, Masashi Sogo. DES: Naoyuki Konno. ANI: Naoyuki Konno. MUS: N/C. PRD: Radix, Studio OX, Kid's Station. 25 mins. x 13 eps. (TV), 4 eps. (v).
When he is mortally wounded in an

accident, Professor Koakishi is restored to life in an android body, believing that a good heart does not deserve to die before its time. But Koakishi's laboratory is attacked one stormy night by an unknown assailant. As his daughter Mitsuko escapes the flames, the whole incident is being watched by a young boy, Jiro, from a vantage point in the forest. Jiro is the last of Koakishi's creations, a robot created to save humankind, Mitsuko in particular. Fighting off the robot minions of the "dark professor" Gill, Jiro transforms into Kikaider, a superpowerful android ready to fight for good. One of **CYBORG 009**–creator Shotaro Ishinomori's most popular live-action creations, *Kikaider* was a relative latecomer to anime, not animated until after its creator's death.

KIKI AND LARA . . .

1989. JPN: *Kiki to Lara*. Video. DIR: Masami Hata. SCR: Asami Watanabe, Kenji Terada. DES: Yukio Abe. ANI: Maya Matsuyama. MUS: Takanori Arisawa. PRD: Sanrio. 30 mins. x 8 eps.

The **HELLO KITTY** team returns for another onslaught of stories based around Sanrio-themed merchandise, on this occasion featuring the loving twins Kiki and Lara. First appearing in a 1989 remake of Maeterlinck's **BLUE BIRD**, they got their own short-lived series of videos in the early 1990s. The children play house, chase after a Pegasus foal, decide they want to be princesses for a day, and try out some magical dance shoes. They also appeared in their own version of the *Hansel and Gretel* story from **GRIMMS' FAIRY TALES**.

KIKI'S DELIVERY SERVICE *

1989. JPN: *Majo no Takkyubin*. AKA: *Witch's Special Express Delivery*. Movie. DIR: Hayao Miyazaki. SCR: Hayao Miyazaki. DES: Katsuya Kondo. ANI: Shinji Otsuka, Yoshifumi Kondo. MUS: Joe Hisaishi. PRD: Studio Ghibli. 102 mins.
Thirteen-year-old Kiki decides to follow in her mother's footsteps. and become a witch, meaning she has to fly away from home and live for a year in a strange town. Accompanied only by her irascible black cat, Jiji, she heads for the seaside and finds the bustling harbor town of Koriko without its own witch. Finding a room at a kindly baker's, she discovers that her ability to fly on a broomstick is a marketable skill and begins delivering packages and messages. Despite minor mishaps and an often-ungrateful clientele, the freelance witch wins hearts all over town, particularly that of would-be pilot Tombo, who is smitten with her. A crisis of confidence causes Kiki to lose her ability to fly, but she regains it in time to save Tombo, who is trapped on a runaway airship. Writing to her mother, Kiki proudly calls Koriko her home.

Like **MY NEIGHBOR TOTORO**, *Kiki* is a world without definable enemies or evil—prissy rich girls may sulk when they get a fish pie for their birthday, but it's hardly an offense, and the only crime the police investigate in the course of the film is a fake one (Tombo pretends he has been robbed). Everyone creates value in their own ways, from the silent baker who melts Kiki's heart with a witch-themed bread sculpture, to the kindly old dog who protects Jiji from a bratty child. Venerable oldsters sigh about how times have changed, but the young generation shouldn't cause them to despair—like Kiki and her artist friend Ursula, they are simply finding their way in their own lives and times.

Miyazaki's follow-up to *Totoro* leaves childhood behind and steps into the early teens in one of the most wonderful films ever made about growing up. Set in a *neverwhere* Europe that combines the look of Stockholm (where Miyazaki had been location-hunting for the canceled 1971 Tokyo Movie Shinsha anime *Pippi Longstocking*) with the light of the Mediterranean, this utterly charming story is based on a book by Eiko Kadono, who also wrote the less well-known **COBBY THE CUTE LITTLE CAT**. The original *Kiki* novel lacked both the crisis of faith and the airborne resolution, which were added for the screen adaptation, initially against the author's wishes. Miyazaki films his witch with the same love of flight that characterizes **NAUSICAÄ**, with views and perspectives impossible from the ground. He imbues her with the independent spirit of Fio from **PORCO ROSSO** but does not shy from having a heroine who can catch cold, feel sorry for herself, and worry about her food budget. The result is arguably one of his best films, the seventh highest-grossing animated film at the Japanese box office, and a character who deserves to be the patron saint of freelancers, students, and motorcycle messengers.

Picked up by Buena Vista for U.S. distribution but not given a theatrical release, *Kiki* became one of the best-selling anime videos in America, trouncing **AKIRA** with sales topping a million. The U.S. dub featured Kirsten Dunst, Janeane Garofolo, and Phil Hartman freely improvising as Jiji in one of his last film roles. An earlier English dub, prepared by Carl Macek's Streamline Pictures for in-flight screenings on JAL trans-Pacific flights, was included on the Japanese Laser Disc but never released in the U.S.

KIKO-CHAN'S SMILE

1996. JPN: *Kiko-chan Smile*. TV series. DIR: Setsuko Shibunnoichi. SCR: Tsubasa Yoshiura. DES: Yukari Kobayashi. ANI: Yukari Kobayashi. MUS: So-Fi. PRD: Magic Bus, TBS. 7 mins. x 51 eps.
In this adaptation of Tsubasa Yoshiura's comedy manga, a sullen, cynical child is born to a pair of lovestruck parents who truly adore each other. Arch comments on the folly of adulthood, in what some might describe as a junior version of *Daria*. Two episodes of *Kiko* bracketed a single episode featuring her pet cat and his feline friends, who develop the power of speech in their own shows, but become mute once more for Kiko's.

KILDIAN

1996. JPN: *Kigurumi Sentai Kildian*. AKA: *Dress-Up Battle-Team Kildian*.

Video. DIR: N/C. SCR: Rei Nekojima.
DES: Rei Nekojima. ANI: N/C. MUS: N/C.
PRD: Pink Pineapple, KSS. 30 mins. x 2
eps.

Twin schoolgirls transform into their
superhero aspects to save the world
from an evil cabal of would-be dictators, but they can only fight for justice
by having lots of sex. This short-lived
porno anime was based on a manga by
the pseudonymous Rei Nekojima—the
only name of any sort attached to this
show in our sources. **N**

KILLIFISH SCHOOL
2001. JPN: *Medaka no Gakko*. Video.
DIR: Hiroyuki Takagi, Ryoji Fujiwara. SCR:
Miho Maruo. DES: Yukie Mori. ANI: Kiyotaka Kiyoyama. MUS: N/C. PRD: Office
Ao. 30 mins. x N/D eps.
Japanese teenage girl Medaka transfers
to a new school, where her homeroom
teacher, Mr. Tanaka, has a fish for a
head. This series is based on the surreal four-panel strip in *Ribbon* magazine
by Yukie Mori and supposedly sold
exclusively through the Internet
(though since you could also phone,
you'd be forgiven for just calling it mail
order).

KIMAGURE ORANGE ROAD *
1987. AKA: *Orange Road Follies*. TV
series, movie, video. DIR: Osamu
Kobayashi, Kazuhiko Kobayashi,
Hiroyuki Yokoyama, Kazuhiko Ikegami.
SCR: Kenji Terada, Sukehiro Tomita,
Shikichi Ohashi. DES: Akemi Takada.
ANI: Masako Goto, Toyomi Sugiyama.
MUS: Shiro Sagisu. PRD: Studio Pierrot,
Nippon TV. 25 mins. x 48 eps. (TV), 25
mins. x 10 eps. (v), 34 mins. (music),
69 mins. (m1), 94 mins. (m2).
Kyosuke Kasuga falls for the pretty
Madoka when her hat blows away in
the wind, but the attractive, musically
minded girl often seems aloof. To complicate matters, Madoka's bubbly
friend Hikaru has fallen for Kyosuke,
and although he likes her as a friend,
he truly has eyes only for Madoka.
Meanwhile, the head of the karate
club, who wants Hikaru for himself, is
mad at Kyosuke, while Kyosuke's irritat-

ing sisters do everything within their
power to make him realize that Hikaru
is the girl for him.

A standard anime love polygon is
exacerbated by a superfluous subplot
revealing that Kyosuke and the rest of
his family have psychic powers. Here,
then, is the reason that Kyosuke is an
eternal transfer student, as his family
tries to outrun public suspicion. Terminally underused in many episodes,
these optional extras merely allow for
some easy getaways from difficult situations, though they are more often likely to backfire, like **DORAEMON**'s
inventions, and get him into still
greater trouble. They also provide
occasions for comedies of manners
and social observations, such as
Kyosuke's mind-reading cousin, who
periodically blurts out people's secret
inner thoughts for comedic effect.

KOR began as a manga in *Shonen
Jump* by Izumi Matsumoto, its 1983 premiere imbuing the entire series with a
deep sense of 1980s nostalgia. Its TV
run was contemporary with **MAISON
IKKOKU**, another drama-comedy about
unsuitable friends becoming unexpected lovers, both made for the **URUSEI
YATSURA** viewing audience as it aged
and found comedy less exciting than
romance. Retained in the anime version is a plethora of 1980s cultural references, chiefly musical, but also
extending to the films of the moment
such as *Top Gun*.

In 1988, the manga was jettisoned
by its publisher and ended early in
Shonen Jump, though the anime continued straight to video for several more
episodes. Studiously tiptoeing around
the TV series continuity, the videos
packed the characters off for stand-
alone episodes including a trip to
Hawaii and a winter skiing trip in the
Japanese Alps. The uneven TV series,
which often flitted from romance to
comedy to sci-fi pranks, was compart-
mentalized into several "specials"
designed to bury the lackluster
episodes and polish the undeniable
jewels in each genre. A 34-minute
music video, *KOR: Music Version*, com-

San leaps into battle in **PRINCESS MONONOKE**.
Though supposedly reared in the wild, her
clothes and mask suggest a connection with
Japan's prehistoric inhabitants. A symbolic conflict between Japan's nature-loving past and its
rapacious, progressive present, Hayao Miyazaki's *PM* is set in the Muromachi era, the time
when humankind began attempting to exert
control over nature. *PM* broke box office
records in Japan, though Miyazaki's follow up,
SPIRITED AWAY, was released as this encyclopedia went to press and already looks sure to
beat it. See entry p. 309.

Princess Mononoke

© 1997 NIBARIKI/TNDG

prised 12 tunes from the series played
over a clip-show of best scenes. The story proper ended with the movie *KOR: I
Want to Return to That Day* (1988).
Directed by Tomomi Mochizuki and
told chiefly in flashback, it discards all
thought of comedy or psychic powers
and concentrates instead on Kyosuke
making a tough decision and breaking
Hikaru's heart. Compare this to the
coy attitudes of its spiritual successor
TENCHI MUYO!, which remains permanently undecided in order to save
everyone's focus-group feelings. Several more video episodes limped along
afterward, two misleadingly premiered
in theaters for those fans who couldn't
accept that there would be no more—
*KOR: Shapeshifting Akane, KOR: I Am a
Cat/I Am a Fish*, and *KOR: Heart on
Fire/Love Stage. KOR*, however, found a
new lease of life in the U.S., where it
was one of the cornerstones of early
video anime fandom, many members
of which were of an age to savor the
1980s nostalgia. It remained a fan
favorite in Japan, too, and eventually
returned for a second ending in *KOR:
And So the Summer Began* (1996), directed by Kunihiko Yuyama. This version
flings the 19-year-old Kyosuke three
years into the future, where his newly
graduated adult self is a cameraman in

Bosnia. With his relationship with Madoka in trouble, and the return of Hikaru, the final *KOR* film presents an opportunity for everyone to live happily ever after—and for the viewers to say a final farewell by seeing their characters do the same, in much the same way as the final **PATLABOR** send-off.

KIMBA THE WHITE LION *

1965. JPN: *Jungle Taitei*. AKA: *Jungle Emperor*. TV series, movie. DIR: Eiichi Yamamoto, Junji Nagashima, Toshio Hirata, Chikao Katsui, Hideaki Kitano. SCR: Masaki Tsuji, Shunichi Yukimuro, Eiichi Yamamoto. DES: Osamu Tezuka. ANI: Chikao Katsui, Hiroshi Saito. MUS: Isao Tomita. PRD: Mushi Pro, Tezuka Pro, Fuji TV. 25 mins. x 52 eps. (TV1), 75 mins. (m1), 25 mins. x 26 eps. (TV2), 25 mins. x 52 eps. (TV3), 98 mins. (m2).

Panja (Caesar), the white lion king of the jungle, is killed by the human hunter Hamegg (Viper Snakely), who captures his mate Eliza (Snowene) alive. Caged on a ship en route to an overseas zoo, Eliza gives birth to their son Leo (Kimba), who escapes by jumping overboard. Eventually returning to the jungle, Leo befriends Mandy (Dan'l Baboon), a wise mandrill counselor, Coco (Pauley Cracker) the parrot, and Tommy (Bucky) the chronically shy deer. They revere him as Panja II, and Leo resolves to keep the jungle forever peaceful by ridding it of Bubu (Claw), his evil, scarred lion adversary, and bumbling hyena minions.

Paid for in part with money from American network NBC, *Kimba* was made with the demands of the foreign market in mind. Hence, **ASTRO BOY**–creator Tezuka was forced to make the story in bite-sized chunks that could be screened out of order without overreaching story arcs. This restriction has severely damaged **DRAGON BALL** and certain other more recent anime that are often shown in a jumbled order by TV channels who can't count. On the bonus side, NBC money secured a high enough budget to leave

monochrome behind, and *Kimba* became the first full-color anime TV series. Several episodes were cut together to make the movie *Jungle Emperor* (1966, *Jungle Taitei*), which was nominated for a Golden Lion for animation at the Venice Film Festival. The name Leo was regarded as unacceptable in the American market, where it was the name of the famous MGM lion; instead, the translators originally intended to name their hero *Simba*, Swahili for "lion." However, this was also rejected on account of a number of African-American trademark applications using the Simba name, though the coincidence would return to haunt the franchise in the 1990s.

Tezuka's original 1950 manga *Jungle Emperor*, serialized in *Manga Shonen*, took the story of Leo much further along, with the white lion growing up, siring his own heir, and eventually laying down his life to save his realm. However, the concept of characters aging was another casualty of the stand-alone episode structure, and the anime Kimba remained permanently a cub. Tezuka redressed this balance with *New Jungle Emperor: Onward, Leo!* (1966, *Shin Jungle Taitei, Susumu Leo!*), a second series that took Leo to adulthood, which was initially intended solely for the Japanese audience. *Onward, Leo!* featured character designs from a young Rintaro and an involving subplot about Mount Moon and a fabled gem—a plot that would later be ripped off for episode six of **POKÉMON**. The adult Kimba/Leo was popular enough to become the mascot of the Seibu Lions baseball team in Japan (see **GO FOR IT, TABUCHI!**), and eventually made it to the States on the Christian Broadcasting Network under the title *Leo the Lion* (1984). By that time, however, Tezuka's studio had filed for bankruptcy, and a litigation tangle had taken the original *Kimba* series off the air.

The series was remade by Tezuka Productions as *New Adventures of Kimba the White Lion* (1989, *Shinsaku Jungle Taitei*), directed by Takashi Ui, taking Leo from his birth up to the moment

when he brings some semblance of order to the jungle. This version was also eventually released in the U.S., but not until after an unexpected brush with controversy in the mid-1990s.

The series had slowly faded from public perception until the release of Disney's *The Lion King* (1994), the tale of a lion called Simba, whose father dies, who just can't wait to be king, who has a mandrill for a counselor, an argumentative parrot-like bird (a hornbill) for a friend, and an evil, scarred lion adversary (plus bumbling hyena minions). Like Kimba, Disney's Simba is also haunted by his father's face in the clouds, a fact lampooned in an episode of *The Simpsons*, when the ghostly apparition of Disney's Mufasa appears to Lisa and mixes up the Simba-Kimba names. Disney representatives made the unlikely assertion that the *entire* production staff of *The Lion King* was unaware of the Tezuka original (including codirector Roger Allers, who, by Disney's own admission, had spent *two years* in Tokyo working on **LITTLE NEMO: ADVENTURES IN SLUMBERLAND**). The controversy was given further fuel when Fumio Suzuki, a creditor who claimed partial ownership of the original 1965 series, authorized the rerelease of eight episodes on video as *Kimba the Lion Prince* (1996), with a new dub that seemed deliberately calculated to imply further, previously nonexistent parallels with the hapless Disney production.

Ironically, the controversy over the Disney film may have pushed Tezuka Productions into making yet another version of its own work, the movie *Kimba the White Lion* (1997, aka, much to the annoyance of encyclopedia compilers, *Jungle Emperor Leo*), released just a little too late to warrant the filmmakers' claims that it was in honor of the original's 30th anniversary. This time directed by Toshio Takeuchi and with character designs by Akio Sugino, the big-budget *Kimba* anime is the last incarnation of the series to date. Disney would inadvertently antagonize the anime audience again with *Atlantis:*

The Lost Empire (2001)—see **SECRET OF BLUE WATER.** *Ill. p. 95.*

KIMERA *

1996. JPN: *Ki-Me-Ra.* Video. DIR: Kazu Yokota. SCR: Kenichi Kanemaki. DES: Kazuma Kodaka. ANI: N/C. MUS: Shiro Sagisu. PRD: Toho. 48 mins.
Legends about vampires and vampirism are finally explained, as strange "lifepods" from space crash in the Western mountains. Their occupants are alien creatures who need humanity to help them propagate their species. A war begins between the space-vampires and their earthly prey, but Terran boy Osamu begins to have feelings for the androgynous Kimera, the vampire sent to kill him. An erotic thriller, based on a manga by Kazuma Kodaka, creator of **KIZUNA,** not to be confused with **CHIMERA.** 🔞

KING ARTHUR AND THE KNIGHTS OF THE ROUND TABLE *

1979. JPN: *Entaku no Kishi Monogatari Moero Arthur.* AKA: *Rage of Arthur; Tales of the Knights of the Round Table.* TV series. DIR: Masayuki Akehi, Tomoharu Katsumata, Masamune Ochiai, Kazumi Fukushima, Teppei Matsuura, Shigeru Omachi. SCR: Michiru Umadori, Akira Nakano, Tsunehisa Ito. DES: Takuo Noda. ANI: Takuo Noda, Yasuhiko Suzuki, Seiji Kikuchi. MUS: Shinichi Tanabe, Shunsuke Kikuchi. PRD: Toei, Fuji TV. 25 mins. x 30 eps., 25 mins. x 22 eps.
When his parents are killed by the evil King Lavic, the three-year-old Arthur is spirited away from Camelot castle by the sorcerer Merlin. Becoming a squire to Sir Ector, at the age of 15 he is able to pull the sword Excalibur from a stone, thus becoming the rightful ruler of the Britons.

A lackluster series that manages to make Arthurian legend look like just another cartoon, it compares unfavorably with anime such as **ESCAFLOWNE** that can make cartoons look like Arthurian legend. Based on Thomas Malory's *Morte D'Arthur,* but only indirectly, through a manga adaptation by

GARAGA-creator Satomi Mikuriya, it was serialized in several children's publications, including *Terebiland* and *Terebi* magazine. The second series, *Prince on a White Horse* (1980, *Moero Arthur Hakuba no Oji*), sinks almost completely into anime cliché, dumping earlier talk of Lancelot, Morgan le Fay, and a Leiji Matsumoto–influenced Lady of the Lake. Instead, it seems to confuse legends of King Arthur with legends of King *Alfred* and a heavy dose of 1970s pulp fantasy, pitting the prince against an invasion of flying Norse longships crewed by the "Zaikings." Accompanied by a young boy with the suitably Old English name of Pete, Arthur must travel undercover, find some secret treasure, and defeat the evil Baron Damiane. In the final episodes, the story reintroduces the Knights of the Round Table and Princess Guinevere, but not before Arthur has met some mermaids, fought off some pirates, and had an encounter with a snow princess straight out of **JAPANESE FOLK TALES.**

Some of the more recognizable episodes were released in a U.S. dub in the 1980s by Family Home Entertainment in a version that provides additional unintentional hilarity as voice-actors attempt English accents with varying degrees of failure. Further dolorous strokes were dealt to British heritage in **MARINA THE MANGA ARTIST GOES TO CAMELOT.**

KING FANG

1978. JPN: *Oyukiyama no Yusha Ha-o.* AKA: *King Fang, Hero of Snowy Mountain.* TV special. DIR: Eiji Okabe. SCR: Ryuzo Nakanishi. DES: Takao Kasai. ANI: Susumu Shiraume. MUS: Ryusuke Onosaki. PRD: Nippon Animation, Fuji TV. 75 mins.
A European wolf and a Sakhalin dog sire five puppies in the wild north of Japan. One day, the canine family is attacked by Gon, the man-eating bear, and the mother is killed. One of the puppies is found by a human girl under a waterfall. She adopts him and names him Taki (Japanese for waterfall), rearing him as a domesticated

dog. However, as in **CALL OF THE WILD,** doubtlessly the inspiration for the Tatsuo Edogawa novel on which this anime is based, Taki's true nature eventually comes out, and he heads for the mountains to return to his own kind.

KING KONG SHOW, THE *

1966. JPN: *Sekai no Osha King Kong Daikai.* AKA: *King Kong Ruler of the World.* TV series. DIR: Hiroshi Ikeda. SCR: Noboshiro Ueno (trans.). DES: Jack Davis, Rod Willis. ANI: Sakei Kitamasa, Tsutomu Shibayama, Osamu Kobayashi, Midori Kusube, Yasuo Maeda, Norio Fukuda. MUS: Yasei Kobayashi. PRD: Toei, Videocraft, Rankin-Bass, NET. 56 mins. (TVm), 8 mins. x 52 eps.
King Kong is a giant ape who lives on an island in the Java Sea. Bobby Bond, whose father is a professor studying the island, meets King Kong and befriends him. Bond father and son cooperate to protect King Kong from the evil Dr. Who, although the large creature can more than hold his own in a fight.

Commissioned by Rankin-Bass from the U.S. company Videocraft, which in turn farmed out the work to Toei in Japan, *King Kong* was the first "anime" to be made specifically for the American market. Though Toei was funding part of it themselves and eventually showed it in Japan, the designs, scripts, storyboards, and voice track were all supplied ready-made from the U.S. As with the American version, episodes of *KK* bookended a single episode of **TOM OF T.H.U.M.B.** to comprise a half-hour show.

KINNIKUMAN: ULTIMATE MUSCLE *

1983 AKA: *Muscleman.* TV series, movie. DIR: Yasuo Yamakichi, Tetsuo Imazawa, Takenori Kawata, Takeshi Shirato. SCR: Haruya Yamazaki, Kenji Terada. DES: Toshio Mori. ANI: Eikichi Takahashi. MUS: Shinsuke Kazato. PRD: Toei, Nippon TV. 25 mins. x 137 eps, 48 mins. x 7 (m).
Superhero Suguru Kinniku, the overmuscled Prince of Planet Kinniku,

wrestles against numerous outlandish opponents, including the Texan Terryman, British lord Robin Mask, and legendary Chinese brawler Ramen Man. The most popular anime superhero of the 1980s, based on the manga in *Shonen Jump* magazine by Tamago Yude, Muscleman also wrestled on the big screen in seven anime features between 1984 and 1988. When his reign in the ring was over, he was replaced by *Fight! Ramen Man* (1988), first as a 26-minute "feature," then as a 35-episode spinoff TV series, directed by Masayuki Akehi, in which the Chinese super-wrestler Mien-Nan hunts down the Poison Snake gang who killed his wrestler parents, employing comedy kung fu in the style of RANMA 1/2. Though unknown for a decade in the West, the wrestlemania appeal of *Muscleman* was too great to resist in the wake of the POKÉMON boom, and a U.S. broadcast was announced as forthcoming in 2001. The toys, however, sneaked abroad long before, released from Mattel as M.U.S.C.L.E. (Millions of Unusual Small Creatures Lurking Everywhere). Kinnikuman's son, Kinnikuman II, appeared in his own short anime movie in 2001.

KIRA KIRA MELODY ACADEMY

2001. JPN: *Kirakira Melody Gakuen.* AKA: *Twinkling Melody Academy.* Video. DIR: Nobuo Tominaga. SCR: Toshimichi Ogawa. DES: N/C. ANI: Narimitsu Tanaka. MUS: N/C. PRD: Media Factory, AIC. 30 mins.
A mystery drama centering on four would-be singer-actresses, students at the Kira Kira Melody Academy and top of a class of 22 who have agreed to intrusive media attention during their studies. The twist lies in the fact that all 22 are based on real girls who volunteered for the "Kira-Melo" talent contest and its subsequent radio, merchandise, and gaming spinoffs. The girls are students at the Melody Academy, a nonexistent drama school on the outskirts of Yokohama, who have been whittled down from the original 2,000 applicants to a reception class of 56

through a year of "exam failures" and "transfers" to 22, and then thinned still further to determine the stars of the anime. In other words, a kind of staged reality TV—the logical, marketing-led conclusion of a long tradition that ran from the animated biography of a pop group in GLORIOUS ANGELS, through artificially engineered singing groups based on anime casts in HUMMINGBIRDS, and up to anime shows built entirely around prefabricated groups such as DEBUTANTE DETECTIVES. The point being that producers can now effectively market-test future stars *while* they train them, which is either very clever or shamelessly exploitative, depending on how seriously you take PERFECT BLUE. As with reality TV itself, throwing two dozen amateurs at an audience may indeed be more entertaining than a lot of fictional drama, but such a situation is an indictment of the depths to which fictional drama has sunk. Compare also to the "real-life" drama of the earlier LEMON ANGEL.

KIRARA

2000. Video. DIR: Kiyoshi Murayama. SCR: Noriko Hayasaka. DES: Shinya Takahashi. ANI: Shinya Takahashi. MUS: N/C. PRD: Ashi Pro, Toho. 39 mins.
Teenager Konpei daydreams about how his future wife might look, only to find her ghost sitting by his bedside. Kirara Imai has traveled back in time from her own death, hoping to rewrite history to keep her and her beloved Konpei together forever. Sure enough, as the apparition predicts, Konpei meets a girl called Kirara Imai and falls in love with her, but he is reluctant to tell her that they are destined to marry in seven years, or that she will be killed in an accident shortly afterward.
A clever variation on the quintessential time-travel story, this video was based on a 1993 *Young Jump* manga by CREAM LEMON's Toshiki Yui. With an older, experienced woman initiating her husband-to-be into romance, and aiding in the seduction of her own younger self, it is a truly mind-bending

set of paradoxes, not unlike the teen years it so subtly surveys. Beyond the story itself, the anime version increased the level of cheesecake and swimwear from the original manga—artful sci-fi or not, teenage boys will never complain about female nudity.
Also available in an extended edition that includes footage of the open casting call in 1998 where amateur actresses read for the part of the young Kirara. Though hyped at the time as a great way of obtaining raw young voices (a tactic also employed in HIS AND HER CIRCUMSTANCES), the *Kirara* production was so delayed that sweet-16 actress Chiaki Ozawa was a strapping 18-year-old by the time the anime was released. **N**

KISHIN CORPS *

1993. JPN: *Kishin Heidan.* AKA: *Machine-God Corps; Geo-Armor.* Video. DIR: Takaaki Ishiyama. SCR: N/C. DES: Masayuki Goto. ANI: Masayuki Goto. MUS: Kaoru Wada. PRD: AIC, Pioneer. 60 mins. x 1 eps., 30 mins. x 6 eps.
An alternate World War II history even more insidious than DEEP BLUE FLEET, suggesting that Japan only invaded Manchuria to protect the world from aliens!
Aliens are attacking Earth, and Japanese scientists have reverse-engineered some of the captured technology to create the Kishin Corps, a group of giant robots who travel in trains, start with hand cranks, and then pummel the opposition into submission—the opposition being the aliens, and those misguided Japanese who have sided with the Nazis.
The story is pure 1940s matinee adventure, with wonderful character stereotypes—the good woman, the femme fatale, the goofy scientist, the dashing flying ace, the dastardly general, and his obedient minions. Real people crop up, or rather have their names borrowed; Eva Braun is included as a top scientist prepared to do anything in the pursuit of knowledge, though in this reality she has an angelic twin sister, Maria. Superb robot

action spread throughout an excellent story and some particularly great chase sequences make up for pacing that is at times painfully slow. One of several retro anime that try to rewrite the lead-up to Pearl Harbor, to be filed with SAKURA WARS and VIRGIN FLEET—doubtless intended as innocent hokum, but somehow distasteful in a country that still avoids telling its schoolchildren the truth about the War, however entertaining the fictions.

KISS XXXX

1991. Video. DIR: N/C. SCR: Maki Kusumoto. DES: Maki Kusumoto. ANI: N/C. MUS: Yurei, Sakana. PRD: Victor Entertainment. 25 mins.
Kanon, the lead vocalist in a band, falls for the doll-like charms of the pretty Kameno-chan. She inspires him to write a love song every day but brings trouble into his life along with the happiness. An image video of scenes from Maki Kusumoto's 1988 manga in *Comic Margaret* magazine set to music from several popular bands of the day.

KITE *

1998. Video. DIR: Yasuomi Umezu. SCR: Yasuomi Umezu. DES: Yasuomi Umezu. ANI: Yuki Iwai. MUS: An Fu. PRD: Beam Entertainment. 30 mins. x 2 eps.
Sawa is a teenage girl and an agent for an underground ring of vigilantes who has been traumatized by the deaths of her parents. Kept in line by drugs and sexual abuse at the hands of corrupt cop Akai, she is sent out armed with explosive bullets to assassinate criminals the law cannot touch. She starts to fall for a boy on a mission with her, but she also comes to realize that the man she now calls father (and lover) is the man who killed her parents.

Excessively violent and featuring scenes of child abuse and underage sex that had to be cut even for the liberal American market, *Kite* draws on several live-action movies for its inspiration. Most notable is John Badham's *Point of No Return* (1993, itself a remake of Luc Besson's earlier *La Femme Nikita*), in which a pretty killer is trapped within

the organization that has made her. There are also tips of the hat to Takashi Miike's *Fudoh* (1996), particularly a vicious restroom shootout. Umezu had formerly treated the same themes and ideas in *Yellow Star*, one of the entries in the COOL DEVICES erotica series. Remade with a longer running time and high-quality animation, he concentrates on balletic, graceful fight choreography amid utter mayhem, and a poignant tale of doomed love between two damaged souls. But as the video-cover panty shots of Sawa attest, *Kite* is far more interested in titillating its audience with sex and violence than it is with condemning them. **LNV**

KITERETSU ENCYCLOPEDIA

1987. JPN: *Kiteretsu Daihyakka*. TV special, TV series. DIR: Takashi Watanabe, Keiji Hayakawa. SCR: Shunichi Yukimuro, Takashi Yamada. DES: Fujiko-Fujio. ANI: Tsukasa Fusanai, Kunihiko Yuyama. MUS: Katsunori Ishida. PRD: Shinei, Fuji TV. 75 mins., 25 mins. x 331 eps.
Kiteretsu and Eiichi love inventing things, but they only ever show their latest creations to Eiichi's girlfriend, Miyoko. Kiteretsu discovers that he is a descendant of the 19th-century inventor Kiteretsu Sai, receiving a copy of Sai's legendary *Encyclopedia of Inventions* from his father. The story returned in 1988 as a full-fledged series, overseen by Hiroshi Kuzuoka. Based on a Fujiko-Fujio manga in *Corocoro Comic* but with its concentration on a group of children getting in and out of trouble with a selection of magical toys, *KE* is little more than a respray of the same creators' earlier and far more successful DORAEMON.

KIZUNA *

1994. AKA: *Bonds*. Video. DIR: Rin Hiro. SCR: Miyo Morita. DES: Ayako Mihashi. ANI: Ayako Mihashi. MUS: Fujio Takano. PRD: Seiji Biblos, Daiei. 30 mins. x 2 eps.
Handsome young man Ranmaru "Ran" Samejima is involved in a hit-and-run "accident" that was really a failed

Benkei vs. Ushiwaka

attempt on the life of his friend Enjoji. As he recovers, the care and attention lavished upon him by Enjoji make him fall deeper in love with him, and the couple move in together. Their friendship is strained by the attentions of a college professor, who tries to seduce Ran. But Enjoji's family are gangsters, his half-brother also wants Ran, and the lothario professor has bitten off more than he can chew. This video was based on the manga created for *Be-Boy* magazine by Kazuma Kodaka, who also created KIMERA. Despite being let down by poor subtitling, it is one of very few openly gay anime available in English, to be filed alongside the more humorous FAKE. **LNV**

KNIGHTS OF RAMUNE *

1990. JPN: *NG Knight Lamune and 40; NG Knight Lamune and 40 EX; NG Knight Lamune and 40 DX*. Video. DIR: Hiroshi Negishi. SCR: Brother Anoppo, Satoru Akahori. DES: Takehiko Ito, Rei Nakahara, Takuya Saito. ANI: N/C. MUS: Tadashige Matsui. PRD: Ashi Pro, TV Tokyo. 25 mins. x 39 eps. (TV1), 30 mins. x 3 (EX), 30 mins. x 3 eps. (DX), 25 mins. x 26 eps. (Fire), 30 mins. x 6 eps. (Fresh).
Japanese schoolboy Ramune is a big fan of the computer game *King Sccash-*

er, until one day the beautiful Princess Milk jumps out of his screen and drags him back to the game-world of A'lala. There, he is hailed as the legendary hero Ramuness, come to save the world from the evil overlord Don Harumage. *N[o] G[ood] Knight Ramune and 40* made a name for Satoru Akahori, who would reprise the formula ad infinitum throughout the decade. Resprays of the same setups and gags would dominate BEAST WARRIORS, MAZE, SORCERER HUNTERS, and many others, while the bold, unshaded splashes of bright color, originally an attempt to simplify designs for less experienced animators in Korea, would appear in many other shows of the 1990s.

The series returned straight to video as *NG Knight Ramune and 40 EX* (1991), directed by Koji Masunari, in which Ramune, now at middle-school, is approached by Milk once more in search of his aid because her world has been attacked by a mysterious giant robot. Before long, the series was back again as *NGR&40 DX* (1993), in which "Ramuness" and his band travel back 5,000 years in time. Adopting a TENCHI MUYO!–style formula of throwing in new cheesecake whenever it ran out of ideas, the series returned to TV as *V[ersu]s Knight Ramune and 40 Fire* (1996). In this incarnation, Ramune's help is solicited by three beautiful androids named Drum, Trumpet, and Cello. By this point, he is a full-grown adult, who Turns To The Dark Side, remaining there for the video sequel *VS Knight Ramune and 40 Fresh* (1997). The only part of the series to be released in English, under the title *Knights of Ramune*, it features busty babes Parfait and Cacao on a quest to bring back the legendary knight Ramuness, only to discover that he's at the helm of the lead ship in an invading alien fleet. With a poverty of ideas typical to late 1990s anime, many of which persist in believing that "zany" means "amateurish," this involves a bit of espionage, spell-casting, and a few gags about how underwear interferes

with the power of magic, as they run around a big spaceship in the company of a mascot that resembles a talking tumor, waiting for the enemy to bring the plot to them.

However, despite being the fifth series in the franchise, *KoR* contains little to confuse audiences—the hours of back story prove to be utterly inconsequential. New director Yoshitaka Fujimoto papers over gaping holes in the plot and action with perfunctory T&A and a few incidences of half-hearted sauciness—because more "mature" viewers can apparently be appeased by a couple of nipples and a bit of suggestive panting. There are some frames of GUNBUSTER-inspired space warfare, and tantalizingly short bursts of excellent animation, but *KoR* is the kind of anime that leads first-time viewers to assume the entire medium is nothing but big eyes, explosions, and weary plot-by-numbers. The U.S. voice cast seem to think so too, contemptuously indulging in over-the-top pseudonyms like Ruby Seedless and Autumn Harvest. **N**

KOBO-CHAN

1990. AKA: *Kobo the Little Rascal*. TV series. DIR: Hiroyuki Torii, Tameo Ogawa. SCR: Noboru Shiroyama. DES: Joji Yanagise. ANI: Hiroyuki Torii, Joji Yanagise, Hisatoshi Motoki. MUS: Noriko Sakai. PRD: Eiken, Yomiuri TV. 12 mins. x 15 eps.
The adventures of a five-year-old boy in the tradition of *Peanuts*, based on Masashi Ueda's four-panel cartoon strip in the *Yomiuri Shinbun* newspaper.

KOIKO'S DAILY LIFE

1989. JPN: *Koiko no Mainichi*. Video. DIR: Noboru Ishiguro. SCR: Akira Miyazaki. DES: Joji Akiyama. ANI: Kiyotoshi Aoii. MUS: N/C. PRD: Nippon Animation. 50 mins. x 2 eps.
In a story that flits between serious drama and comedic farce, Shinjuku gangster Sabu and his young wife Koiko try to live a normal life, despite the interferences of gang politics and criminal deals. After she saves his life, Sabu's

gang-boss, Tominaga, falls in love with Koiko, and sends Sabu into increasingly more dangerous situations, hoping to cause his arrest, and thus obligate himself to "take care" of Koiko while Sabu is in prison. Based on a manga in *Manga Action* magazine by PINK CURTAIN–creator Joji Akiyama, this was also adapted into a TV drama starring Beat Takeshi—years ahead of *The Sopranos*. **NV**

KOJIRO OF THE FUMA CLAN *

1989. JPN: *Fuma no Kojiro*. Video. DIR: Hidehito Ueda. SCR: Takao Koyama. DES: Shingo Araki, Michi Himeno. ANI: Takeshi Tsukasa. MUS: Toshiro Imaizumi. PRD: Animate Film, JC Staff. 30 mins. x 13 eps.
Five young boys are the reincarnations of elemental spirits and replay old tales and enmities from Japanese history in a modern setting. Teenager Kojiro receives a letter from Himeko, the young owner of Hakuo (White Phoenix) High School, who needs help dealing with gang intimidation. Kojiro decides to help her because she's very cute, but gang intimidation is the least of her worries—a rival clan is planning is planning a takeover, and Kojiro must face their champion, Nibu, before dealing with another adversary, Oscar Musashi (see SWORD OF MUSASHI). The inter-clan school struggle is just a cover for the powers of evil, who wish to collect the ten magical swords that determine the balance of power in the universe. It's pretty boys at a ninja high school but with a surprisingly old-fashioned look to the designs and animation. This video was based on a 1982 manga in *Shonen Jump* by Masami Kurumada, who would recycle the same ideas in SAINT SEIYA, though the anime adaptation of the latter preceded this to Japanese screens. **NV**

KONPORA KID

1985. TV series/special. DIR: Juzo Morishita, Yuji Endo, Tatsuo Higashino, Yoshikata Nitta, Shigeyasu Yamauchi. SCR: Takao Koyama, Shigeru Yanagawa, Kenji Yoshida. DES: Yasuhiro Yamaguchi. ANI: Yasuhiro Yamaguchi, Tatsuhiro Nagaki, Masami Shimoda. MUS: Kohei Tanaka. PRD: Toei, TV Asahi. 25 mins. x 26 eps. (TV), 57 mins. (TVm).

In the distant future, merely because someone is eight years old, it doesn't follow that they will have to go to school. In fact, little Daigoro Harumi JR (aka JR) is a teacher at Torad Academy in charge of educating Class Five, whose ages range from a newborn baby to a crusty old grandfather. Partway through the TV series, JR and his class also appeared in a summer TV special, where the flustered eight year old plans on taking a summer vacation with his family in space but ends up chaperoning half his class as well. Based on the manga by Masahide Motohashi, serialized in *Shonen Magazine*, among others.

KOSUKE AND RIKIMARU: DRAGON OF KONPEI ISLAND

1990. JPN: *Kosukesama Rikimarusama: Konpeijima no Ryu*. Video. DIR: Toyoo Ashida. SCR: Toyoo Ashida, Akira Toriyama. DES: Akira Toriyama. ANI: N/C. MUS: N/C. PRD: JC Staff. 45 mins.

Squashed-down samurai Kosuke and Rikimaru must save the world from an evil dragon who wants to rule it for all eternity. This one-off anime, based on an idea by DRAGON BALL and DOCTOR SLUMP–creator Akira Toriyama, was preceded by a 1990 manga in a special

issue of *Shonen Jump* but written originally for the screen.

KOTOWAZA HOUSE

1987. TV series. DIR: Hiroshi Yoshida. SCR: Motoko Misawa, Hiroshi Yoshida. DES: Tadao Wakabayashi. ANI: Tadao Wakabayashi. MUS: N/C. PRD: Eiken, Fuji TV. 5 mins. x 338 eps.

Peter the salaryman lives a very unhealthy lifestyle, starving then bingeing until he feels sick, or slobbing around the house until badgered into taking up exercise, during which he invariably pulls a muscle. In this public-service proverb-of-the-week anime from the same team who made DOTANBA'S MODERN MANNERS, Peter's caring boss and the beautiful Office Lady Sueko drag in a straight-talking doctor and a sprightly granny to educate him about physical and mental health. For the series' first year on-air, the title was simply *KH: Health Edition*, but this was dropped in 1988 to reflect the move toward more general tips and proverbs for well-being.

KUM-KUM *

1975. JPN: *Wanpaku Omukashi Kum-Kum*. AKA: *Naughty Ancient Kum-Kum; Kum-Kum the Caveman*. TV series. DIR: Rintaro, Noboru Ishiguro, Wataru Mizusawa. SCR: Eiichi Tachi, Keisuke Fujikawa, Yoshiaki Yoshida. DES: Yoshikazu Yasuhiko. ANI: Rintaro, Noboru Ishiguro, Minoru Tajima, Akio Sakai. MUS: Masami Uno. PRD: ITC Japan, Mainichi Broadcasting (TBS).

25 mins. x 26 eps.

Kum-kum is a small cave-boy living in the prehistoric mountains that will one day be Japan, where he, his sister Furu-furu, and tag-along companions Chil-chil, Mochi-mochi, and Aron behave the way that their distant descendants would if only modern Japanese children had access to mammoth rides, troublesome dinosaurs, and the opportunity to throw rocks at each other. Kum-kum was an unexpected success on British children's TV in the early 1980s, not for being the first English-language broadcast of work by original creator Yasuhiko, or indeed as an early example of Rintaro's direction, but because its hero didn't wear any pants.

KUROMI-CHAN *

2001. JPN: *Anime Seisaku Shinko Kuromi-chan*. AKA: *Animation Runner Kuromi-chan*. Video. DIR: Akitaro Daichi, Yumi Tamano. SCR: Mitsuru Nagatsuki. DES: Hajime Watanabe. ANI: Hajime Watanabe. MUS: Toshio Masuda. PRD: Yumeta Company. 40 mins.

Self-referential comedy about attractive brunette Mikiko "Kuromi-chan" Okuro getting a job at an anime company and soon finding herself heavily involved in the troubled productions *Ruimond III* (see LUPIN III) and *Time Journeys* (see TIME BOKAN). Based on a four-panel gag strip that appeared in *Anime Station*, the anime industry's in-house magazine—compare to OTAKU NO VIDEO. Released in Japan with English subtitles.

L

LA BLUE GIRL *

1992. JPN: *Inju Gakuen La Blue Girl.*
AKA: *Lust-Beast Academy La Blue Girl.*
Video. DIR: Raizo Kitazawa, Kan Fukumoto. SCR: Megumi Ichiryu. DES: Kinji
Yoshimoto. ANI: Miki Bibanba, Rin Shin.
MUS: Teruo Takahama. PRD: Daiei. 45
mins. x 4 eps., 30 mins. x 4 eps.
Not unlike DEVIL HUNTER YOHKO,
high-school girl Miko Mido and her sister are the heirs to the secrets of an
ancient ninja clan. When they become
embroiled in an interdimensional war
with rapacious demons, they reveal
their secret powers—they are sex-ninja
who cast spells with the power of
orgasm and, hence, cannot get enough
of their enemies' lusty attentions.
Based on an idea by UROTSUKIDOJI-cre-
ator Toshio Maeda, *LBG* continues his
obsession with hormonal chaos, as
demons kidnap the high-school volleyball team, and Miko can only rescue
them (from sexual degradation, naturally) by submitting to the wanton
desires of her demonic enemies. The
series was also released in compiled
feature-length editions and an *Ecstasy*
collection that included only the sex
scenes.

The franchise was rebranded as *La
Blue Girl EX* (1996, released in the U.S.
as *Lady Blue*) for a further four
episodes, taking Miko off to college,
where her crush on a fellow classmate
turns out to be part of a conspiracy, as
her jilted immortal aunt seeks to bring
her ancient lover back from the dead,
predictably by raping Miko. Notorious
in the U.K. market for being refused a
release point-blank by the British censor, *LBG* also caused some controversy
in the U.S., where the Japanese censorship dots were removed prior to
release, revealing half-drawn genitals
which the animators never intended to
be seen, giving the impression that
some of the participants were underage. The franchise was also made as
three live-action films, starting with *Sex
Beast on Campus* (1994), directed by
Kaname Kobayashi, and continuing
with *SBoC: Birth of the Daughter with
Dark Spirit* (1995) and *SBoC: Female
Ninja Hunting* (1996), both directed by
Kaoru Kuramoto. Compare to ANGEL
OF DARKNESS. *Ill. p. 255.* ⓁⓃⓋ

LABYRINTH OF FLAME *

2000. JPN: *En no Labyrinth.* Video. DIR:
Katsuhiko Nishijima. SCR: Kenichi
Kanemaki. DES: Noriyasu Yamauchi,
Hidefumi Kimura. ANI: N/C. MUS: N/C.
PRD: Studio Fantasia, Bandai Visual.
30 mins. x 2 eps.
The secret city of Labyrinth Four was
founded by Japanese citizens of the Aoi
Shigemasa domain, who lost their territory to Russian expansionism in the
19th century. Permitted to exist in
recognition of their support during the
Russian revolution, the secluded
inhabitants have preserved a way of life
unchanged since the samurai era. Now
two of their descendants, hot-blooded
swordsman Garan and princess Natsu
(the unwilling subject of an arranged
marriage), are kicking over the traces
and seeking adventure in the big wide
world. "Swords, Lust and Action in the
mysterious citadel known as the
labyrinth," promise the ads for this
series, which finds a novel way of
explaining the retro fetish also found
in its contemporaries TREE IN THE SUN
and ARMORED CHRONICLE HIO. ⓃⓋ

LADIUS *

1987. JPN: *Makyo Gaiden Le Deus.* AKA:
*Demon Frontier Legend Le Deus; Le
Deus.* Video. DIR: Hiroshi Negishi. SCR:
Hideki Sonoda, Hiroyuki Kitakubo. DES:
Rei Aran. ANI: Hideyuki Motohashi. MUS:
Hiroyuki Nanba. PRD: Ashi Pro. 48
mins.
GUNDAM-meets-*Indiana Jones* as treasure-hunting archaeologists fight over
an ancient energy source. Spunky hero
Riot Geenas travels a postapocalyptic
world accompanied by his dim but
well-intentioned twin-girl companions,
Sulpica and Seneca. He needs the mystic energy Lidorium that's found in the
artifact known as the Eye of Zalem, but
so too do his competitors, the evil
Dempsters. When he finally locates the
Eye, it's being worn around the pretty
neck of bar-owner Yuta la Carradine,
who insists on accompanying him on
his quest until such time as he can pay
for the damages done to the establishment in a brawl with his enemies.
Needless to say, Yuta is the last inheritor of the ancient Kingdom of Quall
who holds the key to unlocking its powers, which are unleashed in a grand
finale involving massive collateral damage amid ancient ruins, the defeat of
the bad guy, and the arrival of the titular war machine, a giant robot hidden
inside a transforming humpback
whale. Derivative hokum, repeated five
years later in the suspiciously similar
BEAST WARRIORS, with which it shares a
director. The last anime translation to
be made in the U.K. by Western Connection and subtitled in that low-budget company's inimitable randomly
timed style.

LADY GEORGIE

1983. TV series. DIR: Shigetsugu Yoshida, Naoto Hashimoto, Satoshi Dezaki,
Kenjiro Yoshida, Tsuneo Tominaga.
SCR: Hiroshi Kaneko, Noboru Shiroyama. DES: Shunsaburo Takahata. ANI:
Junsaburo Takahata, Yoshiaki Kawajiri.
MUS: Takeo Watanabe. PRD: IU, TMS, TV
Asahi. 25 mins. x 45 eps.
In the Australian forest, the Borman
family finds a dying woman who begs
them to take care of her newborn
daughter, Georgie. Despite the opposition of Mrs. Borman, the father agrees,
and the girl is raised as their own, with
no mention of her true parents or that
her father was a British convict. Mr.
Borman dies rescuing Georgie from a
river, and his two sons, Abel and
Arthur, keep their promise to look
after their "sister," though they are
both falling in love with her themselves. When Georgie falls in love with
the Englishman Dowell Gray, Abel confesses his feelings to his mother, who in
her fury blurts out Georgie's true origins. Georgie goes to England to find
her birth father, and her arrival causes
Dowell to dump his fiancée Elise, the
daughter of the powerful Duke Dunkelin. With little evidence but the
bracelet that is the sole memento of
her real mother, Georgie eventually
tracks down her father, who is, of
course, not exactly a convict but the
noble Earl Gerald. Meanwhile, however, the evil Dunkelin has captured
Arthur, who has followed Georgie to
England and accidentally witnessed the
duke's drug-smuggling operation.
Arthur nearly dies from the drugs fed
to him by Dunkelin's men, while Abel
is thrown into the dungeons of the
Tower of London for killing one of
Dunkelin's relatives.

With a Victorian setting, a foundling
heroine, and a long quest for love, *LG*
closely resembles the landmark CANDY
CANDY, all the more for being based on
a manga in *Shojo Comic* by the same
artist, Yumiko Igarashi, though originally written as a novel by Michiru
Isawa. Eventually, everything ends happily with Georgie and her "brothers"

returning to their native Australia,
though the original novel was far more
tragic. As with the same year's TREAS-
URES OF THE SNOW, the anime adaptation builds on the original story, chiefly
with early scenes of the heroine's childhood not in the novel or manga versions. These were perhaps inserted as
an afterthought to justify scenes of
playtime with koala bears, a ubiquitous
feature of early 1980s anime—see THE
NOOZLES.

LADY LADY

1987. TV series. DIR: Hiroshi Shidara,
Yugo Serikawa, Yasuo Yamakichi, Yuji
Endo, Masahisa Ishida. SCR: Michiru
Umadori, Tomoko Konparu, Shigeru
Yanagawa. DES: Takao Sawata, Yoko
Hide. ANI: Kazuya Koshibe. MUS: Kohei
Tanaka. PRD: Toei, TBS, TV Tokyo. 25
mins. x 21 eps. (TV1), 27 mins. (m),
25 mins. x N/D eps. (TV2).
Five-year-old Lynn Midorigawa sets off
for England to meet her Japanese
mother for the first time she can
remember but discovers that her mother has been killed in a car accident.
Her British father remarries, and Lynn
must endure bullying at the hands of
her stepmother, Vivianne, and her
stepsiblings, Mary and Thomas. Her
only friend is the kindly boy Arthur,
who promises to help her become a
true lady. It's another syrupy romance
in the spirit of CANDY CANDY, based on
the manga *Hitomi* by Yoko Hide. The
short 1988 *LL* movie is set a year after
the series and focuses on the heroine's
misery at the mansion of Marquis
Bourbon, where she is forced to work
as a maid to help repay her father's
debts.

The movie bridges the gap between
LL and its sequel, *Hello Lady Lynn*
(1988), for which the franchise moved
to TV Tokyo from TBS. Set three years
after Lynn's original arrival in England, *HLL* packs her off to stay with
Countess Isabelle and attend Saint
Patrick's College for young girls, where
she joins the equestrian club and gets
involved in genteel high jinks in the
spirit of TWINS AT ST CLARE'S. There

The consumptive waif, Tokiko "Key" Mima, is
KEY THE METAL IDOL, a robot performer who
needs the love of 30,000 fans to stay alive. A
modern media variant on the *Pinocchio* story,
mixing the heartfelt tragedy of low self-esteem
with a cunning grab at the audience sympathy
vote—for an audience to show its love is going
to cost in tickets and CD sales, after all. Elements of Key would return at the end of the
1990s in SERIAL EXPERIMENTS LAIN and PERFECT
BLUE. See entry p. 201.

Key the Metal Idol

was also a live-action movie, *Ready!
Lady!* (1989), directed by Kei Ota.

LANDLOCK *

1996. Video. DIR: Yasuhiro Matsumura.
SCR: ORCA. DES: Kazuto Nakazawa,
Masamune Shirow. ANI: Koji Matsuyama. MUS: N/C. PRD: Sega Enterprises.
50 mins. x 2 eps.
In the low-rent Aztec-like fantasyland
of Zer'lue, Chairman San'aku leads an
invading army of seemingly unstoppable Zul'earth warriors. A lone boy,
Lue'der, can stop him, but the chairman's daughter Aga'lee has been sent
to hunt him down before his powers (a
nebulous ability to control the wind)
can truly awaken. Luckily for Lue'der,
who has one normal eye and one red
eye as a mark of the chosen one,
Aga'lee's sister Ansa has a normal eye
and a *blue* eye. He takes this to be some
sort of sign that she should help him
escape, which she duly does. Accompanied by a friendly entomologist(!?),
Lue'der reaches an ancient temple
when he discovers the nature of his
destiny, and that the man Aga'lee
killed was not his real father. He combines the fabled Red and Blue Flows to
become an avatar of the power of the
wind, and then he wins the day.

A horrific mess of an anime, complete with pretentious apostrophes in people's names (inserted for the English version, to be fair), and a *you killed my father, prepare to die* plot unsurprisingly thought up by a committee. This turgid two-parter was rushed out to cash in on the recent success of **GHOST IN THE SHELL** by producers banking on the star-power of Masamune Shirow's name, even though the famous artist's involvement was limited to mere "design assistance." This was enough for distributors in some territories, who eagerly snatched up the chance to release another anime from the successful creator of **BLACK MAGIC** and **APPLESEED**—though they, and their consumers, were to be very disappointed. Four years later, the same criminals would strike again with **GUNDRESS**, another low-rent sci-fi thriller with slight Shirow involvement, even worse than *Landlock* because it was actually released unfinished.

LASERION

1984. JPN: *Video Senshi Laserion*. AKA: *Video Warrior Laserion; Rezarion*. TV series. DIR: Kozo Morishita, Hideki Takayama, Masao Ito, Hiromichi Matano, Shigeyasu Yamauchi. SCR: Kozo Morishita, Akiyoshi Sakai, Takeshi Shudo, Keiji Kubota, Haruya Yamazaki. DES: Hideyuki Motohashi, Koichi Ohata, Akira Hio. ANI: Hideyuki Motohashi, Daisuke Shiozawa, Seiji Kikuchi, Hajime Kaneko. MUS: Michiaki Watanabe. PRD: Toei, Tabac, TBS. 25 mins. x 45 eps.

Laserion, a program created by game-crazed boy Satoshi, is brought to life by an accident that sends the data to Professor Blueheim's teleportation experiment. Luckily, Satoshi soon finds a use for a giant war robot, which, **GIANT ROBO**–style, will only obey his commands, when Earth is invaded by evil lunar-based minions of the evil scientist God Haid, and Satoshi joins the Secret Force to stop them, accompanied by token girl Olivia. Also part of the **GODAIKIN** toy line.

LASSIE

1996. JPN: *Meiken Lassie*. AKA: *Famous Dog Lassie*. TV series. DIR: Sunao Katabuchi, Jiro Fujimoto, Kenichi Nishida. SCR: Aya Matsui, Hideki Mitsui. DES: Satoko Morikawa. ANI: N/C. MUS: N/C. PRD: Nippon Animation, Fuji TV. 25 mins. x 26 eps.

Country-boy John finds a young puppy by the roadside and nurses her back to health. Lassie grows into a fine collie, blessed with almost human intelligence, though her early years are not without their share of odd mishaps, scoldings, and discoveries.

This penultimate **WORLD MASTERPIECE THEATER** anime displays all the hallmarks of the series' decline, most notably a cavalier disregard for the original classic that inspired it, Eric Mowbray Knight's 1940 novel that was expanded from his 1938 short story *Lassie Come Home*. As with **HEIDI** and **TREASURES OF THE SNOW**, the characters' early years, not seen in the original, were used to bulk up the running time, so when the series was ignominiously yanked off the air after just 25 episodes, the novel's central plot had barely begun. Consequently, the extant *Lassie* anime takes its time with the minutiae of Lassie's upbringing, only to rush through her famous long journey home in just three episodes. The unbroadcast final episode, *Run to the Place of Dreams*, was included on the later video release. In a final irony, Knight never lived to see any of the TV or movie incarnations of his much-loved dog—he died in a wartime air crash in Dutch Guiana (modern Surinam).

LAUGHING SALESMAN

1989. TV series, TV special. DIR: Toshiro Kuni, Ryoshi Yometani. SCR: Ichiro Yoshiaki, Kazuya Miyazaki, Kaoru Umeno. DES: Fujiko-Fujio "A." ANI: Tsunehiro Okaseko. MUS: N/C. PRD: Shinei, TBS. 10 mins. x 91 eps., 60 mins.

The miserable life of a salesman whose wife only cares about golf is played for laughs in this long-running series,

based on the manga *Black Salesman* by Motoo Abiko, one half of the Fujiko-Fujio duo who created **DORAEMON**. Splitting from his working partner Hiroshi Fujimoto in the 1980s, he produced several titles under the name Fujiko-Fujio "A," including **PARASOL HENBE**, **LITTLE GOBLIN**, **PROGOLFER SARU**, and **BILLY DOG**. Broadcast as part of the *Gimme a Break* variety show on the TBS channel, which occasionally also showed episodes of Shotaro Ishinomori's **808 DISTRICTS**. Several episodes were also edited into the feature-length TV movie *LS Special* (1990), concentrating on the cheerful way that the psychotic salesman took out his midlife crisis on his coworkers with an extensive campaign of blackmail and extortion. From episode 41 onward, the series was rebranded as *New LS* (1991).

LAUGHING TARGET *

1987. JPN: *Rumic World: Warau Mokuteki*. Video. DIR: Yukihiro Takahashi. SCR: Tomoko Konparu, Hideo Takayashiki. DES: Hidekazu Obara. ANI: N/C. MUS: Kuni Kawauchi. PRD: Studio Pierrot. 50 mins.

Azusa is a girl from a traditional Japanese family, who, through an old-fashioned arranged marriage, has been "promised" to her cousin Yuzuru since the age of five. Growing up in an isolated country mansion, she experiences several bizarre experiences, culminating in the death of her mother. She sets off to snag her long-term betrothed but is shocked to discover that Yuzuru already loves Satomi, a more modern urban girl, and that not even Azusa's beauty is enough to shake his resolve to break the family's pacts. In a sorcerous revenge straight out of **JAPANESE FOLK TALES**, Azusa then reveals that there is more to her family's traditional beliefs than straightforward marriages. The third in the *Rumic World* series based on short manga tales by **URUSEI YATSURA**–creator Rumiko Takahashi. Other entries included **FIRE TRIPPER**, **MERMAID'S FOREST**, and **MARIS THE CHOJO**. **Ⓥ**

LAWS OF DIVORCE AND INHERITANCE

1989. JPN: *Horitsu, Rikon, Sozoku.* Video. DIR: Kazuki Sakaguchi. SCR: N/C. DES: N/C. ANI: Keiichiro Okamoto. MUS: N/C. PRD: Koh Planning, Yang Corporation. 60 mins. x 2 eps.

An unusual public-information series in which helpful lawyer Taro Bengoshi talks the viewer through the fascinating world of divorce relating to marital violence, adultery, and irreconcilable differences, as well as methods for dealing with a partner unwilling to consent to divorce, general procedure, division of assets, compensation, parental rights, and child support. The second episode concentrates on inheritance, planning a will, the rights of legitimate children, rights of children from a former marriage, renouncing the right to inherit, finding missing fortunes, intestate wills, and procedures for dividing assets. One to remember next time someone suggests that anime is nothing but POKÉMON and porn.

LAWS OF THE SUN, THE *

2000. Movie. DIR: Takaaki Ishiyama. SCR: Laws of the Sun Scenario Project. DES: Don Davis. ANI: N/C. MUS: MIZ Music Inc. PRD: Tac. 101 mins.

The Cosmic Consciousness creates the human race on planet Venus, a paradise of wisdom, love, and learning. However, the absence of struggle prevents humanity from striving for perfection, so the entire species is moved to the less hospitable world of Earth, where it is encouraged to seek enlightenment through a process of reincarnation. The early human civilization is smashed up by the dinosaurs, which are luckily killed off by cruel big-game hunters from outer space. Humanity continues to struggle amid several alien assaults. Satan is variously described as leading a revolution against the gods in heaven, leading a revolution in hell, or simply as being an invading alien from the Greater Magellanic Cloud. Mu, Atlantis, Greece, and the Inca civilization all represent peaks of achievement, but are all too soon destroyed by human folly—after, in the case of the Incas, defeating reptilian space invaders with the power of love. Throughout history, however, the same souls are constantly reincarnated, including the wisest humans, such as Jesus, Moses, Confucius, Zoroaster, Buddha, Newton, Thoth, Archimedes, and Hermes. It has now been 2,500 years since Buddha, and the time is right for a new cycle of redemption, handily offered to the audience by the Institute for Research in Human Happiness, the religious cult that funded the film.

Based on a book by Ryuho Okawa (aka "El Cantare"), the leader of the IRH and supposed reincarnation of several notable historical figures. As with his earlier HERMES, the plot is risibly incoherent, mixing myths and pulp sci-fi with such impunity that no writer seems prepared to take responsibility for it. There are, however, some spots of cleverness—particularly the use of reincarnation to ensure that the same point-of-view characters can lead the dumbstruck audience through the 40 *billion* years covered in the feature. As well as doing respectable box-office in Japan, where the IRH faithful flocked to see their leader's latest cinematic outpouring, *Laws of the Sun* was also given a very limited screening in the U.S., chiefly in California, a state not unknown for its readiness to embrace new religions. Director Ishiyama filmed similarly revisionist histories in SAKURA WARS and KISHIN CORPS, while art director Don Davis won an Emmy for his work on Carl Sagan's landmark science *fact* documentary, *Cosmos.* Readers will be pleased to hear that Okawa no longer claims, as he did in the early 1990s, that the end of the world is nigh. One hopes this means that more of his 400 books will be animated soon.

LEAVE IT TO SCRAPPERS

1994. JPN: *Omakase Scrappers.* TV series. DIR: Hideaki Oba. SCR: Hiroyuki Hoshiyama. DES: Satomi Aoki. ANI: Satomi Aoki. MUS: Nagayoshi Yazawa. PRD: ACC Pro, Beam Enterainment, NHK. 25 mins. x 9 eps.

A children's SF series from LUPIN III–creator Monkey Punch, this anime features a boy and his diminutive robot assistants (think *Silent Running,* but played for laughs) attempting to do the right thing, but often creating more trouble for themselves when they take on deceptively easy jobs, such as guarding an idol singer or running a summer camp.

LEDA: FANTASTIC ADVENTURES OF YOKO *

1985. JPN: *Genmu Senki Leda.* AKA: *Dreamwar Chronicle Leda.* Video. DIR: Kunihiko Yuyama. SCR: Junji Takegami, Kunihiko Yuyama. DES: Mutsumi Inomata. ANI: Shigenori Kageyama, Mutsumi Inomata, Mayumi Watanabe. MUS: Shiro Sagisu. PRD: Toho, Kaname Pro. 70 mins.

Yoko Asagiri is a shy teenager who is secretly in love with a schoolmate. She writes a song to express her feelings, only to find that the tune is a bridge to the fantasy world of Ashanti (Leda in the English version). There, the former high priest is making plans to lead his army across to Earth and rule it for all eternity. Aided by warrior-priestess Yoni, a talking dog called Lingam, and a tin man reminiscent of WIZARD OF OZ, Yoko must overcome her fears to become Leda's Warrior and pilot the Wings of Leda into the enemy's floating citadel. Here, her ability to tell between true love and falsehood will be tested to the utmost. A high point of early video anime also shown in theaters in Japan, this video combines many anime staples, including large robots, pilot heroines, battle bikinis, and even a love song to save the world. Fifteen years later, the main crew members would still be in the public eye, directing POKÉMON, designing BRAIN POWERED, and composing the music to EVANGELION.

LEFT OF O'CLOCK

1989. JPN: *Hidari no O'Clock.* Video. DIR: Satoshi Inoue, Hiroaki Sakurai.

SCR: Yugo Serikawa. DES: Osamu Kamijo. ANI: Masami Suda. MUS: N/C. PRD: Toei. 50 mins. x 2 eps.

Disenchanted with life ruled by other people's timekeeping, Yu gets on a motorcycle and rides down the length of Japan from his northern home. While his sister Megumi and girlfriend Aoi fret about him at home, he becomes a different person during his journey, helping out people he meets on the way and falling in love with the pretty Tomo after an accident. A knight-of-the-road tale based on the manga by **AREA 88**–creator Kaoru Shintani and presented as four TV-length "episodes," though these two video incarnations were its only appearance.

LEGEND OF CENTAURUS

1987. JPN: *Centaurus no Densetsu.* Video. DIR: Teruo Ishii. SCR: Junzo Toriumi. DES: Osamu Otake. ANI: Hidemi Kama. MUS: Hatanori Fusayama. PRD: Jin Pro. 95 mins.

The Centaurs are a racing team of 93 bikers from the port city of Yokohama who are named after the legendary Greek horse/men. Arthur and Ken fall out over their love for the same lady, who is unhelpfully called Lady, deciding to settle their competition with a race. Based on a manga by Osamu Otake.

LEGEND OF GALACTIC HEROES

1988. JPN: *Ginga Eiyu Densetsu.* AKA: *Heldensagen von Kosmosinsel.* Video. DIR: Noboru Ishiguro, Akio Sakai, Akihiko Nishimura, Kenichi Imaizumi. SCR: Takeshi Shudo, Shimao Kawanaka, Kazumi Koide. DES: Matsuri Okuda, Masayuki Kato, Studio Nue. ANI: Matsuri Okuda, Keizo Shimizu. MUS: Michiyoshi Inoue (arranger). PRD: Kitty Film. 60 mins., 100 mins. x 28 eps. (109 "episodes" on 28 tapes), 90 mins. (m), 60 mins. (v/*GW*), 100 mins. (v/*Vows*), 100 mins. (v/*Dom, Son*), 100 mins. (*Disgrace*), 100 mins. x 3 eps. (v/*TSTPL*), 100 mins. x 3 eps. (v/*SL*).

In the year A.D. 3597, a hundred and fifty years into the conflict between the Alliance of Independent Worlds and the Galactic Empire, both forces claim victory at the Battle of Astarte. On the Alliance side, the strategic genius Yang Wenli, a former historian dragged into a military life. Fighting for the empire, Reinhardt von Lohengramm, the estranged son of a provincial nobleman, determined to rise through the ranks until he can overthrow the ruling dynasty, whose kaiser bought Reinhardt's sister, Annerose, as a concubine from his dishonorable father. Lohengramm's childhood friend, Kircheis, loves Annerose in a different way.

Yoshiki Tanaka's *magnum opus*, the 18 novels of *LGH* are far superior to his other works, which include **APPLELAND STORY**, **HEROIC LEGEND OF ARSLAN**, and **LEGEND OF THE FOUR KINGS**. *LGH* is a tragic far-future epic, in which two heroes, who would probably have been the best of friends, find themselves on opposing sides in a galactic war. *LGH* has a pathos redolent of Leiji Matsumoto's **COCKPIT** or **CAPTAIN HARLOCK**, and a sympathetic treatment of both sides—though it is also renowned for truly vast space battles with thousands of ships, set to classical music. The imperial forces are part-Nazi, part-stuffy, decadent European aristocracy, while the Alliance is an American-style melting pot. As in WWII itself, which inspires much of the sci-fi, the imperial forces have the best uniforms and the nastiest schemers, but the other side has its fair share of machinations behind the scenes.

The first two episodes were screened as a movie-edit in theaters, with the grossly inferior **ULTIMATE TEACHER** on the same double bill. Released in TV-episodic form but straight to video, *LGH* is one of anime's silent successes, sold chiefly by mail order to a dedicated audience large enough to keep the series running for a whole decade. Ishiguro shoots the anime version like a disaster movie or a Kihachi Okamoto war film (see **EVANGELION**), retaining the novel's cast of thousands and many onscreen titles to remind us who is who. Though the sci-fi trappings are occasionally halfhearted and hokey (there are, mercifully, no transforming robots, although there are hackneyed hovercars and similarly redressed contemporary technology), the execution is still brilliant. If **FIST OF THE NORTH STAR** was animation taken in interesting directions by lack of time and budget, then *LGH*'s need to continuously find new ways to depress its audience has encouraged some masterful writing, most notable in the early episodes. In a scene in which Jessica Edwards is elated to hear of her fiancé's promotion, it takes several seconds for her to register the implication of *posthumous*. But despite the stirring music, gripping plots, and doomed pretty-boy heroes, *LGH* can be too smart for its own good—whereas the anime **LENSMAN** chose the pulp, kiddified sci-fi route, *LGH* keeps to cerebral plotting likely to doom it in the modern anime market.

Another film, *LGH: Overture for a New Conflict* (1993), flashed back to Reinhardt's first great victory at Astarte during the Tiamat War. Promoted to senior admiral, he decides to accept the Lohengramm family title of Count and retire from the military, but he is thwarted by the actions of other officers, who redeploy his efficient subordinates. Sent to Astarte in the company of his adjutant Kircheis, Reinhardt proves himself against the odds.

As befits a series whose sprawling plot makes *Dune* look like *The Cat in the Hat*, there are plenty of other opportunities for video spinoffs. *LGH: Golden Wings* (1992) is adapted from one of the eight flashback novels set apart from the main series continuity, set four years before the beginning of the story proper. Reinhardt and Annerose meet Kircheis for the first time and fight off a group of assassins sent by the court. Similar intrigues await in *LGH: Valley of White Silver* (1997), depicting Reinhardt and Kircheis's first mission after leaving the military academy. They are sent to the front line on the icy planet of Kapturanka and placed under a commander who hates

Annerose because she is favored by the kaiser. Once again, they must deal with assassins without upsetting the status quo. *LGH: Dream of the Morning, Song of the Night* (1997) finds Reinhardt seconded to the military police and sent to investigate a murder at his old school. He undertakes the job, though he is fully aware that he is being framed. The focus shifts to Kircheis for *LGH: Disgrace* (1997), in which the vacationing adjutant rescues an old man, who turns out to be a retired general, forced out of military service after losing a battle. Alliance hero Yang Wenli features in *LGH: A Trillion Stars, A Trillion Points of Light* (1997), in which Schoenkopp, the new commander of the Rosenritter regiment (Knights of the Rose), leads his forces into battle against Runeberg, the *old* commander and his former boss, who has defected to the imperial side and been made a commodore. In the most recent video series to date, *LBH: Spiral Labyrinth* (1999), young Lieutenant Yang Wenli saves the lives of millions of people from an imperial attack and becomes a hero. Soon afterward, he is sent to investigate the murder of Ashby, a retired general. One more tape, the *LGH: Season Four Preview* (1996), is a "making-of . . ." documentary featuring shots of the crew at work and interviews with the voice actors.

LEGEND OF GUSCO BUDORI

1996. JPN: *Gusco Budori no Densetsu.* Movie. DIR: Ryutaro Nakamura. SCR: Ryutaro Nakamura. DES: Shinichi Suzuki. ANI: Shinichi Suzuki. MUS: Yuhiro Kanno. PRD: Bandai Visual. 85 mins.
Another children's story by **NIGHT TRAIN TO THE STARS**–creator Kenji Miyazawa, adapted into an anime as part of the anniversary of the author's birth (see **SPRING AND CHAOS**). Gusco is driven from his home and family by a series of natural disasters but fights back by joining the Iihatov Volcano Deparment. Science brings improvement to the local people, but also causes Gusco's tragic death.

LEGEND OF KAMUI

1969. JPN: *Ninpu Kamui Gaiden.* AKA: *Extra Tales of Kamui the Wind Ninja; Search of the Ninja.* TV series. DIR: Yonehiko Watanabe, Satoshi Murayama, Keisuke Kondo, Kiyoshi Onishi. SCR: Junji Tashiro, Hiroyuki Torii. DES: Sanpei Shirato. ANI: Yoshihide Yamauchi, Toyoo Ashida, Tadashi Maeda, Takashi Oyama. MUS: Ryoichi Mizutani. PRD: Akame Pro, Eiken, Fuji TV. 25 mins. x 26 eps.
Kamui is a new initiate into the world of the ninja, a young boy who wants a normal life, thrown into a society of assassins. He learns the secret tricks of the trade and tries to fight for what he believes in, but the beliefs of his fellow ninja are more mercenary, and liable to cause fatal friction.

Hot on the heels of **MANUAL OF NINJA MARTIAL ARTS**, a 1964 manga by Sanpei Shirato was also adapted, this time for the small screen. Shirato's original ran out with two episodes to go, so the author wrote two further chapters in order to round off the series. The same creator also wrote **SASUKE**. Several TV episodes were also recut into the anime film of the same name, released in 1971. Not to be confused with the unrelated **DAGGER OF KAMUI**.

LEGEND OF LEMNEAR *

1989. JPN: *Kyokuguro no Tsubasa Barukisasu.* AKA: *Jet Black Wings of Valkisas.* Video. DIR: Kinji Yoshimoto. SCR: Kinji Yoshimoto. DES: Satoshi Urushihara. ANI: Kinji Yoshimoto. MUS: Norimasa Yamanaka. PRD: AIC, Nippon Cine TV Corp. 45 mins.
Lemnear, the sole survivor of her village, is a beautiful girl whose destiny is to become the Champion of Silver, the warrior who will lead the people against the invading Dark Lord and his evil minion, the wizard Gardein.

A girl out for revenge, a harem, wobbly breasts, escape, massive fight, bigger fight, the end. Like the same creators' later **PLASTIC LITTLE**, *LoL* suffers from an oversimplification of audience demands—realistically bouncing breasts and massive collateral damage

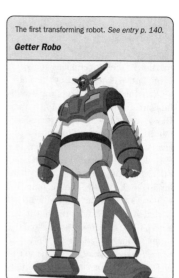

The first transforming robot. *See entry p. 140.*

Getter Robo

will not make an anime work. They can add to its appeal (see **GUNBUSTER**), but more discerning fans demand plot and characterization. Urushihara and Yoshimoto are clearly masters of their craft, but masters to the extent that, when given control of a production, they ignore many important aspects in order to concentrate on their beloved designs. The result is a hodgepodge of incongruities commonplace today in such game-based fantasy anime such as **FINAL FANTASY**—a honky-tonk piano playing in a medieval tavern and a plot so thin that the credits start rolling before the baddie's even cold. There are probably a lot of animators who are using five-second segments from *Lemnear* in their resumés, particularly the highly realistic fire-modeling, but the anime itself is no more than a series of such apprentices' showpieces connected by a half-hearted plot and lovingly drawn cheesecake. The story was also published in manga form, also drawn by Urushihara. *Ill. p. 79.* 🅝🅥

LEGEND OF LYON *

1986. JPN: *Riyon Densetsu Flare.* Video. DIR: Yukihiro Makino. SCR: N/C. DES: Yorihisa Uchida. ANI: Yorihisa Uchida. MUS: Nobuhiko Kajiwara. PRD: Hayama Art, Media Station. 30 mins. x 2 eps., 30 mins. x 2 eps.

Claude leads an army of demons in an invasion of the peaceful kingdom of Lyon, but he is held back by the martial (and marital) powers of the beautiful Flare, mixing the alien rapists of **DEMON BEAST INVASION** with the hokey fantasy plot of **EROTIC TORTURE CHAMBER**. After dispatching the invaders in episode one, the pretty Flare and her sidekick, Neris, discover more of them lurking in the woods, and the tentacled menace is once again dealt with after several scenes of clothes-ripping and high-pitched screams. It was followed by the similarly titled *Legend of Reyon: God of Darkness*, a pastiche in the spirit of **TOURNAMENT OF THE GODS**, in which the hackneyed conventions of beat-'em-up game adaptations (a secret fight arranged to destroy all the bad guy's opponents at once) are adapted for the erotic market. Though *Reyon* was not an actual sequel to *Lyon*, it did recycle the same character designs. **ⒸⓃⓋ**

LEGEND OF ROLLING WHEELS

1987. JPN: *Baribari Densetsu*. Video. DIR: Nagayuki Toriumi, Satoshi Uemura. SCR: Jiyu Watanabe, Asami Watanabe. DES: Shuichi Shigeno. ANI: Noboru Furuse. MUS: Ichiro Nitta. PRD: Studio Pierrot. 30 mins. x 2 eps.

Miyuki Ichinose sees something remarkable—a kid on a 50cc moped outracing a man on a 750cc bike. Since she is the daughter of a motorcycle racing team chief, she wastes no time in inviting the kid, Gun, onto the team. Gun finds it hard to fit in at first, and the rivalry between him and successful rider Hideyoshi makes things even harder. Gun gains confidence, and he and his friends accept Hideyoshi's challenge to enter their team in the world championship. Their team wins, but Hideyoshi's career is interrupted by a tragic accident.

Based on a 1983 manga in *Shonen Magazine* by Shuichi Shigeno, whose need for speed would find a greater outlet in the later **INITIAL D**. This was

made for video but shown in some theaters in its year of release.

LEGEND OF THE BLUE WOLVES

1996. JPN: *Aoki Okamitachi no Densetsu*. Video. DIR: Yasunori Urata. SCR: N/C. DES: Makoto Kobayashi. ANI: N/C. MUS: Masamichi Amano. PRD: Beam Entertainment. 45 mins.

A group of bold young soldiers must defend Earth and its colonies from attacks by an unknown life form, though there is little scope for character development in this one-shot's humble time-frame. A major part of the story's appeal rested on explicit sex scenes—in addition to the 45-minute "X" version, an R-rated version was prepared that ran ten minutes shorter. **ⒸⓃⓋ**

LEGEND OF THE FOREST *

1987. Movie. DIR: Osamu Tezuka. SCR: Osamu Tezuka. DES: Osamu Tezuka. ANI: Takashi Okamura, Yoshiaki Kawajiri. MUS: Peter Tchaikovsky. PRD: Mushi Pro. 23 mins.

In the forest, in the valley, by the river that will eventually flow to the sea, insects buzz among the flowers. Two squirrels fall in love, but the forest is threatened by property developers. The innovation is not in the story, but in the way in which it is told. As with his *Broken Down Film* (see **JUMPING**), Tezuka experiments with the film medium itself, starting with the still frames and limited camera movement on still pictures, before progressing through early monochrome, color, limited TV animation, and Disney-style full animation. In other words, *LotF* takes the viewer through several decades of animation history in just a few minutes. A second, unrelated film follows, in which forest spirits, shown in lush, *Fantasia*-quality animation and coloring, fight off the human building developers (led by a Hitler-lookalike construction boss), who are shown in limited animation with jagged, angular art design and bright, garish colors. Compare to **POMPOKO**, in message if not execution.

LEGEND OF THE FOUR KINGS *

1991. JPN: *Soryuden*. AKA: *Sohryuden; The Endragonning; Legend of the Dragon Kings*. Video. DIR: Norio Kabeshima. SCR: Akinori Endo. DES: Shunji Murata. ANI: Moriyasu Taniguchi, Nobuaki Nagano, Makura Saki (pseud. for Osamu Dezaki). MUS: Hiroyuki Nanba. PRD: Kitty Film. 45 mins. x 12 eps.

Three thousand years in the past, there was a war in the heavenly realm. Betrayed by their allies, the Go clan are banished from heaven and forced to wander Earth as mortals for 117 generations, until the dragons contained within them burst forth once more to begin the battle anew.

Fast forward to the present, where the four Ryudo brothers live in Tokyo but have recently been the subject of several kidnapping attempts. While the brothers are plagued by kidnappers and dreams of dragons, they have to cope with a takeover bid at the family college and dynastic machinations as a mobster tries to marry his son to Matsuri. As if a surname that is Chinese for "Dragon Pavilion" is not enough of a hint, the brothers are the earthly incarnations of the four Dragon Kings of legend, and the powers of their former lives still dwell within them, bestowing superhuman strength and speed. These powers are desired by the "Old Man of Kamakura," who lures them to a firing range by kidnapping their cousin Matsuri. The Old Man is not the only one who wishes to possess the magical powers of the Ryudos—the mad Dr. Tomosawa, famed for live vivisections, and the U.S. military are both keen to kidnap the brothers themselves. The doctor sends cybernetic soldiers in to obtain the brothers, but, as with all the previous assailants, his minions are seen off by the brothers' powers of transformation. One Ryudo, however, is caged and taken to Yokota Air Force Base (see **BLOOD**). The others must rescue him before the cruel experiments awaken the dragon within him and turn him into a monster of awesome destructive capabilities. You can guess the rest.

Dense without being engaging, *LotFK* is based on a series of novels by **LEGEND OF GALACTIC HEROES**–creator Yoshiki Tanaka, but it has none of the virtues of its more illustrious counterpart. A failed attempt to recreate the monthly "video comic" feel of the U.K. distributor's previous **GUYVER**, the dub is particularly poor, with the "Weirdo" brothers speaking a mixture of English and American, and for all their supposed genius, not being able to pronounce each other's names properly. The plot development is confused by the intercutting of disparate scenes from the eight-volume series of novels, patched together with unhelpful voiceovers. The animation itself is often mediocre, barely above the level of later **CRYING FREEMAN** episodes, but the design has a certain special something. From the opening credits that depict the brothers in Chinese dress through to the uncommonly "Asian" features of the characters, *LotFK* is steeped in oriental myth and culture, shamefully occluded by the English-language dubbers, who do not bother to rewrite the Japanese pronunciations of Chinese proper nouns and bungle a whole succession of historical and geographical references. These, however, are minor issues unlikely to rescue an already doomed production. The U.S. subtitled version demonstrates all too clearly that the dub is a surprisingly faithful rendition of the original's tepid tone, with the exception of the story's single funny line ("Don't step in the custard"), which was not present in the Japanese version. Dubbed at the height of Manga Entertainment's beer-and-curry era, *LotFK* even managed to disappoint the lowest-common denominator audience with its failed leap of faith toward hidden depths—the same company would return many years later with a much better version of similar material: its adaptation of CLAMP's **X: THE MOVIE**.

In addition to the *Four Kings* novels, the brothers also appear in the Japanese audio drama *Mirage City* (1995), released on CD with an accompanying manga drawn by CLAMP, who also contributed to the earlier anime adaptation of Tanaka's **HEROIC LEGEND OF ARSLAN**. ●

LEGENDARY IDOL ERIKO

1989. JPN: *Idol Densetsu Eriko*. TV series. DIR: Tetsuro Amino. SCR: Brother Anoppo. DES: N/C. ANI: Noriyasu Yamauchi. MUS: N/C. PRD: Bandai, TV Tokyo. 25 mins. x 51 eps. (TV), 30 mins. (v).

In this popular TV series with a star whose look presaged the girl of the 1990s, **SAILOR MOON** herself, fourteen-year-old Eriko Tamura wants to be a pop star but must compete against her prissy rival, Rei Asagiri. It's scandal and high-pressure performances, as the tropes of the sports anime (e.g., **AIM FOR THE ACE**) are adapted for a show about a hothouse for wannabe stars— the lighter-hearted flipside of artistic pressures that would be so heavily criticized a decade later in **PERFECT BLUE**. *LIE: Music Video* (1989) was, predictably, a ten-song compilation of some of the serial's best tunes, released straight to video.

LEISURE CLUB

1992. JPN: *Yukan Club*. Video. DIR: Satoshi Dezaki. SCR: Machiko Kondo. DES: Yukari Kobayashi. ANI: Yukari Kobayashi. MUS: Toy-Boys. PRD: Pioneer. 35 mins. x 2 eps.

Filthy-rich boys and girls occasionally take time out of their luxurious lifestyle to solve crimes in this short-lived series based on the 1981 manga in *Ribbon* by Yukari Ichijo. For the second episode, the cast relocates to the exotic foreign destination of Hong Kong, where they are dragged into a gangland conspiracy over a stolen microfilm. Compare to **DEBUTANTE DETECTIVES**.

LEMON ANGEL

1987. JPN: *Midnight Anime Lemon Angel*. TV series. DIR: Yasunori Ide, Takashi Akimoto, Susumu Aki, Osamu Yamazaki, Yukio Okazaki, Satoru Namekawa. SCR: Yasunori Ide, Osamu Yamazaki. DES: Kurahito Miyazaki. ANI: Katsu Oyama, Osamu Yamazaki. MUS: Human Company. PRD: Fairy Dust, AIC, Fuji TV. 5 mins. x 37 eps., 5 mins. x 9 eps., 30 mins. x 2 eps.

Three lovely teenagers—and the three actresses who provide their voices— share their midnight confidences and fantasies with the TV audience, as Erika Shima, Miki Emoto, and Tomo Sakurai play "themselves" in a sanitized late-night TV incarnation of the **CREAM LEMON** franchise. Purporting to be studying at the fictitious Lemon Academy (compare to **KIRA KIRA MELODY ACADEMY**), the girls returned the following year for a second season, though it was soon taken off the air. Sakurai's career did not suffer, and she was soon a popular voice actress in mainstream anime such as **EL HAZARD**. The other actresses no longer show up on lists of big names. *Lemon Angel Y[oung] J[unior]* (1990) comprised two toned-down videos made for more censorious times, with Sakurai directed by Tetsuro Amino, who would make her a star in **MACROSS** 7.

LEMON CHUHAI LOVE 30'S

1985. JPN: *Chuhairemon Love 30's*. Video. DIR: Kozo Koizumi. SCR: Ryochi Yagi. DES: Sho Shimura. ANI: Kozo Koizumi. MUS: Yoshikazu Sano, Rob Bird. PRD: Tsuchida Pro. 45 mins.

Bug-eyed Katsumi (known as Chuhai to his friends) is a muscle-bound detective determined to use his strength and pig-headed stupidity to rescue his teenage girlfriend from a succession of embarrassing situations. Based on a manga by Sho Shimura and heavily seeded with background music from the 1960s U.S. hit parade. ●●●

LENSMAN *

1984. JPN: *Galactic Patrol: Lensman*. TV series, movie. DIR: Hiroshi Fukutomi, Yoshiaki Kawajiri, Kazuyuki Hirokawa. SCR: Soji Yoshikawa, Masaki Tsuji, Haruya Yamazaki, Michiru Umadori. DES: Kazuo Tomizawa. ANI: Nobuyuki Kitajima. MUS: Akira Inoue, The Alfee. PRD: MK, Madhouse, TV

Asahi. 25 mins. x 25 eps. (TV), 107 mins. (m).

In A.D. 2742, during a fight to the death in space, the decimated survivors of the Galactic Patrol obtain vital details that could help defeat the evil Boskone Empire. The warship Brittania crashes on the peaceful farm world of M'queie, where the dying pilot passes his lens (a techno-magical power amplifier) to local boy Kim Kinnison. Kim's father, a former patrolman, sacrifices his life to allow Kim to get off-planet, throwing the young farmer into a life of adventure, as he joins forces with the patrol to defeat evil throughout the galaxy.

E. E. "Doc" Smith's *Galactic Patrol* (1937), along with its prequels and sequels, was one of the landmark series in the history of U.S. pulp sci-fi. Shortly after Edmond Hamilton's **CAPTAIN FUTURE** (1940) was turned into an anime in 1978, Smith's classic series was also adapted into the 25-episode *Galactic Patrol: Lensman* TV series, directed by **BATTLE ANGEL ALITA**'s Hiroshi Fukutomi and introducing several new elements in the wake of *Star Wars*. The anime turns Kim Kinnison, originally the superhuman product of a eugenics project dating back to Atlantis, into nothing but a humble farm boy who wants to be a pilot. Nurse Clarissa "Chris" MacDougall, the fiery redhaired product of another breeding program, who eventually becomes the fearsome Red Lensman and gives birth to the immortal *Children of the Lens*, becomes yet another simpering damsel in the anime.

Carl Macek, of **ROBOTECH** fame, picked up the series and dubbed a couple of episodes in a failed attempt to interest U.S. networks. The episodes were eventually cut into the English-language video *Power of the Lens*, while Macek bought the feature-length Japanese theatrical edition instead to release in the U.S. as *Lensman*. As suggested by the 25-minute acts, the film version takes several episodes of the TV series and stitches them together. This makes the "movie" seem strangely paced, with fast action interspersed with overlong *gee-whiz* beauty-passes of the spaceships to allow us to gawp at the incredibly expensive computer graphics, made with the same mega-powerful Cray computers used to animate Jupiter in *2010: Odyssey Two*. Still vaguely recognizable from the book are the Overlords of Delgon, evil creatures whom Kim defeats in the company of the "Dragon Lensman" Worsel, and van Buskirk, a Dutch giant (inexplicably half-bison in the anime). Later scenes set on the "drug planet" Radelix start to go off the rails. Whereas Kim goes deep undercover posing as the drug addict "Wild Bill" in the book *Gray Lensman*, Wild Bill is a character in his own right in the anime, DJ-ing in a dated 1980s disco. By the end, we're in a ho-hum world of final showdown and lighthearted coda, with the baddie predictably still alive; a great disappointment if you've read the books, which feature crashing worlds, maimings, and dismemberments, a revolution on a planet of lesbians, mind-blowing psychic powers, double-, triple-, and quadruple-crossing conspiracies, and gunplay that makes *The Matrix* look like a puppet show.

Instead of reproducing such joys, the anime takes only the characters and most basic of plot outlines, adding the off-the-peg elements that are supposed to guarantee success in the George Lucas mode. The "comic relief" robot Sol, whose appearances are never comic and seldom a relief, is another pointless homage. Ironically, the end result makes *Lensman* look like a cheap knockoff of *Star Wars*, whereas it was originally literally decades ahead of it.

LES MISÉRABLES *

1979. JPN: *Jean Valjean Monogatari*. AKA: *Story of Jean Valjean*. TV special. DIR: Keiji Hisaoka. SCR: Masaki Tsuji. DES: Masami Suda. ANI: Masami Suda. MUS: Yasuo Minami. PRD: Toei, Fuji TV. 75 mins.

Jean Valjean is thrown into prison for stealing a single loaf of bread. Returning to his hometown after several years away, he tries to live an honest life and falls in love with the pretty teacher Mireil. Caught stealing silver, he breaks parole, changes his name, and flees to another town. However, Valjean's past comes back to haunt him in the form of Inspector Javert, who catches him. Once more, Valjean escapes and flees to the big city, where tragedy awaits. An adaptation of the 1862 novel by Victor Hugo, it was released in the U.K. on the Kids Cartoon Collection label and Quebec in a French dub, but this version is unavailable in the U.S.

LESSON OF DARKNESS *

1994. JPN: *Inju Kazoku Kyoshi*. AKA: *Lust-Beast Family Teacher*. Video. DIR: Ben Yabuki. SCR: N/C. DES: Ben Ono. ANI: N/C. MUS: N/C. PRD: Pink Pineapple, KSS. 45 mins. x 4 eps.

Young women are being murdered and desiccated all over Tokyo, their bodies found dried like ancient mummies. Meanwhile, "Nineteen-year-old college student" Miho believes she is being stalked and is surprised to discover that her teacher, who is having an affair with her friend Azusa, is really a monster with large tentacles—a monster whose last rampage decimated the female population of Tokyo 70 years previously, though the plot sounds suspiciously like something from the day before yesterday, and the day before that. **ᴏ🅛🅝🅥**

LESSON XX

1994. Video. DIR: Rin Hiro. SCR: Ei Onagi. DES: Sanae Chikanaga. ANI: Sanae Chikanaga. MUS: N/C. PRD: Tokuma Japan Communications. 50 mins.

Teenager Shizuka is finishing up school and staying at a boardinghouse, but he is confused by his romantic feelings toward another man called Sakura. In a rash moment, he confesses his feelings, though both boys are concerned that once they take the first steps on the road to male love, there may be no going back. A gay-love drama without the gut-wrenching angst that seems almost obligatory with the rest of the genre, based on a manga by Ei Onagi.

LET THE DREAMS NEVER END
1987. JPN: *Yume kara Samenai*. Video. DIR: Satoshi Inoue. SCR: Ran Kawanishi. DES: Yumi Shirakura. ANI: Kazuo Tomizawa. MUS: Kazuhiko Matsuo. PRD: Shaft. 40 mins.
Student Tako is inexorably drawn toward Sao despite class rumors that she has appeared in a porno film. If this were an anime for boys, he wouldn't mind so much, but this is based on a girls' manga by Yumi Shirakura, so it's all dreadfully scandalous. Sao was played by idol singer Ryoko Sano, who also provided the theme tune.

LET'S NUPUNUPU
1998. TV series. DIR: Kazuyoshi Hisakome. SCR: Ko Nanbu. DES: Hiroko Seino. ANI: Yasuto Kaya. MUS: N/C. PRD: Asia-do. 4 mins. x 16 eps.
Schoolteacher Mr. Shidara has trouble keeping his male and female students apart in this comedy broadcast as part of the *Wonderful* slot on TBS, along with shows such as COLORFUL and COOL COUPLE. It was originally based on a four-panel strip in *Shonen Magazine* by Akira Mitsumori.

LEVEL C
1996. JPN: *Level C: Gokuraku no Hoteishiki*. AKA: *Level C: Paradise Equation*. Video. DIR: Yorifusa Yamaguchi. SCR: N/C. DES: Yumi Nakayama. ANI: Yumi Nakayama. MUS: N/C. PRD: Pink Pineapple, KSS. 40 mins.
A story of forbidden love between men, based on a manga by the pseudonymous Futaba Aoi and Mitsuba Kurenai. Not to be confused with EQUATION OF THE ROTTEN TEACHER.

LICCA-CHAN
1990. JPN: *Licca-chan Fushigina Fushigina Unia Monogatari; Licca-chan Fushigina Maho no Ring; Licca-chan no Nichiyobi; Licca-chan the Movie: Licca-chan to Yamaneko, Hoshi no Tabi*. AKA: *Licca and the Mystery of Mysterious Unia; Licca and the Mysterious Magic Ring; Licca's Sunday; Licca the Movie: Licca and the Wildcat: Journey of Dreams; Superdoll Licca-chan*. Video, TV series. DIR: Tomomi Mochizuki, Fumiko Ishii, Tatsuo Sato, Tsutomu Shibayama. SCR: Kazunori Ito, Asami Watanabe. DES: Akemi Takada, Yoshiyuki Kato. ANI: Masako Kato, Takuya Saito. MUS: Mineo Maeda, Kenji Kawai. PRD: Asia-do, Madhouse, TV Asahi. 28 mins. x 2 eps. (v1), 60 mins. (v2), 25 mins. (v3), 78 mins. (v4), 25 mins. x 32 eps. (TV), 10 mins. (m).
Licca is playing the piano when she notices that one of the keys doesn't work. Opening it up to see why, she is transported to the world of Unia with her stuffed toy bird Dodo and Ine the cat. Trying to find her way out of a world that is equal parts ALICE IN WONDERLAND and WIZARD OF OZ, she meets the craftsman who makes dreams and wanders through the Square Pole forest of doppelgangers. A dragon tells her to seek the Amaranth flower at the Tower of Beginning, but Ine has become spoiled by all the fuss he gets and wants to stay. Licca and Dodo are almost trapped in the Maze of Anger by their bad-tempered arguments, but they eventually find their way to the Sky Garden and the Rainbow Bridge that takes them home.
Licca-chan is the Japanese equivalent of Barbie, a child's doll designed in 1967 by Miyako Maki, the wife of CAPTAIN HARLOCK–creator Leiji Matsumoto. Her first video adventure was followed by *Licca and the Magic Ring* (1991), in which a magic ring falls out of the sky into Licca's playground, where she discovers that it can unlock the three seals of Dreams, Shadows, and Death. Less scary antics occupied the third video, *Licca's Sunday* (1992), about her traveling to her auntie's house to play with her cousins. As her 30th birthday grew near, the doll returned to adventure in the video misleadingly and clumsily entitled *Licca the Movie: Licca and the Wildcat: Journey of Dreams* (1994), in which she goes on a country holiday with her father, dreams that she is attending a school

The distinctive lines of a Leiji Matsumoto beauty, also seen in the Daft Punk music videos. See entry p. 317.

Queen Emeraldas

for the stone cats that populate the town, and heads off on a journey through the sky with the largest. The film was also repackaged the same year in a *Special Collection*, including the movie, a selection from 30 years of Licca TV commercials, and an exclusive Licca doll dressed in the uniform of a video-store clerk.

The franchise was revamped for a new generation as *Superdoll Licca-chan* (1998), a TV series featuring new designs from Tetsuya Kumatani and direction from STREET FIGHTER II's Gisaburo Sugii. For the TV version, there are *two* Liccas—the first is a third-grader at St. Therese's School, attacked without warning by Scarecrow, Pul, and Wahya. She discovers that she is the heir to the Doll Kingdom, a human dreamland where dolls live and breathe, though they can become human if loved and cherished for 100 years. Licca is the child of a union between French musician Pierre and "normal human" Orie, who is really the Doll Queen in disguise. Licca's grandmother gives her the magical Call Ring that can summon help and three dolls named Licca, Izumi, and Isamu, the spirits of wisdom, courage and life. Since it is a fundamental problem with shows based on dolls that children often have duplicates of the same ones, this is a clever means of encouraging play with duplicate Liccas, as the child begins her quest to regain her rightful kingdom from the usurper Queen Yaë, her great-aunt. The doll returned again for *Licca-chan: Tale of the Mysterious Sea* (2001), a fully computer-animated short film shown in department stores and amusement parks. For similar doll-inspired action, see RAINBOW ACROSS THE PACIFIC and, frankly, the entire GUNDAM series.

LIGHTSPEED ELECTRON ARBEGAS

1983. JPN: *Kosoku Denshin Arbegas.* TV series. DIR: Kozo Morishita, Masamitsu Sasaki, Masao Ito, Noriyasu Yamauchi, Keiji Hisaoka, Takao Yoshisawa, Masayuki Akehi. SCR: Akiyoshi Sakai. DES: Shigenori Kageyama, Koichi Ohata. ANI: Shigenori Kageyama, Hajime Kaneko, Toshio Mori. MUS: Michiaki Watanabe. PRD: Toei, TV Tokyo. 25 mins. x 45 eps. Earth is invaded by the evil Derringer aliens, who are held off repeatedly by a group of Japanese schoolchildren that have "won the robot prize." These children have inexplicably managed to knock together a giant war machine formed from three combining submachines that can transform in turn into six separate configurations for different missions—electron, magma, space, marine, guard, and sky. Obviously, kids were better at science in the 1980s. Far-fetched, but nothing can surprise an anime viewer after GOLD LIGHTAN. The toys also appeared in the GODAIKIN range and as part of Matchbox's VOLTRON line, though *Arbegas* was completely unrelated.

LILY C.A.T. *

1987. Video. DIR: Hisayuki Toriumi. SCR: Hiroyuki Hoshiyama. DES: Yasuomi Umezu, Yasuhiro Moriki, Yoshitaka Amano. ANI: Toshiyasu Okada. MUS: Akira Inoue. PRD: Studio Pierrot. 70 mins. It's A.D. 2264 and the exploration vessel Saldes is on a 20-year mission to planet L.A.O.3, carrying seven passengers. Not all of them are on the right side of

the law, or totally open about their background and motives—but all of them, and the six-person crew, are in deadly danger. In a blatant rip-off of the first *Alien* movie, death is stalking the ship, picking off the occupants one by one, though the titular cat is revealed to be more than just an excuse to go back out into danger, since it is really the key to the mother computer that will save the day. ⚫NV

LION BOOKS

1983. JPN: *Midori no Neko; Amefuri Koso; Lunn wa Kaze no Naka; Yamataro Kaeru; Adachigahara; Akuemon.* AKA: (see below). TV specials, movies. DIR: Hitoshi Nishimura, Masamitsu Yoshimura, Hisashi Sakaguchi, Makoto Tezuka. SCR: Hitoshi Nishimura, Masamitsu Yoshimura, Hisashi Sakaguchi. DES: Hitoshi Nishimura, Osamu Tezuka, Hisashi Sakaguchi. ANI: Hitoshi Nishimura, Masamitsu Yoshimura, Hisashi Sakaguchi. MUS: Reijiro Komutsu. PRD: Tezuka Pro. 24 mins. x 6 eps. Twenty-four episodes were planned for this series of one-shots, but the hope of ASTRO BOY–creator Osamu Tezuka to animate many of his early short manga was soon dashed by lack of interest. Instead, several were shown as TV "specials," while two more were made for theaters then collected under the *Lion Books* umbrella for release to video in 1997.

In *The Green Cat* (1983), the titular feline is thought to be a good-luck charm but soon brings misfortune to all who come into contact with it. In the second tale, *Rain Boy* (1983), Mouta is on his way home during a storm, when a boy asks if he can have his shoes. The boy is a magical creature who can grant him three wishes after the fashion of ALADDIN's jinni.

Lunn Flies into the Wind (1985) features a boy who falls in love with the girl he sees in an advertisement poster on a wall and goes searching for the original model. *Yamataro Comes Back* (1989) is an *Incredible Journey*–themed adventure about a young bear cub los-

ing his parents and having to survive in the wild. *Adachigahara* (1991) was shown in theaters as a second feature and based on one of the JAPANESE FOLK TALES, though the action is moved into the near future. An old woman meets the young space pilot Jes, exiled for trying to overthrow Earth's pro-independence president Phippo and pining for his girlfriend, Anny. The final story, *Akuemon* (1993), was directed by Tezuka's own son Makoto and shown at the Hong Kong film festival instead of broadcast on Japanese TV. A tale set in old-time Japan, it portrays a fox outwitting a hunter and choosing to live out his life in the shadow of the titular temple gate with his newfound squirrel companion.

LITTL' BITS *

1980. JPN: *Belfy to Lilibet.* AKA: *Belfy and Lillibit.* TV series. DIR: Masayuki Hayashi, Mizuho Nishikubo, Hiroshi Iwata. SCR: Masaru Yamamoto, Kazuo Sato, Takao Oyama, Akiyoshi Sakai, Isao Okishima, Leo Nishimura. DES: Hiromitsu Morita, Akiko Shimomoto. ANI: Hiromitsu Morita. MUS: Takeo Watanabe. PRD: Tatsunoko. 30 mins. x 26 eps. The Fanitt family of fairies protects the forest, even though they are only a few inches tall. Lilbet is a male fairy, happy-go-lucky and always willing to help out. Though the other fairies make fun of him, he never lets it get him down, getting into all manner of adventures in the company of his girlfriend, Belfy, and pals Napoleon, Dokkurin, and Chuchuna. Later episodes of this Tatsunoko fairy story included early jobs for future VIDEO GIRL AI–director Nishikubo and writer Okishima, who also scripted episodes of the live-action *Monkey* TV series.

These *Smurf*-alikes were translated into English and shown on Nickelodeon in 1984, with the location changed to "Foothill Forest." The names were also altered, to a roster including Lillabit, Williebit, Snoozabit, Browniebit, Snagglebit, and the old-timer Elderbit.

LITTLE DEVIL

1989. JPN: *Akuma-kun*. TV series, movie. DIR: Junichi Sato, Shigeyasu Yamauchi, Masayuki Akehi. SCR: Yoshiyuki Suga, Takao Koyama, Nobuaki Kishima. DES: Ginichiro Suzuki. ANI: Fujio Yamamoto, Masami Abe. MUS: Nozomu Aoki. PRD: Toei, TV Asahi. 25 mins. x 42 eps. (TV), 40 mins., 26 mins. (m).

A minor work based on a 1966 manga by SPOOKY KITARO–creator Shigeru Mizuki, in which the Little Devil appears once every ten thousand years (in this case, as Japanese schoolboy Shingo Yamada) to save the world, although his reasons are not too clear considering that he is supposed to be on the side of evil and has 12 "dark apostles" to contend with. Similarly confused renditions of Christian apocalypse turn up for adult audiences in DEVILMAN, UROTSUKIDOJI, and HUMANE SOCIETY, though this anime is most definitely aimed at children. The second "movie," a glorified episode screened as part of the traditional vacation moviegoing season, packs Shingo off to Devil-Land, a Satanic theme park. Come on, Disney, you know you want to.

LITTLE EL CID

1979. JPN: *Little El Cid no Boken*. AKA: *Adventures of Little El Cid*. TV series. DIR: Fumio Kurokawa. SCR: Toshiyuki Kashiwakura. DES: Shuichi Seki. ANI: Takao Kogawa, Akio Sakai. MUS: N/C. PRD: Nippon Animation, TV Tokyo. 25 mins. x 26 eps.

In 10th-century Spain, the Christian inhabitants are fighting a losing battle against the invading Muslim Moors. The young Luis Díaz de Bivar decides to become a knight, but it will be a long time before he becomes the legendary warrior El Cid. A fictitious dramatization of a famous character's youth (compare to ROBIN HOOD), commissioned as a Spanish coproduction but not broadcast in Japan until 1984, long after its Spanish premiere. Curiously, in the original 12th-century *Poema di Mio Cid*, El Cid's name is Rodrigo, not Luis.

LITTLE GHOSTS: ACHI, KOCHI, AND SOCHI

1991. JPN: *Chiisana Obake: Achi, Kochi, Sochi*. AKA: *Little Ghosts: Thither, Hither, and Yon*. TV series. DIR: Osamu Kobayashi. SCR: Yoshio Urasawa, Kazuhiko Koto. DES: N/C. ANI: Hideo Kawauchi. MUS: Takeshi Ike. PRD: Pastel House, Studio Pierrot, Nippon TV. 11 mins. x 100 eps.

Three friendly ghosts play around, make friends, and become involved in mildly surreal adventures, such as delivering donuts to aliens from Venus. Their prime concern, however, is getting lots of lovely food, an orally fixated quest of some appeal to their audience of toddlers.

LITTLE GOBLIN

1968. JPN: *Kaibutsu-kun*. AKA: *Li'l Monster Prince*. TV series, movie. DIR: Masaaki Osumi, Eiji Okabe, Shinichi Suzuki, Hiroshi Fukutomi, Shinji Okuda, Makoto Nakahara. SCR: Haruya Yamazaki, Tsunehisa Ito, Takashi Hayakawa, Takashi Yamada, Hirokazu Mizude, Yoshio Urasawa. DES: Fujiko-Fujio, Tsutomu Shibata. ANI: Norio Kubii, Sadao Tominaga. MUS: Michio Okamoto, Yasei Kobayashi. PRD: Tokyo Movie Shinsha, TBS. 25 mins. x 49 eps. (TV1), 25 mins. x 49 eps. (TV2), 75 mins. (m1), 51 mins. (m2).

Kaibutsu the little goblin appears one day in the apartment next door to average Japanese schoolboy Hiroshi's. He is the prince of Monster Land, sent to Earth to keep him out of trouble, accompanied on occasion by his associates Franken (a junior FRANKENSTEIN), DRACULA, and the Wolfman.

Ghostly goings-on in the tradition of DORORON ENMA, SPOOKY KITARO, and LITTLE DEVIL, based on a 1965 manga by DORAEMON-creator Hiroshi Fujimoto, though credited to the Fujiko-Fujio team of which he was a member. The franchise was brought back in color as the TV series *New Little Goblin* (1980), this time on the TV Asahi channel. The remake lasted far longer than its predecessor, graduating to movie status with *LG in Monster Land* (1981), on a

double bill with the *Doraemon* film *Nobita the Space Colonist*. The character returned for a second film outing with *LG: Sword of the Devil* (1982), set in the rival kingdom of Devil Land, which Kaibutsu is forced to invade in order to save his father's life.

LITTLE HOUSE ON THE PRAIRIE

1975. JPN: *Kusahara no Shojo Laura*. AKA: *Laura the Girl of the Grasslands*. TV series. DIR: Mitsuo Sawazaki, Masaharu Endo. SCR: Iwao Yamazaki, Fumi Takahashi. DES: Yasuji Mori. ANI: Megumi Mizuta. MUS: Akihiko Takashima. PRD: Nippon Animation, TBS. 25 mins. x 26 eps.

Young Laura lives a happy life in Wisconsin but is forced to move west, out of the woods with her family, when a harsh winter makes it impossible to stay in her old home. After encountering American Indians and settling on the Dakota prairie, she has a happy time (again) with her loving family, particularly her sisters, Mary and Carrie.

Not a WORLD MASTERPIECE THEATER production, though made by the WMT studio Nippon Animation, the anime was commissioned and filmed in Japan following the success of the anime HEIDI and the popularity of the U.S. live-action TV series of *LHotP* in Japan. As with the live-action series, the anime version concentrates on adapting the early books in the long sequence of novels by Laura Ingalls Wilder—later volumes would take the child characters into adulthood, way beyond the 1953 volume from which the series takes its name.

LITTLE JUMBO

1977. JPN: *Chiisana Jumbo*. Movie. DIR: Toshio Hirata, Masami Hata. SCR: Takashi Yanase. DES: Takashi Yanase. ANI: Kazuko Nakamura, Shigeru Yamamoto. MUS: Taku Izumi. PRD: Madhouse, Sanrio. 28 mins.

Jumbo the kindhearted elephant arrives at Red Rose island after floating across the sea in a big red box, accompanied by his friend Baloo the elephant-trainer. The pair immediately leap out of the box and begin a series of supposedly cute song-and-dance numbers to entertain the king and his three subjects, although clearly not cute enough for Sanrio, which kept this minor offering from **ANPANMAN**-creator Yanase on the shelf for two years before allowing it to sneak into theaters in 1977.

LITTLE KOALA

1984. JPN: *Koala Boy Kokki.* AKA: *Adventures of the Little Koala.* TV series. DIR: Takashi Tanasawa, Katsuhisa Yamada, Masamitsu Sasaki, Shigeru Omachi. SCR: Toshiro Ueno, Nanako Watanabe, Yoshiaki Yoshida, Toshiaki Imaizumi, Kiichi Takayama, Mamoru Kobe. DES: Kazuyuki Kobayashi. ANI: Kazuyuki Kobayashi, Hidekazu Obara, Yoichi Otabe, Masahiro Yoshida, Megumi Kagawa, Masayuki Uchiyama. MUS: Tsuyoshi Kawano. PRD: Nagata, TV Tokyo. 25 mins. x 26 eps.

Kokki and his twin sister Laura are baby koalas who live in Yukari Village in the countryside. They play with their other animal friends, including Panny the Penguin, but often have to fight to preserve the peace of their village from the predations of the three evil Kangaroo Brothers. Other troubles include a sick whale, invading UFOs, an attacking witch, and other incidents that only go to demonstrate that if your high-concept is so thin as to be nothing more than "Let's do something with koalas," the end result is a mishmash of everything else on TV at the time. Commissioned during the same koala fever that brought us **THE NOOZLES**.

LITTLE KONISHIKI

2000. JPN: *Dotto Koni-chan.* AKA: *Kaboom Koni-chan.* TV series. DIR: Shinichi Watanabe. SCR: Satoru Akahori, Masaharu Amiya. DES: Mitsuhiro Yoneda. ANI: Shinichi Watanabe. MUS: N/C. PRD: Sky PerfecTV. 5 mins. x 20+ eps.

Spoof SF, adventure, and fantasy drama featuring squashed-down child-versions of the sumo wrestler Konishiki, along with his cartoon companions High, Moro, and Nari. Based on a cartoon strip in *The Television* magazine, the series premiered on pay-per-view television before moving to regular broadcasts. Screened within the *Animax* anime-themed schedule strip.

LITTLE LORD FAUNTLEROY *

1988. JPN: *Koshi Ceddie.* AKA: *Young Noble Ceddie; Adventures of the Little Prince.* TV series. DIR: Kozo Kusuba, Fumio Ike. SCR: Shiro Ishimori. DES: Michiyo Sakurai. ANI: Michiyo Sakurai, Hideaki Shimada, Hisatoshi Motoki, Eimi Maeda, Megumi Kagawa, Toshiki Yamazaki. MUS: Koichi Morita. PRD: Nippon Animation, Fuji TV. 25 mins. x 43 eps.

Young American boy Cedric Errol discovers that his late father was English and that he is being deprived of his true inheritance by antiAmerican relatives. Captain Errol, sent away to the U.S. by his resentful father, incurred the wrath of his family by falling in love with a girl in the colonies, and the other Errol family members are determined to keep Cedric out of their lives. Eventually, he returns to his English homeland and the stewardship of Dorincourt Castle. This rags-to-riches tale was based on the 1886 children's book by Frances Hodgson Burnett, who also wrote **A LITTLE PRINCESS** and **THE SECRET GARDEN**. As befits its transatlantic tone, it was released in both British and American dubs, although with a title that has often led to confusion with the unrelated **LITTLE PRINCE**. See also **VIDEO PICTURE BOOK**.

LITTLE LOVE LETTER, A

1981. JPN: *Chiisana Love Letter: Mariko to Nemunoki no Kodomotachi.* AKA: *A Little Love Letter: Mariko and the Children of the Silk Tree.* TV special. DIR: Yuzo Ishida. SCR: Sachiko Akita. DES: Kenzo Koizumi. ANI: Swan Pro. MUS: Nozomu Aoki. PRD: TV Asahi, NOW Planning. 84 mins.

A follow-up to the same studio's **HELEN KELLER** anime, *A Little Love Letter* kept the handicapped theme but focused on a wholly Japanese story. During the 1970s, actress Mariko Miyagi became heavily involved in the Silk Tree Academy, a rehabilitation center for disabled children. She appeared in several live-action films to promote the project, including *The Silk Tree Ballad, Mariko-Mother,* and *Children Drawing Rainbows.* This anime charts the 14-year period of Miyagi's stewardship of the academy and her relationships with several of the children. Divided into four seasonal chapters, the film uses highly realistic character designs based on the actual people involved and features storyboarding from the versatile **STAR BLAZERS**–director Noboru Ishiguro.

LITTLE MERMAID

1975. JPN: *Andersen Monogatari Ningyo Hime.* AKA: *Andersen Story Mermaid Princess.* Movie. DIR: Tomoharu Katsumata. SCR: Yuko Oso, Mieko Koyamauchi. DES: Takashi Abe, Shingo Araki, Kazuo Komatsubara. ANI: Reiko Okuyama. MUS: Hatasu Heikichi. PRD: Toei. 68 mins.

Blonde Marina, the youngest of six mermaid sisters, falls in love with the handsome human Prince Fritz when she sees him one night passing overhead in a boat. The boat is swamped by a large wave, and Marina rescues the man she adores, nursing Fritz back to health with an array of magical potions. He falls in love with her, but if she is to be with him on land, she must lose her tail and her beautiful voice.

The most famous of the **TALES OF HANS CHRISTIAN ANDERSEN**, *LM* was animated to celebrate the centenary of its author's death—bracketed at both ends by live-action footage of Denmark shot by Henning Christiansen. The story was remade in 1995 as a 21-minute fully computer-animated version based on a retelling published by the children's illustrator Chihiro Iwasaki. *Little Mermaid* (1985) was an unrelated three-part collection of pornographic vignettes in the tradition of **LOLITA ANIME**. See also **VIDEO PICTURE BOOK**.

LITTLE MRS. PEPPERPOT

1983. JPN: *Spoon Obaasan.* AKA: *Auntie*

Spoon. TV series. DIR: Keiji Hayakawa. SCR: Maki Nakahara, Tomoko Kawasaki, Keiko Maruo, Masaaki Sakurai, Mamoru Oshii. DES: Koji Nanka. ANI: Noboru Furuse, Toshio Hirata, Kenjiro Yoshida, Naoto Hashimoto, Satoshi Dezaki, Teruo Kigure, Mamoru Oshii. MUS: Koji Nanka, Tachio Akano. PRD: Pierrot, NHK. 10 mins. x 130 mins.
Auntie Spoon (so called because of the strange pendant she wears around her neck) is an old lady loved by everybody. Only local girl Ruri knows Auntie's secret—that she can use her magic pendant to shrink herself to the *size* of a spoon, bringing a whole new perspective to the everyday world. Originally based on a Norwegian folk tale then filtered through Alf Prøysen's retelling of the story as *Little Mrs. Pepperpot* before reaching Japan, this was the first anime series to be serialized on Japan's state channel, NHK.

LITTLE NEMO: ADVENTURES IN SLUMBERLAND *

1989. Movie. DIR: Masami Hata, William Hurtz. SCR: Chris Columbus, Richard Outten, Bruce Schaefer. DES: Jean Giraud, Brian Froud, Paul Julian, Kazuhide Tominaga. ANI: Yasuo Otsuka, Kazuaki Yoshinaga, Nobuo Tominaga. MUS: Richard Sherman, Robert Sherman. PRD: Tokyo Movie Shinsha. 85 mins.
Nemo is a little boy who lives in 1905 New York City. A blimp approaches his house, and the clown who steps out of it informs him that he has been requested as a playmate by the princess of Slumberland. Traveling to Slumberland, the boy is soon involved in a mission to rescue its ruler, who has been kidnapped by the Nightmare King. A tiresome and condescending attempt to reverse-engineer Disney by a studio that reputedly removed members of staff who refused to toe the party line—one of whom was Hayao Miyazaki, whose version of *LN* might well have been vastly superior if he had only been allowed to complete it. As it is, the film is a confusion of good-intentioned but insincere clichés, including

halfhearted musical numbers, far removed from the original 1905 comic strip by Winsor McCay on which it is based. The production features a large number of famous names, including voice actors Mickey Rooney (Flip the Clown) and Rene Auberjonois (Professor Genius). Disney's Frank Thomas, Roger Allers, and Ollie Johnson were among the animators, the songs were written by the Sherman brothers (*Chitty Chitty Bang Bang*), while Jean "Moebius" Giraud provided "conceptual design." However, many of the crew are "ghost" credits symptomatic of a long and troubled production—Ray Bradbury is credited with the "screen concept" but seems to have left the production early on, while the press notes carelessly trumpet the involvement of *Chinatown* scenarist Robert Towne as a "story consultant," a likely sign that Towne had been called in to rescue a failing premise. Both Hayao Miyazaki and Isao Takahata split from the production at an early stage due to "creative differences," while Yoshifumi Kondo stayed to work on the first (1984) pilot. A second (1987) pilot, credited to Osamu Dezaki, also exists, and both are included as bonus items on the Laser Disc release.

LITTLE NORSE PRINCE *

1968. JPN: *Taiyo no Ko Hols no Daiboken.* AKA: *Prince of the Sun: Hols's Great Adventure; The Great Adventure of Little Prince Valiant; Little Norse Prince Valiant.* Movie. DIR: Isao Takahata. SCR: Isao Takahata. DES: Hayao Miyazaki. ANI: Yasuo Otsuka. MUS: Tsuneo Mamiya. PRD: Toei. 82 mins.
Fisherman's son Hols is a brave boy, but when we first meet him, surrounded by a pack of hungry wolves and armed only with an axe, his chances don't look good. He is saved by the intervention of Rockor, a giant of earth and stone awakened from centuries of sleep by the noise of the fight. Hols thanks his new friend by removing a sword wedged deep into the rock of his shoulder; it is the Sword of the Sun, and Rockor predicts that it will help

The titular hero of **ORPHEN: SCION OF SORCERY** is forced to make a difficult choice when his stepsister is transformed into a terrifying beast. A popular fantasy anime in the late 1990s, *Orphen* was based on a long-running series of novels by Yoshinobu Akita, but like many other anime it only reached the U.S. in the wake of the game that was based on it (in this case for PlayStation 2). *See entry p. 288.*

Orphen: Scion of Sorcery

© YOSHINOBU AKITA • YUUYA KUSAKA/KADOKAWA SHOTEN • TBS

him to defeat the evil of Frost King Grunwald. Then Hols's father dies, but on his deathbed he tells his son how they originally came from a fishing village far to the north, and how they were the only survivors when it was destroyed by Grunwald's sorcery. He begs Hols to return to his birthplace and find out what has happened to the other villages. Armed with his axe and his new sword, and accompanied by his pet bear, Coro, Hols heads north.

He is attacked on the way by Grunwald and is almost killed falling off a cliff, but the people of a fishing village find him and care for him. They too are suffering from Grunwald's magic: a giant pike under his dominion is eating all the fish in the area and threatening the village's livelihood. Hols goes after the fish-monster alone and kills it after a titanic battle. This brings him great popularity, and some jealousy, but it further provokes Grunwald, who is determined to destroy all life in the region and sends in another, more stealthy attack. In a deserted village, Hols meets a young girl named Hilda. When he takes her back to the village, she is welcomed for her gentle nature and beautiful singing voice, but as Grunwald's dark sorcery continues to threaten the village, she is revealed as his sister.

Isao Takahata's feature debut shows fluid animation of movement, well-paced action scenes, and a charming style of character design that would become synonymous with the work of the studio he was later to found with his young colleague Hayao Miyazaki, who also assisted on this production. The film received unusually sympathetic treatment from its Western adapters, director Fred Ladd and editor Eli Haviv, who kept the tragic elements of the story intact, including the death of a loved one and the grief that follows. There is no connection with *Prince Valiant*, but the popularity of the comic in Europe led *LNP's* Italian licensees to try and piggyback the film to success, hence the alternate title.

LITTLE PRINCE *

1978. JPN: *Hoshi no Ojisama Puchi Prince*. AKA: *Prince of the Stars: Petit Prince; Adventures of the Little Prince*. TV series. DIR: Takeyuki Kanda, Yoshikazu Yasuhiko, Osamu Sekita, Norio Kabeshima. SCR: Eiichi Tachi, Susumu Yoshida, Tsunehisa Ito, Takero Kaneko, Yoshiaki Yoshida, Masaaki Sakurai. DES: Yasuji Mori, Yoshikazu Yasuhiko, Eiji Tanaka. ANI: Shinnosuke Mina. MUS: Tsuyoshi Kawano. PRD: Knack, TV Asahi. 25 mins. x 39 eps.

The Little Prince is the ruler of a very small planet but also its sole human occupant, so he must sweep the volcano clean and control the roots of the overgrown baobab tree. He talks to springs and butterflies, but his only real friend is the selfish human-shaped Star Rose. One day, the prince has an argument with the rose and sets off to Earth to search for his real friends. Based on the 1943 novella by Antoine de Saint-Exupéry, though little of the French original remains—instead, it is lost almost completely beneath the prince's wanderings after the first episode, concealed still further in the English-language version by a dub that gives Saint-Exupéry a risible French

accent, seemingly modeled on Inspector Clouseau. The series was only broadcast as far as episode 35—the remaining four sneaked out onto video when it was reissued.

LITTLE PRINCE AND THE EIGHT-HEADED DRAGON *

1963. JPN: *Wanpaku Oji to Orochi*. AKA: *Naughty Prince and the Giant Snake*. Movie. DIR: Yugo Serikawa, Isao Takahata, Kimio Yabuki. SCR: Ichiro Ikeda, Kei Iijima. DES: Yasuji Mori. ANI: Sanae Yamamoto, Yasuji Mori, Hideo Furusawa. MUS: Akira Ifukube. PRD: Toei. 76 mins.

Susano (see TAKEGAMI), son of the creators of Japan, Izanami and Izanagi, sets off accompanied by his rabbit assistant Akahana (Red-Nose) to rescue his dead mother, who has gone to the Underworld. After defeating a giant fish and a fire monster, he then witnesses the story of the Sun Goddess Amaterasu, who hides in a cave and needs to be lured out. Falling in love with the earthly princess Kushinada, he discovers that she is to be sacrificed to Orochi, an eight-headed serpent that returns once each year to raid her parents' village until placated by a human sacrifice. All three of these tales are adapted from chapters of the *Nihon Shoki*, an 8th-century chronicle that links the historical emperors with the Japanese gods and demigods, though much of the mythical meaning was lost in the transition to the American kiddie-film. Orochi would also appear in BLUE SEED and YAMATO TAKERU. Note also a rare anime score for Ifukube, better known as the composer for the *Godzilla* films.

LITTLE PRINCESS, A

1985. JPN: *Shokojo Sara*. AKA: *Young Noblewoman Sara; Princess Sarah*. TV series. DIR: Fumio Kurokawa, Takeshi Yamaguchi, Jiro Saito. SCR: Ryuzo Nakanishi, Keiko Mukuroji. DES: Shunji Saita. ANI: Toshiki Yamazaki, Shunji Saita, Kuniyuki Ishii. MUS: Yasuo Higuchi. PRD: Nippon Animation, Fuji TV. 25 mins. x 46 eps.

Fearing that the Indian climate and environment will do more harm than good, Sara Crewe's father sends her away to boarding school in England, where she diligently attends Miss Minchin's academy and dreams that she is a princess. However, her life is shattered when her father dies, and his will reveals that he had no money. Sara is forced to become a servant at her school, reduced to the lowest rung of the social scale, though, as the title already implies, a CINDERELLA-like transformation eventually awaits. The 16th entry in the WORLD MASTERPIECE THEATER series was adapted from the 1888 children's novel *Sarah Crewe* by Frances Hodgson Burnett, who also wrote LITTLE LORD FAUNTLEROY and THE SECRET GARDEN. See also VIDEO PICTURE BOOK.

LITTLE RED [RIDING] HOOD CHA CHA

1995. JPN: *Akazukin Chacha*. Video, TV series. DIR: Yuji Moriyama, Hiroaki Sakurai, Tatsuo Sato, Akitaro Daichi, Kazuhiro Sasaki. SCR: Hiroshi Koda, Takashi Yamada, Shigeru Yanagawa, Hideki Mitsui, Tomoko Kaneko, Ryosuke Takahashi, Hiroshi Yamaguchi. DES: Hajime Watanabe. ANI: Masayuki Onchi, Yoko Konishi. MUS: Toshihiko Sazaki, Osamu Tezuka (b). PRD: Studio Gallop, TV Tokyo. 30 mins. x 3 eps., 25 mins. x 74 eps. (TV).

Twelve-year-old Cha Cha lives in the Mochi-mochi mountains, where she is studying to be a magician. A clumsy student, Cha Cha's spells often backfire on her, though she has the support of her friends Riya (a young werewolf) and Shine, who can help her undergo the magical transformation of Love, Heroism, and Hope. Meanwhile, the great Devil King wants Cha Cha dead in order to lift the curse her grandfather put on his castle, while other rivals include Black Hood and Marine, a competitive mermaid. A spirited SAILOR MOON clone that is more than the sum of its parts, taking much-appreciated time to explore the geography and history of its fantasy world, and thereby making the school/magical-girl antics of its cast all that more appealing. Based on a 1992 manga in *Ribbon* magazine by Min Ayahana.

LITTLE TWINS

1992. Video, movie. DIR: Toshio Hirata, Satoshi Inoue, Yorifusa Yamaguchi. SCR: Junji Takegami. DES: Kazuo Komatsubara. ANI: Shunji Saida, Hiroki Takahashi, Yasuyuki Hirata. MUS: Mash Morse. PRD: Bandai. 25 mins. x 3 eps. (v), 25 mins. (m1).

In these adaptations of Isamu Tsuchida's picture-books for children, Tiffle and Tuffle are two little twins in pointed hats who live on Coracle Island and have a few lighthearted adventures. The "movie" release, *How Our Summer Flew Past*, is of a length and quality to suggest it was merely the fourth video installment, dumped on theaters as a promotional exercise for the tapes.

LITTLE WITCH CHAPPY

1972. JPN: *Mahotsukai Chappi*. TV series. DIR: Yugo Serikawa, Hiroshi Ikeda, Katsutoshi Sasaki, Masayuki Akehi, Osamu Kasai, Keiji Hisaoka, Hideo Furusawa. SCR: Masaki Tsuji, Saburo Taki, Shunichi Yukimuro, Noboru Shiroyama, Jiro Yoshino, Kuniaki Oshikawa. DES: N/C. ANI: Shinya Takahashi, Fusahito Nagaki. MUS: Hiroshi Tsutsui. PRD: Toei, NET. 25 mins. x 39 eps.

Chappy the little witch is sent from her magic kingdom to solve problems on Earth, accompanied by her little brother, Jun, and wielding her family heirloom, a magical baton to help her make the world a better place. A magical-girl tale following on from LITTLE WITCH SALLY and featuring the late addition of the mascot character Don-chan, a cuddly panda that easily dates the show to the panda-hysteria of the early 1970s—see PANDA GO PANDA.

LITTLE WITCH SALLY

1966. JPN: *Mahotsukai Sally*. TV series. DIR: Osamu Kasai. SCR: Akiyoshi Sakai. DES: Yoshiyuki Hane. ANI: Takashi Kasai, Minoru Tajima, Katsuya

Koda, Hideo Furusawa. MUS: Yasei Kobayashi. PRD: Toei, Hikari Pro. 25 mins. x 109 eps. (TV1—1st 18 episodes in b/w), 25 mins. x 88 eps. (TV2), 27 mins. (m), 50 mins. (TVm).

Sally is a trainee witch sent to Earth to study humans and learn how to blend in among them, though she does not always succeed. She befriends Earth children Yotchan and Sumire and fights the corrupt Kabu, who steals from department stores. This was the first of the "magical girl" genre that would extend to the present day through lookalike titles such as CREAMY MAMI, GIGI, and SECRET AKKO-CHAN. Originating in a 1966 manga for *Ribbon* magazine by GIANT ROBO–creator Mitsuteru Yokoyama, the character was originally called Sunny but had her name changed to avoid protests from the car manufacturer Nissan.

Sally returned for a new series in 1989 on TV Asahi, directed by Osamu Kasai, with character designs by Yasuhiro Yamaguchi. In 1990, the new incarnation also appeared in a short 1990 movie and a TV special, *LWS: Mother's Love is Eternal*, which ended the series with Sally's dream that she is to become the new queen of the magical land of Astria and must bid farewell to her friends. Yokoyama's witch, like Tezuka's ASTRO BOY, was one of the defining archetypes of anime, and it is still much imitated to this day—see also his less-successful follow-up, COMET-SAN.

LITTLE WOMEN *

1980. JPN: *Wakakusa no Yon Shimai*. AKA: *Four Sisters of Young Grass*. TV special, TV series. DIR: Yugo Serikawa, Kazumi Fukushima, Fumio Kurokawa, Kozo Kusuba. SCR: Eiichi Konbe, Eiichi Kondo, Akira Miyazaki, Michiru Shimada. DES: Yasuhiro Yamaguchi, Tadaumi Shimogawa, Seiji Kikuchi, Yoshifumi Kondo, Kiharu Sato. ANI: Yasuhiro Yamaguchi Takeshi Shirato, Akira Okuwara. MUS: Nozomu Aoki, Takeo Watanabe; Kazuo Otani, David Silvers. PRD: Toei, Fuji TV, Kokusai Eiga, Toei, Tokyo Channel 12, Nippon Animation,

Fuji TV x 2. 68 mins. (TVm), 25 mins. x 26 eps. (TV1), 25 mins. x 48 eps. (TV2), 25 mins. x 40 eps. (TV3).

In the 1860s, Frederick March goes to fight in the American Civil War, leaving his family behind in Concord, New Hampshire. His daughters, Jo, Meg, Beth, and Amy, help out their mother and try to get along with the Lawrence family next door. The 1868 novel by Louisa May Alcott has appeared in several anime incarnations (all of which are at least partially available in English), the first being this 1980 TV special directed by Yugo Serikawa that seems to rely more on movie versions for its plot than the book itself. The first scene is a case in point when we see Jo fooling around in the snow before throwing a snowball at the window from which her sisters are laughing at her—the same sequence opens the 1949 movie adaptation featuring June Allyson as Jo and Elizabeth Taylor as Amy.

The TV special's true role as a dry run for a series became plain in 1981, when many of the same crew returned with a TV series version. The design for the girls remained the same, but the quality of animation fell considerably, as one might expect from the more relatively limited budgets of TV (especially a TV series than cannot make the cost-cutting economies of recycling transformation footage for robots and superheroes). Alcott's original, however, is subsumed in this version to a patronizing tone that insists on imparting a prepackaged moral to each episode. The series was dubbed in the 1980s and a small number of episodes released on video, featuring new music from usual suspects Haim Saban and Shuki Levy.

The story returned to Fuji TV in 1987 as an all-new TV series, made as the 18th in the WORLD MASTERPIECE THEATER franchise, and featuring character designs by future WHISPER OF THE HEART–director Kondo. Though rather pointlessly setting the action in the new town of "Newcord," the *WMT* version remains the best anime adaptation of Alcott, despite, or perhaps because of, writer Miyazaki's ruthless reordering of the narrative at the scripting stage. The first incident from the novel proper does not arise until episode 18 of the anime, whereas the first line from the novel does not appear until episode 21—instead, this *LW* begins with the Pennsylvania countryside-dwelling Marches forced to flee their burning home, heading for Massachusetts to live with their aunt Marte. An introduction seemingly designed to educate the Japanese audience about the events of the Civil War, while simultaneously extending the possible run of the series in the same manner as the later **CINDERELLA**, the extra sequences eventually click back onto track with the stories of the girls' hopes, dreams, and mild mishaps. Perhaps inspired by similar events in **HUCKLEBERRY FINN** (a book Alcott detested!), this *LW* also features Jim, an escaped slave whom the Marches hide from soldiers, while the female-heavy cast is evened up with David, an extra nephew, and Newcord reporter Anthony. Though the scenes may be cut up and rearranged, the anime remains studiously faithful to the events within them, with the exception of an incident where one of the girls is struck at school—a cause for scandal in the novel, but accepted with traditional Japanese resignation in the anime. One of the few *WMT* serials to be translated for the U.S. market, it was bought by Saban and broadcast on HBO in the 1990s.

A third series was commissioned as a sequel to the second, adapting Alcott's 1871 *Little Men: Life at Plumfield with Jo's Boys* under the title *Story of Young Grasses: Nan and Teacher Jo* (1993, *Wakakusa Monogatari: Nan to Jo Sensei*). However, since the *WMT LW* only adapted the first part of Alcott's original, there is something of a gap between the stories—*LM* takes place ten years later, after Jo has departed for New York, met and married a German professor, and given birth to two children. Inheriting Aunt March's house in Concord (note that it's not Newcord this time,

despite this being a sequel to the second series), Jo sets up a school with her husband, turning both the book and its anime version into a different, more schooling-oriented slice-of-life than the familial predecessor. *LM* features new, softer character designs from another Studio Ghibli alumnus, **MY NEIGHBOR TOTORO**'s Sato, though its approach to the cast seems designed not to disturb the sensibilities of a conservative audience—two disabled characters are mysteriously absent from the anime.

Not to be confused with the unrelated **CHARLOTTE**, whose Japanese title is similar to *LW*'s, or with the *Little Women in Love* broadcast as part of the **MODERN LOVE'S SILLINESS** anthology show. See also **VIDEO PICTURE BOOK**.

LITTLEST WARRIOR, THE *

1961. JPN: *Anju to Zushio-Maru*. AKA: *Anju and Zushio; Orphan Brother*. Movie. DIR: Taiji Yabushita, Yugo Serikawa, Isao Takahata. SCR: Sumie Tanaka. DES: Akira Okuwara, Yasuji Mori. ANI: Sanae Yamamoto, Akira Okuwara, Yasuji Mori, Taku Sugiyama, Reiko Okuyama. MUS: Tadashi Kishimo, Hajime Kaburagi. PRD: Toei. 83 mins. (70 mins. U.S.).

After their father quarrels with local military men, Anju (Anjue) and Zushio (Zooshio) are forced to flee, but they are captured and sold into slavery. When their mother dies, they are sold to Sansho the Bailiff (or Dayu in the U.S. version, which would translate as Bailiff the Bailiff!), a cruel man who subjects them to hideous torments—though his son Saburo secretly shows kindness to the orphans. Anju falls into a lake and is transformed into a swan. Zushio escapes to a nearby temple, is adopted by a nobleman, and, after many trials, grows into a handsome young man. He defeats the Giant Blue Widow Spider that has been terrorizing the village and is appointed to his father's former post as governor. His first act is to subjugate the evil Dayu and his followers then free all the slaves. Reunited with his mother, he then rules wisely and well.

Based on Ogai Mori's novel *Sansho the Bailiff* (*Sansho Dayu*), which was also made into a 1954 live-action film by Kenji Mizoguchi. The original folk tale that inspired the novel was also adapted as one of the **MANGA PICTURES OF JAPAN**.

LOCKE THE SUPERMAN *

1984. JPN: *Chojin Locke*. AKA: *Locke the Superpower; Star Warriors*. Movie. DIR: Hiroshi Fukutomi, Noboru Ishiguro, Takeshi Hirota. SCR: Atsushi Yamatoya, Takeshi Hirota. DES: Yuki Hijiri, Keizo Kobayashi, Susumu Shiraume, Masahiro Sekino. ANI: Susumu Shiraume, Yuji Moriyama, Seiji Okuda, Eimi Maeda, Hideki Tamura, Masahiko Imai, Noboru Takano, Yutaka Kubota. MUS: Goro Omi, Toshiki Ishikawa; Toshiki Hasegawa. PRD: Nippon Animation. 120 mins. (m), 30 mins. x 3 eps. (v1), 50 mins. x 2 eps. (v2), 60 mins. (v3).

Former federation super-soldier Locke is a pacifist psychic who has willed himself to stay eternally young in order to avoid becoming a bellicose man (see **PETER PAN AND WENDY**). He is dragged out of retirement by agent Ryu Yamaki to thwart Lady Cahn, an industrialist secretly training a group of psychics to form the Millennium, a thousand-year dominion over mundane humans.

Surprisingly little of the film centers on its titular hero. Instead, much of it is taken up with Cahn's school for psychics—a bizarre Nazi convent, where Jessica Olin is completing her training. A girl who falsely believes that Locke killed her parents, Jessica is the most powerful of Cahn's new breed, and, after successfully destroying her opponents, she is drafted into a sabotage mission against a government outpost. When her psychic cohorts destroy the base, Cahn's agents start revolts on five outlying planets; the first steps in the foundation of a new order. They then delay Ryu's attempts to return home (though God knows why) by crashing the ship sent to take him home. Ryu rescues Jessica from the wreck, but she has amnesia. Now calling herself

Amelia, she follows him back to Earth, confessing her love for him. Eventually, after all this padding, Locke appears and defeats Cahn. Amelia stays in the arms of her beloved Ryu, while Locke finds love in the form of Cahn's alter ego, schoolmistress Cornelia Prim, only to discover that her personality was removed as punishment for her crime. Alone but satisfied he has saved the universe, he returns home.

Based on the 1979 manga in *Shonen King* by Yuki Hijiri, *Locke* was rushed into production during the post–*Star Wars* boom in sci-fi that also created **CAPTAIN FUTURE** and **LENSMAN**—the ten-minute *Cosmic Game* pilot film for the project was made as early as 1980. It was the first Nippon Animation film made directly for theaters and boasts technical experiments to rival **FIST OF THE NORTH STAR**, including some subtle early computer graphics and actual "live" footage of flames, static, and bubbles. An earnest spectacle that crashes Frank Herbert's *Dune* (Cahn wants to use Holy Mothers to breed a master race) into the thousand-year empire of Isaac Asimov's *Foundation*, with reviled psychic warriors lifted from the *X-Men*, *LtS* is let down by amateurishly clunky dialogue, as twee British-accented voices mispronounce "esper" and "combatant" throughout, confuse planets with stars, and intone priceless lines such as "a small man-made planet in this universe." Ryu Yamaki suffers worst at the hands of Japanese *and* English scripts—a man so outstandingly stupid that he lectures Locke on care of "sheeps," tries to break down a steel door with his own head, and insists on having sex with his ladylove while she is still recuperating in a hospital bed. Released in English with the original names still in place, presumably in a Japan-commissioned translation that explains the poor-quality dub, the "superman" part was dropped in some territories to avoid conflict with DC comics—similar wrangles dogged **MARIS THE CHOJO**.

With plenty more of Hijiri's manga left to adapt, the "industrialist-seeks-power, Locke-leaves-retirement, Locke-loses-girl" plot was rehashed straight to video with *LtS: Lord Leon*, in which the titular cyborg pirate kills the grandson of Great Jugo, a wealthy industrialist whose starship-building project is in financial difficulty. Locke is once more unwillingly pressed into service by Federation Security, only to discover that Leon is the wayward brother of his new girlfriend, Flora, who has sworn vengeance on Jugo for killing the rest of his family. Jugo is responsible for the terrible injuries that caused Leon to have cybernetic augmentation and for the loss of Flora's eyesight. Fearing for his own life, he kidnaps Flora, and Leon sails into a trap while Locke rescues her.

A third incarnation was released as *LtS: New World Battle Team* (1991, *Shin Sekai Sentai*), in which Elena, the leader of the Galactic Alliance, decides to begin an Esper Elimination Project. Locke and four other psychics go on the run but lose their memories. To regain them, they must hunt down the creature known as the Tsar, unless the agents of the Galactic Alliance catch them first.

A sequel, *LtS: Mirroring* (2000), followed after a long hiatus and features new character designs by Junichi Hayama. Elena's "backed-up" cyber-successor Cassandra mutates on the "Galactic" Internet and returns as the mighty "Neon." Locke must round up his old cohorts once more (and why not, the writers just rounded up the old plot, after all). **ⓝⓥ**

LOLICON ANGEL

1985. JPN: *Lolicon Angel: Bishojo Comic Himitsu no Mi*. AKA: *Loli[ta] Co[mplex] Angel: Pretty Girls' Comic: Secret Honey*. Video. DIR: N/C. SCR: N/C. DES: N/C. ANI: N/C. MUS: N/C. PRD: Pumpkin Pie. 25 mins.
While Yuka, Nami, and Aiko are in the shower together, somebody steals Yuka's wallet. The three lesbians set out to investigate at their exclusive girls' school, where everyone seems to harbor secret desires. This anime may

Motoko Kusanagi, a super cool government agent, manipulated by the "Puppet Master" computer virus into a bizarre marriage of minds. A cyberpunk spectacle of computer crime, political intrigue, and speculations on the nature of the soul, **GHOST IN THE SHELL** is a superb science fiction anime. Partly funded by Manga Entertainment in the quest to find "the next **AKIRA**," it artfully adapts and simplifies Masamune Shirow's complex manga, though losing some of the original's political bite in the process. The English-language release also loses the haunting, meaningful closing theme. *See entry p. 141.*

Ghost in the Shell

seem to be a pale imitation of **CREAM LEMON** but actually predates it. However, in the erotic filmmaking stakes, there is rarely a prize for coming first. Even the normally timid *Newtype* comments that, "While there may be hard lesbian action, the animation and story line are considerably below standard." **ⓝ**

LOLITA ANIME

1984. AKA: *Wonder Magazine Series*. Video. DIR: Kuni Toniro, R. Ching, Mickey Soda, Mickey Masuda. SCR: Fumio Nakajima. DES: Fumio Nakajima. ANI: Tatsushi Kurahashi. MUS: N/C. PRD: Wonder Kids. 15 mins. x 4 eps. (1–4), 30 mins. x 3 eps. (5–7), 60 mins. (8), 3 x 30 mins. (Uchiyama).
A collection of underage porn, which, with its cheerful incitement to abuse children, is in its own way far more offensive than **UROTSUKIDOJI**. Based on manga by Fumio Nakajima, the stories range from risqué but unremarkable dramas of sexual awakening to full-blown pedophile rape scenes, with the questionable distinction of being the first erotic anime video release. So it was that after the relative excitement of theatrical outings such as **ARABIAN NIGHTS** and **CLEOPATRA: QUEEN OF SEX**, anime entered a tawdry phase with the

sickening gang-rape of *The Reddening Snow* (#1), in which a group of boys sexually assault a schoolgirl, while the boy who secretly adores her is "forced" to join in. *Girls Tortured with Roses* (#2) is no less shocking—a bondage fable in which older men abuse and assault very young girls—though it pales into insignificance when compared to *Dying for a Girl* (#3), in which the assault of a girl in a playground is offered for the audience's titillation, only to have the neighborhood pervert's intentions thwarted by the timely arrival of a younger man. He then takes the girl back to his place, where, after a shower, she gratefully offers her body to her savior.

The next entry in the series, the lesbian-awakening story *Altar of Sacrifice* (#4), was successful enough to create its own sub-series within the *Lolita Anime* franchise—a form of brand identity that was repeated with greater success within the CREAM LEMON series. *Variations* (#5) was a direct sequel, double the normal length, about one of the girls becoming an artist's model and being invited to postsession dinner where she is drugged and raped.

Another mini-franchise began with *House of Kittens* (#6), in which several schoolgirls are inspired to experiment sexually with each other after witnessing their teacher in the act. However, their friend Miyu prefers to fantasize about having sex with a man. A character whose popularity prefigured that of *Cream Lemon*'s Ami, Miyu returned for *Surfside Dreaming* (#7), about an innocent encounter between two consenting teenagers, and consequently far less disturbing than many of the other *LA* entries. The character returned for the finale, *Seaside Angel Miyu* (#8), a clip-show of earlier episodes, presented as a radio show conducted from orbit, as Earthbound callers telephone Miyu's spaceship and discuss their sexual experiences. The running time is bulked out with four minutes of still images of Miyu at the beach and ends with the "bonus" scene of Miyu having sex with the captain of her spaceship.

Later in 1984, an unrelated *Lolita Anime* was released by Nikkatsu. Directed by Naosuke Kurosawa, it comprised *Aki Feels Ill*, *Milk-Drinking Doll*, and *Gokko Plays Nurse*, all adapted from manga by Aki Uchiyama, an artist who once took Lolicon imagery so far as to eroticize infants in diapers for *Shonen Magazine*. **NV**

LORD OF LORDS: DRAGON KNIGHT

1994. JPN: *Ha-o Taikei Ryu Knight*. AKA: *Adeu's Legend*. TV series, video. DIR: Makoto Ikeda, Toshifumi Kawase. SCR: Katsuyuki Osuzawa, Hiroyuki Hoshiyama. DES: Kazuhiro Soeta. ANI: Kazuhiro Soeta, Tetsuya Yanagawa, Chuichi Iguchi. MUS: Junichi Kanezaki, Michiru Oshima. PRD: Sunrise, TV Tokyo. 25 mins. x 52 eps. (TV), 25 mins. x 13 eps. (v).

A popular show in its day, mixing the role-playing-game feel of RECORD OF LODOSS WAR with the giant-robot combat familiar to so many other Sunrise shows. OUTLAW STAR–creator Takehiko Ito, in collaboration with Sunrise's house pseudonym "Hajime Yadate," posited a standard quest narrative of young Adeu, who sets out to become a knight and ends up saving the universe. When the TV series was released on video, each tape contained at least one unbroadcast episode as a bonus, which is a clever way of dragging in extra customers.

LORDLESS RETAINER TSUKIKAGE

2000. JPN: *Kaze ni Omakase Tsuki-kage*. AKA: *Moonshadow Drifting on the Wind*. TV series. DIR: Akitaro Daichi. SCR: Yosuke Kuroda. DES: Hajime Watanabe. ANI: Takahiro Yoshimatsu. MUS: N/C. PRD: Madhouse, WOWOW. 25 mins. x 13? eps.

In the olde-worlde nostalgia spirit of the turn of the century that also created ARMORED CHRONICLE HIO and TREE IN THE SUN, this anime is a jokey retelling of old samurai dramas, written by JUBEI-CHAN THE NINJA GIRL's Akitaro Daichi, and broadcast on Japanese TV while the latter show was still on-air.

As with *Jubei-chan*, Daichi takes an old favorite (in this case Moonshadow, a wandering samurai originally popularized by heartthrob Jushiro Konoe, star of *Zatoichi Challenged* and *Sworn Brothers*), switches the character's sex, and gives her a gimmicky favorite food in place of any personality. Ran Tsukikage is a wandering samurai *lady*, righting wrongs and doing good deeds all around Japan, accompanied by Miao, a female specialist in Chinese kung fu. Tsukikage likes drinking sake and eating bean-curd dregs (see AKANE-CHAN)—a meal that *Newtype*, without a scrap of irony, recommended its readers eat in front of the TV for the ultimate viewing experience.

LOST UNIVERSE *

1998. TV series. DIR: Takashi Watanabe, Eiichi Sato, Hideki Takayama. SCR: Mayori Sekijima, Jiro Takayama, Sumio Uetake. DES: Shoko Yoshinaka, Tsutomu Suzuki. ANI: Kazuaki Mori, Hikaru Maejima. MUS: Osamu Tezuka (the other one). PRD: IG Film, TV Tokyo. 25 mins. x 26 eps.

Galactic trouble-shooter Kane Blueriver wanders the stars in his sentient ship Sword Breaker, whose artificial intelligence, Carol, is his eternal sparring partner and confidante. A chance meeting forces them to team up with Milly the private eye, an irritating girl determined to be the world's best, though world's best *what* is open to debate.

A lighthearted space opera based on a sequence of novels by SLAYERS-creator Hajime Kanzaka (which were illustrated by designer Yoshinaka) and featuring many of the same cast and crew as the *Slayers* anime. After predictable early beginnings not unlike OUTLAW STAR, the bounty-of-the-week angle falls away to be replaced with a more gripping quest angle as the trio search for the fabled Lost Ships. Despite being written off in its early stages as shallow comedy, the final chapter of *LU* won *Animage*'s Best Individual Episode Award in a year otherwise dominated by NADESICO. Like many other shows of the late 1990s, *LU* featured incongruous amounts of computer graphics designed to distract the viewer from the low-rent cel animation. However. *LU*'s CG, such as the Sword Breaker itself, is consistently below-par—an example of a gimmick backfiring, though the same tactics were used to far greater effect in **COWBOY BEBOP**. *Ill. p. 457.*

LOVE CADETS

1998. JPN: *Ren'ai Kohosei*. AKA: *Starlight Scramble*. Video. DIR: Hideki Tonokatsu. SCR: Hideki Tonokatsu, Osamu Kudo, Katsuhiko Koide. DES: Kenshi Fukube, Masahiro Koyama. ANI: Kenshi Fukube. MUS: N/C. PRD: KSS. 30 mins. x 2 eps.

In a love comedy set in 2149 but rooted very much in the dork-gets-harem spirit of **TENCHI MUYO!** and its 1990s imitators, orphaned Megumi struggles hard at school to qualify as a space pilot, leave behind the space colony, and visit Earth.

LOVE HINA

2000. TV series, TV special. DIR: Shigeru Ueda, Takashi Sudo, Koichi Sugitani. SCR: Kuro Hatsuki, Manabu Ishikawa, Hiroyuki Kawasaki. DES: Makoto Uno, Eiji Yasuhiko. ANI: Makoto Uno, Akio Takami. MUS: N/C. PRD: Xebec, TV Tokyo. 25 mins. x 24 eps., 25 mins.

As a child, Keitaro makes a vow with his sweetheart that they will meet at Japan's prestigious Tokyo University (Todai) when they are older. He doesn't, however, count on failing the exams, or indeed on forgetting his sweetheart's name in the decade that follows. Now in his late teens, he is left by his grandmother to look after a student dorm and meets two students, one of whom he suspects is the long-lost love. As Keitaro attempts to regain his memories of his one true love, he becomes an object of attention among the other girls at the dorm, who are "characterized" by a standard rack of female anime archetypes.

The culmination of a decade of

geek-centered anime, *LH* is based on a manga in *Shonen Magazine* by Ken Akamatsu, but it plays like a combination of **TENCHI MUYO!**, the ronin romance of **SAKURA DIARIES**, and occasional filmic experimentation inspired by **HIS AND HER CIRCUMSTANCES**. The franchise returned for a one-shot TV special in Christmas 2000. Set for U.S. release in 2002 from Bandai.

LOVE POSITION HALLEY

1985. JPN: *Love Position Halley Densetsu*. AKA: *Legend of Love Position Halley; Love Position—Legend of Halley*. Video. DIR: Hideharu Iuchi. SCR: Masaki Tsuji. DES: Hiromi Matsushita, Kunio Aoii, Indori-Koya. ANI: Shinya Takahashi, Isao Kaneko, Kazutoshi Kobayashi, Masashi Maruyama. MUS: Kei Wakakusa. PRD: Tezuka Pro. 93 mins.

A crippled old man recounts his wartime experiences in Vietnam to his son Subaru, telling of his encounter with the young elfin girl Lamina in a temple. He takes a fatherly interest in her after she saves him from the Viet Cong, but she refuses to reveal any details about her past. Fifteen years after he is sent home and leaves her behind, he receives a letter from her announcing that she is coming to the U.S. and desperately needs his help. Since he owes her his life but cannot help her himself, he begs his son to take his place, and a very surprised Subaru discovers that the "teenage" Lamina does not appear to have aged a day. Subaru escorts Lamina across the U.S., where they are pursued by a former vagrant who has been possessed by a killer entity that escaped from a crashing meteorite. Eventually, after a series of escalating battles, Lamina is revealed to be the spirit of Halley's Comet, a messenger sent from the planet/goddess Venus to the sun/goddess Amaterasu, but she is pursued by agents sent by Venus's enemy, Mars. This movie was based on an original idea by **ASTRO BOY**–creator Osamu Tezuka and released to cash in on the real-life reappearance of Halley's

Comet in the skies. Compare to **WIND OF AMNESIA**, a similar road movie with a mystery girl.

LUCKY MAN

1994. JPN: *Tottemo Lucky Man*. AKA: *Really Lucky Man*. TV series. DIR: Hajime Kamegaki, Akira Shigino, Masami Shimoda. SCR: Yoshio Urasawa, Kazuhisa Sakaguchi, Yukichi Hashimoto. DES: Hiroshi Kamo. ANI: Hideyuki Motohashi, Tsuneo Ninomiya. MUS: N/C. PRD: Studio Pierrot, TV Tokyo. 25 mins. x 50 eps.

Yoichi is an unpleasant teenager, but one who can transform at will into the luckiest man in the world—a superpower that he uses freely to get himself out of embarrassing situations. Based on a *Shonen Jump* manga by Hiroshi Kamo and featuring a lead character who resembles a mohawked version of *South Park*'s yammering Canadians, Terrence and Phillip.

LULLABY FOR WEDNESDAY'S CINDERELLA

1987. JPN: *Aitsu to Lullaby Suiyobi no Cinderella*. Video. DIR: Yukihiro Takahashi. SCR: Jiyu Watanabe. DES: Joji Yanagise, Masayoshi Sato. ANI: N/C. MUS: Satoshi Monkura, Takashi Kudo. PRD: Studio Pierrot, Nippon Herald. 50 mins.

Kenji is a motorbike-mad teenager in Yokohama, who just loves his ZII machine, and likes nothing better than grabbing his girl Yumi, skipping school, and motoring down the coast. Hearing from fellow biker Hayase about a fabled racer called Wednesday's Cinderella, Kenji witnesses Hayase on his SRX, squaring off against Cinderella on her Porsche cycle (the synopsis spends more time on the brands than the characters!). Concerned for his friend's safety, Kenji sets off after him, borrowing his friend Kyosuke's Ducatti. Based on a *Shonen Magazine* manga by Michiharu Kusunoki, who also created **SHAKOTAN BOOGIE**. Made for video, but screened on a double bill in cinemas with **LEGEND OF ROLLING WHEELS**, which must have made the day as exciting as changing an oil sump.

LUNA VARGA *

1991. JPN: *Maju Senshi Luna Varga*. AKA: *Demon/Beast Warrior Luna Varga*. Video. DIR: Shigenori Kiyoyama. SCR: Aki Tomato, Yumiko Tsukamoto. DES: Yuji Moriyama. ANI: Kazuhiro Konishi. MUS: Kenji Kawai. PRD: AIC, Studio Hakk. 30 mins. x 4 eps.

The Dunbas Empire tries to conquer a world where humans and beasts have lived in medieval-fantasy harmony for centuries. The three princesses of Rimbell are determined to fight the invaders, but middle sister Luna (the "tomboy princess") does so in a very strange way. Engulfed in a ray of light, the accomplished swordswoman recovers to find herself embedded in the head of a giant tyrannosaur-like beast that communicates with her telepathically, calling her its "brain." To save her land, she has been granted control of the legendary dragon Varga, and even when not in dragon form, she has a reptilian tail. She manages to fight off the Dunban troops but must rescue her sister Vena, who has been kidnapped by the invaders. From the high-concept that posits a princess with a dragon sticking out of her ass (or a dragon with a princess stuck to its forehead, depending on your perspective) to the insanely overblown theme song, *LV* is a madcap comedy to file with **DRAGON HALF**.

LUNATIC NIGHT *

1997. Video. DIR: Shinji Nishiyama, Fuyumi Shirakawa, Teruo Kigure. SCR: Shinji Nishiyama, Haruka Kaio. DES: Kiginmaru Oi. ANI: Taiichi Kitagawa. MUS: Hideyuki Tanaka. PRD: Knack. 35 mins. x 3 eps.

College boy Kanzaki gets a sex-crazed girl for a pet on a moonlit night. She's come to remind him he's the lord of Atlantis and final incarnation of Krishna, forced to fight his satanic schoolmate Mutsuki for control of the world amid innumerable jokey references to classic anime like **GIANT ROBO** and

BABEL II (on which director Kigure worked as an animator) as well as porn-like appearances by characters more familiar from **SAILOR MOON**. In part two, overindulgence has turned all Atlantean men into penises, and incredible power awaits the man who can pass the trials and give Queen Estelle the orgasm of a lifetime. Kanzaki also has to pleasure a giant Amazon who drowns him with her breasts and prompts the meaningful quote, "She's huge! I could stick my whole head in there." The authors would like to apologize for making this sound a lot more interesting than it is. Based on a manga by Akira Mii that was serialized in *Comic Lies*, mercifully, only the first two parts of this anime appear to have been released in the U.S. **LN**

LUPIN III *

1971. JPN: *Lupin Sansei*. AKA: (see below). TV series, movie, video, TV specials. DIR: Masaaki Okuma, Isao Takahata, Hayao Miyazaki. SCR: Tadaaki Yamazaki, Atsushi Yamatoya, Yoshio Urasawa, Yuki Miyata, Yoshio Urasawa, Soji Yoshikawa, Tohru Sawaki. DES: Monkey Punch. ANI: Yasuo Otsuka, Osamu Kobayashi, Hideo Kawauchi, Yoshifumi Kondo, Tameo Ogawa, Norio Yazawa, Minoru Okazaki, Satoshi Dezaki, Tetsuo Imazawa, Yasuhiro Yamaguchi, Koichi Murata. MUS: Takeo Yamashita, Yuji Ono. PRD: Tokyo Movie Shinsha, Nippon TV. 25 mins. x 3 eps. (TV1), 25 mins. x 155 eps. (TV2), 102 mins. (m/*Mamo*), 100 min (m/*Cagliostro*), 25 mins. x 50 eps. (TV3), 100 mins. (m/*Babylon*), 74 mins. (m/*Fuma*), 97 mins. (TVm/*Liberty*), 92 mins. (TVm/*Hemingway*), 90 mins. (TVm/*Napoleon*), 90 mins. (TVm/*Russia*), 90 mins. (*Sword*), 90 mins. (TVm/*Nostradamus*), 90 mins. (TVm/*Harimao*), 90 mins. (*Dead*), 90 mins. (*Twilight*), 90 mins. (TVm/*Walther*), 90 mins. (TVm/*Crisis*), 90 mins. (TVm/*Money*), 90 mins. (TVm/*Alcatraz*).

Lupin is a Japanese criminal with a heart of gold, grandson of the infamous French burglar Arsène Lupin

(see **LUPIN THE MASTER THIEF AND THE ENIGMA OF 813**). His gang includes Lee Marvin–lookalike Daisuke Jigen, a sharpshooter with a 0.3-second quick draw, and Goemon Ishikawa XIII, descendant of the samurai thief first immortalized in the puppet play *Ishikawa Goemon* (ca. 1680). Together with Lupin's occasional girlfriend and frequent rival, the flame-haired Fujiko Mine, they travel the world stealing great treasures while Lupin charms the ladies, Jigen is suspicious of them, and Goemon tries in vain to hold them at arm's length lest they taint his samurai honor. They are pursued all the while by Inspector Zenigata of Interpol (a descendant of Kodo Nomura's samurai-era sleuth Heiji Zenigata, who was the subject of nearly 400 stories and a long-running TV series).

Longer-running than **GUNDAM** and with a pedigree beaten by few anime except perhaps **SAZAE-SAN**, *Lupin III* began as a 1967 *Manga Action* publication by **SCOOPERS**-creator Monkey Punch (pseudonym for Kazuhiko Kato). Adapted by the TMS studio, the series still makes regular appearances 30 years after its debut—largely due to its dogged faith to the camp original, which has endured so long that some of its stories (such as *Mamo*, see below) now outgroove the self-consciously groovy **COWBOY BEBOP** with their *original* kitsch. Yuji Ono's theme music remains one of Japan's best-selling musical exports. *L3* also has many hidden attributes, such as the casting of "famous voices" to draw unseen parallels for the Japanese audience—late Lupin actor Yasuo Yamada used to dub all Clint Eastwood's Japanese dialogue, Jigen actor Kiyoshi Komori "is" the Japanese voice of Lee Marvin, and Goemon's Makio Inoue normally plays the gruff anime hero **CAPTAIN HARLOCK**. There was a certain irony in sharpshooter Jigen getting the "voice of" Lee Marvin, since the actor was a Marine sniper in the Pacific War credited with a number of kills on Japanese soldiers.

After the manga and anime finished their first runs, the franchise continued in the form of the live-action film *L3: Strange Psychokinetic Strategy* (1974, *Nenriki Chin Sakusen*) reuniting all the characters except Goemon. After the original anime series was rebroadcast to popular acclaim, it was revived as the longer-running *New L3* (1977)—as a rule of thumb, the hero's jacket is green in series one, and red in series two, though its pigment varies in the later movies and specials. Monkey Punch claims that only the first series captured the true spirit of his manga, but fan favorites were episodes #145 and #155, written and directed by Tsutomu Teruki (pseudonym for Hayao Miyazaki). In the wake of Miyazaki's later popularity with foreign anime fans, the episodes were released in the U.S. as *L3: Albatross Wings of Death* and *L3: Aloha, Lupin*. The Lupin name, however, was edged from the credits after a legal dispute—the estate of Maurice Leblanc, creator of the original Lupin, discovered the existence of the series when dubbed episodes were broadcast in Australia, and challenged the producers' rights to the name Lupin. Eventually, the courts ruled that, since *L3* had existed uncontested for more than a decade, Leblanc had no right to it in Japan. Such mitigating circumstances, however, do not apply in the rest of the world, and some anime distributors have avoided the wrath of the Leblanc estate by removing all reference to Lupin from the films—the aforementioned episodes renamed *Tales of the Wolf*, with their lead now "Wolf" throughout the script itself. AnimEigo, which subtitled some of the films (see below) instead opted for the safely facetious transliteration of *Rupan III*. The major casualty of the legal upheaval was Rintaro's 22nd-century sci-fi remake, *Lupin VIII*, planned as a Franco-Japanese follow-up to **ULYSSES 31** and regrettably mothballed by TMS and Jean Chalopin's Studio DIC in 1982. Intellectual property issues are likely to haunt the franchise until 2016, when Leblanc's work finally comes out of copyright under current European law.

Meanwhile, the franchise reached theaters with Soji Yoshikawa's *Mystery of Mamo* (1978, *Lupin tai Fukusei Ningen*, aka *Lupin vs. Clone*). At a time when the rest of the world was desperately trying to cash in on *Star Wars*, *Mamo* was a burst of 1960s nostalgia. Fujiko swindles Lupin into stealing the Egyptian "Philosopher's Stone" for her without revealing that she is working for the shadowy would-be dictator Mamo—originally Mameux, though the distributors felt obliged to bring the spelling into line with the inferior transliteration already common in U.S. fandom. As befits its "clone" subplot, *Mamo* plays up the similarities between Lupin and Zenigata. Without his trademark trenchcoat in the Egyptian scenes, Zenigata looks almost identical to Lupin, and the idea reaches its logical conclusion in the final reel, when the two enemies are cuffed together and forced to cooperate to save their skins. The film exists in *three* different dubs—the earliest, made by TMS in 1978 for screenings on Pacific flights, changes Jigen's name to Dan Dunn, Goemon's to simply Samurai, and Mamo's henchman Frenchy to Flinch. As a symptom of its time, it also gives the U.S. president the voice of Jimmy Carter. The second, made in 1995 by Streamline shortly before European legal reforms brought Leblanc back into copyright, calls the hero "Lupin." A third, made in 1996 by Manga Entertainment under the title *Secret of Mamo*, calls him "Wolf" once more, and modernizes some of the dialogue with effective, if anachronistic, rewrites. It leaves in a parody of Henry Kissinger, but lines like "Okay, so I'm not Keanu Reeves" and an in-joke about *Dynasty* can be reasonably expected not to hail from the original Japanese script.

The best-known *L3* film, **CASTLE OF CAGLIOSTRO**, followed in 1979, and though it was an immense success for director Hayao Miyazaki, the aforementioned legal troubles kept a third TV season off the air until *L3: Part III* (1984). Famous live-action director Seijun Suzuki helmed Lupin's last *true* ani-

Nanami and Tico the Orca. Not an adaptation of a European book, despite appearances to the contrary. See entry p. 400.

Tico of the Seven Seas

© 1994 NIPPON ANIMATION CO., LTD.

me movie outing *Gold of Babylon* (1985, *Babylon no Ogon Densetsu*), in which the gang is pursued by the New York mafia, the police, and the elderly bag-lady Rosetta. The trail leads from a hilarious bike chase through Madison Square Garden to the Middle East and back again to New York, pastiching the *Indiana Jones* films, Erich von Däniken, and gangster films, as Lupin searches for buried gold under New York, hidden inside an alien spaceship. Rosetta eventually reveals her true form and Lupin misses out on sex with a space goddess, though the ever-pragmatic Fujiko is simply concerned with getting as much of the gold as possible.

Masayuki Ozeki's superb *L3: Fuma Conspiracy* (1988, *Fuma Ichizoku no Inbo*, aka *Secret Plot of the Fuma Clan*) was originally made for video but given a theatrical release at the last moment. Distinctive for returning the globe-trotting thief to his native Japan, it begins at Goemon's long-delayed wedding, interrupted by the kidnapping of the bride. The mysterious Fuma clan want the Suminawa clan's treasure as a ransom, and Lupin helps out, with an eye on the girl and the chances of loot. Inspector Zenigata, who has abandoned the world and entered a monastery believing Lupin to be dead, soon regains his old lust for life and dogged pursuit of his nemesis. *Fuma Conspiracy* is available in two foreign versions—a very good one from AnimEigo (U.S.) and a very bad one from Western Connection with *manually* timed subtitles (U.K.).

All successive *L3* outings have been made for TV as one-shot specials, though some foreign distributors still like to imply that they are "movies," despite a marked drop in animation budget and great variations in quality. In *Bye Bye Liberty* (1989, aka *Goodbye Lady Liberty*), an Interpol computer has predicted Lupin/Wolf's every movement, so he hangs up his cat-burglar suit and settles down in unwedded bliss with a French floozy, until Jigen drags him back out in search of a treasure hidden inside the Statue of Liberty. Director Osamu Dezaki returned with *Mystery of the Hemingway Papers* (1990, *Hemingway Papers no Nazo*), in which Lupin tracks down a treasure described in clues left in the diaries of Ernest Hemingway that lead him to the tiny Mediterranean island of Colcaca just in time for a coup d'état led by the evil Carlos. Current affairs broke into the series for Dezaki's *Steal Napoleon's Dictionary* (1991, *Napoleon no Jisho o Ubae*), which begins at a G7 conference in New York after the Gulf War, in which delegates blame Lupin for the loss of two trillion dollars from the world economy. Lupin, however, is in Europe for a classic car race, for the prize of the long-lost dictionary used by Napoleon himself, in which the original Arsène Lupin hid a map to his own treasure house. Matters are complicated by the agents of the G7 nations, all intent on avenging their depressed economies on the man who has removed so much money from them.

Dezaki's *From Russia with Love* (1992, *Russia yori Ai o Komete*) concerns Lupin's search for the treasure of the Russian Czars, supposedly lost forever after the murder of the Romanovs in 1917. Only two people can conceivably find the treasure—Princess Anastasia, long rumored to have escaped death,

and the mad monk Rasputin (see also **MASTER OF MOSQUITON**), who has been in hiding for decades and is now seeking the treasure himself by using his powers of telepathy and persuasion.

Masaaki Osumi took over as director for *Order to Assassinate Lupin* (1993, *Lupin Ansatsu Shirei*), an original departure in which the discredited Zenigata is taken off the case and reassigned. The cold-blooded assassin Keith Hayton is set on Lupin's trail, and the thief realizes that the only way to stay alive is to salvage Zenigata's shattered career. Using the stolen Russian nuclear sub Ivanov to infiltrate the criminal gang Shot Shell, Lupin maneuvers them into a position where they can be exposed to Interpol, Zenigata can take the credit, and he can relax without a hitman on his tail. He is not the only one, since the Russian scientist Karen still holds a grudge against Jigen for killing her father, and she is determined to extract her own revenge.

Masaharu Okuwaki's *Burning Zantetsuken* (1994, *Moeyo Zantetsuken*) features a race to find a mysterious dragon statue said to contain the secrets of making weapons like Goemon's sword, a blade that effortlessly cuts through steel. In a story that deliberately concentrates on Goemon, in honor of the fourth centenary of his illustrious ancestor's death in 1594, Chinese gangster Mr. Chan reveals that the statue was last seen setting sail on the Titanic in 1912, and the quest begins.

The following year saw the death of main Lupin voice actor Yasuo Yamada and *two* TV specials. Nobuo Fujisawa's *To Hell with Nostradamus* (1995, *Kutabare Nostradamus*) finds Lupin and Jigen posing as Brazilian soccer players when they are hijacked by a cult, whose leader, Lisely, is determined to bring all of the predictions of Nostradamus to pass. Needless to say, a hunt for treasure soon begins, though it means climbing to the top of a 200-story skyscraper. Barely six months later in Dezaki's *Treasure of Harimao* (1995,

Harimao no Zaiho o Oe), after a mysterious explosion in the English Channel Tunnel, Lloyd's Insurance investigator Archer (see **MASTER KEATON**) and his beautiful archaeologist daughter, Diana, go in search of three statues said to contain clues to the location of the fabled treasure of Harimao. Archer must race a group of neo-Nazis to find them—but, of course, Lupin and Jigen already have plans of their own. *Dead or Alive* (1996), supposedly directed by author Monkey Punch, features Lupin searching for a fabled "drifting island," while simultaneously running from a gang of bounty hunters each after the million-dollar price on his head. It was succeeded in the same year by Gisaburo Sugii's *Secret of Twilight Gemini* (1996, *Twilight Gemini no Himitsu*), which sends Lupin to Morocco in search of a diamond to match the titular stone bequeathed to him by dying mobster Don Dorune. It was a return to the annual schedule with Hiroyuki Yano's *Walther P-38* (1997), in which Lupin's pistol of choice becomes a crucial key in the race to unlock the mysteries of the Tarantula Seal and find the Golden Ghost. Lupin made a rare stop back in his native Japan for Toshiya Shinohara's *Tokyo Crisis* (1998), in a quest to find the legacy of the last shogun, racing against a psychokinetic treasure hunter employed by theme-park millionaire Michael Suzaku. In Shinichi Watanabe's *Love's Da Capo—Fujiko's Unlucky Days* (1999, *Ai no Da Capo*), Fujiko lets Lupin get away with the loot from a Swiss bank job because she is more interested in the Columbus File, a document that can direct her to a 15th-century gem, supposedly connected to **COLUMBUS** himself. The last *Lupin* of the 20th century was *$1 Money Wars* (2000), in which a disguised Lupin completes the swindle of his life, buying a priceless ring at a rigged auction in New York for a single dollar, though the ring's rightful owner, St. Cyr, is prepared to use any means necessary to get it back. Lupin himself soon returned in Hideki Tonokatsu's TV movie *Alcatraz Connection* (2001), in which he battles the Mob for a treasure to be found somewhere in San Francisco Bay. He also appeared in a new video spinoff, *L3: The Magician Lives* (2002). The series was also spoofed in the anime-company comedy **KUROMI-CHAN**, as *Ruimond III*.

LUPIN THE MASTER THIEF AND THE ENIGMA OF 813

1979. JPN: *Kaiketsu Lupin: 813 no Nazo*. TV special. DIR: Hiroshi Sasakawa, Masayuki Akehi. SCR: Akira Miyazaki, N/C. DES: Ippei Kuri, Yoshitaka Amano, N/C. ANI: Sadao Miyamoto, Nobuyuki Kishi. MUS: Nobuyoshi Koshibe, Yoshiki Takaragi. PRD: Herald Enterprises, Tatsunoko, Fuji TV; Toei. 84 mins. (TVm1), 84 mins. (TVm2). Four years after the gentleman thief Arsène Lupin was last seen on the streets of Paris, diamond dealer Kesselbach is found stabbed to death in his hotel room. The police decide that Lupin is the chief suspect, but the master thief himself retrieves a message from Kesselbach containing the mysterious phrase "Napoleon 813." Lupin is forced to team up with Kesselbach's widow to solve the crime before Inspector Lunolman arrests him for the one crime he *hasn't* committed. An adaptation of one of Maurice Leblanc's best-loved Lupin stories, possibly made in a deliberate attempt to annoy Tatsunoko's rival studio TMS, which was experiencing legal difficulties with its **LUPIN III** franchise at the time. This Lupin fable is particularly well-known in Japan, where it was also adapted into the live-action Kenji Mizoguchi film *813: The Adventures of Arsène Lupin* (1923).

Just to rub salt into the wounds, a second Leblanc adaptation followed, this time from another big studio, Toei. In *Lupin vs. Holmes* (1981), the famous English detective Sherlock Holmes is sent to France to track Lupin at the instigation of Baron Autrech, though the baron soon turns up dead, and his priceless blue diamond is missing. *LvH* was based on Leblanc's 1907 series of original stories featuring Holmes, and even includes a famous scene from *The Jewish Lamp* in which the two well-matched rivals face each other on a sinking boat, each daring the other to show the first sign of weakness. In a final karmic irony, the original stories brought protests from Arthur Conan Doyle that Leblanc was using his character without permission, though Leblanc's estate would be just as unforgiving toward Monkey Punch's *Lupin III* many decades later. Leblanc's Lupin has been the subject of dozens of radio dramas, TV series, and movies both in English and French, and even a rumored live-action Hong Kong version, in development from **WICKED CITY**'s Tsui Hark. One of his most recent incarnations was in François Bresson's *Les Aventures de Arsène Lupin* (1996), a French cartoon series dubbed into English as *Nighthood*. Lupin also appeared in **GIGI AND THE FOUNTAIN OF YOUTH**.

MACHINE ROBO *

1986. JPN: *Machine Robo: Chronos no Sotsugeki; MR: Butchigiri Battle Hackers.* AKA: *Machine Robo: Revenge of Chronos, MR: Go for It Battle Hackers.* TV series. DIR: Hiroshi Yoshida, Yoshitaka Fujimoto, Yasuo Hasegawa, Hiroshi Negishi, Yoshinori Nakamura, Kiyoshi Murayama, Yasunori Urata. SCR: Hideki Sonoda, Nobuaki Kishima, Yasushi Hirano, Toshimichi Okawa, Asami Watanabe, Hiroko Naka. DES: Nobuyoshi Habara. ANI: Masami Obari, Norio Hirayama, Yoshiaki Akutagawa, Hajime Inai, Shigeru Omachi, Hiroaki Aida. MUS: Tachio Okano. PRD: Ashi Pro, Plex, TV Tokyo. 25 mins. x 47 eps., 25 mins. x 31 eps., 30 mins. x 3 eps. (v1), 30 mins. (v2).

Gandler space pirates attack Planet Chronos in search of the super-element Hiliveed, but their plans are thwarted by the death of the noble Kirai. His son, Rom Stol, acquires Kirai's "Wolfblade," the key to the secrets of Hiliveed. Accompanied by his sister, Leina, and his friends Rod Drill and Blue Jet, Rom sets out in search of his destiny, finding along the way his ability to transform into the giant robot Vikung-fu.

Conceived by Bandai to promote its Machine Robo toy line, *MR* was nevertheless a success in its own right. The first series was immediately followed by *MR: Battle Hackers* (1987), in which a ship crewed by Earthlings crashes on Chronos. Believing themselves stranded, the crew volunteers to fight alongside the Machine Robos. The second season, however, did not quite live up to the popularity of its predecessor. Realizing that one of the serial's most

popular attributes was not the robots at all but the miniskirted Leina, the series was revived straight to video with a spinoff, *Leina Stol: Legend of the Wolfblade* (1988, *LS: Kenro Densetsu*). In this story, Leina's sister disguises herself as an Earth girl and goes undercover to a typical Japanese school to investigate a series of disappearances. Demonstrating surprising tenacity, the character returned for a last hurrah in a one-shot, *Lightning Trap: Leina and Laika* (1990), about the well-traveled sister on a hijacked plane teaming up with the cyborg Interpol agent Laika to save the day. The songs from the series were also rereleased as "image videos" *MR: Revenge of Chronos Battlefield Memory* (1987) and *Leina Music Video: Thank You for You* (1989).

Some of the original toys were released in the U.S. under the brand name Robo Machine along with the unrelated "Future Machine" from the DX Robo Machine line, which was actually a spinoff model of Cobra's car from SPACE ADVENTURE COBRA.

MACROSS *

1982. JPN: *Chojiku Yosai Macross.* AKA: *Superdimensional Fortress Macross.* TV series, movie, video. DIR: Noboru Ishiguro, Fumihiko Takayama, Masakazu Yasumura, Hiroyuki Yamaga, Kazushi Akiyama, Hiroshi Yoshida, Kazuhito Akiyama. SCR: Kenichi Matsuzaki, Sukehiro Tomita, Hiroyuki Hoshiyama, Shoji Kawamori, Noboru Ishiguro, Kei Onoki, Tatsuya Kasahara. DES: Haruhiko Mikimoto, Kazumasa Miyabe, Shoji Kawamori, Ichiro Itano, Toshihiro Hirano, Eiji Suzuki, Hideaki Shimada. ANI: Noboru Ishiguro, Fumi-

hiko Takayama, Hiroyuki Yamaga, Taro Yamada, Katsuhisa Yamada, Akina Nishimori. MUS: Kentaro Haneda; Yoko Kanno. PRD: Big West, TBS. 25 mins. x 36 eps. (*Macross*), 115 mins. (m), 30 mins. x 6 eps. (*Mac2*), 40 mins. x 4 eps. (*Mac+*), 115 mins. (*Mac+ Movie*), 25 mins. x 49 eps. (*Mac7*), 55 mins. (*Mac7 Encore*), 30 mins. (*Mac7 Galaxy*), 30 mins. x 4 eps. (*Mac7 Dynamite*).

In 1999, a giant space fortress crashes on Earth. Technology salvaged from it changes the face of Terran science, but the military are painfully aware that it is a warship, and that somewhere out in space is the race who built it. Sure enough, the giant Zentraedi arrive to reclaim their errant spacecraft. Attacking just as the recommissioned fortress, now named SDF-1, prepares for take-off, they are thwarted by the brave people on board, who include spunky young pilot Hikaru Ichijo, heroic veteran Roy Fokker, and a ragtag crew of outnumbered Earthlings. During the ensuing conflict out at the edge of the solar system (where SDF-1 has been trapped by a malfunctioning warp engine), the invaders reveal their fatal flaw. Themselves the creations of a far older civilization, the Protoculture, their society knows nothing but war. Zentraedi spies are deeply confused by the concepts of friendship and romance, and entire fleets are driven insane by their first encounter with the dreaded "culture," as transmitted through the love songs of Chinese pop star, Lin Minmei. The fighting is long and hard, with several false truces and partial victories, but eventually humanity wins the day. The Zentraedi volunteer for "micronization" and are reduced in size to interbreed with the human race. It is eventually learned that humans are the descendants of a long-forgotten Protoculture terraforming experiment and, consequently, are just as much children of the Protoculture as the Zentraedi, who were genetically engineered to fight the Protoculture's battles.

Released in the U.S. in a substantially altered form as **ROBOTECH**, *Macross*, along with **STAR BLAZERS** and **GUNDAM**, is one of the three unassailable pillars of anime sci-fi, pioneering the tripartite winning formula of songs, battling robot-planes (the show's famous "Valkyries"), and tense relationships. The series was a success across all media—designer Kawamori insisted on beautiful but practical machinery that was nevertheless exploitable as toys, while the numerous record spinoffs made a star of Minmei's voice actress, Mari Iijima.

After several false starts (see below) the franchise was finally revived in earnest with *Plus* (1994), set in 2040 on the colony world of Eden. Like his spiritual predecessor Ichijo, Isamu Dyson is a maverick pilot, in this case sent back to his homeworld to be a test pilot for a new generation of Valkyries, competing with his former friend Guld Bowman. *M Plus* turns its predecessor on its head, introducing a *broken* love triangle with the return of Myung Fan Lone, a girl over whom the pilots fell out in their teens. A failed singer turned record producer, Myung is in town with the virtual idol Sharon Apple, and studiously trying to avoid dredging up old memories. In their own way, they all face the unemployment line; the pilots because the military are developing an unmanned fighter, and Myung because her artificial songstress (who formerly needed to leech off Myung's talent) can now run on autopilot. *M Plus* concerns itself with the very human fear that machines will take over; ironic considering that much of the hype surrounding its Japanese release concentrated

on extensive computer graphics. Impressive digital effects make regular appearances, though the old-fashioned cinematography of *M Plus* is of very high quality indeed, needing no flashy distractions. Directed by **ESCAFLOWNE**'s Shoji Kawamori, and with a script from **COWBOY BEBOP**'s Keiko Nobumoto, *M Plus* is another excellent example of what anime sci-fi has to offer. The original videos were reedited into *MP: The Movie* (1995), which added some intriguing extra scenes but also removed a substantial portion of the breathtaking battles.

M Plus was released in Japan at the same time as a TV follow-up, *Macross 7* (1994), directed by Tetsuro Amino and incorporating elements of a rejected plot for the original *Macross* series that were to have taken place on a colony ship. Set in a colony fleet heading for the galactic core in 2045, *M7* features Max and Miria Jenius, supporting characters from the original series, as the parents of the love interest Mylene. The fleet is attacked by the soul-vampire race of Protodevlin, eventually revealed to be a race of super-Zentraedi, genetically engineered by the Protoculture and imprisoned for millennia on the distant world of Varauta. Despite a back story that artfully ties up several earlier continuity issues in the series, *M7* is still a mixed bag, let down somewhat by cheap, oft-recycled animation, formulaic menaces-of-the-week, and an overconcentration on hotheaded pilot Basara Nekki and his pop group, Fire Bomber, which seems a little too cynically market-oriented. Whereas the original series actually made the audience believe that a love song could save the world, *M7* featured bizarre sequences of pilots strumming guitars in their cockpits to create weapons. Played for laughs, as in the later **BLACK HEAVEN**, it can work, but not in a show that occasionally wants to be taken seriously. As yet unreleased in English, *M7* was nevertheless popular enough in Japan to spawn several spinoffs, including Haruhiko Mikimoto's manga *M7: Trash* (an excellent study of

Utena and her love interest, the "Rose Bride" Anthy, who holds the key to "revolution." Combining the cross-dressing swordplay of **PRINCESS KNIGHT** and **ROSE OF VERSAILLES**, director Kunihiko Ikuhara concocted an adventurous romance that flourished on television after the tortured apocalypse of **EVANGELION**. *See entry p. 425.*

Utena

Max Jenius's illegitimate son, Shiba), and the spinoff "movie" *M7: The Galaxy Is Calling Me* (1995), in which Basara, now a journeyman musician, is imprisoned on an ice-planet by mysterious forces. There are also two sets of straight-to-video ephemera. The first, *M7: Encore*, simply consists of two unbroadcast TV episodes. *Macross Dynamite 7* (1997) was a new story about Basara going to the isolated planet of Zora, where he meets the elfin alien Elma. Although they have little in common, they communicate through the universal language of song, and Elma's older sister Liza enlists Basara's help in attempting to decode the songs of the interstellar whales that have come to Zora. True to form, Liza is an ace pilot in the *Macross* mold, and there is an all-new love triangle to keep fans of the formula happy.

A fully digital sequel, with the working title of *Macross 3D*, was announced for 2001 as a directorial project for Takeshi Mori. Early reports include a scarred, embittered veteran who goes by the name Redline, a traditional *Macross* heroine in the shape of the red-haired Lorin, and the "mysterious silver-haired" Karno, who seems heavily inspired by **EVANGELION**'s Rei Ayanami.

There are several other spinoffs from the *Macross* series apart from the central plot discussed above. These include the music video *Flashback 2012* (1987), Minmei's "farewell concert," which included bonus epilogue footage of the characters' lives after the show. The theatrical feature *Macross: Do You Remember Love?* (1984, aka *Clash of the Bionoids*) retells much of the original series but with several deviations. The official explanation for this is that it is actually a film made *in* the *Macross* universe *about* the events of the series, taking artistic license with several events. Seen in 2031 by the 15-year-old Myung Fan Lone, it inspires her to become a singer and hence the events of *Macross Plus*! Max's eldest daughter, Comiria, starred in the video game *Macross 2036*, which was followed by another, *Eternal Love Story*. There is also the noncanonical video *Macross II: Lovers Again* (1992), an inferior sequel to the original series, now disowned by its creators. Set 80 years after the original series, this guilty rehash features hotshot journalist Hibiki Kanzaki, who is sent to interview Valkyrie ace Silvie Gena but gets caught up in the action on Earth. A new alien enemy has attacked—the Marduk, who are encouraged in battle by the singing voice of Ishtar, a beautiful girl who switches sides when she falls for Hibiki. A live-action movie version of the original series, *Macross: Final Outpost—Earth*, was planned as a U.S.–Japanese coproduction and reputedly scripted by *Superman*-writer David Newman, but it has been stuck in turnaround for several years. *Ill. p. 121.*

MAD BULL 34 *

1990. Video. DIR: Satoshi Dezaki. SCR: Toshiaki Imaizumi. DES: Keizo Shimizu. ANI: Keizo Shimizu, Hideo Okazaki, Kazunori Iwakura. MUS: Curio, John Michael, James Brown. PRD: Magic Bus. 45 mins. x 4 eps.
America, as we all know, is a land of happy blonde hookers, gun-toting schoolchildren, and roller-skating hoodlums, where self-defense teachers use their classes to scout for potential rape victims, pretty journalists use their bodies as bait to trap molesters, and kindly police get freebies from "high-class" whores. One such hero is "Sleepy," a vast hulk of a police officer also known as Mad Bull. In a series of astoundingly misconceived setups lifted from the worst of U.S. cop shows, Japanese-American rookie Daizaburo is assigned to Mad Bull in New York's 34th precinct, and the older cop shows him the ropes.

While *MB34* is one of the most puerile anime ever made, it is at least partly inspired by American TV itself—a diet of murder and crime-shows genuinely does make America look like this to many foreigners, who could be forgiven for assuming that the U.S. jumped straight from the genteel LITTLE WOMEN to the killing fields of GOLGO 13. Lacking any of the redeeming qualities of the lighter-hearted GUNSMITH CATS, *MB34* presents a stunningly infantile story in which "not doing things by the book" means shooting all suspected perps on sight and the way to snap a traumatized hostage out of shock is to "stick your finger up her ass." Based on a 1985 *Young Jump* manga by Kazuo Koike and Noriyoshi Inoue, the English dub features a new hip-hop music track, which, frankly, is one of the high points of this odious show—the mind boggles at James Brown lending his name to a show that features an episode called "Hit and Rape." The credits thank the *real-life* 34th precinct of the NYPD for unspecified assistance, though the public relations officer must have had a baby when he saw the final result—a ruthless cop hunting down the assassin who has already tried to kill him with poisoned soap, in revenge for the death of the prostitute they share on alternate weekdays. Listen, too, for the British-made dub, which seems to think that referring to civic *dooty* at irregular intervals means you've got a New York accent. **LNV**

MAD OLD BAG

1990. JPN: *O-Batarian*. TV series. DIR: Tetsuro Amino. SCR: Shunichi Yukimuro, Toshiki Inoue. DES: Yoshinobu Shigeno. ANI: N/C. MUS: Yasuo Urakami, Katsuyoshi Kobayashi. PRD: TV Asahi/SPO. 25 mins. x 7 eps.
The misadventures of an unpleasant old woman (compare to NASTY OLD LADY) who embarrasses her family at a school open house, makes a nuisance of herself during a vacation to a hot spring, and lusts after nice young men. Based on the 1984 manga by Katsuhiko Hotta.

MADARA

1991. Video. DIR: Yuji Moriyama. SCR: Akinori Endo. DES: Yuji Moriyama, Junichi Watanabe. ANI: Yuji Moriyama. MUS: The Great Riches. PRD: Animate Film. 60 mins. x 4 eps.
Madara is disowned by his father, King Miroku, who steals his "chakra power" and banishes him to planet Earth, where he is saved by the old man Tatara. Attacked in the forest by Miroku's evil tree-spirits, Madara swears to get back at his father, but he must contend with his brother, sent to Earth to kill him first.

Based on the 1987 manga by Akitaka Tajima, published in *Maru Sho Famicon* magazine. Episode two contains the 36-page Madara Special Edition, a sequel to the fourth volume of the manga.

MADONNA *

1988. JPN: *Madonna: Honoo no Teacher*. AKA: *Madonna: Fiery Teacher*. Video. DIR: Akinori Nagaoka. SCR: Kaori Okamura. DES: Minoru Maeda. ANI: Minoru Maeda. MUS: Minako Honda. PRD: Studio Junio. 50 mins. x 2 eps.
Well-bred young lady Mako Domon decides to be a teacher but is sent to the rough Gyunabe Technical High School, where she is put in charge of a class of juvenile delinquents. She becomes the coach for the school rugby team, which allows this sports anime to repeat the standard clichés of shows in the tradition of AIM FOR THE ACE,

but with the added frisson of a female coach. Based on the popular manga by Ikuko Kujirai, published in *Big Comic Spirits*.

MADOX-01 *

1987 AKA: *Metal Skin Panic Madox 01*. Video. DIR: Shinji Aramaki. SCR: Shinji Aramaki. DES: Hideki Tamura. ANI: Hiroaki Goda. MUS: Ken Yashima. PRD: AIC. 45 mins.

Overworked (but pretty) scientist Miss Kuzumoto sends the new Madox-01 military robot off for more tests, but she carelessly forgets to turn it off. The robot is lost in a crash, falling into the hands of lovable college boy Koji, who tries it on for size. Trapped inside, Koji tries to sneak across Tokyo for a midnight tryst with his estranged girlfriend, Shiori, though he has trouble looking inconspicuous. Realizing that the jealous officer Kilgore will do anything to destroy the Madox, Kuzumoto suits up in another model and tries to find out what Koji wants. All Koji wants, of course, is to get out of the suit, but he conveniently forgets to mention this until large swaths of Tokyo have been turned into smoldering rubble by the ensuing battle.

A weapon-goes-haywire story inferior to its contemporary **BLACK MAGIC**, *Madox* features a robot design also used in the same studio's **BUBBLEGUM CRISIS** but is otherwise unrelated. Tiresomely attempting to compensate for lackluster production with idle moments of "humor" and a couple of references to *Apocalypse Now*, *Madox* also makes some avoidable bloopers in its depiction of the real world—watch for military alarms that go from Defcon Three to Defcon *Four* when trouble escalates. Political types may enjoy the show's shameless characterization of Americans as belligerent morons who revel in destruction with war machines they do not fully comprehend, whereas the Japanese are all mechanically minded innocents with no interest in fighting. "You'd better not turn Tokyo into another Vietnam," Kuzumoto archly warns Kilgore, while

neglecting to mention that none of this would have happened in the first place if she'd bothered to switch the Madox unit off.

MAGIC BOY *

1959. JPN: *Shonen Sarutobi Sasuke*. Movie. DIR: Taiji Yabushita, Akira Okuwara. SCR: Toppei Matsumura. DES: Akira Okuwara, Hideo Furusawa. ANI: Taku Sugiyama, Gisaburo Sugii, Norio Hikone. MUS: Satoshi Funemura. PRD: Toei. 83 mins.

When his pet deer is killed by Princess Yasha, mountain boy Sasuke resolves to go away to Mount Togakushi and study the art of *ninjutsu* under the master Hatsuunsai Tozawa. Bidding farewell to his elder sister Oyu, he heads off, leaving his village prone to attacks from Princess Yasha's agent, Gonkuro, and his gangs of bandits. The local lord, Yukimura Sanada, is unable to deal with the bandit problem because of a spell cast by Yasha, but he teams up with the returning Sasuke to defeat the menace. A flawed film that mixes ninja action with highly idiosyncratic work by several artists who had never worked in anime before. Compare to **SASUGA NO SARUTOBI**.

MAGIC USER'S CLUB *

1996. JPN: *Maho Tsukaitai*. AKA: *Witches' Club; I Wanna Do Magic*. Video, TV series. DIR: Junichi Sato. SCR: Akinori Endo, Chiaki Konaka, Michiko Yokote, Sadayuki Murai. DES: Ikuko Ito, Mahiro Maeda. ANI: Ikuko Ito. MUS: Michiru Oshima. PRD: Madhouse, WOWOW. 30 mins. x 6 eps. (v), 25 mins. x 13 eps. (TV).

Earth has been invaded *again*, by ugly high-performance robots powerful enough to destroy the UN forces with a single blast. Is it the end of the world? Actually, no. The invaders just roam around observing life, don't attack unless provoked, and are very polite. Most people have gotten used to just living around them. But they're still invaders, so somebody obviously has to fight them and save Earth. Cue the members of the Kitanohashi High

School Magic Club. The president, Takeo, is always trying to impress pretty (but clumsy) new recruit Sae. Androgynous vice-president Aburatsubo (who, the titles very carefully inform us, *is* a boy) is devoted to Takeo. Sae's best friend, Nanaka, has a crush on Aburatsubo . . . and remember they're supposed to be fighting the aliens. Takeo is just hoping to impress the girls by leading an attack on the invaders. So far, however, their magic isn't all that good, and with the school's Manga Club taking over their room space, he needs a project to hold the Magic Club together before all the members quit. Then things start to get serious when journalist Minowa begins finding out who these magical kids really are, and Sae finds she feels a bit more for Takeo than the respect of a junior classmate for a senior club leader.

The video series was followed in 1997 by 13 TV episodes focusing on the huge cherry tree Sae creates in the center of town in the final battle to get rid of the aliens. Its petals, far from being a nostalgic seasonal pleasure, are snowing up the roads and causing chaos. In the process of trying to get rid of the tree, the club members discover that it isn't the only unsuitable magical object plaguing the city, and they have a new mission. The video series spun off a manga version by Tami Ota, which ran in *Fantasy DX* magazine. We can think of no reason why the U.S. release title implies there is only one "Magic User," except perhaps a lack of familiarity with English grammar.

MAGIC WOMAN M *

1996. JPN: *Maho Shojo Meryl*. AKA: *Magical Girl Meryl*. Video. DIR: Tougenan, Ahiru Koike. SCR: Hiroshi Ishii. DES: Nekoshita Pong. ANI: Takaichi Hiraizu. MUS: N/C. PRD: Beam Entertainment. 30 mins. x 2 eps.

This video was based on a manga by Nekoshita Pong that was originally serialized in *Monthly Fantazine*. Sexy young witch Meryl Shelk wanders a forest full of rapacious beasts—her only defense, the sorcerous powers she unleashes at the moment of orgasm. **LNV**

MAGICAL EMI

1985. JPN: *Maho no Star Magical Emi.* AKA: *Magical Star Magical Emi.* TV series. DIR: Nobuyasu Furukawa, Kazuyoshi Katayama, Tomomi Mochizuki, Mizuho Nishikubo, Michiru Hongo, Tadayuki Hayashi, Takashi Anno, Fumihiko Takayama. SCR: Hiroshi Kobayakawa, Asami Watanabe, Akinori Endo, Hideki Sonoda, Sukehiro Tomita. DES: Yoshiyuki Kishi, Kazuhiko Kobayashi. ANI: Yoshiyuki Kishi, Yuji Motoyama. MUS: Keiichi Oku. PRD: Studio Pierrot, NTV. 25 mins. x 38 eps. Would-be conjuror Mai Kazuki is playing with her brother Misaki when the fairy Topo offers to grant her a wish. She transforms herself into Magical Emi, a magical girl in the tradition of **CREAMY MAMI**, but who prefers to concentrate on more mundane concerns than her crime-fighting sisters—much of *ME*'s plot concerns her performances at her grandmother's Magicarrot Theater. As with the other magical-girl stories, Mai loses her powers as she leaves childhood behind and becomes an adult in the final episodes. Many of the crew would go on from this obscure work to make many of the best-known anime of the late 1980s and beyond.

MAGICAL GAME

2001. JPN: *Maho Yugi.* Video. DIR: Hiroki Hayashi. SCR: Hideyuki Kurata. DES: Kiyohiko Azuma. ANI: N/C. MUS: N/C. PRD: AIC. 5 mins. x 24 eps. Twelve-year-old girls from different towns in Majokko Land are sent to the central castle to take part in magical duels. The coastal port of Seahaven sends Padodu, a luckless girl who falls into a river and is washed up in the party town of Dancevalley, where she is imprisoned by the mayor, who wants to increase the chances of his own candidate winning the contest. A dejected Padodu shares her cell with Nononon, a former magical-girl candidate defeated by the current incumbent Purirun.

In this combination of the magical-girl genre with game-based fighting anime, Nononon encourages Padodu to persevere and win for the sake of all underdogs. The first fully digital animation from the people who brought you **TENCHI MUYO!**, which similarly combined two disparate genres—can lightning strike twice?

MAGICAL GIRL LALABELLE

1980. JPN: *Maho Shojo Lalabelle.* TV series, movie. DIR: Hiroshi Shidara, Hideo Furusawa, Masahiro Sasaki, Yuji Endo. SCR: Masaki Tsuji, Hirohisa Soda, Noboru Shiroyama, Tomoko Konparu, Tomohiro Ando. DES: Michio Shindo, Eiji Ito. ANI: Hideaki Oroku, Kiyoshi Matsumoto, Masami Abe. MUS: Taku Izumi. PRD: TV Asahi, Toei. 25 mins. x 49 eps., 15 mins. (m). Lalabelle is a magical girl (see **LITTLE WITCH SALLY**) accidentally sent down to the human world. Finding a place to live with old couple Sakuzo and Ume Tachibana, she promises not to use her magic and tries to fit into the human world. She befriends two local children, Toko and Teko, but is continually forced to bend her own self-imposed rules when her town is placed in jeopardy by Viscous, a fame-obsessed conjuror, and his sidekick, Tsumio. Yet another juvenile rehash of *Bewitched*, attached to a heavy-handed moralizing tone, with each episode ending with Lalabelle's Proverb of the Week. Based on a manga by Eiko Fujiwara, better known as the author of *The Infamous Himeko*. Lalabelle also appeared in the theatrical short *MGL: The Sea Calls for a Summer Vacation* (1980).

MAGICAL GIRLCAT TARUTO

2001. JPN: *Maho Shojo Neko Taruto.* TV series. DIR: Tsukasa Sunaga. SCR: Koji Naota. DES: N/C. ANI: N/C. MUS: N/C. PRD: Bandai Visual, Dentsu. 25 mins. x 12 eps. Taruto, one of three cat-eared girls, believes she is the long-lost princess of the Nekomata tribe of feline sorcerers. This cynical mixture of anthropomorphic anime females, the "magical-girl" genre, and a dash of **TENCHI MUYO!** (since she has a shy young master, of course) is based on the manga in *Ultra Jump* magazine by the creators of **STEEL ANGEL KURUMI**.

MAGICAL MAKO-CHAN

1970. JPN: *Maho no Mako-chan.* TV series. DIR: Yugo Serikawa, Yoshio Takami, Minoru Okazaki, Tadaaki Yamazaki. SCR: Masaki Tsuji, Shunichi Yukimuro, Kazuko Yamamoto, Hide Ogawa, Moritada Matsumoto, Kuniaki Oshikawa. DES: N/C. ANI: Toshiyasu Okada, Shinya Takahashi, Fumi Kudo, Nobutaka Nishizawa. MUS: Takeo Watanabe. PRD: TV Asahi, Toei. 25 mins. x 48 eps. Mako, the youngest daughter of the undersea Dragon King, defies her father and comes to the surface world. There, she falls in love with Akira, the first man she has ever seen. She asks a wise old woman to transform her into a human, knowing that she can never go back to being a mermaid. Then she goes to live with the animal-loving Mr. Urashima, longing all the while for another meeting with her beloved Akira. A mixture of **LITTLE MERMAID** and **JAPANESE FOLK TALES**, created for the screen by Masaki Tsuji under the pen-name Shinobu Urakawa.

MAGICAL MEG

1974. JPN: *Majokko Meg-chan.* AKA: *Meg the Witch.* TV series. DIR: Yugo Serikawa, Minoru Okazaki, Hiroshi Shidara, Teruo Kigure, Satoshi Dezaki, Norio Suzuki, Kazuya Miyazaki. SCR: Hiroyasu Yamaura, Shunichi Yukimuro, Masaki Tsuji, Tomohiro Ando, Fumihito Imamura, Kiyoshi Matsuoka. DES: Isamu Tsuchida. ANI: Shingo Araki, Shinya Takahashi, Minoru Maeda. MUS: Takeo Watanabe. PRD: TV Asahi, Toei. 25 mins. x 72 eps. Meg, the oldest child in the Kanzaki family, is forever separating her quarreling brother and sister. She cannot reveal that she is really a witch, sent from Witchland to help the human world fight demons. This magical-girl anime has a distinctly European look, particularly in the streets and houses.

MAGICAL TALRUTO

1979. JPN: *Magical Talruto-kun*. Movie. DIR: Hiroyuki Kadono. SCR: Yoshiyuki Suga. DES: Tatsuya Egawa. ANI: Hisashi Eguchi. MUS: Seiji Yokoyama. PRD: Toei. 40 mins. x 2 eps., 30 mins. x 1 ep.
Talruto escapes a nursery school in the magical dimension and comes to the human world, pursued by teacher Teichianu. In order to save the mother of his friend in human world, Talruto decides to go back to the magical world. Then, a huge robot appears from hell. Based on a manga by Tatsuya Egawa from *Shonen Jump*.

MAGICAL TWILIGHT *

1994. AKA: *The Hex Files*. Video. DIR: Toshiaki Kobayashi, Toshiaki Komura. SCR: "Hisashi Yuki." DES: Junichi Mihara. ANI: Akinobu Takahashi, Toshiaki Komura. MUS: N/C. PRD: Pink Pineapple. 30 mins. x 3 eps.
Tsukasa Tachibana is a student with problems. His exam failures are giving him nightmares; he's dreaming he's about to die. But he's not the only one with exams on his mind. Three young witches have to go to Earth to pass their final exam, and they all have the same project—Tsukasa. They'll affect his life in a weird variety of ways, though black witch Liv fails in her project to kill him after horrendous tortures. This leaves Tsukasa with two young witches on his hands. Guess who's up for hands-on tuition? A cleaned-up U.S. version is available for people who want porn with the porn removed.

MAGNOS *

1976. JPN: *Magne Robo Ga[thering] Keen*. TV series. DIR: Tomoharu Katsumata, Masayuki Akehi, Teppei Matsuura. SCR: Hiroyasu Yamaura, Tomohiro Ando, Keisuke Fujikawa, Hiroyuki Hoshiyama. DES: Kazuo Komatsubara. ANI: Kazuo Komatsubara, Toshio Nitta, Yoshinori Kanemori. MUS: Michiaki

Watanabe. PRD: Japad, Toei, TV Asahi. 25 mins. x 39 eps.
The alien Izzard, former rulers of Earth, have been sleeping beneath its surface for the last two million years. Now they have awakened, and only Professor Hanatsuki of the Earth Research Institute can stop them. Luckily, he has the required teen assistants, including his daughter, Mai, and a square-jawed man named Takeru, who pilot the combining robot Ga Keen. Though Takeru is the nominal hero, the robot cannot move without Mai's presence—that's nepotism for you. A follow-up to the similar STEEL JEEG, reputedly released in the U.S. in a feature-length dub under the *Magnos* title around 1984.

MAHJONG QUEST

1992. Video. DIR: Maru-chan Program Suru. SCR: Kaneyama 6800. DES: ARG, Gekitsuio, Tattakatta. ANI: N/C. MUS: Pinch Pinch. PRD: Kaneyama 6800. 30 mins.
Animated sequences as part of a how-to guide to completing the simulation game *Mahjong Quest*, in which the player gets to see all 25 nubile opponents as well as the ending of the game, for those who weren't good enough to finish it by themselves. Bonus footage of the girls only just qualifies this release as an anime, as opposed to a rather futile spinoff from a video game.

MAHOROMATIC

2001. TV series. DIR: Hiroyuki Yamaga. SCR: Hiroyuki Yamaga. DES: Kazuhiro Takamura. ANI: N/C. MUS: N/C. PRD: Gainax, Shaft, BS-i. 25 mins. x 12 eps.
After a long and faithful service as a Vesper Hyper Soldier fighting alien invaders in outer space, android Mahoro V1046 is permitted to choose her retirement posting. In a triumph for female subservience, she elects to live at her former commanding officer's house and work as a maid for his teenage son. This case of making beds not war was based on a manga in *Comic Gamu* by Monjuro Nakayama and Bo

Chidama (compare to **HANDMAID MAY** or **HANAUKYO MAID TEAM**).

MAICO 2010

1998. AKA: *Androidana Maico 2010; Android Announcer*. TV series. DIR: Kozo Masanari. SCR: Toshimitsu Shimizu. DES: Keiichi Ishiguro. ANI: Keiichi Ishiguro. MUS: N/C. PRD: Pony Canyon, WOWOW. 8 mins. x 24 eps.
In 2010, Nippon Broadcasting tries to increase its ratings by employing Maico the android as a broadcaster. An adaptation of a popular story also made into a radio drama and manga, based on an idea by **AIRBATS**-creator Toshimitsu Shimizu.

MAIDEN OF . . . *

1998. JPN: *Kai no Naka no Kotori*. AKA: *Little Bird in the Shell*. Video. DIR: Hideki Takayama. SCR: Masateru Tsuruoka. DES: N/C. ANI: Hirota Shindo, Makoto Kichizaki. MUS: N/C. PRD: Discovery, Seven Eight. 35 mins. x 5 eps.
An original take on the anime porn genre, set in 19th-century Europe, where a secret society exerts political power, controlling important figures by using a ring of professionally trained prostitutes. The ring is eventually disbanded, but Foster, the man in charge, is approached some time later by

Dread Burton, a railroad tycoon who wants him to train maids to perform very particular duties—cooking, cleaning, and *submitting*. A surprisingly old-fashioned and distinctly British tale of poor waifs abused by rich cads, based on a computer game. In the tradition of the TALES OF . . . series Kitty Films renamed the separate episodes *Maiden of Deception, Desire, Decadence,* and *Destruction.* One episode was not released in the U.S. due to the appearance of underage characters. **LNV**

MAIL ORDER MAIDEN 28 *

1995. JPN: *Nankyoku 28-go.* AKA: *South Pole #28; Dutch Wife 28.* Video. DIR: Hiroshi Midoriyama. SCR: Akira Hatta. DES: Hachi-ko. ANI: Shinya Sasaki, Motokazu Murakami. MUS: N/C. PRD: Sente Studio. 45 mins.
Based on a manga by TALES OF . . . –creator U-jin and pastiching GIGANTOR (i.e., *Tetsujin 28*), this obscure porn title features Aiwa, a typical anime geek, who orders a sex doll and gets more than he bargained for. He opens the package to discover Satomi, a lifelike, sex-crazy android, whose being a robot is a thin excuse for portraying a character who would be otherwise underage. Wild sex ensues, though Aiwa still yearns for his "real" ladylove, the innocent Kozue, who will surely never speak to him again unless he can find Satomi's off-button before she arrives. A predictable rehash of VIDEO GIRL AI, with the flimsy plot papered over, as in ADVENTURE KID, by the hiring of a famous starlet to provide a voice, in this case Mika Yoshino of the "Giri Giri Girls." **N**

MAISON IKKOKU *

1986. TV series, movie. DIR: Kazuo Yamazaki, Naoyuki Yoshinaga, Osamu Sekita, Setsuko Shibunnoichi. SCR: Tokio Tsuchiya, Shigeru Yanagawa, Kazunori Ito, Hideo Takayashiki, Tomoko Konparu. DES: Yuji Moriyama, Akemi Takada. ANI: Masaaki Kawanami, Keiko Fukube, Ryunosuke Otonashi. MUS: Takuo Sugiyama. PRD: Kitty, Fuji TV. 25 mins. x 96 eps., 90 mins. (m).

While he waits for the chance to retake his university entrance exams, Yusaku Godai lives in the Maison Ikkoku dormitory, a strange place peopled by the party-loving Hanae Ichinose, perverse Tom Yotsuya, and free-spirited club hostess Akemi. But Godai soon falls for the new apartment manager, the pretty widow Kyoko Otonashi—a courtship dogged by troubles from the other tenants and from the pressure brought by Godai's rival suitor, Mitaka.
A popular manga from URUSEI YATSURA–creator Rumiko Takahashi, the story is highly regarded in her work, not the least because it has a beginning, a middle, and an end, and not the interminable repetition of RANMA 1/2. *MI* was troubled by early problems—the character designs were changed twice before it truly got underway. It is worth the wait, however, and is an attractive, touching drama that shares a special place in fans' hearts alongside KIMAGURE ORANGE ROAD, a similar tale of almost-unattainable love. The series eventually ends with the movie version, in which plans for the long-awaited wedding are thwarted by whispered rumors that have Godai believing that Kyoko is hiding an incriminating letter from him. Capping the story while the TV series was still running, the movie also featured a cameo from the mystery inhabitant of Room Two, unseen in the TV series. A vacation special was released straight to video as Setsuko Shibunnoichi's *MI Side Story* (1990). *Ill. p. 341.*

MAKOTO-CHAN

1980. Movie. DIR: Tsutomu Shibayama. SCR: Noboru Shiroyama, Masaki Tsuji, Tsunehisa Ito, Tomoko Konparu. DES: Osamu Kobayashi. ANI: Osamu Kobayashi. MUS: Ryo Kawagami. PRD: Tohoku, TMS. 85 mins.
Kindergarten kid Makoto tries hard to be a good boy but is dumped by his nursery-school sweetheart, Anko-chan. Walking through the park feeling sorry for himself, he meets Yuko Daiyu, a grown-up who has also just had her heart broken. They get along well with

each other, but for Yuko, flirting with a little boy is just a game, and Makoto is soon left heartbroken again. Recovering from the experience, he performs a mini-play for his mother on Mother's Day, looks after some sparrow's eggs, and attempts to win the "Good Child" award at his nursery. An unusual comedy based on the short manga *Small Sweetheart, Mother's Day Present, Love Lunch Pack, Sparrow's Eggs,* and *Good Child Award* by BOY WITH CAT'S EYES–creator Kazuo Umezu, who also sings the theme song with his backing group, the Super Police.

MALICE@DOLL

2001. Video. DIR: Keitaro Motonaga. SCR: Chiaki Konaka. DES: Shinobu Nishioka, Yasuhiro Moriki. ANI: N/C. MUS: N/C. PRD: @ Entertainment. 30 mins. x 3 eps.
Androids in a distant future are made for the sexual gratification of their masters, though the manufacture of sentient humanoids calls into question the humanity of their unfeeling creators. A 3-D CG anime revisiting some of the sexual politics of writer Konaka's earlier ARMITAGE III. **NV**

MAMA'S A FOURTH GRADER

1992. JPN: *Mama wa Shogaku Yonensei.* TV series. DIR: Chuichi Iguchi, Kazuki Akane, Nobuyuki Kondo, Nana Harada. SCR: Satoshi Nakamura, Tetsuko Watanabe. DES: Yoshiko Kamimura. ANI: Toshikazu Endo, Kisaraka Yamada, Atsushi Aono. MUS: Hayato Kanbayashi. PRD: Sunrise, Nippon TV. 25 mins. x 36 eps.
Japanese schoolgirl Natsumi gets the fright of her life when her own baby daughter falls through a time warp from 15 years in the future. A comedy with elements of the future offspring of SAILOR MOON and the unwilling babysitter of BABY AND ME. Later episodes veer away from a teen-unwed-mother farce and into science fiction, as Natsumi attempts to return Mirai-chan ("Future") to her rightful time.

MANGA MITO KOMON

1981. TV series. DIR: Kazuyuki Okaseko, Yoshio Nitta, Hiroshi Yoshida. SCR: Tsunehisa Ito, Yoshiaki Yoshida, Masatoshi Fuji. DES: Keisuke Morishita. ANI: Emiko Minowa. MUS: Kentaro Haneda. PRD: Knack, TV Tokyo. 25 mins. x 46 eps.

Though he looks like a humble traveler, this old man is really Mitsukuni Tokugawa (aka Komon Mito [Mito Komon]), the shogun's uncle, traveling Japan incognito in the company of some feisty young heroes—sword master Sasaki, mountain-of-a-man Atsumi, ninja-boy Sutemaru (with Junpei his faithful hound), and pretty maiden Okoto. The group wanders the land in search of trouble, cowing its opponents into submission by brandishing Mito's *inro*, a lacquered case bearing the shogun's crest. A remake of a popular live-action TV series, originally based on the novels of Sanjugo Aoki (1891–1934). The story reached its widest audience through a live-action NTV series in 1954, and its incredibly long-running successor on TBS, which lasted from 1969 to 2000 and wore out three leading men (this anime version was made shortly before Eijiro Higashino was replaced by Hikaru Nishimura in the live version). Budgets kept the live-action version to human-interest stories such as corrupt merchants and samurai, but the anime production was able to introduce more fantastic elements from JAPANESE FOLK TALES. The same set of legends was a distant inspiration for STELLARBUSTERS and ROBOT KING DAIOJA. See also SAMURAI GOLD, another popular story retold in anime form.

MANGA PICTURES OF JAPAN

1977. JPN: *Manga Nippon Emaki*. TV series. DIR: Noboru Ishiguro, Kazuhiko Udagawa, Yasuo Hasegawa. SCR: Kenji Terada, Tomomi Tsutsui. DES: Tsuneo Ninomiya, Kazuo Imura, Takashi Nakamura. ANI: Osamu Kamijo. MUS: Yutaka Soda. PRD: World Television, Anime Room, TBS. 25 mins. x 46 eps.

Deliberately less faithful to fact than JAPANESE HISTORY, this series happily throws in apocryphal anecdotes and legends about the figures it portrays, normally two to an episode. Suitable subjects, famous in Japan though not always famous enough for the internationally minded GREAT PEOPLE series, include many figures from the Heike-Genji War, such as woman warrior Tomoe Gozen, doomed samurai flautist Taira no Atsumori, and Nasu no Yoichi, who shot a fan off a pole to preserve Minamoto honor at the battle of Yashima. Other stories depict Anju and Zushio (see LITTLEST WARRIOR), Iwami no Jutaro's victory against a giant baboon, and the tale, oft-referenced in anime from INU YASHA to USHIO AND TORA, of Fujita no Tawara's fight with a giant centipede.

MANMARU THE NINJA PENGUIN

1997. JPN: *Ninpen Manmaru*. TV series. DIR: Tetsuo Yasumi. SCR: Haruya Yamazaki, Ayako Okina, Masaaki Sakurai. DES: Yuichiro Miyoshi. ANI: Nobuhiro Okaseko, Yoshio Kabashima. MUS: N/C. PRD: Shinei, TV Asahi. 10 mins. x 48 eps.

Manmaru goes to ninja school at Nenga, where foxes and raccoons study the art of assassination under a bear ninja master. He is soon thrown into local rivalry between the Nenga school, the Koga (monkeys), and the Iga (dogs), as well as facing temptations from the Dobe, a group of dropouts from the Nenga. A lighthearted adaptation of ninja folktales, based on a manga by Mikio Igarashi, creator of BONOBONO.

MAN'S AN IDIOT!

1970. JPN: *Otoko do Aho Koshien*. AKA: *Koshien's an Idiot*. TV series. DIR: Akira Nono. SCR: Tajio Tamura, Tadaaki Yamazaki. DES: Shiro Tamura. ANI: Shiro Tamura. MUS: Mamoru Sasaki. PRD: Nippon TV. 25 mins. x 26 eps.

Koshien Fujimura is named after the biannual high-school baseball championship, so it's only natural that he grows up to be absolutely crazy about the sport. Failing a school entrance exam because he has been training too hard, he ends up at party-school Nanba High. Befriending ace catcher Mametan, he decides to join his new school's baseball team but faces opposition from the bad-boys of the school. Based on a manga by DOKABEN-creator Shinji Mizushima, working with Mamoru Sasaki.

MANUAL OF NINJA MARTIAL ARTS

1967. JPN: *Ninja Bugeicho*. Movie. DIR: Nagisa Oshima. SCR: Nagisa Oshima, Mamoru Sasaki. DES: Sanpei Shirato. ANI: Akira Takada (photography). MUS: Hikaru Hayashi. PRD: Sozosha. 117 mins.

A barely animated adaptation of Sanpei Shirato's long-running manga tale retelling the life of Kagemaru, a charismatic ninja leader in Muromachi era Japan. Shirato's art is shown in still montages shot by a rostrum camera. The film was directed by Nagisa Oshima, also known for *Merry Christmas, Mr. Lawrence, Gohatto*, and *In the Realm of the Senses*.

MANXMOUSE *

1979. JPN: *Tondemonezumi Dai Katsuyaku*. AKA: *Overactive Mouse; Legend of M.; Adventures of M.* TV special. DIR: Hiroshi Saito. SCR: Hiroshi Saito. DES: Yasuji Mori, Yoshiyuki Momose. ANI: Yoshiyuki Momose, Noriko Moritomo. MUS: Akira Nakagawa. PRD: Nippon Animation, Fuji TV. 84 mins.

Meyer the English village potter creates a mouse when drunk one night, but the blue, long-eared, tailless Manxmouse comes to life. Setting out to see the world, he leaves Buntingdowndale and is warned on several occasions to beware of the Manx Cat. After helping rescue a friendly circus tiger, Burra Khan, from crooked London pet shop owner Mr. Petman, Manxmouse confronts the fearsome Manx Cat, who turns out to be a gentlemanly creature who invites him to tea. The two decide to stay friends, in contravention of the traditional antagonism between their species as set down in the ancient Book of Destiny. Based on the book by Paul Gallico, written to entertain the late

Grace Kelly (Princess Grace of Monaco, see **CASTLE OF CAGLIOSTRO**) after she gave him one of the first model mice she made in pottery class.

MANY DREAM JOURNEYS OF MEME, THE

1983. JPN: *Meme Iroiro Yume no Tabi*. TV series. DIR: Yoshio Kuroda, Kazuyoshi Yokota, Takayoshi Suzuki. SCR: Yoshio Kuroda, Nobuyuki Isshiki. DES: Shuichi Seki. ANI: Sadahiko Sakamaki. MUS: Takeo Watanabe. PRD: Nippon Animation, TBS. 25 mins. x 129 eps.

Daisuke and Sayaka explore the world of science, accompanied by Meme the pixie, who has popped out of their computer screen. In the second season, they were replaced by a coterie of seven children who spend more time solving mysteries, but the series still had a heavily educational angle, as one might expect for something originally designed to promote the Tsukuba Science Expo.

MAPLETOWN STORIES *

1986. JPN: *Mapletown Monogatari*. TV series, movie. DIR: Junichi Sato, Keiji Hisaoka, Yukio Misawa, Hiroyuki Kadono. SCR: Chifude Asakura, Shigeru Yanagawa, Tomoko Konparu, Keiji Kubota, Keiko Maruo. DES: Tsuneo Ninomiya. ANI: Kazuo Komatsubara, Hiroshi Shidara, Shingo Araki. MUS: Akiko Kosaka. PRD: Toei, TV Asahi. 25 mins. x 52 eps., 25 mins. x 44 eps. (*New*), 24 mins. & 30 mins. ("movies").

Mapletown is a peaceful community of talking animals, where the Hoprabbit family opens a post office. Middle daughter Patty is an innocent female but often caught up in the schemes of the evil Gretel the Wolf. However, Patty is able to triumph with the help of her friends, Bobby the Bear, Diana the Fox, and shy genius Johnny the Dog. A second series, *New MS* (1987), directed by former lead animator Hiroshi Shidara, dumped all the characters except Patty and her sister Lolly, who set off on a journey to the southern resort of Palm-

town to live with the kindly Nurse Jane. Each of the series also had a movie spinoff, though on available evidence, both "movies" appear to have been TV episodes shown in theaters as part of holiday season multiple bills. The series was a very early job for future **SAILOR MOON**–director Junichi Sato. Shown on Nickelodeon in the U.S.

MAPS *

1987. Movie, video. DIR: Keiji Hayakawa. SCR: Kenji Terada. DES: Hatsuki Tsuji. ANI: Hatsuki Tsuji. MUS: Kohei Tanaka. PRD: Studio Gallop (m), KSS (v), 51 mins. (m), 30 mins. x 4 eps. (v).

Teenager Gen Tokishima is abducted with his girlfriend, Hoshimi Kimizuka, by the huge spaceship Lipmira that's shaped like the body of a beautiful woman. Gen is a "map-man," the last descendant of an ancient tribe, on whose body there is a map of a secret route, the Flowing Light of the Nomad Star Tribe. Accompanied by Lipmira, the female space pirate and electronic brain of the ship, Gen begins a search for the Flowing Light, though the galaxy's treasure hunters are soon hunting him, hoping to swipe his birthright.

An incoherent and badly plotted story, supposedly based on a manga by Yuichi Hasegawa but with characters looking quite different from the original. Lipmira's spaceship, however, is a design triumph—a giant flying statue, inspired by the Spirit of Ecstasy found on the hood of every Rolls Royce automobile. A 1994 video remake, directed by Susumu Nishizawa, was the incarnation released in the U.S.

MARCO POLO

1979. JPN: *Marco Polo no Boken*. AKA: *Adventures of Marco Polo*. TV series. DIR: Katsuhiko Fujita, Masami Hata, Kazuyuki Sakai. SCR: Masao Maruyama, Michiru Kaneko, Hideo Takeuchi, Soji Yoshikawa. DES: Akio Sugino. ANI: Masaki Mori, Yoshiaki Kawajiri, Toshio Hirata, Hideo Nishimaki, Hideo Takayanagi. MUS: Takanori Onosaki, Kei

Ogura. PRD: MK, NHK Promote Service, NHK. 25 mins. x 43 eps.

When his mother dies in Venice, young Marco must accompany his merchant father Niccolo and uncle Maffeo on a trip along the Silk Road to the mysterious East. Many years later, when the travelers' wanderings bring them to China, an older, wiser Marco becomes a trusted adviser to the Great Khan, Kublai. An early collaboration by many of the names who would go on to form the Madhouse Studio, this series depicts the man whose writings on the famous "Land of the Rising Sun" would inspire **COLUMBUS** to set out in search of it.

MARGARET VIDEO SERIES

1993. JPN: *Shueisha Margaret Video Series*. Video. DIR: Takuji Endo, Tsukasa Abe, Asami Watanabe, Tomihiko Okubo. SCR: Akinori Endo, Kenichi Araki, Tatsuhiko Urahata. DES: Tomihiko Okubo. ANI: Kazuhiro Soeta, Masaru Kitao. MUS: Satoshi Okada. PRD: Madhouse. 40 mins. x 6 eps.

A series of romantic tales, all adapted from manga originally serialized in the girls' magazine *Margaret*. The first, *A-Plus for the Fashion Boy* (*O-Sharaku Koso wa Hana Maru*), based on a manga by Tsueko Ansei, features Hodaka, a successful young businessman whose life is turned upside down when he falls in love with a 14-year-old schoolgirl. *Singles*, based on a manga by Mari Fujimura, moves the setting to a university, where student Saki is torn with guilt over her feelings for her sister's boyfriend, Yo. She joins the same club to be close to him but is selected to work on a project with another boy, Daichi. Though she feels herself drawn to Daichi, she cannot put thoughts of Yo from her mind. *Pops*, based on a manga by Aya Ikuemi, is an even simpler tale of teenage angst, as two young students fall in love but must endure the pressures of their studies, the opposition of their parents, and the teasing of their classmates. *Sleepless Edo* (*Oedo wa Nemuranai*), based on *Moonlit Night: Starry Dawn* by Noriko Honda, is a period drama set in the Yoshiwara pleasure district of old Tokyo, where a courtesan, a thief, and a doctor become involved in a love triangle. In *Kiss My Eyes* (*Kiss wa Me ni Shite*), based on an original by Noriko Ueda, average schoolgirl Ibuki falls for a handsome exchange student newly arrived from the U.S. For the final episode, *A-Girl*, based on a manga by Fusako Kuramochi, sisters Mariko and May, along with Mariko's bad-tempered boyfriend, become involved with Ichiro, an arrogant, womanizing male model. At the artist's request, *A-Girl* was shown with subtitles, but no dialogue.

MARINA THE MANGA ARTIST GOES TO CAMELOT

1990. JPN: *Mangaka Marina Time Slip Jiken: Ai to Ken no Camelot*. AKA: *Marina the Manga Artist's Time Slip Incident: Love and Swords of Camelot*. Video. DIR: Fumiko Ishii. SCR: Hitomi Fujimoto, Asami Watanabe. DES: Ayume Taniguchi. ANI: Masahiro Koyama. MUS: Kazz Toyama. PRD: Ashi Pro. 45 mins. Marina and her adoring circle of gorgeous young boys are transported back in time to England in the Middle Ages (*sic*), where they help a young King Arthur acquire his sword, Excalibur. Cashing in on the success of Hitomi Fujimoto's popular *Marina the Manga Artist* series of novels for teenage girls, this one-shot was also shown theatrically. Camelot would also appear in the longer-running KING ARTHUR AND THE KNIGHTS OF THE ROUND TABLE.

MARINE BOY *

1966. JPN: *Ganbare Marine Kid*. AKA: *Go for It, Marine Kid*. TV series. DIR: Haruo Osanai, Masaharu Endo, Yoshiyuki Tomino, Suguru Sugiyama. SCR: Hiroshi Yamauchi, Masaki Tsuji, Morimasa Matsumoto, Tomohiro Ando. DES: N/C. ANI: Masaharu Endo. MUS: Tetsuo Tsukahara. PRD: Toei, TBS. 25 mins. x 78 eps. (combined series). Inspired in part by the novel *Deep Range* by Arthur C. Clarke, the Toei Studio made three pilot episodes of

Dolphin Prince, the tale of an undersea boy with a pet dolphin, who swam in a wetsuit with a built-in jetpack and stunned his enemies with an aqua-boomerang. An experiment in color anime that predated KIMBA THE WHITE LION (the first *broadcast* color anime), Suguru Sugiyama's *DP* was shelved but then remade the following year as *Marine Boy*. Marine, whose father, Dr. Mariner, is an oceanographer with the Ocean Patrol, has been genetically altered to have superior underwater swimming abilities and chews Oxygum to supply himself with air underwater. Along with his companion, Whitey the white dolphin (Splasher in the U.S. version), Marine helps his father keep the sea safe. Though originally intended for broadcast on Fuji TV and subsequent sales overseas, the production was dogged by difficulties, and taken off the air after just 13 episodes.

The series returned with the same crew in 1969, retitled *Undersea Boy Marin* (*Kaitei Shonen Marin*), for further adventures about Marine, now equipped with an underwater boomerang, a hydrojet, and a mermaid girlfriend Neptuna (Neptina in the U.S. version). It lasted for a total of 78 episodes, including some recycled from the previous series. Broadcast on TBS, the entire run was not seen until 1971, when it was shown on Nippon TV.

During all this confusion, the series was already doing well in the U.S., where it premiered in 1966. With three episodes dropped for violence, *Marine Boy* still incurred the wrath of the National Association for Better Broadcasting, which claimed it was "one of the very worst animated shows. Child characters in extreme peril. Expresses a relish for torture and destruction of evil characters." Strangely, no mention was made of Neptuna's strategically placed hair, which obscured the fact that she spent the entire series topless, or that the three "violent" episodes were considered harmless enough to be screened when the series was rerun during the 1970s. Though obscure

Yukino Miyazawa, the most popular girl in school, hides a mass of insecurities behind her calm exterior in HIS AND HER CIRCUMSTANCES. A hilarious romantic comedy from the Gainax studio, H&HC featured numerous experimental techniques, including paper cut-outs, a live-action ending sequence, and contradictory subtitles. Disenchanted with the animated medium, the former EVANGELION director, Hideaki Anno, quit the production partway through to work in live-action film. *See entry p. 174.*

His and Her Circumstances

today, *Marine Boy* was a popular anime in its time, outperformed in the 1960s only by SPEED RACER in the U.S. and the first anime to achieve any degree of success in the U.K., though its Japanese origins were occluded. According to popular myth, decades later, the same BBC that screened *Marine Boy* in the 1970s would turn down POKÉMON, claiming that "nobody was interested in Japanese cartoons." In another spurious assertion, the father of the five-year-old Jonathan Clements claimed that "Marine Boy always eats his greens," though none of our Japanese sources support this.

MARINE EXPRESS

1979. JPN: *Kaitei Cho Tokkyu Marine Express*. AKA: *Undersea Super Express: Marine Express*. TV special. DIR: Osamu Dezaki, Satoshi Dezaki. SCR: Osamu Tezuka. DES: Keizo Shimizu. ANI: Shigetaka Kiyoyama, Hitoshi Nishimura. MUS: Yuji Ono. PRD: Tezuka Pro, Nippon TV. 93 mins. Murder on the Transpacific Express, as private investigator Shunsaku Ban boards an undersea train on its inaugural trip from California to Japan in 2002, tracking the killer of the director of the Public Construction Corporation. Meanwhile, architect Dr.

Nasenkopf, much-praised designer of the train, has had a change of heart and now decides he should destroy his creation before it forever changes life in the Pacific. As if that wasn't enough, the feckless Mr. Credit, U.S. Secretary of State, is using fake passenger dummies to smuggle laser weapons, and the train's engineer is convinced that he can see visions of the legendary queen of the undersea empire of Mu (see SUPER ATRAGON). Confused? You will be, because then the train falls through a time tunnel, traveling ten thousand years back to a time before Mu sank beneath the waves. Widely regarded as one of Osamu Tezuka's best works, this TV movie manages to mix Easter Island, invading aliens, time travel, and murder mystery—which just goes to show that not every complex story line needs to be as messy as LAWS OF THE SUN. As seems traditional for Tezuka TV movies, several of his other characters make cameo appearances, including ASTRO BOY (as Adam, robot "son" of Nasenkopf, who is "played" by Dr. Ochanomizu), BLACK JACK, and the THREE-EYED PRINCE, all voiced by their original voice actors. ME, however, crams cameos in to insane levels (Queen Sapphire, Empress of Mu, is actually PRINCESS KNIGHT, who arrives riding on the adult KIMBA THE WHITE LION), and also casts against type, with many of Tezuka's traditional good-guys playing evil roles. The theme tune features vocals from Tommy Snyder of the pop group Godiego, who also contributed to GALAXY EXPRESS 999.

MARINE SNOW

1980. TV special. DIR: Leiji Matsumoto, Fumio Ikeno. SCR: Keisuke Fujikawa. DES: Leiji Matsumoto, Katsumi Sakahashi. ANI: Seiji Yamashita. MUS: Hiroshi Ogasawara. PRD: Studio Uni, Mini Art, Now Planning. 81 mins.
Another tale of underwater expansion, suspiciously similar to the previous year's MARINE EXPRESS. Once again, there is a conflict between the land and sea people, this time caused by a series of underwater cities constructed by the surface-dwellers to ease overcrowding on a future Earth. Construction worker Hiroshi Umino notices that his colleague Nami Shimaoka is behaving suspiciously—shortly afterward, construction is halted by a saboteur's bomb. Someone (no prizes for guessing who) claiming to be Izanami, the Queen of the Sea People, challenges the surface-appointed ruler Zerbert, demanding that the sea people be left in peace. Written and directed by CAPTAIN HARLOCK–creator Leiji Matsumoto.

MARIS THE CHOJO *

1986. JPN: Rumic World: The Supergal. AKA: Supergal; Maris the Wondergirl (U.K.). Video. DIR: Tadamasa Takahashi. SCR: Tomoko Konparu. DES: Katsumi Aoshima. ANI: Tadamasa Takahashi. MUS: Ichiro Arata. PRD: Studio Pierrot. 48 mins.
Space Police Officer Maris comes from Thanatos, a world of incredibly high gravity, so she has to wear a harness to prevent her superhuman strength from damaging people and objects around her—she often causes massive collateral damage nevertheless. She jumps at the chance to wipe out her debts by rescuing Koganemaru Matsushita, a handsome kidnap victim. Her mission forces her (and her alien sidekick, Murphy, the Irish-accented, nine-tailed fox) into a wrestling ring with her old rival, Zombie Sue. The harness comes off for a no-holds-barred showdown, though the entire affair is revealed to have been orchestrated by the bored Matsushita (a cop-out plot twist as unimaginative as "it was all a dream"). Combining intergalactic crime-busting of the DIRTY PAIR with a martial arts comedy from manga creator Rumiko Takahashi, this is one of her weakest offerings. Part of the Rumic World series that also brought us FIRE TRIPPER, LAUGHING TARGET, and MERMAID'S FOREST. As with IRONFIST CHINMI and LOCKE THE SUPERMAN, the original U.S. title was altered in the English-language market to avoid legal conflict with the owners of a U.S. comic character. The production was noted at the time for including fake "outtakes" along with the closing credits—an idea later adopted by Pixar for A Bug's Life.

MARMALADE BOY

1994. TV series, movie. DIR: Akinori Yabe, Atsutoshi Umezawa, Yasuo Yamakichi, Satoshi Yamada. SCR: Aya Matsui, Yumi Kageyama, Motoki Yoshimura. DES: Yoshihiko Umakoshi. ANI: Yoshihiko Umakoshi, Hiroyuki Kawano, Michio Sato. MUS: Keiichi Oku. PRD: Toei, TV Asahi. 25 mins. x 76 eps. (TV), 30 mins. (m).
A bizarre wife-swapping variant on the Brady Bunch, as two married couples decide to exchange partners and live together in an extended family, with their children Miki Koshikawa and Yu Matsura becoming stepsiblings and inevitably falling for each other. Love triangles extend into love polygons, as more male and female characters are introduced, each trying to tempt the lovers from their true desires. The initial premise, however, is stretched to absurd lengths by the series' long broadcast run, with the initial humor of the strange family setup soon fading before seemingly endless rivals in love, breakups over nothing, and reconciliations. The show's quite unexpected success caused it to run ahead of the manga, with new characters and situations not present in the original, causing the plots to diverge. In the spirit of CHILD'S TOY, a genuinely quirky setup whose quiet success far exceeded that of its more famous contemporaries—it ran for three times longer than the "mega-hit" EVANGELION. The story was cleverly completed in a 1995 "movie" that functions as both a prologue and epilogue. Flashing back to the day Yu is first told his parents are to divorce, it reveals that he has worshiped Miki from afar since before the beginning of the series and helps to explain exactly what he really sees in Miki, a mystery that had befuddled many fans for the duration of the series. Based on the 1992 manga by Wataru Yoshizumi.

MARVELOUS MELMO

1971. JPN: *Fushigina Melmo*. AKA: *Mysterious Melmo*. TV series. DIR: Osamu Tezuka, Yoshiyuki Tomino, Fusahito Nagaki. SCR: Osamu Tezuka, Morimasa Matsumoto, Tatsuo Shibayama, Ran Seki. DES: Osamu Tezuka. ANI: Shigeru Yamamoto, Toshiyasu Okada. MUS: Seiichiro Uno. PRD: Tezuka Pro, TBS. 25 mins. x 26 eps.

When her mother "goes to Heaven" after a traffic accident, young Melmo receives a jar of red and blue candy that allows her to magically age ten years and turn into a young woman and also return to her normal age. In ASTRO BOY–creator Tezuka's take on the popular magical-girl genre typified by CREAMY MAMI and LITTLE WITCH SALLY, Melmo decides to use the candy, which was intended to allow her to survive her childhood without an adult protector, for the greater good. As the series progressed, Melmo's age-swings became more pronounced—she comes close to dying of old age or regressing back to "prehuman" fetal states. This allowed her to reorder her cells as she regrew to gain temporary animal characteristics like fur or a strong sense of smell in order to aid her with the task at hand. On the 70th anniversary of Tezuka's birth, the series was rereleased on video as *Melmo: Renewal*, with an all-new voice and music track and Maria Kawamura replacing Reiko Fujita as Melmo. The story was remade again as part of a trilogy of live-action TV specials, *Osamu Tezuka Theater* (2000), along with Tezuka's *Canon* and *Lunn Flies into the Wind* (see LION BOOKS).

MASHURAMBO

2000. AKA: *Shinzo*. TV series. DIR: Tetsuo Imazawa. SCR: Mayori Sekijima. DES: Yoko Kamimura. ANI: Yoko Kamimura. Ken Ueno. MUS: N/C. PRD: Toei, TV Asahi. 25 mins. x 32 eps.

In the far future, the human race has lost a bitter war with the alien Matrixer life forms. Three hundred years after the Matrixer victory, a human boy and girl wake up from cryogenic suspension to discover that the Matrixers have overrun the surface of Earth and they are probably the last humans alive.

MASK OF GLASS

1984. JPN: *Gurasu no Kamen*. TV series. DIR: Gisaburo Sugii, Hideo Makino, Seiji Okuda, Tsuneo Tominaga. SCR: Keisuke Fujikawa, Tomoko Konparu, Tomoko Misawa, Yukifude Asakura. DES: Makoto Kuniho. ANI: Keizo Shimizu, Jiro Tsujino, Masami Abe. MUS: Kazuo Otani. PRD: Eiken, Nippon TV. 25 mins. x 23 eps.

Inspired by Chigusa Tsukikage, a star who retires due to injury, Maya Kitajima resolves to become an actress and joins her idol's theater troupe. Pushed to the limit by Chigusa, who turns out to be a tough taskmistress, Maya trains to perform the infamous Red Angel role solo, all the while repudiating the adoring advances of boy-next-door Masami Hayami and competing with her fierce rival from the Theater Undine, Ayumi Himekawa. Based on the ongoing 1976 *Hana to Yume* manga by Suzue Miuchi, *MoG* is Sugii's tribute to *Flashdance*, but it slips easily into the clichés of sports anime such as AIM FOR THE ACE, even with the sport removed. The titular "mask of glass" is the invisible dramatic energy an actress wears in front of her audience.

MASQUERADE *

1998. JPN: *Gosenzo Sane*. AKA: *Ancestor's Glory*. Video. DIR: Yusuke Yamamoto. SCR: Ryota Yamaguchi. DES: Masaki Kajishima, Kazunori Takahashi. ANI: Kazunori Takahashi. MUS: T. K. Crow. PRD: AIC. 30 mins. x 2 eps.

When his mother dies, Gen Hiraga goes to live with his grandmother, the rich chancellor of an exclusive college. Pursued by Jennifer Collins, a feisty foreign Ph.D. student, he discovers that one of his ancestors discovered the alchemical secrets of immortality. A woman who sleeps with Gen and receives his golden sperm (or "aquapermanence") can prolong her lifespan for a considerable time. Needless to say, this makes Gen popular with the ladies, starting with Beth, a nubile woman who claims to be over 400 years old, though she strangely still works as a maid for his grandmother.

As the TENCHI MUYO! audience *finally* reached puberty, the franchise had its last gasp in a couple of pornographic pastiches. SPACESHIP AGGA RUTER handled the sci-fi end, while *Masquerade* takes the same stereotypes and dumps them in a horror setting. After a suspenseful, artistic beginning that toys with the viewer's expectations for almost a quarter of an hour, the story turns to the requisite sex, falling to pieces in a ludicrous series of assignations as a set of desperate women try to milk Gen for his particular elixir of life. Laughable hokum, helped not a bit by a listless dub spoken by actors who understandably cannot believe what they are saying. **Ⓝ**

MASTER KEATON

1998. TV series. DIR: Masayuki Kojima. SCR: Tatsuhiko Urahata, Tomoko Konparu, Hideo Takayashiki. DES: Kitaro Takasaka. ANI: N/C. MUS: Kuniaki Haishima. PRD: Madhouse, Nippon TV. 25 mins. x 26 eps.

Half-English, half-Japanese ex-soldier Taichi Keaton is a divorced university lecturer and part-time private investigator on behalf of the Lloyds insurance syndicate. His work takes him into many dangerous situations, but his survivalist training always helps him out, as does his plucky daughter, Yuriko. Bravely concentrating on the more cerebral elements of the original 1988 manga by Hokusei Katsushika and Naoki Urasawa, the anime version takes Keaton all around the world, with stops at London's Chinatown (looking suspiciously like Yokohama's, which must have been closer for the studio's picture researchers), Stonehenge, the Middle East, and all over Europe. Combining the wandering, supersmart trouble-shooter of *Indiana Jones* or LUPIN III with an introverted investigator in the mold of Sherlock Holmes (even to the extent of a Baker Street office address), *MK* is also a product of its time, ditching the original Keaton's

Falklands War experience in favor of more up-to-date action in the Gulf. Seemingly influenced by the popularity of *Riverdance*, *Braveheart*, and *Titanic*, the anime production also comes heavily smeared with misplaced Celtic whimsy, particularly in Haishima's folksy musical score.

MASTER OF MOSQUITON *

1996. JPN: *Master Mosquiton*. Video, TV series. DIR: Hiroshi Negishi, Satoru Akahori. SCR: Satoru Akahori. DES: Takahiro Kishida, Kazuya Kuroda. ANI: Hideki Watanabe. MUS: Osamu Tezuka (not *the* Osamu Tezuka!). PRD: Zero-G Room, TV Tokyo. 30 mins. x 6 eps. (v), 25 mins. x 26 eps. (TV).
Tomb-raiding hokum as spunky red-haired Transylvanian schoolgirl Inaho raises the mild-mannered vampire Mosquiton as part of her quest for immortality. Eschewing the simple option of simply letting him suck on her neck, she drags him off on a treasure hunt for the legendary life-prolonging "O-part," in a madcap version of 1920s Europe that soon includes alien invaders in a giant pyramid and battles with Rasputin and the Count de Saint Germaine for control of London. With undertones of a controlling yet adoring parent and angrily dependent child who wants everything to be the same forever, *Mosquiton* shows early promise but soon buries it beneath weak humor (signposted, in typical Satoru Akahori style, by pratfalls from a writer who doubts that the audience will notice it otherwise) and strident bickering from an Inaho voice actress who may once have had depth but comes across in the dub as nothing more than a spoiled brat. The English-language script also seems ignorant of the many historical characters and references, though it does inject some genuinely funny gags, many of which were not present in the original. In Japan, the series was brought back from the dead after its video run as the TV series *Mosquiton 99*—though it was taken off the air in 1998, not surviving to reach the year for which it optimistically named itself.

MATASABURO THE WIND IMP

1988. JPN: *Kaze no Matasaburo*. Video. DIR: Rintaro. SCR: N/C. DES: Yoshinori Kanemori. ANI: Yoshinori Kanemori. MUS: Fujio Miyashita. PRD: Argos, Madhouse. 30 mins.
Heart-rending tale of new student Saburo Takada, who comes to a ramshackle school with only one classroom in a remote valley. By the time he has befriended the shy village children, it is time for a sad farewell. Based on the children's story by Kenji Miyazawa, who also created NIGHT TRAIN TO THE STARS. The same author's *Wildcat and the Acorns* was animated the same year by Toshio Hirata as a 25-minute video.

MATSUGORO THE WOLF

1989. JPN: *Okami Matsugoro*. Video. DIR: Hidetoshi Omori. SCR: Norio Soda. DES: Hidetoshi Omori. ANI: Hidetoshi Omori. MUS: N/C. PRD: Nippon Animation. 50 mins.
Schoolboy gang-leader Matsugoro swears revenge when his lieutenant Koume's house is burned down by a land speculator in an insurance scam. In this unlikely adaptation of the *Shonen Magazine* manga by Minoru Ito, Matsugoro takes on the local gangsters by himself. ◐

MAYA THE BEE *

1975. JPN: *Mitsubachi Maya no Boken*. AKA: *Adventures of Maya the Honeybee*. TV series. DIR: Hiroshi Saito. SCR: Fumi Takahashi. DES: Susumu Shiraume. ANI: Toshio Nobe, Takao Ogawa. MUS: Takashi Ogaki. PRD: Nippon Animation, Peter Film, TV Asahi. 25 mins. x 52 eps.
Flighty young honeybee Maya learns from her teacher, Cassandra, how to fly and collect pollen. But she is so good at her job that she exhausts the supply in the area surrounding her hive and must head out to find a new field of flowers—whereupon she has many adventures with beetles, grasshoppers, and her friend Willy, who is sent by the Queen Bee to find her. It's another tale of a bug's life, similar to HUTCH THE HONEY BEE but based on the 1929 children's book by Waldemar Bonsels and made as a coproduction with the German company Peter Films. The series was shown on Nickelodeon back in the days before a Japanese origin was something to boast of, and, consequently, it is not generally known as "anime." A sequel, *New Maya* (made soon after but not screened until 1982), featured a new crew and was chiefly animated by the inferior Wako Production. It centers on Maya waking from hibernation and discovering that her friend Phillip the Grasshopper's house has been burned during the winter. Meeting Phillip's savior, Mousey the mouse, they begin a series of new adventures.

MAZE *

1996. JPN: *Maze Bakunetsu Jiku*. AKA: *Maze: Exploding Dimension*. Video, TV series. DIR: Akira Suzuki. SCR: Katsumi Hasegawa, Satoru Akahori. DES: Eiji Suganuma, Masayuki Goto. ANI: N/C. MUS: N/C, Seikima-II. PRD: JC Staff, TV Tokyo. 30 mins. x 2 eps. (v), 25 mins. x 25 eps. (TV).
By day, Maze is a girl who wanders the countryside protecting exiled princess Mill of Bartonia, whose kingdom has been over run by the Jaina Holy Group. But by night, she transforms into a brash, annoying, sex-obsessed boy. A lighthearted (and lightweight) cross of RANMA 1/2 with WIZARD OF OZ, featuring the same look, plot, and often gags as Satoru Akahori's earlier BEAST WARRIORS and a stereotypical supporting cast that includes ninja Solude, the demi-hunter (barbarian warrior) Aster, the female knight Rapier, and the old wizard Woll. Their opponent is a pretty-boy cast from the same mold as ESCAFLOWNE's Dilandau and is unabashedly named Gorgeous. The original video series was designed for an audience that had already read the books and listened to the radio show, so it consequently dumps the viewer right into the middle of the

action without any explanation, expecting them to thrill to the self-indulgent quips and breakneck pace, all designed to hide the fact that nothing new is happening. For the older video audience, it is also considerably more risqué, loaded with erotic humor and innuendo. The later TV series takes things a little more slowly and conservatively, opening with Maze's original arrival in this never-never land of giant robots and dueling princes, but even this introduction does little to hide the show's off-the-peg origins, so typical of so many 1990s video anime, although this one did at least survive to reach television. **ᐧ**

MAZINGER Z *

1972. AKA: *TranZor Z*. TV series, movie. DIR: Yugo Serikawa, Tomoharu Katsumata, Fusahito Nagaki, Yasuo Yamakichi, Takeshi Shirato, Masayuki Akehi, Nobutaka Nishizawa (TV 1–2), Yoshio Hayakawa, Hideharu Iuchi (TV3). SCR: Susumu Takahisa, Keisuke Fujikawa (TV1–2), Hiroyuki Onoda, Masaki Tsuji (TV3). DES: Go Nagai (TV1–2), Satoshi Hirayama (TV3). ANI: Koji Uemura, Masamune Ochiai, Keisuke Morishita (TV1–2), Hideyuki Motohashi, Tsutomu Shibayama (TV3). MUS: Hiroaki Watanabe (TV1–2), Kentaro Haneda (TV3). PRD: Dynamic, Toei, Fuji TV (TV1–2), TMS, Nippon TV (TV3). 25 mins. x 92 eps. (TV1/*Mazinger*), 25 mins. x 56 eps. (TV2/*Great Mazinger*), 25 mins. x 23 eps. (TV3/*God Mazinger*). Robot inventor Dr. Hell (Dr. Demon) wants to control the world with his MachineBeasts, who are led into battle by his minions, Baron Ashler/Ashura (Devleen "half man, half woman, and the worst of both"), whose body is literally split down the middle, left side male and right side female, and Count Broken (Count Decapito), a cyborg who carries his head tucked underneath his arm. His attacks are resisted by the Photon Research Institute (Volcanic Research Institute). Photon inventor Dr. Kabuto's grandson, Koji (Tommy Davis), works out how to operate Mazinger Z, Kabuto's giant

super-alloy robot (see **GODAIKIN** and **SHOGUN WARRIORS**), climbing inside its head and using it to fight back against Hell, aided by his stepsister, Yumi Sayaka (Jessica), her robot Aphrodite A (later upgraded to Diana Alpha 1), and Boss Borot (Bobo-bot), a comic-relief machine driven by the local tough-guy, Boss. Based on a 1972 *Shonen Jump* manga by Go Nagai, *Mazinger Z* (*Tran-Zor Z* in the U.S.) was the first "pilotable" robot, not a sentient being like **ASTRO BOY** or a remote-controlled toy like **GIGANTOR**. This changes the relationship between the young hero (and therefore the viewer) and the robot; instead of merely observing its actions, the viewer wears it like a suit of armor and controls it as if he and the robot were one. Secondly, the robot bristled with cool weapons that were all activated by the hero calling out their names ("Rocket Punch!"), which added to the viewer's involvement in the show as well as the play value of the toys. The "gadgets 'n' gimmicks" approach was to have a long life in robot merchandising—see **GUNDAM**, **EVANGELION**, et al.

After the 43-minute crossover movie *Mazinger Z vs.* **DEVILMAN** (1973), the show returned as *Great Mazinger* (1974). With Koji absent in South America, the pilot of the new, improved prototype is Tetsuya Tsurugi, with new token girl Jun Hono (and her token girl robot Venus Ace) and Boss Borot retained from the old series. They were fighting the subterranean army of Mikene and its mechanical monsters, led by Jigoku Daisensei, the reincarnation of Dr. Hell. Koji returned for the grand finale and would also appear in the Nagai robot-series **GRAN-DIZER** along with Boss Borot. The robots appeared again in short cinema outings alongside other Go Nagai creations including *Mazinger Z vs. the General of Darkness* (1974), *Great Mazinger vs.* **GETTER ROBO** *G* (1975), and *Great Mazinger/Grandizer/Getter Robo G: Battle the Great Monster* (1976).

The concept was also rehashed as the short-lived *God Mazinger* (1983).

© A.I.C. • PIONEER LDC

Japanese teen Yamato Hibino is sucked through a time warp into the past, where the dinosaur army of the Dragonia Empire threatens the world, and Queen Aira of Mu (see **SUPER ATRAGON**) needs Yamato to help her fight back with the aid of the guardian God Mazinger, which looks suspiciously like a giant robot. Their chief opponent is the evil Emperor Dorado of Dragonia and his golden-haired son, Prince Eldo, whose vendetta against the dark-haired Yamato was only just beginning when the series was canceled. Though Nagai still drew the tie-in manga, the anime robot was designed in "the Nagai style" by Satoshi Hirayama. More remote tie-ins were the 1988 *Mazinger* manga Nagai wrote and Ken Ishikawa painted for First Comics (the first manga done specifically for U.S. release) and the Mazin Kaiser robot created for Banpresto's *Super Robo Wars* multiplatform game in 1991, which subsequently featured in the video anime *Mazin Kaiser* (2001). Finally, the lead robot in Nagai's **PSY-CHO ARMOR GOBARIAN** bears a staggering resemblance to Mazinger Z.

MD GEIST *

1986. JPN: *Sokihei MD Geist*. AKA: *Armored Devil-Soldier MD Geist*. Video.

DIR: Hayato Ikeda. SCR: Takashi Sanjo. DES: Tsuneo Ninomiya, Koichi Ohata. ANI: Hiroshi Negishi, Kenichi Onuki, Hirotoshi Sano. MUS: Yoichi Takahashi. PRD: Hero Media. 45 mins. x 2 eps. Humankind leaves Earth behind and spreads out among the stars. On the distant world of Jerra, a group of rebels called the Nexrum begin a war of attrition, demanding that Jerra split from Earth's authority and seek its own independence. In the bloody war that ensues, the military devises a series of genetically enhanced superwarriors, the Most Dangerous Soldiers. Combined with their powerful armored exoskeletons, they are unstoppable. For reasons that aren't terribly clear, one particular Most Dangerous Soldier is imprisoned on a satellite, even though the war is still raging. An indeterminate number of years later, he falls back to the surface into a ravaged postapocalyptic wasteland. After killing the leader of a biker gang, Geist (for it is he) decides to lead his new followers to save a beleaguered mobile fortress, which is coincidentally commanded by his old boss, Colonel Krups. The assassination of the president activates a Doomsday machine called Death Force, and the soldiers are on a mission to stop it, lest the world be overrun with legions of robot berserkers. Geist signs up for the final assault, lots of people get killed, and then there's an ending with several twists in it; the last of which makes the whole race-against-time of the previous hour utterly pointless.

With 1980s fashions, squealing guitar music, and simplistic postholocaust bikers-in-a-desert, Geist is a product of the era that gave us *Mad Max*, FIST OF THE NORTH STAR, and VIOLENCE JACK. And there it might have stayed were it not for the U.S. company Central Park Media, which uses Geist in its corporate logo, throwing money at the Japanese to blow the dust off this 1986 stinker and produce the previously canceled *Death Force* sequel (1996)—today, these two awful offerings are most likely to be found conjoined in a full-length "director's cut."

MD Geist is cheap and nasty, featuring some of the world's most half-hearted dialogue and plotting, including a seduction scene where a female character strips solely for the benefit of the camera—not even Geist can be bothered to watch her. The plot is riddled with holes. Why is Krups still alive when Geist returns from suspended animation? Why hasn't the supposedly oppressive Earth government sent reinforcements? Why is Death Force triggered by so inconsequential an event as the death of a president when the world has already been nuked almost to oblivion? There are tiny moments of interest, including a pastiche of *Easy Rider* (1969) when Geist destroys a pocket watch. There are the vaguest hints of subtlety as Krups and Geist duel for the men's respect; Krups by giving them half-hearted pep talks (though that could be the dub, of course), while Geist just "is" the ultimate warrior. And Jason Beck, who plays Geist in the U.S. dub, has a great voice. But these virtues are few and far between in an anime that, despite some respected names in the credits, is one of the medium's more brain-dead offerings. It was, however, the first time that U.S. interest and money resulted in the commissioning of a sequel to an anime video. *Ill. p. 443.* 🅛🅝🅥

ME AND I: THE TWO LOTTES

1991. JPN: *Watashi to Watashi: Futari no Lotte*. TV series. DIR: Kanetsugu Kodama, Yukio Okazaki. SCR: Michiru Shimada. DES: Shuichi Seki. ANI: Hisatoshi Motoki, Toyomi Sugiyama. MUS: Kazuo Otani. PRD: Tokyo Movie Shinsha, Nippon TV. 25 mins. x 29 eps. During summer school, Louise meets Lotte, a girl who looks uncannily like her. Though they initially avoid each other, they eventually become friends and discover that they are twin sisters, raised separately by their divorced parents. Resolving to get their parents back together, they swap families for a while and begin a series of deceptions in order to engineer a reunion that means the chance to live as one family. Adding several new plot threads but remaining ultimately faithful to the original, *Me and I* was based on Erich Kastner's novel *Das Doppelte Lottchen* (1949), which was also adapted into the British film *Twice upon a Time* (1954) and a couple of Hollywood versions, including *The Parent Trap* (1961). In Japan, it was also turned into a musical as well as a live-action film, which starred Hibari Misora as both girls.

MECCANO

1995. JPN: *Mechano Scientific Attack Force*. Video. DIR: Hideyuki Tanaka, Nick Phillip, Yasuaki Matsumoto. SCR: N/C. DES: N/C. ANI: Takeshi Hirota. MUS: Pierre Taki. PRD: Sun Electronics. 29 mins. A short animated collection produced by Pierre Taki of the musical group Denki Groove. It includes the CG Western *Plastic Gun Man*, *World Meccano Triangle*, for which he wrote the music, and the cel animation *Prime Minister of Gray Hill* (*Haiirogaoka no Soridaijin*). The last sequence is a parody of a famous 1977 manga by Akira Mochizuki.

MEDABOT *

1999. JPN: *Medalot Damashii*. AKA: *Medarot Spirits, Techno-Robot Battle Adventure*. TV series. DIR: Katsuhisa Yamada. SCR: Akihiko Inari, Takashi Yamada. DES: N/C. ANI: Hiroyoshi Iida. MUS: N/C. PRD: NAS, TV Tokyo. 25 mins. x 48+ eps. In A.D. 2022, children use their "medabot" robot toys to fight in "robattles." Young boy Ikki finds a medal (a medabot CPU) that has been stolen by the phantom thief Retort. Installing it in a beat-up, secondhand medalot unit, he discovers that it is a rare kind of medallion that imparts superhuman strength to its medabot. With his friends Metabee, Rokusho, Koji, and Arika, he fights off the "bad guys" Fishface, Calamari, Gillguy, and Squidguts in a succession of robot battles. This series is a cash-in on a 1977 Imagineer computer game, with robot combat indebted to PLAWRES SANSHIRO, doubtlessly brought back from the dead in the wake of POKÉMON because there are 222 basic Medalots, and merchandise beckons.

MEGAMI PARADISE *

1995. JPN: *Megami Tengoku*. AKA: *Goddess Paradise*. Video. DIR: Katsuhiko Nishijima. SCR: Katsuhiko Chiba, Mayori Sekijima. DES: Noriyasu Yamauchi. ANI: Noriyasu Yamauchi. MUS: Toshiro Yabuki. PRD: King Record. 30 mins. x 2 eps.

The Megami Paradise is a world of beauty and purity, ruled by the Mother Goddess whose protective influence shields the inhabitants from the corrupt and cruel universe. The reigning Mother Megami is due to step down soon, but her replacement has already been found in the form of the beautiful Lilith. The forces of Darkness, however, are keen on ending the blissful Megami existence once and for all, and it falls to Lilith and her amazonian cohorts to save her world from destruction. Lilith's friends Lulubell, Juliana, and Stasia set out to foil the evil plotters and keep the world safe for lingerie and fan service. Any excuse to show acres of female flesh, from the people who would go on to give us AGENT AIKA. Based on a PC game with distinctly un-PC aims. ◑

MEGAZONE 23 *

1985. Video. DIR: Yasuo Hasegawa, Hiroyuki Kitazume, Ichiro Itano. SCR: Hiroyuki Hoshiyama, Arii Emu ("REM"). DES: Toshihiro Hirano, Haruhiko Mikimoto, Shinji Aramaki, Yasuomi Umezu. ANI: Toshihiro Hirano, Masami Obari, Nobuyuki Kitajima. MUS: Shiro Sagisu. PRD: Aidoru, Artmic. 107 mins. (1), 80 mins. (2), 50 mins. x 2 eps. (3).

Bike-loving Shogo Yahagi obtains the transformable motorcycle-weapon Garland and is soon hotly pursued by the military. While location-hunting for a film he plans to make with his girlfriend's roommate, he wanders into the underground world beneath Tokyo and realizes that he is not in Tokyo at all but a facsimile built inside a spaceship, controlled by the master computer Bahamut. He is in a Megazone, a ship built to hold a billion people, one of many that fled Earth in 2331 as the planet faced imminent environmental collapse. In order to reeducate humankind to avoid making previous mistakes, the Megazones are completely virtual worlds. The occupants are convinced that they are really living in the 20th century, and the central computer, Bahamut, is programmed to maintain the illusion until such time as humankind is ready to repopulate the slowly recovering Earth. However, alien vessels are preparing to attack, and Eve, a virtual idol constructed by Bahamut, contacts Shogo through Garland and begs him to help.

A video anime given a theatrical release in Japan, *Megazone 23* shared many of the same staff as the earlier MACROSS, a fact exploited in the U.S., where it was edited into the unrelated ROBOTECH series as *Robotech: The Movie*.

The sequel, *M23: Tell Me the Secret*, features radically different artwork from new designer Umezu. Set six months later, Shogo collaborates with the Trash motorcycle gang in an attempt to regain Garland from the military. The alien Desarg are causing considerable damage to the technologically inferior crew of *Megazone 23*, but amid the battle, Shogo is reunited with his girlfriend, Yui, in a series of bed scenes cut from the video but left in the theatrical release. Eventually, Shogo saves the day, and it is revealed that *Megazone 23*'s journey has come full circle, and the time is right for humanity to return to Earth.

As the *Megazone* series drew to a graceful close, the anime business was thrown into upheaval by the runaway success of AKIRA. Mere moments after they laid their original story to rest, successfully delivering their characters from a gritty, urban nightmare, the producers turned right around and jammed them back in for the two-part finale *M23: Return of Eve* and *M23: Freedom Day*. Typically, these episodes were released abroad as *Megazone 23* with no reference to the two earlier installments. Instead of the pastoral idyll promised by the end of the original, the story restores the characters to a *Blade Runner*–esque future. Amid mock religious musings about Eve, a virtual idol who shall redeem us all from our sins, life isn't all it's cut out to be in Eden, and new hero Eiji Tanaka is a motorcycle-riding hacker who gets recruited by the government to fight computer terrorism. Except that the terrorists are the good guys, and when Eiji discovers this, he switches sides and leads a revolution from the inside.

News broadcasts make it obvious that the government is lying. People ride around on bikes. There's a conspiracy within a conspiracy. The bad guys aren't necessarily all that bad. But while these elements worked well enough in *Akira*, they leave a nasty taste in the mouth when you know that they're being deliberately swiped in a cynical cash-in—annoying enough for the screenwriter himself to use the Arii Emu pseudonym also seen in the lackluster BUBBLEGUM CRISIS spinoff *Bubblegum Crash*.

MELANCHOLY SLAVE

1997. JPN: *Ai Doru*. AKA: *Idol*. Video. DIR: Raizo Kitagawa. SCR: Yuri Kanai, Naomi Hayakawa. DES: Aidoru Project. ANI: Kazumasa Muraki. MUS: N/C. PRD: Raishin Film. 38 mins.

Bereft at her mother's death, Rachel goes into a convent, only to discover that the contemplative life is not quite as she imagined when she is bound, gagged, and sexually assaulted by lust-crazed lesbian nuns. Based on a story by BEAST CITY–creator Naomi Hayakawa. ◑◐◔

MELLOW

1993. JPN: *Mero*. AKA: *Girl-Boy*. Video. DIR: Teruo Kigure. SCR: Rin Kasahara. DES: Rin Kasahara. ANI: Teruo Kigure. MUS: N/C. PRD: KSS. 45 mins.

Trouble in the classroom when the new teacher turns out to be a transvestite.

Based on the 1991 manga by Rin Kasahara, published in *Shonen Champion*.

MELTY LANCER

1999. Video. DIR: Takeshi Mori. SCR: Hiroshi Yamaguchi. DES: Tomohiro Hirata. ANI: Shoichi Masuo. MUS: Masamichi Amano. PRD: Gonzo. 30 mins. x 5 eps. (planned as 6).

Earth has joined the galactic federation, and humanity has changed beyond all recognition. A religion that sees God in the Internet, alien technology indistinguishable from magic, and a huge Earthbound crime wave of alien crooks. Luckily, we have the Lancers on our side, Galactapol's elite crime-fighting corps, led by a man who's just served a five-year prison sentence and staffed by a gang of dangerous girlies. Sylvie Nimrod is a martial artist, Melvina McGarren only got her job because she's the boss's daughter, and cute little Angela is really an eight-year-old bioweapon. Nana (full name Nanai Nataletion Neinhalten) learned sorcery on her adopted homeworld of Promised Land, and Sakuya is a high priestess of the Arcanest Temple. Jun Kamijo, the team mecha specialist, suspects that Earth's new attackers are her old schoolgirl enemies, a team of women warriors from Mad Scientist College, called the Vanessas. And she's right.

A standard team template, stamped out originally for a PC game before jumping to the Sony PlayStation for *Melty Lancer: Galactic Girl Cops 2086* and the later tie-in game *ML: Third Planet*. A manga spinoff, *ML: Can We Return to Tomorrow?* (1998), was drawn by Akira Matsubara for *Anime V* magazine. The manga, like the anime, preferred to concentrate on gratuitous angles that ogled the female form, rather than attempting to get on with a story.

MEMORIES *

1995. Movie. DIR: Koji Morimoto, Tensai Okamura, Katsuhiro Otomo. SCR: Katsuhiro Otomo, Satoshi Kon. DES: Toshiyuki Inoue, Takashi Watanabe, Hirotsuge Kawasaki, Hidekazu Ohara.

ANI: Yoshiaki Kawajiri. MUS: Takuya Ishino, Yoko Kanno, Jun Miyake, Hiroyuki Nagashima. PRD: Madhouse. 115 mins.

An anthology film in the tradition of **ROBOT CARNIVAL** and **NEO-TOKYO**, hyped further for comprising three stories based on works by Katsuhiro Otomo. For *Magnetic Rose* (*Kanojo no Omoide*, JPN: *Her Memories*, hence the title for the film), a group of space salvage operators find a gravity well in the center of the "Sargasso" area of space. Sensing booty, they investigate, to find that the giant metal rose is the mausoleum of a famous opera singer from the 20th century. Robots and holograms on the ship recreate the events of her life and her bitterness over her rejection by her lover, Carlo; though as the visitors dig deeper, they not only discover more sinister aspects of her past, but also that the mausoleum wants to drag them into the illusions forever. For astronaut Heintz Beckner, haunted by his daughter Emily's death on Earth, this is a tempting prospect, and Morimoto's direction juxtaposes ultramodern sci-fi designs with the stately baroque interiors of the space station and the homespun farmhouse of Beckner's family. Redolent at times of Tarkovsky's *Solaris* (1971) and the poststargate scenes from *2001: A Space Odyssey* (1968), the *Magnetic Rose* sequence is one of the triumphs of anime, helped all the more by liberal extracts of Puccini's *Madame Butterfly* and *Tosca*, which manage to dwarf the other music by Yoko Kanno, Japan's greatest living composer.

The second sequence, *Stink Bomb*, reprises the runaway-weapon theme of Otomo's **ROUJIN Z**. Hapless scientific researcher Nobuo takes an antihistamine, unaware it's an experimental bioweapon that generates a fatal odor. Not realizing there are any ill effects, he heads for Tokyo to report to his bosses, while the military throw every weapon they have at him, and passersby drop dead in his tracks. Eventually, the task is left to foreign soldiers (thinly disguised Americans) whom the

canny Japanese everyman effortlessly outwits. A well-made but lightweight comedy.

The final part, *Cannon Fodder*, was the first anime Otomo directed after **AKIRA**. Originally planned as a 5-minute sequence, it ran well over time and budget, eventually reaching the 15-minute form shown. Set in a steampunk world that recalls the animation sequences of *Pink Floyd's The Wall* (1982), it features a nameless boy living in a town whose entire existence revolves around an unexplained war with a distant foe. He goes to school to learn about gunnery, while his father goes to work on one of the giant cannons, shooting an immense shell over the horizon. Shot in a drained, drab color scheme, *Cannon Fodder* is a stinging indictment of war—the boy knows nothing except fighting and dreams of cartoon soldiers. It is also a masterpiece from Otomo, planned as a single, continuous tracking shot (though this is not sustained for the entire film) and utilizing digital effects and scoring, reputedly as an experiment for *Steam Boy*, a much-delayed project whose arrival has been hotly anticipated for over half a decade.

Memories was shown at several foreign film festivals, but its disjointed nature made it a difficult sell, even to the dedicated anime fans. Reportedly, the attachment of Otomo's name to the production was regarded as such a guarantee of quality that the asking price for the foreign rights was ludicrously high. Unable to find an English-language distributor prepared to pay, the producers eventually released the film on DVD in Japan with an English subtitle track. Currently, this expensive Region 2 edition is the only English version available of one of the best anime of the 1990s.

MEMORU AND HER POINTED HAT

1984. JPN: *Tongari Boshi Memoru*. TV series. DIR: Osamu Kasai, Yukio Misawa, Junichi Sato, Hiroshi Shidara. SCR: Shunichi Yukimuro, Chifude Asakura, Ryoko Takagi. DES: Ginichiro

Suzuki. ANI: Ginichiro Suzuki, Takashi Saijo. MUS: Nozomu Aoki. PRD: Toei, TV Asahi. 25 mins. x 50 eps.

Space travelers from the planet Rilulu crash-land on Earth, where, like the characters in DAGON, they discover that they are tiny compared to the giant local inhabitants. Sneaking away from her parents, Memoru and her friends hitch a ride on the back of an owl and befriend the bedridden child Marielle. Eventually, a Rilulu rescue craft arrives to take them home, but as she prepares to leave, Memoru realizes that her departure will break Marielle's heart, and she decides to stay. The series was followed by a 15-minute "movie" outing, which combined elements of episodes 1, 2, 7, 24, and the reunion of Memoru and Marielle in episode 25.

MEREMANOID

1997. JPN: Shinkai Densetsu Meremanoid. AKA: Deep-Sea Legend Meremanoid. TV series. DIR: Shigeru Morikawa. SCR: Kenji Terada, Nobuaki Kishima. DES: Akehiro Yamada. ANI: Akehiro Yamada, Shigeo Akahori. MUS: N/C. PRD: Triangle Staff, TV Asahi. 25 mins. x 24 eps.

Life has evolved very differently on the distant world of Mere. With the planet's surface almost totally covered by water, human beings have turned themselves into sea-dwellers. The males are called mermen, and the females, for some reason, are now referred to as meremanoids. Queen Ruthmilla broods over evil plans from within the Dark Reef, and Kings Moslem and Akkadia try to thwart her. But only sorceress Misty Jo and her little brother Oz hold the key to stopping Ruthmilla's dark designs. Writer Terada previously used the name "Ruth Miller" for an evil character in BAVI STOCK—his ex-girlfriend, perhaps?

MERMAID'S FOREST *

1991. JPN: Rumic World: Ningyo no Mori. Video. DIR: Takuta Mizutani, Morio Asaka. SCR: Masaichiro Okubo, Tatsuhiko Urahata. DES: Sayuri Isseki, Kumiko Takahashi. ANI: Sayuri Isseki,

Kumiko Takahashi. MUS: Kenji Kawai, Norihiro Tsuru. PRD: Madhouse. 50 mins. x 2 eps.

Yuta is over 500 years old, a former Japanese fisherman who caught and ate the immortality-bestowing flesh of a mermaid. Though it killed his fellow sailors or turned them into feral "Lost Soul" mutants, Yuta has stayed forever young, and now he wanders modern Japan in search of others like him. One such person is Mana, a girl whom Yuta rescues from mermaid crones who intend to restore their own youth by eating her. However, she is also kidnapped by a human woman who has been deformed by ingesting mermaid's blood in an attempt to cure an illness.

Mixing JAPANESE FOLK TALES with a modern vampire analogy seemingly informed by Highlander (1985), the original 1988 Mermaid's Forest manga is one of the darker works from URUSEI YATSURA–creator Rumiko Takahashi. Though parts of the original manga concentrated on Yuta's early wanderings, the anime sequel, Mermaid's Scar (1992), opted for another modern tale. This time, Yuta and Mana arrive in another seaside town where they suspect that another woman living in another secluded mansion (coastal Japan being littered with them, it would seem) is another eater of mermaid flesh. In this they are not mistaken, since the slightly crazed Misa has recovered her beautiful looks with suspicious rapidity after the boating accident that killed her husband. Though at first believing her to be abusing her young son Masato, the pair discover that Masato is the 800-year-old manipulator of a succession of adult foils—Misa, a bereaved mother to whom he fed mermaid flesh during the WWII bombing of Tokyo, is only the latest. However, as happened in its predecessor, Mermaid's Scar's brooding Gothic soon collapses into a succession of gory fights. Its chilling premise is reduced to the straightforward rescue of a damsel in distress, and it suffers somewhat from the same inconsistencies that dog VAMPIRE PRINCESS MIYU—

Patlabor

© 1989 HEADGEAR/EMOTION/TFC

Masato's supply of 800-year-old mermaid flesh seems both inexhaustible and unperishable. Furthermore, the blurb on the box claims that Yuta is tired of immortality and searching for a way to die, though everyone already seems agreed that decapitation or immolation would both do the job nicely. One of the Rumic World series based on Takahashi's short manga tales; other entries included FIRE TRIPPER, LAUGHING TARGET, and MARIS THE CHOJO. Compare to its contemporary 3x3 EYES. ⓃⓋ

METAL ANGEL MARIE *

1995. JPN: Boku no Marie. AKA: My Dear Marie. Video. DIR: Tomomi Mochizuki. SCR: Go Sakamoto. DES: Hirohito Tanaka. ANI: Hirohito Tanaka. MUS: Hisaaki Yasukari. PRD: Victor Entertainment. 30 mins. x 3 eps.

Orphaned techno-geek Hiroshi sublimates his love for unattainable schoolgirl Marie, creating a "surrogate sister" robot who is her exact duplicate. Hiroshi has to keep his "sister's" robot nature secret while chasing the real Marie and trying to fight off all the neighborhood bad girls—who naturally find him incredibly attractive. Robot Marie isn't just a talking blow-up doll with pink hair, her affinity with machines gives her a certain power over electrical objects. She can put cars into spins, track pagers, and open doors—a kind of low-rent superpower that is very handy for keeping your "brother" away from femmes fatales. Despite her robotic limitations, she can do something that Hiroshi never can, and that's have a conversation with the real Marie without blowing a fuse. The two girls become firm friends, much to Hiroshi's chagrin, and his "sister" gets to hear all sorts of inside gossip that he would kill for. In the privacy of the girls' locker room (private, that is, except for the anime cameramen filming fan-service underwear footage), it's the robot who finds out that her twin is still available—rumors that she's dating the high-school hunk are unfounded. Hiroshi discovers that a sure-fire way of standing a better chance with girls is actually *talking* to them, and with his sister's help, he starts to take his first unsteady steps into the adult world. But, like the similar VIDEO GIRL AI, Marie isn't all that keen on helping him attain the love of his life. She'd rather *be* the love of his life, and another anime love triangle is born.

Based on a manga by Sakura Takeuchi in *Young Jump*, *MAM* mixes sports, romantic intrigue, and a slight superheroic twist, coupled with the mid-1990s craze for rearing your own creation, which peaked with TAMAGOTCHI VIDEO ADVENTURES and POKÉMON. But while popular as a manga, its video incarnation died an early death, swamped by the runaway success of the TENCHI MUYO! marketing machine. Renamed *My Dear Marie* for the subtitled version from AD Vision, presumably simply to annoy people compiling encyclopedias. Like Maria in GHOST SWEEPER MIKAMI, the robot's name is a distant homage to the robot girl in Fritz Lang's *Metropolis* (1926).

METAL FIGHTERS MIKU *
1994. JPN: *Metal Fighter Miku*. Video. DIR: Akiyuki Shinbo. SCR: Yasushi Hirano. DES: Takeshi Honda. ANI: Arihiko Sakamaki. MUS: Kenji Kawai. PRD: JC

Staff, TV Tokyo. 25 mins. x 13 eps. In 2061 the latest fad is Women's Neo Pro Wrestling—"neo" because the combatants' natural fighting abilities are augmented with high-tech metal suits. Miku, Ginko, Sayaka, and Nana team up as the Pretty Four, but when they enter a championship tournament, they seek out the help of coach Eiichi Suo, a discredited drunk. After intrigues backstage, Coach Suo rules that the Pretty Four should fight each other in a one-off match. Only a weakling would try to destroy the team by dishonorable means; therefore (obviously!) the guilty party can be hunted down through trial by combat. After this very tongue-in-cheek tale of female fascism, the team gets ready for the next match, but Miku sprains her shoulder. Miku has to overcome her injuries in order to save her team from the invincible Beauties of Nature. Realizing that the Pretty Four are undefeatable in the ring, the father-and-son baddies Shibano and Naoya resolve to destroy the team spirit by making them fight among themselves. Naoya pretends to fall in love with the hapless Miku while simultaneously encouraging Ginko to dump her teammates and head off for new pastures in America.

Wrestling has always been popular in Japan, from the quasi-religious sumo to the adoption of American-style staged matches. *MFM* belongs firmly in the latter camp; although sharp-eyed fans might be able to see more bubbling beneath the surface than straightforward babes in battlesuits. A whole generation of Japanese creators grew up watching wrestling tournaments, and there are many homages within anime (see CRUSHER JOE). One of Japan's most popular wrestling teams was an all-girl combo called the Beauty Pair, hence *MFM*'s Pretty Four, who are, logically speaking, twice as good, and the much more famous DIRTY PAIR, whom we all know to be twice as bad.

METAL JACK
1991. JPN: *Kiko Keisatsu Metal Jack*.

AKA: *Armored Police Metal Jack*. TV series. DIR: Ko Matsuzono, Akihiko Nishiyama, Jun Kamiya, Hideki Tonokatsu. SCR: Hiroyuki Kawasaki, Katsuhiko Chiba, Tsunehisa Arakawa, Ryoei Tsukimura. DES: Yorihisa Uchida, Yukihiro Makino. ANI: Hideyuki Motohashi. MUS: Fuminori Iwasaki. PRD: Sunrise, TV Tokyo. 25 mins. x 37 eps. In 2015, Tokyo is a high-tech "intelligent city," which just means that criminals also have access to even better weapons and equipment to carry out their schemes. When three young men die saving a little boy's life, they become the core of the Tokyo Police's top secret Metal Project as cyborgs who can even the score for the good guys in the fight against crime and, in particular, the criminal network known as Ido. Former police marksman Ken and his cybermutt, F-1 driver Ryo, and wrestler Go are aided and abetted by the mysterious Shadow Jack, survivor of an earlier foreign scheme to use cyborgs in police work, who escaped to Japan and now lives undercover, desperately seeking the human memories his transformation wiped out. Their powerful transforming armor and weaponry achieved its main aim of selling toys for the show's sponsors in this derivative Sunrise show that marries parts of PATLABOR and 8TH MAN to *Robocop* (1987).

METAMORPHOSES/WINDS OF CHANGE *
1978. JPN: *Hoshi no Orpheus*. AKA: *Star of Orpheus; Orpheus of the Stars*. Movie. DIR: "Takashi," Gerry Eisenberg, Richard Hubner, Sadao Miyamoto. SCR: Fujio Akatsuka, Nobuo Fujita. DES: Yukio Abe, et al. ANI: Masami Hata, Shigeru Yamamoto, et al. MUS: Billy Goldenberg, Jim Studer, Steve Tosh, Michael Young (*Meta*), Alec Costandinos (*Winds*). PRD: Sanrio. 95 mins. (U.S. edition, 80 mins.)
An animated version of five of Ovid's Roman versions of Greek myths, this film gives the stories of Actaeon, Orpheus and Eurydice, Herse and Aglauros, Perseus and Medusa, and

Phaethon. Originally planned as a modern *Fantasia* in 70mm, *Metamorphoses* featured original pop music "starring musical performances by Joan Baez, Mick Jagger & The Rolling Stones, [and] The Pointer Sisters." The music and images, however, rarely matched, and the dialogue-free action was simply mystifying to audiences. Matters were not helped by the literary device of having the hero in each of the stories played by the same character, misleading some into thinking the anthology was one long story with a plot too incoherent to follow. The *Winds of Change* version followed in 1979, with music by a single composer and a sardonic narration by Peter Ustinov explaining the adventures of "Wondermaker" as he wanders through the five tales and takes the leading role in each. A product of Sanrio's short-lived Hollywood animation studio, which made the similarly unsuccessful *Mouse and His Child*.

METROPOLIS *

2001. Movie. DIR: Rintaro. SCR: Katsuhiro Otomo. DES: Yasuhiro Nakura. ANI: Yasuhiro Nakura. MUS: Toshiyuki Honda. PRD: Madhouse, Tezuka Pro. Ca. 90 mins.
In a giant future city where robots and humans live together, the greatest construction project of all is the monstrous "Ziggurat." A man is killed in the struggle for power between Duke Red's faction and the black-shirted Marduk party; though on examination, the body is found to be an android. Meanwhile, deep in the bowels of the city where the robots labor on behalf of their masters, agitators are trying to incite rebellion among the workers. A private detective on the trail of international crime syndicate leader Professor Lawton discovers that Lawton has secretly been working on a robotics project of his own.

Tezuka had not seen Fritz Lang's *Metropolis* when he wrote the original manga in 1949, but he had seen a picture of its android Maria (see METAL ANGEL MARIE), which he incorporated into his story. His original Mitchy, who does not realize she is a robot until later in the story, was far ahead of *Blade Runner*'s Rachael, and it only seems fitting that writer Otomo should add *Blade Runner* references such as the ziggurat in this modern remake. S/he (for the original could change sex at the touch of a button) was also a forerunner for Tezuka's ASTRO BOY.

MIAMI GUNS

2000. TV series. DIR: Sadamune Koyama. SCR: To Hirami. DES: Shinichi Masaki. ANI: Hiroka Eto. MUS: N/C. PRD: Toei, Tac, TBS. 25 mins. x 13 eps.
Unlikely adventures in a fantasy version of Miami, a "stateless town" populated almost entirely by Japanese people, as schoolgirl cop Yao Sakurakoji takes on evil power barons with her sharpshooting skills and superhuman athletic abilities. Or so she thinks—like the self-centered beauties of DEBUTANTE DETECTIVES, she is actually a spoiled rich girl who is prepared to do anything to impress, even to the extent of stunning a hostage negotiator so she can force a firefight. In a template stamped straight out of the buddy-movie production line, the maverick Yao is assigned a new partner, police commissioner Amano's daughter Ru, who is cool-headed and always does everything by the book. A series with all the depth of YOU'RE UNDER ARREST!, all the originality of EHRGEIZ, and all the realism of MAD BULL 34.

MICROID S

1973. TV series. DIR: Masayuki Akehi, Hiroshi Shidara, Osamu Kasai, Minoru Okazaki, Masamune Ochiai. SCR: Masaki Tsuji. DES: Osamu Tezuka. ANI: Hiroshi Wagatsuma, Kazuo Komatsubara, Takeshi Shirato. MUS: Ko Misawa. PRD: Tezuka Pro, Toei, TV Asahi. 25 mins. x 26 eps.
Little does the human race realize that it is under threat from the Gidoron, a race of super-intelligent ants who have developed powerful weapons. Butterfly-like Yamma, Ageha, and Mamezo escape from a Gidoron base and convince humans Dr. Mishiji and his son, Manabu, to help them. In a combination of WONDERBEAT SCRAMBLE and the later MICROMAN, the microids continue the war against the ants with full-sized human assistance. Osamu Tezuka's original *Shonen Champion* manga was called *Microid Z*, but the initial letter was changed to "S" at the insistence of the show's sponsor, Seiko watches.

MICROMAN

1999. JPN: *Chiisana Kyojin Microman*. AKA: *Tiny Titan Microman; Micronauts*. TV series. DIR: Noriyuki Abe. SCR: Hiroshi Sakamoto, Yoshio Urasawa. DES: Takashi Wakabayashi. ANI: Hideo Shimosaka. MUS: Seiko Nagaoka. PRD: Studio Pierrot, TV Tokyo. 25 mins. x 52 eps.
Japanese schoolboy Kohei Kuji is understandably surprised when five of his action figures come to life and claim to be Micromen from the planet Micro-Earth, sent on a 30,000-light-year mission to save Earth from the Acroyears—"bad" Micromen who have crashed in Earth's polluted oceans and been transformed into mutants. Bold leader Arthur, blond pretty-boy Isamu, big lunk Walt, bespectacled brain Edison, and veteran tough-guy Odin enlist Kohei's help in their secret battle against the demonic invaders.

A 1980s toy sensation like ZOIDS, Microman figures began life as an economic design decision at former *GI Joe* manufacturer Takara—8-cm action figures meant smaller vehicles and lower production costs than their 30-cm counterparts. With distinctive chrome-colored heads, mounted on top of colored bodies, the toys had interchangeable parts—limbs and attachments could be swapped around by creative kids, one of whom was the young Yukito Kishiro, who cited his childhood Micromen as the inspiration for his own BATTLE ANGEL ALITA. Released in the U.S. in 1976 as the "Micronauts," the Microman line enjoyed a brief popularity before being swamped by the popularity of *Star Wars* action figures, and, as the 1980s wore on, by another Takara line, the TRANS-FORMERS. Memorable tie-ins include Michael Golden's U.S. comic *Micro-nauts* (1979), as well as a 1984 *X-Men* crossover in which the X-Men were shrunk to micro-size, and the *Micro-nauts: New Adventures* (also 1984). Though an anime series was planned in the 1980s by the Artmic studio, it was shelved as the fad of the moment changed. Revived as part of a multimedia promotion for Gameboy and PlayStation releases, Microman finally returned over a decade after it was considered finished. Not only did the new line feature some fabulous gimmicks, like a transforming base that looked like a PlayStation, all the figures were upgraded to "magnepower" status, so they could not only "use a table as a base," but also stick to the fridge and explore the rest of the kitchen, to infinity and beyond.

MIDNIGHT PANTHER *

1998. Video. DIR: Yosei Morino, Hiroshi Kogawa. SCR: Yosei Morino. DES: Rin Shin. ANI: Yosei Morino. MUS: Yosei Morino. PRD: Beam Entertainment. 30 mins. x 2 eps.

During the interdimensional apocalypse of 1999, Kate Sinclair is killed by a dragon from a parallel world. Her biotechnician lover, David Owen, tries to restore her to life, conferring a kind of immortality on himself by continual cloning. Two centuries later, an Owen clone finally finds a way. Inspired by his muse, the exotic dancer "Panther," he combines Kate's DNA with a wildcat's. The experiment is a success, but the Kate-creature kills her former lover. Panther, however, falls in love with the new her and begins murdering humans to bring her fresh meat. A hundred years later, the aged Panther runs her own cartel of assassins, one of whom is the pretty granddaughter of the long-dead Kate. But very little of the above back story is included in the anime, confusing the hell out of many U.S. viewers. Meanwhile . . .

Only boys may rule the Blue Dragon kingdom, which is why Princess Louk-ish's gender is kept secret, even from Crown Prince Bad. But Bad fears that Loukish will become the royal favorite and plots to kill his "brother" anyway. Thrown from the battlements and left for dead, Loukish is found by an old witch and soon becomes part of her traveling minstrel troupe, the Pussy-cats. She loses all memories of her previous life and of her brother's evil deeds—he now exists only as an idolized figure in her dreams.

In fact, the Pussycats are a trio of assassins who use their musical talents as a cover. The spells woven to nurse the half-drowned Lou back to health have wrought some strange side effects. While she may look like a sexy young wench, her exposure to a dragon's blood has left her with super-human strength and virtual invulnerability—though nothing has prepared her for the shocks she will have in her next mission, which is to assassinate Prince Bad himself.

Yu Asagiri's complex manga tale of incestuous family ties across generations is compressed into a 60-minute sword-and-sorcery sex romp. Without the long back story, viewers of the anime are instead thrown into the deep end with the story of little Lou—the titular Panther is actually the nameless, zany old crone who saves her young life. This is a pity, because *MP*, despite all appearances to the contrary, is not the bastard offspring of a short-lived erotic computer game, but the culmination of an artist's lifelong obsession with love, desire, and obsession itself. A terrible adaptation of a lighthearted sex-manga, unleashed upon the English-language market with little attempt to explain its origins, and an awful dub to boot. 🅒🅝🅥

MIDORIYAMA HIGH

1989. JPN: *Midoriyama Koko*. Video. DIR: Shigeru Ikeda. SCR: Shigeru Ikeda. DES: Atsuo Kurisawa. ANI: Shinichi Suzu-ki. MUS: Michiya Katakura. PRD: Balk, Onimaruya. 50 mins. x 10 eps.

The slow route to success of a school baseball team that doesn't know the meaning of the word "teamwork," adapted from the manga in *Young Jump* by Atsui Kurisawa. Over time, the power-hitter Inushima loses his desire to hit everything and concentrates on hitting the ball, while ladies' man Hanaoka devotes just enough time to helping his teammates win before chasing after more skirt. In the same vein as STAR OF THE GIANTS.

MIGHTY ORBOTS *

1985. TV series. DIR: Osamu Dezaki. SCR: Michael Reaves, Hideo Takayashi-ki. DES: Ron Maidenberg, Akio Sugino, Katsuya Kondo. ANI: Hirokata Takahashi, Satoshi Dezaki, Kazuyuki Hirokawa. MUS: Yuji Ono. PRD: Intermedia, Tokyo Movie Shinsha. 25 mins. x 13 eps.

In the 23rd century, the evil Umbra, ruling computer of the Shadow World, tries to conquer Earth, only to be held off by the brave agents of the Galactic Patrol. Though there are humanoid operatives, including the elfin commander Rondu and his beautiful daughter Dia, the GP's last line of defense is the Orbots, a group of android warriors created and led by human cybernetics genius Rob Simmons. Simmons rides in his Beam Car with his flustered robo-assistant, Ono—the other Orbots can function separately or combine to form a mighty super-robot (somehow suddenly 50 feet tall), comprising Tor (torso), Bolt and Crunch (left and right leg), and Bo and Boo (left and right arm). Additionally each of the robots (except Crunch, for some reason) has a special ability—strength, customizable gadgets, energy beams, and teleportation/invisibility, which the whole of the group can access in Mighty Orbot mode.

A rare case of a genuine U.S.–Japan coproduction, blown out of the water by the runaway success of TRANSFORM-ERS and limited to a single season. With the same team's *Galaxy High School*, it was part of a concerted effort by TMS to break into the U.S. market in coalition with producer Fred Silverman.

The inept Bolt and Crunch were added to the lineup purely for "comic" relief, though fans' most frequently asked question was why super-inventor Rob built two bumbling incompetents.

MIGHTY SPACE MINERS *

1994. JPN: *Oira Uchu no Tankofu.* Video. DIR: Umanosuke Iida. SCR: Ritsuko Hayasaka, Tsutomu Iida. DES: Toshihiro Kawamoto, Isamu Imakake. ANI: Toshihiro Kawamoto. MUS: Kenji Kawai. PRD: Triangle Staff, KSS. 30 mins. x 2 eps.

In A.D. 2060, an accident at the Toutatis asteroid mine forces the colonists to survive on their wits alone in the deadly environment of space. A supposedly realistic "hard SF" study of the dangers of zero-gravity life, based on a story by "Horceman Lunchfield." However, such a noble claim is somewhat ruined by having a character who survives exposure to vacuum and another with Big Anime Hair, hardly suitable for tough life in the asteroid belt.

MIKAN'S DIARY

1994. JPN: *Mikan e Nikki.* AKA: *Mikan Picture Diary.* TV series. DIR: Noboru Ishiguro. SCR: Mayumi Koyama. DES: Noboru Sugimitsu. ANI: N/C. MUS: Toshiki Hasegawa. PRD: Bandai. 25 mins. x 31 eps. (pilot, 5 mins.).

A cute kitten keeps a diary about life in the human world. A setup in the style of the more famous I AM A CAT, though this adaptation of Mimei Ogawa's manga in *Lala* magazine is aimed at a far younger audience, with trips to the seaside, Christmas parties, and even a vacation in America. Presumably, a trip to the U.K. was ruled out because "Mikan's Six-Month Quarantine Diary" wasn't catchy enough. When released on video, the final installment included the five-minute pilot film.

MILK HOUSE DREAMING

1987. Video. DIR: Hiroyuki Torii. SCR: Asami Watanabe. DES: Yumiko Kawahara. ANI: Yoshiyuki Momose. MUS: Taeko Onuki. PRD: Kadono Superstation. 43 mins.

An "image video" in the tradition of CIPHER, setting watercolors from Yumiko Kawahara's 1983 manga to a series of 11 pop songs. Made to cash in on the artist winning the Shogakukan Best Young Female Artist Award.

MILKY PASSION

1990. JPN: *Milky Passion: Ai no Shiki.* AKA: *MP: Love in Four Seasons.* Video. DIR: Takashi Imanishi. SCR: Takashi Imanishi. DES: Moriyasu Taniguchi. ANI: Moriyasu Taniguchi. MUS: Natsui Okamoto. PRD: Animation 501. 30 mins.

In this sexy tale based on a manga by Milk Morizono, one of the shining stars of women's erotica, the attractive owner of a love hotel falls in love with her handsome manager. Their different class backgrounds come between them, and she is tempted by the arrival of a rich American hotel magnate; though she eventually returns to the arms of her Motel Mellors. See also HER NEED FOR EMBRACE. Ⓝ

MILLENNIUM ACTRESS *

2001. JPN: *Sennen Joyu.* Movie. DIR: Satoshi Kon. SCR: Sadayuki Mural, Ko Matsuo. DES: Takeshi Honda. ANI: N/C. MUS: N/C. PRD: Genco. 87 mins.

Small-time film producer Genya Tachibana is hired to make a documentary commemorating the 70th anniversary of Gin Ei film Studios. He chooses to interview Chiyoko Fujiwara, a one-time superstar actress who has lived as a recluse for 30 years. Fujiwara's life story combines fragments of 20th-century history (compare to OSHIN) with dramatic incidents from her acting career, blurring the boundaries between reality and fiction in a similar fashion to the same staff's earlier PERFECT BLUE. It also discloses the events behind Fujiwara's fall from favor, leading to inevitable comparisons with the desolate opera star of Katsuhiro Otomo's MEMORIES.

MIRACLE GIANTS

1989. JPN: *Miracle Giants Domu-kun.* TV series. DIR: Takashi Watanabe,

La Blue Girl

© 1992 T. MAEDA / DAIEI CO. LTD.

Koichi Chiaki, Masahito Sato, Masao Ito. SCR: Haruya Yamazaki, Michiru Shimada, Tsunehisa Ito. DES: Hatsuki Tsuji. ANI: Hatsuki Tsuji. MUS: N/C. PRD: Studio Gallop. 25 mins. x 10 eps.

Short-lived baseball story based on a manga by Shotaro Ishinomori, in which fifth-grade baseball prodigy Domu joins his late father's team and plays against anime versions of many real-life stars of Japanese baseball.

MIRACLE GIRLS

1993. TV series. DIR: Takashi Anno, Satoshi Kimura, Hiroyuki Kuzumoto, Akitaro Daichi, Kazuhiro Sasaki. SCR: Hirokazu Kobayashi, Asami Watanabe, Takashi Waguri, Miho Maruo. DES: Masayuki Sekigane. ANI: Ryoko Hata, Mariko Fujita. MUS: Michiru Oshima. PRD: Japan Taps, NAS, Nippon TV. 25 mins. x 51 eps.

The 15-year-old Matsunaga girls are identical twins with very different personalities—the tomboyish Tomomi and the feminine Mikage. Both, however, have the paranormal powers of telepathic communication, limited telekinesis, and teleportation (but only if they both concentrate). The girls are brought closer together when Mikage's boyfriend Kurashige leaves to study in faraway England. They teleport to foil a hijack attempt on his plane, but after this semi-superheroic beginning, the series soon settles into a much more mundane story line. The twins occasionally swap identities, sometimes as a prank, sometimes to help each other out of difficult situations, and use their powers to cheat on the occasional exam or win the occasional sporting event. But as in the similar KIMAGURE ORANGE ROAD, the paranormal elements are swamped by more everyday teenage concerns. Based on the feel-good manga by Nami Akimoto in *Nakayoshi* magazine, *MG* is a sideways look at love and growing up, with occasional detours through time travel, ghost stories, and postmodern japery—in one episode, the voice actresses find other jobs and the twins must get them back to the studio! Episodes also steal from JAPANESE FOLK TALES, and even pastiche *The Red Shoes*, but the characters are so endearing that they more than compensate for the patchwork series of plots. The final episodes add a CINDERELLA twist, where the twins are revealed to be the prophesied saviors of the kingdom of Diamas and must fight the evil Mr. X for control of the country. By the end, everything has returned to normal, the girls are back home, and Mikage continues her chaste epistolary relationship with her absent boyfriend.

MIRACLE OF LOVE
1982. JPN: *Ai no Kiseki: Dr. Norman Monogatari*. AKA: *Miracle of Love: The Story of Dr. Norman*. TV special. DIR: Masami Annai, Yasuo Hasegawa. SCR: Toshi Nagasaki. DES: Yoshitaka Amano. ANI: Hiroshi Yamane, Kazutoshi Kobayashi, Noriko Yazawa, Noboru Furuse. MUS: Chikara Ueda. PRD: Kokusai Eiga, Studio Gallop, TV Asahi. 85 mins.
Dr. Oppenheimer ruins a promising medical career when he kills a small child in a car accident. Hiding from the police, he changes his name to Norman and lives among the people of the slums. When property developers try to clear away the slum-dwellers to build a theme park, Norman defends their rights, though his public good deeds allow Detective Gavan to finally catch up with him. A tale of sin and redemption, screened on Christmas Eve.

MIREI
1995. JPN: *Kotoyoshi Yumisuke Mirei*. AKA: *Yumisuke Kotoyoshi [presents] Mirei*. Video. DIR: Akira Nishimori, Takashi Yoshida. SCR: Yumisuke Kotoyoshi, Nana Okatsu, Masao Oji. DES: Yumisuke Kotoyoshi, Naoki Ohei. ANI: Mitsuharu Miyamae. MUS: N/C. PRD: Reed, TDK Core. 30 mins.
In this adaptation of Yumisuke Kotoyoshi's manga, two beautiful girls are washed ashore on a South Sea island paradise, where they proceed to take their clothes off. ⓝ

MIROKU
1989. JPN: *Kyomu Senshi Miroku*. AKA: *Expunged Chronicle of Miroku*. Video. DIR: Toshio Takeuchi, Junichi Watanabe. SCR: Hideo Takyashiki, Megumi Hiyoshi. DES: Hideyuki Motohashi. ANI: Hideyuki Motohashi. MUS: Michiaki Kato. PRD: Animate Film, Dynamic, JC Staff. 30 mins. x 6 eps.
Psychic ninja fantasy suggesting that the assassins did not die out during the early modern period but burrowed under Japan, where they fought a new war against the alien occupants of a crashed spaceship that has lain undisturbed for several millennia. The shogun Ieyasu is just one of the historical figures who wander into this decidedly unhistorical plot that was based on a story written for *Shonen Captain* magazine by GETTER ROBO–cocreator Ken Ishikawa.

MIRROR OF AREI
1985. JPN: *Arei no Kagami*. Movie. DIR: Kozo Morishita. SCR: Michiru Umadori. DES: Leiji Matsumoto. ANI: Kazuo Komatsubara. MUS: Yuri Nishimura. PRD: Toei. 25 mins.
Meguru and Mayu are two future-wanderers hoping to find the mythical Mirror of Arei that is said to allow all who glimpse it to pass beyond the edge of the universe. Hijacked by renegade android Zero, the trio joins forces when they realize that they are all searching for the same thing. At the edge of our universe they encounter the ethereal being Rin'ne (Japanese for transmigration) and a council of spirits who judge those who wish to enter a new universe. The gatekeeper, Arei, is not impressed with what the travelers' memories tell her of human history. Though the humans try to argue their case, Arei decides to destroy the mirror. Though it will strand them for eternity, the humans use their gravity generator to hold the mirror together so that others may not be denied the opportunity to see it. Arei is impressed by their noble sacrifice and reveals that the mirror was not really destroyed. She sends them home but first permits them a fleeting glimpse of the wonders of the next world. Based on a manga by GALAXY EXPRESS 999–creator Leiji Matsumoto, this film was originally screened at the 1985 World Expo in Tsukuba.

MISHA THE BEAR CUB
1979. JPN: *Koguma no Misha*. TV series. DIR: Yoshikata Nitta. SCR: Shunichi Yukimuro, Yoshiaki Yoshida, Ryuzo Nakanishi. DES: Isamu Noda. ANI: Yutaka Oka, Sadao Tominaga, Takashi Saijo, Yoshiyuki Kishi. MUS: Shunsuke Kikuchi. PRD: Trans Arts, Nippon Animation, TV Asahi. 25 mins. x 26 eps.
Misha the Russian bear cub comes with his parents to a peaceful mountain village full of different kinds of animals. The animals come out to see the train, but Misha's father believes they are a welcoming committee and decides to stay. Misha befriends Natasha (another bear cub) but must avoid the evil local tiger (unimaginatively named Tiger). It's a simple children's series made to cash in on the 1980 Moscow Olympics' Misha mascot. Not quite as successful as the later Olympic anime EAGLE SAM.

MISTER AJIKKO
1987. AKA: *Mr. Flavor*. TV series. DIR:

Yasuhiro Imagawa, Makoto Ikeda, Akihiko Nishiyama, Kunihisa Sugishima, Akio Yamadera, Tatsuo Suzuki, Junichi Sakata, Tetsuro Amino. SCR: Noboru Shiroyama, Akinori Endo, Noboru Aikawa, Yoshikazu Sakata, Ryoei Tsukimura, Yoshinori Watanabe, Toshifumi Kawase. DES: Masahiro Kato. ANI: Nobuhiro Okaseko, Kazuko Yano. MUS: Oku Fujita. PRD: Sunrise, TV Tokyo. 25 mins. x 99 eps.

They call him "Mr. Flavor" because middle-school boy Yoichi is one of the best chefs around, taking on and learning from masters in the many subsets of cooking, including spaghetti, sushi, steak, sardine *gratin*, ramen, omelets, hamburgers, *okonomiyaki*, *bento* boxes, curry, hotpot, and *donburi*. And that's just in the first season. Mr. Flavor returned for two more, until he walked off into the sunset on a quest for even better recipes with a final episode entitled "Gochiso-sama, Mr. Ajikko," the traditional Japanese thanks for a hearty feast. A gourmet anime aimed at a younger audience than the following year's OISHINBO, based on the 1986 *Shonen Magazine* manga by Daisuke Terasawa, who wrote the similarly foody *Ryota's Sushi*.

MISTER HAPPY *
1989. JPN: *Yarukimanman*. AKA: *Ready-to-get-it-on Man; Mad-for-it-man*. Video. DIR: Teruo Kigure, Masamune Ochiai. SCR: Masahito Nishio. DES: Masamichi Yokoyama. ANI: Jiro Sayama. MUS: N/C. PRD: Knack. 26 mins., 45 mins., 40 mins.
Kazua Jinno is the scion of Japan's oldest and most accomplished family of brothel keepers. In preparation for Kazua's taking over the family business, his father, Sopetuen, sends him out into the world to have sex with as many women as possible while always ensuring that the ladies come first (how this is training for running a brothel, Lord knows). He is aided in his erotic misadventures by "Mr. Happy," his talking penis, who provides advice and commentary at relevant moments. The Japanese sales sheet thoughtfully adds,

"The ultimate sex battles developed by his proud penis together with women's juicy vaginas never stop making the lower half of men's bodies hot." Based on the 1977 manga in *Daily Gendai* by "Gyujiro" and AGEMAN AND FUKU-CHAN–creator Masamichi Yokoyama and reputedly screened on a U.S. adult cable channel in the 1990s. ⓛⓝ

MISTER PEN-PEN
1986. TV special. DIR: Ken Baba, Tsukasa Sunaga, Yuzo Yamada, Hiroshi Watanabe. SCR: Kenji Terada. DES: Mayumi Muroyama. ANI: Takahisa Kazukawa. MUS: Takeo Watanabe. PRD: Shinei, TV Asahi. 60 mins. 2 eps.
Pen-Pen, the hat-and-tie-wearing prince of Penguin Land, turns up unexpectedly on little Mika's doorstep and invites himself and his zany penguin friends to stay. Based on a manga written by ASARI-CHAN-creator Mayumi Muroyama for Shogakukan's *Second Grader* magazine and comprising eight 15-minute mini-episodes, these two TV "specials" may be a salvage job from a canceled TV series. It had friends in high places, however—Hideaki Anno would incorporate a genetically engineered penguin called Mr. Pen-Pen into his own EVANGELION.

MIYUKI
1983. TV series. DIR: Mizuho Nishikubo, Hiroko Tokita, Shigeru Omachi, Shigeru Yanagawa, Junichi Sakata. SCR: Michiru Shimada, Shikichi Ohashi. DES: Mitsuru Adachi. ANI: Hayao Nobe, Kazuhiro Oga. MUS: Ryan Merry, Masamichi Amano. PRD: Kitty Film, Fuji TV. 25 mins. x 37 eps.
Two high school students discover they have the same name and become friends, but both fall in love with Masato, a boy who is forced to choose just one. Based on the 1980 *Shonen Sunday* manga by Mitsuru Adachi and the first of his many works to be adapted into anime. Others would include TOUCH, H2, NINE, and SLOW STEP.

MIYUKI-CHAN IN WONDERLAND *
1995. JPN: *Fushigi no Kuni no Miyuki-*

chan. AKA: *Miyuki-chan in the Strange Kingdom*. Video. DIR: Seiko Sayama, Mamoru Hamazu. SCR: Nanase Okawa. DES: Tetsuro Aoki. ANI: N/C. MUS: Toshiyuki Honda. PRD: Animate Film. 29 mins.
A pointlessly kinky retelling of ALICE IN WONDERLAND in which all the characters are sapphically inclined females. Japanese schoolgirl Miyuki is late for school when she is distracted by a bunny-girl on a skateboard. She is dragged into a sex-obsessed Wonderland, complete with strip chess, Humpty Dumpty as a svelte diva, a bondage Queen, and a Cheshire cat resembling a blonde, stockinged Lum from URUSEI YATSURA. Based on the manga by the all-girl collective CLAMP, *MiW* appeared intermittently in *Newtype* over several years, and its absent plot is explained with the age-old get-out clause of it all being a dream. A one-note gag that falls crushingly flat when the clever designs are forced to do more than look good on paper. *Ill. p. 193*. ⓝ

MOBY DICK IN SPACE
1997. JPN: *Hakugei Densetsu*. AKA: *Legend of the White Whale*. TV series. DIR: Osamu Dezaki. SCR: Osamu Dezaki, Akio Sugino. DES: Hirotoshi Takaya. ANI: N/C. MUS: Masahiro Ando. PRD: Image K, Studio Junior, NHK2. 25 mins. x 23 eps.
The Space Federation Police ship White Whale cruises the cosmos in search of pirates ("whale hunters"), tangling with the most infamous—its old nemesis, the one-eyed, one-legged Captain Ahab. A curious sci-fi retelling of Herman Melville's *Moby Dick* from the whale's point of view, its satellite broadcast was split into two sections by financial difficulty, resulting in a year-long hiatus after episode 18.

MOCHI MOCHI TREE, THE
1992. JPN: *Mochi Mochi no Ki*. Video. DIR: Isamu Noda. SCR: Takasuke Saito. DES: N/C. ANI: Susumu Shiraume, Hidekazu Ohara. MUS: Keiichiro Hirano. PRD: Ask Kodansha. 20 mins.
In this adaptation of a lyrical children's

best-seller by Ryusuke Saito and Jiro Takihira, an ailing old man talks about the meaning of life with the shy little boy who keeps him company. The same crew followed with *The Mountain in Full Bloom* (1992, *Hanasaki Yama*), based on another story by the same authors, in which an old woman tells a young girl that a flower opens every time someone does a good deed.

MODERN DOG TALES BOW WOW

1993. JPN: *Heisei Inu Monogatari Bow Wow*. TV series, movie. DIR: Takeshi Kaga. SCR: Yasuhiro Komatsuzaki, Shunichi Yukimuro. DES: Terry Yamamoto. ANI: N/C. MUS: N/C. PRD: Nippon Animation. 25 mins. x 40 eps. (TV), 25 mins. (m).

Based on the manga by Terry Yamamoto in *Big Comic Superior*, here are the comic misadventures of a lovable stray mongrel called Bow Wow and his little-girl owner. The situations are a standard list of food-related story lines, a few interfering cats, and a trawl through the various seasonal events of the Japanese and Western calendar. For the short "movie" version, however, the story sends the couple back to prehistoric times, where they must save a friendly mammoth from an erupting volcano.

MODERN LOVE'S SILLINESS

1999. JPN: *Anime Ai Awa Awa Hour*. AKA: *Anime Lovers' Awa-Awa Hour*. TV series. DIR: Makoto Moriwaki, Kume Issei. SCR: Chika Hojo, Motoki Yoshimura. DES: Yukiko Ohashi, Wataru Yamaguchi, Shuri Nakamura. ANI: N/C. MUS: Minami Toriyama. PRD: Gainax, Pioneer, Tac, DirecTV. 5 mins. x 48? eps.

Three short gag anime presented in a late-night anthology show, aimed at adult women instead of the usual male or fan audiences for anime and produced by Hideaki Anno in the midst of his work on HIS AND HER CIRCUM-STANCES. The first, *Ebichu Minds the House* (*Oruchuban Ebichu*), based on the *Manga Action Pizazz* manga by Risa Ito, portrays modern life from the viewpoint of a hamster, Ebichu, who

observes his Tokyo Office Lady owner's kinky relationship with her slacker boyfriend. Some of the show's controversial sex scenes were cut from the original digital TV broadcast but reinstated in the DVD release.

Little Women in Love (*Ai no Wakakusayama Monogatari*), based on the manga in *Manga Club* by Reiko Terashima, concentrates on unmarried Shizuka, still living with her parents, who fear she will be left perpetually on the shelf.

The final story, based on Mitsue Aoki's manga *Here Comes Koume* (*Koume-chan ga Iku*), switches location to the distinctive accents and attitudes of Osaka (see COMPILER), where Koume works as a designer for the Caramel Ribbon company with a fey boss, an assistant who used to be a bad-girl biker, and a tough-guy boyfriend. ⊕

MOJACKO

1995. TV series. DIR: Tetsuya Endo, Norihiko Sudo, Satoshi Inoue, Masamitsu Hidaka, Masashi Abe. SCR: Raita Okura, Shikichi Ohashi, Hiroshi Koda, Yasuhiro Komatsuzaki, Chika Hojo, Atsuhiro Tomioka. DES: Hidetoshi Owase. ANI: Hidetoshi Owase. MUS: Kei Wakakusa. PRD: OLM, Shogakukan Pro, Tokyo TV. 25 mins. x 73 eps.

Ghost-hunting schoolchildren Sorao, Miki, and Wu-Tang find a crashed spaceship belonging to Mojacko, an alien from the planet Mojamoja, and his robot, Donnoh. He takes them on a journey to the moon (with the aid of handy "air pills"), which is only one of many great adventures—though in exchange, he wants to learn about wacky Earth pursuits like roller-blading, golf, and scuba diving. He also enlists his new friends in a battle against the fearsome Maharaja Moja clan of space pirates. An unremarkable children's anime based on a manga by DORAEMON–cocreator Fujiko F. Fujio, though it was an early voice-acting job for PERFECT BLUE's Junko Iwao. The series would eventually lose its animation director, Endo, to Hong Kong,

where he would work on Tsui Hark's *Chinese Ghost Story* animation. Episodes 60 and 61 were rebroadcast as a one-hour TV movie with the title *Fujio F. Fujiko's Mojacko Christmas Present*.

MOLDIVER *

1993. Video. DIR: Hiroyuki Kitazume. SCR: Ryoei Tsukimura, Manabu Nakamura. DES: Hiroyuki Kitazume. ANI: Hiroyuki Kitazume, Masashi Handa. MUS: Kei Wakakusa. PRD: AIC, Pioneer. 30 mins. x 6 eps.

Tokyo, 2045. Superhero Moldiver rights wrongs and strikes poses all over the city, and pretty Mirai Ozora discovers that Moldiver is actually her brother, Hiroshi. Hiroshi's suit allows the user to repel and defy all laws of physics, which makes flight, bulletproofing, and incredible strength easy. Mirai decides to be a superhero herself, and Hiroshi gets a shock and a half when he finds himself wearing his sister's revealing costume!

Bright, colorful, and fun, *Moldiver* is packed with gentle jibes at the superhero phenomenon and very aware that the only crime in this kind of anime is taking oneself too seriously. With plot lines and characters from a kiddie-cartoon, but a tongue-in-cheek self-awareness aimed at a far older audience, it's also another excellent example of how good English-language translation can be. The humor in Pioneer's dub crosses international borders with deceptive ease. Neophytes might be a little confused by Professor Amagi's attempt to raise the Yamato from the seabed in episode four, but they should be told that this old battleship has many resonances for a slightly older anime audience. It's as famous in Japan as the Titanic in the English-speaking world, with extra baggage brought by its place in military history. For anime fans, of course, it's also the star of STAR BLAZERS, and its appearance here is a tip of the hat from Pioneer's next generation to the classic creators who inspired them to pursue their careers in the first place.

The initial letters of the episode

titles ("Metamorforce," "Overzone," "Longing," "Destruction," "Intruder") spell the name of the series, right up until the final episode ("Verity"), which crams the rest of the title in one go—possibly a sign of an early cancellation.

MOMOKO

1989. Video. DIR: Hideo Norei. SCR: Masahito Nishio. DES: Haru Hosokawa. ANI: N/C. MUS: N/C. PRD: Clion Soft. 45 mins. x 2 eps.

The life of "fashion model and masseuse" Momoko is detailed in this saucy adaptation of Haru Hosokawa's manga in *Comic Be* told in a combination of animated images on live backgrounds. With little else to recommend it, the marketing for this tape declared itself to be a "CVP," a "Comic Video Picture." Compare to MY FAIR MASSEUSE. **N**

MOMOTARO

1989. JPN: *Momotaro Densetsu*. AKA: *Legend of Momotaro*. TV series. DIR: Masamune Ochiai, Yuji Ikeno, Koichi Fujiwara, Teruo Kigure, Akinori Yabe. SCR: Tadaaki Yamazaki, Shunichi Yukimuro. DES: Kazuo Mori, Hideo Okamoto. ANI: Kazuo Mori. MUS: The Peach Boys. PRD: Knack, TV Tokyo. 25 mins. x 48 eps.

A childless woodcutter and his wife adopt Momotaro, a foundling child who springs from the inside of a peach. The superstrong child defeats Lord Brindled Dog, Lord Monkey of the Mountain, and Lord Pheasant of the Moor, who agree to become his traveling companions as he sets out to defeat all the ogres on the nearby island of Onigashima. Perhaps distantly inspired by JOURNEY TO THE WEST, one of the most famous of the JAPANESE FAIRY TALES, and a perennial children's favorite, the story of Momotaro is retold here with some science-fictional elements and a pastiche of Kurosawa's *Seven Samurai*. Pheasant Keeko, dog Pochi, and monkey Monta are asked by harassed villagers to find a hero who can save them—they approach Momotaro, who is famed far and wide for his

naughtiness (guaranteed to annoy ogres everywhere). For the latter half of the series it was rebranded as *New Momotaro (P[each] C[ommand] Shin Momotaro Densetsu)*, in which the stout Japanese boy and his companions head off into space for a more fantastical sequel. See also VIDEO PICTURE BOOK.

MOMOTARO'S DIVINE SEA WARRIORS

1945. JPN: *Momotaro Umi no Shinpei*. Movie. DIR: Mitsuyo Seo. SCR: Kiichiro Kumaki. DES: Mitsuyo Seo. ANI: Mitsuyo Seo, Ichiro Takagi. MUS: Yuji Koseki. PRD: Shochiku, Geijutsu, Japanese Imperial Navy Department of Information. 74 mins. (b/w).

After completing their naval training, a bear cub, a monkey, a puppy, and a pheasant say goodbye to their families. The monkey's young brother plays with his sailor's cap and falls into a river trying to retrieve it. He is rescued by the other animals in the nick of time, before falling over a waterfall. The scene jumps to a South Pacific island, where the rabbit sailors of the Imperial Navy are clearing the jungle to build an airfield. Watched in fascination by the native creatures (who, rather strangely for the South Pacific, include kangaroos, elephants, tigers, leopards, and rhinos), they complete it just in time for the arrival of a fleet of transport planes, bringing the animals from the former sequence, as well as a human boy, Commander MOMOTARO. While the military creatures get acclimated, the puppy teaches the local child-animals a nursery rhyme about the Rising Sun. Training takes a more meaningful turn when recon planes bring pictures of the British base on the other side of the island. The monkey, bear, and puppy begin parachute training, while the pheasant becomes a pilot. Presenting a history lesson using silhouette animation, Momotaro explains that Europeans have stolen Asia from its rightful rulers, and that the time has come to fight back. The animals attack the British base in a jarringly violent change of tone from the

© 1987/1995 BANDAI VISUAL

previous sequences, and the cowardly British ogres each try to get the other to take the responsibility for signing the surrender. Back home in Japan, the animals rejoice at the defeat of the British, while children play at parachuting . . . onto a map of the United States.

A sequel of sorts to the WARTIME ANIME *Momotaro's Sea Eagles* (1943), *MDSW* was Japan's first full-length animated feature, released mere weeks before the end of the war. In a coincidental similarity to many later anime "movies," it has a disjointed quality, seemingly resulting from the output of separate teams; one on the opening pastoral, one on the island sequences, and another on the "why-we-fight" exposition. Inspired by Japanese screenings of *Princess Iron Fan* (a Chinese adaptation of JOURNEY TO THE WEST), Seo keeps to a slow pacing, with time out for comparisons such as paratroopers to falling dandelions. He also appears to have found native English-speakers to play the British in the surrender scene—perhaps prisoners of war?

In 1983, (ironically, a year dominated by the pacifist BAREFOOT GEN), the lost film was rediscovered in Shochiku's Ofuna warehouse and rereleased in 1984. It eventually made it to video, bundled on the same tape as *The Spider and the Tulip* (1943), an unrelated 16-minute short in which a black-faced spider, seemingly modeled on Al Jolson in *The Jazz Singer*, tries to tempt a ladybug into his web. The inclusion of Kichiro Kumaki's film seemed calculated, as in its original year of release, to distract audiences from wartime realities, albeit for different reasons. After the war, director Seo made the featurette *The King's Tail* (1947), before retiring from anime and becoming a children's author and illustrator. Producer Tadahito Mochinaga emigrated to Manchuria shortly before the close of the war. After the Communist revolution, he was instrumental in the foundation of the Shanghai Animation Studio, which would not only rejuvenate the Chinese animation industry, but would also subsequently work as a Japanese subcontractor on many later anime. *Ill. p. 133.*

MONARCH: THE BIG BEAR OF TALLAC

1977. JPN: *Seton Dobutsu Monogatari: Kuma no Ko Jacky.* AKA: *Seton's Animal Tale: Jacky the Bear Cub.* TV series. DIR: Yoshio Kuroda. SCR: Ryuzo Nakanishi, Michio Sato. DES: Yasuji Mori. ANI: Takao Kogawa, Shinichi Tsuji, Koichi Murata, Seiji Okuda, Isao Takahata. MUS: Akehiro Omori. PRD: Nippon Animation, TV Asahi. 25 mins. x 22 eps.

Ran the Native American boy lives high in the Sierra Nevada mountains of California, where he cares for a brother-bear and sister-bear he found as cubs in a cave. Calling them Jacky and Jill, he plays with them and their mother, until the mother bear is killed by Ran's father. Adopting Jacky and Jill as his own, Ran takes them back to his house. An adaptation of one of Ernest SETON'S ANIMAL TALES that was soon to be followed by BANNERTAIL THE SQUIRREL.

MONCHICHI TWINS, THE

1980. JPN: *Futago no Monchichi.* TV series. DIR: Tetsuro Amino, Mariko

Oizumi, Ryoji Fujiwara, Tatsuya Matano. SCR: Akiyoshi Sakai, Masaaki Sakurai, Tomomi Tsutsui. DES: N/C. ANI: Mamoru Tanaka, Minoru Tajima. MUS: N/C. PRD: Ashi Pro, Tokyo 12 Channel. 6 mins. x 130 eps.

Monchichi-kun and Monchichi-chan are simian twins who live in the forest. He "likes to play and she likes to be cute," and they get up to many fairy-tale-inspired adventures in the countryside. A long-running cartoon series made to cash in on the dolls made by the Sekiguchi corporation, which were also released by Mattel for the U.S., where they were accompanied by the less-successful all-American cartoon series *The Monchichis.*

MONCOLLÉ KNIGHTS *

2000. JPN: *Rokumon no Moncollé Knight.* AKA: *Mon[ster] Colle[ction] Knight of Rokumon.* TV series. DIR: Yasunaga Aoki, Akitaro Daichi, Akira Kiyomizu, Shunji Yoshida, Akio Sato. SCR: Katsumi Hasegawa, Satoru Akahori, Reiko Yoshida. DES: Atsuko Nakajima. ANI: Hiroko Sugii, Tetsuhito Saito. MUS: N/C. PRD: Studio Deen, TV Tokyo. 25 mins. x 51+ eps. (TV), 25 mins. (m).

Mondo Oya is a hotheaded 12-year-old schoolboy who just loves playing with his Monster Collection Collectable Card Game. One day, Mondo discovers that Rokumon, the world of the CCG, is actually a real place, when he is co-opted to defend the planet from the predations of mad scientist Duke Collection—described in *Newtype,* rather mysteriously, as "a straightforward homosexual."

A pointless addition to the game cash-in phenomenon of POKÉMON and DIGIMON, artlessly setting itself in the Rokumon "World of Six Gates" to imply a nonexistent connection to its more successful predecessors and tellingly crediting MAZE's Satoru Akahori as a "story generalizer." A theatrical short would pit Mondo against a Fire Dragon and a Lava Chimaera in the magical world of Rokumon, as if anyone cared.

MONEY WARS

1991. JPN: *Money Wars: Nerawareta Waterfront Keikaku.* AKA: Money Wars: Waterfront Project in Peril. Video. DIR: Yusaku Saotome. SCR: Shuichi Miyashita. DES: Chuji Nakajima. ANI: Chuji Nakajima. MUS: N/C. PRD: Gainax. 45 mins.

Everyday life at a finance company is upset when a client turns up murdered, and his death is connected to land ownership after the upcoming handover of Hong Kong to the Chinese in 1997. A financial thriller in an exotic Chinese setting that soon relocates to Japan for further conspiratorial investigations, this anime was based on the manga serialized in *Business Jump* by Soichiro Miyagawa, though the animated story was completely original and did not appear in the print version. **NV**

MONKEY AND THE CRAB, THE

1988. JPN: *Saru Kani Kassen.* AKA: *Fight Between the Monkey and the Crab.* TV special. DIR: Yoshikazu Fujita, Minoru Okazaki. SCR: N/C. DES: Minoru Maeda. ANI: Minoru Maeda. MUS: Bimoth. PRD: Studio Juno, Fuji TV. 25 mins.

The monkey agrees to swap his persimmon seed for the crab's rice ball. The monkey eats the rice ball and is soon hungry again, but the crab plants the seed and grows an entire tree. The monkey steals some of the fruit but refuses to bring any down for the crab, and so the two fight until the crab holds the monkey's tail in his pincers. The monkey promises that, if the crab lets him go, he will give him three hairs from his tail, which is why crabs have three hairs on their claws.

The version listed here, screened as part of the *Ponkiki Kids* children's show, is only one of the more recent appearances of the better-known of the JAPANESE FOLK TALES. An early *Saru Kani Kassen* (1917) by Seitaro Kitayama was the second EARLY ANIME ever to be made, and the tale is often referenced—e.g., in MY NEIGHBOR TOTORO, when Satsuki draws Mei as a crab because she is waiting so intently for her seeds to grow.

MONKEY PUNCH'S WORLD: ALICE

1991. JPN: *Monkey Punch no Sekai: Alice*. Video. DIR: Yuzo Aoki. SCR: Tonori Yoshida. DES: Monkey Punch. ANI: Tatsuo Yanagimachi, Etsuji Yamada. MUS: N/C. PRD: Takahashi Studio. 45 mins. Doctor Stein, a mad scientist, falls in love with his own creation, the female android Alice, though Alice has feelings for the scientist's handsome young son Jiro. In this one-shot adaptation of a minor manga by **LUPIN III**–creator Monkey Punch, Alice flees the doctor's castle but is pursued by Jiro, either to avenge his father's descent into madness or to have her for himself, or perhaps both.

MONSTER MAN BEM

1968. JPN: *Yokai Ningen Bem*. TV series. DIR: Kujiro Yanagida, Seiji Sasaki, Tadao Wakabayashi. SCR: Akira Naritachi. DES: N/C. ANI: Nobuhide Morikawa. MUS: Masahiro Uno. PRD: Daiichi, Fuji TV. 25 mins. x 26 eps. Bem, a gangster with pupil-less eyes, Bero, a young boy, and Bera, a dark, almond-eyed witch, are not humans but creatures from the world of monsters. They wander the Dark Realm as agents of justice, hoping that, by bringing Good into the monster realm, they will eventually be granted the opportunity to become human themselves.

A follow-up to Daiichi's earlier **GOLDEN BAT**, *MMB* was one of the first Korean coproductions in anime, and an early example of the horror genre that would come to be so popular in the medium. Bero's constant catchphrase of "I just can't wait to be human" resulted in chuckles from audience-members of a certain age at Simba's "I just can't wait to be King" in Disney's *The Lion King*.

MONSTER RANCHER *

1999. JPN: *Monster Farm*. TV series. DIR: Hiroyuki Yano, Yuichiro Yano, Fujio Yamauchi. SCR: Satoshi Nakamura,

Masashi Komemura, Takeshi Mochizuki. DES: Minoru Maeda. ANI: Masahiro Sekiguchi. MUS: BMF. PRD: TMS, TBS. 25 mins. x 52? eps. Eleven-year-old Genki is an expert at the video-game *Monster Battle*. When he wins a video game tournament, he's rewarded with a 200x CD-Rom. But the game transports him from the real world to Monster Rancher Land. There, he meets Holly and her own personal monster, Suezo, and together they team up to fight Moo, accompanied by monsters Mocchi (a large, live personification of the Japanese dessert of the same name), Golem (a giant golem), Tiger of the Wind (a talking horned wolf), and Hamm (called Hare in the American dub, presumably because he is one). The personification of evil, Moo is misbehaving by corrupting all the otherwise good monsters. So Genki and his new friends set off on a quest to find the Phoenix, a mysterious creature with the power to change bad monsters into good ones. A hackneyed rip-off of **POKÉMON** and its ilk but swiftly snapped up for U.S. broadcast as a partner to **DIGIMON** on Fox Kids, in spite of poor ratings in Japan. *Ill. p. 37.*

MONTANA JONES

1994. TV series. DIR: Tetsuo Imazawa. SCR: Marco Pagot, Satoshi Nakamura, Megumi Sugiwara. DES: Marco Pagot. ANI: Yoshiaki Okumura, Masamitsu Kudo, Norio Kaneko. MUS: Mario Pagano, Gianni Bobino, The Alfee. PRD: Studio Juno, NHK. 25 mins. x 52 eps. It's the 1930s, and Montana Jones, bored with life as a pilot for Onboro Sea-Air Freight, sets off in search of fortune and adventure. His cousin Alfred would prefer a family life, complete with quiet contemplation, decent music, and copious amounts of spaghetti. They couldn't be more dissimilar, which is exactly why they have been thrown together by the sacred fates of buddy-movie plotting. Accompanying the Jones boys is their talkative interpreter, Melissa Sohn, an annoying girl who is obsessed with shopping but

is endured by the Joneses because she speaks a zillion languages.

The team travels the world in search of treasure on behalf of Baron Gilt, hounded all the way by the evil Lord Zero, who, with the help of the mad scientist Baron Nitro and his idiot assistants, Slim and Slam, aims to steal all the Jones boys' hard-won treasure. Starting in the Mayan jungles, the globe-trotting fortune-seekers head to the Caribbean for a pastiche of *20,000 Leagues under the Sea*, tour Prague in search of an antique bell, search for a hidden chamber in the Taj Mahal, hunt yetis in Tibet, and raid tombs in Egypt.

A fast, furious, and funny Italian anthropomorphic coproduction in the spirit of **SHERLOCK HOUND** but with such a blatant pastiche of the *Indiana Jones* series that we can only assume the series was unreleasable in the U.S. "Homages" go both ways, however, and Marco Pagot was the inspiration for a character created by his former collaborator Hayao Miyazaki: **PORCO ROSSO**. Compare to Disney's similar pulp-serial homage *TaleSpin*.

MOOMINS *

1969. JPN: *Moomin*. TV series, movie. DIR: Masaaki Osumi, Moriyoshi Murano, Masayuki Hayashi, Wataru Mizusawa, Seiji Okuda, Rintaro, Ryosuke Takahashi, Noboru Ishiguro, Toshio Hirata. SCR: Tadaaki Yamazaki, Hisashi Inoue, Yoshiaki Yoshida, Shunichi Yukimuro, Chikara Matsumoto, Keisuke Fujikawa, Kuni Miyajima, Hiroyuki Hoshiyama. DES: Tove Jansson. ANI: Yasuo Otsuka, Tsutomu Shibayama, Toyoo Ashida. MUS: Seiichiro Uno. PRD: Tokyo Movie Shinsha, Mushi Pro, Telescreen, Fuji TV, TV Tokyo. 25 mins. x 26 eps. (TV1), 25 mins. x 49 eps. (TV2), 25 mins. x 104 eps. (TV3), 62 mins. (m). The adventures of a cute little hippo-like troll and his friends, based on the series of children's books written between 1945 and 1971 by the Finnish author Tove Jansson. The relationship of the anime series to Jansson's original, however, was never more than tenuous. The author, angry at anachronisms such as automobiles and moments of minor violence, protested the style of the original TMS series, and production was moved to the Mushi studio for the second *New Moomin* season. While the author was more satisfied with the designs and stories of the new series, it is the TMS version that was the most popular with the *Japanese* audience.

The franchise returned as *Happy Moomin Family* (1990, *Tanoshii Moomin Ikka*), in a remake by Hiroshi Saito, screened on TV Tokyo. The directors changed to Takeyuki Kanda and Tsuneo Tominaga, and the series was renamed *Happy Moomin Family Adventure Diary* (1991, *Tanoshii Moomin Ikka Boken Nikki*) for episodes 79–104, and Jansson's *Comet in Moominland* was brought to the silver screen as Hiroshi Saito and Masayuki Kojima's *Moomin Tani Suisei* (1992), a movie edition that was released on video with ten minutes of extra footage. Twenty-eight episodes of the most recent series were dubbed for the U.K. market by the BBC and broadcast on Hawaii's K5 channel as *Tales of Moomin Valley*, though at time of writing it has yet to reach the U.S. mainland.

MOONLIGHT MASK

1972. JPN: *Gekko Kamen*. TV series. DIR: Nobuhiro Okaseko. SCR: Tsunehisa Ito, Haruya Yamazaki. DES: Sadayoshi Tominaga, Nobuhiro Okaseko. ANI: Tadashi Yamashita. MUS: Goro Misawa. PRD: Ai Planning Center, Knack, Nippon TV. 25 mins. x 39 eps.
Shavanan, the good king of Paradai, is murdered by the man-monster Great Claw of Satan, an evil figure intent on stealing the fabled treasure hidden somewhere in the small country. He only has one of the three golden keys required to reach the treasure, so he hunts down Shavanan's daughter, Fujiko Kuwata, believing her to have another. However, Fujiko is protected by a group of noble detectives and by the "warrior of love and justice," the

mysterious motorcycle-riding superhero Moonlight Mask.

Originating in a 1957 live-action TV series that spun off into four live-action movies, the first two seasons of the anime kept close to the continuity of the TV original, adapting the *Claw of Satan* and *Mammoth Kong* story lines, while the final part was the all-new *Dragon's Tooth* plot. Curiously, the fourth live *MM* movie, *Last of the Devil* (1957, *Akuma no Saigo*), was to feature a plot very similar to that of PATLABOR 2, in which an abandoned soldier decides to avenge himself on the country that betrayed him. Fiercely lampooned in Go Nagai's saucy pastiche KEKKO KAMEN (which featured a Great *Toenail* of Satan as a school principal), in 1981, *MM* returned to the live-action theater screens with a new high-kicking female sidekick—martial arts star Etsuko Shiomi. In 2000, it was also remade as a comedy anime designed to hook the original fans and their own very young children. Directed by Toshio Takeuchi and written by Yoshio Urasawa, *Look! It's Little Moonlight Mask!* featured Naoto, who was a humble schoolboy by day and the nemesis of Satan's Claw in the evenings (before bedtime).

MOONLIGHT PIERCE YUMEMI AND THE KNIGHTS OF THE SILVER ROSE

1991. JPN: *Gekko no P.Y. to Gin no Bara no Kishitai*. Movie. DIR: Takeshi Mori. SCR: Shikichi Ohashi. DES: Katsumi Aoshima. ANI: N/C. MUS: Kyosuke Himuro. PRD: Studio Pierrot. 70 mins.
Seventeen-year-old Yumemi Sato is dragged into an interdimensional conspiracy when her handsome upperclassman Masaki Suzukaga reveals that he is a German were-creature who can use magical powers to change shape at will. Hate it when that happens. A pretty-boy anime based on the best-selling novel of the same name by Hitomi Fujimoto.

MOSAICA

1991. JPN: *Eiyu Yoroiden Mosaica*. AKA: *Heroic Armor Tale Mosaica*. Video. DIR:

Ryosuke Takahashi. SCR: Ryoei Tsukimura. DES: Norio Shioyama. ANI: Hidetoshi Omori, Hideyuki Motohashi. MUS: Kaoru Wada. PRD: Studio Deen. 30 mins. x 4 eps.
The kingdom of Mosaica is on the verge of being overrun by King Sazara when the great warrior Lee Wu Dante is executed for questioning the King of Mosaica's judgment. His son, Lee Wu Talma, decides to save Mosaica in his father's memory, using ancient giant robots that lie dormant in a forgotten valley. Taking the advice of the hermit Ritish, Talma gathers an army but must first rescue Princess Menoza, who has been taken prisoner by his enemies. An SF fantasy deliberately designed to evoke memories of the crew-members' earlier VOTOMS and RONIN WARRIORS.

MOSPEADA *

1983. JPN: *Kiko Soseiki Mospeada*. AKA: *Armored Genesis Mospeada; Genesis Climber Mospeada*. TV series. DIR: Katsuhisa Yamada, Tatsuya Kasahara, Masayuki Kojima, Kazuhito Akiyama, Norio Yazawa. SCR: Sukehiro Tomita, Akira Koson, Kenji Terada. DES: Yoshitaka Amano, Shinji Aramaki, Hideki Kakinuma. ANI: Kazuhiko Udagawa. MUS: Joe Hisaishi, Hiroshi Ogasawara. PRD: Tatsunoko, Fuji TV. 25 mins. x 25 eps.
In the year 2083, the last remnants of the human race on Mars send a military mission to recapture Earth from the Invid, who overran it a generation before. However, all but young fighter pilot Stick Bernard are wiped out. Crash-landing in the Amazon jungle, he resolves to head north and attack the Invid base single-handed, even though this is sure to be a suicide mission. En route, he meets Rei, an inexperienced kid with a natural talent for piloting robots, and the pair hone their skills with the Legioss and Mospeada Ride Armor transforming motorcycles. Slowly, the duo gather other revolutionaries around them in order to fight a guerrilla war against the Invid, though their struggle was

curtailed by poor ratings in Japan. A famous SF anime featuring several famous designers, whose plot was supposedly based on writer Tomita's interpretation of the medieval standoff between Christianity and Islam! However, it also bears an uncanny resemblance to his unproduced story outline for *Terrahawks* (see **THUNDERBIRDS 2086**). The series was cut together with **MACROSS** and **SOUTHERN CROSS** to form the basis for the English-language **ROBOTECH**, long before it was released subtitled in its unadulterated form as part of the *Robotech Perfect Collection*.

Yellow Dancer (Yellow Belmont), a cross-dressing singer from the series, lived on after its cancellation to record an album, *Live from the Pit Inn*, and the *Love, Live, Alive* music video (chiefly comprising recycled footage, as with *Macross Flashback 2012*). *Ill. p. 301.*

MOST SPIRITED MAN IN JAPAN

1999. JPN: *Nihonichi no Otoko no Damashi.* TV series. DIR: Toshio Yoshida. SCR: Masashi Sogo. DES: Masaaki Kawanami. ANI: Bob Shirahata. MUS: N/C. PRD: Studio Deen, TBS. 5 mins. x 48 eps.

Tales of sex and sadomasochism, based on the manga in *Young Sunday* by Masahiko Kikuni, creator of **HEARTBROKEN ANGELS**. Japan's highest-ever-rated late-night anime, with a TV share of 9.1% in the graveyard slot, it was broadcast as part of the *Wonderful* anthology program. ●NV

MOTHER *

1993. JPN: *Mother: Saigo no Shojo Eve.* AKA: *Mother: Eve, the Last Girl.* Movie. DIR: Akira Suzuki. SCR: Soji Yoshikawa. DES: Shuichi Seki. ANI: N/C. MUS: Naoki Nishimura. PRD: Nippon Skyway. 75 mins.

Amnesiac boy Dew and pretty girl Eve set out on a quest to find out how the human race came to die out. An "international version" was reputedly released, dubbed into English with Japanese subtitles.

MUKA-MUKA PARADISE

1993. JPN: *Nauseous/Angry Paradise.* TV series. DIR: Katsuyoshi Yatabe, Kunihisa Sugishima. SCR: Yasushi Hirano, Shikichi Ohashi, Miho Maruo, Mayumi Koyama. DES: Hiromitsu Morita, Masayuki Hiraoka. ANI: Masayuki Hiraoka, Akio Watanabe. MUS: N/C. PRD: Nippon Animation, Mainichi Broadcasting. 25 mins. x 51 eps.

Thanks to a messy accident with the professor's time machine, little Eiba arrives in a world where humans never evolved and cutesy talking dinosaurs still walk Earth. He befriends the baby dinosaur Nikanika, tries to avoid provoking the wrath of Nikanika's father Gojigoji, and is (sort of) adopted by long-lashed brontosaurus mother Dosudosu. Based on a manga by **BONOBONO**-creator Mikio Igarashi.

MUSASHI ROAD

1990. JPN: *Karakuri Kengoden Musashi Road.* AKA: *Tales of the Trickster Swordsmaster Musashi Road.* TV series. DIR: Akira Torino, Satoshi Nishimura, Noriyuki Abe, Akiyuki Shinbo, Yoshitaka Fujimoto. SCR: Akira Torino, Tsunehisa Ito, Isao Shizuoka, Yoshihisa Araki, Shikichi Ohashi. DES: Tsuneo Tominaga, Kunio Okawara. ANI: N/C. MUS: Kenji Kawai. PRD: Studio Pierrot, Nippon TV. 25 mins. x 50 eps.

Musashi and Kojiro are two squashed-down robots in the spoof sci-fi samurai world of Edotopia. This anime carcrashes plots from **JAPANESE FOLK TALES**, historical events and legends, including Empress Himiko (see **ZEGUY**), the Japanese civil war, and the tale of **YAMATO TAKERU**. See also **YOUNG MIYAMOTO MUSASHI**.

MUSHKA AND MISHKA

1979. JPN: *Hokkyoku no Mushka Mishka.* AKA: *Mushka and Mishka of the Arctic.* Movie. DIR: Chikao Katsui. SCR: Akira Kato. DES: Shinichi Tsuji. ANI: N/C. MUS: Reijiro Komutsu. PRD: Mushi Pro, Nikkatsu. 80 mins.

Two polar bears and their friendly seal acquaintance share adventures in this

film supervised by Osamu Tezuka and based on the children's book by Tomiko Inui, also known as the writer of *The Tedious Penguin* and *We Are Kangaroos.*

MUSICAL WANDERINGS OF JIRONAGA KIYOMIZU

2000. JPN: *Anime Rokyoku Kiko Kiyomizu Jironaga.* TV series. DIR: Mitsuo Kobayashi, Tatsuo Suzuki. SCR: Kazuo Kosuga. DES: Mitsuo Kobayashi. ANI: Michishiro Yamada, Nanpei Mitsunori. MUS: N/C. PRD: Piman House, Mainichi Broadcasting. 25 mins. x 27+ eps.

Tales of samurai derring-do, set to old-time tunes for the entertainment of the elderly. The target audience for this anime was the over-sixties, though since it was shown at 5:45 in the morning, it's difficult to imagine that *anyone* saw it at all.

MUTEKING

1980. JPN: *Tondemo Senshi Mutaking.* AKA: *Invincible Warrior Mutaking.* TV series. DIR: Seitaro Hara, Koichi Mashimo, Hiroshi Sasakawa, Shinya Sadamitsu, Kenjiro Yoshida, Kazuo Yamazaki, Yutaka Kagawa. SCR: Kazuo Sato, Akiyoshi Sakai, Haruya Yamazaki, Takeshi Shudo, Masaru Yamamoto. DES: Ippei Kuri, Kunio Okawara. ANI:

Shizuo Kawai. MUS: Koba Hayashi. PRD: Tatsunoko, Fuji TV. 25 mins. x 56 eps.
Law enforcement officer Takuro leaves planet Tako in pursuit of the fugitive Kurodako (Black Octopus) crime family: Takokichi, Takomaro, Takosaku, and Takomi. Arriving on Earth, the octopoid gang disguise themselves as humans and prepare to conquer the planet with their transforming minions. Takoro enlists Earth boy Rin Yuki as his deputy. Rin can now transform into the dashing warrior MuteKing, a superhero (on roller skates) who both fights off the bad guys and wins the heart of Takomi, the female octopus invader who finds his charms irresistible. He also has Takoro's seemingly endless supply of TIME BOKAN–inspired robots at his disposal. Transforming robot vehicles, Las Vegas-inspired musical interludes, and roller-skating superhero action from the usual suspects at the Tatsunoko studio, whose most popular chapter was the "Mute-Queen" incident in which Takoro's transformation ray accidentally misses Rin and makes his girlfriend the hero of the hour—compare to MOLDIVER.

MY ALL-DAY ALL-COLOR

1987. JPN: *Boku no All-Day All-Color*. Video. DIR: Yoji Takatsuki. SCR: Seizo Watase. DES: Seizo Watase. ANI: Seizo Watase, Mikie Maeda. MUS: Tyrone Hashimoto. PRD: Tatsunoko. 30 mins.
Five short manga stories from HEART COCKTAIL–creator Seizo Watase, set to musical standards such as "Fly Me to the Moon" and "Love Me Tender." The tales adapted include *Riding the Wave for Ten Miles, 20 Minutes till Princess Kaguya, 250 Km, A Couple Requesting Gentle Rain*, and *Long-Distance Call from the West Side*. The experiment was repeated the following year with CHALK-COLORED PEOPLE.

MY FAIR MASSEUSE *

1996. JPN: *Soap no Moko-chan*. AKA: *Moko the Soap Girl*. Video. DIR: Shunji Yoshida. SCR: Naruo Kyujukawa. DES: Naruo Kyujukawa. ANI: Kawase

Toshine. MUS: N/C. PRD: Sente Studio. 40 mins.
The perky, sex-starved Moko takes a job in a "soapland" massage parlor, where she cheerfully helps the clientele fulfill their fantasies. This involves sex with old men, a threesome with a couple who want to spice up their love life, and the need to tactfully brush off a priapic grandfather who wants to "save her" from a life she fully enjoys. A porno anime remarkable only for the consensual nature of its sex scenes—a welcome change from the rape and domination that seems to occupy so much space on anime shelves. Based on the manga by Naruo Kyujukawa in *Young Champion* magazine. N

MY FATHER'S DRAGON

1993. JPN: *Elmer no Boken*. AKA: *Elmer's Adventure*. Movie. DIR: Masami Hata. SCR: N/C. DES: Shuichi Seki. ANI: N/C. MUS: Naoto Kine. PRD: Shochiku. 98 mins.
Elmer Elevator runs away with an old alley cat to rescue Boris, a young dragon imprisoned on the faraway Wild Island. The everyday items he needs to help himself include some pink lollipops, rubber bands, chewing gum, and a comb. Based on the children's book by Ruth Stiles Gannett, whose title reflected the original premise that the heroic youngster Elmer is actually the narrator's father as a boy.

MY MY MAI *

1993. JPN: *Sono Ki ni Sasete yo*. AKA: *Get Me In the Mood*. Video. DIR: Osamu Sekita. SCR: Yumi Nakamura, Osamu Sekita. DES: Masakazu Yamaguchi. ANI: N/C. MUS: Koichi Ota, Koji Tajima. PRD: Apple, Beam Entertainment. 22 mins. x 4 eps.
Mai is a psychic investigator who specializes in consultancy jobs—putting members of the public together with the right healer, surgeon, or cure for strange phobias. As with the heroine of the similar PRIVATE PSYCHO LESSON, she prefers hands-on treatment, which she administers with a mix of psychobabble, flashes of her lingerie, and as a

common last resort, her bounteous nude charms. Based on the *Shonen Champion* manga by *Heart Boiled Papa*–creator Masakazu Yamaguchi and presented as four "episodes," though this anime's release only spreads across two tapes. Similar psychosexual investigations turn up in REI REI. *Ill. p. 321.* N

MY NEIGHBOR TOKORO

1990. JPN: *Tonari no Tokoro*. TV series. DIR: Haruya Mizutani. SCR: Joji Tokoro. DES: Joji Tokoro. ANI: Tokuhiro Matsubara. MUS: Hiroaki Nakamura. PRD: Pasteoinc. 40 mins.
Parodies of several JAPANESE FOLK TALES and others, starring an animated version of star-of-the-moment Joji Tokoro, whose bright ideas that was. Originally broadcast as part of the *Not the Real Mr. Tokoro* (*Tokoro-san no Tadamono dewa Nai*) show, these feeble pastiches of *Urashima Taro, Little Red Riding Hood*, and several "comedy" skits were bulked out on video by a "making-of" documentary, once again starring the camera-hungry Mr. Tokoro. The name manages, not quite accidentally enough, to get the show filed next to MY NEIGHBOR TOTORO in both English and Japanese, as if somehow the greatness of the latter would improve its chances. The comedian returned in computerized form as *Mr. Digital Tokoro* (2001).

MY NEIGHBOR TOTORO *

1988. JPN: *Tonari no Totoro*. Movie. DIR: Hayao Miyazaki. SCR: Hayao Miyazaki. DES: Hayao Miyazaki. ANI: Yoshiharu Sato. MUS: Joe Hisaishi. PRD: Studio Ghibli. 86 mins.
While their mother is in the hospital convalescing from a long illness, Satsuki and her little sister, Mei, are taken by their father, Professor Kusakabe, to an old house in the country. They clean the house of lurking "dustbunnies" and turn it into a home. Father takes the bus to the university where he lectures, Satsuki attends the local school, and Mei gets lost in the undergrowth, where she discovers a family of round, fluffy woodland creatures. Mispro-

nouncing "troll," from the *Three Billy-Goats Gruff*, she calls them Totoros. Adults cannot see these Totoros, who befriend the children when Satsuki lends one an umbrella. He returns the favor by growing them a tree with magic acorns and taking them on a magical ride through the countryside on the Catbus—a many-legged feline transport with a Cheshire Cat's grin straight out of ALICE IN WONDERLAND. Mei resolves to take her mother a gift but becomes lost on the way. Fearing the worst, the adults send out search parties, and a distraught Satsuki calls on the Totoros' aid.

Hayao Miyazaki's greatest work, and hence probably the best anime ever made, *MNT* is also a very personal film, set in the disappearing countryside of the creator's childhood and featuring a child's love for a bedridden parent—Miyazaki's own mother suffered from spinal tuberculosis. *MNT* has the widest appeal of any of Miyazaki's films, aimed as it is at an audience so young that it can genuinely be described as family entertainment, unlike his more adult-themed works such as PORCO ROSSO or teen adventures like NAUSI-CAÄ. *MNT* sees everything through the unquestioning, uncritical, undaunted eyes of a child, and it is an uplifting film of unadulterated hope, originally shown on a double bill with its heart-rending opposite, GRAVE OF THE FIRE-FLIES. There are many echoes of other productions from Studio Ghibli, particularly in *MNT*'s depiction of a disappearing pastoral existence, a ghostly rural world superimposed on modern times, much like the studio's more serious POMPOKO. Miyazaki's Japan is a nation very much rooted in its own past, with ancient local shrines overlooking the contemporary action, and the Totoros leading the girls in a stirringly primal fertility ritual. It also mixes the magical with the mundane in the charming style of KIKI'S DELIVERY SERVICE and, like the creator's much more downbeat PRINCESS MONONOKE, refuses to point a formulaic finger at a bad-guy scapegoat. This latter point was of particular importance to Miyazaki, exasperated at modern parents' willingness to use the TV as a babysitter and disgusted with the conflict-based story lines of most modern children's cartoons.

MNT's appeal has not diminished since its appearance. Now the center of a huge industry of tie-in products, it is that rare case of a film whose spinoffs were created *by audience demand* after the fact, instead of generated by the company as part of a publicity offensive. The most recent spinoff is a ten-minute short anime, *Mei and the Kittenbus*, scheduled for premier at Tokyo's new Studio Ghibli Museum in 2001.

At one critical point in the plot, the "next stop" sign on the Catbus revolves to reveal a destination of particular importance. Whereas modern anime distributors would have digitally replaced it with English letters in translation, the dub released in the U.S. in 1994 was actually made in 1989 at a time when such technology was unavailable. Consequently, the Catbus has a warm, fluffy voice to announce the next stop in the English version—provided by Streamline Pictures' producer Carl Macek.

MY NEIGHBORS THE YAMADAS *
1980. JPN: *Ojamanga Yamada-kun; Hohokekyo Tonari no Yamada-kun.* AKA: *Troublesome Manga Yamadas.* TV series, movie. DIR: Hiroe Mitsunobu (TV), Isao Takahata (m). SCR: Masaki Tsuji, Tomoko Konparu, Noboru Shiroyama (TV), Isao Takahata (m). DES: Hisaichi Ishii. ANI: Hikuji Kanezawa (TV), Kenichi Konishi (m). MUS: Makoto Kawanabe (TV), Akiko Yano (m). PRD: Herald, Fuji TV, Studio Ghibli. 25 mins. x 102 eps. (3 stories per ep.).
The Yamada family comprises retired couple Yoshio and Ine, their daughter Yoneko and her husband Komugi, eternal retake student Shigeru (who has failed to pass his university entrance exams three times), hapless high-school baseball player Noboru, early teen Minoru, and toddler Sanae. In addition, the house is often visited by the occupants of the family's dormitory, several university students, and the local doctor—and soon the stork brings Yoneko and Komugi a new baby of their own.

Designer Hisaichi Ishii, who also created GO FOR IT, TABUCHI and FABLED UNDERGROUND PEOPLE, deliberately used flat, two-dimensional artwork for *Meet the Yamadas* (1980, *Ojamanga Yamada-kun*). Scheduled straight after SAZAE-SAN, the show continued the slot of gentle humor, although leavened in this case with chunks of satire, parody, and even science-fiction adventures. Later remade for theaters as *My Neighbors the Yamadas* (1999, *Hohokekyo Tonari no Yamada-kun*) in a deliberately washed-out sketch style. This version was released in Japan with English subtitles on the DVD.

In 1997, Ishii began serializing *Nono-chan*, a follow-up to the original manga. Featuring very similar comic situations but concentrating this time on the misadventures of a cheeky third-grader, *Nono-chan* was picked up for TV broadcast late in 2001. It was directed for Toei Animation by Nobutaka Nishizawa, using fully digital animation in imitation of the *Yamadas* movie, and shown on TV Asahi.

MY SEXUAL HARASSMENT
1994. JPN: *Boku no Sexual Harassment.* Video. DIR: Yosei Morino. SCR: Yosei Morino. DES: Aki Tsunaki. ANI: Aki Tsunaki. MUS: Burnheads. PRD: Seiyo, KSS. 35 mins. x 4 eps.
Jun Mochizuki is one of the best salesmen for his computer company, a position he has achieved by seducing the bosses of the companies to which he sells. He travels Japan and, in a later episode, even heads off to Boston, bedding his colleagues, his superiors, and his clients in a gay pornographic anime. Based on the series of erotic novels by Sakura Momo. ⓝ

MY SKY
1991. JPN: *Ore no Sora: Deka Hen.* AKA: *My Sky: Cop Chapter.* Video. DIR:

Takeshi Shirato. SCR: Hiroshi Motomiya. DES: Masami Suda. ANI: Masami Suda. MUS: Takeshi Yasuda, Chage & Asuka. PRD: APPP. 45 mins. x 2 eps.

A thriller revolving around political connections with a multinational corporation, as a lone cop, son of the company boss, tracks down the murderer of a female university student, finding that there is a conspiracy to prevent him from discovering the truth. Based on the manga in *Young Jump* magazine by **GOODFELLA** and **CLIMBING ON A CLOUD**–creator Hiroshi Motomiya. **Ⓥ**

MYSTERIES OF THE WORLD

1978. JPN: *Sekai no Fushigi Tanken Series*. AKA: *Investigating World Mysteries*. TV series. DIR: Masahiko Soga, Sadao Nozaki. SCR: Keiji Kubota, Takeshi Shudo, Kyoko Tsuruyama, Junji Takegami. DES: N/C. ANI: N/C. MUS: N/C. PRD: Heart Media, TBS. 25 mins. x 10 eps.

Documentaries combining anime with live action, exploring a mixed bag of mysteries and historical topics, including the statues of Easter Island, the search for a lost continent, the Bermuda Triangle, the **NAZCA** Lines, the Sphinx and the Pyramids, the Greenwich Meridian, the Leaning Tower of Pisa, and the Great Buddha of Nara. Confusing in its inability to decide whether it wants to be history, geography, travelogue, or the titular "mysteries."

MYSTERIOUS CITIES OF GOLD *

1982. JPN: *Taiyo no Ko Esteban*. AKA: *Esteban the Child of the Sun; Esteban and the Cities of Gold; Esteban the Sun-Kissed Boy*. TV series. DIR: Eiko Toriumi, Bernard Deyries, Kyosuke Mikuriya, Mizuho Nishikubo. SCR: Michiru Umadori, Michiru Kaneko, Soji Yoshikawa, Jean Chalopin. DES: N/C. ANI: Toshiyasu Okada, Hiroshi Kawanami, Yutaka Oka, Norio Yazawa, Hajime Hasegawa, Mitsuki Nakamura, Shingo Araki, Kazutoshi Kobayashi, Yukihiro Takahashi, Toyoo Ashida, Takashi

Nakamura. MUS: Nobuyoshi Koshibe (Haim Saban, Shuki Levy, Western version). PRD: MK, Studio Pierrot, NHK. 25 mins. x 39 eps.

In 1532, the orphan Esteban sets out from Barcelona in search of the fabled South American Cities of Gold. He's accompanied by the young Inca girl Zia, the adventurous Spaniard Mendoza, who found the baby Esteban adrift on the open sea, and (later) Tao, the last survivor of the sunken kingdom of Heva.

Set in the time when Japan was "discovered" by the West but made at a time when old-fashioned adventure yarns were rediscovered by the *Indiana Jones* mob, *MCoG* was a Franco-Japanese coproduction undertaken after the completion of **ULYSSES 31**. There are a few concessions to kiddie programming, such as an infuriating parrot and some comic-relief bunglers, but there is also much in this series to recommend it. It was loosely based on the books *The King's Fifth* (1966) and *City of Seven Serpents* (so claim the producers, though no work of that name exists in the Library of Congress) by Scott O'Dell, better known in the U.S. as the award-winning author of *Island of the Blue Dolphins* (1961). Full of unexpected changes in gear, *MCoG* starts as a straightforward sea voyage, before giving the first indications of its sci-fi leanings in episode nine when the crew of the Spanish galleon Esperanza jump ship onto the flying ship Solaris. Needless to say, as the quest begins in earnest in South America, Esteban discovers he is the offspring of an Inca princess (with an absent father who turns out to be not so absent)—hence, in true anime tradition, the perfect pilot for the show's supermachine, the solar-powered Golden Condor. Ancient technologies, lost cities, and warring tribes create an exciting mix, and though there are occasional anachronistic bloopers (a tribe of Amazons, *in* the Amazon, for example), the Japanese version closed each episode with a mini historical documentary explaining the actual events and personages

that inspired the fictional characters— explaining the differences between Aztecs, Olmecs, Mayas, and Incas, or filling in the background about Pizarro or Magellan. However, these documentaries were dropped from many foreign-language territories, including the U.K. Though made primarily for the French market, *MCoG* was also popular with the Japanese audience, particularly with those who could spot the irony of staff members from **GOLD LIGHTAN** animating the flight of the Golden Condor using similar glare effects and shot compositions. Perhaps the most compelling element of *MCoG* is the way in which it genuinely conveys a feel for the age. There was, literally, a whole New World to conquer, and the sense of anticipation and adventure is gripping. Predating the similar **SECRET OF BLUE WATER** by several years, *MCoG* remains an original, not the least because it presented a positive, sympathetic view of Native American peoples unique to children's television. When the series was rereleased on French DVD, there were rumors that producer Chalopin was in negotiations with Japan about a remake (or perhaps a sequel, since the children only manage to find one of the seven fabled cities), though there has yet to be any confirmation.

MYSTERY OF THE NECRONOMICON *

1999. JPN: *Kuro no Dansho*. AKA: *Black Fragment*. Video. DIR: Hideki Takayama, Yoshitaka Makino. SCR: Ryo Saga. DES: Yutaka Sunadori. ANI: Koichi Fuyukawa, Masaki Kaneko. MUS: Kazuhiko Izu, Hiroaki Sano. PRD: Discovery/78. 35 mins. x 2 eps.

After a savage mass murder at a remote Nagano ski resort, most of the guests leave the mountain complex. As a storm brings down the phone lines and cuts off the hotel, vacationing private investigator Satoshi Suzusaki hunts down the killer as further murders occur. Accompanied by his foster-daughter Asuka, he interviews a succession of suspects, discovering a web of intrigue that includes blackmail, sexual assault, black magic, and experimental gene therapies.

Despite the usual cavalcade of sick sex and gratuitous violence one would expect from **Urotsukidoji**-director Takayama, the first half of *MotN* is also a simplistic but engaging whodunit. Satoshi collects a number of carefully balanced clues and artifacts, interviewing suspects and collating information that regularly contradicts the viewers' expectations and even prompts suspicion that perhaps *he* is really the murderer. However, with the arrival of his lover, Mina, the dramatic tension snaps. Bearing a satellite phone that allows Satoshi to reconnect to the outside world and the Internet, Mina throws in several extra variables, and

the plot spins wildly out of control. Instead of a sedate unmasking in the drawing room, the finale breaks the rules of detective fiction by keeping several last-minute surprises up its sleeve, stretching the viewer's suspension of disbelief with a series of disguises and linking events to a previously unmentioned gang rape at a distant pharmaceuticals company.

In its continual return to computer-screen research, *MotN* betrays its origin as a game for the Sega Saturn. The characters and their quirks are meticulously distributed—onscreen titles give extra details about people's names and the times of critical events, while sudden revelations come accompanied by fast-forward flashbacks, which are cheap and easy with digital animation.

Asides reveal that this is only the middle chapter in a loosely linked trilogy— Satoshi is the amnesiac survivor of a former crime, and the killer escapes to set up a sequel. If there's any real "mystery," it's what was *cut* for the anime version, as early scenes belabor the point that Asuka's adopted status has been somehow revoked, setting up but forgetting an incestuous subplot, while Abdul Al-Hazred's titular Book of the Dead appears but only as the most tantalizing of McGuffins. A rare case of a game plot that seems to have genuinely required the traditional 30 hours' immersion to make proper sense, reduced here to 60 minutes of sleuthing, dotted with moments of brutal sex and slasher-movie gore. **NV**

N

NADESICO *

1996. JPN: *Kido Senkan Nadesico*. AKA: *Robot Warship Pink (Sweet William); Martian Successor Nadesico*. TV series, movie. DIR: Tatsuo Sato, Nobuyuki Habara, Kenichi Hamasaki. SCR: Noboru Aikawa, Takeshi Shudo, Hiroyuki Kawasaki. DES: Kia Asamiya, Keiji Goto, Takeshi Takakura, Takumi Sakura, Rei Nakahara, Yasuhiro Moriki. ANI: Keiji Goto, Natsuki Egami, Masayuki Hiraoka. MUS: Takayuki Hattori. PRD: Xebec, Studio Tron, TV Tokyo. 25 mins. x 26 eps. (TV), 30 mins. (*Gekiganger*), 90 mins. (m).

In the year 2195, while Earth prevaricates about sending troops to fight invaders from Jupiter, a brave civilian takes matters into her own hands and steals a privately owned warship. With a rogue captain straight out of SILENT SERVICE, an unwinnable war out of GUNBUSTER, and a plaster of irony over any cracks, Earth's last hope against the Jovian "lizards" is the ragtag crew of the Nadesico—a ship named after the *nadeshiko* flower that is said to represent Japanese womanly perfection. Captain Yurika and her mostly female crew are determined to meet the challenge, while their cook (and Yurika's childhood sweetheart) Akito is a former pilot ace on the run from his fears, pilot Jiro Yamada is an anime addict bent on living his favorite show, and the military is out to take control by fair means or foul.

Based on a manga in *Monthly Ace* magazine by Kia Asamiya and supposedly set in the same universe as his SILENT MÖBIUS, *Nadesico* is one of the better 1990s shows, particularly for a hard-core fan audience that can spot

the in-jokes and identify the fine line between a *satire* of cheesy shows and the cheesy shows themselves. Parodies and homages are handled lightly, and the anime's characters and situations are cleverly scripted to avoid the repetitive tedium of TENCHI MUYO!, whose adoring-female-of-the-week policy it often imitates. The most striking example of this is cute moppet Ruri—a mixture of Wednesday Addams and *Tenchi*'s Sasami, marrying intelligence and competence with sullen cynicism.

Often playing like a superfast trailer for a much longer series, the viewer is left dazed by the compression of information, events, and background. Director Sato cuts conversations as if they were fight scenes; tone and mood change without a by-your-leave, and there's an incredible amount of shouting. The camp giant-robot show-within-the-show *Gekiganger Three* is more than mere comic-relief pastiche of GETTER ROBO and its ilk—a viewing experience that turns the crew into anime fans, it eventually becomes a cultural bridge between the warring worlds. With a wink to the fan audience, anime saves the universe in much the same way as the power of song in the earlier MACROSS. The *Gekiganger* segments were compiled and released with extra footage straight to video in 1997.

The movie release *Nadesico: Prince of Darkness* (1998) closes the series with a flash-forward redolent of the second PATLABOR movie. Years after the original series, the two main leads are missing, presumed dead, and an older Ruri is now the commander of the Nadesico B, fighting a new enemy that is not all it seems. *Ill. p. 361.*

NAJICA

2001. JPN: *Najica Dengeki Sakusen*. AKA: *Najica Explosion Battle*. TV series. DIR: Katsuhiko Nishijima, Takeshi Mori. SCR: Takeshi Mori, Kenichi Kanemaki, Kazunori Chiba, Mayori Sekijima. DES: Noriyasu Yamauchi. ANI: Noriyasu Yamauchi. MUS: N/C. PRD: Studio Fantasia, Amber Films. 25 mins. x 12+ eps.

Thirty years after ecological disaster has sunk 17% of Earth's surface below rising seas, 27-year-old perfumier Najica Hiragi moonlights as a secret agent, using her knowledge of 500 different scents to save the world from terrorism. Pretty girls and unlikely plotting from the people who brought you AGENT AIKA.

NANAKO SOS

1983. AKA: *Nana the Supergirl*. TV series. DIR: Akira Shigino, Yoshihiko Yamatani, Yoshinobu Shigino, Tetsuro Amino, Tsukasa Sunaga. SCR: Masaru Yamamoto, Shikichi Ohashi, Asami Watanabe, Tomoko Ishizuka. DES: Tsuneo Ninomiya. ANI: Geki Katsumata, Shiro Murata, Tsuneo Ninomiya, Yoshiyuki Kikuchi, Masami Abe. MUS: Ichiro Nitta. PRD: Kokusai Eiga, Movie International, Fuji TV. 25 mins. x 39 eps.

An alien girl crash-lands on Earth, losing her memory in the process but keeping her superpowers. "Rescued" by a boy, who has a knack for making money, and his dopey friend, she agrees to work for them for room and board. They set up the Supergirl Company investigation agency, and Nana gets to work bringing villains to justice, solving love problems, and dodging the unwanted attentions of a mad scientist out to use her for his own ends. Based on an original *Just Comic* manga by **POLLON**-creator Hideo Azuma, this is one of the most neglected of the magical-girl series, eclipsed in its year of release by the more famous **CREAMY MAMI**. Mercifully, it has nothing whatsoever to do with **AMAZING NURSE NANAKO**.

NANIWA SPIRIT

1992. JPN: *Naniwa Yukyoden*. AKA: Tales of Naniwa Heroism. Video. DIR: Teruo Kigure. SCR: Haruyuki Maeda. DES: Dokuman Pro. ANI: Teruo Kigure. MUS: Jiro Takemura. PRD: Knack. 58 mins. x 2 eps.

Taido Kaimon is the leader of the Kinshu Group gangster syndicate in Japan's Kansai region. His gang is a cluster of wisecracking madmen, eternally running into trouble with the law, each other, and the local girls who give as good as they get. It's a fast and furious Osaka comedy (see **COMPILER**) in an adaptation of the gag manga in *Asahi Geino* magazine by Dokuman Pro. The same year saw the release of a three-part video series based on another Dokuman manga: the Osaka motorcycle gang comedy *Nanbono Monjai*, directed by Masamune Ochiai and written by Yoshihisa Araki. ⓛⓥ

NASTY OLD LADY

1970. JPN: *Ijiwaru Baasan*. AKA: *Bullying Old Woman*. TV series. DIR: Satoshi Murayama, Hiroshi Yamazaki, Yoshio Okamoto, Shoichi Sugiyama. SCR: Susumu Yoshida. DES: Shoichi Hayashi. ANI: Sadayoshi Tominaga, Hiromitsu Morita. MUS: Yasuhiro Koyama. PRD: Knack, Nippon TV. 25 mins. x 40 eps., 25 mins. x 46 eps. (remake).

Based on a 1966 manga by **SAZAE**-**SAN**–creator Machiko Hasegawa, this is another slice-of-everyday-life tale, centered around a spiteful old woman who causes trouble for neighbors with her constant bumbling and grumbling. The first show from anime production house Knack, with a leading "lady" voiced in pantomime-dame fashion by gravely male voice actor Shigeo Taka-

matsu to add to the horror. The story was brought back for a new generation as *New NOL* (1996), a TV remake directed by Yoshimitsu Morita.

NATSUKI CRISIS

1993. Video. DIR: Koichi Chiaki, Junichi Sakata. SCR: Mayori Sekijima. DES: Futoshi Fujikawa. ANI: Futoshi Fujikawa. MUS: Yasuhiko Shigemura. PRD: Madhouse. 30 mins. x 2 eps.

Natsuki is a karate ace in a private high school where martial arts are a major part of the curriculum. There's fierce rivalry between Natsuki's team and another local school's with an even better reputation for fighting skills. A transfer student from the rival school is attacked by her former classmates, the student president authorizes spying missions, and there are romantic complications, too. The designs are attractive, even though contemporary school stories can date fast because the background detail—what to wear, what bags and accessories are cool, how hair is styled—changes very quickly. This one, based on a 1990 manga from *Business Jump* by Hirohisa Tsuruta, has enough heart and punch to retain its charm.

NAUGHTY DETECTIVES

1968. JPN: *Wanpaku Tankentai*. TV series. DIR: Rintaro, Toshio Hirata, Masami Hata, Masami Murano. SCR: Keiji Abe, Aritsune Kato, Masaki Tsuji. DES: Osamu Tezuka. ANI: Kiyomi Numamoto, Akehiro Kaneyama. MUS: Takeo Yamashita. PRD: Mushi Pro, Fuji TV. 25 mins. x 35 eps.

A group of young boys (plus a token girl and her little brother, the obligatory brat) form a detective club, pooling their talents for brain, brawn, invention, and driving skills to solve crimes in Tokyo. Much to the consternation of police chief Nakamura, they often succeed where the professionals fail. The first show made by Tezuka's studio from a non-Tezuka work, this series adapts the juvenile *Boy Detectives Club* stories of Ranpo Edogawa, a 19th-century novelist better known today for his Poe-inspired tales of horror and sus-

CardCaptors

pense, some of which were adapted for the **ANIMATED CLASSICS OF JAPANESE LITERATURE**. A watershed show that transferred the literary penchant for amateur sleuthing into the anime market, setting up a formula that survives to this day in **CONAN THE BOY DETECTIVE** and the **YOUNG KINDAICHI FILES**.

NAUGHTY DOTAKON

1981. JPN: *Mechakko Dotakon*. AKA: *Robot Kid Dotakon*. TV series. DIR: Takeshi Shirato, Kazumi Fukushima. SCR: Masaru Yamamoto, Takao Yotsuji, Kenichi Matsuzaki, Tetsuya Michio. DES: Takeshi Shirato, Iwamitsu Ito, Mitsue Ito. ANI: Takeshi Shirato. MUS: Shunsuke Kikuchi. PRD: Kokusai Eiga, Toei, Fuji TV. 25 mins. x 28 eps.

Geeky genius Michiru has already got her Ph.D. in atomic physics (from a California university) by the age of 11. But she still longs for a little brother, so she builds her own. Robot boy Dotakon is soon joined by their little robot sister, Chopiko, and the trio embarks on a series of fantastic adventures fueled by Michiru's inventions. Luckily for their little town, and the sanity of Michiru's bulky guardian Gorilla Capone, nothing ever gets too out of hand. Eclipsed in its year of release by a far more successful android child, Arale from **DOCTOR SLUMP**.

NAUSICAÄ OF THE VALLEY OF WIND *

1984. JPN: *Kaze no Tani no Nausicaä*. AKA: *Warriors of the Wind*. Movie. DIR: Hayao Miyazaki. SCR: Hayao Miyazaki. DES: Hayao Miyazaki. ANI: Kazuo Komatsubara, Takashi Nakamura, Kazuyoshi Katayama, Hideaki Anno, Takashi Watanabe. MUS: Joe Hisaishi. PRD: Nibariki, Tokuma, Hakuhodo, Toei. 116 mins. (95 mins. as *Warriors of the Wind*).

A thousand years after a great war, in a world dominated by the pollution-induced Sea of Corruption, Princess Nausicaä grows up in a peaceful valley shielded from the devastation by its prevailing winds from the sea. These keep the deadly spores that spread the Sea of Corruption away from its fertile lands—survival by a combination of geographical and meteorological chance. Terrible insect-like creatures roam the Sea of Corruption and the desert lands around. Mightiest of all are the huge crustaceans, the Ohmu. One of these can wipe out most human threats, but in a herd, they are unstoppable. Outside the valley, while smaller communities struggle to survive, factions within the Tolmekian Empire are fighting for supremacy. Princess Kushana of Tolmekia finds one of the superweapons that made the ancient war so terrible, the last God Warrior embryo, and plans to use it to ensure that her people stay on top, even if it means upsetting the fragile balance Nature has struggled to regain after the long-ago war.

When the ship carrying her superweapon crashes in the valley, it brings Kushana's army down on the agrarian enclave to retrieve the terrible cargo. Nausicaä's father dies in the struggle, but she can't give herself up to the lust for vengeance—she is the only one with the vision to see that understanding, tolerance, and patience might give a better outcome than aggression, not only with the Tolmekians, but also with

the Sea of Corruption and its giant denizens. Faced with the God Warrior's awakening, an Ohmu stampede, and even the failure of the wind that has protected her Valley for generations, she must also face up to her own fears and make the ultimate sacrifice to preserve everything she loves.

It would have been easy to make this a hero-villain tale in the Hollywood mold (something the woefully inferior 1986 U.S. edit *Warriors of the Wind* attempts), but what emerges is a far richer, more complex world. Shunning more conventional firepower, Nausicaä uses her brains, her heart, and her courage to find a solution with compassion for everyone involved. The result is a film that is superbly put together on all levels, with messianic and ecological subtexts that don't weigh down a story packed with action and adventure.

After his initial success as a director-for-hire on **CASTLE OF CAGLIOSTRO**, Hayao Miyazaki directed this short segment of his own epic 1982 manga, originally serialized in *Animage* magazine. Despite an ending that seems to owe a debt to David Lynch's movie of *Dune* (1984), *Nausicaä* draws on a variety of other sources, including *The Princess Who Loved Insects* (one of the **JAPANESE FOLK TALES**) and, for its scenes beneath the poisonous-yet-cleansing Sea of Corruption, the 1959 adaptation of Jules Verne's *Journey to the Center of the Earth*. It even pastiches *Bedknobs and Broomsticks* (1971) with an opening montage that ends with Nausicaä in flight where Disney has a witch. As with many of Miyazaki's later characters, there are powerful echoes of the work of British historical fantasy novelist Rosemary Sutcliffe, whose hero-kings are defined by the extent to which they willingly live and die for others. Nausicaä has much in common with Ashitaka, her spiritual heir in **PRINCESS MONONOKE**, and the art direction of both films spares no effort in the quest for perfection. *Nausicaä's* access to cutting-edge technology, however, was more limited; the Ohmu were animated by a range of

techniques which included cut-paper segments. Despite the notoriously short-lived attention spans of the anime-watching public (see **BRAVE SAGA**), *Nausicaä* polled high in Japanese top-ten lists for two decades after its original release. It influenced many imitators, particularly the incoherent eco-babbling of **GREEN LEGEND RAN**, and even films with little direct relation—**WIND OF AMNESIA** and **WINGS OF HONNEAMISE** both had their original titles altered to reflect the cadences of *Nausicaä* in an attempt to inspire Pavlovian ticket-buying in the Japanese audience.

NAYUTA

1986. Video. DIR: Masami Hata. SCR: Akiyoshi Sakai. DES: Akio Sugino. ANI: Akio Sugino. MUS: Masamichi Amano. PRD: Circus Production, Toshiba EMI. 75 mins.

Nayuta is on her way home from high school when she saves a mother and son from an accident and takes them to the hospital. The son, Kiro, wears a strange metal headband and seems to have some extrasensory powers. Then his mother is abducted, and Nayuta finds her good deed has drawn her into conflict with a strange group of activists known as Jarna and aliens called Hazard. Based on Junko Sasaki's 1981 manga published by Flower Comics.

NAZCA *

1998. JPN: *Jiku Tensa Nazca*. AKA: *Time Reincarnation Nazca*. TV series. DIR: Hiroko Tokita. SCR: Tsunehiro Ito. DES: Hirotoshi Sano. ANI: N/C. MUS: Suneyoshi Saito. PRD: Pioneer, TV Tokyo. 25 mins. x 12 eps.

Kyoji is a high-school student who loves kendo and adores his charismatic instructor, art teacher Masanare Tate. He and Tate's fiancée, Yuka, see him transform into an Inca warrior at a kendo match. Long ago they were all Inca nobles, and Kyoji's past self betrayed Tate's just before the conquistadors rolled in and destroyed their empire for good. As history seems set to repeat itself, the two meet again as deadly enemies, dressed in implausibly large feather headdresses and enough spandex to cover a chorus line. Not only this trio but everyone they know in modern Tokyo, right down to Kyoji's dog, has counterparts in 16th-century South America. Flashbacks retell the original fight between Bilka (lieutenant of the last Inca general, Huascar) and Yawaru (lieutenant of his usurper brother, Atahualpa) over both priestess Akulia and the Incan doomsday device Ilya Tesse. In a parallel story line, their reincarnations repeat their previous lives, loves, and conflicts in modern Tokyo, as Tate attempts to revive Ilya Tesse and destroy the modern world.

Amid this hokey plot, screenwriter Ito mixes Aztec and Inca myths and history with impunity, throwing in a spaceship straight out of von Däniken (or **MYSTERIOUS CITIES OF GOLD**) and vague musings about the "close genetic ties" between the Incas and the Japanese. Sano's design work has all the edge he brought to **BOUNTY DOG**, but, as with that show, design alone won't make things work. Also adapted into manga form by the pseudonymous female duo "Akira Hinakawa." As a historical footnote, the real Atahualpa's brother was actually called Manko, presumably omitted from the anime version because *manko* is Japanese for pussy.

NEIGHBORHOOD STORY
1995. JPN: *Gokinjo Monogatari*. TV series. DIR: Atsutoshi Umezawa. SCR: Aya Matsui, Yumi Kageyama, Motoki Yoshimura. DES: Yoshihiko Umakoshi. ANI: Chuji Nakajima. MUS: Masahiro Kawasaki. PRD: Toei, TV Asahi. 25 mins. x 50 eps. (TV), 30 min (m).
One of the freshest and most stylish TV shows of its season, *NS* goes back to the 1960s for its look and atmosphere. Childhood friends and neighbors Mikako and Tsutomu head off to art college (he for photography, she for fashion), where they slowly fall for each other. A bubbly adaptation of the

1995 manga in *Ribbon* magazine by **I'M GONNA BE AN ANGEL**–creator Ai Yazawa, there was also a short theatrical release, *NS: The Movie* (1996). Compare to **HIS AND HER CIRCUMSTANCES**, which tells a similar story, but with a more negative slant.

NEKOJIRU THEATER
1999. JPN: *Nekojiru Gekijo*. TV series, video. DIR: Hiroshi Fukutomi. SCR: Hajime Yamano. DES: Masaaki Yuasa. ANI: Michiko Iwa, Masaaki Yuasa. MUS: N/C. PRD: Kent House, TV Asahi. 10 mins. x 4 eps.
Troubled tales of cat antics, with character designs that resemble the insipid treacle of **HELLO KITTY**, but with far more menacing undertones. Based on the manga written by Hajime Yamano and drawn by his wife "Nekojiru," the series was soon taken off the air because it was considered too hard-hitting even for late-night TV; though it was brought back to video following Nekojiru's suicide in 2000. If anything, this makes the video release, *Nekojiru* (2001), even more disturbing, since the story features a brother cat, Nyaata, who fights to stop Death taking away his sister Nyaako, only for the quarreling boys to tear her in half.

NEO TOKYO *
1987. JPN: *Manie Manie Meikyu Monogatari*. AKA: *Labyrinth Tales*. Movie. DIR: Yoshiaki Kawajiri, Katsuhiro Otomo, Rintaro. SCR: Yoshiaki Kawajiri, Katsuhiro Otomo, Rintaro. DES: Rintaro, Katsuhiro Otomo, Yoshiaki Kawajiri, Takashi Watanabe, Atsuko Fukushima. ANI: Takashi Nakamura, Atsuko Fukushima, Koji Morimoto, Kunihiko Sakurai. MUS: Micky Yoshino. PRD: Project Team Argus, Kadokawa. 50 mins.
A slender anthology brackets two dark shorts by Kawajiri and Otomo inside the titular *Labyrinth*, a chiller by veteran Rintaro. Little Sachiko is warned by her mother about playing with strangers and staring into mirrors, but she ignores the warnings with results as predicted by the Brothers Grimm. She

and her cat stray into a carnival straight out of a Ray Bradbury story—the kind where you don't want to stay after dark but can't find the exit. Otomo's story, *Order to Stop Construction*, is a classic SF essay on the possibilities of chaos inherent in the most efficient automated system. Kawajiri contributes *Running Man*, the tale of a top racing driver who finds he just can't quit. Despite its futuristic trappings, it's anime for the couch-potato audience, a warning against machine addiction that they'll forget while slavering over the gleaming, roaring engines, and the least interesting of the three plot premises. All three selections ooze dark, edgy style. See **ROBOT CARNIVAL** and **MEMORIES** for anthologies on a different theme.

NEORANGA
1998. TV series. DIR: Jun Kamiya. SCR: Noboru Aikawa. DES: Hirohito Tanaka. ANI: N/C. MUS: Kuniaki Haishima. PRD: Studio Pierrot, Pony Canyon, WOWOW. 15 mins. x N/D eps, 5 mins. x N/D eps.
A giant robot, a relic of an ancient South Sea civilization, threatens to destroy Tokyo, but it can be controlled by the three teenage Shimabara sisters, who are descended from its makers. Despite their reservations about inheriting this relic of their previously unknown ancestry, the 18-foot-tall robot becomes "one of the family"— with sometimes comic consequences. Originated by Aikawa, with striking designs, backgrounds, and music, this show begins as a *Godzilla* pastiche but soon transforms into a slice-of-life drama with occasional city-stomping. The short and variable episode lengths stem from its original existence as just one of several anime shown on TV's *Anime Complex* anthology slot, though it is a measure of its quality that it was at least optioned for a follow-up season— few of its fellow short shows shared such success.

NESTING CRANES
1971. JPN: *Tsuru no Sugomori*. AKA: *Cranes in their Nests*. Movie. DIR:

Kazuo Saito (pseudonym for Tsutomu Shibayama). scr: Kazuo Saito. des: Kazuo Saito. ani: Kazuo Saito. mus: Yasuji Kiyose. prd: Japanese Film Collective. 17 mins.

An earnest tale of animal cooperation, as two out-of-place chickens try to make their home on an island inhabited by cranes. When they are attacked by an eagle, their adoptive parent cranes are killed, but the chickens organize a counterstrike. Eventually, peace is restored to the island. Based on a story by Teru Takakura, this anime was made over a three-year period by around 80 members of the Japan Film Broadcasting Industry Association under the pseudonymous lead of Shibayama.

NEW KARATE HELL

1990. JPN: *Shin Karate Jigoku Hen.* Video. dir: Kozo Kusuba, Toshiyuki Sakurai. scr: Hideo Nanbu. des: Kenzo Koizumi, Shunji Saida. ani: Kenzo Koizumi, Shunji Saida. mus: Nobuyuki Nakamura. prd: Nippon Animation. 50 mins. x 2 eps.

A single karate master is all that stands between beautiful women and a group of Neo-Nazi rapists. Hellbent on revenge ever since the Gestapo murdered his father and sister, our hero pursues his quarry from the United States to the Amazon rainforests. Based on a manga by Ikki Kajiwara, creator of KARATE-CRAZY LIFE (with Jiro Tsunoda and Joya Kagemaru), this anime devotes equal screen time not only to the hero's flying fists of vengeance, but also to questionable audience titillation in the form of the baddies' many crimes.

NIEA_7 *

2000. AKA: *Nia Under Seven; NieA_7–Domestic Poor @nimation.* TV series. dir: Takuya Sato, Tomokazu Tokoro. scr: Takuya Sato. des: Yoshitoshi Abe, Yoshiaki Yanagida. ani: Tsuneo Kobayashi. mus: Yoshio Owa. prd: Triangle Staff, WOWOW. 25 mins. x 13 eps.

On an Earth still struggling to come to terms with making contact with aliens, failed college student Mayuko, forced to live in Tokyo while she retakes her exams, shares a flat with a zany alien girl (cat-ears and all) called Niea. But in the sewers and subways of Tokyo, there's a strange underclass that hasn't integrated into this neat near-future society; people call them the Under-7. Made by the same studio as the surreal SERIAL EXPERIMENTS LAIN and intended as a "fantasy sitcom" by original creator Yoshitoshi Abe, a manga version in *Ace Next* magazine preceded the show but was created as a promotional tool rather than existing as an original inspiration.

NIGHT FOR LOVING

1983. JPN: *Ai Shite Night.* AKA: *Kiss Me Licia.* TV series. dir: Osamu Kasai, Kazumi Fukushima, Yugo Serikawa, Shigeo Koshi. scr: Mitsuru Majima, Sukehiro Tomita, Tajio Tamura. des: Yasuhiro Yamaguchi. ani: Yasuhiro Yamaguchi, Akira Kasahara, Tsuneo Komuro. mus: Nozomu Aoki. prd: Toei, TV Asahi. 25 mins. x 42 eps.

Cute schoolgirl Yaeko helps out in the family restaurant in the evenings. Dad disapproves of her friend Satomi, a big fan of the rock band Beehive, and when the pair meet Hashizo, little brother of Beehive's lead singer Takeshi, things get even worse. Yaeko falls for Takeshi and Satomi resents his friend's new infatuation, much to the annoyance of his *own* fiancée. Based on Kaoru Tada's 1981 manga in *Margaret,* and popular in Europe in its day, it has probably passed its sell-by date in the English language.

NIGHT TRAIN TO THE STARS *

1985. JPN: *Ginga Tetsudo no Yoru.* AKA: *Night on the Galactic Railroad.* Movie. dir: Gisaburo Sugii. scr: Minoru Betsuyaku. des: Takao Kodama. ani: Marisuke Eguchi, Koichi Mashimo, Yasunari Maeda. mus: Haruomi Hosono. prd: Hiroshi Masumura, Asahi, Herald, Tac. 115 mins.

Based on Kenji Miyazawa's 1927 novel, this dark but gentle fantasy of life and death is a demanding, rewarding film with some dazzling animation and a script by avant-garde playwright Betsuyaku. Giovanni is a lonely child in unhappy circumstances. Late one night, he boards a strange steam train in a meadow on the outskirts of town. He has no plans or expectations; he's simply along for the ride, and finding his classmate and only friend, Campanella, on board is an unexpected bonus. The fantastic voyage takes them along the Milky Way, through landscapes symbolic of death and rebirth, based on Miyazawa's beliefs as a Nichiren Buddhist and student of Christianity and his background as a naturalist. Only when the train comes full circle and deposits him back at home does Giovanni understand that Campanella's journey had a different destination—in the real world he is dead by his own hand.

Director Sugii isn't afraid to take things slowly or to take liberties with a text when necessary (see TALE OF GENJI). Here he turns all Miyazawa's characters into cats, creating a distancing effect that blurs the edges of the film's tragedy and helps us to accept its overriding sense of wonder and optimism. The imagery of the novel, using a railroad as a metaphor for life's journey, is interpreted with superb attention to detail. The steam train and the stations are as rich and credible as any real-world setting, and the poetic beauty of the imagery combines with this richness to give the long journey a powerful emotional weight. Yellow Magic Orchestra–cofounder Hosono's music perfectly fits this visually stunning film, with its imagery of almost hallucinogenic beauty and power, though even he takes a back seat for Handel's *Hallelujah* chorus. Compare to GALAXY EXPRESS 999, with a similar interstellar train, also pastiched in Tsui Hark's Hong Kong cartoon, *A Chinese Ghost Story* (1999).

NIGHT WALKER: MIDNIGHT DETECTIVE *

1998. JPN: *Mayonaka no Tantei.* TV

series. DIR: Kiyotoshi Sasano, Yutaka Kagawa. SCR: Ryota Yamaguchi. DES: Miho Shimokasa, Ryoichi Makino, Satoshi Isono. ANI: Satoshi Isono, Ikuo Sato. MUS: Akifumi Tada. PRD: AIC, Studio Gazelle, TV Tokyo. 25 mins. x 12 eps.

Half-vampire detective Shido takes a job with Yayoi Matsunaga, a beautiful investigator from the secret NOS government organization, devoted to hunting down the evil "Nightbreed." His orphaned (and lovestruck) assistant, Riho, believes Yayoi and Shido are having an affair, but Yayoi only pays Shido by letting him drink her blood.

Though Buck-Tick's moody industrial rock opening theme disappointingly fades away to reveal yet another man surrounded by adoring girls, NW soon steers clear of the comedy path taken by MASTER OF MOSQUITON—with the possible exception of a pointless devil-Tinkerbell sidekick. A melting pot of contemporary horror influences, particularly Nightbreed (1990) and Buffy the Vampire Slayer (1992), it throws a demons-stalk-Tokyo plot out of WICKED CITY into a conspiracy inspired by the X-Files. Soon, Shido is on the run from the good guys, protecting a human woman bearing a Nightbreed child, facing off against the vampire who created him, and saving Riho's life in a predictable fashion that will link them for all eternity.

Despite a short run on late-night TV like PET SHOP OF HORRORS, NW still manages some original twists, particularly in the second episode that focuses on the suicide of an actress. Selling her soul for fame, she eats human hearts to feed the demon within her and cannot bear to live without her possessor when it dumps her in favor of her understudy. NW has a pragmatic attitude toward the supernatural, running with Ayana Itsuki's original story for Dengeki Comic Gao, and suggesting that anyone who knew what was waiting in the afterlife would stoop to any level to avoid death. In this tale of addiction where life itself is the drug, Shido duels with a sword literally made of his own blood,

all the while fighting the distrust of the NOS.

Such moments clash with less polished incidents, particularly Riho's naïve solo "investigation," in which she hitches a ride with two strangers, hoping to be attacked by a Nightbreed before they can molest her. Shido condescendingly tells Riho that her crucifix is "fake," even though it clearly satisfies the important criterion of being cross-shaped. On several occasions, most notably in a scene lifted from Interview with the Vampire (1994), Shido claims to be unable to endure the sun, even though we have already seen him wandering around in broad daylight. As in PHANTOM QUEST CORP, it would seem that a simple pair of shades will protect modern-day vampires from burning alive. An above-average dub from USMC completes the package, along with a closing theme by rockers Lacrima Christi, who inexplicably sing in Japanese with a Canadian accent. ᴺᵂ

NIGHT WARRIORS: DARKSTALKERS' REVENGE *

1997. JPN: Vampire Hunter. Video. DIR: Shigeru Ikeda. SCR: Tatsuhiko Urahata, Shigeru Ikeda. DES: Shuko Murase. ANI: Shuko Murase, Hiroyuki Tanaka, Hideki Takayama. MUS: Ko Otani. PRD: Madhouse. 40 mins. x 4 eps.

Demitri Maximoff, the most powerful and most feared of vampires, plots to use the psychic energy raised by his human followers to take over the power of the other Darkstalkers, who have always regarded him as an undesirable element. Given that his hair resembles a squeeze of toothpaste, it's hard to blame them completely, but the alternatives aren't so attractive. Meanwhile, the elderly band of advisers to luscious Darkstalker clan chief Morrigan, the girl who put the suck in succubus, is concerned about her general flightiness and the constant in-fighting between clans, which weakens their chances of retaining dominion. But their lady just wants to fight, seeking out Demitri for that purpose and turn-

A last-ditch attempt to recoup money for the troubled Mushi Productions, CLEOPATRA: QUEEN OF SEX failed due to its experimental nature and the rise of the live-action pink eiga soft-porn movie genre in Japan, which killed off "adult" anime until the advent of video in the 1980s. In the U.S., the film was misleadingly advertised as hard-core erotica, disappointing audience members who had paid to see sex on screen and instead found themselves watching the assassination of Julius Caesar reenacted as a kabuki play. See entry p. 63.

Cleopatra: Queen of Sex

© MUSHI PRODUCTIONS

ing the end of episode one into a duel with erotic overtones. Some of the other game characters put in cameo appearances—dour half-Darkstalker Donovan, tiny psychotic Anita, kitten-girl Felicia, and zombie serial killer/rock-star Raptor. Volume two sees Donovan fighting some cursed armor and meeting sisters Hsien-Ko and Ling-Ling, who have become Darkstalkers to help them free their late mother's soul from the dark powers she died fighting.

Amid all the rumbles (which recreate the original game's battles on-screen with real punch and conviction), there is the glimmer of a plot surrounding the Darkstalkers' removal of light from Earth. This has divided humankind into their servants and the rest, preventing the rest from growing much food or making much progress against the faux religiosity that rules their lives. The mysterious Pyron seems to offer humankind the promise of renewed light from his artificial suns, but he's really out to destroy Earth. Things turn very nasty as the Darkstalkers struggle to fight Pyron off before Donovan saves the day.

Films based on games have to overcome major structural problems before they can work as anything but cynical merchandising exercises. *Night Warriors* comes close to sustaining a narrative, but as with **STREET FIGHTER II**, the characters are too firmly embedded in the endless repetitions of gameplay to develop much. There are some interesting subplot possibilities—Donovan's self-hatred and his quest for enlightenment, Morrigan's *Gormenghast* ennui, Anita's shattered childhood, the spiritual and material impoverishment of humankind—but they're flagged rather than explored, relegated to the status of motivation for yet another rumble. **LNV**

NIGHTMARE CAMPUS *

1995. JPN: *Blackboard Jungle: Gaido Gaikuen*. AKA: *Blackboard Jungle: Outerway College*. Video. DIR: Koji Yoshikawa. SCR: Koji Yoshikawa. DES: Keiichi Sato, Kenji Hayama. ANI: Kenji Hayama. MUS: Masamichi Amano. PRD: Phoenix Entertainment. 50 mins. x 5 eps.

Teenager Masao is visiting his father at an archaeological dig in the Himalayas with his mother. When demonic creatures overrun the site, he shoots the one who kills his mother, only to see the corpse turn into his father. A huge earthquake shakes the area, and his school friends back in Japan believe Masao has been killed, but his eventual reappearance is far from the strangest event in school. Masao and his best friend are the embodiment of powerful demonic beings. Other beings, seemingly angelic but in fact completely evil, are trying to take control of the school and the world by unleashing the "demon" in everyone and controlling the powers so released. It's up to the teenage demons to save the world.

Blood, pain, and sadism abound, and there is much nasty sexual content, with the depiction of genitals ranging from the absurdly absent, to suggestive shadows, to explicit realism. The design, art, and animation also vary wildly, with every kind of character style from an Adam Warren-type bimbette to gag-manga goons and retro-styled escapees from early Go Nagai

series such as the similarly themed **DEVILMAN**. The unevenness may be partly blamed on budget problems (even Amano's music budget cuts corners with public-domain Beethoven), but it also indicates Yoshikawa's willingness to experiment with aspects of a genre that can simply be run by the numbers, so uncritical is its audience. This typical (but minor) Toshio Maeda offering has interesting possibilities but sadly never really gets off the ground. The same creator's **UROTSUKIDOJI** was saved from an early finish by export sales (that means us), but this never took off to the same extent in the West, and so the series climaxed prematurely—a fate with which its target audience is probably in sympathy. **LNV**

NIKONIKOPUN

1988. JPN: *Nikonikopun*. TV series. DIR: Yasuo Kageyama. SCR: N/C. DES: Yoshishige Kosako. ANI: Takaaki Ishiyama, Kazuo Iimura, Mitsuo Hikabe. MUS: Takao Ide. PRD: Visual 80, NHK. 23 mins. x 40 eps.

Anime spinoff from a children's show that featured out-of-work actors dressed up as a giant mouse, penguin, and lion, itself part of the Japanese *Watch with Mother* TV strip for the preschool audience. With episode titles like *I Am a Pirate*, *Let's Play*, and *The Picnic March*, the show primed a generation for the later import *Teletubbies*.

NILS' MYSTERIOUS JOURNEY *

1980. JPN: *Nils no Fushigina Tabi*. AKA: *Nils Holgersson*. TV series. DIR: Hisayuki Toriumi, Mamoru Oshii, Yukimatsu Ito. SCR: Narumitsu Taguchi, Ryo Nakahara. DES: Toshiyasu Okada, Mitsuki Nakamura. ANI: Toshiyasu Okada, Noboru Furuse, Jun Tanaka. MUS: Kawauchi Chito. PRD: Studio Pierrot, Gakken, NHK. 25 mins. x 52 eps.

A horrible little boy who torments animals is reduced to the size of a mouse. Rather than seeking revenge, a flock of wild geese take pity on him and ask him along on their migration. In an anime version of Nobel laureate Selma Lagerlof's classic Swedish novel, Nils is

finally restored to his normal size a nicer person. Future **GHOST IN THE SHELL**–director Mamoru Oshii helmed several episodes. Toshiyasu Okada went on to greater things with **MYSTERIOUS CITIES OF GOLD**. The first production for Studio Pierrot.

NINE

1983. Movie, TV special. DIR: Gisaburo Sugii, Hideaki Tsuruta. SCR: Hirokazu Nunose. DES: Mitsuru Adachi. ANI: Minoru Maeda, Hiroshi Wagatsuma. MUS: Hiroaki Serizawa, Yasuo Tsuchida. PRD: Group Tac, Toho, Fuji TV. 83 mins., 80 mins., 71 mins., 75 mins.

Misfit middle-schoolers Karasawa and Katsuya, one a transfer student, sign up for the Seishu school baseball team chiefly because they think it will impress Yuri, the girl they both desire. Before long, their shallow initial reasons have transformed into a burning desire to win the All-Japan championships, in a predictable plotline based on a *Shonen Sunday* manga by Mitsuru Adachi, who also dramatized baseball stories in **H2**, **TOUCH**, **SLOW STEP**, and this show's immediate predecessor **MIYUKI**. The popular movie adaptation was followed by two TV movies the same year, *Nine* and *Nine 2: Declaration of Love*. In 1984, it all ended with *Nine: The Conclusion*, in which Katsuya and his teammates, now high-school juniors, win the regional qualifying tests in an effort to meet Coach Nakao's expectations. However, Karasawa is suffering from a "hitter's block" and is lampooned by school reporter Yoko, who secretly loves him. Inspired by her attention, Karasawa hits a home run just for her, and Katsuya becomes suspicious that his friend has scored with Yuri when he smells that both are using the same shampoo. However, as with all Adachi manga, such minor misunderstandings cannot stop the path of true love, and they all live happily ever after, ending with a double-date at the Koshien baseball stadium.

NINE LOVE STORIES

1992. JPN: *Ai Monogatari*. AKA: *Love*

Stories. Video. DIR: Tomomi Mochizuki, Koji Morimoto, Mamoru Hamazu, Hiroshi Hamazaki, Hidetoshi Omori, Takashi Anno. SCR: Kaiji Kawaguchi. DES: Kaiji Kawaguchi. ANI: N/C. MUS: The Beatles. PRD: Toho. 92 mins.

A feature-length anthology of short romantic tales from the pen of SILENT SERVICE–creator Kaiji Kawaguchi, joined by an underlying theme of Beatles songs. The roster of famous directors is matched by a similarly high-ranking group of voice talents.

NINETEEN

1990. Video. DIR: Takaichi Chiba. SCR: Koji Kawahara. DES: Sho Kitagawa. ANI: N/C. MUS: Toshiku Kadomatsu. PRD: Madhouse, Victor Music. 42 mins.

Kazushi, university student and football player, sees the girl of his dreams in an advertisement. She's really a medical student, who models as a sideline, and one day they meet. As love blossoms against a background of well-to-do student life, can their romance survive the pressures of the 1990s? A tale of yuppie love isn't what most Westerners expect from the Madhouse team, renowned abroad for horror like WICKED CITY, but this exudes quiet charm and elegance. Made for an audience of young, rich Tokyoites, this anime was based on the manga in *Young Jump* by BLUE BUTTERFLY FISH–creator Sho Kitagawa.

NINJA CADETS *

1996. JPN: *Ninja Mono*. Video. DIR: Eiji Suganuma. SCR: Mitsuhiro Yamada. DES: Nobuhito Sue, Keiji Goto. ANI: Fumitomo Kizaki. MUS: N/C. PRD: AIC. 30 mins. x 2 eps.

The Kabuso clan's seizure of Byakuro Castle is marred by the disappearance of the infant princess, who is carried off into hiding by an honorable ninja. Years later, an energetic young group of ninja wannabes are about to be put through their final exam—a mission into the occupied Byakuro Castle to steal the MacGuffin Scrolls of Power. The evil Kabuso clan has hired highly skilled mercenaries to follow them,

knowing that one of the young cadets is actually the missing princess.

Often looking like a spinoff of designer Sue's work on EL HAZARD, *Ninja Cadets* is a lazy afternoon's *D&D* with a sushi flavor—wandering monsters, a bit of comedy business, and a satisfyingly big fight finale. There is a promising monochrome beginning as Byakuro Castle is stormed by evil hordes, but the story soon collapses into a pastoral idyll in which the life of an outcast assassin is presented as a summer camping trip, where you get to play with knives while a mommy ninjette cooks supper. Faced with innumerable foes and a map seemingly drawn by a bored teenage Dungeon Master (you can go any direction you want, as long as it's over the single bridge), the daftest ninja in the world decide it would be a good idea to split up. Then they wander listlessly around the countryside like bored kids on a school trip, which is probably the distant genesis of this whole story.

Luckily, when they reach the impregnable fortress, it's guarded by the daftest samurai in the world, and the scene is set for a walk through all the set pieces of chop-socky ninja films—tiger claws, throwing stars, singing floors, and reconnaissance kites. Our elite assassins try some really smart moves like throwing fire around in a room full of paper scrolls, and voice actress Maria Kawamura steals the show as a suicide-blonde evil minion with an electric-chair hairdo, seemingly inserted at the last minute to inject some much-needed evil into the proceedings. Armed with the Scrolls of Power, the ninja set off to depose the bad guys, just as the ending credits roll—further episodes were not forthcoming. Forgettable fun, but while this does indeed boast both scrolls and ninja, NINJA SCROLL it ain't. ❶

NINJA RESURRECTION: THE REVENGE OF JUBEI *

1997. JPN: *Makai Tensho*. AKA: *Reborn from Hell*. Video. DIR: Yasunori Urata. SCR: Kensei Date. DES: Kenji

Haneyama. ANI: Kenji Haneyama. MUS: Masamichi Amano. PRD: Amuse Video, Phoenix. 40 mins. x 2 eps.

Out of favor, Jubei the ninja roams Japan alone. He believes that a new, dark menace is lurking, waiting to enter the world of men. The great swordsman Musashi, now retired to a monastery, senses the same evil. The Tokugawa shogunate has banned the Western fad of Christianity and is slaughtering its followers. The survivors believe that a new Messiah will be born among them, but the prophecy has a dark side—the Savior could turn bad and become Satan himself. Charismatic Christian leader Shiro Amakusa isn't all he seems, and the believers inside his stronghold are in as much danger from the evil forces within as from the Shogun's armies. Jubei and his associates are sent to infiltrate the Christian citadel of Shimabara, where they find that the peaceful messiah Amakusa has turned to devilry.

Inspired by the same popular novels that informed NINJA SCROLL but misleadingly advertised abroad as a sequel, *NR* is a ninja film for the post-EVANGELION generation, with cruciform explosions in the streets, aliens invading the minds of Japanese citizens, and the use of alien weaponry to fight an alien threat. The eerie, unworldly sight of samurai raising Christian banners and working their foreign magic is truly chilling in this context. Shiro Amakusa's ambiguous position as gentle messiah *and* tormented devil brings echoes of the UROTSUKIDOJI saga—a parallel aided by beautiful music from Masamichi Amano.

NR boasts some classy moments, but the running time is simply too small to contain such multitudes. The mix of fact and fiction is something that really warrants liner notes, and the intense compression of Futaro Yamada's story results in a messy rush of incidental characters. After a promising, portentous beginning with samurai huddling in a Kurosawa rainstorm and turning foreign guns on their convert countrymen, the film rushes headlong into a final battle with no time for a middle act. A completely unnecessary sex scene adds to the collapse of the latter half into substandard anime hackery—described by one of its own producers as "horrendous." The U.S. edition follows the Japanese pattern, with two separate releases, *TROJ* being followed by a second tape, *Hell's Spawn*. In the U.K., both were condensed onto one 80-minute tape. **LNV**

NINJA SCROLL *

1993. JPN: *Jubei Ninpocho*. AKA: *Jubei the Wind Ninja*. Movie. DIR: Yoshiaki Kawajiri. SCR: Yoshiaki Kawajiri. DES: Yutaka Minowa. ANI: Yutaka Minowa. MUS: Kaoru Wada. PRD: Madhouse, Toho, Movic. 94 mins.
After 1603, the people of Japan might as well have lived on another planet for two and a half centuries. Foreign barbarians (that's us) were expelled, along with their corrupting religious influences (Christianity) and their superpowerful, alien weaponry (guns). Under the rule of the Tokugawa family any uprising was ruthlessly suppressed, and stories began to spread about the ninja, a mythical class of superhuman peasants who could beat the samurai through trickery and cunning. Ninja master Jubei occupies a similar position in Japanese popular culture to Robin Hood in ours. A semihistorical figure who mysteriously disappeared, this sword master to the shogun has inspired many plays, novels, and films. It was Jubei's father, Mataemon, who founded the Yagyu clan, and his brother Matajuro who became the hero of a kabuki play, *True Tale of Twin Umbrellas* (1887). It wasn't until the 20th century that his own fan base really grew, stirred up by Futaro Yamada's potboiler novels and turned into anime that eventually made him better known abroad than the rest of his family. In *NS*, he has a set number of superpowered opponents (on this occasion, eight of them) to defeat on a quest for justice against an evil sorcerer. Jubei's ultimate aim is to stop Spanish muskets

from reaching the shogun's enemy and toppling the fragile order.
The same basic plotting can be found in Yamada's *Jubei* novels, the other Jubei anime **NINJA RESURRECTION**, Kinji Fukasaku's live-action Sonny Chiba vehicle *Darkside Reborn* (1981), and its remake, Masakazu Shirai's *Samurai Armageddon* (1996). *NS*, however, beats the cheap special effects of its live-action rivals hands-down and comes complete with a menagerie of flawed heroes, each with distinct magical abilities. The main love interest is one of anime's most interesting female characters, a woman whose very touch is poison. The set pieces are wonderful, from a duel in a bamboo grove to the explosive finale on a sinking ship. Made for a cinema release, *NS* boasts a coherent plot instead of, say, several TV episodes cut together, and a larger budget than many similar anime. The consequently higher production values have made it an enduring anime favorite in the English language. The character has a brief cameo in **JUBEI-CHAN THE NINJA GIRL**, which purports to be a comedy about his modern-day reincarnation. *Ill. p. 69.* **LNV**

NINJA THE WONDERBOY

1964. JPN: *Shonen Ninja Kaze no Fujimaru*. AKA: *Young Fujimaru the Wind Ninja*. TV series. DIR: Daisaku Shirakawa, Kimio Yabuki, Takeshi Shirato, Hiromi Uchida, Michiru Takeda. SCR: Satoshi Iijima, Jiro Yoshino, Daisaku Shirakawa, Minoru Tanaka. DES: N/C. ANI: Daikichi Kusube, Akira Okuwara. MUS: Koichi Fukube. PRD: Toei, NET. 25 mins. x 65 eps.
The first animated version of one of Sanpei Shirato's popular ninja manga about a young boy who is carried away by an eagle and brought up by ninja, who instruct him in secret combat techniques and almost magical fighting arts. The warlords of Japan are fighting over the mystical Book of Dragon Smoke, a scroll detailing how to make special weapons (presumably gunpowder). Fujimaru becomes involved in the conflict with his pacifist love-inter-

est, Midori, and fights against his rival, Jupposai of the Fuma clan, as well as the Iga ninja and the evil southern barbarians.
Shirato was determined to show Japanese life in the Tokugawa shogunate as faithfully as possible, with attention to historical detail, but, although the style of the TV series is quite realistic, it was aimed at a relatively young audience. Shirato's **SASUKE** follows the same pattern, though he would get to appeal to a more adult audience with **LEGEND OF KAMUI**. The original manga in *Bokura* magazine was originally known as *Ninja Clan* but had a name change for the anime designed to associate it closer with the show's sponsor—Fujisawa Pharmaceuticals.

NINJA TRICKERY

1996. JPN: *Ninpo Midare Karakuri*. AKA: *Sowing Disorder the Ninja Way*. Video. DIR: N/C. SCR: Miyasuke Ran. DES: Miyasuke Ran. ANI: N/C. MUS: N/C. PRD: Pink Pineapple, KSS. 30 mins. x 2 eps.
In an erotic anime based on a manga by Miyasuke Ran, Reirei the sex-ninja and her companion Tsukimaru fight injustice and do a lot of humping. Compare to **LA BLUE GIRL**, which has the same idea, but a nastier way of going about it. **N**

NINJAMAN IPPEI

1982. JPN: *Ninjaman Ippei*. TV series. DIR: Hideo Takayashiki, Saburo Hashimoto, Masakazu Yasumura, Yoshihiro Kowata. SCR: Hideo Takayashiki, Masaaki Sakurai, Tomoko Konparu. DES: Saburo Hashimoto, Naoto Hashimoto. ANI: Shunsaburo Takahata. MUS: Kiyoshi Suzuki. PRD: Tokyo Movie Shinsha, Nippon TV. 25 mins. x 13 eps.
Way out in the sticks, the fourth-graders of the local school in Tokio village all come with their own superpowers of doubtful merit, including flying eyeballs and missile-hair. Ippei and his friends study hard at being ninja, but they are constantly under threat from the arrogant cheats

over in the neighboring village of Techno. A strange mix of assassins and school comedy, based on a children's manga by Kazuyoshi Kawai in *100-ten Comics* magazine.

NINKU *

1995. JPN: *Ninku*. TV series, movie. DIR: Noriyuki Abe. SCR: Hiroshi Hashimoto, Ryu Tamura. DES: Tetsuya Nishio, Mari Kitayama, Shigenori Takada. ANI: Kazunori Mizuno. MUS: Yusuke Homma. PRD: Studio Pierrot, Fuji TV. 25 mins. x 55 eps. (IV), 26 mins. (m).

Adapted from Koji Kiriyama's 1993 *Shonen Jump* manga, the anime follows the adventures of the Ninku ninja clan. Since the third year of the Edo period, the clan has brought about a fragile peace through its command of esoteric martial arts, but others are constantly trying to steal their techniques and take over the country. The primary target is Fusuke Ninku, a geeky-looking kid but one of the clan's most vital members; the kidnappers hope he will give them access to its secrets. In the summer "movie" *Ninku: Headstone of a Knife* (1995), screened while the series was still on the air and so separate from its continuity, a gang of impostors is traveling round the country pretending to be the Ninku clan, and the real clan members have to find out what they're up to. The *Ninku* characters also appeared in *Ninku Extra*, a 35-minute video released to popularize the series.

NO GOOD DADDY

1974. JPN: *Dame Oyaji*. AKA: *No Good Daddy*. TV series. DIR: Hisashi Sakaguchi, Fumio Ikeno. SCR: Tomohiro Ando, Susumu Yoshida. DES: Mitsutoshi Furuya. ANI: Fumio Ikeno. MUS: Amp. PRD: Family Planning, Knack, TV Tokyo. 26 mins. x 26 eps.

Poor salaryman Damesuke is married to Onibaba, the Demon-Wife from Hell, who rules him with an iron fist. Every time he tries to assert himself, his family turns on him and beats him up, for they think of him as the world's worst waste of space.

Though in the latter part of the original comic, Dad eventually made good and became the boss of a small company, the anime version was canceled before reaching that point in the story. Created by Mitsutoshi Furuya in 1970 for *Shonen Sunday* magazine, this spiteful, violent series was toned down for an early evening TV audience, and each two-chapter episode involved a greater concentration on son Takobo and his school life. **Ⓥ**

NOBODY'S BOY

1970. JPN: *Chibikko Remi to Meiken Capi; Rittai Anime Ie Naki Ko; Le Naki Ko*. AKA: *Little Remi and His Famous Dog Capi; 3D Animation: Child without a Family; Sans Famille; Homeless Child*. Movie, TV series. DIR: Yugo Serikawa. SCR: Masaharu Segawa. DES: Akira Okuwara. ANI: Akira Okuwara, Yasuji Mori, Katsuya Oda, Akihiro Ogawa. MUS: Tadashi Kishimo. PRD: Toei, TMS, Nippon TV. 81 mins., 25 mins. x 51 eps., 25 mins. x 26 eps.

Hector Malot's 1878 novel *Sans Famille* inspired Tezuka veteran Serikawa to animate the story of little Remi and his search for his lost parents in the early years of the 20th century. Accompanied by his faithful dog, Remi is forced to join a band of traveling players, but after many adventures he finally finds his mother, who thought he was dead, and is no longer a child without a family.

In 1977, a TV series, *3D Animation: Child Without a Home (Ie Naki Ko)*, followed from Tokyo Movie Shinsha. Directed by Osamu Dezaki with character designs by Akio Sugino and a soundtrack by Takeo Watanabe, it covered the same story at much greater length. "3D" was a grandiose claim, but the characters are well designed, and the skill of the animation is considerable, making use of moving backgrounds to give a sense of depth. Another Malot adaptation, NOBODY'S GIRL, followed the next year. In 1980, TMS edited the TV series into another movie, *Child Without a Home*. But the concept still had possibilities—perhaps

The distinctive vulpine features of Masami Obari's character design, shown here from the school beat-'em-up VOLTAGE FIGHTER GOWKAISER. As in many other anime, *VFG* depicts an adult educational institution training its pupils for a hidden purpose. This is less likely to be a feature of the Japanese psyche than of the peculiar demands of the anime industry—freelance artists and writers are more likely to be cynical about traditional career paths. *See entry p. 434.*

Voltage Fighter Gowkaiser

an influence on the success of the live-action OSHIN in 1983, the concept was revived once more, this time with a female lead, as another live-action series, again called *Child Without a Home* (1994). The story was brought back *again* as *Remi: A Child Without a Home* (1996), a 26-episode series directed by Kozo Kusuba for Nippon Animation's WORLD MASTERPIECE THEATER franchise. However, the newest version introduced major changes to the story line, switching Remi's gender and transforming *her* into a child singer in order to showcase the talents of voice actress Mitsuko Horie, for whom the series was a glorified star vehicle. With a shorter running time and such major alterations contravening the worthy spirit of previous shows, the series received the lowest ratings ever for the *WMT* and was the death knell for the franchise. See also a further great boy-and-his-dog epic BELLE AND SEBASTIAN and another oft-adapted tale of an orphan's quest, FROM THE APENNINES TO THE ANDES.

NOBODY'S GIRL

1978. JPN: *Perrine Monogatari*. AKA: *En Famille; Her Own Folk; Story of Perrine*. TV series. DIR: Hiroshi Saito, Shigeo Koshi. SCR: Akira Miyazaki, Kasuke

Sato. DES: Shuichi Seki. ANI: Takao Kogawa. MUS: Takeo Watanabe. PRD: Nippon Animation, Fuji TV. 25 mins. x 53 eps.

Young Perrine travels with her father around Bosnia, where he is a photographer. After his death, Perrine and her mother are forced to move to France, making ends meet with their own photo business, until Perrine's mother also dies. Perrine continues on the journey with only her dog, Baron, for company, heading for the mansion of her rich grandfather Bilfranc. He turns out to be a cruel man, and instead of announcing herself, Perrine takes a job as a humble worker in his string factory. After many trials of cruelty, he comes to trust Perrine, appointing her as his interpreter and awaiting a fairy-tale ending where she reveals that she has been his granddaughter all along.

Another entry in the WORLD MASTERPIECE THEATER series, this family anime was based on an 1893 novel by Hector Malot and is not to be confused with the 1996 sex-change remake of his earlier NOBODY'S BOY. Since Malot's original begins with the death of Perrine's mother, all that precedes it in the above synopsis is the creation of scriptwriter Akira Miyazaki. This was a first-time collaboration between writer Miyazaki and Hiroshi Saito, who would become stalwarts of the *WMT* franchise in the absence of an "old guard," such as Hayao Miyazaki and Isao Takahata, who had gone on to better things. Their next entry in the series would be TOM SAWYER.

NOEL'S MYSTERIOUS ADVENTURE
1983. JPN: *Noel no Fushigina Boken*. Movie. DIR: Tadao Takakuwa, Yasuo Maeda. SCR: Ryohei Suzuki. DES: Iruka. ANI: Nobukazu Otake, Chikao Katsui. MUS: Iruka. PRD: Iruka Office. 72 mins. On a hot summer's day, Noel and his faithful dog, Kinnosuke, get into a plane to buy some ice cream for the sun. En route, they stop off at the planet Kikazari, where dressing up is compulsory. After meeting with the sun, Noel encounters the master of smog, and must wrestle a sludge monster on the bottom of the ocean.

A vehicle for the singer-songwriter Iruka, who wrote the original story and also provides the voice of Noel, while her three-year-old son plays the dog. The film was shown on a double bill with another of the musician's creations, the short film *Iruka's Christmas: Jeremy's Tree*, in which a lonely orphan finds a bird in the snow who tells him that she lost her home when her tree was cut down. Jeremy agrees to steal the tree from a family's living room but is shot in the process. As he loses consciousness, he has a vision of Santa Claus. This story of sub-Wildean pathos was made by *Noel*-assistant director Maeda—a seasonal outing somewhat ruined by being released in April.

NOIR
2001. TV series. DIR: Koichi Mashimo. SCR: Ryoei Tsukimura. DES: Yoko Kikuchi, Minako Shiba. ANI: N/C. MUS: Yuki Kajiura. PRD: B-Train, TV Tokyo. 25 mins. x 26 eps.
Near-future replay of GUNSMITH CATS, as sexy hitwoman Mireille Bouquet, searching the Tokyo underworld for the assassin who killed her parents, teams up with traumatized Japanese girl Kirika Yumura. Neither can remember the full details of their pasts, but both are dragged into a conspiracy that shows that they are linked by more than mere amnesia.

NONOMURA HOSPITAL
1996. JPN: *Nonomura Byoin no Hito-bito*. AKA: *People of Nonomura Hospital*. Video. DIR: Nobuyoshi Ando. SCR: Oji Miyako. DES: Jun Sato. ANI: Jun Sato. MUS: N/C. PRD: Pink Pineapple, KSS. 30 mins. x 2 eps.
After breaking his leg, detective inspector Umihara is sent to Nonomura Hospital to recuperate. When the hospital owner dies, the convalescing Umihara goes to work. Unsure of whether the death was suicide or murder, Umihara questions the victim's beautiful wife, the three attractive nurses, and his charming fellow patient. An anime based on an erotic computer game, it consequently boasts more sex than suspense. **Ⓝ**

NOOZLES, THE *
1984. JPN: *Fushigina Koala Blinky*. AKA: *Blinky the Mysterious Koala; Blinky and Printy*. TV series. DIR: Taku Sugiyama, Noboru Ishiguro. SCR: Taku Sugiyama, Michiru Tanabe. DES: Isamu Noda. ANI: Eimi Maeda. MUS: Reijiro Komutsu. PRD: Nippon Animation, Nippon TV. 25 mins. x 26 eps.
Ten-year-old girl Sandy Brown stays with her grandmother while her archaeologist father is away on a research trip. She is given a toy koala, only to discover that when she "noozles" her nose against it, it transforms into a real koala, Blinky, a refugee from Koalawalla Land. On the run from (literally) a kangaroo court with kangaroo cops, Blinky has come to Earth to hide, his only possession a magical watch that can stop time. His sister, Printy (Pinky in the U.S. dub), also arrives in search of her brother—Printy has a magical makeup compact that can open dimensional gateways. Blinky and Printy take Sandy on many adventures as they study Earth and pop back on occasion to Koalawalla Land, also hiding out from the two evil poachers Frankie and Spike.

Back in the real world, 1984 saw the arrival of six koalas in Japan, sent as goodwill ambassadors by the Australian government. Japan went into a koala frenzy, lapping up this otherwise unremarkable anime and its rival on TV Tokyo, LITTLE KOALA. The same production team specialized in animal cartoons, most notably DOGTANIAN AND THE THREE MUSKEHOUNDS. The series was broadcast on the U.S. children's channel Nickelodeon.

NORA
1985. Video. DIR: Satomi Mikuriya. SCR: Satomi Mikuriya, Reiko Nakada. DES: Satomi Mikuriya, Yuki Motonori. ANI: Masami Suda. MUS: Yuji Ono. PRD: Mik Mak Pro, Toyo Links, Pony Canyon. 56 mins., 45 mins.

In the year 2097, a beautiful girl and two scientists must prevent their frontier space-town's governing computer from going haywire and starting Armageddon. This adaptation differs considerably from the original 1980 manga from **GARAGA**-creator Mikuriya, but, since the creator performed so many tasks on the staff, we can assume the changes were made with her approval. A second episode, *Twinkle Nora Rock Me*, completed the story.

NORAKURO

1970. JPN: *Norakuro-kun*. AKA: *Black Stray*. TV series, movie. DIR: Yonehiko Watanabe, Satoshi Murayama. SCR: Masaki Tsuji, Ichiro Wakabayashi, Shunichi Yukimuro. DES: N/C. ANI: Tsuneo Komuro, Toshitaka Kadota. MUS: Hidehiko Arashino. PRD: TCJ, Fuji TV. 11 mins., 25 mins. x 28 eps., 25 mins. x 48 eps.
Shiho Tagawa's *Norakuro* began as a 1931 manga in *Shonen Club* with the story of a brave stray dog's fight against oppressive monkeys. The popular character was soon put to use promoting Japan's militaristic expansion in the 11-minute short *Corporal Norakuro* (1934, *Norakuro Gocho*), a **WARTIME ANIME** directed by Yasuji Murata, in which the loyal doggy joins the army, beats his monkey allies at rifle practice, has some fun with fireworks, and then wakes up to discover it was all a dream.

The *Norakuro* manga enjoyed a new lease on life during the nostalgia boom that followed the 1968 centenary of the Meiji Restoration. Transferring to *Comic Bon-Bon*, where it ran for another decade, it was brought back for a young audience as the TV series *Norakuro* (1970), in which the low-ranking soldier returned once more, ever jostling for power within an army dominated by General Bull and kept strictly under control by Captain Mole. Playing up the military comedy angle in skits that were crammed two to each episode, Norakuro also had time to fall for Miko, a pretty nurse and troops' pinup.

Never one to admit defeat, the franchise jumped to *Comic Morning* in the 1980s in order to promote Norakuro's latest incarnation, making this one of the earliest retro anime. The original character's grandson was the lead character in *Norakuro-kun* (1987), a lighthearted Studio Pierrot series directed by future **KISHIN CORPS** crew member Takaaki Ishiyama. For this version, the child of a poverty-stricken family is visited by the titular canine, now resembling less a military cartoon than a man in a life-sized Mickey Mouse costume, courtesy of character designs by Yuji Moriyama. The children, however, are soon enlisted in war games, as General Bull arrives and warns of the approaching pig forces of Jimmy Butagawa.

NOTARI MATSUTARO

1990. Video. DIR: Toshio Takeuchi. SCR: Tadaaki Yamazaki, Seiji Matsuoka, Shunichi Yukimuro. DES: Akehiro Kaneyama. ANI: Masayoshi Kitazaki. MUS: Masayoshi Kitazaki. PRD: Mushi Pro. 60 mins. x 6 eps.
A teenage school dropout finds new meaning in his life when he discovers sumo wrestling, heading off to Tokyo for the bright lights and training with an aging master of the sport. Based on a 1973 *Big Comic* manga by **TOMORROW'S JOE**–creator Tetsuya Chiba, *NM* packs two "episodes" into each 60-minute tape to give the impression that it is actually a 12-part TV series, even though it was never broadcast.

NOW AND THEN, HERE AND THERE *

1999. JPN: *Ima, Soko ni Iru Boku*. AKA: *Now I'm There*. TV series. DIR: Akitaro Daichi. SCR: Hideyuki Kurata. DES: Atsushi Oizumi. ANI: Michinori Nishino. MUS: Migaku Iwazaki, Toshio Masuda. PRD: AIC, WOWOW. 25 mins. x N/D eps.
Schoolboy Shu Matsutani climbs a chimney to rescue a girl he sees sitting at its summit, but he falls into an alternate world. There, the damsel he tried to rescue is revealed as Lala Lu, the bearer of a magic pendant that can control the water element in this new world. The evil Hamdo needs Lala's pendant so that he can construct his fortress in a place called Hellyhood—and now Shu isn't just visiting, he's the point man in a war against the forces of darkness. Despite a plot redolent of the comedy **EL HAZARD**, childish designs, and a sub-Miyazaki look, *N&TH&T* is a remarkably adult show that refuses to stint on images of violence and abuse. Shown on more forgiving satellite TV, this anime was compared to Alex Haley's epic *Roots* by screenwriter Kurata—a trifle optimistic from the man who wrote **BATTLE ATHLETES**. Ⓥ

NUBO: THE DISAPPEARING MEDAL

1990. JPN: *Nubo Kieta Medal*. Video. DIR: Hiromitsu Ota. SCR: N/C. DES: N/C. ANI: Hiromitsu Ota. MUS: Hiroaki Ran. PRD: Aubec. 25 mins.
In the green and pleasant village of Nubo, the summer festival is ruined when a gold medal (first prize in the Pie Eating Contest) disappears. All the local inhabitants, who happen to be the mascot characters from the various types of Morinaga chocolate, go hunting for the missing medal. A cynical exercise in product placement, designed to sell chocolate to kids, and, presumably, get them to eat more pies.

NURSE ANGEL LILIKA SOS

1995. TV series. DIR: Akitaro Daichi. SCR: Akitaro Daichi. DES: Koi Ikeno. ANI: Hajime Watanabe. MUS: Shinkichi Mitsumune. PRD: Studio Gallop, TV Tokyo. 25 mins. x 35 eps.
Ten-year-old Ririka is a typical Japanese elementary school heroine—cute, sweet, kindhearted, and always willing to help others. When a very handsome older boy returning from his travels gives her a present from the exotic, mysterious realm of England, it turns out to be the device that transforms her into the latest of a long line of anime heroines dating back to **LITTLE WITCH SALLY**. Earth is under threat from the playing-card-themed forces of

Dark Joker (see also **WILD CARDZ**), and whenever his minions, complete with ace-of-spades tattoos, threaten Earth, Ririka puts on her magic nurse's cap and becomes Lilika, the Nurse Angel. She uses the power bestowed on her to fight evil, extend her powers of healing to the world, and also to sell the many items of product-placement accessories that she wields in the commercially savvy post-**SAILOR MOON** world. At the halfway point, the series suddenly becomes much darker and more unpredictable—heading for a tear-jerker ending with a real twist. A manga was published the same year by Yasushi Akimoto and Koi Ikeno, who also created **TOKIMEKI TONIGHT**.

OCEAN WAVES

1993. JPN: *Umi ga Kikoeru.* AKA: *I Can Hear the Ocean.* TV special. DIR: Tomomi Mochizuki. SCR: N/C. DES: Yoshifumi Kondo. ANI: Katsuya Kondo. MUS: N/C. PRD: Studio Ghibli, Tokuma, Nippon TV. 72 mins.

En route to a high school reunion, Taku Morisaki reflects on his past. Ten years earlier, transfer student Rikako fell for Taku's friend Matsuno, perhaps to hide the alienation she felt at an unwelcoming school. On a trip to Hawaii, her money was stolen, and she surprisingly turned to Taku for help—a simple and possibly innocent act that changed the trio's relationships forever.

Based on a Saeko Himura novel originally serialized in *Animage* magazine, this is Studio Ghibli's only television drama and was made by the studio's younger members for a themed broadcast during the Golden Week holiday. The stress of making *OW* and **HERE IS GREENWOOD** simultaneously would leave director Mochizuki briefly hospitalized. The studio also made two animated shorts to celebrate the 40th anniversary of broadcaster Nippon TV.

ODIN *

1985. JPN: *Odin—Koshi Hansen Starlight.* AKA: *Odin—Photon Ship Starlight; Odin: Photon Space Sailer Starlight.* Movie. DIR: Takeshi Shirato, Toshio Masuda, Eiichi Yamamoto. SCR: Kazuo Kasahara, Toshio Masuda, Eiichi Yamamoto. DES: Geki Katsumata, Shinya Takahashi. ANI: Eiichi Yamamoto, Kazuhito Udagawa. MUS: Hiroshi Miyagawa, Kentaro Haneda, Noboru Takahashi, Masamichi Amano, Fumitaka Anzai, Loudness. PRD: Westcape Corp. 139 mins. (93 mins., English-language version).

The photon ship Starlight sets sail from the orbital space colony City of Einstein, en route for Jupiter. Along the way, crew member Akira picks up Sarah, the last survivor of the spacewreck Alford. Sarah is receiving telepathic messages from what she believes to be an alien spacecraft near one of the moons of Uranus. Disobeying orders, the younger members of the crew change course for the alien craft's distant destination, planet Odin.

A beautifully designed film, its already shaky story line was dealt irreparable damage through the removal of 45 minutes of footage and a dire English-language script and dub. The story of a youthful crew and experienced skipper setting out in a space-going sailing ship on a dangerous mission inspired by a mysterious and beautiful girl had already been done with enormous success in **STAR BLAZERS**, and less so with **THUNDERSUB**. Either producer Yoshinobu Nishizaki wanted to prove that he could repeat that success without help from his former collaborators Leiji Matsumoto and Noboru Ishiguro, or else he is a one-trick pony when it comes to story-lining SF shows. Yet despite the gorgeous design and a skilled crew including Tezuka veteran Yamamoto and "advice" from **NORA**-creator Satomi Mikuriya, Nishizaki's new version never takes off.

OFFICE AFFAIRS *

1996. JPN: *Me Chi Ku.* AKA: *Female Animal, Bitch.* Video. DIR: Mitsuhiro Yoneda. SCR: Rokurota Marabe. DES: Mitsuhiro Yoneda. ANI: Toshiyuki Nishida, Mitsuhiro Yoneda. MUS: Yoshi. PRD: FAI International, YOUC. 30 mins.

Ono is a new publishing recruit, assigned to one of the fastest-rising new titles under editor-in-chief Megumi Sugiyama. His girlfriend since college days, Rie works at the same company, though she's "only in the administration department." Still the two have a good relationship until he gets the hots for his boss. As he gradually "learns the ropes" he is admitted to the department's elite corps of workers who put in overtime satisfying their editor-in-chief's need for sex and humiliation. Eventually Rie finds out and dumps him, and he leaves the company, rationalizing that his boss's kinky sexual needs are the inevitable result of giving women too much responsibility in the workplace.

The tawdry, predictable story line is the benchmark for the standard of work in every department. The most memorable images from this sad video are shots of the door of Ono's apartment, the rejection box into which his manager tosses most of his writing efforts, and the cigarettes and ashtray by his bed—memorable because these are the frames you see most often, with dialogue, orgasmic moans, or panting heard over them to indicate action that's too expensive to draw. Much of the "animation" consists of intercut stills. The characters appear catatonic because they hardly move, even in the grip of passion. For the English dub, Kitty Video gave this lackluster effort as much attention as it deserves, with an undistinguished cast yawning through the tedious script under a director who can't be bothered. **N**

OFFSIDE
1992. JPN: *Offside*. Video. DIR: Takao Yotsuji, Hisashi Abe. SCR: Takao Yotsuji. DES: Hisashi Abe. ANI: Hisashi Abe. MUS: Saburo Takada. PRD: Holly Production, Leona, Visual House Egg. 50 mins.

The world's worst soccer team has never won a single match despite being made up of eager young boys who desperately crave success. Their prayers are answered in the form of new manager Nagisa, who puts them through a sporting regime punched out of the standard AIM FOR THE ACE template. Based on Natsuko Heiuchi's "original" 1987 manga serialized in *Shonen Magazine*, this anime is from the same artist who created the tennis manga *Fifteen-Love*. Compare to CAPTAIN TSUBASA and the actionably similar KICKERS. As the 2002 World Cup approached, the series was revived on Japanese satellite TV in an anime series directed by Seiji Okuda.

O-GENKI CLINIC *
1991. AKA: *Welcome to the O-Genki Clinic; Come to Ogenki Clinic; Return to Ogenki Clinic*. Video. DIR: Takashi Watanabe. SCR: Haruka Inui. DES: Takashi Watanabe. ANI: N/C. MUS: N/C. PRD: AC Create. 45 mins. x 3 eps.

Dr. Ogenki and his pretty assistant, Nurse Tatase, run a clinic specializing in sexual problems. Ever ready to apply hands-on therapy, the doctor and his assistants help those who can't help themselves, with problems varying from the sexually dysfunctional to the just plain weird.

Based on Haruka Inui's manga from *Play Comic*, this somewhat dated tale of everyday working life in a sex clinic has one redeeming feature—everybody in it is obviously a consenting adult, even if their adulthood is signified by the disproportional body shapes in keeping with the art-style of the original manga. Humor plays a central part, leavening the sex scenes with moments

of "comedy," such as Ogenki's talking penis, and Nurse Tatase's ongoing attempts to convince her mother that Ogenki would make a good husband. The stage is set for a series of smutty *Carry On*–style tales where the pair give their all to their professional duties while yearning for each other. Refused a release in the early 1990s by the British Board of Film Classification, it is hence only available in the U.S. The Japanese-language version allegedly features famous voice actors using pseudonyms, but the English dub is poor quality. The live-action porn movie *The Ladies' Phone Sex Club*, also created by Haruka Inui, repeats many of the same jokes. **N**

OGRE SLAYER *
1994. JPN: *Onikirimaru*. Video. DIR: Yoshio Kato. SCR: Norifumi Terada. DES: Masayuki Goto. ANI: Masayuki Goto. MUS: Kazuhiko Sotoyama. PRD: KSS, TBS. 30 mins. x 4 eps.

A young man who is really the child of an ogre is destined to wander Earth slaying his own kind. When he has killed every ogre, he believes he will become fully human; until then, he is known only by the name of the sword he bears, Ogre Slayer. In each separate story, all set in modern Japan, he meets humans in trouble and deals death and destruction to ogres, but he isn't in the business of "happy endings." An episodic, melancholy quest with a resemblance to Tezuka's DORORO but actually inspired by scenes of sword-swinging schoolboys in Paul Schrader's *Mishima* (1985), *OS* has limited animation but attractive artwork and design. The ogres, superbly gross and amoral, are the best things in this short series based on Kei Kusunoki's 1988 manga in *Shonen Sunday* magazine. The same artist also created YAGAMI'S FAMILY TROUBLES and YOMA: CURSE OF THE UNDEAD. **NV**

OH! FAMILY
1986. TV series. DIR: Masamune Ochiai, Takashi Hisaoka, Hideki Tonokatsu. SCR: Shunichi Yukimuro, Yoshiaki Yoshi-

da, Tsunehisa Ito, et al. DES: Fumio Sasaki. ANI: Mikio Tsuchiya, Isao Kaneko, Minoru Kibata. MUS: Tadanori Matsui. PRD: Knack, TV Tokyo. 25 mins. x 26 eps.

A comedy soap based on the everyday lives of the Andersons, a "typical" California household, as seen through the eyes of Taeko Watanabe, on whose 1981 Flower Comic manga *Family* it was based. Mom, Dad, and kids Kay, Tracey, and Fay, along with Fay's boyfriend, Rafe, get on with their lives, though much of the comedy arises from the fact that Kay displays every sign of being gay, and his efforts at concealment cause embarrassment to the family. Meanwhile, Dad starts receiving calls from Jonathan, a stranger who claims to be his long-lost son, much to the consternation of Mrs. Anderson. Shown in Italy, where it was much admired, though one episode was banned. **N**

OH! HARIMANADA
1992. JPN: *Aa Harimanada*. TV series. DIR: Yukio Okazaki. SCR: Shizuo Noha, Shunichi Nakamura, Hitoshi Yasuhira. DES: Yutaka Arai. ANI: Ichiro Fukube, Katsumasa Kanezawa, Yutaka Arai, Shunichi Nakamura. MUS: Masamichi Amano. PRD: Horman Office, EG Film, TV Tokyo. 25 mins. x 23 eps.

The unconventional adventures of Harimanada, a sumo wrestler who attains the top rank of *yokozuna* but fights in a ring that seems to owe a lot more to the masked wrestlers and strange tricks of KINNIKUMAN. As with other sports anime such as AIM FOR THE ACE and TOMORROW'S JOE, the series progresses through hardships (an opponent undefeated through 26 bouts), conflicts outside the ring (the Masked Wrestler's fiancée), forbidden techniques (the Murder Mackerel Snap!), and mysterious challengers (the "Mysterious Wrestler," naturally). Based on the 1988 manga in *Comic Morning* by Kei Sadayasu.

OH MY GODDESS! *
1993. JPN: *Aa Megamisama*. AKA: *Ah!*

My Goddess. Video, movie, TV series. DIR: Hiroaki Goda. SCR: Naoko Hasegawa, Kunihiko Kondo. DES: Hidenori Matsubara, Hiroshi Kato, Atsushi Takeuchi, Osamu Tsuruyama. ANI: Hidenori Matsubara, Nobuyuki Kitajima, Yoshimitsu Ohashi, Masanori Nishii. MUS: Takeshi Yasuda. PRD: AIC, WOWOW. 30 mins. x 4 eps., 40 mins. x 1 ep (v), 8 mins. x 46 eps. (TV), 105 mins. (m).

Hapless student Keiichi phones for takeout and accidentally gets through to the Goddess Helpline. When Belldandy (Verthandi—the Norse embodiment of the concept of Being) turns up in his bedroom and offers to grant him a wish, he wishes for her to be his girlfriend, and they're stuck with each other. In the video series, she's a divine doormat who waits on him hand and foot, exerts her powers very discreetly and then only to make life easier for him, and includes both their siblings in the household without a murmur—a parody of ideal Japanese femininity. The 1988 *Comic Afternoon* manga by Kosuke Fujishima does more justice to all the characters, but the anime compresses the whole tale into a romance between the wettest pair of lovers since Noah, a wimp and a doormat whose excuse is that they were fated to be that way. A soft-soap rendition of alien-spouse drama tradition that traces a line back through URUSEI YATSURA and BELOVED BETTY all the way to the American sitcom *Bewitched*, Kosuke Fujishima's story posits a boy who is pure of heart and gives him the perfect girlfriend, whose role seems to be to look pretty, cook, and clean. The story is sugary enough to rot teeth, but the animation and design are remarkably faithful to Fujishima's stunning original art.

Surprisingly, given the fad for mawkish romance à la TENCHI MUYO!, *OMG* did not graduate to a TV series. While other shows jumped onto its formulaic bandwagon, it was Fujishima's other big manga, YOU'RE UNDER ARREST!, that got a TV broadcast. Instead, fans had to contend with a series of short,

squashed-down comedy skits, *The Adventures of Mini-Goddess* (1998, *OMG: Chichaitte Koto wa Benri da ne!*, aka *The Adventures of Mini-Goddesses in the Handy "Petite" Size*), directed by Yasuhiro Matsumura. Running as part of the *Anime Complex* strand, the series was a predictable rush of sight gags as cartoon versions of Belldandy's sisters Urd and Skuld, accompanied by Gan-chan the rat, rushed through comedy business seemingly inspired by old Warner Bros. cartoons. Belldandy's original voice actress, Kikuko Inoue, is conspicuously absent from the first 14 episodes. There were also, however, brief cameos by *OMG* manga characters not seen in the previous anime version, as well as parodies of contemporary anime, such as BERSERK.

After much hype and delays (reputedly occasioned at one point by a go-slow from animators convinced that the world would end according to the prophecies of Nostradamus, so there was little point in doing overtime!), the feature-length *OMG: The Movie* (2000) was finally released, reuniting director Goda and many of the video staff. Originally planned as an adaptation of the "Welsper" story arc from the manga, the film's plot changed through many rewrites into a simpler setup in which Belldandy is approached by her mentor, Celestin, a one-time member of the Gods' Council. Discredited and imprisoned on the moon, Celestin seeks Belldandy's help, though Keiichi is initially suspicious of her association with the newcomer.

The show was pasticled on many occasions, particularly in erotic variants such as EVOCATION and CAN CAN BUNNY. *Ill. p. 103.*

OH! MY KONBU

1991. TV series. DIR: Tetsuo Imazawa, Mineo Fuji, Shingo Kaneko, Katsunori Kosuga. SCR: Riko Hinokuma, Tatsuhiko Muraame, Aki Tanioka, Shunsuke Suzuki, Yutaka Hayashi, Megumi Sugiwara. DES: Takahiro Kamiya. ANI: Yukio Otaku. MUS: N/C. PRD: Narumi, TBS. 12 mins. x 44 eps.

Ratty, Mole, and Toad in the anime adaptation of Kenneth Grahame's *Wind in the Willows*. Stretching the original across 26 episodes, the anime version pits the creatures of "Willow Town" against Bully the Weasel and Scurry the Ermine, fierce animals from the dark wood who are determined to seize control of the stately Toad Hall for themselves. *See entry p. 445.*

Willow Town

Fifth-grader Konbu Nabeyama is the son of a cook in a slice-of-life gourmet comedy that tries to add an element of adventure to slaving in the kitchen. Konbu helps his father solve problems in the world through the judicious use of seasonings, the right choice of menu, and the pleasing of fickle customers.

OI RYOMA!

1992. AKA: *Hey Ryoma!; Rainbow Samurai.* TV series. DIR: Hiroshi Sasakawa, Yutaka Kagawa. SCR: Masao Ito, Michio Yoshida, Makoto Noriza, Nobuaki Kishima. DES: Katsumi Hashimoto. ANI: Katsumi Hashimoto, Hideo Kawauchi, Takeshi Shirato. MUS: N/C. PRD: Animation 21, NHK. 25 mins. x 13 eps.

In the 19th century, Japan is in the grip of the shogunate, with the shogun wielding power in the name of a puppet emperor. Young Ryoma Sakamoto is growing up with dreams of being a samurai and doing heroic deeds for his country. He witnesses the arrival of Commodore Perry's black ships, and realizes that, although he is a samurai, the time has come to challenge the authority of the shogun, who wishes to keep Japan trapped in a feudal time warp. In this adaptation of a manga by

Tetsuya Takeda and **Go for It, Genki**–creator Yu Koyama, after successfully completing his training, Ryoma leaves Chiba town for a life of adventure.

A famous figure in Japanese history, Ryoma brokered the fateful alliance between the rebel domains of Satsuma and Choshu, and he wrote an eight-point plan for modernizing Japan. His greatest moment was the bloodless coup of 1867, when he and his companions managed to negotiate the "return" of power to the emperor, which ended centuries of rule by the shogunate. Barely a month later, he was assassinated at age 33 without living to see the Japan he helped create. Three weeks after Ryoma's death, the emperor came to power in the Meiji Restoration, beginning Japan's modern era. Ryoma would appear in many other anime, including **Drifting Clouds** and **Armored Chronicle Hio**.

OISHINBO

1988. AKA: *Feast; Taste Quest.* TV series. DIR: Toshio Takeuchi, Kunihisa Sugishima, Masayuki Kojima. SCR: Ryuzo Nakanishi, Yasuo Tahada. DES: Masaaki Kawanami. ANI: Masaaki Kawanami, Shigetaka Kiyoyama. MUS: Kazuo Otani. PRD: Shinei, Nippon TV. 25 mins. x 136 eps.

Banzai! Oishinbo started in 1975 and ran for 25 years. A short slot where celebrities sampled various regional delicacies, it started a craze for gourmet food shows and the 1983 *Big Comic Spirits* manga *Oishinbo* by Tetsu Kariya and Akira Hamasaki. The anime version sticks close to the original, in which two young reporters go in search of the ultimate celebration menu for their newspaper's hundredth anniversary. A live-action movie version followed in 1996. After the resolution of the original quest, the anime story focuses on comedy and romance, as chef Jiro aims for the top in an elegant Tokyo restaurant. Despite Jiro's youth, his boss has put him in sole charge of the menu, and he works hard to

ensure that he deserves such trust. As in the manga, as much care is given to the depiction of food as to Jiro, his lovely costar Yuko, and the other characters. Several interrelated episodes were also edited into TV specials *Oishinbo: Jiro vs. Katsuyama* (#2, 10, 12, and 36) and *Oishinbo: The Ultimate Full Course* (#1, 6, 23, and 62). The characters also appeared in spinoffs, including *Oishinbo: Ultimate Shopping* (1992), which was an animated segment of the *Magical Brain Power* TV quiz game, and the topical TV special *Oishinbo: The U.S.–Japan Rice War* (1993). See also **Mister Ajikko** and the live-action series *Iron Chef* (1993). Original creator Kariya would also inadvertently cook up a giant robot show: **UFO Robot Dai Apollon**. **Cook Daddy**'s unorthodox ingredients put it in a different category despite the similarity of the Japanese title.

OJARUMARU

1999. JPN: *Ojarumaru.* AKA: *Prince Mackaroo.* TV series, Movie. DIR: Akitaro Daichi. SCR: Rin Futomaru. DES: Hajime Watanabe. ANI: N/C. MUS: Harukichi Yamamoto. PRD: Adobe Pictures, Nippon Crown, NHK Educational, NHK. 8 mins. x 270 eps. (TV), 30 mins. (m).

A short series for young children tells the story of a chirpy nobleman's child from Heian-era Japan who time-slips into the modern world. He has wacky adventures living with an ordinary Japanese family, whose son Kazuma becomes his special friend. References to 11th-century culture and modern aspirations mix with artwork that looks naïve but is calculated for comic effect. Like *Teletubbies*, it's paced slowly and simply for easy assimilation by the young. A short film, *Summer of Promises* (2000), introduces Semira, a strange boy who comes to play with Ojaru and his chums and bears a marked resemblance to a boy of the same name who spent a summer with the village elders when they were boys, long ago. A very different blast from the past would characterize director Daichi's **Jubei-chan the Ninja Girl**.

OKAMA REPORT

1991. JPN: *Okama Hakusho.* AKA: *Homosexual Report; Homosexual White Paper.* Video. DIR: Teruo Kigure. SCR: Ippei Yamagami, Sheila Shimazaki. DES: Teruo Kigure. ANI: Jiro Sayama. MUS: Jiro Takemura. PRD: Knack. 45 mins. x 3 eps.

Shinya Okama (a surname that's a Japanese pun on "homosexual") is a university student who gets a part-time job in a gay bar. He puts on a dress and calls himself Catherine, then finds himself falling in love with a pretty customer, Miki. Miki is a real girl—and thinks "Catherine" is, too. The first video was followed by *Okama Report: Midsummer Happening* and a year later by *OR: Man's Decision*, in which Shinya's high-school pal Dan (who doesn't wear dresses) also falls for Miki, presenting Shinya with the dilemma of whether or not he should risk revealing his true nature and losing Miki altogether. Based on the *Young Sunday* manga by Hideo Yamamoto, another of whose sexually themed manga is available in English as *Voyeur*.

OLD CURIOSITY SHOP, THE

1979. JPN: *Sasurai no Shojo Nell.* AKA: *Wanderings of the Girl Nell.* TV series. DIR: Hideo Makino, Katsumi Kosuga, Hajime Sawa, Mineo Fuji, Keinosuke Tsuchiya. SCR: Keisuke Fujikawa, Kazumi Asakura. DES: Norio Kashima. ANI: Norio Kashima, Hiroshi Kuzuoka. MUS: Harumi Ibe. PRD: Dax, TV Tokyo. 25 mins. x 26 eps.

Nell is a perky girl in 19th-century London, who lives with her grandfather, Trent, above his antique shop, while her mother and brother live in a place evocatively named Paradise. When Grandfather loses all his money gambling and the principal creditor wants to marry Nell to his slimy nephew, she has to flee and try to reach her family. A less permanent abode than the Paradise of Charles Dickens's original novel, Nell's destination still takes some hardship to reach, pursued all the while by the feckless Quilp, who wants her for himself. Dickens's *A Christmas*

Carol was also turned into anime as **THE STINGIEST MAN IN TOWN**.

OLD MAN'S SURVIVAL GUIDE, THE

1990. JPN: *Ojisan Kaizo Koza*. Movie. DIR: Tsutomu Shibayama. SCR: Chinami Shimizu. DES: Tsutomu Shibayama. ANI: Kuniyuki Ishii. MUS: Kazz Toyama. PRD: TMS. 92 mins.

In this anime adaptation of the popular *Weekly Bunshun* manga by Chinami Shimizu and Yoshi Furuya, an old man confesses his secrets of business success to an attentive Office Lady, imparting such gems of wisdom as How to Say the Right Thing, Better Commuting, and Etiquette for Meetings. Compare to the same idea from another angle—**SURVIVAL IN THE OFFICE**.

OME-1

1985. JPN: *Ome-1*. Video. DIR: Nobuyoshi Sugita. SCR: N/C. DES: N/C. ANI: Hajime Iwasaki. MUS: N/C. PRD: Towa Creation. 30 mins. x 2 eps.

Two science-fiction adventures attempting (and failing) to cash in on the earlier success of the **CREAM LEMON** and **LOLITA ANIME** releases. In the first, *Torture Chamber at Penius Base*, pretty schoolgirl Momoko is found to be an interstellar spy and punished for her deception. In the second part, *The Model Is a Soap-Girl*, Momoko goes to work at a "soapland" bathhouse/brothel in order to track down her missing friend, Yuko. A low-quality entry in an already low-rent genre. **NV**

ON A PAPER CRANE *

1993. JPN: *Tsuru ni Notte*. AKA: *Riding a Crane*. Movie. DIR: Seiji Arihara. SCR: Seiji Arihara. DES: Yoshio Kabashima. ANI: Takaya Ono. MUS: Reijiro Komutsu. PRD: Mushi Pro. 30 mins.

Modern Japanese schoolgirl Tomoko visits the Hiroshima Peace Memorial Museum, where she has to write a report as part of a school assignment. The twelve-year-old finds the museum's story so shocking that she has to leave, going into the nearby Peace Memorial Park, where children are playing happily. She meets a girl her own age, but when Sadako tells her story, Tomoko realizes she is a ghost. When she was two years old, Sadako Sasaki was exposed to radiation in the bombing of Hiroshima, and she contracted leukemia at the age of six. She folded a paper crane every day in the hope that it would help her recover, but the girl died before reaching her teens. Tomoko comes to understand that the bombings affected far more people than those who were killed and injured at the time, then she wakes up and sees the statue of Sadako. A short film shown on a double bill with **KAYOKO'S DIARY** and sharing much of its crew along with director Arihara, this Hiroshima anime in the spirit of **BAREFOOT GEN** dwells on the long-term effects of radiation poisoning in the fashion of **BENEATH THE BLACK RAIN**. The first part of the story gives what is almost an animated tour of the museum and the last half is devoted to Sadako's flashback autobiography. The animation was inspired by the efforts of Miho Cibot-Shimma, a Japanese woman living in France, who decided to spread the word about the evils of nuclear war after seeing children in her adopted homeland playing "atomic war games." Her Japanese friends started raising funds to make *OAPC* in 1989. Given very limited exposure in the U.S. through subtitled screenings at film festivals.

ON YOUR MARK

1995. Video. DIR: Hayao Miyazaki. SCR: Hayao Miyazaki. DES: Hayao Miyazaki, Masashi Ando. ANI: Masashi Ando. MUS: Chage and Asuka. PRD: Ghibli. 7 mins.

In a futuristic supercity, armed police raid the headquarters of a religious cult. One of them finds an angel chained in a corner, and the winged girl is rushed into quarantine. The officer who found her and his partner break into the science facility to rescue her, but the story then divides into one of two endings. In the first, the officers fall to their deaths as their stolen truck spins off a collapsing bridge. In the second version, the truck develops wings of its own and flies away from the city, revealed to be an oasis amid a desolate, postindustrial polluted landscape. The angel flies free, and the cops return to face the music.

A short promo-video made by Miyazaki for the pop duo Chage and Asuka (whose likenesses can be discerned in the police characters), it was eventually shown in theaters alongside **WHISPER OF THE HEART** and reputedly tested some of the digital techniques he would reuse in **PRINCESS MONONOKE**. It's prettily made, but the reduction of Miyazaki's standard ecological concerns to the time limit and formulae of a pop video makes the story line seem a trifle pretentious. The Japanese video release bulked out the running time with the storyboards and animatics used in production and the live-action video version of the same song.

ONE HUNDRED PER CENT

1990. JPN: *Hyakku Per Cent*. Video. DIR: Yoshihisa Matsumoto. SCR: Oki Ike. DES: Kazuo Iimura. ANI: Akio Takami. MUS: Yuki Nagasaka. PRD: JC Staff. 50 mins.

A pretty 22-year-old girl leaves university and gets her dream job as a TV newscaster, only to discover that life is tough at the top. In this adaptation of the *Young Action* manga by Michio Yanagisawa, she must juggle the demands of her career with her troubled love life. Compare with **WEATHER REPORT GIRL**, which approaches the same idea, but for laughs.

ONE PIECE

1998. TV series, movie. DIR: Goro Taniguchi, Kannosuke Uta. SCR: Michiru Shimada, Atsushi Takegami. DES: Noboru Koizumi. ANI: Hisashi Kagawa. MUS: Kohei Tanaka. PRD: Toei, Fuji TV. 25 mins. x 63+ eps. (TV), 30 mins. (m).

Impetuous, headstrong 16-year-old Monkey D. Rufy eats a piece of magic fruit that renders his whole body elastic and almost invulnerable. Now he wants to be a pirate and find the fabled "One Piece" treasure of Gold Rogers. He saves the life of the red-haired Junx, who gives him his trademark lucky hat. He meets a motley crew of fortune hunters and misfits, and wacky adventures ensue as they hunt the treasure. A movie, also entitled *One Piece*, appeared in summer 2000, in which Rufy and Zorro are captured by the pirate El Dragon and have to escape. Based on Eiichiro Oda's *Shonen Jump* manga, with some debt to JOURNEY TO THE WEST in the lead character.

1+2 = PARADISE

1989. Video. DIR: Junichi Watanabe. SCR: Nobuaki Kishima. DES: Akiyuki Serizawa. ANI: Keiichi Sato. MUS: Jun Watanabe. PRD: Uemura/Toei. 30 mins. x 2 eps.
A strange relationship develops between college-boy Yusuke and the beautiful twins, Yuika and Rika, he saves from a wild dog. The girls fall for their dauntless hero, but Yusuke is pathologically scared of women. The girls eventually overcome his fear, only to find that he's stopped fantasizing about them and has fallen for the new girl in the school—rich corporate heiress Barako.
    A two-part adaptation of Junko Uemura's *Shonen Magazine* series and an early directorial job for SUPER ATRAGON's Watanabe. **N**

ONE POUND GOSPEL *

1988. JPN: *Ichi Pondo no Fukuin*. Video. DIR: Makura Saki (Osamu Dezaki), Masaya Mizutani. SCR: Hideo Takayashiki, Tomoko Konparu. DES: Katsumi Aoshima. ANI: Shojuro Yamauchi. MUS: N/C. PRD: Studio Gallop. 55 mins.
Sister Angela is a novice nun. Kosuke Hatakana is a young boxer who has a problem keeping to his fighting weight, which means that he has never fulfilled his real potential. Angela's concern for Kosuke and his future goes beyond the detached compassion expected of a nun, and his determination to justify her faith in his ability

makes him try to prove himself one more time. His despairing trainer can't believe he really means it this time, but Kosuke has another chance at success and seems ready to take it.
    Manga creator Rumiko Takahashi is better known to American fans for her lighthearted romantic fantasies URUSEI YATSURA and RANMA 1/2, but her heart lies in exploring offbeat events and relationships in the real world, and this is a good example. The director of GOLGO 13 turns in a crisp, professional job on this very different story.

1001 NIGHTS *

1999. Video. DIR: Mike Smith. SCR: Yoshitaka Amano. DES: Yoshitaka Amano. ANI: N/C. MUS: David Newman. PRD: 1001 Nights Prd Cttee, Bell System 24, Hyperion. 25 mins.
The Demon King Darnish plots to ruin the lives of mortals, engineering a meeting between Princess Budhu and Prince Kamahl solely to make the pair fall in love and to heighten the suffering when they are inevitably parted. The princess cannot bear the separation and throws herself from a tower, but is saved by the fairy Mamune. The angry Darnish chases the lovers, who escape forever when they are transformed into a shining star.
    A film commissioned by the Los Angeles Philharmonic Orchestra, featuring music by *The Brave Little Toaster*–composer Newman and showcasing ANGEL'S EGG–creator Amano's artistic talents in the U.S.

ONE-CHOP MANTARO

1990. JPN: *Ippon Hocho Mantaro*. AKA: *One Knife-slice Mantaro*. Video. DIR: Toshio Takeuchi. SCR: Megumi Hikichi. DES: Hidetoshi Omori. ANI: Keiichi Sato. MUS: Kosuke Kanadome. PRD: JC Staff, Animate Film. 45 mins. x 2 eps.
Downtown cook Ginpei's prodigal son Mantaro returns after several years traveling. When he offers to help out in the restaurant, Ginpei notices that the guests eagerly consume Mantaro's pork cutlets but leave his untouched. Mantaro teaches his old-town friends

and family the many tricks he has learned on his travels, before setting off to Osaka for a repeat performance. An anime spinoff of the 1973 *Business Jump* manga *One-Chop Ajimei*, by an artist known as "Big Jo," this kitchen tale was based on an original book by MISTER HAPPY–creator "Gyujiro." The original manga was way ahead of OISHINBO but only made it to anime in the wake of its successor—perhaps this subtle irony is what led the production staff to concentrate on a "new generation."

ONI

1995. JPN: *Toma Kishin Oni*. AKA: *Fighting Devil Divinity Oni*. TV series. DIR: Akira Suzuki. SCR: Natsuko Hayakawa. DES: Masayuki Goto. ANI: N/C. MUS: N/C. PRD: JC Staff, TV Tokyo. 8 mins. x 25 eps.
Human beings can transform into powerful creatures, at which point they fight each other. A series designed to cash in on the Gameboy game of the same name, it was broadcast during the early morning *Anime Asaichi* children's program.

ONIMARU

1990. Video. DIR: Osamu Dezaki. SCR: Osamu Dezaki. DES: Setsuko Shibunnoichi. ANI: Yukari Kobayashi. MUS: Eimi Sakamoto. PRD: Magic Bus. 45 mins.
During the Onin wars in Japan's medieval Muromachi era, five superpowered warriors hire out their services to the highest bidder. Leader Onimaru can beat two hundred mercenaries singlehandedly, Bo handles demolitions, Saru is as agile as a monkey, Osamu is a cool tactician, and Kiri is the obligatory token swordswoman. This prefabricated group (who might as well be a group of superheroes like those in BATTLE OF THE PLANETS for all the difference the period setting makes) gain an extra unwelcome member when Onimaru rescues Princess Aya, who naturally falls in love with him and refuses to go away. Not to be confused with *Onikirimaru*, which was released in English as OGRE SLAYER.

ONLY YESTERDAY

1991. JPN: *Omohide Poroporo*. AKA: *Tearful Thoughts*. Movie. DIR: Isao Takahata. SCR: Isao Takahata. DES: Yoshifumi Kondo, Yoshiharu Sato. ANI: Yoshifumi Kondo. MUS: Joe Hisaishi. PRD: Hayao Miyazaki, Studio Ghibli. 119 mins.

The action skips back and forth between 1966 and 1984 as Office Lady Taeko Okajima, visiting the country for a working sabbatical on a farm, recalls events from her childhood—achievements, embarrassments, hopes, dreams, and people. She's trying to decide whether to return to the city and go on with her career or to marry and settle in the countryside, and her reminiscences, at first seemingly aimless, help to shape her decision just as those events and people helped to shape the person she has become.

Hotaru Okamoto's and Yuko Tone's original 1987 story, serialized in *Myojo* weekly, concentrated on the misadventures of the ten-year-old Taeko—the 1984 framing device was conceived by Takahata solely for the film. Beautiful animation and design are almost taken for granted in a Studio Ghibli production, and the script is excellent. The overall emphasis on the importance of marriage, and the assumption (still widespread in Japan at the time) that a real career and family life are mutually exclusive for women, may offend some viewers. Sexual politics aside, Takahata's tale of one woman's choice recreates everyday life in town and the Yamagata countryside with loving care and a marvelous eye for detail, imparting the weight of a historical document without overwhelming the delicate human story. A U.S. release is a possibility since the Studio Ghibli/Disney deal. Interestingly, Sato was also part of the team working on Disney's *The Tigger Movie* (2000).

ORCHID EMBLEM *

1996. JPN: *Rei-Lan Orchid Emblem*. Video. DIR: Hideaki Kushi. SCR: Toshihiko Kudo, Jutaro Nanase. DES: Taro Taki, Shoichiro Sugiura. ANI: Makoto Fujisake. MUS: Hajime Takakuwa. PRD: Dandelion, Beam Entertainment. 40 mins.

Rei-Lan is a virginal cop on a stakeout of a drug baron when her team is captured and her boyfriend, Doug, is forced to watch while she has wildly enthusiastic sex with crime lord Tojo. Then she stays on Tojo's ship and has more sex with him, naively accepting his word that Doug has "gone ashore." The pair get matching tattoos of great mystical force that make it impossible for either of them to attain ecstasy without the other. Then Rei-Lan finds Doug's body in a barrel on the ship, escapes, goes to live with a cute little lesbian, becomes a top martial artist, and plots revenge on Tojo. But the dragon tattoo is too powerful, and she ends up back with him, carrying on her martial arts career as a sideline.

Based on an erotic novel from the same Napoleon imprint that gave us **EROTIC TORTURE CHAMBER**, you could drive a fleet of very large trucks through the holes in the plot, and the defects are in no way concealed by the average animation. As for the English dub, the pseudonymous actors turn in shamefully wooden work, though Rei-Lan's impressions of a Dalek having an orgasm have some comic value. In their defense, however, given the awful script, any cast picked at random from the greatest classical actors would have struggled to do better.

ORDIAN

2000. JPN: *Ginso Kido Ordian*. AKA: *Attack Armor Ordian; Silver Knight Ordian*. TV series. DIR: Masami Obari. SCR: Kengo Asai, Hiroyuki Kawasaki. DES: Fumihide Sai, Masami Obari, Tsukasa Kotobuki. ANI: Fumihide Sai. MUS: N/C. PRD: Prime, WOWOW. 25 mins. x 24 eps.

High-school student Yu Kananase is crazy about combat, and even though he's never actually fought anything, he's recruited by the International Military Organization as a potential test pilot for new mobile armor. There are other young recruits in the running,

and he has to prove he's the best to achieve his dream. Realizing that game-based anime such as his **FATAL FURY** and **TOSHINDEN** were hardly rocket science, director Obari decided to create his own world, inspired by the mismatched design follies and action-heavy plotting of the genre. Sadly the story isn't hugely original; the low quality of Obari's inspiration causes him to throw his creative efforts behind a show that looks like a hundred other robot serials (see **BRAVE SAGA**), whether inspired by computer games or not. However, the character designs have the pointy-nosed charm of **VIRUS**, albeit without sulky homoerotic pouts.

ORGUSS *

1983. JPN: *Chojiku Seiki Orguss*. AKA: *Superdimensional Century Orguss*. TV series. DIR: Noboru Ishiguro, Yasuyoshi Mikamoto, Kazuhito Akiyama, Osamu Nabeshima, Hiroshi Yoshida, Masakazu Iijima. SCR: Kenichi Matsuzaki, Sukehiro Tomita, Hiroshi Nishimura. DES: Haruhiko Mikimoto, Yoshiyuki Yamamoto. ANI: Haruhiko Mikimoto, Akiyoshi Nishimori. MUS: Kentaro Haneda. PRD: Magic Bus, Big West, TBS. 25 mins. x 35 eps. (TV), 30 mins. x 6 eps. (V).

In 2062, Kei is an officer in one of the

two forces fighting over the latest scientific-military advance, the Orbital Elevator, and he is sent to blow it up to avoid its capture by the enemy. Caught in the blast of his own time-oscillation bomb, he is flung into an alternate world, one of many created by the explosion. There he meets his daughter, conceived on a one-night stand just before his mission. She's now 18, fighting on the other side in a terrible war, and in love with his best friend. He also has problems with cute but not-at-all-disposable alien girlfriend Mimsy. Her species has to mate before they're 17 or not at all, and her ex-boyfriend is still very much on the scene. The fate of the patchwork of worlds fragmented by the bomb, with all their diverse citizens and cultures, and the future of all his relationships hangs in the balance. By now Kei must have realized that casual sex brings its own complications.

One of the big SF series of its day, *Orguss* wasn't cut into **ROBOTECH** (with **MACROSS**, **MOSPEADA**, and **SOUTHERN CROSS**) because, coming from a different studio, it couldn't be bought in the same package. Its Mikimoto-designed characters would have fitted perfectly, and its ethos, a giant-robot show in which robots weren't the only item on the agenda, looks forward to **PATLABOR**, as well as fitting the prevailing fashion for heavy mecha and heavy emotion.

The series returned straight to video as *Orguss 02* (1993), directed by Fumihiko Takayama, featuring character designs "inspired" by Mikimoto's originals from Toshihiro Kawamoto and an industrial rock soundtrack from Torsten Rasch. Set 200 years after the close of the original series, in a steampunk world not dissimilar to that of **WINGS OF HONNEAMISE**, the opposing nations of Zafrin and Revillia send archaeologists to find "Decimators" (giant robots left over from the original series). Though the technology is half-forgotten, the reconditioned robots are important weapons in a fast-approaching war. Lean, a young officer on the Revillan side, is excavating a

Decimator from the sea bed when an ambush forces him into the machine to survive the attack and discover piloting skills he never suspected. He is sent behind enemy lines to destroy their Decimators, and he meets a girl (a distant descendant of Mimsy) who holds the key to a secret and is a target for all sides. As the conflict escalates, he learns that his own prince plans to use the most powerful Decimator ever discovered to subjugate the world, while an ancient stranger (the "General," the only surviving character from the original series) seeks to bring peace once more. There are byzantine court machinations—the queen poisons the ruler to allow her general to rule in the name of a retarded prince. There are even echoes of more recent Japanese history, as soldiers are forced to choose between their allegiance to the throne itself and the throne's current occupant. The script, from **SOL BIANCA**'s Mayori Sekijima and **BLUE SIX**'s Hiroshi Yamaguchi, manages to pull strong political overtones out of a story that would have been good enough if it were just a straightforward actioner. A superior giant-robot series. *Ill. p. 73.*

ORPHEN: SCION OF SORCERY *
1998. JPN: *Majutsushi Orphen*. AKA: *Orphen the Magician; Sorcerous Stabber Orphen*. TV series. DIR: Hiroshi Watanabe, Akira Suzuki. SCR: Mayori Sekijima, Masashi Kubota, Yasushi Yamada, Kenichi Araki, Kenichi Kanemaki. DES: Masahiro Aizawa. ANI: Masahiro Aizawa. MUS: Hatake, Sharan Q. PRD: JC Staff, TBS. 25 mins. x 47 eps.
Growing up in an orphanage after losing his parents at a very young age, "Orphen" and his two adopted elder sisters, Azalea and Letitia, are selected to study sorcery under the famous Childman at the Tower of Fang. At age 15, Orphen becomes a sorcerer to the Royal Family, but his life is plunged into new difficulties when one of Azalea's spells backfires, transforming her into a monster. Even though he has fallen in love with Azalea, Childman is

honor-bound to hunt down the beast that she has become, and Orphen decides to stop him.

Based on a series of over a dozen fantasy novels by Yoshinobu Akita, the *Orphen* TV series begins *in media res* with our hero already a powerful wizard, training a young boy called Majiku. As with **BERSERK**, the majority of the story is told in flashback, as Orphen is threatened by the return of the demon-dragon "Bloody August" only to reveal that it was once the girl he called his sister. Sharing much of the crew of the earlier **SLAYERS**, Orphen fortunately lacks much of its predecessor's comedy, opting instead for hard-core fantasy adventure. However, despite a rocking opening theme from pop group Sharan Q, much of the background music sounds like computer-game filler muzak. *Orphen: The Revenge* (1999) is simply the umbrella title for the "second season" of the last 23 episodes. A game based on the series was the first incarnation to reach the U.S., preceding the anime version by several months. *Ill. p. 223.*

ORUORANE THE CAT PLAYER
1992. JPN: *Nekohiki no Oruorane*. Video. DIR: Mizuho Nishikubo. SCR: Mayori Sekijima. DES: Shunji Murata. ANI: Shunji Murata. MUS: Moto Shiraishi, Kawaji Ishikawa. PRD: JC Staff. 30 mins.
An out-of-work musician mooching round the streets just before Christmas befriends a cat who is fond of good wine. The cat, Iruneido, is one of a feline trio owned by Oruorane, a mysterious old man who can "play" cats as if they were musical instruments. Our hero, always on the lookout for another string to his bow, decides he wants to learn cat-playing for himself. This surreal curio was based on the first novel written by successful writer Baku Yumemakura, who also created **AMON SAGA** and **BATTLE ROYALE HIGH SCHOOL**.

OSHIN
1984. JPN: *Oshin*. Movie. DIR: Eiichi

Yamamoto. SCR: Sugako Hashida. DES: Akio Sugino. ANI: Nobuko Yuasa, Keizo Shimizu. MUS: Koichi Sakata. PRD: Sanrio. 122 mins.

Oshin is a young girl who lives in Japan's northern Yamagata Prefecture at the turn of the 20th century. She endures terrible hardships and poverty, eventually being sold into domestic service at the age of eight. Separated from her mother, she escapes from the timber merchant who treats her like a slave and briefly finds happiness working at a rice shop.

An anime spinoff from one of the landmark Japanese live-action melodramas, Oshin focuses on the early episodes of the 300-part 1983 TV drama, reusing both Sugako Hashida's scripts and the voice of child-star Ayako Kobayashi, who played the young Oshin in the TV version. Supposedly based on true stories, cut-and-pasted from hundreds of letters sent to a women's magazine, the live-action Oshin was an immense hit all around the world, screened in over 40 countries. After the events of the anime version, the character would continue to struggle for many more onscreen decades, through two changes of actress. Accused of stealing from the rice shop, she would be cast out, rescued by a deserting soldier, married to a southern weakling, left penniless by the 1923 Tokyo earthquake, abused by her mother-in-law, and widowed by her husband's suicide caused by his shame at supplying Japan's military machine during the Pacific War. Eventually, she would become the rich boss of a grocery business, but that would not be until her 83rd year—the year in which the original series was screened. A different female experience of Yamagata can be seen in ONLY YESTERDAY, while a very different dramatization of the years around the 1923 earthquake can be found in DOOMED MEGALOPOLIS.

OSOMATSU-KUN

1966. AKA: Young Sextuplets. TV series. DIR: Makoto Nagasawa, Hiroe Mitsunobu. SCR: Fujio Akatsuka, Kon

Kitagawa. DES: Makoto Nagasawa. ANI: Jiro Murata, Kazuo Komatsubara. MUS: Urahito Watanabe. PRD: Fujio Pro, Studio Zero, Children's Corner, NET. 25 mins. x 57 eps. (1966), 25 mins. x 86 eps. (1988).

Osomatsu, Kazumatsu, Karamatsu, Choromatsu, Todomatsu, and Jushimatsu are six identical brothers who are continually making trouble in their town, chasing after the fishmonger's daughter Totoko, and harassing the local snob, Francophile Iyami. Based on a manga in Shonen Sunday by Fujio Akatsuka, who also created GENIUS IDIOT, Osomatsu-kun was derided by the PTA as "one of the worst programs ever made," and was consequently very popular with children; compare to the modern-day excesses of the similarly criticized CRAYON SHIN-CHAN. It was remade in 1988 by Studio Pierrot into 86 episodes, which retained its former popularity, soon gaining a 20% audience rating.

OTAKU NO VIDEO *

1991. JPN: 1982 Otaku no Video; 1985 Zoku Otaku no Video. AKA: Fan's Video; Thy Video. Video. DIR: Takeshi Mori. SCR: Toshio Okada. DES: Kenichi Sonoda. ANI: Hidenori Matsubara. MUS: Kohei Tanaka. PRD: Studio Fantasia, Gainax. 50 and 45 mins.

This fan-favorite fantasy by the Gainax studio, which would also produce WINGS OF HONNEAMISE and EVANGELION, is wry and affectionate, self-parody and wish-fulfillment. Inspired by events from the team's own real-life history, it recounts the story of one ordinary young man's efforts to follow the way of the true fan, or "otaku." He loses his girl, his social standing, and his business. His story is counterpointed by a series of spoof live-action "interviews" with fandom personalities such as a cel thief, a costume freak, and a pornography junky. In the second video, merged with the first for Western release, our hero, his devotion undimmed by age, indignity, and failure, triumphs over the sordid cynicism of the world through the purity of the

fanboy spirit, aspiring to become the Ota-King. An English translation by Shin Kurokawa and the Ledoux/Yoshida team plus AnimEigo's excellent liner notes provide a wonderful snapshot of an era of fandom and allow us to laugh with and cry for the true otaku.

OUTLANDERS *

1986. JPN: Outlanders. Video. DIR: Katsuhisa Yamada. SCR: Kenji Terada. DES: Hiroshi Hamazaki. ANI: Hiroshi Hamazaki. MUS: Kei Wakakusa. PRD: Tatsunoko. 48 mins.

Earth is invaded by the galaxy-spanning Santovasku Empire in its organic spaceships. Princess Kahm first appears slicing up unsuspecting Earthmen as part of her imperial father's great invasion plan; then she falls into the arms of photographer Tetsuya and decides to save him from the destruction that the empire has planned for the rest of humankind. This puts both lovers and their friends in serious danger from Kahm's conquest-mad daddy and his nasty minions. Based on Johji Manabe's 1985 manga for Hakusensha, with affectionate nods to Star Wars and URUSEI YATSURA, the story has considerable charm despite a fairly high violence quotient. Manabe has done little except repeat it since (see RAI and CAPRICORN), but this doesn't detract from the original. 🔞

OUTLAW STAR *

1998. JPN: Seiho Bukyo Outlaw Star. AKA: Stellar Chivalry Outlaw Star. TV series. DIR: Mitsuru Hongo. SCR: Katsuhiko Chiba. DES: Takuya Saito, Junya Ishigaki. ANI: Takuya Saito, Hiroyuki Hataike. MUS: Ko Otani. PRD: Sunrise, Sotsu, TV Tokyo. 25 mins. x 24 eps. Hajime Yadate (Sunrise's name for its in-house idea machine) and Takehiko Ito (ANGEL LINKS) adapted an alternate future from Ito's 1988 Space Hero Tales manga for the late-night slot on TV Tokyo. A loose and unstable galactic alliance is trying to bring order to the chaos of the expanding space frontier. Hot Ice Hilda is on the wrong side of the law, on the run, in disguise, and in search of a fabulous treasure when she runs across Gene Starwind, a Han Solo wannabe running a rather sleazy, jack-of-all-trades business with his 11-year-old "brother," Jim Hawking, who is definitely the brains of the outfit. Gene's career is severely hampered by space phobia; as a child he watched his father die in space, and by a weird coincidence he thinks one of the gangs chasing Hilda is responsible. Hilda hires the duo to help her with a nebulous "repair job," but before long they've gotten aboard a hidden prototype spaceship and its cybernetically engineered living navigation computer, a cute girl named Melfina. Then Hilda gets killed and Gene & Co. suddenly have more enemies than they ever expected. The Outlaw Star and Melfina are targets for every powerful group in the galaxy; it's widely believed that, aside from the value of the ship itself, it contains clues that will lead to the fabled treasure known as Galactic Leyline (refer to SOL BIANCA). As they struggle to survive, they run into comic tropes like Suzuka, a deadly Japanese assassin who's so friendly she joins the crew, and Aisha, a cat-girl who does likewise. The writers rely on such tropes to liven up a plot whose guidance is mostly inertial. Arms mounted on the "grappler" ships turn space combat into something more like a mechanized wrestling match, and, while there are some good flashes of humor (like the OTT opening narrations), this is no competition for COWBOY BEBOP in terms of style, content, or execution. When screened on the Cartoon Network, the anime was edited for nudity, violence, gambling, drinking, and lechery because those things don't happen in America.

OYO MY HUGGABLE CAT

1984. JPN: *Oyoneko Bunichan.* TV series. DIR: Hiroshi Sasakawa, Hiroshi Fujioka, Kenjiro Yoshida, Teruo Kigure, Katsumi Kosuga. SCR: Hiroshi Kaneko, Hideki Sonoda, Tsunehisa Ito, Hideo Takayashiki, Yoshio Urasawa, Miho Maruo, Hiroko Naka. DES: Misako Ichikawa. ANI: Shinichi Suzuki. MUS: Takeo Watanabe. PRD: Shinei, TV Asahi. 25 mins. x 31 eps.

The comical adventures of bad-tempered fat cat Oyoyo who charms his idiot human family but fights an ongoing battle with other neighborhood pets. Based on the manga *Mr. Happy* (*Shiawase-san*) by Misako Ichikawa (no relation to MISTER HAPPY), serialized in several magazines, including *Shojo* and *Ciao.* Unmatched in anime for feline humor until WHAT'S MICHAEL? appeared a year later.

OZ

1992. Video. DIR: Katsuhisa Yamada. SCR: Asami Watanabe. DES: Toyomi Sugiyama. ANI: Toyomi Sugiyama. MUS: Yoichiro Yoshikawa. PRD: Madhouse. 35 mins. x 2 eps.

A nuclear war kills 60% of humanity and splits the U.S. into six warring states. By 2021, a legend has grown amid the hunger, chaos, and devastation—the fabled city of Oz, where high technology has survived to serve humankind, and hunger and war are unknown. Scientist Felicia sets out to find Oz with mercenary Muto and Droid #1019. At the end of the road they find a madman dreaming of world dominion in a military base with enough firepower to create a new nightmare for the world. Natsumi Itsuki's original 1988 manga in *Comic Lala* was based very loosely on WIZARD OF OZ but owed a greater debt to the same studio's WIND OF AMNESIA in this anime adaptation. For reasons known only to the distributor, the *Oz* soundtrack was released in the U.K., though the anime has never been translated.

P

PA-MAN

1967. JPN: *Pa-man*. TV series. DIR: Tadao Nagahama, Eiji Okabe, Shinichi Suzuki. SCR: Fujiko-Fujio, Tadao Nagahama, Masaki Tsuji, Koji Miharu, Tatsuo Tamura. DES: Fujiko-Fujio. ANI: Shinichi Suzuki, Tsutomu Shibayama. MUS: Hiroshi Tsutsui. PRD: Studio Zero, Tokyo Movie Shinsha, TBS. 25 mins. x 54 eps. (b/w), 25 mins. (m), 15 mins. x 526 eps. (color).

Four children and Boobie the chimpanzee are recruited to protect their hometown by a mysterious masked man. He gives them helmets that endow the wearers with superstrength and cloaks that let them fly at 91 kph. Lead male Pa-man #1, chimp superhero Pa-man #2, token female Pa-ko, Osaka-born miser Pa-yan, and baby Pa-bo must try to solve the town's problems, great and small, and help its people. After a brief cameo in the final episode of the same creators' QTARO THE GHOST, Pa-man got his own series in order to keep money rolling in from the TBS sponsors. The franchise was revived many years later for a short film, *Pa-Man: The Coming of Birdman* (1983), directed by Shinichi Suzuki, a former animator on the original series. Inevitably, the film was revealed as a preview of a coming series, the extremely long-running *New Pa-man* that began soon after on TV Asahi. The update revealed Pa-ko's real identity (she is really the pop star Sumi Hoshino) and introduced a new character, Yuki.

PANDA AND THE MAGIC SERPENT*

1958. JPN: *Hakujaden*. AKA: *Legend of the White Serpent; Tale of the White Serpent; The White Snake Enchantress*. Movie. DIR: Taiji Yabushita. SCR: Taiji Yabushita, Soichi Yashiro. DES: Akira Okuwara, Yasuji Mori. ANI: Yasuo Otsuka, Kazuko Nakamura, Reiko Okuyama, Taku Sugiyama, Gisaburo Sugii. MUS: Masayoshi Ikeda. PRD: Toei. 78 mins.

The beautiful snake princess Bai-Niang falls in love with the young boy Xu-Xian. His parents make him put the snake back in the fields where he found her, but he never stops missing his pet. Years later, magically transformed into a beautiful girl during a storm, the snake goddess changes a rainbow fish into her handmaid Xiao Chin, sets up house in the town, and seeks Xu-Xian out again. Both grown up, the two fall in love. Local wizard Fa Hai, convinced Bai-Niang is a vampire out to harm Xu-Xian, tries to break up their romance, and banishes Xu to hard labor in a distant city, reasoning that it's the only way to save him. Xu's two clever pets, Panda and Mimi, set out to follow him and become the leaders of the local animal Mafia, using the gang's skills to find him. Determined to save Xu from what he sees as a terrible supernatural evil, Fa whisks him off to his castle by the ocean, and the devoted Panda and Mimi follow him again through a terrible storm. Xiao has to intervene with the gods to save them, while Bai-Niang fights Fa for Xu's freedom. Even after saving Xu from death, she must give up her magical powers and become human before Fa accepts that her love is genuine. The two young lovers can finally marry, Xiao returns to her true form as a pretty fish, and Panda, Mimi and their animal friends all live happily ever after.

Often regarded as the "first" modern anime, this variant on LITTLE MERMAID was originally adapted from Chinese mythology as a story by Shin Uehara. Featuring uncharacteristically "oriental" character designs and serious trials and hardships for the young lovers and their animal friends, it inspired many others to become animators, including the young Hayao Miyazaki, on whom it made a deep impression. It won honors at the Venice Children's Film Festival in 1959 but reaction to its U.S. release in 1961 was disappointing. Mimi, a small "red" panda, is mistakenly referred to as a cat in some sources.

PANDA GO PANDA *

1972. JPN: *Panda Kopanda*. AKA: *Panda; Panda Cub; Panda and Child*. Movie. DIR: Isao Takahata. SCR: Hayao Miyazaki. DES: Hayao Miyazaki. ANI: Yasuo Otsuka, Yoichi Otabe, Yoshifumi Kondo, Seiji Kitara, Takao Kasai, Minoru Maeda. MUS: Teruhiko Sato. PRD: A-Pro, Tokyo Movie Shinsha. 33 mins., 38 mins.

Miyazaki's first original work as a screenwriter is a charming tale of a little girl who befriends a panda and his cub. Left home alone when her grandmother has to go away for a few days, little Mimiko is surprised to find a panda and his cub moving in. They very soon form a little family of their own, with Father Panda offering the fatherless Mimiko the paternal affection she's always wanted, and Mimiko mothering the motherless cub. Everything is going well until the local policeman discovers exactly who Mimiko's houseguests are. The father-bear, a model of good parenthood foreshadowing Miyazaki's ongoing concern with the parent/child relationship, can also be seen as one of the stages in the creation of MY NEIGHBOR TOTORO, and the young protagonist has much in common with the heroine Miyazaki had sketched for TMS's abortive *Pippi Longstocking* project. The sequel, *Panda Go Panda: Rainy Day Circus*, also directed by Takahata, followed a year later. Pandas were big box office in the 1970s after the arrival of a Chinese panda at Tokyo Zoo, and other unrelated appearances during the period included Yugo Serikawa's *Panda's Great Adventure* (1973) and the Sino-Japanese coproduction TAOTAO THE PANDA. The following decade would see a similar obsession with koalas—see THE NOOZLES.

PANZER DRAGOON *

1996. JPN: *Panzer Dragoon*. Video. DIR: Shinji Takagi. SCR: Yosuke Kuroda. DES: Atsushi Takeuchi, Kazuhiro Kishita. ANI: Atsushi Takeuchi. MUS: Azuma. PRD: Production IG. 30 mins.
Kyle's girl is stolen from him by the Black Dragon, which also kills his obviously expendable fat friend. When he meets blue dragon Blau, Kyle is suspicious, but only Blau can help him save Alita, who will otherwise be enslaved by the Dark Tower and become the catalyst for the destruction of the entire world.

If a bored director and crew copied a few pages from the *Beginner's Book of Fantasy Gaming*, then lost the important bits like plot and characterization, this is what might emerge. The Sega game's distinctive look is matched by what, at the time of release, must have been a truly innovative combination of cel and digital animation. There are set pieces that recall the game itself and quirkily mismatched compositions of technology and magic, setting up a damsel in distress, cross-species buddy business, a rescue, and a big fight in just 30 minutes.

With a fallen empire, a blind sorceress, human/dragon symbiosis, and a quest to defeat the ultimate evil, *Panzer Dragoon* had truly epic potential. People have spun trilogies out of less, but the paltry running time isn't up to it. What little space there is for dialogue that doesn't advance the plot, writer Kuroda fills with poetic meditations on sight and seeing. The blind Alita cannot *see* the color red, instead she must *experience* it. "So this is what the sky feels like!" proclaims Kyle during his first dragon flight—a throwaway line that belongs in a much better story.

AD Vision's dub is far better than the spartan original deserves, but this remains a heroic rescue attempt by both Japanese and U.S. crews, fighting impossible odds of budget and (lack of) inspiration. ◐

PANZER WORLD GALIENT

1984. JPN: *Kikokai Galient*. AKA: *Mechanical Armor World Galient*. TV series, video. DIR: Ryosuke Takahashi. SCR: Ryosuke Takahashi, Hajime Yadate. DES: Norio Shioyama. ANI: Norio Shioyama. MUS: Toru Fuyuki. PRD: Sunrise, Nippon TV. 25 mins. x 26 eps., 55 mins.
Young Jordy is fighting his father, Madar, who is bent on world domination using giant robots. His brother, Hai Shartart, is also fighting Madar, but not to save the people from dominion; instead he plans to take his father's place, and so he sees Jordy and their sister, Chururu, as rivals. Legend tells of a mysterious avenger, known only as the Iron Giant, who will come to overthrow the tyrant. The video, subtitled *Iron Emblem*, covered the same dramatic ground two years later: ruthless ambition, family conflict, and massively overspecified armor.

The golden age of the robot was in full swing in 1984; *God Mazinger* (see MAZINGER Z) and SOUTHERN CROSS among the multitude onscreen, MACROSS in the theaters, and toys everywhere. Takahashi is renowned as one of the prime movers of the "real robot" style spun off from Tomino's

GUNDAM, but the introduction of more realistic elements into future fantasy didn't preclude designs of baroque splendor. The *Galient* robots are among the best—a magnificent fusion of futuristic technology, steam-punk weightiness, and off-the-wall neoclassical design. Robot centaurs—you gotta love 'em. ◐

PAPA MAMA BYE-BYE

1980. JPN: *Papa Mama Bye-Bye*. Movie. DIR: Hiroshi Shidara. SCR: Atsushi Yamagata. DES: Katsumi Aoshima. ANI: Katsumi Aoshima. MUS: Tadahito Mori. PRD: Toei. 75 mins.
Dungaree-wearing teenage tomboy Kaori lives next door to the brothers Ko and Yasu. One day they find an injured pigeon and nurse it back to health. As Kaori is walking to school soon afterward, a U.S. Phantom jet screams overhead and crashes near the boys' house. A heavy-handed juxtaposition of animal hospital and international friendship, inspired by a real-life incident in 1977 when a U.S. jet did indeed make a forced landing in Yokohama. For another U.S. plane ending up where it shouldn't, see SEA OF THE TICONDEROGA.

PAPER TRAIL

1997. JPN: *Isaku*. AKA: *Written Clues, Posthumous Works*. Video. DIR: Katsumasa Kanezawa. SCR: Sakura Momoi. DES: Hiroya Iijima. ANI: N/C. MUS: N/C. PRD: Pink Pineapple, KSS. 30 mins. x 3 eps.
An everyday school is found to have dark secrets—a hidden torture chamber, secret passages, and an insane janitor who has trapped several schoolgirls in the deserted hallways. Five girls, their attractive female teacher, and some token boys star in a schlocky slasher-thriller, with plenty of time out for sexual assault, as befits an anime adapted from an unpleasant computer game. The aim of the original was reputedly to escort the female cast safely off the premises, though many of the players preferred to watch them succumb to the janitor's lust. A similar

mindset seems to have dominated the filmmakers. **◎◐**

PAPUA-KUN

1992. JPN: *Nangoku no Shonen Papuwa-kun.* AKA: *Southern-Kingdom Boy Papua.* TV series, video. DIR: Jun Takagi, Masahiro Hosoda. SCR: Nobuyuki Fujimoto. DES: Hiroshi Takeuchi, Ken Kawai. ANI: Satoshi Takeuchi, Takao Osone. MUS: Nobuyuki Nakamura. PRD: Nippon Animation, TV Asahi. 25 mins. x 42 eps. (TV), 30 mins. x 2 eps., 25 mins. (v).

Papua is a little boy living a quiet life with his dog Chappy on a small island in the South Pacific. Then Shintaro turns up. Not only is he carrying valuable jewelry, but he's being chased by gangsters. When Chappy steals the jewel, the stage is set for insane high jinks of a kind not normally associated with the creators of WORLD MASTERPIECE THEATER. This anime was based on a 1991 manga by Ami Shibata, who also created JIBAKU-KUN, though a similar dogs-and-jewels caper can be found much earlier in HONEY HONEY. The series returned on video with the two-part *Papua-kun Encyclopedia* (1993, *Papua-kun Daihyakka*), which included an "extra" episode, the pilot film for a nonexistent sequel, and some interviews with the cast and crew. A final video release in 1994 comprised an unbroadcast "dream" episode, in which Papua-kun gets a fever and hallucinates a bizarre journey among the stars.

PARADE PARADE *

1996. Video. DIR: Motoaki Isshu. SCR: N/C. DES: Toshimitsu Kobayashi. ANI: N/C. MUS: N/C. PRD: Pink Pineapple, AIC. 30 mins. x 2 eps.

Two short stories, supposedly of an erotic nature, based on Satoshi Akifuji's manga exposé of the entertainment world. In the first, a pop star and her manager pleasure each other after her first concert. In the second, rival stars play a dangerous game that involves avoiding the toilet for as long as possible, with a payoff that may indeed be erotic for someone, somewhere. A similar stretching of the boundaries of good taste can be found in PROFESSOR PAIN. **◐**

PARADISE WITHOUT STARS

1991. JPN: *Hoshikuzu Paradise.* Video. DIR: Masato Namiki. SCR: Takuya Kubo. DES: Fumio Sasaki. ANI: Fumio Sasaki. MUS: Takeshi Kusao. PRD: OB Planning, Pastel. 55 mins.

A love comedy about Hiroshi, a normal teenage boy who discovers after his mother's death that his real father is a famous singer. Moving in with his newfound parent, Hiroshi must cope with having a stepmother who is closer in age to himself than her husband, and who until the previous week, he used to fantasize about whenever he saw her on TV. Based on a *Shonen Sunday* manga by Katsu-Aki, who would also draw the manga adaptation of ESCAFLOWNE several years later. **◐**

PARAPPA THE RAPPER

2001. JPN: *Para Parappa.* TV series. DIR: Hiroaki Sakurai. SCR: N/C. DES: Rodney Alan Greenblat, Takayuki Goto. ANI: N/C. MUS: Masaya Matsuura. PRD: JC Staff, Production IG, Fuji TV. 25 mins. x N/D eps.

The adventures of a happy dancing dog in his ongoing attempts to impress a flower called Sunny. Based on the surreal 1996 PlayStation game, the series features new characters and music from the original designers.

PARASITE HEAVEN

1996. JPN: *Isoro Tengoku.* AKA: *Homestay Heaven; Heaven of a Hanger-on.* Video. DIR: Teruo Kigure. SCR: Satoshi Aoyama. DES: Teru Aranaga. ANI: Kazuyoshi Ota. MUS: N/C. PRD: Beam Entertainment. 30 mins., 40 mins.

Eighteen-year-old Masahiko Kisugi is sent to stay with his Aunt Mizuhara so he can study at a nearby college. In an erotic anime based on the manga by Teru Aranaga in *Comic Lies* magazine, he soon begins an affair with his aunt, and with her three daughters. **◐**

Here are the wards of the titular ARC THE LAD, the savage Pandit with Lieza, the girl who controls him, from an anime unlikely to appeal to anyone who has not previously played the original computer game. Game-based titles began as one-shots like SUPER MARIO BROTHERS, but they grew in stature until they occupied much of the broadcasting slots for TV serials—*AtL's* 26-episode run would have been unthinkably long for a game-based anime in the 1980s. *See entry p. 17.*

Arc the Lad

© SONY COMPUTER ENTERTAINMENT

PARASOL HENBE

1989. JPN: *Parasol Henbe.* TV series. DIR: Masakazu Higuchi, Takami Fujikawa, Shigeru Fujikawa, Masaya Mizutani, Yugo Serikawa. SCR: Megumi Sugiwara, Aya Matsui, Satoru Akahori. DES: Motoo Abiko. ANI: Takao Yamazaki. MUS: Reijiro Komutsu. PRD: Fujiko Studio, NHK. 8 mins. x 109 eps.

Japanese boy Megeru meets Henbe, a strange hippo-like creature from another world. Henbe and his trademark magical parasol have many adventures with Megeru in this series for the very young, with episode titles such as *I Can't Stand the Rain*, *A Broadcast from Parasol World*, *A Butterfly from Another World*, and *The Flying Bicycle*. Based on a manga by BILLY DOG creator Fujiko-Fujio "A," and featuring the screenwriting debut of Satoru Akahori, whose "zany" output would dominate comedy anime for the coming decade.

PASTEL YUMI

1986. JPN: *Maho no Idol Pastel Yumi.* AKA: *Magical Idol Pastel Yumi.* TV series. DIR: Akira Torino, Yutaka Kagawa, Hiroshi Yoshida, Mitsuru Hongo, Toshio Okabe, Miho Maruo, Kazuyoshi Katayama. SCR: Shoji Imai, Azuma Tachibana, Yoshiyuki Suga, Yoshihisa Araki. DES: Yumiko Hirosawa.

ANI: Yumiko Hirosawa. MUS: Koji Makaino. PRD: Studio Pierrot, Nippon TV. 25 mins. x 25 eps.

Schoolgirl Yumi Hanazono lives happily with her parents. She loves nature and all living things. On carnival day, two little imps called Keshimaru and Kakimaru give her a magic baton and a magic ring; anything she draws in the air now becomes real. Using their power, she can transform into the magical idol Pastel Yumi. Another magical-girl story from the people who brought you CREAMY MAMI.

PATALIRO

1982. JPN: Pataliro! Boku Pataliro! AKA: Pataliro! I'm Pataliro! TV series, movie. DIR: Nobutaka Nishizawa, Satoshi Hisaoka, Yugo Serikawa, Hiroshi Shidara, Yasuo Yamakichi. SCR: Masaki Tsuji, Akiyoshi Sakai, Tomomi Tsutsui, Tomoko Konparu. DES: Mineo Maya. ANI: Yasunori Kanemori. MUS: Nozomu Aoki. PRD: Toei, Fuji TV. 25 mins. x 49 eps. (TV), 48 mins. (m).

Based on Mineo Maya's 1978 manga in Hana to Yume magazine, the series was the first to introduce homosexuality to TV anime audiences, and the nudity is reasonably tasteful (allowing for some floral backgrounds) and mostly male. A fantastical plot revolves around Jack Bankolan, a former British agent licensed to kill, who has somehow ended up working on the fabulously wealthy diamond-trading South Sea island of Marinera as a nursemaid to Pataliro VIII, the superpowered brat who is head of state. The joke is that this 007 is gay and the foes he faces are gorgeous men, transposing the machismo of the Bond mythos into lighthearted camp. Originally called just Pataliro!, the longer version of the title was used from episode 27 on. Nishizawa's movie, Pataliro: Stardust Project (1983), featured the titular plan by the international Tarantella crime syndicate to raid Marinera's diamond vaults. Typically, they send in an advance assassin to remove Bankolan, but the tall, handsome Andersen instead falls in love with his quarry. ◐

PATLABOR *

1989. JPN: Kido Keisatsu Patlabor. AKA: Mobile Police Patlabor. Video, TV series, movies. DIR: Mamoru Oshii, Naoyuki Yoshinaga, Fumihiko Takayama, Yasunori Urata. SCR: Kazunori Ito, Mamoru Oshii, Michiko Yokote. DES: Akemi Takada, Yukata Izubuchi, Hiroki Takagi, Yoshinori Sayama. ANI: Hiroki Takagi, Hiroyuki Kitakubo, Kisaraka Yamada. MUS: Kenji Kawai. PRD: Headgear, Sunrise, Nippon TV. 30 mins. x 7 eps., 30 mins. x 16 eps. (video), 25 mins. x 47 eps. (TV), 118 mins. (m1), 113 mins. (m2).

At the close of the 20th century, a rise in global sea levels forces a massive building program in Japan, causing the creation of new "labor" construction robots. In a series that effortlessly incorporates human drama and comedy with hard science fiction, the police set up a Pat[rol] Labor division to deal with the new crime that the new technology brings.

The team behind Patlabor is arguably the finest assembly of talents in modern anime, rivaled only by Hayao Miyazaki's cohorts at Studio Ghibli and the erratic Gainax collective. Written in direct opposition to the gung-ho conflicts of GUNDAM and the postapocalyptic violence of The Road Warrior, Patlabor's creators posit a future world where humanity muddles through regardless, and being a giant-robot pilot is just another job—taken, as with the space-force in WINGS OF HONNEAMISE, by misfits unable to secure work in more glamorous sectors. The tribulations of Special Vehicle Division 2 are consequently dogged by idle bureaucrats, budget cuts, interfering R&D officers, and feuds within the group. Girlish rookie Noa Izumi, disaffected techno-millionaire's son Azuma Shinohara, and ultracool Captain Goto occupy central stage, though the other cast members are some of the most well realized characters in anime. From bad-tempered gun-nut Ota to henpecked husband Shinshi, down to the gentle giant Hiromi and competent-but-snooty half-American

visitor Kanuka Clancy (whose role was greatly expanded from the original manga), all contribute to a truly marvelous ensemble. The series is loaded with subplots that put many live-action shows to shame, including the unrequited love of Goto for his better-qualified opposite number Shinobu (hilariously telegraphed in a spoof episode that featured the pair forced to share a room in a love hotel), Ota's desperately lonely existence (in a Blade Runner pastiche scripted by Oshii), and Noa's deeply respectful love for her "pet" labor Alphonse. Made on video because sponsorship was initially unavailable to make it for TV, the show was soon heading for broadcast and movie success. Some of the TV and video stories are downright goofy, like the white-alligator-in-the-sewers urban myth and a ghost story with spirits that need to be appeased; but there's also a long and carefully evolved story line about industrial espionage between rival labor manufacturers, the exploitation of children, and the lengths people go to for money.

Theatrical outings extend this dark agenda further. Patlabor: The Movie (1990), directed by Oshii, uses a threat of destruction by a suicidal visionary terrorist to examine the extent to which man depends on technology and the dangers involved in that dependency. Noa and the returning American labor captain Kanuka have to overcome their antagonism to save Tokyo from flood and disaster. Patlabor 2 (1993) rounded off the series in a brilliantly contrived manner. Set in 2002, after the original team members have gone their separate ways, it features the attempt of a disaffected ex-soldier to orchestrate a military coup. The former members of the Patlabor team reunite one last time to stop him, and the film includes some real treats for long-term fans, including an explanation for Shinobu's eternal spinsterhood and the rare sight of Goto losing his temper. The second movie secured Oshii's chances of directing GHOST IN THE SHELL and shares with its successor a similar mood, pace, and political cynicism. It also features chilling images of a Japan returning all too swiftly to martial law, a topic that Oshii would approach again in JIN-ROH, as well as "guest" designs from Shoji Kawamori and Hajime Katoki.

Christophe Gans, who directed the live-action movie of CRYING FREEMAN, has reportedly optioned *Patlabor 2* for a remake, impressed with its ability to involve its cast in action to which they always seem to arrive a minute too late. This marginalization of the "little people" is a motif that runs through the entire series and adds to the realism. It is also a fundamental feature of the third *Patlabor* movie *WXIII* (2002), in which Tokyo is threatened by a mutant monster. With Oshii conspicuously absent as director (as he was from the inferior *Jin-Roh*), *WXIII* retells an early story from Masami Yuki's *Patlabor* manga but concentrates on the "guest stars," relegating the central cast almost completely to cameo roles.

Sadly for *Patlabor*, accidents in rights acquisitions have had a similar effect on the series itself. The two movies were well dubbed and promoted by Manga Entertainment but reached a far larger audience than the video and TV incarnations, which were sold to the smaller distributor USMC. The series was also lampooned in the erotic pastiche TOKIO PRIVATE POLICE. *Ill. p. 251.*

PAUL'S MIRACLE WAR

1976. JPN: *Paul no Miracle Daisakusen*. AKA: *Paul's Miraculous Adventures*. TV SERIES. DIR: Hiroshi Sasakawa, Mizuho Nishikubo. SCR: Junzo Toriumi, Masaru Yamamoto. DES: Akiko Shimomoto. ANI: Hayao Nobe. MUS: Shunsuke Kikuchi. PRD: Tatsunoko Pro, Fuji TV. 25 mins. x 50 eps.
Little Paul has a very special cuddly toy—Pakkun is really a spirit from an alternate world under threat from the evil invader Belt Satan. Pakkun has come in search of help from Earth, and Paul is obliged to get involved when Belt Satan kidnaps his friend

Nina. This charming series is hardly in the traditional science-fiction mold of the studio known as the "home of heroes," but for younger viewers, it's magic.

PEACH-COLORED SISTERS

1998. JPN: *Momoiro Sisters*. TV series. DIR: Bob Shirahata. SCR: Satoru Akahori, Satoru Akahori Office. DES: Masaaki Kawanami, Tomoko Kosaka. ANI: N/C. MUS: N/C. PRD: Studio Deen, TBS. 7 mins. x 24 eps.
A love comedy about Momoko ("peach girl"), a hapless 17-year-old who can't seem to snare herself a man, and whose Office Lady sister is very little help at all. Broadcast as part of the *Wonderful* program on TBS, this series of shorts was originally based on a 1993 manga by Tamami Momose. **N**

PEACOCK KING *

1988. JPN: *Kujaku-o; Shin Kujaku-o*. Video. DIR: Katsuhito Akiyama, Ichiro Itano, Rintaro. SCR: Noboru Aikawa, Hajime Inaba, Tatsuhiko Urahata. DES: Takuya Wada, Takahiro Kishida, Ken Koike. ANI: Masahiro Tanaka, Takahiro Kishida. MUS: Satoru Kogura, Kit Kat Club, Yas-Kaz, Toshiyuki Honda. PRD: AIC, Studio 88, Madhouse. 55 mins., 60 mins., 50 mins., 45 mins. x 2 eps. (*True PK*).
Kujaku is a young monk and an avatar, the incarnation of a god. His friend and cute blonde fellow-avatar Ashura, his teacher Ajari, and the leather-clad biker/magic master Onimaru band together to fight the demons released by Tatsuma from the ancient temple statues at Nara. Tatsuma is a powerful psychic, but he's never learned proper control of his abilities, and in seeking to test his powers, he puts humankind in terrible danger in the first episode, *Feast for Returning Demons*. In the second story, *Castle of Illusion*, Onimaru and graduate student Hatsuko are the sole survivors of a team digging up relics of medieval warlord and supposed black magician Nobunaga Oda (see YOTODEN). If the two scrolls found by the team are joined, Azuchi Castle

will rise again and the warlord will unleash hell on Earth. For the third story, *Harvest of Cherry Blossoms*, the threat is undead shogun Ieyasu Tokugawa, who has joined forces with the restless ghost of an actress murdered during WWII and intends to sink Japan beneath the waves.

The story of Kujaku-myo'o (to some esoteric Buddhist sects, a manifestation of Gautama Buddha often depicted riding on a giant peacock) was updated by Makoto Ogino for his 1985 manga in *Young Jump*, using the idea of avatars of the gods as inspiration for a modern-day adventure. The franchise returned as *True PK* (1994, *Shin Kujaku-o*), more faithful to Ogino's original, and it replaced the Madhouse-lookalike animation of AIC with *actual* animation from the Madhouse studio itself, under veteran director Rintaro. His versions throw much of their budget into the movie-quality opening scenes, creating impressive images that soon devolve into less expensive animation. Trawling outside Japan for villains, it features twin avatars, a boy and a girl, born to reincarnate god of light Kujaku-o and god of darkness Tenja-o. The boy, Akira, is a member of a Buddhist sect charged with guarding the Dragon Grail, a mystic vessel that has the power to release Tenja-o into the world. Power-crazed neo-Nazi Siegfried von Mittgard plans to steal the grail and reincarnate himself as Tenja-oh; this will prevent Akira's twin, Tomoko, from fulfilling her destiny, but Siegfried has another role in mind for her.

Like the director's earlier DOOMED MEGALOPOLIS, *PK* suffers in English simply through the weight of the original source material—American actors, working with the Japanese names for the Chinese versions of Buddhist takes on Hindu gods, create a predictably confusing roster, though translators Bill Flanagan and Yuko Sato make a heroic effort to incorporate the original Sanskrit. A live-action Japanese—Hong Kong coproduction, *PK: Legend of the Phoenix* (1988), was directed by

STORY OF RIKI's Nam Nai Choi and starred martial-arts legend Yuen Biao. Another Kujaku appears in CLAMP's RG VEDA. ⬤ⓃⓋ

PEKKLE *

1993. JPN: Ahiru no Pekkle. AKA: Pekkle the Duck. Video. DIR: Akira Shimizu. SCR: Mitsukuni Kumagai. DES: Toshikazu Ishiwatari. ANI: Takashi Asakura, Kennosuke Tokuda. MUS: Yasunori Honda. PRD: Sanrio. 30 mins. x 4 eps.

Another of Sanrio's cute kiddie characters, this time a sweet little duck, accompanied by his girlfriend, Ruby, reenacts tales from the ARABIAN NIGHTS for his U.S. video release—PtD: Aladdin and the Magic Lamp and PtD: Sindbad the Sailor. The final two adventures, unreleased in the U.S., were the shark-infested PtD: Trouble at the Swimming Gala and the Indiana Jones pastiche PtD: In Search of the Secret Treasure. The character, however, was a lame duck when compared to the successes of his Sanrio stablemate HELLO KITTY.

PELICAN ROAD CLUB CULTURE

1986. JPN: Pelican Road Club Culture. Video. DIR: Eiichi Yamamoto. SCR: Eiichi Yamamoto. DES: Koichi Igarashi. ANI: Kazuhiko Udagawa. MUS: Kazuo Kogure. PRD: Studio World, Nippon Columbia. 55 mins.

High-school boy Kenichi Watanabe is crazy about his MBX50 motorcycle. He and his buddies organize a motorcycle club, which they call Culture. In among the engine oil and spark plugs, however, they begin to learn that there's more to life than bikes, chiefly when they are approached by reporter Kanako, who is interested in their stories . . . particularly Kenichi's. Based on Koichi Igarashi's 1982 manga Pelican Road, which was a contemporary of BOMBER BIKERS OF SHONAN in the same Shonen King magazine.

PENDANT

1997. JPN: Pendant. Video. DIR: Yoshihiro Oka. SCR: Kaori Nakase, Takao Nitta. DES: Masaki Takei. ANI: Akio Watanabe. MUS: N/C. PRD: Beam Entertainment. 30 mins. x 3 eps.

Tales of young love, based on a computer game by Masaki Takei, creator of END OF SUMMER, starting with a lonely summer holiday enlivened by a chance meeting of an old flame and building up to a romantic "climax" on Christmas Eve. Unlike many adaptations of games that simply dump a male protagonist into a sea of women in the style of TENCHI MUYO!, this one separates the various female characters into separate stories with different male love interests, which is slightly more realistic, if no less boring. ⓃⓃ

PENGUINS MEMORY

1985. JPN: Penguins Memory Shiawase Monogatari. AKA: Penguins Memory Happy Tale. Movie. DIR: Satoshi Kimura. SCR: Hiroshi Kawano, Ryo Yamazaki, Rei Kuno, Dodekagon. DES: Ginjiro Suzuki. ANI: Norio Hikone, Akinori Nagaoka. MUS: Seiko Matsuda. PRD: Animation Staff Room, CM Land. 101 mins.

Mike, a traumatized penguin who once fought in the Delta War, returns to his hometown of Lake City and takes a job as a librarian. He falls in love with Jill, a would-be singing penguin who is the daughter of the owner of the local penguin hospital. Jill meets a record producer and embarks on a successful career, but Mike waddles away alone— he has discovered that she is engaged to marry Jack the penguin doctor, and he doesn't wish to get in the way.

A film made to cash in on the unexpected popularity of a 1984 series of Suntory Beer commercials that replayed famous American films such as Casablanca and The Deer Hunter but with a cast of cartoon penguins.

PERFECT BLUE *

1997. Movie. DIR: Satoshi Kon. SCR: Sadayuki Murai. DES: Hisashi Eguchi, Hideki Hamazu, Satoshi Kon. ANI: Hideki Hamazu, Hisao Shirai. MUS: Masahiro Ikumi. PRD: Madhouse, Oniro. 82 mins.

Singer Mima Kirigoe leaves the pop trio Cham to become a serious actress. Her change in careers causes a slow decline into insanity, as forces conspire to keep her from changing her public persona, to the extent of interfering directly in her private life. Matters aren't helped by a murderous stalker, egged on by e-mails from someone claiming to be the real Mima. Eventually, Mima's hold on reality is thoroughly undermined as she sinks into the mother of all neuroses. And she's not on her own—this film is told from the viewpoints of three characters, and each one of them is going slowly insane.

Based on a novel by Yoshikazu Takeuchi and originally planned as a live-action film, PB features obvious influences from Hitchcock's Vertigo (1958), Stage Fright (1950), and Dario Argento's Suspiria (1977), but it has ultimately a less bleak and more humane agenda. Murai's script, which adds the film-within-a-film Double Bind to really confuse matters, remains one of anime's best since Kazunori Ito's for PATLABOR. The obsessive fan stalker, who was merely a red herring in the novel, is given a succession of actual murders to perform in the anime version, though the blurred line between fantasy and reality is one of PB's greatest achievements—the director deliberately cut all transition shots that signified dream-sequences or flashbacks, leaving the audience floundering in a confused world cleverly matching the protagonists' own. Kon, the former animator on the surreal JOJO'S BIZARRE ADVENTURES who created environments full of faux-live-action clutter in ROUJIN Z, makes a virtue of a limited animation budget, depicting crowd scenes with empty faces and playing up the ghostly pallor of fluorescent lighting. The cinematography is gorgeous, as loving a rendition of real-life contemporary Tokyo as the dark, glittering forward-projection of the city in AKIRA (whose creator Katsuhiro Otomo has a production credit for introducing the producers to his protégé Kon, although some press releases implied his involvement in *PB* was far greater). The increasing influence of the Internet and cyber-reality on mass perceptions is seriously examined here (and further explored on TV in SERIAL EXPERIMENTS LAIN), but *PB* is also strong on traditional story values—beautifully paced plot development and a craftsman's ability to subvert the conventions of the medium. Most notable and controversial remains a scene in which Mima's character is raped, played out as a pastiche of *The Accused* (1988) but continually taunting the viewer with the question of whether *this* time it is really for real. The prosaic movements of lights and camera, and the whispered apologies of the actor playing one of the rapists who has to stay in position during a shooting break, heighten the surreality precisely because they remind us that Mima is being assaulted in a "respectable" professional context—later in the movie, she is attacked for real.

The English version is excellent despite some inevitable losses in translation. Japan may look like every other modern, industrialized, media-led country, but both language and social interaction are hugely important in this tale of fishes out of water. Some of the bowing, scraping, and statement of the obvious (culturally, an attempt to ingratiate oneself by appearing more clueless than the next person) just seems insincere with American voices. Mima's oft-repeated "Who are you?" loses some of its clout when lip-synching considerations force the actress to add a mitigating "Excuse me." The English dub also loses an extra level of emphasis—two scenes when Mima slips into her native dialect, demonstrating to the Japanese audience that not even the girl we see in private is the real Mima. The city girl-next-door whom the fans worship is actually another mask—a pretty country maid who forgets her elocution lessons when Mom phones from back home. This shift is also heard in the film's final line, when Mima announces that she is "herself"

at last (and uses her native accent, not the well-spoken Tokyo dialect she's been taught to use on TV). Despite these minor cavils, *PB* remains one of the best anime of the late 1990s. The remake rights were optioned by director Darren Aronofsky, who lifted a shot from the film (of Mima crouching in her bathtub) for his live-action movie *Requiem for a Dream* (2000). Director Kon and writer Murai would return with another peek behind dramatic masks: MILLENNIUM ACTRESS. Sequences from *PB* were shown onstage by Madonna as part of her Drowned World concerts in 2001. *Ill. p 117.* **LNV**

PET SHOP OF HORRORS *

1998. TV. DIR: Toshio Hirata, Norihiko Nagahama, Yoshiaki Kawajiri, Satoshi Nishimura. SCR: Yasuhiro Imagawa, Matsuri Akino. DES: Hisashi Abe, Hiroshi Kato. ANI: Hisashi Abe. MUS: N/C. PRD: Madhouse, TBS. 25 mins. x 4 eps.

In Chinatown, in a generic U.S. city (on the Japanese release, *Newtype* magazine claimed it was New York, but *Animage* and *AX* both noted the visual references to Los Angeles), "Count D," a fey Faustian pet shop owner, sells personified desires as "pets" to society's misfits, including a mother who refuses to accept that her own weak will turned her daughter into a drug addict, a faithless husband who cannot admit he drove his bride to suicide, and a proud gangster who wants people to fear his power. Signing deceptively simple contracts, they discover that deals made with the supernatural should never be taken lightly. Leon, a loud-mouth cop who encapsulates several anime stereotypes of Americans, is convinced that the count is up to something, but the count is strangely welcoming and hospitable toward him. The "horrors" happen when purchasers ignore the strict instructions provided for the care of the unusual creatures they buy—*Gremlins* parallels are obvious. Old meets new and East meets West, not just in the mixture of mythologies, but in the

TARO MAEGAMI was one of *two* anime adaptations of Miyoko Matsutani's best-selling children's book, both of which were released in the same year. *See entry p. 393.*

Taro Maegami

© 1979 NIPPON ANIMATION CO., LTD.

mismatched central characters. Everyday laws cannot touch these criminals, but the count cuts through the red tape and delivers punishment where Leon cannot, without fear or favor toward a would-be president, or even a child star prepared to sell his soul for adult fame. Though our wiseacre policeman is too boneheaded to realize it, the count is on his side, transforming the story from a humdrum chiller into a moral *X-Files*, in which hell's own angel teams up with an earthy cop to mete out peculiar justice.

Matsuri Akino's original 1990 manga ran for over a dozen volumes in *Mitzi Comics DX*, and yet this 1999 TBS series was never planned as more than four episodes. Limited animation is bolstered by flashy effects (from some big names, including DOOMED MEGALOPOLIS–director Rintaro on the opening animation), but the biggest mystery is why there was no more. Perhaps wisely, the show canceled itself before the "sin of the week" angle could become too predictable. Compare to similar rough justice in JUDGE. **V**

PETER PAN AND WENDY *

1989. JPN: *Peter Pan no Boken*. AKA: *Peter Pan's Adventure*. TV series. DIR: Yoshio Kuroda, Fumio Kurokawa, Kozo

Kusuba. SCR: Shunichi Yukimuro, Michiru Shimada. DES: Takashi Nakamura, Shohei Kawamoto. ANI: Hirotsuge Kawasaki, Tomihiko Okubo, Moriyasu Taniguchi. MUS: Toshiyuki Watanabe. PRD: Nippon Animation, Fuji TV. 25 mins. x 41 eps.

J.M. Barrie's 1911 novel is given a new twist as Wendy, *not* wanting to grow up, travels with her two little brothers and Peter Pan to Never Land where he must fight the terrible pirate leader Captain Hook and face many other perils, including Darkness, an evil sorcerer who joins forces with Hook. Nakamura's presence may surprise those who know him only from AKIRA and ROBOT CARNIVAL, as would that of future SPRIGGAN-director Kawasaki. A compilation video of the first three episodes was released in the U.K. on an obscure children's label, featuring new music from Haim Saban and Shuki Levy.

PHANTOM BUSTER MIKO

2000. JPN: *Reino Tantei Miko*. AKA: *Spirit Investigator Miko*. Video. DIR: Hiroshi Furuhashi. SCR: Tetsuo Tanaka. DES: Masashi Kojima. ANI: Waki Noguchi. MUS: N/C. PRD: Maxam. 30 mins.
This is a sexually charged variant of the ghostbusting anime typified by PHANTOM QUEST CORP or GHOST SWEEPER MIKAMI, as a sexy exorcist takes on the legions of hell. ⓝ

PHANTOM HEROES

1991. JPN: *Phantom Yusha Densetsu*. AKA: *Legend of the Phantom Heroes*. Video. DIR: Satoshi Dezaki. SCR: Kazumi Koide. DES: Keizo Shimizu. ANI: Toshifumi Takizawa. MUS: Kyan Marie with Medusa. PRD: Magic Bus. 45 mins.
Yazawa, a former aircraft carrier F4 Phantom pilot, becomes embroiled in a South American coup when his lover is killed during a CIA operation in El Salvador. A violent thriller based on a best-selling novel by DARK WARRIOR–creator Sho Takejima, this video was rushed out in the year of his untimely death. ⓝⓥ

PHANTOM QUEST CORP *

1994. JPN: *Yugen Kaisha*. AKA: *Phantom Company/Limited Company, Private Company*. Video. DIR: Koichi Chigira, Morio Asaka, Takuji Endo. SCR: Asami Watanabe, Tatsuhiko Urahata, Satoshi Kimura. DES: Hitoshi Ueda. ANI: Yasuhito Kikuchi. MUS: Junichi Kanezaki. PRD: Madhouse. 30 mins. x 4 eps.
Ayaka is a modern girl running her own successful business—a freelance psychic agency, supplying the power to deal with any problem. Ayaka is also a hopeless lush who can't stay ahead of her finances, blows all her money on designer clothes and karaoke bars, and relies on her child butler, Mamoru, to run her home and her life and to make sure she gets up in the morning. The police's own ghostbusting squad, Section U, headed up by a crumpled-but-cute detective with a soft spot for our heroine, causes even more complications. And as for her staff—she's stuck with a dropout priest, a twisted firestarter, a psychic who only works to supplant her meager pension, and her own rich family's hereditary butler.

Like its longer-running contemporary GHOST SWEEPER MIKAMI, *PQC* is packed with gentle digs at what has become of Japan. The money-culture of the late 1980s produced many unreal phenomena of its own (the bubble economy, Generation X) while simultaneously trying to forget the spiritual past. The title, with a double meaning in the real and ghostly worlds, sets the tone for a witty, wacky post-*X-Files* series, but it didn't get the success it deserved at home or abroad. Takuji Endo and Morio Asaka cram their episodes with innovative jerky camera effects to play up the feel of a horror B-movie, just one of the little touches that made *PQC*, but somehow failed to ignite the audience. Other noticeable presences include Yoshiaki Kawajiri as a "guest" director for the striking opening credits and future TENCHI MUYO!–director Kimura as a humble scriptwriter. Creator Juzo Mutsuki has several other underrated series—the similar ancient-meets-modern clashes

of DEVIL HUNTER YOHKO and CYBER CITY OEDO 808. The dub from Pioneer is of high quality, and even boasts a hilarious English-language version of one of Ayaka's excruciatingly melancholy karaoke sessions—the single thirty-something modern girl singing a widow's song that likens herself to "a riderless horse."

PHAROAH'S SEAL

1988. JPN: *Oka no Monsho*. Movie. DIR: Daisuke Yasaku. SCR: Chieko Hosokawa. DES: Chieko Hosokawa. ANI: N/C. MUS: Joe Hisaishi. PRD: Toei. 40 mins.
Two lovers are caught up in civil unrest in 1000 B.C. Egypt. Based on Chieko Hosokawa's 1977 manga, which has been reprinted over 130 times by its publishers Princess Comics, this is best described as a "costume drama" since, while the setting is ancient Egypt, the characters' concerns speak to any modern schoolgirl, perhaps explaining the series' runaway success in manga form.

PHOTON *

1997. JPN: *Photon*. Video. DIR: Koji Masunari. SCR: Yosuke Kuroda. DES: Masaki Kajishima, Shinya Takahashi, Koji Watanabe. ANI: Shinya Takahashi. MUS: Haruhiko Nishioka. PRD: AIC. 45 mins. x 6 eps.
On Sandy Planet, where the locals are so stupid they worship Magic Markers, chieftain's daughter Aun goes AWOL because she's got a crush on a troubadour, and laconic local boy Photon is sent to find her before she causes trouble. But Photon discovers a crashed spaceship and wakes its beautiful pilot, Keyne, from her cryogenic slumber. Accidentally marrying her by writing the word "Idiot" on her forehead, Photon is forced to protect Keyne from the evil space-faring prince Papacha.

Planned, like its stablemate TENCHI MUYO!, as a multi-media promotion involving animation, radio drama, novels, and a manga, *Photon* is distinguished by BATTLE ATHLETES–director Masunari allowing the designers free rein with their insane visual conceits, from a girl who can stop time in selected places, to levitation garters, wind-powered land-speeders, and a girl trying to proclaim her love through a mouthful of sand. Sadly, the script doesn't live up to the visual promise, relying on puerile nudie gags and a charmless lead, though moments remain when it looks as if a mad scientist has combined **DRAGON HALF** and **NAUSICAÄ** in a secret laboratory. **N**

PIA CARROT *

1997. JPN: *Pia Carrot e Yokoso*. AKA: *Welcome to Pia Carrot*. Video. DIR: Kan Fukumoto, Nobuyoshi Ando. SCR: Katsumasa Kanezawa. DES: Cocktail Soft. ANI: Katsumasa Kanezawa. MUS: N/C. PRD: Pink Pineapple, KSS. 30 mins. x 4 eps., 30 mins. x 2 eps. (six planned).

In an anime based on a computer-dating simulation game, a lusty teenage boy gets a part-time job at a restaurant, where he is soon seducing the waitresses. By episode three, even the crew tired of the setting, and the cast relocates to Okinawa. For the grand finale, manager Kyoko invites the girls back to her place, everyone gets drunk, and formulaic high jinks ensue. After a manga adaptation appeared in *Comic Gao*, the franchise was renewed for *Pia Carrot 2 DX* (1999), in which, predictably, a new branch of the restaurant opens up, a new boy gets a summer job, and a new rack of girls finds him irresistibly attractive. Released in the U.S. as *Welcome to Pia Carrot* (2001). **N**

PICCOLINO

1976. JPN: *Pinocchio Yori: Piccolino no Daiboken*. AKA: *The Adventures of Piccolino, after Pinocchio*. TV series. DIR: Hiroshi Saito, Masaharu Endo, Shigeo Koshi. SCR: Masao Maruyama. DES: Takao Kogawa, Michiyo Sakurai, Marty Murphy. ANI: Takao Kogawa, Michiyo Sakurai, Koichi Murata. MUS: Karel Svoboda. PRD: Nippon Animation, TV Asahi. 25 mins. x 52 eps.

Lonely toy-maker Gepetto constructs a puppet son to keep him company and names him Piccolino. The boy lives as a normal child but yearns to be *real*. This German-Japanese coproduction of Carlo Collodi's 1881 tale involves one of Disney's stalwarts, Marty Murphy. Despite the renaming, the series remains close to the original, with sculpting by old Gepetto, the learning of worldly wisdom, and achieving real humanity—the story is the same. See also **ADVENTURES OF PINOCCHIO**.

PICTURES AT AN EXHIBITION

1966. JPN: *Tenrankai no E*. Movie. DIR: Osamu Tezuka, Shingo Matsuo, Taku Sugiyama. SCR: Osamu Tezuka. DES: Osamu Tezuka. ANI: Akihiro Mori, Shigeru Yamazaki. MUS: Modest Mussorgsky. PRD: Mushi Pro. 34 mins.

This short film by **ASTRO BOY**'s Tezuka sets ten short vignettes of his own devising to music by Mussorgsky originally based on scenes created by a friend of the composer. The Tezuka stories, like the originals, are contemporary social satires: *The Critic, The Artificial Gardener, The Plastic Surgeon, The Factory Owner, The Tough Guy, The Champion, The TV Star, The Zen Funeral, The Soldier,* and *The Finale*. The music is an original arrangement of Mussorgsky's score by Isao Tomita; he was later to make an arrangement of the same work for synthesizer, but this one is fully orchestrated, making for interesting comparisons. Definitely one to file in the "art-house" section of Tezuka's output, here in an unmistakable homage to Disney's *Fantasia* (1940).

PIGGYBACK GHOST

1955. JPN: *Onbu Obake*. AKA: *Knapsack Ghost; Ghost in a Knapsack*. TV series. DIR: Ryuichi Yokoyama. SCR: Ryuichi Yokoyama. DES: Ryuichi Yokoyama. ANI: Mitsuhiro Machiyama. MUS: N/C. PRD: Fuji, Eastman Color, Yomiuri TV (Nippon TV). 55 mins. (m), 25 mins. x 54 eps. (TV).

Green-eyed spirit Onbu is created when lightning strikes jade in a river. He loves swimming through the air but is adopted by Ojie the village blacksmith, who carries him in a knapsack. Onbu plays with the cheeky Kanchan brothers, Ojo the gentle girl, Chinnen the young priest, and the other kindly villagers. Lifting many ideas from **JAPANESE FOLK TALES**, this series was based on a manga by Ryuichi Yokoyama, who also created **FUKU-CHAN**, shared many staff members with the more successful **SAZAE-SAN**, and was remade for TV by Hajime Watanabe at the Eiken Studio in 1966.

PIKKOMAN'S DEVIL TRAINING

1999. JPN: *Pikkoman no Oni Chikudo: Midnight Milk Party*. AKA: *Pikkoman's Way of Devil Taming*. Video. DIR: Rion Kushiro. SCR: Tedokoro Imaike. DES: Piko Fujikatsu (Pikkoman). ANI: Ken Raibi. MUS: N/C. PRD: Tsuyusha, Aka-tonbo. 30 mins.

Teenager Chiho Chino wants to have an adventure before she leaves her school days behind, so she auditions for a role in a schoolgirl porn video, believing that her performance will be of a wholly solo nature. However, when she reaches the set, she is raped on camera. Another of anime's more distasteful offerings, this one based on a manga by Piko Fujikatsu. **NV**

PILOT CANDIDATE *

1999. JPN: *Megami Kohosei*. AKA: *Candidate for Goddess*. TV series. DIR: Mitsuru Hongo. SCR: Akira Oketani, Miho Sakai. DES: Shinichi Yamaoka. ANI: N/C. MUS: N/C. PRD: Production IG, Xebec. 25 mins. x 12 eps.

In the year 4088, a five-girl team (with token male Zero) must learn to pilot the giant robot Ingrid if planet Zion is ever to be a successful space colony for the human race. Aliens with mysterious motives oppose human expansion. This anime was based on a manga in *Comic Gam* by *DNAngel*–creator Yukiru Sugisaki and influenced by the existential musings of **EVANGELION**, but it features slapstick and a cat-girl thrown in for good measure. As with other anime made at the turn of the century (see **DUAL**), the transition to digital animation makes for clever camerawork but a sanitized, "clean" feel to all the art.

PING PONG CLUB *

1995. JPN: *Ike! Inachu Ping-Pong Club.*
AKA: *Let's Go! Inachu Ping Pong Club;
Make Way for the Ping Pong Club.* TV
series. DIR: Masami Hata. SCR: Sukehiro Tomita, Tsunehisa Ito, Kenji Terada,
Yoshihiro Sasa. DES: Minoru Furuya.
ANI: Mamoru Tanaka. MUS: Katsuyoshi
Kobayashi. PRD: Grouper Production,
KSS, TBS. 12 mins. x 47 eps.
The boys' table-tennis club consists of
earnest captain Takeda, school dreamboat Kinoshita, and four deadbeats
who constantly goof off instead of practicing. Their coach, Mr. Shibazaki, is a
pushover for all the other teachers.
The girls' club is a large group of dedicated, gifted young athletes, whose
coach, Mr. Tachikawa, despises the
boys' club and covets its premises. But
the clubroom is about more than just
ping-pong; it's a refuge for a group of
misfits, no-hopers, and adolescents trying to cope with the petty pains and
embarrassments of growing up. To
keep it, the boys will have to find that
old fighting spirit they all seem to
lack—a plan helped by the pretty
Kyoko, who offers a personal "sex pass"
to the highest scorer.

It's hard to describe this short series,
based on Minoru Furuya's 1993 *Young
Magazine* manga, as anything other
than insane. The raging of teenage
male hormones and the nonoperational status of the related brain cells is
conveyed in a fractured visual and
directorial style, complete with a LUPIN
III pastiche, mom-and-pop gags, enka
and taiko, male impersonators, crossdressers, St. Francis Xavier, the legend
of MOMOTARO, volcanic eruptions,
smelly foreigners, feats of *Endurance*,
and every conceivable offensive reference to sexual habits and bodily functions. There are more naked penises in
this low-rent buddy movie than in
many erotic anime—falling out of
shorts, stuffed into bird's heads for a
SWAN LAKE ballet skit, accidentally
revealed during exercise—and all the
tropes normally used to peek at female
nudity, but there's hardly a hint of any
real possibility of sexual action. The

overall effect is as directionless and
futile as the average teenager's life, but
it's hard not to feel a creeping sympathy for its hopeless, dogged solidarity
with those facing hormonal challenge
and social failure.

The throwaway nature is so determinedly pursued as to obscure the solid track record of its crew. This isn't a
team of young punks talking dirty to
their peers (see BITE ME: CHAMELEON),
but a rack of seasoned professionals
with an instinct for video sales. Their
work is full of knowing nudges and
winks, entirely unashamed of itself.
Despite the multitude of monocultural
references, the overall *Beavis and
Butthead* atmosphere would have spoken loud and clear to legions of hormonally challenged males too young to
get most of the cultural digs, but that's
hardly the audience for the subtitled
version that was released in the U.S.
🅛🅝🅥

PINK CURTAIN

1985. JPN: *Pink no Curtain.* Video. DIR:
Yoshiharu Kurahashi. SCR: Masahito
Nishio. DES: N/C. ANI: Minoru Kichoda.
MUS: Hikaru Onda. PRD: Bip. 30 mins.
Virgin boy Okuyama is a stocker at the
supermarket who has no luck with
women. His life is thrown upside down
when his sister Noriko unexpectedly
moves into his house. Okuyama is overcome with lustful thoughts for her, but
she regards him simply as a brother.
With more incest from the era that
gave us CREAM LEMON, this story was
based on the strip in *Manga Action*
magazine by Joji Akiyama, who also
created KOIKO'S DAILY LIFE. 🅝

PIPI THE ALIEN

1965. JPN: *Uchujin Pipi.* TV series. DIR:
Yuichiro Konnai. SCR: Sakyo Komatsu,
Kazumasa Hirai. DES: Toshikazu
Fukuhara. ANI: N/C. MUS: Isao Tomita.
PRD: NHK, TV Doga, NHK. 25 mins. x
52 eps.
Toshihiko and Ryoko meet the gnome-
like alien Pipi and his friends, who
have one year (the length of a lunch
break on Pipi's world) to learn all they

can about planet Earth. Since these
two Japanese children are the first people they have met who are close to
them in size, they tag along with them
as they explore their neighborhood,
repaying them by taking them on fantastic space journeys during their own
school lunch breaks. A series that mixes live action and animation.

PIPI THE FLIGHTLESS FIREFLY

1995. JPN: *Pipi Tobenai Hotaru.* Movie.
DIR: Shinichi Nakada. SCR: Yoshimi
Kato. DES: Akimi Kozawa. ANI: Takaya
Ono. MUS: N/C. PRD: Office CHK, Success Road, Mushi. 90 mins.
In a heavy-handed "educational" film
that also finds the time to tackle environmental issues, a young firefly is bullied by his fellow insects because he
cannot actually fly. Government
approved, it says here.

PLANET BUSTERS *

1984. JPN: *Birth.* AKA: *World of the Talisman.* Video. DIR: Shinya Sadamitsu.
SCR: "Kaname Pro." DES: Koretaku
Kaneda, Makoto Kobayashi. ANI:
Shinya Sadamitsu, Mutsumi Inomata,
Shigenori Kageyama. MUS: Joe Hisaishi
(Randy Miller in U.S. version). PRD: Idol,
Kaname. 80 mins.
Namu Shurugi (Prince Talon) and his
sister Rasa Jupiter (Princess Rasa) are
descended from a race wiped out by
the people of planet Aquaroid (Pandora), who are engaged in a devastating
global war with the android Inorganics
race. They fall into the company of
Bao (Mo) and Kim (Keen), two treasure hunters in search of the mystic talisman. This planet, it seems, is a
"testing ground" to reveal the one destined to become the leader of the
Galactic Empire. In an arrangement
similar to KING ARTHUR AND THE
KNIGHTS OF THE ROUND TABLE, whoever
gets the talisman will become the new
ruler. The fight for the talisman is a
conflict that begins *every* cycle of cosmic existence, as factions compete to
determine whether the dominant life
form throughout the universe will be
flesh or metallic.

Though the American dub unsurprisingly reduces this to the usual simplistic Good Humans vs. Evil Robots, this sci-fi story, which features lots of action, cool machines, and frequent shots of Rasa's cute rear end, is a paradoxical and densely layered parable of reincarnation. This makes it very unsuitable for the audience of under-fives at whom the U.K. video release was aimed. Even with the script revamped to minimize the spiritual dimension and make the goal of their quest the "Planet Buster," a secret weapon made by the creator of the universe (who would really need one, right?), it still makes no sense, but it's fun to watch. Ending with the destruction of this cycle of existence, and only the four main characters preserved in spirit form, it is liable to have befuddled many a preteen viewer, especially with the finale, when two alien superbeings sit down and start debating the transient nature of existence. Made for video but shown in Japanese theaters, a "Special Edition" on video includes the 22-minute *Making of Birth* documentary.

PLANET MASK

1966. JPN: *Yusei Kamen*. TV series. DIR: Yonehiko Watanabe, Tsutomu Yamamoto. SCR: Akira Adachi. DES: Takaji Kusunoki. ANI: Masakazu Tanokura. MUS: Hidehiko Arano. PRD: TCJ, Eiken, Fuji TV. 25 mins. x 39 eps. In the 21st century, the discovery of the inhabited tenth planet, Pineron, out past Pluto, is happy news for the solar system. Earthman Johansen and Pineron girl Maria fall in love and become the proud parents of the first mixed-race child, Peter. Fifteen years later, Earth and Pineron are thrown into a state of war when Pineron warships mistake an Earth vessel in trouble for an attack ship. A lone masked figure riding on a rocket tries to keep the spacefaring powers apart. This Cold War superhero thriller was inspired in equal chunks by the troubles in Vietnam, Japan's conflicts with the USSR over its northern islands, and the chil-

dren of mixed-race parents after WWII—children who would shortly be entering their teens. With typical TV double standards, the theme song cried "stop the war," even as the show encouraged kids to go out and *fight* for peace.

PLASTIC LITTLE *

1994. Video. DIR: Kinji Yoshimoto. SCR: Mayori Sekijima. DES: Satoshi Urushibara, Studio Nue. ANI: Satoshi Urushibara. MUS: Tamiya Terashima. PRD: Animate Film, SME. 45 mins. Orphaned teenager Tita takes over her father's pet shop hunter business, collecting and selling exotic animals from all over the galaxy. In port on planet Yietta (where, to feebly justify the title, there's very *little plastic*) she rescues a young girl who is being pursued by the local authorities. Elysse Nalerov is in big trouble; her father designed a new weapon, she has the arming codes, and the government will stop at nothing to get them. Tita and her crew decide to help her out, and mayhem ensues.

A lightweight but enjoyable sci-fi adventure made, like its predecessor LEGEND OF LEMNEAR, solely to show off the artistic talents of Urushibara and Yoshimoto. While lacking a particularly strong story line, it succeeds most perfectly in the rendition of an individual artist's style into moving pictures. Unfortunately for the genre, Urushibara's style isn't SF illustration but cheesecake. The artist on numerous books of cutie-girl illustrations, he renders lush young flesh with glowing perfection. Yoshimoto transfers this perfection exactly to celluloid and puts a remarkable range of motions onto it, so before they take on the evil overlord, the girls can stop for a bath scene where they can compare their breasts. Not only every jiggle of every curve, but the characters' expressions and movements all give the impression of seeing the creator's original art come to life on the page. When one considers the violence often done to original design art in the cause of simplifying it enough to animate cheaply (see VAM-

Mospeada

PIRE HUNTER D), the achievement is all the more remarkable.

At the time of its release, the creators claimed that it was only a prequel to a set of other stories—though as time passed, the only evidence was a brief *PL* audio drama that described Elysse as a "guest star," thereby implying there was more to come. In 1999, Urushibara and Yoshimoto unveiled artwork from a new project, *Femme Femme Buccaneers*, charting the progress of Ann and Ricorne, a two-piece idol-singer act known collectively as Virginity. Though they promised that these two girls, along with the unshaven male pirates of the Yiettan isle of Espaniola, would soon grace anime screens alongside Tita and her crew, the wait continues, making *PL2* the most delayed project in anime, beating even Otomo's *Steam Boy*. Owing to accidents of international pricing and rights negotiation, *PL* is available in separate U.K. and U.S. translations. *Ill. p. 429.* **NV**

PLAWRES SANSHIRO

1983. TV series. DIR: Kunihiko Yuyama, Masahisa Ishida, Masamune Ochiai, Osamu Sekita, Katsumi Endo, Susumu Ishizaki. SCR: Keisuke Fujikawa, Kenji Terada, Junji Tagami. DES: Mutsumi Inomata, Shigenori Kageyama, Shigeru

Katsumata. ANI: Mutsumi Inomata, Hitoshi Yoshinaga, Kazuhiro Ochi, Hirotoshi Sano, Takashi Sogabe, Satoshi Yamazaki. MUS: Yasunori Tsuchida. PRD: Kaname Productions, TBS. 25 mins. x 37 eps.

Pla[stic] wres[tlers] are miniature robot toys that can be operated to fight each other. Orphan Sanshiro Sugata (see SANSHIRO SUGATA) has inherited a superb plawres from his vanished father and wants to make it a champion, while his grandfather wants him to put away childish things and focus on becoming a judo champion.

The conflict between a child's and an adult's view of "achievement," the symbolism of inheritance, and the way in which toys provide an interface with a world that seems too big and scary to handle directly are interesting concepts for a series. Sadly, the need to keep things on a child's level restricts what Yuyama can do with his material. He can't have minded, though—14 years on, he made POKÉMON. Jiro Uma and Minoru Kamiya produced the spinoff manga in the same year, but strangely enough, the expected toy line didn't materialize.

PLEASE OPEN THE DOOR

1986. JPN: *Tobira o Akete*. Movie. DIR: Keizo Shimizu, Tsuneo Tominaga. SCR: Kazumi Koide, Satoshi Dezaki. DES: Setsuko Shibunnoichi. ANI: Toshihiro Kawamoto, Mayumi Hirota. MUS: Mark Goldenberg. PRD: Kitty Film, Magic Bus. 81 mins.

Miyako Negishi is a seemingly ordinary high-school girl but has amazing powers of ESP, while her friend Keiichiro can transform into a were-lion, and her friend Kaori has the power of teleportation. On a night when the moon is full, they are transported to the alternate "Middle Kingdom," where Miyako is the fair princess Neryura, fighting a losing battle against the Western king Duran III. Forming an alliance with the eastern king Dimida, Miyako and her friends use their powers to save the world, hoping eventually to return home. Based on an SF novel by

Motoko Arai, better known in the English-speaking world for her story *Green Requiem*. Compare to FUSHIGI YUGI.

PLEASE SAVE MY EARTH *

1993. JPN: *Boku no Chikyu o Mamotte*. Video. DIR: Kazuo Yamazaki. SCR: Kazuo Yamazaki. DES: Takayuki Goto, Yuji Ikeda. ANI: Takayuki Goto. MUS: Hajime Mizoguchi. PRD: Victor Entertainment. 30 mins. x 6 eps., 30 mins. (music video).

Seven schoolchildren have a recurring collective dream in which a team of alien scientists on the moon gather data about Earth. Seeking each other's company, they begin to suspect that the dreams are really suppressed memories of their distant past lives. Past relationships replay themselves, as teenage Alice Sakaguchi is desired by eight-year-old Rin, while he in turn is pursued by the mature woman Mokuren. But love is not the only thing that survives reincarnation, as the members of the group discover that their former incarnations ended in tragedy—a tragedy fated to repeat itself.

One of a glut of mid-1990s lunar reincarnation stories, but it is far more mature than the populist SAILOR MOON and better executed than the shoddy BOUNTY DOG. This emotive tale of love, loss, and anger echoing through reincarnation was based on a manga serialized in *Hana to Yume* by Saki Hiwatari, whose other manga works include *A Favor of the Devil* and *Tower of the Future*. Only a fraction of the 21-volume original would fit into the anime, and the story was compressed further into a 100-minute "movie" edit concentrating on the Alice/Rin relationship. There was also an animated music video, comprising eight tracks of the wonderful Mizoguchi music that featured guest contributions from Yoko Kanno. Though released before the series to publicize it, the video actually contained some footage of later chapters and the manga's conclusion, unseen in the anime series proper.

POCHACCO *

1992. TV series. DIR: Masami Hata, Akira Kiyomizu, Katsumasa Kanezawa, Seiichi Mitsuoka. SCR: Kyoko Kuribayashi. DES: Rie Oshima. ANI: N/C. MUS: N/C. PRD: Sanrio. 10 mins. x 4 eps.

Adventures of a cute little puppy and his animal friends from the team that gave you HELLO KITTY and PEKKLE. Pochacco rescues tiny chicks, hunts down a carrot thief, looks for a pink mushroom, and has other adventures to thrill the under-threes. Despite the mushrooms, *Magic Roundabout* fans must look elsewhere for drug references; this is pure, clean, and sweet.

POKÉMON *

1997. JPN: *Pocket Monster*. TV series, movie. DIR: Kunihiko Yuyama, Masamitsu Hidaka, Yoshitaka Fujimoto. SCR: Atsuhiro Tomioka, Takeshi Shudo, Hideki Sonoda, Junji Takegami. DES: Satoshi Tajiri. ANI: Shunya Yamada. MUS: Junji Miyazaki. PRD: SOFTX, TV Tokyo. 25 mins. x 188+ eps., 70 mins. x 4 movies.

Ash (Satoshi) oversleeps and is late for the distribution of the trainers' manual giving details of how to capture and train wild Pocket Monsters (Pokémon), fighting-pets much coveted by children. Since the manual sets out which Pokémon are most desirable and how to find them, the other kids have all the "best" catches, and he is stuck with the only one he can find without help from the manual, an "electric mouse" called Pikachu. After a shaky start, the two soon become firm friends, as Pikachu helps Ash capture many more Pokémon and head toward his goal of becoming the world's greatest Pokémon trainer. However, at every turn, Ash and his friends are dogged by the evil Team Rocket, intent on stealing the best Pokémon for themselves. Officially let off school to hunt their Pokémon, they trek around a safe and supportive world, always finding a bed for the night, and a sisterly type to help out with meals and other necessities. It's a child's dream, with the joys of independence but without the tedium.

Pokémon is a perfectly average TV anime tied into the huge marketing machine of a successful game and, consequently, immeasurably more successful than its contemporaries. Giving children an ongoing adventure, the chance to pit their monsters against each other, and a vast menagerie of creatures guaranteed to befuddle their parents, the game was an immense success, its cross-promotional anime and manga spinoffs reaching the West in record time, arguably creating the most important influence on the medium since Akira. Though the stars of Tamagotchi Video Adventures can claim to be the first "virtual pets," it was the interactive quality of Nintendo's *Pokémon* game that seized the high ground. First broadcast in Japan in April 1997, the *Pokémon* phenomenon came to the notice of the West that December in a news item about strobelike effects in one episode that caused seizures among the Japanese audience (see YAT Budget! Space Tours). Despite this initial stumble, the *Pokémon* juggernaut descended on the Western world, with millions of dollars in advertising eventually generating billions of dollars in sales. Compare this investment with the desultory way Sailor Moon was dumped on the U.S. Though *Pokémon* was undoubtedly a hit, it was also something of a self-fulfilling prophecy. The transition was not completely smooth—several episodes were "lost," chiefly for content comprising the womanizing antics of Ash's friend Brock, or cross-dressing by the zany Team Rocket.

Thanks to the runaway success of *Pokémon* in English, anime became relatively commonplace on American TV. After years of equating the medium with sex and violence, producers suddenly saw it as a cash cow in the children's market. Clone shows Digimon and Monster Rancher swiftly followed, along with unrelated serials such as CardCaptors, Gundam W, and Flint the Time Detective. Early attempts at selling anime for an older

audience foundered, with Escaflowne flopping on American TV, but the early years of the 21st century could well be characterized by a rush to keep the Western *Pokémon* boom generation watching anime as they grow up.

The TV series went through several name changes to reflect the exact brand of game being promoted. After the initial 82 episodes, it became the more-U.S.-friendly *Pokémon: Orange Island* until episode 118, when it returned to previous form in *Pokémon G[old &] S[ilver]*. The franchise also reached theaters in several film outings. *Pokémon the Movie: Mew vs. Mewtwo* (1998) gained Japan's second-largest domestic box office for an animated film, beaten only by Princess Mononoke. It featured a fight against an embittered mutant monster, crazily flipping from promising, cautionary SF in the style of Tezuka's Baghi, through cartoon comedy, to a patronizing moral ending that weakly argued against fighting all the time, even though such activities characterize the rest of the series! The 70-minute film was shown accompanied by the saccharine "let's cooperate" children's short, *Pikachu's Summer Vacation*. Despite a slow decline of interest, the film series continued with *Revelation Lugia* (1999, aka *Power of One*), anime history's *third*-largest Japanese box-office draw, in which yet another very, *very* rare form of Pokémon is the object of the quest. This time, Lugia can only be called forth by bringing three sacred birds together in one spot. The show was accompanied by the short film *Pikachu's Rescue Adventure*. A year later, the *Pokémon* movie was *Emperor of the Crystal Tower* (2000, translated in 2001 as *Spell of the Unkown*), a fairy-tale variant of *Sleeping Beauty* about an imprisoned princess accidentally kidnapping Ash's mother when she wishes for one of her own. The film was accompanied by another short for toddlers, this time *Pichu and Pikachu*, displaying "baby" versions of some of the lead Pokémon. A fourth film, *Encounter Beyond Time*, features the very, very, *very* rare Poké-

mon Celebi from the *GS* game, and opened in July 2001, accompanied by the short *Pikachu's Hide-and-Seek*.

Often held in snooty disregard by a hard-core anime fandom that would prefer its hobby to be forever outside the mainstream, *Pokémon* is nevertheless the most commercially important anime of the 1990s in terms of brand recognition and the investment it attracted to the medium—many more obscure anime and manga translations were funded with Pikachu's profits. As befits a cultural icon, the series has been mercilessly lampooned in other media, most notably as the "Battling Seizure Robots" in an episode of the *The Simpsons*, and the brainwashing Chinpokomon in *South Park. Ill. p. 83.*

POKONYAN

1993. AKA: *Raccoon Miaow; Rocky Rackat*. TV series. DIR: Hiroshi Sasakawa, Seitaro Hara. SCR: N/C. DES: N/C. ANI: N/C. MUS: Man Brothers Band. PRD: Nippon Herald, NHK. 8 mins. x 170 eps.

A Japanese girl discovers a *tanuki* (a Japanese raccoon dog; see Pompoko) in her backpack during a camping trip. He proclaims that she is his sister and follows her everywhere. He can use his powers to turn Amy's dreams into real-life adventures, though his good intentions, like those of the creators' earlier Doraemon, do not always work according to plan. Based on a manga by Fujiko F. Fujio, this anime was also spun off into the *Pokonyan Christmas* and *Pokonyan Summer Holiday* specials.

POLLON

1982. JPN: *Ochamegami Monogatari Korokoro Polon*. AKA: *The Story of Little Goddess Roly-Poly Pollon; Roly-Poly Pollon: The Tallest Tales of the Gods; Little Pollon*. TV series. DIR: Takao Yotsuji. SCR: Masaru Yamamoto, Kenji Terada, Tomohiro Ando. DES: Toshio Takagi, Tsutomu Fujita. ANI: Hirokazu Ishiyuki, Toshio Takagi. MUS: Masayuki Yamamoto. PRD: Kokusai Eiga, Movie International, Fuji TV. 25 mins. x 46 eps.

Pollon, the little daughter of the God Apollo, wants to be a powerful and beautiful goddess when she grows up. Somewhat neglected by her single godly parent, she often assists him in his womanizing ways in the vain hope that she will get a new mommy. With her little friend Eros, she plagues the Olympians in various comical ways as she attempts to earn the trappings of godhood. Sadly (if predictably), her good deeds often backfire, leaving her in hot water with some deity or other and causing chaos for gods and humans alike. But, because she's a kindhearted girl, she will eventually achieve her aim and become a proper, respectable grown-up goddess. This sweet little series for children was the first to be produced in its entirety by Kokusai, based on the manga *Pollon of Olympus* by **NANAKO SOS**–creator Hideo Azuma, originally serialized in *100-ten Comic*. Combining stories about the Greek and Japanese sun gods (with Apollo taking the role of Japan's female Amaterasu for a few tales), the story also contained comic-relief characters absent from Greek mythology, such as the Hollywood-stereotype mad scientist Dr. Nya-ha-ah. Compare to **BIT THE CUPID**.

POLLYANNA

1986. JPN: *Ai Shojo Pollyanna Monogatari*. AKA: *The Story of Loving Child Pollyanna*. TV series. DIR: Kozo Kusuba, Norio Yazawa, Shigeo Koshi, Fumio Kurokawa, Harumi Sugimura. SCR: Saiko Kumasen, Tamao Kunihiro. DES: Yoshiharu Sato, Ken Kawai. ANI: Yoshiharu Sato. MUS: Reijiro Komutsu. PRD: Nippon Animation, Fuji TV. 25 mins. x 51 eps.

Eleven-year-old pastor's daughter Pollyanna is sent to live with her aunt, Polly Harrington, after her father's death in 1920s America. Auntie doesn't like children at all and is brusque and distant, but Pollyanna is an irrepressibly buoyant child and softens her aunt's hard heart with her affectionate, gentle personality. Then she has a tragic accident and loses the use of her

legs. After a dangerous operation, and with the help and encouragement of the friends she's made in her new life, Pollyanna recovers and is able to join the party for her aunt's wedding.

Based on the 1913 novel and its sequel by Eleanor Hodgman Porter, this is part of the **WORLD MASTERPIECE THEATER** series, and in the true *WMT* tradition, ends in happiness all around after a touching, not to say tear-jerking, series of trials. Sato went on to work with Studio Ghibli and has built on his U.S. links, most recently with work for Disney on *The Tigger Movie* (2000).

POLTERGEIST REPORT *

1992. JPN: *Yu Yu Hakusho*. TV series, movie. DIR: Noriyuki Abe, Masakatsu Iijima, Shigeru Ueda, Katsunori Mizuno, Akiyuki Shinbo. SCR: Yoshiyuki Ohashi, Sukehiro Tomita, Katsuyuki Sumizawa, Yoshihiro Togashi. DES: Minoru Yamazawa, Yuji Ikeda. ANI: Saburo Soya, Yoshinori Kanno. MUS: Yusuke Honma. PRD: Studio Pierrot, Fuji TV. 25 mins. x 112 eps., 25 mins. (m1), 93 mins. (m2).

Middle-school tough-guy Yusuke Urameshi is killed trying to save a child in a car accident. In a fustily bureaucratic hell, his name is found to be missing from the Big Book of Dead People, and his "application" is rejected. The son of the ruler of hell (see **DORORON ENMA**) comes to his rescue and offers him a chance to return whence he came. Repatriated to Earth, he teams up with Death, two demons, and his former rival and becomes a psychic investigator, fighting battle after battle against evil spirits.

Based on the 1990 *Young Jump* manga by **HUNTER X HUNTER**–creator Yoshihiro Togashi, *PR* sets up a milieu not dissimilar to the background of **UROTSUKIDOJI**. The human, spirit, and demon worlds coexist, along with a more nebulous, barely glimpsed hell said to be worse than all the others combined. Like the "Wandering Child" Amano, Yusuke does good deeds in the human world, but there the resemblance ends, since *PR* is far more inter-

ested in fight-of-the-week standoffs in the manner of **DRAGON BALL**. A very successful series, particularly by the short runs of many 1990s anime, *PR* returned in the 30-minute short *PR: The Movie* (1993). Shown as part of a triple bill of TV tie-ins, it took the traditional summer-special route, as Yusuke's vacation is interrupted by the kidnapping of his boss, Koenma. The kidnappers demand the King of Hell's seal as ransom, and Yusuke is torn between his loyalty to his friend and savior and his fears of what will happen if the seal falls into the wrong hands.

A full-length feature, *PR: Fight for the Netherworld* (1994), featured the Lord of the Netherworld returning after several millennia to conquer Earth by seizing five power sites around Tokyo. The lush, rich, expensive animation was almost totally wasted on a tired plot, making the *PR* feature look remarkably like a bad remake of several other shows, some of which it actually predated—geomancy from **SILENT MÖBIUS**, a demon invasion à la **SAILOR MOON**, and modern-day ghostbusting straight out of **USHIO AND TORA**. Sadly, this was the only incarnation of the series to reach the English language to date, suffering the usual flaws of movies released out of context: the overlarge, idle cast of **TENCHI MUYO!** and the missing back story of **PATLABOR**. *PR* isn't an outstanding show of its type, but the TV series might well have fared better than the movie on English release.

There were also several half-hour spinoff videos, whose self-indulgence only goes to show just how popular *PR* was in Japan. The best fight scenes were compiled on the two-part video compilation *PR: Arts of Darkness* (1994), followed swiftly by five themed clipshows, compiled as *PR: Image Report* (1995), one for each of the leads. For the ultimate in futile nostalgia, the "next episode" bumpers that closed each episode were released in their own three-part set, *PR: In Next Week's Episode* (1992–94), allowing viewers to spend 90 minutes watching nothing but ads. **Ⓥ**

POMPOKO *

1994. JPN: *Heisei Tanuki Gassen Pompoko*. AKA: *Heisei [Modern-day] Raccoon Wars Pompoko; Defenders of the Forest*. Movie. DIR: Isao Takahata. SCR: Isao Takahata. DES: Megumi Kagawa, Shinji Otsuka. ANI: Shinji Otsuka. MUS: Joe Hisaishi. PRD: Studio Ghibli. 119 mins.

A group of *tanuki* (Japanese raccoon-dogs) finds its country life threatened by the construction of a human New Town. At the instigation of the town elder, these tanuki use their powers of transformation to oppose the human encroachment. Unwilling to declare all-out war on humans (they would miss human food), they fake ghostly hauntings, though the supply of human construction workers appears inexhaustible. An 800-year-old super-tanuki orchestrates a ghostly parade down the main street, but the humans are more intrigued than scared—possibly because some of the "ghosts" include cameo appearances from the stars of Hayao Miyazaki's **PORCO ROSSO**, **MY NEIGHBOR TOTORO**, and **KIKI'S DELIVERY SERVICE**. Any spooky effects are ruined when a local theme park takes credit for the parade, falsely claiming that it was a stunt to showcase its special effects technology. The horrified tanuki discover that the theme park is run by foxes, who have given up fighting humanity and instead live among them in disguise. After outwitting the foxes, the tanuki meet for one last trick, transforming the built-up landscape all too briefly into the virgin countryside it once was. Admitting defeat, they scatter among the human race, though sometimes they meet in secret to briefly walk once more in tanuki form.

Familiar characters from **JAPANESE FOLK TALES**, the mischievous tanuki are used here to tell a touching variant of Studio Ghibli's oft-repeated ecological message—supposedly inspired by the 1960s real-life construction of a suburb in Tama Hills, west of Tokyo. Lamenting the destruction of a way of life in much the same way as **NAUSICAÄ** and **PRINCESS MONONOKE**, it also recalls the happy pastorals of *Totoro*. Tanuki were certainly "in" at this point in the 1990s—the unrelated **POKONYAN** was a big hit at the same time. An English-subtitled print was shown in very limited release in American theaters in advance preparation for a failed attempt to gain the film an Oscar nomination. However, unlike the universal *Totoro*, *Pompoko*'s appeal is, to some extent, ethnocentric. Gags come at the expense of Japanese history and folklore, and some of the humor is a little too earthy for the sanitized Disney market. The end result is often a foreign-language variant on *Watership Down* (1978), with time out for wacky satire, tear-jerking whimsy, and an unforgettable scene in which a tanuki distracts a driver by flattening his testicles against the windshield. Ghibli's usual standard-setting art direction and design are much in evidence. "Pompoko," by the way, is the sound you get when you tap gently on a tummy stretched full of food. The Tama Hills development also featured in **UNTIL THE UNDERSEA CITY** and **WHISPER OF THE HEART**.

PORCO ROSSO *

1992. JPN: *Kurenai no Buta*. AKA: *The Crimson Pig*. Movie. DIR: Hayao Miyazaki. SCR: Hayao Miyazaki. DES: Hayao Miyazaki, Megumi Kagawa, Toshio Kawaguchi, Katsu Hisamura. ANI: Megumi Kagawa, Toshio Kawaguchi, Katsu Hisamura. MUS: Joe Hisaishi. PRD: Studio Ghibli. 93 mins.

The Adriatic, 1929—the Balkans may go up in flames at any moment, and the Fascists are on the rise in Italy. Mercenary pilots, survivors of the last Great War, work for hire defending transports from marauding pirates, and Marco is the best of them. But as his idealistic youth fades behind him, the former handsome flyer has undergone a strange transformation. He has literally turned into a pig, but nobody seems to mind, least of all him. His life is tranquil and simple; he owns a tiny island and when he isn't flying, he's dozing on the beach with his radio, a newspaper, and a cigarette, or he's

X: The Movie

meeting his childhood friend, Gina, now a beautiful widow. But Marco's own world is tipped out of balance by the arrival of an American cad, Curtis, who sets out to make his name by shooting down the Crimson Pig. Taking his beloved plane to Milan for repairs after their duel, Marco meets the irrepressible Fio, just 17 but already an aircraft designer of formidable talent. He also finds the secret police are on his tail, along with a gang of angry aerial pirates who want Marco out of the sky for good. Fio mollifies the pirates by appealing to their sense of pride, reminding them that it took an American to shoot down Marco. The pirates, mortified at this threat to their Italian spirit, wager on a rematch, with a victorious Marco winning the costs of his repairs, whereas a victorious Curtis (already rebuffed by Gina) would win the hand of Fio. As the Italian air force arrive to break up the illegal match, Marco and Curtis prepare to hold them off while the others escape. An epilogue implies that Marco has returned to human form, and that he and Gina live happily ever after.

Miyazaki's most "adult" film, initially conceived for an audience of middle-aged men who had forgotten their youthful aspirations, *PR* was the fourth-biggest animated box-office draw ever in Japan, beaten only by two POKÉMON films and PRINCESS MONONOKE. By turns touching, comic, romantic, and edge-of-the-seat gripping, it is a grown-up's fantasy with a child's directness and innocence. It reflects many of its creator's passions and obsessions and also restates many of his central themes, yet the film has its own freshness and originality. Based loosely on a three-part series Miyazaki wrote in 1990 for *Model Graphix* magazine, *PR* was originally planned as a 45-minute in-flight feature for Japan Air Lines. Eventually produced as a full-length movie, a dub was prepared for the English-language audio channel on JAL flights, and subsequently broadcast on British TV. The idea of porcine transformation would return in Miyazaki's SPIRITED AWAY in which a girl must restore her parents to human form.

POTOMAS THE HIPPO

1988. JPN: *Kaba no Potomas*. Movie. DIR: Taku Sugiyama. SCR: Hitoshi Yokota. DES: N/C. ANI: Shunji Saita. MUS: Takeo Watanabe. PRD: OH Pro. 25 mins.

Potomas the Hippo has a secret—he can speak like a human being, but only the young kids Maki and Toshi realize it. He also wears a bright green T-shirt with a giant letter "P" on it, but this is supposed to be nicely inconspicuous. Momentarily forgetting to keep quiet, Potomas speaks to a child he has just saved from drowning. Rumors soon spread about a talking hippo, and Potomas is forced to go on the run.

POWER DOLLS *

1995. Video. DIR: Tsuneo Tominaga, Masamitsu Hidaka. SCR: Midori Uki, Atsuhiro Tomioka. DES: Masayuki Goto, Yasuhiro Nishinaka. ANI: Masayuki Goto. MUS: Hiroto Saito, Innerbrain. PRD: Kogado Studio, Artmic, VAP. 25 mins. x 2 eps.

It's A.D. 2540, and rebels on the colony world of Omni have been holding out against the Terran government for five years. Without a standing army, the breakaway colonists have fought back by adapting robotic Power Loaders. Originally used to unload spaceships, the machines have been turned into humanoid battle-tanks. A handful of young female pilots (who serve in the Detachment of Limited Line Service to justify the title acronym) is assigned to blow up the dam at Chatteau Village.

Based on a Japanese computer game of the same name, *PD* taps into many well-established conventions designed to appeal to male fans: girls in battledress, girls in robots, girls with guns, girls sniping at other girls. The characters and situations are all stolen stereotypes, and not especially well handled, with competent but limited animation. There's a heroic effort to establish character depth by delving into the parental relationships of one of the lead characters, and there's a passable fight toward the end, but since its appeal in Japan was predicated on a love of the game, it's difficult for a foreign audience to feel anything except cheated. None of them would stand a chance in a fight with Ripley from *Aliens*, however big their power loaders.

A sequel, *PD2,* reunited the girls in another adaptation of a game scenario, this time a mission to recapture a stolen prototype. This episode in particular was further damaged in the English-language version by an overdose of reverb effects in the dubbing studio, though the pointlessly flashy audio matched the halfhearted attempt by the original crew to polish the *visuals* with some unnecessary digital effects. In 1997, the series continued in Japan on CD-ROM with a story set after the war, as the newly free state starts to pick up the pieces. The Power Dolls unit is disbanded but antigovernment rebels start causing trouble, and former leader Hardy Newland starts gathering the old crew for one more mission as poachers-turned-gamekeepers.

POWER STONE *

1999. TV series. DIR: Masahiro Omori.

SCR: Shikichi Ohashi, Masashi Yokoyama, Kenichi Araki. DES: Tadashi Shida. ANI: Yuji Moriyama, Kazuya Miura, Hideyuki Motohashi. MUS: N/C. PRD: Kokusai Eiga, Studio Pierrot, TBS. 25 mins. x 26 eps.

Fokker is on a quest to retrieve the mystical power stones hidden by his father. In a 19th-century world modeled on the foggy London of SHERLOCK HOUND and an olde-worlde Tokyo populated by ninja, Fokker's quest brings him into contact with the British princess Julia, the ninja-girl Ayame, Ryoma the samurai (see OI! RYOMA), Wang Tang the Chinese brawler (actually Won-ton in Japanese, but the jokey name was altered), Garuda the Red Indian (*sic*), and Rouge the belly-dancing dusky maiden. Then they fight.

Based on a popular game from CAPCOM, creators of STREET FIGHTER II, *PS* began as a launch title for the Sega Dreamcast, featuring a true 3D environment packed with useful items and a "power stone" collection theme that allowed the players to transform into more powerful versions of themselves. A few years earlier, such a concept might have barely made it straight to video, but in the late 1990s climate heavy with gaming money and short on options, *PS* became a TV series shown in the prime five-o'clock slot, with the characters regressed from the game to create a slightly younger look designed to appeal to children.

PREFECTURAL EARTH DEFENSE FORCE

1986. JPN: *Kenritsu Chikyu Bogyo Gun*. AKA: *Earth Defense Force*. Video. DIR: Keiji Hayakawa. SCR: Kazunori Ito. DES: Katsumi Aoshima. ANI: Katsumi Aoshima. MUS: Kentaro Haneda. PRD: Shogakukan. 49 mins.

A parody anime in the spirit of writer Ito's URUSEI YATSURA about schoolyard feuds being blown out of all proportion—compare to PROJECT A-KO. Realizing that the ominous-sounding Telegraph Pole Society (who wish to conquer the world) are probably students at his school, Mr. Roberi forms a

Defense Force. Students Shogi Morita
(the handsome blond), Kuho Tasuke
(his beefy dark-haired pal), and token
girl Akiko Ifukube are ranged against
an army of inept ninja. Meanwhile, the
high school's mad scientist, Dr. Inoga-
mi, has turned local boy Kami Sanchin
into a cyborg, and both sides try to
recruit him. While the TPS boasts an
army of ninja, the pretty pink-haired
Captain Baradaga, and "Scope" Tsuza-
ki, a hulking brute with many high-
tech devices, the EDF is somewhat
underfunded—after initial promises of
supervehicles and amazing gadgets,
the best Roberi can rustle up for the
fighters is a ramen cart. The two organizations attempt to steal each other's
secrets and poach each other's members, while, amid much comic angst
about his condition (see CASSHAN or
CYBORG 009), Sanchin tentatively falls
in love with the professor's daughter,
Yuko, who has been similarly cyberized.
Their romance is truncated by their
unerring habit of setting off their built-
in military hardware anytime they get
angry. Once the TPG have been defeated, the professor reluctantly concedes
that he can return the couple to
human form, but the reversion process
accidentally switches their genders.
The couple get used to it, while Morita
starts going out with his former enemy
Baradaga. Based on the 1983 *Shonen
Sunday* manga by Koichiro Yasunaga,
this send-up was presented as three
fake episodes and a fake preview for a
nonexistent episode four.

PRIDE THE MASTER THIEF
1965. JPN: *Kaiketsu Pride*. TV series.
DIR: Yuichi Fujiwara. SCR: Takehiko Mae-
da. DES: Yuichi Fujiwara. ANI: Taku
Sugiyama, Motoyoshi Matsumoto,
Noboru Ishiguro. MUS: Seiichiro Uno.
PRD: TV Doga, Fuji TV. 5 mins. x 115
eps.
Professor Pride and his faithful dog
Dry are masters of crime who boast
that they can steal anything from the
Eiffel Tower to Mount Fuji itself. Pur-
sued across the world by the hapless
Detective Scope, Pride stars in the first-

ever crime-caper anime, a distant
ancestor of the later LUPIN III and
CAT'S EYE. The first anime made by TV
Doga, a company formed in 1963 by a
coalition between the Tokyo advertising company Koei and Fuji TV. The
black-and-white series was completely
remade in color in 1967 but never
broadcast.

PRIME ROSE
1983. JPN: *Time Slip 10,000-nen Prime
Rose*. AKA: *10,000 Year Time Slip
Prime Rose*. TV special. DIR: Osamu
Dezaki, Naoto Hashimoto. SCR:
Keisuke Fujikawa. DES: Osamu Tezuka.
ANI: Keizo Shimizu, Yukari Kobayashi,
Kenichi Onuki. MUS: Yuji Ono. PRD: Magic Bus, Tezuka Pro, Nippon TV. 98
mins.
An accident on the orbiting military
satellite Death Mask wipes out cities in
Japan and America, but the occupants
have not been killed. Danbala Gai, a
member of the time patrol, travels
10,000 years into the future, when
Earth is ruled by strange creatures, and
the occupants of the two cities have
formed their own nations. Though he
is not supposed to interfere, Gai
becomes involved with Prime Rose, a
girl who vows to avenge the murder of
her fiancé by learning to fight and
killing her murderer, Prince Pirar. But
the time patrolman shares her ultimate
goal—the restoration of true peace
to the world. Based loosely on his manga serial in *Shonen Champion*, creator
Tezuka intended the title to refer to
the "primrose" flower, though his pronunciation recalls the old English origins of the word, not its modern
spelling.

PRINCE OF SNOW COUNTRY
1985. JPN: *Yukiguni no Ojisama*. Movie.
DIR: Tomoharu Katsumata. SCR: Yugo
Serikawa, Tadahiro Shimafuji. DES:
Takao Kasai. ANI: Takao Kasai. MUS:
Seiji Yokoyama. PRD: Shinano, Toei. 88
mins.
Koichi and his sister Yuki befriend
Hanaguro, a swan who has flown to
Japan from Siberia. Hanaguro is

attacked by a dog, and the cowardly
Koichi flees, but that night he has a
dream in which he is whisked away to
the Kingdom of the Snow Prince, where
he finds the bravery to help the other
swans. A moral fable from the Buddhist
Soka Gakkai leader Daisaku Ikeda, who
also created RAINBOW ACROSS THE
PACIFIC and FAIRGROUND IN THE STARS.

PRINCE PIRATE
1966. JPN: *Kaizoku Oji*. TV series. DIR:
Yoshio Kuroda, Kimio Yabuki, Kenji Araki. SCR: Jiro Yoshino, Minoru Hamada,
Hiroyasu Yamaura, Yasuo Yamaguchi,
Okichi Harada, Ichiro Wakabayashi.
DES: Shotaro Ishinomori. ANI: Tameo
Ogawa, Eisuke Kondo, Shinichi Suzuki,
Hiroshi Wagatsuma. MUS: Hisayuki
Miyazaki. PRD: Toei, NET. 25 mins. x 31
eps.
Kidd's dying father tells him of Morgan, a pirate who yearns to rule the sev-
en seas. Kidd tracks down Morgan's
ship, the Hurricane, wins over its skipper, an old sailor called Crapp, and
becomes the new captain. However, his
dreams of a life on the open sea are
soon scrapped by the arrival of the Bar-
racuda and its nasty captain, Fugg
Hook.
Mixing equal parts of PETER PAN AND
WENDY with SINDBAD THE SAILOR, and
adapted from CYBORG 009–creator Ishinomori's manga in *Shonen King, PP* also
featured a genuine kid playing Kidd—
the lead voice actor was the 13-year-old
Satoshi Furuya, better known today as
King Philip in ALEXANDER. Captain
Kidd's treasure would also feature in
DAGGER OF KAMUI.

PRINCE PLANET *
1965. JPN: *Yusei Shonen Papi*. AKA:
Planet Boy Papi. TV series. DIR: Tsuto-
mu Yamamoto, Yonehiko Watanabe,
Tadao Wakabayashi, Takeshi
Kawauchi. SCR: Ichiro Kanai, Jusaburo
Futaba, Satoshi Ogura. DES: Hideoki
Inoue. ANI: Tadao Wakabayashi. MUS:
Keiro Miki. PRD: TCJ, Eiken, Fuji TV. 25
mins. x 52 eps.
Unwilling to admit Earth into the
Galactic Council of Planets until its

warlike ways are curbed, the council appoints a prince from the pacifist planet Radion as an Earth-based ambassador. Crash-landing in the American Southwest, he befriends local oil heiress Diana Worthy, who helps him blend in with Earth society. Before long, "Bobby," as he is now known, moves to the urban sprawl of New Metropolis, where his superpowered pendant from Radion bestows superhuman strength and the ability to fly. With his sometime associates Ajababa the magician and wrestler Dan Dynamo, he fights crime in a predictable but earnest cross of **AMAZING THREE** and **ASTRO BOY**. Based on a manga by Hideoki Inoue, a former assistant of Mitsuteru Yokoyama. As was customary in the American market at the time, the original Japanese theme was replaced with a new track, on this occasion by the Carol Lombard Singers.

PRINCESS ANMITSU
1986. JPN: *Anmitsu Hime*. TV series. DIR: Masami Annai, Rei Hidaka, Takaaki Ishiyama. SCR: Yoshio Urasawa, Tomoko Konparu, Hideo Takayashiki, Yoshiyuki Suga, Masaru Yamamoto. DES: Shosuke Kurogane. ANI: Yoshiyuki Kishi. MUS: Hiroshi Ogasawara. PRD: Studio Pierrot, Fuji TV. 25 mins. x 51 eps. A cheeky, vivacious little medieval Japanese princess is bored with life in her father's castle of Amakara. With her best friend Takemaru in sometimes reluctant pursuit, she sets about livening things up. Luckily, as her father's sole heir, she's unlikely to get into real trouble, and since she really loves Takemaru, she'll try and make sure he doesn't either.

Shosuke Kurogane's original manga began in 1949 in *Shojo Comic* magazine, finished in 1955, and was first approached as an anime project in 1961. Abandoned by the inexperienced team because of soaring costs, it took Studio Pierrot to give it all the charm and energy the author hoped for 25 years later, presenting a sweetly fantasized picture of the ideal Japanese childhood, in which preschool- and kindergarten-age children are secure, loved, and much indulged, and their little naughtinesses always innocent and always forgiven.

PRINCESS ARITE
2001. JPN: *Arite-hime*. Movie. DIR: Sunao Katabuchi. SCR: Sunao Katabuchi. DES: Keiko Morikawa. ANI: Kazusane Ozaki. MUS: N/C. PRD: Studio 4°C, Omega Project. Ca. 90 mins. Princess Arite, a little girl who lives in a small room on top of a tower, yearns to learn magic and escape to the town below. This fairy tale from Katabuchi, former assistant to Miyazaki on **KIKI'S DELIVERY SERVICE**, was made inside a computer, though it retains the appearance of traditional cel animation. Based on the novel *The Clever Princess* by Diana Coles.

PRINCESS ARMY
1992. Video. DIR: Osamu Sekita. SCR: Miyuki Kitagawa. DES: Yumi Yamada. ANI: Yumi Yamada. MUS: Yuichi Takahashi. PRD: Group Tack, Animate Film. 30 mins. x 2 eps. Rescued from a drunken attacker by a judoist, Aida Nonoka resolves to become as good as her savior, hoping one day to recognize him by the scar on his back. Transferred to a new high school, she meets two older boys who could possibly be the person to whom she owes her life and wants to give her heart—see **UTENA**. Multiple unrequited yearnings as three judo girls and three judo boys fall in and out of love while they're supposed to be throwing each other around a room—with matters greatly exacerbated by the sudden arrival of a forgotten fiancé from Holland. Based on the manga in *Shojo* magazine by Miyuki Kitagawa, this is an even gentler judo soap opera than **YAWARA**, whose earlier success it was doubtless trying to emulate.

PRINCESS KNIGHT *
1967. JPN: *Ribon no Kishi*. AKA: *Knight of the Ribbon; Choppy and the Princess; The Adventures of Choppy and the Princess; Princesse Saphir*. TV series. DIR: Chikao Katsui, Nobuo Onuki, Yoshiyuki Tomino, Masami Hata, Ryosuke Takahashi, Hideo Makino, Seiji Okuda, Norio Hikone. SCR: Osamu Tezuka, Masaki Tsuji. DES: Kazuko Nakamura, Sadao Miyamoto, Minoru Nishida. ANI: Sadao Miyamoto. MUS: Isao Tomita. PRD: Tezuka Pro, Fuji TV. 25 mins. x 52 eps., 25 mins. (pilot). Thanks to an accident in heaven, where the mischievous cherub Tink is responsible for giving out hearts to babies, Princess Sapphire of Silverland is born with two—a man's *and* a woman's. This is fortunate for her father the king, who proclaims to the populace that the new child is a boy, and, consequently, that any succession problems are over. The secret is kept, since if it becomes known that the heir is a girl, the succession will pass to the corrupt Duke Jeralmin. She grows up as a boy, learning all the masculine skills and doing her utmost to excel and make her father and her people proud. But when she falls in love with the charming prince Franz Charming, she faces a terrible dilemma. Revealing her womanhood would throw away her own achievements, her father's dreams, and the stability of her country—but staying a man means she must sacrifice her dream of love forever.

Beginning as a 1953 manga in *Nakayoshi*, Osamu Tezuka's *PK* was the **ASTRO BOY**–creator's tribute to the many Takarazuka musical revues he saw as a child, where the all-female cast made cross-dressing a narrative necessity. This gem of a series, much loved in Europe, is less well known in the English-speaking world despite several English-language releases, but its enduring influence can be seen in the massive success of its immediate heirs **ROSE OF VERSAILLES** and **UTENA**, as well as in the prevalence of cross-dressing battle-babes throughout anime. It also has powerful links with the magical-girl shows in the princess's masquerade under another identity, her fight against supernatural evil, and her friend and protector-sprite Tink. Its style and pace seem dated now, but the themes, ideas, and plots Tezuka generated are still being reexamined by modern directors and writers who were not even born when it was first broadcast. Versions of *PK* will probably go on being retold forever, but however modern the trappings, they will stand or fall on how they measure up to the power and simplicity of Tezuka's original.

It had a limited American TV release in 1972 under the title *Princess Knight*. Licensees Joe Oriolo and Burt Hecht did better with three episodes edited into a movie entitled *Choppy and the Princess*. With Tink renamed Choppy, this was shown frequently on syndicated TV throughout the U.S. in the 1970s and 1980s. The series also made it onto Australian TV screens, though we haven't been able to find out whether it was shown as *PK* or *CatP*, and a number of 25-minutes episodes were released on British video by two different distributors. Movie Makers released seven episodes under the general title *The Adventures of Choppy and the Princess* and at least three more under individual episode titles without the *AoCatP* surtitle. Tasley Leisure of Leeds released six episodes as *Choppy and the Princess, Adventures 1–6*. The English dubs lose one of Tezuka's beloved jokes—he named the good characters and countries in his fable after precious stones and metals, with the bad guys named after cheap synthetics like nylon and plastic, but the names have been mangled in translation. Following Tezuka's death in 1989, the series was released on Japanese laser disc in 1991, with the original unbroadcast pilot included as a bonus extra. *Ill. p. 373.*

PRINCESS MINERVA *

1995. Video. DIR: Mihiro Yamaguchi. SCR: Hideki Sonoda. DES: Tokuhiro Matsubara. ANI: Tokuhiro Matsubara, Hanchi Rei, Hokukan Sen. MUS: Kenji Kawai. PRD: Pastel. 45 mins.
Without a male heir, the kingdom of Wisler has a girl for its next leader. Minerva is a vain, headstrong, selfish princess who's bored with her role and

wants to excel at combat and spellcasting. Despite the best efforts of her chief guard, Blue Morris, to keep her safe (and keep her in check), she disguises herself to fight in a big tournament for girl fighters. Unfortunately, evil sorceress Dynastar hates Minerva and sets out to kidnap her, but grabs Blue Morris instead. The Princess realizes the error of her ways, gets the warrior girls to help her, and sets out to rescue her long-suffering bodyguard.

PM is sweetly predictable, signaling its next move so far ahead that suspense is not one of its outstanding qualities. Based on a computer game/manga/novel multimedia offensive by Ko Maisaka and Run Ishida, its origins are betrayed in an outsized cast to showcase everyone's favorite from the original. Gently poking fun at **PRINCESS KNIGHT** and other tomboy heroines (at one point, the narrator tries to explain how kindhearted Minerva is, only to choke on his own words), the result is a lackluster cousin to **DRAGON HALF** but without its predecessor's insane charm. The character designs are cute but not very original; ditto the story. Uncritical fans of babes in battle bikinis may be amused.

PRINCESS MONONOKE *

1997. JPN: *Mononoke Hime*. AKA: *Princess Ghost; Phantom Princess*. Movie. DIR: Hayao Miyazaki. SCR: Hayao Miyazaki. DES: Hayao Miyazaki. ANI: Masashi Ando, Kitaro Kosaka, Yoshifumi Kondo. MUS: Joe Hisaishi. PRD: Studio Ghibli. 133 mins.
Young Prince Ashitaka defeats a supernatural beast plaguing the remote Eastern lands in which his tribe dwells but is left with a wound that refuses to heal. Because its origin is supernatural, it has a strange effect that gives Ashitaka superhuman strength and accuracy, enabling his arrows to take the heads or arms off his enemies, but it will also kill him, slowly but surely. Finding that the beast was maddened by an iron ball in its flesh, he goes in search of the culprits, hoping they can provide some way of curing him. As he wanders

© SUNRISE • TVO

through the Western forests, he finds a village of ironworkers, the source of the bullet. Tataraba, the ironworkers' fort, is in conflict with both the local overlord and the creatures of the forest, which are led by a wild girl who rides on a wolf. San, an abandoned child adopted by the wolf god Moro and raised as one of her own cubs, now hates the humans who abandoned her. All her loyalty and devotion is given to her new family, the ancient beast gods whose lands are threatened by the incursions of the growing human population. Eboshi, the tough, pragmatic leader of the ironworkers, is consumed with hatred for San, and Ashitaka, a natural peacemaker whose wish is to see everyone live in harmony, tries in vain to settle their differences. He has another agenda; apart from his hope that he may find healing in the forest, he is falling in love with San. The distant, unseen emperor, who claims to be the Son of Heaven, authorizes the death of Shishigami, the woodland god who is responsible for the natural (and supernatural) resistance to Tataraba. Stealthy humans massacre many of the forest creatures, but the wrath of Shishigami is unstoppable . . . almost.

Purportedly set in medieval Japan but depicting a symbolic *neverwhen* clash of three proto-Japanese races (the Jomon, Yamato, and Emishi), *PM* is the ultimate prequel to Studio Ghibli's ecological concerns in films such as **NAUSICAÄ** and **POMPOKO**. It is set at the very point in time when humankind pushed Nature into submission, toppling the old "natural" order and starting the long chain to the present day, when Nature itself seems under threat of extinction. Twenty years in conception and three in production, the highest-grossing Japanese *movie* in any genre and the first of Miyazaki's films to be released theatrically in America through the Disney/Tokuma marketing deal, *PM* has built a cinematic legend of its own. Born from the creator's own dissatisfaction with the end of *Nausicaä*, which required a miraculous *deus ex machina* to resolve the human/nature conflict, *PM* is consequently far more downbeat and melancholy. Though a minority of critics still regard it as a tedious harangue, even the many who call it Miyazaki's masterpiece agree it's a difficult film for U.S. movie audiences, who are simply unaccustomed either to animation as polemic, or to the level of violence depicted. Preview audiences, not expecting a Tarantino image in a Disney movie, reacted with nervous laughter to a sequence where a man gets his arm shot off. Producer Toshio Suzuki's strict and noble "no cuts" policy may have preserved Miyazaki's creative vision but made the film difficult to sell into markets that still believed cartoons were kids' stuff. Technically, *PM* is a remarkable achievement, especially on the level of art direction and design; the primeval forests of Japan and the first stirrings of industrial society are depicted with ravishing realism. The characters are well drawn in every sense, each with his or her own motivations and needs, not cardboard heroes and villains but humans struggling to get by in a hostile world. This is a grown-up fantasy, and unlike the vast run of anime that gives us stock figures in pretty clothes and wish-fulfillment situations, *PM* presents real people in a

real world that is beautiful and fascinating but must be taken on its own terms.

The U.S. dub, which featured a script rewrite by *Sandman* author Neil Gaiman, was the first theatrical anime production since the **ARMITAGE III** movie to use "name" actors, with a cast including Billy Crudup, Claire Danes, Minnie Driver, and Gillian Anderson. *PM* was widely reported as being Miyazaki's last film, but he has since completed a new production, **SPIRITED AWAY**. *Ill. p. 203.* **Ⓥ**

PRINCESS NINE *
1999. TV series. DIR: Tomomi Mochizuki. SCR: Hiro Maruyama. DES: Akihiko Yamashita, Yoshimi Hashimoto. ANI: Yoshimi Hashimoto. MUS: Masamichi Amano. PRD: Phoenix/NEP21, NHK2. 25 mins. x 22 eps.
Girls don't play baseball, they play softball. But tomboyish Ryo Hayakawa convinces the chairman of the Himuro Corporation to sponsor her baseball team and then talks schoolgirl tennis champion Izumi into changing sports. Rivalries soon break out on and off the field, as the girls fight over token boy Hiroki and corporate sponsorship comes attached to corporate scandal. This typical baseball anime in the fashion of **H2** was dumped onto satellite TV in the impecunious late 1990s as the post-**EVANGELION** anime TV boom turned into a slump.

PRINCESS ROUGE *
1997. AKA: *Legend of the Last Labyrinth*. Video. DIR: Isato Date. SCR: Mamoru Takeuchi. DES: Minoru Yamazawa. ANI: Minoru Yamazawa. MUS: N/C. PRD: Beam Entertainment. 30 mins. x 2 eps.
Recently orphaned teenager Yusuke Mizuki struggles to live alone, until a dimensional portal opens while he is cycling to school, literally dumping a pretty girl in his lap. Reluctantly he takes care of the amnesiac green-haired girl who can only remember her name, Rouge. As a mawkish romance develops between them, **OH**

MY GODDESS! comparisons become actionably obvious, as the couple are besieged by Rouge's supernatural sisters, Kaige and Meige. Discovering that Rouge is a princess of the underworld, the pair are forced to flee from other family members, chiefly a man called Raiga and his sword-wielding minions. Raiga wants Rouge to help him unseal Gaia's Sword, an artifact of great power. As with so many video anime, the cliffhanger ending and lack of followup aren't the fault of Western distributors. Six episodes were projected, but after poor sales, only the two on the American video release were ever made.

PRISM SEASON
1989. JPN: *Nagata Megumi Prism Season*. AKA: *Megumi Nagata's Prism Season*. Video. DIR: Yuichi Ito. SCR: Yuichi Ito. DES: Megumi Nagata. ANI: Yuichi Ito. MUS: Ami Osaki. PRD: Grouper Pro. 30 mins.
In a gentle adaptation of Megumi Nagata's book *Flowers Wait for the Moon*, a girl grows up, falls in love, and becomes a mother, realizing that her childhood is now forever behind her. The same illustrator's distinctive pastels, Victorian-style fairies, and falling flowers could also be seen in later followups, 1994 Japanese-style adaptations of **THUMBELINA**, Mimei Ogawa's children's book *The Coloring Magician*, and *Mermaid and the Red Candle*, though, as a combination of still pictures and narration, none of them is technically anime.

PRIVATE PSYCHO LESSON *
1996. JPN: *U-Jin Kojin Jugyo*. AKA: *U-Jin's Personal Tuition*. Video. DIR: Tetsuro Amino. SCR: Ryusei. DES: Makoto Takahata. ANI: N/C. MUS: N/C. PRD: JC Staff, Blue Mantis. 35 mins. x 2 eps.
Sara Iijima of Stunford (*sic*) University is a psychotherapist working in the field of higher education—which means most of her patients are high-school or college students, coincidentally the target audience for this video. The traditional watch-on-a-chain

method is not for her; to hypnotize patients she whips her top off, gets into a state of sexual excitement, and rotates her breasts in opposite directions. Once the patients are under her hypnotic influence, she regresses them to the point of trauma and sorts it out with a bit of fan service. This sex-solves-everything school of analysis has made her very successful—she travels to assignments in her own helicopter gunship and disciplines inadequate teachers with a few hundred well-aimed bullets. A variant on the elder erotic initiatress also seen in REI REI, but the script's treatment of rape—a punishment for bad Japanese girls dealt out by foreign men—is particularly offensive. U-Jin, who wrote the original manga, knows what his audience wants, but he's capable of delivering it more cleverly; see the TALES OF . . . series. ○LNV○

PROFESSOR PAIN *
1998. JPN: Gakuen Sodom. AKA: Sodom Academy. Video. DIR: Genkuro Shizuka. SCR: Genkuro Shizuka. DES: Saki Kuradama. ANI: Saki Kuradama. MUS: N/C. PRD: Beam Entertainment. 25 mins. x 2 eps.
Frustrated teacher Mr. Ohse plants high explosives all over the school (a university in the U.S. dub), locks his students in the chemistry lab, and subjects them to sexual torments. A female teacher tries to negotiate and becomes Ohse's next victim. Eventually, however, the secret behind Ohse's madness is revealed. Distraught at his sister's suicide after a gang-rape and livid that the press assumed she led her assailants on, Ohse has been encouraged, in a pastiche of the previous year's PERFECT BLUE, to wire up the school and kill his pupils by anonymous e-mails sent by someone posing as his sister. His aim is to create an over-the-top circus of depravity for the media he so despises. In other words, PP wants the best of both worlds—a snide pop at media perversity as an excuse for an hour of orgiastic bondage.
Whereas the original computer

game had one of the hapless boys ("forced" by Ohse to copulate with the girl he secretly adores) as a point-of-view character, Genkuro Shizuka's script concentrates on Ohse himself, though the result is still one of anime's most filthily degenerate videos. Merely summarizing the plot is pushing the boundaries of decency—lowlights include grateful rape victims, sexual assault with a mop, a girl forced to evacuate her bowels at the front of the class, needles stuck into breasts, and a lactating teacher providing nourishment for her pupils. ○LNV○

PROFESSOR POPPEN AND THE SWAMP OF NO RETURN
1982. JPN: Poppen Sensei to Kaerazu no Numa. TV special. DIR: Shiro Ii, Yoshimitsu Morita. SCR: Akiteru Yokomitsu. DES: Shinya Takahashi. ANI: Kazuyoshi Yoshida. MUS: Kuni Kawauchi. PRD: Heruhen, Mainichi, TBS. 90 mins.
The assistant professor of biology at Udo University is dispatched to the local marshes to write a paper on the food chain. However, he is unable to formulate a thesis and angrily decides to stop time. Transforming himself into an insect, he then changes shape into a fish, a kingfisher, and a weasel in order to experience the struggle for life first-hand. Based on the Professor Poppen series of stories by Katsuhiko Funahashi.

PROGOLFER SARU
1982. AKA: Progolfer Monkey. TV special, TV series, movie. DIR: Hiroshi Fukutomi, Junji Nishimura, Minoru Arai, Yasuhiro Imagawa, Tameo Ogawa, Tsukasa Sunaga. SCR: Noboru Shiroyama, Seiji Matsuoka. DES: Shinichi Suzuki. ANI: Toshiyuki Honda, Hideyuki Motohashi. MUS: Hiroshi Tsutsui. PRD: Shinei Doga, TV Asahi. 111 mins. (TVm1), 25 mins. x 147 (TV), 96 mins. (TVm2), 44 mins. (m1), 75 mins. (m2).
Sarumaru Sarutani is a professional golfer, determined to defeat the shadowy Mr. X and his syndicate of evil golfers, including Dragon the kung-fu

golf master. This TV special was based on the 1974 manga by Motoo Abiko, one half of the Fujiko-Fujio duo who created DORAEMON. Splitting from his working partner Hiroshi Fujimoto in the 1980s, he produced several titles under the name Fujiko-Fujio "A," including PARASOL HENBE, LAUGHING SALESMAN, and BILLY DOG—PGS is his longest and most successful creation. Serialized in publications for the very young, such as Mommy, Baby Book, and Corocoro Comic, the story was never intended for the adult audience, except perhaps as a way of making Dad's weekend hobby look more interesting to his children. The hero's much more akin to the Man with No Name than the irrepressible Stone Monkey of JOURNEY TO THE WEST, but these games are played strictly for laughs.
Bringing new meaning to the term "crazy golf," PGS returned as a TV series in 1985, with a series of fantastical tournaments in which players used absurd special powers, and the simian Saru remained determined to triumph. Amid kung-fu masters, dragon warriors, and fairway fairies, his opponents include Death himself. In the midst of these adventures, he went to America in another TV movie PGS: Saru in USA (1985) for a duel against the Native American golf-shaman Hawkwild. The movies beckoned with PGS: Challenge of Super Golf World (1986), set in the eponymous theme park where our hero faced the world greats at a tournament run by the ever-present Mr. X. A second movie, PGS: Koga's Secret Zone—the Shadow Ninja Golfer (1987), took Saru to a hidden valley in the Japanese Alps, where Saru and his family must battle a trio of golf-assassins. More adult golfing activities would be the focus of BEAT SHOT.

PROJECT A-KO *
1986. JPN: Project A-Ko. Movie, video. DIR: Katsuhiko Nishijima; Yuji Moriyama. SCR: Yuji Moriyama, Katsuhiko Nishijima, Tomoko Kawasaki; Takao Koyama. DES: Yuji Moriyama. ANI:

Yuji Moriyama, Tomohiro Hirata. MUS: Richie Zito, Joey Carbone. PRD: APPP, Studio Fantasia. 80 mins. (m), 70 mins., 50 mins., 60 mins., 55 mins. x 2 eps. (all video).

An alien spaceship crashes on Graviton City. Nobody clears it away, people get used to it being there, and gradually the district is rebuilt on an island around the hulk. Years later, two new girls arrive in class—late, as they always will be—at the Graviton Institute for Girls. Eiko ("A-Ko") Magami is a normal Japanese schoolgirl hero, apart from superstrength and superspeed inherited from superparents who are only revealed at the end of the film—one of its many in-jokes. She's cheerful, loyal, and always tries her best. Her best friend, C-Ko Kotobuki, is very, very stupid but so unbelievably cute that she reawakens an intense crush in rich, clever, and beautiful B-Ko Daitokuji. B-Ko decides that she'll break up the friendship between A-Ko and C-Ko, and then C-Ko will be *her* best friend.

Starting out looking like just another girls'-school story in the tradition of **TWINS AT ST. CLARE'S**, *PA* was actually named after Jackie Chan's *Project A* (1984), and the inspiration of the master of slapstick martial-arts mayhem is obvious. The film pokes fun at such anime staples as the heroic **CAPTAIN HARLOCK**, here transformed into a cross-dressing dipsomaniac, and the alien-princess-school-love-triangle so successful in **URUSEI YATSURA**, as well as throwing in foreign jokes like the rotund American fast-food icon Colonel Sanders, in a parody of a scene from **HARMAGEDON** depicting a terrifying warrior emerging from a dark alley toward the hero. (Kentucky Fried Chicken had just opened its franchise in Japan and the lifesize statue of the colonel outside every restaurant became a target for comedians for years—see **JUNK BOY**.) C-Ko isn't what she seems—she is really the princess of a lost alien civilization, and the captain was coming to find her when he accidentally crashed his ship.

In the video sequel *PA2: The Plot of the Daitokuji Corporation* (1987), directed by Moriyama from Koyama's script, B-Ko's millionaire industrialist father, from whom she inherited all her least charming characteristics, is plotting to acquire the alien technology for his own ends, but he reckons without his daughter's determination to win C-Ko's affection or A-Ko's loyalty to her annoying little friend. The pair unite to stop the aliens taking C-Ko home. Moriyama also directed the Kawasaki-scripted video *PA3: Cinderella Rhapsody* (1988), about an unusual love quadrangle forming when A-Ko and B-Ko fall for Kei, who loves C-Ko, who can't stand him because he's taking A-Ko's attention away from her. The whole thing culminates in a huge party on the crashed battlecruiser, which the captain and his crew have converted into the best disco in town. Opening and closing sequences have stunning artwork by Yasuomi Umezu, and the ending reassures us that men come and go, but friends are always friends. Moriyama and Kawasaki teamed up again for *Project A-Ko: Final* (1989, aka *PA4*), in which Kei's matrimonial negotiations with the girls' teacher, C-Ko's origins as an alien princess, and the captain's continuing failure to complete his mission culminate in the arrival of C-Ko's mother in a spaceship modeled on a George Lucas Star Destroyer. But the world's cutest bubble-brain doesn't go home after all, and the video ends, as the first movie began, with our heroines late for school again.

Final wasn't so final after all. A video two-parter, *A-Ko the Versus* (1990, aka *PA5*), took our heroines into an alternate universe to reprise their story with a new twist and new opponents but still the same theme—rivalries, friendships, love, and massive rumbles with bigger collateral damage than most medium-sized wars.

Nishijima and Moriyama (also known as **CREAM LEMON**'s Yuji Motoyama) wrote the story for *PA* with Kasumi Shirasaka reputedly as a pitch for the soft-core franchise, mercifully dropped. Allowed to flourish as comedy instead of erotica, *PA* throws in parodies of and references to just about every area of popular Japanese and American youth culture. Just like its pornographic precursor, *PA* is cunningly telling the same story with the same ingredients, spinning it just enough to hold the audience's attention. The team added two saving graces: good comic timing and a complete failure to comprehend the meaning of the word "excess." The whole canon—especially the first film and *Cinderella Rhapsody*—is still watchable, whether you have seen enough anime to get the in-jokes or just enjoy comedy that goes completely over the top. Nishijima would reprise the character relationships for the 1990s in the less successful **AGENT AIKA**.

PROJECT ARMS

2001. TV series. DIR: Hirotoshi Takaya. SCR: Aya Yoshinaga, Shuichi Miyashita. DES: Masaki Sato. ANI: Masako Shimizu and Hideyuki Motohashi. MUS: N/C. PRD: TMS, TV Tokyo. 25 mins. x 26 eps.

Teenager Ryo Takatsuki almost loses his left arm in an accident, only to discover his wounds taking on a life of their own—he hasn't lost an arm, so much as gained a symbiotic bioweapon. Sub-**GUYVER** action based on the *Shonen Sunday* manga by **SPRIGGAN**-cocreator Ryoji Minagawa. **V**

PSAMMEAD, THE

1985. JPN: *Onegai, Samiadon!* AKA: *Samiadon, I Wish . . . ; Psammead the Sand Imp.* TV series. DIR: Osamu Kobayashi, Hideharu Iuchi, Fumiko Ishii, Tomomi Mochizuki, Mitsuru Hongo, Kazuhiko Kobayashi. SCR: Toshiyuki Yamazaki, Eiichi Tachi, Haruya Yamazaki. DES: Tsutomu Shibayama. ANI: Hideo Kawauchi. MUS: Kentaro Haneda. PRD: Tokyo Movie Shinsha, NHK. 25 mins. x 39 eps. (2 stories per ep.).

In a deserted English chalk quarry, the older siblings of the five Turner children—Jill, Robert, and Jean—find a strange creature buried in the sand

and decide to "take care" of it. It looks like Pikachu in a pointy hat and is allergic to water, but the children have found the powerful and capricious Psammead in this adaptation of E. Nesbit's novel *Five Children and It* (1902). The sand-imp can grant one wish every day, but the wish only lasts until sundown, and like many such magical "advantages" (see **DORAEMON**), it doesn't always work as the wishers intend. The children ask for all sorts of toys and adventures, including becoming a mermaid, going into space, and having a robot of their own. Despite the mishaps some of their wishes bring, they learn valuable lessons from their strange friend.

TMS relocated the story to the present-day "English countryside," a half-timbered neverland of green fields and friendly policemen. The sand-imp character was renamed Samiadon (a Japanese wind spirit) in order to bring an oriental association not present in the original. Several TV episodes were also cut into a feature-length edition for video.

PSIBUSTER

1999. TV series. DIR: Hidehito Ueda. SCR: Hisayuki Toriumi. DES: Takeshi Ito, Yasuhiro Moriki. ANI: N/C. MUS: N/C. PRD: N/C. 25 mins.
In the year 2040, a terrible earthquake in Tokyo shatters time as well as space, causing the titular giant robot to appear from an alternate world. Ken Ando and love-interest Mizuki are great friends who are pulled apart by the events around them and then thrown into the company of the Terran Environmental Protection Agency. Eventually they become two of the ten chosen special operatives charged with investigating the earthquake and its aftermath—the dark shadows that engulf Tokyo's Shinjuku district. Based on a popular computer simulation game, this is one of the stragglers in the rush to imitate **EVANGELION**.

PSYCHIC FORCE

1998. Video. DIR: Fujio Yamauchi. SCR: Hiroyuki Kawasaki, Kenichi Onuki, Katsuhiko Takayama. DES: Kenichi Onuki. ANI: Hideki Araki. MUS: N/C. PRD: Triangle Staff, Broccoli. 40 mins. x 2 eps.
In 2007, the world is under martial law. As telepathic powers manifest in the young, the army begins conducting its own experiments, hoping to create its own elite Psycorps, known as the Psychickers. One day, Keith Evans escapes from the American compound. Evans is taken in by the kindly Griffiths family, but he goes on the run with the Griffiths boy Verne when the family is attacked by soldiers. Griffiths and Evans then fall in with the international Noah cartel, led by the eccentric Richard Wong, and the fight for freedom begins. This anime was based on an arcade fighting game but bizarrely uses Welsh names for the lead characters.

PSYCHIC WARS *

1991. JPN: *Soju Senshi Psychic Wars*. AKA: *Bestial Warrior Psychic Wars*. Video. DIR: Tetsuo Imazawa. SCR: Yasushi Ishiguro. DES: Masami Suda. ANI: Masami Suda. MUS: Tetsuro Kashibuchi. PRD: Toei. 50 mins.
In this disappointingly trite adaptation of Yasuaki Kadota's SF novel, a recently qualified Kyoto doctor discovers that prehistoric Japan was the site of an ancient war between demons and ninja. Injecting Julian May's *Saga of the Exiles* with a Japanese attitude toward honor, obligation, and love, the *PW* novel was clearly optioned for its time-traveling messiah and prehistoric demon wars, as with **DARK MYTH**, hinging on a threat that Japan's ancient enemies are returning to continue a vendetta older than time. But its fascinating take on Japanese history is dumped in a mix of breakneck exposition and supposedly arty pauses. Director Imazawa tries to jolly things along by playing up the rich historicity of the Kansai region and the (literally) many-colored land of the past, but he doesn't

© 1998 GAGA PICTURES/AVEX/JIC

have the time or budget to do it properly. He is not helped in this by a particularly poor U.K. dub that has academics discussing the mysteries of Japan's lost Jomon culture (see **PRINCESS MONONOKE**) without being able to pronounce its name. **Ⓥ**

PSYCHO ARMOR GOBARIAN

1983. TV series. DIR: Seiji Okuda, Satoru Kumazaki, Kazuya Miyazaki, Hiroshi Yoshida, Tatsuya Sasahara, Yasuo Ishigawa, Hiroshi Negishi, Kazuhiro Okaseko. SCR: Yoshihisa Araki, Hideki Sonoda, Katsuhiko Taguchi, Jiyu Watanabe, Tsukasa Takahashi. DES: Kiyoshi Fukuda, Yuki Kinoshita. ANI: Kiyoshi Fukuda, Yuki Kinoshita. MUS: Tatsumi Yano. PRD: Knack, Dynamic, TV Tokyo. 25 mins. x 26 eps.
Sometime in the 21st century, Earth is threatened by the Galadine, evil psychics from another dimension. The world's last line of defense is the giant robot Gobarian and its teenage pilot, Isamu Napoto, who moves the huge weapon using his immense powers of ESP. He's aided in his fight by his companions Kult Buster and Hans in their robots Reido and Garom. If you think that the robot Gobarian and, indeed, the whole setup are strongly reminiscent of **MAZINGER Z**, it won't surprise

you to learn that this is another of Go Nagai's many robot tales—though not one of his best.

PSYCHO DIVER: SOUL SIREN *
1997. JPN: *Psycho Diver Masei Rakuryu*. Video. DIR: Mamoru Kobe. SCR: Toshiaki Kawamura, Tatsuhiko Urahata. DES: Makoto Koga, Masafumi Yamamoto. ANI: Makoto Koga. MUS: Akihiko Hirama, SORMA, TA-1. PRD: Toei, AIC, APPP, Madhouse. 60 mins.
Yuki Kano has it all—fame, wealth, the world at her feet—but she's occasionally unable to sing (and for a pop star, this is probably bad). Enter Bosujima, a "psycho diver" with the capability to enter people's heads and straighten out what's wrong with them. Well, most of the time, anyway. Based on a novel by **AMON SAGA**–creator Baku Yumemakura, this production has a list of distinguished animation houses in its credits as long as your arm. The look is urban-hard, cool, and savvy with just enough retro and pop-culture references; check out the psychodiving machine for echoes of the brain-swap apparatus from cult 1960s series *The Prisoner*. The voice cast is full of fan favorites headed by Junko Iwao as Yuki. **NV**

PUMPKIN WINE
1982. JPN: *The Kabocha Wine*. TV series, movie. DIR: Kimio Yabuki. SCR: Shunichi Yukimuro, Mitsuru Majima, Shinji Shimizu. DES: Megumu Ishiguro, Fumihiro Uchikawa. ANI: Megumu Ishiguro, Akira Shimizu. MUS: Osamu Shoji. PRD: Toei, TV Asahi. 25 mins. x 95 eps. (TV), 60 mins. (TVm), 24 mins.
Shy teenager Shunsuke is terrified of girls. He's grown up surrounded by his sisters, and his mother owns a lingerie shop. When he moves to a new high school thinking it's for boys only but finds it's actually a coed establishment, he's in danger of letting his phobia ruin his schooldays. His fellow pupil, the lovely Natsumi "Call Me L" Asaoka, is a lot bigger than he is in every way. But despite being kindhearted, taller, and stronger, she falls in love with

short, neurotic Shunsuke. And even though he feels he's being run over by a well-meaning bulldozer, he comes to appreciate her finer qualities.
Based on Mitsuru Miura's *Shonen Magazine* manga, the series jars modern audiences because of the dated design and Rubensesque physique of the heroine, but the story has charm, and the French dub was very successful. The TV movie *PW: Is She Really on a Honeymoon with Him!?* (1982) features predictable misunderstandings in a remote ski lodge, following a winter wonderland formula also found in **KIMAGURE ORANGE ROAD** and **URUSEI YATSURA**. A short movie, *PW: Nita's Love Story* (1984), ran on the Toei Manga Matsuri summer double bill alongside **KINNIKUMAN: ULTIMATE MUSCLE**. In it, the titular dog, who lives in the school dormitory at the Sunshine academy, has a puppy sired by the pet of the wealthy Takizawa family. Nita steals milk for her offspring but disappears. While searching for the dog, Natsumi is lured onto the Takizawas' yacht by their wayward son, who claims to have the dog on board but really has designs on Natsumi herself.

PUNI PUNI POEMI
2001. Video. DIR: Shinichi Watanabe. SCR: Yosuke Kuroda. DES: Satoshi Ishino. ANI: Satoshi Ishino. MUS: Toshiro Soda. PRD: JC Staff. 30 mins. x 2 eps.
Poemi Watanabe is a cheerful student at Inunabe elementary school who lives happily with her parents until they are attacked and killed by mysterious aliens. Adopted by the parents of her classmate Futaba Memesu, she finds that the seven Memesu sisters have secret lives as the Earth Protect Unit, defending humankind against the aliens who killed her family and are now popping up in war machines all over the place. The snag is that, like *Thunderbirds'* International Rescue, they are sworn to save life, not threaten it—they can defend but not attack. But Poemi has no such scruples, and, with a bit of magical help, she transforms into Puni Puni Poemi, magical girl

and enemy of Earth's attackers. A spin-off of **EXCEL SAGA**, with Poemi resembling Excel, and Futaba her associate Hyatt.

PUPPET MASTER SAKON
1999. JPN: *Karakuri Soji Sakon*. AKA: *Sakon the Ventriloquist*. TV series. DIR: Hitoyuki Matsui, Hideki Tonokatsu, Kazuo Nogami. SCR: Chiho Katsura, Daisuke Hanebara. DES: Toshimitsu Kobayashi, Tetsu Koga. ANI: Toshimitsu Kobayashi. MUS: Norihiro Tsuru, Yuriko Nakamura. PRD: Kyoiku, Tokyo Movie Shinsha, WOWOW. 25 mins. x 26 eps.
Scooby-Doo meets *Child's Play*? Sakon is following in the footsteps of a master puppeteer who took the art of ventriloquism to undreamed-of levels centuries ago, but not even his studies in these ancient arts and his great talent can explain why his doll Ukon seems to have a life of its own. Realizing that his skills and Ukon's unexpected independence could be very useful in solving mysteries and crimes, Sakon starts to develop a new sideline as an investigator of unusual problems. Based on the 1995 *Shonen Jump* manga by Ken Obata and Maro Sharaku, with attractive designs and an evocative score, *PMS* nonetheless boasts one of the most unlikely premises in detective history. About as believable as Sherlock Holmes talking to a sock puppet, though sleuthing tales such as **CONAN THE BOY DETECTIVE** and **YOUNG KINDAICHI FILES** are hardly less strange. **V**

PUPPET PRINCESS *
2000. JPN: *Karakuri no Kimi*. Video. DIR: N/C. SCR: N/C. DES: N/C. ANI: N/C. MUS: N/C. PRD: N/C. N/D mins.
Lord Ayawatari is not interested in governing his territory or in conflicts between the other warlords but instead only lives to create puppets. Knowing Ayawatari's nature, the evil warlord Sadayoshi Karimata invades Ayawatari's castle and kills almost all his family. Princess Rangiku, the daughter of Ayawatari, is forced to seek out the legendary ninja Danzo Kato to oppose the

evil Karimata, but Danzo's assistance comes at a cost. Together these unlikely heroes must find a way to infiltrate Karimata's castle and restore the mysterious stolen puppet. Based on a *Shonen Sunday* manga by **USHIO AND TORA**–creator Kazuhiro Fujita.

PURE LOVE *

1998. JPN: *Rhythm*. Video. DIR: Miyo Morita. SCR: N/C. DES: N/C. ANI: Chuji Nakajima. MUS: N/C. PRD: Daiei. 30 mins. x 2 eps.

In a fantasy world modeled loosely on medieval Europe, knight Hiro sneaks into the king's secret chambers one evening to meet with the queen. Then, the two of them go at it like rabbits, because this is a porn anime, and she is a nymphomaniac. *Ill. p. 145.* ◐

PURPLE EYES IN THE DARK

1988. JPN: *Yami no Purple Eye*. AKA: *Purple Eye of Darkness*. Video. DIR: Mizuho Nishikubo. SCR: Asami Watanabe. DES: Chie Shinohara. ANI: N/C. MUS: Derek Jackson, Purple Gar, Mayumi Seki. PRD: Youmex, Toei. 30 mins.

Noriko has always had a strange birthmark on her arm but discovers that it indicates she is *not like other girls*. The teenager's young body hides a murderous beast that threatens to transform her at any moment, manifesting itself as glowing, savage purple eyes. An "image video" consisting of images from Chie Shinohara's 1984 *Comic Margaret* manga set to seven musical interludes in the style of **CIPHER THE VIDEO**. A full-blown anime, however, was not forthcoming, since Shinohara's observant fantasy approach to the perils of puberty had already been adapted into a live-action TV drama. The same author created **SEA'S DARKNESS: MOONSHADOW** and *Anatolia Story*, long rumored to be a forthcoming anime project.

PUSS IN BOOTS *

1969. JPN: *Nagagutsu o Haita Neko*. AKA: *Wonderful World of Puss 'n Boots*. Movie. DIR: Kimio Yabuki. SCR: Hisashi Inoue, Morihisa Yamamoto. DES: Yasuo Otsuka. ANI: Yasuji Mori, Reiko Okuyama, Takao Sakano, Hayao Miyazaki, Akio Fukube. MUS: Seiichiro Uno. PRD: Toei. 80 mins. (m1), 53 mins. (m2), 58 mins. (m3), 25 mins. x 26 eps. (TV).

Pierre, youngest of three brothers, befriends Perrault, a cat-musketeer in boots on the run from the henchmen of the evil, rat-loving Nekoboss. Perrault helps Pierre pose as the Marquis of Carabas in order to woo the beautiful Princess Rosa. She, however, is betrothed to the Demon King Lucifer, who kidnaps her on the night of the full moon. Perrault and Pierre set off to rescue Rosa from Lucifer's castle.

This delightful if free version of Charles Perrault's 18th-century fairy tale was given a limited U.S. release to the Saturday-morning kids' market, along with several other Toei anime including **JACK AND THE WITCH** and **TREASURE ISLAND**. Featuring nods to **SWAN LAKE** and *Beauty and the Beast*, it was such a success in Japan that the feline hero became Toei Animation's mascot. The comic elements of the movie owe much to the characterization of the extremely stupid transforming ogre who gets all the best bits of slapstick business. Note the presence of a young Hayao Miyazaki in the lower ranks of the animators.

Tomoharu Katsumata's movie sequel *Three Musketeers in Boots* (1972) dispatched Perrault to the Wild West, where he accompanies the young Annie and Jimmy to Gogo Town, a frontier staging post. Annie's father is killed, and the characters' lives are all endangered when the town boss discovers they know about his counterfeiting operation that he runs out of the basement of the town saloon. Annie is kidnapped, and it is time for a replay of the rescue scenario from the first film, as Perrault and Sheriff Jimmy save her from the bad guys.

A third movie, *PiB: Around the World in 80 Days* (1976), was directed by Hiroshi Shidara for the same film studio—its feline version of Jules Verne a distant precursor of **AROUND THE WORLD WITH WILLY FOGG**. Perrault bets Grumon the pig industrialist that he can travel around the world in 80 days but is pursued by cat assassins, Carter the obstructive hippo, and Grumon's sneaky lupine agent Professor Garigari.

The unrelated TV series *The Adventures of Puss in Boots* (1992) was directed by Susumu Ishizaki and broadcast on TV Tokyo, featuring young boy Hans and his cat Kusuto. Their adventures include cameos by characters from many other fairy tales and stories, including **SNOW WHITE**, **DON QUIXOTE**, *Hansel and Gretel*, **DRACULA**, *The Little Match Girl*, and **THREE MUSKETEERS**. This series is currently being repromoted in the U.S. as *Puss 'n' Boots* along with a 75-minute feature, *the Journey of Puss 'n' Boots*, which is probably three episodes edited together. The original 1969 film was restored in 1998 and shown with **GALAXY EXPRESS 999** as part of the regular Toei Anime Fair theater run. An adaptation of *Puss in Boots* was also included in the anime series **GRIMMS' FAIRY TALES**.

PUTSUN MAKE LOVE

1987. Video. DIR: Minoru Okazaki. SCR: Wataru Amano. DES: Masaki Kajishima. ANI: Masaki Kajishima. MUS: N/C. PRD: Agent 21, Toei. 25 mins. x 6 eps.

The fall and rise of a loving couple's fortunes, in which cute high-school girl Saori begins barely speaking to Yuji, putting him through a series of trials as she slowly realizes that he's the boy for her. As her parents try to fix her up with a husband in an *omiai* ("arranged") marriage meeting, Saori convinces Yuji to impersonate her at the meal, with predictably comedic results. Realizing there is fun to be had in impersonating a girl, Yuji disguises himself again and sneaks into the girls' locker room with a camera, only to be waylaid by his teacher, Miss Akimoto, who confiscates his film. A traditional anime love triangle enters the plot, as Yuji schemes and matchmakes to ensure that Saori's new suitor and the girl who is chasing *him* are maneuvered safely into each other's arms. Yuji and Saori head off to the seaside in the final episode but are kept from consummating their budding relationship by the attentions of their teacher and Yuji's unexpected heroism when he stops a suicidal girl from jumping in front of a train. Based on the manga by Jun Amemiya in *Scholar* magazine, this is an early work for **TENCHI MUYO!**'s Masaki Kajishima in the playful spirit of **SLOW STEP** and **KIMAGURE ORANGE ROAD**.

PYUNPYUNMARU
1967. TV series. DIR: Yugo Serikawa, Yasuo Yamaguchi, Kazuya Miyazaki. SCR: Jiro Yoshino, Tsuneaki Nakane, Kenji Urakawa, Enrico Dolizoni, Tomohiro Ando, Masashi Hayashi, Shunichi Yukimuro. DES: Jiro Tsunoda. ANI: Keijiro Kimura, Hiroshi Wagatsuma, Tetsuhiro Wakabayashi. MUS: Yoshioki Ogawa. PRD: Toei, Shin Production, NET. 25 mins. x 26 eps.
Pyunpyun Maru is a ninja of the Iga clan, in charge of their Nandemo OK (Anything Goes) Office. Lumbered with the crybaby ninja Chibi Maru, downtrodden by his boss, and secretly enamored of the lady ninja Sayuri, Pyunpyun must also fend off the unwelcome advances of Kemeko, the office man-eater. This funny mix of office life and ninja japery was based on the manga *Ninja Awatemaru* by **KARATE FOR IDIOTS**–creator Jiro Tsunoda serialized in *Shonen King* magazine.

Q

QTARO THE GHOST *
1965. JPN: *Obake no Qtaro.* TV series, movie. DIR: Eiji Okabe, Tadao Naga-hama. SCR: Jiro Yoshida, Kuniaki Kashima, Susumu Yoshida, Chikara Matsumoto, Hisashi Oi, Masaki Tsuji, Nanaba Sakai, Seiji Matsuoka, Asako Shiozawa. DES: Fujiko-Fujio. ANI: Dai-kichiro Kusube, Tsutomu Shibayama, Yasuhiro Yamaguchi, Sadayoshi Tomi-naga, Moriyasu Taniguchi, Susumu Shi-raume. MUS: Hiroshi Tsutsui. PRD: Tokyo Movie Shinsha, Shinei, Nippon TV. 25 mins. x 97 eps. (original), 25 mins. x 70 eps. (new), 25 mins. x 96 eps. (*new* new), 13 mins. (m).
Shota Ohara is a klutzy kid who finds an egg that hatches Qtaro, a large big-eyed blob. The Ohara family takes him in, and predictable misunderstandings ensue, with a normal Japanese house-hold gaining an extra member who can fly, make things disappear, and has a whole host of supernatural friends who insist on dropping in. Qtaro's chums include General Godzilla (no relation to the giant monster), the rich Kizao, the Professor, and Doronpa, the comic-relief American ghost. *Qtaro* is a Fujiko-Fujio project that, like the same creators' more successful **DORAEMON**, features an otherworldly playmate foisted on a hapless boy.

The original monochrome series was remade in color as *New Qtaro* (1971) and moved to new production house Shinei after a long hiatus. The second remake, confusingly also called *New Qtaro* (1985), was directed by Shinichi Suzuki and represented a concerted effort to update the postwar character for a new generation. A few episodes of this version were translated by the Hawaiian Japanese-language sta-tion KIKU and shown subtitled in some U.S. TV areas with Japanese communi-ties. In 1986, Qtaro starred in his first "movie," *Jump, Qtaro! BakeBake's Grand Strategem*, which uses 3D technology. Another short film followed in 1987, *Go Qtaro! War at 100th Size*, in which Shota and the Professor try to enlarge a cake but only end up shrinking them-selves, setting up a fantastic voyage across the new terrors of an oversized living room.

QUEEN EMERALDAS *
1998. JPN: *Queen Emeraldas.* Video. DIR: Yuji Asada. SCR: Baku Kamio. DES: Masahito Sawada, Katsumi Itabashi. ANI: Masahito Sawada. MUS: Michiru Oshima. PRD: OLM. 30 mins. x 2 eps.
In the distant future, the Afressians are out to dominate the galaxy, and humankind's only hope for freedom is the pirate known as Queen Emeraldas. Driven by the memory of a long-lost love, she sails the seas of space in her namesake ship, fighting evil on her own terms—more like Robin Hood than a traditional pirate. She is fiercely determined to protect the "good name" of her vocation, and when an Afressian crew flies the Skull and Cross-bones she insists they cease, employing her usual forceful arguments when rea-son fails. In a remote corner of space she meets a young man who has no faith in humanity and a group of ordi-nary folk who do their best to revive that faith. When the Afressians under Captain Eldomain come looking for revenge, they take these ordinary folk hostage as bait for a trap for Emeraldas.

Leiji Matsumoto has spent most of his career constructing a huge person-al universe in which to develop his notions of honor, justice, courage, and what it means to be a real human being. At the center are his two most glorious creations, the heroic pirate-knight **CAPTAIN HARLOCK** and his friend and ally Emeraldas. Around them revolve a huge cast of friends and foes, people who define their own place in the universe by their responses to its trials and hardships. The video series shows us a young boy with a hard, sad past setting out to make a hard, sad future for himself, until pirate queen Emeraldas and an unlike-ly crew of galactic deadbeats show him that an open heart is as vital as courage.

Emeraldas is the active facet of Matsumoto's ideal woman, most fully embodied in Maetel of **GALAXY EXPRESS 999**. In a sense, every Matsumoto story is the same story, and so the viewer always knows what to expect and is drawn into Matsumoto's world without any protest or difficulty. An enticing introduction to Matsumoto's old values and never-changing style, combined here with up-to-the-minute animation techniques. Though limited in places, the animation itself is stylish, and while the computer graphics vary in quality, they don't impede the flow of the story. *Ill. p. 219.*

QUEEN OF A THOUSAND YEARS *
1982. JPN: *Shin Taketori Monogatari Sennen Jo-o.* AKA: *Queen Millennia; Captain Harlock and the Queen of a Thousand Years.* TV series, movie. DIR: Masayuki Akehi. SCR: Keisuke

Fujikawa, Leiji Matsumoto. DES: Yasuhi-ro Yamaguchi, Yoshinori Kanemori, Geki Katsumata. ANI: Yasuhiro Yama-guchi. MUS: Kitaro. PRD: Toei, Fuji TV. 25 mins. x 42 eps. (TV), 121 mins. (m).

Yayoi Yukino seems like any other young woman; she's secretary to the chief of Tsukuba Observatory, and her father owns a noodle bar. Then she commissions Hajime Amemori's father to construct a strange building for her, and Hajime's own house is blown up. The orphaned Hajime learns that she is actually an alien whose home planet is fated to crush Earth at nine minutes and nine seconds past midnight on the ninth day of the ninth month of 1999. She is the Queen of a Thousand Years, and she wants to ensure that Earth will survive into a new millennium. Just as Hajime is beginning to believe her, another alien arrives. Yamori, the Thief of a Thousand Years, tells Hajime that Yayoi is really Earth's enemy, and he no longer knows who to believe. This being a Leiji Matsumoto film, the obvious answer is the one who most resembles Maetel of GALAXY EXPRESS 999, Matsumoto's archetype of perfect womanhood. Based on Matsumoto's manga serialized in the newspaper *Sankei Shinbun*, the TV series was also cut into a movie-length edition that was released in theaters as *Queen of a Thousand Years* (1982) and featured a theme song sung by Neil Sedaka's daughter Della.

It was later acquired by U.S. company Harmony Gold and combined by ROBOTECH's Carl Macek with CAPTAIN HARLOCK to create the 65-episode U.S. series *Captain Harlock and the Queen of a Thousand Years*. Even though they were two different stories from two completely different studios, Macek welded them together by switching the action constantly between two war fronts separated by light-years, thus sidestepping the fact that the major characters could never appear together.

QUIET DON, THE

1990. JPN: *Shizukanaru Don: Yakuza Side Story*. AKA: *The Quietened Don: Yakuza Side Story*. Video. DIR: Hajime Kamegaki. SCR: Kuniaki Oshikawa. DES: Osamu Nabeshima. ANI: Osamu Nabeshima. MUS: Shinji Miyazaki. PRD: TMS. 40 mins.

Soft-spoken, mild-mannered Shizuya works by day at a respected underwear factory but at night leads a double life as the third most-powerful gangster boss in the Tokyo region. Based on the 1988 manga serialized in *Shonen Sunday* magazine by Tatsuo Nitta, this story was also adapted into a live-action TV drama.

R

R.O.D.

2000. JPN: *R.O.D.* AKA: *Read or Die.* Video. DIR: Koji Masunari. SCR: Hideyuki Kurata. DES: Takaru Hane, Shinji Ishihama, Kuniyuki Jinguji. ANI: Shinji Ishihama. MUS: N/C. PRD: Studio Deen, Studio Orfee, SPE Visual Works. 30 mins. x N/D eps.

Bespectacled Yomiko Readman is a teacher whose passion is collecting books. She's also a secret agent for the Royal British Library's Division of Special Operations, a crack squad of bookhunters whose mission is to save literature for posterity. The two sides cross over when she has a run-in with a giant cricket and a strange old man out to steal a book she's just acquired. It's very rare, and the division assigns her a partner to work on finding volume two before the alien bugs get her. We never expected to see the British Library in anime; there's no topic or setting too arcane for the Japanese fantasy romance. Based on a manga in *Ultra Jump* magazine by Hideyuki Kurata and Shutaro Yamada.

RACING BROTHERS LETS AND GO

1996. JPN: *Hasshire Kyodai Lets to Go.* TV series, movie. DIR: Tetsuro Amino, Yoshio Kado. SCR: Hiroyuki Hoshiyama. DES: Akio Takami, Michiru Ishihara. ANI: Akio Takami. MUS: Koji Tsuno. PRD: Xebec, TV Tokyo. 25 mins. x 117 eps. (TV), 81 mins. (m).

Lets and Go are a pair of preteen brothers obsessed with mini-racing cars—half lawn mower, half formula one. In this long-running series based on a manga by Tetsuhiro Koshita, the boys work for genius inventor Professor Tsuchiya to defeat the agents of his rival, Professor Inugami, both on and off the tracks. After the first 51 episodes, the series was rebranded as *L&G: WGP* (1997) and trailed with a feature-length theatrical release. The series proper finished after 98 episodes, but it was brought back as *L&G: MAX* (1998), renumbered back to 1, and featured a new look courtesy of new designer Ishihara. A junior version of CYBERFORMULA GPX, whose sci-fi racing drama was still running when *L&G* began.

RAI: GALACTIC CIVIL WAR CHRONICLE

1994. JPN: *Ginga Sengoku Gunyu Den Rai.* AKA: *Galactic Civil War Rivalry Between Chiefs: Rai; Thunder Jet.* TV series. DIR: Seiji Okuda. SCR: Junzo Toriumi, Satoshi Fujimoto. DES: Makoto Takehoko, Takashi Watabe, Kenji Teraoka, Mitsuki Nakamura. ANI: Makoto Takehoko. MUS: Kaoru Wada. PRD: IG Film, TV Tokyo. 25 mins. x 52 eps.

The Galactic Empire is in shreds after the emperor's death, and the universe is consumed by conflict. Young warrior Rai Ryuga, descendant of an old samurai line, wants to bring peace to the warring clans and enlists the help of Shimon, daughter of the late emperor. A replay of Japan's civil war, but in space with fighting robots, *Rai* was a huge success in its original manga form. Serialized in *Dengeki Comic Gao* magazine by Johji Manabe, it shares character archetypes and graphic style with his earlier OUTLANDERS and sold over two million copies, making the anime adaptation a foregone conclusion. It has a martial feel courtesy of DANCOUGAR-director Okuda and oriental music from KISHIN CORPS' Wada.

RAIJIN-OH

1991. JPN: *Zettai Muteki Raijin-o.* AKA: *Completely Invincible Raijin-o.* TV series, video. DIR: Toshifumi Kawase, Nobuhiro Kondo, Takuya Sato. SCR: Hideki Sonoda, Noriko Hayasaka. DES: Satoshi Takeuchi, Takahiro Yamada, Shige Ikeda. ANI: Shinichi Sakuma, Satoshi Takeuchi. MUS: Kohei Tanaka. PRD: Sunrise, TV Tokyo. 25 mins. x 51 eps., 30 mins. x 3 eps.

Earth is under threat of invasion from another dimension. Balzeb, Taldar, and their shape-shifting underlings, the Akudama (Evil Orbs), create part-cyborg monsters based on problems humankind has created for itself, like pollution, litter, and noise. There is a solution—three robots stored in a secret hangar that can combine to form the mighty fighting machine Raijin-Oh. When a pilot crashes Raijin-oh into an elementary school and is too badly hurt to carry on, he asks the pupils to take his place and become the Earth Defense Group. Once again, the government has no alternative but to put the safety of Earth in the hands of its children. Although 3 of them will be pilots, all 18 classmates have to learn to work together unselfishly for the good of all humanity. With such a large regular cast, one would expect most to be sidelined, but each of the regulars is featured strongly and has his or her own importance to the team and the story.

Another series created by Sunrise house pseudonym Hajime Yadate, *Raijin-Oh* follows in the tradition of giant-robot shows begun by Mitsuteru Yokoyama's **GIGANTOR** and Go Nagai's **MAZINGER Z**, which Sunrise raised to the level of an art form in the late 1970s with shows for a slightly older audience, like **GUNDAM**. Sunrise was also responsible in no small part for the use of very young children—the target audience for merchandising—as heroes in these shows, and the success of *Raijin-Oh* came shortly after the beginning of their long-running **BRAVE SAGA**.

RAIL OF THE STAR *

1993. JPN: *O-hoshisama no Rail.* Movie. DIR: Toshio Hirata. SCR: Tatsuhiko Urahata. DES: Yoshinori Kanemori. ANI: Katsutaka Iizuka. MUS: Koichi Saito. PRD: Madhouse. 79 mins.
As a Japanese national growing up in occupied Korea during World War II, young Chiko learns that soldiers on the battlefield are not the only casualties of armed conflict. As the Japanese Empire reaps the increasingly bitter harvest of a failing war effort, her well-to-do middle-class family is rocked by tragedy, losing friends and loved ones to the everyday domestic hazards of life in the 1940s, before peace brings the greatest danger of all. Korea is divided between the victors, and Chiko's family is in Pyongyang, in the northern half. The Soviet Army begins a search for Japanese veterans like her father, a factory manager called up for military service. Chiko and her surviving relatives embark upon an epic journey to the U.S. Occupied Zone below the 38th parallel. They must rely on the help of the Korean people to get them to safety. Many Koreans suffered during the Japanese colonization, but in this sanitized true-life story (based on a book by Chitose "Chiko" Kobayashi), everything works out tidily. The threadbare but clean and perky-looking Japanese survivors manage to reach safety with the help of forgiving Korean villagers who put human life above race, nationality, or revenge, and Chiko grows up in modern, prosperous Japan, remembering the war through the eyes of a child.

It's not an exclusively Japanese tendency to present war stories in the best possible light—every nation talks about the suffering of its own civilians and the terrible impact of war on children, though sadly only after the event. For this approach, children make the ideal protagonists, since they can't be held responsible for any of the events they observe. A very similar story premise, also based on semiautobiographical memoirs, was transformed into something sublime by the artistry of Studio Ghibli in **GRAVE OF THE FIREFLIES**, whose success encouraged a number of imitators, of which *Rail of the Star* is perhaps the most blinkered. Compared to the deeply romanticized view of war presented in **THE COCKPIT** or the realistic yet humane outlook of **BAREFOOT GEN**, it's pap, used by the Japanese to assure themselves that World War II was some sort of unexpected natural disaster, and that Koreans don't hold much of a grudge for 50 years of colonial rule. Ironically, *RotS*'s artificial worthiness made it more marketable abroad, where American distributors warmed to its deluded cultural relativism, the "bring me your poor" concept of the U.S. zone as refuge, and the opportunity to demonstrate that not all of their anime output was guns and hooters.

RAINBOW ACROSS THE PACIFIC

1992. JPN: *Taiheiyo ni Kakeru Niji.* Video. DIR: Masayuki Akehi. SCR: Yugo Serikawa, Tadahiro Shimafuji. DES: N/C. ANI: Takao Kasai. MUS: Seiji Yokoyama. PRD: Toei. 30 mins.
Schoolgirl Mitsuko tries to protect half-Chinese transfer student Yu-Lian from bullies. That night, she discovers Emily, an old American doll. Given to a Japanese child during an exchange in 1921, it was hidden from the "doll burnings" of the anti-Western war period and saved by a brave young girl (Mitsuko's grandmother) from bayonet practice. At the next day's show-and-tell, Mitsuko tells the story of Emily and encourages Yu-Lian, who has brought her own doll, the beautiful

Feng-Qun. When Feng-Qun's ribbon blows away and is caught in a tree, even the bullies cooperate in retrieving it.

Combining treacly internationalism with inadvertent comedy, especially when a girl donates her underwear to help make a rope, this story also suffers from flabby editing (why have a talking doll *and* a doll fairy?) characteristic of a creator with whom nobody dares argue, in this case Daisaku Ikeda, the leader of the Soka Gakkai Buddhist organization. But it is superior to his **FAIRGROUND IN THE STARS**, cleverly appealing to children by using toys as allegories for human suffering and heroism.

RAINBOW BATTLETEAM ROBIN

1966. JPN: *Rainbow Sentai Robin.* TV series. DIR: Yugo Serikawa, Takeshi Tamiya, Tomoharu Katsumata, Michiru Takeda, Yasuo Yamaguchi. SCR: Kazuhiko Kojima, Hiroshi Ozawa, Minoru Hamada, Hiroaki Hayashi, Michio Suzuki. DES: Studio Zero. ANI: Yoichi Otabe, Keishiro Kimura, Tetsuhiro Wakabayashi, Shinya Takahashi. MUS: Koichi Fukube. PRD: Toei, Studio Zero, NET. 25 mins. x 48 eps.
The people of the dying planet Palta choose Earth as their new home, much to the annoyance of the human race. In an animated pastiche of live-action shows such as **ULTRAMAN,** teenage Robin and his six color-coded friends (nurse-robot Lily, Wolf the werewolf, Benkei the warrior-mage, Bell the cat, the know-it-all Professor, and Pegasus the transforming rocket) form a heroic team to save the planet. Inspired in part by Edmond Hamilton's **CAPTAIN FUTURE** novels, the original concept was thought up by **CYBORG 009**–creator Shotaro Ishinomori, then calling himself Ishimori.

RAINBOW MAN

1982. JPN: *Ai no Senshi Rainbow Man.* AKA: *Love Warrior Rainbow Man.* TV series. DIR: Kazuhiro Okaseko. SCR: Tsunehisa Ito. DES: Yasunori Kawauchi, Kazuhiro Okaseko. ANI: Kazuhiro Okaseko. MUS: Jun Kitahara. PRD: Ai

Planning, Hayama Art, Oscar Studio, Studio Pop, MBS. 25 mins. x 22 eps. Takeshi Yamato has spent years as a student of yogic master Devadatta. He now has superpowers that allow him to transform himself in seven ways and operate seven kinds of machinery. By combining his powers with an organic V Armor, which he can call up at will, he becomes Rainbow Man. In this form, he fights to defend Japan against the evil machinations of the Death-Death Group. This animated adaptation of the live-action SFX series *Rainbow Man* (1972) recreates the feel of the original, even down to the theme song taken from the earlier series. Compare to **ULTRAMAN**, which also has both live-action and anime incarnations.

RAINING FIRE

1988. JPN: *Hi no Ame ga Furu*. Movie. DIR: Seiji Arihara. SCR: Toshiaki Imaizumi, Seiji Arihara. DES: Yoshitsuge Hasegawa. ANI: Takaya Ono. MUS: N/C. PRD: Space, Nikkatsu, Mushi Pro. 80 mins.

On the 19th of June 1945, 230 American B-29s bomb Fukuoka while two horror-struck Japanese children watch the incendiary devices make the night sky look as if it is "raining fire." Funded in part by the Kyushu Film Center, jealous at the attention lavished on other towns in anime such as **GRAVE OF THE FIREFLIES** (Kobe) and **BAREFOOT GEN** (Hiroshima), *RF* fatuously claims to be an antiwar film, though it conveniently neglects to mention that the sleepy harbor town of Fukuoka was actually a major military port. Conventional weaponry killed more Japanese during the war than the much-hyped A-Bombs at Hiroshima and Nagasaki—in addition to Arihara's lookalike follow-up **KAYOKO'S DIARY**, a similar study of the firebombing of civilian and industrial targets was directed by Tsuneharu Otani as *After the Unhealable Wounds: Osaka the Sea of Fire* (1991, *Kiesaranu Kizu Ato: Hi no Umi Osaka*).

RAMAYANA *

1998. AKA: *Ramayana: The Legend of Prince Rama, Prince of Light*. Movie. DIR: Ram Mohan, Yugo Sako. SCR: Krishna Shah. DES: N/C. ANI: Kazuyuki Kobayashi. MUS: N/C. PRD: Nippon Ramayana Film Co. 96 mins.

The God-King Rama and his devoted young wife, Sita, are exiled by political intrigue but determined to prove Rama's right to his ancestral throne. In the course of their long wanderings through the forests and kingdoms of ancient India, they meet many friends and allies, including an old friend of Japanese animation, the Monkey God Hanuman, who was the original template for Monkey King Sun Wu-Kong, hero of **JOURNEY TO THE WEST**. But the beautiful Sita also attracts unwelcome attention from the Demon King Ravana, who kidnaps her and holds her captive in his island fortress. Rama and their friends set out to rescue her and destroy Ravana; before he can recover his throne he must recover his bride. Shapeshifting vampires, flying fortresses, and epic battles provide plenty of action and interest in a film as stuffed with over-the-top weaponry, weird martial arts, and romance as any fantasy anime.

The story, one of the great religious texts of Hinduism, is credited to a half-mythical robber-poet who is said to have given it its present form around 300 B.C. Like the Greek poet Homer, unwitting originator of **ULYSSES 31**, Valmiki could scarcely have suspected where his tale would end up. This first Indian-Japanese coproduction took years of heroic effort on the part of Mohan and Japanese producer Yugo Sako. Licenses from the Hindu religious authorities were required before work on the animation could go ahead in India, and local artists and animators were trained to work to Japanese standards and methods. Every aspect of the story was carefully constructed to avoid any offense to Hindu religious sensibilities. The end result did not score the hoped-for success either in India or Japan or among film-fan Hin-

Osamu Sekita's **MY MY MAI** boasts scientific investigations as overly complex excuses for mild titillation, as its perky heroine gives her all in the pursuit of her patients' well-being. The Japanese title translates as *Get Me in the Mood*, though it is difficult to figure out: "in the mood" for what? Buyers of anime porn are likely to be disappointed by the soft-core antics, while buyers of anime comedy may wonder when the laughs are supposed to start. *See entry p. 264.*

My My Mai

© 1993 YAMAGUCHI MASAKAZU/AKITA SHOTEN/APPLE

di communities overseas. Less faithful adherence to Hindu myth can be found in **RG VEDA**.

RANCE: GUARDIAN OF THE DESERT

1994. JPN: *Rance: Nessa no Guardian*. Video. DIR: Hisashi Fujii. SCR: Satoru Akahori. DES: Kazuto Nakazawa. ANI: Kazuto Nakazawa, Koji Matsuyama. MUS: N/C. PRD: Alice Soft, Tokuma. 50 mins. Lecherous knight Rance decides that all the women in the world belong to him, and that he should start claiming his rights by getting naked with as many of them as possible. This smutty spinoff from a fantasy role-playing computer game featured big names from the mainstream, including **BEAST WARRIORS**' Akahori and **EL HAZARD**'s Nakazawa. ⊘

RANMA 1/2 *

1989. JPN: *Ranma Nibunnoichi*. TV series, movie, video. DIR: Tsutomu Shibayama, Hideharu Iuchi, Akira Suzuki, Junji Nishimura, Kazuhiro Furuhashi. SCR: Shigeru Yanagawa, Ryota Yamaguchi. DES: Atsuko Nakajima, Torao Arai. ANI: Tomomi Mochizuki, Takeshi Mori, Masako Sato, Masamitsu Kudo. MUS: Eiji Mori, Kenji Kawai. PRD: Kitty Film, Studio Deen,

Fuji TV. 25 mins. x 161 eps., 74 mins. and 60 mins. (m), 30 mins. x 9 eps. (v). Ranma (*luan ma*, Chinese for "wild horse") Saotome and his father, martial artist Genma, fall into magical pools while training in a region of China. Henceforth, Ranma will change into a girl whenever doused in cold water and back to a boy when doused in hot. Genma fares even worse—he becomes a giant panda. The pair leave exotic, dangerous China and return home to safe, familiar Japan, where years ago Saotome senior agreed with his old friend Tendo that Ranma would marry one of the Tendo daughters and take over the family dojo. The Tendo girls are underwhelmed by their prospective bridegroom. Youngest sister Akane, who draws the short straw, is a feisty young lady with formidable fighting skills and considerable contempt for the teenage boys who attempt to defeat and date her. She and boy-Ranma (Ranma-kun) strike antagonistic sparks off each other right away. Ranma tries to keep his inadvertent sex changes secret at school by posing as his/her own sibling, resulting in Akane and girl-Ranma (Ranma-chan) becoming rivals for supremacy among their classmates. Ranma-chan attracts unwelcome attention from the guys in class, while Ranma-kun is a babe magnet. The stories revolve around the familiar world of teenage home and school life, with the magical element providing injections of fantasy and romance. Just about every stranger who wanders into town has fallen into some kind of magical pool, and the resulting transformations turn school and dojo into a veritable zoo. Meanwhile Ranma and Akane grow to love each other but can't admit it, their various friends and rivals start to pair off, often unwittingly, and the quest to find a cure for the curse goes on.

Based on a 1988 manga in *Shonen Sunday* from **URUSEI YATSURA**–creator Rumiko Takahashi, *Ranma 1/2* duplicated her earlier success, but this time with a lead character that is both boy and girl and a strangeness that comes not from extraterrestrial origins but from magic. The story was soon picked up for TV, where it lasted for several years despite *Shonen Sunday*'s sales sinking to their lowest-ever ebb while the manga was running in it. Chunks of the TV series are available in the U.S. under the titles *Ranma 1/2, R: Anything Goes Martial Arts, R: Hard Battle,* and *R: Outta Control.* However, real success has come abroad, particularly in Asia, where the kung fu and comedy, dubbed into local languages, make it the most China-friendly anime series. It is even shown in the censorious People's Republic, where its samey, lighthearted obsessions with romance, food, fighting, and sibling rivalries are not regarded as much of a threat to Communism.

The first movie, directed by Iuchi, was not based on incidents from the manga but had a specially created story based on Chinese legend. In *Ranma 1/2 The Movie: Big Trouble In Nekonron, China* (1991), Akane is kidnapped by prince Kirin, who wants to marry her, Ranma and the gang rescue her (in a battle scene that pays open homage to **SAINT SEIYA**, reflecting the involvement of Arai in both movies), and everything ends as usual with the leads refusing to admit their love for each other. The second, *Nihao My Concubine* (1992), directed by Suzuki, has the girls shipwrecked in the South Seas with a crazed young illusionist who forces them to compete in various skill tests to select his bride. To save Akane and the others from this fate worse than death, Ranma-chan has to compete in wacky activities such as survival flower arranging and obstacle-course cooking.

Several video releases also kept the series in the public eye throughout the 1990s, many of which have also been released in English. *Dead Heat Music Match* (1990) started a new career for the three Tendo girls, Ranma-chan, and Chinese interloper Shampoo: they formed the band DoCo and their voice actresses went on to release numerous *Ranma 1/2* music CDs and videos. It was followed in rapid succession by more videos, many of which have been released in English with desperately labored titles punning on famous Western films. Thus it was that the *R Special* video series (1993) was released in America as *Desperately Seeking Shampoo, Like Water for Ranma 1/2,* and *Akane and Her Sisters.* A second video series, *R Super* (1995), was similarly altered into *An Akane to Remember, One Flew Over the Kuno's Nest* (paired with a 30-minute "movie" *Ranma 1/2 Team vs. The Legendary Phoenix*), and *Faster, Kasumi! Kill! Kill!* Nishimura directed most of the videos.

With animation that has not aged as badly as *UY*'s and a seamless dub in the U.S., *Ranma 1/2* has attracted fanatical Western devotees, but Takahashi had already covered the territory thoroughly, and a huge amount of plot and character recycling goes on. She cleverly exploits the factors that made *UY* such a success but with less inventiveness and humor, eventually dumbing down to sheer predictability. Takahashi's talent is far greater than *Ranma 1/2* reveals; but her commercial success comes from giving her audiences exactly what they want, as often as they want it, and the *Ranma 1/2* franchise delivers honestly on that basis. This makes it popular with a young teenage audience, which doubtless appreciates a series so interchangeable that the episodes do not need to be numbered, making little difference whether one is watching a TV episode or a video special. Likely to gain a new lease on life as the **POKÉMON** generation reaches its teens and discovers new obsessions, but for a better measure of Takahashi's work, see **MAISON IKKOKU** and **ONE-POUND GOSPEL**. *Ill. p. 137.*

RANPO

1984. JPN: *Ranpo.* TV series. DIR: Ken Basho, Shin Misawa, Junichi Fukuwara. SCR: Yasushi Hirano, Keiko Maruo, Kenji Terada, Hideki Sonoda, Yoshio Urasawa. DES: Hikuji Kanezawa, Masatoshi Uchizaki. ANI: Hikuji Kanezawa, Toshiyuki Honda, Kaoru Kogawa, Masayuki, Moriyasu Taniguchi. MUS:

Chito Kawauchi. PRD: NAS, Fuji TV. 25 mins. x 20 eps.

Mild-mannered Japanese kid Ranpo is kidnapped by aliens whose UFO-based experiments turn him into a "warp boy" who truly believes that he can do anything. Back at school on Earth, he enlists his classmates in a number of wacky schemes, and comedic misunderstandings ensue. Based on a 1979 manga in *Shonen Champion* magazine by Masatoshi Uchizaki, *Ranpo* was swiftly yanked off the air—though the official excuse was that its slot was required for baseball games, the series never returned. Years after its original release, the only traces it left behind were praise for Hiroshi Watanabe's Beatles-pastiche opening credits and an unbroadcast 21st episode.

RANTARO

1993. JPN: *Nintama Rantaro*. AKA: *Rantaro the Little Ninja*. TV series. DIR: Tsutomu Shibayama. SCR: Yoshio Urasawa. DES: Sobei Amako. ANI: N/C. MUS: Koji Makaino. PRD: Asia-do. 12 mins. x 91 eps. (TV1), 12 mins. x 72 eps., 20 mins. x 18 eps. (TV2), 45 mins. (m).

Well, the ninja have to learn their trade *somewhere*. Rantaro is a little boy who wants to grow up to be a highly trained assassin. So he goes to a ninja school, where he gets to clown around and meet famous people from Japan's civil-war period. Featuring high-profile theme music from bands-of-the-moment Hikaru Genji and Super Monkeys, this lighthearted kids' comedy, based on a manga by Sobei Amako, returned after 91 episodes as *New Rantaro* (1994), which similarly featured ninja whose favorite food was mushrooms, a warrior forced to work part-time at a launderette, and time out from learning about poisons so the gang can go shopping. Several episodes of the second series were "specials" that ran for almost double the time, and the central cast's best moments were later rereleased in the four-part *Rantaro Masterworks* series (1996). The same year saw a short

Rantaro movie, in which the little ninja, trained for cunning and deceit, must somehow convince his elders that he is not responsible for thefts at the school. Compare to **HATTORI THE NINJA**.

RAPEMAN, THE

1994. JPN: *Za (The) Rapeman*. Video. DIR: Kinta Kunte, Kazuo Sawada, Hiroshi Ono. SCR: Shintaro Miyawaki. DES: Keiko Aizaki. ANI: Hidemi Kuma. MUS: N/C. PRD: Pink Pineapple, KSS. 45 mins.

Shotoku and his nephew Keisuke are vigilante rapists. With a company motto of "Righting Wrongs through Penetration," they will don black hockey masks and rape females who have somehow offended their clients by dumping them, refusing their advances, or otherwise treating them inappropriately. After teaching their victims a "good lesson," they donate the money they earn to Keisuke's former home at the Sunflower Orphanage. This deeply offensive series was based on the controversial manga by Shintaro Miyawaki and Keiko Aizaki. The anime version was released roughly halfway through the live-action video series, directed by Takao Nagaishi between 1990 and 1998. **●ⓃⓋ**

RASCAL RACCOON *

1977. JPN: *Araiguma Rascal*. TV series. DIR: Seiji Endo, Shigeo Koshi, Hiroshi Saito. SCR: Akira Miyazaki. DES: Seiji Endo. ANI: Seiji Okuda, Noboru Kameyama, Nobuo Fujisawa, Sadahiko Sakamaki, Yoichi Otabe, Toshiko Nakagawa, Hayao Miyazaki, Hirokazu Ishino. MUS: Takeo Watanabe. PRD: Nippon Animation, Fuji TV. 25 mins. x 52 eps.

Young Sterling lives on a farm in Wisconsin with his parents in the early years of the 20th century. One day, he finds an abandoned baby raccoon in the forest and decides to take it home. The pair soon become inseparable. The raccoon's antics keep the neighborhood in quite a stir, but Sterling also finds his little companion a great comfort in the difficult times of his life, including his mother's illness and the

terrible storm that devastates the farm and threatens the family's livelihood. Based on the writings of Sterling North about his own boyhood, this is part of Nippon Animation's **WORLD MASTERPIECE THEATER** series and includes Hayao Miyazaki among its animators.

RAYEARTH *

1994. JPN: *Maho Kishi Rayearth*. AKA: *Magic Knight Rayearth*. TV series, video. DIR: Toshihiro Hirano, Keitaro Motonaga, Hajime Kamegaki, Koichi Chiaki, Hitoyuki Matsui. SCR: Keiko Maruo, Osamu Nakamura, Nanase Okawa. DES: Atsuko Ishida, Masahiro Yamane. ANI: Atsuko Ishida, Keiji Goto, Hideyuki Motohashi, Masahiro Yamane, Madoka Hiroyama. MUS: Hayato Matsuo. PRD: TMS, Yomiuri TV. 25 mins. x 49 eps., 45 mins. x 3 eps.

Hikaru Shido, Umi Ryuzaki, and Fu Ho-oji are three ordinary Japanese schoolgirls who suddenly find themselves transported to Cephiro, a world of magic and monsters in another dimension. Clef, a very youthful looking ancient wizard, tells them that they have been summoned by the guardian of Cephiro, Princess Emeraude. The princess is a "pillar" of Cephiro, the link that holds the magic kingdom together, but she has been kidnapped by the evil High Priest Zagato. In order to save this fragile world, the three girls must literally win their spurs and become Magic Knights, for only the combined powers of the Knights can hope to challenge Zagato and save the world. Clef helps them from time to time, and they have another friend, the rabbit-like Mokona, whose cuddly exterior hides many secrets. Nothing else is quite as it seems either; the sorcerer is in love with the princess, and each of the girls has her own secret strengths and weaknesses. If they are ever to see Tokyo again, they must work together to save Cephiro.

In the second season, the three girls are once again summoned to Cephiro, once again on the brink of oblivion. With Emeraude absent, the three kingdoms of Autozam, Farhen, and Cizeta begin an invasion of Cephiro to overthrow the pillar system. They must also contend with a girl called Nova, who seems to be Hikaru's nemesis and attacks everything she loves.

The three-part 1997 video series keeps the same basic premise but changes the story. To reflect the change, the title became simply *Rayearth*. Cephiro is slowly materializing in Tokyo and the meeting of two dimensions is causing huge earthquakes on Earth. To avert the impending disaster, Guru Clef and Lantis must find the Magic Knights whose powers can put things right. High-school girl Hikaru is waiting for her friends Umi and Fu under a cherry tree with supposed magic connections when there's another strong quake, and a strangely cute rabbit-like creature, Mokona, falls out. As Hikaru chases the white rabbit and her friends follow, they are all whisked to the Tokyo Tower where they learn that they must summon the Mashin Gods, powerful sentient fighting machines, and use their powers to defeat the sorcerer Eagle Vision and his Mashin if both worlds are to be saved.

Based on a manga in *Nakayoshi* that combined elements of girls' manga with boys' action-adventure, this magical romance was a huge hit for its creators, manga collective CLAMP, whose work has not always been served well on video (see **RG VEDA**) and had considerable success in the U.S. The three heroines, linked specifically with the elements of fire, water, and air, are more "magical" in origin than anything on Cephiro, where many people and places are named for popular Japanese cars. There are references not only to anime tropes, such as destined heroes who alone can control powerful armor, and popular locations, like the Tokyo Tower that features in numerous shows, but also to Western classics—as in **ALICE IN WONDERLAND** and CLAMP's earlier **MIYUKI-CHAN IN WONDERLAND**, the girls are guided by a white rabbit.

READY FOR ADVENTURE
1989. JPN: *Boken Shitemo Ii Goro*. Video. DIR: Masamune Ochiai. SCR: Masaru Yamamoto. DES: Nami Saki. ANI: Akihiro Izumi. MUS: Toshiya Uchida. PRD: Knack. 45 mins. x 3 eps.
Forced to wait a year to retake his university exams, would-be film director Junpei jumps at the chance to leave Hokkaido and head for the big city for a job in the film business. But when he arrives, he discovers he's volunteered to work as a porn actor for the beautiful Apollo Productions director Mika. Rising through the ranks, he becomes a talent scout, "road-testing" would-be actresses in a Harajuku love hotel. Eventually, there is trouble on the set as new star Masako turns out to be understandably afraid of men. Luckily, Junpei is on hand to show her just how nice men can be. This smutty respray of **JUNK BOY** was based on the 1986 manga in *Big Comic Spirits* by Nonki Miyasu. **N**

REAL BOUT HIGH SCHOOL *
2001. AKA: *Samurai Girl*. TV series. DIR: Shinichi Tokaibayashi. SCR: Aya Matsui. DES: Keiji Goto. ANI: Yoshiyuki Kobe. MUS: Takeshi Yasuda. PRD: Gonzo, Kids Station. 25 mins. x 13 eps.
Ryoko Mitsurugi is a bubbly teenager who enjoys martial arts, both in practice and on TV in old samurai shows. The star of the school kendo team, she takes up the all-new K-Fight martial art, and soon beats all-comers. Her training, however, is not as it seems and has a more practical use. One day, time stops, and the surprised Ryoko is forced to defend the frozen world from an attacking monster. Based on a manga in *Dragon* magazine by Reiji Shiga and Sora Inoue.

REAL SCHOOL GHOST STORIES
1996. JPN: *Honto ni Atta Gakko Kaidan*. AKA: *School Ghost Stories That Really Happened*. Video. DIR: Moriyasu Taniguchi, Noriyuki Abe. SCR: Toshimitsu Himeno, Hiroshi Hashimoto. DES: Moriyasu Taniguchi, Masaya Onishi. ANI: Moriyasu Taniguchi. MUS: Satoshi Hirata. PRD: Matsutake Home Video, Studio Pierrot, SPE Special Works, Fuji TV. 30 mins. (v), 25 mins. x N/D eps.
A "true-life" variant of the school ghost stories that characterized the **HERE COMES HANAKO** phenomenon, the idea remained popular into the 21st century, where it was repackaged as simply *School Ghost Story* (2000), a TV series with a larger framing device. Heroic schoolgirl Satsuki must protect her crybaby brother, Keiichiro, from ghosts at their new school while fending off the amorous advances of class lothario Hajime. The trio are accompanied by Momoko, a pallid, withdrawn girl who always attracts the attention of spirits, good and otherwise.

RECORD OF LODOSS WAR *
1990. JPN: *Lodoss to Senki*. Video, TV series. DIR: Akinori Nagaoka. SCR: Asami Watanabe, Akinori Endo. DES: Yutaka Izubuchi, Nobuteru Yuki, Hidetoshi Kaneko. ANI: Eiko Yamauchi. MUS: Mitsuo Hagita. PRD: Madhouse. 30 mins. x 13 eps., 80 mins. (*Crystania Movie*), 40 mins. x 3 eps. (*Crystania*), 30 mins. (*Welcome to Lodoss*), 25 mins. x 27 eps. (*Heroic Knight*).
This video series based on the novels and gaming scenarios created by Ryo Mizuno and Hiroshi Yasuda presents role-playing games as they never were but should have been. In a world still reeling in the aftermath of a war between gods, a classic D&D party of warrior Parn, elf Deedlit, dwarf Ghim, magic-user Slayn, cleric Etoh, and thief Woodchuck set out to seek the aid of Wort the sage, a former adventurer whose early years were chronicled in the spinoff manga *Lady of Pharis*. The land of Lodoss is under threat from a revival of the power of darkness. A heroic king and his noble warlord have been turned to the dark side by an evil counselor, and the heroes of a former struggle are lending what support they can to the new young team as they travel to Wort's stronghold only to learn that he regards himself simply as an observer and is unwilling to use his great power to intervene. The dun-

geon party must travel on, trying to recruit allies for the fight against darkness among exotic kingdoms and dank forests, meeting evil Dark Elves, desert princes, and dragons guarding ancient treasures deep below the earth. At the end of the story, it seems that evil has been stopped in its tracks for the moment, and the young hero Parn has completed his journey from boyhood to manhood, his quest for himself.

The villains are dark and deadly enough to satisfy the keenest good-versus-evil aficionado, but they're neither motiveless nor entirely unsympathetic. One of the most tear-jerking scenes in the whole of anime occurs in episode ten, when tough-guy Ashram the Black Knight, noble servant of dark powers, affirms his eternal love for his elven mistress, Pirotessa, simply in the way he says her name as she dies in his arms. The "little people"—soldiers commanding outpost forts, thieves, and farmers—are shown in a sympathetic light, often more honorable and honest than the great kings and mages, and we learn that some of those who fought for the triumph of Light in days of yore are now on the side of Darkness. In his way the "good" sage Wort is more amoral than his dark counterpart, Karla the Gray Witch, who possesses men and topples empires to keep faith with her unshakable belief that good and evil must be kept in balance, and that when one has ruled for too long the balance must be made to shift.

Seductive music, especially the opening and ending themes, powerful faux-medieval and Art Nouveau design, and strong characters make for an attractive package. There's an effective opening sequence by veteran Rintaro, but the animation is generally undistinguished. The plotting circles and strays in places, and many elements of the dense back story are hinted at though not explored, but the whole is involving enough to carry the viewer over such minor hiccups.

Ryutaro Nakamura's later movie and video sequel *Legend of Crystania* (1995

and 1996) proves less than satisfying. A promising concept is let down by low-rent designs, appalling animation, and editing that verges on the deranged in places—add to this a poor English dub and a different U.S. distributor with a nonexistent numbering policy. Set 300 years after the original and featuring characters who were supposed to be dead last time we looked, Ashram is possessed by the evil god Barbas, while Pirotessa assembles a new band of heroes to fight back. The already confusing plot of warring were-beasts is made even harder to unravel when the tape called "A New Beginning" turns out to be the last episode, coming after "Cave of the Sealed" and "Resurrection of the Gods' King."

The franchise returned briefly for Chiaki Koichi's theatrical short *Welcome to Lodoss Island* (1997), a squashed-down cartoon version rereleased on video with extra footage. In the post-**Evangelion** boom, when producers desperately searched for anything to expand, the franchise was brought back once more, this time as Yoshihiro Takamoto's TV series *Record of Lodoss War: Chronicles of the Heroic Knight* (1998). Set five years after the original video series, *CotHK* features a number of former supporting characters in major roles, along with members of the original cast, who have hardly changed a bit. Young Spark fills the would-be paladin role occupied by Parn, now a bona fide hero, in the original video series. Barely competent mercenaries Shiris and Orson attack a free village and meet apprentice mage Cecil, a prissy, just-masculine version of elfin babe Deedlit from series one. Deedlit and Parn show up in time to stop a bloodbath when gentle giant Orson goes into berserker mode, and grown-up mage Slayn, also from series one, shows up with his wife and daughter in time to fill some of those expository gaps and get everyone organized into a dungeon party without too much bickering. Nothing much has changed in five years. There's another threat to the peace of the island and the

Yuratei, beautiful and deadly leader of the Hau Dragon combine, is bent on world domination; only psychological-wreck Masato Akitsu can stand in her way as the destined pilot of giant mech Zeorymer of the Heavens. Even the threat of nuclear destruction may be less powerful than Masato's own inner demons as he faces seven terrifying foes. In a deliberately dark touch, the hero's adversaries are not the customary invading aliens, but other human beings. *See entry p. 460.*

Zeorymer Hades Project

supremacy of Light. Parn still idolizes the ultracool "mercenary king" Kashue and has no idea how to handle women. Deedlit still isn't sure of their relationship after five *years* of adventuring together. The world is still a reactionary place where Kashue can urge Parn, with complete sincerity, to become a king so that he can have the pleasure of treating him as an equal, and the lip service paid to serious issues with a brief refugee crisis doesn't hold up the real, important action of suborning priests and killing dragons. Despite a wonderful opening sequence, *CotHK* contains all of its predecessor's low-budget faults without any of its earnest, adventuring virtues. Yet the original, loaded with atmosphere and style, still has magic.

RED BARON
1994. TV series. DIR: Akio Saga. SCR: Junji Takegami, Kazuhiko Kobe, et al. DES: Ryu Noguchi. ANI: Satoshi Hirayama. MUS: N/C. PRD: Tokyo Movie Shinsha, NTV. 25 mins. x 49 eps.
In the year 2020, the gladiatorial sport of Mecha Fighting (Metal Fighting in some sources) is the most popular spectator event. One hotheaded boy decides to become the champion pilot, operating his Red Baron robot against

all comers. A remake of a 1973 live-action series that featured men dressed up as giant robots—and they say there's no such thing as progress.

RED SHADOW

1987. JPN: *Kamen no Ninja Akakage*. AKA: *Masked Ninja Red Shadow*. TV series. DIR: Susumu Ishizaki, Kunihisa Sugishima, Tomoharu Katsumata, Kazuhisa Takenouchi. SCR: Yoshiyuki Suga, Toshiki Inoue, Asami Watanabe. DES: Akehiro Kaneyama. ANI: Akehiro Kaneyama, Michio Kondo. MUS: Shunsuke Kikuchi. PRD: Toei, Nippon TV. 25 mins. x 23 eps.

In medieval Japan, young temple boy Gennosuke disguises himself as the Red Shadow in order to fight the Cult of the Golden Eye, teaming up with color-coded allies that include the White and Blue Shadows. Another boy-ninja tale, this was one of the first "retro anime," since this nostalgic production was designed to remind parents of their own youth in 1967, when they could have read Mitsuteru Yokoyama's original manga and watched the live-action spinoff adventure TV series. The story was revived for Hiroyuki Nakano's live-action movie *Red Shadow* (2001).

REI REI *

1993. JPN: *Utsukishiki Sei no Dendoshi Rei Rei*. AKA: *Rei Rei the Sensual Evangelist*. Video. DIR: Yoshiki Yamamoto, Mihiro Yamaguchi. SCR: Michiru Mochizuki. DES: Kenichi Ishimaru. ANI: Oji Suzuki. MUS: Hiroyuki Ishizuka. PRD: KSS, AIC. 30 mins. x 2 eps.

Kaguya is a sexy spirit who wafts down from her home near the moon to solve sexual problems. Aided by cheeky goblin-cum-butler Pipi, she saves humanity from disaster by spreading the gospel of sexual freedom—as long as it's the freedom of *men* to have sex with whomever they choose, as long as they "really love" her. In the first story, schoolboy Mamoru lusts after arrogant Ikuko, who has no time for him since she has been corrupted by her lesbian teacher. Miss Manami, for her part,

lusts after hunky local doctor Okabe, deciding to kill Ikuko so she can run off with him. Kaguya doesn't save the girl, but she does show Manami and Okabe the error of their ways and ensures that Ikuko, now properly appreciative of Mamoru, is restored to life before her cremation. A final scene cut from the Japanese version during production showed Manami and Okabe getting their just desserts—each other.

Kaguya returns to help the nerdy Satoshi, a boy whose heart of gold is concealed under an obsession with astronomy that's boring his girlfriend Mika. No, Kaguya doesn't teach him social skills, just helps him "work through" his breast fixation, before turning him into bathwater so he can experience a girl up close. Everything works out in the end, but not before Satoshi is trapped inside a computer game, and Kaguya must endure the obligatory tentacle-rape to save him. Newly rejuvenated, Satoshi becomes a "real man" at last, ready to treat Mika in a fittingly dominant manner.

With an amusing pseudo-psychotherapy subplot and some semblance of a story, *Rei Rei* compares very favorably to the lackluster erotica of the decade that followed it—thus making it even more of a surprise that this picaresque porno did not return for more than just these two episodes. Based on a manga by **AIRBATS**-creator Toshimitsu Shimizu, *Rei Rei* draws distantly on the *Taketori Monogatari*, one of the more famous **JAPANESE FOLK TALES**—the story of celestial Princess Kaguya whose search for an Earthbound husband proved fruitless. The same legend was pastiched very differently in **QUEEN OF A THOUSAND YEARS** and **GU-GU GUNMO**. ◐

REIKO SHIRATORI I PRESUME

1990. JPN: *Shiratori Reiko de Gozaimasu*. AKA: *I'm Reiko Shiratori*. Video. DIR: Mitsuru Hongo. SCR: Ayako Okina. DES: Yumiko Suzuki. ANI: Keiko Hayashi, Takuya Saito. MUS: N/C. PRD: Asia-do. 40 mins.

Nineteen-year-old Reiko Shiratori is a true material girl, devoted to style, snobbery, and snide put-downs. Thanks to her rich family, she feels superior to everyone she meets, but her high-class schooling has not prepared her for affairs of the heart. Refusing to admit her feelings for classmate Tetsuya Akimoto before it is too late, Reiko pursues him to Tokyo, where she enrolls at his university to try and win him back. Rushed into production to cash in on the live-action TV drama, itself based on a manga by Yumiko Suzuki, *RSIP* encapsulates the spirit of the money-mad 1980s. Compare to the later **HIS AND HER CIRCUMSTANCES**, which also features a homecoming queen whose mask and halo slip.

RELIC ARMOR LEGACIUM

1987. Video. DIR: Hiroyuki Kitazume, Hideki Takayama. SCR: Akinori Endo. DES: Hiroyuki Kitazume, Hidetoshi Omori. ANI: Hiroyuki Kitazume. MUS: Tatsumi Yano. PRD: Atelier Giga. 50 mins.

The inhabitants of planet Libatia are under the mind control of the evil Daats. Professor Grace, escaping from this control, steals the giant robot Legacium and modifies it into a powerful weapon against them. When he is captured, his daughter Arushya manages to flee with the Legacium. Her friends Dorothy and Bric join her to fight Daats and liberate their homeworld.

RENTAMAN

1991. JPN: *Anime V Comic Rentaman*. Video. DIR: Takashi Watanabe, Osamu Tsuruyama, Masakazu Iijima, Eiko Toriumi. SCR: N/A. DES: N/A. ANI: N/A. MUS: N/A. PRD: Studio Pierrot. 74 mins. x 4 eps.

A short-lived, unrepeated experimental concept, *Rentaman* was a video magazine show serializing several short, episodic anime such as **ABASHIRI FAMILIES**, **AKAI HAYATE**, the comedy *Hisashi Eguchi's Hisagoro Show*, and the thriller *Baku Yumemakura's Twilight Theater*. The serials were later compiled into stand-alone tapes, though the episodic nature of their origins goes some way toward explaining the cut-up story-telling of the two available in English.

REPORTER BLUES

1990. TV series. DIR: Kenji Kodama. SCR: Ryuzo Nakanishi, Shuichi Miyashita. DES: Akio Sugino, Yukihiro Yokoyama. ANI: N/C. MUS: Pino Massara. PRD: TMS, Rever, RAI. 25 mins. x 52 eps.

Paris in the 1920s: Toni, a pretty young reporter for a daily newspaper, is crazy about the new jazz music that's sweeping Europe. In her spare time, she plays saxophone in a little jazz cellar. As she goes about her daily work, she keeps running across the trail of one woman, Madame Lapin, who seems to be a very respectable lady, wealthy and influential and yet also involved in other, more dubious events. Toni's nose for a story could get her into serious trouble as she uncovers clues to a dangerous game.

One of the many Japanese-Italian coproductions masterminded by SHER-LOCK HOUND's Marco Pagot, who co-wrote the story with his brother Gi, this ran for two 26-episode series. The jazzy score and attractive designs from the designer of COBRA and CAT'S EYE make it attractive despite the somewhat run-of-the-mill detective stories. Broadcast on Japan's second satellite TV channel in 1991, the series ran on French TV early in the 1990s, but its biggest success has been in Italy.

RG VEDA *

1991. JPN: *Seiden Rg Vega*. AKA: *Holy Scripture R(i)g Veda*. Video. DIR: Hiroyuki Ebata, Takamasa Ikegami. SCR: Nanase Okawa. DES: Mokono Apapa, Tetsuro Aoki, Kiichi Takaoka, Futoshi Fujikawa. ANI: Tetsuro Aoki. MUS: Nick Wood. PRD: Animate Film. 45 mins. x 2 eps.

Ashura the Lord of Heaven is betrayed by his wife and murdered by her lover, his chief general. The usurper rules for 300 years, until the day when the prophesied band of six warriors arrives to defeat him. But there are only five

of them, so they wander around a bit looking for the missing slowpoke, while various people go on about "things that shall be" and "that which is written." By the time they find the latecomer, it's time for the credits to roll.

Based on a manga by the CLAMP artistic collective who gave us CARDCAP-TORS, *RV* is one of many of their works that has been poorly served in anime form. Like many anime designed as ads for much longer manga (e.g., COMPIL-ER), *RV* finishes before it's even begun, with the band of heroes heading off to do great deeds, frustrating English-speaking fans who want to know how the story ends but cannot read the original.

The English dub uses genuinely British accents with mixed success; plummy goddesses ordering around minions sound rather good, but the iconoclastic gang of farting, bickering heroes seem like the Famous Five on safari. Although George Roubicek's script is fine, *Rg Veda* suffers (like many anime) from being transliterated instead of translated. The fact that we're watching a Japanese fantasy retelling of Hindu myth is interesting, but the script keeps names in their Japanese form, so we never find out that Taishakuten is really Indra, Karura is Garuda (see KARULA DANCES), Kujaku is Mahamayuri Vidyarajni (see PEACOCK KING), Kendappa is Gandharva, and Yasha is Yaksha. There are a few nice moments of fantasy, like the butterflies who are "messengers of darkness," and the mad Princess Aizen Myoo (Ragaraja, a red-skinned, three-eyed, six-armed *male* demon in the original), who imprisons Yasha in a castle of ice, but it's all been done better elsewhere—chiefly in the pious Indian coproduction RAMAYANA.

The production company pretentiously used Sanskrit orthography to write the title, not expecting the English distributors to mistake the opening two letters for initials—it's thus pronounced "Rig Veda" not "Argie Veda." *Ill. p. 185.*

RIDING BEAN *

1989. Video. DIR: Yasuo Hasegawa. SCR: Kenichi Sonoda. DES: Kenichi Sonoda, Kinji Yoshimoto, Satoshi Urushibara, L. Lime, Yoshihisa Fujita. ANI: Masahiro Tanaka, Osamu Kamijo, Hiroya Ohira, Jun Okuda. MUS: David Garfield, Phil Perry. PRD: Artmic, AIC. 45 mins.

Bean Bandit is known as the Road-buster; he's one of the best driver/couriers in the business. He makes a living on the outside edge of the law, but he's one of the good guys down deep, a true antihero with a heart of gold. He and his business partner, Rally Vincent, unwittingly get involved with psychotic kidnapper Semmerling, who sets them up to take the rap when her victim is killed, but they fight their way out in a hail of bullets and a screech of brakes. The story ends with nobody the winner and few survivors, but the kidnapper is "retired," permanently, and Bean and Rally live to keep on hustling.

This is one of the most interesting and watchable of anime actioners—made with a real love of Hollywood chase movies including *The Blues Brothers*, *Bullitt*, and *The French Connection*. Watch, too, for Japanese references to such anime as LUPIN III, especially in the cat-and-mouse relationship of cop and criminal. Some of the best car chases in anime are routed along the streets of Sonoda's beloved city of Chicago. Director Hasegawa also lets the darker side of Sonoda's manga show through the lighthearted take on an American genre; the violence and amorality of Semmerling's lifestyle are real and chilling, and her abusive, sadomasochistic relationship with an adoring child-slave is clearly spelled out without any need for sexual explicitness. Following the same studio disputes that truncated BUBBLEGUM CRISIS, ownership of the *Riding Bean* property became difficult to determine, and the franchise seemed finished. However, Sonoda recycled some of the characters and situations in his later GUNSMITH CATS—a radically different Rally becomes a bounty hunter, the child-sex subplot returns in the form of her partner Minnie May, and Bean himself has many cameo roles in the manga, though he does not appear in the anime. ⓁⓋ

RINGING BELL *

1978. JPN: *Chirin no Suzu*. AKA: *Chirin's Bell*. Movie. DIR: Masami Hata. SCR: Takashi Yanase. DES: Takashi Yanase. ANI: Shigeru Yamamoto, Sadao Miyamoto, Toshio Hirata. MUS: Taku Izumi. PRD: Sanrio. 46 mins.
Chirin the lamb is orphaned when the bad wolf Wor (the "Wolf King" in the U.S. dub) kills his mother. Chirin sets out for revenge but has a change of heart. Despairing of his weak nature, he begs the wolf to teach him how to be tough and learns how to be a predator from his parent's killer. Battered, bruised, and half drowned, the lamb is put through a heartless regime of torment until he is toughened into a vicious ram with a "reputation for ruthless killing." Two years later, Chirin is led by Wor in an attack on the farm where he was born. Seeing a ewe vainly fighting to protect her offspring, Chirin is reminded of his mother and turns on the wolf—killing his surrogate father. However, the rest of the flock is afraid of Chirin, and he remains an outcast, forced now to wander without any companionship at all. Chirin is "never seen again," though it is said that sometimes the sheep hear the distant tinkle of the bell around his neck.
A mind-bogglingly disturbing "children's film" that makes *Bambi* look like a comedy, ANPANMAN-creator Takashi Yanase's children's book is an unexpectedly nasty outing for the HELLO KITTY studio Sanrio, featuring sing-along lyrics such as "We will travel, wolf and ram, and we'll ravage all the land." Ⓥ

RISE AND FALL OF THE DINOSAUR KINGDOM, THE

1976. JPN: *Kyoryu Okoku no Kobo*. TV series. DIR: Eiichi Yamamoto. SCR: Eiichi Yamamoto. DES: Shigeo Itahashi. ANI:

N/C. MUS: Hiroki Takaragi. PRD: Eizo Kiroku, Yomiuri TV, Nippon TV. 25 mins. x 6 eps.
After the first life forms evolve on Earth, the world explodes into giant, terrifying action as the dinosaurs arrive. They are the strongest, largest creatures ever to walk on land; their achievements are chronicled in this brief documentary series that mixes diagrams, live-action photography (*not* of dinosaurs), and disappointingly cartoony dinosaur animation closer to *Barney* than *Jurassic Park*.

ROBIN HOOD

1990. JPN: *Robin Hood no Daiboken*. AKA: *Great Adventures of Robin Hood; Robin Hood Junior*. TV series. DIR: Koichi Mashimo. SCR: Tsunehisa Ito, Katsuhiko Chiba, Hiroyuki Kawasaki. DES: Masamitsu Kudo, Tomohiro Hirata, Torao Arai. ANI: Masamitsu Kudo, Chuichi Iguchi. MUS: Fuminori Iwasaki. PRD: NEP, NHK, Tatsunoko. 25 mins. x 52 eps. (TV), 75 mins. (m).
In 12th-century England, the evil Baron Alwine and Abbot Hereford are in league with the devil in their quest for power. Alwine burns the entire Huntingdon family in their castle; only 14-year-old Robin and his three cousins Will, Winifred, and Barbara escape into the forest where they meet Friar Tuck, an old friend of Robin's father. He guides and protects the young orphans as best he can, and when they meet Little John and his band of teenage outlaws, they determine to fight for justice. The beautiful Marian Lancaster, daughter of a noble family, is kidnapped by the abbot, supposedly for marriage but really because he needs the crucifix she wears around her neck to unlock the magical secrets of Sherwood. Robin, Will, and Little John rescue Marian; then the refugees stay in the forest and fight the baron's agents, chiefly Gilbert, the Knight of the Black Rose, who is Robin's rival for Marian's love. A character of contradictions, Gilbert is a good man bound to serve Alwine because the baron saved his sister's life.

Originally broadcast in a 39-episode run, extra episodes were made for the overseas market, particularly Italy and Germany, where the series was a great success. Though written by Tatsunoko producer Ippei Kuri, *RH* claimed to rely on the legend as retold by *Ivanhoe*-creator Walter Scott. It was the first of Tatsunoko's 1990s "fairy tale" series and was soon followed by the same studio's SNOW WHITE. Part of the story was also released as a feature-length movie edit.

ROBIN JUNIOR

1989. JPN: *Seisenshi Robin Jr*. AKA: *Holy Warrior Robin Jr*. TV series. DIR: Masaharu Okuwaki. SCR: Hideki Sonoda, Satoru Nishizono. DES: Minoru Maeda, Satoshi Hirayama. ANI: Kazuyoshi Takeuchi. MUS: Hiroyuki Nanba. PRD: Tokyo Movie Shinsha, TV Tokyo. 25 mins. x 24 eps.
A set of superheroes modeled, as in the case of BIKKURIMAN, on the characters found on packets of candy. Their mission is to fight the attractively labeled Dark Power, a race of aliens intent on conquering the solar system.

ROBOT CARNIVAL *

1987. Video. DIR: Katsuhiro Otomo, Atsuko Fukushima, Hiroyuki Kitazume, Mao Lamdo, Hideyuki Omori, Koji Morimoto, Yasuomi Umezu, Hiroyuki Kitakubo, Takashi Nakamura. SCR: Katsuhiro Otomo, Atsuko Fukushima, Hiroyuki Kitazume, Mao Lamdo, Hideyuki Omori, Koji Morimoto, Yasuomi Umezu, Hiroyuki Kitakubo, Takashi Nakamura. DES: Katsuhiro Otomo, Atsuko Fukushima, Hiroyuki Kitazume, Mao Lamdo, Hideyuki Omori, Koji Morimoto, Yasuomi Umezu, Hiroyuki Kitakubo, Takashi Nakamura. ANI: Katsuhiro Otomo, Atsuko Fukushima, Hiroyuki Kitazume, Mao Lamdo, Hideyuki Omori, Koji Morimoto, Yasuomi Umezu, Hiroyuki Kitakubo, Takashi Nakamura. MUS: Joe Hisaishi, Isaku Fujita, Masahisa Takeshi. PRD: APPP. 90 mins.
This anthology of robot stories is a sampler for some of the big names of

anime and an excellent example of how one theme can be approached in a variety of different ways both in terms of script and design. It's also one of the easiest anime to show to foreign audiences because it has very little dialogue and lots of visual variety. The opening and closing sequences by Otomo and Fukushima take a wry look at what can happen when a seductive new diversion hits a tiny, poor community. A gigantic mechanical carnival rolls into town, a tinsel juggernaut crushing everything in its tracks, all bells and whistles and '30s-style dancing puppets, providing an opportunity for pure whiz-bang pyrotechnics on the part of the animators. The machine itself forms the title lettering, a neat conceit. At the end of the movie, this shimmering shrine to trash self-destructs taking the open-mouthed peasants with it. Kitazume's *Starlight Angel* is a boy-meets-girl-meets-giant-robot love story set in an amusement park and steeped in the style and atmosphere of the early 1980s; all the characters could have stepped straight out of the **Gundam** universe. Mao's *Cloud* is a more abstract piece whose narrative is buried in a series of beautiful, slow-moving images and hypnotic music, as a childlike robot walks slowly through a gathering storm into sunlight. Its purposely retro pencil-sketch and simple monotone pencil-sketch style look surprisingly contemporary in the 21st century. *Deprive* by Omori is another boy-girl-robot romance though with more of a heavy-metal edge. A young girl is torn from the arms of a handsome young man and kidnapped by an evil entity in KISS-type makeup. To rescue her, he must become his true self—a robot. Morimoto's *Franken's Gears* is a funny, quirky look at the limitations of science, in which an inventor overlooks the importance of tidiness and attention to detail and wrecks his own experiment. Kitakubo's *Tale of Two Robots* is a slapstick take on nationalism; a Japanese robot made of wood and operated by a band of kids must fight off the evil intentions of a mad

white scientist and his brick-built alien war machine. *Nightmare* by Nakamura will make you very, very worried about being stranded in town after a drinking binge, as the detritus of urban life takes on ominous new shapes, and a drunk who misses his last train home is forced to watch their rampage and flee their strange leader. Umezu's *Presence* is the crown of a superb collection, a gem of a love story wrapped in a fable about the obsolescence of both people and technology and the responsibilities of the creator to his creation, enhanced by a seductive score whose main theme is unforgettable. The dialogue for this segment was dubbed into laughable "British" by Americans, which is unfortunate, but that's the only flaw in a superbly watchable film that is aging very gracefully, especially in comparison with some of the over-hyped new material. Compare to the same year's **Neo Tokyo** and the later "showcase" anime **Memories**.

ROBOT KING DAIOJA

1981. JPN: *Saikyu Robo Daioja*. AKA: *Strongest Robot Daioja*. TV series. DIR: Katsuyoshi Sasaki. SCR: Hiroyuki Hoshiyama, Yoshihisa Araki, Tsunehisa Ito, Akifumi Yoshida, Kosuke Yoshida, Sukehiro Tomita. DES: Nobuyoshi Sasaemon, Kunio Okawara, Yutaka Izubuchi. ANI: Akehiro Kaneyama. MUS: Michiaki Watanabe. PRD: Sunrise, TV Asahi. 25 mins. x 50 eps.

In the Edon protectorate of some 50 planets, the heir to the throne must make a grand tour of his realm at age 16, the better to serve his subjects. Traveling with Prince Edward Mito are Baron Kaikusu, Duke Skead, and female ninja Flora Shinobu. In their travels they run across many foul plots (the deadliest of which comes in the latter episodes, aimed at the heart of the monarchy itself!) that they unravel in the name of Mito's father, King Tokugar. At these times, Mito's, Kaikusu's, and Skead's small robots combine into one larger unit with the symbol of Edon on its chest—Robot King Daioja.

Mukuzo Imokawa the Doorman

With a federation name that's a pun on Edo and a ruler's that's a pun on Tokugawa, *RKD* was inspired in part by the long-running samurai show *Mito Komon* (see **Manga Mito Komon**). *RKD* used many of the staff from **Unchallengeable Trider G7**, but this show represents the end of the early Sunrise "combining robot" era that began with **Zambot 3**. Sunrise wouldn't produce anything comparable until *Exkaiser* launched the **Brave Saga** in 1990.

ROBOTAN *

1966. TV series. DIR: Hiroshi Ono. SCR: Tsuyoshi Danjo, Takuya Yamaguchi, Kasei Matsubara, Renso Agishita, Takashi Taka. DES: Moriyasu Taniguchi, et al. ANI: Moriyasu Taniguchi. MUS: Robotan Group. PRD: Ohiro, Fuji TV. 25 mins. x 104 eps., 25 mins. x 33 eps. Based on a manga by Kenji Morita, the series revolves around alien household robot Robotan, who comes from planet Roborobo and lives with an everyday Japanese family as a domestic servant and friend to the children. Like **Doraemon**, his good intentions don't always work out, with comic consequences. The original series was made in Osaka by the short-lived Ohiro Planning. Production moved to Tokyo Movie Shinsha for the 20th-anniversary color remake *New Robotan* (1986) under director Masaharu Okuwaki.

ROBOTECH *

1985. JPN: N/A. TV series, video. DIR: Robert Barron, Jim Wager. SCR: Gregory Snegoff, Robert Barron, Greg Finlay, Steve Kramer, Mike Reynolds, Steve Flood, Ardwight Chamberlain. DES: (see original shows). ANI: (see original shows). MUS: Ulpio Minucci. PRD: Tatsunoko Productions, Harmony Gold. 25 mins. x 85 eps. (TV), 80 mins., 90 mins.

In 1999, a giant alien battlecruiser crashes on Earth. The human race decides to stop fighting each other and unite in case the aliens ever come looking for their missing ship. Ten years on, the ship has been renamed the SDF-1 and reconstructed, but the global celebrations are interrupted by an alien attack. Earth's forces under Captain Gloval fight off the threat. As the SDF-1 attempts to save Earth, it uses its untested Spacefold drive and is transported deep into space, where it must fight a prolonged war with the invading Zentraedi fleet. Young pilot Rick Hunter finds himself in a complex triangular relationship with two very different women, ship's officer Lisa Hayes and singing star Lynn Minmay. After 36 episodes, known as the **MACROSS SAGA**, encounters with giant aliens, and big emotional tangles, the soap-in-space ended with the devastation of Earth and the deaths of several important characters. Fifteen years on, the story takes a new turn with the *Robotech Masters* saga. Rick Hunter has set off in SDF-3 to find the world of the Robotech Masters, but the Masters themselves are already heading the other way. Young cadet Dana Sterling, offspring of the first interspecies marriage, is thrown into the thick of the fighting when the Robotech Masters attack Earth in search of their lost "protoculture factory." She and her young comrades encounter a strange man who has spent years with the invaders and whose motives are unclear, but who finally destroys his

own culture to save them. In the interval between this Second Robotech War and the third season, New Generation, the Invid aliens arrive and conquer Earth. Terran defenders are too exhausted to resist, but a generation later, Scott Bernard and his reinforcements arrive to try and liberate their homeworld. Their task seems hopeless, but if they can somehow contact Admiral Rick Hunter and link up with his space fleet, Earth may have a chance.

The *Robotech* phenomenon is a curious hybrid of Japanese material and American ambition.

Originally conceived as a U.S. video release, it was handed to Carl Macek to dub, and the first *Macross* tape, starring Japanese-American hero "Rick Yamada," was premiered at the 1984 World SF Convention. However, Harmony Gold made further deals to bring the show to TV and asked Macek to find a way of expanding it beyond 36 episodes, which is too small for TV syndication. He acquired **SOUTHERN CROSS** and **MOSPEADA** from the same studio, providing another 49 half-hour episodes of *similar* design and background. Macek renamed many of the characters, creating cross-generational links that were absent in the completely unlinked original series, and devised the concept of an ancient alien technology that could generate robots and weapons for space combat, rooted in a mysterious concept called "protoculture." The model-kit company Revell, owners of the *Macross* merchandise rights, already had a trademark line called *Robotech*, and a tie-in was born. The *Robotech* line, having been established before the series was conceived, included robots from shows not involved in Macek's rewrite, like **DOUGRAM** and **ORGUSS**, and did not include anything from *Southern Cross* or *Mospeada*.

The success of the concept led to the construction of *Robotech the Movie*, a dub for the U.S. market of the first part of **MEGAZONE 23**. Since this had absolutely nothing to do with the characters or story lines of any of the three

original series, it was presented as a "side story" happening within the chronology of the Robotech Wars. Extra footage was animated for the film in Japan and included as a bonus on the Japanese *Megazone 23* release.

The story was to have continued in a fourth segment focusing on the forgotten SDF-3. Though all 65 episodes were written for a Japanese-American coproduction, the project was never completed. The footage already shot (four partly completed episodes plus other material) was used to make up a single feature-length video, *Robotech II—The Sentinels*, the last animated installment of the saga.

Robotech gained such a hold on its American fans that it spun off into print with greater success. A series of novels by Jack McKinney (a pseudonym for James Luceno and Brian Daley) fills in many narrative gaps and explores many of the minor characters in greater depth, while *Robotech* comics have been produced by four different publishers over 14 years. Many of the comics and novels are based on the completed scripts for *Sentinels*, even though most were never filmed. The "close" of the *Robotech* saga is the final novel, *End of the Circle*. Similar recycling went on in Japan, where Tatsunoko placed some of the unused designs in the unrelated **ZILLION**.

Robotech attracts passionate response; fans either love or loathe it. Like **NAUSICAÄ**'s U.S. reedit, it is variously viewed as a welcome adaptation of unfamiliar material for a new, less adventurous audience, or a watered-down travesty of its origins. Its supporters cite a complex story line with material rarely seen in U.S. animation—the unexpected deaths of much-loved characters, the fact that the good guys (humans) usually ended up losing, or even the introduction of a cross-dressing hero. Its detractors point out that all this was present in the original Japanese series and that the destruction of the internal logic and character relationships was unnecessary and excessive. The best way to describe it is probably not as anime but as an American reworking of the Japanese original, but, unlike most palimpsests, enough of the original text remains to entice viewers back to the source material.

ROKUDENASHI BLUES

1992. JPN: *Rokudenashi Blues*. Movie. DIR: Takao Yoshisawa. SCR: Yoshiyuki Suga. DES: Masanori Morita. ANI: Yoshitaka Yashima. MUS: Fuminori Iwasaki. PRD: Toei. 25 mins.

A short "movie" based on Masanori Morita's 1988 manga in *Shonen Jump* magazine, in which Taison Maeda determines to be the toughest kid in his school, ruling over his fellow students with the power of his fists. Another distant homage to the U.S. boxer Mike Tyson was carefully buried in **STREET FIGHTER II**.

ROLLING RYOTA

1990. Video. DIR: Masamune Ochiai. SCR: Yuki Kuroiwa. DES: Shinichi Nagasawa. ANI: Natsuki Aikawa, Shinichi Nagasawa. MUS: N/C. PRD: Knack. 45 mins. x 3 eps.

Former biker Takao Ryota becomes a bus driver, causing havoc in the streets by racing his bus against other vehicles. This anime was based on a manga by Hiroyuki Murata, who also created **VOLLEY BOYS**. Ryota, who supports a distinctive gangster punch-perm hairstyle, was originally voiced by Jutaro Kosugi, but he was replaced by Hiroya Ishimaru, the voice of Koji Kabuto in **MAZINGER Z**. ◎◐◑

ROMEO'S BLUE SKY

1995. JPN: *Romeo no Aoi Sora*. AKA: *Romeo and the Black Brothers*. TV series. DIR: Kozo Kusuba, Shinpei Miyashita, Yasuo Iwamoto, Tomomitsu Matsukawa. SCR: Michiru Shimada. DES: Yoshiharu Sato. ANI: Yoshiharu Sato, Ei Inoue, Katsu Oshiro, Masaki Abe. MUS: Kei Wakakusa. PRD: Nippon Animation, Fuji TV. 25 mins. x 33 eps.

Romeo lives happily with his family in the Swiss Alps until a series of crop failures and his father's illness bring about tragic changes. To save his loved ones

from ruin, he sells himself into slavery for 25 francs to Luini, called "God of Death," who travels poor country districts searching for child laborers to fuel the growing cities of Europe. He is taken to Milan and sold to a chimney-sweep, and so becomes one of the "Black Brothers," the boys who keep the city's chimneys clear in great hardship. On the way he meets Alfredo, a boy with a mysterious past whose main aim in life is to find his beloved little sister, Bianca, and the two boys become close friends. In Milan he meets the fragile Angeletta, but her brother Anselmo is part of a local gang, the Wolf Pack, and despite Romeo's overtures of friendship, Anselmo begins a gang war. The Wolf Pack are not the only ones out for blood, as Alfredo is threatened by those who know his secret and will stop at nothing to prevent him claiming his rightful inheritance.

The story was based on the 1941 novel *The Black Brothers* (*Die Schwarzen Brüder*) by Lisa Tetzner, a German forced to flee the Nazi regime to Switzerland because of her husband's Marxist leanings. She wrote her book to highlight the real-life scandal of child slavery in Europe—compare to **24 EYES**, a similar protest. The anime adapted the story freely, though it retained the basic elements of the typical **WORLD MASTERPIECE THEATER** production—a classic tale of emotion and melodrama, set at a safe distance in time and space, with vulnerable but heroic young people enduring testing times in the struggle for survival. The lead character's name was changed from Giorgio, new characters were added, and the plot and conclusion altered, partly to fit a schedule originally planned for 39 episodes but finally forced to squeeze the story into 33. *Ill. p. 99.*

RONIN WARRIORS *

1989. JPN: *Yoiroden Samurai Troopers*. AKA: *Armor Legend Samurai Troopers; Samurai Troopers*. TV series, video. DIR: Makoto Ikeda, Mamoru Hamazu.

SCR: Junzo Toriumi, Yuki Onishi. DES: Norio Shioyama, Hideo Okamoto, Yusho Okada. ANI: Norio Shioyama, Kisaraka Yamada. MUS: Osamu Tezuka. PRD: Sunrise, Nagoya TV. 25 mins. x 39 eps. (TV), 30 mins. x 3 eps. (v1), 30 mins. x 4 eps. (v2), 30 mins. x 5 eps. (v3).

SAINT SEIYA-style action, as the evil Lord Arago (Talpa in the U.S.) sends denizens of the Phantom World to invade Earth, and five teenage pretty-boys are given mystic suits of samurai armor that will enhance their own natural gifts, enabling them to fight back. Wildfire Ryo, Torrent Shin (Cye), Halo Seiji (Sage), Strata Toma (Rowen), and Hardrock Shu (Kento) can unite their suits to form Hariel's White Armor of Fervor. But Arago has already infiltrated the whole world. The boys' suits, plus all those worn by Arago's champions, are parts of a single incredibly powerful battle armor, broken up when Arago was defeated eons ago; now he wants to reunite them and make sure his conquest can't be overturned. The team members must overcome their own fears and weaknesses and face terrible dangers—their friends, too, are liable to be used by Arago as bait or bribes.

Looking suspiciously like an entire unbroadcast season cut into sections, the adventures continued on video with Mamoru Hamazu's *ST: Extra Story* (1989), in which our heroes go to the U.S. to investigate a mysterious news report that may point to new activity from Arago. One of them is captured and tortured by a demon who has teamed up with a human scientist to find the secrets of the Troopers' armor and use them to take over all five suits. A second series, *ST: Empire Legend* (1989), contains another tale of courage against supernatural evil, this time in Africa. In a kabuki-themed story arc redolent of **GASARAKI**, the final adventure of Makoto Ikeda's *ST: Message* (1991) has the boys returning to Japan to investigate mysterious forces at work in Shinjuku. While other members of the team face off against their female adversary Suzunagi, Seiji discovers evidence of an Edo-period play about "five boy warriors."

The series was screened as *Ronin Warriors* (1995) on American TV, with a title change occasioned by two other similarly named shows on the air at the time. Its Japanese origins remain clear, with onscreen Japanese text left in place and the lead character's name unchanged. It's very violent by U.S. standards even though there are few flesh-and-blood casualties, and the overall atmosphere of cruelty and menace is very powerful. **V**

ROOTS SEARCH *

1986. JPN: *Roots Search: Shokushin Buttai X*. AKA: *Roots Search: Life Devourer X*. Video. DIR: Hisashi Sugai, Hiroshi Negishi. SCR: Michiru Shimada. DES: Sanae Kobayashi, Yasushi Moriki. ANI: Sanae Kobayashi. MUS: N/C. PRD: Production Wave. 45 mins.
The Tolmeckius Research Institute is impressed with its latest find, a psychic girl called Moira, who astounds them all when she starts experiencing terrible visions. When the orbital station is approached by a runaway ship, Moira's insight reveals that all is not as it seems. The ship has been occupied by a fearsome alien intelligence that mentally tortures its victims until they beg for the release of death. When the creature proves to be invincible, Moira resolves to make the ultimate sacrifice, although even death, it seems, cannot end the suffering.

There are shades of the more recent hit EVANGELION in this SF tale that mixes Biblical elements with an *Alien* pastiche and a far more sinister interpretation of "God's" purpose. But that is where the resemblance ends for this creaky anime, unreleased in English until 1992, a time on the shelf that did not find it aging gracefully. **O**

ROSE OF VERSAILLES

1979. JPN: *Versailles no Bara*. AKA: *Lady Oscar*. TV series. DIR: Tadao Nagahama, Osamu Dezaki, Yasuo Yamakichi, Minoru Okazaki, Tetsuo Imazawa, Akinori Nagaoka. SCR: Yoshimi Shinozaki, Masahiro Yamada, Yukio Sugie, Hajime Hazama. DES: Shingo Araki, Michi Himeno, Akio Sugino, Ken Kawai, Tadao Kubota. ANI: Shingo Araki, Michi Himeno. MUS: Koji Makaino. PRD: Tokyo Movie Shinsha, Nippon TV. 25 mins. x 40 eps.
In 18th-century France: revolution is in the air, but for Oscar François de Jarjayes, the ties of tradition are all-powerful. Only child of an ancient family, she is given a man's name at birth and becomes the son her father wants. She succeeds so completely that she is soon one of the best fencers in France, promoted to Captain of the Guard of Marie Antoinette, Austrian child-wife of the Crown Prince. Both Oscar and Antoinette are women alone, forced into roles they did not choose and barred from love by duty. The Crown Princess of France loves a foreign nobleman, while the Captain of the Guard loves a childhood friend who is also a servant of her family. Both loves seem doomed, but both women must continue to live artificial public lives concealing real private agonies. A tangle of fascinating subplots and well-developed supporting characters, some historical and some invented, make this one of the most powerful and credible of anime TV series. As in Riyoko Ikeda's original 1972 manga, the sublime tale of love and loss ends with Antoinette going to the scaffold and Oscar leaving her life behind to share the struggle for freedom with her beloved André, dying in the assault on the Bastille.

Yet the two deaths are very different. Oscar's is a triumph of the human spirit, Antoinette's a failure. By stealing private happiness while supporting the feudal system that imprisons her as surely as the peasants, the proud, brave Antoinette has colluded in the lies and injustices that have made revolution inevitable. She dies because of her public role as a glittering cog in an increasingly useless machine, but in finally rejecting a system that separates people with artificial barriers of rank and property, Oscar asserts her own right to be fully human, regardless of gender or status. She dies, not because of, but rather *for* who and what she is. This cleverly subverts the familiar format of forbidden love between beautiful men (which would give birth to the *shonen ai* manga genre) by making one of the pair a woman, but one so gifted in traditionally "masculine" skills that the idea of a truly equal relationship, with no element of dependency or weakness, can still be maintained.

The renowned Araki/Himeno team transformed Ikeda's black-and-white manga art into a colorful fantasy, and while the action is played strong, the romance is played with delicacy and pathos, keeping melodrama in check. Its roots are clearly in Tezuka's magical PRINCESS KNIGHT, and its influence is still strong in the 1990s TV hit UTENA. It is so popular in France that it is still screened regularly on French TV. A live-action musical version is the jewel in the crown of Japan's Takarazuka theater troupe. *Rose of Versailles* deserves its classic rank. Despite its age and technical deficiencies, it still delivers powerful entertainment.

ROUGE

1997. JPN: *Ladies' Comic Video Rouge*. Movie. DIR: N/C. SCR: Haruko Kanzaki, Mizuki Iwase, Kei Misugi, Chika Taniguchi. DES: Haruko Kanzaki, Mizuki Iwase, Kei Misugi, Chika Taniguchi. ANI: N/C. MUS: N/C. PRD: Komine Communications. 40 mins. x 2 eps.
Bereaved strangers lose themselves in a sordid double life of prostitution but find love with each other. A loveless marriage blossoms through bondage. A trainee gets more than she bargained for when the head nurse takes the biology lesson to the limit. And a male beautician uses unorthodox methods to put color in a makeup artist's cheeks. Four erotically charged tales animated for a female audience, based on stories originally printed in the manga magazine *Rouge*. **N**

ROUJIN Z *

1991. AKA: *Old Man Z.* Movie. DIR: Hiroyuki Kitakubo. SCR: Katsuhiro Otomo. DES: Hisashi Eguchi. ANI: Satoshi Kon. MUS: Bun Itakura. PRD: APPP. 80 mins.
Old Mr. Takizawa, unable to care for himself, is selected as the guinea pig for an experimental robot bed designed to administer to his every need. Despite the protests of his nurse Haruko, the project gets underway, but the patient proves to be more trouble than he's worth when he decides to take a trip to the seaside. The bed's true purpose becomes apparent; it's not for the care of the elderly at all, it's the prototype for a military model designed to revolutionize modern warfare. But with Mr. Takizawa at the controls, even the defanged civilian version manages to wreak considerable havoc, with the help of an ornery gang of geriatric hackers and despite the army's efforts to stop it. The ending, an **AKIRA** pastiche in which an ambulance is riddled with cybernetic tentacles, is followed by a surprise, which, on repeat viewing, you will see was planned all along.

There aren't many anime that begin with an old man wetting himself, but that's part of *Roujin Z's* originality. **AKIRA**-creator Otomo took a back seat for this satire on the developed world's aging population, limiting himself to script and design duties. Ridiculing the health service as **HUMMINGBIRDS** lampooned the privatization of the military, *Roujin Z* is entertaining and thought-provoking, with a witty script in the English-language version from George Roubicek. Arguably a superior story, it's fated to remain in *Akira's* shadow owing to a drastically smaller animation budget. Watch for some clever touches, such as an underground battle lit in old-fashioned sepia tones and artificial scan lines on a TV screen, showing real attention to detail. Satoshi Kon worked on the backgrounds and later put this experience of designing lived-in environments to good use as the director of **PERFECT BLUE**.

RUIN EXPLORERS *

1995. JPN: *Hikyo Tantei Fam and Ihrlie.* AKA: *Ruin Explorers Fam and Ihrlie.* Video. DIR: Takeshi Mori. SCR: Takeshi Mori. DES: Toshihisa Umitani. ANI: Toshihisa Umitani, Yoshiaki Yanagida, Takuya Saito. MUS: Masamichi Amano. PRD: Animate Film, Asia-do. 30 mins. x 4 eps.
In a world filled with the relics of fallen civilizations, elf-catgirl Fam and her human companion Ihrlie search for a treasure known as the Ultimate Power. They meet Galuf, a traveler who claims to have a map revealing its location. Since Fam finds it hard to stay focused for more than a few seconds and Ihrie has a "horrible curse," it seems less than likely they will succeed, even if they weren't facing some stiff competition from the greatest evil wizard who ever lived. But they have a serious motive that says more about their friendship than their constant bickering. The Ultimate Power is the only thing that can free Ihrlie from her curse and enable her to fulfill her great magical potential. When she was a young apprentice, her carelessness so annoyed her teacher that he cast a spell to prevent her from using her powers. Every time she does so, she transforms out of human shape. She's been avoiding the problem by taking magical pills that enable her to transform back again, but they're almost all used up, so she can only use her magic in dire emergencies. They usually have to rely on Fam's less powerful magic instead.

Galuf, a sleazy merchant out for treasure himself, is terrified of the various traps and defenses around the Ultimate Power, and he wants our heroines to go in there first. He also hires a crack pair of ruin explorers, sorceress Rasha and swordsman Migel, to make sure the Ultimate Power winds up in his hands. But the Ultimate Power alone won't actually do anything; it must be combined with a magic sword and mirror. Handsome Prince Lyle also wants the Ultimate Power, but for unselfish ends—to fight Rugodorull, a wise cleric corrupted by Dark Powers.

In this publicity shot—the scene never appears in the movie—Lupin is in trouble, which is his natural habitat. Hayao Miyazaki's first movie as writer/director is full of hair-raising moments, and even contains a tiny cameo role (as a Japanese Interpol delegate) by a character with a suspicious resemblance to 1970s photos of the man himself. The French stories starring **LUPIN THE MASTERTHIEF** provided some plot elements, but the design of the heroine, Clarisse, is pure Miyazaki. *CoC* is widely regarded as the best of the **LUPIN III** series, which continues to make annual appearances on television to this day. *See entry p. 56.*

Castle of Cagliostro

Rugodorull has killed everyone else in Lyle's homeland and now wants to destroy all life on Earth. The six finally agree to work together to defeat Rugodorull. Their quest takes them across the seas to a magic island as they try to collect the items that will enable them to summon the Ultimate Power and save the world.

This D&D-style adventure was based on characters created by Kunihiko Tanaka for *Hobby Japan* magazine; compare its more successful contemporary, the lighthearted fantasy **SLAYERS**. The four episodes were released on two tapes by U.S. label ADV, which subtitled the first *Tales IN the Crypt* while the second is *Ruin Explorers 2: Profits and Prophecies.*

RUN MELOS

1981. JPN: *Hashire Melos.* AKA: *Run for Life.* TV special, movie, video. DIR: Tomoharu Katsumata. SCR: Keinosuke Uekusa. DES: Toshio Mori. ANI: Toshio Mori. MUS: Katsuhiro Tsuboiri. PRD: Toei, Visual 80, Fuji TV. 87 mins. (TV), 107 mins. (m).
Melos is a simple Sicilian farmer traveling to see his sister's wedding when he is sentenced to death by Dionysius, the tyrant of Syracuse. He asks for a few days' grace to go to the wedding and

promises to return immediately. The king agrees, but only if Melos can provide a hostage to guarantee his return—to be executed in his place if he fails. His old friend Selinuntius volunteers, and Melos sets off for the wedding. Despite many misadventures and temptations along the way, Melos keeps his word and returns in the nick of time. Dionysius is so impressed by Melos' honesty and Selinuntius' trust in him that he frees them both.

Osamu Dazai's 1940 short story was based on Greek legend filtered through a poem by Schiller, but it has become a classic of *Japanese* literature. The simple story, hinging on the nature of friendship and the ability to keep faith, has a happy resolution that is bitterly ironic when one remembers that Dazai committed suicide.

Toei's TV special was followed in 1992 by a longer theatrical release directed and written by Masaaki Osumi. Despite the overall simplicity of the story, he manages to infuse the film with real tension and urgency, and he has excellent art direction and design to support his work, from the future directors of **PERFECT BLUE** and **JIN-ROH**, Satoshi Kon and Hiroyuki Okiura. Melos runs through ravishing backgrounds by Hiroshi Ono, whose talents also enhance such stellar titles as **KIKI'S DELIVERY SERVICE** and have recently been put to use by Hollywood on *The Tigger Movie*. This movie version was former pop idol Kazumasa Oda's first anime score and also a voice-acting debut for the singer Akina Nakamori, who played Melos' sister. The story was animated twice more for video—for the *Classic Children's Tales* series (1992), as a 30-minute stop-motion short, and again for the *Famous Japanese Fables* series (1997), as a 10-minute short directed by Keisuke Morishita.

RUN=DIM

2001. TV series. DIR: Yasunori Kato. SCR: Shingo Kuwana, Yasunori Kato. DES: Yoshiaki Sato. ANI: N/C. MUS: N/C. PRD: Idea Factory, TV Tokyo. 25 mins. x 12+ eps.

In the 21st century, much of Japan lies underwater after a rise in sea levels. The nation becomes more expansionist in its outlook as it loses more *Lebensraum*, and JESAS, an arm of the military, is implicated in a corruption scandal. Green Frontier, an international ecology organization, discovers that JESAS has been earning foreign currency by taking nuclear disposal contracts but then illegally dumping the waste in space. After such promising sub-**PATLABOR** beginnings, the two sides then start fighting each other with giant robots piloted by 14-year-old children. It's 3-D CG, so the look changes for a new century, if not the plot.

RUNE SOLDIER

2001. JPN: *Maho Senshi Riui*. AKA: *Magical Soldier Riui*. TV series. DIR: Sadamune Koyama. SCR: Katsuhiko Chiba, Nobuaki Kishima, Jiro Takayama. DES: Kazushi Iwaguro. ANI: Yuki Kinoshita. MUS: N/C. PRD: JC Staff, WOWOW. 25 mins. x 24 eps.

Warrior Riui is forced to share his quest with three pretty girls, Melissa, Mirelle, and Janny, in a combination of the role-playing-inspired fantasy adventure of **SLAYERS** with the boy-meets-babes setup of **TENCHI MUYO!** Created by **RECORD OF LODOSS WAR**'s Ryo Mizuno, who should have known better.

RUNNING BOY

1986. JPN: *Running Boy Star Soldier no Himitsu*. AKA: *Running Boy: Secrets of Star Soldier*. Movie. DIR: Tameo Ogawa. SCR: Junichi Ishihara, Kasumi Oka. DES: Oji Suzuki. ANI: Oji Suzuki, Hidemi Kamata. MUS: Yoichi Takahashi. PRD: Toho, Film Link International. 49 mins. Genta Shinoyama is a kindhearted boy and video-game freak who helps drunken Nomoto in the street. Nomoto, a programmer for a major games company, befriends Genta but falls under suspicion when Genta's notes for a computer game are stolen. However, it is not Nomoto but Genta's

friend Hideki who is the thief, a fact proven when Hideki sends the stolen idea to a magazine. Genta challenges Hideki to a duel, his chosen weapon—Nomoto's unfinished computer game *Bee's Hive*. The boys are trapped inside the game and must be guided out by Nomoto, who enlists the help of the famous Master Takahashi.

One of the first in the self-indulgent gaming tie-in subgenre (released the same day as **SUPER MARIO BROTHERS**), this anime was made by Hudson Soft, creators of the *Star Soldier* game, and it features a cameo by their popular designer Takahashi, who also sang the theme songs. It bombed at Japanese theaters, but game-based anime would dominate the 1990s, reaching their apotheosis with **POKÉMON**.

RURO NI KENSHIN *

1996. JPN: *Ruro ni Kenshin*. AKA: *Sword of Ruro; Vagabond Sword; Kenshin the Wanderer; Kenshin the Ronin; Samurai X*. TV series, movie, video. DIR: Kazuhiro Furuhashi, Hatsuki Tsuji. SCR: Michiru Shimada, Yoshiyuki Suga. DES: Hideyoshi Hamazu, Kuniyuki Ishii, Fumie Muroi, Hatsuki Tsuji. ANI: Masami Suda. MUS: Noriyuki Asakura. PRD: Studio Gallop, Studio Deen, Fuji TV. 25 mins. x 94 eps., 90 mins. (m), 30 mins. x 4 eps. (v).

It's 1878 in Japan, 11 years after the Meiji Restoration (see **OI! RYOMA**), and most of the revolutionaries have become just as corrupt as the government they once opposed. "Weakening" foreign influences have become ever stronger, and samurai have lost many of their past rights. Kenshin Himura is a former member of the revolutionary Isshin Shishi group—a reformed assassin who now uses a reverse-bladed sword to avoid ever killing again. He falls for the beautiful Kaoru Kamiya, the impoverished daughter of a swordsmaster whose school has fallen on hard times in the modern age. Kenshin helps her search for her father's killer, a man who claimed to be the infamous killer Hitokiri Battosai. Kaoru is out for revenge, but Kenshin *was* the legendary Battosai, and he wishes to unmask the imposter.

RnK began as a 1994 manga in *Shonen Jump* by Nobuhiro Watsuki, inspired in part by the true-life story of Gensai Kawakami, a 19th-century killer whose good looks often distracted his foes from his cold-blooded nature. Kawakami was useful to Japan's revolutionaries during the pre-Restoration period of civil unrest, but, a danger to the new order, he was imprisoned and executed on trumped-up charges in 1871. To add to the drama, Watsuki threw in a love interest and two more characters, the bratty kid Yahiko (supposedly based on the author's younger self, who was picked last for his school kendo team), and the supertough Sanosuke (based on the semihistorical Sanosuke Harada, hero of Ryotaro Shiba's novel *Burning Sword*). The TV series adapts three major story arcs from the manga, beginning with the "Tokyo" sequence in which Kenshin and Kaoru hunt for her father's killer. This is followed by the "Kyoto" plotline about another former revolutionary, Makoto, plotting to seize power in Japan and being thwarted by Kenshin. The final sequence, "Revenge," introduces a killer determined to avenge the death of his sister, who, it transpires, was a spy sent to tease secrets from the young Kenshin, who fell in love with the boyish samurai but soon died under mysterious circumstances.

Surprisingly popular in the U.S. in spite of featuring a hero who would have happily kicked Americans out of Japan, the *Ruro* TV series occasionally lapses into pointless comedy at the expense of its overall serious tone. The depiction of martial arts, however, while often not realistic, is respectful and detailed. Luckily this doesn't slow down the action; the battle sequences are well staged and directed. Attractive design and characterization, and the emotional and spiritual intensity of the main characters, make this an interesting and involving show. The *RnK* movie (1997) takes the characters to Yokohama, where Kenshin once more faces a figure from his past. He saves the life of a man being attacked by bandits and finds that he and Shigure have a link—in his old, violent life, he killed Shigure's friend. Now, Shigure is planning a coup against the Meiji Government, which he believes to be as corrupt as its precursor, but his revolt has been infiltrated by elements in the government seeking to advance their own position. It fails, and Shigure is killed after he has surrendered by one of his treacherous supporters. Kenshin faces the betrayer of his former enemy and tests his vow never to kill again.

The 1999 video series, released in English as *Samurai X*, is a flashback to Kenshin's youth, detailing the story of how he got the distinctive cross-shaped scar on his cheek. Free of the restrictions of TV broadcast, it is much darker than the TV version. The video series also exists in a 125-minute "movie" edit, with a fake widescreen appearance and cast/crew interviews. During the serial's long run, crucial moments of the plot were rerun in three clip-shows (billed as TV "specials"), while two more compilations of previous footage were rerun as "summer holiday specials." There was also an eight-part video release, *RnK: Popular Characters*, that purported to portray fan-favorite moments, though one is tempted to point out that a "fan" would buy the episodes anyway. A two-part video sequel, *Seisohen* (2001), features an appearance by Kenshin's son. ⓥ

S

SABER MARIONETTES *

1995. Video, TV series. DIR: Masami Shimoda, Koji Masunari. SCR: Mayori Sekijima, Kenichi Kanemaki. DES: Tsukasa Kotobuki, Hidekazu Shimamura, Kazuo Nagai. ANI: Eiji Suganuma. MUS: Parome. PRD: Studio Juno, TV Tokyo. 30 mins. x 3 eps. (v/r), 25 mins. x 25 eps. (TV/J), 25 mins. x 6 eps. (v/J Again), 25 mins. x 26 eps. (TV/J-X; final ep. not broadcast).

In the late 22nd century, humanity spreads out from an overpopulated Earth. The colony ship Mesopotamia crashes on a distant world, and the six male survivors christen the planet Terra 2. Maintaining the species through cloning, the men establish six countries, each ruled by the pure clone of its founder: Japones, Sheien (probably China), New Texas, Peterburg (Russia), Geltland (Germany), and Romana (Italy).

Based on Satoru Akahori's comic novel in *Dragon* magazine, *SM* is a laughable simplification of the same body/soul concepts that informed the same year's GHOST IN THE SHELL. It takes the ADVENTURES OF PINOCCHIO theme buried in so many robot anime and marries it to the ultimate variant on the magical-girlfriend and TENCHI MUYO! genres—a lone boy on a whole world of tailor-made women. It also features the most haphazard release schedule of any anime, jumping from video to TV, back to video, then back to TV, and finally finishing on video again! Two hundred years after mankind's arrival on Terra 2, clones of the originals live on, served by female-form "marionette" androids. Most are simply machines incapable of emotion or thought, but over time some have become more advanced. However the greatest leap—to androids with a "heart"—has yet to be made. An evil scientist and a psychotic villain are out to take over the state and double-cross each other, when the scientist is mowed down by a newly created android, Lime, made for Villey Junior, teenage son of a Romana dignitary. She and her fellow-marionettes Cherry and Bloodberry help Junior to save the day after fighting the bad guys and their powerful, vicious "sexadolls," depraved marionettes who get off on violence rather than sweet submission.

Resetting the plot to zero and recycling the same or similar characters in much the same way as *Tenchi Muyo!*, the series proper began the following year on TV with *Saber Marionette J.* Japonese teenager Otaru discovers the marionette Lime in a hidden basement beneath a deserted museum (refer to the similar discovery of Ifrita in EL HAZARD). Otaru is considered odd because he prefers his relationship with his cute little puppet to the normal male-male relationships on his world. Lime is the first marionette to have a special "girly circuit," like a human heart, which gives her feelings. A little later, Otaru accidentally finds more such marionettes, Cherry and Bloodberry, with the same special circuit. The few marionettes with this circuit are "saber marionettes," and they have a secret purpose. They must achieve spiritual growth, seemingly by playing out the same corny fantasies as countless other anime babes, like getting into bed naked with their embarrassed man, fighting to be top bitch in his pack, participating in "talent" contests, cooking for him, and so on. Should this unlikely program of spiritual discipline enable them to transcend themselves, human females will "revive." The franchise itself revived on video with *SM J Again* (1997), which appeared to be six unbroadcast TV episodes of a tiresomely domestic nature, was released straight to video, and continued straight on from the series. The series bounced back onto TV as *SM J to X* (1998), with the predictable return of the previous series' bad-guy Faust, along with his team of pretty sexadolls. The final episode was not broadcast on TV but is only available on video. **NV**

SABER RIDER AND THE STAR SHERIFFS *

1984. JPN: *Seijushi Bismarck.* AKA: *Star Gunner Bismarck.* TV series. DIR: Masami Annai, Tadamasa Takahashi, Hiroyuki Yokoyama, Norio Kabeshima, Akira Torino, Hiroshi Yoshida, Rei Hidaka. SCR: Michiru Umadori, Tsunehisa Ito, Kazusane Hisajima. DES: Shigeru Kato, Yasushi Moriki. ANI: Tadamasa Takahashi, Moriyasu Taniguchi. MUS: Satoshi Etsuka. PRD: Studio Pierrot, Nippon TV. 25 mins. x 52 eps.

The New Frontier is an untamed region of space where the only law is the Star Sheriffs. From its space station, a team of brave young people—Saber Rider, Colt, Fireball, and April—ride out in their sheriff-shaped giant robot to defend the galaxy from bad guys like the Outriders. Before "versioning" for the U.S. market where, with its Wild West theme, it was inevitably headed, *SR&tSS* was set in the solar system, where the alien Deskula invaders had conquered Ganymede, and Earth was defended by the all-Japanese hero Shinji and his buddies, whose names were regarded (by the Japanese) as suitably Western—Bill, Richard, Marian, and Walter. When the series was altered for U.S. consumption, story editor Marc Handler (who went on to produce **VOLTRON**) had to make teen Texan Colt into the hero and sideline the original lead, Japanese kid Fireball, resulting in some hilarious scenes where other characters are looking at Fireball but supposedly listening to Colt. He also had problems with the amount of teenage drinking in the original, editing out all drunken behavior and moving many scenes from saloons to the "coffee shops" and "soda fountains" that were so much a part of the Old West.

SABU AND ICHI INVESTIGATE

1968. JPN: *Sabu to Ichi Torimonohikae.* TV series. DIR: Rintaro, Mamoru Masaki, Shinichi Suzuki, Fumio Kurokawa, Eiji Kojima, Mami Murano, Kunihiko Okazaki, Masayuki Hayashi, Takeshi Tamiya, Tomoharu Katsumata, Noboru Ishiguro. SCR: Takao Suzuki, Keiichi Abe, Takashi Umebayashi, Yoji Nishikawa. DES: Shotaro Ishinomori. ANI: Akio Sugino, Mami Murano. MUS: Takeo Yamashita. PRD: Mushi, Studio Zero, Toei, NET. 25 mins. x 52 eps. A detective story from Shotaro Ishinomori in which two Sherlock Holmes types solve a range of crimes in old Edo. Sabu, a young man in search of adventure, comes to the big city and becomes assistant to Saheiji, police chief of the Ryusenji quarter, who is almost crippled by rheumatism and spends much of his time bedridden. A local character, the masseur Ichi, turns out to be a very useful contact and helps Sabu in his efforts to keep Edo crime-free on behalf of his boss.

SAILOR MOON *

1992. JPN: *Bishojo Senshi Sailor Moon.* AKA: *Pretty Soldier Sailor Moon.* TV series, movie. DIR: Junichi Sato,

Kazuhisa Takenouchi, Kunihiko Ikuhara, Yuji Endo, Hiroki Shibata, Masahiro Hosoda, Takuya Igarashi. SCR: Sukehiro Tomita, Yoji Enokido, Ryota Yamaguchi, Jun Maekawa, Kazuhiko Kobe, Chitose Mizuno. DES: Kazuko Tadano, Ikuko Ito, Katsumi Igai. ANI: Kazuko Tadano, Ikuko Itoh, Masahiro Ando, Hisashi Kagawa, Hideyuki Motohashi. MUS: Takanori Arisawa, Tetsuo Komuro, Kazuo Sano. PRD: Toei, Aoi, TV Asahi. 25 mins. x 200 eps., 60 mins. x 3 movies, 16 mins. (m/*Ami-chan*), 42 mins. (m/*Make Up*).

Usagi Tsukino (Serena in the U.S. version) is a cheerful but clumsy teenage crybaby. Nevertheless, she is fated to become Sailor Moon, leader of a team of brave girls: Ami (Amy/Mercury), Minako (Mina/Venus), Rei (Raye/Mars), and Makoto (Lita/Jupiter). Collectively, they are known as the Sailor Warriors, or Sailor Scouts in the U.S. She meets a magical cat, Luna, and receives classic magical-girl items (including a wand and tiara) and superpowers to help her transform. In a past life, she was Moon Princess Serenity, beloved of Prince Endymion. That love will be reborn because Endymion has also been reincarnated as a human with the ability to magically transform into dashing hero (and occasional boy-damsel in distress) Tuxedo Kamen (Tuxedo Mask).

SM began as *Codename Sailor V* (1991, often confused with the unrelated **GRADUATION** spinoff *Sailor Victory*), a short-lived manga by Naoko Takeuchi in *Run-Run* magazine in which a teenage girl moonlights as a superhero wearing a distinctive sailor-style Japanese schoolgirl uniform. Rereleased as *SM* in *Nakayoshi* magazine as part of a cross-media promotion with the anime, the refashioned story now featured several color-coded heroines in the fashion of live-action team shows, as well as a supernatural spin—lunar reincarnations would also crop up in its contemporaries **PLEASE SAVE MY EARTH** and **BOUNTY DOG**. There are echoes of *Power Rangers* in the "monster-of-the-week"

© 1981 RUMIKO TAKAHASHI / SHOGAKUKAN • KITTY • FUJI TV

Alien princess Lum, pictured here with her imposing father. His demonic horns and fangs are only visible when she becomes angry. Rumiko Takahashi's **URUSEI YATSURA** dominated Japanese cartoon comedy in the 1980s with a winning formula of domestic farce, up-to-the-minute satire, and intergalactic adventure. Its central conceit, that a hapless boy could unwittingly wed an unearthly beauty, would be taken seriously by a whole subgenre of geek-gets-girl anime in the 1990s. *See entry p. 423.*

Urusei Yatsura

fight sequences in which our heroines take on ever more outrageously costumed baddies, but the show is saved from banality by the strength of its plotting, its earnest, honest romance, and its refusal to talk down to its audience. With reincarnation a given, the show is unafraid of death; the first-season closes with a harrowing assault on the icy lair of the evil Queen Beryl, in which the entire cast is killed off (albeit temporarily). Needless to say, the sanitized U.S. release unconvincingly pretends they have merely been detained elsewhere.

It is unlikely that many of the girls who watched the first season were still glued to their TVs by the last episode in 1996, a ratings disaster the producers attempted to avoid by rebranding and refashioning the series to entice younger audiences. As *SM R[eturns]* in 1993, it introduced new foes from the Black Moon, who intend to destroy present-day Tokyo in order to prevent the founding of Crystal Tokyo in the future. It also introduced Chibi-Usa (Rini), Serena and Endymion's future daughter, who time-travels to stay with the girl who is/was/will be her mother. Rebranded again as Kunihiko Ikuhara's *SM S[uper]* in 1994, it introduced the controversially homoerotic

Sailors Uranus and Neptune, who are in search of three mystic talismans. The talismans must be united to summon the Holy Grail, which is needed to locate the Messiah but must be kept out of the hands of Professor Tomoe and the Death Busters lest it summon the *Dark* Messiah. The new Sailors suspect (rightly) that Sailor Saturn is the Dark Messiah, splitting the group with in-fighting. By 1994's season *SM S[uper] S* (note the easy-to-confuse typography!), the focus of the show was gradually shifting away from Usagi and onto Chibi-Usa, thought to be more appealing to younger girls as the original target audience put childish things (i.e., merchandise) behind them. However, ratings hit an all-time low, partly because Chibi-Usa was unpopular, but also because Ikuhara's growing obsessions with fairy tales and subtexts (see his later **UTENA**) were lost on the target audience. Chibi-Usa befriends Pegasus, a flying horse, who enlists her help in keeping an important Golden Crystal from the evil Queen Nephrenia, leader of the Dead Moon Circus, who needs it to escape from her prison (inside a mirror) and conquer Earth. For the final season, *SM Sailor Stars*, Chibi-Usa returns to the future, Mamoru leaves to study abroad, and the remaining Sailor Scouts must hold off Shadow Galactica, a group of evil Scouts led by Sailor Galaxia. They are aided in this by the Three Lights (aka Sailor Starlight), a boy band who can transform into leather-clad girls in times of need.

There were also several theatrical outings—Ikuhara's *Sailor Moon R* (1993) takes place during the Nega Moon story in the TV series. An alien boy befriends the child who will grow up to be Tuxedo Mask, but, when they meet again as young adults, a misunderstanding leads to tragedy. The same year saw his *Make Up Sailor Senshi!* (aka *Dreaming Moon*), a short film of animated character biographies and gossip. *Sailor Moon S The Movie* (1994) focuses on Luna, Sailor Moon's feline friend, who is rescued by and falls in love with

a young astronomer caught up in the battle to save Earth when evil Princess Kaguya (see **REI REI**) plots to freeze it. Hiroki Shibata's *Sailor Moon SS* (1995) features Chibi-Usa's new friend, a modern-day Pied Piper, who leads all the local children toward a spaceship, and the Sailors must save them from being abducted. On the same bill was the short feature *Ami-chan's First Love* starring Sailor Mercury (always popular with the series' unexpectedly large audience of boys, because she did stuff with computers). The series was eventually brought to the U.S. with an indifferent dub, where it flopped, chiefly because it was shown at an insanely early time of the morning, edged into dead airtime by more powerful local interests. *SM*'s failure was an object lesson in how a multimedia sensation, heavily reliant on merchandising tie-ins, can crash without adequate support—Bandai would not make the same mistake with the later **POKÉMON**. Much imitated in modern anime such as **WEDDING PEACH**, *SM* has also been the subject of erotic parodies in **VENUS FIVE** and *Sailor and the Seven Balls*.

SAINT ELMO: APOSTLE OF LIGHT

1987. JPN: *Saint Elmo Hikari no Raihosha*. TV special. DIR: Tomoharu Katsumata. SCR: Hiroyasu Yamaura. DES: Katsumi Itahashi. ANI: Yasuhiro Yamaguchi. MUS: Michiru Oshima. PRD: Toei, Yomiuri TV. 84 mins.

A Jovian cloud-cruiser disappears in a strange accident, its pilot feared lost. The master "electrician" Issei Yuki is recalled to Osaka from his current project in Africa and dispatched to investigate. He discovers that there are problems on the giant orbital power station Saint Elmo that are creating electrical storms and threatening to plunge Earth into eternal darkness. In order to save his father's great project, and Mayu, the girl he loves, he tries to stop the Saint Elmo from falling into the sun. A very obscure TV anime, not broadcast in the Tokyo area, and therefore unknown to a large proportion of the *Japanese* audience. Despite a devel-

opment credit from **CAPTAIN HARLOCK**–creator Leiji Matsumoto, *Saint Elmo* had its true genesis as a vanity project for the Kansai Electric Company, which wanted to do something to commemorate its 30th anniversary. Apparently, this hokey sci-fi show was it.

SAINT LUMINOUS COLLEGE

1998. JPN: *Sei Luminous Gakuen*. AKA: *St. Luminous Mission High School*. TV series. DIR: Tetsuro Amino. SCR: Akira Oketani. DES: Hisashi Kagawa. ANI: Hisashi Kagawa, Tadashi Yoshida. MUS: Michiya Katakura. PRD: Pioneer, TV Tokyo. 25 mins. x 13 eps.

Two lucky guys become the first male pupils to attend the all-girl St. Luminous College, gaining a seemingly limitless supply of adoring classmates who can't wait to find out about the world of psychic investigation. A predictable rehash of Pioneer's **TENCHI MUYO!** franchise with a cursory *X-Files* twist, this anime was based on an "original" idea by Kenji Terada.

SAINT SEIYA

1986. JPN: *Seitoshi Seiya*. AKA: *Holy Fighters Seiya; Star Arrow; Zodiac Knights*. TV series, movie. DIR: Shigenori Yamauchi, Kozo Morishita, Kazuhito Kikuchi, Masayuki Akehi, et al. SCR: Takao Koyama, Yoshiyuki Suga, Tadaaki Yamazaki, et al. DES: Shingo Araki, Michi Himeno, Masahiro Naoi, Tadao Kubota, Fumihiro Uchikawa. ANI: Shingo Araki, Tetsuro Aoki. MUS: Seiji Yokoyama. PRD: Toei, TV Asahi. 25 mins. x 114 eps. (TV), 45 mins., 45 mins., 75 mins., 45 mins. (m1–4).

Young martial artist Seiya and the Bronze Saints are sworn to protect Saori, the reincarnation of the Goddess Athena. Their magical armor is at the lower end of a divinely initiated pecking order that moves up through Silver and Gold Saints and even encompasses the sinister Black Saints, servants of a dark power who see Athena as the only barrier to their dominion. In the first series, Ikki and his Black Saints steal the legendary Gold armor. The battle to retrieve it seems hopeless, but the boys have their Cosmo, a kind of power in every living being that can be developed for good or evil. Combining their Cosmos with their individual skills and courage, they can beat seemingly invincible powers. Since evil can be reborn, their adversaries can reincarnate to fight them again. A complex plot builds through multiple story arcs in the TV series and the self-contained but linked movies, featuring mythologies from Greece, Scandinavia, China, and Christendom. The series ends with a multiepisode tale in which Poseidon captures Athena as part of a plot to create a new Great Flood; the Saints of Athena must defeat him and save the goddess, to save the world as we know it.

Based on the *Shonen Jump* manga by **B'T X**–creator Masami Kurumada, *SS* was one of the biggest anime phenomena of the late 1980s. Four movie outings followed: the first, Morishita and Kikuchi's *Saint Seiya* (1987, aka *Legend of the Golden Apple*) pitted the boys against Eris, the goddess of Discord. The same year's *SS: Vicious Fight of the Gods* (*Kamigami no Nekki Tatakai*) was designed as the lead-in for the Norse-themed second season of the TV series, moving the action to the frozen wastes of Siberia (not quite Scandinavia, but easier for Japanese kids to find on a map) for a battle with the gods of Midgard over Odin's shield. The only full-length feature was *Legend of the Crimson Youth* (1988, *Makka no Shonen Densetsu*), in which Athena must fight Abel (the reincarnation of her elder brother, the sun god Apollo), and his cohorts Berenice and Jow, who wish to create a "new world of peace" by distinctly unpeaceful methods. Masayuki Akehi's *Armageddon Warriors* (45 mins., 1990) involves the awakening of Lucifer by the powers of the various evil deities Seiya and his companions have sent to Hades. It coincided with the ending of the TV series and proved to be the final outing for the Saints of Athena. Fans hoped for a video series devoted to the later Hades chapters of the manga, but this never materialized;

though an "image CD" was released of music that *might* have accompanied that arc, had it been made. *SS* remains one of the few post-1985 hit series without any made-for-video spinoffs.

Designers Araki and Himeno (**ROSE OF VERSAILLES**) work magic in both the series and movies, except for the last film, where Naoi's design is less successful. Yokoyama's music is suitably grand. Director Yamauchi stretches the series' tension like a bowstring for cliffhanger endings and mid-battle episode breaks that kept audiences coming back for more. But despite its apparent teen appeal, a show that achieves much of its emotional impact through older boys and men fighting brave but naïve teenagers is disturbing, especially when strength and courage are rewarded with ever shinier weapons. *SS* and its close cousin **RONIN WARRIORS** should come with parental warning attached—though their influence, even into the girls' market, can be discerned throughout the **SAILOR MOON**–dominated 1990s. For those old enough to separate the complex strands of the story and keep its brutally seductive heroism in perspective, *SS* has many rewards.

SAINT TAIL *

1995. JPN: *Kaito Saint Tail*. AKA: *Master Thief Saint Tail*. TV series. DIR: Osamu Nabeshima. SCR: Masaaki Sakurai, Masahiro Yokoyama. DES: Junko Abe, Shiro Kobayashi. ANI: Junko Abe. MUS: Seiji Suzuki. PRD: Tokyo Movie Shinsha, TV Asahi. 25 mins. x 43 eps.

Meimi is an ordinary Catholic schoolgirl who transforms at night into the daring thief Saint Tail. It's in the genes, as her mother was a notable burglar before marrying her stage-magician father, but she only steals from those who deserve it, or to help others. Her best friend, Seira, is a novice nun who somewhat heretically hears confessions from troubled parishioners and then blurts out the details to Meimi. Meimi then yells out, "It's showtime!" whereupon God Almighty transforms her

into an angelic superthief in a costume based on a magician's female assistant: top hat, revealing bodysuit, and fishnet stockings. While Saint Tail restores valuable items to their true owners, the hapless police are unable to compete with her divinely assisted crime spree, though Meimi's classmate Asuka is the son of the beleaguered chief of police, determined to track down Saint Tail and hoping to capture Meimi's heart as well. A resurrection of two of the most successful themes of the 1980s—magical girls and TMS's own burglars-for-justice series **CAT'S EYE**—with a dash of Las Vegas showmanship and Catholic guilt. Meimi regrets the embarrassment she causes Asuka's father as she carries out God's work. Based on Megumi Tachikawa's manga.

SAKURA DIARIES *

1997. JPN: *Sakura Tsushin*. AKA: *Sakura Communications*. Video. DIR: Kunitoshi Okajima. SCR: Kenji Terada. DES: Nobuyuki Takeuchi. ANI: Nobuyuki Takeuchi. MUS: Mitsuo Hagita. PRD: Kitty Films, Victor, Shaft. 25 mins. x 12 eps. (rel. on 6 tapes).

Touma Inaba is a dreamer, eager to get into university and began adult life, but cursed to drift permanently around the outskirts. Living in Tokyo with his beautiful cousin Urara, he keeps on retaking the entrance exams but never seems to make the grade. His mother wishes he would just come back to the provinces and get a McJob. When he falls in love with the beautiful but unattainable Mieko Yotsuba, he even starts pretending to be a student in order to win her affection. But cousin Urara wants Touma for herself, and will do anything to get him.

"When it comes to sex, she wrote the book on it," leers the hopeful box blurb, but the very fact that *SD* is released by ADV, rather than their erotic subsidiary brand Soft Cel, speaks volumes about its confused identity. While *SD* looks superficially like a faithful adaptation of the *Young Sunday* manga by U-Jin, the anime loses much of the original's appeal. Despite being U-Jin's most mature and entertaining work, *SD* was clearly optioned with the audience of ANGEL and TALES OF . . . in mind, vacillating between the sex farces of U-Jin's better-known works and the far more involving story of the original.

There are some clever moments that duplicate the spirit of the original. Each episode begins with a striking scene, as little-girl-lost Urara sits at her dresser and contemplates her reflection in the mirror, applying her warpaint and contemplating her next covert operation in this battle of the sexes. For the opening credits, Urara is filmed as if she is the only girl in the world, much the same as in the beginning of VIDEO GIRL AI. As with OH MY GODDESS!, the leads' association begins when they are children, but this is not a simple case of love at first sight—in the manga, it is the seven-year-old Touma who risks his life to protect Urara from her abusive father.

But like so many anime romances aimed at the onanistic male, *SD* paints a picture of a strange viewer, old enough to vote but somehow cursed with the emotional maturity of a child. Consequently, its female characters are dragged down to the level of the wanton Lolitas of CREAM LEMON, while its male lead becomes little more than a priapic TENCHI MUYO! Despite the more sophisticated story line of the original manga, the anime incarnation often slips into tawdriness, seemingly because the production team refused to believe that they can make an U-Jin anime without some eye candy. *Ill. p. 65.* N

SAKURA WARS *

1997. JPN: *Sakura Taisen.* Video, TV series. DIR: Takaaki Ishiyama, Ryutaro Nakamura. SCR: Hiroyuki Kawasaki, Satoru Akahori. DES: Hidenori Matsubara, Kosuke Fujishima. ANI: N/C. MUS: Kohei Tanaka. PRD: Bandai, TBS/MBS. 30 mins. x 4 eps. (v), 25 mins. x 25 eps. (TV).

At the beginning of the 20th century, Earth fends off invading demons from another dimension. Suspecting that another attack is coming, a group of Japanese scientists perfect clunky war machines in the early 1920s, discovering that they can only be effectively piloted by women with the right sort of virtuous energy. Assembling a team of anime archetypes (big-sisterly platoon leader Maria, tomboy Kanna, child Iris, maidenly Sumire, and alien Chinese girl Koh-ran/Hong-Lan), the scientists eventually find their perfect Girl Next Door, Sakura the swordswoman from Sendai. The Tokyo Floral Assault team (since the platoons are chiefly named, Takarazuka theater style, after flowers) then prepares to resist the alien menace.

SW races through four years and a couple of flashbacks in order to set up the beginning of the Sega console game—hence occasional cutaways to the otherwise irrelevant life of Ichiro Ogami, the hapless naval officer who is the player's point of view in the game proper, as well as the introduction of Kanna only to remove her, since she is absent at the beginning of the game. Designed to complement the game, it is nevertheless entertaining in its own right, with an appeal that crosses several anime subgenres—including robot combat, gaggles of girls à la TENCHI MUYO!, retro adventure in the style of SUPER ATRAGON, and hefty multimedia promotion. Fans were asked to buy into a complete "universe," including not just the novelization, but also a CD-ROM encyclopedia, two games, and the Taisho Romantic Society, a fan club of alternate historians with its own magazine. To top it all, the actresses appeared in several live-action musicals, drawing further parallels between the look of the show and the cross-dressing Takarazuka musical tradition (particularly ROSE OF VERSAILLES) that inspired it.

Though *SW* does a masterful job of overcoming its computer-game origins, like KISHIN CORPS and creator Hiroi Oji's later VIRGIN FLEET, its innocuous revisionism leaves a nasty taste in the historian's mouth—in the *real* 1920s, the only aliens the Japanese military were preparing to fight were the hapless inhabitants of Manchuria. Somewhat ironically, the period detail is quite exacting, with obsolete terms used for foreign countries, right-to-left writing in the prewar style, and even a character named Koh-ran, after a Japanese actress who specialized in Chinese roles in prewar propaganda films. The franchise was upgraded to a TV series in 2000, with the team forming a musical comedy troupe and setting off on a nationwide tour. For the game *SW3*, the action shifts to Paris in 1926, where Ichiro Ogami is put in charge of a new team of girls—big-sisterly part-time thief Roberia, tomboy duchess Grecine, Vietnamese child Kokuriko, and girl-next-door Hanabi, a French-born Japanese girl. An anime movie, set in Tokyo during the events of *SW3* in Paris, appeared in late 2001. According to an annual survey by Meiji Life Insurance, Sakura was the most popular name for newborn girls in 2000. Read into that what you will.

SAKYO KOMATSU'S ANIME THEATER

1989. JPN: *Komatsu Sakyo Anime Gekijo.* TV series. DIR: Akira Nishimori. SCR: Sakyo Komatsu. DES: Jun Ishikawa. ANI: Jun Ishikawa. MUS: N/C. PRD: Gainax, MBS. 3 mins. x 27 eps.

A series of adaptations of short stories, this anime's chief source of material is the *Punk Dragon* short-story collection by Sakyo Komatsu, best known for his novels *Japan Sinks* and *Resurrection Day* (the latter adapted into the live-action film *Virus*, 1980). In the anime world, Komatsu also worked with Tezuka on SPACE FIREBIRD and as a voice actor in ARABIAN NIGHTS.

SALAMANDER *

1988. Video. DIR: Hisayuki Toriumi. SCR: Kazuhito Hisajima. DES: Haruhiko Mikimoto, Yasuhiro Moriki. ANI: Toshiyasu Okada. MUS: Tatsushi Umegaki. PRD: Studio Pierrot. 60 mins., 50 mins., 60 mins.

In the year 2381, the aggressive galaxy-devouring parasites known as the Bacterians are heading for planet Gradius. In the first video, *Salamander Basic Saga: Meditating Paola*, ace pilot Stephanie and her teammates, Eddie and Dan, find a beautiful girl in an abandoned spaceship. As she warns of the imminent Bacterian invasion, they wonder if she's an innocent victim or an agent of destruction. The lovely Paola reveals herself to be a Bacterian agent, and Stephanie's father makes the ultimate sacrifice to save Gradius from the invaders. For the second video, *Intermediate Saga*, Dan and Stephanie are called to planet Lotus, whose ruler, Lord British, needs their help. Despite courtly intrigues from rivals embittered at needing foreign aid, the Gradian pilots hold off another invasion. In *Advanced Saga: The Ambition of Gofar*, British comes to Gradius to sign a peace treaty and woo the reluctant Stephanie. She, however, is kidnapped by the Bacterians and taken to their HQ on the artificial sun of Salamander, where they plan to rip out her brain and sew it into the skull of their agent Gofar. Stephanie's father, who has turned to the dark side, figures that her knowledge of the Gradian defenses will turn the battle in the invaders' favor. Needless to say, British and Dan save the day.

A brave stab at adapting the Konami arcade game *Gradius, Salamander* is ultimately defeated by the poverty of its source material. The love triangle between Stephanie and the men is well-handled; she is tempted by riches, royalty, and marriage in the form of British as well as by career and camaraderie in the form of Dan. The ex-refugee Eddie is another intriguing character, drawn to the enemy agent Paola because she too does not really belong. A surprisingly cogent hard-science script and well-realized sequences that duplicate moments of gameplay for the fans are ruined by the worst subtitling in anime history, courtesy of Western Connection.

SAMURAI, THE

1987. Video. DIR: Kazuo Yamazaki. SCR:

Takahiro Miki. DES: Takayuki Goto. ANI: Takayuki Goto. MUS: N/C. PRD: Studio Deen. 45 mins.

Takeshi Chimatsuri is a young martial artist whose rare sword is a gift from his father. He won it in a fair fight from the brilliant swordsman Kagemaru Akari, who was killed in the struggle. Now Akari's twin sons, Toki and Kagedi, have come looking for Takeshi to avenge their father's death and retake the sword. Based on the manga serialized in *Young Jump* by Mitsuhiro Harunichi, this samurai soap opera fast devolves into a love comedy.

SAMURAI GIANTS

1973. AKA: *The Star Pitcher*. TV series. DIR: Tadao Nagahama, Satoshi Dezaki, Osamu Dezaki, Yoshiyuki Tomino. SCR: Seiji Matsuoka, Satoshi Dezaki, Haruya Yamazaki, Tomohiro Ando, Asako Tani. DES: Hideo Kawauchi. ANI: Yasuo Otsuka. MUS: Shunsuke Kikuchi. PRD: Eiken, TMS, Yomiuri TV (Nippon TV). 25 mins. x 46 eps.

The Giants baseball team is scouting for new talent and find a high school player who can hit one massive home run after another. But the school star's great physical strength has a balancing weakness—he lacks control and can't pitch to save his life. Worried about this basic problem, he's not sure whether he should join the team or forget baseball and look for another, more conventional career. His girlfriend convinces him that he should join the Giants and work with the team on his weak point. With her encouragement, he's determined to become a star pitcher. Based on yet another baseball manga by STAR OF THE GIANTS–creator Ikki Kajiwara, working here with Ko Inoue.

SAMURAI GOLD *

1988. JPN: *Toyamazakura Uchucho Yatsu no Na wa Gold*. AKA: *Cosmic Commander of the Toyama Cherry Trees; The Guy's Name Is Gold*. Video. DIR: Atsutoshi Umezawa. SCR: Akiyoshi Sakai. DES: Hiroyuki Kitazume. ANI: Hiroyuki Kitazume. MUS: Kentaro Hane-

Lonely widow Kyoko seeks comfort in the arms of her tenant Godai, a would-be student living at the **MAISON IKKOKU** dormitory. A mature work from Rumiko Takahashi. *See entry p. 240.*

Maison Ikkoku

© 1996 RUMIKO TAKAHASHI/SHOGAKUKAN • KITTY • FUJI TELEVISION

da. PRD: Toei. 60 mins.

Late in the 21st century, Earth and its colonies are controlled by five Overseers working through EDO, a vast computer system. When Overseer Redklaad Mount is wounded by a would-be assassin, his estranged son, Gold, is dragged from a seedy downtown bar to investigate. On the space colony of Fedovar, Gold discovers that Redklaad is implicated in the death of the local ruler Duke Plenmatz, who died when the liner Ovconia crashed on its maiden voyage. After fighting with Plenmatz's vengeful son, Ion (his girlfriend Midi's brother), Gold goes missing, presumed dead. Posing as Gold, Ion returns to Earth, where he almost succeeds in sentencing Redklaad to death. Gold saves the day by baring his unique cherry-blossom tattoo, thus unmasking Ion's deception. Gold reveals that all the Overseers, not just his father, are guilty of orchestrating the crash of the Ovconia and murdering the shipbuilders who arranged it. Having challenged his rulers, Gold prepares to commit suicide but is stopped by EDO herself, who admits that she ordered the removal of Plenmatz without thinking of the consequences. EDO exonerates the Overseers, who were only following her orders, and sentences herself to deactivation. Gold becomes an Overseer, but still has time to return to his favorite bar, where Midi plays the piano, Ion serves the drinks, and Ion's former henchman, the Gay Blade, waits on tables.

A lighthearted sci-fi romp, distantly inspired by the life of Kinshiro Toyama, a figure who lived from 1793 to 1855. The character was popularized first in the kabuki play *Toyama no Kinsan* (1893), in which he is portrayed as a tattooed playboy who makes good when he becomes a magistrate, fighting corruption in Edo (old-time Tokyo) in the style of MANGA MITO KOMON. Dramatized by several novelists, including *SG*'s credited Tatsuro Jinde (who died in 1986) and Kyosuke Yuki, the character is best known in Japan through several live-action TV series. *SG*, however, is just an excuse for some laser swordplay and mild detective work, rounded off by an overlong courtroom finale. Very 1980s in both good and bad senses—Gold boasts a hideous mullet haircut, and the Gay Blade takes camp beyond the funny into the insulting, but Kitazume's stark pop-art colors and designs still retain a certain freshness. Similar samurai retellings occur in JUBEI-CHAN THE NINJA GIRL and CYBER CITY OEDO 808, while Toyama was parodied again in U-JIN BRAND.

SAMURAI PIZZA CATS *

1990. JPN: *Kyatto Ninden Teyande*. AKA: *Stealth Tales of the Kool Kat Gang*. TV series. DIR: Kunitoshi Okajima, Takeshi Serizawa, Shinji Sakai, Katsumi Kosuga. SCR: Satoru Akahori, Mayori Sekijima, Yumi Kageyama, Hiroyuki Kawasaki. DES: Noritaka Suzuki, Mayori Sekijima. ANI: Noritaka Suzuki, Yoshio Kabashima. MUS: Kenji Kawai (Shuki Levy, Haim Saban in Western version). PRD: Tatsunoko, TV Tokyo. 25 mins. x 54 eps. (TV).

In the high-tech streets of Edolopolis (Little Tokyo), a fox (a rat in the English-language version) who has found his perfect role in life, cross-dressing politician Ko'on-no-Kami (Big

Cheese), and his avian sidekicks, Karamaru and Gennari-sai (Bad Bird and Jerry Atrick), plot against Shogun Iei-Iei Tokugawa (Emperor Fred) and his ditzy, romance-obsessed rabbit daughter, Usa-hime (Princess Vi). To save the city from their evil plans, loyal dog retainer Wanko-no-kami (Big Al Dentei) calls for help from the Ninja Team Nyanki (Samurai Pizza Cats), who moonlight as superheroes while making and delivering the best pizza in town. Yattaro (Speedy Cerviche) is the leader of the team and fights with the unbeatable Magical Ginzu Sword. Sukoshii (Guido Anchovy), his smooth-talking comrade in arms and rival for the love of the beautiful Miss Omitsu (Lucille), fights with the Samurai Sunspot Umbrella. Pururun (Polly Esther), the hotheaded sex-kitten of the trio, uses the Cat's Paw Attraction technique, raising her paw like the "beckoning cat" statues in Japanese shops, while electromagnetic waves (represented by streams of fluttering hearts) pull her victims to her. She also throws heart-shaped *shuriken*. In a sly reference to the live-action show *Cyber Ninja*, for most of their missions, the Pizza Cats are launched from a giant revolver on the roof of the Pizza Parlor by their loyal (and frequently sarcastic) assistant, Otama (Francine.) When they need extra clout they can use their own magnificent armored vehicle, Nyago-sphinx (Golden Sphinx); it can even transform into a giant robot, Nyago-king (The Great Catatonic).

With pizza-loving martial artists inspired by the *Teenage Mutant Ninja Turtles*, early writing credits for Satoru "Mr. Zany" Akahori, and even music from GHOST IN THE SHELL's Kenji Kawai in the original version, *SPC* is an anime classic. Many shows are ruined in translation, but *SPC* simply shrugged off the change of language and stayed insanely itself—in one memorable scene in the English version, the characters panic *because* they have been sent a note in Japanese. Brought to the West by Saban soon after its release, *SPC* was

perhaps one of the last "translations" in the old 1970s *let's-just-make-it-up* style (see ROBOTECH). The improvised nature of the English-language version is, by definition, a very bad translation, but, luckily, one that succeeds in retaining the madcap spirit of the original. Saban International, execrated in many quarters for its editing jobs on Asian material, brought together a team that not only understood what the show needed but actually seems to have enjoyed itself—an object lesson for the bored crews of many English anime dubs with grander pretensions. Edited episodes of the TV series were released on video in the U.S. as *SPC The Movie* (1991). The series made it into U.S. syndication in 1996; it had already been screened in Canada and Britain with some success and remains a fan favorite. Subsequent French, Spanish, and German editions were based on the English version, which means that a true translation of *SPC* has yet to be attempted in any Western language.

SAMURAI SHODOWN: THE MOTION PICTURE *

1993. JPN: *Samurai Spirits*. TV special, video. DIR: Hiroshi Ishiodori, Kazuhiro Sasaki. SCR: Nobuaki Kishima, Masamuro Takimoto. DES: Kazunori Iwakura, Aoi Nanase. ANI: Kazunori Iwakura. MUS: Osamu Tezuka (the other one). PRD: SNK, Asia-do. 80 mins. (TVm), 30 mins. x 2 eps. (v).

One hundred years after their deaths at the hands of a former colleague, six legendary holy warriors are reborn to seek justice against the teammate who betrayed them into the hands of an evil god. Charlotte, Wan Fu, Nakoruru, Galford, and Tam Tam search the feudal province of Edo questing for their lost comrade, Haohmaru, and their sworn nemesis, Shiro Amakusa (see NINJA RESURRECTION). Will the followers of the divine light triumph over the forces of the dark, or is the course of history destined to repeat itself? Yes to both, as our heroes fight and fight again. Based on a video game by SNK for the Neo Geo, this video series edited into a "movie" was widely considered a disappointment by game fans. Instead of blood, characters leak a milky white liquid, and the violence levels have been watered down to match. American fans suffered even worse—the androgynous lead villain was rewritten as a woman for the U.S. release.

In the video sequel *SS: Defeat of Ashura* (1999), spiky-haired Haohmaru is back with Rimururu, Nakoruru, and Galford and they're faced with a problem. Shiki, an old enemy of theirs, shows up badly hurt. Nakoruru wants to take her in, but Galford and Rimururu have other plans. They believe she should be destroyed because she's working for an agent of corruption that could destroy them all. Haomaru takes up his sword once again, to save Shiki's life and destroy the dark influence.

SAMURAI: SPIRIT OF THE SWORD *

1999. JPN: *Kaito Ranma*. AKA: *Swift-Blade Ranma 1/2*. Video. DIR: Masahiro Sekino. SCR: Mitsuhiro Yamada. DES: Hidekazu Shimamura. ANI: Hidekazu Shimamura. MUS: N/C. PRD: AIC, Animate Film. 30 mins. x 2 eps.
Edo-era swashbuckling with a touch of romance, based on a PC and PlayStation game. ❶

SAMURAIDER

1991. Video. DIR: Hideaki Oba. SCR: Masaru Yamamoto. DES: Moriyasu Taniguchi. ANI: Moriyasu Taniguchi. MUS: Mitsuo Takahama. PRD: Studio TV. 50 mins.
In a weak combination of samurai movie and **BOMBER BIKERS OF SHONAN**, Tokyo street-punk Masao buys a treasured FZR "katana" motorcycle and becomes a knight of the road, attacking criminals with a genuine *katana* sword. Based on the manga by Shinichi Sugimura in *Young Magazine*.

SANCTUARY *

1996. Video. DIR: Takashi Watanabe. SCR: Kenishi Terada. DES: Hidemi

Kuma, Hiroshi Kato. ANI: Hidemi Kuma. MUS: N/C. PRD: OB Planning, Toho. 70 mins.
Two Japanese survivors of the Khmer Rouge massacres in Cambodia vow to find a sanctuary even if they have to build it themselves. Returning to Japan, they take seemingly opposite paths—one becomes a politician, the other a gangster. As Asami and Hojo work their way through the linked worlds of politics and crime in modern Japan, they don't hesitate to do anything necessary to secure their own positions and stay true to their vow. Loyal to no one else, they find their friendship increasingly tested as they rise in their chosen fields. A prequel to the 1990 *Big Comic* manga by Sho Fumimura and **CRYING FREEMAN**-creator Ryoichi Ikegami, the style is glossy and international, the protagonists two sharp-suited young sharks navigating the murky seas of the 1990s without a scruple. It was also made as a live-action film. ❶❷

SANPEI THE FISHERMAN

1980. JPN: *Tsurikichi Sanpei*. TV series. DIR: Eiji Okabe, Yoshimichi Nitta, Tameo Ogawa, Kiyoshi Harada, Yasuhiro Yamaguchi, Kazuyoshi Yokota, Fumio Kurokawa, Katsuhiko Yamazaki, Shigeo Koshi, Yasuhiro Imagawa. SCR: Michiru Umadori, Tajio Tamura, Sukehiro Tomita. DES: Takao Yaguchi. ANI: Kazuyuki Okaseko, Takashi Saijo, Hidehito Kojima. MUS: Tatsuaki Sone, Hideyuki Yamamoto. PRD: Nippon Animation, Fuji TV. 25 mins. x 109 eps.
Having grown up in a distant mountain village in northeastern Japan, Sanpei Nihira is a gifted teenage fisherman, and this long-running series is the story of his struggle to catch as many fish as possible, all over Japan and even overseas. The bigger and meaner, the better he likes it, as he invents new techniques and exploits old ones learned from seasoned anglers to their limits in pursuit of more and more powerful fishy opponents. Based on Takao Yaguchi's 1973 manga that ran in both the weekly and monthly edi-

tions of *Shonen Magazine*—among the few attempts to present fishing as a combat sport (also see **GRANDAR**).

SANPEI THE KAPPA

1992. JPN: *Kappa no Sanpei*. Movie. DIR: Toshio Hirata. SCR: Shunichi Yukimuro. DES: Shigeru Mizuki. ANI: Tatsuo Kitahara. MUS: Kazuki Kuriyama. PRD: Nikkatsu. 90 mins.
Japanese boy Sanpei befriends a *kappa* water-sprite and is soon accepted into a world of spiritual fun that lurks beneath the surface of modern Japan (see **POMPOKO**). This movie was based on the 1962 manga by **SPOOKY KITARO**-creator Shigeru Mizuki and selected by the Japanese Ministry of Education as a worthy title.

SANSHIRO SUGATA

1981. JPN: *Sugata Sanshiro*. AKA: *Judo Story*. TV special. DIR: Kyomi Mikamoto. SCR: Fumio Shinbo, Kiyohide Ohara. DES: Monkey Punch. ANI: Kazuhide Yoshinaga. MUS: Talisman, Susumu Akitagawa. PRD: Tokyo Movie Shinsha, Fuji TV. 84 mins.
In the Tokyo of 1882, Sanshiro is a promising young martial artist who seeks a worthy teacher. He proves his ability by defeating 39 masters of jujitsu (who ridicule his choosing judo) and is taken in by their teacher, who continually tests him. He falls for local girl Sayo Murai and must fight her father at judo before defeating his greatest rival on the plain of Ukyogahara. Based on a novel by Tsuneo Tomita, best-known in the West through its 1943 movie adaptation by a young Akira Kurosawa—though Kurosawa's version lacks the anime's comic-relief cat. The story, also included in **ANIMATED CLASSICS OF JAPANESE LITERATURE**, was an inspiration for the toy combat serial **PLAWRES SANSHIRO**, which supposedly starred the grandson of the original. Kurosawa's 1945 sequel was pastiched in later episodes of **IRONFIST CHINMI**, when Chinmi fights a foreign sailor. For more judo fun, see **YAWARA**.

SASUGA NO SARUTOBI

1982. AKA: *Idiot Ninja*. TV series. DIR: Koichi Sasaki, Masahisa Ishida. SCR: Takeshi Shudo, Masaki Tsuji, Tomoko Komparu, Shigeru Yanagawa. DES: Hiroshi Kanezawa, Jiro Kono. ANI: Hiroshi Kanezawa, Mutsumi Inomata, Masayuki, Shinichi Suzuki, Moriyasu Taniguchi. MUS: Joe Hisaishi. PRD: NAS, Tsuchida Pro, Fuji TV. 25 mins. x 69 eps.

Sarutobi is the best pupil in his ninja school, but to look at him you'd never know it—he's as round as a butterball, and his superb fighting abilities are masked under a dozy demeanor. Both Mako, the prettiest girl in the school, and local bad-girl Mika see through his appearance to the hero underneath. Rivalry with the neighboring Spiner martial arts school is intense, but Sarutobi and his chums always come out on top. This cheerful comedy was based on Fujihiko Hosono's manga for Shogakukan, itself inspired by the earlier SASUKE and MAGIC BOY.

SASUKE

1968. JPN: *Sasuke*. TV series. DIR: Kiyoshi Onishi, Takeshi Kawanai. SCR: Junzo Tashiro. DES: Sanpei Shirato. ANI: Toyoo Ashida. MUS: Masashi Tanaka. PRD: TCJ, TBS. 25 mins. x 29 eps.

Sasuke's father sends him away to learn ninja techniques to defend the oppressed of feudal Japan from their overlords, the Tokugawa shogunate. Although just a little boy, he must fight the best warriors, armed to the teeth with swords, *shuriken*, nunchaku, and other deadly weapons. Based on the 1961 manga by Sanpei Shirato, which in its turn was inspired by a novel by Kazuo Den, the story of Sasuke was remade by Eiji Okabe for a much younger audience as *Manga Sarutobi Sasuke* (1979), a 24-episode series on Tokyo Channel 12, concentrating on Sasuke's feud with the rival ninja of the Iga clan.

SAVE ME, GUARDIAN SHAOLIN

1998. Mamotte Shugogetten. AKA: *Protect Me Shugogetten*. TV series, video. DIR: Tatsuo Misawa, Satoshi Yamada, Keiji Hayakawa, Tetsuya Watanabe. SCR: Kenichi Yamada, Yasutoshi Yamada. DES: Ken Ueno. ANI: Masayuki Takagi, Hideyuki Motohashi. MUS: N/C. PRD: Toei, TV Asahi. 25 mins. x 22 eps. (TV), 30 mins. x 5 eps. (v).

Teenager Tasuke Shichiri is home alone while his parents travel China. His father sends occasional presents; the first is a ring with a note—if someone of pure heart peers into it, a guardian from heaven will appear to protect them. No surprise that the heavenly body is a gorgeous teenage girl called Shaolin, whose sole destiny is to protect the "master" who releases her from 4,000 years of imprisonment. However, her naiveté about the modern world causes Tasuke more trouble (in the style of DORAEMON). Still, she has access to powerful spirits called Star Gods, who can use their special skills to help her. Father's second package contains a rod found in the same place as the ring, containing another spirit, also a gorgeous teenage girl whose sole destiny is to please her "master." Lu-An, confined for 1,652 years, can bring inanimate objects to life. By another strange coincidence, she and Shaolin are sworn rivals, often getting into fights over Tasuke. To complicate matters even further, several of Tasuke's friends fall for the girls and do all in their power to entice the goddesses away, while a younger girl at Tasuke's school has a huge crush on him and is constantly trying to get rid of his supernaturally stacked slaves.

Based on the manga written by Sakurano Minene for *Shonen GanGan*, the similarity to OH MY GODDESS! reaches actionable proportions when a third goddess, Huang-Long, shows up to give Tasuke challenges (presumably to strengthen his character, which is normally the scriptwriter's job). Amazing—an average Japanese boy waits all through junior high school for a goddess to worship him, and then three show up at once! A video series, *New Legend: SMGS* (2000), further augmented by five CD dramas and a weekly radio show hosted by the characters, make up the grandly titled *Shugogetten Millennium Project*.

SAZAE-SAN

1969. TV series. DIR: Kazuo Kobayashi, Satoshi Murayama, Takeshi Yamamoto, Yonehiko Watanabe. SCR: Masaki Tsuji, Noboru Shiroyama, Shunichi Yukimuro. DES: Toshiyuki Osumi. ANI: N/C. MUS: Nobuyoshi Koshibe. PRD: Fuji TV. 25 mins. x 1600+ eps.

Sazae Isono, her husband, Masato, their two children, and her mother live together in a small house in a quiet suburb of Tokyo. Each episode is simply a snippet of their daily life, running the gamut of putting up with noisy neighbors, sharing a public phone, or being polite to unwanted visitors.

Based on a 1946 manga serialized in the *Asahi Shinbun* newspaper until 1974, *Sazae-san* was the most successful work by NASTY OLD LADY–creator Machiko Hasegawa. Still running 32 years later, the program has outlived both its manga incarnation and its creator, who died in 1992. Appealing to a vast mainstream audience who do not otherwise watch animation, it remains the highest-rated anime on Japanese television, consistently maintaining an audience share around 25% (POKÉMON can barely manage 14%, while major hits like CHIBI MARUKO-CHAN and CONAN THE BOY DETECTIVE hover around the 13% mark). *Sazae-san* is thus the most popular anime in Japan and makes a mockery of *The Simpsons'* claim to be the longest-running TV cartoon series in the world as it enters its fifth decade of continuous, quiet, small-screen triumph. Compare to the similar tone of MY NEIGHBORS THE YAMADAS.

SCARLET DEMON

1989. JPN: *Shuri Iro no Yoma*. Video. DIR: Wayu Suzumiya. SCR: Wayu Suzumiya. DES: Wayu Suzumiya, Atsushi Matoba. ANI: Atsushi Matoba. MUS: Kaoru Wada. PRD: Mushi. 20 mins. x 4 eps.

A "video comic" based on Wayu Suzu-miya's manga about twin boys born to mixed human and dragon-god parent-age. Passing their happy teens at a nor-mal Japanese school, they are forced to defend their classmates from demonic attackers—a task made easier by their magical blood. Compare to LEGEND OF THE FOUR KINGS.

SCARLET SANSHIRO

1969. JPN: *Kurenai Sanshiro*. AKA: *Judo Boy*. TV series. DIR: Junzo Toriumi, Ippei Kuri, Hiroshi Sasakawa. SCR: Junzo Toriumi. DES: Eiji Tanaka, Mitsuki Naka-mura. ANI: Eiji Tanaka. MUS: Nobuyoshi Koshibe. PRD: Tatsunoko, Fuji TV. 25 mins. x 26 eps.

Saburo's father is a martial artist who dies in a fight with a mysterious one-eyed man outside the city gates. The boy sets out in search of his father's killer with only one clue: the killer left his glass eye at the scene of the crime. He meets, and fights, a lot of one-eyed people before he finally reaches the end of his quest, accompanied by his blood-red motorcycle, his mischievous junior pal Ken, and his faithful canine companion, Stupid. A run-of-the-mill adventure series of combat against mutants and mummies, characterized by some innovative filming techniques from Tatsunoko, including limited rotoscoping, strobe effects, and clever lighting.

SCHOOL FOR THIEVES

1998. JPN: *Dorobo Gakko*. Video. DIR: Katsumi Hashimoto. SCR: Naoyuki Sakai. DES: Satoshi Hako. ANI: Katsumi Hashimoto, Kenzo Koizumi. MUS: Kenichi Kamio. PRD: Toei. 20 mins.
Based on a best-selling children's book by Satoshi Hako, this short features the self-explanatory goings-on at an educa-tional institute with a difference. Also released as a double cassette with the same crew's 20-minute *Mr. Crow the Baker* (*Karasu no Panya-san*), another Hako story.

SCHOOL SPIRITS

1995. JPN: *Gakko no Yurei*. AKA: *Spir-*its/*Ghosts of the School*. Movie. DIR: Norio Kabeshima. SCR: Masatoshi Kimura, Shigenori Kurii. DES: Shigenori Kurii. ANI: Shigenori Kurii. MUS: N/C. PRD: Toei. 45 mins. x 6 eps.
Another entry in the spooky-school genre typified by HERE COMES HANAKO, this anime is presented as short vignettes split roughly 50/50 between animation and live action. Based origi-nally on chilling tales written for *My Birthday* magazine, it was disgracefully repackaged after the rental release as ten 15-minute tapes for retail. See also REAL SCHOOL GHOST STORIES.

SCI-FI HARRY

2000. TV series. DIR: Yasuhito Kikuchi, Katsuyuki Odera. SCR: Kenichi Takashima, Mitsuhiro Yamada, Takeo Tsutsui. DES: Shinya Takahashi. ANI: Yuji Shigekuni, Keiji Tani. MUS: Jeanne D'Arc, Luca. PRD: APPP, TV Asahi. 25 mins. x 11+ eps.
Harry McQueen is a shy 17-year-old who gets picked on by school bully Chris and his gang because they know he won't fight back. Harry's imagina-tion is his escape route; fantasizing that he's the hero of one of his favorite TV shows, he retreats behind the screen into an imaginary world where he can kick Chris's butt. Then we begin to see another side to Harry. When his friend Kate, who has always stood up for him, is kidnapped by the bullies, Harry sud-denly appears to save her, though he has no idea how or why. And then a bizarre series of murders occur. Based on the manga by *Night-Head*–creator Joji "George" Iida and Asami Tojo, set in the fantasy land of the U.S. (and loaded with American names, clearly aimed squarely at a foreign release from the get-go), this might at first sight seem an unlikely project for the studio that brought you JOJO'S BIZARRE ADVENTURES, but events soon take a turn for the surreal.

SCOOPERS

1987. Video. DIR: Jun Hirabayashi, Hideo Watanabe. SCR: Monkey Punch. DES: Monkey Punch, Masakazu Abe.

Star Blazers

STAR BLAZERS © IS A REGISTERED TRADEMARK OF VOYAGER ENTERTAINMENT, INC.

ANI: Hirohide Yashikijima. MUS: N/C. PRD: ACC, Video Tech. 58 mins.
It's 2016, and Shambhala city reporter Yoko and her android boyfriend/body-guard/cameraman Vito are hunting the enigmatic criminal Mr. X. Their search leads them to the Rainbow Tow-er, where Yoko is taken hostage and Vito must battle to save her by destroy-ing the program of the Tower's central computer to prevent X's escape. Based on a manga by LUPIN III–creator Mon-key Punch.

SCRYED

2001. TV series. DIR: Goro Taniguchi. SCR: Yosuke Kuroda. DES: Hisashi Hirai. ANI: N/C. MUS: N/C. PRD: Sunrise. 25 mins. x 26 eps.
In the near future, Kanagawa Prefec-ture becomes the "Lost Ground," an alternate reality where light and dark-ness duel for control of the locals' hearts. Sixteen-year-old Kazuma is an "Inner," a child who has never left the world of the Lost Ground, forced into conflict with powerful beings known as the Altered. Announced as forthcom-ing in Japan at the time of our dead-line.

SEA OF THE TICONDEROGA

1991. JPN: *Ticonderonga no iru Umi*.

Movie. DIR: Yuji Nichimaki. SCR: Koji Kawakita. DES: Takao Kasai. ANI: Takao Kasai. MUS: N/C. PRD: Urban Project, Asmik, Kobushi Pro. 28 mins.

On December 5, 1965, a U.S. aircraft carrier is en route from Vietnam to Yokosuka, Japan. While conducting training exercises 80 miles off Okinawa, an A4 strike aircraft is loaded with a B43 hydrogen bomb, but it falls overboard and sinks in 16,000 feet of water. Based on the true story of the USS Ticonderoga, which reached Japan two days later (on the anniversary of Pearl Harbor; nice touch). Neither side revealed the incident, nor that she was carrying atomic weapons in contravention of U.S. treaties with Japan. The plane, its pilot, and the bomb were never recovered, and the incident was only declassified in 1989, causing an outcry in Japan and resulting in this environmentally themed anime. The extra "n" in *Ticonderonga* may be a genuine error in transcription or an attempt to distance the story from real events, since the anime continues with Ashika, a boy from a Japanese fishing town, contacted by telepathic whales who bring him visions of fearful sea-monsters. Then again, if you were a whale given a choice between nuclear contamination and talking to Japanese fishermen, which would you choose? For more fun with the U.S. navy, see SPACE FAMILY CARLVINSON.

SEA PRINCE AND THE FIRE CHILD *

1981. JPN: *Sirius no Densetsu*. AKA: *Legend of Sirius*. Movie. DIR: Masami Hata, Takuo Suzuki. SCR: Chiho Katsura. DES: Shigeru Yamamoto. ANI: Shigeru Yamamoto, Mikiharu Akabori. MUS: Koichi Sugiyama. PRD: Sanrio. 108 mins.

Prince Sirius comes from a family of water spirits and Princess Malta, daughter of Hyperia, from a family of fire spirits. The long and bitter war between the two makes the love of the two young protagonists impossible. When Sirius and Malta try to escape their parents' wrath, they are enveloped in a powerful storm conjured by the evil Algorac, Lord of the Winds. The Disneyesque animation style looks charming.

SEA'S DARKNESS: MOON'S SHADOW

1988. JPN: *Umi no Yami, Tsuki no Kage*. AKA: *Darkness of the Sea, Shadow of the Moon*. Video. DIR: Satoshi Dezaki. SCR: Hirokazu Mizude. DES: Setsuko Shibunnoichi. ANI: Akio Sugino, Yukari Kobayashi. MUS: N/C. PRD: Visual 80. 40 mins. x 3 eps.

These SF-horror adventures that were based on the 1987 manga in *Shojo Comic* by PURPLE EYES IN THE DARK–creator Chie Shinohara feature twin girls Ryusui and Ryufu, who discover they have unearthly powers that increase as the moon waxes. As a bonus, tape two contains a ten-minute anime based on Miyuki Kitagawa's *That Girl Is 1,000%* (*Ano Ko wa 1,000%*), a similar tale of haunting romance.

SECRET AKKO-CHAN *

1969. JPN: *Himitsu no Akko-Chan*. AKA: *Akko-chan's Secret*. TV series. DIR: Hiroshi Ikeda, Keiji Hisaoka, Masayuki Akehi, Takeshi Tamiya, Yoshio Takami. SCR: Shunichi Yukimuro, Tomohiro Ando, Masaki Tsuji, Tadaaki Yamazaki. DES: Fujio Akatsuka. ANI: Shinya Takahashi. MUS: Yasei Kobayashi. PRD: Toei, NET. 30 mins. x 94 eps.

Helpful ten-year-old Akko usually takes good care of her belongings, especially her old mirror, brought back as a present from India by her father. She polishes it carefully every night before she goes to bed, but one night she accidentally breaks it. Very sad, she buries the pieces in the garden. That night, the spirit of the mirror wakes her and gives her another mirror to thank her for cherishing the old one. Her new present is a compact with the power to transform the owner into any person or animal she chooses if she says a magical word; but the fairy warns Akko that she must keep the spell, and the powers of the mirror, a secret. Akko uses her new powers to solve the problems of friends and neighbors in her quiet hometown, and, as her confidence grows, she transforms into animal shapes and even goes to other countries. Based on the 1962 manga series by Fujio Akatsuka, who also created OSOMATSU-KUN and GENIUS IDIOT BAKABON, *SA* was the next "magical girl" series after LITTLE WITCH SALLY and confirmed the appeal of the formula. The series was remade for Fuji TV in 1988, with Hiroki Shibata as director and new character designs from Yoshinori Kanemori. Shibata returned for a *third* 28-episode TV season on TV Asahi in 1998, with character designs from Toshio Deguchi.

SECRET ANIMA SERIES *

1997. AKA: (see below). Video. DIR: Kunimitsu Ikeda, Kaoru Tomioka, Hachi Saiga. SCR: Susumu Nanase, Doctor Emu. DES: Ran Hiryu, Protonsaurus, Mon-Mon, Yokihi, Yoshimasa Watanabe. ANI: Ruthie Tanaka, Jiro Makigata. MUS: N/C. PRD: Beam Entertainment. 30 mins. x 8 eps.

An umbrella series of adaptations of pornographic manga, which, unlike the similar COOL DEVICES, was broken up and released abroad as *separate* titles. *Mama* (#1–2, released in the U.S. as *Mama Mia*) was based on a manga by Ran Hiryu and features Yuichi, an orphaned boy who discovers that his frisky stepsister Mika has been seducing her own mother to prevent her getting her kicks from making any more porn videos. For the second part, a completely different boy (confusingly also called Yuichi) loses his adoptive father in the same traffic accident that leaves his adoptive mother in a wheelchair. Now the man of the house, Yuichi discovers that Dad used to play pervy games with Mom and Rika the maid, and Yuichi carries on the noble family tradition. *Chu*^{2} (#3) consists of three far shorter tableaux from Protonsaurus, with a similar S/M theme to his work in *Cool Devices*. For U.S. release, it was combined with *Momone* (#4, aka *The Naughty Professor*), another tale of bondage from Kazu Yoshinaga, under the title *Twisted Tales of Tokyo*. In *Dream Hazard* (#5), based on a manga from CREAM LEMON's Mon-Mon, timid schoolgirl Kaori buys a virtual-reality date in order to sublimate her desires for an upperclassman. Needless to say, things go horribly wrong, and she finds herself "virtually" subjected to the usual porn anime cavalcade of abuse, assault, rape, and torture. In *Four Play* (#6–7), based on the manga *2x1* by ETCHIIS-creator Yokihi, two boys are sent to an absent classmate's home to deliver notes. However, the malingering Noriko instead seduces the sporty Junichi and eventually succumbs to the geekier charms of his quiet friend Satoshi. All three of them begin a series of sexual experiments, scandalizing their contemporaries in a Tokyo suburb. After several different scenes of naughtiness the foursome (Junichi's sister Miyuki turning up as an afterthought) agree that it's okay to do whatever they want, as long as nobody gets hurt. Junichi delivers an impassioned speech to that effect (at least, it might have been impassioned before the dubbers got hold of it) and the credits roll. In *Pianist* (#8), based on a manga by Yoshimasa Watanabe, concert pianist Seiji injures his wrist (sure he does) in a car accident, develops a crush on his robot nurse, and buys a slave-robot to remind him of her. When robot Yuna turns out to be a piano prodigy, he tries to secure her a record deal, only to discover that prejudice exists against nonhuman musicians. Finally, in Serina Kamuro's *Love2Police* (#9), three girls carry out secret missions in order to rescue boys from their virginity and any other frustrations.

Unsurprisingly, these titles register a very low level of interest from all parties concerned—starting with the original creators, since only *Pianist* has a remotely interesting plot, and even that is riddled with holes. The sex is even less entertaining, let down by substandard animation. Most noticeable is the overuse of flashbacks, a relatively easy trick using digital animation, allowing, for example, multiple scenes of video playback as *Mama Mia*'s protagonist watches his stepmother's porno appearances on tape. The low budget also shows in traditional ways, such as very limited backgrounds in several episodes and heavy reliance on pans across single images. With such bad workmanship at the Japanese end, it comes as little surprise that the U.S. dubbing crews seem similarly disinterested in their material—both *Dream Hazard* and *Mama Mia* feature particularly bad performances from actors who clearly wish they were somewhere else. Producing porn will always be a thankless task, but *Secret Anima* is a particularly low-rent example of the genre, unlikely to satisfy fans of anime or erotica. ●LNV

SECRET GARDEN, THE

1991. JPN: *Anime Himitsu no Hanazono*. AKA: *Anime Secret Garden*. TV series. DIR: Tameo Ogawa. SCR: Kaoru Umeno. DES: Hidemi Kuma, Aiko Katsumata. ANI: Hideki Kubo, Hiroshi Suzuki. MUS: Masaaki Matsumoto, Shiro Sagisu. PRD: Aubec, NHK. 25 mins. x 39 eps.

Plain, awkward Mary is neglected by her pretty mother and military father. Orphaned in India, she is sent to live with her uncle in the north of England. She discovers that her cousin Colin is as lonely as she is—after his mother's death while giving birth to him, he is both indulged and neglected by his heartbroken father and often kept locked away. But Mary's company and the fascinating project she has uncovered—finding and reviving his mother's secret garden—soon gets Colin back on his feet. When her uncle finally comes home, he finds a welcome he never imagined. Frances Hodgson Burnett's 1909 novel has been filmed many times in the West, and even made into a Broadway musical. The same author wrote LITTLE LORD FAUNTLEROY and A LITTLE PRINCESS.

SECRET OF BLUE WATER, THE *

1990. JPN: *Fushigi na Umi no Nadia*. AKA: *Nadia of the Mysterious Seas; Nadia*. TV series, movie. DIR: Hideaki Anno, Shigeru Morikawa, Masayuki, Koji Masunari, Takeshi Mori. SCR: Toshio Okada, Hisao Okawa, Kaoru Umeno. DES: Yoshiyuki Sadamoto. ANI: Kazuto Nakazawa, Shunji Suzuki, Kazunori Matsubara, Yoshiaki Yanagida, Hideaki Anno. MUS: Shiro Sagisu. PRD: Gainax, Group Tac, NHK. 25 mins. x 39 eps. (TV), 90 mins. (m).

Paris 1889 is the scene of the International Exposition. Young inventor Jean meets circus acrobat Nadia. He rescues her from a strange gang of comical villains out to steal her necklace, and the pair set off on an amazing adventure that takes them far beneath the seas, and all around the world. They face racism in France and cold-blooded killing on a remote Pacific island, see a flying contest with Chitty-Chitty Bang-Bang as one of the entrants, and share a dream sequence in which they ride in something suspiciously like Thunderbird 2 (see THUNDERBIRDS 2086). They face the last remnants of Atlantis and join the fight to save the world from domination by a mad genius. Along the way they learn that their origins are less important than what they make of themselves, and that while love can conquer all, it doesn't guarantee a happy ending. The 1993 movie *Nadia of the Mysterious Seas the Movie: Fuzzy's Secret* takes up the story some years later, with Jean rescuing a mysterious girl and the impact this has on his stormy relationship with Nadia

While working at Toho Studios in the 1970s, the young Hayao Miyazaki pitched a scenario to his bosses inspired by Jules Verne, creator of ADRIFT IN THE PACIFIC. Set in the late 19th century, *Around the World in 80 Days by Sea* would use two Vernean concepts—a trip around the world by two plucky characters on the run from bad guys, and the mighty submarine Nautilus, commanded by Captain Nemo, who has a secret past of his own. Toho didn't make the series but held onto the option. Miyazaki later used various elements of the idea in FUTURE BOY CONAN and CASTLE IN THE SKY, but it wasn't until the critical triumph of WINGS OF HONNEAMISE that Toho dusted off the outline and approached Gainax to turn it into a TV series.

SBW was conceived as a blatant pitch to the mass audience. Very rarely has this approach produced a show of such enduring charm and emotional validity. The combination of Vernean adventure, Dickensian richness of characterization (particularly in the comical semivillains Grandis, Sanson, and Hanson), nods and winks to more contemporary classics, and steam-punk technology was irresistible, propelling the series to success and Nadia to an enduring place in the list of fans' favorite characters. In Nadia, the Gainax team created a heroine who was beautiful and independent yet alone and unsure of her place in the world, capable of anger and courage yet completely opposed to killing, a heroine of color and an animal rights advocate ahead of her time. Young hero Jean, a brilliant but naïve kid with total faith in technology and innocent of the world's deceits and cruelties, is an orphan as she is. The two are bonded by loss and alienation; despite the sunny color palette of the show and its upbeat pacing and music, the audience quickly realizes that a dark and terrible fate is always waiting just out of shot, threatening to engulf the young couple—the same team's later hit EVANGELION brought the lurking darkness into the foreground. The impact of several violent scenes—which are never gratuitous but likely to be shocking to a modern Western audience in a children's series—foiled an attempt in the mid-1990s to get the show onto U.K. television screens. *SoBW* was rereleased on DVD as *Nadia: SoBW* in the U.S. in 2001, just in time to invite insidious comparisons between it and the new Disney cartoon *Atlantis: The Lost Empire.* Though the film-makers admitted to an interest in the works of Hayao Miyazaki, they denied any knowledge

of *SoBW*—compare to the controversy surrounding KIMBA THE WHITE LION. *Ill. p. 33.* ◐

SECRET OF THE SEAL, THE *

1991. JPN: *Tottoi.* Movie. DIR: Noboru Ishiguro. SCR: Ryuzo Nakanishi. DES: Haruhiko Mikomoto, Masamichi Takano. ANI: Haruhiko Mikimoto. MUS: Koichi Sakata. PRD: Nippon Animation, Nikken Academy. 90 mins.
After the death of his mother, little Alexander moves with his father and sister to the Mediterranean island of Sardinia, where he is nicknamed Tottoi. In a grotto by the sea, he finds a baby seal and its mother. They've been thought extinct in the area for ten years, and he fears that if discovered they'll be shut up in an aquarium for scientific study or experimentation. But he is not sure he can even trust his friends among the islanders to help him keep the rare animals safe. Based on the novel by Gianni Padoan, the story has very strong similarities to FLY PEEK, although the character style is more naturalistic.

SECRETS OF THE TELEPHONE CLUB

1991. JPN: *Terekura no Himitsu.* Movie. DIR: Kan Fukumoto. SCR: Satoshi Yagi. DES: Akira Narita. ANI: Kan Fukumoto. MUS: N/C. PRD: Japan Home Video. 45 mins. x 2 eps.
A lonely man discovers the seedy world of the telephone club, where he can wait to receive calls from women desperate for sex. Soon he becomes a happy escort, taking the virginity of an appreciative client and helping an unhappy housewife find fulfillment. Sometimes they just want to talk, but this adaptation of Akira Narita's manga doesn't dwell for too long on those ones. Compare to CALL ME TONIGHT.◐

SEIZE THE WIND

1988. JPN: *Kaze o Nuke.* Video. DIR: Kazunori Ikegami, Noboru Furuse. SCR: Noboru Aikawa. DES: Noboru Furuse. ANI: Noboru Furuse. MUS: Masahiro Takami. PRD: Madhouse. 60 mins.

In a sports anime that takes place in the world of motocross, 16-year-old Satoshi Ichimonji fights his way from the novice grade up to the Junior Cross championship. Motorcycle trickery abounds, alongside sporting hardships, and, of course, feckless foreign rival Jeff Anemoth. Based on the manga by SWORD OF MUSASHI–creator Motoka Murakami in *Shonen Sunday.*

SENBON MATSUBARA

1992. Movie. DIR: Satoshi Dezaki. SCR: Tetsuaki Imaizumi. DES: Setsuko Shibunnoichi. ANI: Keizo Shimizu. MUS: Masato Nichiyoshi. PRD: Magic Bus. 100 mins.
After suffering severe floods in 1753, the people of Senbon Matsubara in Shizuoka cooperate on flood prevention around the Kiso, Nagara, and Yuhi rivers. The people of Satsuma (Kumamoto Prefecture) endure great hardships after being forced to undertake the work by the central government, a subtle indication of the bad feeling that would foment into open rebellion the following century—see OI RYOMA!

SENSUALIST, THE *

1990. JPN: *Ihara Saikaku: Koshoku Ichidai Otoko.* AKA: *Ihara Saikaku's Life of an Amorous Man.* Video. DIR: Yukio Abe. SCR: Eiichi Yamamoto. DES: Yukio Abe. ANI: Tomoko Ogawa, Masaharu Endo, Hiroyuki Kondo. MUS: Keiji Ishikawa. PRD: Groupier Productions. 53 mins.
The merchant Yonosuke decides to help his underling Juzo, a comical peasant who has made an unwise bet with a malicious acquaintance. The fool has bet his manhood that he will sleep with the famous courtesan Komurasaki on their first meeting, when any cultured person would know she would not dream of doing so for the richest and most intelligent man in the land, let alone this hayseed. Yonosuke has known her for a long time, and at his request, she agrees to help the poor fool out, not only giving him

a night beyond his wildest dreams, but even writing a certificate of the event on his underwear in her most elegant calligraphy. Novelist Saikaku Ihara chronicled the follies and dramas of old-time Japan in his works. This film was based on just part of his *Life of an Amorous Man* (1682), retelling a few of the adventures of Yonosuke. The exquisite, jewel-like animation makes use of techniques that recall the traditional crafts of old Japan. Cels were not simply painted but embossed with the textures of leaves or fine fabrics. Genitals are not just pixilated or blacked out, they are transformed into symbolic representations from old woodcuts—a penis becomes the head of a tortoise, a vagina a splitting fruit or unfolding flower. Director Abe's pace is as slow and precisely calculated as a courtesan's every move, producing a hothouse atmosphere of elegant eroticism as far removed from the teenage crudities of most porn anime as Edo is from modern Tokyo. A beautiful anime. **◐**

SENTIMENTAL JOURNEY

1998. TV series. DIR: Kazuyoshi Katayama, Keiichi Sato. SCR: Tsunehisa Arakawa. DES: Keiichi Sato, Madoka Hirayama. ANI: Madoka Hirayama. MUS: Toshiyuki Okada. PRD: Sunrise, TV Tokyo. 25 mins. x 12 eps.
Twelve friends are the heroines of this high-school romance series, based on the game *Sentimental Graffiti*. Each episode focuses on one of them and her boyfriend problems—getting one, keeping one, making sure he's the right one. Aki is a violinist, Chie wants to be a folk guitarist, Chiho is the tough, sporty daughter of an *okonomiyaki* chef, Wakaba is an archer, Asako wants to be an artist, and Miyuki is fascinated with old-fashioned clothes. Players/viewers who insist on something out of the ordinary can plump for Emiru, who can see ghosts, or Honoka, who is afraid of *all* men. If that's not good enough for you, there are plenty of wounded souls to nurture—Yu pines for the man she last saw

eight years ago, while Manami is consumptive, weak, and in need of a good cuddle. Asuka is a perky events manager whose bright exterior conceals a broken heart, while Rurika is bullied at school. A show about the everyday lives and little romantic problems of 12 teenage girls isn't exactly what we expect from the Sunrise studio, but since over a dozen GUNDAM kits have been sold for every inhabitant of Japan, doubtless there was an ulterior motive: selling new models and figurines to the chiefly male target audience. The same motivation inspires game-anime tie-ins like TO HEART and SERAPHIM CALL.

SERAPHIM CALL

1999. TV series. DIR: Tomomi Mochizuki. SCR: Go Sakamoto, Sadayuki Murai. DES: Aoi Nanase, Maki Fujii. ANI: Maki Fujii. MUS: Akifumi Oda. PRD: Media works, Sunrise, TV Tokyo. 25 mins. x 12 eps.
A sci-fi respray of SENTIMENTAL JOURNEY, in which 11 beautiful girls between the ages of 12 and 25—the Seraphim—live in the future city of Yokohama Neo Acropolis. Each of them has a different talent or hangup (in place of characterization), and each has a story devoted to her. Yukina is a high-school science genius, but she's so afraid of men that she can't so much as pick up a pencil when one of them is looking at her. Tanpopo is 12, collects stuffed animals, and worries about growing up. Chinami is 16 and wants to open her own bakery and bring her divorced parents back together. Hatsumi is a sporty tomboy who's never been seen in a skirt in all her 18 years, but she's suddenly asked to model for an artist. Sakura and Shion are 16-year-old twins worried that romance may drive them apart. Their classmate Kurumi is a wannabe cartoonist in a slump, while Urara, also 16, is the daughter of the man who designed Neo Acropolis, and she loves him so much that she can't love a boy just yet. Ayaka is a spoiled rich kid whose father decides she needs to

The sexy superhero **KEKKO KAMEN**, who reduces the eye-candy formula to an absurd degree by going almost completely naked, thereby ensuring that nobody looks at her face. It's a winning combination of smut, satire, and arch cynicism, as she fights the evil school principal Great Toenail of Satan. Inspired by **MOONLIGHT MASK**, and based on a manga by Go Nagai, which has also been influential in the giant-robot genre of **MAZINGER Z** and the satanic superheroism of **DEVILMAN**. *See entry p. 200.*

Kekko Kamen

learn the value of money by getting a job at the age of 14. Saeno is the oldest at 25, an English teacher whose true passion is mathematics, but who runs into an equation she can't solve unless she uses her heart. The eleventh girl is a legend: 18-year-old Kasumi, the goddess of Acropolis whom no one has ever seen. But on Christmas Eve all the Seraphim gather at the Acropolis Tower, hoping for their personal miracles to happen.... This collection of adolescent fantasies, some with an SF twist like Yukina's *Turn-A* GUNDAM parody robot, is designed to promote a game and sell related merchandise. Players can pick their favorite Seraph and get the idol card, *gachapon* toy (see VILLGUST), action figure, and so on.

SERENDIPITY THE PINK DRAGON *

1983. JPN: *Serendipity Monogatari yori, Pure Shima no Nakamatachi.* AKA: *The Story of Serendipity: Friends of Pure Island.* TV series, movie. DIR: Nobuo Onuki, Masayoshi Osaki, Mitsuo Hikabe, Susumu Ishizaki, Keiji Hayakawa, Shigeru Omachi, Hiroyuki Yokoyama, Satoshi Inoue. SCR: Takeshi Matsuki, Tsunehisa Ito, Himiko Nakao. DES: Kazuo Tomizawa, Yoichi Otabe, Yoshiniki Nishi. ANI: Kazuo Tomizawa, Yutaka Oka. MUS: Takeo Watanabe.

PRD: Hokuto, Zuiyo Enterprise, Nippon TV. 25 mins. x 26 eps. (TV), 90 mins. Based on an illustrated book by Steven Cosgrove and Robin James, this children's series tells the story of Corna, a little boy separated from his parents after an accident at sea washed him ashore on a remote South Pacific island with a large pink egg. The egg hatches and a cute little pink creature is born that soon grows into a large dragon. It's Serendipity, who is really a sea spirit, and who becomes the lost boy's friend. Corna's new home is governed by a queen who allows him to stay. A pretty little mermaid called Laura and many strange creatures live there. When the island is threatened by a pirate band come to steal its fabled treasure, the Mermaid's Tears, Corna and his comical friends fight to protect their home. Several episodes were also compiled into a 90-minute "movie" in 1989.

The theatrical release and TV series production were started by a subsidiary of Mizutaka Enterprises, but work was abandoned with 10 episodes in the can. Only after the completion of a further 16 episodes were the series and movie released. Both have been screened in Europe, and the movie is available on video in the U.S.

SERIAL EXPERIMENTS LAIN *

1998. TV series. DIR: Ryutaro Nakamura, Shigeru Ueda, Akihiko Nishiyama, Masahiko Murata, Johei Matsuura. SCR: Chiaki Konaka. DES: Takahiro Kishida, Yoshitoshi Abe, Hiroshi Kato. ANI: Yuichi Tanaka, Masahiro Sekiguchi, Yoshihiro Sugai. MUS: Reichi Nakaido, Bôa. PRD: Pioneer, Triangle Staff, TV Tokyo. 25 mins. x 13 eps.
Shy 14-year-old Rein Iwakura meets a school friend on the Wired, a super-Internet that allows almost total immersion in cyberspace—but Chisa died by her own hand days ago. Now she says God is in the Wired. Understandably shaken, Rein is further baffled by a strange encounter in a club, where a junkie is so scared by her sudden, chilling response to his pestering

that he kills himself. Rein learns more about the Wired, drawing her further into another existence, one where Lain, her second self, lives an independent life in the electronic impulses. In an identity crisis redolent of PERFECT BLUE, Lain starts putting in appearances in the real world, causing her double to wonder which of them is real. Uncertain of her true origins or existence, or of reality itself, Rein/Lain crosses paths with the godlike entity Deus (creator of the Wired, now dwelling inside it) in a surreal struggle. The listless analogue world of the late 20th century and the digital dream of the Wired combine to present a vision of the dominance of technology so nihilistic that at times it makes EVANGELION look almost sunny.

Real originality is rare in any field, but *SEL* skillfully perverts the two-as-one magical-girl tradition in an interesting Internet-inspired direction, fused with a paranoid Luddite technophobia. Much of the credit goes to ARMITAGE III–veteran Konaka and newcomer Abe, who has since created NIEA_7. Director Nakamura deliberately plays up the low-budget animation, making a virtue of 1990s cost-cutting by contrasting Rein's flat, unnatural daily life with the luxuriant, swirling CG images of the Wired itself. Much of the "action" takes place in cyberspace or inside Rein/Lain's skull, and the blurring of links and walls between objective and subjective reality is chillingly effective. Unlike in KEY THE METAL IDOL, Rein finds ordinary life messy and banal; weighing the so-called advantages of humanity, she is prepared to trade up, a sentiment guaranteed to appeal to troubled teens.

SETON'S ANIMAL TALES

1989. JPN: *Seton Dobutsuki*. TV series. DIR: Takeshi Shirato, Eiji Okabe, Keiji Kawanami, Hiromitsu Morita, Masao Ito. Yoshikata Nitta. SCR: Yu Mizugi, Haruya Yamazaki, Sukehiro Tomita, Haruya Yamazaki, Tsunehisa Ito. DES: N/C. ANI: Kazutoshi Kobayashi, Hiro-

hide Yashikijima. MUS: N/C. PRD: Nippon Animation, Eiken, TV Asahi. 25 mins. x 45 eps.
A series of stories taken from the work of Ernest "Black Wolf" Thompson Seton, the creator of BANNERTAIL THE SQUIRREL and MONARCH, THE BIG BEAR OF TALLACH. Born in England but a Canadian emigrant, Seton was the leader of the North American Boy Scout movement from 1910 to 1915, until he left over disagreements about the "military" aspects promoted by Lord Baden-Powell and James West. Setting up the "Woodcraft League," he promoted the healthy outdoor life with his 60 books and over 400 short stories and articles. A fraction of these were adapted for this anime series, including *Monarch* (again), *Wari the Fox, Bingo the Famous Dog, Link the Puppy, The Beaver of the Poplar Tree, Fox of Springfield, Snap the Heroic Puppy, Wolf of the Badlands,* and *Silver Fox of Yellowstone,* among others.

SEVEN CITIES

1994. JPN: *Nanatoshi Monogatari*. AKA: *Story of Seven Cities*. Video. DIR: Akinori Nagaoka. SCR: Tomomi Nobe. DES: Katsumi Matsuda. ANI: Kasumi Matsuda. MUS: Hiroshi Sato. PRD: Sony Music Entertainment. 30 mins. x 2 eps.
In 2099, Earth has shifted off its axis and begins to rotate at an angle of 90% to the 20th-century equator. Three years of natural disasters follow, and when things settle down, Earth's ten billion population has died and only two million moon colonists remain. Some return to begin the repopulation of the world in seven new cities. The remaining colonists on the moon fear that their former neighbors might pose a threat and construct a ring of defense satellites to trap them on the newly repopulated homeworld—the Olympus system destroys anything that travels more than 500 meters above the surface. Then the lunar colonists are wiped out by plague. Trapped beneath a defensive ring that will operate automatically for the next 200 years, the seven newly founded cities begin to

fight one another. Moorbridge Jr., the son of the exiled ruler of Aquionia, becomes the ruler of New Camelot and leads a force to recapture his homeland. His superior tactician, Kenneth Guildford, leads an attack on an Aquionian supply base, but his victorious troops are subject to a counter-attack by the Aquionian hero Almaric Ashvail—compare to the similar well-matched foes of LEGEND OF GALACTIC HEROES, based on another novel by ToSC creator Yoshiki Tanaka.

SEXORCIST *

1996. JPN: Ningyo Tsukai. AKA: Puppet Masters. Video. DIR: Shigeru Yazaki. SCR: Kazuhiko Godo. DES: Kenji Teraoka, Kenichi Harada. ANI: Masao Tsutsumi. MUS: Kazuhiko Izu. PRD: Sente Studio. 45 mins.

The Silhouette robots of 2114 are virtual-reality "puppets" whose sensations of pleasure and pain can be passed on to their human operators. Enter Rika, a beautiful Silhouette manipulator thrown into a corporate underworld where Silhouette-gladiators fight in death-matches, and women are forced to endure assaults through the machines to which they are wired.

Despite being another smut-session of screaming girls and leering perverts, Sexorcist has a lot to teach other game adaptations. The SF/erotica combination gives two extra angles to the dreary combat of TEKKEN or TOSHINDEN. Avoiding the halfhearted hackery of most porn, it really makes use of the SF setting—particularly in the separation of body and mind. In one chilling moment, Rika sees herself through the eyes of the Silhouette she is operating and notices that an assailant is sneaking up behind her.

In legal terms, the Silhouettes are not human, so they can perform more explicit acts than normally allowed by the Japanese censor. They also speak without moving their lips, allowing the animators to concentrate their budget on the fights and naked flesh. But while it may be an outstanding exam-

ple of the genre, the genre is porn, and this offering also features bondage, tentacles, hypnotism, drugs, electric whips, and ceremonial rape. The PC game sequel to the original, featuring Rika's granddaughter, was released in the U.K. as Bishojo Fighter. **NV**

SHADOW SKILL *

1995. JPN: Kagewaza/Shadow Skill. Video, TV series. DIR: Hiroshi Negishi, Hiroyuki Kuroda, Tsukasa Sunaga. SCR: Mayori Sekijima, Masashi Sogo. DES: Toshinari Yamashita, Fumitoshi Kizaki. ANI: Yoshio Murata, Fumitoshi Kizaki. MUS: Osamu Tezuka (the other one), Tsutomu Ohira. PRD: Zero-G Room, Shadow Skill Project; Studio Deen, TV Tokyo. 45 mins. (v1), 30 mins. x 3 eps. (v2), 25 mins. x 26 eps. (TV).

In the kingdom of Kuldar (Karuta in the dub), there is only one way out of servitude—by becoming a gladiator in the arena (a thinly disguised Colosseum). Gladiators can become shavals (sevilles), the chosen knights of the kingdom. Ele Rag is the youngest of the 59 shavals, a mistress of the secret fighting art known as the Shadow Skill. She cares for Gau Ban of the Black Howling, a traumatized young orphan she found four years earlier. But Gau lives in a secret internal turmoil of honor and duty, watching Ele Rag's every move so that he may learn the Shadow Skill and become the brother she deserves.

SS was based on the 1992 Comic Gamma manga by Megumu Okada, praised in Japan for its meticulous internal logic. Okada has some great ideas, such as the Shadow Skill itself (a psychic martial art for slaves whose hands are bound) and magic in which each spell must be engaged in conversation before being unleashed. Okada's clan terminology creates "families" of people who aren't really related, defending the memories of "fathers" who weren't necessarily their biological parents. Like sumo wrestlers, clan adoption brings a new name, and like the samurai codes of old, the ignoble

death of one's master forces a period of exile while the outcast seeks revenge. It also forbids the exile to use his or her former name, so SS contains a lot of people with very long and cumbersome handles. The man known as Screep Lohengrin of the White Running in the original manga is just plain "Louie" here, for example. Similar compressions devalue the rest of the production: mere moments after we're told that Gau is mute, he breaks his vow of silence to chat with the first stranger he meets. The anime SS is reduced to a simple kung-fu revenge tragedy, as a party that consists of two warriors (Ele and Gau), a magic-user (Fowari), and a ranger/cleric (Kiao Yu) square off against people who killed their fathers, and now must prepare to die (etc.). We're occasionally reminded of the original's evil Sorphan Empire, with tales of the King of the Moon or shots of a young Gau hunting a centaur, but the invaders are greatly underused.

The one-shot video SS soon made it to the U.K. through Manga Entertainment. It performed way beyond expectations in Japan and was followed in 1996 by an additional three-part series, also released in English, though cut into the feature-length SS the Movie. The dub was done in Wales, a land known for its own arcane language, though that's no excuse for the clunky dialogue or the outrageous moment when Kiao yells away soundlessly, presumably because nobody was paying attention to the visuals. The 1998 TV series, produced after the manga had switched publication to Comic Dragon Junior, was screened in a late-night slot and restored much of the manga's back story. However, it still awaits English-language release. **LNV**

SHAKOTAN BOOGIE

1991. Video. DIR: Hiromitsu Sato, Junichi Tokaibayashi. SCR: Shikichi Ohashi. DES: Hiroyuki Horiuchi. ANI: Hiroyuki Horiuchi, Hirotaka Kinoshita. MUS: Noriyuki Asakura. PRD: Studio Pierrot. 55 mins. x 4 eps.

It's girls, gangs, and cars in this adaptation of the 1985 manga in *Young Magazine*, by **LULLABY FOR WEDNESDAY'S CINDERELLA**–creator Michiharu Kusunoki. Local tough guys steal cars, switch the plates, and sell them, but not without racing them for a while against rival gangs. The anime continues the story where the 1987 live-action version starring Kazuya Kimura left off. Compare to **INITIAL D**.

SHAMANIC PRINCESS *

1996. Video. DIR: Mitsuru Hongo, Hiroyuki Nishimura. SCR: Asami Watanabe. DES: Atsuko Ishida. ANI: Atsuko Ishida, Masahiko Ogura, Hiroyuki Nishimura. MUS: Yoshikazu Suo. PRD: Bandai, Movic, Animate Film. 30 mins. x 6 eps.

Accompanied by Japolo, her ermine-like familiar (or "Partner"), Princess Tiara is sent from the Guardian World into our own dimension to prevent an imbalance in the cosmos. As a Magic User, this is her royal duty, since the Guardians must police the actions of indestructible, unpredictable Shadows. Disguised as a schoolgirl, Tiara must find Kagetsu, a being loyal to Yord, the godlike entity that is the Guardian World's source of power. Not only has Kagetsu stolen the Throne of Yord (a direct link to unfathomable powers), but he is also her ex-beloved, and the brother of her missing best friend, Sara.

SP refers on occasion to the story of Daphne, who in Greek mythology was turned into a laurel tree to avoid the advances of Apollo—Sarah is actually trapped inside the Throne, which looks like a painting of laurel trees. But such literary pretensions are a red herring in themselves, since the six-strong committee that provided *SP*'s "story concept" are more interested in providing good-looking images. With painstakingly animated CG rose petals in the opening credits and ribbon-like adornments worthy of **OH MY GODDESS!**, they are not unsuccessful; girls duel with swords made of shadows and Tiara's luscious red hair transforms into unearthly wings beneath the light

of the moon (a "moon-tree" in Japanese is a laurel). There are faint echoes of **KIKI'S DELIVERY SERVICE** in the European setting and mundane witchery, but *SP* is very much a designer's film, with sharp characters from **RAYEARTH**'s Ishida and lush green backgrounds from **SPRIGGAN**'s Hajime Matsuoka. It also has magical powers entrapped in sigils on the sorcerers' own skins, a peculiar fad from the mid-1990s also found in **TATTOO MASTER**. The switch in directors for the final two episodes also brings a switch in plotting—parts five and six are a prequel to the first four, creating an intriguing circular structure that plays with ideas of memory, dream, and reality.

SHAME ON MISS MACHIKO

1981. JPN: *Maitchingu Machiko Sensei*. TV series. DIR: Masami Annai, Keiichiro Mochizuki. SCR: Seiko Taguchi, Chiho Shioda, Kenji Terada, Yasuko Hoshikawa. DES: Kazuya Kaminashi, Keiko Aono. ANI: Kazuya Kaminashi, Norio Hirayama. MUS: N/C. PRD: Studio Pierrot, Studio Gallop, TV Tokyo. 25 mins. x 95 eps.

Machiko is a young elementary-school teacher who does her utmost to solve the everyday problems faced by her little pupils. Unfortunately the situations and traps created by the little moppets always seem to involve Teacher losing some or all of her clothes, much to the delight of her class, and the utter disapproval of the Japanese PTA, which fulminated against lechery in a "children's" show (albeit one broadcast at 7:30 p.m.). The later **CRAYON SHINCHAN** would bring similar criticisms. ◐

SHAMEFUL *

1999. JPN: *Shusaku*. Video. DIR: Jun Fukuda. SCR: Sakura Momoi. DES: Toshihide Masudate. ANI: Toshihide Masudate. MUS: N/C. PRD: Pink Pineapple, KSS. 30 mins. x 3 eps.

Secret lusts abound in a music school, where the teacher instructs his students in more than just carrying a tune. Based on a computer game by "Elf," and shamefully similar to **WAKE**

UP ARIA. Released in the U.S. as *Shusaku* (2001). ◐

SHAMELESS SCHOOL

1995. JPN: *Heisei Harenchi Gakuen*. AKA: *Modern-Era Shameless School*. Video. DIR: Koichi Kobayashi. SCR: N/C. DES: Go Nagai. ANI: Kimiyo Ono, Taseiko Hamazu. MUS: N/C. PRD: Pink Pineapple, KSS. 47 mins.

Yamanegi is determined to enjoy his school days—a desire made easier by attending a place of learning where the teachers are more interested in looking at girls' underwear and the classes are a nonstop party. This one-shot anime revived Go Nagai's controversial 1968 manga, originally run in *Shonen Jump*, much to the annoyance of PTA organizations all over Japan. Compare to Nagai's equally silly **KEKKO KAMEN**. ◐

SHERLOCK HOUND *

1984. JPN: *Meitantei Holmes*. AKA: *Famous Detective Holmes*. TV series, movie. DIR: Hayao Miyazaki, Keiji Hayakawa, Seiji Okuda. SCR: Toshiyuki Yamazaki, Yoshihisa Araki, Hayao Miyazaki, Tsunehisa Ito. DES: Yoshifumi Kondo. ANI: Tsukasa Tannai, Seiji Kitahara. MUS: Kentaro Haneda. PRD: Tokyo Movie Shinsha, RAI, TV Asahi. 25 mins. x 26 eps. (TV), 45 mins. x 2 (m).

The great detective Sherlock Holmes and his faithful friend Dr. John Watson are in constant demand in Edwardian London to foil the evil schemes of Professor Moriarty, who is constantly out to steal some exotic treasure or cause havoc with his minions, Todd and Smiley. In this charming adventure series for children, they are transformed into anthropomorphic dogs (see also **DOGTANIAN AND THE THREE MUSKEHOUNDS**). Their adventures are full of charm, wit, and energy as they search for a missing train, track three mysterious lobsters, and defeat a "monster" in the Thames that is more than it seems. Adapted by **MONTANA JONES**–creator Marco Pagot from the original novels by Arthur Conan Doyle, this was Pagot's first work with Ghibli's giants. The series was very popular on TV in the U.K.

and is still available on video in the U.S. The episodes *Blue Carbuncle* (#5) and *Sunken Treasure* (#9) were combined to make a 1984 theatrical release shown on a double bill with Miyazaki's NAUSICAÄ. A further two, *The Kidnapping of Mrs. Hudson* (#4) and *Air War Over the Cliffs of Dover* (#10), were combined to create a 1986 "movie" shown on a double bill with CASTLE IN THE SKY. A more realistic Sherlock Holmes would get on the trail of a French master thief: see LUPIN THE MASTERTHIEF AND THE ENIGMA OF 813. The first episode also exists in an alternate dub made by TMS for promotional purposes, which showcases more realistic British accents and renames Todd and Smiley as Nigel and Bruce.

SHE'S NO ANGEL

1994. JPN: *Tenshi Nanka Janai*. AKA: *Somewhat Unangelic*. Video. DIR: Hiroko Tokita. SCR: Tomoko Konparu. DES: Yasuomi Umezu. ANI: Chuji Nakajima. MUS: Fujio Takano. PRD: Group Tac. 30 mins.
Based on the manga in *Ribbon* magazine by NEIGHBORHOOD STORY–creator Ai Yazawa, this anime features the drama and romance centering on one girl's attempt to transfer schools.

SHIBAI TAROKA

1993. JPN: *Shibai Taroka*. AKA: *Puttin' it On*. Video. DIR: Teruo Kigure. SCR: Shunsuke Amemura. DES: Shigeru Koshiba. ANI: Teruo Kigure. MUS: Toshio Okazawa. PRD: Toei, Knack. 30 mins. x 2 eps.
Hard-faced tough-guy Kusuta transfers to the Osaka area, where everyone is a hard-faced tough guy (see COMPILER). But appearances can be deceptive: he likes flowers and fairy stories. The girls love him, the guys hate him. There's trouble. Based on the 1993 manga in *Young Champion* by Shigeru Koshiba.

SHIBUYA HONKY TONK

1988. Video. DIR: Masamune Ochiai. SCR: Masaru Yamamoto. DES: N/C. ANI: Tadashi Abiko. MUS: BORO. PRD: Tokuma Japan, Knack. 35 mins. x 4 eps.

Set in 1945, this is the story of teenager Naoya Abe, who comes from a good family but is fixated by the seeming glamour of organized crime. He manages to talk his way into working for the Todogumi, the clan that controls Tokyo's fashionable Shibuya area, but it's a lot tougher and less glamorous than he hoped. When his girlfriend is threatened and he kills a rival clan member, he decides to escape to London. Volume two sees him working in London as an assistant to photographer Aoki, but he manages to get himself involved in the theft of military secrets. When his criminal past comes to light, he's sent back to Japan to face the music, but he survives and rises through the ranks of the Todogumi. Based on the semiautobiographical novel by Joji Abe, who also appears in a live-action section.

SHIHO-CHAN

1996. JPN: *Maho no Shiho-chan*. AKA: *Magical Shiho-chan*. Video. DIR: Takashi Abe. SCR: N/C. DES: Minato Koimoro. ANI: Yasuhito Kikuchi. MUS: N/C. PRD: Pink Pineapple, KSS. 30 mins. 2 eps.
Released from an icy tomb in the Antarctic, Vaj the talking penguin goes in search of a girl to protect Earth from danger by transforming into a more "adult" version of herself. This porno based on a *Young Magazine* manga by Minato Koimoro contains oblique references to EVANGELION that serve no purpose whatsoever. Ⓝ

SHIN HAKKENDEN

1999. JPN: *God Hakkenden*. TV series. DIR: Katsuyoshi Yatabe, Toshiaki Suzuki, Kenji Yoshida. SCR: Yasushi Hirano. DES: Atsuko Ishida, Masahiko Okura. ANI: Moriyasu Taniguchi, Shinichiro Minami. MUS: N/C. PRD: Beam Entertainment, TV Tokyo. 25 mins. x 21 eps.
The year is 2588 in the system of Godworld and its eight satellites. Humanity came here in the distant past, after a long journey across the stars from Earth. Now the system is ruled by a loose coalition of powerful families:

The most powerful robot in the world will only obey the commands of Japanese schoolboy Daisaku Kusama. The generation weaned on ASTRO BOY had their own children in the 1990s, encouraging a "retro" fad for nostalgic remakes that attempted to appeal to both generations at once. Paramount among these was Yasuhiro Imagawa's GIANT ROBO, made in a 1960s style but for a 1990s audience. The show mixed exuberant camp and techno paranoia, but alienated some of its audience through a long-delayed finale. *See entry p. 142.*

Giant Robo

© 1992/1995 HIKARI PRODUCTIONS/AMUSE VIDEO/PLEX/ATLANTIS

House Owari, House Meed, and House Iigy. The story begins when Kai, the heir to House Owari, attacks an icy planet. Living in a humble village on the surface is Ko, a young boy who is perpetually arguing with his father. When Kai's navy arrives, Ko takes his father's mighty Murasame sword to fight back, and his adventures begin. A sci-fi remake of HAKKENDEN. (Not to be confused with Pioneer's continuation of the original *H* series, *Shin [New] Hakkenden*).

SHINESMAN *

1995. JPN: *Tokumu Sentai Shinesman*. AKA: *Special Duty Battle Team Shinesman*. Video. DIR: Shinya Sadamitsu. SCR: Hideki Sonoda. DES: Kiyoharu Ishii, Atsuo Kobu. ANI: Kiyoharu Ishii. MUS: N/C. PRD: Sony, Animate Film. 30 mins. x 2 eps.
Hiroya Matsumoto is a bright young salesman working for Right Trading Company, devoted to his job and to his younger brother, Yota. But after work he swaps his business suit for red combat armor and puts in overtime as leader of the company's Special Duty Combat Unit division. He and his four colleagues Ryoichi Hayami (green), Shojo Yamadera (gray), Shotaro Ono (sepia), and Riko Hidaka (pink) are

the Shinesman team. They're under the command of Kyoko Sakakibara of Human Resources and helped by support staff Hitomi Kasahara and Tsukasa Nakamura, and their sworn mission is to defend the Right Trading Company and the world from the invaders from Planet Voice, who are bent on conquering Earth. Sasaki, the prince of Voice, and his strategist sidekick, Seki, are already on Earth implementing the devious plan—through their company Science Electronics, they plan to take over the world through building a great business empire. They've started out with theme parks and a TV show that's wowing kids everywhere; Yota is one of its biggest fans. This is a bizarre combination of *Power Rangers* and *Wall Street*, based on Minamu Tachibana's manga in *Comic Bokke*. Bad acting, recycled footage, silly dialogue, and insane plotting are presented as a satire—though since one gets plenty of that in anime anyway, it's tempting to suggest this is the same old same-old, just presented "ironically." Another allegory of corporate competition, this time about video formats, can be discerned beneath the surface of **ARMITAGE III**.

SHINSENGUMI FARCE
1989. JPN: *Shogeki Shinsengumi*. Video. DIR: Hiromi Noda, Takenori Kawata. SCR: Hiromi Noda. DES: Hiromi Noda. ANI: Michi Sato. MUS: N/C. PRD: ACC, Tanihara Studio, Random. 30 mins.
A comical depiction of the unrest caused by the arrival of Commodore Perry's black ships in 1853, as nationalists and *ultra*-nationalists fight over who should rule Japan in the name of the emperor (see **OI RYOMA!**). As the rival domains of Satsuma and Choshu jostle for power, the Shinsengumi organization becomes the emperor's "protectors" in Kyoto. Hyped on release as "the Shinsengumi as you've never seen them before," somewhat ironically since anime *never* seems to have portrayed the Shinsengumi as the vigilante extremists they actually were. Similarly sanitized versions would appear in

ZEGUY and in Nagisa Oshima's live-action *Gohatto* (2000), which romanticized them as sexually confused pretty-boys.

SHOCKING PINK GIRL MOMOKO
1990. Video. DIR: Masakatsu Tonokawa. SCR: Tetsuya Aikawa. DES: Tetsuya Aikawa. ANI: Hiroyoshi Sugawara. MUS: N/C. PRD: Apollon, Mook, Central AV. 30 mins. x 2 eps.
The misadventures of a large-chested bimbo, based on Tetsuya Aikawa's manga in *Manga Sunday* magazine. She wants to be a star like Marilyn Monroe, but it's a tough route to the top, and it unsurprisingly involves taking off her clothes. ◐

SHOGUN WARRIORS
1977.
This is not an anime show, but it was the first major impact of anime robots on U.S. consciousness since **ASTRO BOY**. It's a brand name created by Mattel for a range of unrelated anime robot toys imported from Japan. Monogram also produced plastic kits of the toys, and in 1979 Marvel acquired permission to produce a comic book featuring the first three robots licensed, although the story lines and characters bear no relationship to the original Japanese series. The comic ran for 20 issues. By 1980, the line was at an end, but it was massively influential at the time; when **FORCE FIVE** was advertised in 1981, Jim Terry Productions' flier for the show labeled it "for the kids who have already bought $75 million worth of these Super Robot toys marketed by Mattel under the name of *The Shogun Warriors*." See also **GODAIKIN**. The names used in the U.S. included (in order of U.S. release) Raydeen (*Brave Reideen*, see **BRAVE RAIDEEN**), Combatra (**COMBATTLER V**), Dangard Ace (**DANGARD ACE**), Mazinga and Great Mazinga (see **MAZINGER Z**), Daimos (see **STARBIRDS**), Dragun, Raider, and Poseidon (see **GETTER ROBO** G), **GRANDIZER**, and Voltus V (**VOLTUS**).

SHOOT!
1994. JPN: *Aoi Densetsu Shoot*. AKA: *Blues Legend Shoot*. TV series, movie. DIR: Daisuke Nishio, Akinori Yabe, Takenori Kawata, Masahiro Hosoda, Tatsuo Misawa, Hiroyuki Kadono. SCR: Junji Takegami, Kazuhiko Kobe. DES: Shingo Araki. ANI: Shingo Araki, Masami Abe, Toshio Takahashi. MUS: Yusuke Honma. PRD: Toei, Fuji TV. 25 mins. x 58 eps. (TV), 25 mins. (m).
Toshi joins his high-school soccer team and is enjoying the training and social life to the full. Then, in the middle of the series, Kubo, the popular captain of the team, has a cardiac arrest on the pitch and dies. The rest of the series is the story of how Toshi and his teammates cope with this shattering loss (see **TOUCH** for a baseball drama along the same lines). The short film of the same title, also released in 1994, brings back many memories for the team members of their match against a squad from Germany, including an old friend of Kubo's. Based on the 1990 *Shonen Sunday* manga by Tsukasa Oshima.

SHOYONOID MAKO-CHAN
1998. Video. DIR: Sassai Ima. SCR: Sassai Ima. DES: Sassai Ima. ANI: Sassai Ima. MUS: N/C. PRD: JVD. 30 mins. x 2 eps.
A deceased superheroine is brought back from the dead when her inventor father combines her with the body of a slightly underage-seeming android. Then she takes her clothes off. ◐

SHURATO
1989. JPN: *Tenku no Senki Shurato*. AKA: *Heavenly Chronicle Shurato*. TV series, video. DIR: Mizuho Nishikubo, Takao Koyama, Ippei Kuri, Kazuhiro Mori, Shinji Takahashi, Satoshi Okada, Kiyoshi Murayama, Koji Masunari. SCR: Mayori Sekijima, Takao Koyama, Akinori Endo, Go Mihara. DES: Matsuri Okada, Masaki Nakao, Ammonite, Torao Arai. ANI: Masaki Nakao, Nobuyoshi Habara, Kenichi Okazaki. MUS: Hiroya Watanabe. PRD: Tatsunoko, TV Tokyo. 25 mins. x 36 eps. (TV), 30 mins. x 6 eps. (v).

Close friends Shurato and Gai are fighting in a martial-arts tournament in modern-day Tokyo when they are hauled into another dimension and find that they have new powers bestowed by Asian gods and by *shakti*, animal totems with strange powers of their own. Shurato is one of the Eight Warriors of Vishnu, whose celestial kingdom is under threat of invasion from Asura. Gai is also one of these mystic warriors, but when Vishnu's treacherous general, Indra, turns the goddess into a statue and blames Shurato, Gai sides with Indra. The two close friends are now mortal enemies. Branded a traitor, can Shurato save Vishnu, her kingdom, and his friend? Can the two get back to their own lives? The series ended tragically, but six further episodes were released on video in 1991 and 1992, extending the story.

Though possessing a Hindu-mythos setting redolent of RG VEDA, this is a series aimed squarely at the teenage boy market; a decade on, transforming the shakti into flying skateboards looks like a mistake. With the guiding hand of Tatsunoko's legendary producer Ippei Kuri on the tiller, *Shurato* delivers the goods. It was the number-one series in Japan in its year of release.

SHUTENDOJI *

1989. AKA: *Star Hand Kid; Star Demon*. Video. DIR: Junji Nishimura, Masaaki Sudo, Jun Kawagoe. SCR: Masashi Sogo. DES: Satoshi Hirayama. ANI: Hideyuki Motohashi. MUS: Fumitaka Anzai. PRD: Dynamic Planning, Studio Signal. 50 mins. x 4 eps.
The childless Mr. and Mrs. Shutendo are praying for divine intervention at a shrine when two giant ogres crash through the space-time continuum. One of them is carrying a baby in his mouth, leaving it with them and promising to return in 15 years. Jiro, as they call the child, grows up to be a fine young man (albeit one who casts a giant, horned shadow) and is reluctant to return to his real parents when the allotted time expires.

Based on Go Nagai's 1977 manga for *Shonen Magazine, Shutendoji* replays the creator's earlier DEVILMAN but with solely Japanese mythical references. Drawing on one of the JAPANESE FOLK TALES in which Minamoto no Yorimitsu and several other warriors defeated an ogre who abducted a local maid, *Shutendoji* begins with two monsters fighting across time, crashing from medieval Kyoto, past the mystified crew of a spaceship, before ending up in modern Japan. The first two episodes are concerned with Jiro's attempts to come to terms with his heritage and fight off his supernatural relatives. His teacher, possessed by evil, kidnaps Jiro's girlfriend, Miyuki, intending to use her as a sacrifice to open the interdimensional barrier that holds back the demons. He must also kill off the evil monk Jawanbo, whose son swears vengeance. By this point, however, Jiro has been thrown forward to the year 2100. He arrives in time to save the Iron Kaiser, a war cyborg sent on a suicide mission to protect its ship, the Alfard. Captain Persis Mahmoud (a CUTEY HONEY lookalike) promises to help return Jiro to his own time; a plan delayed by the revelation that Iron Kaiser is Jawanbo's son, whose life has been prolonged for decades with cybernetic implants, as he waits for the chance to avenge his father's death. For the finale, Jiro and his band must fight their way out of hell, while his adoptive human mother goes slowly insane, decorating the walls of her cell with pictures of hell, until Jiro's adoptive father destroys the pictures and saves Jiro's life. One of the better adaptations of Nagai's work, with a clever script, chilling visuals, and inspired plot twists that bridge time and space. *Ill. p. 423.* ⚫Ⓝ⚫

SIAMESE CAT

2001. JPN: *Siam Cat*. Movie. DIR: Masahiro Hosoda. SCR: Kihiro Ono. DES: Shingo Araki, Michi Himeno. ANI: Masuo Nakayama. MUS: Nao Kisugi. PRD: Buyu. N/D mins.
Jun and Naomi are two pretty disc-jock-

eys who comprise "Siamese Cat," a secret government antiterrorist rapid-response team. Jun handles guns and martial arts, Naomi does communications and demolitions, while Mr. Kuritagachi, vice-president of the Cabinet Research Room, is their government contact. When the terrorist Shunsuke Kaido (aka Asian Tiger), kidnaps the Japanese prime minister, Siamese Cat goes into action, competing against a rival government's special force, Major Isurugi's Mighty Dog. *Charlie's Angels*, Japanese style, courtesy of LUPIN III–creator Monkey Punch.

SIGN OF THE OTAKU

1994. JPN: *Otaku no Seiza*. AKA: *Fanboy Constellation*. Video. DIR: Junji Nishimura, Akira Nishimori. SCR: Masashi Sogo. DES: Hisashi Eguchi, Noboru Furuse, Hiroshi Motomiya. ANI: Tatsuo Okano. MUS: Aurora 5. PRD: KSS. 30 mins. x 2 eps.
A new idol group, the Aurora Girls, are the greatest threat to humankind ever known. They plan to wipe out civilization by spreading the otaku disease, a deadly virus that transforms ordinary people into hard-core anime fans. Packed with anime parodies, including affectionate homages to OTAKU NO VIDEO, this was based on an NES game that featured designs from Hisaishi Eguchi and Hiroshi Motomiya, better known for ROUJIN Z and MY SKY.

SILENT MÖBIUS *

1991. Movie, TV series. DIR: Kazuo Tomizawa, Michitaka Kikuchi, Hideki Tonokatsu, Kunitoshi Okajima. SCR: Michitaka Kikuchi, Kei Shigema, Hiroyuki Kawasaki, Kenichi Kanemaki, Nami Narita, Katsuhiko Takayama. DES: Kia Asamiya (pseudonym for Michitaka Kikuchi), Michitaka Kikuchi, Yasuhiro Moriki, Yutaka Izubuchi, Masaki Tanaka. ANI: Michitaka Kikuchi, Masahide Yanasawa, Kunihiro Abe, Tetsuro Aoki, Nobuyuki Kitajima, Moriyasu Taniguchi. MUS: Kaoru Wada. PRD: AIC; Radix, TV Tokyo. 54 mins., 60 mins. (m), 25 mins. x 26 eps. (TV).
In the year 2028, Tokyo is overcrowd-

ed, polluted, and (unlike present-day Tokyo) occasionally attacked by demonic entities known as the Lucifer Hawks, who are using Japan's luckless capital as an interdimensional portal. Hence the formation of the Attacked Mystification Police Department, a unit designed to prevent the Lucifer Hawks from causing havoc. In a setup not dissimilar to **BUBBLEGUM CRISIS**, the tough half-human leader Rally Cheyenne heads a group of uniformed beauties—cybernetic medium Lebia Maverick, Australian cyborg Kiddy Phenil, old-school Japanese mystic Nami Yamigumo, psychic dispatcher Yuki Saiko, and newest recruit Katsumi Liqueur, daughter of the arch-mage Gigelf and wielder of his sword Grospoliner. In mixing a cyberpunk look with occult imagery, *SM: The Motion Picture* is a visual feast. This is a dark, brooding anime aimed at an audience familiar with Kia Asamiya's original 1988 manga in *Comic Comp*, an assumption that may leave the uninitiated viewer feeling confused. Matters are not helped by the extensive use of flashbacks—as with the manga, the narrative pattern is one of introducing "present-day" action in order to bracket a story from a character's past. Thus, for part of the action, Katsumi Liqueur is a hardened Lucifer-Hawk hunter and a member of the team, though several scenes also depict her as a fresh-faced arrival in 2024, unaware of the secrets that will be imparted to her by her dying mother. Though the first film ends in 2028, *SM 2* (1992), released on a triple bill with **WEATHERING CONTINENT** and the second part of **HEROIC LEGEND OF ARSLAN**, continues in 2025, with Katsumi's permission to leave Tokyo revoked, and her reluctant recruitment into the AMPD. Both movies share the same dark, brooding elegance; the ambience is definitely that of *Blade Runner*, with "spinner" vehicles flying through an almost permanently rain-swept Tokyo hiding terrors under its shiny carapace. They are triumphs of mood and atmosphere, with little in the way of narrative variety but lashings of cyber-noir style.

There was also a 54-minute *Making of SM* video in the same year—*SM* was *very* popular in the Japanese fan community, which lapped up not only the manga and movies, but several novels, including a series of spinoffs set in the 19th century (during the last invasion of the Lucifer Hawks), a computer game from Gainax, and a series of CD dramas.

As studios scrambled for TV product in the wake of the success of **EVANGELION**, many old favorites were snapped up. *SM* was one of them, but the opportunity to reset to zero and remake the series was somewhat defeated by the low budgets of 1990s TV. Though 13 hours of running time allow for better fleshing-out of character backgrounds, the TV version disappointingly dumps much of the movies' style without adding much substance. Its animation and scripting are trite and undistinguished, limited time and budget watering down the impressive look of manga and movies; even the terrifying Lucifer Hawks now looks more **ULTRAMAN** than Asamiya.

SILENT SERVICE, THE *

1995. JPN: *Chinmoku no Kantai*. TV special, video. DIR: Ryosuke Takahashi, Masamitsu Hidaka, Koji Koshigoe. SCR: Soji Yoshikawa, Akira Nishimori, Takeshi Ashizawa. DES: Shigeru Kato, Hisashi Hirai, Kimitoshi Yamane. ANI: Shigeru Kato, Keizo Shimizu, Hisashi Hirai. MUS: Akira Senju. PRD: Sunrise, Video Champ, TBS. 100 mins. (TVm), 57 mins., 60 mins. (v).

As part of the surrender terms set at the end of WWII, Japan does not have an army so much as a "Defense Force." However, various interests have been developing the Seabat—a secret nuclear submarine created by both U.S. and Japanese ingenuity. It's on the cutting edge of military technology, armed with 50 of the most powerful nuclear weapons ever developed, manned by a crew believed to be dead, and led by Shiro Kaieda, an officer so devoted to the principle of peace that he will go to any lengths to uphold it.

His ideas, however, differ somewhat from his superiors', as he steals the Seabat, renames it Yamato (see **STAR BLAZERS**), and declares it to be an independent nation. Now former Japanese comrades and U.S. allies alike are equally determined to capture or destroy them. Kaieda is playing for the ultimate prize, by the rules he learned from America, with the most powerful weapon in the world to back him up.

Based on Kaiji Kawaguchi's controversial 1988 manga in *Comic Morning*, *SS* asked pertinent questions about Japan's role in the modern world, when, during the bubble economy of the 1980s, it was a major player on the world stage but hamstrung and embarrassed by its reliance on the unpredictable U.S. for defense (see **SEA OF THE TICONDEROGA** and **PAPA MAMA BYE-BYE**). The anime version, however, was made after a succession of events that diluted the stirring message of the original, commencing with the collapse of the Soviet Union. After the Gulf War, from which the resource-hungry Japan benefited at the expense of other nations' soldiers, Japan was "invited" to join policing actions in Cambodia, negating much of the impact of the postwar restrictions on sending troops abroad. The war in the Balkans (a heavy influence on **GASARAKI**), with its succession of broken truces and pyrrhic victories, made foreign military involvement look distinctly unappealing. Accordingly, the pacifist movement in Japan now had two factions, those who opposed war itself on moral grounds (see **BAREFOOT GEN**) and a growing number who simply couldn't see the point in wasting any money on it when the U.S. was doing such a fine job on its own. In other words, by the time *SS* got its premier as a TV movie on TBS, it had already been overtaken by history—though still a chilling controversy redolent of **WARTIME ANIME**, it was less of an anti-American manifesto than a modern-day **DEEP BLUE FLEET**—the opportunity to set up war-gaming scenarios between nominally friendly nations. Two further installments went straight to video but were not released abroad. Two other Kawaguchi manga, **NINE LOVE STORIES** and **HARD AND LOOSE**, were also adapted for anime. The flagship of the U.S. 7th Fleet, the Carl Vinson, would appear again in **SPACE FAMILY CARLVINSON.**

SILVER FANG

1986. JPN: *Ginya: Nagareboshi Gin.* AKA: *Silver Tooth: Shooting Star Silver.* TV series. DIR: Tomoharu Katsumata, Yugo Serikawa, Kazumasa Horikawa, Nobutaka Nishizawa, Masayuki Akehi, Tatsuo Higashino. SCR: Michiru Umadori, Kenji Terada. DES: Joji Yanagise. ANI: Koji Yanagise, Masaharu Endo, Tetsuro Aoki. MUS: Goro Omi. PRD: Toei, TV Asahi. 25 mins. x 21 eps. Gin, a beautiful dog with a silver-white coat, is third in a line of attack dogs trained by their master Gobei to fight with Aka Kabuto, the fearsome bear of the mountain. While hunting with Gobei, Gin meets his father, Riki, now the amnesiac leader of a pack of wild dogs determined to kill Aka Kabuto. The wild Riki and the domesticated Gin join forces and go in search of other brave dogs. Yoshihiro Takahashi's manga from *Shonen Jump* ran for several years, but the anime didn't do as well as other shaggy-dog tales like **CALL OF THE WILD.**

SIN: THE MOVIE *

2001. Video. DIR: Yasunori Urata. SCR: Carl Macek. DES: Dan Kongoji, Makoto Kobayashi. ANI: Dan Kongoji. MUS: Masamichi Amano. PRD: ADV Films, Phoenix Entertainment. 60 mins. Late in the 21st century, Freeport is plagued by crime and corruption. Crack paramilitary unit HARDCORPS is there to sort it out. Hardman Colonel John Blade comes up against an enemy worthy of his steel in his latest case. Ruthless mogul Elixis Sinclaire, founder of multimillion-dollar biotechnology corporation SinTEK, has recently been developing something really big; at the same time, a wave of kidnappings in the city is baffling the regular law enforcement ser-

vice. A U.S.–Japanese coproduction with two different subtitle scripts giving two story lines, this is an interesting experiment that's at least an effort to do something new with DVD's many possibilities. The original *Sin* computer game was bundled onto the same DVD.

SINDBAD THE SAILOR *

1962. JPN: *Arabian Night Sindbad no Boken.* AKA: *Arabian Night Sindbad Adventure.* Movie. DIR: Taiji Yabushita, Yoshio Kuroda. SCR: Osamu Tezuka, Morio Kita. DES: Yasuo Otsuka. ANI: Sanae Yamamoto. MUS: Isao Tomita, Masao Yoneyama. PRD: Toei. 81 mins. Sindbad and his friend Ali meet an old man on the seashore who gives them the map to an island of treasure. They sail off in search of it but are imprisoned in one of the countries they visit. Released through the efforts of the beautiful Princess Samir, they head off once more but are pursued by the evil Grand Vizier, who wants the treasure for himself.

After this popular, big-name movie inspired by the **ARABIAN NIGHTS**, Sindbad would return for the unrelated *Arabian Nights: Sindbad's Adventure* (1975, *Sindbad no Boken*), a 52-episode Nippon Animation series on Fuji TV, directed by Fumio Kurokawa. Though aimed at a younger audience, the series crammed in more of the original, including the stories of Ali Baba (see **ALIBABA'S REVENGE**) and **ALADDIN AND THE WONDERFUL LAMP.**

SINS OF THE SISTERS *

1990. JPN: *Sei Michaela no Gakuen Hyoryuki.* AKA: *Tales of Saint Michaela's Academy.* Video. DIR: Hiroshi Fukutomi, Yorifusa Yamaguchi. SCR: Ryo Motohira, Masaru Yamamoto. DES: Michitaka Kikuchi. ANI: Tetsuro Aoki, Mitsuru Takanashi. MUS: N/C. PRD: Visual SD, Production Eureka, OL Production. 40 mins. x 2 eps., 45 mins. x 2 eps. During the ill-fated Children's Crusade of A.D. 1212, Pope Innocent III double-crosses the loyal Christian soldiers and sells them to African slavers. Distraught

Left to right: Feral cat-girl Meryl, rakish prince Van, and lost Japanese schoolgirl Hitomi, from Kazuki Akane's wonderful **ESCAFLOWNE.** Deliberately engineered to appeal to both the male and female audiences, *Escaflowne* combines war and romance in a fantasy world, all seen through the eyes of a refugee from Earth. One of the best anime TV series of recent years, it was mercilessly hacked to bits by misguided broadcasters determined to make it "suitable" for the U.S. market. *See entry p. 115.*

Escaflowne

© SUNRISE • TX

at his betrayal by the very church he is sworn to serve, the children's leader, Hans, throws himself into the sea. Centuries later, he is reincarnated as a hermaphrodite in a convent school, where he seduces the girls and leads them in a bloody revolt against the oppressive nuns. Seizing control of the nuns' time tunnel, Hans (now called Aiko) and his/her chums travel back to Japan's Amakusa Rebellion (see **NINJA RESURRECTION**), where they fight the evil Christians. Eventually, all religions are wiped out in a worldwide atheist jihad, and the battle-hardened schoolgirls decide to go back in time again to save the original Hans from the slavers. Meanwhile, Hans/Aiko's lesbian lover, Rika, is brought back to life by Aron/Yuki, an evil nun out to retrieve her kamikaze pilot boyfriend from hell.

An everyday story of multiverse revenge, bare-breasted zombies, mass murder, and kung-fu schoolgirls— prime candidate for the most mind-boggling plot in anime, further mangled on U.S. release when only the final two episodes were released. Thus, the opening half of Hide Takatori's original novel is only discernable through flashbacks and occasional asides, while the complex (and paradoxical) rewrite of both European and Japanese history is buried amid a flurry of leaden dialogue and lesbian titillation. One of the funniest anime since **DRAGON HALF**, albeit unintentionally, with immortal lines like, "I must avert Yuki's evil plot, or else I will evaporate!" **N**

SISTER PRINCESS

2001. TV series. DIR: Kiyoshi Ohata, Kazuo Nogami. SCR: Masaharu Amiya, Koichi Taki. DES: Yasunari Nitta. ANI: Osamu Kobayashi, Yasuo Okawara. MUS: N/C. PRD: Sunrise, TV Tokyo. 25 mins. x 26 eps.
Disgraced when he fails his high-school entrance exam, Wataru Minakami is sent by his father to a remote island school, where he is the sole boy in a population of 12 pretty girls. A bizarre mixture of **TENCHI MUYO!** and *The Prisoner* ensues.

SKYERS 5

1967. TV series. DIR: Seiji Sasaki, Takeshi Yamamoto, Takeshi Kawauchi, Satoshi Murayama. SCR: Norimasa Mayumi, Kenji Nakano. DES: Noboru Kawasaki. ANI: Shuichi Seki. MUS: Ichiro Tsukasa, Sanpei Akasaka. PRD: TCJ, Eiken, TBS. 25 mins. x 12 eps.
When he receives a microfilm from a dying man, Shotaro becomes the target of the international arms syndicate Ghost, which kills his mother and sister. He is enlisted in Japanese International Secret Police, along with the agents Captain, Polka, Yuri, and Sampson. With Shotaro as their fifth team member, they form the "Skyers," a group of secret agents with high-tech gadgets, ready for the (almost) impossible mission of defeating Ghost's plans for world domination. Perhaps the earliest anime to introduce a five-strong team of Hero, Rogue, Big Guy, Comic Relief, and Token Girl (see **BATTLE OF THE PLANETS**). In 1971, the series was remade in color.

SLAM DUNK

1994. TV series, movie, TV specials. DIR: Hiromichi Matano, Nobuaki

Nishizawa, Hiroyuki Kadono, Masayuki Akehi, Kazuhisa Takenouchi, Satoshi Nakamura. SCR: Yoshiyuki Suga, Nobuaki Kishima. DES: Masaki Sato, Hidemi Kuma. ANI: Masaki Sato, Yoichi Onishi, Takahiro Kagami. MUS: Takanobu Soda, BMF. PRD: Toei, TV Asahi. 25 mins. x 130 eps. (TV); 30 mins., 48 mins., 45 mins., 40 mins. (m); 50 mins. x 3 (TVm).
Hanamichi Sakuragi joins Shohoku High School as a senior and falls in love with gorgeous Haruko Akagi. But his romantic record in junior high was terrible—he's been dumped by 50 girls. This could have something to do with the fact that he's tall and skinny, with red hair, an attitude with very little respect for others, and tremendous fighting abilities; but whatever it is, he's determined to overcome his problem and win Haruko. She already has a boyfriend, Kaede Ryukawa, who's crazy about hoops, and when Hanamichi learns that her beloved older brother, Takenori, is captain of the Shohoku basketball team, he decides to take up the sport. He gradually learns that there's a lot more to basketball than he ever imagined, and as he gets more and more involved with his teammates, he starts to use his strength for something other than fist-fights.

Like Takehiko Inoue's original 1990 manga in *Shonen Jump*, *SD* depicts basketball games with loving realism, but with character development and plotting good enough to interest nonaddicts. More of the same would follow in the movie editions, *Slam Dunk* (1994), *SD: National Championships, Hanamichi Sakuragi* (1994, *SD: Zenkoku Seiha Da! Sakuragi Hanamichi*), *Shohoku's Biggest Crisis: Enter the Hanamichi* (1995, *Shohoku Saida no Kiki: Moero Sakuragi Hanamich*), and *Roaring Basketman Soul! Hanamichi and Ryukawa's Hot Summer* (1995, *Hoero Basketman Damashi: Hanamichi to Ryukawa no Nekki Natsumi*). There were also three "TV specials"—*SD: Decisions at Shohoku Basketball Club* (1994, *Ketsui no Shohoku Basuke-bu*); reedited versions of episodes 40 and 41, *SD: King of the*

Rebound (1995, *Rebound-O*); and episodes 62 and 63, *SD Special* (1995).

SLAYERS *

1995. TV series, movie, video. DIR: Takashi Watanabe, Susumu Ishizaki, Kazuo Yamazaki, Masahito Sato, Yoshiaki Iwasaki, Moto Kawaguchi, Seiji Mizushima, Eiji Sato. SCR: Takao Koyama, Katsuhiko Chiba, Jiro Takayama, Tetsuko Watanabe, Yasushi Yamada, Katsumi Hasegawa. DES: Naomi Miyata, Kenji Teraoka, Toshihasa Higashi. ANI: Naomi Miyata, Kazuhiro Sasaki, Seiji Kikuchi, Mitsuru Abunai. MUS: Osamu Tezuka (the other one), Vink. PRD: IG Film, SoftX, TV Tokyo. 25 mins. x 78 eps., (TV), 65 mins. (m1), 85 mins. (m2), 80 mins. (m3), 64 mins. (m4), 40 mins. (m5), 30 mins. x 3 eps. (v1), 30 mins. x 3 eps. (v2).
Hoping to obtain the Sword of Light, a powerful artifact wielded by the slow-witted Gourry Gabriev, flat-chested teen sorceress Lina Inverse decides to accompany him on his travels. The pair wander a sub-D&D world in search of fortune, helped and hindered by a changing stock company of sidekicks and adversaries, which include Amelia, a self-proclaimed Champion of Justice, the cursed swordsman Zelgadis, and the priestly prankster Xelloss. One of the most popular anime franchises of the 1990s, along with **TENCHI MUYO!**, *Slayers* remained a popular choice throughout the teens of its original 12-year-old target audience, leaping from Hajime Kanzaka's original 1989 short stories in *Dragon* magazine, illustrated by Rui Araizumi, to a long-running set of novels and the inevitable manga and anime spinoffs, eventually sliding from TV to video. Set in a complicated fantasyland supposedly in a neighboring plane of existence to the same creator's **LOST UNIVERSE**, it is the antidote to the deadly serious **RECORD OF LODOSS WAR**, with a cynical cast modeled on argumentative role-players. *Slayers* makes light of its own lumpen predictability, with the characters constantly bickering about food, being double-crossed by feckless clients, and

lamenting the formulaic setups they face. Ridiculing its own shortcomings, *Slayers* has successfully kept a strong following that watches for what some might call biting satire, and others bad workmen blaming their tools.

The three 26-episode TV seasons (branded *Slayers*, *S Next*, and *S Try*) also came accompanied by a set of theatrical releases, beginning with *Slayers: The Movie* (1995). In order not to disturb the continuity of the ongoing TV series, writer/director Kazuo Yamazaki opted for a story from a spinoff continuity, the *S Special* tales set two years before Lina's first meeting with Gourry. While the TV show contained many running "gags" about breasts and the effect of menstruation on magic powers, it remained essentially asexual. However, with the absence of TV restrictions, the first and subsequent movies retain Naga from the stories, a large-breasted, cackling sorceress and self-appointed traveling companion for the young Lina, her one-time enemy and sometime sidekick. Four further films followed: *S Return* (1996), *S Great* (1997), *S Gorgeous* (1998), and *S Premium* (2001). Meanwhile, the prequels also made it straight to video with *S Special* (1996, released in the U.S. as *S Dragon Slave* and *S Explosion Array*, aka *S Book of Spells* on DVD) and *S Excellent* (1998). Naga and her breasts have become three very popular characters in the series, and long-term fans of the series wait eagerly to see how the writers can explain not only her disappearance between the end of *S Special* and the beginning of the original series, but also why she is never even mentioned after the events of the videos. Other spinoffs include the *Slayers* game for the SNES and *S Royal* for the Sega Saturn, the CD *S Etcetera*, and the CD-ROM *S Hyper*. In a final irony, the *Slayers* universe was sold as an add-on to the *Magius* role-playing game, bringing it full circle to the format that originally inspired it. *Ill. p. 61.*

SLEAZY ANGELS *
1998. JPN: *Koin Tenshi*. Video. DIR: Sas-

sai Ima. SCR: Sassai Ima. DES: Sassai Ima. ANI: Sassai Ima. MUS: N/C. PRD: Uill Animation, JVD. 30 mins.
Three pretty girls decide to make their own erotic video, are unsurprisingly surprised to find that they enjoy it, and want to do it again. ◉

SLIGHT FEVER SYNDROME *
1996. JPN: *Binetsubyo Kogun*. Video. DIR: Taiichi Kitagawa, Kozo Shirakawa. SCR: Rumi Miyamoto. DES: Kazunami Ota. ANI: Kazunami Ota. MUS: Hideyuki Tanaka. PRD: Yang Corporation, Karasu Communications, Knack. 45 mins. x 2 eps.
Nubile, easily stimulated Mizuki combines the roles of nurse and health education teacher at a private high school (or "college" in the U.S. version). In other words, a feeble framing device for a succession of pornographic scenes in which students and teachers alike confess their experiences or seek her "help" with sexual problems. Mizuki tends to use a very hands-on approach with her students, especially when demonstrating all the various functions of the female anatomy. Then she starts to fall for Kirishima, one of her very attractive male students. In the second video, Mizuki catches him peeping at her sex session with a female colleague. She invites him to her apartment, finally starting to bring her work home with her. Based on the erotic manga by Rumi Miyamoto in *Penguin Club*. ◉

SLIPPY DANDY
1987. TV series. DIR: Tameo Ogawa. SCR: N/C. DES: N/C. ANI: Hisatoshi Motoki. MUS: N/C. PRD: Meruhen, Fuji TV. 5 mins. x 4 eps.
Farcical thievery in the style of CAT'S EYE, as the pretty blonde photographer Audrey pursues the burglar Slippy Dandy, unaware that he is really Steve, the young college boy who worships her from afar. This series of shorts was shown as part of the variety show *Midnight Treasure Chamber* and made in a deliberately "American" style (meaning brashly bright colors and redundant

sound effects plastered over the action in the style of the 1960s TV *Batman*).

SLOW STEP *
1991. Video. DIR: Kunihiko Yuyama. SCR: Toshimichi Saeki, Kenji Terada. DES: Tokuhiro Matsubara. ANI: Tokuhiro Matsubara. MUS: Hiroya Watanabe. PRD: Pastel, Youmex, OB. 45 mins. x 5 eps.
Minatsu is a lively, popular teenager and star of the girls' softball team. Her chief admirers are her childhood sweetheart, Akiba, and her perverse softball coach, Yamazakura. But while Minatsu falls for Kadomatsu, the boxing champ from a rival school, he is not interested in her. In fact, he is only interested in "Maria," a pretty girl with glasses, though he is unaware that "Maria" is really a disguise Minatsu uses to avoid a gang of thugs that's intent on getting back at her for reporting them in a hit-and-run incident. Kadomatsu and Akiba soon come to blows over their love for the same girl, and Coach Yamazakura, a former high-school boxer himself, agrees to teach Akiba how to defend himself. Meanwhile, Coach's orphaned niece, Chika, is determined to find a wife for him so she can have a new mommy *and* daddy. Throw into this mix Somei, the newest teacher at the school, who's a gorgeous hunk but is scared of *all* women ... except Sawamura, the school bad-girl who wants Yamazakura for herself.

An addictive blend of softball, boxing, and nostalgic school-day intrigues that adapts the entirety of the short 1987 manga by Mitsuru Adachi in *Ciao* magazine. Not as well known as the same creator's TOUCH, **H2**, **NINE**, or **MIYUKI**, *SS* remains unavailable in the U.S. and has achieved the questionable distinction of being the U.K.'s worst-selling anime from 1995 to 2000, a record broken only by the release of the KIMAGURE ORANGE ROAD videos. This is a great shame because it retains Adachi's masterful qualities of character interaction and observational comedy. The early episodes of quick-change farce are soon discarded for a complex mating dance, as Minatsu deftly deals with her suitors and tries to decide which (if any) to choose. Needless to say, after much comedy business divided, like the original manga, into seasonal chapters, the show ends happily with a spring wedding attended by several couples formed from the supporting cast.

SS is fascinating both for its portrayal of everyday Japan and for the "everyday" aspects that seem so alien to the Western viewer. These include the Japanese attitude toward smoking and sexual harassment, teen rebellion expressed through littering or (the horror!) buying alcohol from a vending machine, as well as the Japanese concept of what makes a man marriage-material, and what aspirations a 17-year-old schoolgirl should have. A charmingly conservative story, with beautiful backgrounds and some wonderful humor, including the boys' vehement complaints about the service at a holiday resort, chiefly because they are unable to peek at the girls bathing. Parts three and four were run together as a single feature-length episode in the British version in a feeble attempt to avoid having to pay the classification board for two separate titles.

SMART-SAN

1978. JPN: *Haikara-san ga Toru*. AKA: *Miss "High Collar"; Fashionable Girl Passing By*. TV series. DIR: Yoshihiko Umakoshi, Kazuyoshi Yokota. SCR: Fumi Takahashi. DES: Tsutomu Shibayama. ANI: Tatsuhiro Nagaki, Eiji Tanaka, Takashi Saijo. MUS: Masuhiro Yamaguchi. PRD: Nippon Animation, TV Asahi. 25 mins. x 44 eps.
Early in the 20th century, pretty teenage tomboy Benio Hanamura is the spoiled only child of a major in the army. She studies martial arts and is much more direct than is considered proper for a young lady, even if it is the modern fashion. Benio is caught up in Japan's conflict between progress and tradition when her father decides to arrange her marriage to rich boy Shinobu, much against her will. According to custom, she is sent to her future

husband's family home, but he is called up for war service and sent to the Russian front. Soon his family hears that he is missing, believed dead. Benio eventually becomes a journalist and is astounded to meet Shinobu again some years later; he has lost his memory and believes he is Mikhailov, the husband of a Russian noblewoman. Benio becomes engaged to another man, but on their wedding day, Shinobu arrives at the ceremony, memory restored, to reclaim his bride just as a terrible earthquake hits the capital (see DOOMED MEGALOPOLIS).

Waki Yamato's original 1975 manga in *Shojo Friend* was hugely successful, but the anime didn't do as well; Nippon Animation cut it short earlier than planned. *Haikara* ("high collar") is a mild term of ridicule in 1920s Japanese slang—a fashion-victim who slavishly adopts Western trends and fads.

SNOW WHITE

1994. JPN: *Shiroyuki-hime no Densetsu*. AKA: *Story of Princess Snow White*. TV series. DIR: Kunitoshi Okajima. SCR: Tsunehisa Arakawa. DES: Yoshio Kabeshima. ANI: N/C. MUS: N/C. PRD: Tatsunoko, NHK2. 25 mins. x 52 eps.
The evil Lady Crystal is affronted to hear that she is not "the fairest of them all" and orders the hunter Sampson to take her stepdaughter Snow White out into the forest and kill her. But Snow White escapes into the forest and hides with seven dwarves, hoping that some day her prince Richard will come to save her and restore justice in the kingdom. This retelling of one of the most famous of GRIMMS' FAIRY TALES, like the same studio's later CINDERELLA, expands the original to fill out an extended running time. In this case, Tatsunoko ensures that Snow White meets her prince charming early on in the events so that her intrigues, letters, and clandestine meetings with him allow for plenty of extra action. The finale returns to the original, poisoned apple and all. See also VIDEO PICTURE BOOK and HELLO KITTY.

SAILOR MOON–director Junichi Sato would also create the "new *SW* story" *Preytia* (2001, *Shin Shiroyuki-hime Densetsu Preytia*), first as a manga drawn by Kaori Naruse for *Asuka* magazine, then as a TV anime. Refracting the legend through the prism of UTENA, it features Himeno Awayuki, a Japanese teenager who discovers she is the "Snow Princess," fated to save the world from evil, assisted by seven bold "knights," who are, of course, fearsomely pretty boys.

SOCCER FEVER

1994. TV series. DIR: Hitoshi Oda. SCR: Marco Pagot. DES: N/C. ANI: Kazuyoshi Takeuchi. MUS: N/C. PRD: RAI, Tokyo Movie Shinsha, NHK2. 26 mins. x 52 eps.
In the year of the World Cup tournament in the U.S., this series features British journalist Brian Thompson recounting anecdotes from various earlier World Cup games in other countries. Created by Marco Pagot (SHERLOCK HOUND, REPORTER BLUES), the animation of this Japanese-Italian coproduction has much in common with European styles and shows characters considerably older than the usual school or college-age heroes like CAPTAIN TSUBASA. Korean animators followed the same lead with a special called *Spin Kicker* (1997) to cash in on the run-up to the 2002 World Cup.

SOL BIANCA *

1990. Video. DIR: Katsuhito Akiyama, Hiroki Hayashi, Hiroyuki Ochi. SCR: Mayori Sekijima, Hideki Mitsui. DES: Naoyuki Onda, Atsushi Takeuchi, Koji Watanabe, Kenji Teraoka, Satoshi Shimura. ANI: Kazuhiro Konishi, Naoyuki Onda, Koichi Arai, Takashi Takeuchi. MUS: Toru Hirano, Kosei Kenjo, Seiko Nagaoka. PRD: AIC; Pioneer. 60 mins. x 2 eps., 30 mins. x 6 eps.
Rim Delapaz wants to rescue his mother from the evil dictator Battros. He disobeys his father, stows away on a cruiser, and hopes that the rest of a plan will come to him before he arrives. But the cruiser is hijacked by

pirates, the crew of the Sol Bianca, who are ready to throw Rim out of the air-lock before he tempts them with the treasure that lies in Battros's vaults. The pirates decide to help Rim in his mission, but their landing team is ambushed by Battros's minions. As their fellow buccaneers mount a rescue mission, Rim's father decides it's time to mount a revolution, in which the crew of the Sol Bianca are caught.

Take a bunch of girls and a space-ship and you have a very wide range of possibilities. Luckily not all of them are pornographic (though see SPACESHIP AGGA RUTER). Strangely redolent of *Blake's 7*'s Liberator, Sol Bianca is an alien ship faster than any other vehicle in space, while its pirate crew, in the eye-candy tradition of BUBBLEGUM CRISIS, are all female: laid-back, wine-drinking captain Feb; butch Janny, good with weapons but inclined to fly off the handle; complex, tough-but-fair April; intelligent but reserved June, whose empathic link with the ship and its guidance computer, G, has mysteri-ous origins; and the very young May, with a penchant for frilly clothes but an ace engineer in the bargain. After the promising beginning, the second *SB* video slid into anime hackery, with the girls chased around by a rival pirate whose gun can disintegrate their clothes, and the ship overrun by clunky "viruses" that look like cybernetic worms. Though it ends on a cliffhang-er with the suggestion that the Sol Bianca's original builders want her back, a third chapter of *Sol Bianca* nev-er arrived—this is despite a popular reception in the English-speaking world, where it's available in two trans-lations, of which Kiseki's, in the U.K., is the better. In the U.S., AD Vision pub-lished a short-lived spinoff comic called *SB: Treasure of the Lost Sun*, which featured the girls in an *Indiana Jones*–style treasure hunt, with no men-tion of their video antics.

Pioneer remade the series from scratch with *SB: The Legacy* (1999), fea-turing all-new character designs from Onda, a new script from Hideki Mitsui,

and contributions from two stalwarts of the company's 1990s success: ARMITAGE III–director Ochi and EL HAZARD–com-poser Nagaoka. The revamped version takes the concept from the earlier series that Earth is semilegendary to the people of the far future, and then postulates a group of religious fanatics, the "Earthians," determined to pre-serve artifacts from the homeworld. This turns the crew of the Sol Bianca, somewhat pointlessly, from devil-may-care pirates into iconoclastic art thieves. *SB: The Legacy* also "updates" the characters, mostly ignoring the precedents of the first series. April is now captain, having found the Sol Bianca and put together a crew. Janny is still the muscle. June is still the brains, with a powerful symbiotic rela-tionship with the ship and its comput-er. The biggest changes are in Feb, who still drinks but doesn't really seem to have a role in the crew, and May (now Meiyo), who supplants Rim as a stowaway and ship's mascot, though she too can link with the computer as June does. The computer can also take the form of a huge, shadowy woman, sometimes resembling the Christian Madonna and sometimes the goddess Diana. As with most TV anime of the late 1990s, digital animation gives the show an overly "clean" look, though it adds considerable charm to the space-ships. Released almost simultaneously in Japan and the U.S., *SB: The Legacy* was derided in Japan for "smelling of butter"; in other words, it was a little too Americanized for Japanese tastes—though art connoisseurs will find a treasure trove of cultural references, from Dante's *Inferno* to Alphonse Mucha paintings.

SONG OF RAIYANTSUURI
1993. JPN: *Raiyantsuuri no Uta*. AKA: *Song of Liang Chu Li* [?]. Movie. DIR: Seiji Arihara. SCR: Seiji Arihara, Toshia-ki Imaizumi. DES: N/C. ANI: Takaya Ono. MUS: N/C. PRD: Mushi, Ringoro. 90 mins.
An indentured Chinese laborer, brought to Japan to work in a coal

Ditzy Captain Yurika prepares to defend the Earth from Jovian lizard invaders, or so she thinks. Tatsuo Sato's NADESICO accentuated the parodic elements of its predecessor EVANGELION, suggesting that, in the future, anime itself might become a religion, and anime fans its zealous missionaries. The series also spawned the comedy spinoff *Gekiganger Three*, a crazy, over-the-top homage to the square-jawed robot pilots of yesteryear. *See entry p. 268.*

Nadesico

© XEBEC/PROJECT NADESICO • TV TOKYO

mine during WWII, manages to escape his captors. He hides out in the Japa-nese countryside, so far from human habitation that he does not realize when the war ends, with ultimately tragic results. Based on a story by Yoichi Takashi.

SONG OF THE BASEBALL ENTHUSIAST
1977. JPN: *Yakyukyu no Uta*. TV spe-cial, TV series, movie. DIR: Tameo Ogawa, Eiji Okabe, Hiroshi Fukutomi. SCR: Eiji Okabe, Haruya Yamazaki, Ryu-zo Nakanishi, Shunichi Yukimuro. DES: Shinji Mizushima. ANI: Hidenori Kondo. MUS: Michiaki Watanabe. PRD: Nippon Animation, Fuji TV. 50 mins. (TVm), 25 mins. x 24 eps. (TV), 90 mins. (m).
Yuki Mizuhara is a teenage southpaw pitcher with outstanding ability, spot-ted by a talent scout for the Tokyo Mets. Brought into the team, "Yuki" is forced to reveal that he is really a she, but *Yuko* Mizuhara soon wins the affec-tions of the scandalized players when she helps them in their ongoing feud against their rivals, the Hanshin Tigers. Based on the 1977 manga by MAN'S AN IDIOT–creator Shinji Mizushima, *SotBE* began as a double-length pilot episode released as a TV special just before Christmas, with the series proper start-

ing in May of the following year. Episodes 3–6 were also screened as full-length "specials" before being retailored as standard 25-minute chapters. Later episodes tried to move away from the Mizuhara story line (which was only one part of the original), but tales about other players on the team did not attract the same ratings—25 years on, it's the Mizuhara episodes that are still available on video. A movie, shown on a double bill with FUTURE BOY CONAN in 1979, focused on two players, the Northern Wolf and the Southern Tiger, whose rivalry gathers extra drama when it is revealed that they are twins separated at birth.

SONG OF THE CHIMNEY GHOSTS

1993. JPN: Obake Entotsu no Uta. Movie. DIR: Yutaka Ozawa. SCR: Yoko Yamamoto. DES: Takao Kasai. ANI: Takao Kasai. MUS: N/C. PRD: Asmik. 42 mins.

One day in 1945, children in Tokyo mistake the distant factory smoke of Shitamachi for ghosts in the sky, though their happy playtime is soon destroyed by the arrival of American bombers. Yet another childhood-inno-cence-obliterated-by-heartless-Allied-cruelty movie, this one based on a story by Katsumoto Saotome. Compare to the worthy BAREFOOT GEN or GRAVE-YARD OF THE FIREFLIES, and their many inferior successors.

SONG OF THE LADYBUGS

1974. JPN: Tento Mushi no Uta. TV series. DIR: Masami Annai, Yukihiro Takahashi. SCR: Akiyoshi Sakai. DES: Noboru Kawasaki. ANI: N/C. MUS: Shun-suke Kikuchi. PRD: Tatsunoko, Fuji TV. 25 mins. x 104 eps.

Seven orphaned children decide to stay together and earn their own living. Even though their grandfather is very wealthy, he does nothing to help them, so they struggle to survive in difficult conditions. Based on the 1974 manga by STAR OF THE GIANTS–creator Noboru Kawasaki, another of whose works, Inakappe Taisho, was animated by Tatsunoko in 1970. No relation to the Can-

dies pop trio's 1970s nuptial ditty "Ladybug Samba," sung in karaoke form at a wedding scene in EVANGELION.

SONG OF WIND AND TREES

1987. JPN: Kaze to Ki no Uta: Sei ni Naru ka na. AKA: Song of Wind and Trees: Sanctus—Can This Be Holy? Video. DIR: Yoshikazu Yasuhiko, Tatsuya Hiramatsu. SCR: Keiko Takemiya. DES: Keiko Takemiya, Yoshikazu Yasuhiko. ANI: Yoko Kamimura. MUS: Nobuyuki Nakamura. PRD: Studio Gallop, Konami Kogyo, Herald. 60 mins.

At the end of the 19th century, a new academic year starts in a European boarding school for boys. Serious, devoutly religious Serge finds himself sharing a room with beautiful blond Gilbert Cocteau, an incorrigible flirt whom Serge correctly suspects of being homosexual. Gilbert's sweet nature and considerable physical charms gradually win over his suspicious and hostile roommate, and the pair become friends and lovers. But their relationship is under pressure from Serge's religious convictions and Gilbert's naturally flirtatious personality, which attracts plenty of offers from other boys, staff, and visitors. This tender, starry-eyed romantic melodrama was based on the 1976 manga by TOWARD THE TERRA–creator Keiko Takemiya.

SONIC SOLDIER BORGMAN *

1988. JPN: Cho-on Senshi Borgman. AKA: Borgman; Supersonic Soldier Borgman. TV series, movie, video. DIR: Hiroshi Negishi, Hiroshi Yoshida, Kiyoshi Murayama. SCR: Hideki Sono-da, Nobuaki Kishima, Noboru Aikawa, Kiyoshi Murayama. DES: Michitaka Kikuchi, Koichi Ohata, Torao Arai, Take-hiro Yamada. ANI: Masamitsu Kudo, Hideyuki Motohashi. MUS: Hiromoto Tobisawa. PRD: Ashi Pro, Nippon TV. 25 mins. x 35 eps. (TV), 25 mins. (m), 60 mins., 30 mins. x 3 eps. (v).

In the late 1990s, Tokyo is destroyed by four meteorites. In 2030, Megalo City in Tokyo Bay is infiltrated by a secret organization. Check: natural disaster,

rebuilding, sinister organization—now all we need is a group of armored vigilantes. Our heroes Anice, Chuck, and Ryo are actually cyborgs (hence Borgman) created for a peaceful international deep-space probe, but the project head, Memory Geen, is the first to have been infiltrated by the alien Yoma, who plan to inherit the Earth since their own world is dying. The five battle-suited female cops of the World Criminal Police at first distrust and oppose the Borgman team, since fighting the Yoma is what they've been specially created and trained to do. Sound familiar? Post-BUBBLEGUM CRISIS but curiously more old-fashioned, Borgman is a stylistic bridge between earlier team shows and the dystopian heroes ushered in by Alien, Blade Runner, and Terminator, though none of them used a teaching career as cover for their hard-suited heroes. If you can ignore the presence of the annoying infants that this tactic welds into the story line and the somewhat simplistic characterization, this is a pleasant enough adventure for teens. Originator Kikuchi's design skills, helped by Ohata's monsters, propelled the show to success in Japan and a video revival four years later. The first video, Midnight Gigs, is a music compilation from the series, with some cast and crew information. The video release The Borgman: The Last Battle (1989), Murayama's movie Lover's Rain (1990), and the three-part video series Borgman 2: New Century 2058 (1993, B2: Shinseiki 2058) carry the story forward to 2058 and a new Yoma conflict unite with new allies to fight the old battles. Compare to the similarly themed VIRUS.

SONIC THE HEDGEHOG *

1996. Video. DIR: Kazunori Ikegami. SCR: Mayori Sekijima. DES: Tsuneo Ninomiya, Haruo Miyakawa. ANI: Tsu-neo Ninomiya. MUS: Mitsuhiro Oda. PRD: Sega, Taki Corporation. 25 mins. x 2 eps.

Sonic the Hedgehog's archnemesis, Dr. Robotnik, has been banished from the

Land of Darkness by an evil Metal Robotnik. He tells Sonic that the Robot Generator has been sabotaged and will blow Planet Freedom to kingdom come. Sonic is reluctant to get involved until the president's daughter Sara turns on the charm, but as he sets off on his mission, he must defeat the Hyper Metal Sonic, a robot hedgehog (and *Terminator 2* homage) who's after his girl and his life.

Based on the video-game series of the same name, the anime was released in English as *Sonic the Movie* to imply a budget and quality that simply weren't there. *StH* retains many favorites from the original, though Sonic's original hedgehog girlfriend, Amy, is replaced with the more human Sara.

SORAN THE SPACE BOY

1965. JPN: *Uchu Shonen Soran.* TV series. DIR: Tatsuo Ono. SCR: Kazuya Fujimoto, Ryu Mitsuse, Morimasa Matsumoto, Shota Fujimura, Masaki Tsuji. DES: N/C. ANI: Shizuko Sumeoka, Norio Yazawa. MUS: Kazuo Iba, Taku Izumi. PRD: TCJ, Eiken, TBS. 25 mins. x 96 eps.
Professor Tachibana invents the Antisolar Bomb. Fearing it might be "put to the wrong uses" (it's a bomb!), he flees from Earth with his wife and child, but an accident befalls their capsule, and their son is the sole survivor. Raised by aliens on the planet Soran, the boy returns to Earth 15 times stronger than humans. Accompanied by his sidekick, Chappy the space squirrel, Soran rights wrongs on Earth, searching all the while for his long-lost sister. A muddled mixture of *Superman* and the James Bond movies.

SORCERER HUNTERS *

1995. JPN: *Bakuretsu Hunter.* AKA: *Explosion Hunter.* TV series, video. DIR: Koichi Mashimo, Nobuyoshi Habara. SCR: Satoru Akahori, Hiroyuki Kawasaki, Masaharu Amiya. DES: Keiji Goto, Toshihisa Kogawa. ANI: N/C. MUS: Kenji Kawai. PRD: Xebec. 25 mins. x 26 eps. (TV), 30 mins. x 3 eps. (v).
The place is the Spooner Continent.

The benevolent Big Mama's last lot of defenders of peace and justice, the Haz Knights, failed to rid the land of evil sorcerers. Instead, she finds some unlikely replacements and names them the Sorcerer Hunters. Two are brothers, goofy lecher Carrot Glace, who's always hungry, and Marron Glace, who's quiet and refined. Despite their constant backbiting, they're devoted to each other. Then there's a big blond hunk named Gateau Mocha, who may be gay and secretly lusting after prettyboy Marron. The other two are sisters, Tira Misu and Chocolate Misu, who dress in S/M style clothing when they go to work, complete with spike-heeled shoes and whips. They're both fixated on Carrot but don't fight over him because they're devoted to each other. They're all theoretically named after desserts, though to Western palates it's stretching things to call carrot ice a dessert.

The plot is riddled with internal contradictions. Many of the people our heroes are called on to help are stupid, superstition-ridden chumps not much better than the sorcerers who plague them. The supreme being, despite having a reassuringly maternal name and a sidekick whose name sounds like Daughter, has not been entirely honest with them. She's actually using each mission she gives them to train them for a bigger mission, one that will save the whole world from destruction, and she hasn't told them that Carrot is the ultimate weapon. Carrot (like innocent Rushe Lenlen in **BASTARD**) has the ultimate evil locked inside him. He can transform into a monster of enormous power, but he is completely unaware of this power and unable to control it. It only emerges when those he loves—his brother and their friends—are in danger. The bad guy, Sacher Torte, is actually an ex-good guy, one of the Haz Knights who was driven to the dark side by despair over their failure to save the world from evil last time around. He knows about Carrot's power and wants to use it to destroy everything and start again with a clean slate.

The survival of a planet depends on a hormonally challenged kid and his love for his brother and friends. No wonder Big Mama is keeping it to herself. The three-episode video series is somewhat saucier than the TV anime, with more flesh on show and more gags. The first episode is a hot-springs story in which an unnaturally advanced child chases Tira and Chocolate while Carrot goes after his unnaturally youthful mother; amid all the fan service the producers allow the child to break the fourth wall repeatedly, getting into heated debate with the narrator. Episode two brings in the leader of the Haz Knights, swordswoman Milfey Yu, and once again shows the difference between TV and video; the restrained androgyne of the series is a gleeful, girl-fondling pervert. Carrot's multiple manga transformations, ignored in the TV series, are also showcased in the climactic final fight. The final episode flashes back to the characters' early lives but also provides comic relief, including Big Mama's karaoke turn.

Based on a manga in *Dengeki Comic Gao* by Satoru Akahori and Rei Omishi, *SH* is actually a rather enjoyable series, with more on offer than its slapstick wrappings indicate, including fun characters and wild designs. Though individual episodes may often stray into the banal territory that Akahori has done his utmost to claim, there are some interesting premises and plot twists like Sacher's origins, the Gateau-Marron relationship, and the genuine devotion between the two sisters competing for Carrot's affections. The second season of the TV series, which features Sacher's attempts to waken the destructive god slumbering inside Carrot, was renamed *Spell Wars; Sorcerer Hunters' Revenge* in the U.S.

SORCERER ON THE ROCKS *

1999. JPN: *Chivas 123.* Video. DIR: Kazuhiro Ozawa. SCR: Hiroyuki Kawasaki. DES: Yuki Mirai. ANI: Hisashi Abe. MUS: Nobuo Ito. PRD: Toho Video. 30 mins. x 2 eps.
Chivas Scotch is a loud, self-centered

Chasemancer (magical bounty hunter) determined to tame the god Loki for a big reward, accompanied by his shapeshifting servant Kiss and nurse-out-of-water (and occasional bunny girl) Gin Phase. Beginning life in *Comic Gao* as yet another off-the-peg creation from BEAST WARRIORS' Satoru Akahori and pseudonymous collaborator Yuki Mirai, it nevertheless stayed on video. In the cutthroat conditions of the early 21st century, it would take something more than 60 minutes of hackneyed magic to win a lucrative TV contract . . . we hope. Bought for translation by ADV Films, though the name had to be changed in the U.S., where Chivas is a trademark.

SOUL HUNTER *
1999. JPN: *Sendai den Hoshin Engi.* AKA: *Immortal Tales of Hoshin Engi; Fengshen Yanyi.* TV series. DIR: Junji Nishimura. SCR: Koji Ueda, Atsuhiro Tomioka, Masashi Sogo. DES: Masashi Kojima. ANI: N/C. MUS: Ryo Sakai. PRD: Studio Deen. 25 mins. x 26 eps.
In the 11th century A.D., the world is divided into two realms that coexist without any problem: Earth for humans and Heaven for immortals. Heaven has conferred on the priest Takuin the mission of delivering Earth from the threat of the diabolical Daji, by capturing the 365 demons who are rampaging all over China. She and her aides have taken Emperor Chou and in his name are bringing misfortune, famine, and slavery to the land. Takuin sets out to find warriors to support him in his mission and is joined by "Thunderbolt" and Naza, while at the Imperial Palace Wenzon and general Fun-Faze seek to protect the imperial princes.

Based on Ryu Fujisaki's 1996 manga for *Shonen Jump*, which adapted a Chinese ghost story for a modern Japanese audience, it was noteworthy for the originality of his characters and his remarkable graphic treatment of drapery and costume. Although set in a specific time, everything seems deliberately incoherent, notably the

presence of a hi-fi setup during festivals (also seen in the *Monkey* live-action series). Occasional laziness in the animation is obscured behind flashy computer graphics.

SOUL TAKER, THE
2001. TV series. DIR: Akinori Arafusa. SCR: Mayori Sekijima. DES: Akio Watanabe, Noriaki Tetsura. ANI: Haruo Sotozaki, Toshiaki Aida. MUS: N/C. PRD: Tatsunoko, WOWOW. 25 mins. x 10+ eps.
Kyosuke Date comes home on a visit from his college dormitory to a devastating scene. His mother, Mio, has been assaulted and is dying in a sea of blood, a knife gripped in her shaking hand. Beautiful Maya Misaki is somehow or other on hand to help. The bemused Kyosuke learns things he never knew about his family. He has a twin sister, Runa, who has a group of "other selves," beings called Flickers. She's on the run from both the mysterious organization known as Hospital, men in white with seemingly magical powers, and from robots sent by Kirihara Kontzern, a giant corporation. Kyosuke has to find his sister so that he can find out why their mother died, and why so much mystery surrounds his family.

SOUND OF MUSIC, THE
1991. JPN: *Trapp Ikka Monogatari.* AKA: *Story of the Trapp Family.* TV series. DIR: Kozo Kusuba, Jiro Saito, Fujino Sadohara, Nobuaki Nakanishi. SCR: Ayo Shiroya. DES: Shuichi Seki. ANI: Katsu Oshiro, Hiromi Kato, Nobuhiro Hosoi, Koji Ito, et al. MUS: Shinsuke Kazato. PRD: Nippon Animation, Fuji TV. 25 mins. x 40 eps.
In pre-WWII Austria lives the von Trapp family—widowed Baron Georg and his seven children—who find their lives transformed by their new nanny, who reinforces their love of music, and eventually helps them escape the Nazis. This anime was based on Maria Augusta Kutschera von Trapp's account of her family's struggles that was published as *The Story of the Trapp Family Singers* (1949) and made world-

famous by the 1959 Rodgers and Hammerstein musical and the subsequent 1965 film starring Julie Andrews, which fictionalized the events considerably. Part of the WORLD MASTERPIECE THEATER series, this anime also takes many liberties with the story, chiefly to make it palatable to a younger audience. The series was also cut down into an 85-minute feature-length TV movie that covered roughly the same pacing and ground as the live-action movie.

SOUTHERN CROSS *
1984. JPN: *Chojiku Kitai Southern Cross.* AKA: *Superdimensional Cavalry Southern Cross.* TV series. DIR: Yasuo Hasegawa, Tsukasa Sunaga, Masakazu Yasumura, Katsuhisa Yamada, Hiroshi Yoshida. SCR: Junzo Toriumi, Hisato Kaganai, Tomoko Kawasaki, Kenji Terada. DES: Miya Sonoda, Hiroshi Ogawa, Hiroyuki Kitazume. ANI: Yutaka Arai. MUS: Tsutomu Sato. PRD: Tatsunoko, TBS. 25 mins. x 23 eps.
The human colony world of Grolier is attacked by the savage alien Zor. Jeanne Francaix, hotheaded commander of the 15th Squadron of the Southern Cross army, is on the front line. Her close friend Bowie Emerson, a passionate music-lover, is one of her troop, and when he is taken prisoner by the Zor, he falls in love with alien singer Musika. Believing that most of the Zor don't want war but are being forced into it by their commanders, he escapes, promising Musika that he will come back for her. Meanwhile Jeanne has fallen in love with Seifrietti Weisse, an enemy pilot who has been captured in battle and lost his memory. She convinces him that he should join the human side and enlists him in her squadron despite the protests of her commander, who is not convinced by his courage and success in battle. The lovers find new hope in a hidden outcrop of beautiful, thriving flowers uncontaminated by the devastation that both races have wrought. They also learn that the leaders of Zor are planning the total extinction of humanity. Seifrietti's memory returns,

and he decides to return to the Zor base alone and eliminate the leaders in the hope that his people can live in peace with humans and that their world can survive.

SC was only one of a rich crop of robot series from this period, and not the most successful, but it achieved fame in the West when it became part of ROBOTECH, with changes to character names and relationships made to support the new continuity. Jeanne became Dana, half-breed daughter of Max and Miriya Sterling from the *Macross Saga* segment. It would be more than a decade before Max and Miriya's "real" daughter, Mylene Jenius, took to the screen in MACROSS 7. The rewrite also brought a different kind of ecological emphasis. Carl Macek's *SC* removed one of Grolier's moons in order to claim the story was set on a polluted Earth: as in GUNBUSTER, it is humans, not aliens who now present the greatest threat to the environment. Humanity is presented as a race of shortsighted idiots whose fight for survival obscures the fact that they have wrecked their own planet, forcing other species into extinction just as the Zor leaders seek to wipe them out.

SOUTHERN RAINBOW
1982. JPN: *Minami no Niji no Lucy*. AKA: *Lucy of the Southern Rainbow*. TV series. DIR: Hiroshi Saito, Shigeo Koshi, Kozo Kusuba, Takayoshi Suzuki. SCR: Akira Miyazaki. DES: Shuichi Seki. ANI: Eimi Maeda, Koichi Murata, Fumiko Morimoto, Noboru Takano. MUS: Koichi Sakata. PRD: Nippon Animation, Fuji TV. 25 mins. x 50 eps.
Lucy May is the youngest daughter of the Popple family. In 1836, she sets out with her mother, father, brothers Ben and Tob, and sisters Clara and Kate on the long voyage from England to Australia, which was then a mysterious and hazardous continent where colonists faced hardship but had the opportunity to become rich in their new homeland. The series covers four years during which, after many struggles, the family sets up a successful business in

the new city of Adelaide. Part of the WORLD MASTERPIECE THEATER series, this anime was based on a novel by Phyllis Piddington serialized in the Japanese magazine *Living Book*.

SPACE ACE *
1965. JPN: *Uchu no Ace*. AKA: *Ring-O*. TV series. DIR: Hiroshi Sasakawa, Toshio Kinoshita, Ippei Kuri, Tatsuo Yoshida, Seiji Okuda. SCR: Junzo Toriumi. DES: Tatsuo Yoshida. ANI: Akiyuki Kuma, Tatsuo Yoshida, Seiji Okuda. MUS: Taku Izumi. PRD: Tatsunoko, Fuji TV. 25 mins. x 52 eps. (b/w).
The survivors of an alien race set out in search of an uninhabited planet where their civilization can be rebuilt. During the voyage, a single ship piloted by one little alien leaves the convoy and lands on Earth. Professor Tatsunoko of the Tatsunoko Institute discovers what he thinks is a giant shell on the sea bed and opens it to find the childlike pilot. A creature from planet Parum, "Ace" can use "space fuse" energy to perform amazing feats of strength and can fly through the air on a silver ring. With the professor's daughter Asari (Ginger), cub reporter Yadokari (Flash Scoop), and Ebo (Ibo) the robot dog, Space Ace fights off alien monsters and invaders by using a high-energy food supply maintained by Asari and stored in Ebo's flip-top nose. The Tatsunoko Studio's first production, planned as an answer to Osamu Tezuka's ASTRO BOY. *SA* featured Rei Osumi as a "science fiction adviser"—the author took the studio's money in return for such suggestions as shooting one's way out of trouble with a "platina ray." Broadcast on Australian TV; the first episode was remade in color in an unsuccessful attempt to gain a U.S. sale. Not to be confused with the American animation by Don Bluth for the wholly unconnected *Space Ace* game.

SPACE ADVENTURE COBRA *
1982. JPN: *Space Cobra* (TV); *Space Adventure Cobra* (m). TV series, movie. DIR: Osamu Dezaki, Toshio Takeuchi, Shunji Oga, Masaharu Okuwaki. SCR:

After cybernetic augmentation, a police officer is left with only his tongue to remind him he was once human. As fashions changed in anime sci-fi post-*Robocop*, the stylish poses of BUBBLEGUM CRISIS gave way to the grittier, harder-hitting prequel AD POLICE. Despite outrageous misogyny and sexism, the short-lived vi) series features some thoughtful musings on the nature of humanity, later used to better effect in GHOST IN THE SHELL. *See entry p. 4.*

AD Police

© AIC/TOSHIBA EMI/EMOTION

Kenji Terada, Haruya Yamazaki, Kazuo Terada. DES: Akio Sugino, Shinji Otsuka. ANI: Akio Sugino, Koji Morimoto, Ryutaro Nakamura, Atsuko Fukushima, Chuji Nakajima, Jun Kawagoe, Hideo Nanba, Takuya Wada. MUS: Kentaro Haneda (TV), Osamu Tokaibayashi (m). PRD: Tokyo Movie Shinsha, Fuji TV. 25 mins. x 31 eps. (TV) 99 mins. (m).
Bored 24th-century salaryman Mr. Johnson buys a virtual vacation at the Trip Movie Corporation only to discover that his chosen holiday (the life of a space pirate) triggers real memories that he has suppressed. He discovers that he really *is* Cobra, a rogue with a price on his head who has a false arm hiding the mentally powered "psychogun." Fleeing the Galactic Guild, he encounters beautiful bounty hunter Jane Royale (Jane Flower), who has part of a treasure map tattooed on her shapely back. Her sisters Dominique and Catherine have the other pieces that reveal the location of the Supreme Weapon. Cobra springs Catherine from prison before tracking down Dominique, a police officer who has infiltrated the all-female Snow Guerrillas gang. Though Cobra claims to want the Supreme Weapon (and, like any Buichi Terasawa hero worth his salt, to

see the girls naked), he is also intent on protecting the ladies from Crystal Boy, his golden cyborg rival, who lacks Cobra's qualms about skinning them alive to make the map more portable.

Keeping relatively close to Buichi Terasawa's 1978 manga in *Shonen Jump* magazine, the first season's quest for the McGuffin Supreme Weapon ends with Cobra recruited by Dominique for undercover work. Investigating Guild drug-smuggling on planet Laloux, he joins the Red Saxons, a sports team that plays the rugby/baseball hybrid *rugball*. Amid violent matches reminiscent of *Rollerball* (1975), he rises through the ranks to crack the case and win the championship. The series ends with a third arc, as Cobra locates Salamander, the entity behind the guild that's revealed to be an energy field controlled by the spirit of Adolf Hitler.

Predating *Total Recall* with its original premise, *SAC* is typical Terasawa, crammed full of leggy, disposable beauties who turn up, wiggle their assets, snog the hero, and then get shot. It's got plenty of ray-gun action, as well as the artist's other trademark—madly futurist designs based on contemporary technologies like motorcycles, cars, and planes.

The TV series was preceded by a feature, with a script written by Terasawa himself and Haruya Yamazaki—Miyazaki's amanuensis on **CASTLE OF CAGLIOSTRO**. The movie script shuffles the characters into a slightly different setting—in this version Jane Flower and her sisters Catherine and Dominique form the three aspects of the Empress of the Universe, ruler of the planet Myras, who will manifest when all fall in love with the same man (guess who?). Crystal Boy (aka Necron) is now the personification of Death itself, tracking Cobra as he springs Catherine from jail and encounters Dominique on the Planet of the Snow Guerrillas. Clearly a dry-run for the later series, changes made between the two include a new composer and the replacement of the origi-

nal Cobra voice actor Shigeru Matsuzaki with Nachi Nozawa. *SAC* also steals from many SF movies, including *Barbarella* (1967), *Flash Gordon* (1980), the Genesis project from *Star Trek: Wrath of Khan* (1982), and the carbonite-freezing episode from *The Empire Strikes Back* (1980). The movie is often claimed as a sequel set two years *after* the TV events, though it requires remarkable suspension of disbelief to accept that Cobra would meet two trios of virtually identical girls with the same names, occupations, and troubles. Similarly, the movie version does not allude to Mr. Johnson's induction at the Trip Movie Corporation; Japanese audiences familiar with the manga could disregard any of the film's more far-fetched or hallucinatory episodes as yet more evidence that this is all "really a dream"—not an option available to most English-speaking viewers. When dubbed for the U.K. market, Manga Entertainment replaced the Japanese soundtrack with all-new material from the group Yello. The decision gained *SAC* extra press coverage and papered over the cracks to make this antique film seem up-to-date, while the 1995 copyright date for the new score helped imply it was newer than it really was.

The series is popular to this day and has an ardent fan following in Japan and Europe. Scenes from the feature were also recycled for Matthew Sweet's pop promo "Girlfriend." However, its influence was strongest in Korea, where Cobra's relationship with Jane was shoddily rehashed with Hyesong and Marie Kim in Lee Hyun-se's *Armageddon* (1996). Other Terasawa works adapted as anime include **GOKU: MIDNIGHT EYE** and **KABUTO**.

SPACE DEFENSE OFFICER TAA-BO

1991. JPN: *Uchu Jieitai Taa-bo.* AKA: *Space Self Defense Force Taa-bo.* Movie, Video. DIR: Masami Hata. SCR: Joji Iida, Anzu Nemuru. DES: Koichi Kadowaki. ANI: Toshiharu Akahori. MUS: Toyomi Kojima. PRD: Sanrio. 34 mins., 30 mins.

Interstellar crime-fighter Taa-bo fights

the evil Scorpion Brothers in a short-lived attempt to introduce a more traditional hero to the Sanrio lineup. After his movie debut *Taa-Bo on the Planet of the Dragon Pavilion* (1991, *Taa-bo no Ryumiyasei Daitanken*), the character devolved to video, where he disappeared from view after *Taa-Bo on the Planet Where Time Stopped* (1993, *Taa-bo no Toki no Tomatta Sei*). The "movie" was also bundled onto a Sanrio anthology tape with mini-features of more popular stars **HELLO KITTY** and **KEROPPI**.

SPACE FAMILY CARLVINSON

1988. JPN: *Uchu Kazoku Carlbinson.* Video. DIR: Kimio Yabuki, Tatsuo Suzuki. SCR: Michiru Shimada. DES: Yoshito Asari. ANI: Masahiro Kanno. MUS: Hiroya Watanabe. PRD: Toei. 45 mins.

A traveling-show troupe of aliens are playing cards when a vessel comes out of warp space and nearly crashes into their ship before crashing on planet Anika. The only survivor is a baby human girl, Corona. They decide to look after her, at least until somebody shows up to claim her. In order to equip themselves to play the part of the "normal" human family and friends the baby will need, they research information from the crashed ship's data banks and embark on one of the longest-running shows of their entire career. But they identify more and more with their roles, and when a ship comes for Corona five years later, they have *become* her family and friends.

Yoshito Asari's 1985 manga in *Shonen Captain* was a revamp of the popular **SWISS FAMILY ROBINSON** castaway theme that also inspired the U.S. comic *Space Family Robinson*, later known as *Lost in Space*. Mysteriously, the Nimitz-class U.S. aircraft carrier Carl Vinson visited Japan in the 1980s, though it seems likely that the use of its name is either coincidence or one of those meaningless puns that the Japanese find so entertaining (see **SORCERER HUNTERS**). As Chairman of the House Naval Affairs Committee from 1931 to 1947, the original Carl Vinson could be said to be personally responsible for the support and maintenance of the U.S. Navy during WWII, which hardly seems likely to have endeared him to the Japanese.

SPACE FIREBIRD *

1980. JPN: *Hi no Tori 2772: Ai no Cosmozone*. AKA: *Firebird 2772: Love's Cosmozone; Phoenix 2772*. Movie. DIR: Taku Sugiyama. SCR: Osamu Tezuka, Taku Sugiyama. DES: Shinji Ito, Tsuyoshi Matsumoto, Noboru Ishiguro. ANI: Kazuko Nakamura, Noboru Ishiguro. MUS: Yasuo Higuchi. PRD: Kadokawa, Tohoku Shinsha. 122 mins. In the 22nd century, humans are bred to order, raised in laboratories, and selected for their roles from birth by a tyrannical government exploiting the planet to the verge of ecological collapse. Godot is lucky enough to be raised by the robot Olga, a warm, gentle mother-figure who looks like a fetishist's dream girl in her shiny red outfit and can transform into a whole range of fabulous toys and vehicles. He grows up to be a sensitive and intelligent young man who rebels against the harshness and cruelty of his society. While training to be a space pilot, he learns that he has a brother, Rock, who is one of the ruling class, selected for his intelligence and ruthlessness. He also falls in love with Lena, an upper-class girl, and, because this is a crime against the State (and against Rock, her fiancé!), he is sent to a harsh prison-planet. He is offered his freedom if he will capture the Space Firebird, a mystical creature whose blood can bestow immortality and everlasting power. The faithful Olga, who has followed him through all his troubles, joins him on his mission; she has always loved him and is determined to help him use the powers of the Firebird to revive the dying Earth.

Based on Osamu Tezuka's long-running series of 12 interlinked tales first begun in 1967 in the manga magazine *Com*, this magical love story contains many elements common in his work—the recycling of characters (**BLACK JACK** is the prison planet commandant), the use of comic characters and musical numbers straight out of Disney, the contrast between inner beauty and outer sham, supportive and exploitative relationships, and the visual inventiveness that makes every frame a pleasure. There are unexpected roles for Frederik L. Schodt and his fellow translator Jared Cook, credited along with SF writer Sakyo Komatsu as "planning brains."

The phoenix in *Space Firebird* is an eternal being who visits all parts of space and time in the course of the long-running *Phoenix* manga, which only finished in 1988, shortly before Tezuka's death in February 1989. The earliest chapters, created at the height of Tezuka's powers when he was also writing **ASTRO BOY**, are said to be the best. The third, fourth, and fifth chapters of the original were also animated for video by the Madhouse studio. The 48-minute one-shots were supervised by Rintaro and seem to be a short-lived attempt to follow *SF* with the ten remaining chapters, though only these three were made. Rintaro's *Phoenix: Karma* (1986), also shown in cinemas on a double bill with **TIME STRANGER**, features the firebird's manifestation in ancient India, where it witnesses a conflict between a pirate king and a sculptor, who is, of course, making a statue of a phoenix. Toshio Hirata's *Phoenix: Yamato* (1987) moves to Japan for a retelling of the story of **YAMATO TAKERU**. The last episode, Yoshiaki Kawajiri's *Phoenix: Future* (1988), features the Earthbound starship ZFX-302 finding an icy planet whose occupants prefer death to life.

SPACE PATROL HOPPER

1965. JPN: *Uchu Patrol Hopper*. AKA: (see below). TV series. DIR: Taiji Yabushita, Yoshio Ishihara, Yoshio Kuroda, Hiroshi Shidara, Masayuki Akehi. SCR: Taiji Yabushita, Susumu Ginga, Fumi Takahashi. DES: N/C. ANI: Masao Kumogawa. MUS: Shunsuke Kikuchi. PRD: Toei, NET. 25 mins. x 44 eps.

After being severely injured in a space accident, Earth boy Jun is saved by the Hopper Aliens, who give him a new cyborg body. With superhuman powers, Jun signs up for the space patrol along with fellow operatives Donkey, Pooh, Dar, Hook, and Professor Doc. After episode 27, the title was changed to *Patrol Team: Space Boy Jun (Patrol Tai: Uchukko Jun)*. One of many 1960s also-rans in the wake of **ASTRO BOY**, including **PRINCE PLANET**, **SORAN THE SPACE BOY**, and **SPACE ACE**.

SPACE RUNAWAY IDEON

1980. JPN: *Densetsu Kyoshin Ideon*. AKA: *Legendary God-Giant Ideon*. TV series, movie. DIR: Yoshiyuki Tomino, Masanori Miura, Toshifumi Takizawa. SCR: Sukehiro Tomita, Jiyu Watanabe, Arata Koga. DES: Yukien Kogawa, Submarine. ANI: Yukien Kogawa. MUS: Koichi Sugiyama. PRD: Sunrise, TV Tokyo. 25 mins. x 38 eps. (TV), 90 mins. (m). In 2400, the human race and the Buff Clan are at war, but one young pilot believes that peace can be made between the two enemies. Meanwhile humankind has one last line of defense: advanced war machines retrieved from the destroyed colony world Solo, which can be combined into the super-robot Ideon—piloted, of course, by children, Cosmo Yuki, Casha Imhof, Sherril Formosa, and Bes Jordan. Devised by Yoshiyuki Tomino in large part as a reworking of his popular **GUNDAM**, *SRI* had an even more outrageous main robot. It was formed from three giant trucks (Sol-Amber, Sol-Vainer, and Sol-Conver), each of which could become an independent war machine (Ideo-Delta, Ideo-Nova, or Ideo-Buster) and was armed with massive quantities of weaponry, including a small black-hole cannon. Any fan would call that serious play value, but the merchandising of *SRI* never took off as *Gundam's* did. Two films followed in 1982, shown on the same double bill. The first was a digest of episodes 1–32, the second of episodes 35–38. Within five years, the coming of video would make such "movies" much rarer, and less popular with audiences—witness the outrage at the discovery that much of the EVANGELION DEATH AND REBIRTH double bill was recycled TV footage.

SPACE SAGITTARIUS

1986. JPN: *Uchusen Sagittarius*. AKA: *Spaceship Sagittarius*. TV series. DIR: Kazuyoshi Yokota, Jiro Saito, Keiji Hayakawa. SCR: Nobuyuki Isshiki, Nobuyuki Fujimoto. DES: Sadahiko Sakamaki, Shuichi Seki, Noboru Takano. ANI: Hiroyoshi Sugawara. MUS: Haruki Mino. PRD: Nippon Animation, TV Asahi. 25 mins. x 77 eps.
Mr. Giraffe, a scientist, commissions Toppie and Lana, a mouse and frog with their own space haulage company, to take him in search of his teacher Anne, who disappeared while trying to prove her scientific theories on the dangerous planet Vega III. The pilots are dragged away from their loved ones (in Toppie's case, his pregnant wife, while Lana simply kisses his lasagne goodbye), and they are soon in trouble when facing a death sentence on the first planet they reach. Saved by the minstrel Sibip, they continue their journey. Based on the Italian comic *Altri Mondi* by Andrea Romoli, this charming little fantasy series brings together three animal astronauts who cruise the galaxy in the good ship Sagittarius, with anthropomorphic adventures in the style of SHERLOCK HOUND and MONTANA JONES.

SPACE TRAVELERS: THE ANIMATION *

2000. Video. DIR: Takashi Ui. SCR: Katsuhiko Koide. DES: Chikara Okazaki. ANI: Noboru Takahashi. MUS: Toshiyuki Watanabe. PRD: Amuse Video, Fuji TV, Robot. 60 mins.
Plucky hero Hayabusa Jetter, his ingenue sidekick Irene Bear, muscle-mountain Crush Bomber, slimy Chinese trader Hoi, slinky femme fatale Gold Papillon, boomerang-throwing kid Black Cat, unstoppable space samurai Dragon Attack, mechanic Electric Sunny, and funky cyberhipster Karl Hendrix fight to restore the honor of planet Earth after an apocalyptic interstellar incident. A parody of the giant-robot space operas of the 1980s, with homages to *Star Wars* and *Star Trek* thrown in, *ST* is cheap and derivative, though the producers would argue that this was at least *part* of the plan.

It began as a throwaway gag in Katsuyuki Motohiro's popular live-action movie *Space Travelers* (2000) in which a Tokyo bank robbery goes disastrously wrong. As the police surround the building, the staff and hostages volunteer to help the robbers bluff their way out; each is given a code name based on a character from the robbers' favorite cartoon, a nonexistent show called *Space Travelers*—hence the ridiculously large cast of anime archetypes. Scraps of animation were made as inserts for the original movie and are reused here—hence the strange pacing of the overlong opening credits that were not originally intended to be shown in this manner. The plot is a tired succession of fight-scenes, a ludicrous transformation sequence, and an in-joke as the crew flies past the ruins of the Fuji TV building. An afterthought following the movie's success, *ST* was reputedly inspired by Motohiro's love of STAR BLAZERS, GUNDAM, and EVANGELION, though in execution it is a pale imitation of the 1970s hacksploitation of COWBOY BEBOP and all too obviously a product of the terminally low budgets of many 1990s anime. Ironically, it was Motohiro's previous film *Bayside Shakedown* (1999) that was said to have sounded the death knell for anime—not understanding its appeal to the teen audience, certain producers backed away from making shows for that age group, only to discover that Motohiro's follow-up was just that.

SPACE WARRIORS *

1980. JPN: *Uchu Senshi Baldios*. AKA: *Space Warrior Baldios; Baldios*. TV series, Movie. DIR: Kazuyuki Hirokawa, Takao Yotsuji, Kunihiko Yuyama, Kazuya Yamazaki, Seiji Yamamuro, Jun-ji Nishimura, Osamu Sekita. SCR: Akiyoshi Sakai, Junzo Toriumi, Tomomi Tsutsui, Takeshi Shudo. DES: Osamu Kamijo, Hajime Kamegaki. ANI: Takeshi Tanaka, Toyoo Ashida. MUS: Kentaro Haneda. PRD: Ashi Productions, Tokyo 12 Channel. 25 mins. x 31 eps. (TV), 117 mins. (m).
Marin Reagan, a native of planet S1, flees a radioactive atmosphere and the persecutions of dictator Gattler, making his way to Earth. Gattler and the S-1 armies are on their way to take over the planet as a replacement for their hopelessly polluted homeworld, and Marin joins the team working to defend Earth from alien attack as the pilot of super-robot Baldios. Earth and S-1 are fated to come into final conflict, and the love-hate relationship between Marin and Aphrodia, commander of the S-1 forces, will finally be resolved. The show went off the air with another eight episodes to go, leading to protests from Japanese fans. The partly completed finale was assembled with some new footage from Toyoo Ashida to make a movie release, *Space Warrior Baldios* (1981, aka *Revenge of the Space Warriors*, aka *SW: Battle for Earth Station S-1*), showing the last battle between Gattler's spaceship Aldebaran and the Earth satellite base Blue Fixer under Commander Tsukikage. Gattler offers Aphrodia the chance to avenge her dead brother by killing Marin, but she can't do it and commits suicide. The ensuing battle destroys both armies and their weapons, and Marin, the sole survivor, is left to return to a devastated Earth with the body of the woman he truly loved. A 98-minute version of the movie was screened in Japan and is also available on video in the U.S.

SPACEKETEERS *

1978. JPN: *SF Saiyuki Starzinger*. AKA: *SF Journey to the West Starzinger*. TV series. DIR: Yugo Serikawa, Kozo Morishita, Kazumi Fukushima. SCR: Tatsuo Tamura, Michiru Umadori, Sukehiro Tomita. DES: Masami Suda. ANI: Masami Suda, Satoshi Kamimiya. MUS:

Shunsuke Kikuchi. PRD: Toei, Fuji TV. 25 mins. x 73 eps.

As the Queen of the Great Planet at the center of the universe grows old, the harmony of the universe becomes unbalanced. Minerals and planets transform into evil starmen and attack other planets. In order to restore peace, the old queen must be replaced with a young, strong ruler who can keep her subjects in order. Princess Aurora is saved by scientist Dr. Kitty when the starmen attack the moon. He knows that she has the power to restore the harmony of the universe as the new ruler of the Great Planet, so she sets out in the spaceship Cosmos Queen with three companions charged to keep her safe: Sir Jogo (Arimos) from the planet of water, Don Hakka (Porkos) from the planet of fire, and rebel cyborg Jan Kugo (Jesse Dart), who wears a control circlet around his head. The starmen and other monsters try to stop them, but Aurora won't allow any creatures who were originally peaceful to be killed. She knows that if she fulfills her destiny, they will be restored to their former shapes and will once again live in harmony with their fellow beings.

Based on the *Terebi* magazine manga by **CAPTAIN HARLOCK**–creator Leiji Matsumoto, this SF retelling of **JOURNEY TO THE WEST** was rebranded as *SFSS "II"* for its final nine episodes, in which the four have replenished the galactic energy provided by the old queen and go to the solar system of Girara, which is still unbalanced and needs Princess Aurora to restore it to normalcy. This time, the farewell to their princess is a final one, and her three companions must take their leave of her, but all of them (especially Kogo) leave their hearts in her keeping. Edited down to 26 episodes for U.S. release as part of the **FORCE FIVE** series, Jim Terry's new title and character names now misleadingly implied a space-going **THREE MUSKETEERS**. For the U.S. version, the characters are on a mission to the Dekos Star System, whose evil power source has caused the once-peaceful

creatures of the universe to change into evil mutants.

SPACESHIP AGGA RUTER *

1998. JPN: *Space Opera Agga Ruter*. Video. DIR: Shigeru Yazaki. SCR: Masaki Kajishima, Hideyuki Kurata. DES: Masaki Kajishima, Kenji Teraoka. ANI: Katsuhisa Ito. MUS: T.K. Crow. PRD: AIC, Beam Entertainment. 30 mins. x 4 eps.

The evil Shiunk kills Taiyo's parents and leaves him to die in space. Rescued by the kindly android Kei, Taiyo is raised without human companionship for 15 years aboard her ship the Agga Ruter. Kei tells Taiyo to call her "Mother" and instructs him in the arts of love in a succession of Oedipally suspect scenes. When captured by the shrill space pirate Janis (who has been hired by Shiunk to steal the Agga Ruter), the pair prove to be perkily cooperative hostages, volunteering to cook and clean, rummaging in her underwear drawer, and reading out the funny bits from her diary. Janis is a descendant of Re-Formed Humans, ancient members of the Fighter civilization who recombined their DNA to survive on hostile worlds. Though she appears human, she turns into a weretiger when reminded of abuse at the hands of her circus-ringmaster stepfather. Endowed with superhuman strength *and* bedroom prowess, Taiyo is the only man who can satisfy her, and the sexually sated Janis agrees to switch sides. The Agga Ruter, itself a Fighter relic (see the similar **SOL BIANCA**), lacks a vital component, which has been mistaken for a precious gem and put on display on the Millennium Mule cruise liner. The gang sneak in to steal it, but Shiunk (now disguised as the Joker with a bad blond wig) has followed them and arranged for their capture by a vicious green-eyed blonde, who is luckily not immune to Taiyo's charms.

A sci-fi porno made by the thinly disguised cast and crew of the **TENCHI MUYO!** series, whose audience was probably old enough by this point to

Kagetsuya, the devil's advocate—an angel sent to Earth to determine if the human race deserves to survive, in Nobuyasu Furukawa's **EARTHIAN**. Like most other depictions of angels, both in Christian iconography and Yun Koga's original manga, Kagetsuya has blond, Aryan features. However, the story's true hero is his ideological opposite Chihaya, whose dark hair establishes him as an angelic underdog but with obvious appeal to the original Japanese target audience. *See entry p. 109.*

Earthian

appreciate the "joke." Even the humor is familiar, with Kei setting up a mock Japanese living room on the bridge of Janis's warship in order to teach her how to be a good wife (sexually available and a great cook). Taiyo is a dead ringer for the older but still passive hero of *Tenchi in Tokyo*, the Agga Ruter is a ship with all the weird properties of Jurai vessels, and the females are cookie-cutter *Tenchi* girlies. Compare to **MASQUERADE**, which also appears to be reheated leftovers from the franchise.

SPARKLING PHANTOM

1990. JPN: *Sparkling Phantom: Runohara Meikyu*. AKA: *SP: Runohara Labyrinth*. Video. DIR: Narumi Kakinouchi. SCR: Narumi Kakinouchi. DES: Kana Hoshino. ANI: N/C. MUS: N/C. PRD: Victor Entertainment. 45 mins.

This SF fantasy about a Japanese girl who is transported to an alternate world populated by fairies was based on the manga in *Hana to Yume* magazine by Kana Hoshino.

SPECTRAL FORCE

1998. JPN: Spectral Force. Video. DIR: Yoshiaki Sato. SCR: N/C. DES: Jinnosuke Hibino, Tatsunori Nakamura. ANI: Katsuaki Tsubata. MUS: Satoshi

Kobayashi. PRD: Idea Factory. 30 mins. x 2 eps.

This heroic fantasy has fighters duel for supremacy in the world of Neverland (no relation to **PETER PAN AND WENDY**). Featuring copious computer graphics, it was based on the *Spectral Force* video game.

SPECTRE

1991. JPN: *Hosai Sengoku Shi Spectre/Requiem*. AKA: *Racing Civil War Chronicle Spectre/Requiem*. Video. DIR: Yoichiro Shimatani. SCR: Yoichirio Shimatani, Ranko Ono. DES: Fumihide Sai, Hiroshi Kiyomizudera. ANI: Fumihide Sai. MUS: Takahiko Kanemaru. PRD: Apples, Miyuki Pro. 45 mins. x 2 eps.

Modern-day bikers make and break alliances with neighboring gangs, fight over the right to use a local petrol station, and are eventually united under a powerful leader. It's a replay of the events of Japan's 16th-century civil war, but with bikes instead of horses and knives instead of swords. Based on the manga by Jiro Ueno in *Weekly Playboy*.
🅥

SPEED RACER *

1967. JPN: *Mach Go Go Go*. AKA: *Mach 5, Go Go!* TV series. DIR: Tatsuo Yoshida, Ippei Kuri, Hiroshi Sasakawa, Seitaro Hara, Hiroyuki Fukushima. SCR: Junzo Toriumi, Tadashi Hirose, Takashi Hayakawa, Masaaki Sakurai, Masashi Kubota. DES: Ippei Kuri, Hiroshi Sasakawa. ANI: Masami Suda, Takashi Saijo. MUS: Nobuyoshi Koshibe, Michiru Oshima. PRD: Tatsunoko, Fuji TV, Tatsunoko, TV Tokyo. 25 mins. x 52 eps. (TV1), 25 mins. x 34 eps.

Go Mifune (Speed) is a young racing driver for his father Daisuke's (Pops Racer) Mifune Motors team (nameless in the U.S. version). His mother Aya (Mom Racer), irritating kid brother Kuo (Sprite), and pet monkey Senpei (Chim Chim) all work on the team along with Go's girlfriend, Michi (Trixie), and mechanic Sabu (Sparks). Go's success and the superb engineering of his racing car the Mach Five lead other jealous racers to try and put a spanner in the works, but they are foiled by the mysterious Masked Racer (Racer X), who also fends off master criminals and foreign spies. He's really Go's older brother Kenichi (Rex), a government agent who, for a variety of top-secret reasons, is compelled to work anonymously and cut himself off from his family. The series contained a surprising amount of violence and tension, and it had all the technical limitations of 1960s TV animation, but since distributors K. Fujita had successfully sold **MARINE BOY** to U.S. company Trans-Lux, it had a ready market for this new product.

Accepted by many of its fans as an American product from the first American TV screening in 1967, *Speed Racer* amended the Japanese original considerably. Actor/writer Peter Fernandez was entrusted with the task of toning down the Japanese version for U.S. consumption, and he ensured that no *Speed Racer* villain was ever killed by amending the scripts and inserting shots of stunned bad guys with cartoon planets and stars circling their heads.

A revival on MTV led to the making of a new 13-episode series, *The New Adventures of Speed Racer* (1993) by Fred Wolf Films in 1993; this really *was* an American cartoon. A proposed live-action feature film didn't get beyond concept stage, but 1994 brought us *Speed Racer the Movie*—a compilation of two series episodes with an episode of *Colonel Bleep* interspersed with classic animated TV commercials of the 1960s to bulk out the running time to 80 minutes. Speed would also appear in a commercial for Volkswagen and a music video for Ghost-Face Killah. He returned to Japan, this time to TV Tokyo, in a 34-episode "30th anniversary" remake in 1997, with Pops renamed Daisuke Hibiki and new character Mai Kazami (photographer/love interest) along with her brother, Wataru (brat). The final season neglected the racing plot in favor of time travel. After hitting 555 kph while trying to outrun a tornado, Speed is catapulted through time to the year 2555, when the world is ruled by the evil dictator Handler. With his car newly converted to a fully operational time machine, Speed and the gang set off in search of the Ezekiel Wheel, an energy source that can change the future.

SPIRIT OF WONDER *

1992. JPN: *Spirit of Wonder China-san no Yutsu*. AKA: *SoW: Miss China's Melancholy; SoW: Miss China's Ring*. Video. DIR: Mitsuru Hongo, Takashi Anno. SCR: Michiru Shimada. DES: Yoshiaki Yanagida. ANI: Yoshiaki Yanagida. MUS: Kohei Tanaka. PRD: EMI, Asia-do. 45 mins. (v1), 45 mins. x 2 eps. (v2).

Miss China runs a bar and boarding house in a small town. Her long-term residents are mad scientist Professor Breckenridge and his assistant, Jim Floyd (named for Heywood Floyd in *2001: A Space Odyssey*), whom she secretly loves. But she thinks Jim is smitten with local florist Lily and that her love is hopeless, until, for her birthday, he flies her to the moon and gives her a real moonstone ring.

Based on Kenji Tsuruta's delicately beautiful manga short stories serialized in *Afternoon* from 1986 onward, *SoW* harks back to a bygone age of Jules Verne, H.G. Wells, and similar Victorian-era science fiction. Tsuruta's output is fearfully slow, so it was little surprise that the anime incarnation was similarly tardy. A second *SoW* release, the *Scientific Boys' Club* (2001, *SoW: Shonen Kagaku Kurabu*), chiefly features Wendy Lindberg, a leading interplanetary ether theorist, who believes that light oscillates in "ether" just as sound oscillates in air and that one can therefore travel in space by airship using "ether convection." Her father, Gordon, and his eccentric old buddies from the Scientific Boys' Club plan to celebrate the club's 50th anniversary by flying to Mars using this method, a crackpot idea, which, like other insanely romantic schemes in Tsuruta's universe, pays off eventually. The two 35-minute *SBC* episodes each came with a 10-minute short to tie them in with the original 1992 video titled *Chi-na-san's Reduction* (*C-san no Shukusho*). Yanagida, who turned Tsuruta's fragile art into animation with such skill, returns on character design and art direction, and Anno directs.

SPIRITED AWAY *

2001. JPN: *Sen to Chihiro no Kamikakushi*. AKA: *Sen and Chihiro's Spirited Away*. Movie. DIR: Hayao Miyazaki. SCR: Hayao Miyazaki. DES: Hayao Miyazaki. ANI: Masashi Ando. MUS: Joe Hisaishi. PRD: Studio Ghibli. Ca. 90 mins.

Young girl Chihiro must journey from modern-day Japan to the Spirit World in order to rescue her parents, who have been turned into pigs. This is a surreal mixture of the childhood adventure of **MY NEIGHBOR TOTORO** with the threatening other-world of **PRINCESS MONONOKE** and the transformations of **PORCO ROSSO**.

SPOOKY KITARO

1968. JPN: *Gegege no Kitaro*. AKA: *Spooky Ooky Kitaro*. TV series, movie. DIR: Yoshio Kuroda, Masao Murayama, Yasuo Yamaguchi, Yoshio Takami, Masayuki Akehi, Hiroshi Shidara, Keiji Hisaoka, Fusahito Nagaki, Hideo Furu-sawa, Masamune Ochiai, Hiroshi Wagatsuma, Tomoharu Katsumata, Isao Takahata, Takeshi Tamiya. SCR: Susumu Takahisa, Masaki Tsuji, Shu-nichi Yukimuro, Tomohiro Ando. DES: Shigeru Mizuki, Yoshinori Kanemori. ANI: Mitsuo Hosoda, Masamune Ochiai, Hiroshi Wagatsuma, Shinya Takahashi. MUS: Taku Izumi. PRD: Toei, Fuji TV. 25 mins. x 65 eps. (TV1, b/w), 25 mins. x 45 eps. (TV2, color), 25 mins. x 108 eps. (TV3), 25 mins. x 7 eps. (TV4), 24 mins. (m1), 40 mins. (m2), 49 mins. (m3), 48 mins. (m4), 25 mins. x 92 eps. (TV5), 50 mins. (m5), 30 mins. (m6), 24 mins. (m7).

Kitaro is a little boy who lives with a gang of phantoms and figures from **JAPANESE FOLK TALES**, including his friends Rat Man, Cat Girl, and Piece-of-Paper. The spirit of his father possesses one of his eyeballs, which has grown tiny arms and legs and can climb about from its perch in his hair. His life may be strange in some of its details, but Kitaro is actually just a nice, ordinary Japanese boy who uses various magical artifacts, like his traditional coat and wooden shoes, to assist him in helping his human and nonhuman friends to resolve the problems that arise in their lives. Despite (or perhaps because of) reprising basic magical-girl and school-story concepts (the great thing about ghosts, of course, is that they *don't* have to go to school, as the theme song glee-fully informs us), the series is charming and funny, with Kitaro's supernatural surrogate family presented as regular folks whose ditherings, weaknesses, and prosaic good-heartedness wouldn't be *too* out of place in **SAZAE-SAN**. **LITTLE DEVIL**–creator Shigeru Mizuki's 1965 manga in *Shonen Magazine* led to the first TV series, which then returned in color in 1971. The fashion for ghoulies and ghosties at the time was influenced by American TV and inspired other anime like **VAMPIRE, LITTLE GOBLIN**, and **MONSTER MAN BEM**. After a long hiatus, *SK* returned for a third series in 1985, now overseen by Osamu Kasai and Hiroki Shibata—in many ways a complete remake of the preceding two versions but with a few nods to the modern audience, such as the intro-duction of super-deformed "SD" scenes of a squashed-down Kitaro at humor-ous moments. Some later stories were all-new ideas based on viewer sugges-tions. During the same period, Toei also took the franchise into movie the-aters, commencing with *SOK* (1985), which drew less on the original manga than on Mizuki's picaresque *Ghoulish Travels in Kitaro's World* (*Kitaro no Sekai o Bake Ryoko*), then running in *Shonen King* magazine. Three more short movies followed in 1986: *Great Ghost War* (*Yokai Daisakusen*), featuring cameos from **DRACULA, FRANKENSTEIN,** and the Wolfman, *Great Ghost Army—Destructive Monsters Arrive in Japan* (*Saikyo Yokai Guntai! Nippon Joriku*), and *The Big Revolt of Monsters from Another Dimension* (*Kyojigen Yokai no Dai Hanran*). The short-lived TV series *SOK: Hell Chapter* (1988, *Jigoku Hen*) retold the story of Kitaro's origins, prompted by the opportunity to meet his parents' ghosts in the underworld. After that, the franchise lay dormant again until revived in 1996 by director Daisuke Nishio. This most recent incar-nation, confusingly termed the "fourth" TV series, though technically being the fifth, also spun off into three more movies, Tomoharu Katsumata's *Giant Sea Monster* (1996, *Dai Kaiju*), Junichi Sato's *Ghost Knighter* (1997, *Obake Knighter*), and Takao Yoshizawa's *Monster Express! Ghost Train* (1997, *Yokai Tokkyu! Maboroshi no Kisha*). There was also a brief live-action series featuring Mizuki in a cameo role.

SPRIGGAN *

1998. AKA: *Striker*. Movie. DIR: Hiro-tsuge Kawasaki. SCR: Katsuhiro Oto-mo, Hirotsuge Kawasaki, Yasutaka Ito. DES: Hisashi Eguchi. ANI: Hisashi Eguchi. MUS: Kuniaki Haishima. PRD: TBS, Toho, Bandai, Studio 4°C. Ca. 90 mins.

Explorers in Turkey find "Noah's Ark," a spaceship frozen in layers of ice. The clandestine ARCAM research organiza-tion, dedicated to recovering the arti-facts of a lost prehistoric civilization, sends in its researchers but comes under attack from American agents who want the Ark's secrets for them-selves. Yu Ominae, a Japanese school-boy who is really one of ARCAM's elite "Spriggan" agents, heads for Turkey for a battle of wits against the Pentagon's high-powered Machiners Platoon led by the supersoldiers Fatman and Little Boy. They, however, report to the evil McDougal, a child prodigy whose pow-ers are dangerously out of control. McDougal has realized that the Ark is a weather control device, and he intends to start a new Ice Age.

Inspired by the final shot of *Raiders of the Lost Ark* (itself an homage to *Citi-zen Kane*), Hiroshi Takashige and **PRO-JECT ARMS**–creator Ryoji Minagawa's 1989 manga in *Shonen Sunday* posited a secret society fighting to claim all the world's paranormal artifacts for good, with agents named after Celtic fairies that "protect important treasures in ancient ruins."

From the English lettering to the Chinese theme song, this is an anime made with the foreign audience in mind—the script was translated before the film was made in an attempt to secure foreign backing. The manga was originally translated into English as *Striker*, in a version that hid its strong anti-Americanism, though the film was made and released in the U.S. amid a post-*X Files* willingness to cast the Pentagon as the bad guy. The anime project began life as a video of *Spriggan*'s "Berserker" chapters but was changed to the Ark plot line and upgraded to a theatrical release—close up it still looks like a video production inflated with extra capital. In a succession of bloody battles punctuated with Biblical apocalypse and government conspiracy, director Kawasaki recalls the whip-like cuts of **GHOST IN THE SHELL**, tearing from shot to shot to distract us from the sparse animation—*Spriggan* has less than a third of **AKIRA**'s cel count, which it hides with a breakneck pace worthy of Tsui Hark. "Superviser" Katsuhiro Otomo's influence is clearest in the design of the Ark and the portrayal of the evil McDougal. Like the mutant children of *Akira*, he has a bluish pallor, a vocabulary that belies his age, and a voice provided by a genuine child actor. *Ill. p. 391.*

SPRING AND CHAOS *

1996. JPN: *Ihatov no Kenso: Kenji no Haru*. AKA: *Iwate Fantasy: Kenji's Spring*. TV special. DIR: Shoji Kawamori. SCR: Shoji Kawamori. DES: Takahiro Kishida. ANI: Takahiro Kishida. MUS: Shang-Shang Typhoon. PRD: Group Tac, Magic Bus, Animal, Triangle Staff, NTV. 53 mins.
A brief survey of the life and works of Kenji Miyazawa, animated for theatrical screenings in his hometown of Iwate during the centenary of his birth but only combined in this form for a December TV special. As in the adapta-

tion of the same author's earlier **NIGHT ON THE GALACTIC RAILROAD**, the main roles are taken by cats, and all visible signs are written in Esperanto in honor of the author's devotion to the artificial language—hence Ihatov and not Iwate. Young Kenji, a pacifist, is at odds with Japan's increasingly militaristic society in the days before WWII. He is also determined to pursue a career as an author and poet, much to the chagrin of his levelheaded father. The story of Miyazawa's brief life (he died in his thirties) is punctuated by brief interludes from his stories, in a style similar to the **DIARY OF ANNE FRANK**. Director Kawamori is better known today for **ESCAFLOWNE** and **MACROSS**.

SPRITE: BETWEEN TWO WORLDS *

1996. JPN: *Manami to Nami Sprite*. AKA: *Manami and Nami Sprite*. Video. DIR: Takeshi Yamaguchi. SCR: Tsutomu Senogai. DES: Shinobu Arimura. ANI: Takashi Wada. MUS: Plectrum. PRD: Toei. 40 mins. x 2 eps.
When his mother is taken ill, the irritating Toru is packed off to stay with "relatives" in Tokyo, where he meets the shapely Manami. Immediately smitten, he discovers that this demure girl next door has a hidden side, a second bad-girl personality called Nami who's ready to put out at the drop of a hat.

Ever since the early days of **CREAM LEMON**, the tawdry genre of anime Lolita porn has suggested that inside every underage girl there's a sexually mature adult bursting to get out, if only the right boy comes along with the magic password. You couldn't get much better than Toru—so pathologically shy he can only search for sexual partners among his own family. And he's not the only one—this adaptation of Shinobu Arimura's manga alludes to a victim of childhood abuse, returning to the scene of the crime to face her demons. Blink and you'll miss it: a moment when Manami compares the size of Toru's member to her father's.

Where animation is limited, as it is here, voices have to carry a lot of emotional weight, but the dubbing

crew simply can't be bothered. The end result contains many silent hiatuses as the cast seemingly waits for canned laughter that never comes, and though **DEEP BLUE FLEET**–director Takeshi Yamaguchi tries to inject some arty moments (schoolgirls fighting with martial-arts moves based on common sports, waving grasses as lovers talk by a river), this is, like so many others of its ilk, a morally dubious attempt to package human pain as entertainment. **ⒸⓃ**

SPT LAYZNER

1985. JPN: *Aoki Ryusei SPT Layzner*. AKA: *Blue Meteor SPT Layzner*. TV series, video. DIR: Ryosuke Takahashi, Tetsuro Amino, Takashi Imanishi, Toshifumi Takizawa, Yoshitaka Fujimoto. SCR: Hiroyuki Hoshiyama, Fuyunori Gobu, Yasushi Hirano, Tsunehisa Ito, Ryosuke Takahashi. DES: Moriyasu Taniguchi, Kunio Okawara. ANI: Moriyasu Taniguchi. MUS: Hiroki Inui. PRD: Sunrise, Nippon TV. 25 mins. x 38 eps. (TV), 55 mins. x 3 eps. (v).
In 1996, Mars has been colonized by humans, with Russia and the U.S. both having established settlements on the planet. A group of Russian students, including Anna, David, Simone, and Arthur, is welcomed to an American base as part of a student exchange program. Eiji Asuka, child of a human father and a mother from planet Glados, is caught up in the beginnings of hostilities between the Americans and Russians and manages to save most of the students, but when Glados attacks Earth, he comes under suspicion purely because of his mixed blood. He and his giant robot, the "Blue Meteor" SPT (Super Powered Tracer) Layzner, are fated to play a key role in the conflict between planets. He is imprisoned by the Americans, considered a traitor by Glados, and has to fight his own sister Julia in a war that results in the occupation of Earth under Glados leader Le Kain. The second part of the TV series begins on Earth in 1999, when three years of oppression have all but crushed human culture; the books, art, and

learning of humankind are destroyed wherever they are found. Eiji and his young friends are living a hand-to-mouth existence as part of the resistance, while Julia has become the leader of a cult and a target for the aliens. As Eiji and Kain face each other for the last battle, Julia prepares to use her mystic powers to save Earth. The series is laden with emotional tension, with a dark emphasis on the cruelty of war and the corrupting effects of power. The early deaths of innocent civilians—including one of the original school party—set the tone; these are battles where nobody really wins and the good don't always survive. The series was taken off the air after episode 38, resulting in a confusing ending with Eiji simply left floating in space and a complex transfer to video. Initially, the series was released as three tapes: *Eiji 1996* and *Lu Kain 1999* (digests of episodes 1–24 and 26–37 respectively), incorporating extra, previously unseen footage, and *Act III: Seal 2000*, which contained the unbroadcast episodes 39 and 40. Set after the end of the war, Kain is still spoiling for a fight and prepares to reopen hostilities, but he is killed by his son Lu who takes control of Glados. Lu faces off against Eiji, but Julia manages to stop the fighting by warping Earth to a different part of the universe. *SPTL* was also released as another video series, the first two tapes comprising episodes 1–4, while the third contained episodes 15 and 28, supposedly because they were fan favorites. The entire 38-episode broadcast run was not released on video until 1997.

SPY OF DARKNESS *

1996. JPN: *Inju vs. Onna Spy*. AKA: *Lust-Beast vs. Female Spy*. Video. DIR: Hisashi Tomii, Tai Fujimoto. SCR: N/C. DES: N/C. ANI: Hideki Araki. MUS: N/C. PRD: Pink Pineapple, KSS. 45 mins. When the government develops a high-tech cyborg as a secret military weapon, a failure in gene manipulation causes the experimental creature to become a sex beast, fueled only by

its insatiable lust for women and utter destruction. The creature escapes and starts to abduct women, so the government assigns Anne, a sexy spy, to solve the crimes. When Anne finds the hideout where the creature is keeping the abducted women, she is caught in "an erotic battle of the sexes!" Another one for the pile. ⓁⓃⓋ

SRUNGLE *

1983. JPN: *Aku Dai Sakusen Srungle*. AKA: *Great Subspace War Srungle; Gorilla Force*. TV series. DIR: Kazuya Miyazaki, Kenzo Koizumi, Tatsuya Kasahara. SCR: Masaru Yamamoto, Juzo Tsubota. DES: Yoshitaka Amano, MIC Group. ANI: Asao Takahashi, Satoshi Yamaguchi, Tsukasa Dokite. MUS: Masayuki Yamamoto. PRD: Kokusai Eiga, TV Asahi. 25 mins. x 53 eps.
Garrick Space Town, built in the habitable zone between the twin planets Baxas, is under threat from a criminal organization, calling itself, rather pathetically, Crime. Led by an android known as Fork-Razor, the police are powerless against its daring exploits. To help the forces of law to contain this android crime wave, Doctor Mandi (Captain Chance) forms the Gorilla team of brave space cops Jet, Sexy, Superstar, Magician, and Baby's-Face, equipped with powerful robotic weapons like the mighty Srungle. In this golden age of robot shows, there was plenty of dross around; with a TV run starting the week before Tomino's magical **DUNBINE**, this pedestrian cop show was never likely to fly. It isn't one of the more frequently highlighted entries on Amano's resume. However, it was picked up by Saban, crashed into another show, dressed up with a Top 40 soundtrack, and syndicated on American TV in 1985 as *Macron One* (see **GOSHOGUN**).

STAFF-ROOM AFTER SCHOOL

1994. JPN: *Hokago Shokuinshitsu*. AKA: *Staff-room after Class*. Video. DIR: Kazuko Hirose. SCR: Mieko Koide. DES: Masayoshi Sudo. ANI: Masayoshi Sudo.

Princess Knight

© TEZUKA PRODUCTIONS • MUSHI PRODUCTIONS

MUS: N/C. PRD: Daiei, Tokuma. 30 mins. x 2 eps.
Despite his normal appearance, schoolteacher Mitsuo is a whirlwind of homosexual lusts, and he can contain his desires no longer when, on his birthday, he blurts out his feelings to fellow art teacher Toshiaki. A secret romance develops, but, a year later, Mitsuo's parents try to fix him up with a nice girl. Based on the pretty-boy manga by Mieko Koide, who also wrote the script. Ⓝ

STAINLESS NIGHT *

1995. Video. DIR: Ryunosuke Otonashi. SCR: Akira Takano. DES: Ryunosuke Otonashi, Yuriko Chihane. ANI: Ryunosuke Otonashi. MUS: N/C. PRD: Pink Pineapple, KSS. 30 mins. x 2 eps.
In the year 2020, hiking teenagers Mirei and Sayaka find a broken android in the mountains. It is the beautiful Linnear, who, once repaired, repays their kindness by having lesbian sex with them. Based on the manga by Kei Amaki, whose erotic works also appear in the **CREAM LEMON** collection. Ⓝ

STAR BLAZERS *

1974. JPN: *Uchu Senkan Yamato*. AKA: *Space Cruiser Yamato; Space Battle-*

ship Yamato. TV series, movie, video.
DIR: Noboru Ishiguro, Leiji Matsumoto,
Eiichi Yamamoto, Yoshinobu Nishizaki,
Takeshi Shiraji, Toshio Sodota. SCR:
Keisuke Fujikawa, Maru Tamura, Eiichi
Yamamoto, Yasushi Hirano. DES: Leiji
Matsumoto, Studio Nue, Kazuyuki
Okaseko, Toshiyuki Kubooka, Hiroyuki
Kitazume, Aki Tsunaki, Nobuaki
Nagano, Makoto Kobayashi, Atsushi
Takeuchi, Keiji Hashimoto, Syd Mead.
ANI: Toyoo Ashida, Yoshikazu Yasuhiko,
Takeshi Shirato. MUS: Hiroshi Miya-
gawa, Kentaro Haneda. PRD: Westcape,
Studio Take Off, Yomiuri TV (Nippon
TV). 25 mins. x 26 eps. (TV1), 25
mins. x 26 eps. (TV2), 25 mins. x 25
eps. (TV3), 130 min. (m1), 151 mins.
(m2), 93 mins. (TVm/m3), 93 mins.,
145 mins. (m4), 163 mins. (m5), 30
mins. x 3 eps. (v).

In 2199, the evil emperor Desslar
(Desslock) orders the destruction of
Earth. Radiation bombs from his planet Gamilas (Gamilon) have devastated
the planet's surface and will make it
uninhabitable within a year. Enemy
cruisers have Earth under heavy sur-
veillance so there's no chance to build
a starship to fight back or escape. But
the radiation that has dried up the
oceans has exposed many old hulks,
including the 250-year-old wreck of the
WWII battleship Yamato (Argo). Tunneling under the surface, the authorities have secretly built a starship within
the old hull. When Queen Starsha
from the distant world of Iscandar
offers Earth a device that can rid them
of the deadly radiation if they'll just
send a ship to fetch it, Captain Okita
(Avatar) and a handpicked crew set
out on the hazardous journey in the
reborn Yamato. Young pilot Susumu
Kodai (Derek Wildstar) has a grudge
against the captain, who survived the
battle that claimed Kodai's beloved
older brother, Mamoru (Alex), but as
time goes on, Kodai and the whole
crew come to see the captain as a heroic father-figure whose responsibility to
do everything in his power to save
Earth is a heavy burden.

Despite looking faintly ridiculous to
modern eyes, *Space Battleship Yamato* is
one of the watersheds in anime history.
A Japanese respray of *Star Trek*, it
replaces pioneer exploration (or gun-
boat diplomacy) with oblique references to WWII—a desperate suicide
mission, hounded by enemy vessels in
red, white, and blue. The titular ship
itself is the most obvious—at the time
the greatest battleship ever built, it was
sunk during a one-way mission to hold
off the U.S. attack on Okinawa in 1945.
Naval and aerial battle sequences are
clumsily transposed to a space setting:
ships "list" when holed in the hull and
fighters are shot "down," although in
space there isn't supposed to be a
"down." Beyond the risible pseudo-
physics, however, *SBY* contained a
supremely strong story line. *SBY*
changed the way TV programmers
thought about SF; previously it had
been supposed that only very young
audiences watched TV anime, and so
there was no point in screening anything but giant-robot and *sentai* shows.
The influence of the original series on
a whole generation of Japanese animators is incredible, and it resulted in
homages and cameos for the ship in
many anime works. The green-skinned
aliens seem to have inspired the design
of the Zentraedi in **MACROSS**, while the
teacher-pupil relationship of Okita and
Kodai, born out of the captain's guilt
over the loss of the pilot's close relation, never had a better reprise than in
GUNBUSTER, where Coach Ota played
the captain role to the full, even to the
extent of dying before the end.

The show was the brainchild of
writer Eiichi Yamamoto and **THUNDER-
SUB**-producer Yoshinobu Nishizaki,
who poached many staff from his former employers Mushi Pro. It also features heavy involvement from **CAPTAIN
HARLOCK**–creator Matsumoto, who
drew many of the initial designs and
also the spinoff manga. The planned
52 episodes were cut to 26 after a lukewarm ratings reception on TV, but, as
the series drew to a close in 1977, the
advent of *Star Wars* rejuvenated network interest in sci-fi. The first movie,

SBY (1977), is a compilation of the first
TV series that gained a new lease on
life abroad as *Space Cruiser*, with the
Gamilas hordes renamed the Gorgons.
Back in Japan for the TV series *SBY 2*
(1978), Earth's new age of peace is disrupted in 2201 by Emperor Zorder's
Comet Empire. The sequel to *this*
series came in movie form with the first
SBY feature to comprise all-new
footage: Tomoharu Katsumata's
Farewell to SBY: In the Name of Love
(1978, *Saraba Uchusenkan Yamato: Ai no
Senshitachi*, aka *SBY: Warriors of Love*).
This was soon followed by Takeshi Shirato's *SBY: The New Voyage* (1979, *USY:
Arataranu Tabitachi*), a 95-minute TV
special broadcast on Fuji TV, in which
the Yamato has the chance to come to
the aid of Earth's savior Queen Starsha
when she suffers attacks by the Black
Star Cluster Empire and the Gamilon
Dessler. *The New Voyage* was shown in
1981 in theaters on a double bill with
the next genuine movie edition, Katsumata's *Be Forever Yamato* (1980, *Yamato
yo Towa ni*), featuring Kodai and a crew
that includes Starsha and Mamoru's
daughter, Sasha, traveling in time to
defeat the invading forces of commander Kazan of the Dark Empire.

However, *SBY*'s reissue as *Space
Cruiser* was by no means the last of its
English-language incarnations. The
series made it to American TV screens
as *Star Blazers* (1979). Claster Studios
had acquired the first two series with its
sights on marketing tie-ins for its toy
division, Hasbro. Some changes were
made for the U.S. market, notably to
character names. Comic relief robot
Analyzer and cyborg mechanic Sandor
had been created well in advance of
George Lucas's knockabout robot duo
in *Star Wars*, but Analyzer was named
IQ-9 in imitation of C-3PO. Some
changes were made to cushion U.S.
sensibilities; violence was toned down,
and Dr. Sado's copious drinking
became nonalcoholic. Despite an early
lukewarm reception, American anime
fans, as passionately loyal as their Japanese counterparts to the show they
loved, began to screen episodes in con-

vention video rooms. Its classic status on both sides of the Pacific was secured by fan interest and activity, to the extent where the full series and all five movies are still selling on video in the U.S. and Japan.

In 1980, a third Japanese TV series (also brought to the U.S.) moved the action further forward again to the year 2205, when new danger appeared in the Bolar Wars. During a battle between Galman Gamilas and the Bolar Commonwealth, a stray missile flies into the sun and renders it unstable. With only a year before the sun explodes, Kodai must restaff the Yamato with a crew fresh out of the academy and find a new Earth for the human race. In fact, by the end, the sun's stability is restored, leaving the grande finale of the Yamato's adventures to Takeshi Shirato's movie release *Final Yamato* (1983, USY: *Kanketsu*). For this conclusion, Okita (returned from the dead as an admiral) takes command of the ship in 2203 to defend Earth from Lugarl, priest-king of the water planet Aquarius, whose people are flooding the rest of the galaxy. The Aquarians are descendants of an advanced race that fled Earth during Noah's flood, and now they want to come home. The Yamato saves the galaxy once again, then sinks into the watery grave from which it was raised at the very beginning of the saga, there to remain until *Blade Runner*–futurist Syd Mead resurrected it in his much-trumpeted designs for the video series *Yamato 2520* (1995). Top-heavy with directors (Shirato, Nishizaki, and Shigenori Kageyama) and adding a stellar design team to rework Matsumoto and Kitazume's originals, this relaunch of the old ship failed to fly. It looks pretty, but the repetition of the teens-save-Earth concept lacks the passion and conviction of the old series. Sometimes the latest fashion just can't compete with the classics. The *New SBY* movie (planned for 2002) is reputedly based on the later manga in *Comic Gotta*. Set in 3199, it features the descendants of the crew, recruited by an ethereal

beauty, Aya Haguro, for a new mission. Another galaxy is fated to clash with the Milky Way, and Aya leads the crew in a quest to fight off the Dark Queen and her metallic Metanoid subjects. *Ill. p. 345.*

STAR DUST
1992. Video. DIR: Ichiro Itano. SCR: N/C. DES: Kazutoshi Kobayashi. ANI: Kazutoshi Kobayashi. MUS: Junichi Kanezaki. PRD: Yoyogi Animation Gakuin. 30 mins.
A misguided sci-fi tale of ecological police keeping *space* free from pollution in 2061. The quality of this anime is at least partly forgivable, though, for being an apprentice film made by students at the Yoyogi Animation academy. Only a few years later, budgets would become so tight in the anime business that members of the same college would become cheap labor on the far longer-running but equally amateurish GANDHARA.

STAR OCEAN EX
2001. TV series. DIR: Hiroshi Watanabe. SCR: Mayori Sekijima, Kenichi Kanemaki. DES: Ayako Kuroda. ANI: Ryoko Hata, Akira Matsushima. MUS: N/C. PRD: Studio Deen, TV Tokyo. 25 mins. x 26 eps.
Claude is transported to Exvel, a world beyond time, where the fantasy adventures are what one might expect of an anime adaptation of a novel adaptation of a PlayStation game. This anime was based on *Star Ocean Second Story* serialized in *Shonen Gan Gan* magazine.

STAR OF DAVIDE
1989. JPN: *Davide no Hoshi*. Video. DIR: Yoichiro Shimatani. SCR: Akio Sato, Yoichiro Shimatani, Ranko Ono. DES: Masaaki Sato. ANI: Tatsuya Sotomaru. MUS: Takahiko Kanemaru. PRD: Apples, Miyuki Pro. 45 mins. x 5 eps.
Lustful creatures from another dimension are invading Earth, starting with the women, for a change. Based on the manga by Masaaki Sato, the fifth episode of this video series was rebranded *New SoD* (1991) and moved

the sex and violence to the English countryside. A less fantastic (but equally distasteful) version of the story was also turned into *Star of David: Beauty Hunter* (1979), a live-action film directed by Norifumi Suzuki. **NV**

STAR OF THE GIANTS
1968. JPN: *Kyojin no Hoshi*. TV series, movie. DIR: Tadao Nagahama, Yoshio Kabashima (TV1); Tetsuro Imazawa, Satoshi Dezaki, Minoru Okazaki, Akinori Nagaoka (TV2). SCR: Tadaaki Yamazaki, Mamoru Sasaki, Masaki Tsuji, Ryohei Suzuki, Sumiko Hayashi, Tsunehisa Ito, Toru Sawaki, Yoshiaki Yoshida, Seiji Matsuoka (TV1); Toshiaki Imaizumi, Noboru Shiroyama, Yoshihisa Araki (TV2). DES: Noboru Kawasaki. ANI: Daikichiro Kusube, Hideo Kawauchi, Yasuo Otsuka, Yoshifumi Kondo, Tetsuo Imazawa, Toshiyuki Honda, Tetsuro Wakabayashi, Noboru Ishiguro, Soji Yoshikawa, Masaru Inoue, Shingo Araki, Takao Kasai. MUS: Takeo Watanabe. PRD: Tokyo Movie (Shinsha), Magic Bus, Yomiuri TV (Nippon TV). 25 mins. x 181 eps. (TV), 88 mins. (m1), 70 mins. (m2), 61 mins. (m3), 25 mins. x 75 eps. (TV2).
Hyuma Hoshi is a promising young baseball player who dreams of becoming a top star like his father before him. When he joins the famous Giants team, his father and friends all do their utmost to make sure he achieves his full potential of becoming the star of the Giants. Based on the 1966 *Shonen Magazine* manga by Noboru Kawasaki and Ikki Kajiwara, *SotG* was the first sports anime, the direct ancestor of the rest of the genre, including Kawasaki's later ANIMAL 1, as well as the girls' variants AIM FOR THE ACE, ATTACK NUMBER ONE, and their many imitators. In bringing a sports plot to a medium previously dominated by juvenile adventure and sci-fi, it paved the way for other aspects of manga's diversity to cross over into animation. During the course of the original TV run, several reedits were screened in theaters as part of vacation anime festivals. The first, *SotG* (1969), was billed as the only

chance for many viewers to see their favorite show in *color*—black-and-white TV sets being more common at the time. Other movie edits included *SotG: Big League* (1970, *Dai League Ball*), and the final game against the Yakult Swallows, *SotG: Confrontation at Shinjuku* (1970, *Shinjuku no Taiketsu*). Though *SotG* was popular in Japan, the mundane nature of its struggles, albeit leavened with some far-fetched training techniques lifted from martial arts, left it unlikely to be exported to the West. Hyuma's only appearance in the English-language was in the 30-minute TV special *Star of the Giants vs. the Mighty Atom* (1969), a friendly match between the Giants and the characters from **ASTRO BOY**, which reached the U.S. as part of the latter series—renamed *Astro Boy vs. the Giants*. The series was followed by **SAMURAI GIANTS**, adapted from another Kawasaki manga, and by a later, much less successful sequel. *New [Shin] SotG* (1977) is set five years after the original and was broadcast at a time when the Yomiuri Giants were facing anime competition from the Tokyo Mets (see **SONG OF THE BASEBALL ENTHUSIAST**) and the Seibu Lions (see **GO FOR IT, TABUCHI**). The final 23 episodes, rebranded as *New SotG II* (1979), deviated most from the original manga, introducing new regular characters, dumping Hyuma's girlfriend, and even killing off his father in the final episode, much to the original creators' annoyance.

STAR OF THE SEINE

1975. JPN: *La Seine no Hoshi*. AKA: *Star of La Seine; The Black Tulip*. TV series. DIR: Masaaki Osumi, Yoshiyuki Tomino, Satoshi Dezaki. SCR: Soji Yoshikawa, Michiru Umadori. DES: Akio Sugino. ANI: Kazuo Yamazaki, Toshio Takagi. MUS: Shunsuke Kikuchi. PRD: Unimax, Fuji TV. 25 mins. x 39 eps.
Simone, illegitimate daughter of the King of Austria and an opera singer, is taken from court as a baby into the care of a Parisian florist and grows up as just another working-class girl in the French capital at the end of the 1700s.

When the king's old friend the Comte de Voudrel recognizes her, he adopts her, and she discovers the secret of her birth. She learns to fence and teams up with the comte's son Robert, who secretly helps out the poor and needy using his secret identity as the Black Tulip. Thus is born the Star of La Seine, heroine of the Revolution. But despite her support of the people in their struggle to overthrow the nobility, Simone also has sympathy for her half-sister, Queen Marie Antoinette, and when the Revolution finally overthrows the monarchy, she and Robert rescue the queen's children and adopt them as their own. A popular adventure series that leaves the nods to historical accuracy to **ROSE OF VERSAILLES** (the heroine of the Revolution dresses in hotpants and boots more suited to 1970s disco than 1780s swordfights), *SotS* did well in Europe, though Italy made Robert rather than Simone the titular hero. The *Black Tulip* title seems to have been engineered to imply an association with an unrelated 1850 novel of the same name by **THREE MUSKETEERS**–creator Alexandre Dumas.

STARBIRDS *

1978. JPN: *Tosho Daimos*. AKA: *Fighter/Champion Daimos; Fighting General Daimos*. TV series. DIR: Tadao Nagahama, Yoshikazu Yasuhiko, Kazuo Terada, Yoshihiro Takahashi. SCR: Masaki Tsuji, Fuyunori Gobu, Masaaki Sakurai. DES: Akehiro Kaneyama, Studio Nue, Yutaka Izubuchi. ANI: Akehiro Kaneyama. MUS: Shunsuke Kikuchi. PRD: Sunrise, Toei, TV Asahi. 25 mins. x 44 eps. (TV).
Winged aliens from the dying planet Baam decide to conquer Earth and make it their new home. Heading up the resistance is Kazuya Ryusaku in the giant robot Daimos. During an enemy attack, Kazuya saves a girl called Erika. She's lost her memory, so both are completely unaware that she's the princess of the invading aliens, and they fall in love. When the truth emerges, she returns to her people to try and stop the war, while Kazuya is

considered a traitor by his own people because he supports her wish for peace. The evil Emperor Olbam compels Erika to shoot her human lover; he survives and, not knowing that she is being forced to act against her will, decides to destroy the alien base in revenge. *Romeo and Juliet* with giant robots, the series didn't achieve the stellar popularity of Go Nagai's robot epics like **GRANDIZER**, its one claim to fame being the debut of **PATLABOR**'s Yutaka Izubuchi as a guest robot designer on one episode. A 1980 "movie" was simply a theatrical showing of episode 24. In the U.S., the show was also edited into a 90-minute feature by New Hope Productions (see **VOLTUS**), broadcast on the Showtime cable network under the title *Starbirds*, with the robot renamed Dynamo and a new soundtrack deliberately redolent of *Star Wars*. See also **SHOGUN WARRIORS**.

STARCAT FULL HOUSE

1989. JPN: *Hoshineko Full House*. Video. DIR: Noboru Ishiguro. SCR: Noboru Ishiguro. DES: Noboru Sugimitsu, Haruhiko Mikimoto. ANI: Masahito Kitagawa. MUS: Kaoru Wada. PRD: Artland. 30 mins. x 4 eps.
This slapstick comedy is about three pretty girls struggling to earn a living as pilots of the Iron Goblin delivery vessel. The computer answers back, the space pirates are on their tail, and romantic entanglements with their clients cause friction in the trio. The final episode throws the alien Eterna race into the mix, but it's hardly **GUNBUSTER**.

STARLIGHT NOCTURNE

1989. JPN: *Gasei Yakyoku*. Video. DIR: Osamu Dezaki. SCR: Toshiaki Imaizumi. DES: Akio Sugino. ANI: Akio Sugino. MUS: Akira Mioka. PRD: Magic Bus. 30 mins. x 4 eps.
Complicated romance in early 20th-century Japan, as a baron's only daughter switches places with the maid who shares her birthday, causing confusion when each is more attracted to a man

from the other's social background. The 1923 Tokyo earthquake (see **DOOMED MEGALOPOLIS**) brings matters to a close. Based on the manga by Masako Hirata.

STARSHIP GIRL YAMAMOTO YOHKO *

1995. JPN: *Sore Yuke! Uchu Senkan Yamamoto Yoko*. AKA: *Go! Space Cruiser Yoko Yamamoto*. Video. DIR: Akiyuki Shinbo. SCR: Yuji Kawahara, Mayori Sekijima, Masashi Kubota. DES: Kashiro Akaishi, Kazuto Nakazawa (v) Akio Watanabe (TV). ANI: Hiroyuki Morinobu. MUS: N/C. PRD: JC Staff, Tee-Up, TV Osaka. 30 mins. x 7 eps. (v), 25 mins. x 26 eps. (TV).

In A.D. 2990, the human race has been split into two space faring empires, Terra and Ness. With Terra on a losing streak in the ritualized "war games," scientist Rosen creates a time machine, sending emissaries back to 20th-century Earth to recruit new warriors by testing them with familiar-looking arcade games. He finds schoolgirl Yoko and friends and convinces them to time-travel after school to the battlefront. This is yet another spin on *The Last Starfighter* (see also **BATTLE ATHLETES**), with video-game style duels in advanced machines that look like a cross between a Formula One racing car and a goldfish. The alleged "girl power" is presented, in the tradition of **GUNBUSTER**, for the titillation of a male audience, but there are a few fun visual tricks, like cockpits that disappear in battle leaving the pilot apparently floating in space. Based on a novel by Taku Atsushi, also adapted as an audio drama. Episode four is renumbered "episode zero," and reintroduces the characters for the second "season." *YY* returned as a TV series in 1999.

STARSHIP TROOPERS

1988. JPN: *Uchu no Senshi*. AKA: *Space Warriors*. Video. DIR: Tetsuro Amino. SCR: Tsunehisa Ito, Noboru Aikawa. DES: Hiroyuki Kitakubo, Yutaka Izubuchi, Kazumasa Miyabe, Studio Nue. ANI: Yoshinobu Inano. MUS: Hiro

Tsunoda. PRD: Sunrise, Bandai. 50 mins. x 3 eps.

Johnnie Rico loves the beautiful, willful Carmen, his high-school sweetheart. When she signs up for the war against Earth's alien assailants, he follows suit in the hope of impressing her, but they get different assignments—she as a trainee pilot, he as an infantry grunt. From the studio that brought you **GUNDAM**, cited by its creator Tomino as one of his inspirations, this is an animated version of the Hugo-award winning 1959 novel by Robert Heinlein. Amino's version retains the scenes of training and combat but also focuses on time off the battlefield. His soldiers get into barroom brawls with disgruntled civvies, bury one of their comrades, and are then forced to attend his girlfriend's wedding to a new lover. The romance between Johnnie and Carmen becomes more central, ending with their tearful reunion in the hospital, to which they have both been evacuated with injuries. Carmen, absent for the bulk of the novel, has regular appearances in the anime to remind viewers what Johnnie is fighting for. In addition, each episode closes with Carmen bouncing along a beach in a bikini.

Johnnie's mother, Maria, also has a larger part to play. In the anime, she opposes Johnnie's enlistment, slapping his face as he prepares to leave. Her death is also made far more immediate; Amino's version keeps the trainees closer to Earth so that we see Johnnie and his platoon fighting fires at the Fall of Buenos Aires, unaware that his mother is breathing her last nearby. The only Japanese character in the original book, Private Shujumi, is not present in the anime, perhaps because a Japanese audience would not warm to a stereotypical martial artist. He is replaced by the jug-eared, happy-go-lucky Private Azuma, who has "dead meat" written all over him from day one.

Directing the adaptation amid the post-*Top Gun* glut of gung-ho Hollywood movies, Amino tried to de-fang

A pretty baseball player reveals all off screen, and a baseball team can't believe its luck, in a moment from U-Jin's **TALES OF** . . . . The bulging eyes are a staple of American cartoon comedy stretching back to Looney Toons, but the bloody nose is uniquely Japanese and indicates sexual frustration. Other anime symbols include a cross-shaped bulging vein in the forehead that denotes anger and a sweat droplet on the temple that suggests extreme nervousness. *See entry p. 391.*

Tales of Sintillation

© 1992 U-JIN (LEED COMICS)/SOEISHINSHA

Heinlein's militarist text with some home truths about the evils of war, but he still ran into criticism at home for "over-Americanizing" the anime. Maybe he shouldn't have turned his Filipino hero into an all-American blond, but Paul Verhoeven's live-action *Starship Troopers* (1997) later followed the same route with Caspar van Dien looking about as Filipino as Bugs Bunny. One of Heinlein's references to his own military past managed to survive untouched in the anime; Johnnie's ship, the Rodger Young, is named after a real-life Ohio private who was posthumously decorated for singlehandedly destroying a Japanese gun emplacement in 1943.

STARZAN S

1984. JPN: *Okawari Boy Starzan S*. AKA: *Transforming Boy Starzan S*. TV series. DIR: Hidehito Ueda, Hiroyuki Tanaka, Mazakazu Higuchi, Shinya Sadamitsu, Masayuki Kojima, Takaaki Ishiyama. SCR: Takao Koyama, Mayori Sekijima, Yoshiyuki Suga, Miho Maruo. DES: Yoshitaka Amano, Ammonite. ANI: Masayuki Hayashi. MUS: Kazunori Ishida. PRD: Tatsunoko, Fuji TV. 25 mins. x 32 eps.

The beautiful Jun Yagami sets out in search of her father, Mamoru, who was last seen searching for the world of Paratopia, where nobody ever grows old. Caught in a space storm with a group of feckless bounty hunters, she lands on the unexplored world of Kirakira. The world is riven by a war between the Zenobi tribe and a group of evil robots led by the metallic Darth Bellow. The bounty hunters join forces with Darth Bellow, while Jun supports the Zenobi and their "forest god," the human boy Starzan, who possesses a transforming vehicle known as the Tobida Star. Conceived as a rather obvious mixture of *Star Wars* and *Tarzan*, this anime had robot toy tie-in potential ahead of the TRANSFORMERS sensation the following year.

STEALTH! KARATE CLUB

1990. JPN: *Onin! Karate-bu*. Video. DIR: Osamu Sekita. SCR: Hideo Nanbu. DES: Koichi Endo. ANI: Koichi Endo. MUS: Akira Yamazaki. PRD: JC Staff, Nippon Eizo. 50 mins. x 4 eps.
Supertough high-school kids duke it out in the Osaka area (see COMPILER), which, naturally, means that they're all in league with gangsters. Based on the 1985 manga by Koji Takahashi in *Young Jump* magazine. **◊**

STEAM DETECTIVES *

1998. JPN: *Kaiketsu Shoki Tanteidan*. AKA: *Handsome Steam Detectives*. TV series. DIR: Kiyoshi Murayama. SCR: Tsunehisa Arakawa, Kenichi Araki. DES: Akio Takami, Satoshi Hashimoto. ANI: Akio Takami. MUS: N/C. PRD: Xebec, TV Tokyo. 25 mins. x 26 eps.
Ten-year-old smartass Narutaki fights crime in the steampunk environs of Steam City. He is assisted by his loyal butler (shades of *Batman*) who has looked after him since his parents were killed by the malevolent Phantom Menace, and also by curvy 16-year-old nurse Ling Ling, daughter of a dead scientist, who not only shops, cooks, and wears a cute uniform, but also has her own magnificently clunky giant robot, Goriki. This intriguing mix of the diminutive CONAN THE BOY DETECTIVE with the nostalgic technology of

GIANT ROBO is frittered away with low-quality animation and poorly conceived plots. Based on the 1995 manga by SILENT MÖBIUS–creator Kia Asamiya in *Ultra Jump*.

STEEL ANGEL KURUMI *

1999. JPN: *Kotetsu Tenshi Kurumi*. TV series. DIR: Naohito Takahashi, Kazuya Murata, Norihiko Sudo. SCR: Tsunehisa Arakawa. DES: Yuriko Senba, Takeshi Ito, Toshihiko Sato. ANI: Yuriko Senba. MUS: N/C. PRD: Kadokawa, Pony Canyon, WOWOW. 15 mins. x 26 eps.
In a 1920s Japan not unlike that of SAKURA WARS, a mad scientist (we know he's mad because he's called Professor Demon) has devoted the full power of his weird science to producing a robot whose deadly weapons are pink hair, a cute voice, and a French maid outfit. When a teenage boy sneaks into the basement for a peek, Kurumi decides *he's* her master. The 15-minute running time restricts what can be done to move the story along, but the audience's short attention span might work in favor of a concept that was hackneyed about three TENCHI MUYO! clones back. Realizing that a respray was all the audience's low expectations required, the producers returned in 2001 with a new series, which was just like the old one but set in the present day, with everyone's name now bearing the suffix "Mark Two." That was worth it.

STEEL DEVIL

1987. JPN: *Daimaju Gekito Hagane no Oni*. AKA: *Violent Encounter Demon of Steel*. Video. DIR: Toshihiro Hirano. SCR: Noboru Aikawa. DES: Naoyuki Onda, Koichi Ohata. ANI: Koichi Ohata. MUS: Masahiro Kawasaki. PRD: AIC, Tokuma Japan Communications. 60 mins.
An experimental laser brings down a UFO on a remote island, and scientists Haruka and Takuya risk their lives to investigate. Accidentally opening a door to another dimension, Haruka is transformed into a giant mechanical warrior. In this derivative apocalyptic anime from ICZER-ONE-creator Hirano,

ancient entities rise from their slumber of ages and fight in the sky above Shinjuku to herald the end of the rule of humanity. See also CYGUARD and GENOCYBER.

STEEL JEEG

1975. JPN: *Kotetsu Jeeg*. TV series. DIR: Masayuki Akehi, Yoshio Nitta, Kazuya Miyazaki, Masayuki Akehi, Yugo Serikawa, Masamune Ochiai, Nobutaka Nishizawa, Yasuo Yamakichi. SCR: Hiroyasu Yamaura, Keisuke Fujikawa, Tomohiro Suto. DES: Kazuo Nakamura, Geki Katsumata. ANI: Kazuo Nakamura, Seiji Kikuchi, Koji Uemura, Sadao Tominaga. MUS: Michiaki Watanabe. PRD: Toei, NET. 25 mins. x 46 eps.
Hiroshi Shima is mortally injured in a racing accident but restored to life as a cyborg by his scientist father. Professor Shima is also investigating the relics of the ancient Jamatai kingdom, and he is murdered by the henchmen of their Queen Himika when he discovers a tiny bronze bell with supposed sorcerous powers. The modern inhabitants of Japan are attacked by the bell's ancient makers, but Hiroshi holds them off by interfacing with the head of a giant robot, Steel Robot Jeeg, also created by his father (a multitalented physiologist-cum-archaeologist-cum-robot designer, it would seem). To complete its body and launch into space, he needs parts released by the space-jet Big Shooter, piloted by his father's lovely assistant, Miwa Satsuki. The enemy has huge *haniwa* robots, called "clay phantoms," buried under the soil of Japan, and only Jeeg can destroy them and save the world; but can cyborg Hiroshi suppress his human feelings for Miwa? After episode 29, the Jamatai invaders were replaced by a new enemy, the Ryoma Empire. Based on an idea by Tatsuya Yasuda and Go Nagai, creator of GRANDIZER, GETTER ROBO, and MAZINGER Z, *SJ* also ran as a manga in several children's publications. *Haniwa* in Japanese archaeology are literally "circles of clay"—barrel-shaped terracotta cylinders topped

by sculptures, used to mark the borders of burial grounds in ancient Japan. They date from the period when Queen *Himiko* ruled the state of *Yamatai* in the 3rd century A.D. (see **DARK MYTH**). Compare to similar ghosts of the past in **PSYCHIC WARS** and **BLUE SEED**.

STELLARBUSTERS

1999. JPN: *Uchu Kaizoku Mito no Daiboken*. AKA: *Great Adventures of Space Pirate Mito*. TV series. DIR: Takashi Watanabe, Koji Yasuda, Yoshio Nitta, Masahiko Murata, Shigeru Ueda, Kunitoshi Okajima. SCR: Hidefumi Kimura, Junko Okazaki. DES: Reibanji Ishigami. ANI: Masahiro Sekiguchi, Hitoshi Kanezawa. MUS: Hikaru Nanase. PRD: Sunrise, TV Tokyo. 25 mins. x 26 eps.

Fifteen-year-old Aoi discovers that his mother is not a model working abroad at all. He discovers this when she is attacked in the cemetery by members of the space patrol, where she reveals that her adult body harbors Mito, a childlike female space pirate. Mito is his real mother, but, because she is an alien, she does not appear old enough to be. She reveals that Aoi is actually the heir to the throne of the Great Kingdom of the Milky Way, and they are chased by Lanban, the corrupt leader of the space patrol, who wants an artifact that can make *him* king of the galaxy instead. A sci-fi take on the stories of Mitsukuni Tokugawa (see **MANGA MITO KOMON**), with a space pirate straight out of **TENCHI MUYO!**, this series only got more bizarre for its second season. After episode 13, Aoi suddenly transforms into a girl. The newly female Aoi becomes Queen of the Milky Way but also continues to attend Japanese high school in disguise. The former Queen, Hikari, returns as a ghost and demands her throne back, setting the stage for more space piracy (in the name of the established order) and motherly interference from Mito (who seems to have been passed over in the succession). When released on DVD, the series also included a bonus short, *Mito Wars*, an early experiment in full digital animation.

STINGIEST MAN IN TOWN, THE *

1978. JPN: *Machi Ichiban Kechinbo*. TV special. DIR: Katsuhisa Yamada. SCR: Romeo Muller. DES: Paul Coker Jr. ANI: Kazuyuki Komori. MUS: Fred Spielman. PRD: Top Craft, Rankin-Bass, TV Asahi. 55 mins.

On a cold Christmas Eve in 1880s London, notorious miser Ebenezer Scrooge is visited in his sleep by three ghostly apparitions who teach him the errors of his ways and the meaning of Christmas. This U.S.–Japan coproduction based on Charles Dickens's 1843 novel *A Christmas Carol* was designed as a musical for the American market and made to order by the Japanese from a prerecorded voice and music track. Character designer Coker seems to have worked almost solely on festive cartoons back in the U.S., including *Frosty's Winter Wonderland* and *The Year without a Santa Claus*—he is better known as one of the artists on *Mad* magazine and an old hand at designing greetings cards for Hallmark. For the subsequent Japanese version, a new script was synchronized to the existing pictures: a rare case of an anime that genuinely has been *dubbed* in Japanese. The Japanese edition was broadcast on Christmas Eve 1978, a mere 24 hours after the U.S. premiere. Director Yamada would go on to make a variety of more obviously Japanese cartoons, including the high-spirited **JUNK BOY** and the spirit-slaying **DEVIL HUNTER YOHKO**. Dickens's **OLD CURIOSITY SHOP** was animated the following year by an unconnected crew.

STOP HIBARI-KUN

1983. JPN: *Stop Hibari-kun*. TV series. DIR: Satoshi Hisaoka, Tetsuo Imazawa, Yoshiaki Kawajiri, Hiroshi Sasakawa. SCR: Shigeru Yanagawa, Hiromi Asano, Tokio Tsuchiya, Hiroshi Koda, Tomomi Tsutsui, Takeshi Shudo. DES: Yoshinori Kanemori. ANI: Makoto Ito, Kazuo Tomizawa, Kiyoshi Matsumoto, Takao Kasai, Yasuomi Umezu. MUS: Koji Nishimura. PRD: Toei, Fuji TV. 25 mins. x 35 eps.

Yusaku Sakamoto is sent to live with a friend of the family after his mother's death—or should that be, a friend of the Family. Now he's living with Ibari Ozora, head of the Ozora crime syndicate, and Ozora's pretty daughters Tsugumi, Tsubame, Suzume, and Ko-chan. The prettiest "girl" of all, however, is Hibari, Ozora's eldest son, who has decided he likes life better if he dresses as a girl. This bizarre forerunner of **TENCHI MUYO!** combined with a cross-dressing *Godfather* was based on the 1982 manga in *Shonen Jump* by **EIJI**-creator Hisashi Eguchi.

STORIES FROM A STREET CORNER *

1962. JPN: *Aru Machikado no Monogatari*. Movie. DIR: Eiichi Yamamoto. SCR: Osamu Tezuka. DES: Osamu Tezuka. ANI: Shigeyuki Hayashi (Rintaro), Masaharu Mitsuyama, Tetsuro Amino, Gisaburo Sugii. MUS: Tatsuo Takai. PRD: Mushi Pro. 38 mins.

Posters on a street corner each tell their own story—a circus poster and several advertisements briefly come to life, and a pianist and a violinist from separate pictures fall in love. Meanwhile, a little girl in a nearby garret apartment loses her doll, which finds a new friend in the mouse, playing in the gutter, who saves it from being swept away in a rainstorm. Military posters are slapped over the peacetime images, and the buildings are destroyed by enemy bombs. However, in the aftermath, the girl, the mouse, and her doll are all safe, and the military posters have blown away, revealing the originals underneath. There is no dialogue; the film tells its stories visually. The first work to be produced by Tezuka's Mushi Productions; the second would be **ASTRO BOY**. See also **STREET CORNER FAIRYTALES**.

STORY OF DONBE

1981. JPN: *Donbe Monogatari*. TV special. DIR: Fusahito Nagaki. SCR: Shota Tatsumachi, Keisuke Fujikawa. DES:

Takashi Keuchi, Akira Fukuda. ANI: Akira Fukuda. MUS: Hiroshi Takada, Kiyoshi Suzuki. PRD: Eiken, NTV. 84 mins.

Researcher Mutsugoro takes his family to a remote and uninhabited island near Hokkaido, to study the local population of wild bears. Nearby poachers make his life difficult, and he "inherits" an orphaned bear cub, whom the family call Donbe and raise as one of their own. A dramatization of one Tadashi Hata's essays from his book *The Hokkaido Animal Kingdom*, the author himself provided authentic bear impersonations for the voice track, and is hence credited as Donbe's "voice actor."

STORY OF LITTLE LOVE
1984. JPN: *Chiisana Koi no Monogatari*. TV special. DIR: Toshio Hirata, Satoshi Dezaki. SCR: Shunichi Yukimuro. DES: Yoshiyuki Momose. ANI: Yoshishige Kosako. MUS: Shinsuke Kazato. PRD: Visual 80, MK, TBS. 84 mins.
Tiny schoolgirl Chiiko develops a crush on older boy Saly and believes herself to be his girlfriend, although Saly is already involved in a love triangle with Tonko, the girl he met on his summer vacation in the mountains. Based on a 1962 manga by Chikako Mitsuhashi.

STORY OF RIKI
1989. JPN: *Riki-O*. AKA: *Power King; King Riki*. Video. DIR: Satoshi Dezaki. SCR: Kazumi Koide. DES: Akio Sugino. ANI: Yasuhiro Seo. MUS: Yoshimasa Nakajima. PRD: Magic Bus. 45 mins. x 2 eps.
In the near future, supertough-guy Riki is sent to a private prison for a crime he didn't commit. He thrives, however, in the ultraviolent prison environment, fighting his way to the top of the pack and then out to freedom. Based on a manga by Masahiko Takakumi in *Business Jump*, this story was also made into Nam Nai Choi's live-action Hong Kong film *Story of Riki* (1992). ❷

STORY OF SUPERCONDUCTORS
1988. JPN: *Chodendo Monogatari*. TV special. DIR: Masayuki Oseki, Kenji Naito. SCR: Takashi Yamada, Hiroshi Aoki. DES: Isao Oji. ANI: Isao Oji. MUS: N/C. PRD: Studio Twinkle, Tokai TV. 60 mins.
The science department of the *Tosai Shinbun* newspaper investigates a story on superconductors, learning all about the mysterious world of subzero electrical conductivity, the Meissner Effect, Brian Josephson's work on "tunneling" (flow across an insulating layer without application of voltage), and implications for super-*computer* technology in the 21st century. Meanwhile, attractive reporter Miss Ohashi begins to find bespectacled scientist Dr. Arai rather attractive.

STORY OF THE SOYA
1984. JPN: *Soya Monogatari*. TV series. DIR: N/C. SCR: Masaru Yamamoto. DES: Shiro Murata, Hiroki Hayashi. ANI: Shiro Murata. MUS: Toshi Fukui. PRD: Kokusai Eiga, TV Tokyo. 25 mins. x 21 eps.
In 1978, the Antarctic survey vessel Soya calls in at Yamaguchi Prefecture's Moji port on her final voyage. Watching are Susumu Kozaki, a shipbuilder's son who was born on the day the Soya was launched, and his own son, Hiroshi. Susumu tells Hiroshi the story of the Soya, how it was commissioned by the Russians, and how the contract was canceled soon after launch. Renamed the Jishin Maru, the Soya bears witness to the events of the 1930s, as the dark clouds of war gather.

STRANGE DAWN
2000. TV series. DIR: Shogo Kawamoto, Junichi Sato. SCR: Michiko Yokote. DES: Akihiko Yamashita. ANI: Miho Shimokasa. MUS: Kaoru Wada. PRD: HAL Filmmakers, WOWOW. 25 mins. x 13 eps.
Eri and Yuko are high-school girls summoned into another world by Queen Aria. Her kingdom, Guriania, is at war with neighboring Barujitan, and she believes the two girls are witches that can use their mighty powers to end the conflict. But they don't have any powers, don't like each other, and don't want to work together—except that it seems like it's the only way they can get back to their own world. Predictably cute character designs, including a couple of childlike fantasy creatures that at least make a change from the usual magical animal sidekicks. The story by Junichi Sato is so like EL HAZARD that the makers should blush to call it original.

STRANGE LOVE *
1996. JPN: *Hen*. AKA: *Strange*. Video. DIR: Oji Suzuki. SCR: Mayori Sekijima. DES: Yasuomi Umezu. ANI: Chuji Nakajima. MUS: Koji Tsuno. PRD: Group Tac. 40 mins. x 2 eps.
Nerdy teacher (sorry, college professor) Sushiaki develops an obsession with one of his pupils, the impossibly proportioned Chizuru Yoshida. Torn with conflicting feelings in the hypocritical manner of HOMEROOM AFFAIRS, he discovers that she has been secretly appearing in commercials, in contravention of a school (sorry, college) rule that specifies no part-time jobs. Hoping to use this to his advantage, he realizes too late that he has become the plaything of a masterful tease. The "virginal" Chizuru is already sleeping with a rock star, but both men are left in the lurch when Chizuru falls for a *female* transfer student, Azumi Yamida. Despite several notable names in the crew, this is a creatively barren and often incoherent jailbait fantasy in the spirit of CREAM LEMON, complete with a few halfhearted homages to other anime such as PROJECT A-KO. Based on just part of the 1991 manga in *Young Jump* by Hiroya Oku, which sold more than five million copies, the story (and viewers) deserved better than this. Though the USMC release labels this as only *possibly* unsuitable for minors, it's probably unsuitable for anyone. ❷

STRAWBERRY EGG
2001. JPN: *Ai! Mai! Mi! Strawberry Egg*. TV series. DIR: Yuji Yamaguchi. SCR: Yasuko Kobayashi. DES: Maki Fujii. ANI: Tetsuya Yanasawa. MUS: Keiichi Nozaki. PRD: TNK, WOWOW. 25 mins. x 13 eps.

Twenty-three-year-old hothead Hibiki Amawa is a boy from the far north of the Japanese mainland, who wants to be a schoolteacher. With funds running low, he accepts the first job he can find, teaching (in drag!) at an all-girls' school. TENCHI MUYO! has a lot to answer for.

STREET CORNER FAIRYTALES
1984. JPN: *Machikado no Meruhen.* Video. DIR: Mizuho Nishikubo. SCR: Takeshi Shudo. DES: Yoshitaka Amano. ANI: Heihachi Tanaka. MUS: Virgin VS. PRD: Kitty Film. 52 mins.
Hiroshi, a student in a Shinjuku high school, dreams of one day writing a children's book and is working hard to save enough money so that he can do it. He falls in love with a girl he meets by chance on the subway, and Hiroko becomes very important to the eventual realization of his dreams. Set to 17 pop tunes in the style of CIPHER, this is not to be confused with Tezuka's STORIES FROM A STREET CORNER, though the producers rather hoped it would be.

STREET FIGHTER II *
1994. JPN: *Street Fighter II; Street Fighter II Victory; SF Zero.* AKA: *Street Fighter II: The Movie; SF II TV; SF Alpha.* Movie, TV series, video. DIR: Gisaburo Sugii (m/TV); Eiichi Sato, Takuya Sato, Yukio Takahashi, Kuniaki Komura, Hideaki Shimada, Shigeru Yamazaki, Yutaka Arai (TV); Shigeyasu Yamauchi (v). SCR: Kenichi Imai, Gisaburo Sugii (m); Reiko Yoshida, Naoyuki Sakai (TV). DES: Shuko Murase, Minoru Maeda (m); Akira Kano, Junichiro Nishikawa, Yasuhiro Oshima, Satoshi Matsuoka (TV); Yoshihiko Umakoshi (v). ANI: Minoru Maeda (m); Yoshihiko Umakoshi. MUS: Tetsuya Komuro (m/TV); Chage & Asuka, Hayato Matsuo, Masahiro Shimada (TV). PRD: Group Tac. 104 mins. (m), 25 mins. x 29 eps. (TV), 45 mins. x 2 eps. (v).
Evil Vega (M. Bison) is one of the leaders of the Shadowlaw organization intent on world domination. He is brainwashing martial artists in order to use them as secret agents and has kidnapped Ken Masters, a prominent street fighter. Ken's former sparring partner, Ryu, teams up with Interpol to track him down.

A film based on the sequel to CAPCOM's original computer *game, SFII*'s thin premise is a weak hook on which to hang a succession of fight scenes. However, Sugii's theatrical release sets the standard for the entire game-adaptation subgenre and has been much imitated by titles including TOSHINDEN, ART OF FIGHTING, FATAL FURY, and SEXORCIST. Though not the first game-based anime (see SUPER MARIO BROTHERS), *SFII* was arguably the most successful until POKÉMON. Many anime "movies" such as TEKKEN aren't "motion pictures" at all but straight-to-video nonsense given a pretentious title for foreign release. *SFII*, however, is a genuine theatrical feature, with computer graphics, lifelike fight animation, and a big budget. Unlike the live-action version released the same year starring Kylie Minogue and Jean-Claude Van Damme, the anime didn't have to try for a younger audience by cutting out the fights, nor was it limited by some cast members without any martial arts experience—the fights in *SFII* were coordinated by real-life fight choreographer Shinichi Shoji, and, since this is animated, every one's superb.

The derivative plot is a cunning conceit to gain as much of the feel of the game as possible without wasting too much time. Stealing from *Enter the Dragon* (1973), *SFII* maneuvers its characters into a set of standoffs engineered through a fighting contest and the idea that several of them are working as secret agents or in law enforcement. It also adds two elements that would become staples of fighting-game adaptations—a mind-control subplot to orchestrate fights between supposed allies, and a shower scene to showcase a female character in the nude.

Characters' billing comes partly determined by their popularity among

See entry p. 386.
Scramble Wars

SCRAMBLE WARS © 1992 ARTMIC, TEN LITTLE GALL FORCE © 1988 MOVIC/SONEY M.E.

fans and partly from their seniority. The American Ken and Japanese Ryu are two characters from the first game (1987), and the two gave the filmmakers the chance to have a male American in distress getting rescued by a hunky Japanese guy. Chun-Li and Guile (Interpol agents in the anime) were popular characters from the *SFII* game (1991), while Cammy's cameo role (as a brainwashed assassin) was largely determined by her standing with fans. Though a relative latecomer in *Super SFII* (1993), she gets to climb further up the billing by virtue of being a girl. The other characters get a chance to show their special moves in various bouts, but most of the film belongs to this central cast. Each featured character gets an obligatory rumble, but Sugii creates moments of genuine drama, most notably in a marvelously choreographed fight between Chun Li and Balrog (Vega), enhancing the tension with most of the violence offscreen or in partial shot. As in the game, the bad guys' names have been confusingly shuffled for legal reasons—M(ike) Bison, originally the name of the big African-American boxer character, was assigned to the supreme baddie in the Western release, while M. Bison's name is changed to Balrog, and Balrog's to Vega.

The TV series *Streetfighter II V* (1995) serves as a prequel to the game, in which teen versions of Ryu and Ken are trounced by a young Guile and set off on an around-the-world trip to learn from "the best of the best." Though there is a heroic effort to introduce deeper back-stories for the kung-fu clothes-horses of the game (Chun Li is a young Hong Kong tour guide, Fei Long is an action-film star, etc.), the TV series is undistinguished, and even Sugii's direction rarely rises above the barely necessary. Matters are not helped by an English dub that persistently mispronounces "Ryu" throughout—an achievement roughly equivalent to dubbing *Star Wars* with Han *Sulu*. However, amid the relatively undemanding audience of fighting-game fans, the TV series could be considered a success—it certainly outlasted many of its more "popular" contemporaries.

A final incarnation of the franchise was the two-part video series *SF Zero* (1999, renamed *SF Alpha* in the West, like its game incarnation). With a new director and scenarist better known for **FLOWERS BEFORE BOYS**, *Zero* keeps the "early years" aspect of the TV series, focusing on an even younger audience by introducing the game's popular schoolgirl fighter Sakura, as well as Ryu's previously unmentioned brother, Shun, who arrives from Brazil. Somewhat cynically dumping the previous continuity (Chun Li and Ryu meet for the first time, *again*, as if the producers do not expect any of the original audience to still be watching), *Zero* runs through a predictable set of clichés, as Ryu discovers his father's evil secret, is tempted by the dark side, and avenges the death of his teacher. *Zero* was partly funded by U.S. distributor Manga Entertainment, which edited it into a single feature-length edition in the expectation it would do as well as its predecessor. But while it often matches the kinetic action of its illustrious ancestor, complete with some good

backgrounds, after half a decade of inferior copies of the original *SFII* movie, *Zero* simply looks like just another one. *Ill. pp. 29, 181.* **Ⓥ**

STUMBLING WITCH DOREMI

1999. JPN: *Ojamajo Doremi*. TV series. DIR: Junichi Sato, Takuya Igarashi, Akinori Yabe. SCR: Reiko Yoshida, Yumi Kageyama, Atsushi Yamatoya, Midori Kuriyama. DES: N/C. ANI: Yoshihiko Umakoshi, Chuji Nakajima. MUS: N/C. PRD: Toei, TV Asahi. 25 mins. x 46+ eps.

Doremi is an average third-grade girl who wishes she could be a witch. She meets Lika, the owner of a magic shop, and correctly guesses that she is a genuine witch. Unfortunately, the lucky guess transforms Lika into a frog, and Doremi can only transform her back by becoming a qualified witch herself. Doremi minds the store with her schoolmates Hazuki and Aiko, beginning her adventures in witchery. This child-oriented variant on **SAILOR MOON** features innovative crayon and watercolor backgrounds in the style of children's books. The third season, which began in 2001, transforms the girls' magic shop into a bakery and introduces a "funny" American, Momoko, who only speaks halting Japanese.

SUBMARINE 707

1996. JPN: *Shinkai no Guntai Submarine 707F*. AKA: *Undersea Fleet Submarine 707F*. Video. DIR: Teruo Kigure, Jiro. SCR: Satoru Ozawa. DES: Masaaki Sudo. ANI: Masaaki Sudo, Teruo Kigure. MUS: N/C. PRD: Knack. 45 mins. x 2 eps.

Investigating a "Bermuda triangle" effect in the Pacific, the damaged submarine 707 is led to a vast undersea cavern by a white whale. 707 rests on the sea bed for repairs but sinks beneath it to find the lost undersea empire of Mu (see **SUPER ATRAGON**). Queen Chiaka, ruler of Mu, has been thrown into a conflict with the surface world by bad-guy Red Silver's illegal drilling operations near her kingdom, and the crew of 707 must end the crisis

before it destroys the world. An old-fashioned yarn based on Satoru Ozawa's 1963 submarine manga in *Shonen Sunday*, it was revived for the 1990s thanks to the dual influence of the nostalgic "retro" fashion ushered in by **GIANT ROBO** and the new-found popularity of submarine dramas post–**SILENT SERVICE**. A year later, Ozawa's **BLUE SUBMARINE NO. SIX** was also adapted into an anime, with far greater success.

SUE CAT

1980. TV series. DIR: Takao Yotsuji. SCR: Tsunehisa Ito. DES: Front Publicity. ANI: Shinnosuke Mina. MUS: Akira Ito. PRD: Knack, Tokyo 12 Channel. 15 mins. x 40 eps.

Sue is a suburban Tokyo cat who enjoys climbing up on the roof to scat sing, beating out the rhythm with her tail, hoping that one day she'll become a star singer just like the human vocalists on TV. She talks her way onto the set of the NTV talent show *Who's the Star?* and becomes an overnight celebrity, soon forgetting all about her past life. As her life becomes a whirl of music hits, recording contracts, and product endorsements, she begins to wonder if she has sacrificed her personal life for stardom. As she reminisces about her happy kittenhood, she is found by her sisters, Lan and Miki, who convince her to return home to obscurity.

NTV and Crown Records, both real-life companies, have manufactured starlets before, so it's no surprise that they should do the same with a cat. This silly anthropomorphic "star is born" series was broadcast in double chunks in the Kansai region, and hence is listed as "30 mins. x 20 eps." in some sources. Later, very different satires of the idol-singer's life include **PERFECT BLUE** and **HUMMINGBIRDS**, while *Mis Print* (1997) was a much shorter-lived anime series about feline pop stars.

SUIKODEN *

1993. JPN: *Yokai Seki Suikoden*. AKA: *Demon Century Water Margin*. Video. DIR: Hiroshi Negishi. SCR: Mayori Sekijima. DES: Noboyuki Tsuru. ANI: Nobuyuki Tsuru. MUS: N/C. PRD: JC Staff. 46 mins.

Hotheaded country boy Nobuteru Sugo goes to town when his sister is abducted by an evil gang boss who is trying to buy up land in Shinjuku by blackmail and intimidation. Sugo meets other heroes who help him in his quest: one is a crossdressing martial artist who can disable a man without breaking a fingernail; another a Christian priest who believes in muscular, not to say aggressive, evangelism; and yet another a psychotic nun who is gentle as a lamb with orphan children but freaks out if anyone catches a glimpse of her tattoo.

Based on a story by IRRESPONSIBLE CAPTAIN TYLOR–creator Hitoshi Yoshioka that retold Shi Nai-an and Luo Guanzhong's 14th-century Chinese novel *Water Margin* in a sci-fi setting, the final scene reveals that the characters are the reincarnations of the novel's Lin Chung, Hu San-Niang, and company, but this allusion is left unclear in an English dub that appears ignorant of the distant literary origins. Mitsuteru Yokoyama's unrelated 1969 *Water Margin* manga in *Kibo Life* was much more faithful to the original. It was never animated, but several of the characters are lifted wholesale for the later GIANT ROBO. For another rehash of the *Water Margin*, see HAKKENDEN. **NV**

SUKEBAN DEKA *

1991. JPN: *Sukeban Deka*. AKA: *Bad Girl Cop*. Video. DIR: Takeshi Hirota. SCR: Takeshi Hirota. DES: Nobuteru Yuki. ANI: Masahiro Kase. MUS: Takashi Takao. PRD: JH Project, SIDO. 50 mins. x 2 eps.

Former high-school tearaway Saki Asamiya soon ends up on the wrong side of the law and is stuck in the slammer just like her wayward mother. She is offered the chance to redeem herself by returning to school as an undercover agent to spy on the Mizuchi sisters' crime ring. It's an offer she can't refuse since it's the only way to gain her

mother a reprieve from Death Row. Armed only with a police-issue yo-yo and a very bad attitude, Saki goes back to school and finds herself facing the Mizuchis and their father, a criminal hiding behind a cloak of respectability. As allies she has only a boy so fixated on her that he shaves his head to get her attention and Junk, an innocent young artist whose talents make her a target for one of the sisters.

Played in a deadly serious, deadpan manner that only accentuates its essential silliness, *SD* is an entertaining one-joke knockabout. Based on a 1976 manga by Shinji Wada in *Hana to Yume* magazine, it was soon co-opted for the male gaze in Hideo Tanaka's live-action TV series the same year. The anime version was released partway through a later series of live-action movie adaptations that also showcased cute young actresses in school uniforms. Ultimately, however, like its female lead, it's too bad to be good, and too good to be bad.

SUNNY BOARDINGHOUSE

1987. JPN: *Yo Atari Ryoko*. AKA: *Ray of Sunshine; Staring into the Sun*. TV series, movie. DIR: Hiroko Tokita, Gisaburo Sugii, Satoshi Inoue, Hayato Ikeda, Mitsuru Hongo. SCR: Satoshi Yagi, Michiru Shimada, Tomoko Konparu, Higashi Shimizu, Hiroko Naka. DES: Minoru Maeda. ANI: Yoshihiro Kawamura, Kazuya Takeda, Kazuyuki Okaseko. MUS: Hiroaki Serizawa (TV), Kohei Tanaka (m). PRD: Group Tac, Fuji TV. 25 mins. x 48 eps. (TV), 70 mins. (m).

Kasumi lives in a student hostel run by her aunt while studying and enjoying her other passion, running. Her fiancé, Kazuhiko, is at college in America. As she makes friends in the hostel, one boy, Yusaku, becomes especially close to her. Their friendship develops through comic moments, misunderstandings, and day-to-day events, with Kasumi's betrothal hanging over them like the Sword of Damocles. Based on a 1979 manga by Fumi Yamazaki and Mitsuru Adachi (creator of TOUCH),

this is another of Adachi's specialty soap operas with sympathetic female characters, often with a sporting connection and a relationship dilemma. The movie finale *You Were in My Dreams Kasumi* (1988, *Kasumi Yume no Naka Kimi ga Ita*), shown on what must have been a weepy double bill with the KIMAGURE ORANGE ROAD feature, has the tanned Kazuhiko returning from the U.S. to become a motorcycle racer and demanding to marry Kasumi right away. Yusaku tries to keep a low profile, but at the last moment—literally, on the steps of the altar in church—he finally tells her he loves her, and she realizes that she really loves him. Luckily Kazuhiko is a good sport and encourages them to be together. Though credited to Sugii, the bulk of the movie was actually a directorial debut for Kimiharu Ono, Sugii's assistant on TALE OF GENJI.

SUNSET GUARDSMAN

1968. JPN: *Yuyake Bancho*. TV series. DIR: Renzo Kinoshita, Yoshiyuki Tomino. SCR: Yoshiaki Yoshida, Shunichi Yukimuro. DES: Renzo Kinoshita. ANI: Renzo Kinoshita, Kazuhiro Okaseko. MUS: Kenjiro Hirose. PRD: Tokyo TV Doga, Nippon TV. 10 mins. x 156 eps.

Tadaharu Akagi is a small but tough boy, transferred to Kiso Junior High, which is infamous for its badly behaved children. He is literally from the wrong side of the tracks—orphaned, he lives with his grandfather in a ramshackle house near the railway. One day at school, two of his classmates ask for his help in dealing with bullies. Though he is a strong fighter, he refuses, until the bullying becomes intolerable and he loses his temper. Samurai ethics at a modern school, as a bold hero resists violence and gets dewy-eyed whenever he sees a sunset.

SUPER ATRAGON *

1995. JPN: *Shin Kaitei Gunkan*. AKA: *New Undersea Battleship*. Video. DIR: Kazuyoshi Katayama, Michio Fukuda. SCR: Nobuaki Kishima. DES: Yoshikazu Yasuhiko, Makoto Kobayashi, Masami

Kosone. ANI: N/C. MUS: Masamichi Amano. PRD: Toho. 50 mins. x 2 eps. In the troubled 1930s, the alien inhabitants of the sunken Pacific kingdom of Mu test the people of Earth by giving them a huge power source and waiting to see if they use it for good or evil. This classic case of bad timing leads to the U.S. and Japan each building a supersubmarine. Consumed with grief over his brother's death at Hiroshima (see BAREFOOT GEN), a gunner on the prototype battlesub Ra disobeys his captain's orders and opens fire on the American sub Liberty. The Ra and the Liberty ram each other and sink, and the Mu experiment is called off for fifty years.

Fast forward to the present, where Mu attack craft are spotted at the north and south poles. The United Nations prepare for battle, unaware that they have no chance of defeating the Mu battleships. Only the Ra itself, lovingly restored in secret by the surviving first mate and his patriotic colleagues, can save the day, captained by the son of the original captain. Go, whose father went missing when he was a small child, is on a UN vessel sent to investigate the Mu weapons and is rescued by the Ra. Needless to say, he is troubled by the thought that the remote, forbidding "captain" may be his missing father, as the Ra takes on its enemy in naval action that recalls both SILENT SERVICE and STAR BLAZERS.

Shunro Oshikawa's original novel *Kaitei Gunkan* (1900) was a militaristic scientific romance, as if Jules Verne's Captain Nemo had decided to wage war on the Western powers in the Pacific. Combined with *Undersea Kingdom* (*Kaitei Okoku*), an unrelated "lost civilization" story by Shigeru Komatsuzaki, it was adapted into Ishiro Honda's live-action *Atragon* (1963, *Kaitei Gunkan*, aka *Atoragan the Flying Supersub*), which featured special effects by Eiji Tsuburaya (see ULTRAMAN) and designs by Komatsuzaki, who was also one of Toho's senior illustrators.

Made in the middle of the retro boom ushered in by GIANT ROBO, the

1995 anime version keeps WWII, but now has to include three generations of the hero's family in the story in order to establish a link with Japan's martial past. As well as supremely Vernean technology like gravity lenses, *SA* injects an ambiguous note of 1990s conspiracy, suggesting that the battle between Terrans and Mu-ites is an accident in communication. Annette, exiled from Mu since the 1940s and prepared to help the Terrans, suggests that the entire conflict is a misunderstanding engendered by Avatar, the unbalanced Earth envoy of the Mu Empire. Sadly, however, none of these questions are answered, since *SA* is left open-ended, with the crew of the Ra preparing to dive beneath the sea and go in search of the Mu Empire itself. This was not in either of the previous versions of the story, and, although a journey to the center of the Earth seems quite fitting, *SA* never made it beyond episode two. Mu (or Lemuria) is a "lost continent" in the Pacific that was originally suggested as an explanation for the distribution of Polynesians before Thor Heyerdahl's 1947 Kon-Tiki expedition demonstrated that they had probably scattered across the ocean on boats. As Asia's Atlantis, the place appears in many anime, including WHITE WHALE OF MU, SUBMARINE 707, BRAVE RAIDEEN, MARINE EXPRESS, and FIGHT! OSPA.

SUPER BABY
1994. JPN: *Osawaga Super Baby.* Movie. DIR: Junichi Sato. SCR: Junichi Sato. DES: Akira Inagami. ANI: Akira Inagami. MUS: N/C. PRD: Toei. 30 mins. Kazuyoshi the bratty baby causes trouble for his long-suffering mother and elder sister, though he is often placated by his grandfather's creations—toy animals that can come to life. Then, when that plot idea seems to run out of steam, he transforms into Super Baby to fight crime. One of the few theatrical outings so forgettable as to never get a release on video.

SUPER JETTER
1965. JPN: *Super Jetter Mirai kara Kita Shonen.* AKA: *Super Jetter, the Boy from the Future.* TV series. DIR: N/C. SCR: Ichiro Kanai, Takao Tsutsui, Masao Yamamura, Masaki Tsuji. DES: N/C. ANI: Kiyoshi Onishi. MUS: Takeo Yamashita. PRD: TCJ, Eiken, TBS. 25 mins. x 52 eps.
Time patrolman Jetter comes back from the 30th century in pursuit of the evil criminal Jagger, enlisting the help of pretty contemporary photographer Kaori Mizushima and her friend Professor Nishigoro. He fights crime in our time with three of the professor's inventions—a paralyzer ray, an anti-gravity belt, and a device that can stop time for 30 seconds.

SUPER MARIO BROTHERS
1986. JPN: *SMB Peach Hime Kyushutsu Dai Sakusen.* AKA: *SMB: Struggle to Rescue Princess Peach.* Movie. DIR: Masami Hata. SCR: Hideo Takayashiki. DES: Nintendo, Shigeru Miyamoto, Takashi Tezuka. ANI: Maya Matsuyama. MUS: Toshiyuki Kimori. PRD: Nintendo. 60 mins.
Italian plumber Mario is playing a computer game when Princess Peach calls out to him from the screen, begging him for help. He dives in to help save her from the evil Turtle tribe, aided by his loyal brother, Luigi. He must head for the game's Mushroom land, there to seek advice from the Mushroom sage. Released on the same day as RUNNING BOY, hence tied in the race to become the first anime based on a video game, *SMB* features the lovable character who first appeared in Nintendo's hit game *Donkey Kong*. A slightly different plot, involving the characters' efforts to save Princess *Daisy* from *dinosaurs*, would form the basis for Rocky Morton's live-action *SMB* (1993), starring Bob Hoskins. The franchise also returned as a short-lived three-part video anime in 1989, pointlessly retelling the fairy tales of MOMOTARO, SNOW WHITE, and *Rumplestiltskin*, but with the cast of the game.

SUPER MILK-CHAN

1998. JPN: *Oh! Super Milk-chan*. TV series. DIR: Hideyuki Tanaka, Yoshio Nitta. SCR: Kiki Shiina. DES: Hideyuki Tanaka. ANI: Atsuko Nakajima. MUS: N/C. PRD: Pioneer, Fuji TV. 5 mins. x 14 eps., 25 mins. x N/D eps.

This spoof on 1970s spy thrillers and Bond movies has the cute and childlike Milk, a greedy, immoral brat with a passion for sushi, battling invading aliens, toxic monsters, and enemy snipers. After starting life as a short segment in the late-night *Flyer TV* show, Milk's adventures moved up to full half-hour status on satellite, with the same gang of regulars augmented by new characters like ghastly genius Professor Eyepatch. As the new series opens, Milk is holed up in her apartment with her two sidekicks, bottle-shaped and somewhat paranoid robot Tetsuko and little green blob Hanage ("nose hair"), who resembles a particularly cute booger, complete with round eyes, bright pink nose, and stringy black mustache. Milk is beset by creditors and can't pay the rent. After her inept attempt at extortion from the local ant family fails, she is saved by a job offer from the president himself. He wants her to catch a counterfeiter with a Belgian waffle fixation. Visiting Eyepatch, who may have been Tetsuko's creator but now has a new toy, Robodog, a sniffer hound that can detect fakes, our little band sets up a roadside waffle stand to lure the villain into their net.

SUPER PIG *

1994. JPN: *Ai to Yuki no Pig-Girl Tonde Burin*. AKA: *Pig Girl of Love and Justice—Fly Burin*. TV series. DIR: Takayoshi Suzuki, Tatsuya Hirakawa, Masahiro Hosoda, Masahito Kitagawa, Kunihisa Sugishima, Teppei Matsuura. SCR: Minori Ikeno, Tomoko Ishizuka. DES: Hiromi Kato, Masamichi Takano. ANI: Kazuyoshi Sekiyuki, Takao Yamazaki, Kenichi Imaizumi. MUS: Goro Omi. PRD: Nippon Animation, Mainichi Broadcasting (MBS). 25 mins. x 51 eps.

Young Karin receives magical powers from a pig. Of all the magical girls, she gets the roughest deal, since instead of transforming her into a curvy, long-legged singing idol or magician, she gets to be the Pig of Justice. Not too happy at first, she buckles down and makes the best of her new powers. Everyone in town loves their cute little pink hero, and every time she does a good deed, she gets a magic pearl. When she's collected enough, she'll be allowed to choose her own transformation. But her father, a reporter, has sworn to find Pig's true identity. Based on a manga in *Ciao* magazine from Taeko Ikeda and Mari Mori, it's a somewhat original take on the magical-girl genre of LITTLE WITCH SALLY.

SUPER ROBOT GALATT

1984. JPN: *Choriku Robo Galatt*. AKA: *Change Robo Galatt*. TV series. DIR: Takeyuki Kanda, Osamu Sekita, Tetsuro Amino, Mamoru Hamazu, Hiroshi Negishi, Hideki Tonokatsu, Susumu Ishizaki, Shinya Sadamitsu. SCR: Hiroyuki Hoshiyama, Tsunehisa Ito, Yasushi Hirano, Takao Koyama. DES: Toyoo Ashida, Kunio Okawara, Koichi Ohata. ANI: Toyoo Ashida, Hiroshi Watanabe, Megumu Ishiguro. MUS: Masanori Sasaroku. PRD: Sunrise, Fuji TV. 25 mins. x 25 eps.

Ceaselessly inventing for 30 years in spite of recriminations and complaints from his neighbors, mad scientist Dr. Kiwi finally cooks up an "expanding super alloy" (see GODAIKIN) by combining scrap iron, sugar, Japanese radish, and boogers. He builds Jamboo, a supercharge roboid, to ferry young Michael Marsh to and from school. Michael's associates Patty Pumpkin and Camille Cashmere have their own robots, too. But Jamboo changes into the powerful robot Galatt to fight the minions of the Space Real Estate Company, which plans to parcel Earth up and sell it on the open market. Not one of Sunrise's longer-running robot shows, *SRG* treats giant-robot combat primarily as a topic for gag and parody—compare to PREFECTURAL EARTH DEFENSE FORCE.

3x3 Eyes

SUPER ZUCAN

1992. JPN: *Midnight Gamble Anime Super Zucan*. TV series. DIR: Junji Nishimura. SCR: N/C. DES: N/C. ANI: N/C. MUS: Haruo Mitsunami. PRD: Kitty Film, Fuji TV. 12 mins. x 42 eps.

This late-night mahjong anime using many of the staff from RANMA 1/2 dredges through the clichés of sporting anime but adds more girls in states of undress. Based on a manga by Sayuki Katayama.

SUPERBOOK: VIDEO BIBLE *

1981. JPN: *Anime Oyako Gekijo*. AKA: *Anime Mother and Child Theater*. TV series. DIR: Masakazu Higuchi, Kenjiro Yoshida, Osamu Sekita, Susumu Ishizaki, Norio Yazawa. SCR: Akiyoshi Sakai, Kiichi Takayama, Tomomi Tsutsui, Kazuo Sato. DES: Akiko Shimomoto, Hajime Fukuoka. ANI: Kenjiro Yoshida, Osamu Sekita. MUS: Masashi Maruyama, Hiro Takada. PRD: Tatsunoko, Production Roots, TV Tokyo. 25 mins. x 26 eps. (TV1), 25 mins. x 52 eps. (TV2), 25 mins. x 26 eps. (TV3).

Professor's son Sho (Christopher) and his girlfriend, Azusa (Joy), are cleaning the attic when they discover an old Bible among the scattered books. A magical "Time Bible," it transports them to the Old Testament era, where they watch the greatest story ever told as it happens around them.

A different take on Biblical studies from Tezuka's IN THE BEGINNING, this series was seemingly made to cash in on the Bible's status as a worthy international bestseller rather than through any overt religious impetus. The writers introduced Zenmaijikake (Gizmo), a wind-up crusader toy that is brought to life by the Time Bible, and attempted to involve the children in the stories, though events are predestined, so all they can do is *try* to change them—for example, Eve bites into the apple because Zenmaijikake's clockwork winds down before he can stop her, and, though he shoots up a flare to warn Sho, the children cannot get there in time to stop Adam from taking a bite himself.

Bought for the U.S. market and reedited for the Christian Broadcast Network under the title *Superbook*, by the time the series reached video, its Japanese origins were almost completely occluded, though the voice actors in the English version included many from the cast of SPEED RACER. It was discredited in Christian circles for the introduction of modern characters—instead of making the original more accessible, it was more likely to confuse its young audience who were disappointed not to find robots and time-travelers in the *real* Bible.

A sequel the following year, *Adventures at Tondera [Flying] House*, kept the same TIME BOKAN–inspired kids-and-robot lineup for another 52 episodes; this time young Gen and female foil Kanna are caught in the rain and find shelter in a Western-style house in the forest. The guardian robot Kandenchin is building a time machine that, when struck by lightning, catapults the group into the past, where they witness further Biblical events up to and including the story of Christ (though the Nativity and Resurrection had already been included in the former series). The sequel, *PC Travel Detectives* (1983, aka *Trouble Shooters*), was set five years after their original adventures with the Time Bible, with an older Chris and Joy, accompanied by Chris's younger brother, Hisashi, thrown into the past by a magic computer.

SUPERCAR GATTIGER *

1977. JPN: *Cho Supercar Gattaiger*. TV series. DIR: Yukihiro Takahashi, Tadashi Hosono, Tsutomu Murai. SCR: Michiru Umadori, Sukehiro Tomita, Haruya Yamazaki, Hideharu Iuchi, Hisashi Chiaki. DES: Shiro Yamaguchi (pseudonym for Shiro Murata), Mechaman. ANI: Shiro Yamaguchi (pseudonym for Shiro Murata). MUS: Hiroya Ishikawa. PRD: Eiwa, Tokyo 12 Channel. 25 mins. x 26 eps.

Racing driver Jo Kabuki is abandoned by his mother soon after his birth, and his scientist father dies in strange circumstances when a bomb explodes under his car. Now Jo is a member of the five-man Tiger Team—Hiroki, Ken, Katsumi, and, as in SPEED RACER, a token girl who is the professor's daughter, in this case Sachiyo Tabuchi, daughter of the inventor of the 300-mph Solar Energy engines. When not racing all around the world, the team's supervehicles combine to form Gattiger, a mighty weapon that fights those of evil intent. Many of their races bring them up against the Demon Empire, whose leader, Emperor Black Demon, is not only Jo's grandfather, but also his father's murderer. Jo's mother, Queen Demon, was compelled to leave her loved ones out of loyalty to her own father. She works to support the Empire's semi-evil schemes (Black Demon only wants to conquer the world to put an end to war, though his assistant, Erich Bergen, has his own sadistic motives), but at moments of extreme danger, she shows up masked and disguised to save her son. Even though she always obeys her father (as a good daughter should), she still protects her child (as a good mother should)—for instance, when ordered to shoot Jo through the heart while Black Demon watches, she uses a tranquilizer instead of a bullet. Much loved by early American fandom for its hilariously over-the-top melodrama, it was based on an original idea by Hitoshi Chiaki and given a limited U.S. broadcast on some local TV stations for the Japanese community. Compare to CYBERFORMULA GPX.

SUPER-DEFORMED DOUBLE FEATURE *

1988. JPN: *Scramble Wars To'Hasshire! Genom Trophy Rally*. AKA: *Scramble Wars Get Going! Race for the Genom Trophy Rally; Scramble Wars; Ten Little Gall Force*. Video. DIR: Kenichi Yatagai, Hiroyuki Fukushima. SCR: N/C. DES: Kenichi Sonoda, Kimitoshi Yamane, Hiroyuki Kitazume. ANI: Toshiko Sasaki. MUS: Takehito Nakazawa. PRD: Artmic, Movic. 67 mins.

GENOM, the malevolent corporation of BUBBLEGUM CRISIS, is sponsoring a road race through the desert to the town of Bangor. "Super-deformed" (i.e., cute and squashed-down) versions of characters from *BGC*, GALL FORCE, GENESIS SURVIVOR GAIARTH, and AD POLICE are all taking part, and they all mean to win. The ensuing mayhem is straight out of *Wacky Races*, parodying the original shows with insane humor. The *GF* gals return in *Ten Little Gall Force*, a 1992 parody in which more super-deformed characters return to the studio to make a documentary about the making of their movie and interact with animated versions of the crew.

The Western release combines the two completely separate Japanese videos of just over half an hour each, linked by their super-deformed art style of characters with heads out of all proportion to their squat, comical bodies. It's pure coincidence that the British release company also had its headquarters in a town called Bangor, though Wales has no deserts at present. *Ill. p. 381.*

SUPERDIMENSION ROMANESQUE SAMY

1986. JPN: *Chojiku Romanesque Samy Missing 99*. Video. DIR: Seiji Okuda,

Hidemi Kama. SCR: Seiji Okuda. DES: Moriyasu Taniguchi, Toru Yoshida. ANI: Yutaka Arai, Moriyasu Taniguchi. MUS: Hideo Goto. PRD: Aubec, Anime R. 59 mins.

The universe created by God is not eternal but can collapse if Satan has his way. Luckily, the forces of good are lined up to save the cosmos. This is all news to average Japanese teenager Samy, who is chased by supernatural pursuers and escapes from them into a place "beyond time." Samy and her friends Tokyo, Silver, and Dews must oppose the might of the evil Noa, with the aid of swords, sorcery, and cybernetic battle-suits. A mixture of ALICE IN WONDERLAND and PLANET BUSTERS.

SURFSIDE HIGH SCHOOL

1999. TV series. DIR: Nobuyoshi Yoshida, Kenichi Maejima. SCR: N/C. DES: Tsutomu Ishigaki. ANI: N/C. MUS: N/C. PRD: Shogakukan, PolyGram, TBS. 7 mins. x 16 eps.

Late-night lineup of high-school surfer dudes who dress like gangsters for TBS's after-midnight series of shorts. Drawn in a hard-edged caricature style, this series of shorts was based on a 1996 *Young Sunday* manga by Ken Sawai and screened as part of the *Wonderful* program.

SURVIVAL IN THE OFFICE

1990. JPN: *OL Kaizo Koza.* AKA: *O(ffice) L(adies) Remodeling Lecture.* Video. DIR: Hajime Ishigaki. SCR: Megumi Hikichi, Hiroshi Hashimoto. DES: Shinobu Arima. ANI: Yasushi Nagaoka. MUS: Michiru Oshima. PRD: TMS. 91 mins.

An Office Lady forgets to make a single photocopy, threatening the very fabric of existence in a Japanese company— or not. She muses on the ways to get through the week, including helpful advice on Goofing Off on Different Weekdays and The Right Thing to Say to Your Boss. Inspired by the column *Drop Dead! Stupid Office Ladies* in *Monthly Gendai* magazine. Released straight to video shortly after the same studio's OLD MAN'S SURVIVAL GUIDE, this is not

to be confused with Risu Akizuki's manga *Survival in the Office* (*OL Shinka Ron*), which was released in English.

SUSIE AND MARVIE

1999. JPN: *Susie to Marvie.* TV series. DIR: Shinya Sadamitsu, Scott Frazier. SCR: Noma Sabear. DES: Sonomi Makino. ANI: Nobuyoshi Habara. MUS: N/C. PRD: ShoPro, Xebec, NHK. 4 mins. x 104 eps.

Ten-year-old Susie is a daydreamer, while her one-year-old brother, Marvie, is a mischievous scatterbrain. They like to play with their neighbor Aunt Nana, and her lovable golden retriever, Hana. They also like to play with Professor Peabney, a dachshund inventor with a remarkable resemblance to *Rocky and Bullwinkle*'s Professor Peabody. In the style of DORAEMON, the professor's inventions never quite go according to plan. These happy-go-lucky playtime adventures in a 1950s style were based on the 1994 manga by Noma Sabear serialized in *Sunshine* magazine.

SWAN LAKE *

1981. JPN: *Hakudori no Mizuumi.* Movie. DIR: Kimio Yabuki. SCR: Hirokazu Fuse. DES: N/C. ANI: Takuo Noda, Hiroshi Wagatsuma, Shunji Saita, Takashi Abe. MUS: Peter Tchaikovsky. PRD: Toei. 75 mins.

Princess Odette is bewitched by the wicked magician Rothbart; by day she is a swan, by night a girl. Prince Siegfried sees her transformation and falls in love with her. He vows to break the spell and save the princess, but the spell may only be broken by the man who proclaims his undying love for her. At a ball, Siegfried dances with several girls, eventually finding the one whom he assumes to be Odette. Proclaiming his love, he discovers too late that it is Odile, Rothbart's daughter, breaking Odette's heart. Toei's animated version of Tchaikovsky's 1877 ballet won an award at the 1981 Moscow Film Festival. In a backhanded compliment to its artistic merits, 2,500 cels were stolen during production.

SWEET MINT

1990. JPN: *Maho no Angel Sweet Mint.* AKA: *Magical Angel Sweet Mint.* TV series. DIR: Toshitaro Oba, Norio Takase, Kazuhiro Ozawa. SCR: Takao Koyama, Aya Matsui, Yoshimasa Takahashi, Masaharu Amiya. DES: Toshiyuki Tsuru. ANI: Himiko Ito, Hiroaki Sakurai, Yoshitaka Fujimoto. MUS: Osamu Morizuka. PRD: Ashi Pro, TV Tokyo. 25 mins. x 47 eps.

Another magical-girl series whose sweet heroine has a cute little bluebird as her magical friend and uses a magic compact (harking back to SECRET AKKO-CHAN) that transforms into anything she needs. The compact is a gift from Grandmother Herbe; when 12-year-old Mint opens the lid, the design of a crossbow engraved there actually turns into a bow whose arrow is tipped with a crystal heart. When she fires the arrow, the streaks of light from its facets transform her into a Magical Angel. From the studio that brought you GIGI, Mint has a similar origin— she is really a princess from the land of magic, sent to Earth to bring happiness to humans, taking up residence in the "Happy Shop" in the little town of Toal so she can carry out her mission.

SWEET SPOT

1991. Video. DIR: Gisaburo Sugii. SCR: N/C. DES: Kiyosuke Eguchi. ANI: Kiyosuke Eguchi. MUS: N/C. PRD: Tomason, Group Tac. 45 mins.

These "amusing" adventures of a golf-crazy Office Lady were based on a manga from *Weekly Spa!* magazine by Yutsuko Chudoji.

SWIMMY

1991. JPN: *Ganbare Swimmy.* AKA: *Go for It, Swimmy!* Movie. DIR: Hidetoshi Omori. SCR: Hideharu Iguchi. DES: Hidetoshi Omori. ANI: Hidetoshi Omori. MUS: Hideo Sato. PRD: OH Productions. 26 mins.

Swimmy, a black fish born into a shoal of red fish, tries to fit in amid adventures as he is chased by tuna and must evade the Great Octopus. Originally based on a children's picture book.

SWISS FAMILY ROBINSON *

1981. JPN: *Kazoku Robinson Hyoryuki: Fushigi na Shima no Flowne*. AKA: *Swiss Family Robinson: Mysterious Island of Flowne*. TV series. DIR: Yoshio Kuroda, Seiji Okuda, Michiyo Sakurai, Shigeo Koshi, Fumio Kurokawa, Hideo Fukuzawa, Fumio Ikeno, Takayoshi Suzuki, Taku Sugiyama. SCR: Shozo Matsuda. DES: Shuichi Seki. ANI: Michiyo Sakurai, Koichi Murata. MUS: Koichi Sakata. PRD: Nippon Animation, Fuji TV. 25 mins. x 50 eps.

The Robinsons leave Switzerland for Australia, but shipwreck strands them alone on a Pacific island. Gradually they build a home and a life there, but then find they are not alone—an old sailor and a young aborigine are also on the island. Helped by their new friends, they build a raft to try and reach Australia. One of Nippon Animation's WORLD MASTERPIECE THEATER series, this retelling of Johann David Wyss's 19th-century shipwreck tale has been adapted for TV and film many times before, but rarely with such charm. A series with moments of real beauty, owing much to Masahiro Ioka's backgrounds. See also SPACE FAMILY CARLVINSON. Dubbed by Saban and broadcast on the Family Channel (later known as Fox Family Channel).

SWORD FOR TRUTH *

1990. JPN: *Shuranosuke Zanmaken*. AKA: *Demon-slaying Sword of Shuranosuke*. Video. DIR: Osamu Dezaki. SCR: Jo Toriumi. DES: Akio Sugino. ANI: Akio Sugino. MUS: Toshiyuki Watanabe. PRD: Toei. 50 mins.

Lone samurai Shuranosuke strolls into 1636 Edo (the capital of Ieyasu, first Tokugawa shogun) and with one swipe of his legendary blade Onimaru, nonchalantly dispatches the giant white tiger that has been terrorizing the citizenry. The tiger is only the first wave of an assault by evil forces using demonic powers to kidnap Princess Mio then swap her for a magical dagger. Shuranosuke agrees to make the exchange but must then get the princess safely past a series of magical traps to return her to her no less treacherous household. But while the enemy has magic on its side, he has his own superb skills and the love of beautiful ninja-thief Orin.

Based on a novel by YOTODEN-creator Jo Toriumi, *SfT* oozes style and mystery, with gorgeous art direction by Yukio Abe. However, the limited animation that characterizes Dezaki's direction (e.g., BLACK JACK) lets it down—though optioned by Manga Entertainment in the hope it would be another NINJA SCROLL, it is nowhere near as good. To add insult to injury, the anime was infamously advertised with the fiendishly inaccurate line, "Ancient feudal Japan was ruled by clans of shoguns." A live-action version, *Legend of the Devil* (1998), directed by Masaru Tsushima and starring the incandescently gorgeous Masaki Kyomoto as Shuranosuke, contains more of our hero's story than *SfT*, and retains plenty of the sex scenes, but has less convincing supernatural perils. *Ill. p. 239.* **ⓝⓥ**

SWORD OF MUSASHI

1985. JPN: *Musashi no Ken*. AKA: *Sword of Musashi*. TV series. DIR: Toshio Kadota, Katsumi Minoguchi, Masamune Ochiai, Yuji Asada, Akinori Yabe, Hideki Tonokatsu, Kazutoshi Kobayashi, Kenjiro Yoshida. SCR: Masaru Yamamoto, Haruya Yamazaki. DES: Motoka Murakami. ANI: Makoto Kuniyoshi. MUS: Hidemi Sakashita. PRD: Eiken, TV Tokyo. 25 mins. x 72 eps. (TV1), 25 mins. x 72 eps. (TV2).

Born on the same day as Japan's legendary "Sword Saint" and named after him, too, the young Natsuki Musashi hopes one day to become as good with a sword as his famous namesake. Training hard at kendo at his home in Iwate, he is devastated by his father's death and transfers to a new dojo. There, however, he encounters not only new challenges, but also the bitter enmity of a new rival. Based on a manga by SEIZE THE WIND–creator Motoka Murakami in *Shonen Sunday*, *SoM* was rebranded after episode 49 as *SoM: The Teen Years* (1986, *Seishun-hen*), featuring Musashi's ongoing feuds with rival "samurai" from neighboring high schools. All set in the present day, this mixture of the clichés of sports anime and samurai period drama drew its inspiration from the life of Musashi Miyamoto (see YOUNG MIYAMOTO MUSASHI).

SWORD OF THE DESTROYER

1992. JPN: *Hayo no Ken*. AKA: *Sword of the Destructive Phantom*. Video. DIR: Setsuko Shibunnoichi, Shinichiro Kimura. SCR: Kazumi Koide. DES: Yukari Kobayashi. ANI: Yukari Kobayashi. MUS: Makihiko Araki. PRD: Magic Bus. 30 mins. x 2 eps.

Heroic fantasy in the ancient kingdom of Gandia, as the Fairy and Human realms choose their Princess of the Red Lotus, the only one who may wield the Sword of the Destroyer. Lots of Talking With Capital Letters, as battlemaid Raethril takes on the minions of the Prince of Darkness, rather unfortunately named Redial. Based on a bestselling novel by Shuko Maeda. **ⓥ**

SYMPHONY DREAM STORY

1985. JPN: *Symphony Yume Monogatari*. Video. DIR: Dojiro, Satoshi Harada, Yutaka Kuramoto. SCR: Gokiburi, Yuka Kurokawa. DES: N/C. ANI: N/C. MUS: N/C. PRD: Nippon Soft System. 75 mins.

Three short pornographic tales in the tradition of CREAM LEMON: *Shining May*, in which an idol singer takes to the spotlight in more ways than one; *Telepathist Love Q315*, in which Earth can only be saved from alien invaders by the nubile bodies of young telepaths; and, finally, *Barefoot after Class*, in which two school girls find something else to do with each other beyond helping with their homework. Supposedly "humorous." **ⓝ**

T

TA-CHAN KING OF THE JUNGLE
1994. JPN: *Jungle no Osama Ta-chan.* TV series. DIR: Hitoshi Nanba, Akitaro Daichi, Shigeru Ueda, Teppei Matsu-ura, Takaaki Ishiyama. SCR: Junzo Toriu-mi, Akihiro Arashima, Satoshi Fujimoto, Toshiyuki Otaki, Takeshi Ito. DES: Hiroka Kudo. ANI: Shigeru Kato, Chuji Nakajima, Kiyoshi Matsumoto, Masahiko Murata. MUS: Masatake Yamada. PRD: Amuse, TV Tokyo. 25 mins. x 50 eps.
A muscle-bound man in a loincloth fights evil kung-fu masters and vam-pires in darkest Africa. Though distant-ly inspired by Edgar Rice Burroughs's *Tarzan of the Apes* (1912), this series was filtered through a popular *Shonen Jump* manga by Masaya Tokuhiro.

TAIMAN BLUES
1987. Video. DIR: Satoshi Dezaki. SCR: Machiko Kondo. DES: Yukari Kobayashi. ANI: Yukari Kobayashi. MUS: N/C. PRD: Magic Bus. 30 mins. x 5 eps.
A series grouping together two differ-ent stories linked by the biker theme. The three-part *Naoto Shimizu Chapter* is a tale of rivalry between two gangs, MND and Laku, and the personal vendetta between MND's Naoto and Laku's Yota, which lands Naoto in prison in the second (1988) episode. The third part of his story, his life after prison, was released in 1989. *Lady's Chapter* (1990) is devoted to a different set of characters, this time focusing on biker girls. Fifteen-year-old Mayumi has to move to the rough end of Osaka when her parents split and remarry. She meets Noriko, who helps her settle into her new life, and eventually moves in with her. Through Noriko's job at a

petrol station, they get to know regular customer Big Bear and his biker gang, and eventually get into their own gang of girl racers. Based on a manga by Yu Furusawa.

TAITO ROAD
1996. JPN: *Shinken Densetsu Taito Road.* AKA: *True Fighting Legend Taito Road.* TV series. DIR: Tatsuo Misawa. SCR: Kenichi Kanemaki, Kazuhiko Kobe, Yoshihiko Tomizawa. DES: Michio Fukuda. ANI: Masahiro Masai. MUS: Koji Tsunoda. PRD: Toei, TV Tokyo. 25 mins. x 13 eps.
In a lackluster picaresque that tries to cash in on the successful STREET FIGHT-ER II franchise, a young man sets out to fight lots of people. **Ⓥ**

TAKAMARU
1991. JPN: *Cho-Bakumatsu Shonen Seiki Takamaru.* AKA: *Super 19th-Centu-ry Boy Takamaru.* Video. DIR: Toyoo Ashida, Satoshi Nishimura. SCR: Toyoo Ashida, "Mindanao," Yuichiro Takeda. DES: Toyoo Ashida. ANI: Takahiro Yoshi-matsu. MUS: Kohei Tanaka. PRD: JC Staff, Studio Live. 25 mins. x 6 eps.
Set in the world of the Champion Kingdom, an imaginary island whose inhabitants follow a traditional samurai lifestyle, this is a tale of friendship and courage aimed at preteens. Based on director Ashida's manga in *Animedia* magazine. Compare to SHINSENGUMI FARCE.

TAKE THE X TRAIN
1987. JPN: *X Densha de Iko.* AKA: *Let's Take the X Train.* Video. DIR: Rintaro, Tatsuhiko Urahata. SCR: Rintaro, Yoshio Urasawa. DES: Yoshinori Kanemori. ANI:

Yoshinori Kanemori. MUS: Yosuke Yamashita. PRD: Madhouse. 50 mins.
Public-relations man Toru Nishihara is waiting on an underground station platform when he sees a phantom train. Ghosts are about to invade the human world, and Toru is co-opted by a secret military unit that has gathered the world's psychics to hold them off. Toru is threatened and cajoled into taking part, though the phantom train lays waste to the armed forces in a cata-clysmic battle. The jazz number "Take the A-Train," whose title inspired Koichi Yamano's original short story, appears at several points in this elegant little chiller and is sung over the clos-ing credits by Akiko Yano.

TAKEGAMI *
1990. JPN: *Ankoku Shinden Takegami.* AKA: *Guardian of Darkness Takegami.* Video. DIR: Osamu Yamazaki. SCR: Osamu Yamazaki. DES: Masami Obari. ANI: Masanori Nishii. MUS: Seiko Naga-oka. PRD: JC Staff. 45 mins. x 3 eps.
The lonely, homely Terumi has a crush on Koichi and sells her soul for beauty, agreeing to be possessed by an ancient dragon lord, who in return will make her more popular at school. Now everywhere she goes she is greeted by hissing cats and wilting flowers. And next time the school bullies come call-ing, she tears their souls apart. But Koichi has also been possessed, by a "kindly" spirit called Susano, although he (and anyone else who knows their JAPANESE FOLK TALES) has his doubts about who the good guys are, as the powerful beings fight an age-old war in modern Tokyo.

Despite a U.S. dub that adds to the

suspense by not scrimping on the demonic voice effects, *Takegami* is a derivative tale of violent transformations that sits somewhere between **GUYVER** and **SHUTENDOJI**, with a dose of misogyny and lackluster fight scenes. Compare to **LEGEND OF THE FOUR KINGS** and **DARK MYTH**, which similarly retell ancient myth in a modern setting, but not as an excuse for getting into fights with girls. **NV**

TALE OF GENJI *

1987. JPN: *Murasaki Shikibu Genji Monogatari*. AKA: *Murasaki Shikibu's Tale of Genji*. Movie. DIR: Gisaburo Sugii, Kimiharu Ono, Naoto Hashimoto. SCR: Tomomi Tsutsui. DES: Yasuhiro Nakura. ANI: Yasuo Maeda, Masahiko Murata, Masayuki, Yoshiyuki Sadamoto, Minoru Maeda, Mahiro Maeda. MUS: Haruomi Hosono. PRD: Tac, Herald. 110 mins.

Hikaru Genji, son of Japan's Kiritsubo Emperor , is a brilliant and gifted young man stifled by the conventions of Heian court life, which offers no real outlet for his talent and energy except the arts and illicit love affairs. He is also haunted by memories of his mother, Lady Kiritsubo, who died when he was very young. He falls in love with his father's consort, Fujitsubo, but his own wife, Lady Aoi, and another lover, Lady Rokujo, will not give him up. The battle for sole possession of his heart is at the core of this film; despite being fought with courtly grace, it's a vicious and ultimately fatal contest, observed by the child Murasaki Shikibu, an orphan in Genji's care who will later become one of his loves.

Facetiously advertised as a "faithful adaptation" of Murasaki Shikibu's 11th-century novel, *ToG* was commissioned to mark the centenary of the *Asahi Shinbun* newspaper and the minor anniversaries for some of its affiliates. It unsurprisingly ditches most of the 1,000-page original, concentrating on a love triangle that formed just chapters 4–10 out of a total of 54. Though highly compromised by a recognizably modern script featuring several anachronisms of manner and etiquette, it is nevertheless a brave representation of the *spirit* of the original, and it is as stylistically rich as **THE SENSUALIST**. Sometimes, however, its attempt to be faithful can backfire—most notably in the confusingly "real" predominance of black hair, demonstrating all too well why so many anime prefer to differentiate characters with brighter colors and styles. Director Sugii takes enormous risks with pacing, composition, and narrative flow; he utilizes early computer graphics and live-action footage of flames and cherry blossoms. Many scenes are composed of static shots, and the exquisite delicacy of the imagery is given plenty of time to sink in—this film is *slow*. Heavy with the beauty and mood of a vanished age, the hothouse emotions of the court reflect Genji's own emotional turmoil, somewhat ill-served by a translation and U.S. release that plays up the original's classical credentials but shies from offering any notes on the surviving poetic allusions. However, the true value of *ToG* does not lie in its relation to the original book at all but in its position as one of the small number of available anime that demonstrate the true diversity of the medium. Composer Hosono was one-third of the Yellow Magic Orchestra with Ryuichi Sakamoto and Yukihiro Takahashi. An erotic pastiche, "Bareskin Gen-chan," appeared as one of the stories in the historical porn series *Classical Sex-Zone* (1988).

TALE OF HIKARI

1986. JPN: *Hikari no Densetsu*. TV series. DIR: Tomomi Mochizuki, Shinya Sadamitsu, Toriyasu Furusawa, Tetsuya Komori, Hirotsugu Hamazaki. SCR: Hideki Sonoda, Mayori Sekijima, Asami Watanabe, Yasushi Hirano. DES: Toyoko Hashimoto, Ammonite. ANI: Chuichi Iguchi. MUS: Koji Kawamura. PRD: Tatsunoko, TV Asahi. 30 mins. x 19 eps.

Teenage gymnast Hikari struggles to succeed in bitter rivalry with school supergymnast Diana Groichiva. A typical sports anime in the tradition of **AIM FOR THE ACE**, the series was taken off the air before finishing the standard 26-episode run despite injecting a contrived romance with a young rock star. Based on the 1985 manga in *Comic Margaret* by Izumi Aso.

TALE OF JUKYO'S FALLEN SAVAGERY

1999. JPN: *To Kyo Ju Kyo Den*. Video. DIR: Hikaru Takanashi. SCR: Tetsuya Oishi. DES: Sawako Yamamoto. ANI: Sawako Yamamoto. MUS: N/C. PRD: Beam Entertainment. 40 mins. x 3 eps.

In turn-of-the-century Tokyo, the human world is under attack from demons determined to seize control of Earth (see **SILENT MÖBIUS**). Only a single high-school transfer student, orphaned as a child when demons killed her parents, holds the key to saving the universe. Based on an "original" novel by Taku Atsushi, though if this outline is anything to go by, it all sounds tiresomely familiar. A new series was announced as forthcoming in 2001.

TALE OF THE NINJA RYUKEN

1991. JPN: *Ninja Ryuken Den*. Video. DIR: Mamoru Kobe, Minoru Okazaki. SCR: Katsuhiko Nobe. DES: Satoshi Horiuchi. ANI: Satoshi Horiuchi. MUS: Toshiya Okuda. PRD: Studio Juno. 50 mins.

The scene is New York, where bioresearcher Ned Freidman announces a cure for cancer, although there are rumors of strange goings-on—screams are heard from his house, and large crates are transported from there to his laboratory. Modern-day ninja Ryu, along with CIA operative Robert and his team, go to investigate. But Ryu is really the avatar of ancient dragon gods, and this is only another stage in the eternal battle between good and evil.

Based on the video game known in the U.S. as *Ninja Gaiden*, *TNR*'s action is its biggest selling point. The beginning of the story, a running midnight brawl, is fluid and well depicted, with no dialogue, just the sound of footsteps and blade on blade. The characterization can be strange—if presenting feisty game character Irene as quiet and shy seems a contradiction in terms, making her a CIA operative scared to fire a gun is downright silly. There's an underdeveloped romantic subplot, and Robert gets more emphasis than game stars Ryu and Irene, as well as the video's best line, "Men love three things. We love fighting, we love alcohol, and we love women." **⊘**

TALES FOR SLEEPLESS NIGHTS

1992. JPN: *Nemurenu no Chiisana Ohanashi.* AKA: *Small Stories for Sleepless Nights.* Video. DIR: Kimiharu Ono. SCR: Eto Mori. DES: Shinji Nomura. ANI: Shinji Nomura. MUS: Yuko Hara. PRD: Group Tac, Victor Music Production. 33 mins. x 3 eps.

Three videos about cats—*Cat's Best Friend, Cat's Adventure,* and *Cat's Christmas*—each containing three smaller stories of feline fun. Based on a 1989 column in *Monthly Kadokawa* magazine by Yuko Hara, better known as the keyboard player/vocalist with the Southern All-Stars.

TALES OF . . . *

1990. JPN: *Konai Shasei.* AKA: *Pictures from High School.* Video. DIR: Toshiyuki Sakurai, Takamasa Ikegami. SCR: Toshiyuki Sakurai. DES: Yuji Moriyama, Kinji Yoshimoto, Satoshi Urushihara. ANI: Yuji Moriyama, Kinji Yoshimoto, Satoshi Urushihara, Satoshi Hirayama. Masamune Ochiai. MUS: Takeshi Yasuda. PRD: Studio Fantasia. 40 mins. x 3 eps.

Bare-faced and bawdy anime porn based on short manga from **SAKURA DIARIES**–creator U-Jin. Broken into several short tableaux, it includes the infamous spoof **ULTRAMAN** episode where a giant businessman humps skyscrapers until a giant schoolgirl helps him out. It's the one with the naughty nurse looking for a soft spot in a bodybuilder, the college girls who will do absolutely *anything* for a free pizza, and the little match-girl who turns out to be the

Ghost of Christmas Porn. Humor is the order of the day, with pastiches of **AIM FOR THE ACE** and **ASTRO BOY**—U-Jin is not afraid to laugh at himself, and at other dirty old men. His male characters are pathetic, hormonal losers in thrall to capricious little minxes. Everybody is desperate for sex, although, in a refreshing change from the rape fantasies that characterize so much anime porn, everybody has a good time. Strangely, the U.S. distributors have switched the running order, so that the second Japanese release is actually the first in the translated version. This means that the salaryman we see growing into a giant monster and being destroyed in "Sailor Warrior Akko" is inexplicably brought back from the dead for his cameo role on the train in "Lusty Long-Distance Commute." But since this anime is still on sale in Japan 11 years after its original release, whereas lesser erotica are swiftly deleted, such minor continuity bloopers are unlikely to put off the U.S. audience. Released in America as *Tales of Misbehavior, Tales of Titillation,* and *Tales of Sintillation. Ill. p. 377.* **Ⓝ**

TALES OF ETERNIA *

2001. TV series. DIR: Shigeru Ueda, Takeshi Nagasawa, Satoshi Sato. SCR: Hiroyuki Kawasaki, Satoru Nishizono, Katshuiko Takayama. DES: Akihisa Maeda, Mutsumi Inomata. ANI: Akihisa Maeda, Miko Nakajima. MUS: N/C. PRD: Xebec, Production IG, WOWOW. 25 mins. x 13 eps.

Inferia and Celestia are in the midst of a religious war, which the locals (with the arrogance of religious fanatics everywhere) call the Extreme Light War. As diplomacy breaks down and things get nasty, a young girl meets three teenagers near the borders of Inferia. She is Meldy, a Celestian, and according to her, both countries face a disaster called Grand Fall if they don't stop fighting. Eighteen-year-old Lid Harshel and his 17-year-old friends, Keal Zaibel and Fara Elstead, agree to help her, and together they set off for Belcarnu, legendary isle of everlasting

Child prodigy General McDougal unleashes his psychic powers in the service of the Pentagon, in Hirotsuge Kawasaki's **SPRIGGAN**. The only thing that can stop him is ARCAM, an international foundation whose agents include heroic Japanese schoolboy Yu Ominae. With his bluish skin and paranormal abilities, McDougal strongly resembles the experimental test subjects of **AKIRA**, a parallel made all the more likely by the presence of Katsuhiro Otomo as scenarist and designer on the *Spriggan* movie. The earlier translation of the manga tried to cover up the Pentagon's role as the adversary. See entry p. 371.

Spriggan

© 1998 HIROSHI TOKOSHIGE • RYOJI MINOGAWA/SHOGAKUKAN • BANDAI VISUAL • TBS • TOHO

summer, in search of a solution. Based on the PlayStation RPG of the same name, a follow-up to *Tales of Fantasia* and *Tales of Destiny,* the series credits Toshinori Otsuki as "Exclusive Production Director." No, we don't know what that means either.

TALES OF HANS CHRISTIAN ANDERSEN *

1968. JPN: *Andersen Monogatari.* AKA: *Andersen Tales; The World of Hans Christian Andersen.* Movie, TV series. DIR: Kimio Yabuki (m), Masami Hata, Ichiro Fujita, Taku Sugiyama, Noboru Ishiguro, Makura Saki (pseudonym for Osamu Dezaki), Satoshi Dezaki (TV). SCR: Hisashi Inoue, Morihisa Yamamoto (m), Yoshiaki Yoshida, Shunichi Yukimuro, Eiichi Tachi, Koji Ito, Haruya Yamazaki, Seiji Matsuoka, Takeyuki Kanda, Keisuke Fujikawa. DES: Reiji Koyama (m), Toshihide Takeuchi, Shuichi Seki, Keiichi Makino (TV). ANI: Akira Okuwara (m), Masami Hata. Shuichi Seki (TV). MUS: Seiichiro Uno (both). PRD: Toei (m), Zuiyo (Nippon Animation), Fuji TV. 80 mins. (m), 25 mins. x 52 eps. (TV).

Toei's 1968 movie interweaves the most famous of Andersen's stories into a Disneyesque musical around the tale of young Hans trying to get a ticket for the opera and gradually discovering his talent for telling stories. It focuses particularly on *The Red Shoes* and *The Little Match Girl*. A 73-minute version was dubbed for U.S. release as *The World of Hans Christian Andersen* (1971). Toei would mine Andersen's works for two further movies, **LITTLE MERMAID** and a version of **THUMBELINA** in 1978.

The 1971 TV series, also entitled *Andersen Monogatari*, retold many of the best-loved fairy tales collected by the Danish author, some in a single episode and some as an extended tale over several episodes. It employs the framing device of Candy, a girl who wishes to enter the Magic University and must collect 100 cards to do so by performing 100 good deeds—one shudders to think to what uses such a concept would be put post-**POKÉMON**. The large number of different staff members were encouraged to vary their styles (see **JAPANESE HISTORY**). This led to a wide range of looks and moods (some episodes are light-hearted, some darker) and some interesting stylistic experimentation. Compare to **GRIMMS' FAIRY TALES**.

TALES OF YAJIKITA COLLEGE

1991. JPN: *Yajikita Gakuen Dochuki.* Video. DIR: Osamu Yamazaki, Yoshihisa Matsumoto. SCR: Ayumu Watanabe. DES: Minoru Yamazawa. ANI: Minoru Yamazawa. MUS: Nobuhiko Kajiwara. PRD: JC Staff. 40 mins. x 2 eps. Forbidden love triangles at Mura'ame College, as Junko and Reiko become involved with boys they shouldn't, then discover that they are the last inheritors of the secrets of the ninja. Your average, everyday mix of romance and assassins, based on the 1982 girls' manga in *Bonita* magazine by Ryoko Shito.

TAMA AND FRIENDS *

1994. JPN: *Uchi no Tama Shirimasen ka.* AKA: *Have You Seen/Do You Know My Tama?* TV series. DIR: Hiroshi Takefuji, Seiko Sayama (TV), Hitoshi Nanba (m). SCR: Masumi Hirayanagi, Shige Sotoyama. DES: N/C. ANI: N/C. MUS:

Michiko Yamakawa. PRD: Sony, TBS. 12 mins. x 36 eps. (TV), 40 mins. (m). Puppies and kittens hang out together in an infants' playground, where they get involved in numerous saccharine adventures. Tama, Doozle, Tiggle, and Momo then "share in fun-filled adventures that impart important social values." The anime was aimed at the very young and marketed in Japan as a kind of "Where's Waldo?"—its posters demanding "Have You Seen My Tama?" That it was optioned and "re-imagined" for broadcast in the U.S. by 4Kids almost makes one wish for the days of tentacle porn once more.

TAMAGOTCHI VIDEO ADVENTURES *

1997. JPN: *Eiga Tamagotchi Honto no Hanashi.* AKA: *True Tamagotchi Tales.* TV series. DIR: Masami Hata, Mitsuo Hashimoto. SCR: Hideki Mitsui, Narimi Narita. DES: Kenji Watanabe, Hideki Inoue. ANI: Kenji Watanabe. MUS: N/C. PRD: Bandai, Fuji TV. 9 mins. x 2 mins. The Tamagotchi Museum doesn't have a display from Earth, so a group of Tamagotchi friends decide to go and collect appliances and artifacts from our world to make a display before the Great Gotchi realizes there isn't one. A blatant cash-in broadcast on Japanese TV in the wake of the Tamagotchi "virtual pet" boom, which combined the get-a-life-factor of pet rocks with the sonic irritation of other people's mobile phones. They were a brief fad in the mid-1990s, soon superseded by their "third generation" fighting versions, the **DIGIMON**. Both, however, were trounced in the marketplace by the multimedia phenomenon of Nintendo's **POKÉMON**.

TANSA 5

1979. JPN: *Kagaku Boken Tai Tansa 5.* AKA: *Science Adventure Command Tansa 5.* TV series. DIR: Shigeru Suzuki, Tameo Ogawa, Akira Suzuki, Kunihiko Okazaki, Osamu Sekita, Toshifumi Takizawa. SCR: Yoshihisa Araki, Sukehiro Tomita, Hiroyuki Hoshiyama, Tsune-

hisa Ito, Kenichi Matsuzaki, Takao Yotsuji, Jiyu Watanabe. DES: Michiru Suzuki, DM Design. ANI: Michiru Suzuki. MUS: Goro Omi. PRD: Sunrise, TV Tokyo. 25 mins. x 33 eps.

Tansa 5 is a five-member patrol team comprising Ryu, Daichi, Rui, Yumeto, and Hajime, whose Land, Aqua, and Sky Tansa vehicles can combine to form the predictably giant robot, Big Tansa. They also have the Time Tansa, a vehicle that allows them to travel an hour into the past, though they must return within their time limit or risk creating a paradox and leaving them lost forever. Their opponents are relics of the past—the forgotten civilization of Lemuria (see **SUPER ATRAGON**), found to be responsible for the statues on Easter Island—a handy ad for sister-company Bandai, which use the statues as the logo for its Emotion video range. In the tradition of team shows dating back to **BATTLE OF THE PLANETS**, one of the team members was doomed, in this case Yumeto, who was replaced halfway through the run by new team member Johnny.

TAOTAO THE PANDA

1981. JPN: *Shunmao (Xiong Mao) Monogatari Taotao.* AKA: *Panda Story Taotao.* Movie, TV series. DIR: Tatsuo Shimamura (m), Shuichi Nakahara, Kazuhiko Ikegami, Taku Sugiyama. SCR: Takeshi Takahashi (m), Keiji Kubota, Takeshi Shudo, Nobuko Morita, Osamu Kagami. DES: Shuichi Nakahara. ANI: Yusaku Sakamoto (m), Masao Kumagawa (TV). MUS: Masaru Sato (m), Yasuo Tsuchida (TV). PRD: Shunmao, Shunmao, TV Osaka. 90 mins., 25 mins. x 50 eps.

Chinese panda Taotao and his mate, Ang, are forced to flee when humans encroach on their natural habitat in Sichuan. Trapped and taken to a zoo in Europe, he becomes popular with the visitors, though animal psychologist Marie realizes that he is pining for his homeland. The first ever Sino-Japanese coproduction, this harks back to the panda boom of the 1970s (see **PANDA GO PANDA**) and was shown on a double bill with the live-action film *Tora-san's Promise* (see **TORA-SAN: THE ANIME**). Many of the same team went on to make the German coproduction *Taotao's Library—World Animal Stories* (1983, *Taotao Ehonkan Sekai Dobutsu Banashi*), in which a baby panda, coincidentally called Taotao, hears a number of stories at his mother's knee.

TARO MAEGAMI
1979. JPN: *Maegami Taro.* TV special. DIR: Hiroshi Saito. SCR: Akira Miyazaki. DES: Yoshiyuki Momose. ANI: Yoshiyuki Momose. MUS: Shinichi Tanabe. PRD: Nippon Animation, Fuji TV. 70 mins.
An elderly couple, childless through many years of love and sacrifice, is finally rewarded by the birth of a son whom they name Taro. Determined to help his impoverished home village, young Taro travels the world in search of the Water of Life, which legend says brings both peace and wealth. But the water is guarded by an evil serpent, which uses its powers as a weapon. Based on the book by Miyoko Matsutani considered a children's masterpiece, this story was also adapted into another anime—**TARO THE DRAGON BOY**. *Ill. p. 297.*

TARO THE DRAGON BOY *
1979. JPN: *Ryu no Ko Taro.* AKA: *Taro the Dragon's Son.* Movie. DIR: Kirio Urayama. SCR: Kirio Urayama, Takashi Mitsui. DES: Yoichi Otabe, Reiko Okuyama. ANI: Yoichi Otabe, Yuji Endo, Osamu Kasai. MUS: Riichiro Manabe. PRD: Toei. 75 mins.
A young mountain boy named Taro searches for his mother who has been changed into a dragon. During his dangerous quest, he risks his own life to save others and fulfill his mission. Finally, Taro engages in a ferocious battle with the enchanted dragon. A beautifully animated film featuring animation from Otabe, who also worked on the Miyazaki/Takahata **HEIDI**. Released on video in the U.S. in 1985, it was based on the same Miyoko Matsutani book adapted into **TARO**

MAEGAMI, a TV special screened the following month. For another suspicious case of "simultaneous creation," see **WIZARD OF OZ**.

TATTOON MASTER *
1996. Video. DIR: Kazuyuki Hirokawa. SCR: Yosuke Kuroda. DES: Hiroyoshi Iida. ANI: Hideki Araki. MUS: Harukichi Yamamoto. PRD: AIC, KSS. 30 mins. x 2 eps.
While his anthropologist mother is off studying the remote Tattoon tribe, Hibio (Eric) sulkily does the housework for his inept father, a pornographic filmmaker. He believes his mother to be dead, and she very nearly was, since she angered the Tattoons, who were ready to kill her. Unbeknownst to Hibio, his mother has bought her life by offering his hand in marriage to the Tattoon chieftainess Nima (Bala), who arrives in Tokyo weapons in hand, magical powers at the ready, and all set to marry him. This is not a welcome thought to the misogynist Hibio, whose sole experience of women has been his father's models, his feckless mother, and his militant feminist class president Fujimatsu (Lisa), a keen archer who carries her bow everywhere, and, for reasons utterly incomprehensible, wants Hibio for herself. Yet another alien-girl-adores-geek scenario, it traces a long line back to **URUSEI YATSURA** but is sadly lacking any of its predecessor's virtues—a failed attempt to take the well-worn clichés in a new direction resulting in a uniformly unlikable cast. Based on a manga in *Ultra Jump* by Masahisa Tadanari.

TEACHER TANK ENGINE
1996. JPN: *Kikan Kuruma Sensei.* Movie. DIR: Kozo Kusuba. SCR: Takuro Fukuda. DES: Shuichi Seki. ANI: Shunji Saita. MUS: N/C. PRD: Nippon Animation. 100 mins.
A modern spin on **BOTCHAN**, as a clueless city boy becomes a supply teacher on a remote Japanese island, slowly gaining the trust of the canny locals. Based on a novel by Shizuka Ijuin, the

anime features live-action stars as many of the voices, including Yumi Adachi, Kin Sugai, and Shigeru Muroi.

TEACHER'S PET *
2000. JPN: *Natural.* Video. DIR: Kan Fukumoto. SCR: Fairy Tale. DES: Mizuki Sakisaka. ANI: Tadaji Tamori. MUS: N/C. PRD: Beam Entertainment, Green Bunny. 30 mins. x 2 eps.
A predictable combination of **HOMEROOM AFFAIRS** and **CINDERELLA EXPRESS**, as new teacher Haruhiko falls for pretty student Chisa, who, to complicate matters, is also his girlfriend's younger sister. Not to be confused with Izumi Aso's 1989 romantic manga of the same name. ◐

TECHNOPOLICE 21C *
1982. JPN: *Technopolis 21C.* AKA: *Techno Police.* Movie. DIR: Masashi Matsumoto, Shoji Kawamori. SCR: Mamoru Sasaki, Kenichi Matsuzaki, Masaru Yamamoto, Hiroyuki Hoshiyama. DES: Yoshitaka Amano, Kazumasa Miyabe. ANI: Norio Hirayama, Kogi Okawa. MUS: Joe Hisaishi. PRD: Studio Nue, Artmic, Toho, Dragon Production. 79 mins.
In the year 2001 (which still seemed quite a long way off in 1982), the police force uses robots to minimize risk to human personnel in fighting crime. The Technopolice is the special squad of cops and robots set up to use the new technology to its best effect. But a crime wave is sweeping Centinel City, and the police have almost lost control. When a powerful experimental tank is hijacked, hotheaded rookie cop Kyosuke (Ken) is thrown in at the deep end. In a high-tech Road Ranger car (a step up from his own beloved Lotus Seven, which he proudly describes as a "collector's item"), he sets out on a death-defying chase through the streets. Luckily he's got the best Techroid (Technoid) backup on the force, three superb robots: his own Blader (Blade), who throws a pair of cuffs to catch villains as they flee; pretty Scanny, the computer hacker partner of token girl Eleanor; and Vigoras (Vigorish), a big, strong robot to

partner his big, strong sidekick Kosuga. With their help, he may just manage to stay alive long enough to capture the crooks, disarm the tank, and save Eleanor; but not even his instinct for outguessing the criminals can help him outwit the political machinations behind the hijack and bring the culprits to justice. Based on an idea by Toshimitsu Suzuki, who would return in **BUBBLEGUM CRISIS** with hard-suits bearing a certain resemblance to the Techroids. Also note the cameo appearance of two cute girl traffic cops in a small car, distantly foreshadowing **YOU'RE UNDER ARREST!**

TEKKAMAN *

1975. JPN: *Uchu Kishi Tekkaman*. AKA: *Tekkaman the Space Knight; Space Knight Tekkaman*. TV series, Video. DIR: Hiroshi Sasakawa, Hideo Nishimaki, Eiko Toriumi, Seitaro Hara (TV1), Hiroshi Negishi, Akihiko Nishiyama, Kazuya Yamazaki, Hideki Tonokatsu (TV2), Hideki Tonokatsu (v). SCR: Junzo Toriumi, Akiyoshi Sakai, Hiroshi Sakamoto (TV1), Mayori Sekijima, Hiroyuki Kawasaki, Satoru Akahori, Tetsuko Watanabe, Katsuhiko Chiba (TV2), Hiroyuki Kawasaki (v). DES: Yoshitaka Amano, Kunio Okawara (TV1), Yoshinori Sayama Hirotoshi Sano, TO III O (sic) (TV2), Hirotoshi Sano, Yoshinori Sayama, Rei Nakahara (v). ANI: Masami Suda, Tsuneo Ninomiya (TV1), Shigeru Kato (TV2), Akira Kano (v). MUS: Bob Sakuma (TV1), Kaoru Wada (TV2), Shigeki Kuwara (v). PRD: Tatsunoko, NET (now TV Asahi) (TV1), Tatsunoko, TV Tokyo (TV2). 25 mins. x 26 eps. (TV1), 25 mins. x 49 eps. (TV2), 30 mins. x 6 eps. (v).

A space-borne version of **BATTLE OF THE PLANETS**, as the invading Waldstar aliens (Waldarians in the U.S. dub) are opposed by Joji Minami (Barry Gallagher), a young man who can wear the powerful Tekkaman battle armor designed by Professor Amachi (Dr. Edward Richardson). The professor's daughter, Hiromi (Patricia), the teleporting alien Andro Umeda, and space furball Mutan support him in his fight on the starship Terra Azzura. Not unlike Vega in **HARMAGEDON**, Andro is a survivor from another world ravaged by the enemy, helping humans avert a similar disaster on their own world. In the Japanese version, the situation was considerably more desperate, since Earth is on the verge of ecological collapse, and the human race will perish without a new home. Conversely, in the U.S. version, the human ships that first encounter the Waldarians are simply looking for new worlds to colonize. Created by Junzo Toriumi and Akira Toyama from an idea by Ippei Kuri, the original TV series ends with Earth saved, but at the price of the hero's life—though it is highly likely that his "death" was only a cliffhanger that would have been revealed as a red herring in episode 27, had the unpopular series not been pulled off the air only halfway through its original planned run of 52 episodes.

The concept was revived for a new series, *SK Tekkaman Blade* (1992), screened in the U.S. as *Teknoman*. This time, the alien Radamu kidnap humans to use them as living weapons, almost invincible once they conjure up the alien Tekkaman armor. One such human, known only as D-Boy, escapes from their control and makes his way to Earth, whose defenders, undecided as to how far to trust him, still need his armor and its power to have a chance of saving the planet. The classic team-show jealousies, misunderstandings, and romantic love tangles back up a plot with plenty of fighting action, and D-Boy's past tragedy is gradually revealed. In the video series *SK Tekkaman Blade 2* (1994), ten years have elapsed since the events of the second TV series, and D-Boy returns to save Earth again. The marketing-led emphasis on starlets in the 1990s means that this time the Tekkaman Support Team consists of several beautiful young girls, each of whose voice actresses made a tie-in single. **ⓥ**

TEKKEN *

1998. AKA: *Iron Fist*. Video. DIR: Kunihisa Sugishima. SCR: Ryota Yamaguchi. DES: Masaaki Kawabata. ANI: Masaaki Kawabata. MUS: Kazuhiko Sotoyama. PRD: Foursome. 30 mins. x 2 eps., 58 mins.

Sometime in the near future, cloning has been outlawed by the Darwin Treaty, but an international crime-fighting organization suspects that super-rich weapons magnate Heihachi Mishima is planning something nasty. Meanwhile Kazuya, Mishima's son, is out to kill him. Mishima thought the best way to train his gentle, good-hearted son was by throwing him into a ravine. The boy survived only thanks to his raging thirst for revenge and has now become a superb martial artist in his own right. A prestigious martial arts tournament on Mishima's private island off Hong Kong, attended by the best fighters from all over the world, offers Kazuya the chance to achieve his aims. His childhood friend Jun wants to bring him back from his chosen path of hatred, but his father aims to Turn Him To The Dark Side.

This game-based anime incorporates characters from all three *Tekken* versions then available. *Tekken* pays lip-service to the police thriller angle exploited in the past by **STREET FIGHTER II**, casting Jun Kazama as a lady investigator with an international crime-busting syndicate. Both in anticipation of the large Chinese market and in recognition of the ideal way to engineer as many fight-scenes as possible, it also pastiches Bruce Lee movies—hence the martial arts tournament on a millionaire's private island, the promised fight through the floors of a central tower, and the Hong Kong setting. Though the plot meanders toward a massive fight at Mishima's lair, which would, of course, be the tournament featured in the game itself, the events of the game only take place off-screen for a few fleeting seconds. The script takes the macho posturing of games to mind-boggling extremes, and as a rundown of all the available clichés, *Tekken* has the lot, including a childhood flashback, bad dreams, sibling rivalry, a shower scene, an evil corporation, a female assassin, a psychic girl agent, graphic breaking bones, a gentle giant, a girl in a sailor suit, a broken punching bag, incompetent minions, Russian androids, a self-destruct sequence, and a baddie who lives to fight another day. As a small bonus, it also includes stealth dinosaurs and a boxing kangaroo. As well as adding the pretentious subtitle "the motion picture," the English-language release replaced the original soundtrack with music from popular beat combos, including Offspring and Corrosion of Conformity. **Ⓥ**

TEN LITTLE FROGS

1998. JPN: *10-piki no Kaeru*. Video. DIR: Masahiro Hosoda. SCR: Miyako Ando. DES: Hirokazu Ishiyuki. ANI: Hirokazu Ishiyuki. MUS: Kenichi Kamio. PRD: Toei, Trans Arts. 20 mins. x 2 eps.
Ten frogs set out in search of adventure in their swamp, sailing in a boat made from a running shoe. Based on the children's book by Hisako Madokoro and Michiko Nakagawa, the story of the frogs returned in a second episode, in which they went to a summer festival.

TEN TOP TIPS FOR PRO BASEBALL

1983. JPN: *Proyakyu o 10 Tanoshiku Miru Hoho*. AKA: *How to Make Pro Baseball Ten Times More Exciting*. Movie. DIR: Kiyoshi Suzuki. SCR: Junichi Ishihara, Toshiharu Iwaida. DES: Hisaichi Ishii. ANI: Tsutomu Shibayama, Osamu Kobayashi, Satoshi Dezaki, Tsukasa Sunaga. MUS: Kazuo Otani. PRD: Tokyo Movie Shinsha for Film Link (1), Magic Bus for Film Link (2). 95 mins., 106 mins.
Based on the two books of career reminiscences by real-life Hanshin Tigers baseball star Takenori Emoto. Mixing live action and animation to tell humorous anecdotes from professional baseball (nine short tales in nine "innings"), the film was followed by a sequel in 1984.

TENAMONYA VOYAGERS *

1999. Video. DIR: Katsuhito Akiyama, Akiyuki Shinbo. SCR: Ryoei Tsukimura. DES: Masashi Ishihama, Noriaki Tetsura, Naoyuki Konno. ANI: Takashi Azuhara. MUS: Masamichi Amano. PRD: Studio Pierrot. 30 mins. x 4 eps.
Rookie schoolteacher Ayako Hanabishi volunteers for a posting in the middle of nowhere only to find that the school has closed down before she arrives. Far from home with no money, she meets Wakana Nanamiya, a Japanese girl on a sports scholarship, who is also stranded. The brash, tough girl Paraila has never seen the girls' homeland, and she inspires the others to pool their resources and head for home. However, their train is attacked en route, and the girls realize too late that Paraila is wanted by the police and using them as cover. So begins a road-movie setup that would make a perfect live-action film of the week, somewhat redundantly transformed into an anime space opera. Compare to **AWOL**, which similarly augmented a real-world drama with pointless sci-fi trappings. An inferior Japanese fish-out-of-water comedy to Tsukimura's earlier **EL HAZARD**, *TV* mixes obvious quick-fixes (a spacegoing *bullet*-train after **GALAXY EXPRESS 999**) with halfhearted visual gags (spaceships like battering rams that deposit a 20th-century police car inside a criminal's ship). There are regular breaks for cheesy shots of Tatsue Yokoyama, the dogged police officer who never quite catches them—the filmmakers would have you believe that this is an "homage" to pulp detective shows of the 1970s, though it looks suspiciously like a poverty of ideas masquerading as irony. There are some genuinely funny moments born of the onscreen ensemble, and occasionally some tongue-in-cheek observations in the style of a poor man's **GUNBUSTER**, but like so many 1990s anime comedies, *TV* thinks it's a lot funnier than it really is (see also **JUBEI-CHAN THE NINJA GIRL**), and it stops abruptly with a cynical narration that unhelpfully adds, "And for some reason, this is the end."

Eagle Ken stands beneath the God-Phoenix, transport vehicle for the *Science Ninja Team Gatchaman*. Better known by their American name G-Force, Team Gatchaman have appeared in several U.S. incarnations, most memorably in **BATTLE OF THE PLANETS**. Their five-strong cast roster of strong leader, maverick deputy, big lunk, childish clown, and token girl would be repeated in many other team shows, although recent years have seen more females as eye candy for the male viewer. *See entry p. 29.*

© 1978 SANDY FRANK SYNDICATION, INC.

Battle of the Planets

It will, however, remain forever in the anime history books as the first to be released in the U.S. straight to DVD without ever gracing the old-fashioned VHS format.

TENCHI MUYO! *

1992. JPN: *Tenchi Muyo! Ryo Oh Ki*. AKA: *This Way Up!; No-Good Tenchi; No Need for Tenchi; Heaven and Earth Prince*. Video, TV series, movie. DIR: Hiroki Hayashi, Kenichi Yatagai, Kazuhiro Ozawa, Yoshiaki Iwasaki, Shinichi Kimura, Koji Masunari, Satoshi Kimura. SCR: Naoko Hasegawa, Masaki Kajishima, Hiroki Hayashi, Ryoei Tsukimura, Yosuke Kuroda, Satoru Nishizono. DES: Masaki Kajishima, Atsushi Takeuchi, Takeshi Waki. ANI: Takehiro Nakayama, Wataru Abe. MUS: Seiko Nagaoka, Christopher Franke, Ko Otani. PRD: AIC, Pioneer, TV Tokyo. 30 mins. x 13 eps. (v), 40 mins., 45 mins. (v special), 25 mins. x 26 eps. (TV1), 25 mins. x 26 eps. (TV2/TV3), 95 mins. x 3 (m).
Tenchi Masaki is a quiet, average teenager who lives in the family shrine with his father and grandfather, goes to school, and does nothing much—until the day he accidentally releases a malevolent creature from the family shrine (compare to **USHIO AND TORA**).

It transforms into a hot babe, space pirate Ryoko, and her hots are aimed at Tenchi. Then another alien babe, Jurai Princess Ayeka, arrives with her sweet little sister, Sasami. She too fancies Tenchi, but she's got another reason for hating Ryoko—a past tragedy that robbed her of her intended husband. When ditzy Space Officer Mihoshi falls out of the skies onto the Masaki household and pink-haired alien professor Wasshu shows up, the scene is set for a romantic farce in which the girls fight for Tenchi's affections while he fights off various galactic threats and gradually uncovers the truth about his family. There's also a mascot "cabbit" (cat/rabbit), the titular Ryo-Oh-Ki, which likes carrots and will one day grow into a spaceship.

The "unwelcome guest" genre, in which a hapless boy is saddled with a magical babe, is a popular high-concept in anime. It's a genre rich in mind-boggling situation comedies: girlfriend-as-alien (**URUSEI YATSURA**), girlfriend-as-elfin-nymphomaniac (**ADVENTURE KID**), girlfriend-as-the-Norse-embodiment-of-the-concept-of-Being (**OH MY GODDESS!**), girlfriend-as-time-traveling-ghost-of-future-dead-wife (**KIRARA**). *Tenchi* is its 1990s apotheosis; a show about a boy stuck with more girls than he can shake a stick at, every one of them feverishly competing for a chaste peck on the cheek. Originally conceived as a spoof vacation episode of **BUBBLEGUM CRISIS**, *Tenchi* reached screens in this heavily rewritten form—however, along with the girl-heavy cast, the idea that it was okay to just goof off for an episode or two became ingrained. Sasami's regular plea that things can always stay the same "forever and ever" is perhaps the most bowel-emptyingly fearsome line in televisual history, striking greater dread into the audience than any horror movie. Though the first video series of *Tenchi* was witty, funny, and charming, the premise was repeated *ad nauseam* by a creative team happy to simply coast along. Later incarna-

tions of the series reorder a few plot elements into what some might call alternate universes, and others lazy continuity.

The Pioneer corporation, searching for an easily repeatable franchise to rival Sunrise's **BRAVE SAGA** or Tatsunoko's **TIME BOKAN**, hyped *Tenchi* to insane extremes, and someone eventually believed it—the series clambered onto TV screens with the new-look *Tenchi Universe* (Ryoko *crashes* on Earth while being *pursued* by Mihoshi; see the subtle difference?), which moves the action into space for its second season. A further TV series, *Tenchi in Tokyo*, packed our boy off to college—but a dimensional portal let his harem pop up for "unexpected" visits. At the time of its U.S. release, Pioneer's blurb proclaimed it was the "same old Tenchi," which was at least honest.

The series proper "ended" with three expensive movies, beginning with *Tenchi Muyo in Love* (1996), which paid out for music from *Babylon 5*–composer Christopher Franke. Shamelessly ripping off *Back to the Future*, Tenchi must travel back in time to unite his courting parents. Despite high production values and an involving plot, the movie is let down by the serial's vastly overpopulated cast—the number of characters demanding a scene to steal often makes it resemble crowded game-based anime like **STREET FIGHTER II**. In typical *Tenchi* style, the movie *Daughter of Darkness* (1997, aka *Midsummer's Eve*) halfheartedly inverts the previous plot, featuring the cast visited by a character from the *future*, claiming to be Tenchi's daughter. The final movie, *Tenchi Forever* (1999), features Tenchi kidnapped by yet another obsessive female and spirited into a parallel world where his adoring harem have to find him. Though the public breathed a collective sigh of relief that it was all over, press releases from Pioneer now threaten a return of the series to video in 2002.

With both the appeal and dogged staying power of a mutant cockroach, the franchise might not necessarily

have pleased the crowds (ratings were unremarkable), but it certainly pleased studio executives. *Tenchi* was a fertile breeding ground for other shows during the 1990s—most notably the superior **EL HAZARD**, which was made by bored staffers Hayashi and Tsukimura, and the pornographic pastiches **SPACESHIP AGGA RUTER** and **MASQUERADE**. Two video "specials" also introduced a superheroine, who returned in her own video series *Magical Princess Pretty Sammy*, which followed the classic magical-girl-show pattern (see **LITTLE WITCH SALLY**), and, predictably, ran a string of subplots about the grown-up girls competing for first place in Tenchi's affections. Little Sasami, however, was safely remodeled as his sister, allowing an 8-year-old girl to adore a 17-year-old guy without a hint of impropriety and simultaneously securing her claim to be big bro's Number One. The series has some enjoyable moments—one episode is a wholly unsubtle dig at Bill Gates's Microsoft empire—but ultimately it's a show about cute little girls for much older boys who really should know better. The video series was itself rehashed for Japanese TV as the jaw-droppingly camp 26-episode *Magical Girl Pretty Sammy* (*Magical Project S*). The relationships and premises are completely reworked, but this time, apart from the odd cameo appearance, Tenchi and friends are sidelined. Sammy has a mother and father and a whole bunch of elementary school friends and is more interested in talking to her best friend Misa (who is also her unwitting adversary Pixie Misa) than mooning over boys. Marketed in Japan for the little-girl audience, the series received inexplicably high ratings in Nagoya but has proved unpopular with Western *Tenchi* fans, perhaps because it abandons most of the series' established tropes in favor of those of standard magical-girl shows. *Ill. p. 109.* ◐

TENMARU THE LITTLE TENGU
1983. JPN: *Kotengu Tenmaru*. TV series. DIR: Hiroshi Shidara, Yuji Endo,

Atsutoshi Umezawa, Takeshi Shirato, Junichi Sato. SCR: Tadaaki Yamazaki, Akiyoshi Sakai, Katsuhiko Taguchi. DES: Kiichiro Suzuki. ANI: Masami Abe, Takeshi Shirato. MUS: Hiroshi Tsutsui. PRD: Toei, Fuji TV. 25 mins. x 19 eps. Prince Tenmaru leaves the land of the tengu (crow-spirits) in pursuit of 108 evil creatures who have invaded the human realm. He hides out at the apartment of pretty Earth girl Yoko. A mixture of the gentle humor of DORAE-MON with the ghost-busting of DORO-RON ENMA, *Tenmaru* was the anime debut of future SAILOR MOON–director Junichi Sato.

TEPPEN
1995. AKA: *Summit.* Video. DIR: Yota Minagawa, Fumi Shirakawa. SCR: Tomo-hiro Ando, Masashi Reishi. DES: Masashi Yusono. ANI: Hidemizu Kita. MUS: N/C. PRD: Toei. 50 mins. x 2 eps. In an adaptation of Takanori Onari's manga from *Young Jump* magazine, teenage tough-guy Satoshi gets into fights at school and has run-ins with the police. **Ⓥ**

THAT'LL DO NICELY
1991. JPN: *Nyuin Bokki Monogatari: O Daiji ni.* AKA: *Hospitalization Surprise Story: That'll Do Nicely.* Video. DIR: Sadamune Koyama, Naoko Kuzumi. SCR: Sadamune Koyama. DES: Koichi Arai. ANI: Yoshio Mizumura. MUS: Michiya Katakura. PRD: Tokyo Kids. 45 mins. x 2 eps. Ayumu Nerima is hospitalized after a motorcycle accident, but he soon perks up when he discovers that everyone on the ward is desperate for sex, from the nurses to the unwed-teenager mother next door. A predictable farce based on a manga by Maki Otsubo in *Manga Action* magazine—compare to O-GENKI CLINIC. **Ⓝ**

THERE GOES SHURA
1994. JPN: *Shura ga Yuku.* Video. DIR: Masamune Ochiai. SCR: Yu Kawanabe. DES: Aiko Kamada. ANI: Teruo Kigure. MUS: Hideyuki Tanaka. PRD: Knack. 50 mins. x 2 eps.

The assassination of a Shinjuku gang boss starts a trail of blood-soaked revenge, ending with a nasty shootout between yakuza in Kyushu. Based on the original manga in *Comic Goraku* by Yu Kawanabe (who also wrote EMPEROR OF THE SOUTH SIDE) and Masato Yamaguchi. **Ⓥ**

THERE GOES TOMOE
1991. JPN: *Tomoe ga Yuku.* Video. DIR: Takaaki Ishiyama. SCR: Asami Wata-nabe. DES: Matsuri Okuda. ANI: Masayu-ki Goto. MUS: Katsuhiro Kunimoto. PRD: Beam Entertainment. 45 mins. x 2 eps. In this adaptation of Yumi Tamura's manga from *Bessatsu Shojo Comic*, Tomoe Oshima is a bad-girl biker who cherishes a hidden love for stuntman Tokoro. Since the heroine takes her name from Tomoe Gozen, the famous 12th-century woman-warrior, it might be prudent to file this story with SPEC-TRE, another adaptation of Japanese history into a modern setting.

THEY WERE ELEVEN *
1986. JPN: *Juichi-nin Iru.* Movie. DIR: Satoshi Dezaki, Tsuneo Tominaga. SCR: Toshikai Imaizumi, Katsumi Koide. DES: Akio Sugino, Keizo Shimizu. ANI: Keizo Shimizu, Yukari Kobayashi, Kenichi Maejima. MUS: Hirohiko Fukuda. PRD: Kitty Film. 91 mins. An interplanetary group of 10 military academy cadets set out on their end-of-course test. They have to take an elder-ly spaceship out into space and survive 53 days without outside help. Any one of them can give up, but if so, they all fail. Then they find there are 11 peo-ple on board. One of them is an imposter, and they can't contact the academy to find out who it is or whether it's all part of the test. A series of incidents and accidents, trivial at first, grow increasingly threatening, and their personal strengths and weak-nesses, as well as the social and politi-cal agendas of their different races, have a wider impact than on the out-come of this test alone. The anime ver-sion of Moto Hagio's suspenseful 1978

manga is delicate but powerful, a miniature gem.

30,000 MILES UNDER THE SEA
1970. JPN: *Kaitei Sanman Mile.* Movie. DIR: Takeshi Tamiya. SCR: Katsumi Okamoto. DES: Makoto Yamazaki. ANI: Reiko Okayama, Sadao Kikuchi, Torihi-ro Kaneyama. MUS: Takeo Watanabe. PRD: Toei. 60 mins. Returning home from an ocean trip, young Isamu meets the beautiful sea-dweller Angel on a volcanic island. Attacked by a fiery dragon, Isamu and Angel escape on the observation boat See Through (a punning reference to the Sea View in Irwin Allen's 1961 *Voy-age to the Bottom of the Sea*), and Angel invites Isamu to see her undersea king-dom of Atlas. As Isamu is preparing to return to dry land, Atlas is attacked by the evil king, Magma VII, who reveals that he is planning to use the dragon to seize control of the surface world. The fate of Earth and Ocean is placed in the hands of Isamu and Angel for the final battle against the invading king.
This was the fourth Toei adaptation of a Shotaro Ishinomori story (the pre-vious one was FLYING GHOST SHIP), but this popular manga artist's work con-tinues to appear in a variety of differ-ent anime for many decades to come, from the SF of CYBORG 009 to the eco-nomics education of JAPAN INC. Direc-tor Tamiya would go on to direct another kids-save-world extravaganza in 1973 with BABEL II.

THOSE WHO HUNT ELVES *
1996. JPN: *Elf o Karu Monotachi.* AKA: *Elf Hunters.* TV series. DIR: Kazuyoshi Katayama, Tatsuo Okazaki, Hiroshi Fukutomi. SCR: Masaharu Amiya, Masashi Kubota. DES: Keiji Goto, Akira Furuya. ANI: Keiji Goto. MUS: Susumu Akitagawa. PRD: Group Tac, TV Tokyo. 25 mins. x 24 eps. A trio of adventurers is transported (with their T-74 tank) to a world inhab-ited by elves. Elven leader Celcia acci-dentally destroys the spell to send them back. Luckily fragments were copied

onto the skin of five elves (and you can bet they aren't fat, old male elves, either) so fighter Junpei, actress Airi, and schoolgirl tank pilot Ritsuko must find them to get home. Crashing quest into skin-flick, with the emphasis on stripping the elves rather than skinning them, there are a few plot twists designed to amuse *Beavis and Butthead* viewers (firebrand Celcia transforms herself into an ugly dog and gets stuck, ho ho) and some with wider appeal (all the spell fragments our heroes find are easily visible without removing a stitch of clothing from their hosts.) There are nods to **DOMINION** in Ritsuko's devotion to her tank, and **EL HAZARD** in Junpei's obsession with finding decent curry in this alien world. Based on an "original" manga by Yutaka Yagami in *Dengeki Comic Gao. Ill. p. 113.* **CN**

THREE MUSKETEERS, THE

1987. JPN: *Anime Sanjushi*. TV series, TV special, movie. DIR: Kunihiko Yuyama, Tetsuro Amino, Takashi Watanabe, Keiji Hayakawa, et al. SCR: Yasuo Tanami, Jack Production. DES: Mitsuki Nakamura, Shingo Ozaki, Hatsuki Tsuji. ANI: Hatsuki Tsuji, Shojuro Yamauchi. MUS: Kohei Tanaka. PRD: Studio Gallop, Gakken, Toei, NHK. 25 mins. (TVm), 25 mins. x 52 eps. (TV), 45 mins. (m). In 17th-century France, young D'Artagnan leaves his home village to travel to Paris and find fame and fortune, serving his King as a Musketeer like his father before him. So far, so close to the 1844 novel by Alexandre Dumas *père*. In Paris, he defeats the plots of evil Cardinal Richelieu and Milady against Louis XIII, aided by his fellow-Musketeers and mentors Athos, Porthos, and Aramis, and by the queen's beautiful maid, Constance. The familiar Dumas tale was popularized in Japan by *D'Artagnan's Story*, an 11-volume series of novels by Yoshihiro Suzuki, with accompanying artwork by **LUPIN III**–creator Monkey Punch. The *3M* anime adapts the first volume of this version, with two major additions to the Dumas original—D'Artagnan's orphan boy-assistant Jean, and the fact

that Aramis is actually a *woman*, in a cross-dressing homage to **ROSE OF VERSAILLES**. The series, which began in October, was piloted the previous May with a 25-minute TV special *Chase the Iron Mask* (*Tekkamen o Oe*). For the latter half of the series, the animators would draw on the same events, from Dumas' *Man in the Iron Mask* through the tenth book in Suzuki's series. The series was recut again into the movie *Aramis' Adventure* (1989, *Aramis no Boken*), which rearranged flashbacks with new footage set a year after the final episode. Lune is a 16-year-old girl from the Swiss Alps, who falls in love with François, a young man she meets in the forest. Believing him to have been murdered, she adopts a man's disguise and changes her name to Aramis, hoping to track down the man who ordered his death. Naturally, this turns out to have been his twin brother, Louis XIII, in a surprise that dovetails beautifully with the original source material. For very different animated versions, see **DOGTANIAN AND THE THREE MUSKEHOUNDS**, **KEROPPI**, and **PUSS IN BOOTS**.

3X3 EYES *

1991. JPN: *Sazan Eyes*. Video. DIR: Daisuke Nishio, Kazuhisa Takenouchi. SCR: Akinori Endo, Yuzo Takada. DES: Koichi Arai, Tetsuya Kumagai, Hiroshi Kato. ANI: Koichi Arai, Tetsuya Kumagai. MUS: Kaoru Wada. PRD: Tabac, Toei. 30 mins. x 4 eps., 45 mins. x 3 eps.
Yakumo Fuji loses his father in an accident in Tibet but gains a new responsibility. He must help a 300-year-old immortal, the last of the race that once ruled Earth, who lives in a symbiotic relationship with a 16-year-old girl called Pai. Yakumo is killed rescuing Pai but is brought back to life as her zombie protector. Now both of them begin a quest to become human.

Creator Yuzo Takada began as an assistant to **JUDGE**'s Fujihiko Hosono, and here combines the "walking dead" hero of **ULTRAMAN** with the ancient immortals of Tezuka's **THREE-EYED PRINCE**. Takada's *3x3 Eyes* manga suggests that all myths are the vestigial race-memory of a great conflict between extra-dimensional entities. Mixing the treasure-hunting elements of *Indiana Jones* with a mythopoeic buddy-movie, Pai and Yakumo search the world for artifacts that might help them. The mawkish romance between the two (made frankly irritating in an English dub that gives Pai a grating screech in place of a voice) is nicely contrasted with their magical personae—shy-boy Yakumo is an indestructible zombie, and puppy-fat ingenue Pai disappears completely when her third eye opens, revealing a powerful being with a demonic disregard for human life. In this way, *3x3 Eyes* is perhaps the most dramatically interesting spinoff from **CREAM LEMON**'s schizophrenic "Lolita" concept and is mercifully asexual.

A second series followed in 1995 after Takada's successful **BLUE SEED**, with Pai losing her memory in Hong Kong and living as a schoolgirl in Japan. The new story, featuring input from Takada himself, takes the pair to Mount Kunlun, China's version of Olympus, where they join forces with some priests and a man with a really bad Australian accent to find the "key" to Pai's dimension. Covering only the first five volumes of the ongoing original, *3x3 Eyes* remains one of those truncated anime series consistently beset with rumors of its imminent return to the screen. *Ill. p. 385.*

THREE-EYED PRINCE

1985. JPN: *Mitsume ga Toru; Akumajima no Prince Mitsume ga Toru*. AKA: *The Three-eyed Prince on Devil's Island*. TV special, TV series. DIR: Yugo Serikawa (TVm), Hidehito Ueda, Yusaku Saotome, Keiichiro Mochizuki, Shichi Matsumi (TV). SCR: Haruya Yamazaki (TVm), Mayori Sekijima, Reiko Naka, Tsunehisa Arakawa. DES: Osamu Tezuka (TVm), Kazuhiko Udagawa (TV). ANI: Shigetaka Kiyoyama, Hiroshi Wagatsuma, Masami Abe (TVm), Kazuhiko Udagawa, Yoshiaki

Matsuhira (TV). MUS: Kazuo Otani (TVm), Toshiyuki Watanabe (TV). PRD: Toei, Tezuka Pro, Nippon TV, Tezuka Pro, TV Tokyo. 85 mins. (TVm), 25 mins. x 47 eps. (TV).

Sharaku is a high-school student but his naïve manner, youthful face, and bald head make him look like a kindergarten kid, and he usually has some kind of bandage or dressing on his forehead. If he didn't, the world would be in trouble, for he is the last descendant of a three-eyed race who once ruled the world with advanced technology and vast intelligence. His mother left him to be raised at Dr. Inumochi's home shortly before she was killed by a mysterious lightning blast. Sharaku's friend is the local priest's daughter, Wato, a tomboy and aikido expert who knows his secret. She loves his "true" self, an arrogant but lonely superbeing, and looks after and protects his childlike human persona. She's also the one who usually has to take off his third-eye covering so he can save the situation when they get into some kind of trouble with magical phenomena, and she puts it back on again to prevent him taking over the world once the danger is past. Based on a manga by Osamu Tezuka, in which he hoped to combine the look of Elmer Fudd with the adventures of Sherlock Holmes—note an investigative character "Sha-rak," whose faithful assistant is addressed as "Watsan." A heavy influence on the later **3x3 EYES.**

THUMBELINA

1978. JPN: *Andersen Dowa: Oyayubi-hime.* AKA: *Andersen's Tale: Thumbelina; Princess Thumb.* Movie, TV series. DIR: Yugo Serikawa (m), Hiromitsu Morita, et al. (TV2). SCR: Yuko Oyabu (m), Akiyoshi Sakai, Shigeru Yanagawa, Yu Mizugi (TV1). DES: Osamu Tezuka, Satoshi Fukumoto (m), Usagi Morino (TV). ANI: Tatsuji Kino (m), Usagi Morino (TV). MUS: Shunsuke Kikuchi (m), N/C (TV). PRD: Toei, Tezuka Pro (m), Enoki Film, TV Tokyo (TV). 64 mins. (m), 25 mins. x 26 eps. (TV).

The movie made by Tezuka's studio for

Toei is a straightforward adaptation of the classic fairy tale. A tiny girl, only as long as a man's thumb, is born to a childless woman, abducted by frogs who want her to marry their son, but escaping instead (with the help of a kindly bumblebee, a Tezuka addition) to find a real prince without having to kiss the frog first. It's utterly charming. One of the ever-popular **TALES OF HANS CHRISTIAN ANDERSEN**, the story was adapted again by Megumi Nagata (see **PRISM SEASON**), and again as a TV series, *The Story of Princess Thumbelina* (1994, *Oyayubi-hime Monogatari*). A feature-length edit of this series was apparently released on home video in the U.S. as *Thumbelina.* The series was also shown in Spanish on Puerto Rican TV.

THUNDERBIRDS 2086 *

1982. JPN: *Kagaku Kyujotai Technovoyager.* AKA: *Scientific Rescue Team Technovoyager.* TV series. DIR: Noboru Ishiguro, Yasuo Hasegawa, Katsuhito Akiyama, Hiromichi Matano, Shigeo Koshi. SCR: Hideki Sonoda, Noboru Ishiguro, Kazuo Yoshioka, Takayuki Kase, Shiro Ishimori, Keiji Kubota. DES: Kenzo Koizumi, Kunio Aoii, Kazuto Ishikawa. ANI: Katsu Amamizu, Mitsuru Ishii, Yasushi Nakamura. MUS: Kentaro Haneda, Koji Makaino. PRD: Jin, Green Box, AIC, Tohoku Shinsha, Fuji TV. 25 mins. x 24 eps.

In 2066, the World Federation Supreme Council appoints former astronaut Dr. Gerard Simpson (pointlessly renamed Warren Simpson in the U.S. dub) to run the International Rescue Organization. Based on a remote Pacific Island, he leads a group of kids who pilot the "Techno Voyager" vehicles to save people in danger—Captains Raiji Hidaka (Dylan Beyda) in One, Sammy Edkins Jr. (Johnathan Jordan Jr.) and Eric Jones (Jesse Rigel) in Two, Gran Hanson (Gran Hansen) in Three, Catherine Heywood (Kallan James) in Four, and token brat Paul Simpson ("Skipper" Simpson) getting under everyone's feet.

The concept of the five-strong team

Stock hero Ran and stock "mysterious girl" Aira head out into the desert wilderness, leaving their oasis and its towering Holy Mother spaceship behind them. Satoshi Saga's **GREEN LEGEND RAN** is a well-made but derivative eco-saga, only let down by illogical plotting, which starts with a *deus ex machina* and then waits patiently for another one. *See entry p. 155.*

Green Legend Ran

© A.I.C. • PIONEER LDC

had already been popularized in anime by **BATTLE OF THE PLANETS,** but the other similarities between *Technovoyager* and the British cult puppet show *Thunderbirds* (1966) might be considered actionably obvious. Luckily for him, producer Banjiro Uemura was head of Tohoku Shinsha and also of ITC Japan, part of the international corporation that owned the Thunderbirds copyright—*if* he found the resemblance too close for comfort, he would have had to sue *himself.* Uemura had already made **ZERO TESTER,** which by his own cautious admission "learned from" *Thunderbirds.* In 1977, he had held extensive talks with *Thunderbirds*-creator Gerry Anderson about a new animated series to be called *Terrahawks: Order to Recapture Earth.* During the outlining process, much of Anderson's original idea was discarded in favor of new plot elements from Sukehiro Tomita and designs from Yoshikazu Yasuhiko. Set in the year 2085, it was to be the story of second-generation immigrants from the rest of the solar system, returning to reconquer their homeworld, which has been overrun by aliens led by the evil "Queen Mother." The show stalled in the early stages, because the Japanese network MBS claimed there was no call for sci-fi. *Star Wars* opened in Japan just a few months later, by which time the project was already canceled.

However, several parties reused elements of the proposal in later shows—writer Tomita with **MOSPEADA**, Anderson with his puppet-show *Terrahawks* (1983), and Uemura with *Technovoyager*.

Technovoyager flopped in Japan (only 18 episodes were screened on its initial run), but in his capacity as head of ITC Japan, Uemura was able to sell it to ITC's American arm, and, in 1983, the full run was broadcast in America as "*Thunderbirds 2086*, an ITC Entertainment Production"—transformed into a *bona fide* ITC production after the fact. The new title recognized the show's debt to *Thunderbirds*, but where the British only allowed for a handful of rescue craft, the Japanese team could call on no less than 17, enabling them to investigate crime and save lives on land, under the sea, in the air, and in space. The coincidental and remarkably convenient confusion of the letters B and V in Japanese allowed for the "Techno Voyager" vehicles to have the letters "TB" on their sides. The extensive vehicle lineup and stock hero team characters were close to the Japanese *Terrahawks* outline, while the *Terrahawks* puppet series released in Britain reputedly had many elements of the British outline—with the Queen Mother renamed Zelda. In another moment of chance cross-cultural pollination, both *Terrahawks*' Zeroids and **GUNDAM**'s Haro were spherical robots.

The confusion continued when the six unbroadcast episodes of *Technovoyager* were exported back to Japan as part of *Thunderbirds 2086*, two 90-minute videos with the U.S. dub (by **SPEED RACER**'s Peter Fernandez) left intact for added exoticism. Meanwhile, in a final irony, an "anime" version of *Terrahawks* did eventually reach Japanese screens; when the puppet show was broadcast in Japan, its opening sequence was replaced with new Japanese-made animated footage, directed by Satoshi Dezaki. Hideaki Anno, a big

enough fan of the original *TB* to produce the Japanese-made documentary *The Complete Thunderbirds*, would acknowledge his own debt to Gerry Anderson with numerous homages in **EVANGELION**.

THUNDERBOYS

1995. JPN: *Itsuka no Main*. AKA: *Forever Main*. Video. DIR: Hiromichi Matano. SCR: Isao Shizudani. DES: Shushi Mizuho. ANI: Mitsuharu Otani. MUS: Teppei Sato. PRD: Toei. 45 mins. Tokyo bikers race and fight, and race, and fight. Based on the manga in *Young Jump* by Shushi Mizuho. ●⊘

THUNDERSUB *

1979. JPN: *Uchu Kubo Blue Noah*. AKA: *Space Carrier Blue Noah*. TV series. DIR: Kazunori Takahashi, Tomoharo Katsumata, Masahiro Sasaki, Kunihiko Okazaki, Shiro Murata, Teppei Matsuura. SCR: Hideaki Yamamoto, Kiyoshi Matsuoka, Takashi Yamada. DES: Akinobu Hane. ANI: Kenzo Koizumi. MUS: Masaaki Hirao. PRD: Westcape Corporation, Yomiuri TV (Nippon TV). 25 mins. x 27 eps.
In the year 2050, Earth is invaded by the alien Godom race, known rather more grandly in the Western version as the Force of Death. Ninety percent of humanity is wiped out, but their last hope lies in the secret Point N1 Base on Minamidori Island. There, the great aircraft carrier Blue Noah is nearing completion. With a young crew led by the inventor's son Makoto Kusaka (Earth commander's son Colin Collins in the U.S. version), it launches fighters to save the world, but the project isn't yet complete, and the ship must get to other secret Points to complete its construction, powered by a pendant passed on to the hero by his dying father.

As if taking a WWII battleship and sending it on a star trek wasn't ludicrous enough, this Earthbound follow-up to **STAR BLAZERS** somehow failed to recapture the magic of its predecessor. It wasn't until episode 21 that the ship justified its "Space Carrier" title, pick-

ing up a star drive at Point N9 that finally allowed it to get out of the water. Though 27 episodes were made, the first 4 were not shown in their original form but cut together into a feature-length "TV special" to open the series. Unlike the Yamato, however, the Blue Noah did not return for a sequel. See also **ODIN**, another attempt by producer Yoshinobu Nishizaki to make money out of ships sailing in space.

TICO OF THE SEVEN SEAS

1994. JPN: *Nanatsu no Umi no Tico*. AKA: *Tico and Nanami*. TV series. DIR: Jun Takagi, Jiro Fujimoto, Shinpei Miyashita, Kozo Kuzuba, et al. SCR: Hideki Mitsui, Aya Matsui, Noriyuki Aoyama, Asako Ikeda, Toru Nobuto. DES: Satoko Morikawa, Shigeru Morimoto, Kazue Ito. ANI: Yoshiharu Sato, Masaru Oshiro, Koichiro Saotome, Ei Inoue, Azumayami Sugiyama. MUS: Hibiki Mikazu. PRD: Nippon Animation, Fuji TV. 25 mins. x 39 eps.
Little Nanami travels the world's oceans with her father, Scott Simpson, an oceanographer, in search of adventure and on the track of a legendary luminous whale said to have played a vital role in the evolution of life on Earth. Their captain is Alphonso, a brave fishermen and the owner of the good ship Peperonchino. Rich, beautiful Cheryl Melville talks her way on board in search of adventure, with her butler, and refuses to leave. Nanami's special friend, the orca Tico, swims alongside their boat as they search for the whale through the seven seas. When an unscrupulous team of scientists gets to the whale first, Nanami and Tico rescue it in the hope of learning its secrets and sharing them with the rest of the world. This is one of Nippon Animation's rare series *not* based on a classic novel; the story was created for the company by Akira Hiroo. Beautiful designs and a plot combining adventure with ecological correctness make a charming children's series. Episode 31 was not broadcast but included on the laser-disc release.

TIES OF LOVE

1992. JPN: *Ai no Kusabi*. AKA: *Ties of Affection, Bonds of Love*. Video. DIR: Akira Nishimori, Kazuhito Akiyama. SCR: Naoko Hasegawa, Reiko Yoshiwara. DES: Katsumi Michihara, Naoyuki Onda. ANI: Koichi Arai, Takeyoshi Nakayama. MUS: Toshio Yabuki. PRD: AIC. 60 mins. x 2 eps.

The future city of Tanagra is governed by a computer entity known as Jupiter but administered by the Parthia syndicate, whose members are drawn from the aristocratic group known as Blondys. Social tensions bubble under its serene, ordered surface; disaffected political groups are plotting to kill the most important syndicate member, Jason Mink. But there's an even more pressing destabilizing factor in Jason's life: he has fallen deeply and embarrassingly in love with his "pet" Riki, a boy from the wrong side of the tracks who, like many young men and women with no other options, has voluntarily become a sex slave. Neither Jason nor Riki can admit the ties that hold them, even to themselves; leaving aside their pride, both would be outcasts. Jason gives Riki a vacation, a chance to go back to the slums and find his old friends again, but a meeting with his former lover leads to tragedy.

Based on the novel by Reiko Yoshiwara, which was illustrated by JOKER's Katsumi Michihara, *ToL's* society is reminiscent of ancient Greece; not only are the institutions of power restricted to a certain class, but women are completely excluded from significant roles. All the key power relationships we see, including sexual ones, are between men. Ironically, the Jupiter computer manifests as feminine: like Kusanagi in GHOST IN THE SHELL, she's a man-made idea of the female in a world run by masculine elites. There is sexually explicit material but the violence is mostly emotional. Like all anime about homosexual love, this was originally made for a *female* audience. ❶❷❸

TIGER MASK

1969. TV series, movie. DIR: Takeshi

Tamiya, Kimio Yabuki, Tomoharu Katsumata, Fusahito Nagaki, Hiroshi Shidara, Yoshio Kuroda, Yasuo Yamaguchi (TV1), Kozo Morishita, Shigenori Yamauchi, Hideki Takayama, Tomoharu Katsumata, Masayuki Akehi, Kazuo Yamazaki, Osamu Sekita (TV2). SCR: Masaki Tsuji, Tadashi Kondo, Tomohiro Ando (TV1), Haruya Yamazaki (TV2). DES: Naoki Tsuji. ANI: Keijiro Kimura, Koichi Murata (TV1), Tsukasa Abe (TV2). MUS: Shunsuke Kikuchi (both). PRD: Toei, Yomiuri TV (Nippon TV) (TV1), Toei, TV Asahi (TV2). 25 mins. x 105 eps. (TV1), 47 mins., 53 mins., 25 mins. (m), 25 mins. x 33 eps. (TV2).

Naoto Date has a secret identity as masked wrestler Tiger Mask, part of a crude school of fighting that is more violence than art. Overcome by guilt when an opponent's death puts his little son in an orphanage, the hard man devotes himself to the well-being of the orphans and works to improve their lives in the only way he knows how—by fighting. He also aims to raise the standards of the ring and ensure that fighting is recognized as an honorable art, not mere violence.

Based on a 1968 manga in *Bokura* magazine by KARATE-CRAZY LIFE's Ikki Kajiwara and ZERO SEN HAYATO–creator Naoki Tsuji, *TM* soon made it to theaters, as episodes were edited into seasonal "movies"—*TM* (1970, #9), *TM: War Against the League of Masked Wrestlers* (1970, #23, 25 and 26), and *TM: The Black Demon* (1971, #56).

A 1981 follow-up series is set after Naoto's death—he was killed saving the life of a child. A new opponent, Outer Space Mask, not endorsed by any of the national wrestling federations, bullies his way into the ring and injures a young wrestler. Tatsuo, a great fan of Tiger Mask who once lived in the orphanage he supported, intervenes wearing his hero's old mask and is accepted into the fraternity of masked wrestlers, where he becomes a major star. Champion of the oppressed and weak, he hides his secret wrestling identity under the everyday clothes of a sports journalist, echoing

that other champion of the weak, *Superman*. ❶

TIME BOKAN

1975. AKA: *Time Fighters, Time Machine*. TV series. DIR: Hiroshi Sasakawa, Takao Koyama, Katsuhisa Yamada, Hideo Nishimaki (TV1), Seitaro Hara (TV2), Takao Yotsuji (TV4). SCR: Junzo Toriumi, Haruya Yamazaki, Keiji Kubota, Tsunehisa Ito, Shigeru Yanagawa (TV1), Akiyoshi Sakai (TV2), Masaru Yamamoto (TV4), Satoru Akahori. DES: Tatsuo Yoshida, Yoshitaka Amano, Kunio Okawara. ANI: Eiji Tanaka, Hidemi Kama, Hitoshi Sakaguchi. MUS: Masayuki Yamamoto, Masaaki Jinbo. PRD: Tatsunoko, Fuji TV. 25 mins. x 61 eps. (TV1), 25 mins. x 108 eps. (TV2), 25 mins. x 53 eps. (TV3), 25 mins. x 52 eps. (TV4), 25 mins. x 52 eps. (TV5), 25 mins. x 58 eps. (TV6), 25 mins. x 20 eps. (TV7), 30 mins. x 2 eps. (v), 25 mins. x 26 eps. (TV8).

Junko and Tanpei are the grandchildren of a mad inventor who produced a time machine, went off into history, and simply vanished. They're determined to find him, but they're not the only ones. The scandalously dressed villain Madame Margot, with her hapless sidekicks, Birba and Sgrinfia, are also on his trail, and on the trail of a massive diamond lost somewhere in time. The ending could be viewed as an anticlimax—the professor returns to the present under his own steam—but in this case the journey, with its slapstick perils, crazy creatures, and interventions by wicked but inept villains, is more than the destination.

Time Bokan was only the first chapter in an epic saga of insanity on every level: design, characterization, and plot. With often-cited similarities to *Wacky Races*, and machines and performances that went further and further over the top, Ippei Kuri produced the first series based for Tatsunoko and remained in charge throughout its increasingly silly but lovable progress to classic status.

Like Sunrise's BRAVE SAGA, both the crew and central concept of the series remained through successive sequels, with only superficial changes. Only the characters' looks and the wonderful machines, designed to spin off into toy merchandising, displayed any variation—the robots and vehicles became so lucrative that a new one was introduced every episode.

Its successor, *TB Series Yattaman* (1977), came only a week later. Ganchan, descendant of a line of inventors, has made his own robot car, Yatta One, and takes his girlfriend and mechanic for a celebratory meal. Unfortunately they go to a restaurant run by sexy Miss Doronjo and her comic sidekicks, Tonzura and Boyakei. They are members of a gang under orders to find a powerful artifact, the Dokurostone (Skullstone), which can locate hidden treasure and is really the head of a mighty extraterrestrial called Dokurobei, who is just using the crooks to retrieve it. Ganchan and his friends must stop the crooks, but the quest takes them all over the world and through time. Though the plot is an obvious respray, art directors Toyoo Ashida, Kazuhiko Itada, and Takashi Nakamura brought *visual* freshness and invention.

Once again, as one series ended another began, the following year's *TBS Zendaman* (1978). This time young Tetsu and his girlfriend Sakura race through time in their robots, Zendalion and Zendagorilla, to fight the trio of villains headed by sexy Miss Mujo. A short *Zendaman* movie premiered in spring 1980, but the new series *TBS Time Patrol Tai [Team] Otasukeman* was already on the air. In an achingly familiar setup, Miss Atasha, Dovalski, and Sekovitch are seeking an artifact that will enable the shadowy Tonmanomanto to dominate the world. Hikaru and Nana spring to the rescue in their increasingly incredible machines, chasing or chased by the villains through time and space. An *Otasukeman* movie was screened in spring 1981 as once again the new series *TBS Yattodetaman* had just begun on TV. Princess Domenica's rule is challenged

by the theft of the Cosmopavone, a magical bird whose powers (like Tezuka's SPACE FIREBIRD) can bring peace and healing. She calls on two of her ancestors, a boy and a girl from the 1980s, for help against hot-tempered Princess Mirenjo and her henchmen.

The sixth series, *TBS Gyakuten Ippatsuman* (1982, aka *Ippatsuman Returns*), revolved around Homuran and Harubo, owners of the time delivery company Timelease, who set off to make a delivery to another era and find themselves pursued by Munmun, Kosuinen, and Kyokanchin, representatives of rival firm Sharecowbellies, who are now calling themselves the Clean Aku Trio. Then Ippatsukiman shows up to help Timelease, and they realize that there's more to this job than they thought. The final series, *TBS Itadakiman* (1983), moves the starting point for the journey to Oshaka Academy, where the headmaster orders three students, Hoshi, Sagosen, and Hatsuo, to find the pieces of an artifact called the Oshakapuzzle, now scattered throughout the world. Meanwhile three "ronin" (students waiting to retake entrance exams) called Yanyan, Dasainen, and Tonmentan are also looking for the puzzle, which will give the finder strange powers. As before, the titular hero comes to the aid of the good guys.

Falling ratings brought the show to an end after reasonably long innings, though it returned to video once its young audience were old enough to rent. Members of the original crew reunited one last time for the *Wacky Races* homage *Time Bokan Royal Revival* (1993), which pits all seven trios of villains from the original series in a race against each other. The prize is supposedly the leading role in the next episode.

However, there was no next episode until *Thieving Kiramekiman* (2000, *Kaito Kiramekiman*), an eighth series that reordered the archetypes to make good-natured criminals the protagonists. The handsome Puff is sent back

500 years to our time to rescue his ancestor, Professor Rikkid. Everybody needs the treasure known as the Gold Eye, and Puff teams up with the pretty teenager Lips to form the Kiramekiman cat-burglar team. They are pursued by a trio of bumbling French cops, while Lips' own father is the chief of police—a combination of elements of CAT'S EYE and LUPIN III. This most recent incarnation in the franchise was shown on TV Tokyo. There was also an unrelated Fuji TV series *Time Travel Tondekeman* (1989), directed by Kunihiko Yuyama.

TIME STRANGER

1986. JPN: *Toki no Tabibito Time Stranger*. AKA: *Time Traveler Time Stranger*. Video. DIR: Mamoru Masaki. SCR: Atsushi Yamatoya, Mamoru Masaki, Toshio Takeuchi. DES: Moto Hagio, Koji Morimoto. ANI: Takuo Noda, Hiroshi Fukutomi, Toshio Hirata, Yoshiaki Kawajiri, Kunihiko Sakurai, Yasuomi Umezu. MUS: Ryoichi Kuniyoshi. PRD: Project Team Argos, Madhouse. 91 mins.

A minibusload of modern-day teenagers is hijacked by Jiro Agino, a time-traveler from the future, who drags them back to WWII Tokyo, and then to feudal Japan. They arrive at Azuchi Castle in 1582, just before the surprise attack that will/did/could result in the death of Nobunaga Oda. Jiro has determined that this is a critical moment in history, and that, had Nobunaga survived, Japan would have been spared the seclusion and stagnation of the Tokugawa period—forecasting that when Western powers arrived in the 19th century they would not have been able to treat Japan as a second-class nation. This in turn would have created a better political climate in the Pacific, and averted Japan's involvement in WWII! The gang is faced with a dilemma—to change history by warning Nobunaga (portrayed with a sympathy rare in his other anime appearances such as YOTODEN), or to keep quiet and risk dying in the coming "surprise" attack. Meanwhile, far-future assassin Toshito Kutajima arrives to terminate Jiro's meddling, while schoolgirl Tetsuko "Teko" Hayasaka unhelpfully falls in love with Nobunaga's page-boy Ranmaru. Sometimes confused with **GOSHOGUN** spinoff *Etranger*, this has more in common with **FIRE TRIPPER** minus the cute infant. Considering the famous names all over the crew (note **THEY WERE ELEVEN**'s Hagio designing alongside future **MEMORIES**-director Morimoto), it's a real mystery why this was never picked up for U.S. release. Based on a young adult SF novel by Taku Mayumura.

TIME TRIO
1988. JPN: *Zukkoke Sanningumi Zukkoke Jiku Boken*. AKA: *Bumbling Trio's Time Travel Adventure*. Video. DIR: Hidehito Umeda. SCR: Takao Koyama. DES: Kazuo Maekawa. ANI: Takashi Saijo. MUS: Masayuki Yamamoto. PRD: Tama. 57 mins.
Hachibe, Mochan, and Hakase are three young newshounds for their elementary school newspaper. While trying to spy on their pretty teacher, Yukiko, they are flung back into the Edo period where they meet another beautiful authority figure, this time a princess struggling to control her domains. Based on a best-selling children's book by Masayoshi Nasu. Compare to **ZEGUY**.

TIMID VENUS
1986. JPN: *Okubyo Venus*. Video. DIR: Hiroyuki Kadono. SCR: Koichi Arai. DES: Hiroyuki Kitakubo, Shingo Araki, Michi Himeno. ANI: Michi Himeno. MUS: Ami Osaki. PRD: Victor. 20 mins.
Young singer Hiromi is packed off to New York shortly after the release of her debut single and told to train hard for her first concert. A short anime made with a semidocumentary feel.

TO HEART
2000. TV series. DIR: Naohito Takahashi. SCR: Hiroshi Yamaguchi. DES: Yuriko Senba. ANI: Shichiro Kobayashi. MUS: N/C. PRD: KSS, Sun TV. 25 mins. x 13 eps.

Akari and her boyfriend, Hiroyuki, walk to high school together every day. In the evenings, Akari chats to her old friend Shiho on the phone, or the two girls hang out at restaurants and karaoke bars. Their classmates include a rich girl who belongs to the school's Black Magic Club and a robot maid sent to school to collect data on Japanese student behavior. So it's just another typical Japanese high school, and Hiroyuki is just another typical Japanese high-school boy who, despite being a nice quiet guy with no outstanding talents, finds himself surrounded by pretty girls who would do anything for him. But the trouble is, they don't seem to have much idea of anything *to* do. Episode one revolves around selecting seating assignments for the class, which involves much making and ripping up of lists. Episode two shows extended footage of Akari getting ready for a date with Hiroyuki, but those anticipating fan service should note she spends most of the time brushing her teeth and their date consists of drinking coffee and talking. Created by a group of artists calling itself **AQUAPLUS**, this is another anime based on a 1997 "love simulation game" (see also **SERAPHIM CALL**) for the PlayStation and designed to sell merchandise depicting the cute characters. The anime shifts the original's focus from Hiroyuki to Akari, presumably to lure in a female audience who wouldn't take kindly to being regarded as the "prize" in a game. It's not overtly sexual; rather it creates the fantasy life most lonely Japanese teenagers would apparently like to have, which, on the evidence of this show, is a quiet one.

TOBIDAZE BATCHIRI
1966. AKA: *Jump to It, Batchiri*. TV series. DIR: Kumi Yamamoto. SCR: Hitoshi Narihashi. DES: Mitsuteru Okamoto. ANI: Batchiri Group. MUS: Kunio Miyauchi. PRD: Nippon TV. 10 mins. x 132 eps.
The adventures of jug-eared schoolboy detective Batchiri, who can solve cases that baffle the police, thanks to his bril-

Equalizer Ryo Saeba metes out his own form of rough justice. Popular all over the world, **CITY HUNTER** flits between vigilante thriller and mild comedy. It shares the same setting as two other manga by creator Tsukasa Hojo, increasing the likelihood of cameos from the gentlewoman thieves of **CAT'S EYE** or the reformed assassin of *Angel Heart*. The live-action Hong Kong version featured Jackie Chan as Saeba. *See entry p. 61.*

City Hunter

© TSUKASA HOJO/SHUEISHA • YTV • SUNRISE

liantly ingenious mind. An early precursor of **CONAN THE BOY DETECTIVE**.

TOBIWAO IS TAKEN ILL
1982. JPN: *Tobiwao no Boya wa Byoki Desu*. AKA: *The Boy Tobiwa Is Taken Ill*. Movie. DIR: Kazuya Miyazaki. SCR: Tomiko Inui. DES: Renzo Kinoshita. ANI: Tatsuhiro Nagaki. MUS: Tadashi Kinoshita. PRD: Mushi. 19 mins.
Flying fish Tobiwao is happily frolicking in the waters of the Pacific when there is a bright flash in the sky and white ash starts to rain down on him. He dives for cover beneath the sea, but that night, he goes to his mother complaining of feeling very ill indeed. An anthropomorphic parable, set on March 1, 1954—the day of the infamous Bikini Bomb Test. The same event prompted producer Ishiro Honda to wonder if the test could do so much damage to fish, what would it do to other animals? The result of his speculation was released as *Godzilla* (1954).

TOKAIDO GHOST STORIES
1981. JPN: *Tokaido Yotsuya Kaidan*. AKA: *Ghost Stories of Tokaido/Yotsuya*. TV special. DIR: Hajime Suzuki. SCR: Sadatoshi Yasunaga. DES: N/C. ANI: N/C. MUS: N/C. PRD: TMS, Telecom, Fuji TV. 54 mins.

Set in 1636, this is the story of Iemon, who plans to kill his wife, Oiwa, hoping to inherit her wealth and marry his new, rich ladylove. Though his slow poisoning scheme pays off, he escapes justice in this world but not in the next, as Oiwa's shade returns to haunt him at every turn. A TV special based on Japanese ghost stories, for which one segment consisted of an animated tale.

TOKIMEKI MEMORIAL

1999. AKA: *Heartbeat Memorial*. Video. DIR: Hajime Kamegaki, Akira Nishizawa. SCR: Yosuke Kuroda. DES: Hideyuki Motohashi. ANI: Hideyuki Motohashi, Yasunori Tokiya. MUS: N/C. PRD: Studio Pierrot. 40 mins. x 2 eps.

Kirameki High School has a beautiful romantic legend. If on graduation day a girl confesses her love to a boy under the old tree in the school grounds, the two will have a long and happy life together. Twelve girls are in their last five months before graduation: Shiori Fujisaki, the principal character; her best friend Megumi Mikuhara; the beautiful but vain Mira Kagami; and the others consisting of Saki Nijino, Ayako Katagiri, Nozomi Kiyokawa, Yuko Asahina, Yuina Himoo, Yukari Koshikii, Yumi Saotome, and Miharu Tatebayashi. The first episode is essentially an introduction to all the characters, but in the second, as Rei Ijuin's Christmas party approaches, Shiori must decide whether to let her beloved know her true feelings.

Based on a 1994 dating game by Konami, which required the player to win one of the girls' hearts over a game span that was supposed to occupy three years of high school and end at graduation, this video spinoff matches the game story closely and uses the same voice actresses, though the character designs are slightly different. Launched for the PC Engine, the original game spun off ten further titles in PlayStation, Sega Saturn, Game Boy, PC, Mac, and arcade incarnations, plus a radio chat show, radio dramas, and a long list of merchandise.

TOKIMEKI TONIGHT

1982. AKA: *Heartbeat Tonight*. TV series. DIR: Hiroshi Sasakawa, Akinori Nagaoka, Tsutomu Shibayama, Teruo Kigure, Hideo Yoshisawa, Noboru Ishiguro, Tomomi Mochizuki. SCR: Toshio Okabe, Takao Koyama, Tomomi Tsutsui, Fuyunori Gobu, Akiyoshi Sakai. DES: Koi Ikeno. ANI: Keiichi Takahashi, Keiko Yoshimoto, Gisaburo Sugii. MUS: Kazuo Otani. PRD: Group Tac, Nippon TV. 25 mins. x 34 eps.

Ranze looks like any other teenage girl, but she's the daughter of a vampire and a female werewolf. You can imagine how that would cramp your style bringing friends home after school, so she leaves her family to try and live a normal life. But then, just as she's enjoying falling in love with school hunk Shinpeki, she begins to manifest powers of her own. Strict laws forbid creatures of the night from marrying humans, and it seems that everything's going to go wrong for her—but in the end, luckily, Shinpeki turns out to be the long-lost son of Satan. Based on the 1982 manga by **NURSE ANGEL LILIKA SOS**–creator Koi Ikeno.

TOKIO PRIVATE POLICE *

1997. JPN: *Tokio Kido Police*. AKA: *Tokio Mobile Police*. Video. DIR: Moriichi Higashi. SCR: Yu Yamato. DES: Harunaga Kazuki, Satoshi Teraoka. ANI: Harunaga Kazuki. MUS: An Fu. PRD: Beam Entertainment. 30 mins. x 2 eps.

In 2034, Tokyo is beset by a giant robot crime wave. Section One of the police's Robot Division is on hand to deal with the problems, but they spend most of their time screwing each other in the office. New recruit Kazuko manages to get through the whole of her team on day one, enthusiastically bonding with her new colleagues. This "parody" of **PATLABOR** misses everything that made the original so emotionally powerful—suppressed longings and unstated desires simply don't exist here—and offers nothing to replace the comedy, action, and humanity it jettisons. Ⓝ

TOKYO BABYLON *

1992. Video. DIR: Koichi Chiaki, Kumiko Takahashi. SCR: Tatsuhiko Urahata, Hiroaki Jinno. DES: Kumiko Takahashi. ANI: Kumiko Takahashi. MUS: Toshiyuki Honda. PRD: Animate Film. 50 mins., 55 mins.

Subaru Sumeragi lives in Tokyo with his twin sister, Hokuto. A fey, gentle young man, he's a psychic by heritage and by trade, often called on by the police to assist on investigations that stump all normal crime-fighting methods. Each of the two videos (the second appeared in 1994) focuses on one case: the first a murder for power and money that is complicated when a bereaved young woman, out for revenge, unleashes psychic forces she can't control; and the other a genuinely chilling look into the world of a psychopathic serial killer. The stories contrast Subaru's unworldly gentleness with the cynical and self-seeking city dwellers around him. The religious symbols are leftover 1980s fashion statements rather than deep philosophical references—a superficial quality only emphasized by a truly awful English-language musical interlude. The real importance of *TB* is its part in the movement of elements from girls' manga into the commercial mainstream—though the U.K. distributors did hype it by falsely claiming that the tape contained scenes of phone sex! Both videos are enjoyable in their own right but are only fragmentary glimpses of CLAMP's much larger manga universe, missing many of its facets. Subaru has a part in the earthshaking events of **X: THE MOVIE**, in which the genial vet who has been his friend, suitor, and mentor, reveals his darker side, and the ancestral links between their two families are finally resolved. *Ill. p. 439.*

TOKYO REVELATION *

1995. JPN: *Shin Megami Tensei: Tokyo Mokushiroku*. AKA: *True Goddess Reborn: Tokyo Revelation*. Video. DIR: Osamu Yamazaki. SCR: Mamiya Fujimura. DES: Kenichi Onuki. ANI: Minoru

Yamazawa. MUS: Hiroshi Ikeyori. PRD: JC Staff. 29 mins. x 2 eps.

Pale loner Akito Kobayashi sells his soul to Satan, and swears to assemble large quantities of the element Magnetite in order to open a gateway to hell. He transfers to a new school, where he swiftly turns all the local girls into vessels of demonic possession and sets his sights on class beauty Saki, whose pliant young body contains massive amounts of Magnetite. Ranged against him are a motley crew of schoolkids, including two ninja in disguise, a teen witch, and handsome occult hobbyist Kojiro. This junior version of UROTSUKIDOJI has sorcerous computer geeks summoning devils through the Internet, necromantic heavy petting, a harpy who's an obvious rip-off of DEVILMAN's Silene, a clueless cast who don't know their Hecate from their athame, and some of the cheesiest dialogue known to man, including, "It's not every day I meet ninjas who are demon slayers. . . . I wouldn't be surprised if you were the reincarnation of some great goddess." Kojiro is the reincarnation of Tokyo's guardian deity Masakado (see DOOMED MEGALOPOLIS), his golden retriever has been possessed by the Hound of Hell (see CARD CAPTORS), and, if the plot wasn't trashy enough for you, it's actually a remake—this is a slightly more faithful adaptation of the novel and computer game already available in anime form as DIGITAL DEVIL STORY. Before you can say "Buffy," Satan is stalking Tokyo, Kyoko's been excommunicated for performing sex magic, and there's a faint whiff of homoeroticism redolent of the later X: THE MOVIE, as Akito confesses his love for Kojiro, albeit in a doomed, unrequited sort of way. The whole thing is tied up in a fiendishly rushed ending, with the characters yelling plot details at each other while the credits roll over them.

In 2000, the franchise was revived to promote a new version of the game on the Nintendo Gameboy. In *Goddess Reborn Devichil* (*Shin Megami Tensei Devichil*), 11-year-old soccer-loving

schoolboy Setsuna flees indoors when rocks begin to rain from the sky. He meets token female Mirai Kaname and her scientist father, Kokai, who explains that the raining rocks are a sign that Magical King Lucifer has returned to terrorize the planet and is trying to break out of the parallel "magic" Earth to subdue the everyday world. Mirai, however, is one of the "Devil Children," a carrier of the "Devil Genome" that will allow her to fight Lucifer in the style of Go Nagai's *Devilman*. As demonstrated by the younger age group, the early morning broadcast, and the availability of the game in "Black" and "Red" editions, the new generation of the franchise has more in common with POKÉMON than with the story that originally inspired it. **LV**

TOKYO VICE *

1988. Video. DIR: Osamu Yamazaki. SCR: Minami Machi Bugyosho. DES: Kenichi Onuki. ANI: Osamu Tsuruyama. MUS: Karioka. PRD:, Minami Machi Bugyosho. 60 mins.

Teenagers Junpei, Akira, and Keiko get involved in corruption on a grand scale when one of them is slipped a computer disk in a Shinjuku club by someone whose life is just about to be terminated. The bad guys are prepared to do anything to recover the disk, including tracking Junpei with a military satellite, kidnapping his sister Kumiko, chasing him in a helicopter gunship, and suppressing all media coverage of the cataclysmic aftermath. As usual, the police (in the form of Inspector Sakamoto and his team) are some way behind the young heroes in getting to the root of the problem, which leads to an explosive showdown with the corrupt corporation's secret weapon, a heavily armed robot. Like its U.S. inspiration *Miami Vice*, TV flirts with low life but is basically clean-cut, cute, and earnest. The action (the main point of an action show) is rather patchy; apart from the admittedly good final fight, there's a motorcycle/helicopter chase and a shootout with some suits, and that's

your lot. We know that real investigators spend most of their time playing with computers and questioning suspects, but we don't necessarily want to watch the whole process.

TOM OF T.H.U.M.B. *

1967. JPN: *001/7 Oyayubi Tom*. AKA: *Tom Thumb, 001/7*. TV series. DIR: Yasuji Mori. SCR: Toshio Shino (translator). DES: N/C. ANI: Yasuji Mori, Takao Kasai. MUS: Yasei Kobayashi. PRD: Toei, Videocraft, NET. 25 mins. x 26 eps.

Secret agent Tom and his faithful assistant, Swinging Jack, are accidentally zapped by a Miniaturization Ray, and are now small enough to fit into pockets. This actually makes them more, not less, effective as secret agents, and they become employees of the Tiny Humans Underground Military Bureau. From their new secret hideaway inside a desk, they pop out in a tiny sportscar, ready to battle against MAD, an organization hellbent on world conquest.

A diminutive variant on James Bond, with the U.S. title a reference to *The Man From U.N.C.L.E.*, ToT was a coproduction between Toei Animation and the U.S. company Videocraft, made as a companion piece to THE KING KONG SHOW. The same companies also produced several other cartoons, including *The Mouse on the Mayflower* and *The Smokey Bear Show*. Among the many other "American" shows that technically qualify as anime are MIGHTY ORBOTS, the ROBOTECH sequel *Sentinels*, and THE STINGIEST MAN IN TOWN.

TOM SAWYER *

1980. JPN: *Tom Sawyer no Boken*. AKA: *Adventures of Tom Sawyer; Tom and Huck*. Movie, video, TV series. DIR: Hiroshi Saito, Shigeo Koshi, Takayoshi Suzuki. SCR: Akira Miyazaki, Mei Kato, Yoshiaki Tomita, Tadahiko Isogai, Takeshi Shise, Seijiro Kamiyama. DES: Shuichi Seki. ANI: Yoshishige Kosako, Yoshitaka Gokami, Noboru Takano, Michiyo Sakurai, Akio Sugino. MUS: Katsuhisa Hattori. PRD: Nippon Animation, Fuji TV. 25 mins. x 49 eps., 105 mins. (m).

Tom is a boy who lives in a small town on the banks of the Mississippi River in 19th-century America. He and his best friend, orphan Huck, hang out together and make mischief in and out of school. Their shenanigans include a balloon ride, a river trip, and a rescue of an innocent person from the false accusations of Indian Joe. Based on Mark Twain's 1876 novel, this WORLD MASTERPIECE THEATER series was edited into a feature-length movie entitled *Tom and Huck* for U.S. video release. An English dub of the series by Saban was shown as part of HBO's Family Showcase, alternating in the 7:30 a.m. timeslot with LITTLE WOMEN. Twain's follow-up, HUCKLEBERRY FINN, was also turned into an anime.

TOMATO-MAN

1992. JPN: *Sarada Ju Yushi Tomato Man.* AKA: *Tomato-man and the Knights of the Salad Table.* TV series. DIR: Hiroshi Sasakawa, Teppei Matsuura, Shinichi Watanabe, Hiromichi Matano. SCR: Masaaki Sakurai, Shikichi Ohashi. DES: Futako Kamikita, Yoshiko Hashimoto. ANI: Michio Shindo, Hiroshi Kagawa. MUS: N/C. PRD: Animation 21, TV Tokyo. 25 mins. x 50 eps.

The Kingdom of Salad is a beautiful dreamland where vegetables, fruits, and insects try, often unsuccessfully, to live together in peace and harmony. When the wicked Bug-Bug gang casts an evil sleep spell on beautiful Princess Peach, King Boo-Melon sends for "the Withered Plum," an old hermit believed to have magical powers, to awaken the princess from her eternal sleep. To help protect the king, Plum uses his magical powers to create a group of mighty warriors from ordinary food, the Knights of the Salad Table. Tomato-man, the last of the knights created by Plum, is the hero of the show. One of the few TV shows to attribute disruptive political intent to fruit and vegetables.

TOMORROW'S ELEVEN

1979. JPN: *Ashita no Yusha Tachi.* AKA: *Heroes of Tomorrow.* TV special. DIR: Kozo Morishita. SCR: Seiji Matsuoka. DES: Hiroshi Motomiya. ANI: Susumu Shiraume. MUS: N/C. PRD: Toho, Nippon TV. 85 mins.

In 1978, as the World Under-21 Soccer Championships draw near, amateur Jiro Ipponji is still living on a Hokkaido ranch with his sister Yuki, caring for his beloved horse, Golden Leg, and romancing his girlfriend, Yoko. The withdrawn loner is approached by Shin Mizuki and coach Matsumoto to play for Japan's national team. He agrees, becoming a formidable attacker. I think they make him leave his horse at home, though. Made as part of the hype for the 1979 championships, which were held in Japan. Compare to CAPTAIN TSUBASA.

TOMORROW'S JOE

1970. JPN: *Ashita no Joe.* AKA: *Rocky Joe.* TV series, Movie. DIR: Osamu Dezaki, Hideo Makino, Seiji Okuda, Yuki Kobayashi, Toshio Hirata. SCR: Shunichi Yukimuro, Tadaaki Yamazaki, Seiji Matsuoka, Haruya Yamazaki, Hiroshi Saito, Tsunehisa Ito. DES: Akio Sugino, Hiroaki Kaneyama, Shingo Araki. ANI: Akio Sugino, Hiroaki Kaneyama, Shingo Araki. MUS: Tadao Yagi (TV1); Ichiro Araki (TV2). PRD: Mushi, Fuji TV; TMS, Nippon TV. 25 mins. x 79 eps. (TV1), 153 mins. (m1), 25 mins. x 47 eps., 120 mins. (m2).

One of anime's great sporting legends, this is the story of Joe Yabuki, a 15-year-old from the wrong side of the tracks living by his wits in Tokyo, who meets Danbei, a once-great boxing coach now seeking refuge from his past in drink. Both see something they need in the other—Joe a source of free meals, Danbei a potentially great fighter and a reason to live. Under the cloak of training with Danbei, Joe carries on a life of petty crime, eventually getting caught and sent to prison. Over a year inside, he finally realizes that Danbei was offering him both friend-

ship and a future, and he carries on with the training regime the two had set up. On his release, he begins a successful boxing career. As he rises through the ranks, his main rival is Riki Ishi, a prison acquaintance, who dies tragically in a bout with Joe at the end of the series, leaving the champion devastated.

TJ is the most famous creation of Tetsuya Chiba, also known for WEATHER PERMITTING, I'M TEPPEI, and NOTARI MATSUTARO. His 1968 *Shonen Magazine* manga, drawn from a script by KARATE-CRAZY LIFE's Ikki Kajiwara, continued to attract readers after the series it inspired had ended, and in 1980, with a second series in production for Nippon TV, the first series was edited to feature length for theatrical release, providing background for new fans and a reminder of the story for older ones. Though many of the old crew returned to work on the sequel, *TJ2* also featured new directors, including Mizuho Nishikubo and Toshio Takeuchi. It opens as Joe, having given up boxing after Riki's death, is brought back to the ring through the encouragement of his friends. This time, as in the manga, the tragic death at the end of the series is Joe's own, and fans were inconsolable. The second movie, premiered in 1981, was an edit of this series. The title *Rocky Joe* was adopted for Western sale in an attempt to cash in on the popularity of Sylvester Stallone's live-action film series, obscuring the fact that Joe was there first. **Ⓥ**

TONDE MON PE

1982. JPN: *TondeMon Pe.* AKA: *Mon-Pe.* TV series. DIR: Shigetsugu Yoshida, Junzo Aoki, Hideharu Iuchi, Saburo Kawashima, Masaharu Okuwaki. SCR: Chifude Asakura, Yoshiaki Yoshida, Masaaki Sakurai, Kenji Terada. DES: Kazu Mitsui. ANI: Takao Kasai. MUS: Yuikihide Takekawa. PRD: Tokyo Movie Shinsha, TV Asahi. 25 mins. x 42 eps.

Fifteen-year-old country girl Mon-Mon dreams of being a fashion designer and gets a job as an au pair to a rising star designer, Mrs. Kano, her baby girl

PePe, and her silly writer husband. But PePe can make toys and animals do very odd things. Mon's employers don't seem to notice anything odd is going on, and she finds her dream job turning into a chaotically cute trial of wits she has no chance of winning. She's a sweet girl, hardworking and kind, but very unsophisticated and simply not used to walking teddy bears and talking stuffed animals. She eventually decides to leave her job and go home, but psychic baby PePe, who has come to love her, finds a way to make sure she stays.

TOPO GIGIO

1988. TV series. DIR: Shigeo Koshi, Noboru Ishiguro, Masahito Kitagawa, Shigeru Omachi. SCR: Noboru Ishiguro, Chiyu Tadaoki. DES: Susumu Shiraume. ANI: Tadaichi Iguchi, Hirokazu Ishino. MUS: Nobuyoshi Koshibe. PRD: Nippon Animation, TV Asahi. 25 mins. x 34 eps.

By the 25th century, mice have evolved into a sentient species, gaining bigger heads, shorter tails, and the power of speech. Topo Gigio is a mouse space pilot sent on an exploration mission who accidentally returns to the 20th century, before the establishment of peaceful diplomatic relations between humans and mice. Landing in Santa Catalina City, he finds that humans still think of mice as either pets or pests, cats are still the enemy, and mouse society is still underground, but a nine-year-old girl, Jean, learns his secret and helps him.

Created by the Italian author Maria Perego, the famous mouse was introduced to Japanese children in a series of adventures getting his friends into and out of trouble (compare to future cat DORAEMON). These included rescuing mouse rebel Kurt and his fat friend Per from numerous scrapes, foiling the plots of head cat Megalo, helping mouse inventor Doc with his devices, and even meeting with Dracula. After episode 21, the series was rebranded as *Dreaming Topo Gigio (Yume Miru Topo Gigio)*.

TOPPUKU VIOLENT RACERS

1996. JPN: *Toppuku Kyoso Kyoku*. AKA: *Symphony of Violent Racers in Battledress*. Video. DIR: Yoshimasa Yamazaki. SCR: Narihiko Tatsumiya. DES: Kenzo Koizumi. ANI: Kenzo Koizumi. MUS: N/C. PRD: Taki. 42 mins. x 2 eps.

The Sea Monkey biker gang fights over its turf. Yet another bikers-beat-each-other-up anime, this one based on a manga by Yu Furuzawa. Compare to **BOMBER BIKERS OF SHONAN**. **LV**

TOPSTRIKER

1991. JPN: *Moero Topstriker!* AKA: *Burn Topstriker; Enter the Topstriker*. TV series. DIR: Ryo Yasumura, Akira Kiyomizu, Shigeru Yamazaki, Masahito Kitagawa. SCR: Yoshiyuki Suga, Yoshimasa Takahashi. DES: Kazuyuki Okaseko. ANI: Kazuyuki Okaseko. MUS: N/C. PRD: Nippon Animation, TV Tokyo. 25 mins. x 49 eps.

Hikari Yoshikawa arrives in Italy to develop his soccer skills with the Columbus team under top trainer Bertini and Dr. Robson, who used to be a top-level English player—he is, as anyone acquainted with the current state of the English game would realize, rather old. Hikari has some problems with rival player Cesare but eventually leads the team to the final, losing with honor, and is selected by Robson for a new international team, the Jupiter Wings. This consists of talented players from all over the world who haven't been selected for their national teams. The aim is to compete with the best at the international level, but with so many strong personalities involved, it will take time and effort to get them to work together. The story has a similar premise to 1992's **FREE KICK FOR TOMORROW**, but without the focus on the family relationships of the hero; the presentation of the game itself was more realistic than in many earlier series. It was screened in France as *School for Champions*, with Hikari renamed Benjamin, Cesare called Mark, and almost every Japanese name removed from the credits—a yellow

Inspired by the actions of his heroes, a Japanese *tanuki* flies out to sea and fights off an invading army of pigs, stealing an enemy gun and using it to shoot at the images of Popeye and Stalin in the clouds. The nine-minute **WARTIME ANIME** *Aerial Ace*, was completed more than two years before Pearl Harbor and demonstrates all too well that Japan was expecting a coming conflict with American and the Soviet Union. The same tanuki character appeared in the earlier fairy tale *Chinkoro Peipei's Treasure Box* (1936). *See entry p. 438.*

Aerial Ace

card for local boy Thibault Chatel for crediting himself as director.

TORA-SAN: THE ANIME

1998. JPN: *Otoko wa Tsurai yo: Torajiro no Wasurenakusa*. AKA: *It's Tough to Be a Man: Torajiro's Forget-Me-Not*. TV special. DIR: Setsuko Shibunnoichi, Satoshi Dezaki. SCR: Tadao Hayashi. DES: Kenichiro Takai. ANI: Kenichiro Takai. MUS: Naoki Yamamoto. PRD: Eiken, TBS. 95 mins.

Torajiro Kuruma is an itinerant peddler, eternally unlucky in relationships but forever prepared to help others in need. In this case it is the singer Madonna Lily, who asks for his aid in Hokkaido but rejects his offer of love. A tragicomedy spun off from Yoji Yamada's long-running "Tora-san" series, which produced 48 movies, starting with *It's Tough to Be a Man* (1969, *Otoko wa Tsurai yo*) The franchise, arguably the most successful movie series on the planet, was thrown into chaos by the death of its leading man Kiyoshi Atsumi late in 1996. The character had a brief cameo, played by a double, in Yamada's live-action *The Man Who Caught the Rainbow* (1997), but this anime version can be seen as an attempt to move into a medium where the absence of the star would be less noticeable. The original was pastiched in the anthropomorphic anime **DORATARO**, and its 28th installment was shown on a double bill with **TAO-TAO THE PANDA**.

TOSHINDEN *

1996. JPN: *Toshinden*. Video. DIR: Masami Obari. SCR: Masaharu Amiya, Jiro Takayama. DES: Tsukasa Kotobuki, Kazuto Nakazawa, Masahiro Yamane. ANI: Hiroshi Kato. MUS: Kensuke Shina. PRD: Animate Film. 30 mins. x 2 eps.
Uranus, leader of a powerful secret organization cleverly called "The Organization," wants to build an army of indestructible, invincible warriors. To foil the plan, the world's indestructible, invincible warriors reunite. Eiji, Sophia, and tooth-rottingly cute little Ellis are among the chosen ones, but Uranus' minions are gradually picking off the opposition and time is running out. Yet another game-based clone in the **STREET FIGHTER II** mode—a large cast of two-dimensional video game "characters" brought to the screen in a cynical promotion, each given barely enough screentime to have a fight and use their little combat catchphrases or moves. Meanwhile, the big-haired Eiji embarks on a halfhearted quest for his missing brother, with risible attempts at depth resulting in immortal dialogue like, "We both know your brother killed my dad."

Obari's direction starts off well, with a line of soldiers aiming guns upstaged by a journalist aiming a camera. He pastiches the **AKIRA** manga as the robotic Sho takes on a U.S. aircraft carrier, then shifts the scene to a Chinatown setup redolent of his later **VIRUS**. But this remains an anime-by-numbers that ticks every perfunctory box of a game adaptation—including a female character in a shower scene (Sofia actually manages to put her clothes back on while jumping through a window), fights between allies engineered through "mind-control," and a big fight at a secret hideout (in this case, two nicely inconspicuous skyscrapers).

Ⓥ

TOUCH

1985. TV series, movies, TV special. DIR: Gisaburo Sugii, Hiroko Tokita, Naoto Hashimoto, Akinori Nagaoka. SCR: Yumiko Takahoshi, Shigeru Yanagawa, Tomoko Konparu. DES: Minoru Maeda, Shichiro Kobayashi. ANI: Yasuo Maeda, Masako Goto, Hajime Watanabe. MUS: Hiroaki Serizawa. PRD: Toho, Group TAC, Fuji TV. 25 mins. x 101 eps. (TV), 93 mins., 80 mins., 85 mins. (m), 60 mins. x 2 (TVm).
When his popular twin brother is killed in an accident, Tatsuya tries to fill his shoes, both on their high-school baseball team and romantically with Minami, the team's manager. A moving and involving story based on the 1981 manga in *Shonen Sunday* by **SLOW STEP**–creator Mitsuru Adachi. *Touch* the anime was a huge hit, both in Japan, where its rating topped 30%, and in Europe. The series transferred into theaters for three movie editions—*T: Ace without a Backstop* (1986, *Senbango no Nai Ace*), *T2: Goodbye Gift* (1986, *Sayonara Okurimono*), and *T3: You Are Too Right* (1987, *Kimi wa Torisugi Daa to ni*)—ending with the team about to play the national championship finals and Tatsuya asking himself if he has succeeded either on the field or in love. The closing credits of the series rolled without showing fans the outcome of the big game, or giving answers to either of Tatsuya's questions. Over a decade later, released in a period that also saw the long-delayed ending of **KIMAGURE ORANGE ROAD**, the TV special *Miss Lonely Yesterday—Are kara, Kimi wa . . .* (1998, *MLY: Since Then, You've . . .*) takes place three years after that fateful match and shows us how Tatsuya and Minami have dealt with life and their own relationships outside the protective routines of school days. Series director Sugii and original designer Maeda returned for this follow-up. After it gained outstanding 23.3% ratings, it was only a matter of time before a further follow-up was announced: *Crossroads: Whereabouts of the Wind* (2001, *Crossroads: Kaze no Yukue*). In this latest installment, Tatsuya joins the

minor U.S. team the Emeralds, and he soon finds himself courted by the team owner's young daughter, Alice Vormont. Meanwhile, Minami becomes a sports photographer's assistant, and the two nonlovers' paths are fated to cross once again. Adachi's baseball manga also reached anime in **H2**, **MIYUKI**, and **NINE**.

TOURNAMENT OF THE GODS *

1997. JPN: *Toshin Toshi II*. AKA: *Battle City II*. Video. DIR: Takehiro Nakayama. SCR: Takehiro Nakayama. DES: Takehiro Nakayama. ANI: Takehiro Nakayama. MUS: N/C. PRD: Pink Pineapple, KSS. 30 mins. x 3 eps.
At the Battle Tournament, fighters struggle to become proclaimed the supreme "Battle God." The victor of each gladiatorial bout gets the possessions of the vanquished, including their female partner. Sid, a mere fourth-level fighter, enters the tournament not because he wants to find his way through the maze and become an "angel eater" (use your imagination), but rather because he wants to win the hand of his beloved Azuki. Even though Sid wins the day with his pure heart, he is infected with a bizarre drug by the evil Aqruss and becomes subject to incredible sexual urges that must be satisfied by copulation with angels. Though the superior **SEXORCIST** got there first, this erotic anime is based on a computer game that came even closer to the original inspiration—even the Japanese title is designed to look almost, but not quite, exactly like **TOSHINDEN**. ⓁⓃⓋ

TOWARD THE TERRA *

1980. JPN: *Terra e*. Movie. DIR: Hideo Onchi. SCR: Hideo Onchi, Chiho Shioda. DES: Masami Suda. ANI: Masami Suda. MUS: Masaru Sato. PRD: Toei. 119 mins.
Earth is a distant memory. Five hundred years after a revolution replaced human government with computer-aided totalitarianism, machines control every aspect of human life. Artificially created children are examined on

reaching adulthood—telepaths are weeded out and destroyed. These "Mu" rejects marshal their strength in a desperate attempt to escape this hostile environment. They need a dynamic leader who can take them to a world of their own, where they can live without fear of persecution. Meanwhile the computers declare that a fugitive Mu is at large, and Keith, one of the elite caste who work for the computers, realizes that his servant Jonah is more than he seems to be.

Keiko Takemiya, author of SONG OF WIND AND TREES, wrote this science-fiction epic for *Manga Shonen* in 1977, and the anime remains close to the original style—boys' manga from a girls' artist. Despite the old-fashioned character designs, the film has held up well. The story handles familiar science fiction concepts with assurance: Orwellian social and political oppression, computers that dictate humankind's every move, mutant monsters shunned and hunted by humans, and pilgrims braving danger for a freer world. The film does not shy away from death, and, though violence and gore are kept low-key, some scenes are disturbing. **Ⓝ**

TO-Y

1987. Video. DIR: Mamoru Hamazu. SCR: Izo Hashimoto. DES: Naoyuki Onda. ANI: Naoyuki Onda. MUS: Masayuki Matsuura. PRD: Studio Gallop. 60 mins.
To-Y, leader of the up-and-coming band Gasp, has an intense rivalry with another young musician, Yoji. An ambitious manager, Miss Kato, tries to use this to persuade him to dump his band and let her manage his solo career. She plays him and Yoji off against each other and threatens to stop Gasp playing a big open-air concert that is vital to their career. In the end To-Y decides that playing his own kind of music with his own kind of people is more important than manufactured pop success, and this commitment pays off when he and Gasp set up their own gig near the open-air concert and draw a good crowd. An enjoyable pop soap opera

based on Atsushi Kamijo's 1985 manga from *Shonen Sunday Comics Wide*, it had added cred thanks to music director Matsuura, a member of hit band PSY-S, who also have a single on the soundtrack, along with Zelda, Barbee Boys, Street Sliders, Kujira, and more.

TP TIME PATROL BON

1989. TV series. DIR: Kunihiko Yuyama. SCR: Shunichi Yukimuro. DES: Tsukasa Fusanai. ANI: Tsukasa Fusanai. MUS: Hiroshi Tsutsui. PRD: Studio Gallop. 25 mins. x 26 eps.
A lackluster TIME BOKAN rip-off from DORAEMON-creators Fujiko-Fujio, in which Japanese schoolboy Heibon is enlisted in the efforts of the time patrol to keep the past out of trouble. Compare to FLINT THE TIME DETECTIVE.

TRAGEDY OF BELLADONNA

1973. JPN: *Kanashimi no Belladonna.* Movie. DIR: Eiichi Yamamoto. SCR: Eiichi Yamamoto, Yoshiyuki Fukuda. DES: Kuni Fukai. ANI: Gisaburo Sugii, Shinichi Tsuji, Yasuo Maeda. MUS: Nobuhiko Sato. PRD: Mushi. 89 mins.
In medieval France, country-boy Jean falls in love with country-girl Jeanne. As part of a strange ritual, the local landlord forces himself on Jeanne, and then allows his soldiers to gang rape her. Jean's hand is cut off when he fails to raise enough funds for the war coffers. Losing faith in God, Jeanne starts to have conversations with the Devil. Both Jean and the villagers throw her out, believing her to be possessed, and the disillusioned girl devotes herself to the Devil. Based on the 1862 novel *La Sorcière* by Jules Michelet, it adapts the story of Joan of Arc for an adult arthouse audience, using a combination of still frames and full animation deliberately aimed at breaking free of the full-animation mold and extending anime's "artistic" potential. Compare this with THE SENSUALIST, aimed at the same kind of artsy audience, and HEROIC LEGEND OF ARSLAN, which uses the still-frame device with considerable artistic invention purely to reduce costs. It is the last of three films made

for an adult audience by Mushi, though before production began, Osamu Tezuka had already lost control of the company. New president Eiichi Kawabata appointed Yamamoto to direct *Belladonna*, and the result is different in mood and tone from ARABIAN NIGHTS and CLEOPATRA: QUEEN OF SEX, made by Mushi under Tezuka. **Ⓝ**

TRANSFORMERS *

1985. JPN: *Tatakae Cho Robot Seimetai Transformers.* AKA: *Fight Super Living Robots Transformers.* TV series, movie. DIR: (Japan) Takayuki Nakano, Shoji Tajima (TV1–2), Katsutoshi Sasaki, Takao Yoshizawa (TV3–5), Mika Iwanami (*BW*), Osamu Sekita (*Car-Robot*). SCR: (Japan) Katsushige Hirata (translator, TV1–2), Keisuke Fujikawa (TV3–5) Tomohiro Ando (v), Mika Iwanami (*BW*). DES: (Japan) (TV1–2), Ban Magami (TV3–5, v). ANI: N/C. MUS: Shiro Sagisu (TV1–2), Kazunori Ishida (TV3–5, v). PRD: Toei, Nippon Animation, Toei; TV Asahi; TV Tokyo. 25 mins. x 64 eps. (TV1), 25 mins. x 30 eps. (TV2), 25 mins. x 35 eps. (TV3), 25 mins. x 35 eps. (TV4), 25 mins. x 35 eps. (TV5), 25 mins. x 36 eps. (*Beast Wars* TV1), 25 mins. x 36 eps. (*BW* TV2), 25 mins. x 36 eps. (*BW* TV3), 25 mins. x 39 eps. (*Car-Robot*), 25 mins. x N/D eps. (*Powerful Cars*), N/D mins. (m).
Far out in the galaxy is a planet where life has evolved in mechanical, rather than organic, form: Cybertron, a world of intelligent transforming robots. Two forces struggle for control of the planet—the evil Destrons (Decepticons in the U.S. version) led by Galvatron (Megatron in the U.S. version), and the heroic Cybertrons (Autobots), led by Convoy (Optimus Prime). The energy that sustains the planet is running out and the good guys build a huge starship, the Ark, to look for new energy sources. The Destron too have their own starship, and after their plotting leads to both ships being flung far back in time to Earth, good and bad robots are buried under the crust of our planet until, in the 20th century, they are

awakened by the eruption of a volcano. Remodeling themselves to allow transformation into automobiles, jets, and other indigenous technology so as to conceal their presence from the local population, they plan to carry on their war on Earth. The Cybertrons team up with a few humans who stumble across their base, but the Destrons see humankind as inferiors to be enslaved or removed.

A U.S.–Japanese coproduction and the POKÉMON of its day, *Transformers* was originally made to order by Toei from scripts and designs prepared in the U.S. It was based on a toy line by Takara that was not originally known as *Transformers* until it was licensed to Hasbro for Western markets. Though nothing particularly new (MACROSS was way ahead of the game with transforming robots) or believable (a consistent sense of scale disappearing for good), the concept of two-toys-in-one wormed its way into boys' hearts, and there it stayed.

Transformers: The Movie (1986) was notable for a voice cast including Orson Welles, Eric Idle, and Leonard Nimoy. It moved the action back to the robots' homeworld in 2005. Supposedly designed to bridge the gap between the first and second series, it was not shown in Japan, creating the first wobbles of confusion that would eventually split the franchise into four distinct and contradictory continuities. Optimus Prime dies, handing on leadership of the Cybertrons to Ultra Magnus, who in turn passes on the leadership to Rodimus Prime. On the dark side, Megatron is remodeled by the mighty Unicron, an even nastier Force of Evil that goes around the galaxy eating planets, into a new leader named Galvatron—possibly after his Japanese self, who appeared in a new TV series the same year.

Transformers 2010 (1986) continued the story without reference to the movie continuity, ending with another heroic self-sacrifice for Convoy and featuring a whole range of new transforming toys. The format of "new

transformations to fight new battles" was set, and from here on the complications multiplied, with U.S. and British comics from Marvel taking the story in separate directions, while the animated version continued in Japan. Originated completely in Japan, the third series, *Transformers Headmasters* (1987), has the goodies led by Fortress Maximus and Galvatron still leading the Destrons, as the search for new energy sources goes on across the galaxy.

The fourth series, *Transformers Chojin Master Force* (1988), introduces a new breed of robots, known as Pretenders, that can mix with human beings. The Destron have been driven off Earth, but under their leader Metalhawk, the few remaining Cybertron Pretenders are fighting to defend humans from a demonic force. The transformations that sold toys were still paramount, with the robot characters changing into other forms such as starfighters. The fifth season, *Transformers: Victory* (1989), focuses around Star Saber, the Galaxy's greatest swordsman, who leads the Cybertron to protect Earth from the menace of Deathsaurus.

Transformers Z[one] (1990), in which a supernatural evil has resurrected the Destron, was canceled, and instead it was released straight to video as a 25-minute special. The series returned with a vengeance as *Beast Wars* (1998) on TV Tokyo, which reduplicated its checkered origins for a whole new generation. Though now using computer animation (from *ReBoot* creators Mainframe) the franchise began once more as a U.S.–Japan coproduction, which was then continued in Japan as the rebranded *Beast Wars Neo* (1999) and *Beast Machines* (2000). A twist was borrowed from *Jurassic Park*: as the two opposing robot ships crashed on planet Gaea and the good guys merged with local animals, while the bad guys linked up with fossil dinosaur DNA, enabling the protagonists to transform into cyber-versions of the local fauna both alive and extinct. The Destron

(Predacon in the English version) under souped-up T-Rex Galvatron (Megatron) want the planet's mysterious energy source, and the Cybertron (Maximals) under Live-Convoy (giant gorilla Optimus Primal) mean to stop them.

Transformers: Car-Robot (2000) returned to cel animation and the basic vehicle-to-robot transformation on which the series originally made its name. At the beginning of 2001, it was rebranded as *Transformers: Powerful Cars*. With the concept still selling toys to a new generation of six-year-old fans, and "vintage" 1980s items acquiring collectible status, it seems the *Transformers* concept will run and run. Edits of various series were also rebroadcast as seven "TV specials" throughout the period and were also shown as *Beast Wars* "movies" in 1998 and 1999.

TREASURE ISLAND *

1965. JPN: *Shin Tarakajima; Dobutsu Takarajima*. AKA: *New Treasure Island; Animal Treasure Island*. TV special. DIR: Osamu Tezuka (TVm), Hiroshi Ikeda (m1), Osamu Dezaki, Toshio Takeuchi, Hideo Takayashiki (TV1). SCR: Osamu Tezuka (TVm), Satoshi Iijima, Hiroshi Ikeda (m1), Haruya Yamazaki, Hajime Shinozaki (TV1). DES: Osamu Tezuka (TVm), Yasuji Mori (m1), Akio Sugino (TV1). ANI: Gisaburo Sugii (TVm), Yasuji Mori (m1), Akio Sugino (TV1). MUS: Isao Tomita (TVm), Naoki Yamamoto (m1), Kentaro Haneda (TV1). PRD: Mushi, Fuji TV (TVm), Toei (m1); Tokyo Movie Shinsha, Nippon TV (TV1). 52 mins. (TVm), 78 mins. (m1), 25 mins. x 26 eps. (TV1), 90 mins. (m2).

Jack the wolf sea-pirate is killed in a harbor inn. The innkeeper's rabbit son, Jim, finds a treasure map on the old sea-wolf and sets out to find the booty, berthing on a ship crewed by other animals, chartered by the deer Dr. Livesay and financed by the pig Squire Trelawney. He befriends Silver, another wolf, who is revealed as the leader of the local pirates when they seize control of the ship. Eventually, the pirates find the island on the map and go in search of buried treasure. The anime then deviates from Robert Louis Stevenson's original 1881 story, in a style that not only contains elements of creator Osamu Tezuka's occasional heavy-handed moralizing, but also his genius. As the animals near the treasure, they lose their anthropomorphic characteristics, devolving back to a feral state and running off into the jungle. Eventually, only Silver and Jack are left, and Silver struggles between the two states. Reasoning that no treasure is worth losing one's "humanity" to animal greed, Silver and Jack leave the treasure behind. This anthropomorphic adaptation should not be confused with Shima Sakai and Osamu Tezuka's 1947 manga *Shin Takarajima*, which shares the title but not the concept. Some sources list this as the first-ever anime "TV special," a somewhat pointless distinction since it was not the first one-shot anime to be broadcast—see **INSTANT HISTORY**. The U.S. release was colorized for Fred Ladd by animators in Seoul, who ensured that it was the South Korean flag, not the Japanese one, that the animals accidentally raise in a throwaway visual gag.

Hiroshi Ikeda's *Animal Treasure Island* (1971, *Dobutsu Takarajima*) deviated further from the original. The human Jim Hawkins and his mouse companion Lex set sail in a toy boat, pursued by a porcine Long John Silver (perhaps thanks to animator Hayao Miyazaki, who worked on the production). Jim also joins forces with a third party in search of the map, Captain Flint's granddaughter Cathy. At the climax, the treasure is found to be at the bottom of a drained lake, a conceit later reused in Miyazaki's **CASTLE OF CAGLIOSTRO** and ripped off in other anime, including **LADIUS** and **BEAST WARRIORS**. It was released in the U.S. as just plain *Treasure Island*, coincidentally featuring many of the same voice actors from the U.S. dub of the earlier version.

A more faithful version came in the form of the TV series *Treasure Island* (1978), director Dezaki's follow-up to his **NOBODY'S BOY** for TMS. This version restored the human characters from the original but did insist on giving Jim Hawkins a leopard cub for a pet. As well as directing, Dezaki provided storyboards under his pseudonym of Makura Saki, and this version was also reedited into a "movie" release, with Takeuchi credited as director and Dezaki as assistant. The series has been screened in Europe and run in Spanish on Puerto Rican TV.

TREASURES OF THE SNOW
1983. JPN: *Alps Monogatari: Watashi no Annette*. AKA: *My Annette: Story of the Alps*. TV series. DIR: Kozo Kusuba. SCR: Kenji Yoshida. DES: Issei Takematsu. ANI: Issei Takematsu, Eimi Maeda, Yoshiharu Saito. MUS: Ryohei Hirose. PRD: Nippon Animation, Fuji TV. 25 mins. x 48 eps.
In the remote Swiss village of Rossiniere, local bully Lucien causes Annette's younger brother Dani to fall into a valley and break his leg. The 13-year-old Annette vows revenge on Lucien, determined to damage his life in any way she can, although she eventually realizes that a truly good person should forgive others, even if they do wrong to them. Based on the 1950 children's book with a heavy Christian subtext by Patricia M. St. John, the anime version added many sequences not found in the original story, taking several episodes, for example, to cover the years leading up to the fateful leg-breaking incident. Compare to another **WORLD MASTERPIECE THEATER** Alpine story, Johanna Spyri's **HEIDI**.

TREE IN THE SUN, A
2000. JPN: *Hidamari no Ki*. TV series. DIR: Gisaburo Sugii, Rei Mizuno. SCR: Tatsuhiko Urahata. DES: Marisuke Eguchi. ANI: Noriyuki Fukuda, Masahiro Kitazaki. MUS: Reiko Matsui. PRD: Madhouse, Nippon TV. 25 mins. x 25 eps.
At the end of the Tokugawa period, as Americans enter feudal Japan, two young men come of age. Manjiro Ibu-

Haruka has a reputation for his excellent rapport with patients, but will he ever win the heart of the pretty nurse Miyuki? *See entry p. 94.*

Doctor Surprise

© FUJIHIKO HOSONO/SHOGAKUKAN • FUJI TV • SPE VISUAL WORKS • ST. PIERROT

tani is a samurai through and through, beholden to his lord and obliged to lay down his life before his honor. But Manjiro's code is put to the test by a succession of humiliations, such as guarding the U.S. consul and commanding a unit composed of lowly farmers. Eventually, Manjiro becomes one of the fundamentalists who refuse to modernize (see **OI RYOMA!**); he is unable to survive in the brave new world of the late 19th century. But Ryoan, the doctor who tends his wounds, is very different. Ryoan has studied Western-style medicine and appreciates all the good that can be learned from the foreign powers. Both love their country and want to help their people, but in very different ways—compare to **SANCTUARY**, which similarly observes life from two very different perspectives. Based on the 1981 manga by Osamu Tezuka and partly inspired by the life of his own great-grandfather, Ryoan Tezuka, a 19th-century doctor.

TRIANGLE *
1998. JPN: *Terra Story*. Video. DIR: Yukihiro Makino. SCR: Yutaka Hidaka. DES: Hiro Asano. ANI: Hiro Asano. MUS: N/C. PRD: Daiei. 30 mins. x 2 eps.
Nineteen-year-old Keisuke gets a whirl-

wind education in the art of love from several enthusiastic ladies. Will they help him win the woman of his dreams? And will she mind some extra company? Based on a computer game, so the answers are probably yes and no. **Ⓝ**

TRIANGLE SESSION *

2001. JPN: *Chance! Triangle Session.* Video. DIR: Susumu Kudo. SCR: Kazuhiko Soma. DES: Fumie Muroi. ANI: Kunio Kazuki, Yumiko Ishii. MUS: Avex, Goro Matsui. PRD: Madhouse, TV Tokyo. 25 mins. x 13 eps.

A group of girls hope to make it as performers—16-year-old street busker Yuki, large-breasted 17-year-old Akari, and prissy company director's daughter Nozomi. Based on a 1999 radio drama.

TRIGUN *

1998. JPN: *Trigun.* TV series. DIR: Satoshi Nishimura. SCR: Yosuke Kuroda. DES: Takahiro Yoshimatsu. ANI: Yoshimitsu Ohashi. MUS: Tsuneo Imahori. PRD: Madhouse, TV Tokyo. 25 mins. x 26 eps.

A space Western in the style of EAT-MAN, set in one of those star systems that look exactly like the fantasy American West, if you ignore the two suns and the presence of a pair of female insurance investigators. Derringer Meryl and Stungun Millie, both as cute as pie, are there to keep an eye on a one-man destruction machine named Vash the Stampede, to try and minimize the collateral damage and expense of his shootouts. But Vash, a fabled gunman chased by every bounty hunter in the area, is not just another bad guy. He avoids killing at any cost and only fires off one of his mighty weapons to prevent injury to others. When you get right down to it, he's just a skinny geek with spiky hair and a good nature, whose main passions in life are food and girls. With hot lead flying from just about every other direction, Vash doesn't fire a single shot until episode five. He also raises issues such as exploitation of natural resources and the ethics of murder.

And in Nicholas Wolfwood, a sexy young Christian priest whose weapons (wielded only in a good cause) include a portable confessional and a huge cross packed with weaponry, he's created an unusual antagonist. Later episodes gain a darker tone, as it is revealed that the terraforming of the desert planet has stalled, and that the world will become uninhabitable unless Vash can repair the wrecked Seed Ships. Ranged against him are his real enemies, the Gung-Ho Guns, determined to blacken his reputation and keep him from gaining any support. Based on Yasuhiro Nightow's original manga in *Young King Ours.* **Ⓥ**

TRITON OF THE SEA

1972. JPN: *Umi no Triton.* TV series, movie. DIR: Yoshiyuki Tomino. SCR: Seiji Matsuoka, Masaki Tsuji, Yuki Miyata, Chikara Matsumoto, Minoru Onotani. DES: Osamu Tezuka. ANI: Akiyoshi Hane. MUS: Yoshimasa Suzuki. PRD: Animation Staff Room, Westcape; Office Academy. 25 mins. x 27 eps. (TV), 74 mins. (m).

Poseidon rules the depths of the sea cruelly, imposing his will through armies of vicious creatures. Little Triton's parents died resisting him, and now the boy carries on their struggle, helped by the intelligent and gentle female dolphin Lukar and by little mermaid Pipi. *Triton* began life as a 1969 manga in the *Sankei Shinbun* and was first animated as the unreleased eight-minute pilot *Blue Triton* (1971, *Aoi Triton*). Taken from Osamu Tezuka by skullduggery behind-the-scenes, both *Triton* and WANSA-KUN may have been birthed by the ASTRO BOY creator, but they were reared by other hands.

TRI-ZENON

2000. JPN: *Muteki Trizenon.* TV series. DIR: Takashi Watabe, Matsuo Asami, Hiroshi Kimura. SCR: Katsumi Hasegawa, Takao Yoshioka. DES: Naomi Miyata, Rei Nakahara. ANI: Naomi Miyata, Naoko Yamamoto. MUS: Kenji Kawai. PRD: Ganges, Kadokawa, TBS. 25 mins. x 22 eps.

"Hot-blooded and straightforward" Akira Kamui lives with his father and kid brother, Ai. His mother is mysteriously missing, and Japan is under threat from alien invaders. To fight the enemy, Akira has help from his childhood friend Kana, with whom he constantly squabbles, his dog Gon, the enigmatic but cute Shizuku, and sisters Uma and Riku (complete opposites), as well as Rama, a girl from an old Japanese family, and Umu, the standoffish singer of a local amateur band. Akira's rival Jin, who is strong, handsome, cool, and really nice, and Jin's sister Ena make up the rest of the team. Conceived as a multimedia project by Rui Araizumi, its publicity claims that *Tri-Zenon* will simultaneously encompass manga, anime, and novels, with each freestanding enough to be enjoyed independently, but together forming a complex interweaving story. A man's reach should exceed his grasp, but this may be rather too ambitious for the creator and team that gave us SLAYERS.

TROUBLE CHOCOLATE

1999. TV series. DIR: Tsuneo Tominaga. SCR: Hideki Sonoda. DES: Sachiko Hikabe. ANI: Robot, Junichi Takaoka. MUS: N/C. PRD: AIC, TV Asahi. 25? mins. x 20 eps.

Timid teenager Cacao, a student at the Microgrand Academy, spends more time lusting after gorgeous green-haired Hinano next door than studying, even though the classes on offer include magic. His magic professor, Professor Garner, reveals that, since he's over 120 years old, it's time for him to stop goofing around and move on to the next stage of his magical education. As Cacao slowly starts to regain his memory, he recalls that not only has he already achieved his ends with Hinano, but also isn't quite as human as she seems. Most males forget how old they are at some point, but very few forget who they've slept with, so Cacao isn't the brightest apple in the barrel, and his continuing progress may be problematic.

TROUBLED TIMES

1991. JPN: *Michiteru Kuru Toki no Muko ni.* AKA: *Toward a Time of Trouble.* TV special. DIR: Eiko Toriumi. SCR: Eiko Toriumi. DES: Takayuki Goto. ANI: Hisatoshi Motoki. MUS: Teruhiko Sato. PRD: Studio Pierrot, Nippon TV. 80 mins.

It's a fantasy adventure as tribal boy Bokudo, his red-deer guardian spirit, and the chieftain's pretty daughter Faya go hunting in the Gobi Desert. A one-shot adaptation of Koji Suzuki's novel *Paradise*, which won the 1991 Japan Fantasy Novel Award.

TRUSTY GINJIRO

1991. JPN: *Koha Ginjiro.* Video. DIR: Koichi Ishiguro. SCR: Hirokazu Mizude. DES: Kazuya Takeda. ANI: Kazuya Takeda. MUS: N/C. PRD: Animate Film, Visual 80. 45 mins. x 3 eps.

After the death of his elder brother, Ginjiro Yamazaki appoints himself his parents' protector. Transferred to a new school, he gets into a lot of fights, as one might expect in an anime from **MY SKY**–creator Hiroshi Motomiya, this one based on a 1975 manga originally serialized in *Shonen Jump.* **V**

TSURU-HIME

1990. JPN: *Tsuru Hime Jaaaa!* AKA: *Princess Tsuru, Crane Princess.* TV series. DIR: Tameo Ogawa, Yoshihiro Yamaguchi, Yoshiko Sasaki, Shigeru Ueda, Koichi Sasaki. SCR: Hirokazu Mizude, Tadashi Hayakawa, Tameo Ogawa. DES: Yoshiko Tsuchida. ANI: Hiromi Muranaka. MUS: N/C. PRD: Aubec, Nippon TV. 17 mins. x 67 eps.

The ugly Princess Tsuru makes life hell for everyone in the samurai-era Hagemasu Castle. This gag anime was based on the manga in *Margaret* magazine by Yoshiko Tsuchida.

TSURUPIKA HAGEMARUKUN

1988. AKA: *Little Baldy Hagemaru.* TV series. DIR: Hiroshi Sasakawa, Tetsuo Yasumi, Tsukasa Sunaga, Hiroyuki Sasaki, Teruo Kigure, Koichi Sasaki, Junji Nishimura. SCR: Masaaki Sakurai. DES: Munekatsu Fujita. ANI: Akira Kawa-

jima, Katsuhiko Yamazaki. MUS: Kuni Kawauchi. PRD: Shinei Doga. 25 mins. x 58 eps.

In this adaptation of the four-panel gag strip by Shinbo Nomura, ten-year-old brat Hagemaru Hageda causes mischief all over his small Japanese suburb.

TWD EXPRESS: ROLLING TAKEOFF

1987. Video. DIR: Kunihiko Yuyama. SCR: Izo Hashimoto. DES: Kazuyuki Kobayashi. ANI: Kazuyuki Kobayashi. MUS: Minoru Yamazaki. PRD: Gakken, Shochiku. 55 mins.

Space cargo workers Ken Kato, Duke Stern, and Ivan Sernikov run the Tiger Wolf Dragon Express service, but they land themselves in big trouble when they rescue the beautiful android Rina. She is being pursued by the evil Baron Gohdam, who wants her so he can seize control of the superpowerful Hydra. Based on a manga in *Comic Nora* by Yuki Hijiri, it was also shown in some theaters on a double bill with the **MAPS** movie.

TWELVE MONTHS *

1980. JPN: *Mori wa Ikiteiru.* AKA: *The Forest Is Alive.* Movie. DIR: Kimio Yabuki, Tetsuo Imazawa. SCR: Tomoe Takashi, Kimio Yabuki. DES: Yasuhiro Yamaguchi. ANI: Takashi Abe, Takao Kasai, Shinya Takahashi. MUS: Vladimir Grifutsov. PRD: Toei. 65 mins.

Sent out to collect spring flowers in midwinter by the wicked queen, Anya believes her life is lost, but she is saved by the spirit of her mother, who chases the snow from the forest. Anya is helped by the twelve spirits of the months of the year, each one a handsome prince, and within an hour, the once-barren winter wood is awash with the colors of spring. A Cinderella-like fairy tale based on a story by Soviet poet Samuel Marshack and featuring powerful orchestrations from the Leningrad Symphony Orchestra.

24 EYES

1980. JPN: *Nijushi no Hitomi.* TV special. DIR: Akio Jissoji, Shigetsugu Yoshida. SCR: Sumie Tanaka. DES: Kazuyuki

Honma. ANI: Shunsaburo Takahata, Hiromi Yokoyama, Kanetsugu Kodama. MUS: Takeo Watanabe. PRD: TMS, Fuji TV. 84 mins.

Young Miss Oishi is the new school teacher on the island of Shodoshima in 1928. When she injures her leg, her 12 students visit her at home and discover that she cycles nine miles every day to teach them. Miss Oishi transfers to a new school in time to see her students five years later (1933). In 1941, the boys go off to war, preferring a glorious military career to a humdrum life at home. Four years later, a widowed Miss Oishi comes out of retirement to teach once again—her new students including a sister and a daughter of the original class. The surviving class of 1928 arrange a reunion and buy her a new bicycle.

Based on the book by Sakae Tsuboi, *24 Eyes* draws lightly on Tsuboi's years at the periphery of Japanese anarchist counterculture and her disgust that "pacifist" Japan was rearming during the Korean war. The book was also adapted into a live-action film by former propagandist Keisuke Kinoshita in 1954. Made after the previous year's **DIARY OF ANNE FRANK** made WWII an acceptable subject for TV, this anime remake mixes animation with live action (old Tsuburaya studio hand Jissoji handling the former, **HELLO SPANK**–director Yoshida the latter) to depict different times of Miss Oishi's life. The story was remade again as the fully live-action *Children on the Island* (1987). Many other anime would copy *24 Eyes'* concentration on children, recognizing that a cast too young to have started WWII need not be held accountable for those who really did. Hideaki Anno would pay homage to *24 Eyes* in **GUNBUSTER** with a scene in which a teacher bids farewell to a class including the daughter of her former classmate.

21 EMON WELCOME TO SPACE

1981. JPN: *21 Emon: Uchu e Irasshai.* Movie. DIR: Tsutomu Shibayama. SCR: Masaki Tsuji. DES: Yuko Yamamoto. ANI:

Michishiro Yamada. MUS: Shunsuke Kikuchi. PRD: Fujiko F, Shogakukan, Shinei. 93 mins.

In the 21st century, would-be space pilot Emon discovers that he is the sole heir to the dilapidated Tsuzureya Inn in Tokyo. But the inn hasn't changed since the 19th century, and customers no longer find it quaint. Realizing that Emon can be "persuaded," the owners of the Galaxy Hotel chain invite him on a space holiday to get him away from his inheritance. Emon is accompanied on the trip by his wacky potato-digging robot, Gonsuke, and the all-powerful alien, Monga.

The Fujiko-Fujio team behind **ESPER MAMI** and **MOJACKO** were heavily involved in this adaptation of their series from *Corocoro Comic*, even to the extent of singing the theme song themselves. The film was shown on a double bill with another Fujiko-Fujio production, the **DORAEMON** short *What Am I for Momotaro?*, and reuses the footage for one scene in which Doraemon and Emon briefly share each other's movie.

TWILIGHT OF THE COCKROACHES *

1987. JPN: *Gokiburi no Tasogare*. AKA: *Cockroach*. Movie. DIR: Hiroaki Yoshida. SCR: Hiroaki Yoshida. DES: Yoshinori Kanemori. ANI: Toshio Hirata. MUS: Morgan Fisher. PRD: TYO, Kitty Film. 105 mins.

Naomi, an attractive young cockroach, enjoys the easy life with her boyfriend, Ichiro, and other roaches in Mr. Saito's apartment. This is because the lazy Saito lets the roaches eat the scraps from his table and never tries to hurt them. Hans, a hard-bitten fighter-roach from the other side of the yard, is a rival for Naomi's affections, but he eventually returns to his own people. Naomi embarks on the long quest across the yard (50 human feet, an incredible distance) to find him. There, she discovers that Hans did not lie, and that other humans are engaged in an all-out war to exterminate the roaches; Hans and his people are fighting a suicidal battle they can-

not win. The unthinkable happens when Momoko, the woman across the yard, moves in with Saito—a newly house-proud Saito kills off the roaches. Soon, only Ichiro and the pregnant Naomi are left, then he too is killed. Naomi escapes to give birth to a new litter, and a new generation of cockroaches, just that little bit more resistant to human poisons, is ready for a rematch.

A very *Japanese* insect movie that mixes a neighborly human romance with the anthropomorphized characters of *Hoppity Goes to Town* and the apocalyptic Armageddon of WWII—*A Bug's Death*, if you will. Beginning with Naomi's first encounter with the human female, the film is chiefly told in flashback, lending it the weight of inevitable tragedy that also characterizes **GRAVE OF THE FIREFLIES**. Shot in a mixture of live action (the humans) and animation (the roaches) that is all the more impressive in these days of digital easy-fixes, it mixes the comic spectacle of humans battling their only serious rivals for planetary domination, with the heroic defensive actions of a tiny community facing impossible odds. The director reportedly thought of his cockroaches as a metaphor for the way the Japanese appear to the rest of the world—he meant as selfish, parasitical trading partners, though many foreign critics saw other parallels, particularly in *TotC*'s glorification of fanatical suicide missions and its insect cast's self-assured belief that they will, eventually, become the masters of Earth. A fascinating and unexpectedly entertaining experiment. **V**

TWILIGHT OF THE DARK MASTER *

1997. JPN: *Shihaisha no Tasogare*. AKA: *Twilight of the Master*. Video. DIR: Akiyuki Shinbo. SCR: Duanne Dell'Amico, Tatsuhiko Urahata. DES: Hisashi Abe. ANI: Hisashi Abe. MUS: Keiji Urata. PRD: Madhouse. 46 mins.

In the beginning, the Great Mother created a Demon Master, an adversary designed to test the mettle of human beings. However, the Demon Master

exceeded its design specifications, and the Great Mother had to create a Guardian to protect humankind. Eons later, in the year 2089, a strange force transforms the Japanese Eiji—he turns on his lover Shizuka, mutilates her, and escapes into the city. Determined to give her mutated fiancé the release of death, Shizuka pursues him, accompanied by a police detective and Shijo, an androgynous man who is the current Guardian. As in **DOOMED MEGALOPOLIS**, the monster terrorizing the city is simply a pawn of the true evil, in this case the Demon Master himself, who is asserting his powers through a new illegal muscle-enhancement drug. This predictable sci-fi gorefest was based on the manga by Saki Okuse and originally serialized in *Wings* magazine. **LNV**

TWILIGHT Q

1987. JPN: *Twilight Q Toki no Musibume—Reflection; Twilight Q 2—Meikyu Bukken File 538*. AKA: *TQ: A Knot in Time; TQ2 Labyrinth Article File 538*. Video. DIR: Tomomi Mochizuki, Mamoru Oshii. SCR: Kazunori Ito. DES: Akemi Takada, Katsuya Kondo. ANI: Shinji Otsuka. MUS: Kenji Kawai. PRD: Studio Deen. 30 mins. x 2 eps.

Mayumi is on holiday when she finds an old camera while swimming. Out of curiosity she has the film developed—only one frame can be saved. The picture shows her with a young man she has never met. Returning to her holiday base to investigate, she learns from the camera manufacturer that this model hasn't even been made yet. She finds herself caught up in weird events that take her back in time to WWII and forward to her own graveside. This unsettling paradoxical tale is seemingly without meaning, a bizarre entry in the girls' anime catalog. The second story takes matters even further into fantasy, opening with the transformation of an airship into a giant carp and focusing on a small girl, seemingly the reincarnation of a powerful deity, and a mysterious detective in shades. He's a Tokyo detective who wants to find out why every aircraft over his town has suddenly vanished without a trace. The magic of the transformation sequence is unforgettable, but there's little that could be described as action.

The surreal goings-on in this short-lived "twilight zone" were made by the crew of **PATLABOR** but owe a heavy debt to the 1960s live-action show *Ultra Q[uestion]* (a forerunner of **ULTRAMAN**). Whereas its predecessor threatened to "apart your soul and going into the mystery zone [*sic*]," this modern update preferred to "take over your reality and disable the stop button."

TWIN

1989. JPN: *Hassai Circuit Roman Twin*. AKA: *Racing Circuit Romance Twin*. Video. DIR: Noboru Ishiguro, Osamu Sekita. SCR: Takashi Yamada. DES: Tsuneo Ninomiya. ANI: Tsuneo Ninomiya, Koichi Endo. MUS: N/C. PRD: Japan Home Video. 80 mins.
Hyo Hibino grows up a confused orphan after his mother dies giving birth to him—alternately blaming himself for her death and believing himself to be invulnerable. He gets the perfect opportunity to prove it when he becomes a motorcycle racer. An anime based on the 1986 *Young Sunday* manga by **F** and **DASH KAPPEI**–creator Noboru Rokuda.

TWIN BEE PARADISE

1999. Video. DIR: Kazuhiro Takamoto. SCR: Yasunori Ide. DES: Akihiro Asanuma. ANI: Akihiro Asanuma. MUS: N/C. PRD: Public & Basic, Beam Entertainment. 30 mins. x 3 eps.
Fresh from the video game that spawned them, the Twin Bee team is carted off for an intergalactic adventure, complete with big hair, babies, and UFOs. The series was preceded by a 1994 "episode zero," which must have made for one of the slowest anime productions in history.

TWIN DOLLS *

1994. JPN: *Seijuden Twin Dolls; Inju Seisen Twin Angels*. AKA: *Holy Beast Story Twin Dolls; Lust Beast Crusade Twin Angels*. Video. DIR: Kan Fukumoto.

SCR: Oji Miyako. DES: Rin Shin. ANI: Akira Ojo. MUS: Teruo Takahama. PRD: Dandelion. 45 mins. x 2 eps. (*Dolls*), 30 mins. x 4 eps. (*Angels*).
The one thing you can be pretty sure of in anime is that people who look like ordinary high-school girls rarely are. Mai and Ai are professional demon hunters, descended from an immortal being, dedicated to defending mankind (and, in particular, high-school grrrl-kind) from the demons of the Pleasure Underworld. They are appointed guardians of the infant Messiah who will save the world. For once tentacles aren't used as penis substitutes—instead the crew animates optimistic renditions of the real thing. This openness doesn't last long as the story introduces one of the most meretricious of all plot devices, the "orb of orgasm"; pop it in a woman's mouth and she'll *enjoy* being raped. Historical and mythical figures are used as set dressing in the background of an unpleasant exercise in taking money for old rope.

For reasons we've never been quite able to fathom, the franchise not only changed its Japanese title to *Twin Angels*, but also gained itself a new U.S. distributor, moving from Softcel to Anime 18 for the distribution of the 1995 sequel.

For *Angels*, the sorcerer-nuns must defend their charge, Lord Onimaro (who is 21, allegedly), from another demon assault, when Kama and Sutra, the King and Queen of Seduction, drag him off to a ritual orgy. Onimaro's guardian Dekinobu worries that if he succumbs to his demonic heritage, he will become the Demon King and his legion of sex-crazed monsters will subdue the world. He makes a predictable choice and has the twins stripped and tortured for his pleasure, planning to have them sacrificed. But Dekinobu is determined to rescue Onimaro from his destiny, even if it costs him his life.

Angels adds staggering naiveté to its other offenses—what hormonally normal male, offered the career choice of

Yoma: Curse of the Undead

© 1989 TOHO CO., LTD. • MPS

ordinary human or Demon King with ultimate power, is going to be persuaded into the paths of righteousness by two "19-year-old" bimbos who can't even find sensible underwear? It is difficult, however, to completely write off any show that has immortal dialogue like, "Commence creation of an evil sex barrier!" and a scene featuring two miniskirted girls on a stormy school roof trying to hang onto a magic staff while lightning transforms it into a giant penis. ●**NV**

TWIN SIGNAL

1995. Video. DIR: Takashi Sogabe. SCR: N/C. DES: Toshiko Sasaki. ANI: Toshiko Sasaki. MUS: Takeshi Suzuki. PRD: Tokyo Kids. 28 mins. x 3 eps.
A-S Signal is the newest, most sophisticated Human Formed Robot (HFR) in the Atrandom series, created by Professor Shinnosuke Otoi, a brilliant engineer. Signal looks like a cute 16-year-old boy, programmed to be "big brother" to the professor's grandson, Nobuhiko. Made of the revolutionary material MIRA by a secret process, Signal is the constant target of kidnap attempts and other efforts to steal the Professor's secrets. But there's one small problem with the process—whenever Nobuhiko sneezes, Signal

transforms from a normal teenage boy into a sweet three-year-old super-deformed dwarf who can fit into the palm of your hand. Chibi Signal, as he's known in this state, is phenomenally cute and obsessed with eating chocolate, but his powers as a bodyguard are severely compromised.

Luckily, lots of pretty-boy robots pop up to help Signal out. They are earlier models in the Atrandom series. Signal's older brother and prototype, Pulse, also lives with the Otoi family as does Code, a robot bird also made by the same secret techniques. Based on the early chapters of the *Shonen Gan-Gan* manga by Sachi Oshimizu, which has also spun off novels and drama CDs.

TWINKLE HEART
1986. Video. DIR: Seiji Okuda. SCR: Kenji Terada. DES: Sachiko Yamamoto. ANI: Moriyasu Taniguchi. MUS: N/C. PRD: Project Team Argos. 45 mins.
On a distant planet, the treasure of Love is being sought by planetary ruler Ogod. Three insufferably cute aliens—Cherry, Lemon, and Berry—join in the search and finally reach Earth. In order to look for information about the treasure, they decide that the best course would be to turn their spaceship into a hamburger bar, so as to blend in with the natives and listen for any intelligence. A comedy, in case you were wondering.

TWINS AT ST. CLARE'S
1991. JPN: *Ochamen Futago Clare Gakuen Monogatari*. AKA: *Story of Mischievous Twins at Clare College*. TV series. DIR: Masaharu Okuwaki, et al. SCR: Haruya Yamazaki, Michiru Shimada. DES: Shuichi Seki. ANI: Keiko Sasaki, Satoshi Hirayama, Toshiharu Mizutani. MUS: Masahiro Kawasaki. PRD: Tokyo Movie Shinsha, Nippon TV. 25 mins. x 26 eps.
Patricia and Isabel are identical twins whose rich parents decide that their girls should learn the true values of life. They don't feel their expensive, luxurious school is making a very good

job of this, so instead they send them to St. Clare's, a much simpler school. At first the girls resent this, seeing it as a step down the social ladder. Their privileged background doesn't help them adjust to life as members of a community unimpressed by wealth. They are determined to win respect, but because they're completely unused to communal life, they rebel against the rules, going on strike, stealing, and causing all sorts of trouble. Instead of the school's best students they become its biggest troublemakers, but they eventually settle down, make friends, and learn to value and respect others while having lots of fun. Midnight feasts, adventures, all the things people do at boarding school in novels like the 1941 book by Enid Blyton that inspired this series. Unfortunately real English boarding schools were never so exciting, but Japanese audiences didn't care; nor did those across Europe. TMS followed with another twin story, **ME AND I: THE TWO LOTTES**.

TWO DOWN, FULL BASE
1982. AKA: *Two Out, Bases Loaded*. TV special. DIR: Tsutomu Shibayama. SCR: Seiichi Yashiro. DES: Michishiro Yamada, Hideo Kawauchi. ANI: Tsutomu Shibayama, Kenichi Onuki. MUS: Takeyoshi Hoguchi, Joe Hisaishi. PRD: Group Tac, Asia-do, Toho, Fuji TV. 85 mins.
Musuke "Shorty" Sato is a shortstop for the local junior baseball team, the Eggs, who is asked by his mother to look after some money for her. He foolishly lends it to Tower and Dump, the school bad-boys, and must enlist the help of the pitcher's pretty little sister.

TWO ON THE ROAD
1992. JPN: *Itsumo Futari*. AKA: *Always the Two of Us*. Video. DIR: Hirotoshi Hayasaka, Seizo Watase. SCR: Seizo Watase. DES: Seizo Watase. ANI: N/C. MUS: BEGIN. PRD: Cure. 37 mins., 30 mins.
Two anthologies of short stories, 13 in all, based on originals by **CHALK COL-**

ORED PEOPLE–creator Seizo Watase. As with other adaptations of Watase's work, they are set to music—stories here include *Ashes of Love*, *White Fish/Blue Fish*, *Dance on the Sands*, *Glider*, *Handbag Mirror*, *Blue Snow*, and *Living in the World*. Though several early ones were broadcast on the WOWOW satellite channel, this qualifies more as a video production.

TWO TAKAS, THE
1984. JPN: *Futari no Taka*. TV series. DIR: Takao Yotsuji, Hiroko Tokita, Junichi Sakata, Hiroshi Negishi. SCR: Sukehiro Tomita, Hideo Takayashiki, Jiyu Watanabe, Yasushi Hirano. DES: Shiro Murata, Akira Nakanishi. ANI: Shiro Murata, Yasuhiro Moriguchi. MUS: Joe Hisaishi. PRD: Movie International, Fuji TV. 25 mins. x 32 eps.
Two boys both named Taka ("Hawk") are both passionate motorcyclists and both determined to be champions. The similarity ends there; one's a rich kid from a good family, one's from the wrong side of the tracks, constantly fighting with his mother. Then they learn that, following a fire in the maternity unit where they were born, two babies were accidentally swapped over. Based on Kaoru "**AREA 88**" Shintani's 1981 manga in *Shonen Sunday*, this was the last Movie International production. The studio closed down before it could be completed, so only by reading the manga could fans find out how the story ended; but the series gave them Hisaishi's music by way of compensation.

2001 NIGHTS
1987. JPN: *Space Fantasia 2001 Nights*. Video. DIR: Toshio Takeuchi. SCR: Chiho Katsura. DES: Akio Sugino, Takashi Watanabe. ANI: Hisatoshi Motoki, Noboru Tatsuike. MUS: Satoshi Kadokura. PRD: TMS. 57 mins.
In 2085, a sleeper ship carrying the embryos of the "Robinson Family" launches for planet Ozma. A community begins to thrive onboard the ship, and when it reaches Ozma 375 years later, the terraformed planet is settled

peacefully. Then, a second ship arrives, captained by yet another Robinson, who urges the colonists to help spread the human race even further into space. Owing much more to *2001: A Space Odyssey* than SWISS FAMILY ROBINSON, this majestic video was shot in "Super Perspective Technique" (whatever that is) to capture the photo-real quality of Yukinobu Hoshino's original 1984 *Action Comics* manga. Note also the homages to WIZARD OF OZ.

TWO'S COMPANY
1998. JPN: *Futari Kurashi*. AKA: *Two People Living Together*. TV series. DIR: Futa Morita. SCR: Fumihiko Shimori. DES: Masayuki Hirooka. ANI: Masayuki Hirooka. MUS: Katsuo Ono. PRD: TBS. 5 mins. x 36 eps.
The romantic misadventures of an out-of-work manga artist, based on a manga by working manga artist Kenjiro Kakimoto. These shorts were broadcast as part of the late-night *Wonderful* program. ◑

TYPHOON IN ISE BAY
1989. JPN: *Ise-wan Taifun Monogatari*. AKA: *Story of the Typhoon in Ise Bay*. Movie. DIR: Seijiro Kamiyama, Yasuo Iwamoto. SCR: Seijiro Kamiyama. DES: Masahiro Kitazaki. ANI: Masahiro Kitazaki. MUS: Masao Haryu. PRD: Mushi. 90 mins.
This self-explanatory true story of a 1959 storm that decimated Western Japan was directed by Kamiyama, who also wrote the original book.

U

UFO ROBOT DAI APOLLON *

1976. JPN: *UFO Senshi Dai Apollon*. AKA: *UFO Warrior Dai Apollon, Shadow World*. TV series. DIR: Tatsuo Ono. SCR: Takao Koyama, Okihara Matsumoto, Noboru Shiroyama, Soji Yoshikawa, Seiji Matsuoka. DES: Toyoo Ashida. ANI: Keijiro Kimura, Takashi Kakuta, Konio Okoto, Toyoo Ashida, et al. MUS: Masahisa Takeshi. PRD: Eiken, TBS. 25 mins. x 39 eps.

Sixteen-year-old Takeshi forms a football team at the Blue Sky Orphanage. One day after a game, he's alone on the field when a warrior of light on a mighty steed appears and points his sword at Takeshi's chest. Takeshi loses consciousness, waking later to find a mark in the shape of a sun over his heart. He is really the son of the king of planet Apollon, spirited away to Earth by his father's faithful retainer, Rabi, in order to avoid the prince's death at the hands of the usurper General Dazaan. His heart contains the "Key Energy" of his planet, which allows him to control the space ship Rabi cunningly hid on the ocean floor—it contains several flying saucers, a dart-shaped flyer with detachable motorcycle, and the three component vehicles Edda (Head), Trangu (Trunk), and Legga (Leg) that combine to form the giant robot Dai Apollon. Using his Key Energy, Takeshi can painfully synchronize with the robot, allowing him to operate it as an extension of his own body. The separate vehicles are piloted by his teammates Miki, Choko, and Goro, whose clothes magically change into their football jerseys whenever they shout "U! F! O!" Using the robot, Takeshi

hopes to set his planet free and release his mother from imprisonment. Based on the 1974 *Shonen King* manga by OISHINBO-creator Tetsu Kariya and Shigeru Tsuchiyama, though since the original featured a 15-year-old orphan called Akira defeating demons with the powers of 108 heroes (see SUIKODEN), and no giant robot anywhere to be seen, it's a wonder the producers bothered to pay for the rights at all.

U-JIN BRAND *

1991. Video. DIR: Osamu Sekita. SCR: Satoru Akahori. DES: Yumi Nakayama. ANI: Yumi Nakayama. MUS: Nobuo Ito. PRD: JC Staff, Animate. 45 mins.

Three short stories based on U-Jin's erotic manga, similar in style to ANGEL and TALES OF. . . . In the first story, a songwriter can produce hits for teenage idol singers—but only after he gets to know the girl *really* well. Despite his constant calendar of seductions, he secretly loves innocent Akiyo, with whom he must one day work and try on his irresistible charm. The other two chapters are linked tales of Toyama no Benbo, a righter of wrongs in the tradition of Toyama no Kinsan (see SAMURAI GOLD). In the first, he is called in to avenge a girl wronged by a serial seducer, who claims he will still respect her if they do the deed then dumps her because she is no longer a virgin. In the second, he is brought in to solve the problem of a young man who doesn't want to dump his career prospects along with his unwelcome engagement to the boss's daughter. *Ill. p. 57.* ⓝ

ULTIMATE SUPERMAN R

1991. JPN: *Kyukyoko Chojin R*. Video.

DIR: Ayumi Shibuki. SCR: Toshiko Uehara. DES: Toyomi Sugiyama. ANI: Toyomi Sugiyama. MUS: Masayuki Yamamoto. PRD: Studio Core. 75 mins.

Average Japanese teenager Ichiro Tanaka is really an android, programmed to take over the world by mad scientist Hiroshi Narihara. He enlists the help of the school photography club, which is probably a bad idea. Based on the comedy manga by PATLABOR-creator Masami Yuki, this anime was also spun off into several audio dramas.

ULTIMATE TEACHER *

1988. JPN: *Kyofun no Bio-Ningen: Saishu Kyoshi*. AKA: *Fearsome Bio-Human: The Last Teacher*. Video. DIR: Toyoo Ashida. SCR: Monta Ibu. DES: Atsuji Yamamoto, Mandrill Club. ANI: Noriyasu Yamauchi. MUS: Miyuki Otani. PRD: Studio Live, SME. 60 mins.

Ganpachi Chabane, half-man, half-cockroach, is the result of a genetic experiment. This makes him a natural teacher in the eyes of many teenagers, so when he escapes from the lab where he was created, he heads straight for Emperor High School and installs himself on the staff. His idea of education agrees with that of the pupils—both see it as a battleground where only the strong survive. The school is overrun by student gangs; Chabane has to defeat the leader of the strongest gang, pretty martial artist Hinako Shiratori, if he's to keep his class in line. Luckily Hinako has a weakness; if she isn't wearing her lucky blue bloomers emblazoned with a cute white cat, she has no confidence at all in her fighting skills and changes from powerhouse to pushover. The U.S. translation calls these "lucky gym shorts," but the U.K. version's "velvet pussy panties" is much more in line with the crude tone of the whole package. Mystifyingly released in theaters on a double bill with the LEGEND OF GALACTIC HEROES movie, it features a theme song by famous Japanese pop band the Kome-Kome Club. Atsuji Yamamoto also wrote a manga version for *Animage Comics.* ♥

ULTRA B

1987. TV series, movie. DIR: Hiroshi Sasakawa, Tetsuo Yasumi, Teruo Kigure, Kazuhiro Mori, Fusahito Nagaki. SCR: Masaaki Sakurai, Masaru Yamamoto, Nobuaki Kishima, Hirokazu Mizude. DES: Fujiko-Fujio "A." ANI: Keisuke Mori. MUS: Shunsuke Kikuchi. PRD: Shinei Doga, TV Asahi. 25 mins. x 51 eps., 20 mins. (m).

One night, Michio chases a UFO to see where it lands. He is taken inside it and encounters a mysterious baby, Ultra B (aka UB). Though at first the only strange thing about him is his pathological obsession with drinking milk, UB soon reveals that he has superpowers when he moves in with Michio's family—a fact that causes humorous misunderstandings in the style of DORAEMON. Based on a manga by Fujiko-Fujio "A" for *Fujiko-Fujio Land* magazine, its appearance in a glorified vanity publication perhaps explaining the tiredness of the idea. The 1988 "movie" outing *UB: Dictator B.B. from the Black Hole* featured the arrival of the evil, pterodactyl-riding "Black Baby," whom UB defeats with the aid of his cohorts Super Baby Robot and Muscle Bird. Another work from PROGOLFER SARU–creator Motoo Abiko, formerly half of the Fujiko-Fujio duo.

ULTRA GRAN

1982. JPN: *Hitotsuboshi-ke no Ultra Baa-san.* AKA: *Ultra Granny of the Hitotsuboshi Family; Super Grandma.* TV series. DIR: Kenji Hirata, Satoshi Inoue. SCR: Yoshiyuki Suga, Shigeru Mizuno, Hiroko Naka. DES: Toshio Kitahara. ANI: Takumi Manabe, Takao Yamazaki. MUS:

Masayuki Yamamoto. PRD: Knack, Yomiuri TV (Nippon TV). 25 mins. x 13 eps. Seventy-year-old Granny Hitotsuboshi acts like a teenager and cares nothing about the effect her quick tongue and accident-prone nature have on those around her. Her crazy schemes create chaos for her family, which includes hard-pressed salaryman Eitaro, examobsessed mother Kinuko, consumptive grandson Kenichi, toddler Todome, and Antonio the local tramp. Based on a gag manga by Meme Akutagawa—compare to SAZAE-SAN and MY NEIGHBORS THE YAMADAS.

ULTRAMAN *

1979. JPN: *The Ultraman.* Movie, TV series. DIR: Eiko Toriumi, Masahisa Ishida, Takashi Anno, Katsuyuki Tsuji, Takeshi Shirato, et al. (TV1), Masayoshi Ozaki (TV2), Mitsuo Hikabe (*USA, Company*), Hiroshi Sasakawa (v), Tetsuro Amino (*Tsuifun*), Mitsuo Hikabe (*Company*), Hiroko Tokita (*Love and Peace*). SCR: Keiichi Abe, Soji Yoshikawa, Hiroyuki Hoshiyama, Yasushi Hirano (TV1), Hiroko Naka, Keiji Kubota (TV2), John Eric Seward (*USA*), Hiroshi Hashimoto (v). DES: Tsuneo Ninomiya, Kunio Okawara, Shoji Kawamori (TV1), Yoshihiko Shinozaki (TV2), Kazuo Iimura (*USA*), Tsuneo Ninomiya (v), N/C (*Love and Peace*). ANI: Tsuneo Ninomiya (TV1), Osamu Kamijo (TV2), Kazuo Iimura (*USA*), Tsuneo Ninomiya, Hiroko Minamimoto (v), Yutaka Miya (*Tsuifun*), Noriko Nishimiya (*Company*), Haruo Takahashi (*Love and Peace*). MUS: Kunio Miyauchi (TV1, TV2), Shinsuke Kazato (*USA*), N/C. PRD: Sunrise, Tsuburaya, TBS, Tsuburaya, NHK2, Tsuburaya, Hanna-Barbera, Tsuburaya, Triangle Staff. 30 mins. x 50 eps. (TV1) , 25 mins. (*Kids* m), 10 mins. x 26 eps. (TV2/*Kids*), 10 mins. x 26 eps. (TV3/*Mother*), 80 mins. (*USA*), 30 x 6 eps. (v), 30 mins. (*Tsuifun*), 60 mins. (*Company*), 80 mins. (*Love and Peace*).

After an apprenticeship in special effects on films ranging from *The War at Sea from Hawaii to Malaya* (see WARTIME ANIME) through the original

What's Michael?

Godzilla to Kurosawa's *Throne of Blood* (for which he made the forest move), Eiji Tsuburaya started the famed "monster studio" that bears his name. The live-action *Ultraman*, one of the enduring icons of Japanese TV, evolved from *Ultra Q* (1966), an SF drama series in the *X-Files* mode featuring the investigation of mysterious beings and events. As *Ultraman* (also 1966), it was taken over by the monsters and became a battle between the heroic Ultrans, citizens of Nebula M78, and their human allies, against often absurd but compelling monster opponents. It is still one of the most popular toy lines in Japan, with legions of new plastic monsters released every year.

The Ultraman (1979), broadcast during the period that reruns of the live-action series prepared the audience for *Ultraman 80*, commences with glowing symbols appearing over major cities like Tokyo, Paris, and New York. A new tactical team, the Space Garrison, is set up by the Earth Defense Force and discovers they are signs of a higher civilization from another dimension, the Ultrans, who came to Earth in ancient times. To fight evil in our dimension, they need human help. Young pilot Hikari flies out into space to investigate and is transported by a beam of light into another dimension, where he meets an Ultran and agrees to the merging of their life forces. Hikari can now use the star-shaped "Beam Flasher" on his forehead to transform into Ultraman Joneas (aka Joe). He can fight the monsters and aliens that menace Earth, and thanks to the lower cost of animation, he has a much wider range of power-rays than any of his live-action brothers. Episodes from this series were edited into a feature-length video, *The Adventures of Ultraman* (1982), for the U.S. market only. It focuses on Hikari's journey and meeting with the Ultran, and the space warfare elements. A few translated episodes were also released in the U.S. video market on one tape as *Ultraman II.*

Ultraman Kids (1984) was more humorous, a short movie of cute kiddie versions of the Ultraman family and their monster rivals. In April 1986 they got their own series, *Ultraman Kids Proverb Stories* (U.K.: *Kotowaza Monogatari*), in which Ultraman Zoffy and friends reenact wise maxims for little ones. The two final episodes were not broadcast. A second kids' series moved from Ultraman's home on TBS to the NHK2 satellite channel—the **FROM THE APENNINES TO THE ANDES** pastiche *30 Million Light Years in Search of Mother* (1991, U.K.: *Haha o Tazunete 3,000 Man Konen*).

The serious movie *Ultraman: The Adventure Begins* (1987; retitled *Ultraman USA* in Japan) was a Japanese-American coproduction between Tsubaraya and Hanna-Barbera and based on a story by Noboru Tsubaraya. Three stunt pilots survive a fatal crash thanks to three aliens from M78, who have linked life forces with the pilots and made them part of the Ultra-Force. The aliens' mission is to destroy four evil Sorkin Monsters hatched from asteroids that have crashed onto New Orleans, San Francisco, Denver, and New York. Ultra-Scott, Ultra-Chuck, and token woman Ultra-Beth now have a secret base inside Mount Rushmore and another under a golf

course, plus three robots to help them out.

The video series *Ultraman Graffiti* (1990) featured more cartoony adventures for mini-versions of the Ultra brothers—a style that continues to dominate the franchise, at least in its animated incarnation. It was followed by Tetsuro Amino's video release *Ultra-Violent Battle—Comet War-God Tsuifun* (1996, *Chotoshi Gekiden—Suisei Senshin Tsuifun*). In the late 1990s, the live-action *Ultraman* was influenced by the postmodern angst of **EVANGELION**, resulting in the more serious *Ultraman Gaia* TV series, written in part by **SERIAL EXPERIMENTS LAIN**'s Chiaki Konaka. The sturm-und-drang of the *Gaia* movies was balanced in theaters by new cartoon Ultrakids features, Mitsuo Hikabe's *Ultraman Company* (1996) and Hiroko Tokita's *Ultraman: Love and Peace* (1999), featuring animation by Triangle Staff. This is the most recent animated incarnation of the series to date, though the original is often referenced in shows including **BIRDY THE MIGHTY**, **PROJECT A-KO**, **URUSEI YATSURA**, **PATLABOR**, **DOCTOR SLUMP**, and the feline parody *Ultranyan* (1997).

ULYSSES 31 *

1981. JPN: *Uchu Densetsu Ulysses 31.* AKA: *Space Legend Ulysses 31.* TV series. DIR: Bernard Deyries, Tadao Nagahama, Kazuo Terada, Seiji Okuda. SCR: Ryohei Suzuki, Jean Chalopin, Nina Wolmark. DES: Shingo Araki, Michi Himeno, Studio Nue, Manchu, Noboru Tatsuike, Shinji Ito, Yuki Motonori. ANI: Shingo Araki, Toyoo Ashida. MUS: Kei Wakakusa (Denny Crockett, Ike Egan, Haim Saban, Shuki Levy for Western version). PRD: DIC, Tokyo Movie Shinsha, TV Nagoya (TV Asahi). 25 mins. x 26 eps. (only 12 shown in Japanese broadcast, 1988).

Preparing for a routine journey back to his home on 31st-century Earth, starship captain Ulysses runs into trouble on planet Troy when his son, Telemachus, is captured by the disciples of the Cyclops. Killing the Cyclops to save Telemachus, Ulysses brings

down the wrath of the god Zeus, who puts his crew into suspended animation and wipes the navigation systems of his ship, the Odyssey. Accompanied only by Telemachus, Numinor, and Yumi, the alien siblings from planet Zotra, and the intensely annoying robot No-no, Ulysses must wander the stars in search of the Kingdom of Hades to awaken his crew and find the way back home.

A ridiculously contrived sci-fi reworking of Homer's *Odyssey*, accomplished in such an endearing and exciting fashion as to become one of the best-loved anime in Europe, *Ulysses 31* was the first French-Japanese coproduction. It was also the last for **ROSE OF VERSAILLES**' Tadao Nagahama, who died during production. Producer Jean Chalopin would return with the equally memorable **MYSTERIOUS CITIES OF GOLD**, before his output sank into the financially lucrative but creatively impoverished doldrums of the toy tie-ins *Rainbow Brite* (also made with Japanese staff) and *Care Bears*. He next surfaced in the anime world when his Studio DIC provided the English dub of **SAILOR MOON**.

The basis of the story (the gods, their human servants, and the obstacles they place in Ulysses' way) has hardly changed, except that Telemachus accompanies our hero rather than staying at home to fight off his mother Penelope's suitors as he did in the original. The addition of new characters doesn't jar; there are so many fantastic beings in the story already that a sweet alien telepath and an annoying robot with an appetite for metal fit right in. The design team makes the best of what it has, with classy machines from Manchu (aka French designer Phillippe Bouchet), reworked by Studio Nue and **SAINT SEIYA**–designer Araki. His version of Ulysses had to be toned down by Deyries at final approval stage; the director wanted a pacifist hero, so most of the Japanese-originated futuristic sidearm designs were discarded. The show remains deservedly popular, despite the annoying little robot—most notable among its many achievements, a Homeric episode in which the SF Ulysses travels back in time to meet the Greek original and the faithful Penelope. For this episode alone, *Ulysses 31* is an anime classic.

UNCHALLENGEABLE TRIDER G7

1980. JPN: *Muteki Robo Trider G7*. AKA: *Invincible Robo (T) Rider G7*. TV series. DIR: Katsutoshi Sasaki, Seiji Kikuchi, Akira Suzuki, Takao Yoshikawa. SCR: Hiroyuki Hoshiyama, Tsunehisa Ito, Kenichi Matsuzaki, Katsutoshi Sasaki, Sukehiro Tomita, Fuyunori Gobu. DES: Nobuyoshi Sasakado, Kunio Okawara, Yutaka Izubuchi. ANI: Nobuyoshi Sasakado, Akehiro Kaneyama, Keijiro Kimura, Norio Shioyama. MUS: Kurodo Kaya. PRD: Sotsu Agency (Sunrise), TV Nagoya (TV Asahi). 25 mins. x 50 eps. When his father dies in 1985, young Watta Takeo inherits the family space transport firm. Despite the fact that the president is just a schoolkid, the company has to fight for survival in a competitive world with rivals and space pirates at every turn. Watta manages to succeed and keep the company going thanks to Professor Navarone's giant robot, Trider G7. Looking forward to the workhorse robots of PATLABOR and back to the boy-and-his-bot sagas of Go Nagai, the series mixes school and home scenarios with space battles—compare to John Stanley's American comic *O.G. Whiz*, which similarly featured a boy "dragged" away from school and forced to play with expensive supertoys.

UNDERSEA ENCOUNTER *

1981. JPN: *Kaitei Daisenso Ai no Niman Mile*. AKA: *War Beneath the Sea: 20,000 Miles for Love*. TV special. DIR: Ippei Kuri. SCR: Mamoru Sasaki. DES: Akemi Takada, Kunio Okawara. ANI: Takashi Saijo. MUS: Hiroaki Suzuki. PRD: Tatsunoko, Nippon TV. 72 mins. All the nations of Earth are crumbling before the might of Darius, ruler of the Gabia Empire. Meanwhile, childhood friends Ben and Ricky are sailing on

the oceans in search of the lost city of Atlantis. When their ship is sunk, they are rescued by Captain Nemo in his submarine Nautilus. The captain reveals that he knows the location of Atlantis and offers to take them there.

Dubbed in the early 1980s by Harmony Gold and broadcast as afternoon filler in several U.S. cities, this obscure TV movie was two years in the making, shot on 35mm film, and the first lead design job for PATLABOR's Akemi Takada. Directorial assistant Koichi Mashimo would later be given charge of another ship's commander, the less heroic IRRESPONSIBLE CAPTAIN TYLOR. The character of Nemo would reappear in SECRET OF BLUE WATER, an even freer adaptation of Jules Verne's original story.

UNICO *

1981. Video, movie. DIR: Toshio Hirata, Mami Murano. SCR: Masaki Tsuji. DES: Osamu Tezuka. ANI: Shigeru Yamamoto, Akio Sugino, Yoshiaki Kawajiri, Kazuo Tomizawa. MUS: Yukihide Takakawa, Micky Yoshino, Godiego, Ryo Kitayama, Iruka. PRD: Madhouse, Sanrio Eiga, Tezuka Pro. 25 mins. (v), 90 mins. x 2 (m).
Exiled from Paradise by a malevolent goddess, Unico the baby unicorn is blown on the West Wind, finding troubled souls and helping them before he moves on again. Originally appearing as a color Osamu Tezuka manga in *Lyrica* magazine, Unico first showed up on TV in the pilot *U: Black Cloud, White Feather* (1979, *Kuroi Kumo Shiroi Hane*), eventually released straight to video. In this version, he arrives in a heavily polluted city, where he is befriended by a rat. While sharing a meager meal with the rat, Unico finds out that the sick girl upstairs can only be cured by the destruction of the local factories and chemical plants. As soon as Unico has brought sunlight back to the town, the West Wind returns to carry him away, before depositing him in yet another desolate place, alone and with no memory of the past.

The TV series wasn't picked up, but

the movie *Fantastic Adventures of Unico* (1981) presents the back story, showing the gods jealous of baby Unico's happiness. They command the West Wind to take him away from his mother and abandon him on the Hill of Oblivion, but the West Wind hasn't the heart to do it, instead leaving Unico in the Land of Mists. When the gods learn of the deception, they send the evil Night Wind to finish the job, and the West Wind saves Unico's life by racing to the Land of Mists and snatching Unico away from the friends he has made there. A second movie, *U in the Land of Magic* (1983, *Maho no Shima e*), again opens with the amnesiac Unico in a strange place, once more making friends thanks to his open, happy nature and willingness to help those in trouble. This time a puppet, maltreated by humans, has been brought to life and given magical powers by the mysterious energy of sunlight. Kuruku has vowed to revenge himself on all humanity by turning humans and animals into puppets and imprisoning them on his magical island. Helped by a little girl and boy, Unico tries to save Kuruku but cannot convince him there is more to life than hate. As Unico's new friends are reunited with their families, he is once again torn away by the West Wind, who tells him the gods will soon find him because of the happiness he has created. Given such a bleak scenario, it's perhaps not surprising that the TV series was not picked up, but the movies—whose art style is not the same as the pilot episode—have acquired their own overseas following thanks to U.S. video release. Compare to similar Sanrio-sponsored misery in RINGING BELL.

UNINHABITED ISLAND, THE *

1998. JPN: *Mujin Shima Monogatari X*. AKA: *Story of X the Uninhabited Island*. Video. DIR: Hiroshi Ogawa. SCR: Mirin Takefuji. DES: Hirohito Kato. ANI: Shigenori Kurii. MUS: N/C. PRD: Pink Pineapple, KSS. 50 mins. x 2 eps. Seven beautiful Japanese girls are shipwrecked on a deserted island, where they are overcome with madness and desire, much to the benefit of the men who have arranged for their castaway status. Released in the U.S. as *Desert Island Story*. **N**

UNTIL THE MOONRISE
1991. JPN: *Takeda Tetsuya Tsuki Noboru made ni*. AKA: *Tetsuya Takeda, Until the Moonrise*. Video. DIR: Eiichi Yamamoto. SCR: Eiichi Yamamoto. DES: Kazuo Tomozawa. ANI: Kazuo Tomozawa, Sai Imazaki, Neri Mimana. MUS: N/C. PRD: Grouper Productions. 40 mins.
A father and daughter in Japan climb to the top of a ridge to watch the moonrise. As they wait, an old man tells them his story. An adaptation of Tetsuya Takeda's story about the relationship between a Japanese child and an American soldier.

UNTIL THE UNDERSEA CITY
1969. JPN: *Kaitei Toshi ga Dekiru made (31 Nen no Nippon)*. AKA: *Until the Undersea City: Japan in 31 Years*. TV special. DIR: Eiichi Yamamoto, Yusaku Sakamoto. SCR: Tadaaki Yamazaki. DES: Shuji Kimura. ANI: Jiro Fujimoto. MUS: N/C. PRD: Mushi, Nippon TV. 45 mins.
Taro Yamamoto has devoted his life to designing an undersea city. In 1972, he joins Tokyo Electronics, where he meets and eventually marries the pretty submariner Kazuko. He moves out to Tama New Town (see **POMPOKO**) and is present at the launch of the submarine Mambo in 1983. In 1986, construction finally begins on the undersea city of Oceanacopia. It is completed in 1997, and three years later, in the futuristic-sounding year of 2000, Taro finally gets to gaze on his creation.

URBAN SQUARE
1985. JPN: *Urban Square Kohaku no Tsuigeki*. AKA: *Urban Square: Chasing Amber*. Video. DIR: Akira Nishimori. SCR: Kazunori Ito. DES: Akemi Takada, Chiharu Sato. ANI: Hideyuki Motohashi. MUS: Chicken Chuck. PRD: Network. 55 mins.
Ryu Matsumoto is a screenwriter who

sees a murder in Kobe, but his testimony is ignored by police because the body has vanished without a trace. Eager to prove he's not crazy and worried that he may have attracted the attention of the murderers, Ryu hires private detective Mochizuki to protect him and investigate. Similarities with cult live-action movie *Blow-Up* (1966) are unlikely to be coincidental. **V**

URIQPEN: ANIMAL RESCUE LEAGUE *
1974. JPN: *Uriqpen Kyudotai*. TV series. DIR: Hiroshi Sasakawa, Seitaro Hara. SCR: Junzo Toriumi. DES: Akio Sugino. ANI: Jun Tanaka. MUS: Shunsuke Kikuchi. PRD: Tatsunoko, Fuji TV. 5 mins. x 156 eps. (also broadcast as 26 30-min. strips).
Four young animals, rabbit Seitaro Usagi, squirrel Risu, bear Kuma, and penguin Penguin (U-Ri-Ku-Pen), are part of a team of brave young animals that rescues others in peril—a sort of animal **THUNDERBIRDS 2086**. Other team members included a dog, a boar, a deer, a koala, a mouse, a seagull, and a lion, but the title would have become too unwieldy even for such a long-running show if they'd all been included in the acronym, although it would have been fun listening to announcers say, "And now, it's time for *Uriqpen-inu-bu-shi-ko-nezu-kamome-shi*." The animals would win a prize for completing a mission, as would the viewers, who were encouraged to write in and guess which of the creatures would save the world by each Friday (a single mission stretched over a week of TV). Created by Mitsuru Kaneko, this show was given a limited broadcast on some American local TV stations for the Japanese community.

UROTSUKIDOJI *
1987. JPN: *Chojin Densetsu Urotsuki-doji*. AKA: *Legend of the Overfiend: Wandering Child; Wandering Kid*. Video, movie. DIR: Hideki Takayama. SCR: Noboru Aikawa, Goro Sanyo, et al. DES: Rikizo Sekime, Shiro Kasami, Sumito Ioi, Keiichi Sato, Tetsuya Yana-

sawa. ANI: Tetsuya Yanasawa. MUS: Masamichi Amano. PRD: JAVN, Angel. 45 mins., 55 mins. x 3 eps., 50 mins. (v1), 108 mins., 88 mins. (m), 60 mins., 50 mins. x 3 eps. (v2), 40 mins. x 4 eps. (v3).
Every three thousand years, a superbeing is born who will unite the three separate dimensions of humans, demons, and Jujin "man-beasts," bringing about a new world. Man-beast Amanojaku is determined to track down this "Chojin," and after 300 years of wandering, locates demonic forces at work in 1993 Japan. Teenager Nagumo impregnates schoolgirl Akemi, rupturing the fabric of the universe and ushering in the apocalypse. Akemi goes into hibernation for a century to await the birth of her child (the Chojin), and Earth is ravaged by a nuclear war. Decades later, in a Japan ruled by former industrialist Caesar, the Chojin is born early because of the arrival in Tokyo of his diametrical opposite, the Kyo-O (translated variously as Mad King, or Lord of Chaos). Buju, a man-beast hybrid, elopes with Caesar's daughter, Alecto, and finds the Kyo-O in a temple shortly before he is killed. Buju is brought back to life by the Kyo-O (a young girl called Himi whose growth is rapidly accelerated) and overthrows Caesar. He vows to take Himi to Osaka to confront the Chojin. Despite the efforts of the Chojin to stop him, he eventually succeeds—Chojin drinks a drop of the blood from Himi's first menstruation, and the world is restored to normality.
Based on the violent and pornographic 1985 manga by Toshio Maeda for *Wani* magazine, **UROTSUKIDOJI** is the best-known of the anime "nasties" released in English in the 1990s. A fiercely complex cycle of rape and redemption, it even seems to have confused its Japanese crew—the first three episodes take place in Osaka, the next two are set *before* the third episode, with the same characters inexplicably moved to Tokyo. This leap backward seems designed to incorporate the Kyo-O subplot, vital to the rest of the series,

but unnecessary if the series were to end early; though considering that the series has a fiendishly cyclical plot (like its contemporary **GALL FORCE**), it is conceivable that one is set several eons after the other! Perplexity continued in the English-language market, where the series was dubbed by three different companies using different actors and contradictory translations. The first five-part video series was edited into the two "movies," *Legend of the Overfiend* and *Legend of the Demon Womb*. In the U.S., all five video episodes appeared, numbered 1 to 5 in order of release, not action, to add to the confusion. The massive and (to the Japanese originators) completely unexpected success of the series in English led to the making of two sequels. The four-part *Return of the Overfiend* (1993) featured the postholocaust chapters, followed by *Inferno Road* (1995), which concludes the saga in three parts. However, though the series is complete in the U.S., *Inferno Road* was delayed by the British censor for three years. Eventually, the final chapter alone was permitted a release in 2001—the British DVD sheepishly includes the scripts of the banned episodes to compensate.

Urotsukidoji amply achieves Maeda's overriding narrative aim—to demonstrate that the only way to win in this world is to die young before your dreams are shattered. The question for his critics, in both the pro- and anticensorship lobbies, is whether the poetry of the end justifies the gross extremity of the means. Since *Urotsukidoji*, many other Maeda works have been adapted, including **DEMON BEAST INVASION**, **ADVENTURE KID**, **LA BLUE GIRL**, **NIGHTMARE CAMPUS**, and **DEMON WARRIOR KOJI**. Though the *Urotsukidoji* saga is now complete in manga form, recent spinoffs have included stories of the Chojin's earlier manifestations in human history, leaving a rich vein of material for potential further anime installments. Scenes from *Urotsukidoji*, **MD GEIST**, and **PERFECT BLUE** were shown onstage as part of Madonna's Drowned World tour in 2001, **CNV**

URUSEI YATSURA *

1981. AKA: *Those Obnoxious Aliens; Weird Folk from Planet Uru; Noisy People*. TV series, movie, video. DIR: Mamoru Oshii, Keiji Hayakawa, Tameo Ogawa, Kazuo Yamazaki, Satoshi Dezaki, Katsuhisa Yamada, Setsuko Shibunnoichi. SCR: Hiroyuki Hoshiyama, Masaru Yamamoto, Shunsuke Kaneko, Ichiro Izumi, Takao Koyama, Kazunori Ito, Michiru Shimada, Tomoko Konparu, Hideo Takayashiki. DES: Akemi Takada, Torao Arai, Setsuko Shibunoichi, Kumiko Takahashi. ANI: Katsumi Aoshima, Yuichi Endo, Tsukasa Dokite, Yukari Kobayashi, Kumiko Takahashi. MUS: Shinsuke Kazato, Izumi Kobayashi, Fumitaka Anzai, Masamichi Amano, Toshiyuki Omori, Mitsuru Kotaki. PRD: Studio Pierrot, Kitty Film, Fuji TV. 25 mins. x 218 eps. (TV), 101 mins., 98 mins., 90 mins., 95 mins., 85 mins., 77 mins. (m), 45 mins. x 2 eps., 57 mins., 30 mins. x 2 eps., 25 mins. x 6 eps. (v). The alien Oni race decide to invade Earth but offer to leave if Earth's champion can defeat theirs at a game of tag. But the randomly selected Earth champion is Ataru Moroboshi, a hapless Japanese teenage lecher. Racing the beautiful Princess Lum, Ataru tricks her by stealing her bikini top and wins the game. Earth is saved, but he has gained an alien fiancée living in his closet. She may be sexy, but she has the power to electrocute him if he goes near another girl and is fiercely jealous of his many love interests, including his Earth-girl paramour, Shinobu.

One of Western fandom's favorites, based on the 1978 *Shonen Sunday* manga by Rumiko Takahashi, this romantic comedy mixes sci-fi with **JAPANESE FOLK TALES** and suburban life. Takahashi has a dark side, but she keeps it for her horror stories like **MERMAID'S FOREST**; in most of her work, creatures of all planets share the same failings and desires, and there is more of a gulf between male and female than there can ever be between human and alien.

The TV series (sadly showing its age

Flung a century into the future, demon-child Jiro is revived by the friendly crew of a passing spaceship, unaware that his sworn enemy lurks nearby. Go Nagai's **SHUTENDOJI** cleverly interweaves folktales of foundling children and demonic underworlds with a superheroic story line akin to his earlier **DEVILMAN**. But in keeping to specifically Japanese lore, *Shutendoji* avoids the multimyth mess of its predecessor, resulting in a tale that is by turns gripping and chilling. *Shutendoji* also cleverly exploits the confusion and alienation of an adolescent audience, in a more subtle manner than the more infamous **UROTSUKIDOJI**. *See entry p. 355.*

Shutendoji

© 1989 GO NAGAI/DYNAMIC PLANNING, INC. • NIPPON COLUMBIA CO., LTD.

in terms of animation quality) introduces us to Lum, her unlikely beloved Ataru, the unluckiest, laziest, and most lecherous boy on Earth, and their associates, including his helplessly uncomprehending parents, her dreamboat ex-boyfriend, Rei, her bratty cousin, Ten-chan, and her many pretty friends. The original series is loaded with topical domestic humor in the manner of a Japanese *Simpsons*, but though little of this survives translation, the fresh, funny slapstick and situations do, along with an educational quantity unforeseen by the original filmmakers. *UY's* depiction of mundane *Japanese* life is a window onto a culture alien to many Western fans, a fact cleverly exploited in the studiously annotated subtitled releases from AnimEigo. The TV series is a delight from beginning to end and absolutely deserves its fan-favorite status; its stablemate **RANMA 1/2**, originally made for an audience too young to remember the early *UY*, has attained a similar status simply by copying it.

The movies and videos are all variations on the same theme—love, and the crazy deceptions we play in its name. The first two movies are directed by **GHOST IN THE SHELL**'s Mamoru Oshii and designed by Kazuo Yamazaki. *Only You* (1983) introduces another alien fiancée for Ataru, and shows Lum's desperate attempts to save him from walking to the altar with Elle, a girl who rules a planet with décor straight out of a rose-strewn Harlequin fantasy. In the surreal *Beautiful Dreamer* (1984), the characters are caught up in Ataru's recurring dream, enabling Oshii to play with perceptions of reality within the conventional format of a romantic comedy. Yamazaki moved up to direct *Remember My Love* (1985) with character designs by Takada. This tale of transdimensional travel, obsessive love, and the line between childhood and adulthood remains, for all its lunatic wrappings (such as Ataru transformed into a pink hippo and a Bradburyesque nightmare circus that later showed up in NEO-TOKYO and SAILOR MOON), the purest SF story ever achieved by the *UY* team. *Lum the Forever* (1986) was again directed by Yamazaki and designed by Takeda, with DIRTY PAIR's Dokite directing the animation. The gang is making a film, with Lum as the star, but all the surrounding activity, including the cutting down of an ancient cherry tree, has awakened a curse that may change their lives forever and lead to the loss of the things they value most. *UY The Final Chapter* (1988, *Kanketsuhen*) puts the romantic boot on the other foot; instead of Ataru running after some cute girl, Lum is carried off by an alien hunk named Lupa, to whom, it appears, her grandfather promised her in marriage when she was still a baby. Neither Ataru nor Carla (Lupa's girlfriend) is pleased, and the chaos culminates in yet another game of tag to decide the fate of Earth. Dezaki directed Konparu's screenplay with designs by Shibunnoichi. Typically, the "final chapter" wasn't—the last *UY* movie was actually *Always (Itsudatte) My Darling* (1991), made when *UY* had been supplanted on TV by *Ranma*, reversing the previous plot for a kidnap tale in which Ataru is carried off by an alien princess named Lupica, and Lum sets out to get him back with a little help from biker goddess Benten and snow princess

Oyuki. It was made by a new team, with Yamada in the director's chair, Takayashiki joining Konparu on screenplay, another Takahashi (Kumiko) designing and directing the animation, and music from Koteki.

The ever-increasing cost of moviemaking coincided with the rise of the video format that started with DALLOS in 1983. In 1986, the Japanese *UY* fan club began screening "exclusive" minimovies at public events, soon revealed to be advance copies of the straight-to-video *UY* releases *Ryoko's September Tea Party* and *Memorial Album*. Both stories used flashback footage from the series with about 15 minutes of new framing animation to recount the past history of the characters and episodes from the story line—a useful way of hooking new video buyers to boost TV series sales on video. A new story, *Inaba The Dream Maker* (1987), featured a transdimensional white rabbit and answered the question of what happens when you unlock doors in time and space without knowing where they lead. Next up was the insanely funny *Raging Sherbet* (1988), in which flying alien icecream cones carry out kamikaze revenge attacks on Lum's greedy girlfriend Ran. Ghost love story *Nagisa's Fiancé* appeared the same year. Then 1989 brought four new romantic-comedy stories. *I Howl at the Moon* has Ataru gobbling Lum's cooking and turning into a wolf. *Catch the Heart* has hardnosed Ran involved in chaos when a spirit gives her a candy that makes capturing the heart of the one you love a breeze. *Goat and Cheese* shows the problems of ancient and incomprehensible family curses when Mendo's father breaks one by taking a picture in front of the statue of great-grandfather's goat, and *The Electric Household Guard* gives Mendo a new servant with eyes only for his sister, Kyoko. In 1991 the series was rounded off with *Terror of Girly-eye Measles*, in which Ataru's womanizing ways spread an alien virus all over town, and *Date with a Spirit*, in which he tries to date a pretty ghost haunting sorceress Sakura's fiancé. An

improvisational dub of two episodes by minor British celebrities was screened as *Lum the Invader Girl* (2000) as part of a "Japan Night" on a U.K. cable channel. *Ill. p. 337.*

USHIO AND TORA *

1992. JPN: *Ushio to Tora*. Video. DIR: Kunihiko Yuyama. SCR: Kenji Terada, Kunihiko Yuyama. DES: Tokuhiro Matsubara. ANI: Tokuhiro Matsubara. MUS: Shiro Sagisu. PRD: Pastel, Toho. 30 mins. x 11 eps.

Ushio Aotsuki is the grandson of a priest and guardian of an ancient temple, where (so he is told) the malevolent spirit Nagatobimaru (Lord Long-Flyer) has been imprisoned for centuries, impaled on the magical Spear of Beast. He discovers the old legends are true when he inadvertently releases the spirit. Invisible to others, Tora (as Ushio calls Nagatobimaru) claims he would dearly love to eat Ushio but cannot get close to him while Ushio hangs onto the spear. The second-sight provided by the spear allows Ushio to see a whole world of spirits living amid our own, and, in an unlikely team with Tora, he sets out busting ghosts in the neighborhood. These include a stone centipede in a school storeroom, sickle-carrying weasels, a group of flying heads, and floating clouds of bad vibes.

Combining a reluctant-buddies/unwelcome-guest plot with modern rewrites of JAPANESE FOLK TALES, *U&T* began as a 1990 *Shonen Sunday* manga by Kazuhiro Fujita, only parts of which are adapted here. Despite the obvious potential for a long-running TV series (the manga tops 30 volumes), *U&T* stayed on video and fizzled out in the mid-1990s, while its inferior contemporary TENCHI MUYO! ripped off its premise before swapping the ghostbusting for interminable flirting. The show comes laden with arch observations on modern Japan in the style of POMPOKO— the samurai-era Tora cannot eat today's people because they daub themselves with sickly perfumes; the sickle-weasels must disguise themselves as humans to survive; and a sea monster made of drowned souls is rendered invulnerable by modern pollution. As in **DEVIL HUNTER YOHKO**, new construction disturbs the ancient dead, while modern children are their inheritors and saviors—Ushio is the descendant of a warrior-mage, and his friend Mayuko the reincarnation of an exorcist. This anime also features some unexpected changes of tone—despite their antagonism, Ushio and Tora complement each other like signs of the Chinese zodiac (*ushi*/ox and *tora*/tiger), and it is Ushio who leaps to Tora's defense when he is pursued by talisman master Piao, a Cantonese exorcist who mistakenly believes Tora killed his family. Similarly, while Ushio spars constantly with local tomboy Asako, he is prepared to fight for her against Tsubura, the spirit of a water wheel who wishes to carry her away (this episode is the only one not taken directly from the manga). The series ends with a spoof episode, the *C[omical] D[eforme] Theater*, in which cartoon versions of the characters fight, sing songs, and eventually appear in their own zany silent movie. There was also an audio spinoff on the *U&T Original Album*, which featured music "inspired by" the series from Seikima-II guitarist Ace Shimizu (see **HUMANE SOCIETY**).

A welcome antidote to the teen wish-fulfillment pap that dominated much of the anime market throughout the 1990s, *U&T* is by turns funny, exciting, and reflective, distinguished by two separate translations, of which the U.S. version by ADV is the superior. **ⒹⓋ**

UTENA *

1997. JPN: *Shojo Kakumei Utena*. AKA: *Revolutionary Girl Utena; La Fillette Revolutionnaire Utena; Ursula's Kiss*. TV series, movie. DIR: Kunihiko Ikuhara, Shingo Kaneko, Toru Takahashi, Tatsuo Okazaki, Akihiko Nishiyama, Katsushi Sakurabi, Takafumi Hoshikawa, Shigeo Koshi, Hiroaki Sakurai. SCR: Yoji Enokido, Noboru

Higa, Kazuhiro Uemura, Ryoei Tsukimura. DES: Chiho Saito, Shinya Hasegawa. ANI: Shinya Hasegawa, Tomoko Kawasaki, Yuji Matsukura. MUS: Shinkichi Mitsumune, J.A. Seazar. PRD: Be-Papas, JC Staff, TV Tokyo. 25 mins. x 39 eps. (TV), 75 mins. (m).

Pink-haired tomboy Utena Tenjo (a surname infuriatingly mispronounced throughout the U.S. dub) is an eighth grader at Otori Academy. She clings to the memory of her childhood encounter with a mysterious "prince" as she wept by the grave of her parents. Though she cannot remember his face (refer to **CANDY CANDY**), she treasures the rose signet ring he gave her and, for reasons not totally clear, resolves to dress and behave as a boy until she finds him again.

Otori is a teen fantasy, where teachers live in fear of the student council and sputter impotently at pupils' "witty" comebacks, the boys and girls are all beautiful, and dueling is the number-one occupation. Fencers regularly meet for ritual combat within a gargantuan hall (part of the school, yet also a separate dimension), where they fight for the right to the hand of Anthy, the "Rose Bride" whose body is a living sheath for a sword. Victorious in battle, Utena becomes Anthy's betrothed, though the student council do what they can to topple her because they are searching for the ultimate duelist who will summon forth the divine power known as "Dios."

Portentous and pretentious in equal amounts, *Utena* quite literally invests teenage crushes and schoolgirl intrigues with world-shattering significance. Created by director Ikuhara, with several other staffers from his earlier **SAILOR MOON** S, and Chiho Saito, who drew the *Utena* manga for *Ciao* magazine, it artfully perverts mundane school life into a quest of fantastic proportions. It also features swordplay and cross-dressing in the swashbuckling tradition of **PRINCESS KNIGHT** and **ROSE OF VERSAILLES**, to which it owes a heavy aesthetic debt. Director Ikuhara acknowledges a strong influence from

TRAGEDY OF BELLADONNA, the film that inspired him to work in anime. Like the tarot-themed episodes of **ESCAFLOWNE**, *Utena* presents its heroine with a series of subtext-laden duels to test her mettle, forging her into a suitable messiah. Highly sensual though rarely explicit, its premise is ironically close to that of an **UROTSUKIDOJI** that replaces sex and violence with pure, infinite yearning. On Japanese TV, *Utena* thrived in the vacuum left by the conclusion of **EVANGELION**, though it was not without controversy—in a ludicrous outbreak of racism, the TV Tokyo switchboard received complaints that love interest Anthy was "black."

Many better-known fairy tales are mixed and matched with situation comedy: one character proudly displays a "designer pendant" that is nothing more than a cowbell, then slowly transforms into a cow before the others' eyes. In another, tomboy Utena and twee Anthy swap personalities after a particularly hot curry. Amid all the school high jinks, the central story continues, as girls pine for their princes, boys for their princesses, and a plot with the vague aims of "bringing revolution and attaining eternity" advances ever onward. Ikuhara brings sensibilities and themes from his own *Sailor Moon S* episodes to this unlikely confection of swords and roses, mirroring the rollercoaster of teenage emotions in a whirl of seductive imagery. Unlike **SLAYERS,** which mixes "real" elements into its fantasy world for comic effect, *Utena* coats the real world in fantasy but lets the sharp edges show through. Beautiful clothes and skill with a sword can't ward off the pain of inadequacy and loss—though they certainly *look* good. The series too places increasing emphasis on style over substance as it progresses, becoming ever more surreal, with additional digital effects in the last season.

The movie *Adolescence of Utena* (1999) wraps up the story with a fantasy that summarizes its main themes in a succession of vignettes rather than providing a logical conclusion. It's therefore incomprehensible to anyone who has not seen the preceding series; a hallucinogenic whirl of tortured relationships, floating roses, flying cars, flashing blades, and gorgeous costumes. *Ill. p. 235.*

UTSUNOMIKO

1989. AKA: *Celestial Prince.* Movie, video. DIR: Fumio Kurokawa (m), Tetsuo Imazawa (v). SCR: Kenji Terada, Sukehiro Tomita (m), Junji Takegami, Sukehiro Tomita (v). DES: Mutsumi Inomata (m), Teruyoshi Yamazaki (v). ANI: Chuichi Iguchi, Kazuya Kise. MUS: Chiyoshi Kawano (m), Masahiro Kawasaki (v). PRD: Nippon Animation, Toei Animation. 83 mins. (m1), 30 mins. x 13 eps., 75 mins. (m2).

Based on Keisuke Fujikawa's novel of mythical 7th-century Japan, the first movie, subtitled *Earth Chapter*, introduces the divine child Utsunomiko, born with a tiny horn on his head but otherwise a normal mystic hero. Trained with a group of friends by the mysterious priest Ojino, he is a fine fighter but will only ever use a bamboo staff. When the group is forced to fight a cruel overlord and his diabolical allies, they must prove their courage and strength to save their friends. In the video series, subtitled *Heaven Chapter*, Imazawa used Inomata's designs but completely changed the staff. Yamazaki redesigned the characters, and new music was provided by Kawasaki. Ojino gives the friends a magic Phoenix ship that takes them to heaven, but Utsunomiko finds the gods can be just as cruel as humans, and he fights them for the rights of the people, eventually changing into his god-form as the only way to win and finally meet his father, the supreme lord of heaven. The clash between the "new" Buddhist practices and native Shinto spirits, as well as the civil disorders of the time, form the backdrop to a series of richly designed adventures, and the video animation is (unusually) better than that of the 1988 film, allowing for better appreciation of the subtlety of Inomata's work. The 1990 film *U: Heaven Chapter* was a short reworking of the video series.

V

VAMPIRE

1968. TV series. DIR: Tsutomu Yamada, Tei Mabune. SCR: Yasuhiro Yamaura, Masaki Tsuji, Toshiro Fujinami, Tomohiro Ando, Shunichi Yukimuro, Yoshiyuki Fukuda. DES: Osamu Tezuka. ANI: Renzo Kinoshita. MUS: Hikaru Hayashi. PRD: Mushi Pro, Fuji TV. 25 mins. x 26 eps.
Toppei Tachibana is an everyday worker at the Mushi Pro company, who is secretly one of the Clan of Night's Weeping, a were-creature. Mr. Morimura, a reporter from the *Daily Times* researching vampires, discovers that Toppei transforms into a wolf whenever he sees a full moon and starts to chronicle both his activities and his secret feud with other clan members. A self-referential series from Tezuka, disastrously mixing animated supernatural creatures with live-action footage, shot in and around his own studios—the ASTRO BOY–creator would later do his best to edge *Vampire* out of his biography. Tezuka, Toppei's boss in real life and onscreen, plays himself in the series, while behind the scenes are several staff borrowed from ULTRAMAN's Tsuburaya studios and respected arthouse animator Renzo Kinoshita (see WARTIME ANIME). Compare to the later BORN FREE.

VAMPIRE HUNTER D *

1985. JPN: *Vampire Hunter D.* Movie. DIR: Toyoo Ashida. SCR: Yasushi Hirano. DES: Yoshitaka Amano, Noriyasu Yamaura. ANI: Hiromi Matsushita. MUS: Tetsuya Komuro. PRD: Ashi Pro. 80 mins., ca. 120 mins.
Ten thousand years in the future, humanity lives in a quasi-medieval society overrun by the vampires who keep them in a state of feudal subjugation and terror. When Count Lee claims Doris as his next bride, a mysterious cloaked stranger in a big hat, known only as "D," rides into town on a huge horse and saves her. The townspeople want to give her up to pacify the count, but Doris has fallen in love with her vampire-hunter savior. "D" has to clean out the nest of vampires, but he's not without problems of his own. His hand has an independent life and nags him mercilessly, and his own background as a half-vampire is the cause of much inner conflict.

The film is based on a long series of novels by Hideyuki Kikuchi, who also created WIND OF AMNESIA, WICKED CITY, and DARKSIDE BLUES. Despite the Hammer-horror trappings, at heart *VHD* is more like a vampire Western. The character designs, based on Amano's illustrations for the novels, may entice lovers of his smoky, elegant watercolors and baroque game characters, but they were radically simplified to cut animation costs, with only traces of the artist's hand remaining, mostly in still frames. Technically it's showing its age, but a U.S.–Japanese coproduction planned for release in 2001 may fare better among modern fans.

Based on Kikuchi's third novel, *D: Demon Deathchase*, and shown unfinished and unedited as a "work in progress" at the Fantasia 2000 festival, the new version, *VHD Bloodlust*, is directed and scripted by NINJA SCROLL's Yoshiaki Kawajiri. As with the original, the story is based on part of Kikuchi's epic novel series but adds a greater emphasis on action. D, revealed as a half-vampire or "dhampir," is one of several hunters hired to rescue Charlotte, the daughter of a wealthy family, who has been kidnapped by a vampire; but she has fallen in love with her captor. Does he kill them both, or allow her to escape the misery of human life and flee to another planet with her lover? Characters are designed by Yutaka Minowa, monsters by Yasushi Nirasawa, and animation is by Madhouse. **NV**

VAMPIRE PRINCESS MIYU *

1988. JPN: *Kyuketsuki Miyu.* AKA: *Vampire Miyu.* Video, TV series. DIR: Toshihiro Hirano. SCR: Noboru Aikawa, Yuji Hayami. DES: Narumi Kakinouchi, Yasuhiro Moriki (v), Megumi Kadonosono, Kenji Teraoka (TV). ANI: Narumi Kakinouchi, Masahiro Nishii. MUS: Kenji Kawai. PRD: AIC, Pony Canyon. 30 mins. x 4 eps. (v), 25 mins. x 25 eps. (TV).
Himiko is a cynical, charlatan "medium" faced with a real-life case of demonic possession in Japan's former capital of Kyoto. There, amid sleepy, leafy lanes, she witnesses a battle between the Shinma, evil "demon-god" creatures from another dimension, and Earth's only protector, a vampire princess called Miyu.

Like Claudia in Anne Rice's *Interview with the Vampire*, Miyu is a former human who bears a vampire curse, trapped forever in a world of teenage angst. Motivated sometimes less by a sense of justice than by her own raging hormones, she pushes a succubus away from a man she secretly wants herself, parades Lolita-fashion around her devoted servant (and former enemy) Larva, and slowly worms her way into

Himiko's life. Like PET SHOP OF HOR-RORS, *VPM* features the ghostbusting odd-couple of a mundane person from our world and a flashy spellcaster from the next. The olde-worlde charm of Kyoto makes a nice change from the sprawling city of Tokyo, particularly when the animation has aged so well. But amid the long, long silences and dark, meaningful glances, *VPM* is a mass of contradictions. As Himiko points out in a rare moment of lucidity, Miyu walks around in daylight, licks up holy water, and can crush a crucifix in her bare hands—so for the peculiarly picky audience of vampire folklorists, *VPM* is little more convincing than the execrable BEAST CITY. Furthermore, since she often seems only to be protecting people so she can chow down on their jugular veins, what exactly makes her any better than the creatures she is supposed to be fighting? Don't expect any answers, because Miyu (and, it would seem, her creator Narumi Kakinouchi) would rather smile condescendingly and tell you that you could never understand rather than admit they don't know either.

Sometimes this approach pays off, especially when the story reverses the roles of the sexes. It makes a change to see a predatory succubus chasing after a young *male* virgin, or indeed to see a vain pretty-*boy* selling his soul to the devil to keep his looks forever. There are some great ideas, such as the girl who loses her mind because she is kept alive by blood transfusions from her dying parents, or alien parasites that feed off people's dreams. But such moments are few, making for an elegantly chilling and curiously watchable anime that constantly promises more than it delivers.

The video series is based on Kaki-nouchi's 1988 manga and directed by her husband, one of Japan's masters of horror and creator of ICZER-ONE. In 1997, it was snapped up for TV adaptation amid the post-EVANGELION boom when so many old video shows were reborn as cheap but at least *partly* mar-ket-tested TV. The TV series, conceived by Kakinouchi, Hirano, and Yuji Hayanami, introduced new characters such as Miyu's little bat-winged rabbit Shina, and another servant, Reiha, a snow demon who detests Miyu and also has the power to send Shinma back to the shadows. Reiha confides in her doll while chirpy human schoolgirl Chisato balances Miyu's coldness and further enhances the disturbing links between magic and childhood. Megumi Kadonosono reworks the character designs without obvious disharmony, and Kenji Kawai's music is just as evoca-tive and elegant. Hirano (by this point using his real first name of Toshiki) dis-liked some of the changes required by Japanese TV censorship, including the removal of much of the projected sec-ond episode story line, and restored the deletions for the video release in 1998. Another Kakinouchi project, *Vampire Princess Yui*, the story of a girl whose mother was bitten by Miyu while pregnant, is due out on video from the same team. **Ⓥ**

VAMPIRE WARS *
1990. Video. DIR: Kazuhisa Takenouchi. SCR: Hiroyuki Hoshiyama. DES: Hideki Hamazu, Hiroyuki Kitazume. ANI: Hideki Hamazu. MUS: Kazz Toyama. PRD: Toei. 50 mins. Japanese agent Kosaburo Kuki (sort of) hides out in Paris in the company of dialogue-challenged whores and meets Lamia Vindaw, a girl who's sort of chummy with "vampires," who are really a galaxy-spanning alien race that have achieved immortality by storing life-giving energy in their bodies. Human blood provides a weak source of this energy, but Lamia's altered body chemistry has a uniquely powerful ver-sion. It's just what the aliens need to revive their king, trapped in a deep sleep in Transylvania ever since the visi-tors arrived five thousand years ago. Meanwhile, Monsieur Lassar of the French Secret Service thinks there is a connection between a terrorist attack on a NASA base in Arizona and the murder of a CIA man in Paris, and he hires Kuki to find out. Naturally, it's Lamia that is the key, though the more interesting elements of the back story are only revealed in the final moments of this awful anime, which is little more than an ad for the opening chapters of the best-selling Kiyoshi Kasai novel on which it is based. Most but not all ani-me novel adaptations suffer in the tran-sition, mainly from being cut down to fit a 50-minute running time—barely enough to contain the average short story. However, such bastard children of the industry are often sold off at a bargain price to foreign companies (for obvious reasons), though any who pay for them discover at their cost that there is negligible pressure to rush out the next part—thus the interminable wait over the next episodes of HEROIC LEGEND OF ARSLAN.

The original Lamia of vampire leg-end was Queen of Libya and one of Zeus's many lovers. She was trans-formed into a child-eating monster, giv-ing her name to a race of ghoulish female demons with a craving for blood. This tired story does no credit to its ancient antecedents. **ⒸⓁⓃⓋ**

VANDREAD *
2001. TV series. DIR: Takeshi Mori, Hitoyuki Matsui. SCR: Atsuhiro Tomio-ka, Natsuko Takahashi. DES: Mahiro Maeda, Kazuya Kuroda, Tomohiro Kawahara. ANI: Takahiro Fujii, Satoshi Kawano. MUS: N/C. PRD: Gonzo, Media Factory, WOWOW. 25 mins. x 13 eps. War has been raging for generations between the all-male planet Talac and the all-female planet Majel. Suspend disbelief as to how they keep this up, then imagine that they are invaded by a common enemy and forced to settle their differences for a united counter-attack. The first meeting of 16-year-old Talac engineer Hibiki Tokai and Majel babe Dirda is unplanned; he gets tired of his mundane job assembling robots and plots to steal one of his own. He stows away on a Talac immigration ship, but then the ship is attacked by a Majel pirate. But, despite their races' history of separate development, Hibi-

ki and Dirda will eventually work things out. The script cleverly exploits the mutual attraction/repulsion of teenagers of opposite sexes, though the visuals resort to standard fan-service ogling of female charms.

VANILLA SERIES *
1999. JPN: *Kiss Yori; Rosoku no Yashiki; Shimei Ijiri; Mei King; Ikenie*. AKA: *More Than a Kiss; House of Wax; Interfering With Sisters; Mei King; Holy Sacrifice (Sins of the Flesh)*. Video. DIR: Rion Kujo, Norihiko Nagahama, Teruaki Murakami. SCR: N/C. DES: Raihiken. ANI: Raihiken, Tetsuya Ono. MUS: N/C. PRD: Vanilla. 30 mins. x 10 eps.
An umbrella title for several unrelated porno anime in the style of **COOL DEVICES** or **SECRET ANIMA**—all based on lecherous computer/video games. The Sega Saturn–originated *Kiss Yori* (#1–3) features Masato, an aspiring novelist who moves to a seaside town for a working vacation while looking for candidates for a summertime fling. Masato's friend Oka finds his dream girl working at a restaurant, but Masato rekindles his love with his high-school sweetheart, Chisato, before juggling her with a succession of other girls in the style of an erotic **TENCHI MUYO!** Released in three seasonally themed chapters, *Kiss Yori*'s English-language release featured a title change to *Summer Heat, Autumn Heat*, and *Winter Heat*. *House of Wax* (#4–5), a tale based on a PC game, features extensive scenes of bondage in a secluded forest mansion between a father and his daughters. Similar sibling seductions occur in *Interfering with Sisters* (#6–7), in which a perverse grandfather orders two girls to behave as if they are his dolls. *Mei King* (#8–9) is another outbreak of the **CREAM LEMON** virus, as a man called Cane falls in love with a spirit trapped inside the body of a young girl called Charlotte. In *Holy Sacrifice* (#10, released in English as *Sins of the Flesh*), talented artist Adolfo wants to enter the Church and live out his days painting angels, though temptations of the flesh present themselves in the form of

the country girl Michaela, with predictable results. Though episodes #4–9 are unavailable in English at time of writing, they are likely to be sooner rather than later.

VARIABLE GEO *
1996. Video. DIR: Toru Yoshida. SCR: Yosuke Kuroda. DES: Takahiro Kimura. ANI: Takahiro Kimura. MUS: Harukichi Yamamoto. PRD: KSS. 30 mins. x 3 eps.
This ridiculously puerile anime was based on a video game that must have seemed like a really good idea at the time. Waitresses from rival restaurants meet in public fighting bouts in which they pound each other into submission (see **STREET FIGHTER II**). The ultimate winner gets $10 million and some prime real estate in the city of her choice. The loser must strip off her clothes and humiliate herself in front of the audience (see **SEXORCIST**). Meanwhile, a shadowy secret organization (see **TOSHINDEN**) is planning to use the ultimate winner's DNA to breed the ultimate warrior (see **TEKKEN**). Plucky heroine Yuka Takeuchi punches and kicks her way through a series of opponents from the game (see all of the above), in a succession of ludicrous set pieces that show off fighting catchphrases and special moves (ditto). Working conditions in the fighting-evil trade have obviously gone downhill—this never happened to the Knight Sabers. It lasts 90 minutes. Life's too short, really. Trust us.

VENUS FIVE *
1994. JPN: *Sailor Senshi Venus Five*. AKA: *Sailor Warriors Venus Five*. Video. DIR: Satoshi Inoue, Kan Fukumoto. SCR: Wataru Amano. DES: Rin Shin. ANI: N/C. MUS: N/C. PRD: Daiei. 45 mins. x 2 eps.
Five beautiful teenage girls are destined to battle the evil Inma Empire led by the perverted Necros. The empire aims to revive the god Apollo from his ten-thousand-year slumber in order to gain his near-infinite power. And the only thing that will revive a

god is . . . yes, you've guessed it, the sexual secretions of certain beautiful high-school girls. Unfortunately for the bad guys, our heroines have been recruited by the Goddess of Love to ensure that the power of evil doesn't triumph, and Aphrodite has even sent them a talking cat to help them. A shameless **SAILOR MOON** parody based on a manga by Jin Ara, *V5* is aimed straight at the fans who dream of seeing more than just a flash of thigh in those transformation sequences. The girls mimic the Sailor Scouts every way they can—fighting poses, speeches, costumes, all are so close to the original that they could be twins. There, however, all similarity ends, as the cat talks dirty, the tentacles multiply, and the smut takes over. This is for all those out there who snicker at a bad guy called Count Uranus, as well as connoisseurs of Immortal Dialogue like, "Let me entice you to the very summit of lust."

VENUS WARS *
1989. JPN: *Venus Senki*. AKA: *Venus War Chronicle*. Movie. DIR: Yoshikazu Yasuhiko. SCR: Yuichi Sasamoto, Yoshikazu Yasuhiko. DES: Hiroyoshi Yokoyama, Yoshikazu Yasuhiko, Sachiko Kamimura, Hirotoshi Sano,

Makoto Kobayashi, Shichiro Kobayashi. ANI: Yoko Kamimura. MUS: Joe Hisaishi. PRD: Triangle Staff, Kugatsu-sha. 104 mins.

Young journalist Susan Sommers arrives on Venus to cover the war between its two nation-states just before the troops of Ishtar take the capital and overcome the armies of Aphrodia. She meets a group of young motorcycle punks, the Killer Commandos, led by Hiro. Previously engaged in racing other gangs around a makeshift circuit in scenes reminiscent of *Rollerball*, Hiro and some of his team fight a guerrilla action against the occupying forces of Ishtar, and Susan soon loses her journalistic objectivity as she is drawn into the struggle. Based on one of Yasuhiko's own manga, and with music by the man who has given both Hayao Miyazaki and Beat Takeshi some unforgettable themes, this glossily produced and well-designed film ought to be a classic, but it just misses the mark. Sasamoto contributes an intelligent script in which our young hotheads learn that not all adults are brain-dead, not all organization is tyranny, and not all action is sensible. There's plenty to interest the genre fan, including some good action sequences and fine mecha designs, yet the film lacks the emotional edge and perverse power of Yasuhiko's earlier ARION. A similar Venusian Cold War standoff would appear in BLACK MAGIC.

VICKY THE VIKING *

1974. JPN: *Chiisana Viking Vickie*. AKA: *Vickie the Little Viking*. TV series. DIR: Hiroshi Saito, Noboru Ishiguro, Kiyoshi Harada. SCR: Yuji Fusano, Hiroshi Kaneko, Akira Saiga, Takeshi Hidaka, Chikao Katsui. DES: Shuichi Seki. ANI: Shinichi Tsuji. MUS: Seiichiro Uno. PRD: Zuiyo, Taurus Film, Fuji TV. 25 mins. x 77 eps.

Vicky is the son of Halvar, chief of a little Viking village. He'd rather play than learn to fight, but he is compelled to go on one of the village's raiding expeditions where he manages to foil the plans of the enemy, Sven the Terri-

ble, through his quick wits and courage. Adapted from a series of stories by Runer Jonsson, this German-Japanese coproduction holds the seeds of a great tradition—Zuiyo later became Nippon Animation, whose WORLD MASTERPIECE THEATER series was dedicated to bringing classic stories from the West to Japanese TV.

VICTORY PITCHER

1987. JPN: *Shori Tosha*. Video. DIR: Hiroki Shibata. SCR: Akane Nishiura. DES: Noriko Umeda. ANI: Katsumi Aodori. MUS: Akihiko Matsumoto. PRD: Toei. 72 mins.

Baseball coach Hoshiyama offers a chance to turn professional to Katsumi Kunimasa, a star member of the student squad that won the summer tournament. The young girl becomes a star pitcher for the Chunichi Dragons (conveniently, the team her father owns), and, after a year of triumphs, she leads them to victory in the national championships at legendary Koshien Stadium. Based on the manga by Noriko Umeda, this anime may be compared to the other girl-playing-baseball story SONG OF THE BASEBALL ENTHUSIAST. The Dragons team members are all based on the real-life team, though their opponents are fictional. At the time, the real-life Hoshiyama was a commentator, but fact was eventually true to fiction, and he became the manager for the real-life Dragons.

VIDEO GIRL AI *

1992. JPN: *Denno Shojo Ai*. AKA: *Cyber Girl Ai; Electric Girl Ai*. Video. DIR: Mizuho Nishikubo. SCR: Satoru Akahori. DES: Takayuki Goto. ANI: Takayuki Goto. MUS: Nobuyuki Shimizu. PRD: Production IG, Tatsunoko. 30 mins. x 6 eps.

Average-guy Yota loves girl-next-door Moemi. But Moemi has a crush on local hero Takashi, and to make it worse, Takashi is a nice guy and Yota's best friend. Enter Ai, a disposable alien girl who escapes from a dating video and resolves to get Yota together with his true love. But before you can say "Cyrano de Bergerac," Ai secretly longs

for Yota, too. Ai is a "video girl," designed to distract and amuse, programmed, like all video, with a definite time limit. When her relationship with Yota moves from being a disposable, casual entertainment into more dangerous territory, the "copyright authorities" step in. Yota, Moemi, Ai, and their friends move through the tortuous dance of teenage emotion and sexual longing, beautifully conveying the agonies of alienation and embarrassment inherent in growing up, and also learning that time will not always be on their side.

An unwelcome guest/magical girlfriend tale in the tradition of URUSEI YATSURA and OH MY GODDESS!, playing straight to the gallery with fan-service asides and a loving appreciation of the loser male psyche. Satoru Akahori's script masterfully recreates a world of teenage desperation, far from the madcap comedies for which he is normally known. From the opening shot in which Ai addresses the audience directly, through the regular stuck-record repetition of Moemi's declaration of love for the wrong man, Akahori demonstrates that there's more to him than the slapstick of SORCERER HUNTERS. But occasional moments of unnecessary physical comedy intrude on what could have been a great emotional farce, and sporadic outbreaks of Katsura's trademark panty shots further undermine a show that, at heart, is all heart. After shoving the couple together, Ai immediately breaks them up—a schizophrenic characterization that is one of *Ai*'s biggest flaws. She fluctuates unevenly between bitchy best friend, infuriating tease, and doormat mother-substitute, while Moemi is part drippy little girl, part sassy schemer. Yota himself is half lovable dork, half *annoying* dork, his own wavering interest in his love objects often reduced to comparisons of breast size or cooking ability.

Director Nishikubo's clever camerawork fades the entire world into the background so that only the self-obsessed leads get any screen time, overexposing shots of school life to turn every dingy corridor into a pathway of dreamy bright nostalgia. He puts similar thought into the opening credits, which feature a fully rendered Ai skipping through a world that's often only half-formed, as if the camera itself has eyes only for her. Nishikubo's pauses emphasize the secret language of women, lingering for long moments as Ai and Moemi alternate between friendship and rivalry. The series considerately ends before outstaying its welcome (see **TENCHI MUYO!**), and an excellent dub completes the package.

VIDEO PICTURE BOOK
1988. JPN: *Video Anime E-Bon*. Video. DIR: Noriaki Kairo. SCR: Noriaki Kairo, Shin Yukuba. DES: N/C. ANI: Shunji Saita. MUS: Masahito Maekawa. PRD: Mushi Pro. 12 mins. x 50 eps.
A vast library of classic tales animated in bite-sized chunks, including a number from **AESOP'S FABLES**, **GRIMMS' FAIRY TALES**, **TALES OF HANS CHRISTIAN ANDERSEN**, and the **ARABIAN NIGHTS**. Some of the titles include **JOURNEY TO THE WEST**, *Jack and the Beanstalk*, **CINDERELLA**, **ALICE IN WONDERLAND**, **SNOW WHITE**, **A LITTLE PRINCESS**, **WIZARD OF OZ**, **LITTLE WOMEN**, *Little Red Riding Hood*, *Hansel and Gretel*, **LITTLE MERMAID**, *The Ugly Duckling*, **HEIDI**, **TREASURE ISLAND**, **PETER PAN AND WENDY**, *The Little Match Girl*, *Gulliver's Travels*, **DADDY LONG-LEGS**, **ROBIN HOOD**, **LITTLE LORD FAUNTLEROY**, **SECRET GARDEN**, *Frog Prince*, **THREE MUSKETEERS**, **NOBODY'S BOY**, **NOBODY'S GIRL**, and **ADRIFT IN THE PACIFIC**. A similar concept was on sale at the same time in Aubec's 26-volume *Video Anime Picture Book Theatre: World Masterpiece Children's Stories*.

VIFAM
1983. JPN: *Ginga Hyoryo Vifam*. AKA: *Galactic Tales of Vifam; Galactic Wanderer Vifam; Round Vernian Vifam*. TV series. DIR: Takeyuki Kanda, Susumu Ishizaki, Tetsuro Amino, Osamu Sekita, Seiji Okuda, Junji Nishimura, Kazuo Yamazaki. SCR: Hiroyuki Hoshiyama,

Yasushi Hirano, Tsunehisa Ito. DES: Toyoo Ashida, Kunio Okawara, Shoji Sato. ANI: Toyoo Ashida, Hiroshi Watanabe, Hideyuki Motohashi, Yasushi Nagaoka, Makoto Ito. MUS: Toshiyuki Watanabe. PRD: Sunrise, TBS. 25 mins. x 46 eps. (TV), 50 mins. x 4 eps. (v), 25 mins. x 12 eps. (TV2).
The Terran colony of Kreado is attacked by alien Kuktonian invaders, and when the adult crew of its orbiting space station are all killed, it is up to their 13 surviving children to fight back. Eventually, they reactivate the old starship Janus from dry-dock and prepare to head for their homeworld—a trip fraught with perils both on the planets they pass and within the labyrinthine corridors of the Janus itself. It's a sci-fi remake of **ADRIFT IN THE PACIFIC**, and *Vifam*'s ludicrously overpopulated cast returned in 1984 for video adventures *V: News from Catcher* (*Catcher kara no Benri*), *V: Gathering of the Thirteen* (*Atsumatta Jusanbito*), *V: The 12 Fade Away* (*Kieta Junibito*, also shown in theaters), and *V: Kate's Reflections* (*Kate no Kioku*). The fact that the 4 video episodes follow on from the TV series, break down into eight 25-minute acts, and would have taken the series to a full year's 52 episodes makes it likely that they were the final unbroadcast episodes of the series.
The series was remade by Toshifumi Kawase as *Vifam 13* (1998), reuniting many of the old crew for a production that used previously unfilmed scripts as its basis. For the *V13* story arc, the crew rescue baby Kukto twins from a derelict ship and are forced to juggle child-care with their continuing mission.

VILLGUST
1992. JPN: *Kyoryu Densetsu Villgust*. AKA: *Armored Dragon Legend Villgust*. Video. DIR: Katsuhiko Nishijima. SCR: Satoru Akahori. DES: Katsuhiko Nishijima. ANI: Katsuhiko Nishijima. MUS: Kohei Tanaka. PRD: Animate Film. 30 mins. x 2 eps.
Two separate groups of adventurers meet up in a faux-medieval European

village in the alternate universe of Villgust. Wannabe paladins Kui, Yuta, and cute girls Kris and Fanna are full of high ambitions to protect the land and rid it from evil, while catgirl Ryugia, Marobo the dog-man, Bostof the elf, and cute little girl Lemi are more interested in finding something to eat. They've actually been sent by the presiding goddess of the land to rid Villgust of a dark, evil force that looks suspiciously like Jabba the Hutt. Gabadi is a wicked oppressor with a large band of thoroughly nasty disposable minions, but he's devoted only to his pet frog, Antoinette. Gabadi succeeds in tricking Kui and company into fighting Ryugia (who has a penchant for bikini-style armor, an infantile food fetish, and a set of claws borrowed from X-Man Wolverine) and her friends—the very people intended by Heaven to be their allies! He wants them to destroy each other so that there is no opposition to his evil plans. More through luck than judgment, our heroes eventually start fighting his minions instead of each other, and they battle their way through a tornado, flying slabs of rock, snake-headed monsters, and tentacles to rid the land of his evil and bring peace back to Villgust.
Bandai originated the *gachapon* concept—small plastic toys enclosed in egg-shaped cases and sold for small change in street-corner vending machines. The name is said to be the sound of the egg-shaped cases falling from the machine. These sweet little creatures influenced video games, card games, and manga—Nintendo created the *Villgust* role-playing game based on them, and from that came this video series. So if anyone asks you which came first, it was definitely the egg.

VIOLENCE JACK *
1986. JPN: *Violence Jack Harlem Bomber; Violence Jack Jigokugai; Violence Jack Hell's Wind*. AKA: *VJ Slumking; VJ Hell Town [Evil Town]; VJ Hell's Wind*. Video. DIR: Seiji Okuda, Ichiro Itano. SCR: Noboru Aikawa, Takuya

Wada, Makio Matsushita. DES: Takuya Wada, Moriyasu Taniguchi. ANI: Takuya Wada, Moriyasu Taniguchi. MUS: Hiroshi Ogasawara. PRD: Ashi Pro, Studio 88, Dynamic Planning. 30 mins. x 2 eps. (*Harlem/Slumking*), 30 mins. x 2 eps. (*Hell Town*), 60 mins. (*Hell's Wind*).

A comet strikes Earth and causes a chain reaction of other cataclysms. In Japan, the fault line gives way in the mother of all earthquakes, while the long-dormant volcano Mount Fuji erupts in a spectacular cloud of ash and lava. Survivors trapped in the Tokyo subway system turn into savage tunnel tribes. Gangs of motorcycle bandits roam the land in search of resources. And through the midst of it all walks Violence Jack, a mountain of a man with superhuman strength, inhuman fangs, and absolutely no scruples. Jack is an elemental force, wandering the desolate land like hell's own lawman, coming to the rescue of the assaulted, raped, and injured survivors, but not before the camera has permitted us a long, lingering look at their torments. These include stabbings, shootings, eviscerations, chainsaw decapitation, and someone eating his dead lover.

Often thought to be an inferior remake of FIST OF THE NORTH STAR, *VJ* actually predates it, starting as a 1973 manga in *Goraku* magazine, as the sequel to Go Nagai's DEVILMAN. The video necessarily condensed much of the epic original (Nagai's longest) into a broader, more basic, and much less shocking package, though it remains extremely violent and nasty even when censored—the U.K. running time is considerably shorter than the original. The lead character, with "the strength of a gorilla and teeth of a wolf, blood boiling with the fire of prehistory," is named for the huge jackknife he carries, and the anime focuses on his volcanic nature rather than the tangle of subplots and reincarnations of the manga. The basic postapocalyptic plots of the video version (with knowing winks to *Mad Max*) were originally intended to have some internal coherence but were released in the wrong order outside Japan. The first episode, showing the comet hitting Earth and explaining that Jack is the personification of the Grim Reaper, born from a mound of skulls, is actually *Slumking*, which was inexplicably the *last* episode to be released in the English version. To be fair, the muddled running order hardly makes any difference. The then boss of U.K.'s Manga Entertainment, Mike Preece, coined the term "beer-and-curry movie" for those anime destined to be watched by a group of inebriated teenage boys in search of sex and violence, and *VJ* is exactly what he meant. Those with higher hopes for the anime industry find the show embarrassingly infantile, including the English-language voice cast, who all appear to be using pseudonyms. **CNV**

VIOLINIST OF HAMELIN, THE

1996. JPN: *Hamelun no Violin*. AKA: *Violin of Hamelin*. Movie, TV series. DIR: Takashi Imanishi, Junji Nishimura, Hiroshi Morioka, Akira Kiyomizu. SCR: Takashi Imanishi, Yasuhiro Imagawa. DES: Toshimi Kato. ANI: Toshimi Kato. MUS: Kohei Tanaka. PRD: Nippon Animation, Studio Deen, TV Tokyo. 50 mins. (m), 25 mins. x 25 eps. (TV).

Fifteen years ago, Queen Horn of Sforzando tried to shut evil out of the world of Staccato with a powerful spell, but not even the strongest spell lasts forever, and now Horn's strength is failing. Evil Hell King Bass is trying to break through the barrier and release the "supreme leader" Great Chestra (in Japanese "Oh-kestra"), a dark being of unparalleled power who is trapped somewhere in Staccato. Horn's estranged daughter, Flute, is the only person who can save Sforzando from the inrush of darkness. She's been in hiding for 15 years, but now she is called by her mother to return to Sforzando. She sets out for the capital with her childhood friend and guardian, Hamel, but on the way they have many strange adventures and meet old and new friends. Hamel learns more about the mystery of his past and the strange horn on his head.

Based on a 1991 manga in *Shonen GanGan* by Michiaki Watanabe, *VoH* mixes tragedy and suspense with humor. On the way to becoming a moving picture the story developed a split personality. In 1996, it became a funny movie and was followed soon after by a much darker and more serious TV series—insofar as anything can be dark and serious when the protagonists' main weapons, as well as their names, are musical instruments. The animation in the TV series is noticeably low-budget, too, which caused controversy when the director himself publicly complained about the limited materials he had to work with.

VIOLIN OF THE STARRY SKY

1995. JPN: *Hoshizora no Violin*. Movie. DIR: Setsuo Nakayama. SCR: Toshikai Imaizumi. DES: Mitsuharu Miyamae. ANI: Kazunori Tanabashi. MUS: Kazuki Kuriyama. PRD: Takahashi Studio. 90 mins.

Based on Noboru Wada's true story of the life of the Shinshu violinmaker Kikuji Ozawa (1916–98), who pursued his dream to make and play violins even as the clouds gathered for World War II. Violin music is provided by soloist Mio Umezu.

VIRAGO IN DUNGEON

1991. JPN: *Ozanari Dungeon*. AKA: *Perfunctory Dungeon*. Video. DIR: Hiroshi Aoyama. SCR: Hideki Sonoda. DES: Minoru Maeda. ANI: Yoshikazu Takiguchi, Yasuo Otsuka. MUS: Kazz Toyama and Secret Plans. PRD: Tokyo Movie Shinsha. 30 mins. x 3 eps.

Three adventurers are hired by King Gazelle to steal the Dragon Head relic from the Shrine of Fire. Mocha (sexy elf-babe warrior), Blueman (funny animal cat-thief), and Kilieman (dog-wizard) are startled out of their larcenous intentions when the relic introduces itself to them as Morrow and asks to be taken, not to Gazelle's Tower of Fire, but to the Tower of Wind. Morrow is an organic program that can transform the Tower of Wind into an ultimate weapon called the Space Dragon. Gazelle, he says, is just a frontman for the real enemy, a mysterious being out to control the Space Dragon and destroy the world. Based on the 1987 *Comic Nora* manga by Motoo Koyama, who named the characters after the brands of coffee he was drinking while drawing the series–Mocha, Blue Mountain, and Kilimanjaro.

VIRGIN FLEET *
1991. JPN: *Seishojo Kantai Virgin Fleet.* AKA: *Holy Maiden Fleet Virgin Fleet.* Video. DIR: Masahiro Hosoda. SCR: Yasuhiro Imagawa. DES: Hiroyuki Kitazume. ANI: Hiroyuki Kitazume. MUS: Masanobu Ito. PRD: Beam Entertainment. 30 mins. x 3 eps.
In the 1930s, a group of teenage girls in a Japanese military academy train with a mysterious psychic energy that includes, among other things, weather control and telekinesis and can only be controlled by a few young female virgins. Many years before in WWI, a similar team called the 36 minstrels somehow succeeded in controlling this force and was able to put an end to the fighting. With the political situation growing ever more tense, Russia spying on its neighbors and trying to steal military secrets, and internal squabbling between the leaders of Japan, the nation desperately needs that power once more. A survivor of the Minstrel force is now highly placed in the military command and her daughter heads the academy—but she hasn't inherited her mother's power, which causes some friction between them. And out of the squabbling, shallow band of young ladies in her care, the one who emerges as able to release virgin energy is Shiokaze, who is engaged and whose boyfriend is pressuring her to leave the academy and marry him right away. Sadly, he's not the only man in the story who takes sexism to comic levels—the local military leaders trot out all the clichés about a woman's place in war without any sense of irony, though in the U.S.

dub the director and actors substitute a level of overacting that approaches talent in itself.

VF is part of the subgenre that includes creator Hiroi Oji's earlier **SAKURA WARS**, in which 20th-century military history isn't quite the way the West remembers it. In Oji's cute, squeaky-clean universe, Japan only wants to unleash the massive destructive force of virgin energy to *prevent* more killing—compare to similarly far-fetched avoidances of history in **KISHIN CORPS** and **SUPER ATRAGON**. However, this anime remains curiously endearing, full, like **GUNBUSTER**, of the martial enthusiasm of an undefeated Japan (see **WARTIME ANIME**), with well-animated backgrounds, sepia-toned flashbacks, and intriguing *neverwhen* aircraft designs. The story has some interesting moments and makes a few pointed observations on the real thoughts and feelings of teenagers about jealousy, love, and sex, but like many video anime, it starts a whole raft of subplots that don't go anywhere.

VIRTUA CALL 2 *
1997. Video. DIR: Kaoru Tomioka. SCR: Tetsuya Oseki. DES: N/C. ANI: Mitsuru Fujii. MUS: N/C. PRD: Fairy Dust. 45 mins. x 2 eps.
Virtuacall is the latest development in phone-sex clubs—a virtual meeting service that lets you see, hear, and even touch the man or woman of your dreams. Emily decides to use the service to help Hasegawa, a friend from her apartment building. She desires him, but he seems reluctant to make a move. She plans to assist in building his confidence and improving his chances of scoring by introducing him to Virtuacall for some online practice sessions. The anime is based on a Sega Saturn game; compare to similar cybersex in **SECRET ANIMA**'s *Dream Hazard.* Ⓝ

VIRTUA FIGHTER *
1995. TV series. DIR: Hideki Tonokatsu. SCR: Tsutomu Kamishiro, Kuniaki Kasai, Natsuko Chizumu. DES:

Bubblegum Crisis

© A.I.C. INC. & TOSHIBA, INC.

Ryo Tanaka, Hiroshi Ono. ANI: Ryo Tanaka. MUS: Kaori Ohori. PRD: Tokyo Movie Shinsha, TV Tokyo. 25 mins. x 35 eps.
Based on Sega's successful video game, the story hinges around young martial artist Akira Yuki and his travels in search of his inner self. This involves lots of fighting. Luckily he meets lots of other people who also want to find themselves through fighting. He teams up with Pai Chan, a Chinese girl who is fighting to find her fiancé, and Jacky, who is fighting to find his sister Sara, and they fight lots of people "for honor, love, and revenge." The almost concurrent appearance of the **STREET FIGHTER II** TV series obviously had nothing to do with it, and an artist like Ono, who did the ravishing backgrounds for **DOG OF FLANDERS**, is wasted here. Ⓥ

VIRUS
1997. JPN: *Virus Buster Serge.* TV series. DIR: Masami Obari. SCR: Masami Obari, Jiro Kaneko, et al. DES: Masami Obari, Natsuki Mamiya. ANI: Masami Obari, Kazuto Nakazawa. MUS: Toshiyuki Omori. PRD: JC Staff, Plum, TV Tokyo. 30 mins. x 13 eps.
In 2097 Hong Kong, virtuality is preferable to the real world. The Internet has

a mind of its own. Cloning is outlawed. Vast supercomputers run on biological software, but the combination of genetics and cybernetics places human beings at the mercy of digital viruses, some of which are accidents, some of which are the work of the infamous "Incubator." The STAND is an elite task force that terminates viruses with extreme prejudice. Serge is a brainwashed assassin, plotting the death of STAND captain Raven. But when Serge is "cured" of his desire for vengeance, he joins the team. Impossibly proportioned token female Erika is just dying to get to know him better. But Serge is less popular with the two gunslinging officers, Macus and Joichiro, who don't want an ex-assassin for backup. The team must learn to work together and to exorcise the demons from their own past—the viruses feed on skeletons in the mental closet.

With its possessed human hosts, *Virus* shares themes with **GHOST IN THE SHELL** and glossy horror moods out of **SILENT MÖBIUS**. It combines the angst of **EVANGELION** and the superheroes of **SONIC SOLDIER BORGMAN**, artfully concealing a tiny budget and breakneck schedule with great splashes of special effects, clever uses of shadow, and superfast cuts. Its appeal to audiences is nicely, if perhaps cynically, manufactured; the makers assume that a male SF audience is already guaranteed, so they concentrate on the brooding, pouting, pretty-boys to drag in female fans. Fight scenes are carefully interwoven with character development; the end-of-episode cliffhanger is just as likely to be a terrifying revelation from the past as a physical threat. However, like the equally beautiful **DARKSIDE BLUES**, *Virus* has a frustrating tangle of subplots and relationships running into dead ends with no time to resolve them. For those who really can't wait to get more of the high-tensile battle action and the darkly erotic aura of the male cast, the Sega Saturn game and later PlayStation spinoff *Virus: The Battle Field* use the original cast voices and design. The hip-hop group Dragon

Ash had its big break with the anime's opening theme, going on to record music for **DT EIGHTRON** and Kinji Fukasaku's live-action *Battle Royale* (2001). **V**

VISIONARY *
1995. Video. DIR: Teruo Kigure, Taiichi Kitagawa. SCR: Ryo Saga. DES: Tomohiro Ando. ANI: Tomohiro Ando. MUS: Masahiko Kikuchi. PRD: Knack, Beam Entertainment. 30 mins., 45 mins., 30 mins.
Ujita is a geeky high-school boy who has no luck whatever with women and gets grief from the local bully, until he hits the wrong key on his computer by mistake. Up pops sexy Doreimon, back from the future to solve all his problems in a cheeky parody of **DORAEMON** with no panties. Just like the hapless robot cat, she can answer all of Ujita's prayers, but things don't always work out as she plans or he hopes. Later episodes continue the short pornographic comedies in the style of creator U-Jin's similar **TALES OF . . .** , with scenes including nymphomaniac vampires on a college campus and skydiving love. **NV**

VISITOR
1998. TV series. DIR: Atsushi Tokuda. SCR: Kazunori Ito. DES: Akemi Takada. ANI: N/C. MUS: Keiichi Matsuzaki. PRD: COM NT, WOWOW. 50 mins. x 3 eps.
In the year 2099, one of NASA's Apollo rocket capsules is found in the Mongolian desert, where it appears to have been for 65 million years. Meanwhile on Mars, a strange black artifact of unknown origins is eating one of the planet's moons. Earth ship Davide is sent to investigate and is sucked into the vortex. Lila Mochizuki and her companions are suddenly a long, long way from home. Entirely computer-generated animation faintly reminiscent of Supermarionation is one of the earliest in a style of animation likely to dominate the medium in the 21st century—motion-capture against CG backgrounds fast becoming the only viable means of making anime in an age of

atrophied artistic skills and cheap computer power. This anime was intended for video but premiered on the satellite channel WOWOW. Later repackaged as a feature-length movie-edit. Compare to **A.LI.CE** and **AURORA**. *Ill. p. 313.*

VOLLEY BOYS
1996. Video. DIR: Kunihiko Yuyama. SCR: Hiroshi Koda. DES: Hiroyuki Murata. ANI: N/C. MUS: N/C. PRD: Toho. 50 mins. x 2 eps.
Sex-starved teenage boys at Kudo high school sign up for the *girls'* volleyball team—hoping that if they build it, the girls will come, to a year that has no girls in it at all. This spinoff from Hiroyuki Murata's 1988 manga in *Young Magazine* mixes *Field of Dreams* with **PING PONG CLUB**.

VOLTAGE FIGHTER GOWKAISER *
1996. JPN: *Shojin Gakuen Gowkaiser*. AKA: *Superhuman Academy Gowkaiser*. Video. DIR: Masami Obari. SCR: Kengo Asai. DES: Masami Obari. ANI: Masahiro Yamane. MUS: Airs. PRD: JC Staff, GaGa. 45 mins. x 2 eps.
Isato Kaiza's (Isato Goka's) athletic skills have won him a place at the Belnar Institute, a school for those with some outstanding gift, and this being an Obari anime, all the female students have at least two. But the institute's mysterious founder has a hidden agenda—he is using the arcane powers of his Caizer Stones to control his students by giving them superhuman fighting skills, while he is controlled by a beautiful, seemingly female but definitely inhuman entity. Isato's friend Kash has given him a Caizer Stone and with it the power to transform into armored hero Gowkaizer; he learns that just about everyone else he knows has similar powers of transformation. Alas, the script doesn't. It starts with some interesting ideas, but many never develop. A subplot about incest between a brother and sister at school is well developed, largely because it provides an excuse for more sex and fighting; another, about a teacher's

involvement in the government's attempts to keep an eye on things at the institute, is more or less ignored because it doesn't. The interesting relationship between the founder and his control remains unexplained. Perhaps the plan was to take all these ideas further if the video had spun off into a TV series, but it never happened. Based on a computer game (though it only uses some of the characters), with plenty of action and plenty of Obari's trademark fan service, *Gowkaizer* remains just another beat-'em-up with fantasy tropes thrown in. *Ill. p. 277.* **OOV**

VOLTRON *

1981. JPN: *Hyakujuo Go-Lion, Kiko Kantai Dairugger XV*. AKA: *Beast Centurion Go-Lion, Machine Platoon Dairugger XV; Lion Force Voltron*. TV series. DIR: Katsuhiko Taguchi, Kazuyuki Okaseko, Kazushi Nomura, Hiroshi Sasakawa. SCR: Susumu Takahisa, Ryo Nakahara, Masaaki Sakurai. DES: Kazuo Nakamura. ANI: Kazuo Nakamura, Moriyasu Taniguchi, Akira Saijo. MUS: Masahisa Takeshi. PRD: Toei, Tokyo 12 Channel. 25 mins. x 125 eps.

Reptile Emperor Dai Bazal of planet Garla (aka Zarkon of planet Doom in the American version) has built a galaxy-conquering army by transforming kidnapped enemies into fighting monsters. On a mission to Earth his forces kidnap some of its people, including our unsuspecting heroes Akira, Takashi, Tsuyoshi, Isamu, and Hiroshi. They are carried off to a conquered world for transformation. Stealing an enemy ship, they escape and manage to reach the palace of Princess Fara, where they learn that five ancient robot lions can combine to form one mighty robot. Impressed by their courage, the dead emperor (in hologram form) gives them the power to operate the machines, form the robot, and free the galaxy from the forces of evil in just 52 episodes.

In the U.S. version, Earth was the headquarters of the peace-loving planetary federation known as the Galaxy Alliance, and Sven, Keith, Lance, Pidge, and Hunk were Space Explorers sent on a mission to planet Arus, recently devastated by Zarkon. Their objective was the Lion Force, Arus's five greatest weapons, which could merge to form the super-robot Voltron. They find that Princess Allura has survived the devastation of her world and is struggling to overthrow Zarkon's evil rule, and they join her as the pilots of the five robot lions that combine to make up Voltron. In the original story Akira is killed in battle (Sven is merely wounded, since American heroes can't die) and Fara/Allura takes his place on the team.

The *Golion* series was bought for U.S. syndication as *Voltron: Defender of the Universe!*, with scripts "written" by Jameson Brewer and Howard Albrecht. preempting the later treatment of ROBOTECH, it was combined with an unrelated show to bulk out the running time. *Dairugger XV* (1982) was a 56-episode show, also from Toei, renamed *Vehicle Team Voltron* in the U.S. In the original Japanese version, Earth is enjoying a period of unparalleled prosperity thanks to its alliances with the people of the planets Mila and Sara. The president of the Terran League initiates a mission to explore space beyond our galaxy, and the starship Rugger-Guard sets out on its mission. Attacked by a ship of the Galveston Empire, Rugger-Guard sends out its best line of defense—Dairugger XV, a giant robot made up of 15 different mecha, each with its own pilot. As with GOLD LIGHTAN and other shows of the period, there is a far-fetched origin—15 players on a team in rugby, a sport whose only other anime appearance is in WARTIME ANIME.

In the U.S. version, Voltron technology was brought back to Earth after the struggle with Zarkon in the earlier *Lion Force Voltron* segment of the series. The Galaxy Alliance used it to build their own, even larger Voltron made up of 15 smaller robots and sent it out of our galaxy on the spaceship Explorer to find habitable new planets. The Drule dictatorship, whose homeworld was dying of pollution, sent ships to tag along behind the Explorer and try to steal any habitable worlds for themselves. The 15 pilots of the Explorer had to do battle both with natural forces like volcanoes on the worlds they discovered and with the Drule. Eventually the Drule population revolted, the planet exploded, and the "good" Drule were rescued by Voltron and relocated to new homes.

The producers intended to refashion LIGHTSPEED ELECTRON ARBEGAS as the third part of the series, but the show was canceled. However, merchandising by U.S. toy distributors Matchbox further confused matters by including the "stackable" robot hero from *Arbegas* as "Voltron II." The toy boxes show stills from all three anime, with Dairugger as "Voltron I" and GoLion as "Voltron III," claiming that the Arbegas robot is part of the Voltron story line, though he never appears in the TV show. Riding on the momentum created by *Star Wars* and sales of space battle toys, *Voltron* was successfully rerun on U.S. cable TV in the early 1990s. World Events Productions ran a 90-minute special in 1983 then syndicated the series as a half-hour daily show, tied into the merchandising of toy weaponry. *Lion Force* did better than *Vehicle Team Voltron* with its new audience, to the extent that new episodes were commissioned from Japan specially for the American market—creating a total run for the combined *Voltron* series of 125 episodes. In one of these, the "recovered" Sven rejoined the team just in time to help defeat Zarkon. The sequel *Voltron: The Third Dimension* (1998, aka *Voltron 3D*) was an all-American 3-D CG motion-capture version made by *Babylon 5*'s effects company Netter Digital. In this version, the team is joined by Zarkon himself, who has seen the error of his ways, and fights to defeat Zarkon's evil son Lotor—you can tell he's evil because he has a *scar*.

VOLTUS *

1977. JPN: *Cho Denji Machine Voltes V.*

AKA: *Super Electromagnetic Machine Voltes 5.* TV series. DIR: Tadao Nagahama, Yoshiyuki Tomino, Yukihiro Takahashi. SCR: Koichi Taguchi, Masaki Tsuji, Fuyunori Gobu. DES: Akehiro Kaneyama, Nobuyoshi Sasakado. ANI: Akehiro Kaneyama. MUS: Hiroshi Tsutsui. PRD: Sunrise, Toei, TV Asahi. 25 mins. x 40 eps.

The three Go brothers, Kenichi, Daijiro, and Hiyoshi, and their friends Ippei Mine and Megumi Oka pilot the giant robot Voltes V in the battle against the people of planet Bozan, who are trying to add Earth to their galactic empire. But the prince of Bozan, Hainel, claims to be the Go boys' half-brother; he says their father was an alien, sent to Earth many years before. How can they fight their own flesh and blood, can Earth trust them, and might this point to a way forward for both peoples?

After Sunrise made **COMBATTLER V** for Toei, it followed up with this repeat performance—the undisputed star of which is Hainel, the first baddie to be a real hit with the female audience, who wrote in demanding that he survive. Originally dubbed in Japan by William Ross for a U.S. theatrical release, the relatively faithful version was scrapped by new owners "New Hope Productions," which replaced it with a soundtrack more like *Star Wars* and eventually sold it to the Christian Broadcast Network. The company similarly tried to capitalize on George Lucas' success by refashioning **STARBIRDS**.

VOOGIE'S ANGEL *

1997. JPN: *Denno Sentai Voogie's Angel.* AKA: *Cyber Battle Team Voogie's Angel.* Video. DIR: Mamoru Takeuchi. SCR: Mamoru Takeuchi. DES: Masami Obari. ANI: Masami Obari. MUS: Satoshi Yuyama. PRD: JC Staff, Beam Entertainment. 30 mins. x 3 eps.

A hundred years after Earth is invaded by aliens, the last remnants of the human race dwell in underwater "Aqua Bases." A team of five cybernetically enhanced women is trained for the purpose of carrying out guerrilla attacks against the occupying forces. Earth's last best hope for salvation is Voogie's Angel. Playing like a warped version of *Stingray*, *VA* delivers some interesting moments. The cutesy-conventional girl cyborg team (good sort, tough girl, kid sister, nice Japanese girl) and their scientist father-figure go from the aliens-invade-earth scenario, via space battles and embarrassing "comic" scenes, to the extremely violent fight in the second episode in which our heroes are smashed almost to a pulp. Then there's the black-and-white **GUNBUSTER** homage in episode three, which shows how each of the cyborgs died tragically and was then rebuilt in enhanced form. The fight for human freedom shows the cyborgs what it means to be truly human but doesn't explain why cyber-enhanced women usually have gravity-defying breasts or why swimwear is the battle dress of preference in Obari-designed shows. A radio and CD drama in 1996 preceded the video release. Spinoffs include a manga in *Comic Gamma* and a "side story" *Onward! Super Angels* that features the characters in superdeformed (see **SUPER-DEFORMED DOUBLE FEATURE**) mode. The series was also released on DVD in the 70-minute feature-length "director's cut" *VA: Forever and Ever* (1998), containing extra footage. **V**

VOTOMS *

1983. JPN: *Sokokihei Votoms.* AKA: *Armored Trooper Votoms; ScopeDog.* TV series, video. DIR: Ryosuke Takahashi, Haruka Miyako, Tatsuya Matsuno, Toshifumi Takizawa, Hiroshi Yoshida, Yukihiro Takahashi, Masakazu Yasumura. SCR: Fuyunori Gobu, Soji Yoshikawa, Junzo Toriumi, Ryosuke Takahashi, Takashi Imanishi. DES: Norio Shioyama, Ryosuke Takahashi, Kunio Okawara (TV, v), Yutaka Izubuchi (v94). ANI: Norio Shioyama. MUS: Hiroki Inui. PRD: Sunrise, TV Tokyo. 25 mins. x 52 eps. (TV), 60 mins. x 3 eps. (v), 30 mins. x 4 (v94).

On a distant world, the Perfect Soldier is finally created after genetic manipulation and a breeding program lasting centuries, but by the time this happens, the war has almost ended. The politicians and scientists who bred him either want him dead or want to use him in other, more sinister ways. But Chirico Cuve isn't a machine—he's a human being, and he's determined to find out who is responsible for all this. As the war ends he is separated from his unit, thrown into a series of desperate situations, enslaved, used as a gladiator in robot combat, enlisted as a mercenary, and meets the love of his life, only to discover that she too is a Perfect Soldier.

The first video, *The Last Red Shoulder* (1985), is a continuation of the story after the end of the TV series. Chirico leaves Udo City in search of his beloved Fiana. In *Big Battle* (1986), he finds her being held hostage by Bararant in an experimental facility near Koba City, and he and his comrades have to fight their way in to save her. 1987's *Red Shoulder Document: The Roots of Treachery* is a prequel to the TV series and shows Chirico's origins as part of a genetic experiment and recruitment into the Red Shoulder group. In 1994 Takahashi brought the same team together for a four-part video adventure set 32 years after the end of the TV series. Chirico and Fiana have been in cryo-sleep together for all that time, but now a new threat has arisen, and it's time for them to fight again. An extra item on the first tape, *Votoms Briefing*, filled in the back story for those who missed the series 11 years earlier.

The "real robot" concept was born out of a conviction that the weapons of the future would not be made of shiny metal in clean, bright primary colors. Designer Okawara wanted to create suits that looked as if they could be made in a 20th-century factory, designed so that the toys that would inevitably be spun off the series could be posed and moved exactly like their animated inspirations (unlike many of the suits he'd designed for **GUNDAM**) and smaller in scale than his designs for **DOUGRAM**.

Robots, which started out in anime primarily as cool toys to even up the odds for the little guy (children, the human race, or the Japanese) against a big, hostile world (adults, alien invaders, or foreign competition), had been seen right from the first as having as much potential for destruction as for good. **GIGANTOR** could be used by evil men just as easily as by perky little Jimmy Sparks—the power lay in the hands of whoever held the remote control. Takahashi and his fellow writers and directors extended this idea into the whole range of future military technology (Vertical One-man Tank for Offensive Maneuvers), showing robots and scientifically enhanced superbeings as just another weapon in the arsenal of the politicians, and war as a vicious, dehumanizing process in which honor and courage came from the individual, rather than any religion or value system and could be crushed as easily as an insect (see **GREY: DIGITAL TARGET**). It also didn't hurt that *Votoms'* hero resembled Steve McQueen (lead character in the Western *Junior Bonner*, an early inspiration for the anime), whose laconic combination of little-boy charm and man's-man toughness was hugely popular with Japanese audiences.

The concept and the appealingly gritty realism of Takahashi's future war vision spun off another video series set in the same universe, as the title signals. Written by Takahashi but directed by Takeyuki Kanda, *Armored Trooper Votoms: Armor Hunter Merowlink* (1988, *Kiko Ryohei Merowlink*) is the story of a young rookie who is the sole survivor of a platoon cut down by bungling and treachery higher up the ranks. Framed for desertion and the deaths of his colleagues, he vows to avenge them; each of the six 50-minute episodes shows one act of vengeance on an individual betrayer. A brilliantly paced series richly meriting a Western release, it combines good character development and edge-of-the-seat tension. There are points when *Merowlink* doesn't simply suspend disbelief but knocks it out cold, especially in the final episode with an escape sequence as silly on calm reflection as it is absolutely convincing while you watch. Sequences of extreme violence and deliberate cruelty are carefully calculated to enhance the effect of this stunning rite-of-passage tale. The series was a major inspiration for the *Heavy Gear* role-playing war- and video-game franchise, which now has its own CGI cartoon series. **LV**

VOYAGE OF THE TSUSHIMA
1982. JPN: *Tsushima-maru: Sayonara Okinawa*. AKA: *The Tsushima: Farewell Okinawa*. Movie. DIR: Osamu Kobayashi. SCR: Shoichiro Okubo, Koji Senno. DES: Osamu Kobayashi. ANI: Tsutomu Shibayama, Hideo Kawauchi. MUS: Haruya Sugita. PRD: Asia-do. 70 mins.
On August 22, 1944, the Japanese freighter Tsushima Maru flees Okinawa for the mainland with a cargo consisting primarily of evacuees, the crew divided over whether to steer a zigzag course or simply to steam at full speed for safety. Her luck runs out off Akuseki Island, Kagoshima, when she is struck three times by torpedoes from an American submarine. The ship sinks with the loss of 1,484 lives, including 738 children. Based on a true story dramatized by Tatsuhiro Oshiro in book form in 1961, this movie ends with a roll call of those who did not survive. The wreck of the Tsushima Maru itself was not located until 1997.

WAKE UP ARIA *

1998. Video. DIR: Komari Yukino. SCR: N/C. DES: N/C. ANI: Hideo Ura. MUS: N/C. PRD: Cosmos Plan. 30 mins.
Pretty young musician Aria goes to Golden Breast Island in search of an education and finds herself in the company of several other pretty, musically minded girls, including the Chinese Yang, Hiren, and the Indian twins Luna and Monica. However, the Royal Elegance Music School is just a front for the lusts of its principal and vice-principal, Mr. Karma and Ms. Shinbi. Every student they see ends up brainwashed into performing sexual acts for and with the perverse pair. Aria must escape the island alive, but not before she gets a good "education" in this predictable porno. ❶Ⓝ

WANDERING SUN

1971. JPN: Sasurai no Taiyo. TV series. DIR: Chikao Katsui, Yoshiyuki Tomino, Masayuki Hayashi, Ryosuke Takahashi. SCR: Hiroyuki Hoshiyama, Shunichi Yukimuro, Michio Suzuki, Tadaaki Yamazaki, Haruya Yamazaki, Tsunehisa Ito, Isao Okishima. DES: Yoshikazu Yasuhiko. ANI: Hayao Nobe. MUS: Taku Izumi. PRD: Mushi, Fuji TV. 25 mins. x 26 eps.
Miki and Nozomi are two would-be singers. Miki's rich parents will go to any lengths to give their little princess her heart's desire, but the more talented Nozomi comes from a deprived background. The daughter of a deceased noodle seller, Nozomi must struggle to support her blind mother and make sacrifices on the way to achieving the success that her natural guitar-strumming ability deserves.

Based on a manga in *Shojo Comic* by Keisuke Fujiwara and Mayumi Suzuki.

WANNA-BE'S *

1986. Video. DIR: Yasuo Hasegawa. SCR: Toshimichi Suzuki. DES: Kenichi Sonoda, Yoshiharu Shimizu, Shinji Araki, Kimitoshi Yamane, Hideki Kakinuma. ANI: Yoshiharu Shimizu. MUS: Hiroshi Arakawa, Seikima-II. PRD: Artmic, Animate Film, AIC. 45 mins.
Eri Fuma and Miki Morita, are young female pro-wrestlers who fight under the professional name Wanna-Be's. They struggle to rise through the ranks and challenge the champions, not realizing that they are embroiled in a plot to test a secret muscle-enhancing drug. Will it be enough to help them defeat mutated monsters, though? A hilarious look at the sport that's so popular in Japan, with some thinly disguised "guest appearances" by real girl wrestling stars—compare to the similar wrestling in-jokery of CRUSHER JOE and METAL FIGHTERS MIKU.

WANSA-KUN

1973. AKA: Little Wansa. TV series. DIR: Eiichi Yamamoto, Minoru Tanaka, Masami Hata, Noboru Ishiguro, Norio Yazawa, Minami Asa. SCR: Keisuke Fujikawa, Maru Tamura, Fumio Ikeno, Eiichi Yamamoto, Hitoshi Hidaka. DES: Shinji Nagashima. ANI: Hiromitsu Morita, Toyoo Ashida. MUS: Yasushi Miyakawa. PRD: Tomi Pro, Anime Room, Mushi, Fuji TV. 25 mins. x 26 eps.
Wansa the little white dog comes to town and befriends neighborhood boy Kota. His "people," however, are the neighborhood dogs, who introduce him to a hidden life of triumph and

tragedy as the local canines fight a vicious turf war with their cat enemies. Wansa falls in love with local puppy Midori and pines for his mother, *presumed* dead in typical anime fashion. Based on the 1971 manga written by Tezuka for *Tezuka Magazine Leo* and starring the mascot character of the Sanwa Bank, this musical comedy, faintly redolent of *Lady and the Tramp*, was the last TV series made by the beleaguered Mushi studio. It, along with TRITON OF THE SEA, was effectively lost to its creator through copyright foul-ups and is not a "true" Tezuka work.

WARTIME ANIME

As Japan invaded China in the 1930s, the fairy tales and fables of EARLY ANIME were gradually co-opted into the military machine, tempted by offers of funding and, for the first time, wide distribution. The animators answered with a series of works that promoted Japan's right to establish an East Asian "co-prosperity sphere" and her right to interfere in the affairs of other countries in order to overthrow Western imperialism. The first example was Yasuji Murata's *Aerial Momotaro* (1931, *Sora no Momotaro*), featuring a war between penguins and albatrosses on a remote island near the South Pole, broken up by the timely arrival of the Japanese hero MOMOTARO. In the wake of the League of Nations' condemnation of Japan's expansion into Manchuria, attacks on foreign powers became more blatant. In Takao Nakano's *Black Cat Banzai* (1933, *Kuroneko Banzai*), a peaceful parade of toys is disrupted by a fleet of flying bat-bombers, each ridden by a clone of Mickey Mouse. Snake-marines with machine-gun mouths land on the beach, and the invaders kidnap a little doll. The islanders beg for help from a book of JAPANESE FOLK TALES, which obligingly disgorges Momotaro, Kintaro, and several other heroes to save the day. The story ends with a celebration, as all the dead trees sprout cherry blossoms. Shiho Tagawa's popular manga character NORAKURO joined up in Yasuji Murata's *Corporal Norakuro* (1934, *Norakuro Gocho*), and the emphasis on humor continued with the uncredited *Sky Over the Shanghai Battle-Line* (1938, *Sora no Shanhai Sensen*), featuring two comical Japanese pilots observing the Chinese war theater in a biplane. Similarly, Nobuo Ofuji's *Aerial Ace* (1938, *Sora no Arawashi*) starred another pilot fighting giant clouds in the shape of Popeye and Stalin.

The onset of war with America in 1941 brought greater funding, but also high pressures on all filmmakers. Kajiro Yamamoto's live-action *War at Sea from Hawaii to Malaya* (1942, *Hawaii-Marei Okikaisen*), which recreated Pearl Harbor with special-effects footage by ULTRAMAN's Eiji Tsuburaya, was completed in six months, prompting the Imperial Navy to order Mitsuyo Seo to make *Momotaro's Sea Eagles* (1943, *Momotaro no Umiwashi*) in just three. Retelling the *Momotaro* folk tale with enemy caricatures, the film pushed the boundaries of animation in Japan with an unprecedented running time of 37 minutes. With animation cels in short supply (cellulose was a crucial ingredient in gunpowder), Seo's animators were forced to wash and reuse their materials for this retelling of the bombing of Pearl Harbor in fairy-tale form, destroying the original artwork even as they shot each frame of animation. In order to get the right voice for a caricature of *Popeye's* Bluto, seen on the deck of a sinking ship, they also sampled the original straight from a reel of the American print—copyright law hardly being an

issue at the time. The film was immensely popular with children on release and was even screened in the palace for Prince Akihito (the current Heisei Emperor). The Navy authorized Seo to make an even longer sequel, and the result was Japan's first full-length animated feature, MOMOTARO'S DIVINE SEA WARRIORS.

Other anime of the 1940s show signs of increasing desperation, as Japanese defeats became harder to ignore. Sanae Yamamoto's *Defeat of the Spies* (1942, *Spy Gekimetsu*) depicts Roosevelt and Churchill sending three agents onto Japanese soil—although they are swiftly unmasked. In Ryotaro Kuwata's *Human Rugby Bullets* (1943, *Tokyu Nikudan Sen*), a sports match between Japanese dogs and foreign monkeys attempts to make light of Japan's use of the *taiatari* ramming attack—a chilling precursor of the following year's kamikaze. Animation was also a major component of the ten-minute short *Nippon Banzai* (1943), best described as Japan's *Why We Fight*. In it, evil British soldiers are shown oppressing the natives of Asia beneath a hot sun, which segues into the rising sun of Japan's flag. Cartoon fish dance in and out of the wreck of the *HMS Prince of Wales*, while Chiang Kai-Shek is first displayed as a marionette (with his wife, operated by Allied "advisers"), then as a gleeful child with a toy plane (a snide reference to the Flying Tigers). The anime sequence ends with Roosevelt impeached and Churchill's trademark cigar falling from his mouth in shock, before returning to live-action footage exhorting young men to join up.

After Japan's crushing defeat, the war remained a taboo subject for a generation, with the anomalous exception of ZERO SEN HAYATO and occasional references as origin stories in shows such GIGANTOR and BIG X. As the baby-boomers reached maturity, several anime began alluding to the war through future allegories such as STAR BLAZERS, and the devastation wrought by the giant aliens of MACROSS.

The sensitive, timid sorcerer Subaru, whose magic powers and incongruous 1980s fashion choices loom large in Koichi Chiaki's TOKYO BABYLON. Clearly planned as pilots for a psychic investigation series, *TB* instead faded from view, its only memorable legacy being the astonishingly misleading British sleeve notes. The manga incarnation eventually segued into *X: 1999*, resulting in Subaru's return to the anime screen in X: THE MOVIE several years later. See entry p. 404.

Tokyo Babylon

© 1992 CLAMP/SHINSHOKAN/MOVIC/SONY MUSIC ENTERTAINMENT (JAPAN) INC.

After the success of the anime DIARY OF ANNE FRANK, producers realized the value of children as protagonists—caught up in a conflict not of their own making, the brutalized innocents of BAREFOOT GEN, GRAVE OF THE FIREFLIES, and their many imitators allowed history without discussion of responsibility. The Hiroshima Peace Festival film prize became dominated by Renzo Kinoshita, whose short anime included *Pica-Don* (1978, the nickname of the bomb that destroyed Hiroshima), TOBIWAO IS TAKEN ILL, *Last Air Raid Kumagaya* (1990), and the unfinished project *Okinawa*. Outside the art-house theaters however, popular representations of the war became increasingly fantastic, as a nostalgic craze for "retro" anime transformed into an obsession with rewriting history—KISHIN CORPS and SAKURA WARS would have met with joyous approval from the government censor in 1941. *Ill. pp. 41, 407, 461.*

WAT PO AND US

1988. JPN: *Wat Po to Bokura no Ohanashi*. AKA: *The Story of Us and Wat Po*. Video. DIR: Shigenori Kageyama. SCR: Shozo Uehara. DES: Mutsumi Inomata, Shohei Kohara, Takahiro Tomoyasu, Torao Arai. ANI: Mutsumi

Inomata. MUS: Satoshi Kadokura. PRD: Diva, Konami. 55 mins.

The life of a tiny fishing village is disrupted when Wat Po, a horned white whale who is the village's guardian spirit, vanishes. The creature used to attract fish for the people to catch. Local boy Jam, hearing strange music wafting down from the mountains, sets out with three friends and his dog in search of the sound. Attacks by monsters scare his friends away, but he finds a mountain lake where a lovely young girl called Selene is playing music to Wat Po. At first she's afraid and tries to flee in winged armor. Her people, the Birdoes, are technologically far in advance of the village folk, but they hid inside the mountain generations ago after a terrible war devastated and polluted the land. They used their power of flight to bring Wat Po from the sea to the landlocked lake. Selene and Jam decide to rescue Wat Po and try to bring their peoples back together, but Jam's disappearance is arousing old hatreds and may even rekindle the long-ago war.

An eco-saga with a strong antiwar message in the vein of FUTURE BOY CONAN and GREEN LEGEND RAN, it fails to match up to the same team's work on WINDARIA and LEDA: FANTASTIC ADVENTURES OF YOKO.

WATARU

1988. JPN: *Majin Eiyuden Wataru*. AKA: *Legend of Devilish Heroism Wataru*. TV series, Video. DIR: Hideharu Iuchi, Michio Fukuda, Masamitsu Hidaka, Nobuhiro Kondo, Katsuoshi Yatabe, Yutaka Kagawa. SCR: Yoshiaki Takahashi, Ryosuke Takahashi, Hiroyuki Kawasaki, Takao Koyama, Hiroko Naka. DES: Toyoo Ashida, Kazunori Nakazawa. ANI: Toyoo Ashida. MUS: Junichi Kanezaki, Satoshi Kadokura. PRD: Sunrise, Nippon TV. 25 mins. x 45 eps., 25 mins. x 28 eps., 30 mins. x 4 eps. (v).

After school, ten-year-old Wataru doesn't go straight home—instead he slips into an alternate world where he is the pilot of a huge super-deformed comi-

cal robot and fights to deliver the world from the oppression of an evil magician with the help of the cute but overexciteable Tora-chan. Luckily these adventures only last a few seconds in our world, or his mother would wonder why he was late for dinner. A huge success in Japan, the first series spun off a remake series with the prefix *Cho* [*Super*] and the four part video series *W: Tales of Endless Time* (*W: Owarinaki Toki no Monogatari*).

WATCH WITH MOTHER

1988. JPN: *Mama Ohanashi o Shikikasete*. TV series. DIR: Keiji Hayakawa. SCR: Shunichi Yukimuro. DES: Yuzo Sato. ANI: N/C. MUS: N/C. PRD: Staff 21, Nippon TV. 8 mins. x 15 eps.

Short animated films of well-known JAPANESE FOLK TALES, including the stories of TARO MAEGAMI, *The Riceball Family*, *The Master of Catching Stars*, *Thunder Is the Bridegroom*, and *The Elephant's Sneeze*. Shown as part of the children's variety program, *Tondeke Gutchonpa*.

WAVE OF RAGE

1998. JPN: *Soliton no Akuma*. AKA: *Sea of Angels—Waves of Devils; Devil of the Solitons*. Movie. DIR: Toshio Takeuchi, Jun Kawagoe. SCR: Masashi Sogo. DES: Hisatoshi Motoki. ANI: Hisatoshi Motoki. MUS: N/C. PRD: Locomotion, Japan Cinema Associates. 90 mins.

Deep below the sea off the coast of Okinawa, the Ocean Technopolis is at the forefront of humankind's efforts to adapt to catastrophically rising sea levels, but it's caught in the middle of escalating tensions between Japan and Taiwan. Taiwan is already blaming Japan for the disappearance of its submarine Shui Long, though the vessel was actually destroyed by an underwater monster enraged by the testing of a new Japanese holophonic sonar device. Fleeing the creature, the Japanese submarine Hatsushio inadvertently leads its pursuer to Technopolis. The serpentine creature attacks the underwater city, trapping several tourists on the sea

floor. Atsushi Kurase, head of the nearby Helios Oil underwater drilling rig, is trying to organize a rescue operation—his estranged wife and daughter, Qiu Hua and Mei Ling, are trapped on a stricken tour submarine. He sees the Hatsushio and calls on it for aid. The sub cannot publicly refuse, but its commander is given orders that if Atsushi or any rescuees should realize the top-secret nature of its mission, they are to have a "fatal accident." Though the tourists are saved, the cast is now trapped on the damaged Sea Turtle 200, Helios Oil's underwater platform. They are contacted by the Solitons, underwater creatures made from pure energy, who reveal that a rogue one of their race is responsible for the attacks and that only a human mutated into Soliton form can stop it. To save his daughter, Kurase volunteers, destroying the menace with the aid of the Hatsushio. This derivative combination of *The Abyss* and *The Hunt for Red October* was redeemed in Japanese eyes by its well-conceived setting—a 21st-century Asia riven by international tension, with Japan, Taiwan, and China provocatively cast as superpowers in a new Cold War. Based on the 1995 novel by Katsufumi Umehara. For more underwater action, see BLUE SUBMARINE NO. SIX and SILENT SERVICE. **◯**

WEATHER PERMITTING

1984. JPN: *Ashita Tenki ni Naare*. AKA: *Tomorrow If the Weather Holds*. TV series. DIR: Hisaya Takabayashi, Hiroe Mitsunobu, Kenjiro Yoshida. SCR: Noboru Shiroyama. DES: Tetsuya Chiba. ANI: Hikuji Kanezawa, Kazuo Tomizawa, Akira Kasahara. MUS: Masakazu Togo. PRD: Fuji TV, NAS. 25 mins. x 47 eps.

Taro is a short, fat food-addict who is obsessed with golf—the one sport that doesn't object if its players meander around the field slowly. He astounds observers with his golfing skill but eventually becomes so devoted to the game that he excludes everything else from his life. Based on a 1980 manga by TOMORROW'S JOE–creator Tetsuya Chiba.

WEATHER REPORT GIRL *

1994. JPN: *Otenki Oneesan*. AKA: *Weather Woman*. Video. DIR: Kunihiko Yuyama, Takashi Watanabe. SCR: Kunihiko Yuyama. DES: Naomi Miyata. ANI: Shinji Sato. MUS: Fumihiko Kurihara. PRD: OB Planning, Toho. 45 mins. x 2 eps.

A determined young woman gets her big break in TV when the regular weather girl goes on vacation. Regardless of the barometer, Keiko sets temperatures and ratings soaring as she uses her clothing, or lack of it, to illustrate the trends and turns the serious stuff of the weather report into a song and dance routine. When the original weather girl gets back from her holiday and finds her replacement so popular, the fur begins to fly! Not everyone at the TV station likes the new-style weather report, though, and rivals in the boardroom and on the screen are out to end Keiko's career. Based on the 1992 manga in *Young Magazine* by Tetsu Adachi, *WRG* also spawned the live-action film *Weather Woman*, directed by Tomoaki Hosoyama, starring Kei Mizutani as the exhibitionist heroine. *Ill. p. 263.* Ⓝ

WEATHERING CONTINENT, THE

1992. JPN: *Kaze no Tairiku*. AKA: *Continent of Wind*. Movie. DIR: Koichi Mashimo. SCR: Koichi Mashimo. DES: Mutsumi Inomata, Nobuteru Yuki. ANI: Kazuya Yokose. MUS: Michiru Oshima. PRD: IG, Kadokawa. 60 mins.

The long history of the continent of Atlantis is coming to an end; its once-great cities are crumbling to dust, and it is almost completely deserted after a series of natural disasters. Its few surviving people are under constant threat from scavengers and bandits. Water is increasingly scarce; the winds that scour the land carry no rainclouds, and most of the rivers and springs have long dried up. Across this desolate landscape walk three travelers: Tieh, an androgynous young mystic devoted to the Moon Goddess, Boyce, a mercenary warrior, and Lakshi, a feisty young person who is really the princess Lakshi Arun Ard. Through a series of strange events, they find themselves in a long-dead city where they face the anger of departed souls disturbed by a group of pirates plundering their comfortable afterlife. Tieh and Lakshi must confront their own demons, and all three of the companions must fight to escape the grip of Death and return to a world that, while dying, still has something to offer them.

Originally released on a triple bill with SILENT MÖBIUS 2 and HEROIC LEGEND OF ARSLAN 2, this hypnotically slow tale was based on a novel by Sei Takekawa with illustrations by Mutsumi Inomata, on which Yuki's character designs are based. A manga by Masaeda Hashimoto followed in *Dragon* magazine.

WEB DIVER

2001. JPN: *Denno Boken-ki Web Diver*. AKA: *Cyber Adventure Web Diver*. TV series. DIR: Hiroshi Negishi, Kunitoshi Okajima. SCR: Mayori Sekijima. DES: Shigetsugu Takahashi. ANI: N/C. MUS: N/C. PRD: NAS, Radix, TV Tokyo. 25 mins. x N/D eps.

In the year 2100, children are able to transform themselves into data, allowing them to interact in a "magical" cyberworld. When the cyberworld is attacked by the evil Wills Program Deletron, Japanese kids Kenta and Aoi hold them off with the aid of the Web Knight Gradion, which looks uncannily like a giant robot.

WEDDING PEACH

1995. JPN: *Ai Tenshi Densetsu Wedding Peach*. AKA: *Legend of Love Angel WP*. TV series, Video. DIR: Kunihiko Yuyama, Norihiko Sudo, Yuji Asano, Toshiaki Suzuki, Yoshitaka Fujimoto. SCR: Sukehiro Tomita, Kenji Terada, Hideki Sonoda, Shikichi Ohashi. DES: Kazuko Tadano. ANI: Yuri Isseki, Mariko Fujita, Moriyasu Taniguchi. MUS: Toshiki Hasegawa. PRD: NAS, KSS, TV Tokyo. 25 mins. x 51 eps., 30 mins. x 4 eps. (v).

Three adolescent girls—one good, one bad, one silly—band together to fight evil as the Love Angel and her, er, bridesmaids. Yes, where SAILOR MOON fought evil with the power of love and makeup, *WP* uses bridal finery. Naturally, the ditzy one (Momoko, aka Wedding Peach) is the bride and lead fighter of evil, with the intellectual and the bad girl (Yuri and Hinagiku, aka Angel Lily and Angel Daisy, respectively) as her sidekicks. All this has its roots in an ancient battle between the devils, led by Reine Devilla, who wants to banish all love from Earth, and the angels, led by Queen Aphrodite, who wants to preserve it. So the queen picked three ordinary high-school girls and gave them magical items to enable them to transform into their wedding-day alter egos. Unlike most magical girls, they transform in three stages—from school uniform to wedding dress or bridesmaid's outfit to sexy lightly armored battlesuits. (Why wedding dress, you ask? To build up the power of Love, *obviously!*) The series ended with the world made safe for Love, but in 1997 our heroes returned in the four-part video series *WP DX;* they're enjoying a quiet vacation when a monster attacks Earth, and Aphrodite gives them back their powers to fight once more for love and truth. Tomita, who wrote the manga of *WP* for *Ciao* magazine, was also a writer on SAILOR MOON, and Tadano worked as a designer on the first two *SM* TV series.

WEISS KREUZ

1998. AKA: *White Cross; Night Hunters*. TV series, video. DIR: Kiyoshi Egami, Masami Obari. SCR: Isao Shizuoka, Shigeru Yanagawa, Sukehiro Tomita. DES: Tetsuya Yanasawa. ANI: Tetsuya Yanasawa. MUS: Weiss. PRD: Animate Film, TV Tokyo. 25 mins. x 25 eps. (TV), 25 mins. x 2 eps. (v).

Why *shouldn't* four pretty teenage male florists fight evil when the shop closes for the night? Our heroes hate the crime and murder stalking the big city and harming the innocent, so they roam the night streets offing as many of the bad guys as they can—and I do mean permanently; they may be florists, but they're no shrinking violets when it comes to pest control. Unlike the Knight Sabers (but like *Charlie's Angels*), they have an external authority—a mystery man known only as Persia. As the series progresses they find that more of the drug rings and terrorist factions they take out are connected to one hugely powerful family, pointing to a coldly planned conspiracy.

With a concept straight from **Bubblegum Crisis** and a cast out of **Saint Seiya** via **Gundam W**, *WK* was made to promote Weiss, a band manufactured from four young voice actors, purportedly based on an idea by their lead singer, Takehito Koyasu, and first serialized as a novel in *Animage*. A number of interesting *Doomwatch*-style SF concepts lurk in the plotlines (like the attempt to infest the water supply with flesh-eating bacteria), but relentless cuteness always wins out, and every episode has a downbeat ending designed to pluck at the heartstrings of the intended junior-high-school-girl audience. Giving one of the boys a Wolverine-style steel claw and making him a biker jock isn't enough to give the show real teeth; it loses out in the crime-fighter stakes to *BGC* and can't compete with **Zetsuai** for angst. For sheer prettiness, though, the characters take some beating, and the series is fabulous eye-candy.

WE'RE MANGA ARTISTS: TOKIWA VILLA

1981. JPN: *Bokura Mangaka: Tokiwa So Monogatari*. AKA: *WMA: Tokiwa Villa Story*. TV special. DIR: Shinichi Suzuki, Kazumi Fukushima, Atsutoshi Umezawa. SCR: Masaki Tsuji, Kazuo Koike. DES: Shotaro Ishinomori. ANI: Takao Kasai. MUS: Nozomu Aoki. PRD: Toei, Aoi, TBS. 84 mins.
Possibly the single most influential address in the postwar history of Japanese comics, Tokiwa was the apartment complex where a group of stellar artists lived in 1953. Hiro Terada, Motoo Abiko and Hiroshi Fujimoto (the pair who worked as Fujio-Fujiko), Shotaro Ishinomori (then plain Ishimori), and Fujio Akatsuka shared the trials and tribulations of being struggling young

artists and writers with no money and no luck with editors or girls, with a spirit of insane youthful enthusiasm that enabled them to survive the lean years and emerge as stars of the manga firmament. The Tokiwa building was demolished in 1981, prompting both this anime and NHK's rival live-action documentary *Tokiwa Villa of My Youth*. In allowing the manga characters to come to life for some sequences, the anime version was the greater success. The story was revived for Jun Ichikawa's live-action movie *Tokiwa: The Manga Apartment* (1996).

WHAT'S MICHAEL?

1985. Video, TV series. DIR: Yuichi Higuchi, Katsumi Kosuga, Norio Yazawa, Kunitoshi Okajima, Hideki Hirojima, Satoshi Okada, Seiji Okuda. SCR: Masaaki Sakurai, Yoshio Urasawa, Koji Tanaka, Osamu Nakamura, Nobuaki Kishima, Mayumi Shimazaki, Tomoko Konparu, Megumi Sugiwara. DES: Norio Kabeshima, Katsuyoshi Kanemura. ANI: Norio Kabeshima. MUS: Makoto Kobayashi, Koji Makaino. PRD: Kitty Film, TV Tokyo. 56 mins., 60 mins. (v), 25 mins. x 45 eps. (TV).
Michael is a fat orange cat who lives with a pair of well-meaning but very stupid humans who fondly imagine he is their pet. But Michael's own daily life is rich in all kinds of little incidents and upheavals—avoiding local bad cat Nyazilla, a monster against whom Michael knows he'll always come out worse, scrounging food from local stores, meeting up with his animal friends, and keeping the humans amused as best he can. And Michael also has a fantasy life even his fellow feline Garfield would envy, with cat corporations, cat nightclubs, and his own imitation of a dancing American megastar also called Michael. His adventures continued in 1988 with another video and a TV series. Based on the 1984 manga in *Comic Morning* by Makoto Kobayashi, itself the happy musings of an indulgent pet-owner rather than the more biting satire of **I Am a Cat**. *WM* was the first show to

begin on video and then transfer to TV, and it is a must for cat-lovers and fans of observational humor. *Ill. p. 419.*

WHAT'S UP MECHADOC?

1984. JPN: *Yoroshiku Mechadoc*. TV series. DIR: Hidehito Ueda, Takaaki Ishiyama, Hiroyuki Tanaka, Masayuki Kojima, Shinya Sadamitsu. SCR: Kenji Terada, Hirohisa Soda, Takao Koyama, Mayori Sekijima. DES: Tatsunoko Anime Office, Ammonite. ANI: Hideyuki Motohashi, Chuichi Iguchi. MUS: Hirokazu Takahashi. PRD: Tatsunoko, Fuji TV. 25 mins. x 30 eps.
Jun Kazama is crazy about cars and loves to tune their engines to top performance; he can make even a standard manufacturer's model run above spec. With Kazumichi Nakamura and Kiyoshi Noro, he sets up a tuning shop called Mechadoc in Yokohama, helped by Kanzaki, the owner of the nearby Paddock teashop. Competing with a rival store owned by the scheming Wataru Hochi, they tune up biker gangs and befriend female car-nut Reiko Ono. Eventually Jun is so drawn into the world of custom cars that he races against rival mechanics' masterpieces—compare to the much later **Initial D**. Based on the 1982 *Shonen Jump* manga by Ryuji Tsugihara.

WHISPER OF THE HEART *

1995. JPN: *Mimi o Sumaseba*. AKA: *Prick Up Your Ears; If You Listen Closely/Carefully*. Movie. DIR: Yoshifumi Kondo. SCR: Hayao Miyazaki. DES: Yoshifumi Kondo, Satoshi Kuroda. ANI: Kitaro Kosaka. MUS: Yuji Nomi. PRD: Studio Ghibli. 111 mins.
Imaginative, intelligent 14-year-old Shizuku Tsukishima secretly longs to be a writer, reading anything she can lay her hands on. Observing that the same name continually crops up on the borrower's lists of books she takes from both the school library and from the public library where her father works, she wonders who this Seiji Amasawa, who shares her taste in reading, might be. When they do finally meet, Seiji upsets her by criticizing her work,

and she storms off in a temper. Idly following a cat she sees getting off her train, she finds herself in a chic residential area. Wandering into an antique store, she befriends the shopkeeper (eventually revealed as Seiji's grandfather) and becomes intrigued by Baron, an elegantly dressed German cat-doll. Shizuku and Seiji learn that they share a love of music, and with his violin playing and her singing, they soon become closer.

Baron himself appears in Shizuku's dream and shows her a magical fantasy world, which Shizuku begins to turn into a story. Grandfather encourages her to continue writing, while reminiscing about his prewar youth in Germany, where he loved and lost the owner of Baron's lady-doll companion. But Seiji's future plans threaten their growing friendship—he is taking two months off school to have special violin tuition. If he shows promise, his father has agreed to let him go to Italy and study to become a professional musician. Meanwhile, their friendship and her writing project are distracting Shizuku from her schoolwork and may even mean she fails her exams.

A gentle, beautifully executed movie based on a manga by Aoi Hiragi, which, like KIKI'S DELIVERY SERVICE, juxtaposes flights of fantasy (Shizuku's daydreams of journeys with Baron) with commonplace realities (Shizuku's "failure" in the eyes of her teachers). It revolves around the stresses of love and ambition, the need to lay the groundwork of both careers and relationships, and the difficulty of balancing it all when your head and heart are awhirl. It marries the lush production values common to Studio Ghibli productions with a new directorial vision that, sadly, developed no further. Director Kondo died, tragically just into his forties, soon after the film was released. A sequel, *Happy Times* (*Shiawase na Jikan*), exists in manga form, while the real-world location, Tama Hills, also got the Ghibli treatment in POMPOKO. Released in Japan on DVD with English subtitles.

WHITE FANG

1982. JPN: *Shiroi Kiba White Fang Monogatari*. AKA: White Fang Story. TV special. DIR: Soji Yoshikawa, Takeyuki Yokoyama. SCR: Shiro Hagiwara. DES: Yoshikazu Yasuhiko. ANI: Yoshikazu Yasuhiko, Tsuneo Ninomiya. MUS: Hitoshi Komuro. PRD: Sunrise, TBS. 85 mins.

A hunter living in the forests of North America rears and trains a superb white wolf to become his faithful companion. Based on the classic novel by Jack London, author of CALL OF THE WILD, this was the first non-SF show from GUNDAM studio Sunrise.

WHITE WHALE OF MU, THE

1980. JPN: *Mu no Hakugei*. AKA: *Moby Dick 5*. TV series. DIR: Tetsuo Imazawa, Yasuo Yamakichi, Akinori Nagaoka, Minoru Okazaki, Satoshi Dezaki. SCR: Hiroyuki Hoshiyama, Kenichi Matsuzaki, Masaaki Sakurai, Hideo Takayashiki. DES: Shunzo Aoki. ANI: Takao Kasai. MUS: Kentaro Haneda. PRD: Toyko Movie Shinsha, Yomiuri TV (Nippon TV). 25 mins. x 26 eps.

The people of Atlantis are defeated by the people of Mu (see SUPER ATRAGON) and send their planet through a time slip to escape. Thirty thousand years later, at the end of the 20th century, the White Whale, last remnant of the forgotten civilization of Mu, awakes from her slumber, causing massive natural disasters all over Earth. The escaped Atlanteans have emerged from their time tunnel, and the flying cybernetic White Whale assembles a group of young children on Easter Island to protect the Earth. Ken (the leader), Mamoru (the cocky one), Rei (the token girl), Shin (the fat one), and Manabu (the bratty brain) serve Princess Madora, daughter of King La-Mu. This far-fetched mixture of BATTLE OF THE PLANETS and BLUE SUBMARINE NO. SIX was based on an original story by Motoo Fukuo and is infamous in early U.S. fandom for its naked winged cherub, who was quite obviously male. A transforming whale would also appear in LADIUS.

The ultimate warrior squints out from behind his battle armor as he prepares to save the world. A forgettable, microcephalic macho throwback, Hayato Ikeda's **MD GEIST** gained a new lease on life when its titular "Most Dangerous" hero became the corporate logo for an American anime company. It attained a further place in the history books when it became the first aborted anime video series to be revived through foreign interest—U.S. backers funded a sequel in 1996. *See entry p. 247.*

MD Geist

© 1986 HIRO MEDIA/PRODUCTION WAVE

WICKED CITY *

1987. JPN: *Yoju Toshi*. AKA: *Demon Beast City; Supernatural Beast City; Monster City*. Video. DIR: Yoshiaki Kawajiri. SCR: Kisei Cho. DES: Yoshiaki Kawajiri, Masao Maruyama, Kazuo Oga. ANI: Kenichi Ishikawa. MUS: Takeshi Nakazawa, Hironobu Kagoshima. PRD: Madhouse. 80 mins.

A state of stalemate exists between our world and the next dimension, and while "Black Guard" agents from both sides play a game of espionage, representatives from the two worlds prepare to sign a treaty. Renzaburo Taki is an undercover human, forced to partner up with the sexy, deadly Makie. Charged with guarding the uncooperative and lecherous old ambassador Giuseppe Maiyart, the pair become attracted to each other, though relationships between a human and a denizen of the Dark Realm are most inadvisable. In the climactic final battle between good and evil they learn that they are vital to the future of both worlds, and the love they have developed is more than just coincidence.

Made for the theaters with a relatively large budget, *WC* is vastly superior to the later straight-to-video DEMON CITY SHINJUKU, with which it is often confused, and indeed shares a writer, director, and studio. However, it still comes lumbered with risible *"Oh Taki!"/ "Oh, Makie!"* dialogue, perfunctory sex scenes, and a misogynistic obsession with Bad Girls From The Dark World. The final showdown in a church also throws in a contrived twist to wrap up the story, tearing vast holes in the preceding plot as it does so.

DARKSIDE BLUES–creator Hideyuki Kikuchi's original novel cleverly exploited the fantasies of bored businessmen. Taking the viewer from bar to office to airport to hotel, it walks through the scenery of a company rep's humdrum life, enlivening each familiar place with dangerous sex and vicarious violence. *WC* was the first film to show the distinctive style of **NINJA SCROLL**'s Kawajiri, whose trademark blue-red lighting is leavened here with artful fog effects and moody shadows. The first set piece says it all: a fight to the death beneath the wheels of a taxiing jumbojet, with superfast fists making a virtue of the low animation cel count, an imitation shaky-cam effect right out of a Sam Raimi film, and superfast cutting to hide the joins, borrowed from Hong Kong action master Tsui Hark. Tsui would repay the compliment in 1993 when he produced a live-action version of *WC* in Hong Kong, featuring Leon Lai as Taki and Michele Reis as Makie.

Amid the dark palette and piano-wire tension, Kawajiri demonstrates a marvelously gothic sense of the unbreakable link between sex and death. The predatory nature of most sexual relationships, set out in Taki's opening encounter with a spider-woman whose vagina is lined with teeth, is contrasted in true Hammer-horror fashion with the purity of his relationship with Makie, whose inner self is affected but not changed by the sexual horrors she endures. For Makie, transformation and transcendence come when the deadly power of her fighting skill is lifted to another level by motherhood; Death and the Madonna become one. **LNV**

WILD ARMS *
1999. TV series. DIR: Toshiaki Kawasaki. SCR: Aya Matsui, Hideki Mitsui. DES: Kanami Sekiguchi, Yasuo Miyazawa. ANI: Minoru Yamazawa, Kanami Sekiguchi. MUS: Miyuki Otani. PRD: B-Train, WOWOW. 25 mins. x 24 eps.
On the planet Far Gaia, Loretta, a dark and deadly Crest Sorceress who wields a powerful magic based on tarot cards (flavor of the month since **ESCAFLOWNE** and **CARDCAPTORS**) leads a team of strange talents. Shaian looks like a little boy, but he's really a 25-year-old scientist and a sharpshooter of no mean skill. His main aim is to get his grown-up body back. But he's not the only one around who conceals his age—team genius Jerusha is a cute pink bunnykin who won't see 5,000 again. Even cute little turquoise-haired Mirabelle is really a Noble Red Vampire under that sweet exterior. A "macaroni" Western that mixes cute fantasy and frontier adventure based on the PlayStation RPG, this doesn't have the same protagonists as the game; producer Sony decided to throw in a few little kids.

WILD CARDZ *
1997. JPN: *The Crown Knights: Jaja Uma Quartet.* AKA: *Crown Knights: Wild Horse Quartet.* Video. DIR: Yasushi Nagaoka. SCR: Hideki Sonoda, Hiromitsu Amano. DES: Noritaka Suzuki. ANI: Keisuke Watanabe. MUS: N/C. PRD: Animate Film. 25 mins. x 2 eps.
The story follows the four defenders of the Card Kingdom as they try to defend it from a series of game-themed aggressors such as battle mecha shaped like giant chessmen and oversize mahjong tiles. As usual, the four defenders are girls of high-school age and uniform cuteness who possess supernatural powers. The two episodes released form one long battle sequence, giving the impression that they come from the middle of a much longer story that might as a whole possess some substance. Or it might not.

WILD 7 *
1994. Video. DIR: Kiyoshi Egami. SCR:

Ginzo Choshiya. DES: Hisashi Hirai, Akira Takeuchi. ANI: Hisashi Hirai. MUS: Kazushi Umezu. PRD: Animate Film. 50 mins. x 2 eps.
A team of seven killers from Death Row, led by a reform school escapee, is equipped with motorcycles and a license to terminate with extreme prejudice, Police Captain Kusanami showing touching but wholly unjustified faith in their ability to discriminate between bad guys and innocent bystanders. Their first assignment, bringing in a gang of bank robbers, turns into a running firefight through downtown Tokyo that piles taxpayers' bodies on the sidewalks. *W7: Biker Knights* followed in 1995. A shady politician and his crime-lord buddy decide to discredit our heroes even more by forming their own lookalike gang which will race through Tokyo and—here's the twist—kill innocent bystanders *deliberately*. Based on a 1969 manga by Mikiya Mochizuki, inspired by the *Dirty Dozen* (1967), and predating **CYBER CITY OEDO 808**, the anime version does its utmost to outgross **MAD BULL 34**, with which it also shares the same standard of writing and English dubbing—so bad it's almost good. **V**

WILD SWANS, THE *
1977. JPN: *Hakucho no Oji.* AKA: *Swan Princes.* Movie. DIR: Nobutaka Nishizawa, Yuji Endo. SCR: Tomoe Ryu. DES: Takashi Abe, Hideo Chiba. ANI: Takashi Abe. MUS: Akihiro Komori. PRD: Toei Animation. 62 mins.
A widowed king remarries, but his frequent visits to his six sons and daughter annoy his new bride. Since she's the daughter of a witch, she is in a position to solve the problem in an interesting way; her spell transforms the six brothers into swans. Only their sister, Elisa, escapes, and she must follow her brothers and find a way to break the spell and bring them home. Based on a dark story found in both the **TALES OF HANS CHRISTIAN ANDERSEN** and **GRIMMS' FAIRY TALES**.

WILLFUL IDOL

1990. JPN: *Kimama ni Idol*. Video. DIR: Junichi Sato. SCR: Koichi Yomogi. DES: Kenichi Koya. ANI: Seiji Kikuchi. MUS: Toshitaro. PRD: Tabac. 50 mins.

Three pretty girls want to make it big as pop stars, but it's tough on their way to the top. Based on a manga in *Comic Burger* by Kenichi Koya, *WI* was distinguished by a marketing gimmick that had the three lead voice actresses taking to the stage for real in an early attempt at multimedia promotion. Compare to the earlier GLORIOUS ANGELS, which didn't try to manufacture its own hype, or the later PERFECT BLUE, which documented what can happen when you do.

WILLOW TOWN

1993. JPN: *Tanoshii Willow Town*. AKA: *Happy Willow Town; Wind in the Willows*. TV series. DIR: Tameo Ogawa, Masahito Sato, Yasuo Yamakichi, Shigeru Omachi, Yutaka Kagawa. SCR: Takao Koyama, Hideki Mitsui, Yoshimasa Takahashi, Yumi Kageyama, Toshiyuki Machida, Kenichi Yamada. DES: Toshiyasu Okada. ANI: N/C. MUS: N/C. PRD: Enoki Films, TV Tokyo. 25 mins. x 25 eps.

Kenneth Grahame's enchanting novel *The Wind in the Willows* (1908) is the basis for a series about the happy little world of the animals who live along the riverbank. Toad's boastful nature and the evil ferrets and weasels who live in the Wild Wood threaten everyone's quiet lives until the brave Ratty, Mole, Badger, and Toad band together to ensure that they can all live happily ever after. The series ends with them all saying their farewells before hibernating for the winter. *Ill. p. 283.*

WIND NAMED AMNESIA, A *

1990. JPN: *Kaze no Na wa Amnesia*. AKA: *The Wind's Name Was Amnesia; Wind of Amnesia*. Movie. DIR: Kazuo Yamazaki. SCR: Kazuo Yamazaki, Yoshiaki Kawajiri. DES: Satoru Nakamura, Morifumi Naka. ANI: Satoru Nakamura. MUS: Kazz Toyama, Hidenobu Takemoto. PRD: Madhouse. 80 mins.

In 1997, a mysterious wind wipes the minds of most of the human race. In a Montana research facility, crippled cyborg Johnny retains human memories; when he is saved from an attack by a bestial human, he names his rescuer Wataru ("drifter") and starts teaching him to talk. When Johnny dies, Wataru sets off to search for other survivors. In San Francisco, he meets Sophia, who listens to his story and pointedly refuses to tell him hers. They wander across America until Sophia feels like telling Wataru the story behind the wind, 20 minutes before the end. Then there's a showdown with a law-enforcement robot that's been stalking Wataru since San Francisco, a perfunctory sex scene, and a finale that implies there's hope, even when the rest of the film has demonstrated that there isn't.

Wind of Amnesia has a fascinating "high-concept," based on a novel by DARKSIDE BLUES–creator Hideyuki Kikuchi, but after the bold, broad strokes of the original idea (coincidentally similar to Thomas Calvert McClary's 1934 story *Rebirth*), it swiftly devolves into mundane cliché little better than FIST OF THE NORTH STAR. Transforming into an aimless road movie, it shifts gear into a quest to rescue a damsel in distress whose people still have the intelligence of chimps but have nonetheless managed to set up a society based around ritual human sacrifice. Wataru then teaches a former policeman how to be human again (by showing him how to use a shotgun), before making a brief stop at the obligatory "false paradise." In other words, despite being made for the movies as a stand-alone production, it still has the picaresque feel of a cut-up TV series, amateurishly crashing George R. Stewart's *Earth Abides* (1949) into Harlan Ellison's *A Boy and His Dog* (1969). The script suggests early on that the "wind" could be a psionic experiment gone wrong, or perhaps even rather stupid aliens who prefer to wipe humanity's mind as part of a preemptive strike, but there's no mystery here. Despite having the answers to everything,

Sophia refuses to tell Wataru (or us) for a full 60 minutes, preferring instead to play devil's advocate with mind-boggling inconsistency, railing against the civilized charade of a computer-controlled city in the Nevada desert but vigorously defending the rights of savages who want to sacrifice virgins. Quite possibly, she is simply too embarrassed to tell the truth about an alien intervention plot device whose incoherence would not be matched until GREEN LEGEND RAN. The rest of the script is similarly shoddy—no thought is given as to why people wear clothes, considering that they have forgotten what they were for, and an "Eternal City" is supposedly built "at the beginning of the 21st century" when we've already been told that the film is set in 1999. There is a brief treatment of the idea that humanity might be better off this way, but it was done far more convincingly in GREY: DIGITAL TARGET. Artistically, this is a departure for the Madhouse studio, full of airy, wide-open spaces that are a far cry from the dark urban sprawls of WICKED CITY. **NV**

WINDARIA *

1986. JPN: *Windaria Senki Densetsu*. AKA: *Legend of Windaria Chronicle; Once Upon a Time*. Movie. DIR: Kunihiko Yuyama. SCR: Keisuke Fujikawa. DES: Mutsumi Inomata, Shigenori Kageyama, Shohei Kohara, Shigeru Katsumata, Toshihiko Sato. ANI: Mutsumi Inomata. MUS: Satoshi Kadokura. PRD: Kaname Pro. 101 mins.

After centuries of peace, the Kingdom of Paro (the Shadowlands) is under the reign of an arrogant king, Draco, who sees himself as a mighty conqueror. The neighboring Kingdom of Isa (Lunaria), realizing that it would be the first target for any expansionist plans, tries to keep Paro peacefully under control by rationing the fresh water flowing through Isa's system of locks and canals. As war looms, their heirs Prince Jil (Roland) and Princess Aanasu (Veronica) love one another, but family loyalty makes their union impossible; she chooses death for both in a twist on *Romeo and Juliet*. A happily married farming couple, Izu (Alan) and Malin (Marie), are drawn into the conflict when the agents of both countries try to buy Izu's services. Seeing a chance for adventure and wealth working for Paro, he tries to sneak out of his home in the middle of the night, but Malin wakes and makes him promise to return to her even as she promises to wait for him, no matter what happens. His betrayal of his country and his marriage buys him the sophisticated toys he covets—elegant clothes, a fast bike, an upper-class girl who would never look at a mere farmer—but costs him dearly. His new masters try to have him killed; when he runs for home he finds it destroyed, his village devastated, most of his old friends dead. Only the ghost of his beautiful wife lingers to say a final farewell. Painfully, he learns that he can't buy his way back into the past he has betrayed. Presiding over the conflict between tradition and modernity, a huge "tree of life" symbolizes the enduring power of nature.

Based on Keisuke Fujikawa's novel, written at a time when Japan was beginning to realize how much it had already thrown away in its rush to modernize, this Asian romance has wider meaning for a world whose small economies and ecosystems are increasingly under threat. Katsumata's backgrounds are pure delight, and although the robots of Windaria are rarely mentioned among its many pleasures, this is partly because Kohara does such a good job of integrating them carefully into their faux-feudal societies. This genuinely thoughtful fantasy has a good mix of action and reflection and a score whose sweeping grandeur reflects the beauty of the visuals.

WINGMAN

1984. JPN: *Yume Senshi Wingman*. AKA: *Dream Warrior Wingman*. TV series. DIR: Tomoharu Katsumata, Yugo Serikawa, Masayuki Akehi, Hideo Watanabe, Hiroyuki Kadono, Shigeo Koshi. SCR: Akiyoshi Sakai, Sukehiro Tomita, Shigeru Yanagawa. DES: Yoshinori Kanemori. ANI: Masamune Ochiai. MUS: Keiichi Oku. PRD: Toei, TV Asahi. 25 mins. x 47 eps.

Some of the greatest battles take place, not in the waking world, but in dreams. Warriors capable of transforming into powerful armored beings can intervene in our world to save those in danger. When superhero-obsessed teenager Kenta sees a girl literally fall out of the sky, he has no idea what's about to happen. Aoi has a "dream note," a kind of promissory paper: whatever you write on it will come true. Kenta writes that he wants to be the superhero Wingman, protecting everyone from the evil Rimel, ruler of the fourth-dimensional land of Powdream. And it happens—he's a superhero! But Rimel sends his minions into the real world in disguise to steal the dream note and so prevent Wingman from foiling his plans. He also wants to break up the growing friendship between Kenta and Aoi. Based on the 1983 *Shonen Jump* manga by Masakazu Katsura, creator of VIDEO GIRL AI and DNA2.

WINGS OF HONNEAMISE *

1987. JPN: *Oneamisu no Tsubasa*. AKA: *Royal Space Force*. Movie. DIR: Hiroyuki Yamaga. SCR: Hiroyuki Yamaga, Hiroshi Onogi. DES: Yoshiyuki Sadamoto. ANI: Hideaki Anno, Yuji Moriyama, Fumio Iida, Yoshiyuki Sadamoto. MUS: Ryuichi Sakamoto, Yuji Nomi, Koji Ueno. PRD: Bandai, Gainax. 120 mins.

Shiro Lhadatt is a dropout, a wannabe pilot who wasn't good enough to get into the navy air corps. Instead, he joins the only organization that will have him, a ragtag group of misfits called the Royal Space Force. Underfunded, undermotivated, and under extreme pressure, they race to get a man in space, but nobody believes it's possible. Nobody, that is, except for Shiro and his would-be girlfriend, a religious zealot called Lequinni. Space is waiting for humanity as a whole, but the project to reach it is the result of two nations' political and military agendas. Our hero joins up for all the wrong reasons but eventually realizes that he can turn the "fake dream" of his government's PR campaign into a real dream, and he becomes the first man in space. Despite the political skullduggery that follows, he refuses to let go of the hope that the reality just might redeem all the failure and sacrifice of history and give us another chance to soar.

One of anime's greatest successes and greatest failures, *WoH* is a peculiarly Japanese take on the U.S.–Soviet space race—an outsider's view of the gung-ho ideals of *The Right Stuff*, moved to an alien world to emphasize the viewer's own alienation. Made by the young, fiendishly talented Gainax collective, it was so expensive and so badly received in Japan that it didn't break even until 1994. One of the shining examples of how cerebral and intelligent anime can be, it's far removed from the sex and violence that stuffs Western anime catalogues. It's a film that rewards repeat viewings if only for the meticulous design of every aspect of its world. The language, the names, the maps, and even the telegraph poles all scream to be recognized as triumphs of world-building almost unequalled elsewhere in science-fiction film. Even the minutiae of everyday life are knocked ever-so-slightly out of kilter, with little touches like triangular spoons, unidentifiable foods, and sunrise in the north.

Gainax, which later made GUNBUSTER and EVANGELION, is made up of *true* science-fiction fans. Space is their religion; they fervently believe that it's humankind's destiny to leave the cradle of Earth and spread out among the stars. The film's closing moments are their manifesto: a march of progress from the earliest times until the climactic moment, a final leap into space as war rages around the launchpad. *WoH* is a marvelous film, improved all the more by music from *Merry Christmas, Mr. Lawrence*'s Ryuichi

Sakamoto and a fluent adaptation (though allegedly far removed from the original) from LA Hero, which was bought out during production and rebranded as the American arm of Manga Entertainment. A sequel, *Blue Uru*, has been promised for a decade but thus far has only materialized in the form of a Gainax video game. *WoH* also exists in an ill-fated 1987 dub version from Go East, under the title *Star Quest*—which rearranged some scenes, changed some names, and was reputedly so bad that it was hidden from sight after its poorly received LA premiere. Compare to the similarly unfortunate treatment suffered by **NAUSICAÄ** as *Warriors of the Wind. Ill. p. 259.* ⊙

WITCHES
1992. JPN: *Nozomi Witches*. Video. DIR: Gisaburo Sugii. SCR: Gisaburo Sugii. DES: Kosuke Eguchi. ANI: Kosuke Eguchi. MUS: Hiroaki Serizawa. PRD: Tac. 45 mins. x 2 eps.
Ryutaro is an average high-school student until the beautiful Nozomi takes an interest in him. Clever, a superb athlete, and fancied by every boy in class, she decides that Ryutaro has real potential, and her belief in him soon pushes him all the way to the Olympic boxing trials. But does she see him as anything but a sporting project? Based on the *Young Jump* manga by Toshio Nobe. ⊙

WIZARD OF OZ, THE *
1984. JPN: *Oz no Maho Tsukai*. Movie, TV series. DIR: Masaru Tenkauchi, Masaharu Endo, Hiromitsu Morita. SCR: Akira Miyazaki, Takafumi Nagamine, Hiroshi Saito. DES: Shuichi Seki (TV), N/C (m). ANI: Shinya Takahashi, Minoru Kobata, Akio Sakai, Joji Yanase, Toshio Kaneko. MUS: K. S. Yoshimura (TV), Joe Hisaishi (m). PRD: Itoman, Panmedia, TV Tokyo. 25 mins. x 52 eps. (TV), 60 mins. (m, 78 mins. in the U.S.).
Brunette Kansas girl Dorothy Gale and her dog, Toto, are whisked away to the magical land of Oz, where she joins forces with a Tin Woodman, a Scarecrow, and a Cowardly Lion, following

the Yellow Brick Road to the Emerald City, from whence she hopes to return home. Based on *The Wonderful Wizard of Oz* (1900), *The Marvelous Land of Oz* (1904), *Ozma of Oz* (1907), and *The Emerald City of Oz* (1910) from L. Frank Baum's 14-volume series, *WoO* was first broadcast abroad in 1984 but not shown in Japan until 1986. It was dropped by NHK and eventually screened on TV Tokyo, though the final two episodes were crammed into an hour-long special. On video, the separate story arcs were condensed into 90 minutes each and released across four two-tape sets—thereby existing in feature-length chunks, often leading to their confusion with the Fumihiko Takayama anime movie version. The Takayama *Wizard of Oz* (1982, though not released in Japan until 1986) is a 60-minute movie (78 in the U.S.) with a blonde Dorothy. It keeps closer to the plot of the first book only, just like the famous live-action 1939 Judy Garland adaptation. Curiously, Akira Miyazaki is credited as a screenwriter in both blonde and brunette versions, which, despite the contradictory international release dates, must have begun production almost simultaneously! Both were seen in the U.S. before being shown in Japan.

A video of a Japanese Oz puppet show, *WoO: Dorothy's Adventure* (1991, *Dorothy no Daiboken*), is also filed in some anime sources. See also the sci-fi remake **GALAXY ADVENTURES OF SPACE OZ**, the distantly related **OZ**, and **VIDEO PICTURE BOOK**.

WIZARDRY
1990. Video. DIR: Shunsuke Shinohara. SCR: Masaru Terajima. DES: Satoshi Hirayama, Yasushi Hirayama. ANI: Yasushi Nagaoka. MUS: Soji Kawamura. PRD: TMS. 50 mins.
Evil wizard Werdna has stolen a powerful amulet from crazy King Trebor and constructed a ten-level dungeon right under the king's own castle, where he and the amulet are hiding. The king offers a reward for the recovery of his

Dirty Pair

© TAKACHIHO & STUDIO NUE • SUNRISE

property, so hero Shin Garland takes up the challenge and joins a band of adventurers to descend into the wizard's lair. Based on the computer game of the same name designed by AnimEigo founder Robert Woodhead and Roe R. Adams III.

WOLF GUY
1992. Video. DIR: Naoyuki Yoshinaga. SCR: Toshikazu Fujii. DES: Osamu Tsuruyama. ANI: Atsushi Aono. MUS: Kenji Kawai. PRD: JC Staff. 30 mins. x 6 eps.
Akira Inugami is infected with a terrible poison. The only known antidote has an unfortunate side effect—it turns him into a werewolf. He opts for survival but then has to cope with his new desires and with the attention of the military, which is interested in using his affliction for its own purposes. Based on the series of novels by Kazumasa Hirai, who also wrote **HARMAGEDON** and episodes of **8TH MAN**.

WONDERBEAT SCRAMBLE
1986. JPN: *Wonderbeat S*. TV series. DIR: Satoshi Dezaki, Seiji Arihara. SCR: Toshiaki Imaizumi, Kazumi Koide, Noboru Shiroyama, Hideo Takayashiki, Toshiyuki Tanabe, Yoshihisa Araki. DES: Setsuko Shibunnoichi, Keizo Shimizu, Yuichi Higuchi. ANI: Toshio Nitta. MUS:

Ko Komemitsu. PRD: Mushi, Magic Bus, TBS. 25 mins. x 24 eps.
In the year 2121, Professor Sugida disappears during an experiment in medical miniaturization, for which he has been inserted within a patient's body. His son, Susumu, is allowed to join the White Pegasus team sent to rescue him and is miniaturized to board the minivessel Wonderbeat. The seven-man crew discovers that the professor, far from being dead, has been kidnapped by the alien creature Hieu as the first step in its quest for world domination. It's anime's homage to *Fantastic Voyage* (1966), or, if you'd rather, *Invasion of the Body Snatchers* (1956), seen from the inside out. Each episode finishes with a live-action mini medical lecture, from **ASTRO BOY**'s Osamu Tezuka, who was also the executive producer. Compare to the similar **MICROID S**.

WONDERFUL GENIE FAMILY *

1969. JPN: *Hakushon Daimao*. AKA: *Bad King Haxion/Atchoo*. TV series. DIR: Hiroshi Sasakawa, Tsuneo Ninomiya. SCR: Junzo Toriumi. DES: Tatsuo Yoshida. ANI: Shigeru Yamamoto, Yukihiro Takahashi, Takashi Saijo. MUS: Shosuke Ishikawa. PRD: Tatsunoko, Fuji TV. 25 mins. x 52 eps.
In this modern-day parody of **ALADDIN AND THE WONDERFUL LAMP**, a jinni and his family can be summoned from their imprisoning bottle by a Sneeze (Dad), a Sniff (Mom), and a Yawn (the eternally tired daughter). Created by producer Tatsuo Yoshida.

WOOF WOOF 47 RONIN

1963. JPN: *Wan Wan Chushingura*. AKA: *Woof Woof Chushingura; Doggie March*. Movie. DIR: Daisaku Shirakawa, Hiroshi Ikeda. SCR: Satoshi Iijima, Daisaku Shirakawa. DES: Seiichi Toriizuka. ANI: Akira Okuwara, Hayao Miyazaki. MUS: Urahito Watanabe. PRD: Toei. 81 mins.
Lock the puppy lives happily in the peaceful forest until outlaws Kira the tiger and Akamimi the fox murder his mother. Lock enlists Goro, an aging stray dog, to help him in his quest for revenge, and they assemble a band of dogs to bring justice against the killers where the law has failed. Based an idea by executive producer Osamu Tezuka, itself inspired by the kabuki play *Chushingura* (which exists in many forms, the earliest known dating from 1706), also known as *Treasury of Loyal Retainers* or *The 47 Ronin*.

The original story dates from 1701, when Lord Asano of Ako Castle was provoked into drawing his sword and wounding his guest, the high-ranking samurai Kira. Asano was forced to commit suicide, but the castle steward Oishi assembled 46 loyal retainers, who murdered Kira, and then committed ritual suicide in 1703. The anime version is far simpler, dumping matters of etiquette and loyalty in favor of an archetypal quest for revenge, with only Oishi (Lock) and Kira surviving in any recognizable form. The final showdown in the snow, also present in the original, made the film ideal for its release just before Christmas. Compare to the similarly canine **DOGTANIAN AND THE THREE MUSKEHOUNDS**. A young Hayao Miyazaki was one of the animators.

WORDS WORTH *

1999. Video. DIR: Kan Fukumoto. SCR: N/C. DES: Rin Shin. ANI: Rin Shin. MUS: N/C. PRD: Beam Entertainment, Green Bunny. 30 mins. x 5 eps.
The forces of light and darkness fight to obtain the scattered pieces of the Words Worth, a stone monolith with magical powers. This sensual fantasy epic was based on the pornographic computer game from Elf. As per usual, there is a prophecy about a legendary swordsman, ladies in diaphanous veils, and lots of shagging. **N**

WORLD MASTERPIECE THEATER

After the success of Isao Takahata and Hayao Miyazaki's **HEIDI**, Nippon Animation began a long-term project to adapt numerous Western children's favorites into anime. Originally sponsored by the soft drink company Calpis, the *WMT* (*Sekai Meisaku Gekijou*) series began in 1975 with **DOG OF FLANDERS**. The Calpis sponsorship continued in the following years with **FROM THE APENNINES TO THE ANDES**, **RASCAL RACCOON**, and **NOBODY'S GIRL**. Without Calpis, but firmly established as Nippon Animation's yearly cash cow by 1979 (compare to Tatsunoko's **TIME BOKAN**, Sunrise's **HERO SERIES** and **GUNDAM**, or Tokyo Movie Shinsha's **LUPIN III**), the *WMT* series continued with **ANNE OF GREEN GABLES**, **TOM SAWYER**, **SWISS FAMILY ROBINSON**, **SOUTHERN RAINBOW**, **TREASURES OF THE SNOW**, **KATRI THE MILKMAID**, **A LITTLE PRINCESS**, **POLLYANNA**, **LITTLE WOMEN**, **LITTLE LORD FAUNTLEROY**, **PETER PAN AND WENDY**, **DADDY LONG-LEGS**, **THE SOUND OF MUSIC**, **THE BUSHBABY**, **LITTLE MEN**, **TICO OF THE SEVEN SEAS**, and **ROMEO'S BLUE SKY**. By 1996, however, the franchise was showing signs of increasing strain—**LASSIE** was taken off the air and replaced with *Remi: A Child without a Home*, a remake of **NOBODY'S BOY** that deviated so far from the original as to betray the entire raison d'etre of the franchise. The *WMT* never recovered and was laid to rest after 21 years, though the earlier shows were soon given a new lease on life through video. Though the English-language market has been dominated in successive waves by the likes of **ROBOTECH**, **AKIRA**, **UROTSUKIDOJI**, and **POKÉMON**, anime in Europe is far more likely to be known through the high-quality children's entertainment for which the *WMT* became justly famous.

WORLD OF AIKA-CHAN, THE

1993. JPN: *Aika-chan no Chikyu*. Video. DIR: Kusa Sugiyama. SCR: Kusa Sugiyama. DES: Shunji Saita. ANI: Shunji Saita. MUS: N/C. PRD: Tech. 33 mins.
The author of the manga *Secrets of the World* was only 12 years old, and she died only days after completing it. Aika Tsubota's parents published her environmentally themed story in her memory, and this one-shot anime was the eventual result, sponsored in part by a charity opposing the pollution of the oceans. In 1995, *Secrets of the World* itself

was animated as a two-part video series under the auspices of the Japanese Department of the Environment.

WORLD OF AKIRA TORIYAMA, THE

1990. JPN: *Pink Mizudorobo Amedorobo; Kennosuke-sama.* AKA: *Pink Thieves Water and Rain; Kennosuke-sama.* Movie. DIR: Toyoo Ashida, Minoru Okazaki. SCR: Aya Matsui. DES: Akira Toriyama. ANI: Toyoo Ashida, Katsuyoshi Nakatsuru. MUS: Takeshi Kazuchi. PRD: Toei. 31 mins. x 2 eps.
Two minor works from **DRAGON BALL**–creator Toriyama, shown on their own dedicated double bill under this umbrella title. *Pink*, the first story, is set in a town where no rain has fallen for three years. The corrupt Silver Company has monopolized the water supply and charges high prices even for drinking water. Bath-loving girl Pink starts stealing water from Silver Company's tankers, soon teaming up with spiky-haired guy Cobalt Blue to rob from the water-rich and give to the poor. The second story, *Kennosuke-sama*, is a squashed-down cartoon comedy about a family of old-fashioned samurai living in modern-day Tokyo whose young son has to head out for an important date.

WOUNDED MAN

1986. JPN: *Kizuoibito.* Video. DIR: Satoshi Dezaki, Takao Takeuchi. SCR: Tetsuaki Imaizumi, Kazuo Koike. DES: Keizo Shimizu. ANI: Keizo Shimizu. MUS: Noriaki Yamanaka. PRD: Toei, Magic Bus. 30 mins. x 5 eps.
TV reporter Yuko Soka visits gold-rush Brazil in order to interview Keisuke Ibaragi, aka Rio Baraki, the quarterback of the football team. After predictably becoming lovers, the pair go in search of an Amazon treasure in the company of Peggy, a shipbuilder. The girls eventually meet with death for the crime of being eye-candy in a macho anime—this one based on a manga by the same team of Kazuo Koike and Ryoichi Ikegami that produced **CRYING FREEMAN** and **SANCTUARY**. Keisuke discovers that his mother, Natsuko, Yuko, and Peggy were killed by the mysterious secret group GPX. Boiling with revenge, he finally confronts the two men responsible for a showdown on a sinking aircraft carrier. ●ⓃⓋ

WOW! MR. MASARU!

1998. JPN: *Sexy Commando Gaiden! Wow! Masaru-san.* AKA: *Sexy Commando Side Story!; Wow! Mr. Masaru.* TV series. DIR: Akitaro Daichi. SCR: Kyosuke Usuta. DES: Toshihide Masudate. ANI: Toshihide Masudate. MUS: Harukichi Yamamoto. PRD: M-BAS, TBS. 10 mins. x 48 eps.
Teenager Masaru is already the top fighter at his school in a number of martial arts—karate, judo, boxing, and more. But he wants to get even better. He goes off into the mountains for three months and returns transformed into the "Sexy Commando." His new special technique is to stun opponents with his weird fighting poses, then attack before they can gather their wits. Based on the 1995 *Shonen Jump* manga by Kyosuke Usuta, these shorts were serialized as part of the *Wonderful* variety program. Ⓥ

X

X: THE MOVIE *

1998. JPN: *X: 1999*. Movie. DIR: Rintaro. SCR: Nanase Okawa, Asami Watanabe. DES: Nobuteru Yuki. ANI: Nobuteru Yuki. MUS: Yasuaki Shimizu, X-Japan. PRD: Madhouse. 98 mins.

Two groups of psychic warriors, known as the Seven Seals of the Earth Dragon and the Seven Harbingers of the Heaven Dragon, fight to save the world or destroy it. The battle is fought in modern Tokyo but draws on landmarks of the city's historic and spiritual past as both shields for Earth and levers to trigger its destruction. Subaru and Seishiro (characters from CLAMP's earlier **TOKYO BABYLON**) fight on opposing sides and end up by destroying each other without resolving the struggle. Kamui, a psychic of enormous power, witnesses the fight and is so devastated that he flees Tokyo. But running can't save him; it is his destiny to join one side or the other and decide the fate of Earth. He finally returns to Tokyo to avenge the death of his mother, but to protect his friends Fuma and Kotori (whom he has loved since childhood), he refuses to take sides in the decisive battle. But Fate has decided otherwise. Fuma is Kamui's opposite number, the balance to his powers in the scales of destiny. When Fuma is seduced by the Earth Dragon's powers and kills his own sister, Kotori, Kamui finally joins the other side. The two friends must fight each other to decide if the world survives or ends.

Based on the manga in *Asuka* magazine from the CLAMP collective, *X* was preceded by lots of hype and a 25-minute music video made with the rock group X-Japan, suitably titled *X2*.

But the amount that has to be cut from a huge, unfinished saga to make it into a coherent feature-length script can destroy the subtlety of a story and alienate fans of the original. Faced with compressing the massive melodrama without upsetting its fans, director Rintaro opted for style and emotion over clarity and substance. The look and mood of the original are there, just don't expect it to make much sense in terms of plot. The "1999" was dropped from the title for its English-language release since it didn't reach video until 2000. A 24-episode *X* TV series was announced soon afterward as a forthcoming project from Yoshiaki Kawajiri, for which a video prequel was released in August 2001. *Ill. p. 305.*

XABUNGLE

1982. JPN: *Sento Mecha Xabungle*. AKA: *Battle Mecha Xabungle; The Bungler*. TV series, movie. DIR: Yoshiyuki Tomino, Toshifumi Takizawa, Osamu Sekita, Akira Suzuki, Yasuhiro Imagawa. SCR: Tsunehisa Ito, Soji Yoshikawa. DES: Kunio Okawara, Yutaka Izubuchi. ANI: Tomonori Kogawa, Akehiro Kaneyama. MUS: Koji Makaino. PRD: Sunrise, TV Asahi. 25 mins. x 50 eps. (TV), 86 mins. (m).

On planet Zola, the purebred Innocents live inside a sealed dome, unable to survive in the inhospitable environment. The Civilian underclass, who live out in the wilderness, regard the Innocents' rocket launches as "ascensions of light" and do not question their assigned roles as rockmen (bluestone miners), freighters (traders), and sandrats (desert-dwellers). Civilian Jiron Amos believes his rockman father was

murdered and steals the new Walker Machine Xabungle, quarrelling all the way with the pretty land-ship captain Elche. He sets out on the land-ship Iron Gear to learn the truth about his father's death, but the whole planet has another truth to learn. For generations all Zolans have believed that they were descended from colonists from the planet Earth, but they never left the homeworld—Zola *is* the Earth, devastated by centuries of exploitation.

A more jocular robot show than its contemporaries, *Xabungle* (i.e., "The Bungler") featured an inept hero and giant robot battles often played for laughs, set against a background that mixes parts of **GREY** and **NAUSICAÄ** with Westerns—homages extend as far as having a Clint Eastwood clone among the characters, along with a lookalike of Sunrise's all-time great antihero Char Aznable. A deliberate attempt to break the serious mold of Sunrise robot shows (by Tomino, the man whose name remains synonymous with **GUNDAM**), it also predates **PATLABOR** in its depiction of robots as everyday working tools. The story reappeared in 1983 in a feature-length edit, *Xabungle Graffiti*, screened alongside the two **DOUGRAM** short movies. The Wild West imagery would return years later in **TRIGUN** and **EAT-MAN**.

XANADU: LEGEND OF DRAGONSLAYER

1988. JPN: *Xanadu Dragonslayer Densetsu*. Video. DIR: Atsutoshi Umezawa. SCR: Haruya Yamazaki. DES: Koichi Arai. ANI: Koichi Arai. MUS: Seiji Yokoyama. PRD: Nippon Falcom, Toei. 50 mins.

The evil magician Reichswar has killed the King to gain possession of a magic crystal; now he means to use its power to rule the whole of Xanadu. Then the widowed Queen Rieru is kidnapped. One brave young warrior, wielding the magic blade Dragonslayer, goes to her rescue. It's all based on the role-playing game *Xanadu*, as if you couldn't guess.

X-TREME TEAM
1998. JPN: *Totsugeki! Pappara Tai*. AKA: *Attack! Sprinkle Squad*. TV series. DIR: Kenichi Maejima. SCR: Natsuki Matsuzawa. DES: Yukari Kobayashi. ANI: N/C. MUS: N/C. PRD: Mediaworks, TV Tokyo. 25 mins. x 26 eps.
This spoof of anime's teens-save-Earth genre starts with rumors of an imminent alien invasion. The world mobilizes to establish the United Earth Defense Forces, the most powerful of whom are, of course, in Japan. When the promised alien invasion doesn't arrive, however, the SWAT teams resort to mercenary activities, fighting crime, chasing terrorists, and even delivering valuables as security guards. They also organize "friendly" competitions with rival defense teams. A tongue-in-cheek comedy about what might have happened if, say, the cast of **EVANGELION** was all ready for the Angels, but the Angels forgot to come.

Y

YADAMON

1992. TV series. DIR: Kiyoshi Harada, Masaya Mizutani, Yoshiko Sasaki, Koichi Takada. SCR: Minami Okii. DES: SUEZEN. ANI: Masahiko Murata, Hideaki Sakamoto, Kenichi Shimizu. MUS: Koji Makaino. PRD: Group Tac, NHK. 8 mins. x 170 eps.

Yadamon is a little witch who lives with Jan and his parents in the near future. Maria, Jan's mother, is a biologist and spends her time performing experiments. Yadamon is an inquisitive girl, and, like most magical friends (see DORAEMON), she frequently gets Jan into trouble. Like all good magical girls, she has a cute little magical pet, Taimon, who can not only talk but also stop time for a short while. The series aired every weekday; the 21-week first run accounted for 110 episodes. Starting out on NHK, the second series aired on NHK's Educational Channel in 1993. For the linguistically curious, *iya-damon* is a cute way for little girls to say "no," which might be useful for the heroine of YOIKO.

YAGAMI'S FAMILY TROUBLES

1990. JPN: *Yagami-kun no Katei no Jijo.* AKA: *Yagami's Family Circumstances; Affairs at the House of Yagami.* Video. DIR: Shinya Sadamitsu. SCR: N/C. DES: Kei Kusunoki, Kazuya Yokose. ANI: Kazuya Yokose. MUS: Ichiro Nitta. PRD: IG Tatsunoko, Kitty Film. 30 mins. x 3 eps., 55 mins.

Yagami's mother looks as if she's just 16 and is as cute as anything; despite finding this embarrassing, he can't help lusting after her in a combination of Oedipus *and* Lolita complexes! All his classmates, and his teacher, and the local delinquent, are in love with his mother; as well as fighting each other over who loves her most, they get together to plot ways of getting rid of their common enemy, Yagami's father. Dad has problems of his own as the love object of a secretary in his office, but once his coworker discovers he has such a pretty "young" wife, she turns her affections instead to Yagami. No wonder the poor boy's confused. Things could hardly get worse when a new student who looks almost exactly like Yagami's mother joins his class—and it's a boy. The 1986 *Shonen Sunday* manga by OGRE SLAYER–creator Kei Kusunoki pushed the envelope of family values, but the spinoff video is a low-budget effort aimed at exploiting the manga fan base. The series was repackaged into an edited one-shot *Decisions* (*Yorinuki*) the same year.

YAIBA

1993. JPN: *Kenyu Densetsu Yaiba.* AKA: *Legend of Brave Swordsman Yaiba.* TV series. DIR: Kunihiko Yuyama, Norihiko Sudo, Sadao Suzuki, Hiroshi Yoshida, Osamu Sekita, Akitaro Daichi, Kazuya Murata, Yasuhiro Matsumura, Eiichi Sato. SCR: Kenji Terada, Shikichi Ohashi, Isao Shizuoka. DES: Tokuhiro Matsubara, Katsuyoshi Kanemura. ANI: Tokuhiro Matsubara, Tadashi Hirota, Kazuto Nakazawa. MUS: Kohei Tanaka. PRD: Pastel, TV Tokyo. 25 mins. x 52 eps.

Leaving the distant isle where he and his father studied samurai skills, Yaiba Kurogane comes home with his animal friends—a tiger and a vulture. He stays with his father's old adversary, Raizo, and Raizo's cute daughter, Sayaka, enrolling in her high school. Here he has to face school kendo champion Takeshi Onimaru, possessor of a demonic sword. Yaiba goes into the mountains to learn from ancient sword master Musashi (see YOUNG MIYAMOTO MUSASHI) and gets not just new skills but also a magic sword of his own, the legendary Sword of the Thunder God. All he has to do is stay true to the samurai spirit within him and collect seven magic spheres to enhance his sword's power, and then he can vanquish all evil. But he and Takeshi aren't the only people with conquest in mind. Princess Moon, the Thunder God's old adversary, is out to conquer Earth, and Yaiba and Takeshi must forget their quarrel and unite to save the world. Adapted from the first successful manga by CONAN THE BOY DETECTIVE–creator Gosho Aoyama, *Yaiba* has many similarities with its smarter younger brother, mixing action, drama, and humor.

YAKUMO TATSU

1997. Video. DIR: Tomomi Mochizuki. SCR: Go Sakamoto. DES: Yukiko Kusumoto. ANI: Yukiko Kusumoto. MUS: Hajime Mizoguchi. PRD: Studio Pierrot. 30 mins. x 2 eps.

Kuraki Fuzuchi and Takeo Nanichi are not only Japanese schoolboys, but also the reincarnations of an ancient shrine-maiden and a swordsmith. They fight off evil spirits and unwelcome female attention as they attempt to collect sacred swords and preserve them from evil. Based on a manga by Natsumi Itsuki (OZ), the anime covers only the first collected volume of the manga, originally published in *Hana to*

Yume magazine. It also comes complete with moody evocations of Japan's past (see **DARK MYTH**) and a homoerotically charged buddy-relationship, deliberately aimed at Japan's large female audience of pretty-boy aficionados.

YAMATO TAKERU

1994. JPN: *Yamato Takeru*. TV series. DIR: Hideharu Iuchi, Shinichi Masaki, Nobuhiro Kondo, Jiro Saito, Takeshi Yoshimoto. SCR: Masaharu Amiya, Kenichi Araki. DES: Koichi Ohata. ANI: Takahiro Kishida, Moriyasu Taniguchi, Akira Kasahara. MUS: Takahiro Kishida. PRD: Nippon Animation, TBS. 25 mins. x 39 eps.

On planet Yamato, a twin birth is a bad omen for the throne, so when two brothers are born to the queen, one of them must be killed. But Takeru is saved through the intervention of the gods and survives to return and claim the throne (and the beautiful princess) as fate has decreed. For this sci-fi clash of robotic armor indistinguishable from "magic," creator Masami Yuki took his inspiration from one of Japan's oldest stories. The original Yamato Takeru's epic expedition was recorded in two of Japan's oldest historical texts, the *Kojiki* (A.D. 712) and *Nihon Shoki* (A.D. 720), and he and Princess Ototachibana are jointly credited as founders of many real shrines. Ancient sources sometimes embroider the bare cloth of supposed history— Takeru is alleged to have defeated Kumaso warriors by disguising himself as a woman and getting them drunk, and he was to have saved the plains from Ainu arsonists by cutting away the burning brush with his sword. The weapon, known thenceforth as *Kusanagi* ("Grass-Cutter"), became one of the Imperial Treasures of Japan, lending its name to several anime protagonists, most notably Motoko Kusanagi in **GHOST IN THE SHELL**.

The final two episodes were not broadcast but released on video in 1997. The beginning of a fourth season that never materialized, they are set three years after the original, with

Takeru now 16 years old, having to defend his homeworld from samurai-style robot invaders from planet Izumo in a "flying magic fortress." See also **LITTLE PRINCE AND THE EIGHT-HEADED DRAGON** and the live-action version of the legend released in the West as *Orochi the Eight-Headed Dragon*.

YAMAZAKI KING OF SCHOOL

1997. JPN: *Gakko O Yamazaki*. AKA: *School King Yamazaki*. TV series. DIR: Tsuneo Tominaga. SCR: Kazumi Koide, Taku Ichikawa. DES: Hiroshi Ikeda. ANI: Shinichi Suzuki. MUS: N/C. PRD: Bandai, TV Tokyo. 25 mins. x 33 eps.

A bratty six-year-old declares himself the "King of School." In a rip-off of the earlier **CRAYON SHIN-CHAN**, this adaptation of Manabu Kashimoto's manga from *Corocoro Comic* features kleptomania, disobedience, and fighting.

YANBO, NINBO AND TONBO

1995. JPN: *Yanbo Ninbo Tonbo*. TV series. DIR: Seitaro Hara, Tatsuo Okazaki, Shigeo Koshi, Mamoru Kobe. SCR: Satoshi Nakamura. DES: Takumi Izawa. ANI: Katsumi Hashimoto, Hiroshi Kagawa, Kazuhiko Udagawa. MUS: N/C. PRD: Image K, NHK2. 25 mins. x 39 eps.

An old 1950s NHK radio-drama featuring the three titular monkey brothers, this anime updates the story for the '90s audience of the original broadcasters' new satellite channel. The brothers try some crow soup, start a fire on the mountain, and race the king of the Pig People—like kids do.

YANKI: RIDE LIKE THE WIND

1989. JPN: *Yanki Reppu Tai*. AKA: *Yanki Wind Gang*. Video. DIR: Tetsuro Imazawa. SCR: Ryunosuke Ono, Yasushi Ishikura. DES: Masahide Hashimoto. ANI: Hideki Kakinuma. MUS: Tetsuro Kashibuchi. PRD: Toei. 50 mins. x 6 eps.

Impossibly tough and hairsprayed biker boys and girls fight turf wars in the streets, with much revving of motors and "you killed my buddy, prepare to die" dialogue. This lackluster latecom-

Sworn to protect the Kushinada lineage of ancient times, Mamoru Kusanagi races to the rescue in Yuzo Takada's **BLUE SEED**. Positing a Japan besieged by creatures from its mythological past, *BS* recycles local folktales in homage to **ULTRAMAN**'s monster of the week, with a conspiracy redolent of the *X-Files* thrown in for good measure. Like Motoko Kusanagi from **GHOST IN THE SHELL**, Mamoru takes his name from "Grass-Cutter," a legendary sword wielded by **YAMATO TAKERU**. See entry p. 39.

Blue Seed

er to the genre typified by **BOMBER BIKERS OF SHONAN** was based on the *Shonen Magazine* manga by Masahide Hashimoto, whose hero was *so* tough that he transferred schools 20 times. Only a Japanese tough guy would continue to go at all! **LV**

YASUJI'S PORNORAMA

1971. JPN: *Yasuji no Pornorama Yachimae!* AKA: *Yasuji's Pornorama: How About That!* Movie. DIR: Takamitsu Mitsunori. SCR: Yoshiaki Yoshida. DES: Yasuji Tanioka. ANI: Michiru Suzuki. MUS: Kiyoshi Hashijo. PRD: TV Tokyo. 101 mins.

Three incidents in the life of Busuo ("Fatso"), the lecherous hero of Yasuji Tanioka's anarchic 1970 manga *Yasuji's Course on Being an Utter Brat* (*Yasuji no Metameta Gaki Michi Koza*). Though produced by TV Tokyo, these cartoon erotica were "too hot for television" and screened instead in theaters. With the failure of **CLEOPATRA: QUEEN OF SEX** the previous year, anime pornography would disappear for a generation after this, until straight-to-video releases made **LOLITA ANIME** possible.

YAT BUDGET! SPACE TOURS

1996. JPN: *YAT Anshin! Uchu Ryoko*. TV series. DIR: Hitoshi Nanba, Takuya

Sato, Tsuneo Kobayashi, Kazuhiro Sasaki. SCR: Keiko Hagiwara, Ryo Motohira, Mineo Hayashi, Yutaka Hirata. DES: Hiroka Kudo. ANI: Hiroka Kudo. MUS: Kenji Kawai. PRD: Tac, NHKEP. 25 mins. x 75 eps.

The Yamamoto Anshin Travel Company's latest luxury space tour hits an unexpected setback when the ship warps into an unknown part of space, ruled by a race of fishlike humanoids called the Gannon, who don't like their visitors. "Luxury" is a misnomer; the ship is a pile of junk, the captain is fat and grumpy, and, with the exception of the stewardess—his daughter Katsura—and the boy who's crazy about her, most of the crew are robots or aliens, and all of them are weird. Beset by pretty shark-boys out for their blood, with restless passengers, and the normally quiet Katsura ready to bash someone with her monkey wrench, how will our gang of misfits get their passengers home? To make matters worse, they've got a stowaway—squirrel-girl Marron, who can turn herself into a little pink ball but doesn't seem to have many other useful survival skills. This cute, colorful slapstick SF show, created by Shinji Nishikawa, was a departure for NHK's educational division. Something the anime industry *itself* should have learned from was a stroboscopic sequence in the final episode, which produced fainting and convulsions in some viewers in March 1997. Nine months later, a similar sequence in POKÉMON would make international headlines.

YAWARA!

1989. JPN: *Yawara! The Gentle Judo Girl*. TV series, movie, TV special. DIR: Hiroko Tokita, Katsuhisa Yamada, Akio Sakai, Junichi Sakata. SCR: Toshiki Inoue, Yoshiyuki Suga. DES: Yoshinori Kanemori. ANI: Kunihiko Sakurai, Hirotsugu Yamazaki. MUS: Eiji Mori. PRD: Kitty Film, Yomiuri TV. 25 mins. x 124 eps. (TV), 60 mins. (m), 90 mins. (TVm).

Teenage judo genius Yawara Inokuma (who shares the surname of the gold medalist from the 1960 Tokyo Olympics) wants to get to the Barcelona Olympics and fulfill her grandfather Jigoro's dream of making her a judo champion under his coaching. But she also wants a life of her own outside of training schedules and competitions—her best friend, the plain Fujiko, also strives hard to be a top-class sportswoman. Yawara attracts two suitors, playboy Kasamatsuri and young sports reporter Matsuda. With them come rivals to create anime love polygons—Matsuda is also desired by the buxom photographer Kuniko, while rich-bitch judoist Sayaka sees herself as the perfect companion to Kazamatsuri. To make matters even more complicated, Sayaka's trainer is Yawara's own estranged father, Kojiro—determined that his daughter is toughened by a truly worthy opponent.

Based on the 1986 manga in *Big Comics Spirits* by MASTER KEATON–creator Naoki Urasawa, *Yawara* is one of the better successors to AIM FOR THE ACE, always ready to lay sports aside for more human-interest drama. Her love for her crusty old grandfather is equal to her determination to go to school, have fun with her friends, and maybe even fall in love; this is the main cause of conflict in both manga and anime. The first season ends, in true sports-anime style, with Yawara's defeat of her Soviet rival, Tereshkova, as *glasnost* takes hold. The series was a hit with more than just the female audience. Life imitated art as it drew to a close with Tokita's movie *Wiggle Your Hips* (1992, *Soreyuke Koshinuke Kids*), shown on a double bill with the RANMA 1/2 feature *Nihao My Concubine*. As the anime Yawara went off to the Barcelona Olympics in 1992, 16-year-old real-life judoist Ryoko Tamura won a silver medal at the actual Barcelona games and was immediately christened "Yawara-chan" by the Japanese media. Four years later, the series was revived for a feature-length TV special, Morio Asaka's *Yawara: Only You* (*Y: Zutto Kimi no Koto ga . . .*), in which Yawara defeats Sayaka in Atlanta and faces

another of her father's protégés in the finals, the French Marceau. The real-life Tamura dutifully obliged by winning another silver at the real-life Atlanta Olympics. Four more years later, Tamura finally won gold in Sydney, wearing the fictional Yawara's trademark yellow ribbon in her hair. For other judo-related struggles, see SANSHIRO SUGATA.

YEARLING, THE

1983. JPN: *Koshika Monogatari*. AKA: *Little Deer Story*. TV series. DIR: Masaaki Osumi. SCR: Shunichi Yukimuro, Eiichi Tachi, Michiru Umadori, Soji Yoshikawa. DES: Shuichi Seki. ANI: Shuichi Seki. MUS: Koichi Sugiyama. PRD: MK Production, NHK. 25 mins. x 52 eps.

Based on the book by Marjorie Kinnan Rawlings about an orphaned fawn and the 12-year-old boy who finds it and rears it. Jody lives in grinding poverty on an isolated homestead in the Florida swamps in 1807. As he grows toward manhood and the fawn grows into an adult deer, Jody struggles with the difficulties of keeping a relationship going with a wild thing while still respecting its own nature. *The Yearling* was Osumi's last anime directing job—he left to work in the theater.

YESTERDAY ONCE MORE

1997. JPN: *Dosokai Y.O.M*. AKA: *Same Window Club: Y.O.M*. Video. DIR: Kan Fukumoto. SCR: Miyuki Takahashi. DES: Shinichi Takagi. ANI: Shinichi Takagi. MUS: N/C. PRD: Pink Pineapple, KSS. 30 mins. x 4 eps.

Meeting for a reunion after a long time apart, the former members of a school tennis club discover new, forbidden pleasures in each other's company and agree to meet again, to catch up on old times, of course. Based on the erotic computer game from Fairy Tale, in the style of END OF SUMMER.

YOIKO

1998. AKA: *Pretty Girl, Pretty Child*. TV series. DIR: Takahiro Omori, Jun Matsumoto, Kiyotaka Matsumoto, Kenichi

Takeshita. SCR: Sukehiro Tomita, Shikichi Ohashi, Shigeru Yanagawa. DES: Yugo Ishikawa. ANI: N/C. MUS: Shigeru Chiba. PRD: Studio Pierrot, TBS. 25 mins. x 20 eps.

The agenda of this late-night series is hinted at by the title's wordplay. Kazahana Ezumi is just a little girl at elementary school, but her body is almost that of a grown woman. This gets her into all kinds of problematic situations that a little girl her age isn't equipped to handle. Same old same-old (see **CREAM LEMON**) gets new names, faces, and clothes. Based on Yugo Ishikawa's *Big Spirits* manga, this anime incongruously mixes childish schoolroom gags with prurient nudity. **⓪**

YOKOHAMA SHOPPING

1998. JPN: *Yokohama Kaidashi Kiko.* AKA: *Going Shopping in Yokohama.* Video. DIR: Takashi Anno. SCR: Takashi Anno. DES: Atsushi Yamagata. ANI: Atsushi Yamagata. MUS: Gontiti. PRD: Asia-do. 29 mins. x 2 eps.

This is either a sweet tale of a young girl's everyday life in a quiet suburb or a mold-breaking SF adventure in which an android searches for meaning in a world plagued by global warming. Alpha Hasseno is a humanoid robot girl who lives in the countryside of a future Japan, near what used to be Yokohama. Though Yokohama today is a big coastal city partly built on reclaimed marshland, in this future much of Japan's urban infrastructure has been destroyed as global warming has put much of the world underwater. Her area is safe for the moment, but storms and floods are a constant threat. She runs a coffee shop, Café Alpha, in the absence of her owner, but she doesn't know where he is or when he will return. She's happy to wait, meanwhile serving coffee to the local characters. But in the course of her daily life and her shopping trip into Yokohama city—a trip that shows us how her world differs from ours— she meets other people, even another robot, and starts to wonder about her own life and purpose. The arrival of a

parcel containing her creator's diary adds to the mystery. Based on the 1994 manga by Hitoshi Ashinano in *Afternoon* magazine.

YOKOHAMA THUGS

1993. JPN: *Yokohama Bakurettai.* Video. DIR: Mineo Goto, Masamune Ochiai. SCR: Shunsuke Amemura. DES: Satoshi Kuzumoto. ANI: N/C. MUS: N/C. PRD: Toei. 50 mins. x 4 eps.

It's all gags and fighting as gangster Tsunematsu Narita (the "biggest idiot in Yokohama") causes havoc in the neighborhood with his two henchmen. Based on the *Shonen Champion* manga by Satoshi Kuzumoto. **⓿**

YOKOHAMA'S FAMOUS KATAYAMA

1992. JPN: *Yokohama Meibutsu Otoko Katayamagumi.* AKA: *Yokohama's Famous Male Katayama Gang.* Video. DIR: Yoshinori Nakamura, Osamu Sekita. SCR: Hideo Nanba. DES: Masafumi Yamamoto. ANI: Masafumi Yamamoto. MUS: Quarter Moon. PRD: JC Staff, Nippon Eizo. 50 mins. x 2 eps.

Motorcycle gangsters with "a comical touch," as Hiromi Katayama, leader of the Yokohama biker gang Crazy Babies, tries to proclaim a one-month moratorium on violence while he trains new recruits, though his Tokyo rival, the Mad Emperor, has other ideas. Based on the manga in *Shonen Magazine* by Akira Yazawa. Compare to **BOMBER BIKERS OF SHONAN**.

YOMA: CURSE OF THE UNDEAD *

1988. JPN: *Yoma.* AKA: *Blood Reign; Curse of the Undead.* Video. DIR: Takashi Anno. SCR: Noboru Aikawa. DES: Matsuri Okuda. ANI: Matsuri Okuda. MUS: Hiroya Watanabe. PRD: Animate Film, JC Staff. 40 mins. x 2 eps.

In medieval Japan, the constant battles between rival warlords have left the land ravaged and prey to evil; the spirit world is ever-present. When the great warlord Shingen Takeda dies, one of his ninja, Maro, tries to escape from the clan, and his best friend, Hikage, is sent to hunt him down. He comes to a village where people seem to have no

memory of their earlier lives, and he falls in love with Aya, a woman he meets there; but he learns that it's really just a fattening ground for people who don't want to live because of past sadness. They are kept in a state of happy forgetfulness while being held as sacrificial food for a demonic giant spider that has drawn Maro into its coils. When he destroys the god and breaks the spell, his beloved Aya remembers her past sorrows and kills herself. The second part of the story, *Maro's Evil Fang*, released in 1989, reveals that the spider god was only part of a huge conspiracy to allow the Demon Kings of the Land and Sea to unite as one and unleash all the devils in the world on mankind. Through a ninja girl named Aya, who looks exactly like his dead love, and the ghost of Maro's beloved Kotone, Hikage learns that only by killing his friend can he prevent this evil, but Maro offers him the chance to become a Lord of Hell. After a final bloody battle, it seems that evil has been defeated; but on the road, Aya and Hikage take a baby from the arms of a dead woman and see that it looks exactly like Maro. Is evil simply reborn again and again? Based on an original story by Kei Kusunoki, creator of **OGRE SLAYER** and **YAGAMI'S FAMILY TROUBLES**, this is an elegant and chilling story, much subtler than the blockbuster **UROTSUKIDOJI**, with which it shares the rebirth-of-evil theory. *Ill. p. 415.* **⓿**

YOTODEN *

1987. JPN: *Sengoku Kitan Yotoden.* AKA: *Civil War Chronicle of the Magic Blades; Wrath of the Ninja.* Video. DIR: Osamu Yamazaki. SCR: Noboru Aikawa. DES: Kenichi Onuki, Junichi Watanabe. ANI: Kenichi Onuki. MUS: Seiji Hano. PRD: MTV, JC Staff. 40 mins. x 3 eps.

In 1582, demons possess the warlord Nobunaga Oda, acting through his adviser Ranmaru Mori. The only weapons that can fight the demons are three magical weapons—a sword, a pike, and a dagger—each in the possession of a different ninja clan. The Kasami clan holds the dagger, and when the demons wipe out the rest of her family, teenage Ayame assumes the masculine name Ayanosuke and sets out to avenge her clan. Sakon of the Hyuga clan has the sword, and Ryoma of the Hakagure clan the pike. As the demons try to prevent them from using the magic weapons, their loved ones are killed and their homes destroyed. They think they have foiled the plot by killing Nobunaga and Ranmaru, but the dead were only impersonators. Ranmaru has a master plan, centuries in the making, to build a bridge between hell and Earth and give the world over to the rule of the Demon God. The three blades reunite in a titanic battle at Azuchi Castle, where victory is won at a terrible cost (compare to TIME STRANGER, which approaches the same events from a science-fictional viewpoint).

As with most ninja stories, SWORD FOR TRUTH–creator Jo Toriumi's original *Yotoden* novel owes more to 20th-century fiction than 16th-century fact. Treading the same ground as NINJA SCROLL, it assumes that the real-life events of Japan's civil war went hand-in-hand with black magic, and that Nobunaga united Japan, not with the foreign guns of the history books, but with demon armies. Ninja with '80s haircuts duck and dive their way in and out of real historical events like super-powered Forrest Gumps with throwing-stars, led by an ice-cool heroine whose gorgeous voice is from the refreshingly unsqueaky Keiko Toda. The story ends with a demonic battle that carries visceral, ultraviolent overtones of the contemporary UROTSUKIDOJI series, also written by scenarist Aikawa. **ÑV**

YOUNG ASHIBE
1991. JPN: *Shonen Ashibe*. TV series, video. DIR: Noboru Ishiguro. SCR: Oki Ike, Toshiaki Sasae, Katsuhide Motoki. DES: Hiromi Morishita. ANI: Kiyotoshi Aoii. MUS: Toshiyuki Arakawa. PRD: Nippon Eizo, TBS. 8 mins. x 75 eps.
The story of a cute little boy and his pet white sea lion was a successful

Young Jump 4-panel strip by Hiromi Morishita, selling five million copies of its six collected volumes by the end of 1992. The first TV series starring Chika Sakamoto in the leading role spun off 25 more episodes of *YA2* in 1992, with Minami Takayama taking over the role. The fourth season (#64–75) was not broadcast on TV but released straight to video.

YOUNG KINDAICHI FILES
1996. JPN: *Kindaichi Shonen no Jiken Bo*. AKA: *Young Kindaichi's Casebook*. Movie, TV series. DIR: Daisuke Nishio. SCR: Takeya Nishioka, Michiru Shimada, Hiroshi Motohashi, Akinori Endo, Toshiki Inoue. DES: Shingo Araki; Hidemi Kuma. ANI: Shingo Araki. MUS: Kaoru Wada. PRD: Toei Animation, Nippon TV. 90 mins. (m), 25 mins. x 148 eps., 90 mins. (m).
Hajime Kindaichi, grandson of a famous detective, swears on the name of his grandfather to solve every murder case he finds. He's 17, a bit of a delinquent with a bad record of attendance at his high school, but he's got a mind like a steel trap, a gift for sleight-of-hand, and a lot of help from childhood friend, Miyuki Nanase.

Based on the 1992 manga in *Shonen Magazine* by Yozaburo Kanari and Fumiya Sato, *YKF* features the descendant of a famous sleuth—the Kosuke Kindaichi created by crime novelist Seishi Yokomizo in 1946, whose most famous cases include *The Man with Three Fingers* and the live-action movie *The House of Inugami* (1976). As with LUPIN III, there were legal wrangles with the indignant executors of the original, though these were resolved with an out-of-court settlement as the series' popularity steadily increased. The manga spun off into a 1995 live-action TV series, and the first volume was adapted into Nishio's anime movie *YKF: Murder at the Hotel Opera* (1996). *YKF* rode a post-*X-Files* wave of interest in detective stories, making it and rival CONAN THE BOY DETECTIVE two of the greatest anime hits of the 1990s. Rather than limiting the mysteries to

the 25-minute sessions of single episodes, writers favored two- and three-part dramas, increasing the suspense and readily lending themselves to feature-length video releases. Just some of Kindaichi's TV cases include *The Waxworks Murders, Death by the Devil's Symphony*, and *The Killer on the Haunted Train*. Araki's designs for the 1997 TV series were revamped by Hidemi Kama for the 1999 movie *Deep Blue Slaughter*, in which Kindaichi hunts a murderer stalking a newly built Okinawa beach-resort.

YOUNG MIYAMOTO MUSASHI
1982. JPN: *Shonen Miyamoto Musashi: Wanpaku Nitoryu*. AKA: *Young Miyamoto Musashi: Naughty Way of Two Swords*. TV special. DIR: Yugo Serikawa, Hideo Watanabe. SCR: Shizuo Nonami. DES: Kazumi Fukube, Hiroshi Wagatsuma. ANI: Hiroshi Wagatsuma, Moriyasu Yamaguchi, Satoshi Hirayama. MUS: N/C. PRD: Toei, Fuji TV. 84 mins.
Four-year-old Bennosuke sees his father, a great swordmaster, killed by an even better man, Hirata. Since he knows he isn't old enough or skilled enough to take revenge, he becomes Hirata's disciple. When he's mastered the secrets of the sword and invented the technique of fighting with two at once, he kills Hirata and assumes the name Musashi. Based on the life of Musashi Miyamoto (Miyamoto Musashi, 1584–1645), often said to be the greatest swordsman in Japanese history, author of *The Book of Five Rings*, and subject of Eiji Yoshikawa's famous series of novels. In this incarnation, however, his life bears an uncanny similarity to the plot of RINGING BELL. This anime version of Musashi's life was based on Renzaburo Shibata's novel *The Duellist*, with character designs lifted from Kazumi Fukube's later manga adaptation. See SWORD OF MUSASHI.

YOUNG PRINCESS DIANA
1986. JPN: *Niji no Kanata e: Shojo Diana-hi Monogatari*. AKA: *End of the Rainbow: Young Princess Diana Story*. TV special. DIR: Hidemi Kama. SCR: Seiji

Matsuoka. DES: Yutaka Arai. ANI: Oji Suzuki, Animation 501. MUS: N/C. PRD: Tachyon, Aubec, NTV, TV Asahi. 114 mins.

Born in 1961, Diana Spencer is a child of the British aristocracy. Her parents divorce when she is six years old, and she goes to live with her father and grandmother. Sent away to boarding school, Diana is shy and withdrawn, but a sweet-natured girl who helps the maid with the washing-up and excels at pet care—winning the best-guinea-pig contest. Isolated when her father remarries, Diana throws herself into swimming and ballet, hoping that one day her prince will come. Then she meets Charles, the heir to the throne, never imagining that one day she will become his wife.

Screened a few days before the arrival of the real-life Charles and Diana on a royal visit to Japan, this could well be described as the highlight of scenarist Matsuoka's career—his later **KAMA SUTRA** hardly compares! The early life of the late Princess Diana is plundered with, in anime terms, only minor alterations; voiced by **NAUSICAÄ**-actress Sumi Shimamoto. The mind boggles at how this might have been "improved" with a few giant robots and invading aliens, but sadly it was not to be. The appeal is obvious to a Japanese audience reared on **CINDERELLA** and denied intrusive media access to their own royals—though the upbeat ending is particularly ironic considering the protagonist's later fate.

YOU'RE UNDER ARREST! *
1994. JPN: *Taiho Shichauzo*. Video, TV series, movie. DIR: Hiroshi Watanabe, Kazuhiro Furuhashi, Junji Nishimura, Takeshi Mori. SCR: Michiru Shimada, Michiko Yokote, Kazuhisa Sakaguchi (TV), Masashi Sogo (m). DES: Atsuko Nakajima, Toshihiro Murata, Hiroshi Kato. ANI: Yasuhiro Aoki. MUS: Ko Otani (TV), Kenji Kawai (m). PRD: Studio Deen, Toei, TBS. 30 mins. x 4 eps., 25 mins. x 47 eps. (TV), 6 mins. x 20 eps. (special), 90 mins. (m).
Miyuki is a gentle, reserved young woman, but for all that she's an ace driver in her working life as one of Tokyo's police officers. Natsumi is hot-headed, impulsive, and disorganized. She too is a Tokyo police officer, in the motorcycle division, and, when the two are teamed up, she doesn't think she and Miyuki will ever hit it off. But from their first important case, a pursuit of a reckless driver with a deadly agenda, they come to rely on each other and value each other's good qualities.

This pretty, innocuous, and astoundingly sanitized cop show takes the mismatched-partners cliché, removes almost all jeopardy, and hopes to muddle through on infantile foolery, female flesh, and an anal attention to audio effects—particularly engine noises. Based on the manga by **OH MY GODDESS!**-creator Kosuke Fujishima, *YuA* flips incessantly between car chases and mawkish flirting at the station house, creating a peculiar combination of *CHiPs* and a school disco. The 1996 TV series that followed the four videos—quite literally, with the first episode numbered as episode five—is pure soap opera, following day-to-day life at the station and expanding the roles of their colleagues, in particular Officer Ken Nakajima, whose romance with Miyuki forms an ongoing subplot. The episodes pack in much fan service and even a little violence, like Miyuki trying to electrocute a pervert, but there's nothing to merit real concern on these counts. A new series, *YuA: Special* (1999), comprised much shorter episodes, screened as part of the *Wonderful* program. The 1999 movie, directed by Nishimura, did much the same thing with a bigger budget for its story of an abandoned car full of weaponry and the danger that arises from its discovery. The series also spun off into audio dramas, wittily written by former **PATLABOR**-scenarist Michiko Yokote, including *Police Stories* and *Only One*. The latter CD features the girls getting jobs as the pop group "Tokyo Policewoman Duo," in which guise they record the worst song ever made, the "We Are Policewomen" rap. In tak-

Lost Universe

© TV TOKYO/SOFTX

ing the genre that gave us "Cop Killer" and using it to extol the virtues of driving safely, the song is the perfect summary of the series as a whole. It returned for a 26-episode TV season in spring 2001. *Ill. p. 91.*

YS
1989. Video. DIR: Jun Kamiya, Takashi Watanabe. SCR: Tadashi Hayakawa, Katsuhiko Chiba. DES: Tetsuya Ishikawa, Hideaki Matsuoka, Hiroyuki Nishimura. ANI: Tetsuya Ishikawa, Hiroyuki Nishimura. MUS: Michio Fujisawa. PRD: Urban Project; Tokyo Kids. 30 mins. x 7 eps. (v), 30 mins. x 4 eps. (v2).
Adol, a young swordsman in the magical kingdom of Esteria, must save the world from demonic destruction by gathering six sacred books and bringing them to the Goddesses on Precious Mountain. Based on the NES game by Nippon Falcom that has also spun off a manga by Sho Hagoromo, a series of novels, and other merchandise. *Ys: Palace of the Celestial Gods* (1992, *Tenku no Shinden*) was a second video series based on the events of the second game. Set on the flying island of Ys, it featured Adol in another quest. There was also a 60-minute animated music video, *Ys Special Collection: All About Falcom.*

YUGI-OH *
1998. AKA: *King of Games*. TV series, movie. DIR: Hiroyuki Kadono, Yoko Ikeda, Satoshi Nakamura, Keiji Hayakawa, Kunihisa Sugishima. SCR: Junji Takegami, Toshiki Inoue, Yasuko Kobayashi, Kenichi Kanemaki, Katsuhiko Chiba. DES: Shingo Araki, Michi Himeno. ANI: Masayuki Takagi. MUS: BMF. PRD: Studio Gallop, Nippon Animation, TV Asahi. 25 mins. x 27 eps. (TV1), 25 mins. x 40+ eps. (TV2), 25 mins. (m).
Game-mad Japanese boy Yugi is victimized by the school bullies and obsessed with an ancient Egyptian Millennium Puzzle. The successful player acquires a second thoroughly evil and nasty persona. Yugi can now transform into a vengeful, powerful figure; he can bring game monsters to life and deal out retribution to local evildoers, as well as to those who used to bully him, by forcing them to play a "dark game" on his terms. When he accidentally awakens the Guardian of Darkness, he and his friends are dragged into an adventure that features his own father reincarnated as a Pegasus and a showdown at a real-world gaming convention against his archenemy, who in our dimension is the president of the Industrial Illusion Company. Armed with another Egyptian artifact, the Millennium Eye, Yugi becomes the strongest duelist, in an anime/manga/collectible card game tie-in commissioned in the wake of POKÉMON. Based on the manga by Kazuki Takahashi serialized in *Shonen Jump*, it was followed by a second season, *YO: Duel Fighters*, still running at the time of writing. This is a kids-get-even fantasy so some sequences are quite violent—like the one where our hero pours petrol down the trousers of an armed robber and keeps him at bay with a cigarette lighter. A 30-minute movie formed part of 1999's Toei Anime Fair bill. **V**

YUKI
1981. Movie. DIR: Tadashi Imai. SCR: Akira Miyazaki. DES: Tetsuya Chiba. ANI: Shinichi Tsuji. MUS: Chito Kawauchi. PRD: Mushi, Nikkatsu. 89 mins.
Demons threaten the peaceful existence of a group of peasants who live in Japan's far north during the Muromachi period (1338–1573). However, the villagers have the aid of Yuki, a snow fairy who dwells among them in human form, and her beloved horse, Fubuki (Snowstorm). Though based on the story by Takasuke Saito, itself drawing on JAPANESE FOLK TALES, elements of this anime seem to coincidentally foreshadow the far more famous PRINCESS MONONOKE.

YU-NO *
1998. Video. DIR: Katsumasa Kanezawa. SCR: Osamu Kudo. DES: Tetsuro Aoki. ANI: Takeo Takahashi, Yasushi Nagaoka. MUS: N/C. PRD: Pink Pineapple, KSS. 30 mins. x 4 eps.
Takuya falls for the woman his father marries after his mother's death. Yes, it's yet another almost-but-not-quite incest story; compare to CREAM LEMON and COOL DEVICES. Announced as forthcoming in the U.S. from Nu-Tech at the time of our deadline. **N**

YUN-YUN PARADISE
1995. JPN: *YunYun Paradise*. Video. DIR: Hiroshi Yamakawa. SCR: N/C. DES: N/C. ANI: Inatsugi Kiyomizu. MUS: N/C. PRD: Pink Pineapple, AIC. 30 mins.
This "love comedy" features Yun-Yun, a suspiciously young-looking Chinese girl, falling in love with a Japanese boy. Based on a novel from the same Napoleon imprint that gave us EROTIC TORTURE CHAMBER. **N**

Z

ZAMBOT 3

1977. JPN: *Muteki Chojin Robot Zambot 3*. AKA: *Invincible Superman Zambot 3*. TV series. DIR: Yoshiyuki Tomino, Minoru Onodani, Susumu Yukita, Takao Yotsuji, Shinya Sadamitsu, Kazuyuki Hirokawa, Kazuya Yamazaki. SCR: Fuyunori Gobu, Yoshihisa Araki, Soji Yoshikawa. DES: Yoshikazu Yasuhiko, Ryoji Hirayama, Studio Nue. ANI: Tadaichi Iuchi, Green Box, Kazuo Tomozawa. MUS: Takeo Watanabe, Hiroshi Matsuyama. PRD: Sunrise, Nagoya TV (TV Asahi). 25 mins. x 23 eps.

The last descendants of an extraterrestrial race take refuge on 19th-century Earth when their homeworld of Bial is destroyed by the treacherous Gaizoku. Several generations later, a Gaizoku advance force led by "Killer the Butcher" attacks Earth, and the local population accuses the descendants of the original refugees of bringing down trouble on the planet. They decide to use the ships their fathers arrived in to fight the mechanical monsters. These ships include the giant robot Zambot 3, made up by combining three different machines. Young Kappei, the robot's pilot, is assisted by Uchita and Keiko. The enemy has a very nasty way of killing; they implant explosive devices in their prisoners' bodies and can set them off at any time, even after the prisoners have returned to their homes and families. The tragic climax has Uchita and Keiko killed in a valiant effort to fight off the enemy, presaging the angst to come in Tomino's GUNDAM, for which this can reasonably be regarded as a test run. Notable for beginning as a lighthearted parody of earlier robot shows, before descending into tragedy—compare with GUNBUSTER and EVANGELION. ⓥ

ZANKAN

1996. AKA: *Killer Mischief*. Video. DIR: Motoaki Isshu. SCR: N/C. DES: N/C. ANI: Sugiko Enkai. MUS: N/C. PRD: Pink Pineapple, KSS. 30 mins. x 2 eps.

At the turn of the 21st century, Earth is conquered by demons, and only the two sexy "Riot" girls can save the universe, by having lots of sex. That's a surprise. Based on a manga by EVOCATION-creator Ryoga Ryuen. ⓝ

ZEGUY *

1992. JPN: *Unkai no Meikyu Zeguy*. AKA: *Labyrinth of the Sea Clouds: Zeguy*. Video. DIR: Shigenori Kageyama. SCR: Shigenori Kageyama. DES: Aki Tsunaki. ANI: Akinobu Takahashi. MUS: Soichiro Harada. PRD: KSS. 40 mins. x 2 eps.

Time-traveling trouble-shooters Toshizo and Gennai (from the ultranationalist Shinsengumi organization of 19th-century Japan) must prevent the evil Himiko (Japan's ancient ruler, see DARK MYTH) from opening a gateway to our world. They have two sailor-suited schoolgirls to help them but are lined up against a squad of smart enemies, including Leonardo da Vinci. Sadly, however, da Vinci is one of the only historical references that have survived in the dub version of this comedy romp—many of the clever references of the original script are sanded away by a distributor uneasy with "ethnocentric" allusions. Fun despite the dumbing-down, it's notable for a rare moment in a Manga Entertainment release when a character is chastised for using a rude word.

ZENKI: THE DEMON PRINCE *

1995. JPN: *Kishin Doji Zenki*. AKA: *Demon-God Boy Zenki*. TV series. DIR: Junji Nishimura. SCR: Ryota Yamaguchi, Masashi Sogo, Hitoshi Tokimura. DES: Hideyuki Motohashi, Torao Arai. ANI: Hideyuki Motohashi. MUS: Koji Tsuno. PRD: Studio Deen, Kitty Film, TV Tokyo. 25 mins. x 51 eps.

A thousand years ago, a sorcerer sealed the demon Zenki in stone to protect the world. Chiaki, a direct descendant, lives in modern Tokyo, where her grandmother has taught her the forbidden spell that breaks Zenki's bonds. To save her own world, she must use the spell, set Zenki free, and try to harness his power to fight off the spirits that are attacking modern Japan. The problem is, this involves his living with her in the family temple, and when he isn't casting spells as a superb hunk of menacing magical manhood, he takes the form of an annoying little brat who's every girl's worst nightmare of a kid brother. The director of RANMA 1/2 must know something about milking a franchise for its last drop of humor, but he doesn't have much to work with here—just an average kids' TV series and not a patch on USHIO AND TORA. Based on the manga in *Shonen Jump* by Hide Taniguchi and Yoshihiro Kuroiwa.

ZENO: LOVE WITHOUT LIMITS

1999. JPN: *Zeno: Kagirinaki Ai ni*. Movie. DIR: Takashi Ui. SCR: Takashi Ui, Shigeki Chiba. DES: N/C. ANI: Satoshi Mutsukura. MUS: N/C. PRD: Robot, Media Vision. 90 mins.

Father Zeno is a Polish priest who lived in Japan during the 1930s and fell in love with the land and its people. In the aftermath of World War II, he comes back with a mission to help the children of Japan who have been orphaned by war, fire, flood, or earthquake.

ZEORYMER HADES PROJECT *

1988. JPN: *Meio Kikaku Zeorymer*. AKA: *Hades Project Zeorymer*. Video. DIR: Toshihiro Hirano. SCR: Noboru Aikawa. DES: Michitaka Kikuchi, Yasuhiro Moriki. ANI: Michitaka Kikuchi. MUS: Eiji Kawamura. PRD: AIC, Artmic. 30 mins. x 4 eps.

Scientist Masaki Kihara rebels against his employers, the Haudragon crime syndicate. He destroys seven of the huge Hakkeshu robots he created for their top-secret Hades Project and hides the eighth and most powerful, the Zeorymer. Fifteen years later, the Haudragon have almost rebuilt the Hakkeshu, but the government has the Zeorymer and means to use it to thwart the criminals' plans. It needs the right pilot—a clone of its creator. Luckily, the government has one it had made earlier. Fifteen-year-old Masato is about to find out that his whole life so far has been a lie, and that he was created in a test tube for the sole purpose of going into battle as the pilot of the greatest war machine the world has ever seen. Unless he can destroy the Hakkeshu and thwart Haudragon's plans, the world will plunge into an abyss of nuclear destruction.

Hirano gives this dark, tense scenario all the menace and nastiness that he brought to ICZER-ONE a year earlier, while the atmosphere and design work foreshadow Kikuchi's later SILENT MÖBIUS. But there are no nasty alien invaders here—all the evil and suffering, as well as all the near-magical technology that created the magnificently spiky robots, is the work of humans; like GUNDAM, this reminds us that science fiction doesn't need aliens. Masato's emotional struggle and the near-disintegration of his personality are por-

trayed with melodramatic emphasis. This is a minor work by the standards of its stellar team but still has much of interest to offer. *Ill. p. 325.* ◐◑

ZERO SEN HAYATO

1964. TV series. DIR: Kazuo Hoshino, Tomio Sagisu. SCR: Satoru Kuramoto, Tomio Sagisu. DES: Tomio Sagisu. ANI: Saburo Sakamoto, Fujio Watanabe. MUS: Takeo Watanabe. PRD: P Productions, Oricomi, Fuji TV. 25 mins. x 41 eps.

Hayato Azuma, grandson of one of the Iga ninja clan, becomes a Zero-sen fighter pilot in the South Seas. Launching from Atsugi Island, he and his 34 ace pilot associates (including other descendants of ninja) fight as the Bakufu Team, under their commander Miyamoto, against a large number of opponents from nations whose insignia and nationality remain coyly unidentified. The only postwar anime for a generation after WARTIME ANIME to refer to WWII itself, this was based on the manga by TIGER MASK–creator Naoki Tsuji. In one memorable scene, the animators used footage from the live-action *War at Sea from Hawaii to Malaya* (see ULTRAMAN) as a background.

ZERO TESTER

1973. TV series. DIR: Ryosuke Takahashi, Yoshiyuki Tomino, Seiji Okuda. SCR: Fuyunori Gobu, Haruya Yamazaki, Kazushi Inoue, Soji Yoshikawa. DES: John Dettault, Crystal Art Studio. ANI: Kazuo Nakamura, Kazuhiko Udagawa, Yoshikazu Yasuhiko. MUS: Naoki Yamamoto. PRD: Tohoku Shinsha, Soei, Kansai TV (Fuji TV). 25 mins. x 66 eps.

A series of space accidents turn out to be the work of the Armanoid aliens, who plan to conquer Earth. Professor Tachibana gathers a team around him at the Future Science Invention Center and prepares five state-of-the-art vehicles for Shin, Go, Lisa, and Captain Kenmotsu. Three of the Tester vehicles combine to make the giant Zero Tester robot, which successfully sees off the Armanoid invasion in 39 episodes. The rest of the series, retitled *ZT: Save the*

Earth! (*Chikyu o Mamotte!*), was aimed at a younger age group and featured an attack by the new Gallos aliens.

An early gathering of many of anime's future greats, particularly for the GUNDAM series, this Gerry Anderson "homage" escaped complaint from the Japanese division of ITC because *Thunderbirds* (1965) was distributed in Japan by Tohoku Shinsha, who also produced *ZT!* Tohoku producer Banjiro Uemura would eventually work with Gerry Anderson himself on the abortive *Terrahawks* anime, and he would go it alone with the blatant THUNDERBIRDS 2086. Crystal Art was eventually renamed Studio Nue.

ZETSUAI *

1992. JPN: *Zetsuai 1989*. AKA: *Desperate Love 1989; Everlasting Love 1989*. Video. DIR: Takuji Endo, Kazuo Yamazaki. SCR: Tatsuhiko Urahata. DES: Tetsuro Aoki, Kazuya Kise. ANI: Tetsuro Aoki. MUS: Kenji Kawai, Yasunori Honda. PRD: Madhouse. 45 mins., 33 mins., 45 mins.

Takuto Izumi, a high-school soccer star, has a dark family secret—his mother's obsessive love for his father led to murder. Superstar idol singer Koji Nanjo has a terrible family background, with longstanding animosity between him and his eldest brother, and his middle sibling clinging to the elder. With their problems, the two should never even contemplate a relationship, but Koji has fancied Izumi since he first saw him; even when he finds out Izumi isn't, as he thought, a girl, he can't get him out of his mind. His obsessive love is the last thing Izumi needs, but as Koji pursues the relationship and Koji's friend Katsumi Shibuya becomes a friend to Izumi, too, love grows between the desperately needy pair despite Izumi's reluctance to accept it. It's tested by the hostility of Koji's family, which doesn't hesitate to threaten Izumi's chance of an international soccer career.

Bronze Cathexis (1994), a 33-minute "image" video concentrating on Koji, features five pop promos set to animation (as with **Cipher**) directed by some of the star directors of the Madhouse studio: Katsuyuki Kodera, Yoshiaki Kawajiri (who storyboarded *Zetsuai*), Koichi Chiaki, Toshio Hirata, and Rintaro.

A further video, *Bronze: Zetsuai since 1989* (1996), directed by Yamazaki and designed by Kise, shows Izumi leaving for a soccer tour. When Koji doesn't show up to see him off, he gets worried and starts to wonder why. In fact, Koji has had a minor car accident, but as a result Izumi starts pondering over their whole relationship.

Based on the ongoing 1990 manga in *Margaret* by Minami Ozaki, *Zetsuai* is one of the greatest icons of *shonen ai*—gay erotica for a female audience. The video versions show only a tiny segment of the angst-ridden multicharacter story, and though there's not much explicit sex, there is a lot of blood—accidents and self-inflicted wounds abound. Koji and Izumi have become *shonen ai*'s Romeo and Juliet, and a similarly tragic ending probably awaits. "Everlasting Love" is Ozaki's preferred English title, either through deliberate irony or simply poor translation. **ⓃⓋ**

ZILLION *

1987. JPN: *Akai Kodan Zillion*. AKA: *Red Tracer Zillion; Red Photon Zillion*. TV series, video. DIR: Hiroshi Hamazaki, Tetsuya Kobayashi. SCR: Tsunehisa Ito, Mayori Sekijima. DES: Mizuho Nishikubo, Kunio Aoii, Ammonite. ANI: Takayuki Sato. MUS: Jun Irie. PRD: Tatsunoko, Nippon TV. 25 mins. x 31 eps., 45 mins. (v).

In the year 2387, a group of human colonists live on the planet Maris, hailed as a "second Earth." However, the colonists are attacked by the Noza aliens—Maris' only hope is a captured alien weapon system known as the "Zillion Gun." Three of these fall into the hands of the defenders, and a team of brave young freedom fighters calling themselves the White Nauts/Nuts (White Knights in the U.S. release) fight for their people's survival. The 1988 video release *Burning Night* was a

one-shot written and directed by Nishikubo, set in the peacetime after the aliens have been seen off. Former comrades Champ, Dave, JJ, and cute girl Apple form a rock band (see **Dancougar**) but have to call on their old combat skills again when Apple is kidnapped by a criminal gang. Made just after **Robotech** *Sentinels* was canceled, *Zillion* incorporated some of the design work undertaken for the aborted project by Tatsunoko. The whole series was based on a toy—a photoelectric gun used for Lazer Tag—and only 5 of the 31 episodes, plus *Burning Night* (released as *Zillon Special: BN*) appeared on video in the U.S.

Z-MINE *

1999. JPN: *Omoharuki Shojo Gattai Robo Zee-Mine*. AKA: Spring Term Pretty-Girl Synchro Robot Z-Mine. Video. DIR: Yasuhiro Matsumura. SCR: Fuyunori Gobu. DES: Kamo Manimaru, Kenta Aoki. ANI: N/C. MUS: Toshiki Inoue. PRD: Sunrise. 25 mins. x 6 eps.

Ayame, on her way home from viewing the cherry blossoms, is attacked by strange men and dragged, along with three other girls, into a new role as a transforming-robot pilot. It was made in a deliberate 1970s style (compare to the '60s retro of **Gate Keepers**), even down to a mysterious male who pops up to give advice (shades of *Charlie's Angels*). Displaying all the hallmarks of an **Evangelion** clone that arrived too late, only to discover that the TV boom had slumped, it sidled out sheepishly onto video. Announced as forthcoming by Bandai in the U.S.

ZOIDS

1999. TV series. DIR: Yoshio Kado, Nobuyoshi Habara, Shingo Kobayashi. SCR: Kazuhiko Sumizawa, Kazuhiko Koide. DES: Tadashi Sakazaki. ANI: Taro Ikegami. MUS: Akira Takahashi. PRD: Xebec, Sho-Pro, MRS, JRK, TBS. 25 mins. x 67 eps. (TV1), 25 mins. x 26 (TV2).

Van is just an ordinary kid, but his life changes forever when a capsule crashes outside his village and he defends it

Cunningly wearing a mask so that his true identity is never revealed, an unidentified foreign rodent threatens an innocent rag doll on a South Pacific beach. The **Wartime Anime** *Black Cat Banzai* was made in 1934, after the annexation of Manchuria, but only released in 1936. It was one of several anime that depicted the foreign threat to islanders who seek Japanese "help"—a reference to Japan's mandate over the Inner South Pacific region, which was revoked by the League of Nations in 1935. *See entry p. 438.*

Black Cat Banzai

from bandits. The occupants are a sleek metallic dinosaur and a beautiful girl. The girl, Phina, says that her companion, Jeek, is a zoid. Van sets off with them on an adventure he could never have imagined, a battle against Deathsaura.

Promoting toys is what kids' robot shows are all about; Bandai's **Gundam** franchise is just one example. Here, though, is a show that starts out with a range of toys that have been on sale since 1982, a motor-driven range of construction kit toys by Tomy, with a name made from a Japlish combination of *ju* ("beast") and "android," making *ju-oids*. The artwork has a split personality, using CG on the Zoids (under the supervision of Nobuyoshi Habara) but aiming for a cel-animated look overall. At the beginning of 2001, the series was rebranded as *New Century Zoid Slash Zero* (*Zoid Shinseki/0*) with episode 68, moving away from the martial theme of the earlier episodes and concentrating instead on gladiatorial zoid combat. A manga spinoff was serialized in *Corocoro Comic*.

ZONE OF ENDERS

2001. Video, TV series. DIR: Tetsuya Watanabe. SCR: Shin Yoshida. DES: Madoka Hirayama, Tsutomu Suzuki,

Tsutomu Miyazawa. ANI: Kumi Horii. MUS: Hikaru Nanase. PRD: Sunrise, TV Tokyo. 55 mins. x N/D eps. (v)., 25 mins. x 26 eps.

In A.D. 2167, humankind has established colonies in space. Jupiter colony Antilla is the farthest human settlement from Earth, so its residents are called Enders. Leo Stenbuck, an introverted Ender, goes along with his friends (who bully him most of the time) to a UN Space Force facility to steal from their junkyard, but he gets caught. At the same time, fanatical Martian military ruling party Z.O.E. hijacks the Antilla colony. His home turned into a battlefield, Leo witnesses the deaths of his friends. Scared and weighed down with guilt, he runs from the scene determined to find the reasons behind the attack. In April 2001, the video *ZoE 2167* and the *ZoE Dolores* TV series were both released alongside the PlayStation game, which itself has a solid crew including **GUNDAM** and *Metal Gear Solid* veteran Nobuyoshi Nishimura. The anime version is set five years before the events of the game.

ZOO WITHOUT AN ELEPHANT

1982. JPN: *Zo no Inai Dobutsuen.* Movie. DIR: Yasuo Maeda. SCR: Hikaru Saito. DES: Junji Nagashima. ANI: Minoru Aoki. MUS: Kuni Kawauchi. PRD: Tac, Herald. 80 mins.

After the war, concerned brother Hide promises his critically ill sister Miyoko that he will arrange for her to see a real elephant. But when he goes to the zoo to find one, an old man tells him of the tragic day when the zoo animals were slaughtered. Compare to **GOOD-BYE LITTLE HIPPO**, a similar tale of wartime deprivation.

ZORRO THE MAGNIFICENT

1996. JPN: *Kaiketsu Zorro.* AKA: *Magnificent Zorro; Z for Zorro.* TV series. DIR: Katsumi Minoguchi, Kenichi Hirano, Yasuhiro Matsumura, Masakazu Amiya, Takeshi Yamaguchi, Akiyuki Shinbo. SCR: Sukehiro Tomita, Yasushi Hirano, Takashi Yamada, Hideki Sonoda, Isao Shizuoka. DES: Hisashi Kagawa. ANI: Hirotoshi Takaya, Masaaki Endo. MUS: N/C. PRD: Tohoku, Ashi productions, NHK2. 25 mins. x 52 eps.

Based on the stories by Johnston McCulley, which first appeared in *All-Story Weekly* in 1919, the series chronicles the adventures of a heroic freedom fighter (*El Zorro*. "The Fox") struggling to defend the independence of the people of 19th-century California from their Spanish rulers. Like the Hollywood feature film *Mask of Zorro* (1999), *ZtM* is set a generation later, with Zorro's son taking up the mantle and rapier. The idea has previous history in animation—Hayao Miyazaki planned a *Kaiketsu Zorro* series in 1982 but it never appeared. Other animated adventures of Zorro include the 1981 Filmation series and a 2000 Warner Bros. remake. *Zorori the Magnificent* (1993, *Kaiketsu no Zorori*) is an unrelated 30-minute feature directed by Toshio Takeuchi, which featured two popular episodes from a Zorro-pastiche children's book by Miho Mizushima, with animals in all the main roles. Zorro, of course, is played by a fox.

Selected Bibliography

Indexes

Names and Studios

Film Titles

SELECTED BIBLIOGRAPHY

BOOKS

Akiyama, F. *Current Japanese Robots and Heroes.* Volume. 1. Tokyo: privately published, 1993.

Animage. *The Art of Japanese Animation I: 25 Years of Television Cartoons.* Tokyo: Tokuma Shoten, 1989.

_____. *The Art of Japanese Animation II: 70 Years of Theatrical Films.* Tokyo: Tokuma Shoten, 1989.

Cremin, S. *The Asian Film Library Reference to Japanese Film.* 2 vols. London: Asian Film Library, 1998.

Galbraith, S. *Japanese Science Fiction, Fantasy, and Horror Films.* Jefferson, North Carolina: McFarland, 1994.

Haraguchi, M., ed. *Animage Pocket Data Notes.* Annual. Tokyo: Tokuma Shoten, 1989–2000.

Inoue, S., ed. *Anime DVD Kanzen* [Complete] *Catalogue 2000.* Tokyo: Kadokawa Shoten, 2000.

Inoue, T., ed. *Niju Seiki Anime Daizen* [Encyclopedia of 20th-Century Anime]. Tokyo: Futabasha, 2000.

Kondo, T., ed. *Nihon-ichi no Manga o Sagase!* [Find the Best Manga in Japan!]. Tokyo: Bessatsu Takarajima (#316), 1996.

Ledoux, T., and D. Ranney, eds. *The Complete Anime Guide: Japanese Animation Video Directory and Resource Guide.* Issaquah, Washington: Tiger Mountain Press, 1996.

_____ et al. (eds.) *Anime Interviews: The First Five Years of Animerica Anime and Manga Monthly.* San Francisco: Cadence Books, 1997.

Lent, J., ed. *Animation in Asia and the Pacific.* Eastleigh, U.K.: John Libbey, 2001.

Levi, A. *Samurai from Outer Space: Understanding Japanese Animation.* Chicago: Open Court Press, 1996.

Okada, T. *Otakugaku Nyumon* [Introduction to Otakuology]. Tokyo:

Ota, 1996.

Otani, R., ed. *Anime Video Sogo* [General] *Catalogue '99.* Tokyo: Hinode, 1999.

Schodt, F. *Manga! Manga! The World of Japanese Comics.* Tokyo: Kodansha International, 1984.

_____. *Dreamland Japan: Writings on Modern Manga.* Berkeley: Stone Bridge Press, 1996.

Schilling, M. *Encyclopedia of Japanese Pop Culture.* New York: Weatherhill, 1997.

_____. *Contemporary Japanese Film.* New York: Weatherhill, 1999.

Smith, T., and M. Graham, eds. *Japanese Animation Information: Baycon Guide.* Bay Area Animation Society (California), 1986.

Sunrise. *Sunrise Anime Super Data File.* Tokyo: Tatsumi Shuppan, 1997.

Takefuji, T. *Newtype Animesoft Kanzen* [Complete] *Catalog.* Tokyo: Kadokawa Shoten, 1993.

Tatsunoko. *Tatsunoko*

Pro Anime Super Data File. Tokyo: Tatsumi Shuppan, 1999.

Tezuka Productions. *Tezuka Osamu Gekijo* [The Animation Filmography of Osamu Tezuka]. Tokyo: Tezuka Productions, 1991.

Tokyo Movie Shinsha. *TMS Anime Super Data File.* Tokyo: Tatsumi Shuppan, 1998.

Weisser, T., and Y. M. Weisser. *Japanese Cinema Encyclopedia: Horror, Fantasy, Science Fiction.* Miami: Vital Books, 1997.

MAGAZINES

Animage (Japan). 1978–.

Anime UK/Anime FX (U.K.). 1991–96.

Animeland (France) 1991–.

Animerica (U.S.). 1993–.

AX (Japan). 1998–2001.

Manga Mania/Manga Max (U.K.). 1993–2000.

Newtype (Japan). 1984–.

Protoculture Addicts (Canada). 1988–.

INDEX

NAMES AND STUDIOS

This index, like the anime-title index, is alphabetized by the "word first" method, in which, for example, the name Ai Planning Center comes before the listing for AIC.

Arihara, Seiji, 199, 285, 321, 361, 447
Arima, Ichiro, 175
Arima, Katsumi, 58
Arima, Shinobu, 387
Arimasa, Toshihiko, 164
Arimura, Shinobu, 372
Arisawa, Hiroaki, 135
Arisawa, Takanori, 35, 75, 90, 202, 337
Ariseki, Toshihiko, 32
Aronofsky, Darren, 297
Artland, 42, 165, 168, 376
Artmic, 4, 30, 48, 100, 104, 134, 138, 249, 254, 306, 327, 384, 393, 438, 460
Asa, Minami, 438
Asada, Tetsuya, 135
Asada, Yuji, 60, 317, 388
Asagawa, Tomoyuki, 124
Asagiri, Yu, 254
Asahi International, 120, 272
Asai, Kengo, 287, 434
Asaka, Morio, 55, 126, 133, 251, 298, 454
Asakawa, Miya, 137
Asakura, Chifude, 242, 250, 406
Asakura, Daisuke, 154
Asakura, Kazumi, 284
Asakura, Noriyuki, 334, 351
Asakura, Takashi, 296
Asakura, Yukifude, 245
Asami, Matsuo, 412
Asami, Takashi, 42
Asamiya, Kia (pseud. for Michitaka Kikuchi), 66, 69, 268, 355, 378
Asano, Hiro, 411
Asano, Hiromi, 379
Asano, Megumi, 109
Asano, Shingo, 171
Asano, Yuji, 441
Asanuma, Akihiro, 415
Asari, Yoshito, 90, 366
Ashi Pro, 6, 7, 9, 15, 41, 51, 80, 92, 96, 125, 128, 136, 143, 151, 181, 188, 191, 195, 206, 210, 234, 260, 362, 368, 387, 427, 432, 462
Ashibe, Yuho, 47, 83
Ashida, Hiroshi, 183
Ashida, Toyoo, 6, 38, 74, 89, 93, 100, 123, 128, 136, 143, 153, 209, 215,

261, 266, 344, 368, 374, 385, 389, 402, 418, 420, 427, 431, 438, 440, 449
Ashinano, Hitoshi, 455
Ashizawa, Kazunori, 138
Ashizawa, Takeshi, 356
Asia Do, 45, 81, 147, 198, 219, 323, 326, 333, 342, 370, 416, 437, 455
Asimov, Isaac, 34, 227
Asmic, 74, 136, 150, 189, 346, 362
Aso, Izumi, 390, 393
Association to Protect Children from Comics, 12
Astaire, Fred, 78
Atelier Giga, 326
Atsumi, Kiyoshi, 407
Atsushi, Taku, 377, 390
Aubec, 52, 75, 83, 279, 347, 387, 413, 431, 457
Auberjonois, Rene, 223
Aubrey, Cecile, 32
Aurora 5, 355
Austrian Tourist Board, 194
Avalon, Frankie, 192
Avex, 412
AVN, 136
Awai, Shigenori, 127
Aya, Hideo, 174
Ayahana, Min, 225
Aznavour, Charles, 159
Azuhara, Takashi, 395
Azuki, Yu, 9, 181
Azuma (MUS), 292
Azuma, Hideo, 269, 304
Azuma, Ichiro, 14
Azuma, Kiyohiko, 238
Azuma, Masayoshi, 25, 68

B Pro, 97, 166
B2 Pro, 36
Baba, Ken, 257
Baba, Noboru, 112
Baba, Toshiko, 152
Bach, Johann Sebastian, 154
Baden-Powell, Robert, 350
Badham, John, 207
Baer, Dale, 10
Baer, Jane, 10
Baez, Joan, 253
Bakewell, Michael, 193
Bakin, Kyokutei, 163
Balk, 119, 254
Bandai Visual, 7, 10, 11, 13, 40, 42, 58, 62, 69, 79,

145, 152, 184, 193, 210, 215, 217, 225, 234, 238, 255, 338, 352, 371, 377, 392, 431, 446, 453, 461
Bang Heads, 119
Banpresto, 247
Barbee Boys, 409
Barrie, J. M., 298
Barron, Robert, 330
Barter, Michael, 82
Basho, Ken, 322
Batchiri Group, 403
Batow, Zhiemay, 46
Baxter, Les, 192
BB Queens, 59
BBC, 243, 262
Be Bo, 155
Be Factory, 44
Beam Entertainment, 4, 31, 42, 46, 50, 59, 68, 87, 121, 127, 156, 207, 213, 216, 237, 254, 264, 287, 293, 296, 310, 346, 353, 369, 390, 393, 397, 404, 415, 433, 436, 448
Beat Club, 56
Beat Takeshi. See Kitano, "Beat" Takeshi
Beatles, The, 275, 323
Beck, Jason, 248
Bee Media, 200
Beethoven, Ludwig van, 102, 150, 154, 274
BEGIN, 416
Bell System 24
Belmondo, Jean-Paul, 17
Be-Papas, 425
Berié, Albert, 69
Berkley, Elizabeth, 19
Berriere, Marc, 60
Besson, Luc, 207
BeStock, 23, 110, 166
Betsuyaku, Minoru, 272
Beyond Two, 144
Bibanba, Miki, 210
Big Bang, 33, 85, 154
Big Jo, 286
Big West, 185, 234, 287
Bimoth, 260
Bip, 300
Bird, Rob, 217
Black Point, 150
Blair, Linda, 26
Blue Mantis, 310
Bluth, Don, 365
Blyton, Enid, 416
BMF, 169, 261, 358, 458

Bôa (pop group), 350
Bobino, Gianni, 261
Bogart, Humphrey, 108
Bond, Dennis, 79
BONES, 13, 20
Bonsels, Waldemar, 246
Boomerang, 61
BORO, 353
Bradbury, Ray, 18, 271
BRB, 20
Bresson, Francois, 233
Brewer, Jameson, 435
British Board of Film Classification (BBFC), 176, 200, 210, 282
Broccoli, 123, 313
Brooks, Margaret, 50
Brother Anoppo, 207, 217
Brothers Grime, 71
Brown, James, 236
BS-I, 239
B-train, 17, 278, 444
Buck-Tick, 273
Buena Vista, 202
Burgess, Thornton W., 190
Burnett, Frances Hodgson, 222, 224, 347
Burnheads, 265
Buronson, 123
Burroughs, Edgar Rice, 389
Burton, Tim
Buyu, 355

C&D Distribution, 59, 67
Calpis, 448
Cameron, James, 37, 86, 169
Candies, The, 362
Cansino, Richard, 30
Canyon, 78
Capcom, 191, 306, 381
Carbone, Joey, 312
Carol Lombard Singers, 308
Caron, Leslie, 78
Carroll, Lewis (pseud. for Charles Dodgson), 10
Cartoon Network, 30, 290
CBS, 60
Celebrity Home Entertainment, 192
Central AV, 354
Central Park Media/CPM, 172, 248
Centre, 12
Cervantes, Miguel de, 96
Chage & Asuka, 266, 285,

Anime whose titles begin with numerals are listed *twice* in this index, at the very beginning in numerical order and within the alphabetical entries according to spelling based on pronunciation; e.g., the anime *1001 Nights* appears at the beginning of the listings as well as under the (reasonably assumed) pronunciation/spelling *One Thousand and One Nights*. Alphabeticization is by the "word first" method, so that the anime *Ai Oboeteimasu ka* is listed before *Aika*. **Boldface type** indicates a main text entry for an anime that has been released in English. **Boldface** numerals are used with Japanese and alternative English titles to lead you to their corresponding main entries; cross-references follow in normal type. Italicized numbers in parentheses—e.g., *(385)*—indicate locations of illustrations; illustrations are also listed alphabetically after the Contents page. This index also includes some rare but known alternative titles that are not listed in the main text, as well as books, magazines, and other creative works.

VIEWING NOTES

VIEWING NOTES

VIEWING NOTES

VIEWING NOTES

VIEWING NOTES

VIEWING NOTES

VIEWING NOTES

VIEWING NOTES

VIEWING NOTES

VIEWING NOTES

VIEWING NOTES

ABOUT THE AUTHORS

JONATHAN CLEMENTS was formerly the editor of *Manga Max* magazine and contributing editor to the online edition of *Newtype*. He has worked as a voice actor, dubbing director, or translator on dozens of anime productions including *The Cockpit, Sol Bianca, Hummingbirds, Samurai Gold, Slow Step,* and *Plastic Little.* Other translation projects have included songs from *Tenchi Muyo,* part of the *Cowboy Bebop* story *Ural Terpsichore,* and ancient Chinese ballads. He wrote scripts for the *Halcyon Sun* series and is the author of *The Moon in the Pines, Chinese Life, The Teachings of Confucius,* and *A Kid's Guide to the Movies.*

A leading figure in early British anime fandom, HELEN MCCARTHY was the founding editor of *Anime UK/FX* magazine and subsequently editor of *Manga Mania.* She has also appeared as a voice actress in several anime and produced the U.K. release of *Beast Warriors.* She is the author of several other books on Japanese animation, including *Anime! A Beginner's Guide* (the first English-language book on the medium), *The Anime Movie Guide, The Erotic Anime Movie Guide* (with Jonathan Clements), and *Hayao Miyazaki: Master of Japanese Animation.*